The Criminal Appeal Reports (Sentencing)

Volume 1 of 2005

AUSTRALIA
LBC Information Services
Sydney

CANADA AND USA
Carswell
Toronto

HONG KONG
Sweet & Maxwell Asia

NEW ZEALAND
Brooker's
Aukland

SINGAPORE AND MALAYSIA
Sweet & Maxwell Asia
Singapore and Kuala Lumpur

The Criminal Appeal Reports (Sentencing) 2005

Editor
David Thomas, Q.C., LL.D.

Editorial Contributor
T. Rees, M.A., LL.M., Barrister

Volume 1

London • Sweet & Maxwell
2005

This volume should be cited as [2005] 1 Cr.App.R.(S.)

ISBN-10 0-421-92480-2
ISBN-13 978-0-421-92480-2

Criminal Appeal Reports (Sentencing) will continue to develop its position as
the most authoritative and accessible source in practice of full text reports of
cases involving sentencing questions.

Printed and Bound in United Kingdom by Butler and Tanner, Frome, Somerset

No natural forests were destroyed to make this product; only farmed timber was
used and re-planted.

Appellants

v

Table of Statutes

Table of Statutory Instruments

Table of Cases

xiii

R. v RICHARD THOMPSON

Court of Appeal (Lord Justice Thomas, Mr Justice Holland and Judge Michael Baker Q.C.): March 26, 2004

[2004] EWCA Crim 669; [2005] 1 Cr.App.R.(S.) 1

(LT) Computers; Indecent photographs of children; Indictments; Internet; Sentence length; Sentencing guidelines

H1   *Possessing indecent photographs of children—length of sentence—real and pseudo-photographs—guidance on drafting indictments where numerous images alleged*

H2   **Editor's note:** where a defendant is charged with offences of possessing indecent photographs of children, the indictment should be so drawn as to identify the number of images at each level of gravity alleged to be in the possession of the defendant, whether they are photographs or pseudo-photographs, and if possible the estimated age range of the children involved. If individual counts relate to particular images, the image should be identified.

H3   The appellant pleaded guilty to 12 counts of possessing indecent photographs or pseudo-photographs of children contrary to the Criminal Justice Act 1988, s.160. Eleven counts related to specific images, while the last count related to 3,735 other images. A search warrant was executed at the appellant's home address and his computer was seized. It was found to have contained over 3,700 indecent images of children which had been downloaded from commercial sites on the internet, but subsequently deleted. The appellant eventually admitted that he had downloaded them. Sentenced to two years' imprisonment on each count concurrent.

H4   **Held:** the sentencing judge described the photographs identified in the 11 specific counts as showing young children engaging in sexual activity and referred to the other photographs, some of which involved pictures of category four which involved penetrative sexual activity between children and adults. The indictment did not indicate whether the images were photographs or pseudo-photographs. In *Oliver* [2003] 2 Cr.App.R.(S.) 15 (p.64), the Court had indicated that possession including downloading of artificially created pseudo-photographs should generally be treated as being at a lower level of seriousness than possessing or making photographic images of real children, although there might be exceptional cases in which the possession of a pseudo-photograph was as serious as the possession of a photograph of a real child. It would usually be desirable that the charge or count in the indictment should specify whether photographs or pseudo-photographs were involved. In the appellant's case, the indictment did not identify whether the photographs in question were real photographs or pseudo-photographs, but it was accepted by the appellant that the images were real photographs. The indictment did not identify clearly which count related to which image, and no information was provided in the indictment as to the categorisation of the remaining 3,735 images which were not the subject of specific counts. The sentencing judge had been placed in a difficult position by not being told the approximate number of images at each level contained in the general count relating to the 3,735 further images, so that he could properly proceed to sentence in accordance with the guidelines set out in *Oliver*. The situation was not uncommon. The Court suggested that in cases of this kind the following practices should be adopted in the drafting of indictments or the presentation of information in summary proceedings:

(1) In cases where there were significant numbers of photographs, in addition to the specific counts, the inclusion of a comprehensive count covering the remainder was a practice that should be followed.

(2) The photographs used in the specific counts should so far as was practical be selected so as to be broadly representative of the images in the comprehensive count. If agreement could be reached between the parties about the number of images at each level, the need for a judge to view the entirety of the offending material might be avoided.

(3) Where it was impractical to present the court with specific counts that were agreed to be representative of the comprehensive count, there must be available to the court an approximate breakdown of the number of images at each of the levels. This might best be achieved by the prosecution providing a schedule setting out the information and ensuring that the defence had an opportunity of viewing the images and checking the accuracy of the schedule.

(4) Each of the specific counts should make clear whether the image in question was a real image or a pseudo image. The same count should not charge both.

(5) Each image charged in a specific count should be identified by a reference so that it was clear with which image the specific count was dealing.

(6) The estimated age range of the child shown in each of the images should where possible be provided.

H5   Taking into account the lack of information before the Court, the fact that all the images had been deleted from the computer by the appellant, the fact that he was not involved in distribution, and the personal mitigation, the Court would substitute a sentence of nine months' imprisonment.

H6   **References:** indecent images, *Current Sentencing Practice* B 10-1

H7   *N. Casey* for the appellant.

JUDGMENT

1   **THOMAS L.J.:**   On October 31, 2003 the appellant pleaded guilty to 12 counts of possession of indecent photographs or pseudo photographs of children contrary to s.160(1) and (2A) of the Criminal Justice Act 1988; 11 of those counts related to specific images while the last count related to 3,735 other images in the appellant's possession. On November 28, 2003 he was sentenced by H.H. Judge Lockhart at Basildon Crown Court to two years' imprisonment on each count, such sentences being concurrent with each other. He appeals against that sentence with leave of the single judge.

2   The facts can be briefly summarised. The appellant was a man of 52 years of age. He ran his own business of fitting windscreens to buses. He was married with three children. One of those was aged 11, but the others were adults.

3   On March 26, 2003 a search warrant was executed at the appellant's home address. His computer was seized. When it was examined, it was found to have contained over 3,700 indecent images of children which had been downloaded from commercial sites on the internet, but subsequently deleted. When being interviewed he initially denied knowledge of the images but at a second interview in July 2003 admitted possession of the images. He said he had downloaded them from the internet, but then deleted them.

4   As a consequence of his arrest and the discovery of the indecent photographs, he has been rejected by his family. He was of previous good character. There were two reports before the court which sentenced him; one of those was from a social worker who had been conducting individual sessions which he had attended. There was before us, in addition, a report from the prison at which the appellant was serving his sentence. This was a positive report which showed he had been making good use of his time in prison.

5   In sentencing the appellant the learned Judge referred to the photographs which he had seen which related to the 11 specific counts. He described them as showing:

> "in very unpleasant focus and close up, young girls engaging in sexual activity — intercourse — with other people (some adult, certainly). It is gross behaviour to be adopted towards any young child. In this case, two of the children were aged between five and six. It really does not bear thinking about as to what those little girls are going to make of their lives in later years, because each of them is a victim. Whether they will ever be able to recover from this is something that none of us will know".

6   He then referred to the fact that not only was he dealing with those specific images, but

> "with another 3,735 cases — some of which (and I do not know how many) being category 4, in other words towards the more serious end of the scale of offending of this sort."

7   In his reference to category 4, the learned Judge was referring to the guideline case of *Oliver* [2002] EWCA Crim 2766; [2003] 2 Cr.App.R.(S.) 15 (p.64) where

at para.[10], Rose L.J. giving the judgment of the Court categorised the levels of pornographic images of children as:

> "(1)　images depicting erotic posing with no sexual activity;
> (2)　sexual activity between children, or solo masturbation by a child;
> (3)　non-penetrative sexual activity between adults and children;
> (4)　penetrative sexual activity between children and adults;
> (5)　sadism or bestiality."

8　　　The Court made clear that among the factors to be taken into account in sentencing in such cases were whether the images were photographs or pseudo-photographs and the quantity of images at the different levels that the defendant had in his possession:

> "15. Possession, including down-loading, of artificially created pseudo-photographs and the making of such images, should generally be treated as being at a lower level of seriousness than possessing or making photographic images of real children. But there may be exceptional cases in which the possession of a pseudo-photograph is as serious as the possession of a photograph of a real child: for example, where the pseudo-photograph provides a particularly grotesque image generally beyond the scope of a photograph. It is also to be borne in mind that, although pseudo-photographs lack the historical element of likely corruption of real children depicted in photographs, pseudo-photographs may be as likely as real photographs to fall into the hands of, or to be shown to, the vulnerable, and there to have equally corrupting effect. It will usually be desirable that a charge or count in an indictment specifies whether photographs or pseudo-photographs are involved.
>
> . . . .
>
> "17. In relation to more serious offences, a custodial sentence between 12 months and three years will generally be appropriate for (a) possessing a large quantity of material at levels 4 or 5, even if there was no showing or distribution of it to others; or (b) showing or distributing a large number of images at level 3; or (c) producing or trading in material at levels 1 to 3"
>
> . . .

9　　　In this particular case:

> i)　The indictment did not identify whether the photographs in question were real photographs or pseudo-photographs, but it was accepted on the appellant's behalf that the images were real photographs.
> ii)　Save for one count, the indictment did not identify by its "jpg" or similar reference which count in the indictment related to which image; again counsel was able to agree which the images were when we viewed them.
> iii)　In respect of the count in the indictment which covered possession of 3,735 other photographs, there was no information whether by way of schedule, admission or otherwise, as to the number of photographs which fell into each of the levels identified by this Court in *Oliver*.

iv) Although the charge sheet which was provided to us to enable us to identify the photographs when we viewed them gave an indication of the age
of the children in question by reference to "under 5" in one case and
"under 10" or "under 12" or "under 16" in other cases, there was
nothing before the judge which contained any agreement on the age of
the child. Again it was accepted on behalf of the appellant that the
judge had correctly identified the age of the children in two of the images
as referred to in para.[5] above.

10   Although three of the issues to which we have referred were resolved by counsel's acceptance on behalf of the appellant of the position described, the position
was different on the important issue as to the breakdown of the 3,735 images into
the quantities at the different levels. Enquiries made on our behalf confirmed that
the prosecution had not provided any schedule listing the 3,735 images and no
question was raised by the judge as to the deficiency in the information provided
in respect of these images; it seems to us that the judge allowed himself to be
placed in a very difficult position in this case by not requiring to be told of the
approximate number of images at each level contained in the count relating to
the 3,735 images, so that he could properly proceed to sentence in accordance
with the guidelines set out in *Oliver*.

11   In the light of the experience of some of the members of this constitution of the
Court and questions we raised with counsel, it appears that the situation that arose
in this case is not uncommon. We would therefore suggest that in each case of this
kind the following practices should be adopted in the drafting of indictments. The
same practices might also be adopted in the selection of images for presentation
in summary proceedings:

i) In cases where there are significant numbers of photographs, in addition
to the specific counts, the inclusion of a comprehensive count covering
the remainder is a practice that should be followed.
ii) The photographs used in the specific counts should, if it is practicable, be
selected so as to be broadly representative of the images in the comprehensive count. If agreement can then be reached between the parties that
(say) 5 images at level 2, 10 at level 3, and 2 at level 4 represent 500 level
2, 100 level 3 and 200 level 4 images in the comprehensive count of 800
images, the need for the judge to view the entirety of the offending
material may be avoided.
iii) Where it is impractical to present the court with specific counts that are
agreed to be representative of the comprehensive count there must be
available to the court an approximate breakdown of the number of images
at each of the levels. This may best be achieved by the prosecution providing the defence with a schedule setting out the information and
ensuring that the defence have an opportunity, well in advance of the sentencing hearing, of viewing the images and checking the accuracy of the
schedule.
iv) Each of the specific counts should, in accordance with what was stated by
this Court in *Oliver*,make it clear whether the image in question is a real

image or a pseudo-image; the same count should not charge both. As this Court pointed out in *Oliver*, there may be a significant difference between the two and where there is a dispute, then there should be alternative counts. In the majority of cases there will be no doubt as to whether the image in question should be dealt with either as a real image or a pseudo-image.

  v) Each image charged in a specific count should be identified by reference to its "jpg" or other reference so that it is clear with which image the specific count is dealing.

  vi) The estimated age range of the child shown in each of the images should where possible be provided to the Court.

12   We make these observations because, in our view, the judge was placed in a position as regards this appellant where he had no information (apart from the 11 images set out in the counts dealing with specific images) as to the approximate quantity of the images at the different levels. There was no basis on which he could find on the information before him that there were any at level 4. Counsel for the appellant has taken the point that as the prosecution failed to identify the levels of the 3,735 other images and no request was made by the judge prior to sentence for those to be identified, it would not be right to make an assumption against his client as to the number of images at the different levels which were encompassed within the 3,735 other images.

13   It is because we see the force of that submission that we have set out the good practice in para.[11] above which we consider should have been followed in this case.

14   Taking into account the unfortunate lack of information before the court, the fact that all the images were deleted from the computer by the appellant, that he was not in any way involved in distribution and that the images were used for his own personal purposes and the personal mitigation to which we have referred, we consider that the sentence passed by the learned trial judge was too long. On the information before him, the judge could not properly conclude that the appellant was in possession of a large quantity of material at level 4. In the circumstances, we consider that the appropriate sentence for this offence should have been nine months' imprisonment. We accordingly quash the sentence of imprisonment of two years and substitute one of nine months.

15   There is one other matter. The judge also stated in his sentencing remarks:

> "I make a Restraining Order in the terms as represented to me and I order that on release from prison you will register under the Sex Offenders Act . . .".

16   We enquired into the restraining order that is said to have been made by the learned judge. No copy of the order was recorded on the court computer system and none could be found on the file. Enquiries were made of the court and of the Crown Prosecution Service (as counsel who had appeared for the prosecution at trial was overseas). None could recall to what the judge was referring. This is another unfortunate aspect of the case. It is accepted on behalf of counsel for

the appellant that an order should have been made disqualifying the appellant from working with children, having regard to the sentence he passed and to s.28 of the Criminal Justice and Court Services Act 2000. It may be that the judge was referring to this but no such order was made. We do not ourselves make such an order because the sentence of ninemonths which we substitute for the sentence at trial is not a qualifying sentence for such an order.

R. v CRAIG MICHAEL ALLEN

COURT OF APPEAL (Lord Justice Rose (Vice President, Court of Appeal, Criminal Division), Mr Justice Crane and Mr Justice Hunt): April 5, 2004

[2004] EWCA Crim 1030; [2005] 1 Cr.App.R.(S.) 2

LT Brain damage; Detention; Extended sentences; Grievous bodily harm; Young offenders

H1   *Causing grievous bodily harm with intent—eighteen-year-old offender kicking and stamping on head of victim so as to cause brain damage and consequential injuries—whether a longer than commensurate sentence justified*

H2   Ten years' detention in a young offender institution, passed as a longer than commensurate sentence for causing grievous bodily harm with intent by kicking and stamping on a man's head so as to cause grave injuries, varied to an extended sentence with a custodial term of seven years and an extension period of three years.

H3   The appellant, aged 18, pleaded guilty to causing grievous bodily harm with intent to do so. The appellant and two co-accused went to a night club where they encountered two older men. There was an altercation between the appellant and one of the men, who became the victim of the offence. Later the appellant and his friends left, but they encountered the two men. There was an exchange of words and the appellant and the victim squared off. The victim punched the appellant in the face; the appellant punched the victim so that he fell. As the victim fell backwards the appellant kicked him a number of times to the head and stamped on his head. The victim was later found to have traumatic brain damage. Some months after the incident he required continuous care. He had lost much of the sight in one eye. He was paralysed down one side and had lost the ability to read normally and was unable to write. He was depressed at the thought that he would be unable to live a normal life. The appellant pleaded guilty on the basis that he had been struck by the victim and he had struck back at the victim, knocking him backwards. When the victim fell to the ground, the appellant kicked him on the head four or five times and stamped once on his head. Sentenced to 10 years' detention in a young offender institution, passed as a longer than commensurate sentence under the Powers of Criminal Courts (Sentencing) Act 2000, s.80(2)(b.).

H4   **Held:** (considering *Crow and Pennington* (1995) 16 Cr.App.R.(S.) 409, *Nelson* [2002] 1 Cr.App.R.(S.) 134 (p.565)) the Court accepted the submission that a longer than commensurate sentence was not necessary. It was sufficient to impose an extended sentence consisting of a custodial term of seven years and an extension period of three years.

H5   **Cases cited:** *Crow and Pennington* (1995) 16 Cr.App.R.(S.) 409, *Nelson* [2002] 1 Cr.App.R.(S.) 134 (p.565)

H6   **References:** causing grievous bodily harm with intent, *Current Sentencing Practice* E 2-4

H7   *O.D. Woolhouse* for the appellant.
        B. Linnehan for the Crown.

JUDGMENT

1   **HUNT J.:**   Craig Michael Allen is now 19, though he was 18 at both offence and sentence. He is a young man with numerous previous convictions for violence.

2   On October 23, 2003, in the Crown Court at Wolverhampton, he pleaded guilty and was sentenced on December 5 by H.H. Judge Chapman to 10 years' detention in a young offender institution under s.80(2)(b) of the Powers of Criminal Courts (Sentencing) Act 2000, for causing grievous bodily harm with intent to do grievous bodily harm. He now appeals against sentence by leave of the single judge.

3   There were two co-accused, a young man called Kevin Harrison, aged 16, and a young man called Mark Hill, aged 18, who were each sentenced to six months' detention in a young offender institution.

4   The facts of the offending were that at about 10.45 on a Saturday night in August 2003, the appellant and the co-accused went into a nightclub in Bilston with two females. In there were 38-year-old Glen Parkes (the victim of count 1) who was there with a young man called Patel, who was 33. At some time in that nightclub there was some sort of altercation between the appellant and Parkes but door staff prevented that getting out of hand.

5   At about 2 o'clock in the morning, on the Sunday that is, the appellant's group left and went to get some food from a take-away. They then walked back towards the club, eventually stopping at a bench area outside the public house. At about 2.30am Parkes and Patel left the nightclub. They bought some food from a chip shop and began to walk home. That took them past the appellant's group. The appellant and Parkes exchanged words. They squared up to each other. Patel attempted to pull Parkes away and the appellant's girlfriend attempted to pull the appellant away. Parkes punched the appellant in the face. The appellant retaliated by punching Parkes in the face. As Parkes fell backwards the appellant

kicked him a number of times to the head and body. Parkes fell to the floor and remained still, making no attempt to get up or defend himself.

6   That is when the real gravamen of this offence occurred. The appellant stamped on Parkes' head. It was alleged at one point that he jumped in the air and landed with both feet on Parkes' head. That he denied. But Parkes was left unconscious in a pool of blood. Meanwhile, Patel was assaulted by the co-accused who punched him and then kicked him.

7   The emergency services were summoned. Parkes and Patel were taken to hospital. Parkes was extremely seriously injured. He was found to have a traumatic brain injury, with a haematoma in the front left frontal lobe, a fractured skull of the left orbit, the phenoid bone and the floor of the anterior cranial fossa on the left. There was extensive skull swelling, mainly on the left side and associated with tissue of the face.

8   As at October 28, 2003 Parkes remained an in-patient. That, of course, was the case when the appellant pleaded guilty. After 11 weeks he had made good progress, particularly with motor functions. His immediate long-term and potential problems included epilepsy, personality changes and a lack of drive, insight and higher cognitive functions. He would be handicapped in the community. He required and requires long-term rehabilitation.

9   There was a statement from his sister indicating that he had been home for a few weeks as at the time of the appellant's sentence. He required 24-hour care. He suffered from epilepsy and he had lost much of the sight in his left eye. He is paralysed down the left side and unable to walk unaided. He had limited mobility and his speech had been affected. He had lost the ability to read normally and was unable to write. He had some memory loss. He was depressed and as he recovered became more so knowing that he was not going to lead a normal life. It is explained that the incident has affected the whole family, who have had to arrange their life around caring for him. It was felt not only had his life been taken away but also theirs.

10   The appellant had been arrested on August 15, Harrison on the 17th. When interviewed the appellant fully admitted that he had indeed stamped on Parkes' head. Hill and Harrison made other limited admissions. He pleaded guilty on the basis of his fifth police interview, that is that on the night in question he had been approached by Parkes, who had shouted towards his group and approached them. Parkes was abusive, saying that he wanted to "fuck him up the arse", and Parkes had taken off his jacket and punched him in the mouth causing him to bleed and, believing Parkes was going to hit him again, he had struck him to the face, knocking him backwards. When Parkes fell to the ground, the appellant kicked him to keep him down. He kicked Parkes four or five times to the head and to the body and he stamped on his head with one foot, twice, before his girlfriend pulled him away. That was the basis of plea that seems to have been accepted.

11   In sentencing him the learned judge said, and very rightly, that this case demonstrated just how tragically street fighting could end up. Parkes, he said, was not totally blameless. He had been prepared to fight and it appears that Parkes made the first move. Having knocked Parkes to the ground the appellant had barbarically kicked and stamped on him leading to Parkes' present disablement. The

judge took account of the fact that Parkes struck him first. The judge said that he took account of his age and the fact that he pleaded guilty at an early stage. He had a long-standing violent nature and there was a high risk of re-offending. That conclusion was inevitable bearing in mind although he was only 18 this appellant had two previous convictions for inflicting grievous bodily harm, two for inflicting actual bodily harm and two for common assault.

12   The single judge, in granting leave, reflected that it was arguable that it was not necessary to pass a longer than commensurate sentence, the learned judge having come to the conclusion that the commensurate sentence was seven years and the full Court might consider that the sentence should be extended for licence purposes. In that way, behaviour after release could continue to be monitored.

13   In a skeleton argument before this Court Mr Woolhouse has set out the relevant authorities. Mr Woolhouse's submission is indeed reflected in the comments of the single judge and in those authorities. He submitted that it is not every case of violence or sex offending which requires that s.80(2)(b) should be invoked. If, for example, there is no reason to fear a substantial risk of further violence the subsection would not apply.

14   In *Crow and Pennington* (1995) 16 Cr.App.R.(S.) 409 those views were expressed. It was said that the learned judge did not take into sufficient consideration the fact that there was ample information in the following terms to suggest that the future risk in this case was not a substantial one. The appellant had acknowledged his wrongdoing and expressed genuine remorse. He had written to the judge, recognising that it was time that he broke his offending cycle and he had already, at that stage, nominated himself for such treatment. He had shown a willingness to act by way of involvement during his last a term of detention.

15   Mr Woolhouse submits that the proper way of dealing with this would be by passing a sentence which was the proper sentence for this offender together with an extended licence period of three years, which brings it up to the same period of 10 years. We reflect, as Mr Woolhouse pointed out in his skeleton, that in *Nelson* [2002] 1 Cr.App.R.(S.) 134 (p.565), at [14], my Lord, Rose L.J. said this:

> "As to whether a longer than commensurate sentence is necessary, it is to be noted that the risk of further offences being committed by the offender does not justify a longer than commensurate term unless those further offences may cause death or some physical or psychological injury. Also, there may be cases in which, because of the power to impose an extended licence period, a longer than commensurate sentence may not be necessary."

Mr Woolhouse submitted that that was apposite in this case. He also referred us to the remarks of Rix L.J. in the case of *Briggs* [2003] 2 Cr.App.R.(S.) 103 (p.615) at [17], where it was said:

> "The purpose of the extended licence is not to impose an additional immediate sentence upon an offender but to hold above his head, for the protection

of the public and for his own rehabilitation, the sword of recall from his licence in the event of further offending."

It is not necessary to quote further.

16   As my Lord, the Vice-President, has indicated already, we accept Mr Woolhouse's submission. We shall substitute a sentence of seven years with an extended licence period of three years. The effect, of course, though it is not always appreciated, is not to change the length of sentence, but it will affect the period of time which this appellant spends in custody and the period thereafter during which he will be on licence. To that extent, and to that extent only, this appeal succeeds.

ATTORNEY GENERAL'S REFERENCE NO.81 OF 2003 (MOHAMMED ATTIQ)

COURT OF APPEAL (Lord Justice Keene, Mr Justice Penry-Davey and Mr Justice Fulford): April 7, 2004

[2004] EWCA Crim 994; [2005] 1 Cr.App.R.(S.) 3

⟨LT⟩ Aggravating features; Possession with intent to supply; Undue leniency

H1   *Possessing heroin with intent to supply—possessing equivalent of almost one kilogram of pure heroin as courier—length of sentence*

H2   Five years' imprisonment for possessing the equivalent of almost one kilogram of pure heroin as a courier, increased to eight years.

H3   The offender was convicted of possessing a Class A controlled drug, heroin, with intent to supply. The offender was driving in his taxi when he was stopped by police officers. A bag containing 4.1kg of powder containing heroin was found in the car. The prosecution alleged that the offender was acting as a courier of the drugs. The offender maintained that the bag had been left in his taxi by passengers. Sentenced to five years' imprisonment. The Attorney General asked the Court to review the sentence on the ground that it was unduly lenient.

H4   **Held:** for the Attorney General it was submitted that the offence was aggravated by the quantity of heroin found, equivalent to almost 1kg at 100 per cent purity. The Court recognised that the quantity of the drugs in question was not the whole of the story. It was necessary to consider how high up the chain of distribution the offender was. The two matters were related. Anyone who was permitted by a major supplier to have sole possession of heroin worth nearly a quarter of a million pounds was clearly a very well-trusted courier. Taking into account the previous decisions of the Court, the sentence was unduly lenient. The offender had contested the matter over a three-day trial. At first instance, an appropriate sentence would not have been less than nine years. Making allowance for the element of double jeopardy, the Court would substitute a sentence of eight years' imprisonment.

H5 **Cases cited:** Aramah (1982) 4 Cr.App.R.(S.) 407, *Bilinski* (1987) 9 Cr.App.R.(S.) 360, *Aranguren* (1994) 99 Cr.App.R. 347, *Attorney General's References Nos 64 and 65 of 1997 (O'Gorman and Hibbard)* [1999] 1 Cr.App.R.(S.) 237, *Attorney General's Reference No.146 of 2002* [2003] 2 Cr.App.R.(S.) 107 (p.640)

H6 **References:** possessing heroin with intent to supply, *Current Sentencing Practice* B 11-2.3B

H7 *T. Adebayo* for the Attorney General.
    B. Singh for the offender.

JUDGMENT

1   **KEENE L.J.:**   This is an application under s.36 of the Criminal Justice Act 1988 by Her Majesty's Attorney General for leave to refer a sentence to this Court because it appears to him to be unduly lenient. We grant leave and we treat this as being the hearing of the reference.

2   On October 23, 2003, at Doncaster Crown Court, before Mr Recorder Woolman, the offender was convicted after a trial of one count of possessing a Class A drug, that is to say heroin, with intent to supply. He was sentenced on the same date to five years' imprisonment.

3   The offence in question occurred on the morning of June 7, 2003 in Doncaster. The offender was the driver and sole occupant of a taxi cab which was stopped by police who were acting on information received. When the cab was searched, the police officers found a bag in the passenger footwell which contained some 4.12kg of heroin. The Crown's case was that the offender was a courier of the drugs, and, indeed, it was on that basis that the offender was sentenced.

4   He denied at trial knowing anything about the drugs. He had told the police that a passenger had left the bag in the taxi. During his interviews he gave "no comment" replies. He maintained his story that a passenger had left the bag when he gave evidence at trial. Despite evidence that he was a highly respected member of the community, his evidence patently was not believed by the jury.

5   In sentencing him, the recorder approached the case on the basis that this was a single instance of ferrying drugs around. He noted that this consignment had a street value of nearly a quarter of a million pounds and that the only mitigation was the offender's previous good character.

6   That is a factor which is acknowledged by the Attorney General in his reference, but he points to the quantity of Class A drugs involved as being the aggravating feature of the case. There were 11 packages in all, containing heroin (within a brown powder) at varying levels of purity. These ranged from 2 per cent to 39 per cent. In all, the 4.12kg of powder had an average purity of around 23.25

per cent, the equivalent of almost 1 kilo at 100 per cent purity—to be more precise, 959g at 100 per cent purity.

7   Mr Adebayo, who appears on behalf of the Attorney General, submits that the sentence of five years' imprisonment was unduly lenient because it failed to mark the gravity of the offence, the need for deterrence and the public concern in relation to dealing in Class A drugs.

8   Reliance is placed on a number of authorities, beginning with Aramah (1982) 4 Cr.App.R.(S.) 407and *Bilinski* (1987) 9 Cr.App.R.(S.) 360. We need not take time on those well known decisions. But in particular Mr Adebayo refers the Court to three somewhat more recent decisions of other constitutions of this Court. Those are *Aranguren and others* (1994) 99 Cr.App.R. 347, *Attorney General's Reference Nos 64 and 65 of 1997 (O'Gorman and Hibbard)* [1999] 1 Cr.App.R.(S.) 237, and finally, *Attorney General's Reference No.146 of 2002 (Stewart)* [2003] 2 Cr.App.R.(S.) 107 (p.640). In the light of those decisions, it is contended that the sentence here of five years' imprisonment was significantly out of line with the authorities and was and is unduly lenient.

9   On behalf of the offender, Mr Singh submits that the offender may not have been trusted by those at the top of the distribution chain. Somebody tipped off the police and that may indicate a lack of trust on the part of those involved higher up the distribution chain. Mr Singh also emphasises that the offender was merely a courier, whereas those in *Attorney General Reference Nos 64 and 65 of 1997* were minders as well as couriers and must have been regarded as higher up the chain than this offender. The starting band, it is submitted, should be between six and eight years for this quantity in a contested case because the offender in the circumstances here should be regarded as someone near the bottom of the chain. That being so, five years' imprisonment should not be regarded as unduly lenient or, if so, should be so marginally unduly lenient that this Court in its discretion should not interfere.

10   Mohammed Attiq is aged 31. He has no previous convictions, and, indeed, there are a number of character references before the Court. Nonetheless, given the serious nature of this offence and the absence of any plea of guilty, a substantial prison sentence was clearly inevitable. We have already indicated that at 100 per cent purity the quantity of heroin in the possession of this offender was almost 1kg, with a street value of nearly a quarter of a million pounds.

11   In the case of offences involving distribution, we recognise that sheer quantity of the drugs in question is not the whole story: it is also important to consider how high up the chain of distribution the offender was. But we emphasise that these two matters are not unrelated. Anyone who is permitted by a major supplier to have sole possession of nearly a quarter of a million pounds worth of heroin and to convey it is clearly a well-trusted courier. We reject the argument that the tip-off to the police undermines that point. Whoever entrusted this man with these drugs would not want to be losing a quarter of a million pounds worth of heroin simply to implicate this offender.

12   In *Aranguren* this Court, presided over by the then Lord Chief Justice, Lord Taylor, dealt with the range of sentences appropriate for the importation of Class A drugs. As a guideline, it was suggested that where the weight of the

drugs involved at 100 per cent purity is half a kilo or more, then sentences of 10 years' imprisonment and upwards would be appropriate in a contested case at first instance. Although that was an importation case except in respect of one of the appellants, it is a decision which has been treated by this Court on previous occasions as providing helpful guidance in cases involving the supply of heroin: see, for example, *Robb and Akram* [1996] 2 Cr.App.R.(S.) 414.

13   The *Attorney General's Reference Nos 64 and 65 of 1997* are also clearly relevant. Both offenders there had pleaded guilty at the earliest opportunity to conspiracy to supply heroin. Both were treated as couriers and minders of the drugs, and both were of previous good character. The amount of heroin involved was about 1.5kg at 100 per cent purity. The offenders were originally sentenced at first instance to 30 months' imprisonment. This Court, on the reference, emphasised that couriers or minders are still people in the supply chain and because of the scale of the drugs involved the sentences there were increased to six years' imprisonment in each case. Those sentences made allowance both for the very early pleas of guilty and for the double jeopardy arising on a reference.

14   Finally, we refer to *Attorney General's Reference No.146 of 2002 (Stewart)*, where the offender again had pleaded guilty at a very early stage and again had done so on the basis that he was a courier. The amount involved was 363g of heroin, which he believed was cannabis, and he was sentenced on that basis. This Court increased his sentence from two years' imprisonment to four years, to allow for his plea of guilty, his belief that the drugs were cannabis and for the element of double jeopardy. It was indicated that five years' imprisonment would have been appropriate at first instance given the plea and of the order of seven and a half years or higher if the matter had been contested.

15   When one takes those three decisions into account, it is clear, in our judgment, that the five years imposed here was lenient and unduly so. There was no plea of guilty here—the matter was contested over a three-day trial—and so no credit could be given for that. The offender was a knowing courier of heroin, and the amount involved was very substantial—well over twice the quantity involved in the case of *Stewart*. He was, as we have already said, to be regarded as a highly trusted courier. Lengthy sentences are necessary in such cases to deter people from engaging in this horrendous, life-wrecking trade.

16   We take account of his previous good character and the other points made on his behalf by Mr Singh, but we have come to the conclusion that at first instance the appropriate sentence here could not have been less than nine years' imprisonment. Making allowance for the element of double jeopardy which arises on a reference, we set aside the sentence imposed below and in its place we shall substitute one of eight years' imprisonment.

R. v CHRISTOPHER PETER EYRE

COURT OF APPEAL (Lord Justice Scott Baker, Mr Justice Hunt and Judge Radford): April 21, 2004

[2004] EWCA Crim 1114; [2005] 1 Cr.App.R.(S.) 4

(LT) Abuse of position of trust; Children; Disqualification from working with children; Indecent exposure; Teachers

H1   *Abuse of trust—schoolteacher exposing penis to nine year old girl—length of sentence*

H2   Fifteen months' imprisonment for abuse of trust upheld on a school teacher who exposed his penis to a nine-year-old girl.

H3   The appellant was convicted of abusing a position of trust, contrary to the Sexual Offences (Amendment) Act 2000, s.3(1)(b). The appellant was a teacher at a primary school. He exposed his penis to a nine-year-old girl who was a pupil at the school, and told her that she should not tell anyone what had happened. The child told the headmistress. Sentenced to 15 months' imprisonment and disqualified from working with children.

H4   **Held:** the appellant was of previous good character. In the Court's view an immediate custodial sentence was inevitable, and the sentence of 15 months was not manifestly excessive.

H5   **Case cited:**   *MacNicol* [2004] 2 Cr.App.R.(S). 2 (p.6)

H6   **References:** abuse of trust, *Current Sentencing Practice* B 4-10

H7   *M. McNiff* for the applicant.

JUDGMENT

1   **SCOTT BAKER L.J.:**   On August 21, 2003, in the Crown Court at Norwich, before H.H. Judge Curl, this applicant was convicted of one count of abusing a position of trust contrary to s.3(1)(b) of the Sexual Offences (Amendment) Act 2000. He was acquitted of another count alleging the same offence. He was sentenced to 15 months' imprisonment, required to register for 10 years under the Sex Offenders Act 1997, and disqualified for five years from working with children, pursuant to s.28 of the Criminal Justice and Court Services Act 2000. He renews his application for leave to appeal against sentence after refusal by the single judge.

2   The facts of the case can be shortly stated. The applicant was a teacher at a primary school in Norfolk. During the lunch hour on October 11, 2002, the nine-year-old victim went to the classroom in a small mobile unit where the applicant was in order to see her sister and friend. When she arrived, the applicant asked her sister and the friend to leave whilst she was asked to stay. He took her into a cloakroom and whilst alone with her in the cloakroom, removed his penis from his clothing and exposed it to her before putting it back in his clothing. Other children began to return to the classroom. The victim became upset and burst into tears. The applicant told her that she was not to tell anyone, that it was their secret, and that he was sorry. She went to the headmistress with her sister and eventually revealed what had happened.

3   Following his arrest the applicant was interviewed. He declined to comment. In due course he pleaded not guilty and contested the allegation at the trial.

4   An offence under this section carries a maximum penalty of five years' imprisonment. The applicant is 29 years of age, of previous good character, and has a daughter aged five. The court had before it two reports: a pre-sentence report and a psychiatric report. The pre-sentence report told the Judge that the applicant qualified as a teacher in 1996 and had worked since then at various schools in Norfolk. Once the offence became public knowledge the applicant's life became increasingly difficult. He was shunned by many of his friends and received verbal abuse from others on a regular basis. He found that he could not leave his house and decided to move back to Derbyshire where his parents live. His partner and his child also moved back to Derbyshire. They live separately in a mortgaged property. At the time of the trial the applicant intended to return to live with his partner and child. His partner is supportive of him, but at the time of the trial the applicant was suffering from feelings of anxiety and depression. The judge had in mind that if the applicant does move back with his partner and child, the Social Services will have to undertake an investigation into such risk as he may present to his daughter. The applicant has realised that his teaching career is now at an end.

5   The trial judge also had a psychiatric report which he had ordered. In the event it seems to us that the psychiatric report adds little to the material information before the judge. However, it indicates that the applicant developed an acute stress reaction when the allegation was made against him and that anxiety symptoms persisted for some time.

6   When he came to pass sentence, the judge had clearly in mind that the applicant had been acquitted on a further count, the circumstances of which illustrated some of the background to the commission of the count 1 offence. But the judge made it absolutely clear that he was not sentencing the applicant on the allegations in the second count in respect of which the jury had acquitted him.

7   The question that arises for us is whether the sentence of 15 months' imprisonment, following as it did a contested trial, is either manifestly excessive or wrong in principle. The judge said that the case did not present an easy sentencing problem. The reason that he reached that conclusion is because there was no authority to give him any indication as to the appropriate level of sentence. The only case that we have been able to find is *MacNicol* [2004] 2 Cr.App.R.(S). 2 (p.6),

reported in *Current Sentencing News* for March 24, 2004, where a custodial term of 15 months, passed as part of an extended sentence for two offences of abuse of trust by a school teacher who engaged in sexual acts with two 16-year-old pupils, was upheld. The circumstances there were very different from those in the present case.

8   The judge had in mind that, as a result of the conviction, the applicant's family life was in jeopardy and that there would be a likely investigation by the Social Services with regard to the suitability of the applicant's five-year-old daughter living in the same household. He also had in mind the depression that the applicant had suffered since the matters had come to light. But that, in our judgment, is not the whole of the picture. The judge also had to reflect on the gravity of the offence and, most particularly, the effect it had had on the victim. We have seen a letter dated October 9 written by the girls' mother to the judge which illustrates very plainly just the kind of damage that is caused by serious offences of this nature.

9   We have given very careful consideration to the sentence that was passed by the judge in this case. In our view an immediate custodial sentence was inevitable. Mr McNiff, for the applicant, has submitted that the judge alighted on a sentence in excess of 12 months because he was determined to ensure that the applicant was disqualified from working with children. In our judgment, the judge was entitled to enquire of counsel what the minimum sentence was that would have that consequence. But the real question that he had to decide was: what was the appropriate sentence of imprisonment for the circumstances of this particular offence?

10   We have come to the clear conclusion that not only was an immediate custodial sentence inevitable, but also that the sentence that the judge passed of 15 months was in no way manifestly excessive. We can see nothing wrong with the sentence of 15 months' imprisonment after a trial. Indeed, in our judgment, if anything it was on the low side. In these circumstances this renewed application for leave to appeal must be refused.

R. v WILLIAM STEWARD

COURT OF APPEAL (Lord Justice Rose (Vice President, Court of Appeal, Criminal Division), Mr Justice Hughes and Mrs Justice Cox): April 21, 2004

[2004] EWCA Crim 1093; [2005] 1 Cr.App.R.(S.) 5

LT Aggravating features; Forcible entry; Intoxication; Rape; Sentence length; Threatening to kill; Violence

H1 *Rape—rape with multiple aggravating factors—length of sentence*

H2 Twelve years' imprisonment upheld for rape where the appellant forced his way into a hotel bedroom, raped a young woman several times and subjected her to violence, threats of death and oral sex.

H3 The appellant was convicted on four counts of rape. The appellant forced his way into to a hotel bedroom occupied by a young woman. He placed a hand over her mouth and threatened her with violence. He pinned her to the bed and threatened to kill her. When the woman attempted to escape, the appellant caught her and pulled the telephone out of its socket. He then required the woman to undress and raped her twice anally and twice vaginally. He forced her to perform oral sex on him and ejaculated in her vagina. He then left the hotel and was arrested shortly afterwards. The incident lasted about two hours. The appellant claimed in interview that the victim had consented. Sentenced to 12 years' imprisonment.

H4 **Held:** (considering *Millberry* [2003] 2 Cr.App.R.(S.) 31 (p.142)) five or six of the aggravating factors mentioned in *Millberry* were present. Violence was used over and above the force necessary to commit the offence; the victim suffered serious mental effects and was unable to continue with work which required her to stay in hotels; the victim had feared for a substantial period that she had been infected with HIV; the victim had been forced to participate in oral sex; the offender had broken into her hotel bedroom. All of these features were capable of aggravating the offence significantly above the eight-year starting point which was initially appropriate. The sentence of 12 years was severe but could not be said to be manifestly excessive. The appeal would be dismissed.

H5 **Case cited:** *Millberry* [2003] 2 Cr.App.R.(S.) 31 (p.142)

H6 **References:** rape, *Current Sentencing Practice* B 4-1

H7 *P. Fortune* for the appellant.

JUDGMENT

1   **ROSE L.J.:**   On June 19, 2003 at Lewes Crown Court, the appellant was convicted on four counts of rape and was sentenced by Aikens J. to 12 years' imprisonment on each count concurrently. Against that sentence he appeals by leave of the single judge.

2   The facts were these. On November 8, 2002, at about 4.00am, a 24-year-old woman, who was an IT consultant, was staying in a bedroom on the sixth floor of a hotel in Brighton. She was awakened by noise from the direction of the door of her room. She went to the door and opened it a little. The appellant was lying on the floor of the corridor outside. He put his foot in the door where it was ajar and prevented the victim (as she became) from shutting it. She asked what he was doing. He said he needed to get into his friend's room to get some money. When the young woman tried to close the door the appellant jumped to his feet and forced his way in. She screamed. He put his hand over her mouth and his other arm round her body. He said she must not scream or he would break her jaw. He threatened to smash her head against the wall and to kill her. He pinned her to the bed. He threatened to kill her with a gun. He locked the door and told her to get under the bed covers. At that stage he wandered round the room, rummaging through the young woman's belongings. She made a run for the door. The appellant caught her and dragged her back to the bed. She tried to reach the telephone. He pulled it out of its socket. He said that, if she tried to do that again, he would kill her.

3   He told her that he thought she was a prostitute. He told her to remove her pyjamas and put on her day clothes. She did so. He then told her to undress as he was going to rape her. She undressed. He raped her twice anally and twice vaginally. In addition, he forced her to perform oral sex upon him. He ejaculated in her vagina. After this he began to talk to her. He said he was desperate for a cigarette. She persuaded him to go with her to the reception in the hotel where she said she would buy some cigarettes. This happened and the appellant left the hotel with the cigarettes. The young woman contacted the hotel staff. The police were called, just before 6.00am. This incident had taken about two hours.

4   A few minutes after 6 o'clock police saw the appellant walking not far from the hotel and he was arrested. In interview, he gave a number of different accounts, but claimed to have had consensual intercourse with the young woman and he claimed she had given him her room number earlier in the evening when she had seen him in the street. He had assumed she was a prostitute.

5   The learned judge, in passing sentence, referred to the fact that the appellant at the time was under the influence of alcohol and drugs, and to that aspect in a moment we shall return. The judge commented that the hotel was a highly respectable one and, by some means, the appellant had reached its sixth floor. The judge referred to the ordeal lasting two hours and to the victim's presence of mind which had led to be able to get rid of the appellant. He referred to the significant effect on her physically and mentally, and to that, in a moment, we shall return.

6   The judge referred also to the use of violence to prevent the young woman escaping and the attack on the telephone, which was part of the violence. The judge accepted that the offences of rape had not been long planned but, said the judge, the appellant had gone to the hotel hoping to find someone he could either persuade or force to have intercourse with him. The influence of alcohol and drugs, said the judge, was not really a mitigating factor.

7   The judge referred to the appellant's difficult upbringing and criminal career starting when he was 14 years of age and to two particular relevant previous convictions, one of false imprisonment and robbery in 1997 and the other of wounding in 2001. To those also we shall return.

8   The judge concluded his sentencing observations by saying, having been referred to the relevant authority of *Millberry* [2003] 2 Cr.App.R.(S.) 31 (p.142) that there had to be an eight-year starting point because the attack involved repeated rapes and there were a number of aggravating features, namely the threats to kill, the use of violence over and above what was needed for the offences, the serious effect of the attack on the victim, the further degradation imposed upon her by forced oral sex, the fact that he had, effectively, broken into her room and the appellant's history of violent offences. The only mitigating features, the judge said, were, first, the appellant's age, and secondly, his lack of previous convictions for offences of rape.

9   On the appellant's behalf, Mr Fortune submits that 12 years was too long a sentence having regard, first, to the judge's inadequate regard to the level of intoxication. The appellant was apparently approximately three times over the alcohol legal limit for driving and, in addition, he had taken a considerable cocktail of drugs, some lawfully prescribed, but others including ecstasy, which were not. That drink and drug impact on the appellant, said Mr Fortune, was borne out by the statement made by the victim which referred to the changeability of the appellant's behaviour. Mr Fortune stressed that there was no planning of an offence of rape which was, he submitted, opportunistic. To those features, he said, the judge paid inadequate addition.

10   Secondly, Mr Fortune submitted that the judge's starting point of eight years, although a proper one, in the light of two of the matters identified at [20] of the judgment in *Millberry*, namely, the holding captive of the victim and the repeated rapes in the course of one attack, did not justify the sentence of 12 years which the learned judge imposed.

11   Mr Fortune also submitted that there was some overlap, at least, in the impact on the victim, as both an aggravating feature and as one of the two factors justifying the eight-year starting point. He accepted that the requirement for oral sex was one of the aggravating features identified at [32] of the *Millberry* judgment but he said that was a comparatively brief episode. No weapon was used, or in fact carried. There was no significant physical injury to the victim and the judge, Mr Fortune submitted, accorded too much weight to the appellant's previous offences. In relation to the first he was sentenced to five years' detention in a young offender institution at the age of 17, having pleaded guilty to falsely imprisoning and robbing a cab driver. The second resulted in a six-month sentence of

imprisonment, following a plea of guilty to wounding, in 2001, when the appellant had broken into premises armed with a gas canister and a baseball bat.

12 So far as the victim's impact statement is concerned, Mr Fortune points out, as is clearly the case, that the victim was an articulate young woman. He accepted that she must have endured a terrifying experience but she had in fact been believed by the jury which she had feared, at the time of that statement made about a week before the trial, might not be the case. Mr Fortune also told the Court, on the express instructions of the appellant, that he is determined to abandon his life of crime and he is presently having treatment by way of a sex offenders course in prison.

13 To all of these matters we have regard. It is to be noted that of the aggravating features identified at para.[32] of the judgment in *Millberry*, some five or six are present in this case. Violence was used over and above the force necessary to commit the offence. There was an especially serious mental effect on the victim, whose job required her to stay frequently in hotel bedrooms: in consequence of these offences, she had to leave the project that she was working on and, at the time of trial, could not contemplate staying in a hotel bedroom. The appellant, in the course of these offences, refused to wear a condom and the victim lived, for a substantial period, in the fear that she might, by reason of this, have been infected with HIV. There was the further degradation arising from the forced oral sex. There was the fact that the offender had broken into her bedroom and there was the history of violence reflected in the two offences to which we have referred. All of those features were capable, as it seems to us, of aggravating this offence so that the judge was entirely right to impose a sentence significantly above the eight-year starting point which was initially appropriate. There is no doubt that 12 years was a severe sentence. As it seems to us, it cannot be said that it was manifestly excessive and, in those circumstances, this appeal is dismissed.

[Paragraphs [14] and [15] have been omitted.]

R. (ON THE APPLICATION OF D) v ACTON YOUTH COURT, THE DIRECTOR OF PUBLIC PROSECUTIONS

DIVISIONAL COURT (Maurice Kay L.J. and Crane J.): April 21, 2004

[2004] EWHC 948 (Admin); [2005] 1 Cr.App.R.(S.) 6

Age; Indictable offences; Jurisdiction; Magistrates courts; Remittal for sentence; Young offenders; Youth courts

H1   *Youth court—defendant attaining age of 18 before conviction of offence triable only on indictment—whether youth court has power to remit defendant to adult magistrates' court*

H2   Where a defendant charged with an offence which is triable only on indictment before a youth court attains the age of 18 before he is convicted, the youth court should not remit him to an adult magistrates' court for sentence.

H3   The claimant was charged with an attempted robbery committed in July 2002, when he was 17. He appeared before a youth court in August 2002 when he pleaded not guilty. The trial was delayed and he was convicted of the offence in August 2003, by which time he was 18. The youth court adjourned sentence and remitted him to an adult magistrates' court, under the Powers of Criminal Courts (Sentencing) Act 2000, s.9(1). Under s.9(2)(b), an offender remitted under s.9(1) could be dealt with by the adult magistrates' court as if all the proceedings which had taken place before the youth court had taken place before the adult court. The issue arose as to the jurisdiction of the adult magistrates' court to deal with the claimant for an offence which was triable only on indictment in the case of an adult, and in relation to which the adult magistrates' court had no sentencing powers. The deputy district judge considered that the order of remittal was lawful because s.9(1) was not limited to "either way" offences. However, she considered herself to have no jurisdiction to deal with the claimant for an offence which was not triable summarily in the case of an adult. She considered that she had no power to return the case to the youth court as the claimant was now 18, and had no power to commit him to the Crown Court for sentence as the relevant provisions (Powers of Criminal Courts (Sentencing) Act 2000, ss.3 to 6) applied only to offences triable either way. Accordingly she adjourned the matter and invited the youth court to reconsider the order to remit, acting in accordance with the Magistrates Courts Act 1980, s.142(1). In the youth court, the claimant objected to any such reconsideration and applied to the Divisional Court for judicial review.

H4 **Held:** it was argued on behalf of the claimant that s.142 could not apply in the present case. It was argued on behalf of the prosecution that although s.9(1) of the 2000 Act did not in terms exclude indictable only offences from the power to remit to the adult court, it made no sense to remit a person to an adult court for sentence if the adult court had no power to sentence him. It was implicit from the wording of s.9(2)(b) that any such remit must be legally defective. Whether the defect was one of illegality or unreasonableness, it ought to lead to the quashing of the remittal with the result that the matter remained in the youth court where it began and belonged. The remittal would be quashed and the youth court would deal with the claimant. It was not necessary to deal with the question, but in the court's view, an order under s.9 of the 2000 Act was "an order made when dealing with an offender" and it was clear from the language of the Magistrates' Courts Act 1980, s.142, that a youth court could rescind a remittal under that section and could have done so in the present case. The adult court had not proceeded to sentence the claimant. The Court would quash the remittal order made by the youth court and direct that the matter be listed for sentence in the youth court as soon as possible. It would be helpful to youth courts and their advisers to have their attention drawn to the judgment, whose effect was that a youth court should never remit under s.9 in relation to an offence which would be triable only on indictment in the case of an adult. Unless the offence was such that it warranted committal to the Crown Court for trial, even in the case of a young person, it must be completed in the youth court. Whether this apparent lacuna was desirable was a matter which Parliament might wish to consider.

H5 **References:** remitment for sentence, *Current Sentencing Practice* L 13-1

H6 **Commentary:** [2004] Crim.L.R. 959

H7 *D. Bunting* for the claimant.
A. Ramsubhag for the Crown Prosecution Service.

JUDGMENT

1 **MAURICE KAY L.J.:** R D was born on June 15, 1985. He was charged with an offence of attempted robbery, alleged to have been committed on July 2, 2002 (at which time he was aged 17). At Acton Youth Court on August 27, 2002 he entered a plea of not guilty. For reasons which have not been fully explained, and for which it is difficult to believe that there can be an acceptable justification, he was not tried in the youth court for over a year.

2 The eventual finding of guilt in the youth court was on August 6, 2003 (by which time he was aged 18). The youth court then adjourned sentence and remitted him to Ealing Magistrates' Court, as the local adult court. That remittal was said to be pursuant to s.9(1) of the Powers of the Criminal Court (Sentencing) Act 2000, which provides:

"Where a person who appears or is brought before a youth court charged with an offence subsequently attains the age of 18, the youth court may, at any time after conviction and before sentence, remit him for sentence to a magistrates' court (other than a youth court) acting for the same petty sessions area as the youth court."

Section 9(2)(b) then provides:

"Where an offender is remitted under subsection (1) above the youth court shall adjourn proceedings in relation to the offence and . . .
    (b) . . . the court to which the offender is remitted . . . may deal with the
        case in any way in which it would have power to deal with it if all
        proceedings relating to the offence which took place before the
        youth court had taken place before the other court."

3   An issue then arose concerning the jurisdiction of the adult court. The case was listed for legal argument before a Deputy District Judge on October 13, 2003. The issue related to the jurisdiction of the adult court in view of the fact that the offence of attempted robbery is not an either way offence: in the case of an adult it is triable only on indictment. An adult magistrates' court has no sentencing powers in relation to it.

4   The Deputy District Judge considered that the order of remittal from the youth court had been lawful because the wording of s.9(1) of the 2000 Act is not limited to "either way" offences. However, she considered herself to be without jurisdiction in relation to an offence which, as regards an adult, is not triable summarily. She further considered herself powerless to remit the case back to the youth court for sentence as the offender was now aged 18, and powerless to commit him to the Crown Court for sentence because ss.3 to 6 of the 2000 Act apply only to "either way" offences. She therefore adjourned the matter in the adult court to November 10, remanding the claimant on conditional bail, whilst, at the same time, inviting the youth court in the meantime to reconsider the order to remit. She had established that the youth court could list the matter for reconsideration on the next day, October 14. She had in mind that such reconsideration might take place pursuant to s.142(1) of the Magistrates' Courts Act 1980 as amended. Section 142(1) provides that a magistrates' court:

". . . may vary or rescind a sentence or other order imposed or made by it when dealing with an offender; and it is hereby declared that this power extends to replacing a sentence or order which for any reason appears to be invalid by another which the court has power to impose or make."

5   At one time for that section to be resorted to the exercise of the power had to take place within a period of 28 days following the original sentence or order. However, that time limit has been removed by subsequent amendment.

6   On October 14 in the youth court objection was taken on behalf of the claimant to any such reconsideration. The matter was adjourned to enable an application to be made to this Court for judicial review. On January 2, 2004 Beatson J. granted

permission for such an application. The primary basis of that application was that s.142 does not apply in the present circumstances.

7   In his skeleton argument on behalf of the prosecution, as an interested party, Mr Ramsubhag sought to raise an issue about the lawfulness of the original order of the youth court to remit to the adult court for sentence.

8   It had been the case for the prosecution before the Deputy District Judge that the remittal was unlawful but she had not agreed. Mr Bunting, on behalf of the claimant, concedes that he is not taken by surprise by the matter being re-opened at this stage. He is in a position to deal with it without the need for an adjournment. We have indicated to counsel the view of the Court that we ought to allow the issue to be argued before us, notwithstanding that the youth court, as defendant, may not be on notice as to it. It is common for magistrates' courts, and similar bodies of a judicial nature, not to participate in proceedings such as this. The youth court as defendant has shown no previous sign of participating in these proceedings, although there is before us a witness statement of the Deputy District Judge who sat in the adult court.

9   The point made by Mr Ramsubhag is a fundamental one: although s.9 does not, in terms, exclude indictable only offences from the power to remit to the adult court, it plainly makes no sense to remit a person to an adult court for the specific purpose of sentence when, as is common ground, the adult court has no power to sentence him. I can envisage no circumstances in which it would be appropriate to remit (by reference to s.9) in the case of an offence triable only on indictment. In my judgment, it is implicit from the wording of s.9(2)(b) that any such remittal must be legally defective.

10   Mr Bunting's submission is that whilst he concedes that the remittal in the present case was *Wednesbury* unreasonable, it was not inherently unlawful so as to render it a nullity, and that the most that this Court should do at this stage is to declare the defect without returning the claimant to the youth court for sentence.

11   I do not accept this submission. Whether the defect is one of illegality or unreasonableness—and I take the view that it is primarily the former—in my judgment it ought to lead to the quashing of the remittal with the result that the matter remains in the youth court where it began and belongs.

12   Relief is of course a matter of discretion but, notwithstanding the passage of time, I can see no good reason why the public interest in seeing those convicted of offences sentenced for them should not be fully respected in the circumstances of this case. As it is, we know nothing of the circumstances of the offence, save that by definition it is a serious one, or the personal history of the claimant, save for his age. They are matters to be taken into consideration by the sentencing court, which can only give such weight as it sees fit for the delay. Again the reasons for it are not wholly within our cognisance, although it seems that at least some of the delay between remittal and the hearing before the Deputy District Judge was the fault of the claimant himself.

13   The quashing of the remittal, on the grounds to which I have referred, effectively disposes of this case. However, it is appropriate to address the points raised by Mr Bunting in his original application. They were to the effect that it would not have been open to the youth court to rescind the remittal pursuant to

s.142 because an order of remittal under s.9 is not "a sentence or other order imposed or made by it when dealing with an offender", and/or because the youth court had ceased to be seised of the case once it had made the order or, at the latest, once the adult court had become involved and, for example, granted bail.

14   In my judgment, a remittal under s.9 is "an order . . . made . . . when dealing with an offender." I do not accept that it is merely a lesser step of a preparatory or procedural nature, as Mr Bunting suggests. It is clear from the language of s.142 that "sentence" and "other order" are disjunctively linked by the word "or" and that whereas sentences are "imposed" other orders are "made". It is significant that they both relate to a time "when dealing with an offender". I have no doubt that, all other things being equal, a youth court can rescind a remittal by reference to s.142 and could have done so in this case.

15   I agree with Mr Bunting when he submits that a point will come when the youth court cannot re-visit the case under s.142 because it has been overtaken by the adult court. However, I do not accept that that point had been reached in this case. From the moment the adult court took up the case it did so on the basis that there was an issue, effectively one of jurisdiction, to be resolved before it could proceed further. It never reached the stage of considering sentence. All it did was arrange a hearing date for legal argument; determine that argument in the way I have described; adjourn and grant bail. In my view, that did not put s.142 beyond the reach of the youth court, especially when the adult court itself was encouraging the youth court to resort to s.142 and creating the circumstances in which it might do so.

16   In summary, I would refuse the application for judicial review as sought by the claimant, but would quash the remittal order for the reasons I have given. I would direct that the matter be listed in the youth court for sentence as soon as possible and further direct that the claimant attend when it is so listed. Failure to attend in such circumstances would be punishable as a contempt of this Court. The result of such orders would be to render further proceedings in the adult court nugatory.

17   It may be helpful to youth courts and their advisers to have their attention drawn to this judgment, the effect of which is that they should never remit under s.9 in relation to an offence which would be triable only on indictment in the case of an adult. Unless the offence is such that it warrants committal to the Crown Court for trial, even in the case of a young person, it must be completed in the youth court. Whether this apparent lacuna is desirable is a matter which Parliament may wish to consider.

18   **CRANE J.:**   I agree with the decision, the reasoning and the proposed order.
     [Paragraphs [19]–[27] have been omitted.]

R. v ARMANA LTD

COURT OF APPEAL (Lord Justice Kay, Mr Justice Roderick Evans
and Mr Justice Pitchers): April 22, 2004

[2004] EWCA Crim 1069; [2005] 1 Cr.App.R.(S.) 7

(LT) Fines; Fishing vessels; Offshore installations; Reasonable precautions;
Safety at sea; Strict liability

H1   *Public safety offences—owner of vessel entering safety zone around offshore
installation—plea of guilty on basis of strict liability—amount of fine*

H2   A fine of £40,000 imposed on the owner of a fishing vessel which entered the
safety zone around an offshore installation and collided with the installation
reduced to £15,000, on the basis that the owner had taken all reasonable precautions to avoid such an incident and pleaded guilty on the basis of strict
liability.

H3   The appellant company pleaded guilty before a magistrates' court to being the
owner of a fishing vessel which entered the safety zone around an offshore installation, contrary to the Petroleum Act 1987, s.23(2). The company was committed
to the Crown Court for sentence. The company owned a trawler which was underway to fishing grounds in the North Sea when it struck a gas platform, causing
damage to the platform and to the trawler. No injuries were caused. The master
of the vessel had 28 years' experience of which 12 were as a first class deck officer and master. There was a crew of 21. The company had implemented a safety
management system. Shortly before the incident, the master had handed over the
bridge to the second mate, giving him the instructions to watch out for gas installations. Subsequently visibility was reduced due to fog. The second mate did not
follow instructions to reduce speed. For some unexplained reason the vessel
changed course. When the installation was seen by a lookout, an attempt was
made to avoid a collision, but the trawler struck the installation a glancing
blow. The cost of putting right the damage to the installation, including the evacuation of the 128 personnel, amounted to more than £650,000. Sentenced to a fine
of £40,000 and ordered to pay £15,000 prosecution costs.

H4   **Held:** in passing sentence the sentencing judge acknowledged that the offence
with which the company was charged was one of strict liability, and that the guilty
plea had been entered on that basis. It was submitted that the fine failed to reflect
the level of culpability of the company and failed to take into account the company's financial circumstances. It was apparent that the level of the company's
culpability was at the bottom of the scale. There were no significant aggravating
features so far as the company was concerned. The company was not aware of a
likely breach and did not encourage or acquiesce in any breach of safety regu-

lations. The company had employed an experienced crew and officers, and organised and operated their vessels in such a way as to reduce the risk of breaches of safety procedures. The breach of the safety zone and subsequent collision did not arise through any operational failure of the safety management system. The appellants had a clear safety record with no cautions or previous convictions. They had co-operated fully with the investigating authorities and had suffered significant financial losses due to breach of the safety zone. In the year ending 2003, the company had lost more than £400,000. In fixing the fine in cases such as this, the court had to have regard to the level of culpability, the financial circumstances of the defendant and the consequences and potential consequences to others of the breach of safety which the court was examining. Bearing these matters in mind, it appeared to the Court that the fine was manifestly excessive. An appropriate level of sentence would be a fine of £15,000.

H5   **References:** public safety offences, *Current Sentencing Practice* B 13-2

H6   *I. Lawrie* for the appellants.

JUDGMENT

1   **RODERICK EVANS J.:**   On June 19, 2003 before the magistrates in the Kingston upon Hull & Holderness Magistrates' Court, in a prosecution brought by the Health & Safety Executive, the appellant company pleaded guilty to a charge of being the owner of a fishing vessel which entered the established 500-metre safety zone around an offshore installation contrary to s.23(2) of the Petroleum Act 1987. The installation in this case was a gas platform in the North Sea. The company was committed by the magistrates to the Crown Court for sentence and on August 19, 2003 in the Crown Court at Kingston upon Hull the company was fined £40,000 and ordered to pay £15,000 towards the costs of the prosecution. The company now appeals against that fine by leave of the single judge.

2   The prosecution arose out of an incident that occurred on May 8, 2002 when a trawler, the MFV *Marbella*, then underway in the North Sea from Hull to fishing grounds off Spitzbergen, struck the gas installation in what is known as the Rough Gas Field. As a result the installation suffered damage to two "boat bumpers" attached to a leg, and substantial damage was caused to the bow of the trawler, putting it out of operation for two months. No personal injuries resulted from this collision.

3   The appellant company are the owners of the MFV *Marbella*, which is a 14-year-old stern freezer trawler of 2,280 gross tonnage operating out of Kingston upon Hull.

4   On May 8 Captain Waddy was the master of the vessel. He had 28 years' trawling experience, with 15 years' deck officer certification, 12 of which were as a deck officer first class and master. The second mate was Mr Trevor Atkinson, a full deck certificated officer, with 13 years of trawling and seagoing experience,

who had frequently been employed by Armana on other vessels. There was also a crew of 21.

5   Armana Ltd had implemented a safety management system based on codes which were in place for merchant fleet vessels. Watchkeeping instructions, including proceedings when sailing in fog, were incorporated in the system. According to these, when sailing in fog speed should be reduced, the fog signal activated and the skipper called.

6   While the modern practice of passage planning in the form of a "staged and detailed plotted course" is advocated it was not adhered to by Captain Waddy. However, had the intended plot line marked on a chart been followed the collision would not have occurred and the vessel, so we are told, would have passed to the west of the safety zone by a small margin, but with a north west tide that would have been acceptable.

7   On the day in question the *Marbella* left Hull at 4.25am. At an appropriate point Captain Waddy handed over the bridge to the second mate, Mr Atkinson, explaining the radar set-up to make sure he was happy with everything on the bridge. As part of the handover Captain Waddy made it clear that he must watch out for gas installations in the Rough Gas Field and the installation was pointed out to him. The first mate also conducted a handover procedure and he saw the installations appear on the 12-mile radar and pointed it out to Mr Atkinson, who said that he would give them a wide berth. No complaint is made, nor could one be made, about the handover procedures that we have just mentioned.

8   Visibility at the time of the handover was good and clear at one to two miles, but due to fog it deteriorated to less than 200 yards. It appears that the second mate did not follow the instructions to reduce speed, sound the fog signal or call the master's assistance.

9   By 9.30am the vessel was proceeding at 13 knots and its course was plotted by radar on two other installations from which it appeared it would have passed outside the safety zone. However, for some unexplained reason the trawler changed course about 1.2 nautical miles from the installation. The change of course appears to have been unanticipated and unnecessary, and Mr Lawrie who appears before us on the part of the appellant company says that the only sensible explanation for that must have been human error.

10   The safety standby vessel for the field picked up the *Marbella* on radar but did not alert her to the fact that she was approaching the safety zone, apparently due to a faulty radio on the standby vessel. It appears that the second mate subsequently saw what he thought was another ship on the radar and shouted to the lookout, who replied that it was an installation and to pull the helm hard over. This was attempted, but it was too late and the starboard side of the *Marbella* struck the installation a glancing blow.

11   The subsequent cost of putting right the damage to the installation, the evacuation of its 128 personnel, a structural survey and remedial work on the installation was put at over £650,000.

12   Captain Waddy was subsequently interviewed by the Marine & Coastguard Agency and the Health & Safety Executive. The former informed the solicitors that they intended to take no further action other than to indicate a caution was

appropriate in the case of the master and a notification of concern in the case of the company. The Health & Safety Executive, however, proceeded to lay informations.

13   Captain Waddy entered a guilty plea to a charge similar to that which faced the appellants. He did that before the magistrates, was committed to the Crown Court for sentence and was fined £3,000.

14   The second mate, Trevor Atkinson, was prosecuted by the Marine & Coastguard Agency. He pleaded guilty on October 21 to a charge of failing to prevent a collision, contrary to the Merchant Shipping (Distress Signals & Prevention of Collisions) Regulations 1996 (SI 1996/75), and he was fined £1,000.

15   In passing sentence upon this company the recorder acknowledged that the offence with which the company was charged was one of strict liability and it was on that basis that the guilty plea had been entered.

16   Mr Lawrie submits that the fine imposed upon this company is manifestly excessive. It fails, he submits, to reflect the level of culpability of this company and the matters of mitigation which were available to it. Furthermore, he submits that the fine fails to take into account the financial circumstances of this particular company.

17   From the narration of the facts underlying this case it becomes apparent that the level of culpability of this company was at the bottom of the scale. There were numerous matters of mitigation upon which the company did, and did properly, rely. First of all, there were no significant aggravating features as far as the company were concerned. The company was not aware of a likely breach and did not encourage or acquiesce in any breach of safety regulations. The company had employed an experienced crew and deck officers, and organised and operated their vessels in such a way so as to reduce the risk of breaches of safety procedures occurring. Indeed the company had in operation a voluntary safety management system. The breach of a safety zone and the subsequent collision in this case did not arise through any operational failure of the safety management system put in place by the appellants. The appellants had a clean safety record, with no cautions or previous convictions recorded against it. Furthermore, as far as the proceedings were concerned they had cooperated fully with the investigating authorities and had indicated a guilty plea at a very early opportunity.

18   The company itself has suffered significant financial losses due to the breach of the safety zone. There was a loss of catch revenue of approximately £1 million, the repair costs before insurance cover operated was in the region of £30,000, and there was an additional £22,000 to be paid by way of insurance premium.

19   As far as the company itself is concerned and its financial circumstances, draft management accounts for the year ending 2003 showed the company to be in a parlous state. There was a loss before taxation of a little over £218,000 and a total loss on the year set at £449,557. The equity shareholders deficiency exceeded £800,000. Looked at in the round the company's finances were merely a reflection of the UK fishing fleet generally, and the future of that industry did not give any grounds for optimism as to signs of significant improvement.

20   In fixing the fine in cases such as this amongst the features that the court has to have regard to are the level of culpability, the financial circumstances of the

defendant, and the consequences and potential consequences to others of the breach of safety which the court is examining. Bearing those matters in mind in this case, together with the matters of mitigation to which we have referred it appears to us that this fine is indeed manifestly excessive. An appropriate level of sentence, in our view, is one of £15,000. Accordingly we quash the fine of £40,000 and in its place impose a fine of £15,000. To that extent the appeal is allowed.

[Paragraphs [21]–[32] have been omitted.]

R. v ANTHONY MALCOLM VITTLES

COURT OF APPEAL (Lord Justice Rose (Vice President, Court of Appeal, Criminal Division), Mr Justice Hughes and Mrs Justice Gloster): April 22, 2004

[2004] EWCA Crim 1089; [2005] 1 Cr.App.R.(S.) 8

LT Anti social behaviour orders; Area; Duration; Theft

H1 *Antisocial behaviour order on conviction—Crime and Disorder Act 1998, s.1C— order prohibiting offender indefinitely from entering particular district council area except to attend court—whether order appropriate*

H2   An order under the Crime and Disorder Act 1998, s.1C prohibiting an offender indefinitely from entering a particular district council area except to attend court approved in principle in the circumstances of the case but reduced in length to five years.

H3   The appellant pleaded guilty before a magistrates' court to theft, driving while disqualified and using a vehicle with no insurance. Twelve offences of theft and three of attempted theft were taken into consideration. The appellant was committed to the Crown Court for sentence under the Powers of Criminal Courts (Sentencing) Act 2000, ss.3 and 6. The appellant, who was a heavy drug user, admitted breaking into between 10 and 30 vehicles belonging to American servicemen who lived off airbases used by American forces. Such cars were readily identifiable. The offences involved theft of items from the owners of the motor cars, to a value of over £3,500. Sentenced to a total of three years and 10 months' imprisonment, with an order under the Crime and Disorder 1998, s.1C preventing the appellant for an indefinite period from entering a specified district council area except to attend court.

H4   **Held:** the sentencing judge observed that the appellant had a terrible criminal record, predominantly for theft from vehicles. The offences for which he was sentenced involved plundering the vehicles of American servicemen and their families in the specified local government area. The Court did not accept the submission that the total sentence was longer than it should have been. It was accepted that the order under s.1C was not open to criticism in principle, but it was submitted that it was not justifiable to impose a lifetime disqualification from entering the area concerned. The Court considered that it was not possible to specify the geographical area within which the order applied more precisely than in the order and took the view that an order preventing the appellant from entering the specified district council area save for the purposes of attending court was a proper sorder to make. The Court did not consider that an indefinite period was appropriate. The Court would quash the length of the antisocial behaviour order made by the judge and substitute an order for a period of five years running from the date on which the appellant was sentenced.

H5   **Case cited:** *Parkin* [2004] 2 Cr.App.R.(S.) 63 (p.343)

H6   **References:** orders under the Crime and Disorder Act 1998, s.1C, *Current Sentencing Practice* H 10

H7   *R. Potts* for the appellant.
R. Sadd for the Crown.

JUDGMENT

1   **ROSE L.J.:**   On October 2, 2003 at Northwest Suffolk Magistrates' Court, this applicant pleaded guilty and was committed to the Crown Court under s.3 of the Powers of Criminal Courts (Sentencing) Act 2000, in relation to the first two offences and under s.6 of the same Act in relation to the third offence. On November 6, 2003, at Ipswich Crown Court, he was sentenced by Bell J. in relation to offence No.1, which was theft, to three and a half years' imprisonment; offence No.2, driving while disqualified, four months' imprisonment consecutively; for offence No.3, using a vehicle with no insurance, no separate penalty was imposed. Twelve offences of theft and three of attempted theft were taken into consideration. The total sentence was therefore one of three years and 10 months' imprisonment. But, in addition, an antisocial behaviour order, under s.1 of the Crime and Disorder Act 1998, was made preventing the applicant from entering the Forest Heath District Council area, except to attend court, for an indefinite period. He was also disqualified from driving for three years. He renews to this Full Court his application for leave to appeal against sentence following refusal by the single judge.

2   The circumstances were that, during the night of June 2, 2003, the applicant broke into a car parked in the driveway of a home and stole a tool which was worth £20. The 15 offences which he asked to have taken into consideration all related to similar offences in which he had stolen over £3,500 worth of goods, of various kinds, from parked cars.

3   In interview, he admitted these offences. The prosecution case was that offence No.1 was a specimen offence, based on the admissions.

4   He had broken into somewhere between 10 and 30 vehicles, at night, in an area he knew well, particularly Lakenheath. He was a heavy drug user, requiring something of the order of £900 a week to feed his habit and he had, as he admitted, deliberately targeted cars belonging to American servicemen and their dependants who lived off the air bases at Lakenheath and Mildenhall and worked there. Such cars were, we are told by Mr Sadd, who has attended on behalf of the prosecution in this Court, readily identifiable because of a particular form of pink certificate which they carried within them.

5   The driving whiledisqualified came to light because, on September 26, 2003, a plain clothes police officer saw the applicant driving a car. He was stopped and, at that time, he was on bail for the theft offences to which we have referred.

6   In passing sentence, the judge said that the applicant had an absolutely terrible criminal record, predominantly for theft from vehicles and, occasionally, for driving while disqualified. It is apparent that his criminal record extends back to 1987 and bristles with offences of dishonesty, particularly, in recent times, thefts from motor vehicles of a kind similarly targeted to those in the present case.

7   The learned judge pointed out, rightly, that community sentences had not worked in the past and therefore a substantial custodial sentence was justified to deter the applicant and to give the public, from whom he stole, the protection which they deserved. He was, as the judge pointed out, plundering the vehicles of American servicemen and their families in this area. It was for those reasons, also, that the learned judge made the antisocial behaviour order to which earlier we have referred.

8   On behalf of the applicant Mr Potts submits, first, although a consecutive sentence for driving while disqualified, while on bail, could not be challenged in principle, a total resulting sentence of three years and 10 months was longer than it should have been. With that submission we do not agree. The learned judge, as it seems to us, having regard to the scope of this applicant's criminality, appropriately tailored the custodial term in relation to the theft offences and the driving while disqualified to a figure which still rendered the applicant a short-term prisoner. As it seems to us, no possible complaint can be made about that.

9   However, in relation to the antisocial behaviour order, Mr Potts submits that, although an order intended to protect those working at and living in the vicinity of the two American air bases could not be criticised in principle, the lifetime disqualification imposed by the learned judge is not supportable.

10   That submission, as it seems to us, is correct. Accordingly, we grant leave to appeal against that part of the judge's sentence and grant the necessary extension of time.

11   We have been referred to *Parkin* [2004] EWCA Crim 287; [2004] 2 Cr.App.R.(S.) 63 (p.343). But we take the view that the transient, vulnerable, nature of the American population specifically targeted by the appellant makes its appropriate that, exceptionally, an antisocial behaviour order should here be made, notwithstanding the imposition of a substantial prison sentence.

12   The question was canvassed with counsel on both sides, in the course of their helpful submissions to this Court, as to whether it might be possible, geographically, to limit the area of any antisocial behaviour order made, more closely than

the limitation imposed by the learned judge. Having considered that matter and a map of the area, we are not persuaded that, in practicable terms, a more sensible limitation could be imposed. We take the view that an order preventing the appellant (as he now is) from entering the Forest Heath District Council area, save for the purpose of attending court, was a proper order to make.

13   We do not, however, take the view, that an indefinite period is appropriate. We do, of course, bear in mind the statutory provision which enables the appellant to seek a discharge of such an order, after two years of its currency have lapsed.

14   In all the circumstances, we quash the length of the antisocial behaviour order made by the learned judge and we substitute, for the indefinite order, a period of five years, to run from November 6, 2003, on which date the appellant was sentenced. To that extent, this appeal is allowed.

[Paragraphs [15]–[16] have been omitted.]

R. v JOHN ANTHONY THOMAS

COURT OF APPEAL (Mr Justice Owen and Mr Justice Fulford):
April 22, 2004

[2004] EWCA Crim 1173; [2005] 1 Cr.App.R.(S.) 9

(LT) Anti social behaviour orders; Breach; Imprisonment; Return to custody;
Sentence length

H1   *Antisocial behaviour order—breach of order—second breach of order following release from custodial sentence imposed for earlier breach—length of sentence*

H2   Eighteen months' imprisonment upheld for breach of an antisocial behaviour by an offender who had just been released from a custodial sentence imposed for breach of the same order on an earlier occasion.

H3   The appellant was made subject to an anti-social behaviour order by a magistrates' court in June 2003. The order prohibited the appellant from entering four stores in a particular town until further order. The order was made on the basis that the appellant had entered the stores when drunk, stolen from them, refused to leave when asked to do so and had been abusive and threatening to staff at the premises. The appellant appeared before the magistrates' court for breach of the order and was sentenced to five months' imprisonment. Following his release from that sentence, he entered one of three specified stores and placed an item under his coat. He subsequently appeared before a magistrates' court where he admitted this second breach of the order and an offence of theft. He was committed to the Crown Court for sentence, where he was sentenced to 18 months' imprisonment for breach of the anti-social behaviour order, with one month's imprisonment concurrent for theft, the sentence to run consecutively to an order returning him to custody in respect of the first sentence.

H4   **Held:** the sentence was justified. The appellant had an appalling record and persisted in his criminal and anti-social behaviour, despite attempts by the courts to break the pattern of offending. He showed a flagrant disregard of the anti-social behaviour order by breaching it within weeks of it being made, and again within a matter of days after his release.

H5   **References:** breach of order, *Current Sentencing Practice* B 3-7

H6   *J. Jones* for the appellant.

JUDGMENT

1   **OWEN J.:**   On November 14, 2003, the appellant appeared at the Cardiff Magistrates' Court where he admitted breach of an antisocial behaviour order and pleaded guilty to an offence of theft. He was committed to the Crown Court for sentence. On December 5, 2003, in the Crown Court at Cardiff, he was sentenced to 18 months' imprisonment for breach of the antisocial behaviour order and one month imprisonment concurrent for the offence of theft. The sentencing judge directed that those sentences be served consecutively to the 69 days of licence recall. The appellant now appeals against sentence with the leave of the single judge.

2   The antisocial behaviour order was made on June 17, 2003 by the Cardiff Magistrates' Court. It prohibited the appellant from entering four stores in Llandaff North, Aquapets, the Co-operative store, Victoria Wine and Blockbusters, until further order. It was made on the basis that the appellant had stolen from those premises, had entered them when drunk, had refused to leave when asked to do so, had been abusive and threatening to staff at those premises and had loitered outside them when drunk.

3   The appellant is an alcoholic with an appalling record of petty offending. As the learned judge said in passing sentence upon him:

> "Your list of previous convictions is the longest by far of any list of previous convictions that I have ever seen. It contains 237 convictions for 451 offences, 263 of which are for offences of shoplifting or theft. That, undoubtedly is an aggravating feature so far as these offences are concerned."

4   On July 31, 2003, six weeks after the antisocial behaviour order was made, the Cardiff Magistrates' Court imposed a community rehabilitation order for offences of theft and of common assault. That order was breached four days later, on August 3. On September 1 the appellant again appeared before the Cardiff Magistrates' Court for breach of the antisocial behaviour order, having entered the Co-operative store Llandaff North. He was sentenced to five months' imprisonment. He was released on licence on October 17, 2003. Eight days later, on October 25, he again entered the Co-operative store, Llandaff North in further breach of the antisocial behaviour order. The store supervisor saw him in one of the aisles holding a can of beer with something under his coat. She approached

him and took from him a teddy bear valued at £19.99, which he had placed under his coat. After being ejected from the store, she saw him a short distance away holding a small, cuddly toy valued at £9.99. That was the breach for which he was sentenced at the Crown Court.

5   The offence of theft for which he was also sentenced was committed on November 13, 2003 when he entered a Tesco store (not one of those he was prohibited from entering under the antisocial behaviour order), took a joint of meat valued at £8.28 from a display counter and walked through the check-out without paying.

6   When he was interviewed in relation to these offences he said he thought that the antisocial behaviour order had expired and admitted the offence of shoplifting. Both the breach of the antisocial behaviour order and the offence of theft were committed whilst the appellant was on licence.

7   It is submitted by Mr Jones that the sentence of 18 months' imprisonment was manifestly excessive in that it failed adequately to reflect four matters: first, that the appellant had pleaded guilty at the earliest opportunity; secondly, that although on licence, he was not on bail for any offence at the time of committing the offences; thirdly, that there was no ancillary conviction to the breach on October 25; and fourthly, that the appellant had not shown any hostility or resistance to the shop manager on October 25. Mr Jones sought to amplify those points in his submission to us, suggesting that the sentence imposed was disproportionate to the offence in the sense that the behaviour of the appellant on October 25 did not in substance amount to the type of behaviour for which the order had been imposed in the first place.

8   In our judgment, and notwithstanding the manful efforts that Mr Jones has made on behalf of the appellant, we do not consider that there is substance to this appeal. As to the plea of guilty, the appellant had little choice but to admit his breach and to plead to the shoplifting. Secondly, that he was not on bail at the time of these offences affords scant mitigation, given that he was on licence. The proposition that the breach was mitigated by the fact that he did not, in addition, commit any other offences does not, in our judgment, weigh in his favour. Finally, the fact that he did not show any hostility or resistance when ejected from the Co-operative store affords little mitigation.

9   We consider that the sentence imposed by the learned judge was fully justified. The appellant has an appalling record. He persists in his criminal and antisocial behaviour, despite every attempt by the courts to break the pattern of his offending by the deployment of the entire range of sentencing options. He showed a flagrant disregard of the antisocial behaviour order, breaching it within weeks and breaching it again a matter of days after release on licence. He also showed a complete disregard of the community rehabilitation order imposed on July 31, breaching it within four days. In our judgment, the sentence of 18 months' imprisonment was entirely appropriate. Furthermore, the learned judge cannot be criticised for directing that it should be served consecutively to the term of recall to prison. It follows that this appeal must be dismissed.

R. v JC, MARCUS ARTRY

Court of Appeal (Lord Justice Latham, Mr Justice Aikens and
Judge Peter Beaumont Q.C.): April 22, 2004

[2004] EWCA Crim 1367; [2005] 1 Cr.App.R.(S.) 10

LT Age; Children; Detention; Indecency; Indecent assault; Rape; Sentencing
powers; Unlawful sentences; Young offenders

H1   *Long term detention of juvenile—rape and other sexual offences—availability of*
detention under the Powers of Criminal Courts (Sentencing) Act 2000, s.91

H2   Sentences totalling nine years' detention under the Powers of Criminal Courts
(Sentencing) Act 2000, s.91, imposed on two offenders aged under 18 for rape
and other sexual offences varied to a sentence of nine years' detention for
rape, with other sentences made concurrent or subject to no separate penalty.

H3   The appellants, aged respectively 13 or 14 and 17 at the time of the offences,
were convicted of rape, and pleaded guilty to other offences of indecent assault
and indecency with a child. The appellants met two women and succeeded in
separating them. The two appellants pushed one of the women up a road until
she fell into the road with her head against the pavement. Each of the appellants
raped the woman, one anally and one vaginally, while she lay in the gutter. The
victim was in pain and screamed. Neighbours in the street came out of their
houses and saw what was happening. The appellants ran off but were arrested.
Each claimed that the victim had consented to sexual intercourse for money.
The appellants were each convicted separately of rape and acquitted of aiding
and abetting the rape committed by the other. The appellants pleaded guilty to
other offences of indecent assault and indecency with a child, arising out of incidents in which girls were forced to take part in sexual acts against their wishes.
Sentenced in each case to a total of nine years' detention under the Powers of
Criminal Courts (Sentencing) Act 2000, s.91, made up of terms of seven
years' detention for rape and consecutive terms for the other offences.

H4   **Held:** so far as the rape was concerned, the offence was a case of a stranger rape
committed at night in a public street, in humiliating and demeaning circumstances for the victim and in a brutal and cynical manner. Consecutive
sentences of detention under s.91 were imposed on the first appellant for one
offence of indecent assault and two offences of indecency with a child. It was
now accepted that the sentence for indecency with a child was unlawful, as the
power to order to detention under s.91 did not apply to that offence. So far as
the second appellant was concerned the same problem arose. In the Court's
view, if the rape had been committed by two adults, the starting point would
have been eight years. Even though it was not a joint enterprise, the appellants

were acting together and it was a case of repeated rapes in the course of one attack. If the appellants had been adults, the offence would have attracted a sentence of 10 years or more after trial. It was accepted that each sentence should be discounted by reference to the age of the appellants. In relation to the other offences, difficulties arose because the offence of indecency with a child did not attract detention under s.91. It was now accepted that where an offender was to be sentenced for a number of offences, for some of which the power to order detention under s.91 was available, and for some of which it was not, the proper course was to order the offender to be detained for those offences in respect of which the power under s.91 was available for a term which was commensurate with the seriousness of all of the offences for which the sentence was being passed, and to impose no separate penalty for the offences in respect of which the power under s.91 was not available. In the Court's view, the offences taken together fully merited a total sentence of nine years' detention in the case of each appellant. The Court had considered the Criminal Appeal Act 1968, s.11(3) and concluded that if the overall justice of the case required a sentence of nine years' detention, it was within the power of the Court to impose such a sentence on both appellants. Accordingly the proper approach in relation to each appellant would be to substitute a sentence of nine years' detention under the Powers of Criminal Courts (Sentencing) Act 2000, s.91, for the offences of rape, to order the sentences for indecent assault to run concurrently, and to impose no separate penalty in respect of the offences of indecency with a child.

H5   **Cases cited:** *Millberry* [2003] 2 Cr.App.R.(S.) 31 (p.142), *Hayward and Hayward* [2001] 2 Cr.App.R.(S.) 31 (p.149), *Ghafoor* [2003] 1 Cr.App.R.(S.) 84 (p.428), *L.M.* [2003] 2 Cr.App.R.(S.) 26 (p.124), *Mills* [1998] 2 Cr.App.R.(S.) 128

H6   **References:** long term detention—rape, *Current Sentencing Practice* E4

H7   *G. Rees Q.C.* for the appellant C.
       Miss S. Wass Q.C. for the appellant Artry.
       Miss E. Broadbent for the Crown.

JUDGMENT

1   **AIKENS J.:**   J C is now aged 15 and a half. He was 13 and 14 at the time of the offences with which this appeal is concerned. He was just 15 at the time when he was sentenced. Marcus Artry is now aged 18. He was aged 17 at the time of the offences and was still 17, but only just, when he was convicted. On September 17, 2003 at Inner London Crown Court before H.H. Judge Smith Q.C. and a jury, C and Artry were both convicted of the rape of the same woman, who we shall refer to as MW, on February 8, 2003. The two appellants also pleaded guilty to a total of five other sexual offences on other girls in circumstances we shall mention. On November 7, 2003 the two appellants were each sentenced by H.H. Judge Smith to a total of nine years in a young offender institution.

2   The two appellants now appeal their sentences with the leave of the single judge. We understand from the submissions of Mr Rees Q.C. and Miss Wass Q.C. that the appeals are principally aimed at the sentences imposed on each young man for the rape of MW. However, issues arise in relation to the other sentences.

3   We will deal first of all with the facts relating to the rape of MW. In the evening of February 8, 2003, MW and a friend, who lived in the Woolwich area, had some alcohol and then decided to go out socially. MW was not particularly affected by the alcohol. The appellants approached the two women, whom the appellants had never met before. The appellants chatted to the two women and Artry kept the victim MW away from the other woman and gave MW his telephone number. Together they pushed MW up the road. In doing this C took the lead. The victim tried to run away but she was pushed and fell onto the road with her head against the pavement. She screamed, but then she was raped by each defendant in turn. Artry raped her anally and C raped her vaginally. At the time she was defenceless and on the ground. She was literally in the gutter of a public road in a residential area. She cried in pain and screamed. The judge said in his sentencing remarks that this all caused a lot of commotion in the street as neighbours came out and saw what was going on. One young child, A, witnessed the rapes and subsequently gave evidence at the trial.

4   The two appellants ran off eventually, leaving the victim to fend for herself as best she could in the street. The police were called. The appellants were caught and arrested. In interview they tried to suggest that MW had consented to sex in return for money. That defence was run at the trial and was clearly rejected by the jury.

5   Those facts gave rise to counts 18 and 19 on the indictment. Count 18 alleged anal rape by Artry as a principal and C was accused of aiding and abetting. Count 19 alleged vaginal rape by C as a principal and Artry was accused of aiding and abetting. As we have said, the defendants were convicted (as principals) of those two offences by the jury, although each was acquitted of the charge of being an aider and abettor of the rape by the other.

6   The other offences to which the two appellants pleaded guilty shortly before the trial all relate to two girls who were both known to each of the appellants. We will refer to the girls as RM and SC.

7   We deal first with the offences committed by C against RM. C wanted RM, who was 15 at the time, to go out with him. She refused. He pestered her to do so. She became frightened of him. The first offence concerning C was committed on July 11, 2002. On that occasion RM was with a friend. She was chased by C and two other youths, one of whom, Perry Wright, was a co-defendant at the trial. Wright was 17 at the time. C got RM in a headlock and took her into an alleyway where he forced his hand down her trousers, touched her bottom and tried to go round to her front. Eventually she got away from the youths, but when she got to her friend's house she was physically sick. That offence of indecent assault formed count 3 on the indictment.

8   Next we deal with the offences committed by both C and Artry against another girl who we will call SC. She was 14 at the time. SC knew Perry Wright who lived

across the road from her. Through him she got to know both appellants and another co-accused at the trial, Kyle Reid, who was also 17 at the time of these offences. At first they were on friendly social terms, but then the youths began to treat SC as a sex object.

9   On November 22, 2002, SC was taken by Kyle Reid to Plumstead Station. SC was told to take a train to Woolwich Docks Station. There she was met by Artry, C and Perry Wright. C was carrying a baseball bat. He told SC that she was going to lose her virginity that day. SC was taken to a male public lavatory. C decided that he, Artry and Wright should each be allotted five minutes with SC. C took her into one of the cubicles and there he forced her to perform oral sex on him. That was count 5 on the indictment. Wright then entered the cubicle. He had sexual intercourse with SC, which formed the subject matter of count 21 on the indictment (sexual intercourse with a girl under 16) with which we are not concerned. When Wright's allotted time was up, Artry entered the cubicle and he forced SC to perform oral sex on him. He then masturbated and ejaculated over her jacket. Those facts formed the basis of count 7 on the indictment, an offence of indecency with a child.

10   On January 18, 2003 C telephoned SC and told her to meet him. She did not wish to do so but went out after some threats from C. In an alleyway near a block of flats C forced her to perform oral sex on him. He then masturbated and wiped his penis on her jacket. Those facts formed the basis of count 16, indecency with a child. That was against C alone.

11   C then took SC to his home. They were joined by Artry and Reid. Reid was carrying a baseball bat and he threatened SC. The three took her into the flats. On a balcony Reid had both vaginal and anal intercourse with SC. Artry then forced SC to perform oral sex on him whilst they were still on the balcony. This was witnessed by the residents of the flats. Those facts gave rise to count 20 against Artry, which was an accusation of indecent assault.

12   We can attempt to summarise the offences committed by the two appellants, the sentences given to each and their pleas, as follows. First, dealing with JC. Count 3 was the indecent assault on RM, committed on July 11, 2002, to which he pleaded guilty. He was given six months in a young offender institution, purportedly under s.91 of the Powers of Criminal Courts (Sentencing) Act 2000. Again dealing with C, on count 5, indecency with SC on November 22, 2002, to which he pleaded guilty, he was sentenced to 12 months in a young offender institution, again purportedly under s.91 of the 2000 Act. On count 16, a charge of indecency with SC on January 18, 2003, he pleaded guilty and was sentenced purportedly to two years in a young offender institution under s.91. On count 19, vaginal rape on MW on February 8, 2003, he was convicted of that offence and sentenced to seven years under s.91.

13   In relation to Artry: on count 7, indecency with SC on November 22, 2002, he pleaded guilty and was sentenced to 12 months in a young offender institution. On count 18, anal rape on MW on February 8, 2003, he was convicted and sentenced to seven years in a young offender institution. On count 20, indecent assault on January 18, 2003 against SC, he pleaded guilty and was sentenced to two years in a young offender institution.

14   In passing sentence the judge dealt with the rape offences first. He referred to the guideline case of *Millberry* [2003] 2 Cr.App.R.(S.) 31 (p.142). The judge noted that in the present case:

       (1)   this was a case of stranger rape;

       (2)   it was at night in a public street;

       (3)   the rapes occurred in humiliating and demeaning circumstances for the victim;

       (4)   the rapes were carried out in a brutal and cynical manner. However he also concluded that the force used was not more than that necessary to commit the offence itself.

15   The judge concluded that the rapes demonstrated that the two appellants presented a risk of causing serious sexual harm to young women.

16   In relation to the offences against RM and SC, the judge concluded that the victims were targeted by the two appellants. He noted that SC was already an extremely vulnerable young person. The judge had before him, as we have, victim impact statements from all three complainants. It is very clear that these offences were deeply traumatic for the victims. Their lives have been dramatically altered for the worse as a result of these offences.

17   In relation to C, the judge noted that although he was the younger of the offenders with which we are concerned, he had taken the lead in all these events. However, he noted that on the authority of *Millberry*, C's youth meant he should receive a significantly shorter sentence than he would otherwise do for the offence of rape. The judge also took account of the fact that C had pleaded guilty to the offences committed against RM and SC.

18   In relation to Artry, the judge accepted that he had played a lesser part in these offences, although ultimately the judge concluded that he could find no difference in Artry's culpability relating to the rape offence. He also noted that Artry was older than C, that he was of previous good character and that he had pleaded guilty to the two offences involving SC.

19   In passing sentence on C the judge specifically stated that the seven years in a young offender institution for the offence of rape was imposed under s.91 of the Powers of Criminal Courts (Sentencing) Act 2000. The judge also purported to invoke s.91 to impose the other shorter sentences of detention in a young offender institution for one offence of indecent assault and two offences of indecency with a child. In relation to the offences of indecency with a child, those were, as is now accepted by all counsel involved, unlawful sentences. That is because, for an adult, the maximum sentence for that offence under s.1 of the Indecency with Children Act 1960 is 10 years. It is not 14 years or more, which is the qualifying condition before s.91 can be invoked in relation to offenders under 18. The judge was apparently not reminded of (1) the provisions of s.100 of the Powers of Criminal Courts (Sentencing) Act 2000, dealing with the regime of detention and training orders in relation to offenders under 18, nor (2) the case law which has laid down that a detention and training order should not be imposed to run consecutively to an order made under s.91 of the Powers of Criminal Courts (Sentencing) Act 2000—see *Hayward and Hayward* [2001] 2

Cr.App.R.(S.) 31 (p.149). There does seem to have been some limited discussion of the approach to be adopted on sentencing young persons who cross a relevant age barrier between the time of commission of an offence and the date of conviction—see for example *Ghafoor* [2003] 1 Cr.App.R.(S.) 84 (p.428); *L.M.* [2003] 2 Cr.App.R.(S.) 26 (p.124). This might have been important in the case of C who was 14 at the time of the offences. A DTO regime cannot be invoked for a 14-year-old unless the court is satisfied that he is a "persistent offender"—see s.101(2)(a) of the Powers of Criminal Courts (Sentencing) Act 2000. We shall return to this issue later.

20   In passing sentence on Artry the judge said that the sentence in relation to the rape would be seven years' "appropriate detention". As Artry was 17 at the time we take this to mean seven years' detention under s.91. In relation to the offence of indecency with a child against SC, the judge appeared to sentence Artry to a period of 12 months' detention in a young offender institution, apparently under s.91. Again the same problem that we have identified in relation to C also arises in relation to that sentence.

21   The single ground of appeal raised and the single argument advanced by Mr Rees Q.C. today on behalf of C was that the judge gave insufficient discount for his age. He submitted that in all the circumstances of this case a greater discount than that which the judge said he was giving would have been appropriate.

22   On behalf of Artry, Miss Wass Q.C. in her grounds of appeal and submissions today submitted first that the judge erred in treating this as a rape involving two persons. She submitted that the judge should have regarded this as two single rapes, one after the other. She relied upon the fact that the jury had acquitted the two appellants of being aiders and abettors of the other's rape. She submitted that this meant that the jury had concluded that there was no joint enterprise to rape between the two offenders and so this meant that this was not a case of rape by two people acting together. Secondly, Miss Wass submitted that the judge should not have regarded the fact that this was the rape of a stranger as an aggravating factor. She submitted that it is clear from his sentencing remarks that the judge did so. Thirdly, Miss Wass submitted that the judge did not give sufficient weight to the fact that Artry was a juvenile at the time of the offence. Fourthly, she submitted that the judge did not give sufficient weight to Artry's good character. Lastly, she submitted that in general the judge failed to give sufficient weight to the principle of totality.

23   All counsel accepted that we must be guided by the case of *Millberry* [2003] 2 Cr.App.R.(S.) 31 (p.142) in relation to the sentence to be imposed for the offences of rape. In that case the Lord Chief Justice set out the basic principle at [8], saying that there were three dimensions to consider in assessing the gravity of an individual offence of rape. The first is the degree of harm to the victim; the second is the level of culpability of the offender; and the third is the level of risk posed to society by the offender. The Lord Chief Justice went on to indicate that there were four "starting points" in relation to sentences for rape. Those are dealt with at paras [19] to [23] of the judgment.

24   In our view if the rape had been committed by two adults in this case then this would have been an eight-year "starting point" case. Even if, strictly speaking,

this was not a joint enterprise, these two were undoubtedly acting together; they were at the scene together; the rapes were conducted literally one after the other. This was, in our view, a case of repeated rapes in the course of one attack on that young woman. In our view, if these offenders had been adults their offences of rape would have attracted a sentence of 10 years or perhaps more after a trial.

25   In *Millberry* the Lord Chief Justice considered the impact of the age of the defendant on sentence, in particular when a young offender is involved. It is clear from para.[30] of the judgment in *Millberry* that the sentence for a young offender must be significantly shorter than it would have been if the offender had been an adult. However, as we have already noted, in this case the judge concluded that although C was the younger, he was the ringleader. The effect of that was that the discount to be given to each young offender should be the same. Miss Wass, on behalf of Artry, accepts that this approach was correct.

26   In relation to the other offences, the problem that we have to deal with concerns the age of the appellants and the fact that they were charged with offences of indecency with a child. In relation to C, as we have said, he was only 14 at the time of the offences and 15 at the time of conviction and sentence. That meant that the regime to be invoked would normally have been that of a DTO. However, it is clear, as we have pointed out, that a DTO cannot be added as a consecutive sentence to a sentence of detention in a young offender institution.

27   It is now accepted that what should have been done in this case is as set out in the case of *Mills* [1998] 2 Cr.App.R.(S.) 128, referred to at *Archbold* para.5–284, p.639. The principle is that where an offender is to be sentenced for a number of offences, for some of which the power to order detention (under s.91 of the 2000 Act) is available and for some of which it is not, the proper course is to order the offender to be detained (under s.91) for those offences in respect of which the power under s.91 is available, but to impose a term of detention which is commensurate with the seriousness of all the offences for which sentence is being passed. Thus no separate penalty will be imposed for those offences for which the s.91 power cannot be used.

28   What is our view of these offences? First of all we consider the rape offences. In relation to C we have come to the conclusion that the learned judge was absolutely right in his approach and we do not accept the submission made by Mr Rees that the judge failed to take sufficient account of the youth of the offender. However, there is a problem in relation to C because of the unlawfulness of the sentences that have been passed in relation to the offences of indecency with a child—that is to say those in relation to counts 5 and 16. The effect of this unlawfulness would be to reduce overall the sentence of the court to one of seven and a half years, that is to say seven years for the offence of rape and six months consecutive for the offence of indecent assault on RM. We must consider what the Court should do in relation to that in a moment.

29   As to the appellant Artry, we have also concluded that there can be absolutely no complaint about the judge's approach in relation to the sentence of seven years for the offence of rape. In his case the judge also imposed a sentence of two years consecutive in relation to the indecent assault on SC, under count 20. Accordingly, the total sentence for Artry was one of nine years. However, given the

view that we take, in line with that of the judge, that the culpability of both C and Artry in relation to the rape is the same, we have to consider what the consequences of our conclusion in relation to C are for both C and Artry.

30   Our view overall is that these offences taken together fully merited a total sentence of nine years' detention on each of the two appellants. Given that conclusion, the question which then arises is whether or not this Court has the power to see that the justice of these cases can be met by this Court. We were referred to s.11(3) of the Criminal Appeal Act 1968 which sets out the powers of this Court. That provides that:

> "On an appeal against sentence the Court of Appeal, if they consider that the appellant should be sentenced differently for an offence for which he was dealt with by the court below may—
> (a) quash any sentence or order which is the subject of the appeal; and
> (b) in place of it pass such sentence or make such order as they think appropriate for the case and as the court below had power to pass or make when dealing with him for the offence;
> but the Court shall so exercise their powers under this subsection that, taking the case as a whole, the appellant is not more severely dealt with on appeal than he was dealt with by the court below."

31   That subsection was considered by this Court in the case of *Sandwell* (1985) 80 Cr.App.R. 78. The facts of that case need not concern us. The question there which arose was whether or not the Court could increase the period of disqualification of a driver where the court had passed unlawful periods of disqualification in relation to offences committed. Glidewell J. (as he then was) giving the judgment of the Court, considered the effect of s.11(3) at p.81 of the judgment. He said:

> "'Taking the case as a whole' means, in our view, taking the totality of the matters in respect of which this appellant was being dealt with by the Crown Court at Bedford [that was the Crown Court in that case] on the one day. This Court, as Dunn LJ has pointed out not infrequently, substitutes, say for two consecutive sentences each of 12 months' imprisonment a concurrent sentence of say 18 months or two years on each count, having the same, or a lesser total effect. In our view precisely the same can be done with regard to disqualification from driving."

32   We have decided that in this case, if we conclude that the overall justice of the case is met by a sentence of nine years, it is within our power to impose such a sentence on both appellants. Accordingly, having regard to the principle set out in *Mills* [1998] 2 Cr.App.R.(S.) 128(to which we have already referred), we have concluded that the proper approach in relation to C should be as follows: for the offence of rape against MW, the sentence of seven years in a young offender should be quashed and for that a sentence of nine years should be substituted. The sentence of six months' detention in a young offender institution imposed in relation to indecent assault on RM on count 3, which the judge said should run consecutively to the rape sentence, will be quashed and instead

there will be substituted a sentence of six months in a young offender institution imposed under s.91 of the Powers of Criminal Courts (Sentencing) Act 2000. That term will run concurrently with the term of nine years imposed in relation to the rape offence. With regard to the two offences of indecency with a child committed against SC, there will be no separate penalty. Therefore, the total sentence on JC will be one of nine years' detention in a young offender institution.

33   In relation to Marcus Artry, we have concluded that because the culpability of Artry and C are the same in relation to the rape offence, the sentence of seven years for the rape of MW should be quashed. In its place a sentence of nine years (imposed under s.91 of the 2000 Act) should be substituted. However, in relation to the offence of indecent assault on SC, the sentence of two years in a young offender institution, which the judge said should run consecutively to the sentence in relation to the rape, will be quashed. Instead there will be substituted a sentence of two years' detention in a young offender institution, imposed under s.91 of the 2000 Act, such term to run concurrently with the term imposed in relation to the rape offence. In respect of the offence of indecency with a child against SC, there will be no separate penalty imposed on Artry.

34   To that limited extent the appeals in this case are allowed.

R. v ROBERT YOUNG

COURT OF APPEAL (Mr Justice Owen and Mr Justice Fulford):
April 23, 2004

[2004] EWCA Crim 1183; [2005] 1 Cr.App.R.(S.) 11

Guilty pleas; Learning difficulties; Sentence length; Sexual offences against mentally disordered persons

H1   *Sexual intercourse with defective—length of sentence*

H2   Fifteen months' imprisonment imposed on a man who had intercourse with a woman aged 27 who had severe learning difficulties reduced to nine months.

H3   The appellant pleaded guilty to having sexual intercourse with a defective, contrary to the Sexual Offences Act 1956, s.7(1). The appellant and another man knocked on the door of a house occupied by a woman aged 27 who had severe learning difficulties. The appellant and the other man pushed their way into the house and demanded sexual favours. The appellant had sexual intercourse with the woman. Sentenced to 15 months' imprisonment.

H4   **Held:** (considering *Adcock* [2000] 1 Cr.App.R.(S.) 563) no real distinction could be drawn between the facts of *Adcock* and those of the present case. The Court had come to the conclusion in the light of that decision that the sentence imposed on the appellant was excessive. A sentence of nine months' imprisonment would be substituted.

H5   **Case cited:**   *Adcock* [2000] 1 Cr.App.R.(S.) 563

H6   **References:** intercourse with defective, *Current Sentencing Practice* B 4-4

H7   *C.P.D. Dorman-O'Gowan* for the appellant.

JUDGMENT

1   **OWEN J.:**   On December 8, 2003, the appellant pleaded guilty to an offence of sexual intercourse with a defective contrary to s.7(1) of the Sexual Offences Act 1956 in the Crown Court at Newcastle. On January 12, 2004, he was sentenced to 15 months' imprisonment. His co-accused, Gary Sproston, pleaded guilty to aiding and abetting sexual intercourse with a defective and was sentenced to eight months' imprisonment. The appellant now appeals against sentence by leave of the single judge.

2   Their victim was a woman aged 27 who has severe learning difficulties (having the level of understanding of a six- or seven-year-old). In the early hours of May 19, 2003 she was awakened by a knock on her door. When she opened the door she found the appellant, whom she knew, and his co-accused on her door step. They pushed their way in and demanded sexual favours. The appellant then had sexual intercourse with her. The co-accused assisted him and also inserted his fingers into her vagina several times.

3   The offence came to light when the victim picked her seven-year-old daughter up from school later that day and told the head teacher what had happened.

4   It is submitted that the sentence imposed upon the appellant was manifestly excessive bearing in mind the mitigating factors, namely his previous good character, his remorse and shame and his plea at the earliest opportunity.

5   The prison report to this Court recorded that when his motivation for committing the offence was explored, he was unable to demonstrate any victim empathy, saying that he was not interested in how his victim was coping with the aftermath of the abuse. But this morning Mr Dorman-O'Gowan, for whose submissions we are grateful, explained the context in which that statement had been made. In essence what the appellant was saying to the probation officer was that he wanted to get on with his life, and wanted to leave her to get on with hers. In those circumstances we accept that the remorse that was expressed on his behalf before the sentencing judge was genuine.

6   It is also submitted on behalf of the appellant that he was not in a position of trust in relation to the victim. That is the case, but he was well aware of her learning difficulties. He went to her house that night, knowing her to be vulnerable and for the express purpose of having sexual intercourse with her.

7   This was a disgraceful episode. The appellant and his co-accused took advantage of their victim in a shameful manner. Furthermore, and as the learned judge observed, the offence was aggravated to a degree by the fact that to the knowledge

of the appellant their victim had a young daughter who was likely to be present in the house whilst they satisfied their sexual appetites on her mother.

8   In the course of his submissions this morning, Mr Dorman-O'Gowan drew our attention to the decision of this Court in the case of *Adcock* [2000] 1 Cr.App.R.(S.) 563. In that case the appellant pleaded guilty to indecent assault on a female and having sexual intercourse with a defective. The appellant was a night porter at a hotel. A woman aged 49, with learning difficulties, who was naive in sexual matters, obtained work as a cleaner at the hotel. The appellant indecently assaulted her by sucking her breast and touching her between the legs. A week later he locked the woman in a lavatory cubicle and had sexual intercourse with her. He claimed that she had consented on each occasion. He was sentenced to four months' imprisonment for indecent assault and to 18 months' imprisonment concurrently for unlawful sexual intercourse with a defective. He appealed to this Court. The judgment of the Court was given by Jackson J. He addressed the second submission advanced on behalf of the appellant, namely that the sentence imposed in relation to the offence of sexual intercourse with a defective was manifestly excessive, in the following terms:

> "Section 7 of the Sexual Offences Act 1956 provides that the maximum sentence for an offence of having sexual intercourse with a defective is two years' imprisonment. The points are made in this appeal that there are a number of mitigating factors: first, the appellant's previous good character; secondly, his plea of guilty; thirdly, his remorse and shame; fourthly, that, although serious, this was not the most serious offence of its kind because the appellant was not responsible for the complainant's care or otherwise in a position of trust in relation to her; and finally, from the statement of the social workers who were responsible for the complainant's care, it can be seen that she was not as seriously disabled as many persons falling within the protection of section 7 of the Sexual Offences Act 1956."

He continued:

> "We see considerable force in these submissions. As previously mentioned, the maximum sentence under the Act is two years' imprisonment. Having regard to the circumstances of this case, an appropriate sentence after trial for the appellant would have been between 13 and 14 months. A discount must be made for the fact that he pleaded guilty, sparing the complainant the need to attend court and give evidence. This court concludes that after making that discount the appropriate sentence on count 4 is one of nine months' imprisonment."

9   Mr Dorman-O'Gowan submits, correctly in our judgment, that no real distinction can be drawn between the facts of *Adcock* and those of the instant case. As in *Adcock*, the appellant is of good character; secondly, he has pleaded guilty to this offence, thereby sparing the complainant the ordeal of attending at court to give evidence; thirdly, he shows genuine remorse and shame for this unpleasant offence; and fourthly, this was not the most serious offence of its kind, given that the appellant was not in a position of trust in relation to the victim.

10   In those circumstances we have come to the conclusion that in the light of the decision of this Court in *Adcock* the sentence imposed upon the appellant was excessive. In our judgment, the appropriate sentence is one of nine months' imprisonment. Accordingly, this appeal will be allowed by quashing the sentence imposed at the Newcastle Crown Court and substituting for it a sentence of nine months' imprisonment.

R. v JACKSON CANN

COURT OF APPEAL (Mr Justice Roderick Evans and Mr Justice Pitchers): April 27, 2004

[2004] EWCA Crim 1075; [2005] 1 Cr.App.R.(S.) 12

LT Bomb hoaxing; Deterrence; Sentence length

H1   *Bomb hoax—falsely reporting bomb to police on three occasions—length of sentence*

H2   Thirty months' imprisonment for falsely reporting bombs to the police on three occasions reduced to 21 months.

H3   The appellant pleaded guilty before a magistrates' court to three offences of communicating a bomb hoax. He was committed to the Crown Court for sentence. On three occasions over a short period of time the appellant telephoned the police from a mobile telephone, giving a false name and saying that a bomb had been planted. Sentenced to 30 months' imprisonment.

H4   **Held:** (considering *Smith* [2002] EWCA Crim 1946, *Spencer*, unreported, June 29, 1998, *Enright and Cooper* [2001] EWCA Crim 62, *Walters* [2002] EWCA Crim 1114, *Hall* [2003] EWCA Crim 1714) offences of this kind had always to be regarded as of great seriousness and requiring deterrent sentences. The sight of the police deploying to deal with a perceived bomb threat caused alarm to members of the public, and police resources were wasted. The question was whether the judge had set the level too high. Having regard to the cases which had been cited, and giving full credit for the plea of guilty entered at an early opportunity, the Court considered that the appropriate total sentence would be 21 months' imprisonment.

H5   **Cases cited:**   *Smith* [2002] EWCA Crim 1946, *Spencer*, unreported, June 29, 1998, *Enright and Cooper* [2001] EWCA Crim 62, *Walters* [2002] EWCA Crim 1114, *Hall* [2003] EWCA Crim 1714

H6   **References:** communicating bomb hoax, *Current Sentencing Practice* B 7-3.3

H7   *N. Ham* for the appellant.
       R. Pearce for the Crown.

JUDGMENT

1   **PITCHERS J.:**   On August 15, 2003 this appellant pleaded guilty in the
magistrates' court to three offences of communicating a bomb hoax. He was
committed for sentence and at the Crown Court at Isleworth received a total sentence of 30 months. He appeals against that sentence with leave of the single
judge.

2   The facts were these. So far as the first count was concerned, on the evening of
June 1 he made a 999 call stating that there was a pink bag in a bin near a church in
Hounslow. Police officers put in place procedures, and resources were gathered
and officers deployed to the scene. He rang again later the same evening saying
that the police were not dealing with the bomb very well and that the bomb was
sensitive and if it were not touched it would go off in an hour. He gave a false
name.

3   Count 2: the following day, during the afternoon he telephoned the police to
say that there was a bomb in a black Mercedes car parked in the street. He
gave the same false name and was ringing from the same mobile telephone.
Again the police deployed the necessary resources and made enquiries to trace
the subscriber of the telephone.

4   Count 3: the following day again, at about midday, he telephoned on the same
mobile telephone, again gave the same name and again said that there was a bomb
in a black Mercedes. He said the vehicle was in an alleyway and had been abandoned and set alight the previous day. He gave the general location and said the
bomb would go off if it were touched.

5   The police were able to trace the mobile telephone, and attended at his house
and arrested him. When he was interviewed, he said that he had sold the telephone
and its SIM card to his neighbour and it was not he who had made the phone calls
but by implication must have been that neighbour. The neighbour was interviewed by the police. She agreed that she had bought the mobile telephone but
said that it did not include the SIM card, which had remained with the appellant.
He acknowledged, of course, by his pleas that it was indeed him.

6   He was a man of 22 and had no previous convictions.

7   There was personal mitigation, although the authorities are clear that that is of
limited weight in a case such as the present.

8   Two grounds of appeal were drafted by counsel, the second of which is only
rather faintly advanced today and we deal with it first. It was suggested that
the judge had wrongly taken into account something that he should not have
taken into account based upon this comment in his sentencing remarks (p.3,
line 17 of the transcript):

   "I have heard much about the defendant's personal position, but that comes
   in second place to the public interest in making clear that such offences do

mean custody, particularly in the present circumstances of a heightened awareness about public safety from possible bomb threats."

It is suggested that that comment indicates that he was taking into account the changed world circumstances following the events of September 11, 2001. This Court made clear in the case of *Smith* [2002] EWCA Crim 1946 that that was not appropriate, where Ouseley J., giving the judgment of the Court, said this:

> "It is, in our judgment, not appropriate for there to be any general increase in sentences for offences of this sort committed after September 11th 2001. It needs to be remembered that the previous cases concerning bomb hoaxes would have been committed during periods when the IRA and other terrorists were engaged in bombing on the mainland. Nor in this case was there any specific reference to the September 11th incident by the appellant so as to increase the fear and panic which the bomb hoax might have created, nor were these offences committed in the immediate aftermath of a particular incident nearby creating a greater than normal disruption."

9   In our judgment the words used by the judge in the present case fell far short of the kind of consideration which the Court was saying was wrong in *Smith*, and there is nothing in this ground.

10   The main ground of appeal is that the sentence was manifestly excessive. These sorts of offences have always in modern times to be regarded of great seriousness and requiring deterrent sentences. There are two broad reasons for that: one, the sight of the police deploying to deal with a perceived bomb threat causes great alarm to members of the public; and two, police resources, desperately needed in case of genuine threats, are diverted to time-wasting hoaxes.

11   We have been taken through a series of authorities helpfully by Mr Ham, who appears for the appellant today. We simply list them by name because of course each depends upon its own facts: *Spencer*, unreported, June 29, 1998; *Enright and Cooper* [2001] EWCA Crim 62; *Walters* [2002] EWCA Crim 1114; *Stuart Smith*, to which we have already referred; and, finally, *Hall* [2003] EWCA Crim 1714.

12   The question for us is whether, in pursuit of the legitimate sentencing aims of punishment and deterrence, the judge has in the present case set the level too high.

13   We have some sympathy for the judge in passing the sentence he did because, unguided by previous decisions of this Court, we might ourselves have passed very similar sentences. However the cases to which we have referred, although not in any sense guideline cases and each depending upon its own particular facts, do set out a general level of sentencing which indicates that, following an early guilty plea, the sentence of 30 months was too high. We have come to the conclusion that the appropriate sentence in the present case for these offences, giving full credit for the plea of guilty entered at an early opportunity, would be one of 21 months in total. The sentences of 21 months will take the place of the sentencing imposed by the judge below, giving a total of 21 months. To that extent this appeal is allowed.

R. v JAMIE JOHN FRANKS

COURT OF APPEAL (Lord Justice Rose (Vice President, Court of Appeal, Criminal Division), Mr Justice Hughes and Mrs Justice Gloster): April 28, 2004

[2004] EWCA Crim 1241; [2005] 1 Cr.App.R.(S.) 13

LT Cars; Detention; False statements; Jury directions; Manslaughter; Totality of sentence; Young offenders

H1   *Detention in a young offender institution—manslaughter—swerving car into man to prevent apprehension of accomplice—length of sentence*

H2   Ten years' detention in a young offender institution for manslaughter by swerving a car into a man to prevent the apprehension of an accomplice reduced to nine years (total sentence reduced from 12 years to 10).

H3   The appellant was convicted of manslaughter on an indictment charging him with murder. The appellant and three others were driving in a stolen car. They had been drinking and the appellant had taken various quantities of cocaine during the day. In the evening, they stole a mobile telephone from a person sitting at an adjoining table in a public house. The loser of the telephone and his associates went in pursuit. There was a struggle. Two of the appellant's companions reached the car in which the appellant was already sitting, but a third did not. The appellant drove off at speed, but returned a few moments later to fetch the third person, who broke free from those who were holding him and ran off down the road. He was pursued by one of those who had detained him. The appellant drove at speed in pursuit of the two running men and swerved suddenly to the left, striking the pursuing man with a car. The impact caused severe injuries from which he died. The appellant swung back and drove off. He lost control of the car and hit a wall. Later he set fire to the car in an attempt to destroy the evidence, but gave himself up to the police when he learned that the man he had hit had died. The appellant denied that he had steered the car towards the deceased. The jury was directed that if they were satisfied that the appellant deliberately swerved towards the deceased without the intention to kill or to do serious bodily harm, he would be guilty of manslaughter. Sentenced to 10 years' detention in a young offender institution for manslaughter, with 12 months consecutive for perverting justice and a total of 12 months, also consecutive, for dangerous driving and theft (total sentence, 12 years' detention in a young offender institution).

H4   **Held:** (considering *Gault* (1995) 16 Cr.App.R.(S.) 1013, *Ripley* [1997] 1 Cr.App.R.(S.) 19, *Attorney General's Reference No.64 of 1999* [2002] 1 Cr.App.R.(S.) 94 (p.409)) this was a serious case of manslaughter by the use of the car as a weapon. The car was aimed deliberately at the deceased, albeit with an intention to frighten or injure less than gravely. The car had been stolen and the appellant had taken quantities of alcohol and cocaine throughout the day. He was using it as part of an escape from a deliberate theft. The cases to which the Court had been referred suggested sentences after a plea of guilty of the order of six years in cases of this kind. That was consistent with a sentence following a trial of the order of nine years or more. The Court was impressed by the fact that the appellant was 18 with only relatively minor previous convictions and that there was the risk that the consecutive sentences for the other offences involved taking the facts of those offences into account twice. In the circumstances the Court had been persuaded that the sentence for manslaughter should be reduced to nine years, and the sentences for dangerous driving and theft would be ordered to run concurrently. The sentence of 12 months for perverting the course of justice would remain consecutive, with the result that the total sentence would be 10 years rather than 12 years.

H5 **Cases cited:** *Gault* (1995) 16 Cr.App.R.(S.) 1013, *Ripley* [1997] 1 Cr.App.R.(S.) 19, *Attorney General's Reference No.64 of 1999* [2002] 1 Cr.App.R.(S.) 94 (p.409)

H6 **References:** detention in a young offender institution, manslaughter, *Current Sentencing Practice* E 2-4

H7 *B. Cox* for the appellant.

JUDGMENT

1   **HUGHES J.:** This is a renewed application for leave to appeal against conviction and sentence.

2   The applicant, who is now 19, was convicted in the Crown Court at Leeds on August 20, 2003 of the offence of manslaughter on an indictment which charged murder. He contends that he should have leave to appeal his conviction on grounds which relate to the judge's directions concerning the jury's approach to lies told by him and also to expert evidence. The single judge refused leave.

3   On December 11, 2002, in company with a friend called Walker and two girls, the applicant was driving about Leeds in a stolen car on which he and Walker had put false number plates chosen as ones which matched the make, model and colour of the stolen vehicle. They had been drinking and, in the appellant's case at least, taking various quantities of cocaine on and off throughout the day.

4   In the evening, as a group of four, they stole a mobile telephone from somebody who happened to be sitting at an adjoining table in a public house. Whilst the applicant went out to get into the car in order to launch a getaway, one of the girls pretended to want to borrow the telephone and made off with it. The loser of the telephone, who was with a number of friends, realised what was happening. He and his associates went in pursuit. There was a struggle involving Walker and the girls, on the one hand, and the loser and his friends on the

other. In the ensuing commotion the girls successfully reached the applicant in the getaway car but Walker did not. The applicant thereupon drove off dangerously and at speed but a few moments later he returned in an effort to fetch Walker. Walker was by then being held by the friends of the loser and they included the man who was later killed, David Gellan. Walker managed to break free and he ran off down the road. The applicant sped after him. The deceased chased Walker on foot down the road, first down the right-hand side, as the applicant drove, and then, when Walker crossed, on the left. As the applicant drove, at considerable speed, in pursuit of those two running figures, he swerved suddenly to the left and struck Gellan with the car, just before Gellan reached the nearside pavement. The impact caused severe injuries from which Gellan died.

5   The track which the applicant adopted had taken the car into line with a parked car on the nearside but, after hitting Gellan, the applicant swung back to his offside, missing the parked car and drove off. He lost control subsequently, a little further on, and hit a wall, but he made good his escape. Later, he set fire to the car in an attempt to destroy the evidence. Subsequently, when he heard that the man he had hit had died, he gave himself up to the police.

6   When he was interviewed by the police the applicant gave an account which was false in several ways, although he admitted being the driver of the car. By the time of the trial he had pleaded guilty to a number of offences. They included the theft of the telephone, dangerous driving when first he had left the public house and, in addition, causing death by dangerous driving in the manoeuvre just described. That last plea was entered, as his leading counsel explicitly explained to the judge, on the basis of speed and failure to keep a lookout and failure to avoid a collision. The applicant disputed, at all times, that he had deliberately steered left at all. His account to the police and in due course his evidence at the trial, was that he had driven at speed in an effort to pick up Walker, that he had had no intention of driving at or near the deceased but that he had either coughed or blinked and suddenly found that he had hit him, when he had no idea that he was in his path.

7   In due course the jury was directed that, if they were satisfied that the applicant had deliberately swerved towards the deceased, that would result in a conviction for murder, providing he did it with the intention of killing or causing serious bodily harm to the deceased, and would give rise to a conviction of manslaughter if he did it with some lesser intention. If, lastly, the jury was not sure that he deliberately swerved towards the deceased, that would be the offence of causing death by dangerous driving, to which he had pleaded guilty, but would be neither murder nor manslaughter. There is and can be no complaint about that direction. The jury acquitted of murder but convicted of manslaughter.

         [Paragraphs [8]–[19] have been omitted.]

20   The total sentence passed was one of 12 years' detention. The applicant was, at the time of sentence, 18. He had some previous convictions of a comparatively minor kind. He had taken somebody else's car and driven it without insurance or driving licence on one occasion, and he had been dealt with on a second, for being drunk and disorderly. He had not previously been subject to any form of

custodial sentence. He had either had an attendance centre order or he had been conditionally discharged.

21   The total sentence of 12 years was made up as follows. For the manslaughter, 10 years: that was concurrent to sentences for driving while disqualified on this occasion, and for making off without making payment from a garage earlier in the day but it was consecutive to other sentences. Those were: for firing the car (perverting the course of justice), 12 months; for dangerous driving on the occasion immediately after leaving the public house, nine months and for the theft of the mobile telephone, three months. Thus, in addition to the manslaughter, a total of two further years, making 12 in all.

22   This was a serious case of manslaughter by use of a car as a weapon. The car was aimed deliberately at the deceased, albeit with an intention to frighten or to injure lesser than gravely. It was, in addition, a stolen car, of which the applicant had been making free use and it was driven by a man who had taken quantities of alcohol and cocaine throughout the day, and who was using it as part of an escape from a concerted and deliberate theft. There could be no reduction for a plea of guilty. Although, of course, the applicant pleaded guilty to causing death by dangerous driving, he put in issue and always denied the critical allegation that he had deliberately driven at the deceased. That is what he was convicted of doing.

23   We have looked at Mr Cox's invitation at a number of reported cases, beginning with *Gault* (1995) 16 Cr.App.R.(S.) 1013 and including also *Ripley* [1997] 1 Cr.App.R.(S.) 19 and *Attorney General's Reference No.64 of 1999* [2002] 1 Cr.App.R.(S.) 94 (p.409). Those cases suggest sentences, after a plea of guilty, of the order of six years or so in cases of this kind. That, in turn, is consistent with a sentence, following a trial, of the order of nine years or perhaps more. This case had, as we have said, the aggravating features that we have mentioned.

24   We are, however, impressed by two submissions. The first is that the defendant who fell to be sentenced was 18, with only the comparatively minor previous convictions that we have mentioned. The second is that, whilst the sentence for the offence of perverting the course of justice had, as a matter of principle, to be consecutive, the sentences for dangerous driving and theft of the telephone did not need to be and, if they were made consecutive, there was a real risk of taking the facts of those offences into account twice. First, as features aggravating the manslaughter, and secondly, by way of consecutive sentence.

25   In those circumstances, we are persuaded that we should grant leave to appeal against sentence and should allow the appeal to this extent. The sentences of nine months and three months respectively for dangerous driving and for theft of the mobile telephone will stand but will be made concurrent rather than consecutive to the sentence for manslaughter, and the sentence for manslaughter will be reduced to nine years. The net result of that is that the total sentence becomes one of 10 years rather than one of 12 years. The applicant, we are conscious, is not here, but Mr Cox has been able to agree to our dealing with the appeal against sentence on this occasion, and accordingly we do so. To that extent this appeal is allowed.

[Paragraphs [26] and [27] have been omitted.]

ATTORNEY GENERAL'S REFERENCE NO.2 OF 2004 (DANIEL JOHN NEVILLE)

COURT OF APPEAL (Lord Justice Latham, Mrs Justice Cox and Judge Beaumont Q.C.): April 28, 2004

[2004] EWCA Crim 1280; [2005] 1 Cr.App.R.(S.) 14

ᴌᴛ Community punishment and rehabilitation orders; False imprisonment; Handcuffing; Undue leniency

H1 *False imprisonment—offender detaining former girlfriend for six hours— whether community punishment and rehabilitation order adequate*

H2   A community punishment and rehabilitation order for false imprisonment imposed on a man who detained his girlfriend in his flat and kept her naked and handcuffed for six hours varied to 18 months' imprisonment.

H3   The offender, aged 21 at the time of the offence, was convicted of false impri- sonment. The offender formed a relationship with a young woman of the same age whom he had met about three weeks before the offence. The young woman went to stay at the offender's flat, but the relationship ran into difficulties and she removed her belongings from the flat. They subsequently arranged to meet at a public house and returned to the offender's flat, where an argument began. When the young woman tried to leave, the offender prevented her from leaving by sitting astride her, pressing her throat and slapping and punching her. The assault lasted about 45 minutes. The offender then pulled the young woman into his bedroom, stripped her naked and then handcuffed her to the bed. He committed further assaults while she was handcuffed. The young woman remained handcuffed for about six hours until she was released by the offender. Sentenced to a community punishment and rehabilitation order requir- ing 100 hours' work and two years' supervision. The Attorney General asked the Court to review the sentence on the ground that it was unduly lenient.

H4   **Held:** it was suggested for the Attorney General that the appropriate bracket for the offence in the light of the authorities was between two and three years' imprisonment. For the offender it was submitted that the offence arose out of an existing relationship, and was therefore at the lower end of the scale of kidnap- ping offences. The offender did not have the benefit of a plea of guilty. The Court considered that the Attorney General's submission was right and that the appro- priate bracket was two to three years' imprisonment. Taking into account the element of double jeopardy and the fact that the offender had completed 100 hours of community service, the Court would substitute sentence of 18 months' imprisonment.

H5   **Case cited:**   *Spence and Thomas* (1984) 5 Cr.App.R.(S.) 413

H6   **References:** False imprisonment, *Current Sentencing Practice* B 3-4

H7   *Miss S. Whitehouse* for the Attorney General.
        Miss H. Valley for the offender.

JUDGMENT

1   **LATHAM L.J.:**   This is an application by Her Majesty's Attorney General for leave to refer to this Court a sentence imposed on December 5, 2003 on the offender for an offence of false imprisonment for which he received a sentence of a community punishment order of 100 hours and a community rehabilitation order for two years.

2   The offender is now 22 years of age. At the time of the offence he was 21 years of age. He had formed a relationship with the victim, TR. She was the same age as him and they had met about three weeks before the offence. Within a short time the victim had begun to stay at the offender's flat; but unhappily the relationship ran into difficulties because, according to Miss R, the offender was possessive. On July 2, 2002, which was the date of the offenders's birthday, she removed her belongings from the flat.

3   There was then a telephone conversation two days later between the victim and the offender as a result of which they arranged to meet at a public house. They there had an argument because the offender learnt that Miss R had been kissed by a friend of his on the day of his, that is the offender's, birthday. Despite the fact that they had had the argument they went back to the offender's flat. There the offender accused the victim of having had a sexual relationship with that friend; he had discovered the friend's telephone number in the memory of the victim's mobile telephone.

4   There was then predictably an argument. The victim tried to leave. The offender prevented her from leaving by sitting astride her. He pressed her windpipe, slapped her, punched her on the face, legs and stomach; and this assault lasted, according to her, approximately 45 minutes. He then pulled her into his bedroom and stripped her naked. He handcuffed her, first to himself and then to the bed. She was terrified that he was going to rape her. In fact he never did. Whilst she was in the handcuffs she was subjected to further assaults. She was grabbed by the throat; and he put his hands over her mouth. She remained in that condition from about 1 o'clock in the morning until 7 o'clock in the morning. She was then released from the handcuffs by the offender and they then left the home on the basis that the offender indicated that they should go to his mother's. As they left she managed to escape and ran to a safe house.

5   She was examined by a police doctor and was found to have areas of swelling on her face, back and right of side of her head and a significant bruise over her left hipbone.

6   The offender had no previous convictions and was at the time of sentence a man who was in work.

7   The Attorney General submits that the length of time over which the victim was held and the circumstances in which she was held, were such that it was inappropriate for any other sentence than a custodial sentence to have been imposed, despite the fact that the offender had no previous convictions and was relatively young at the time that the offence was committed.

8   We have been referred to a number of authorities which suggest, it is submitted, that the appropriate bracket for sentence would have been somewhere between two and three years' imprisonment.

9   Miss Valley, on behalf of the offender, points out, as was pointed out to the sentencing recorder, that the events arose out of a relationship—this was not a case of a person being snatched from the street; it occurred at the end of a row between people who had been in a relationship and therefore, it is said, it falls within the category of offence which was described by the then Lord Chief Justice, Lord Lane, in *Spence and Thomas* (1984) 5 Cr.App.R.(S.) 413 as at the lowest end of the scale of kidnapping offences which, as the Lord Chief Justice put it, very often arise as a sequel to family tiffs or lovers' disputes. He suggested that those incidents seldom required anything more than 18 months' imprisonment and sometimes a great deal less. In those circumstances, Miss Valley submits, although a community penalty might be considered to be lenient, it could not properly be described as unduly lenient.

10   It seems to us that the difficulty for Miss Valley in making good that submission is that the offender did not have the benefit of a plea of guilty to his credit. In these types of case a plea of guilty and clear remorse might well justify a course which would otherwise be inappropriate.

11   We consider that the Attorney General's submission is right, that the appropriate bracket in this case was two to three years' imprisonment. But clearly we have today to take into account not only the element of double jeopardy but also the fact that the offender has completed the 100 hours of community service which he was ordered to serve. In those circumstances it seems to us that the right sentence today is one of 18 months' imprisonment.

    [Paragraphs [12]–[15] have been omitted.]

ATTORNEY GENERAL'S REFERENCE NO.25 OF 2004 (ALAN THOMAS GAY)

COURT OF APPEAL (Lord Justice Rose (Vice President, Court of Appeal, Criminal Division), Mr Justice Hughes and Mrs Justice Gloster): April 28, 2004

[2004] EWCA Crim 1203; [2005] 1 Cr.App.R.(S.) 15

⌐LT⌐ Community punishment and rehabilitation orders; False imprisonment; Mental illness; Threatening to kill; Undue leniency

H1   *False imprisonment—lodger imprisoning landlady in her house for an hour and a half and threatening to kill her—whether community punishment and rehabilitation order adequate*

H2   A community punishment and rehabilitation order for false imprisonment, where a former lodger imprisoned his landlady in her house for an hour and a half and threatened to kill her, considered unduly lenient but not varied in the exercise of the Court's discretion.

H3   The offender pleaded guilty to one count of false imprisonment and asked for an offence of common assault to be taken into consideration. The offender moved into the victim's house as a lodger. He had previously known the victim for some years. The victim went out with a male friend to celebrate her birthday, and subsequently returned home with the friend. The offender became jealous. When the victim asked him what was wrong, the offender slapped her with his open hand and slapped her again when she slapped him in return. The police were called and the offender was arrested. The victim complained to the police that the offender had indecently assaulted her some days earlier. The offender was charged with indecent assault. He appeared at a magistrates' court and was bailed on condition that he did not enter the county in which the victim lived. Three days later the offender telephoned the victim and later forced his way into her house, pushed another lodger out of the house and locked the doors. The victim tried to call the police but the offender tore out the telephone wires. The offender detained the victim until the police arrived after about one and a half hours. He threatened to commit suicide and to kill the victim. He put the blade of a knife to her throat and another knife to his own throat. These actions were demonstrated to the police. Eventually the victim was able to escape from an open first-floor window. The offender was eventually overpowered by police and taken to hospital. The offender had various previous convictions for offences of dishonesty, but none for violence. The offender maintained throughout that he had intended no harm to the victim or her children. Sentenced to a community punishment and rehabilitation order, with 100 hours' work and two years' supervision. The

Attorney General asked the Court to review the sentence on the ground that it was unduly lenient.

H4   **Held:** (considering *Brown* (1994) 15 Cr.App.R.(S.) 337, *Butterworth* (1993) 14 Cr.App.R.(S.) 674, *Hibbert* [2002] 2 Cr.App.R.(S.) 29 (p.106), *Ashbridge* [2002] 2 Cr.App.R.(S.) 89 (p.408)) for the Attorney General it was submitted that the offence was aggravated by the fact that it was a second offence directed towards the victim, it involved an invasion of the family home and took place in breach of conditions of bail. The offender made an immediate admission of the offence and pleaded guilty at the earliest opportunity. In the Court's view, the sentencing judge had an extremely difficult task. If there were no exceptional mitigating circumstances, a sentence of the order of three years' imprisonment would have been appropriate on a guilty plea. It followed that the sentence imposed was an unduly lenient sentence. However the Court had formed the view that the public interest did not require that the offender should be sent to prison. Although the Court considered that the sentence was at first blush unduly lenient, the Court did not think it right to interfere with it.

H5   **Cases cited:** *Brown* (1994) 15 Cr.App.R.(S.) 337, *Butterworth* (1993) 14 Cr.App.R.(S.) 674, *Hibbert* [2002] 2 Cr.App.R.(S.) 29 (p.106), *Ashbridge* [2002] 2 Cr.App.R.(S.) 89 (p.408)

H6   **References:** false imprisonment, *Current Sentencing Practice* B 3-4

H7   *A. Derbyshire* for the Attorney General.
      G. Aspden for the offender.

JUDGMENT

1   **ROSE L.J.:**   The Attorney General seeks the leave of the Court, under s.36 of the Criminal Justice Act 1988, to refer a sentence which is said to be unduly lenient. We grant leave.

2   The offender was born in June 1957 and is therefore 46 years of age. On December 19, 2003 he pleaded guilty to a single count of false imprisonment and asked for a further offence of common assault to be taken into consideration. Sentence was adjourned for the preparation of pre-sentence and psychiatric reports. On February 6, 2004 he was sentenced by H.H. Judge Machin, at Lincoln Crown Court, to a 100-hour community punishment order and to a community rehabilitation order for two years.

3   The circumstances, in outline, were that the offender assaulted his landlady at the house where he lived as a lodger. He was arrested and charged with offences against her and granted bail, subject to conditions that he should not return to the area and he should not contact her. Three days after bail was granted, he returned to the house and imprisoned his landlady inside. He too was inside and, at one point, he put a knife to her throat. She was there for about an hour. She escaped through an upstairs window.

4   In a little more detail, the victim lived with her two children, who were aged 13 and 11, in a house in Market Deeping, in Lincolnshire. She took in lodgers to pay the rent. There was another lodger there in his sixties, and in poor health.

5   On October 1, 2003 the offender, who had previously lodged with the victim's friend, moved to the victim's house as a second lodger. He and the victim had known each other for two or three years. According to the victim, the offender would behave strangely and, at first, she put that down to medication which she understood him to be taking for depression. It appears that he had developed an affection for the victim which she did not reciprocate and he, in consequence, was frustrated and anxious.

6   On the evening of November 24, 2003 the victim, having been out celebrating her birthday, returned home with a male friend. They put on music and danced. The offender and the 13-year-old child were also in the house. The offender was jealous. He began to behave oddly, coming downstairs and then going back upstairs and mumbling and, at one stage, he left the house, carrying his socks and shoes. He went out by the front door but came back immediately by the back door.

7   The victim spoke to him to find out what was wrong. He told her to go away. He then suddenly slapped her with his open hand and she slapped him back. He slapped her again, harder, causing her to reel back. Her male friend stood up to stop any further violence and the offender said that "if he was to start he would kill him". The offender went into the kitchen and closed the door, where he could be heard opening drawers and removing knives. Understandably, the victim was afraid. Her daughter telephoned the police.

8   When they arrived, the offender was lying face down on the kitchen floor, bare chested. He was lying on top of a wooden curtail pole which he had broken from the kitchen window. There were two knives near his head and others on the work top surfaces. There was a brief struggle. He was arrested.

9   In a statement which she made the following day, the victim described these matters and said that she was very frightened, both for herself and her children. She packed up his possessions for collection and she did not want him back in her house or to contact her in any way. She also described an indecent assault on her, in her home, by the offender on November 18. She had not previously complained about that but now she wanted to pursue the matter and the offender was charged. The offence of indecent assault was remitted to the magistrates' court on December 19, 2003, which was the date on which the offender pleaded guilty to the false imprisonment charge. There had been a defect in the procedure remitting the matter to the Crown Court.

10   The offender had appeared at the magistrates' court on November 25, charged with indecent assault and common assault. He was bailed, on condition that he lived at his sister's in Peterborough and did not enter Lincolnshire.

11   There was no further contact between the victim and the offender until three days later, on November 28. At about 3.30 that afternoon, he telephoned her and spoke to her. She could not understand what he was talking about and put the telephone down. He rang again and asked to speak to the other lodger. Again, she put the telephone down and she went out. She returned about an

hour later and was sitting in the living room with the other lodger. The offender burst in, by the back door, which he locked behind him, pushed the other lodger out of the front door and locked that. The victim tried to call the police but the offender tore out the telephone wires. The victim was very scared, crying and shaking.

12   Her nine-year-old son returned home. The offender let him in. He told him to stand in the living room and let the offender know when his sister came back. The offender said to the boy that he would not hurt his mother. The sister came back a few minutes later but, when she was inside the house, the offender pushed her and her brother out again. He then told the victim to sit down and he removed his upper clothing. He picked up some knives and tied them round himself with string, first, sitting in an armchair and, then, tying himself to the bannister. He said that he did not care about his life any more but he was not going to hurt her. The doors were locked and the keys thrown by the offender onto the staircase so that they were inaccessible to the victim.

13   Police arrived shortly after 5.00pm. The offender was shouting and irate. He told the victim to speak to them from the window and tell them to go back to the station until she rang, otherwise he was going to take both their lives. The victim thought that the offender meant what he said. He squashed her against the wall by a window and stood with his arms around her. He put the blade of the knife to her throat and another knife to his own throat. These acts were demonstrated to the police, who were watching below. The offender was described as "very agitated" and holding the knife to the victim's throat for about two minutes. Then he released her. He ordered her to go upstairs. He followed her. He told her to speak to the officers through the upstairs window, which she did. When he returned downstairs she was able to escape through the open first floor window and to climb down over a small adjacent roof.

14   The offender appeared at the front of the house wielding a knife. Later he was seen at the rear, shouting at police officers and occasionally throwing objects at them. He was eventually rendered unconscious by the police using a Taser gun. He was taken to hospital.

15   In the statement which she made later that day, the victim described, on her part, a great amount of fear and being terrified in her own home and thinking he would kill her. She also found, after the offender had been arrested, that he had turned the house upside down.

16   In interview, on November 29, the offender said that on the 28th he had consumed a large amount of alcohol at a public house and become highly agitated. He decided to return to the house to retrieve some clothing and to clarify what had happened on the night of the 24th and to see if the victim would withdraw the charges against him. Once at her house, he never intended to harm her but he had made what he described as an empty threat. In general, he did not disagree with her account of events.

17   He had, he said, mental problems which caused him to be violent. He would have taken his own life on that day but he would not have hurt his victim. He was sorry for his actions. He had been affected by a combination of medication and alcohol, albeit aware of what he was doing.

18   There was, in fact, no physical injury to the victim.

19   The offender has previous convictions, having regularly appeared before the courts for minor offences of dishonesty between 1984 and 1988, when non-custodial sentences were passed. He was also fined for shoplifting in 1994. In January 2002 he was convicted of making false representations, contrary to the Job Seekers Act 1995 and conditionally discharged for 12 months. In December 2002 he was sentenced to a 40-hour community punishment order, in relation to each of two charges, one of theft and the other of obtaining by deception. He had also been sentenced for the dishonesty offences for which he was conditionally discharged the previous January. For that there was another community punishment order for 40 hours, so the total sentence, on that occasion, in December 2002, was of 120 hours' community punishment. That had not been completed by the time of these events in November 2003. He had not complied with the order because he was acting as a carer for a friend who was terminally ill. The offender has only one conviction for any sort of violence; in 1986, he was sentenced to three months for assault occasioning actual bodily harm.

20   There was before the learned sentencing judge, as there is before this Court, a psychiatrist's report from Dr Diane Tamlyn of Rampton Hospital. That report is dated February 2, 2004. It clearly had a significant impact upon the judge's mind when considering the appropriate sentence in this case. It contains, at p.2, in the fifth paragraph, the following passage:

> "He has no history of violence towards women, false imprisonment or sexual fantasies. At the time of the index offence he was suffering from a bereavement reaction and being treated with antidepressant medication by his general practitioner. His judgment is likely to have been impaired by mental illness and his emotional attachment to the complainant and his reckless behaviour precipitated by unaccustomed consumption of alcohol. In conclusion he does not represent a serious risk of re-offending of this nature, nor does he represent a risk to the complainant or women in general. He is at risk of impulsive and ill-judged behaviour when under the influence of alcohol but this could be of any description, not necessarily amounting to criminal behaviour. The offender will benefit from offence focused work on alcohol, thinking skills and relationship skills while in custody. He will also require on going treatment and counselling for prolonged bereavement reaction."

21   The pre-sentence report before the judge indicated that the offender demonstrated insight into the harm his behaviour had caused the victim and her family, and showed considerable remorse. The offender was adamant that he had intended no harm to the victim or her children and his consideration for the consequences of his behaviour on November 28 had been outweighed by the anger he was experiencing.

22   The report concluded that the offender struggled to employ appropriate coping strategies and may remain at medium to high risk of offending and harm unless he is able to learnnew strategies. There was no evidence, the report said, that the offender presented a direct risk towards other members of the public. The report

indicated suitability for a community punishment and/or rehabilitation order, designed to address the offender's deficits in thinking skills about decision-making.

23   The judge, in passing sentence, referred to the 10 weeks which the offender had spent in custody prior to sentence. He referred to the "unimaginable" anxiety and fear caused to the victim. But the judge accepted that the offender was "far from being yourself at the time" and still suffered from a residue of bereavement. The judge went on to say that he regarded the offender as a quite exceptional case and he had behaved in a way clearly quite out of character.

24   The submissions to this Court on behalf of the Attorney General and on behalf of the offender have been, if we may say so, distinguished by their clarity, brevity and forcefulness. On behalf of the Attorney, Mr Derbyshire drew attention to what he submits are three primary aggravating features. First, there was a second offence directed towards the same victim. Secondly, it involved an invasion of the family home and an element of vandalisation of it. Thirdly, the offence took place in breach of conditions of bail, specifically imposed for the purpose of protecting the victim.

25   Mr Derbyshire refers to three secondary aggravating features. First, the vulnerability, in different ways, of the victim in her home, her young children and the elderly and frail other lodger. Secondly, weapons were employed, accompanied by threats to kill. Thirdly, the offender was, at the time, subject to an order of the court imposed many months previously for quite different offences.

26   Mr Derbyshire draws attention to two mitigating features. First, the offender's immediate admission of the offence and expression of remorse and his plea of guilty at the earliest opportunity. Secondly, the minor mental illness in the form of a bereavement reaction which contributed to him acting as he did. Mr Derbyshire also accepts that the judge correctly described this conduct as being out of character.

27   Mr Derbyshire drew attention to several authorities. In particular, in *Brown* (1994) 15 Cr.App.R.(S.) 337, a sentence of three years was upheld, following a guilty plea, by a man with a very bad record, in relation to an offence the circumstances of which bear some similarity to the present. In some respects, Mr Derbyshire submits, the circumstances there were not as serious in the present case, where the fear of being killed, the ejection of the other lodger and the display and use of knives constituted aggravating features not found in *Brown*.

28   Mr Derbyshire also referred to *Butterworth* (1993) 14 Cr.App.R.(S.) 674 where, following a trial, a sentence of four years was reduced to three years, defendant's former girlfriend having been driven round at pistol point for half an hour. He also referred to *Hibbert* [2002] 2 Cr.App.R.(S.) 29 (p.106), where a sentence of three and a half years was upheld, following a plea of guilty to an offence involving imprisonment for some 13 hours.

29   Mr Derbyshire's central submission is that a community penalty failed adequately to reflect the gravity of the offence and the aggravating features which we have described. In commenting on the authority of *Ashbridge* [2002] 2 Cr.App.R.(S.) 89 (p.408) Mr Derbyshire drew attention to the features in the present case, not to be found in the authorities referred to in *Ashbridge*, of a

repeated invasion of a home in breach of bail. He submitted that a starting point for an offence of false imprisonment of this kind must be a substantial term of imprisonment. The judge was not justified in taking the exceptional course that he did by reason either of the defendant's frustration or anger or depression, or the fact that he was acting entirely out of character.

30   On behalf of the offender, Mr Aspden made six points. First, he conceded that, for this type of offence, immediate custody of some length must be the sentence, failing exceptional circumstances. Secondly, he relied on *Ashbridge* (at [18]) as identifying a tariff of between 18 months and three years as appropriate in a normal case where no exceptional circumstances arise. Thirdly, he said there were here three unexceptional circumstances, namely the earliest possible guilty plea, genuine remorse and the absence from the offender's record of similar previous convictions. Fourthly, he said that there was one exceptional circumstance of mitigation to be found in the report of Dr Tamlyn, in particular the paragraph which we have earlier set out. He stresses that the judge was—and this is clearly right—anxious to reflect that circumstance in the sentence which he passed, which took into account the 10 weeks spent in custody. Fifthly, Mr Aspden submitted that, if the sentence passed was unduly lenient, this Court should exercise its discretion not to interfere with the sentence passed, bearing in mind that the offender has performed more than a quarter of the community punishment which was imposed by the learned judge and his performance, in that regard, is said to have been excellent. It would be particularly harsh to return the offender to prison at this stage, bearing in mind the non-custodial sentence initially passed, and the Court must have regard to the element of double jeopardy involved in sentencing the offender a second time. Mr Aspden's final submission was that, if the Court took the view that a custodial term should now be imposed, it ought to be scaled down, having regard to the three matters identified in his fifth submission.

31   To all of those factors we have regard. As it seems to us, this was an extremely difficult sentencing exercise. We have no doubt that, if there were no exceptional circumstances mitigating the sentence it would properly have been, in the court below, of the order of three years' imprisonment on a guilty plea. We say that bearing in mind the very great anxiety which clearly must have been caused to this victim by this offence, in the circumstances which we have outlined. That said, it follows that, on the face of it, this was an unduly lenient sentence.

32   However, we have to consider whether the public interest, as well as the offender's interest, would now be served by sending this offender to prison. In our judgment, it would not, having regard to the progress which the offender has made in carrying out a significant part of the community punishment order which was made, having regard to the non-custodial penalty which was imposed in the first place and having regard to double jeopardy. We also add this, as this Court has said on many previous occasions: sentencing is an art not a science. Where a Crown Court judge has a proper basis for imposing a lenient sentence and even, it may be, in some cases, an unduly lenient sentence, this Court ought not lightly to interfere. There was, as it seems to us, a two-fold proper basis for the judge to take the exceptional course which he did. First, the fact that this conduct, so far as this offender is concerned, was entirely out of charac-

ter. Secondly, and more importantly, the terms of the psychiatrist's report, which plainly asserted an absence of risk to women in general and this victim, in particular, from the offender.

33 Taking all of those matters into account, although, as we have said, the sentence passed was, at first blush, unduly lenient, it is not one with which this Court thinks it right to interfere.

R. v TERRENCE MARK DONOVAN

COURT OF APPEAL (Lord Justice Rose (Vice President, Court of Appeal, Criminal Division), Mr Justice Hughes and Mrs Justice Gloster): April 28, 2004

[2004] EWCA Crim 1237; [2005] 1 Cr.App.R.(S.) 16

Mitigation; Possession with intent to supply; Sentence length

H1 *Possession of cannabis with intent to supply—possession of 409g—length of sentence*

H2 Twelve months' imprisonment for possession of 409g of cannabis with intent to supply reduced to six months.

H3 The appellant was convicted of possessing 409.9g of cannabis with intent to supply, and possessing two further quantities of cannabis. He was acquitted of possessing the further quantities with intent to supply. Police stopped a vehicle being driven by the appellant and noticed a smell of cannabis. The appellant admitted being in possession of cannabis and was arrested. A search of the appellant revealed two small wraps of cannabis. A search of his home resulted in the discovery of the three other small quantities of cannabis and a case containing a total of 409.9g of cannabis in cling film packages. Sentenced to 12 months' imprisonment for possession of cannabis with intent to supply, with no separate penalty on the other counts, and an order to pay £363 towards the costs of the prosecution.

H4 **Held:** (considering Doyle [1996] 1 Cr.App.R.(S.) 409) the evidence did not suggest that the appellant was a drug dealer on any significant scale. His case throughout the trial was that he had the cannabis for personal use. The sentencing judge agreed to deal with the appellant as if he had pleaded guilty. In the Court's judgment, possession of cannabis with intent to supply was an offence which almost inevitably attracted a custodial sentence. This was not affected by the fact that cannabis had been reclassified as a class C drug, as the maximum penalty for supply of a class C drug had been increased from 5 to 14 years, so that the maximum penalty for supply of cannabis remained as it always had been. In the Court's judgment, having regard to the fact that the judge treated the appellant as though he had pleaded guilty on all three counts and the very limited extent to which the appellant was involved in supplying, the sentence of 12 months was excessive, and a sentence of six months would be substituted.

H5   **Case cited:**   *Doyle* [1996] 1 Cr.App.R.(S.) 409

H6   **References:** distributing cannabis, *Current Sentencing Practice*, B 11-1.3D

H7   *P. Caldwell* for the appellant.

JUDGMENT

1   **GLOSTER J.:**   On January 7, 1994, in the Crown Court at Kingston, before Mr Recorder Donne, the appellant, Terrence Donovan, then aged 25, was convicted of two counts of possession of a then Class B controlled drug, namely cannabis, in amounts of 218.2g and 5.61g respectively and on a third count of possession of 409.9g of cannabis with intent to supply. Originally Donovan had been charged with possession with intent to supply on all three counts, to which he pleaded not guilty, but he accepted that, on his own evidence, he must in any event be found guilty of the lesser offence of possession. The jury acquitted on the first two counts of possession with intent to supply, returning a guilty verdict on the lesser offence of possession, but convicted him on the third count of possession with intent to supply in respect of 409.9g of cannabis. The appellant had also pleaded guilty to possessing a controlled drug of Class A, namely 0.665g of a substance containing cocaine. Sentence was adjourned for a pre-sentence report. On February 6, 2004 the appellant was sentenced by the trial judge, Mr Recorder Donne Q.C., to 12 months' imprisonment on the count of possession of 409.9g of cannabis with intent to supply. No separate penalty was imposed in respect of the remaining counts. The judge made the usual orders for forfeiture and disposal of the drugs. He made no order for recovery of defence costs but ordered the appellant to pay £363.50 towards the costs of the prosecution, this money being already held by the police.

2   The appellant now appeals against that sentence by leave of the single judge.

3   The facts can be briefly stated as follows. On November 27, 2002 police stopped a vehicle being driven by the appellant because of the defective rear light and noticed a strong smell of cannabis from the vehicle. The appellant admitted being in possession of cannabis and was arrested. He was searched at the police station and a bag containing two wraps of cannabis, weighing 5.61g, was recovered from the back of his trousers. These were the subject of the second count referred to above.

4   The appellant's home was searched. On the sofa in the living room was found a red plastic bag containing two bags of herbal cannabis weighing 43g, a carrier bag in the refrigerator containing 62.6g of cannabis and a clingfilm package in the freezer containing 112g of damp cannabis. These drugs were the subject-matter of the first count referred to above. In the main bedroom the police found a drum case containing a plastic carrier bag, which held the following: 10

single-layered clingfilm packages containing 278g of cannabis, two double-layered clingfilm packages containing a total of 55.6g and three plastic bags containing a total of 76.3g. These drugs totalling 409.9g were the subject of the third count referred to above. Police also found a cannabis grinder and a roll of clingfilm in the living room. A further roll of clingfilm was found in the kitchen. The appellant's fingerprints were found on the carrier bag and the drum case and there was evidence that the rolls of clingfilm had been used to wrap some of the cannabis.

5   In interview the appellant declined to answer questions, save to say that he worked as a percussionist and had suffered some injuries to his wrist and fingers.

6   The evidence of the financial resources available to the appellant and of his life-style did not suggest that he was a drug dealer on any or any significant scale. His flat was modest and poorly furnished. His car, a Honda Civic, was described by the police as battered and in poor condition. He was able to show that he received money throughout 2002 from a trust fund of which he had been the beneficiary. The police confirmed that the appellant had not been in receipt of benefit. On the day of his arrest, the police found £363.50 in cash on his person, which he said was the balance of £400 rent given to him by his lodger. No money was found at his flat, nor were any "client lists" or scales found.

7   The appellant's case at trial was that all of the cannabis found was for his own use. He stated that he was a heavy user of cannabis for recreational purposes. He also said that he used the cannabis to alleviate the systems of a chronic medical condition which caused severe pain to his wrist. He acknowledged that this condition was exacerbated by his occupation as a drummer and was determined to pursue his musical career. He accepted that even on his own case he must be found guilty by the jury of the offence of simple possession of cannabis.

8   The appellant stated that he smoked approximately an ounce of cannabis every week and that he also cooked with it. He maintained that taking cannabis in cooked form had a more potent effect in relieving pain.

9   Before his counsel made submissions in mitigation the judge indicated that, because the appellant had never disputed possession of all the cannabis for his personal use and had been acquitted of the more serious charge of intent to supply on two of the three counts, the judge was prepared, in effect, to deal with him on the basis of a guilty plea. That, perhaps, was a somewhat surprising approach for the judge to take but we deal with this appeal on the basis that he did so approach the matter.

10   In view of the jury's findings, the judge also indicated to the appellant that he would view the appellant as someone who subsidised his own consumption of cannabis by dealing in a comparatively small way. The judge also bore in mind that the appellant lived and worked in the music industry where consumption of drugs was commonplace. The judge took the view that the appellant was also effectively of good character, his previous convictions for possession of drugs, in 1997, and 1998 having resulted in a small fine, conditional discharges and reprimands. However, the judge said that, notwithstanding the new reclassification of cannabis, it was still an offence to possess it with intent to supply. In sentencing the appellant to 12 months' imprisonment the judge said that he bore

in mind the mitigation, character references, the lack of positive information of profit or high living from drug dealing and the appellant's effective admission to possession.

11   In our judgment, possession of cannabis with intent to supply is an offence which almost inevitably attracts a custodial sentence (see *Doyle* [1996] 1 Cr.App.R.(S.) 409). That is so even though cannabis has now been reclassified as a Class C drug. That is reflected by the fact that the maximum penalty for supply of a Class C drug has been increased from five years to 14 years, so that the maximum penalty for the supply of cannabis remains as it always has been (see Sch.28 to the Criminal Justice Act 2003).

12   Mr Caldwell, on behalf of the appellant, concedes that a custodial sentence was appropriate in this case. His principal submission is that, taking into account the limited extent of the appellant's supply activities for the purpose of supporting his own use and his good character, the sentence of 12 months in this case was excessive.

13   In our judgment, having regard to the fact that the learned judge treated this matter as though the appellant had plead guilty on all three counts, and taking into account the very limited extent to which the appellant was involved in supply and his previous effectively good character, supported by impressive character references, a sentence of 12 months was excessive in all the circumstances. The view which we have come to is that the appropriate sentence in this case is six months' imprisonment. The sentence of 12 months will therefore be quashed and a sentence of six months substituted. To that extent this appeal is allowed.

ATTORNEY GENERAL'S REFERENCE NO.87 OF 2003 (NICHOLAS LEER)

COURT OF APPEAL (Lord Justice Latham, Mrs Justice Cox and Judge Peter Beaumont Q.C.):   April 28, 2004

[2004] EWCA Crim 1144; [2005] 1 Cr.App.R.(S.) 17

LT Community punishment and rehabilitation orders; Harassment; Undue leniency; Wounding with intent

H1   *Wounding with intent—attacking man with iced lollipop so as to cause lacerations to head—revenge attack—whether community order adequate*

H2   A community punishment and rehabilitation order for wounding with intent and harassment causing fear of violence, where the offender attacked the victim with two iced lollipops in the belief that the victim was engaged in a relationship with the offender's girlfriend, and then threatened him with violence, varied to two years' imprisonment.

H3   The offender was convicted of wounding with intent to cause grievous bodily harm, and of putting a person in fear of violence by harassment, contrary to the Protection from Harassment Act 1997, s.4(1). The victim made the acquaintance of the offender's girl friend, and over a period of time exchanged text messages with her. The offender became jealous. The offender came into a store where the victim was working and attacked him with two ice lollipops, which were in effect shards of ice encased in plastic. The offender struck the victim four of five times, causing two five centimetre lacerations to the head. Later, the offender made a number of telephone calls to the victim, threatening to kill him. Subsequently the victim and the offender met by chance, and the offender pointed a knife at the victim. Sentenced to a community punishment and rehabilitation order, requiring 100 hours' work and 18 months' supervision. The Attorney General asked the Court to review the sentence on the grounds that it was unduly lenient.

H4   **Held:** the sentencing judge accepted that the offender believed that the victim had had a relationship with the offender's girlfriend, who had been his partner for 11 years and with whom he had two children. She accepted that the ice lollipops had not been purchased with a view to use as a weapon, although the attack had been planned to some degree. For the Attorney General it was submitted that the attack was a revenge attack involving the use of a weapon and an element of planning. The Court reached the conclusion that the sentence was unduly lenient, and although the offence was towards the lower end of the bracket of offences of wounding with intent, it should have attracted a sentence of imprisonment of at least two years, taking into account the mitigating factors. The offence of harassment should be marked with a consecutive sentence of one year's imprisonment, making a total minimum sentence of three years. Taking into account the fact that the offender had completed the community punishment order, and the element of double jeopardy, the Court would substitute a total sentence of two years' imprisonment.

H5   **Case cited:** *Attorney General's References Nos 59, 60 and 63 of 1998* [1999] 2 Cr.App.R.(S.) 128

H6   **References:** wounding with intent, *Current Sentencing Practice* B 2-2

H7   *E. Brown* for the Attorney General.
H. Lodge for the offender.

JUDGMENT

1   **LATHAM L.J.:**   This is an application by Her Majesty's Attorney General to refer to this Court a sentence which was imposed on the offender Nicholas Leer on November 14, 2003. He was on that date sentenced to a community punishment and rehabilitation order of 100 hours' unpaid work and 18 months' probation, on two counts of which he had been convicted by a jury, those sentences to be served concurrently.

2   The offences of which he was convicted were an offence of wounding with intent to cause grievous bodily harm contrary to s.18 of the Offences Against the Persons Act and putting a person in fear of violence by harassment contrary to s.4(1) of the Protection of Harassment Act.

3   The facts of the offences disclose that the victim and the offender lived in a relatively close knit community and it is clear that the victim had made the acquaintance of the [offender's] girlfriend in circumstances which are not relevant, but that their acquaintance developed into a relationship in the sense that they exchanged, it would appear, text messages with each other. There were regular and frequent messages over a period of months. It is apparent that the offender became intensely jealous and indeed suspected that there was more to the relationship than merely the sending of text messages.

4   On January 6, 2003, the victim was at work in his uncle's shop pricing groceries. Whilst he was doing so, the offender came into the shop, went straight up to him and, without warning, took out of a bag two ice lollipops, known as ice pops, which were in effect shards of ice encased in plastic about six to eight inches long, and struck the victim over the head with them four or five times with sufficient force to cause a five-centimetre laceration over the left frontal region of the head which required five stitches and a five-centimetre laceration on the right side which required four stitches.

5   The offender left the shop threatening, according to the evidence, to kill the victim. A closed circuit television film which showed at least part of the incident showed him stopping, turning and standing in an aggressive stance as he left the shop.

6   Thereafter the victim was telephoned by the offender on a number of occasions in which phone calls the offender threatened him in a similar way to the threats that he had uttered as he left the shop.

7   On March 20, 2003 the victim and the offender met by chance in the stairwell of a block of flats. The offender approached the victim and said "Have you got anything to tell me?" and held a Stanley knife with the blade protruding pointed at the victim. He told the victim to follow him to his flat where he said they would sort the matter out. The conversation ended with the offender threatening the victim, at which point the victim ran off and the incident then came to an end. It was that incident which formed the subject-matter of the second count of which this offender was convicted.

8   The recorder in sentencing the offender indicated that she accepted that the offender had indeed believed that the victim had had a relationship or was having a relationship with his girlfriend, who had been his partner for 11 years and with whom he had two children and with whom he lived. She concluded that nonetheless the attack was an unprovoked attack, that it was premeditated in the sense that he had deliberately gone into the shop in order to attack the victim. She however accepted that the two iced lollies had not been purchased with a view to their being used as a weapon—he had bought the lollies for his children and they were simply used as a weapon when the opportunity to attack the victim arose. She accordingly concluded that the attack, although planned to some degree, was

not planned in the sense that the offender had taken to the scene deliberately a weapon with which to commit the assault.

9   She also accepted that the second count of harassment arose out of circumstances which had arisen by chance. There was no premeditation in the meeting in question. Nonetheless, she referred to the fact that the victim had clearly been extremely frightened by the use of the knife. She said that the combined effect of the attack, the phone calls and the incident of harassment indicated that the offender was someone who had been unable to control his anger at the time; she formed an unfavourable view of his truthfulness, but she considered that he would find it difficult to survive in prison and that the risk of reoffending was small. She treated him as a man of good character and bearing in mind the particular problems which the offender had and indeed has, namely that he is a man with profound learning difficulties, with severe dyslexia, the circumstances did not justify, she thought, a custodial sentence. She was, in those circumstances, prepared to sentence the offender as she did, indicating that clearly if she had not accepted the mitigation to the extent that she had the offences would have justified a custodial sentence.

10   It is right to say that the offender has now completed the sentence in so far as it required him to do 100 hours of unpaid work. That was not only completed but completed satisfactorily by March 19, 2004, we have been informed by Mr Lodge on his behalf.

11   Her Majesty's Attorney General nonetheless submits to us that the recorder imposed not merely a lenient but an unduly lenient sentence.

12   Mr Brown on his behalf submits that the attack was a revenge attack involving the use of a weapon, where there was an element of planning and where the offender continued to harass and threaten the victim following the attack. In the circumstances, although accepting that the offender has learning difficulties and is dyslexic and has no convictions of any relevance, nonetheless the offence of wounding with intent to cause grievous bodily harm was one which should inevitably have resulted in a sentence of imprisonment.

13   He has referred us to a number of authorities. Perhaps the leading authority being that of *Attorney General's Reference Nos 59, 60 and 63 of 1998* [1999] 2 Cr.App.R.(S.) 128, where the Court, presided over by Lord Bingham, dealt with a number of cases involving offenders who had been convicted of offences under s.18 of the Offences Against the Person Act. He has referred us to the passages in that judgment which make it plain that the Lord Chief Justice was indicating clearly that wherever the court is confronted with an offender who has either admitted or been found guilty of an offence involving the intention to cause grievous bodily harm, it will only be in the most special circumstances that a sentence of imprisonment will not be appropriate. Indeed, the authorities to which he drew our attention apart from that authority underline that particular policy of the courts. He submits that given that a custodial sentence was the only proper course in this case, it follows that the sentence that was imposed was unduly lenient.

14   We consider that the arguments of Mr Brown justify our granting leave for this sentence to be referred to this Court and turn to consider, therefore, the extent to

which it can be said, in the light of all the material before us, that the sentence was indeed unduly lenient.

15   Mr Lodge, on behalf of the offender, has put before us, in an extremely effective submission in mitigation, a number of factors which he submits justified the recorder in the course that she took, at least to the extent that he can properly say to us that albeit lenient the sentence was not unduly lenient. He has pointed out that the lollipops were not dangerous weapons in themselves; they were used as weapons simply because they were to hand. They had not been, as the recorder accepted, deliberately purchased or brought to the scene in order to be used as weapons. Accordingly, he submits that realistically this attack can be equated to an attack with the bare fists which Lord Bingham, in the case to which we have referred, indicated would be at the lower end of the spectrum of seriousness for offences of this sort.

16   He points out, as is obviously correct, that the recorder was in the best position to assess the seriousness of the incident, having heard the evidence, indeed having had the opportunity of seeing the closed circuit television material and having heard the evidence in particular of the offender himself. She had, as a result, an opportunity to gauge the extent to which the harassment which followed from the attack was harassment which could properly have been said to have frightened the victim and in that context it is said that she would have had the opportunity to appreciate that the victim was significantly taller than the offender. He points to the fact, as we have already related, that the offender has severe learning difficulties which obviously make it the more difficult for him, perhaps, to come to terms with the vicissitudes of life and in particular to come to terms with what must have been, as it appeared to him, a serious blow to his happiness and self esteem in that there appeared to be a relationship which could undermine what to him was his family life with his partner and his two children. Unhappily these offences have in fact resulted in his partner leaving and his being unable to have contact with his children. That, Mr Lodge submits, is a matter which we should bear in mind, as we should the fact that he has satisfactorily completed the community service which was ordered, as part of our assessment on what course this Court should adopt today. He also points out that there has been no recurrence of any incidents so far as the Court is aware, despite the fact that both the offender and the victim have remained in the same relatively close knit community.

17   Having considered with care all those submissions by Mr Lodge, we nonetheless take the view that Her Majesty's Attorney General is correct in his submissions that the sentence imposed on this offender was indeed unduly lenient. In our judgment, although we accept that in the spectrum of offences under s.18 this is towards the lower end of the bracket, it nonetheless should have attracted a sentence of imprisonment and we consider that the minimum appropriate sentence which could have been imposed, taking into account the mitigating factors, was two years' imprisonment and that the recorder should have marked the offence of harassment with a consecutive sentence of one year's imprisonment, making a total minimum sentence of three years' imprisonment. But we have to take into account that the offender has completed his

community order and reflect in our order the element of double jeopardy. We consider that we can properly do so by reducing the sentence which is appropriate to one of one and a half years' imprisonment for the offence under s.18 of the Offences Against the Person Act and six months' imprisonment to be served consecutively for the offence under s.4 of the Protection of Harassment Act. The sentence accordingly will be one of two years' imprisonment.

[Paragraphs [18]–[22] have been omitted.]

ATTORNEY GENERAL'S REFERENCE NO.19 OF 2004 (BRETT CHARLTON)

COURT OF APPEAL (Lord Justice Latham, Mrs Justice Cox and Judge Peter Beaumont Q.C.: April 28, 2004

[2004] EWCA Crim 1239; [2005] 1 Cr.App.R.(S.) 18

(LT Courts duties; Guilty pleas; Judicial indications; Racially aggravated offences; Undue leniency; Unlawful wounding

H1   *Racially aggravated unlawful wounding—adequacy of sentence—plea of guilty—plea made following indication as to sentence by sentencing judge— whether Attorney General precluded from referring sentence for review on the ground that it was unduly lenient*

H2   Leave to refer a sentence for review on the ground of undue leniency given to the Attorney General, although the sentencing judge had given an indication of the likely sentence before the plea was entered, on the ground that prosecuting counsel did not act in such a way as to lead the offender to expect the sentence indicated.

H3   A sentence of 10 months' imprisonment for racially aggravated unlawful wounding, where the victim was slashed in the neck and subjected to verbal racial abuse, increased to three years.

H4   The offender pleaded guilty to racially aggravated unlawful wounding, on an indictment charging him with wounding with intent to cause grievous bodily harm. The offender was with a girlfriend at a railway station, when the victim, who had been at school with the girlfriend, said "hello" to her. The offender became aggressive to the victim and addressed words of racial abuse to him. The offender then produced a knife from his pocket and slashed the victim across the side of the neck, causing a wound which required 18 stitches. The offender had a significant record of convictions and had been subjected to a drug treatment and testing order for burglary a few weeks before the offence. On his first appearance in the Crown Court, he pleaded not guilty to wounding with intent to cause grievous bodily harm. At a later stage, the offender's counsel asked the judge to indicate what the judge would do if the offender pleaded guilty to unlawful wounding contrary to the Offences against the Person Act 1861, s.20. The offender had been in custody at that stage for six months. The judge indicated that on such a plea he would not impose a further custodial sentence. Prosecuting counsel indicated that he could not indicate what the attitude of the prosecution would be to such a plea. At a subsequent hearing prosecuting counsel informed the offender's counsel that the prosecution would be prepared to accept a plea to racially aggravated unlawful wounding but not to unlawful wounding. Both counsel went to see the judge in chambers and the judge was asked whether a plea to racially aggravated wounding would make any difference to the indication previously given. The sentencing judge indicated that it would not, and that he considered that it was important to pass such a sentence as would allow the offender's immediate release so that the offender could continue to benefit from the drug treatment and testing order. Prosecuting counsel did not indicate any view as to the prosecution's position. The sentencing judge sentenced the offender to 10 months' imprisonment for racially aggravated unlawful wounding and re-imposed the drug treatment and testing order. The probation service considered that the drug treatment and testing order was inappropriate in view of the nature of the offence and the matter was relisted. The sentencing judge substituted a sentence of three years' imprisonment for the offence in respect of which the drug treatment and testing order had been made. The Attorney General asked the Court to review the sentence on the ground that it was unduly lenient.

H5   **Held:** (considering *Attorney General's Reference No.4 of 1996 (Robinson)* [1997] 1 Cr.App.R.(S.) 357, *Attorney General's Reference No.17 of 1998 (Stokes)* [1999] 1 Cr.App.R.(S.) 407, *Attorney General's Reference Nos 8, 9 and 10 of 2002 (Mohammed and others)* [2003] 1 Cr.App.R.(S.) 57 (p.272), *Attorney General's Reference Nos 86 and 87 of 1999* [2001] 1 Cr.App.R.(S.) 141 (p.505), *Saunders* [2000] 2 Cr.App.R.(S.) 71, and *Kelly and Donnelly* [2001] 2 Cr.App.R.(S.) 73 (p.341)) it was submitted for the Attorney General that the Attorney General was entitled to refer the matter to the Court, notwithstanding that the judge had given a sentencing indication which resulted in the offender changing his plea. For the offender, it was said that the prosecution had effectively acquiesced in the course which the judge proposed to adopt and that in those circumstances the Attorney General should be precluded from asking the Court to interfere with the sentence. It seemed to the Court that it was undoubtedly right that if the prosecution acted in such a way that it could be said to have played a part in giving the offender the relevant expectation, it could not be appropriate for the Court of Appeal to permit the Attorney General to argue that the sentence imposed was unduly lenient. The principle had to be considered in the light of the facts of each particular case. On the facts of the present case, it seemed to the Court that the prosecution did not act in a way which could be said to amount to playing a part in giving the offender an expectation as to sentence. In the first instance, counsel for the offender was seeking an indication on the basis of a plea to simple unlawful wounding, and the indication was given. On the second appearance, the prosecution indicated that it was not prepared for the matter to be dealt with on the basis proposed by the offender's counsel. The sentencing judge made it clear what his view was; prosecuting counsel was confronted with a *fait accompli* and accepted the inevitable. In those circumstances, the Court did not consider that the case fell within the category which precluded the Attorney General from asking the Court to consider the sentence on the basis that it was unduly lenient. Turning to the sentence, the Court had indicated in *Saunders* [2000] 2 Cr.App.R.(S.) 71 how racially aggravated offences should be disposed of. The message had been reinforced in *Kelly and Donnelly* [2001] 2 Cr.App.R.(S.) 73 (p.341). The level of sentencing for offences of this kind would clearly depend both on the seriousness of the wound itself and the extent to which it could be said that the racial element did aggravate the seriousness of that offence. In the present case there was a substantial wound which might have had more serious consequences, caused by a folded knife which the offender had in his pocket. In relation to the assault itself, on a plea of guilty the offence would have attracted a sentence of two and a half years or upwards. The element of racial aggravation should have led to an increase of the sentence by one and a half years. Bearing in mind the element of double jeopardy the Court considered that the right sentence to impose now was three years' imprisonment, incorporating an element of two years for the wounding and an additional one year for the element of racial aggravation.

H6 **Cases cited:** *Attorney General's Reference No.4 of 1996 (Robinson)* [1997] 1 Cr.App.R.(S.) 357, *Attorney General's Reference No.17 of 1998 (Stokes)* [1999] 1 Cr.App.R.(S.) 407, *Attorney General's References Nos 8,9 and 10 of 2002 (Mohammed and others)* [2003] 1 Cr.App.R.(S.) 57 (p.272), *Attorney General's Reference Nos 86 and 87 of 1999* [2001] 1 Cr.App.R.(S.) 141 (p.505), *Saunders* [2000] 2 Cr.App.R.(S.) 71, *Kelly and Donnelly* [2001] 2 Cr.App.R.(S.) 73 (p.341)

H7 **References:** racially aggravated wounding, *Current Sentencing Practice* B 2-3; plea discussions, *Current Sentencing Practice* L 1-1E

H8 *R. Horwell* and *E. Brown* for the Attorney General.
Miss S. Munro Q.C. for the offender.

JUDGMENT

1 **LATHAM L.J.:** This is an application by Her Majesty's Attorney General for leave to refer to this Court a sentence imposed on the offender Brett Charlton, who is 27 years of age, on January 22, 2004. On that day he pleaded guilty to an offence of racially aggravated wounding, he having been charged originally with an offence of wounding with intent to cause grievous bodily harm. The judge sentenced him in relation to that offence to 10 months' imprisonment. At the same time he revoked an earlier drug treatment and testing order which had been made in relation to a charge of burglary and then re-imposed that order with effect from that day.

2   The facts of the offence to which the offender pleaded guilty on that occasion were as follows. At about 10.00pm on the evening of July 30, 2003, a 16-year-old black youth, Alhassan Kamara, was with two black friends at Worthing Railway Station. They were sitting on some railings near to a stairway leading to one of the platforms. Mr Kamara saw a girl with whom he had been at school. This girl was in fact with the offender. He said "hello" to her but she told him to "fuck off". The offender then came up to Mr Kamara and asked why he had spoken to his girlfriend. Mr Kamara explained that he had been to school with her. The offender became aggressive and threatening and said words which were generally to this effect: "You fucking black monkey." At that the girlfriend sought to pull the offender away and told him to stop, but he shrugged her off, went towards Mr Kamara, putting his hand into his jacket pocket, from which he produced a knife which he opened; and although Mr Kamara tried to escape he was unable to do so and the offender slashed Mr Kamara across the left side of the neck, caus-ing a significant wound which required 18 stitches and which from the photographs that we have seen was clearly a wound which was close to but for-tunately did not affect vital parts such as the jugular vein.

3   In order to understand the circumstances in which this reference is made and the issues which it raises, it is necessary just to say something about the history of the matter and in particular refer to what occurred during two hearings in cham-bers before the trial judge, H.H. Judge Thorpe.

4   The offender is a man with a significant record of previous convictions. The first relevant one that we need to refer to was a conviction for burglary on May 21, 1999 for which he received a sentence of five years' imprisonment. On his release from that sentence of imprisonment he offended again on February 19, 2003. That was within the licence period. For that offence he received a 12-month drug treatment and testing order on July 3, 2003 which was imposed by H.H. Judge Thorpe who did not give effect to the breach of the licence by any separate order. The drug treatment and testing order that he made at that time reflected an extremely positive report from the probation service to the effect that the offender's drug-taking was the undoubted background to his previous offending behaviour and he at last was prepared to face up to that and to seek to keep himself free from drugs. An indication of how persuasive that report must have been to the judge is the fact that the offender's co-defendant on that occasion was sentenced to four years' imprisonment for that offence.

5   It can be seen that unhappily it was only some four weeks or so later that the offender committed the offence with which we are concerned. By that time no work had in fact been done with the offender in relation to the drug treatment and testing order.

6   After his arrest he was remanded in custody. When first arraigned on November 24, 2003, he pleaded not guilty to the count of wounding with intent. There were thereafter directions hearings at one of which, on January 13, 2004, the judge raised for the offender's counsel's consideration a concern that he had about the fact that the offender had not been given an immediate opportunity of an interview by the British Transport Police, who were the prosecuting constabu-lary. The offender had apparently been offered interviews at times and places

which were unacceptable to the solicitor whom the offender wished to instruct. The judge suggested that this might provide the basis for an application to stay on the grounds of an abuse of process. That was a somewhat surprising suggestion for the judge to have made; but it would appear that it reflected a concern that he had about the way in which the British Transport Police had dealt with other prosecutions with which he had dealt.

7   On January 19, 2004 there was a further directions hearing at which again the issue of abuse of process was raised; but then, at the end of the proceedings in open court, counsel acting for the offender at that stage indicated that he would wish if possible to see the judge in chambers. The judge acceded to that request. During the course of the hearing in chambers, the offender's counsel asked in effect what the judge would do if the offender pleaded guilty to an offence of wounding under s.20 of the Offences Against the Person Act. The judge indicated that his concern at that time was that the drug treatment and testing order that he had imposed in July had not in fact had a chance to take effect and said at p.20 of the transcript that we have:

> "On the basis that he has been inside six months, he has served a 12 month sentence, has he not? I think I would take the view that subject to anything else, were this a plea to section 20 on that basis, I think he has served long enough. I would not interfere with the drug treatment and testing order but give it a chance to run. Of course if he breaches that then I would deal with him for the domestic burglary and he would be facing a substantial sentence there."

8   Prosecuting counsel indicated that he was in no position at that time to indicate what the attitude of the prosecution would be to a plea to simple s.20.

9   The parties returned to court on January 22, 2004 with a different prosecuting counsel present. Prosecuting counsel then instructed was Mr Cherrill. He informed the offender's counsel, Mr Shapiro, that the prosecution would be prepared to accept a plea to racially aggravated unlawful wounding and not to simple wounding under s.20.

10   Both counsel then went in to chambers to see the judge. The offender's counsel informed the judge as to what the position of the prosecution was and specifically asked the judge whether or not a plea to racially aggravated wounding, as opposed to simple wounding, would make any difference to the indication that the judge had previously given. The judge said as follows (p.23):

> "You know my views on racially aggravated matters. I think the world has gone PC mad and I say it advisedly having mixed race grandchildren with a black son-in-law. I think the legislation should be used and worked. I cannot really design for a drunken episode such as 'fucking black monkey'. If you are asking whether it would make any difference to the sentence, the answer is no. If that is what you are actually asking me."

The offender's counsel indicated that that was precisely what he was asking. The judge then reiterated the fact that so far as he was concerned the important point was to pass a sentence which would allow the offender's immediate release so that he could then impose a drug treatment and testing order and enable the offender to obtain the benefit of that order which was what he had hoped would have already happened in July.

11   There was no indication given by prosecuting counsel at any stage before the judge indicated his views as to the prosecution's position; but as the parties left the room Mr Cherrill said:

"Your Honour, it sounds, therefore, as if the matter can be resolved."

12   The indictment was thereafter amended to add the second count in the form to which prosecuting counsel had indicated he would be prepared to accept a plea; and the matter proceeded on the basis of the offender's plea then of guilty.

13   The judge, as we have indicated, sentenced the offender to 10 months' imprisonment for the offence with which we are concerned and, as we have already indicated, re-imposed the drug treatment and testing order to take effect from the new sentencing date.

14   However, the probation service, on considering the matter, concluded that it was inappropriate for a drug treatment and testing order to be made in the light of the offender's plea to the offence of violence with which we are concerned. The matter then had to come back before the judge. It will be noted that the judge had at no stage until making the drug treatment and testing order asked the probation service for their views in the light of the changed circumstances. He had relied simply on the material which had persuaded him to make that order in the first instance.

15   In those circumstances when the matter came back before the judge, the judge appreciated that, even though the probation service recommended as an alternative to a drug treatment and testing order a community rehabilitation order, he had no option but to impose a sentence of imprisonment and accordingly on February 20, 2004 the offender was sentenced for the burglary to three years' imprisonment, which is the sentence which he is now serving.

16   Counsel for the Attorney General, Mr Horwell, has submitted that although the offender had been given an indication as to sentence by the judge which resulted in his changing his plea and accordingly changing his position, he is nonetheless entitled to refer the matter to this Court for us to consider the appropriateness of the sentence which was imposed. He relies in that regard primarily on the authority of *Attorney General's Reference No.4 of 1996 (Robinson)* [1997] 1 Cr.App.R.(S.) 357. In that case this Court, presided over by the then Lord Chief Justice, Lord Bingham, made it clear that when the judge in circumstances such as the present has given an indication as to sentence, that does not preclude the Attorney General from bringing the matter before this court for it to consider whether or not the sentence was unduly lenient. However, the indication given by the judge will be an important matter for the Court to take into consideration when deciding how to dispose of that reference.

17   The matter was dealt with again in *Attorney General's Reference No.17 of 1998 (Stokes)* [1999] 1 Cr.App.R.(S.) 407. In that case the Court was presided over by Rose L.J. and the issue was again raised as to the effect of an indication given by a judge as to sentence. The argument was that the Court should not follow the

decision in *Robinson* on the basis that it was *per incuriam*, which might have been thought to be an ambitious submission. Rose L.J. said as follows at 411:

> ". . . if it were the position that a legitimate expectation of a lenient sentence prior to a plea of guilty, was a sufficient reason for this Court not to exercise its powers under section 36. . . the whole purpose of those powers would, as it seems to us, be set at naught. Anyone who pleads guilty to an offence . . . must. . . be taken to do so in recognition of the risk that, if a lenient sentence is passed, that may give rise to an Attorney-General's Reference to this Court, on which this Court may increase the sentence passed . . . It follows that we do not accept that the case of Robinson was decided *per incuriam*."

18   Despite those statements of principle, Miss Munro Q.C. on behalf of the offender has directed our attention to a number of cases which the Attorney General himself acknowledges are cases in which those principles have been said to be subject to some modification. It is said on the offender's behalf by Miss Munro that the authorities upon which she relied are authority for the proposition that wherever the prosecution has in effect acquiesced in the indication given by a judge, then it would be an abuse for the Attorney General, who stands in the shoes of the original prosecution, then to turn round and suggest to this Court that the course in which the prosecution had acquiesced was inappropriate on the basis that it would result in a sentence which was unduly lenient.

19   Perhaps the high watermark of the authorities upon which Miss Munro bases that argument is the case of *Attorney General's Reference Nos 8, 9 and 10 of 2002 (Mohammed and others)* [2003] 1 Cr.App.R.(S.) 57 (p.272). That was a case in which this Court was presided over by Kennedy L.J. In that case the Attorney General had sought to refer conditional discharges granted to three men for kidnapping a young woman with a view to preventing her from continuing a relationship with a non-Muslim. The result of an indication by the judge was that the offenders pleaded guilty to those offences. Before the offenders pleaded guilty, the judge had asked to see counsel in chambers and indicated that he was not thinking of a custodial sentence. The offenders entered pleas of guilty and the Crown offered no evidence against three of the co-defendants. The circumstances were such that the Court considered that the prosecution had acquiesced in the course that was suggested by the judge so as to justify the conclusion that although in fact in that case it was prepared to grant leave to refer, it was nonetheless not prepared to intervene. The way the issue of principle was put by the Court was as follows, at 277:

> "The problem of an Attorney General's Reference against the background of a judicial indication that there might be some non-custodial disposal is one which has troubled this Court on a number of occasions in the past. In *Attorney General's Reference Nos 86 and 87 of 1999* [2001] 1 Cr.App.R (S) 141 (p505), this Court considered a number of authorities in relation to this area of the law and said at paragraph 31 on page 512:
>
> > '. . . we consider that where an indication is given by a trial judge as to the level of sentencing and that indication is one which prosecuting counsel

considers to be inappropriate, or would have considered to be inappropriate if he or she had applied his mind to it, prosecuting counsel should register dissent and should invite the attention of the Court to any relevant authorities as indicated by the Lord Chief Justice in the case of Thompson and Rogers, otherwise if the offender does act to his detriment on the indication which has been given this Court may well find it difficult to intervene in response to a reference made by the Attorney-General.'".

20   In the present case Miss Munro submits that the position in front of the judge in chambers on the day when the prosecution indicated that they would be prepared to accept a plea of guilty to racially aggravated wounding was precisely the situation envisaged by Kennedy L.J. in that passage. It was a situation where prosecuting counsel, if he considered the sentence that the judge suggested to be inappropriate, had an obligation so to inform the judge or, as it might be put, forever hold his peace. The consequence, it is said, is that the prosecution has effectively acquiesced in the course that the judge proposed to adopt and the principle to which we have just referred is one which should preclude the Attorney General from being able to ask this Court to interfere with the sentence in question.

21   It seems to us that the passage upon which Miss Munro relies is a passage which must be considered with some care. It clearly has to be read in conjunction with what Lord Bingham said in *Robinson* and what Rose L.J. said in *Stokes*. It is undoubtedly right that if the prosecution has acted in ways in which it could be said that it had played a part in giving the offender the relevant expectation, then clearly it would not be appropriate for this Court to permit the Attorney General to argue that the sentence which was imposed, partly as a result of what the prosecution had said or done, was unduly lenient. But we have, it seems to us, to look in the light of that principle at the facts of each particular case. On the facts that we have related as to what happened in this case, it seems to us that the prosecution did not act in a way in which it could properly be said that it had played a part in giving the offender the relevant expectation as to sentence upon which Miss Munro relies. The position was this: in the first instance counsel for the offender was seeking an indication on the basis of simple wounding and the indication was given. When the prosecution returned to court on the second occasion, its stance clearly indicated that it was not prepared for the matter to be dealt with on the basis proposed by the offender's counsel and upon which the judge's indication had been given. What occurred in chambers makes it abundantly plain that the judge, without any reference to counsel at all, made it clear, and indeed crystal clear, what his view was. Prosecuting counsel in those circumstances, whilst there is no doubt that as a counsel of perfection he should have indicated to the judge the problems of approaching the case as the judge intended to, by reason of the authorities to which we will refer later as to the appropriateness of sentencing for racially aggravated offences, was in the unenviable position of being confronted with a "*fait accompli*" by the judge. What happened thereafter does not seem to us to have changed that situation. Prosecuting counsel was sim-

ply accepting what was clearly inevitable. He could not properly resile from the indication he had given as to the acceptability of the plea.

22   In those circumstances we do not consider that this is a case which falls into the category of case which precludes the Attorney General from asking this Court to consider the sentence on the basis that it is unduly lenient and we accordingly give leave to refer.

23   Turning then to the sentence itself, the first and most important fact to remind ourselves of is the nature of the offence which was charged and the way that this Court has consistently indicated that racially aggravated offences should be disposed of. The position was made abundantly plain by Rose L.J. in *Saunders* [2000] 2 Cr.App.R.(S.) 71. The passage, which seems to us to be a passage which should be in the forefront of the minds of all who sentence in such circumstances, comes at the bottom of 74:

> "One of the most important lessons of this century, as it nears its end, is that racism must not be allowed to flourish. The message must be received and understood in every corner of our society, in our streets and prisons, in the services, in the workplace, on public transport, in our hospitals, public houses and clubs, that racism is evil. It cannot coexist with fairness and justice. It is incompatible with democratic civilisation. The courts must do all they can, in accordance with Parliament's recently expressed intention, to convey that message clearly, by the sentences which they pass in relation to racially aggravated offences. Those who indulge in racially aggravated violence must expect to be punished severely, in order to discourage the repetition of that behaviour by them or others."

The message has been reinforced by the decision of this Court in the case of *Kelly and Donnelly* [2001] 2 Cr.App.R.(S) 73 (p.341), again a court presided over by Rose L.J., when he considered the advice that had been given to this Court by the Sentencing Advisory Panel in July 2000. The recommendation which he accepted was that the court in cases such as the present should identify what is the appropriate sentence for the offence leaving aside the element of racial aggravation and then add an appropriate amount to reflect the racial aggravation involved and that that exercise should be done transparently—in other words that the court should indicate each element of the overall sentence. It does not need saying that of course in the present case that was clearly not done by this judge.

24   The level of sentencing for offences of this nature will clearly depend upon both the seriousness of the wounding itself and the extent to which it can be said that the racial element did indeed aggravate the seriousness of that offence. In the present case the wound was a substantial wound to a vulnerable part of the victim. As the judge himself accepted, it was a wound which could well have had far more serious consequences. The wound was caused by a folded knife which the offender had had in his pocket and which he opened for the purposes of the attack. Whether or not it was unprovoked may be a matter of some debate; but on its face the fact that the offender's girlfriend tried to stop him indicates what others there thought of his behaviour. He was a man with a bad record. It

follows that in relation to the assault itself one would have expected that a wounding of this nature on a plea of guilty would have attracted a sentence of two and a half years or upwards in the circumstances. The racial aggravation described by the judge as merely a "drunken remark", was in fact a clear statement of racial bias; it was offensive; it was in the context of there being other black friends with the victim; and one of the circumstances which this Court has to take into account is the effect that the racial remark or remarks may have on those who are in the vicinity. In our view the judge should have been considering that a sentence of one and a half years or so as an appropriate figure to add in order to reflect the racially aggravated features of this particular case.

25   The problem here was, as the history that we have related indicates, that the judge had become blinkered by his original determination in July 2003 to provide a drug treatment and testing order for this offender. One can only commend his hopes in that regard at that time; but events had overtaken the position by July 2003. The judge needed to pause, which he did not, in order to ensure that even if a drug treatment and testing order were even remotely appropriate for this sort of offence, it was one which the probation service was still prepared to recommend. Had he considered the matter with care he would have appreciated that a drug treatment and testing order was inappropriate in the circumstances where there was an offence of violence in the background. Accordingly, he allowed himself to be diverted from imposing a sentence which in our judgment it was his duty to impose, which was a significant sentence of imprisonment for this offence.

26   In determining how we should deal with the matter today, we bear in mind in particular the element of double jeopardy. We also bear in mind the mitigation which has been urged before us, which is firstly that he had pleaded guilty; secondly, that he had clearly impressed the probation service as to his genuineness in relation to an intent to clear himself from drugs in 2003; and thirdly, and in particular, that he had been given an indication which had resulted in the plea of guilty. We consider that the right sentence is one of three years' imprisonment: two years for the wounding itself and one year for the element of racial aggravation.

27   We have been asked to consider whether or not to depart from the normal form of order which is that the sentence that we impose today should run from today in accordance with para.10 of Sch.3 to the Criminal Justice Act 1988, but we consider that there is no reason why we should do so and accordingly the sentence will run from today. That means it will be being served concurrently with the sentence which he is at present serving.

[Paragraphs [28]–[29] have been omitted.]

ATTORNEY GENERAL'S REFERENCE NO.6 OF 2004 (PLAKICI)

Court of Appeal (Lord Justice Latham, Mrs Justice Cox and Judge
Peter Beaumont Q.C.): April 29, 2004

[2004] EWCA Crim 1275; [2005] 1 Cr.App.R.(S.) 19

 Assisting illegal entry; Coercion; Consecutive sentences; Corruption;
Incitement; Kidnapping; Living on prostitution; Rape; Trafficking for sexual
exploitation; Undue leniency

H1 *Facilitating illegal entry and living on the earnings of prostitution—length of
sentence*

H2   Sentences totalling 10 years for facilitating illegal entry, living on the earnings
of prostitution, kidnapping and incitement to rape in the case of a man who was
concerned in arranging the illegal entry into the United Kingdom of a number of
women who were then required to work as prostitutes increased to a total of 23
years.

H3   The offender pleaded guilty to seven counts of assisting unlawful immigration,
contrary to the Immigration Act 1971, s.25, and was convicted of three counts of
living on the earnings of prostitution, three counts of kidnapping and one count of
incitement to rape. The prosecution case against the offender was that he had
arranged the illegal entry into the country of a number of girls or young
women, and then compelled them to act as prostitutes. One witness, aged 24,
said that she and her 17-year-old sister were approached in Romania and persuaded to come to England with a promise of work in a bar. They were introduced to
the offender and then brought into England by two other men. When they arrived
at the offender's home in London the two girls were required to act as prostitutes
and detained at different addresses. The witness was able to escape before being
required to have sexual intercourse with a client. The offender threatened the sister with violence if she did not submit to intercourse with another man, which she
eventually did. The offender's premises were searched and two other girls were
found who had been brought to the United Kingdom in a similar manner. A third
girl had been brought to the United Kingdom at the age of 16 and had been
required to work as a prostitute for about two years, eventually marrying the
offender. Another girl aged 16 had also been brought to the country where she
was effectively sold by the offender to another man and subsequently worked
as a prostitute for the offender. A further girl had been helped by the offender
to enter the United Kingdom with a false passport, and subsequently required
to work as a prostitute. Investigations established that in the three years before
his arrest, a total of more than £200,000 had been deposited in the offender's
bank accounts. Sentenced to two years' imprisonment concurrent in respect of

the offences of assisting illegal immigration, a total of three years for living on the earnings of prostitution and ten years on each count of kidnapping, all concurrent. The Attorney General asked the Court to review the sentences on the ground that they were unduly lenient.

H4   **Held:** the evidence established that the offender occupied a principal position in a well organised and international enterprise concerned with the illegal trafficking of women into the United Kingdom. So far as assisting unlawful immigration was concerned, there was guidance in *Van Binh Le and Stark* [1999] 1 Cr.App.R.(S.) 422 to the effect that the appropriate sentencing bracket would be between two and a half years' and five years' imprisonment, depending on the circumstances. Where there was a commercial element the appropriate figure would be five years' imprisonment. This guidance was in the context of a maximum sentence of seven years' imprisonment, which had subsequently been increased to 10 years. The offender fell into the category of commercial exploitation of illegal immigrants for whom a sentence of five years was wholly appropriate despite his pleas of guilty. For offences of living on immoral earnings, the case of *Farrugia* (1979) 69 Cr.App.R. 108 established that a sentence of two years might be appropriate where there had been no coercion or corruption, but that five years might be appropriate where there was coercion or corruption but not otherwise. This had been confirmed in *Powell* [2001] 1 Cr.App.R.(S.) 76 (p.261). So far as one of three victims of the offence of living on the earnings of prostitution was concerned, there was evidence of coercion and corruption which would have justified a sentence of five years' imprisonment. In the case of two other victims, who had lived with the offender for a significant period of time, there was some justification for treating their case as different, but there was evidence of coercion and corruption such as to justify a sentence of three years' imprisonment in respect of the offences against them. So far as the offence of kidnapping was concerned it was clear from *Spence and Thomas* (1983) 5 Cr.App.R.(S.) 413 that a sentence in excess of eight years' imprisonment could be expected. In those circumstances, bearing in mind that three witnesses had been held against their will, a sentence of 10 years' imprisonment was not inappropriate. For the offence of incitement to rape of which the offender was convicted in relation to one victim, a sentence of at least eight years' imprisonment was appropriate in the light of *Millberry* [2003] 2 Cr.App.R.(S.) 31 (p.142). It followed that the Court did not consider that the sentences imposed by a judge adequately reflected the guidance to be found in the decisions and that the total sentence of 10 years did not adequately reflect the criminality of the case or the need for a substantial deterrent sentence. In respect of the first victim the appropriate sentence would be five years for facilitating illegal entry and three years for living on the earnings of prostitution. So far as the second victim was concerned the sentence for illegal entry would be five years, for kidnapping, 10 years, and for living on the earnings of prostitution, five years' imprisonment. The sentences on three of the counts would be served consecutively so as to make a total of 20 years' imprisonment. The total sentences imposed in respect of the victim who had been forced to submit to sexual intercourse would be increased to 23 years' imprisonment, which would be the overall sentence.

H5 **Cases cited:** *Van Binh Le and Stark* [1999] 1 Cr.App.R.(S.) 422, *Farrugia* (1979) 69 Cr.App.R. 108, *Powell* [2001] 1 Cr.App.R.(S.) 76 (p.261), *Spence and Thomas* (1983) 5 Cr.App.R.(S.) 413, *Millberry* [2003] 2 Cr.App.R.(S.) 31 (p.142)

H6 **References:** facilitating illegal entry, *Current Sentencing Practice* B 9-5; living on the earnings of prostitution, *Current Sentencing Practice* B5

H7 *R. Horwell* for the Attorney General.
B.Waylen for the offender.

JUDGMENT

1   **LATHAM L.J.:**   This is an application by Her Majesty's Attorney General for leave to refer to this Court sentences which were imposed upon the offender after trial at the Wood Green Crown Court when on November 22, 2003 he was sentenced to a total of 10 years' imprisonment for offences relating to the trafficking in young girls. As Mr Horwell on behalf of the Attorney General has indicated, this is the first occasion upon which this Court has had to consider a story of human trafficking of this nature and accordingly we give leave for the sentences to be referred.

2   Human trafficking is a problem which confronts not only this country but many other countries in the world. It is an activity which is degrading and produces untold misery to girls all over the world. As Mr Horwell has said, some parts of the story in this case have echoes of the days of slavery with girls being sold by one procurer to another. Sadly the story which is disclosed by this case is now only too familiar from the newspaper reports which have put a spotlight on this trade in the last few years. Accordingly, it is clearly important that courts which deal with these offences have well in mind the need for a message to be sent that this type of activity is despicable, cannot be tolerated by a civilised society and that those involved in it will be sentenced to lengthy sentences of imprisonment.

3   With that introduction we turn to the story in this case.

4   The offender is an Albanian by birth, although now a British citizen, is 26 years of age and effectively of previous good character. The story involves seven young girls all of whom were brought here at the hands, in part at least, of the offender in breach of our immigration laws. As a result he faced seven counts of assisting unlawful immigration contrary to s.25 of the Immigration Act 1971. He did not deny his involvement in those offences. He pleaded guilty to them and he was sentenced to two years' imprisonment in respect of each of them to be served concurrently.

5   The trial, which was presided over by the sentencing judge, related to his pleas of not guilty to the offences which the prosecution claimed followed from the

girls having been brought into this country. As far as three of those girls were concerned, after coming into this country they worked as prostitutes, each having given evidence that in one way or another they were corrupted by the offender or coerced by the offender so as to prostitute themselves. In relation to those offences, which were of living off immoral earnings, the offender was sentenced in relation to two of the girls to 12 months' imprisonment and to one of the girls to three years' imprisonment. We will return to the reason for the distinction later.

6   So far as one of those girls was concerned, her story made it clear that she had been brought to this country on false promises and was originally held here against her will. In addition to her account, there was an account from two sisters which told a similar tale of being brought here by promises of lawful employment which, when they arrived, here it became apparent were wholly untrue; they were being brought here to become prostitutes and were held against their will in order to persuade them to become prostitutes. In relation to those three girls the offender was charged with kidnapping and received sentences of 10 years' imprisonment which were essentially the substantive sentences upon which the judge based the overall sentence.

7   One of those three girls gave a graphic account of having been forced to submit to the sexual advances of a colleague of the offender and in relation to that he was charged with incitement to rape and sentenced to eight years' imprisonment. The remaining two girls were, fortunately for them, found on the offender's premises when the police raided them ultimately in October 2002, before the offender had in fact done any more than assist to bring them into this country and was providing them with accommodation in his flat.

8   That then is a general description of the nature of the offences which this offender faced as charges in the trial and of which he was found guilty.

9   The evidence which the jury heard and upon which they convicted the offender started with the investigation which was triggered by a girl Claudia E, whom we shall refer to as Claudia, being found in the street on October 29, 2002 in Green Lanes, London. She waved down a passing police car and complained that she had been raped. It was her story which lifted the lid on the offender's activities. It transpired that she, who was then 24 years of age, and her sister Arabella, aged 17, were approached by a man in Romania where they lived and were persuaded to come to this country being promised work in an English bar. They were taken to Prague where they met the offender who took them to Italy from where they were driven in a car to England by two Italian men. Eventually they arrived at the offender's home at 3c Middleton Road in London where they were assaulted by the offender and informed that they would be separated. He told Arabella that she would now have to work as a prostitute. She was threatened that water and food would be withheld until she complied. They were offered, during the time that they were together, to various men, one of whom they knew by the name of Plummi. The sisters were then separated. Arabella was taken to premises where she learnt that she had been sold to Plummi. She was told that she would have to have sexual intercourse and oral sex with men. She did not submit and was then locked into a room. Three men then came and undressed and demanded sexual intercourse and oral sex. She again refused. She was threatened. She

responded by saying that she would throw herself out of the window rather than submit. Plummi who was there, confronted by her intransigence, telephoned the offender. He arrived together with the girl called Alexandra L, to whom we will refer shortly, who acted as interpreter because he was unable to speak Romanian. Through her he threatened to beat Arabella and leave her for dead unless she did whatever Plummi demanded of her. The offender and Alexandra L then left. Arabella then ultimately was forced to submit to sexual intercourse by Plummi. She was terrified.

10   Claudia had meanwhile been taken to another address where she was kept prisoner. She was told that she would have to have sex with clients the next day. It was fortunate that she was able to escape from that address into the street and, as we have indicated, wave down a passing police car before she was subjected to any sexual indignities.

11   The information that she had enabled the police to identify the offender's address at 3c Middleton Road. They went straight to that address where they found the offender. The offender, it is right to say, at that stage indicated to the police that he would be able to get Arabella released and he telephoned Plummi. Arabella was indeed, as a result of that telephone call, released, but simply into the street where she was ultimately found by the police in a state of distress.

12   The offender's address was searched and the paraphernalia of prostitution was found. Hundreds of condoms, lubricants and guides to massage parlours were discovered and it was plain that the premises had been used to house prostitutes before they went to brothels in London, Reading, Luton and elsewhere. Also in the premises were the two girls Andrea S and Alina B who were in possession of false Italian passports. They were illegal immigrants from Romania and were cousins. They had originally left Romania to work as waitresses in Italy. They were, as they described it, bought by a man in Italy and they were driven to the United Kingdom where they were met by the offender and Alexandra L and were taken to the offender's address. It was apparent that the girl Alina B had in fact been in this country previously and had been forced into prostitution but had agreed to go to Italy to collect her cousin and to bring her back to this country for the same purpose, which was the reason that they were together in the offender's address at that time.

13   Also at that address was the girl Alexandra L. She left Moldavia in July 2000, aged 16, and entered this country with the assistance of the offender and other people. She had been taken first to Romania and then met up with another of the girls involved in this case, Natasha B. They met the offender in Yugoslavia and were brought to this country. When they were here the offender told them that he had had to spend a substantial amount of money to bring them to this country and they would have to repay him by working as prostitutes. For at least two years Alexandra L did so, working as a prostitute in London, Reading, Luton and Bedford. Alexandra L in fact married the offender on March 7, 2001. She told the police and the court that she felt coerced both into prostitution and into the marriage, but it is right to say that she continued to live with the offender right through the period from the time she came to this country to the time that the police went to the offender's home on October 29, 2002 and indeed played the

part that we have described in the story told by Arabella. She said that the offender had lived off her earnings in the sense that they shared expenses from pooled finances.

14   The girl she came over to this country with, Natasha B, was also just 16 years of age. She said that after she was brought to this country she was sold by the offender for £7,000 to a pimp in Brighton. She was then told that she would have to repay that sum by having to work as a prostitute. She stayed in Brighton for a time but then she came back to London and thereafter worked as a prostitute for the offender. He subjected her to assaults and other forms of mistreatment and throughout kept a close watch on her. She received between £600 and £1,000 per day, all of which was given to the offender or those who worked for him. She was simply provided with pocket money. She subsequently managed to escape from the offender, was traced by the police and gave the account which we have just described.

15   Finally, so far as the girls themselves are concerned, was the girl Alla O. She was a Moldavian national who grew up with Alexandra L. She heard of what was happening to Alexandra L and came to this country to be with her. The offender helped her to obtain entry. She was at first turned back at Dover when she was attempting to use a false Czech passport, but that did not deter either the offender or her; a false Belgian passport was then procured and she managed to enter this country through the Channel Tunnel later. She was 20 years of age. On her arrival, which was in July 2002, the offender told her that she would have to reimburse him for the £7,000 it had cost to bring her to England and he made her work for him as a prostitute for some five months before the arrests were made. Her account was that she lived with Alexandra L and the offender at the offender's home and they all shared household expenses.

16   The investigation by the police was able to establish that a sum of £204,396 could be traced through bank deposits which the offender controlled in the three years or so from 1999 to October 2002 and it is plain from the accounts that were given by the girls, and from the offender himself, that he lived extravagantly. He travelled extensively, he wore designer clothes and at the time of his arrest he was in possession of a Ferrari and a BMW.

17   The evidence therefore established that the offender occupied a principal position in a well-organised and international enterprise concerned in the illegal trafficking of women into the United Kingdom and the pattern which was disclosed by these girls is a pattern recognisable in accounts given by others in the material which has been exposed, as we have indicated, in the press.

18   There is no doubt that the judge was faced with a difficult sentencing exercise in the sense that there was no guidance from this Court or from the Sentencing Panel dealing with human trafficking and in those circumstances the judge was, we accept, faced with a relatively clean piece of paper. However, sufficient guidance can be gleaned from the authorities to which we have been referred by counsel on behalf of the Attorney General, to provide a secure basis for placing these offences in their appropriate sentencing brackets.

19   So far as assisting the unlawful immigration into this country is concerned, Lord Bingham, Lord Chief Justice, in *Van Binh Le and Stark* [1999] 1 Cr.App.R

(S) 422 gave guidance to the effect that the appropriate sentencing bracket would be between two and a half and five years' imprisonment, depending upon the circumstances of the case. The Lord Chief Justice made it clear that in cases where there was a commercial element the appropriate figure would be one of five years' imprisonment and that was in the context of a maximum of seven years' imprisonment which was the regime in place at the time. In the case of this offender the maximum sentence available to the court was one of 10 years' imprisonment and there is no doubt at all that his offending in this regard falls into the category of commercial exploitation of illegal entrants where a sentence of five years is wholly appropriate despite his pleas of guilty, bearing in mind the number of offences.

20   The next category of offence is the offence of living on immoral earnings contrary to s.30 of the Sexual Offences Act 1956. In such cases the authorities establish that where there has been no coercion or corruption a sentence of two years may be appropriate. This Court said that as long ago as 1979 in *Farrugia* (1979) 69 Cr.App.R 108 where it was said that five years might be appropriate where there was coercion or corruption but not otherwise. In the case of *Powell* [2001] 1 Cr.App.R.(S.) 76 (p.261), this Court considered that where there was coercion the appropriate figure was indeed five years' imprisonment. In the present case, as far as this offender is concerned, the evidence establishes, it seems to us, that Natasha B was certainly subject to coercion and corruption and that in the case of the charges in relation to her which were firstly procuring a girl under the age of 21 to have unlawful sexual intercourse, and count 8, living on prostitution, that fact had to be taken into account by the sentencing judge. So far as procuring was concerned, the maximum was two years' imprisonment. The judge sentenced him to 18 months' imprisonment and that was an appropriate sentence for that offence. However, as far as living on immoral earnings was concerned, it appears to us that the facts justified a sentence of five years' imprisonment.

21   So far as Alexandra L and Alla O were concerned, it may be said that their position was different. They clearly lived with the offender for a significant period of time and that was the basis of the charge of living on immoral earnings. There was therefore some justification in treating their cases differently. But in the evidence of both girls there was sufficient to justify the conclusion that there was an element of coercion and corruption and in the overall context of the story an appropriate sentence for them would have been one of three years' imprisonment.

22   We then turn to the offence of kidnapping. It is plain that where there is serious kidnapping of this sort a sentence in excess of eight years' imprisonment can be expected. That was clearly spelt out by Lord Lane in *Spence and Thomas* (1983) 5 Cr.App.R.(S.) 413. In those circumstances, bearing in mind the evidence of Natasha, Claudia and Arabella, it is plain that the sentence must reflect the fact that each of them was not only tricked into coming here but also held here against their will and indeed so far as Natasha was concerned sold under circumstances that we have described. It follows that a sentence of 10 years' imprisonment was not inappropriate and we shall have to return to that question when considering the way in which the overall sentences should be constructed.

23   The next and final offence as to which there is guidance is the offence of incitement to rape which was the offence which the offender faced in relation to Arabella. The case of *Millberry* [2003] 2 Cr.App.R.(S.) 31 (p.142) does not directly deal with incitement to rape, but clearly incitement to rape in the circumstances of this case must carry with it a sentence of at least eight years' imprisonment, bearing in mind the nature of the account given by Arabella. Indeed, if it was taken by itself that offence would have merited a substantially greater sentence of imprisonment.

24   Finally, we are properly reminded that in the case of *Millberry* it was said that for campaigns of rape sentences of 15 years' imprisonment and upwards can be expected; and the story that we have related carries with it the characteristics of a campaign of rape, bearing in mind the consequences to these young girls brought over here unwillingly so far as prostitution is concerned.

25   It follows that we do not consider that the sentences imposed by the judge adequately reflected the guidance given to which we have referred in respect of each of the individual counts in the indictment, nor do we consider that 10 years' imprisonment in total in any way adequately reflects the criminality in this case or the need for a substantial and deterrent sentence. However, clearly some allowance has to be made in order to adjust the sentences by making them concurrent to recognise what would otherwise be a total sentence of too great a length, and to take into account the element of double jeopardy.

26   We consider the right approach to sentencing in this case is as follows. In relation to Alexandra, that is counts 1 and 4, the offender should receive a sentence of five years' imprisonment on count 1 and three years' imprisonment on count 4. Those sentences are to be served consecutively in order to reflect the fact that there are two separate sets of criminal activities involved in what the offender did.

27   So far as Natasha is concerned, on count 5, relating to illegal entry, the sentence is five years' imprisonment; on count 6, the offence of kidnapping, 10 years imprisonment; on count 7 for procuring her for sexual intercourse, that will remain at 18 months' imprisonment and for living on immoral earnings, five years' imprisonment. Counts 5 and 6 will be served consecutively; counts 7 and 8 will be served concurrently but consecutively to counts 5 and 6, making a total of 20 years' imprisonment.

28   So far as Alla is concerned, in relation to the illegal entry count the sentence will be five years' imprisonment and on count 14, immoral earnings, three years' imprisonment to be served concurrently, as in the case of Alexandra, making a total of eight years' imprisonment.

29   So far as Claudia is concerned, count 16, the offence of kidnapping, the proper sentence is one of 10 years' imprisonment as imposed by the judge, but as far as count 22 is concerned, which is assisting illegal entry, the sentence should be five years' imprisonment. Those sentences are to be served consecutively making a total of 15 years' imprisonment.

30   So far as Arabella is concerned, count 18, incitement to rape, we consider that that should be restricted to the sentence imposed by the judge, that is one of eight years' imprisonment, and the sentence on count 19 for kidnapping should like-

wise be restricted to the sentence imposed by the judge of 10 years' imprisonment. However, so far as count 23 is concerned of assisting illegal entry, that
will be increased to five years' imprisonment. We restrict the sentences in
relation to counts 18 and 19 because in our judgment all three counts should
be served consecutively, making a total of 23 years' imprisonment.

31   So far as Andrea L and Alina O are concerned, that is the remaining counts 24
and 25, in respect of each of those counts of assisting illegal entry there will be
sentences of five years' imprisonment, as in the case of all the others.

32   The overall sentence we therefore impose is one of 23 years' imprisonment.

ATTORNEY GENERAL'S REFERENCE NO.10 OF 2004 (SIMON WALKER TEESDALE)

COURT OF APPEAL (Lord Justice Kay, Mr Justice Roderick Evans
and Mr Justice Pitchers): April 29, 2004

[2004] EWCA Crim 1530; [2005] 1 Cr.App.R.(S.) 20

⟨LT⟩ Causing death by dangerous driving; Diabetes; Drugs; Knowledge; Undue
leniency

H1   *Causing death by dangerous driving—driver suffering from diabetes driving with
knowledge that his insulin requirement was unstable—colliding with pedestrian
while suffering hypoglycaemic attack—adequacy of sentence*

H2   A sentence of 18 months' imprisonment for causing death by dangerous driving, where a driver suffering from diabetes drove with the knowledge that his
insulin requirement was unstable and collided with a pedestrian while suffering
a hypoglycaemic attack, increased to two years' imprisonment.

H3   The offender pleaded guilty to causing death by dangerous driving. The
offender, aged 33, had been an insulin-dependent diabetic since the age of
eight. He had become addicted to heroin and had suffered an infection which
required treatment with antibiotics, which affected his insulin requirements.
He had not held a driving licence since January 1998, but a few days before
the incident bought a motor vehicle, but did not obtain insurance to drive it.
The offender left his home one morning with his baby daughter in a baby seat,
saying that he was going to visit his mother. He later telephoned his wife to
say that his mother was not at home. Some hours later his car was seen being driven in an erratic manner. As it proceeded down a road subject to a 30mph speed
limit, it swerved into the path of oncoming traffic, returned to its own lane, mounted the pavement and collided with a pedestrian who suffered severe head injuries
and later died. The offender's car continued and eventually collided with a brick
wall. The offender reversed the vehicle and continued along the road until the
vehicle broke down. When police officers arrived, the offender collapsed. He

was found to have a very low blood sugar level and was taken to hospital. The offender's blood was found to contain amphetamines and diazepam, which could be incompatible with driving. The offender attributed the accident to a hypoglycaemic attack. Sentenced to 18 months' imprisonment and disqualified from driving for four years. The Attorney General asked the Court to review the sentence on the ground that it was unduly lenient.

H4   **Held:** the essence of the case was that the offender drove having taken drugs which, whilst not necessarily affecting his ability to drive, might have had an effect on his ability to manage his diabetes at a time when he knew that the antibiotics he was taking for an infection made his daily insulin requirement unstable. For the Attorney General it was submitted that the offence was aggravated by the fact that the offender drove when he knew that his control requirement was unstable, that he drove after taking drugs which might have affected his judgment, and that he must have known that he was unfit to drive on the morning of the incident, that the offender did not have insurance or a driving licence and that he had endangered the life of his baby daughter by taking her as a passenger. It was submitted for the Attorney General that the case came into the higher culpability bracket identified in *Cooksley* [2003] 1 Cr.App.R.(S.) 1 (p.1), and that the starting point in a contested case would have been within the range of four to five years. The Court accepted that the case presented a difficult sentencing problem. The Court had reached the conclusion that the sentence was unduly lenient. The offender's driving was appalling, but the factor of diabetes mitigated the serious nature of the way in which the driving occurred. Where bad driving resulted from a failure properly to manage the offender's own condition, this was a serious aggravating factor in an offence of this kind. In the light of the guidance in *Cooksley*, the Court considered that the case had to be considered as coming into the top category, where the appropriate starting point in a contested case would be of the order of five years. The offender had driven at a time when he knew that there were problems with his diabetes and his control of it, and had exhibited a failure to take proper care to make sure that he would not represent a substantial risk to others if he drove his vehicle. The taking of drugs was not a feature which would in itself have called for a long sentence, as the level of drugs was not such as to be likely to cause a greater risk of harm, but the drugs had to be seen in the context of the management of the offender's condition. The offender must have known that the taking of drugs made it considerably more difficult for him to manage his diabetes, and that any failure to manage his diabetes coupled with driving represented a serious risk to other road users. It seemed to the Court that the proper sentence on a contested trial would have been of the order of four to four and a half years' imprisonment. Making allowance for the mitigation and discounting the sentence for the guilty pleas, it seemed that the judge could properly conclude that the sentence could be reduced to the level of two and a half to three years, but that the sentence could not further be discounted below that level. The Court accordingly concluded that the sentence was unduly lenient. Taking into account the element of double jeopardy, the Court would substitute a sentence of two years' imprisonment. The period of disqualification would not be changed.

H5   **Cases cited:**   *Cooksley* [2003] 1 Cr.AppR.(S.) 1 (p.1), *Davies* [2002] 1 Cr.App.R.(S.) 135 (p.579)

H6   **References:** causing death by dangerous driving, *Current Sentencing Practice* B 1-7

H7   *S. Denison* for the Attorney General.
      R.P. Johnson for the offender.

JUDGMENT

1   **KAY L.J.:**   Her Majesty's Attorney General seeks the leave of the Court to refer to it a sentence which he considers to be unduly lenient pursuant to s.36 of the Criminal Justice Act 1988. We grant leave.

2   The offender is aged 33. On December 1, 2003 he pleaded guilty to an offence of causing death by dangerous driving. On January 9, 2004 he was sentenced by H.H. Judge King, sitting at the Reading Crown Court, to 18 months' imprisonment and he was disqualified from holding a driving licence for four years.

3   In summary, the offender is a diabetic who drove after having taken drugs which, whilst not necessarily affecting his ability to drive a vehicle, may have affected his ability to manage his diabetes at a time when he knew that his daily insulin requirement was unstable. He was driving his new car for the first time. He had no driving licence and he was not insured. He had his 10-week-old child in the front passenger seat. He suffered hypoglycaemia and collided with a pedestrian, causing the death of that unfortunate person.

4   In more detail the facts were these. The deceased was a 16-year-old. The offender has been an insulin-dependent diabetic since he was eight years old. In early March 2003 he had suffered an infection to his arm which required surgery and was treated with antibiotics. That was having an effect on his insulin requirement at the time of the incident. The offender has also been addicted to heroin since May 2002 and he had voluntarily attended a course for his addiction. He has not held a driving licence since January 1998. A few days before this incident he bought a Toyota Hilux 4 × 4 vehicle, but he did not obtain insurance in order to drive it.

5   On March 20, 2003 he left his home in Langley, Slough, at about 9.00am. He drove his new car with his 10-week-old daughter in a baby seat in the front passenger seat. He had told his wife that he was going to see his mother. He phoned her at 9.30am to say that his mother was not home and that he would see her later.

6   His movements until about 12.15pm are not known. At about 12.15pm he visited Mothercare at a retail park on the A4 near Slough. He left at 12.35pm. Shortly thereafter he was driving on the dual carriageway which is a part of the A4. He stopped at a traffic light at a roundabout. When the light turned to green his car did not move. It rolled a few feet forward on to the junction, then stopped

again and the light turned back to red. The car was blocking the junction. When the light again turned to green the offender's car shot forward, almost hitting the back of the vehicle in front. It then swerved across the two lanes of a dual carriageway, bouncing off the kerb and the central reservation. As it approached Langley Road on its left, it almost passed the junction, before swerving round into Langley Road. The driver of the vehicle behind was sufficiently concerned at the offender's driving to divert from his own route and follow the offender.

7   Langley Road is a two-carriageway road with a 30mph speed limit. The unfortunate Usman Akhtar was walking on the pavement in the same direction as the offender on the offender's nearside. As the car proceeded down Langley Road at about 35 to 40mph it swerved out into the path of the oncoming traffic, then back into its own lane. It then mounted the pavement and struck Mr Akhtar and a low wall to the left of the pavement. There was no sign of the offender having applied the brakes.

8   Mr Akhtar was propelled beyond the wall into a hedge. He suffered severe head injuries and died on March 26, 2003. The offender's car did not stop, but continued along Langley Road in the same manner. As it approached Langley High Street it swerved into the path of an on-coming vehicle, then back again and mounted the pavement. It hit a brick wall and a signpost, badly damaging the front of the vehicle. The offender reversed it off the signpost and back into the road, and then continued on into Langley High Street. It then turned left into Common Road. The front nearside wheel was by then at an angle and making a screeching noise as it drove. The car broke down in Common Road and stopped, with smoke and steam coming out of the bonnet. The offender remained in the driver's seat for a few minutes, leaning over to the baby seat in the front passenger seat. He then went round to the passenger door and leant in towards the baby seat. He was unable to unbuckle the seat belt. His behaviour seemed strange to passers-by who saw him, and he then slumped against the car. When the police arrived he collapsed to the ground. There was a small amount of frothy saliva on his lips and his eyes were staring and fixed. His blood sugar level was found to be very low. He was treated at the scene and was then taken to hospital, where the level was found still to be very low. After further treatment there he was discharged into police custody.

9   When he was seen by a doctor at Amersham Police Station that evening, he said that he was on antibiotics for an infection to his right upper arm which affected his diabetic control. He admitted using opiates but had only taken dihydrocodeine that day. He said that he had not taken any heroin for two days, but he had smoked cannabis in the previous 24 hours. Although his memory of the incident was poor, he did remember driving to his doctor's surgery in the morning to seek help with his diabetic control as he knew he was not well.

10   A sample of his blood taken that day was found to contain amphetamine at the level of 0.11 micrograms per millilitre of blood, and diazepam and its major breakdown product, desmethyldiazepam, at concentrations of 0.14 and 0.13 micrograms per millilitre of blood respectively. The effect of these drugs can be incompatible with driving.

11   In interview on March 21, 2003 the offender said that the only thing he remembered of the previous day was being in Mothercare in the morning and drinking a
bottle of Lucozade and knowing that he had to get to his doctor's surgery. He said
that he had been intending to get insurance for the car that morning. That day was
the first time he had driven the car. He said that he had held a full driving licence
since he was aged 17 and had never had it taken away. He claimed to be unaware
that his licence had expired in 1998. He said that the accident happened because
he had suffered a hypoglycaemic attack. He went on to say that he had been waiting for 14 months to get help for his drug addiction. He did not know when he had
last taken drugs.

12   When he was interviewed on May 10, 2003 he was asked about the findings
from the analysis of his blood. He denied that he had taken amphetamine and
could not explain how it came to be in his blood. He said that he was prescribed
diazepam by his doctor and remembered taking one tablet two days before the
accident.

13   In summary, the offender drove having taken drugs which, whilst not necessarily affecting his ability to drive a vehicle, might have had an effect on his ability
to manage his diabetes at a time when he knew that, because of the antibiotics he
was taking for his infection in his arm, his daily insulin requirement was unstable.

14   Against that factual background Mr Denison on behalf of the Attorney General
submits that there were a number of aggravating features. He submits that the
offender drove at a time when he knew that his diabetic control requirement
was unstable because of the antibiotics that he was taking. Secondly, he contends
that it is a further aggravating feature that he drove and killed a person after
having taken drugs which might have affected his judgment at a time when he
knew that his diabetic control requirement was unstable because of the antibiotics
that he was taking. Thirdly, the offender must have known that he was unfit to
drive that morning as he felt sufficiently unwell before the hypoglycaemic attack
to feel it necessary to attend his doctor's surgery. Fourthly, he drove and killed
without having insurance and without having a driving licence since January
1998. Finally, in the circumstances to which we have already referred, it is submitted that the offender endangered not only the life of others but also the life of
his 10-week-old child by driving with her as a passenger in the front seat of the
car.

15   On the other hand it is recognised that there were a number of mitigating features. The first is that the offender had pleaded guilty: it was not at the first
possible opportunity, but the judge thought it right nonetheless to give him full
credit in the particular circumstances for his plea of guilty. Secondly, it was
accepted that he had shown remorse and that that remorse was genuine. Thirdly,
he had no previous convictions for driving offences. Fourthly, he had always in
the past successfully controlled his diabetes.

16   Against those aggravating and mitigating factors it is submitted that the sentence of 18 months' imprisonment with the four-year disqualification from
driving was unduly lenient, in that it did not adequately reflect the gravity of
the offence in view of the aggravating features and in consequence it failed to pro-

vide the necessary levels of punishment and deterrence required for offences of this type.

17   We have had our attention drawn to two cases. The first, unsurprisingly, is the guidance given by this Court in the case of *Cooksley and others and the Attorney-General's Reference No 152 of 2002* [2003] 1 Cr.App.R.(S.) 1 (p.1). There the Court sought to lay down, consequent upon advice given to it by the Sentencing Advisory Panel, the appropriate level of sentencing for offences of causing death by dangerous driving. In its advice to the Court the Sentencing Advisory Panel had set out a number of aggravating factors, splitting them into a first category of those which it described as "highly culpable standards of driving at time of the offence". They included, at para.(a), "the consumption of drugs (including legal medication known to cause drowsiness) or of alcohol, ranging from a couple of drinks to a 'motorised pub crawl'". Further, at para.(g), it included "driving when knowingly suffering from a medical condition which significantly impairs the offender's driving skills". The second category of aggravating features was "driving habitually below acceptable standard," in relation to which para.(j) read:

> "Other offences committed at the same time, such as driving without ever having held a licence; driving while disqualified; driving without insurance; driving while a learner without supervision; taking a vehicle without consent; driving a stolen vehicle."

It is submitted to us that paras (a) and paragraph (g) have a relevance to this case—and we will return to them shortly—and also that the absence of the licence and the absence of insurance brought the matter to be considered under para.(j) as well.

18   The guidance given by the Court as to the level of sentencing was to split the possible offending into three categories of seriousness: first, those with no aggravating circumstances, secondly, those described as intermediate culpability, and, thirdly, those of higher culpability. So far as higher culpability was concerned, the Panel had recommended that the approach should be that a case came into that category:

> "When the standard of the offender's driving is more highly dangerous (as would be indicated, for example, by the presence of one or two of factors (a) to (i) the Panel suggests that the appropriate starting point would be a custodial sentence within the range from two to five years. The exact level of sentence would be determined by the dangerousness of the driving and by the presence or absence of other aggravating or mitigating factors."

The Court accepted in principle that there should be a category of the kind suggested, but came to the conclusion that the band of two to five years was simply too wide and that the starting point ought to be to consider a much narrower band of four to five years in relation to a contested case of this type. That was to be contrasted with the acceptance by the Court of a range of two to three years where there was intermediate culpability.

19   It is submitted on behalf of the Attorney General that this case came into the higher culpability bracket so that the starting point on a contested matter ought to have been within the range of four to five years and that if one started from a point such as that, even having regard to the mitigating features in this case and particularly the guilty plea, it was not possible for a judge properly to end at a figure of 18 months' imprisonment. It is for that reason that it is submitted that the sentence has to be viewed as being unduly lenient.

20   The other case, which was drawn to our attention really by way of illustration of the problems that arise where the dangerous driving results from a diabetic condition, is the case of *Davies* [2002] 1 Cr.App.R.(S.) 135 (p.579). That was a case in which a lorry driver caused the death of three persons. He had driven at a time when he had a history of diabetes and he suffered a hypoglycaemic attack whilst driving. That was because he had failed to take proper precautions to ensure that he would not suffer such an attack. It had an aggravating feature that it was not the first time that he had driven and suffered such an attack so that he was particularly aware of the dangers. He had been sentenced to three years' imprisonment and the Court concluded that that sentence was not manifestly excessive.

21   It is not suggested that that case factually can be equated to this case one way or the other because there are different factors that militate in one direction in respect of some matters and in the other direction in respect of others, but it indicates, so it is submitted, the broad approach of the court to cases of this kind.

22   The submissions made on behalf of the offender by Mr Johnson in his helpful skeleton argument and in his useful address to the Court are that the sentence was one within the proper range that was open to the judge. He accepts that it may be viewed as being a lenient sentence, but he submits that it cannot be characterised as being unduly lenient.

23   The first point that he makes is one with which we wholeheartedly agree: the sentencing exercise for the judge was a particularly difficult one. We think that this was a case where there was little guidance for the judge over and above the matters to which we have already referred and that the particular circumstances of this case really have not been replicated in other cases. We think it is right that the judge in those circumstances was, as is suggested, dealing with a matter which was peculiarly difficult.

24   It is submitted that, notwithstanding those problems, the sentencing judge very carefully considered all the factors, properly took into account the guidance given by this Court in *Cooksley* and reached his conclusion, giving considerable weight to the mitigation that there had been in this case. It is submitted in those circumstances that a sentence of 18 months can be seen as a proper sentence within the range, even if it was at the lenient end of the range.

25   If at the end of the day the Court reaches a conclusion that it was unduly lenient, Mr Johnson rightly invites the Court to bear in mind that this is the second occasion on which the offender's sentence has to be considered and to make the normal allowance that is to be made for what has come to be known as double jeopardy.

26   We have anxiously considered this case for the reasons that we have already made clear as to the difficulty that it represents. At the end of the day we have reached a conclusion that this sentence was unduly lenient. We make clear though that we are not over-critical of the judge in reaching that difficult decision. The driving on this occasion was, on any view of it, appalling. That in itself would be a very serious matter were it not for the factor of diabetes. The factor of diabetes explained why driving of this dreadful standard in fact took place and to that extent it mitigates the serious nature of the way in which the driving occurred. However, where such bad driving results from a failure properly to manage the offender's own condition that, as *Cooksley* makes clear, is a seriously aggravating feature of an offence of this kind. In the light of the guidance given by this Court in *Cooksley*, we think this has to be viewed as being a case that does come in that top category, where the appropriate starting point would be, if the matter was contested, a sentence of the order of four to five years. The offender had driven at a time when he knew that there were problems with his diabetes and his control of it, and he had exhibited a failure to take proper care to make sure that that would not represent a substantial risk to others if he drove his vehicle. The taking of the drugs was not in this case a factor which in itself ought to have called for a longer sentence, in that the level of drugs was not such as to be likely to cause a greater risk of harm. But they also have to be seen in the separate context of his management of his condition. He must have known that the taking of drugs would make it considerably more difficult for him to manage his diabetes and that any failure to manage his diabetes coupled with driving represented a serious risk for other road users. We debated with counsel during the course of the hearing whether this is properly to be seen as a case with two aggravating features, both (a) and (g) on the list to which we have referred, or whether it really is simply a case in which one looks at (g). It seems to us unnecessary to resolve that matter. Clearly it is a matter of relevance that there were the drugs, but it is not relevant in the way that it normally is because they did not in themselves represent the danger, they only represented the danger when they were coupled with the condition.

27   Nonetheless it seems to us that this is a case in which the proper sentence on a contested matter would have been a sentence of the order of four to four and a half years' imprisonment. Making every allowance that one can for the mitigation that there was and certainly discounting the sentence for the guilty pleas, which the judge thought attracted a full discount, it seems to us that the judge could properly conclude that the sentence could be reduced to a sentence of the order of two-and-a-half to three years but that it could not further be discounted below that level. Accordingly, we view that as being the appropriate level of sentencing in the circumstances of this case and if we had been passing sentence at first instance a sentence in that bracket would have seemed appropriate to us.

28   We now have to consider what should be done following our conclusion that this sentence is unduly lenient. It is clearly right that we should follow the normal practice of discounting the sentence we otherwise would have deemed to be appropriate. Having considered the matter carefully, we think that this is a case in which we are obliged to interfere with the sentence passed by the judge but

that it should not be a great interference because of the element of double jeopardy. For those reasons we have concluded that we should set aside the sentence of 18 months' imprisonment and substitute for it a sentence of two years' imprisonment. We make clear that that is not the sentence we would have deemed appropriate if the matter had been heard at first instance.

[Paragraphs [29]–[32] have been omitted.]

R. v PAUL MICHAEL REECE

COURT OF APPEAL (Lord Justice Scott Baker, Mr Justice Hunt and Judge Radford): April 30, 2004

[2004] EWCA Crim 1387; [2005] 1 Cr.App.R.(S.) 21

⟨LT⟩ Criminal intent; Manslaughter; Sentence length

H1   *Detention in a young offender institution—manslaughter—manslaughter of friend by kicking while drunk—length of sentence*

H2   Six and a half years' detention in a young offender institution for the manslaughter of a friend by kicking him while he lay on the ground reduced to five years.

H3   The appellant, aged 19 at the time of the offence, pleaded guilty to manslaughter on an indictment for murder. The appellant and the deceased, who were friends, went to a public house together with their respective partners. They were joined by others during the course of the evening. Members of the party left the public house at different times; the appellant and the deceased were the last to leave the public house and they left together. A witness heard them shouting and then saw the deceased fall to the ground. Subsequently, the appellant kicked the deceased at least once while he lay on the ground; the blow left a bruise and the impression of a shoe on the deceased's cheek. The deceased subsequently died from a subarachnoid haemorrhage due to a rupture of the left vertebral artery caused by the kick. The appellant and the deceased were very drunk at the time of the incident. Sentenced to six and a half years' detention in a young offender institution.

H4   **Held:** (considering *Eaton* (1989) 11 Cr.App.R.(S.) 475, *Redfern* [2001] 2 Cr.App.R.(S.) 33 (p.155), *Small* (1994) 15 Cr.App.R.(S.) 534, *Morbey* (1994) 15 Cr.App.R.(S.) 53) the Court considered a number of authorities. In this case, there was one kick of moderate severity. A kick with a shod foot was just as serious as the use of a weapon. The appellant had previous convictions for offences of causing alarm or distress and racially aggravated common assault. However, the case was not sufficiently high up the scale of gravity of manslaughter, when there was no specific intent to cause really serious injury, to justify a sentence of six and a half years' detention. The Court concluded that the right sentence would have been five years' detention.

H5   **Cases cited:** *Eaton* (1989) 11 Cr.App.R.(S.) 475, *Redfern* [2001] 2 Cr.App.R.(S.) 33 (p.155), *Small* (1994) 15 Cr.App.R.(S.) 534, *Morbey* (1994) 15 Cr.App.R.(S.) 53

H6   **References:** detention in a young offender institution, manslaughter, *Current Sentencing Practice* E 2-4

H7   *D.J. Desmond* for the appellant.

JUDGMENT

1   **SCOTT BAKER L.J.:** The appellant, aged 20, appeals with the leave of the single judge against a sentence of six and a half years' detention in a young offender institution imposed by Curtis J. in the Crown Court at Stafford on November 5, 2003. The appellant had pleaded guilty to manslaughter on an indictment for murder. At the time of the offence in February of last year the appellant was aged 19. The deceased was aged 25. Both lived in the Leegomery area of Telford. They were apparently friends.

2   The facts of the offence were these. On Friday February 14, 2003 the deceased, Carl Jones, together with his partner, Jane Lloyd, left their home with the appellant and his partner, Donna Flanagan, to go to a public house. Later that evening they were joined by others, including Brian Hancox and David, the appellant's brother.

3   At about closing time they all began to leave at different times in order to walk back to the deceased's home. The appellant and the deceased were the last to leave the public house and they left together. They caught up with Miss Flanagan, and as she started walking towards the house she heard them shouting. She told them to be quiet and carried on walking. When she looked back she saw the deceased swaying and then fall to the ground.

4   Kevin Hill, who was Miss Lloyd's former husband, was babysitting their children at the deceased's house. Miss Lloyd and David arrived home first. A few minutes later the appellant arrived and Hill heard him say that the deceased was in the road. Hill went outside and saw the deceased staggering. The appellant went up to the deceased and started a conversation. Hill could not make out what they were saying as they were both extremely drunk, but he heard the appellant say that he was going to hit the deceased again. He tried to intervene to separate them, but was getting nowhere and so went back to the house to tell David. When they went back outside the deceased was lying on the ground.

5   The evidence is that the appellant had kicked the deceased at least once whilst he was on the ground. The blow was of sufficient strength to leave a bruise and a shoe impression on the deceased's cheek. Efforts were made to revive him and an ambulance was called, but, unfortunately, he died early the following day. The

cause of death was a subarachnoid haemorrhage due to the rupture of the left vertebral artery, which, it appears, was caused by the kick that we have described.

6   The appellant was arrested at the scene. When he was interviewed he recalled going to the public house, but had no recollection of the incident, no doubt because of the very substantial quantity of drink that he had consumed.

7   The appellant has two relevant previous convictions. On March 31, 2000 for, amongst other things, causing intentional harassment alarm or distress he was made the subject of a supervision order for 18 months. On May 2, 2001 for racially aggravated common assault he was made the subject of a 100-hour community punishment order and made to pay compensation.

8   The learned judge had the advantage of a pre-sentence report. It told him that the deceased was a friend of the appellant and that the appellant could recall nothing of the relevant events because he had consumed about 13 pints of beer or lager that night. He was in the habit of excessive drinking and also taking ecstasy and cannabis. This had taken its toll on such employments as the appellant had had. The indicators were that the appellant presented a high risk of reoffending. He was distressed at having caused the death of a man that he considered to be his friend. That distress was compounded by his inability to recall his behaviour that had led to the death.

9   The judge in passing sentence referred to the two previous convictions for violence. He described the appellant's behaviour in kicking the deceased when on the ground and leaving a footprint near his jaw as "high up on the scale of criminal responsibility required for the offence of manslaughter" albeit that the offence was committed without the intention of causing really serious injury. The judge took into account the appellant's youth and the fact that this was his first custodial sentence, and also his plea of guilty at the first practical opportunity, but, nevertheless, emphasised again that this was a bad case.

10   We have been referred by Mr Desmond, who has appeared for the appellant, to a number of authorities. We are indebted to him for the clarity and succinctness with which he has advanced this appeal. He has made a forceful case for reducing the sentence and, indeed, has persuaded the Court to reduce the sentence by a little more than we had originally in mind having considered the papers.

11   First the case of *Eaton* (1989) 11 Cr.App.R.(S.) 475. In that case a sentence of seven years was reduced to one of five and a half years. In the course of his judgment the then Lord Chief Justice, Lord Lane, said this at 478:

> "If one inspects the various cases to which our attention has been drawn, one can see that sentences varying from two years to seven years or more have been imposed in respect of offences of involuntary manslaughter arising out of fights in the streets, similar to the situation which was presented to the judge in the present case. Some of the cases differ very little from accidental death: for instance where the victim is discovered to have an abnormally thin skull, and where consequently, by falling to the ground and hitting his head, the skull has been fractured. At the other end of the scale are cases where a knife or other weapon has been used, where the distinction between manslaughter and murder is wafer-thin.

The present offence is unhappily an example of the comparatively recent manifestation of brute violence starting off with excessive drinking by young men in their late teens or early twenties, and developing into a group attack, each member of the group stimulating the others to violence, a sort of 'wolf pack' syndrome, the violence to be wreaked upon another group, because of some supposed slight.

The problem of course lies very largely on the amount of alcohol which has been consumed. That is not a matter over which this Court has any jurisdiction. All we can do is to make it clear that this sort of violence in these sort of circumstances will, if it causes death, lead to a substantial term of imprisonment, in the hope that it may possibly reduce the amount of alcohol which people in these circumstances seem to drink, and may reduce the incentive to resort to violence at the end of an evening's entertainment."

12   This case, too, has a very plain background of excessive drinking. We have been told by Mr Desmond that the appellant has taken a positive decision that he is never going to drink again and has taken steps to become enrolled on an alcohol awareness course and to seek the assistance of Alcoholics Anonymous. It is, in our judgment, clear that the appellant does have considerable remorse for his serious offence.

13   The case of *Eaton* was distinguished by Mr Desmond on a number of grounds, the most significant appearing to us to be that there were a number of assailants involved. Eaton himself had committed violent disorder shortly before the offence and again was on bail at the time the offence was committed.

14   Then there is *Redfern* [2001] 2 Cr.App.R.(S.) 33 (p.155), where another division of this Court reduced a sentence of six and a half years to one of five and a half years. Curiously the trial judge in that case was also Curtis J. The Court in *Redfern* expressly said that they were not giving an opinion as to whether the sentence of sentence of six and a half years imposed by the trial judge was manifestly excessive. The sentence was reduced to five and a half years primarily on the basis that there was a possible misunderstanding between counsel and the judge about the relevance of *Eaton* and the sentence that had there been substituted by the Court of Appeal to the appropriate sentence in *Redfern*. In any event, it seems to us that on the facts *Redfern* fell a little higher up the scale than the present case. There were three men involved in the attack. It was a violent beating and the assault was unprovoked.

15   We were also referred to the case of *Small* (1994) 15 Cr.App.R.(S.) 534. There a sentence of seven years' imprisonment was reduced to four years' imprisonment following a plea of guilty, but the defendant was a man of previous good character. The death was caused, as here, by a kick on the side of the face. The case of *Small* establishes, in our view, that seven years is an appropriate sentence for more serious and tenacious attacks than that which occurred in the present case.

16   Finally there is *Morbey* ((1994) 15 Cr.App.R.(S.) 53, and our attention has, in particular, been drawn to a passage from the judgment of Beldam L.J. at 56 where he said:

"We consider that the range of sentences which is disclosed by those reported cases in which, on the highest authority, the various decided cases were considered and reconciled show that unless there is some exceptional feature, which was not in the present case, five years is a sentence which can properly be imposed for manslaughter of this kind."

17   In *Morbey* the Court declined to intervene with a sentence of four and a half years where the appellant had been kicked on the head or hit on the head.

18   The factors that, in our judgment, are relevant in the present case are first that there was one kick of moderate severity. A kick with the shod foot is just as serious in our view as the use of a weapon. Second that the appellant had the two previous convictions that we have described.

19   That said, however, we have come to the clear conclusion that this case was not sufficiently high up the scale of gravity of manslaughter when there is no specific intent to cause really serious injury to justify a sentence of six and a half years' detention. We have come to the conclusion in the light of the authorities that the right sentence in this case would have been one of five years' detention. Accordingly, the appeal will be allowed and the sentence of five years' detention substituted for that of six and a half years.

R. v KERRIE JANE COLLINS

COURT OF APPEAL (Lord Justice Scott Baker, Mr Justice Hunt and Judge Radford): May 4, 2004

[2004] EWCA Crim 1269; [2005] 1 Cr.App.R.(S.) 22

(LT) Making false statements; Perverting the course of justice; Sentence length

H1   *Perverting justice—making false witness statement implicating two people in murder—people implicated detained in custody—length of sentence*

H2   A sentence of 18 months' detention in a young offender institution for perverting justice, where a young woman made a false witness statement implicating two people in murder, as a result of which they were detained in custody, reduced to nine months, partly on the grounds of personal mitigation.

H3   The appellant, aged 19, pleaded guilty to doing an act tending or intended to pervert the course of justice. An incident took place in the course of which the owner of a van which was being stolen was run over by the thieves and died from the injuries he suffered. The appellant's boyfriend was suspected of involvement in the offence. The appellant made a number of statements to the police, in one of which she said that a friend of the boyfriend was responsible for running over the victim and that her boyfriend had been involved in the theft of the van. She claimed to have overheard a conversation to this effect. The boyfriend and his friend were charged with murder as a result of this statement. Subsequently the appellant changed her statement and said that she had not overheard the conversation. Her boyfriend and his friend spent respectively five weeks and two weeks in custody as a result of her statement. The proceedings against the boyfriend and his friend were subsequently discontinued. Sentenced to 18 months' detention in a young offender institution.

H4   **Held:** (considering *Evans* [1998] 2 Cr.App.R.(S.) 72) the appellant was unable to give any comprehensive explanation as to why she had made a false statement. She claimed to have been confused; she was in the early stages of labour when the statement was made and had a history of depression. The sentencing judge referred to the fact that the false witness statement had hampered a murder inquiry and resulted in two people being charged with murder and kept in custody. The Court was in no doubt that a custodial sentence was not wrong in principle. Making a witness statement implicating two people in an offence of murder struck at the heart of the administration of justice and had led to two people being kept in custody. In the light of the appellant's personal mitigation, the sentence of 18 months' detention in a young offender institution was manifestly excessive. At the time of the offence the appellant was in an advanced stage of pregnancy; she was young and of previous good character. She pleaded guilty at an early stage in the proceedings. The custodial sentence kept a young mother away from her young children. In the circumstances, the Court would substitute a sentence of nine months' detention in a young offender institution.

H5   **Case cited:** *Evans* [1998] 2 Cr.App.R.(S.) 72

H6   **References:** perverting justice, *Current Sentencing Practice* B 8-2

H7   *D. Mason* for the appellant.
R. Atkins for the Crown.

JUDGMENT

1   **JUDGE RADFORD:**   This appellant, who is aged 19 having been born on May 23, 1984, pleaded guilty at the Crown Court at Warwick on January 8, 2004, on rearraignment, to the one offence that she faced in the indictment, namely an offence of doing an act tending or intended to pervert the course of public justice. She was subsequently sentenced on February 13 by the learned judge, H.H. Judge Coates, to a sentence of 18 months' detention in a young offender institution. She now appeals against the length of that sentence by leave of the single judge.

2   The facts of this offence can be stated shortly. On January 13, 2003 a Ford transit van was stolen in Birmingham. Whilst the van was stolen the owner of the van was run over by the thieves who had taken it and sadly he died from the injuries which he suffered. The appellant's boyfriend was one of a number of people who had been identified in the course of the police investigation into that fatality as possibly being responsible for the incident and he was spoken to about his move-

ments on the day of the offence. He was suspected of involvement because it was said that he had made a 999 call to the police concerning the incident.

3   On May 8, 2003 the appellant was seen by police and she provided a preliminary statement in which she said that she had been aware of the incident having heard about it on television. She said she had not talked to her boyfriend about it.

4   The boyfriend was arrested on suspicion of committing the offence of murder on July 8. In interview he admitted making the 999 call but denied any involvement in any of the offences in respect of which he was interviewed. On the same day, July 8, the appellant made a further statement under the provisions of s.9 of the Criminal Justice Act 1967 to the police. In the course of that statement she said that the personality of her boyfriend had changed and he had been observed by her as being unable to sleep and having been distressed. She gave details in the statement about the police having visited him and having obtained a statement from him about his movements on the day of the offence. She said in the statement that after the day in question she had confronted her boyfriend that something was wrong and that he had hidden something about this matter from her. She said in her statement that her boyfriend had told her that he had gone out with a friend of his to, in the words she recounted, "do a little tickle", which she knew meant that they had gone out to steal cars. She recounted in the statement that it was known to her that the friend of her boyfriend had admitted running over the victim and that her boyfriend had been the person responsible thereafter for telephoning the ambulance in relation to what had occurred. She said that she had been very shocked by what she had been told and she detailed in the statement a conversation that she said she had overheard between her boyfriend and his friend talking about their involvement in the matter. As a result of the statement she made, both the appellant's boyfriend and the co-accused (as he became), his friend, were charged with the offence of murder.

5   On September 2, 2003 the appellant, with a legal representative, met police officers and said that she wished to change part of her statement relating to the conversation that she had recounted as having overheard between her boyfriend and the boyfriend's friend talking about, so she had claimed, their respective parts in the offence. In what she had to say to the police on September 2 the appellant said that that conversation which she recounted in her witness statement had in fact never happened and that she had lied. She was informed that further enquiries should be made.

6   As a result, it should be noted, of the original statement that the appellant had made, the two people she had implicated—her boyfriend and his friend—had been kept in custody. So far as the friend of the boyfriend was concerned he spent two weeks in custody, whilst her boyfriend spent five weeks in custody until granted bail by the High Court.

7   On September 17 the police interviewed the appellant about her false witness statement under caution. In the interview that took place the appellant admitted that all of the contents of her original witness statement made on July 8 were untrue and were in effect lies, except, she said, the fact that her boyfriend had told her that he had telephoned for the ambulance service after the incident concerned.

8   Following those admissions on September 22 the appellant was arrested for the offence for which she was subsequently prosecuted of doing an act tending or intended to pervert the course of public justice. She was interviewed under caution again and she again indicated she had lied when making the original witness statement on July 8. In the course of that interview she was unable really to give any comprehensive explanation as to why she had made the false witness statement. She said that she had been confused. There was, it seems clear, a great deal of uncertainty as to what her responses to the questions posed in that interview in reality amounted to.

9   It should be noted that some time prior to the proceedings against her, following the police discovering from the appellant that her witness statement contained lies, the two people she had implicated had proceedings against them discontinued.

10   When she appeared for sentencing in respect of this matter the appellant was someone who had no convictions recorded against her. In the pre-sentence report, dated February 9, 2004, that was before the learned sentencing judge, there was reference in the course of it to the appellant's assertion that she had not deliberately misled the police. There was reference too to the fact that the appellant had been in the early stages of labour at the time of the full statement made in July and the probation officer writing the report expressed the view that that may certainly have had an impact on her ability to concentrate fully in the course of making that statement. That was a consideration which was referred to expressly in the pre-sentence report. The report also referred to the fact the appellant had two small children then aged two and a half years and five and a half months respectively. The reporting officer referred to the fact that the appellant suffered from depression and was on medication, and had in the past on two occasions attempted suicide.

11   There were medical reports also available, which were before the learned judge who sentenced the appellant, which corroborated what had been written in the pre-sentence report as to the history of depression from which the appellant suffered and medication having been prescribed for some time in respect of that, and confirmed too that she indeed had taken overdoses of drugs prescribed to her on previous occasions.

12   There was also a letter from the appellant's boyfriend in which he wished to make clear, so he stated, that he believed that nothing that the appellant had done had caused him to be imprisoned. He did not hold anything against her and that he had been aware that when she had made the false witness statement the appellant had only been a few days away from giving birth to their child and had been under enormous pressure. He expressed concern about the welfare of the two children should the appellant be given a custodial sentence.

13   In sentencing the appellant, the learned judge referred to the fact that in not telling the truth in the witness statement the appellant had hampered a very serious murder enquiry which had resulted in two people being charged with that grave offence and being kept in custody. The learned judge stated in his sentencing observations that it was not the court's job to understand why the appellant had changed her account or why she had lied in the first place. But it was the case,

so the learned judge observed, that by changing her mind as to what truthfully had happened, the alleged murder had never been pursued to the point of a trial by a judge and jury. The learned judge stated that this was an extremely grave charge and went beyond consideration of the appellant's personal situation. The learned judge stated that taking account of the appellant's age and previous good character, nevertheless a custodial sentence had to be passed and the least sentence in his view that should be passed was 18 months' detention in a young offender institution.

14 In the grounds of appeal against that sentence, and in submissions to us this morning, it has been argued that the sentence of 18 months was manifestly excessive in all the circumstances of the case, having in mind the matters of personal mitigation which were available to the appellant and the length of sentence normally passed for offences of this kind. We are in possession of a report from the prison in which the appellant has been kept and it is right to note that not only has the appellant been cooperative with the prison service but it is plain from what we read that she has found it very difficult being separated from her two young children and that plainly has made her time in custody more distressing than it would be for someone not in her situation.

15 We are in no doubt that there was nothing wrong in principle in a custodial sentence being passed in this case. It is quite obvious that an offence of making a witness statement implicating people in an offence of murder, falsely, strikes at the heart of the administration of justice and it has led in this case to the two men that she implicated in that statement being charged with the grave offence of murder. That led to them being held in custody for some weeks, one of them for as long as five weeks. It is clear too that as a result of the appellant later informing the police that her witness statement was untrue, that led to the discontinuance of the proceedings brought against those two men for murder.

16 In assessing the seriousness of the appellant's behaviour, it is of relevance, we judge, to weigh in the balance the fact that her false witness statement was made, as she well knew, in the course of a police investigation into such a grave crime as murder. But what this appeal is really about, in our judgment, is whether in the light of the appellant's personal mitigation the sentence of 18 months' detention in a young offender institution was manifestly excessive.

17 We have drawn attention to the case of *Evans* [1998] 2 Cr.App.R.(S.) 72 where this Court found persuasive in the context of sentencing for the common law offence of doing an act tending to pervert the course of public justice by making a false witness statement under the provisions of s.9 of the Criminal Justice Act 1967, as a prosecution witness, that Parliament by s.89 of the same Act had provided for a maximum sentence of two years' custody for that statutory offence of wilfully making a s.9 statement material in criminal proceedings which the witness knew or did not believe to be true.

18 We also have consideration for the personal circumstances of the appellant. We have taken account of the fact that at the time the offence was committed the appellant was plainly somewhat vulnerable, being at an advanced stage of pregnancy. We note too her young age at the time of the offence and her previous good character. We find too that given, as has been confirmed to us this morning, that

the appellant pleaded guilty on rearraignment a considerable time ahead of any date for trial being fixed in the matter, she deserves significant credit for her plea of guilty, though it was not tendered on first arraignment. We are conscious too that a custodial sentence on a young mother kept away from her young children means, as we have learnt from the report from the prison, the impact of such a sentence is worse than it would be for someone else not in that situation committing the same offence.

19   In all the circumstances we find that the length of sentence is manifestly excessive and we are satisfied that the appropriate sentence that should be substituted for it is one of nine months' detention in a young offender institution. To that extent and in that way this appeal is allowed.

ATTORNEY GENERAL'S REFERENCE NO.4 OF 2004 (JOSEPH GREEN)

COURT OF APPEAL (Lord Justice Latham, Mrs Justice Cox and Judge Beaumont Q.C.): May 4, 2004

[2004] EWCA Crim 1197; [2005] 1 Cr.App.R.(S.) 23

(LT) Aggravated burglary; Knives; Robbery; Undue leniency; Violence

H1   *Robbery—robbery of residents—robbery of flat by men armed with knives—length of sentence*

H2   Four years' imprisonment for robbery of the residents of a flat by one of three men who went to the flat armed with knives and threatened the residents varied to six years.

H3   The offender was convicted of aggravated burglary and two counts of robbery. The offender went with two others to a block of flats and rang the doorbell of one of them. When an occupier answered the door, two of the men produced knives and demanded money. They entered the flat and threatened another man with a knife and demanded money and other items. The first man was again threatened with knives and various items were stolen before the offender and his accomplices left the flat. The registration number of the offender's car was taken by a neighbour and he was arrested. Sentenced to four years' imprisonment. The Attorney General asked the Court to review the sentence on the ground that it was unduly lenient.

H4   **Held:** (considering *Attorney General's Reference No.35 of 2001* [2002] 1 Cr.App.R.(S.) 44 (p.187), *Harrison* [2002] 1 Cr.App.R.(S.) 107 (p.471), and *Brady* [2000] 1 Cr.App.R.(S.) 410) this was clearly a planned offence by three men who went to the premises by night and used a knife to cause injury, albeit of a superficial kind. The Court had no doubt that the sentence of four years' imprisonment was unduly lenient. An appropriate sentence in the absence of a guilty plea would have been in the region of eight years' imprisonment. The Court would substitute a sentence of six years' imprisonment, having regard to the offender's behaviour in prison under sentence.

H5   **Cases cited:**   *Attorney General's Reference No.35 of 2001* [2002] 1 Cr.App.R.(S.) 44 (p.187), *Harrison* [2002] 1 Cr.App.R.(S.) 107 (p.471), *Brady* [2000] 1 Cr.App.R.(S.) 410

H6   **References:** robbery, *Current Sentencing Practice* B 6-2

H7   *Miss Z. Johnson* for the Attorney General.
R. Pearce for the Crown.

JUDGMENT

1   **LATHAM L.J.:**   This is an application by HM Attorney General for leave to refer to this Court the sentence imposed on the offender on December 12, 2003 of 4 years' imprisonment for offences of aggravated burglary and two counts of robbery of which he was convicted at the Kingston Crown Court. We give leave to the Attorney General to refer this sentence.

2   The offender is 32 years of age. He has not served a previous custodial sentence. On January 29, 2003, together with two others, the offender went to a block of flats in Sutton. They rang the door bell. One of the men inside the flat went to answer. When he opened the door he was confronted by the three men, two of whom were armed with knives; one of those was the offender. They demanded money. The person who opened the door was pushed against the wall. When he denied having any money, he was pushed to one side as the intruders entered the flat and went upstairs.

3   The offender then confronted the other occupant of the flat, grabbed him by the throat, pushed him down onto the bed, threatened him with a knife and ordered him to remove his watch. He demanded money and when the man denied that he had any, the offender attempted to slash at his face, threatening to stab his eye out. He terrified him. One of the other intruders ripped a gold chain from the man's neck. There were further threats, in particular in relation to the cannabis which it was apparent the two occupants of the flat were smoking. When it had been identified one of the three intruders took it. There were persistent demands for money.

4   The offender then turned his attention to the other occupant of the flat whom he pushed against the wall and pressed a knife to the side of his face towards his mouth. The intruders then picked up a set of keys, took a portable television set, an electronic game machine, mobile telephones, jewellery and the cannabis. They then left. They had clearly terrified both occupants of that flat.

5   Fortunately the offender and those with him were seen escaping from the flat and getting into a car. The registration number was taken by a local shopkeeper

which enabled the police to go to the offender's home address where he was arrested. He was identified later by both occupants at an identification parade.

6   At the trial he sought to blame those in the flat for burglary, saying that all he had intended to do was to obtain items which had been stolen from him. The offender had 13 previous convictions, but had never received a custodial sentence. In a pre-sentence report he denied having carried a knife. The probation officer assessed him as posing a risk of harm to known adults but not to the public at large.

7   This was clearly a planned offence by three men who went armed to the premises in question. The use of the knife did cause injury although it was a relatively superficial injury. The offence took place during the hours of darkness.

8   Miss Johnson, on behalf of the Attorney General, has referred us to three authorities, which it is submitted provide guidance to this Court as to the appropriate level of sentencing for offences such as these. The first is the case of *Attorney General's Reference No.35 of 2001* [2002] 1 Cr.App.R.(S.) 44 (p.187). In that case the Court was confronted with an offender who had burgled the home of a man aged 72 with a knife. He had been sentenced to three and a half years' imprisonment after a plea of guilty. In giving judgment the Court said:

> "What would a proper sentence have been? In our view, no less than six years on a plea of guilty, that is to say, giving credit (and substantial credit) for the plea of guilty."

9   In *Harrison* [2002] 1 Cr.App.R.(S.) 107 (p.471) this Court upheld a sentence of five years' imprisonment imposed following a plea of guilty for an offence of aggravated burglary (where the offender was carrying a knife). In *Brady* [2000] 1 Cr.App.R.(S.) 410 this Court upheld a sentence of seven years' imprisonment for aggravated burglary on premises occupied by a 70-year-old. From those authorities counsel for the Attorney General derives the submission that the appropriate sentence in this case, where there was no credit to be given for a plea of guilty, must have been in the region of eight years. With that submission we agree. The question therefore is, what should this Court do?

10   There is no doubt that the sentence of four years' imprisonment was unduly lenient, but we have to take into account the matter of double jeopardy. In the present circumstances we also take into account, as Mr Pearce on behalf of the offender has submitted we should, the material set out in a letter from the offender which we have had an opportunity to read.

11   It is plain that the result of this offence has destroyed the offender's life. He has lost his wife and children in that his marriage has now come to an end and he has not been given an opportunity to see his children whilst he has been in prison. It is clear from what he says that, whilst in prison, he has impressed. He is now an enhanced prisoner; and there was an incident in which he behaved with conspicuous bravery. That enables us to say that we can properly discount from the sentence of eight years' imprisonment, which would otherwise be appropriate, to a sentence of six years' imprisonment. We consider that that is the most that we can do by way of mitigating the appropriate sentence in this case.

12   Accordingly the sentence we impose is one of six years' imprisonment.

R. v HENRY JOSEPH LUNNON

Court of Appeal (Lord Justice Kay, Mr Justice Eady and Mr Justice Royce): May 5, 2004

[2004] EWCA Crim 1125; [2005] 1 Cr.App.R.(S.) 24

(LT) Basis of plea; Concessions; Confiscation orders; Drug trafficking; Justice

H1   *Confiscation order—Drug Trafficking Act 1994—basis of plea accepted by prosecution and sentencing judge for purposes of sentence—application of required assumptions producing result inconsistent with basis of plea— whether serious risk of injustice if assumption made*

H2   Where the defendant pleaded guilty to an offence of conspiring to supply cannabis on a particular basis which was accepted by both the prosecution and the sentencing judge for the purpose of sentence, there was a serious risk of injustice in making the assumptions required by the Drug Trafficking Act 1994, s.4, if they were inconsistent with the basis of plea.

H3   The appellant pleaded guilty to conspiring to supply a Class B drug, cannabis. The appellant was concerned with others in importing a consignment of cannabis concealed in a lorry carrying scrap metal. The consignment of scrap metal was transferred from one lorry to another, and driven to a scrap yard in the second lorry, which followed a car in which the appellant and another man were travelling. As the second lorry was being unloaded, police officers entered the yard and the defendants were arrested. The appellant was arrested a short while afterwards. Cannabis weighing approximately 1,892kg was found. The appellant pleaded guilty on the basis that he had flown to Holland to take a quantity of cash to one of the co-defendants. He had agreed to drive the first lorry to its destination. The appellant had derived no financial benefit from his involvement in the conspiracy. It was accepted by the Crown that the appellant had no prior involvement in drug trafficking before the conspiracy. Sentenced to 13 months' imprisonment, with a confiscation order under the Drug Trafficking Act 1994 in the amount of £12,371. The appeal was limited to the confiscation order.

H4   **Held:** the sentencing judge determined the appellant's benefit by making the required assumptions under s.4(3) of the 1994 Act. Section 4(4) provided that the court should not make any required assumption if the court was satisfied that there would be a serious risk of injustice in the defendant's case if the assumption were to be made. This provision had been considered in *Benjafield* [2002] 2 Cr.App.R.(S.) 71 (p.313). The sentencing judge had accepted the appellant's basis of plea in relation to the length of the prison sentence. He did not consider the basis of plea in relation to the application of the required assumptions. For the

Crown it was argued that a defendant might properly be sentenced on the basis that he had not previously been involved in drug trafficking, yet have the confiscation order made against him in relation to previous drug trafficking. It could be perfectly proper for a judge to conclude that the defendant was a first time dealer when sentencing for the offence, yet make a confiscation order against him on the basis of prior drug dealing. The House of Lords in *Benjafield* approached the process of making a confiscation order as part of the sentencing process. Circumstances could be envisaged in which the Crown had discovered prior to the conclusion of a confiscation hearing that a concession had been wrongly made, in the light of further information. In such circumstances, the appropriate course would be for the Crown to notify the defendant that the concession had been withdrawn, and that he would have the choice of proving on the balance of probability that he was a first time offender, or of inviting the court to be satisfied that there would be a serious risk of injustice if the statutory assumptions were to be applied. What was unacceptable was for the concession to be made for part of the sentencing process, without qualification, but for reliance to be placed on the assumptions when it came to the confiscation hearing. The court's obligation was to stand back and make an independent assessment of the risk of injustice. Once the Crown had made a concession, unless and until it was withdrawn, there would be an apparent injustice in the court's ignoring it for the purposes of a confiscation hearing. At least, when the court stood back to consider the risk of injustice, a fully reasoned explanation would be required as to why the statutory assumptions should apply. The confiscation order would be quashed.

H5   **Case cited:** *Benjafield* [2002] 2 Cr.App.R.(S.) 71 (p.313), *Rezvi* [2002] 2 Cr.App.R.(S.) 70 (p.300)

H6   **References:** confiscation order, *Current Sentencing Practice* J7, *Archbold* 5-444a

H7   **Commentary:** [2004] Crim.L.R. 678

H8   *Lord Thomas Q.C.* for the appellant.
       K. Talbot for the Crown.

JUDGMENT

1   **EADY J.:**   On February 6, 2003 at the Sheffield Crown Court the appellant pleaded guilty to conspiring to supply a Class B drug (cannabis), on re-arraignment, after the jury had been sworn. He was sentenced to 13 months' imprisonment. On May 14, 2003 H.H. Judge Swanson made a confiscation order under s.6 of the Drug Trafficking Offences Act 1986 in the sum of £12,371.29 with a default sentence of eight months' imprisonment consecutive. The appellant now appeals against the confiscation order by leave of the single judge.

2   By way of background, it is necessary to record that there were four co-accused. Jesse Richards, Anthony Wood and Walter Hawker all pleaded guilty to the conspiracy on re-arraignment. Richards and Wood were sentenced to six years' imprisonment and Hawker to four years. Samuel Richards was found not guilty by the jury on the judge's direction.

3   In view of the way the grounds of appeal have been formulated, it is necessary to set out in broad terms the nature of the conspiracy and the appellant's role within it. On September 12 and 13, 2002, officers from the National Crime Squad kept observation on the activities of the appellant and his co-accused. Cannabis was concealed within a lorry containing a consignment of scrap metal. This was driven from Holland to Sheffield, where the consignment was unloaded and put on another lorry. This was driven to another scrap yard by Hawker, who followed a car in which this appellant and Jesse Richards were travelling. On arrival, the co-accused were seen to unload sacks from the lorry. At that point officers entered the yard and all the co-accused were arrested. The appellant had driven out of the yard in the car but he was arrested a short while later.

4   Upon examination, the sacks were found to contain 7,666 blocks of cannabis weighing a total of approximately 1,892.66kg. They had a wholesale value of between £1,703,394 and £2,271,192. The corresponding street value ranged between £4,731,650 and £5,677,980. When he was interviewed, this appellant said that he had been asked by Anthony Wood to accompany Walter Hawker from Holland to the United Kingdom, but he had no idea that the arrangement was anything to do with the drugs seized. It is important to record the precise basis upon which the appellant pleaded guilty:

   i) He flew to Schiphol airport on September 11, 2002, having been asked by Jesse Richards to bring him a quantity of cash. The appellant accepts that the money was to be applied for the purchase and subsequent importation of cannabis. He was told that his fare would be paid and that he would receive £200 for his trouble. Originally, he understood that this was to be the limit of his involvement.

   ii) It had then been agreed that the appellant would return to the United Kingdom with Walter Hawker in the hire van. He was unaware that the lorry carrying the cannabis was on the same ferry.

   iii) It was originally intended that the appellant would be collected from Anthony Wood's house in Loughton, but on the journey between Dover and Loughton he was asked by Woods to take the van to Sheffield. He agreed, knowing that he was becoming further involved in the enterprise, but without detailed knowledge of the arrangements. There was no discussion regarding any additional payment.

   iv) Once in Sheffield, the appellant acted under the direction of Jesse Richards and Anthony Woods in the knowledge that he was becoming further involved in a criminal enterprise.

   v) At the time of his arrest, the appellant's part in the enterprise was over and he was leaving the premises in his father's car.

vi) The appellant has had no financial benefit from his involvement in the conspiracy.

5   The appellant's counsel offered to put the basis of the plea in writing, but it was said by counsel for the Crown that this was not necessary (although it was insisted that a written basis of plea be provided from the other defendants). It was, however, accepted by the Crown that this appellant prior to the incident in question had no previous involvement in drug trafficking.

6   We turn to the statutory framework under which the order was made. In particular, it is necessary to have in mind the provisions of ss.2 and 4 of the Drug Trafficking Act 1994. This represents, in effect, the consolidated form of the 1986 Act, as amended by the Criminal Justice Act 1993. In so far as relevant, the terms of s.2 are as follows:

> "(1) Subject to subsection (7) below, where a defendant appears before the Crown Court to be sentenced in respect of one or more drug trafficking offences (and has not previously been sentenced or otherwise dealt with in respect of his conviction for the offence or, as the case may be, any of the offences concerned), then—(a) if the prosecutor asks the court to proceed under this section, or (b) if the court considers that, even though the prosecutor has not asked it to do so, it is appropriate for it to proceed under this section, it shall act as follows.
>
> (2) The court shall first determine whether the defendant has benefited from drug trafficking.
>
> (3) For the purposes of this Act, a person has benefited from drug trafficking if he has at any time (whether before or after the commencement of this Act) received payment or other reward in connection with drug trafficking carried on by him or another person.
>
> (4) If the court determines that the defendant has so benefited, the court shall . . . determine in accordance with section 5 of this Act the amount to be recovered in his case by virtue of this section
>
> . . .
>
> (8) The standard of proof required to determine any question arising under this Act as to—(a) whether a person has benefited from drug trafficking, or (b) the amount to be recovered in his case by virtue of this section, shall be that applicable in civil proceedings."

7   The provisions of s.4 are as follows:

> "4 (1) For the purposes of this Act—(a) any payments or other rewards received by a person at any time (whether before or after the commencement of this Act) in connection with drug trafficking carried on by him or another person are his proceeds of drug trafficking: and (b) the value of his proceeds of drug trafficking is the aggregate of the values of the payments or other rewards.
>
> (2) Subject to subsections (4) and (5) below, the Crown Court shall, for the purpose—(a) of determining whether the defendant has benefited

from drug trafficking, and (b) if he has, of assessing the value of his proceeds of drug trafficking, make the required assumptions.

(3) The required assumptions are—(a) that any property appearing to the court—(i) to have been held by the defendant at any time since his conviction, or (ii) to have been transferred to him at any time since the beginning of the period of six years ending when the proceedings were instituted against him, was received by him, at the earliest time at which he appears to the court to have held it, as a payment or reward in connection with drug trafficking carried on by him; (b) that any expenditure of his since the beginning of that period was met out of payments received by him in connection with drug trafficking carried on by him; and (c) that, for the purpose of valuing any property received or assumed to have been received by him at any time as such a reward, he received the property free of any other interests in it.

(4) The court shall not make any required assumptions in relation to any particular property or expenditure if—(a) that assumption is shown to be incorrect in the defendant's case; or (b) *the court is satisfied that there would be a serious risk of injustice in the defendant's case if the assumption were to be made*; and where, by virtue of this subsection, the court does not make one or more of the required assumptions, it shall state its reasons" (emphasis supplied).

8   Judge Swanson reminded himself at the hearing below that he was concerned with the civil standard of proof and that he not only could, but should, rely upon the statutory assumptions contained in s.4(3) of the 1994 Act unless, in accordance with s.4(4), any required assumption was shown to be incorrect or the court was satisfied "that there would be a serious risk of injustice in the defendant's case if the assumption were to be made".

9   The learned judge correctly identified the relevant assumptions for present purposes in accordance with s.4(3) of the Act and held that there was nothing to displace those assumptions in the light of the fact that the appellant had admitted telling lies and, also, that there was a notable paucity of documentation in respect of his business. It is thus apparent that the learned judge put to one side in this context the agreed basis of plea and, in particular, the acknowledgement by the Crown that the appellant had no previous involvement in drug trafficking.

10   In referring to the appellant's "lying", what the learned judge had in mind were the lies told by him and his wife in relation to the ownership of a Golf car. He had originally denied that it was his and claimed that it belonged to his father until a late stage in the proceedings when he admitted the contrary. In the transcript of his ruling the judge addressed the significance of these lies in the following terms:

"The lies told by the Defendant, admitted as lies, and indeed admitted by his wife, about the ownership of the Golf, are of course conclusive of nothing, other than the fact that they lied. However, in a case which depends, as this does, on their credibility it can do the Defendant's case nothing but harm. In short, there is little of the defence evidence that I can, on the balance of probabilities, accept".

11   Our attention was drawn to the consideration given by the House of Lords to the terms of s.4(3) of the 1994 Act, and especially to the requirement that the assumptions should be displaced if ". . . the court is satisfied that there would be a serious risk of injustice in the defendant's case if the assumption were to be made". In *Benjafield* [2002] 2 Cr.App.R.(S.) 71 (p.313) their Lordships were concerned with the issue of compatibility between Art.6 of the European Convention on Human Rights and Fundamental Freedoms and the comparable provisions for confiscation under s.72AA of the Criminal Justice Act 1988. It was recognised by Lord Steyn in para.[15] of his judgment in the linked case of *Rezvi* [2002] 2 Cr.App.R.(S.) 70 (p.300) that those provisions were passed in furtherance of a legitimate aim and that the measures were rationally connected with that aim. It had been submitted before their Lordships that the means adopted were disproportionate to the objective, in so far as a persuasive burden was placed upon the defendant. He expressed agreement with the Court of Appeal: see at [2001] 3 W.L.R. 75 at 103. Specifically, Lord Steyn recognised the responsibility placed by Parliament upon the courts not to make a confiscation order where there was a serious risk of injustice. It is clear that the court, whenever it is necessary to decide whether a confiscation order should be made, should stand back and determine whether there is or might be a risk of serious or real injustice and, if there is, or might be, then such an order should not be made.

12   It is also clear from Lord Steyn's observation at [13] in *Rezvi* (at p.307) that ". . . confiscation proceedings are part of the sentencing process following a conviction and do not involve a fresh criminal charge".

13   For the appellant here, Lord Thomas of Gresford Q.C. has submitted that the learned judge failed to take account of the obligation imposed by Parliament upon the courts by s.4(4). As Lord Steyn observed in *Benjafield* at [8] (at p.316):

> "The 1994 Act pursues an important objective in the public interest and the legislative measures are rationally connected with the furtherance of this objective. The procedure devised by Parliament is a fair and proportionate response to the need to protect the public interest. The critical point is that under the 1994 Act, as under the 1988 Act, the judge must be astute to avoid injustice. If there is or might be a serious or real risk of injustice, he must not make a confiscation order".

14   Lord Thomas argues that, if the judge had stood back and made an assessment as required, he would have been bound to take into account the fact that the Crown had accepted that this appellant had no previous involvement with drug trafficking. In this context it is important to note that, at the outset of his ruling on May 14, 2003, he appears to have recognised the significance of the Crown's concession:

> "Also, prior to the sentence of imprisonment, I was told that the Crown accepted the basis of his plea which was substantially concerned with the

length of the prison sentence imposed but was relevant to these proceedings in two regards. Firstly, the indication was given by the Crown that he had no previous involvement with drug trafficking and, secondly, that the Crown had no information from any other source that that was untrue. I'll refer to this later".

Unfortunately, despite this assurance, the learned judge never did return to the subject. Accordingly, it is simply not possible to identify any strand of reasoning on the basis of which the judge thought it appropriate to ignore, for confiscation purposes, the Crown's concession and to rely simply upon the statutory assumptions.

15   The Crown sought to overcome these formidable difficulties, on appeal, by arguing that the appellant's grounds rested upon a fundamental misconception. It was argued that the statutory regime is such that ". . . a defendant may properly be sentenced on the basis that he has not previously been involved in drug trafficking, yet have a confiscation order made against him relating to previous drug trafficking". It was said to be ". . . perfectly proper, indeed inevitable in certain cases, that the judge may conclude that the defendant is a first time drug dealer when sentencing him for the offence of which he is convicted, yet make a substantial confiscation order against him on the basis of prior drug dealing".

16   It has already been pointed out that the House of Lords approached the process of making a confiscation order as part of the sentencing process (see above at [12]). It would always be open to a defendant to prove on the balance of probabilities that he had no previous involvement in drug trafficking, but why should he where the Crown has explicitly conceded this to be the position?

17   No doubt one could envisage circumstances where the Crown has discovered prior to the conclusion of a confiscation hearing that such a concession has been wrongly made. Further information may have come to light which demonstrates this to have been the case. In such circumstances, the appropriate course would be for the Crown to notify the defendant that the concession has been withdrawn and that, accordingly, he will have the choice of proving on the balance of probabilities that he was, after all, a first-time offender, or of inviting the court to be satisfied that there would be a serious risk of injustice, for some other reason, if the statutory assumptions were to be applied. What is plainly unacceptable is for the concession to be made for part of the sentencing process, without qualification, but for reliance to be placed, tacitly, on the assumptions when it comes to the confiscation hearing.

18   It is clear from the House of Lords' decision in *Benjafield* that the obligation upon the court under s.4(4)(b) to "stand back" and make its own independent assessment is of fundamental importance, since this is what renders the reverse burden of proof compatible with the requirements of Art.6 of the European Convention. The Crown has submitted before this Court that it cannot be unjust to make the assumptions because ". . . the court's power to make a confiscation order in these sort of circumstances is the very power Parliament intended to confer". Such an argument diminishes, however, the importance of the requirement

to stand back and make an independent assessment. Once the Crown has made a concession, such as in this case, unless and until it is withdrawn, there would be an apparent injustice in the court's ignoring it for the purposes of a confiscation hearing. At least, when the court stands back to consider the risk of injustice, a fully reasoned explanation would be required as to why the statutory assumptions should nevertheless apply. Here the judge omitted to give any such explanation, and the Court is not in a position to evaluate his reasoning.

19   It was submitted by the Crown before this Court that there was ". . . no reason to think that the judge did not apply his mind to the justice of the case in the round". There is, however, in the view of this Court every reason to come to that conclusion because the Crown's concession was simply not addressed.

20   As we indicated at the conclusion of the hearing, the appeal will be allowed and the confiscation order accordingly quashed.

ATTORNEY GENERAL'S REFERENCE NO.26 OF 2004 (JAMEEL KHAN)

COURT OF APPEAL (Lord Justice Rose (Vice President, Court of Appeal Criminal Division), Mr Justice Hughes and Mrs Justice Gloster): May 6, 2004

[2004] EWCA Crim 1384; [2005] 1 Cr.App.R.(S.) 25

LT Aggravating features; Knives; Undue leniency; Wounding with intent

H1   *Wounding with intent to cause grievous bodily harm—stabbing victim to head in premeditated attack following dispute over loan—length of sentence*

H2   Three years and nine months' imprisonment for wounding with intent to cause grievous bodily harm, where the offender stabbed the victim to the head in a premeditated attack following a dispute over a loan, varied to six years.

H3   The offender was convicted of wounding with intent to cause grievous bodily harm. The offender claimed that the victim of the offence owed him money and went to the victim's home in company with another man to confront the victim. After an argument they left but returned a few minutes later. When the offender again asked for the money, the victim picked up a walking stick to defend himself. The offender's companion took the walking stick from him and the offender struck the victim to the left side of the neck with a knife and then struck him again in the head. The offender then hit the victim several times with the walking stick. The victim was taken to hospital where it was found that he had a three-inch wound to the neck and a four-inch wound to the back of the head. Sentenced to three years and nine months' imprisonment. The Attorney General asked the Court to review the sentence on the ground that it was unduly lenient.

H4   **Held:** (considering *Attorney General's Reference No.4 of 1998 (Ward)* [1998]
2 Cr.App.R.(S.) 388, *Attorney General's References Nos 59, 60 and 63 of 1998*
[1999] 2 Cr.App.R.(S.) 128, *Attorney General's Reference No.52 of 2001
(Lamoon)* [2001] EWCA Crim 1906, and *Attorney General's Reference No.18
of 2002 (Hughes)* [2003] 1 Cr.App.R.(S.) 9 (p.35)) for the Attorney General it
was submitted that the offence involved the use of a knife to attack an unarmed
man in his own home, with a degree of premeditation; potentially fatal wounds
had been inflicted and there was persistence in the attack. It was submitted that
the sentence was at the bottom of the proper sentencing bracket. In the Court's
judgment, this was a serious case of wounding with intent, having regard to
the fact that it took place in the victim's home, the degree of premeditation,
the disarming of the victim before the attack took place and the repeated attacks
on vulnerable parts of the body. The Court would have expected a sentence of at
least seven years for the offence; taking into account the element of double jeopardy, the Court would substitute a sentence of six years' imprisonment.

H5   **Cases cited:**   *Attorney General's Reference No.4 of 1998 (Ward)* [1998] 2
Cr.App.R.(S.) 388, *Attorney General's References Nos 59, 60 and 63 of 1998*
[1999] 2 Cr.App.R.(S.) 128, *Attorney General's Reference No.52 of 2001
(Lamoon)* [2001] EWCA Crim 1906, *Attorney General's Reference No.18 of
2002 (Hughes)* [2003] 2 Cr.App.R.(S.) 9 (p.35)

H6   **References:** wounding with intent to cause grievous bodily harm, *Current Sentencing Practice* B 2-2

H7   *Miss B. Cheema* for the Attorney General.
Miss J. Dyer for the offender.

JUDGMENT

1   **ROSE L.J.:**   The Attorney-General seeks the leave of the Court, under s.36
of the Criminal Justice Act 1988, to refer a sentence said to be unduly lenient. We
grant leave.
2   The offender is 35 years of age, having been born in April 1969. In January
2004 he was convicted by the jury at Preston Crown Court of an offence of
wounding with intent, contrary to s.18 of the Offences Against the Person Act
1861. On February 9 he was sentenced by H.H. Judge Badeley, after pre-sentence
reports had been prepared, to three years and nine months' imprisonment.
3   In brief outline the offender and a friend, who was an older man, went to the
home of the victim, a Mr Mohammed Afzal Khan. The offender alleged that
Mr Khan owed him money. There was an argument. The offender left. He
returned soon afterwards carrying a knife with a seven-inch blade concealed in
his jacket. The argument resumed. Without warning, the offender stabbed the
victim in the neck. When he tried to escape, the offender stabbed him from behind
in the head.
4   A substantial amount of blood was lost. There was permanent scarring.

5   In a little more detail, the offender and victim had known each other and had, at one stage, been good friends. But, in recent times, the offender claimed, contrary to the victim's denial, that the victim owed him money. This led to a fallout between the two of them. The incident which gave rise to this indictment took place at about 9.30 on the evening of April 25, 2003.

6   Then, the offender and the older man went to confront the victim in the victim's home about the money. After an argument the visitors left. They returned two or three minutes later and the victim invited them into the house. Again, the offender asked for money, to which the reply from the victim was that he had no money and he was unemployed. The victim was fearful that the offender had a weapon and, in consequence, he picked up a walking stick to defend himself. The older man, who had accompanied the offender, took the walking stick from him saying that they had not come for a fight. Thereupon, the offender took out a knife, which we have earlier described, and struck the first blow to the left side of the victim's neck. The victim pushed the offender away and tried to run out of the house. The offender pursued him and, from behind, struck him in the head a second time. Then, for good measure, the offender hit the victim on the head and body with the walking stick, several times, with such force to cause it to break.

7   The wounds, as we have said, bled profusely and the victim was taken by a neighbour to hospital. In the meantime, the offender and his accomplice made off in a motorcar. The knife was never recovered but the walking stick was found in a broken and bloodstained condition in the victim's house.

8   The offender was arrested a few days later. In interview, he agreed he had been at the victim's flat asking for money but claimed that it was the victim who had attacked him with the walking stick. He denied having a knife.

9   At trial, he claimed that some other person must have attacked the complainant after he, the offender, had left him in an undamaged condition.

10   The injuries were a three-inch wound to the neck requiring eight stitches, and a four-inch wound to the back of the head, requiring 15 stitches. The complainant was in hospital for two days. In the victim impact statement which he made, he described his fear in his own home, his physical scarring, his nightmares, at that time continuing and requiring the use of sleeping pills, and severe headaches especially in cold weather. He also had experienced some memory loss and pain in the neck and shoulder. He had to give up the college course which he was attending and, at the time of the statement, felt that his future, in consequence, had been ruined.

11   On behalf of the Attorney General Miss Cheema draws attention to a number of what she submits are aggravating features. First, the use of a knife. Secondly, the attack on an unarmed man in his own home. Thirdly, the premeditation implicit in the history which we have rehearsed. Fourthly, the ferocious and sustained nature of the attack involving stab wounds to particularly vulnerable parts of the body, which might have been fatal. Fifthly, the attack was persisted in despite the victim's attempt to escape. Sixthly, the victim had been disarmed prior to the attack. Seventhly, there was no sign of remorse exhibited by the offender and eighthly, knife offences are, sadly, very prevalent.

12   Miss Cheema draws attention to the mitigating features to be found in the offender's previous good character; the fact that, happily, there was no serious permanent physical disability; the fact that the incident was an isolated one; the possibility that the offender, because of language difficulties and some history of depression, may experience unusual problems in prison; finally, the low risk of re-offending, as assessed in the pre-sentence report and the fact that the offender is father of five children, one of whom is unwell.

13   Miss Cheema drew attention to four authorities, *Attorney General's Reference No.4 of 1998 (Ward)* [1998] 2 Cr.App.R.(S.) 388, *Attorney General's References Nos 59, 60 and 63 of 1998* [1999] 2 Cr.App.R.(S.) 128, *Attorney General's Reference No.52 of 2001 (Lamoon)* 2001 EWCA Crim 1906 and *Attorney General's Reference No.18 of 2002 (Hughes)* [2003] 2 Cr.App.R.(S.) 9 (p.35). She submits that the sentence of three years and nine months passed by the learned judge was unduly lenient, placing it at the bottom of the bracket of three to eight years, indicated in the last of those authorities as being appropriate in relation to an offence of this kind. Such a placement, Miss Cheema submits, was unjustified having regard to the absence of any plea of guilty and the presence of the aggravating features to which she draws attention.

14   On behalf of the offender, Mr Dyer accepts that the sentence passed was a lenient one and that the bracket for offences of this kind is indeed between three and eight years. He submits that the sentence was not unduly lenient. He emphasises that the trial judge has a discretion in relation to sentencing and is generally best placed to assess the seriousness of a particular offence. Mr Dyer stresses the good character of the offender, who has been in this country for some 10 years. He submits that it is comparatively rare for offences of this kind to be committed by persons of good character. We have some difficulty in accepting that part of Mr Dyer's submission: unhappily, even such serious offences are, not infrequently, committed by people of good character, although it is right to say that, in the four authorities to which Miss Cheema drew attention, some though not all of the offenders had previous convictions for violence.

15   Mr Dyer accepts that this was a serious offence, having regard to the site of the blows. He points out that there was no long-term physical disability, although he concedes, having regard to the site of the blow, that there might have been. He also points out that the scarring is by no means as severe as in some cases, one of the wounds having been inflicted in the hairline.

16   Mr Dyer also invites the Court, if it takes the view that this sentence was unduly lenient, to take into account the element of double jeopardy involved in the second sentencing process which is a feature of all Attorney General's References. To all of these factors we have regard.

17   In our judgment, this was a very serious case of wounding with intent, having regard to where it took place, namely the victim's home, the degree of premeditation which involved going to fetch a weapon, the disarming of the victim before the attack took place and the repeated attack on vulnerable parts of the body.

18   Having regard to those matters in particular, but also taking into account the mitigating factors to which reference has already been made, we would have expected, following a trial, a sentence in the court below of at least seven

years for this offence. Taking into account double jeopardy, we quash the sentence of three years and nine months passed by the learned judge and substitute for it a sentence of six years' imprisonment.

R. v HALEY NICOLA ONLEY

COURT OF APPEAL (Lord Justice Rose (Vice President, Court of Appeal Criminal Division), Mr Justice Hughes and Mrs Justice Gloster): May 6, 2004

[2004] EWCA Crim 1383; [2005] 1 Cr.App.R.(S.) 26

(LT) Child cruelty; Manslaughter by gross negligence; Sentence length

H1   *Detention in a young offender institution—manslaughter—manslaughter of young child by neglect—length of sentence*

H2   Six years' detention in a young offender institution upheld for manslaughter by neglect of a child aged 18 months by his mother.

H3   The applicant, aged 20, pleaded guilty to the manslaughter of her son aged 18 months. The applicant became pregnant but separated from the father of the child shortly before the child's birth. She moved out of her mother's home to live on her own in a rented flat. The applicant began to experience financial difficulties and began working as a prostitute for an escort agency. She began to neglect the child, who was left alone in her flat for long periods without anyone to look after him or to check up on him. The child suffered from nappy rash of increasing severity as result of being left alone in a soiled state and suffered significant fluid loss as a result. On the day of the child's death, the applicant left him alone at 11.00am and did not return until 6.45pm, when she discovered that the child was dead. A post-mortem indicated that the most likely cause of death was dehydration associated with severe nappy rash and lack of drinking. The applicant pleaded guilty to manslaughter by virtue of gross negligence on the basis that she had not physically assaulted the child. Sentenced to six years' detention in a young offender institution.

H4   **Held:** (considering *Watts* [2002] 1 Cr.App.R.(S.) 56 (p.228)) the Court did not accept the submission that the sentence of six years' detention in a young offender institution for manslaughter by gross negligence was excessive. The child was grossly neglected for a period of at least a week before its death. The sentence of six years was well within the appropriate range. In the Court's judgment, the sentence was within the band of the sentencing judge's discretion and there was no reason to interfere with it.

H5   **Case cited:**   *Watts* [2002] 1 Cr.App.R.(S.) 56 (p.228)

H6   **References:** detention in a young offender institution—manslaughter, *Current Sentencing Practice* E 2-4

H7   *N. Lithman Q.C.* and *A. Compton* for the applicant.

JUDGMENT

1   **GLOSTER J.:**   On November 20, 2003, in the Crown Court at Chelmsford, the applicant, Haley Onley, pleaded guilty to manslaughter of her son, Ryan, who was then aged 18 months. She was sentenced by H.H. Judge Ball to six years' detention in a young offender institution. The single judge refused her application for leave to appeal against sentence and she renews her application to this Court.

2   The facts may be briefly stated as follows. The applicant was a single mother aged 20 at the time of her son's death on May 31, 2003. She had received a diploma in nursery nursing and NNEB in October 2001, one month before the birth of her son. She was, therefore, as a result of her qualification, well aware of the needs of a very young child. She had become pregnant shortly before qualifying, the natural father being her then boyfriend, from whom she separated shortly before Ryan's birth.

3   She lived with her mother and brother when the child was first born but she then moved out to live in a rented flat of her own. The mother, brother and grandparents appear to have been supportive and the natural father attempted to maintain contact with Ryan, although that contact appeared to have ceased some time before Ryan's death because of tensions between the father and the applicant over access.

4   Prior to the beginning of May 2003, the applicant worked on a part-time basis as a clerical assistant approximately three days a week. Although she had suffered from postnatal depression after the birth of Ryan, she appeared to be coping adequately with the baby during the first four months of 2003. The prosecution accepted that, until the beginning of May the applicant was a caring, attentive mother who was, whatever her difficulties, not, at that stage, abusive of the child. Although the medical records maintained by her GP showed that on February 19, 2003 the applicant was reporting symptoms of slight depression associated with the demands of looking after a small child, entries in the GP's records relating to visits by the applicant on May 2 and May 5 related exclusively to her physical problems and made no reference to her reporting any psychological problems or symptoms associated with depression. Certainly, the applicant appeared to be able, during the early months of 2003, to maintain her lifestyle of socialising with her friends in pubs and clubs, notwithstanding also having to look after her child.

5   At some time about the beginning of May, the applicant, who had got into debt and had financial difficulties in supporting her lifestyle, began working at an escort agency as a prostitute. She started a relationship with a Nigel Davidge, a driver employed by the escort agency to take her to appointments with her cli-

ents. From that time on, the evidence displays an increasing neglect of Ryan by the applicant. By May 12, when the applicant took Ryan to her GP, Ryan was suffering from a cough, high temperature and bad nappy rash. In the last week of his life the applicant left him for long periods of time in his cot, in her flat, both during the day and at night, without anyone having been there to look after him and without the applicant having made any arrangements for a baby-sitter to look after the baby or for anybody even to check up on him. Although on occasions she told her mother that she had in fact made arrangements for other people to look after the baby, the reality was that she left Ryan wholly on his own with bottles of milk, orange juice and food placed in his cot, but with no one to change his nappies or care for him during her long periods of absence. During the last week of his life the nappy rash increased in severity because he was being left alone to lie in his soiled cot, such that by May 31 the rash was a source of significant fluid loss. The flat itself, and the room where the child was sleeping, was also left in a terrible mess, littered with remnants of out-of-date food, soiled nappies, dirty clothing and other detritus.

6   On May 31, the last day of the child's life, the applicant left Ryan alone at about 11.00am. She went to a hairdressers nearby, which she frequently visited and, where, according to the evidence, she appeared to be happy enough. Then, without first checking up on the baby, she visited a friend nearby and then had lunch and spent the rest of the day with Davidge.

7   When she returned at about 6.45pm she discovered that Ryan was lifeless in his cot. She took him out into the street but her, Davidge's and a passerby's attempts to revive him, both in the street and subsequently by hospital staff at the hospital, failed. A post-mortem conducted by Professor Risden considered the most likely cause of death to be dehydration. He later confirmed that the excoriation of the skin associated with the severe nappy rash, coupled with the fact that Ryan had been in a hot environment, because of this warm day, possibly without drinking, led to a situation where potentially fatal dehydration could develop. Subsequent reports obtained by the defence confirmed the conclusions of Professor Risden.

8   The applicant was interviewed on a number of occasions on June 1. During those interviews, she asserted that she left Ryan assuming that baby-sitters were on their way. That was not true, because, as we have already said, the applicant had in fact made no arrangements for baby-sitters to attend. She said that Ryan had a bad nappy rash but she had been treating it.

9   On June 3 the applicant was interviewed again. During those interviews she did admit that she had been leaving Ryan for long periods on his own while she worked for the escort agency or was otherwise enjoying herself. She stated that she was tired, ill, not getting any help and suffering from depression. It was almost exclusively from her admissions that the prosecution were able to build up the detail of the times that Ryan had been left alone in the week before his death.

10   The basis on which the applicant pleaded guilty to the charge of manslaughter by virtue of gross negligence was agreed with the prosecution. She pleaded on the basis, which again was accepted, there had been no long-term abuse to the child and that there had appeared to be no significant problems prior to ones occurring

before Ryan's death. She also pleaded on the basis that there was no evidence that
she had physically assaulted the child.

11   Counsel for the applicant, Mr Lithman Q.C., submits that the sentence of six
years' detention was excessive. He criticises the judge for not giving the applicant sufficient credit for her guilty plea. In our view, there is nothing in this
submission. The judge specifically said, in his sentencing comments, that he
gave her credit for the fact that she had now, despite earlier attempts to deflect
responsibility, pleaded guilty. His reference to earlier attempts to deflect
responsibility was not a reference to the lateness of her plea (because the plea
was not in effect late) but simply to her attempts to suggest that the reason
why the child had been left alone, on the date of his death was because a baby-
sitter had failed to turn up.

12   Secondly, Mr Lithman submits, by reference to various authorities, that a sentence of six years in this case of manslaughter, by virtue of gross negligence, is
excessive. We do not agree. In a case such as this one, the sentence is critically
dependent on its own facts. Here, even accepting that up until May, the child
was adequately looked after, there was nonetheless during the last six or seven
days of this boy's life appalling and gross neglect for a period of at least a week.

13   In our judgment, the six years' detention which was imposed by the judge was
well within an appropriate range in a case of this sort. Mr Lithman made reference
to the case of *Watts* [2002] 1 Cr.App.R.(S.) 56 (p.228), where the Court of Appeal
reduced a life sentence to 10 years' imprisonment on a young mother, likewise in
a case of neglect. The fact of this case may not be as serious as those in *Watts* but,
nonetheless, this case, in our judgment, was clearly a case where a substantial
period of detention was justified.

14   Thirdly, in his written submissions, counsel submitted that the judge had paid
insufficient regard to a number of features relating to the applicant's personal circumstances, including her age, her previous good character and the evidence that,
prior to the last week of Ryan's life, the appellant was a caring and attentive
mother.

15   In our judgment, it is clear from the sentencing remarks of the learned judge
that he took all these matters into account and that the sentence he passed was
well within the bands of his discretion in this unfortunate and sad case. We see
no reason to interfere with this sentence and accordingly this application must
be refused.

R. v DMYTRO TORKONIAK

COURT OF APPEAL (Mr Justice Hughes and Mrs Justice Gloster):
May 7, 2004

[2004] EWCA Crim 1402; [2005] 1 Cr.App.R.(S.) 27

(LT) Abuse of position of trust; Client accounts; Legal aid; Making false statements; Obtaining property by deception; Solicitors; Theft; Totality of sentence

H1 *Theft—theft by solicitor from clients and others—sums in excess of £300,000 stolen or otherwise obtained—length of sentence*

H2 Sentences totalling eight years upheld in the case of a solicitor who stole or obtained sums in excess of £300,000 from clients and others.

H3 The applicant was convicted of 15 counts of theft, two counts of obtaining a money transfer by deception, one count of false accounting, two counts of obtaining property by deception, one count of forgery, and one count of perjury. The applicant was in practice as a solicitor. He negotiated a settlement of £100,000 for a client who suffered personal injuries. The applicant told the client that the amount awarded was £18,000 and retained at least £75,000 for himself. In the case of another client, the applicant retained £3,000 out of an award of £18,000, and failed to repay costs to the Legal Services Commission of £10,000 which the applicant had recovered from insurance. Various other amounts were stolen from clients in a variety of circumstances. Substantial amounts were obtained from the Legal Services Commission. The applicant received payments over a period of nine years in respect of a client's pension after the client had died. The total amount obtained was in excess of £300,000. Sentenced to a total of eight years' imprisonment.

H4 **Held:** (considering *Bingham* (1992) 13 Cr.App.R.(S.) 45, *Wheeler* (1992) 13 Cr.App.R.(S.) 73, *Cove* (1993) 14 Cr.App.R.(S.) 498, *Chisnall* (1994) 15 Cr.App.R.(S.) 230, *Clark* [1998] 2 Cr.App.R.(S.) 95, and *Barrick* (1985) 7 Cr.App.R.(S.) 142) in the Court's view, the overall sentence of eight years' imprisonment could not be regarded as manifestly excessive. This was a particularly bad case of breach of trust by a solicitor. The amount of money stolen was important but not the only factor. The victims of the applicant's crimes were vulnerable members of society and had to be able to repose confidence and trust in the applicant. The offences of theft, taken on their own, fully justified a total sentence of seven years' imprisonment and the offences of forgery and perjury justified the consecutive sentence of one year. The fact that the money stolen by the applicant was potentially realisable was no justification for a reduction in sentence. Leave to appeal would be refused.

H5   **Cases cited:** *Bingham* (1992) 13 Cr.App.R.(S.) 45, *Wheeler* (1992) 13 Cr.App.R.(S.) 73, *Cove* (1993) 14 Cr.App.R.(S.) 498, *Chisnall* (1994) 15 Cr.App.R.(S.) 230, *Clark* [1998] 2 Cr.App.R.(S.) 95, *Barrick* (1985) 7 Cr.App.R.(S.) 142

H6   **References:** theft, *Current Sentencing Practice* B 6-1

H7   *M. Sharpe* for the applicant.

JUDGMENT

1   **GLOSTER J.:**   On November 13, 2003, following a seven-week trial at the Crown Court at Lincoln, the applicant, a solicitor then aged 36, with a substantial legal aid practice in the Derby area, was convicted and sentenced to a total of eight years' imprisonment for 21 offences involving or related to theft of sums totalling something in excess of £300,000 from his clients, the Legal Services Commission and the DHSS and, in addition, for one offence of perjury.

2   In detail, the sentences he received were as follows: on 14 counts of theft, he received three years' imprisonment on each, to run concurrently with each other but consecutive to a sentence of four years, on what was count nine in the indictment, which related to a theft from a client called Buckley; on two counts of obtaining a money transfer by deception, he received three years concurrent; on one count of false accounting, he received three years' imprisonment again concurrent; on two counts of obtaining property by deception, he received a sentence of three years' imprisonment, again concurrent; on a count of forgery, he received a sentence of three years' imprisonment concurrent; and, on a count of perjury, relating to a lie, which he made in an affidavit sworn by him, in proceedings taken by The Law Society, he received a sentence of one year's imprisonment consecutive to the theft and other counts. As we have said, in total his sentence was one of eight years' imprisonment.

3   The facts may be summarised as follows. Whilst the applicant was in practice as a solicitor in Derby, he stole in excess of £300,000 from his clients, the Legal Services Commission Aid Fund and the DSS. In addition, when defending legal proceedings brought against himself, he committed perjury. The most serious offence was committed against a man called Buckley, who fell off a girder and sustained multiple injuries and fractures. He was hospitalised for weeks and suffered severe psychological damage as a result of the accident. These included continuous flashbacks of the fall, severe post traumatic stress disorder, sleep impairment, depression and irritation as a result of which his family relationships suffered.

4   The applicant was engaged to obtain compensation for Buckley and succeeded in negotiating a settlement of £100,000. When Buckley came along to the applicant's offices to collect the compensation award from the applicant, the latter pretended that Buckley had only been awarded £18,000 and kept at least £75,000 for himself out of the total compensation award, which he put in an offshore bond in his own name.

5   Another offence related to a young man who was injured by a exploding fire-work. Again, out of the £18,000 compensation that the applicant managed to obtain for this claimant, the applicant retained some £3,000 for himself, without informing the claimant and failed to repay the Legal Services Commission some £10,000 in costs, which the applicant had recovered from insurers.

6   Another offence related to theft of £1,100 from the estate of a dead man, whose only beneficiary was the priest who had baptised the applicant's children. A further offence related to the sum of £1,500, stolen from the proceeds of compensation paid, or intended to be paid, to an injured laboratory assistant. The applicant also stole £3,500 from the Legal Services Commission, when his costs had in fact been paid by the other side. The applicant was also convicted of theft of £14,300, out of the estate of a dead man whose relatives spoke no English, and he made a false entry in a ledger to cover it up before charging the relative £4,200 to transfer the property into her own name, when the actual fees were one-tenth of that amount.

7   Another offence related to the theft of £10,000 from a total settlement of £15,000, intended to be received by a man who had been injured in a road accident. In relation to that case, the applicant falsely claimed £1,600 costs from the Legal Services Commission.

8   Another offence related to the theft of £800 from the estate of his godfather. In connection with that theft the applicant forged an invoice from a firm of local printers in order to pay the money to himself. A further offence related to theft of an award intended for people who had been injured. In relation to that offence, the applicant stole £1,100 out of a total settlement of £7,500.

9   A further offence related to the theft of at least £5,000, out of a total settlement of £23,500, intended for an Asian woman who had received severe facial injuries in a car accident and who spoke and wrote no English. He also stole over £5,000 from the Legal Services Commission on this occasion.

10   Another offence related to a false claim by the applicant for costs from a client and a further offence related to theft of half of a £25,000 compensation claim. Yet another offence related to a false claim for costs from a client where the applicant received £950. A further offence related to the receipt by him of approximately £113,000 in costs from the Legal Services Commission, in order to pursue a claim of child abuse against the local authority. But, when the case was settled, his firm was in fact paid £132,500 in costs by the local authority. The applicant did not return the £113,000 to the Legal Services Commission.

11   Another offence related to the deliberate failure by the applicant to inform the DSS of the death of one of the applicant's clients and the Department continued to pay the client's pension which the applicant received and paid into an offshore account which involved theft of nearly £40,000 in respect of this pension over a nine-year period.

12   Proceedings were finally brought against him by The Law Society following his arrest. The applicant lied on oath in an affidavit which he swore in those proceedings, relating to possession of papers in the case of Buckley. The applicant stated that he did not have certain papers in Buckley's case, when, in fact, such papers were, to his knowledge, in the boot of his car.

13   In sentencing, the trial judge, in addition to referring to the facts relating to the
        offences, as have been summarised above, made the following comments:

> "At your trial you pretended that you were entitled to do so as part of your
> agreement in merging with another firm of solicitors. You accused two other
> solicitors, effectively of lying, at a time the partnership was suffering such a
> financial crisis that no partner was taking drawings, except you, in the form
> of a massive amount of costs which were not yours to take. Your partners
> were having to take out loans from the bank while you had over half a mil-
> lion pounds in offshore bonds and you were adding to them."
>
> Anyone who lies on oath can expect a consecutive sentence and an officer
> of the Court expect a longer one.
>
> You tried to cover up your dishonesty not only by lying on oath but by
> removing index cards, files, and chequebook stubs. During the course of
> the fraud you made false entry in the books, misled clients, and dictated fic-
> titious letters and file notes to cover up your thefts. Your dishonesty over a
> period of nearly three years netted you over £300,000 on the indictment, and
> almost certainly a great deal more but I am only sentencing you on the mat-
> ters upon which the Jury have convicted you.
>
> Although the Police have succeeded in tracing most of the money, you
> have made serious efforts to remove it from the jurisdiction and keep it
> away from your colleagues. The effect of the fraud has been to ruin one
> of your former partners, Shamin Khan, who was left holding the liabilities
> and the title of the firm which is left in ashes and only the stench of dis-
> honesty remaining.
>
> I can give you no credit for a guilty plea. I do not punish you further for the
> way that you conducted your defence, but you either directly or by inference
> accused everyone, apart from your defence team, the Jury, and myself, of
> lying. It was obvious to anyone that you shifted your evidence to suit the
> state of your case. There can be little doubt that you are a very talented Cos-
> sack dancer and that you may have considerable skills in the entertainment
> and promotion business. No doubt you could have made a decent living in
> that profession and undoubtedly you had skills as a solicitor. All of this pales
> into the background, as does your character, in light of the cold blooded and
> callous hearted dishonesty which you have exhibited.
>
> I take into account the other matters that are urged upon me: the end of
> your careers both in law and entertainment, the family position, particularly
> in relation to your children and parents. These must be subordinated to the
> seriousness of your crimes. I have looked individually and at the totality of
> the sentence that I must pass."

14   In support of the applicant's application for leave to appeal against sentence,
        counsel has submitted that the sentence of eight years in total was manifestly
        excessive. He accepts that the sentencing remarks made by the judge cannot
        be criticised and counsel also accepts that the aggravating factors were correctly
        identified by the learned judge. Counsel also accepts that the structure of the sen-
        tences (that is to say the fact that some sentences were concurrent and some were

consecutive) cannot be criticised overall. However what he submits, in essence, is that, overall a sentence of eight years was too long. He has referred in support of his submission to a number of cases by way of comparison and analogy. He submits that, given the amount involved, that is to say, just over £300,000, eight years was excessive.

15   In particular Mr Sharpe referred to the following cases: *Bingham* (1992) 13 Cr.App.R.(S.) 45, a plea of guilty by a solicitor; *Wheeler* (1992) 13 Cr.App.R.(S.) 73, a plea of guilty by a director and major shareholder; *Cove* (1993) 14 Cr.App.R.(S.) 498, a case involving a solicitor; and *Chisnall* (1994) 15 Cr.App.R.(S.) 230, a plea of guilty by a solicitor.

16   We should say that we have also considered, in so far as they are relevant to an appeal against sentence, the points made in the applicant's own letter to this Court, dated April 27, 2004 and in the accompanying materials. Mr Sharpe has not adopted the submissions made by the applicant in that letter but has invited us, on instructions, to have regard to such matters therein as may assist us on this application.

17   In our judgment, taking into account the relevant circumstances surrounding the offences, the overall sentence of eight years cannot be regarded as manifestly excessive. Moreover, we derive no support for a reduction in the applicant's sentence from the cases to which Mr Sharpe has referred. They involved different circumstances; in many cases where a plea of guilty had been made, attracting the inevitable discount against the full sentence. In *Clark* [1998] 2 Cr.App.R. 137, this Court laid down guidelines for appropriate sentences involving theft, where there had been a breach of trust, which updated the previous guidelines that had been given by this Court in *Barrick* (1985) 81 Cr.App.R. 78. In *Clark*, at 142, Rose L.J., giving the judgment of the Court, said, as follows:

> "In the light of all these considerations we make the following suggestions. We stress that they are by way of guidelines only, and that many factors other than the amount involved may affect sentence. Where the amount is not small, but is less than £17,500, terms of imprisonment from the very short up to 21 months will be appropriate; cases involving sums between £17,500 and £100,000, will merit two to three years; cases involving sums between £100,000 and £250,000, will merit three to four years; cases involving sums between £250,000 and £1 million will merit between five and nine years; cases involving 1 million or more, will merit 10 years or more. These terms are appropriate for contested cases. Pleas of guilty will attract an appropriate discount. Where the sums involved are exceptionally large, and not stolen on a single occasion, or the dishonesty is directed at more than one victim or group of victims, consecutive sentences may be called for."

18   It is clear that, even allowing for inflation, this case involving a theft of over £300,000, falls within the bracket of cases meriting between five and nine years' imprisonment. Moreover, in the earlier case of *Barrick*, Lane L.C.J., at 81 and following in the judgment of the Court, identified certain factors which

the Court would no doubt wish to pay regard in determining what a proper level of sentence should be in cases involving breach of trust:

19   The Lord Chief Justice, Lord Lane, said, as follows:

> "The following are some of the matters to which the Court will no doubt wish to pay regard in determining what the proper level of sentence should be: (i) the quality and degree of trust reposed in the offender including his rank; (ii) the period over which the fraud or the thefts have been perpetrated; (iii) the use to which the money or property dishonestly taken was put; (iv) the effect upon the victim; (v) the impact of the offences on the public and public confidence; (vi) the effect on fellow-employees or partners; (vii) the effect on the offender himself; (viii) his own history; (ix) those matters of mitigation special to himself such as illness; being placed under great strain by excessive responsibility or the like; where as sometimes happens, there has been a long delay, say over two years, between his being confronted with his dishonesty by his professional body or the police and the start of his trial; finally, any help given by him to the police."

This passage was quoted with approval by Rose L.J. in *Clark*.

The aggravating features of this case which reflect the factors as identified in *Barrick* were correctly identified by the learned judge. Those aggravating features were considerable.

20   Of course, in all cases of theft by solicitors there is, as Steyn L.J. (as he then was) said in *Cove*, considerable damage to the public confidence in the legal system which potentially affects the reliance that members of the public will place in the legal profession. It is, therefore, a matter of the greatest public interest that the court should take a severe and stern view of such offences.

21   In our judgment, this was a particularly bad case of breach of trust by a solicitor. Of course, the amount of money stolen in cases such as these is an important factor, but it is not the only factor. Here, the other important feature and which, as is clear from his sentencing remarks, was clearly taken into account by the learned judge, was the deplorable extent of the applicant's abuse of his position of trust. The victims of this applicant's crimes were vulnerable and weak members of society, who had a particular need to be able to repose absolute confidence and trust in the applicant as their solicitor and, likewise, to be able to repose confidence in the system of obtaining compensation. Likewise, the applicant's cynical abuse of the procedures of the Legal Services Commission and the DHSS were reprehensible and amounted, in our judgment, to a particularly gross breach of trust by an officer of the court.

22   In our judgment, the offences of theft, taken on their own, clearly justified a total sentence of seven years' imprisonment, which was well within the *Clark* guidelines of offences involving sums of this nature. In addition, the offences of forgery and perjury were particularly serious in circumstances where they were committed by an officer of the court. Accordingly the consecutive sentence of one year for perjury was clearly right as a matter of principle.

23   The fact that, as submitted by counsel, the money stolen by the applicant is potentially realisable because it was secreted offshore rather than dissipated in

living expenses, is, in our judgment, no justification whatsoever for any reduction in sentence. Nor does it support the submission that the sentence was excessive. That some of the stolen money was fortunately preserved was only as a result of freezing orders obtained by The Law Society, or the police, shortly after the applicant's offences were discovered. His attempt to conceal the proceeds of his crime in offshore jurisdictions and the fact that, because he had done so, they were available to be realised and to pay compensation cannot, in our judgment, possibly be relied upon as a factor in mitigation on his behalf. Accordingly, this application for leave to appeal against sentence is dismissed.

R. v ARAN BOWERS

COURT OF APPEAL (Lord Justice Clarke, Mr Justice Elias and Judge Rivlin Q.C.): May 12, 2004

[2004] EWCA Crim 1247; [2005] 1 Cr.App.R.(S.) 28

LT Actual bodily harm; Assault; Basis of plea; Mistake; Sentence length

H1   *Detention in a young offender institution—assault occasioning actual bodily harm—attack involving single punch to man intervening to calm situation— length of term of detention*

H2   Eighteen months' detention in a young offender institution for assault occasioning actual bodily harm, imposed on a young man of 19 who punched in the face a man who tried to calm him down, reduced to eight months.

H3   The appellant, aged 19, pleaded guilty to assault occasioning actual bodily harm. The appellant became involved in an argument in a public house which led to his being banned. He returned to offer an apology to those involved and this led to a further altercation. He was later seen in the road standing with a brick in his hand challenging someone to fight. A man who was acquainted with the appellant approached him in an attempt to calm him down. The appellant struck the man, who fell to the ground and hit his head, suffering a fracture around the eye socket. The appellant pleaded guilty on the basis that he had left the public house under the impression that he was being followed, and that he believed that the victim was one of those following him. Sentenced to 18 months' detention in a young offender institution.

H4   **Held:** the sentencing judge commented that the assault involved a vicious punch to a man who was not trying to fight the appellant. The Court was satisfied that the sentence was out of line with the authorities and did not take account of the mitigating features. The Court considered that an appropriate sentence would be eight months' detention.

H5 **Cases cited:** *Blewitt* (1994) 15 Cr.App.R.(S.) 132, *Marpels* [1998] 1 Cr.App.R.(S.) 335

H6 **References:** detention in a young offender institution, assault occasioning actual bodily harm, *Current Sentencing Practice* E 2-4

H7 *Miss L. Sayers* for the appellant.

JUDGMENT

1   **ELIAS J.:**   On December 8, 2003 at the Crown Court at Chester the appellant pleaded guilty to a count of assault occasioning actual bodily harm. He was sentenced the following day by H.H. Judge Edwards at the Knutsford Crown Court to 18 months' detention in a young offender institution. He now appeals against sentence by leave of the single judge.

2   The background, briefly, was as follows. During the early evening of Sunday June 15, 2003 the appellant, then aged 19, was involved in an argument which led to him being banned from the White Lion public house in the Disley area of Cheshire. At about 8.15 that same evening he returned and tried to offer an apology to the landlord and the person with whom he had been arguing. Unfortunately he was unsuccessful. An altercation followed and the appellant again left the public house.

3   He was seen in an agitated state. He stood with a brick in his hand on the main road, the A6. Anthony Connor, the complainant in this case, saw the appellant shouting at a group, "Come on if you want a fight". The comment appeared in particular to be directed to a man called Redfern. Connor had been aware of the appellant for about three months. He had been pointed out to Connor on a number of occasions. He was also aware that there was some bad feeling between the appellant and Redfern. There had been an incident on the previous day when they had come to blows and he believed that he was simply seeing a continuation of this same running dispute.

4   Connor was concerned that the appellant was in danger; he might get hit by a car or alternatively by the group that he was provoking. He decided to go and talk to the appellant in an attempt to calm him down. Connor approached the appellant and said, "If you want a fight put the brick down". Connor placed himself between the appellant and the group and said again, "Look, just put the brick down and calm down". But the appellant continued to be aggressive. He was jigging from foot to foot; he appeared very tense. He shouted at Connor, "Who the fuck are you? What's it got to do with you?" Connor raised his right arm and said, "Look, just go, get out of here". At that point the appellant struck Connor, who fell to the floor and hit his head. He suffered a small cut and bruising above his left eye and he suffered a minor fracture around the eye socket. There was temporary double vision and extreme constant headaches and soreness. As a consequence Connor had to take unpaid time from work.

5   The appellant was arrested on July 25, 2003. Initially he said that Connor was part of the group that was threatening to attack him. Connor had come up to him,

pushed him and said that he would knock him out. He also said that Connor had punched him to the face and that he had hit Connor once and run off.

6   Subsequently, however, he retracted much of that account. He pleaded guilty on the basis of a specific basis of plea, which was as follows:

> "(1) Following an altercation in the White Lion public house, he left with the impression that he was being followed and that harm would be done to him.
> (2) He was approached by Mr Connor and mistakenly believed he was part of those following and struck him to the eye causing his injury. Connor offered no provocation.
> (3) He then ran and telephoned the police.
> (4) He recognised that his actions went beyond self-defence; and
> (5) He wished to apologise for his behaviour and the distress he had caused."

7   We should note that we have had the advantage of seeing the transcript of the telephone conversation which he had with the police, and of course it is quite unusual for the attacker to contact the police in this way. Suffice it to say that it is quite plain that he was very distressed at the time and, indeed, at one point in the conversation he was apparently sobbing. This transcript was not before the sentencing judge.

8   In passing sentence the judge commented that although it was only one punch, it was a vicious punch to a man who was not trying to fight him and Connor was therefore extremely vulnerable. The judge commented that the blow could have had far more serious consequences. The appellant, he said, was a vicious young man and had to learn the hard way that society was not going to put up with this kind of conduct. He had a significant record of violence. There had been four occasions where he had been convicted of various assaults.

9   There are a number of grounds of appeal. We have had the benefit of an extremely helpful skeleton argument by counsel acting on the appellant's behalf, Miss Sayers. She puts at the forefront of her appeal that the sentence imposed by the judge was simply too high. She has referred us to a whole series of cases which she says demonstrates this, but focuses in particular upon two cases: *Blewitt* (1994) 15 Cr.App.R.(S.) 132 and *Marpels* [1998] 1 Cr.App.R.(S.) 335. Both these cases involved adult appellants who pleaded guilty to s.47 assaults. In *Blewitt* there was an unprovoked attack involving a punch to the victim's head. The victim suffered a swollen eye and a fractured cheekbone and this Court reduced the 12 months' imprisonment to six months. In *Marpels* the appellant was waiting in a taxi queue. There was an altercation and a man intervened to calm the appellant down. The victim was struck in the face, fracturing his nose, and in that case six months was reduced to four months.

10   Miss Sayers submits that on the basis of these authorities, dealing with this appellant, who was only 19 years old at the time and given the fact that this was his first custodial sentence, 18 months was plainly too high. She also commented that, although he did have a record of four assaults, they were somewhat unusual, in that only one of them involved a stranger, and that was

an incident of spitting at a motorist. That occurred on the day of the appellant's grandmother's funeral when he had been drinking and was in an emotional state; and another of the incidents involved two punches to a boy who was known to the appellant and who, it was alleged, had been bullying the appellant's younger brother.

11   In addition, Miss Sayers submits that the sentence imposed by the judge simply did not take account of the basis of plea. In particular, there was the fact that the appellant thought that he might potentially be attacked by the victim, albeit that he was wrong about that. There was also some personal mitigation: there was evidence that the defendant was seeking to reduce his potential aggression, which was frequently fuelled by alcohol, and he had developed a recent relationship and had a young baby.

12   Having regard to all these factors, we are satisfied that the sentence imposed in this case was plainly too high. Not only is it out of line with the authorities, but there were these particular mitigating features here which we consider ought to weigh quite heavily when considering the appropriate sentence. Of especial importance is the fact that this was the first custodial sentence for this appellant and there is no doubt, as we have indicated, that he was in a very highly emotional and distressed state when this particular incident took place. Accordingly we propose to reduce the sentence of 18 months that was imposed. We recognise that it was an unprovoked attack on the [victim] and also at the time when this incident occurred the appellant was undertaking a community punishment order and that, of course, was terminated when he was sent to prison. Taking all these matters into consideration we think that the appropriate sentence here, given the guilty plea and the other factors, is one of eight months' imprisonment. Accordingly we quash the sentence of 18 months and substitute a sentence of eight months. To that extent this appeal succeeds.

R. v LEE MICHAEL KHAIR

COURT OF APPEAL (Lord Justice Waller, Mr Justice Davis and Mr Justice David Clarke): May 12, 2004

[2004] EWCA Crim 1296; [2005] 1 Cr.App.R.(S.) 29

(LT) Child cruelty; Manslaughter; Sentence length

H1   *Manslaughter—manslaughter of two-year-old by father—death apparently resulting from unexplained blow to the head—length of sentence*

H2   Seven years' imprisonment upheld for manslaughter of a two-year-old boy by his father, where death resulted from an unexplained blow to the head.

H3   The appellant was convicted of manslaughter of his child, aged two years. The appellant had had a brief relationship with a woman who gave birth to the child.

The appellant subsequently learned of the birth of the child and, when it was confirmed that he was the father, paid child support and played an active role in the parenting of the child. It was arranged that the appellant would look after the child while the mother was on holiday. He took the child to the child's mother's home to spend the night there before travelling to his family home. Early the next morning the appellant called for an ambulance. He claimed that he had found the child at the foot of the stairs and had tried to revive him. The child was found to have bruises to the head and body and a severe swelling to his brain. The child died from injuries two days later. The cause of death was identified as a blow to the back of the head, causing bleeding in the brain. The injuries to the child were consistent with non-accidental injury, and included further bruises to the body. The bruising was consistent with the child having been gripped and shaken. The appellant denied harming the child. Sentenced to seven years' imprisonment.

H4 **Held:** (considering *Brannan* (1995) 16 Cr.App.R.(S.) 766, *Yates* [2001] 1 Cr.App.R.(S.) 124 (p.428), *Piggott* [1999] 1 Cr.App.R.(S.) 392) the question for the Court was whether the sentence of seven years' imprisonment was manifestly excessive. The sentencing judge had considered the authorities and had heard the evidence. There was no explanation of what happened and how a serious blow came to be delivered to the small child. The sentence was at the top end of the scale, but the Court could not say that it was manifestly excessive.

H5 **Cases cited:** *Brannan* (1995) 16 Cr.App.R.(S.) 766, *Yates* [2001] 1 Cr.App.R.(S.) 124 (p.428), *Piggott* [1999] 1 Cr.App.R.(S.) 392

H6 **References:** manslaughter, *Current Sentencing Practice* B 1-3.3E

H7 *J. Aspinall Q.C.* for the appellant.
G. Bebb Q.C. for the Crown.

JUDGMENT

1   **WALLER L.J.:** On October 28, 2003, in the Crown Court at Winchester, before Steel J. and a jury, the appellant was convicted of manslaughter. On December 12, 2003, he was sentenced to seven years' imprisonment. He now appeals against that sentence by leave of the single judge.

2   The facts were these. The appellant was a serving soldier. At the time of the offence he was based in Hereford. Previously he had been based in Blandford and whilst there had had a brief relationship with the mother of his child. The mother became pregnant and on February 11, 2000 she gave birth to a son.

3   The appellant learned of the birth of his son in October 2000, although he did not know at that stage that he was the father. Ultimately it was confirmed that he was the father. Thereafter he paid child support and played an active role in the parenthood of him.

4   On the weekend of May 25/26, 2002 it was arranged for the appellant to look after the child while the mother left to go on holiday. The appellant picked the

child up from the mother's parents' house on May 26. He took him to the mother's home in Blandford, where he and the child were to spend the night before travelling to Sheffield the next day, where the appellant's family were expecting them.

5   At 6.30am on May 27 the appellant called for an ambulance, stating that he had found the child in a semi-conscious state. When the paramedics arrived they found the child with bruising to his head and body. The appellant claimed that he had been woken by the alarm clock at 5.30am, found the child at the foot of the stairs and that he had tried to revive him. It was thus his case that he did not call an ambulance for at least an hour. The prosecution case was that the delay was nearer two hours. The child was taken to hospital where the appellant could not account for the child's injuries, other than to suggest, as he did at the trial, that the child must have fallen down the stairs.

6   The child had severe swelling to his brain. He died from his injuries on May 29. The pathologist's report identified the cause of death as a blow to the back of the head, which caused bleeding in the brain. A post-mortem report also showed that the injuries to the child were consistent with non-accidental injury. The injuries included further bruising to the child's body. No explanation could be given for that bruising, but it was consistent with the child having been gripped and shaken.

7   On September 24, 2002 the appellant was arrested. He was initially charged with murder. He always denied harming the child. The jury convicted the appellant of manslaughter. The judge in his sentencing remarks said this:

> ". . . despite the verdict of the jury following a detailed trial, you are still unable to acknowledge any responsibility for [the child's] death. The truth is that only you know what happened that fatal night. I must proceed on the basis that you have simply chosen to remain silent. Nothing I can say will bring any comfort to Ryan's mother or his grandparents."

The judge recorded the verdict of the jury being supported by compelling evidence. He said:

> ". . .. I am driven to the conclusion that, maybe tired, [the child] somehow caused you to lose your temper and your control. Moreover, I cannot but refer to the fact that there were a very large number of bruises on [the child's] body when the ambulance was finally called and one thing I do know is that there was prolonged delay in seeking medical help."

He referred to the loving relationship between the appellant and the child. He referred to the appellant's career in the army and of the successful reports that he had in relation to that career. He then said that he had had careful regard to the sentences in similar cases reviewed by the Court of Appeal, which were produced for his assistance by Mr Aspinall Q.C. who represented the appellant in the court below as well as here. He then said:

> "The court has an obligation to seek to protect young children who are so vulnerable to violent assault that it would be completely unrealistic for anyone in this court, let alone a member of the family, to expect that the term of

years which you will have to serve in custody will begin to match the loss of life involved.

The sentence, having regard to your very young age, is one of 7 years."

8   The question for this Court is whether that sentence of seven years is manifestly excessive. We must remember, in reviewing the sentence, the advantage that the judge had in hearing all the evidence at a full trial. Furthermore, he had reviewed the authorities, of which there are a number in this area. He was accordingly aware of the range of sentences which had been considered by the Court of Appeal. At the lower end of the scale is *Brannan* (1995) 16 Cr.App.R.(S.) 766, where the child had been thrown at a settee which had a wooden frame. There the appellant had pleaded guilty to manslaughter. That plea was accepted. In that case a sentence of 42 months was reduced to 30. In *Yates* [2001] 1 Cr.App.R.(S.) 124 (p.428), Roch L.J. referred to the range of sentences in this type of case being between two and five years. Mr Aspinall accepted that the range of two to five years followed a plea of guilty. In *Piggott* [1999] 1 Cr.App.R.(S.) 392, the appellant had offered a plea to manslaughter which the Crown would not accept. He was ultimately found guilty of manslaughter. It was a case in which the appellant admitted a blow with his hand or fist. The judge had imposed 10 years, but this Court, emphasising that in reality there had been a plea, reduced the sentence to six years. Mr Aspinall submits that in that case there were exceptionally aggravating features. He referred us to pages 392 and 393 where it was pointed out that the appellant had been drinking, had shown complete disregard for the feelings of the mother and others, and had shown no remorse for what he had done to the child. However, when the Court reduced the sentence from 10 years to six, it was not saying that the reduction to six rather than five was on the basis of any aggravating features. In *Bennett* [2003] EWCA Crim 2446, a small baby died from a severe shaking and probably a blow of considerable severity. The appellant pleaded not guilty and he was convicted of manslaughter. The judge ruled that the basis on which he had been convicted was that the Crown had failed to disprove provocation. Further, the appellant, very unattractively, had blamed the mother for the child's death. A sentence of nine years was imposed by the judge and the Court of Appeal upheld that sentence. Mr Aspinall very properly points out that in that case, on the basis on which sentence was passed, the judge must have found that there was an intention to cause grievous bodily harm and that therefore that was a more serious case. On that he must be right.

9   With that range of authority in mind, with the judge's knowledge of this case, and with the need to protect children, it seems to us that this sentence cannot be said to be manifestly excessive. It seems to us that there was here an incident which places this case very high in the range of these kind of cases. We do not have an explanation of what happened and how this serious blow came to be delivered to this small child. Nor do we have an explanation of how the bruises came to be on his body. It seems to us that this sentence is at the top end of the scale, but it is one that this Court cannot possibly say is manifestly excessive. This appeal must be dismissed.

R. v JOHN CLUGSTON

Court of Appeal (Lord Justice Buxton, Mrs Justice Rafferty and
Mr Justice Roderick Evans): May 13, 2004

[2004] EWCA Crim 1324; [2005] 1 Cr.App.R.(S.) 30

LT Guilty pleas; Obtaining property by deception; Totality of sentence

H1   *Obtaining by deception—confidence tricks—obtaining a total of £26,725 by
falsely pretending to have cheap champagne for sale—length of sentence*

H2   Six years' imprisonment for obtaining a total of £26,725 by falsely pretending
to have cheap champagne for sale reduced to four years.

H3   The appellant pleaded guilty to eight charges of obtaining property by deception and was committed to the Crown Court for sentence. The appellant on a
number of occasions approached people in commercial premises, telling them
that he had surplus champagne which he could sell them at a favourable price.
The people would agree to buy the champagne and the appellant received
money but did not provide the champagne. The total amount obtained by the
appellant in respect of the offences to which he pleaded guilty was £26,725.
The appellant had 16 previous appearances for a total of 78 offences, and had
served numerous sentences of imprisonment. Sentenced to six years' imprisonment on each count concurrent.

H4   **Held:** the Court asked itself whether the offences would have justified a total
term of nine years if the appellant had contested the charges and concluded that it
would not. An appropriate total sentence would be four years' imprisonment.

H5   **References:** obtaining by deception, *Current Sentencing Practice* B 6-3

H6   *A. Goh* for the appellant.

JUDGMENT

1   **RODERICK EVANS J.:**   This appellant appeals with the leave of the single
judge against a sentence of six years' imprisonment imposed at the Crown Court
at Blackfriars on October 17, 2003.

2   On February 13, 2003 before the West London Magistrates' Court the appellant pleaded guilty to three charges of obtaining property by deception and was
then committed to the Crown Court for sentence. On September 18, 2003 before
the City of London magistrates he pleaded guilty to five further charges of obtaining property by deception and was again committed to the Crown Court for

sentence. It was on October 17 that he appeared for sentence and was sentenced to concurrent terms of six years' imprisonment on each charge. The Court was then asked to consider 19 other offences when sentence was passed. That was done.

3   This appellant is a skilled professional confidence trickster. He uses a similar method in his deceptions. He would find commercial premises fairly close to a local restaurant. He would research the premises and would get to know the names of the people who were employed there. He would then visit commercial premises and pretend to be connected in some way with the restaurant, either as an employee of the restaurant or as a supplier of wine to the restaurant. He would tell people in the commercial premises that he had some surplus champagne in stock and could let them have cases of champagne at a favourable price. That, of course, would be an attractive offer and people would agree to buy the cut price champagne. On more than one occasion he actually went to the bank with somebody from the firm to collect cash. He would then say he was going off to sort out the delivery but he would not come back. By that means he obtained money for the champagne which, of course, he had no intention of supplying.

4   The three offences in the first committal and 11 of the offences taken into consideration by the court took place between October 2002 and January 2003. The appellant obtained £2,675 from three charged offences and £7,550 from the offences taken into consideration: a total on those offences, therefore, of £10,225. In relation to those matters he was arrested on January 19, 2003 and, somewhat surprisingly, was granted bail.

5   He thereafter, between March and September 2002, committed the five offences in the second set of charges, together with eight other offences considered by the court. In relation to those offences he obtained £8,800 in respect of the offences themselves and £7,700 in respect of those offences that were considered.

6   The total amount, therefore, obtained by this appellant in respect of all the charged offences and the other offences considered was £26,725.

7   In interview the appellant admitted the offences and pointed out that he had a gambling problem.

8   There was some money available to compensate the losers. Amongst the appellant's property when he was arrested there was found a betting slip which had a pay out value of £6,000. In addition to that sum, £1,200 was seized from him on his arrest.

9   The appellant is 57 years of age. He has been before the courts on 16 previous occasions for a total of 78 offences, plus, of course, numerous offences considered by the courts on the various occasions. His offending has mainly been for theft and obtaining by deception and he has received numerous periods in prison. In 1990 he was sentenced to a total of three years' imprisonment; in 1994 to two years' imprisonment; in 1996 three years' imprisonment; and four years' imprisonment was imposed on February 26, 1999. From that sentence he was released on licence on March 10, 2002 and the present offences were committed while he was subject to the at risk period of that last sentence. We have no information, however, of when that sentence was due to expire and, therefore, cannot say how much he was liable to serve from that last sentence.

10   The judge when passing sentence had the benefit of a pre-sentence report. That reported that the appellant showed little remorse or sympathy for the victims. The risk of reoffending was considered to be high because nothing appeared to deter him from continuing his offending. His gambling problem appeared to be a causative factor behind this offending and he had made some attempt at addressing this by trying to arrange a placement at Gordon House Hostel and by attending Gamblers Anonymous when in Ford Prison. However, the reporting officer considered that he lacked the persistence and determination to overcome his gambling. However, were the court to consider an alternative to custody a community punishment and rehabilitation order was proposed with a condition that the appellant attend a Think First Programme as part of the rehabilitation order. Such a programme, it was thought, had a "slight" chance of reducing the risk of reoffending.

11   There was an addendum report also before the judge; that is dated October 16, 2003. That stated that an assessment of the appellant had been completed and he had been accepted for a residential bail assessment at Gordon House. The judge, however, was not prepared to consider a community rehabilitation order or any further adjournment for any further assessment, and he imposed the sentence of six years that we have mentioned. He concluded that he would be failing in his public duty if he acceded to the request for a community rehabilitation order. He had no doubt that a lengthy prison sentence was required in this case.

12   The first ground of appeal is that the judge failed to give sufficient weight to the proposal in the pre-sentence report for a community rehabilitation order. That has not been persisted in before us, we think for good reason. There is no merit in it. The judge's conclusion was correct.

13   The second ground of appeal, however, has more merit. It is that a total of six years' imprisonment was simply too long for this appellant's offending, bearing in mind in particular that he had entered guilty pleas at the earliest possible opportunity.

14   It is, of course, correct that there were a number of aggravating features in this case. First, that the offences were committed whilst the appellant was liable to serve part of his last sentence. He was fortunate, perhaps, that the judge did not make him serve that period. Secondly, that the second set of offences were committed whilst he was on bail. Thirdly, of course, the appellant's previous offending.

15   We have asked ourselves whether this offending would have justified a total term of imprisonment in the region of nine years had the appellant contested the charges. We conclude that it would not. The total sentence here is too long. An appropriate total sentence would be one in our view of four years. Accordingly, we quash the sentences of six years and in their place impose terms of four years, which, in our view, adequately reflects the mitigation available to this appellant. To that extent this appeal is allowed.

R. v ANTONY DANIEL ELLIS

COURT OF APPEAL (Lord Justice Waller, Mr Justice Jack and Mr
Justice David Clarke): May 17, 2004

[2004] EWCA Crim 1355; [2005] 1 Cr.App.R.(S.) 31

(LT) Assault; Findings of fact; Justice; Sentencing powers; Violent disorder

H1   *Factual basis for sentence—defendant convicted of violent disorder—whether
sentencing judge entitled to sentence on the basis that defendant was
responsible for specific acts of violence occurring in the course of the disorder*

H2   Where a defendant was convicted of violent disorder, but was not charged with
any specific offence of violence, the sentencing judge was entitled to pass sentence on the basis that the defendant was responsible for specific acts of
violence which occurred during the disorder.

H3   The appellant was convicted of violent disorder. The appellant was involved in
a violent incident in which a woman was kicked in the head and another woman
was punched in the face. The sentencing judge passed sentence on the basis that
the appellant was responsible for the attacks on both women. Sentenced to four
years' imprisonment.

H4   **Held:** (considering *Stosiek* (1982) 4 Cr.App.R.(S.) 205 and *McGlade* (1990)
12 Cr.App.R.(S.) 105) it was argued for the appellant that the sentencing judge
was not entitled to proceed on the basis that the appellant was personally responsible for the two attacks in the absence of convictions for causing or inflicting
grievous bodily harm. The appellant did not give evidence. There was evidence
on which the sentencing judge could conclude that the appellant was the person
responsible for the attacks. It seemed to the Court that the sentencing judge was
entitled to make his own factual findings, having presided at the trial, heard the
evidence and heard the speeches to the jury. It was established that if the verdict of
the jury left open an important issue which might affect sentence, the sentencing
judge was free to come to a conclusion on the evidence. That principle remained
unchallenged. The sentence was not manifestly excessive.

H5   **Cases cited:** *Stosiek* (1982) 4 Cr.App.R.(S.) 205, *McGlade* (1990) 12
Cr.App.R.(S.) 105

H6   **References:** factual basis for sentence, *Current Sentencing Practice* L2, *Archbold* 5–16

H7   *M. Shelley* for the appellant.
T. Brown for the Crown.

JUDGMENT

1   **DAVID CLARKE J.:** On June 25, 2003, in the Crown Court at Norwich, the appellant, Antony Daniel Ellis, who is aged 22, was convicted of an offence of violent disorder. In due course he and his co-defendants who had pleaded guilty were sentenced for that offence. The appellant received four years' imprisonment. His two co-defendants, James Wilks, aged 21, and Patrick Molloy, aged 20, who had pleaded guilty to the offence, were sentenced to two and a half years' imprisonment and detention in a young offender institution respectively. The appellant now appeals against sentence by leave of the full court granted following refusal by the single judge.

2   The facts on which the prosecution case of violent disorder against the three men was based are these. On the evening of January 22, 2003, a young woman, who was a student studying in Cambridge, went to a concert. At the end of the concert she and her friends met up with some people who included one of the members of the band, John Loughlin. He invited them to a party in their tour bus which was parked behind the establishment at which they had been performing. On their way there Loughlin and the young woman, Miss Elder, hung back from the others. At that stage she became aware of two men running. The two men were the appellant and a youth whom he was chasing. When he caught up with the youth the appellant appeared to strike him, at which Mr Loughlin intervened to ask him what he was doing. The appellant said that he did not want any trouble. The prosecution case as it developed at the trial was that he (the appellant) then launched a flying kick at Miss Elder's head, which smashed into her jaw. She was taken to hospital, where she had two metal plates inserted into her jaw which will remain there indefinitely. There was a complaint of permanent disfigurement as a result of this very vicious assault.

3   The case for the prosecution was that the appellant was then joined in the violence by his two co-defendants. They attacked Mr Loughlin, punching and kicking him. Another young woman was punched in the face by the appellant. Mr Loughlin broke free from his attackers and sought refuge. Other people present saw the three co-defendants acting in a very aggressive manner. There was still punching and kicking going on. Stones were being thrown at the people in the club. The police were called and the three men, who were making their way away from the scene, were in due course arrested. The two co-defendants having pleaded guilty, the appellant was convicted by the jury.

4   The judge dealing with sentence considered the previous record of convictions of the appellant, which included four previous convictions for affray, two for assault on the police, two for common assault, and one for assault occasioning actual bodily harm. Indeed he and his friends had been out that night drinking, celebrating his release from prison from his previous sentence. There was a pre-sentence report before the court which recognised the likelihood of a custodial sentence but indicated that a community rehabilitation order was available to the judge. Appropriate work would be needed to address the appellant's aggression and drinking. There was a high risk of re-offending. However, he had expressed remorse and he regretted his actions.

5   In lengthy sentencing remarks the trial judge referred to the defendants having gone out to celebrate the appellant's release from prison, but said that this was a disgraceful and violent incident started by the appellant's actions. The judge held that the factual basis of sentence was that the appellant had launched a flying kick to Miss Elder's face, smashing her jaw, after which the three of them had launched an attack on the male victim and in the course of what followed he had punched the second female victim in the face. The judge referred to the fact that the later stages of the episode had been recorded by a person with a video camera, the film of which had been shown in the course of the trial (over objection from the appellant's advocate). In his sentencing remarks the judge held that the appellant was responsible for the events of the night. He did not have the advantage of mitigation for a guilty plea. He was responsible for the attacks on both the women. The attack on the first woman was particularly cowardly. The judge went on to pass the sentence to which we have referred.

6   The application having been refused by the single judge, Mr Shelley appeared before the Full Court and was granted leave in these terms:

> ". . . leave to argue whether the judge was entitled to sentence in the way that he did as though the applicant was guilty of specific assaults when the prosecution have proceeded by way of the advantage of violent disorder, which did not require them to prove specific assaults."

7   The case has been argued carefully and realistically by Mr Shelley today. We have had the advantage also of Mr Brown, who appeared at the trial for the Crown and who has prepared a skeleton argument for us today, appearing before us.

8   The position seems to be this. The appellant was sentenced on a particular factual basis. The argument is that he had not been charged with the offence of causing Laura Elder grievous bodily harm. Indeed it seems clear to us that if there had been such a charge, it would have been a charge of causing grievous bodily harm with intent contrary to s.18 of the Offences against the Person Act 1861. Mr Brown tells us that, before the start of the trial, the evidence was not considered sufficiently clear to establish the link between the descriptions of the person who delivered the kick and the appellant. However, such evidence emerged during the course of the trial. At the end of the prosecution case it was the Crown's case that the appellant (the only one in the light top), was the one who delivered the kick to Miss Elder.

9   The argument is that since the conviction was for violent disorder rather than for causing grievous bodily harm, the judge was not entitled to proceed on that factual basis of sentence. Furthermore, on the facts it is argued that there was evidence that the kick was delivered by a person wearing white trainers, whereas it is common ground that on that night the appellant was wearing brown shoes.

10   We were referred to a number of cases in which this Court has deplored the inappropriate use of Public Order Act offences when charging cases more appropriately dealt with by specific assault charges of one form or another under the Offences against the Person Act 1861—cases in which charges of affray, for example, have been brought against people who have assaulted police officers in private premises. But this is not such a case. The charge against these three

men was that they were responsible for an episode of serious public disorder whereby bystanders were likely to be put in fear and it was not, in our judgment, inappropriate to proceed in this way, particularly on an analysis of the state of the evidence as gleaned from the papers. It seems to us that there is no injustice to the defence in it being dealt with in this way since issues of participation arise in Public Order Act offences: issues of self-defence arise and the jury can reach proper conclusions.

11   The real question here is whether there is any justification for the appellant's complaint of the actual basis upon which the judge sentenced the appellant. The appellant did not give evidence in the trial. The evidence, including the police evidence relating to the arrest, was that he was the man in the light top. There was evidence, as Mr Shelley concedes, upon which the judge could conclude that it was the one in the light top who delivered that particular kick, even though he draws attention to other aspects of the evidence which he says should have cast some doubt on that.

12   It seems to us that the learned judge was fully entitled to make his own factual findings and to make them clear, having presided over the trial, having heard the evidence and speeches to the jury and having formed his own conclusions as to the facts which the jury must be taken to have accepted.

13   Mr Shelley has referred us to the decision of this Court in *Stosiek* (1982) 4 Cr.App.R.(S.) 205, which sets out the principle that where an accused person is convicted by the jury, but the verdict is consistent with more than one version of the facts, a sentencer may reach his own conclusion on the evidence; he is not bound to reach the most favourable version of the facts, but he must give any benefit of any doubts that there may be to the defendant whom he is sentencing. It seems to us clear that in the present case the judge made clear that he was not in any doubt as to the particular participation of the appellant.

14   In *McGlade* (1990) 12 Cr.App.R.(S.) 105, a somewhat similar question arose as to the factual basis of sentencing following a trial. Taylor L.J. said this:

"There is clear authority that if the verdict of a jury leads inexorably to one version of the facts being found and only one version, the learned judge is bound to sentence upon that basis. But if the verdict of a jury leaves open some important issue which may affect sentence, then the learned judge, having heard all the evidence himself in the course of the trial, is free and, indeed, it is his duty to come to a conclusion, if he can, upon where the truth lies. Of course if the learned judge is unable, on the evidence, to be sure, in the circumstances of this case or one like it, there was not consent then he would have to deal with the matter on the basis that there was consent. But here the learned judge made it perfectly clear that on the evidence that he had heard he came to the conclusion that this act of buggery was committed without consent."

15   The present case concerns factual findings of a very different nature from those involved in that case, but the principle, in our judgment, remains unchallenged. The judge was entitled, in our view, to reach this conclusion.

16   The next ground upon which Mr Shelley seeks to argue the case is that four
years' imprisonment for this offence of violent disorder, being only one year
short of the maximum prescribed for that offence, was itself manifestly excessive. We do not accept that submission. Indeed if the appellant had been convicted,
as he might have been in other circumstances depending on the state of the evidence, of causing grievous bodily harm with intent, on the facts of this case a four-
year sentence would in our judgment have been a lenient sentence. It must also be
remembered that the learned judge imposed two-and-a-half year sentences on the
co-defendants who had pleaded guilty. They are not before this Court.

17   In all the circumstances we are wholly unpersuaded that this sentence was
manifestly excessive. The appeal against that sentence must therefore be dismissed.

ATTORNEY GENERAL'S REFERENCE NO.12 OF 2004 (ALFRED WASHINGTON WEEKES)

COURT OF APPEAL (Lord Justice Rose (Vice President, Court of Appeal Criminal Division), Mr Justice Grigson and Mr Justice Andrew Smith): May 19, 2004

[2004] EWCA Crim 1623; [2005] 1 Cr.App.R.(S.) 32

LT Domestic violence; Grievous bodily harm; Undue leniency; Wounding with intent

H1 *Wounding with intent to cause grievous bodily harm—husband attacking wife with hammer—length of sentence*

H2   Three years' imprisonment for wounding with intent to cause grievous bodily harm imposed on a man who attacked his wife with a hammer, causing fractures to the skull, increased to four and a half years.

H3   The offender pleaded guilty to causing grievous bodily harm to his wife with intent. The offender had been married for about eight years. After some years of marriage the offender began to threaten his wife with violence. On the night of the offence, there was an argument during which the offender's wife fell and skidded along a corridor. She asked the offender to call for an ambulance but the offender did not do so. The wife lay on the floor for some time and then tried to sit up: as she did so, the offender attacked her with a hammer, striking her a number of blows to the head. The victim was found to have multiple lacerations of the scalp and two depressed compound skull fractures. Sentenced to three years' imprisonment. The Attorney General asked the Court to review the sentence on the ground that it was unduly lenient.

H4   **Held:** (considering *Hudson* [2003] 2 Cr.App.R.(S.) 52 (p.327), *Attorney General's Reference No.98 of 2002 (Bishop)* [2003] 2 Cr.App.R.(S.) 95 (p.563), *Attorney General's Reference No.32 of 1994 (Dawson)* (1995) 16 Cr.App.R.(S.) 710, *Attorney General's Reference No.19 of 1994 (Arnold)* (1995) 16 Cr.App.R.(S.) 541, *Davies* (1986) 8 Cr.App.R.(S.) 97, *Mannion* [1999] 2 Cr.App.R.(S.) 240, *Attorney General's Reference No.68 of 2002 (Catterall)* [2003] 1 Cr.App.R.(S.) 94 (p.498)) for the Attorney General it was submitted that the offence was aggravated by the fact that the victim was attacked in her own home while her children were asleep; the attack was unprovoked when the victim was lying defenceless on the floor; a hammer was used to her head, and the attack ceased only when one of the children intervened. In the Court's view, a sentence of the order of five and a half to six years' imprisonment would have been appropriate in the court below. Taking into account the element of double jeopardy, the Court would substitute a sentence of four and a half years' imprisonment.

H5   **Cases cited:**   *Hudson* [2003] 2 Cr.App.R.(S.) 52 (p.327), *Attorney General's Reference No.98 of 2002 (Bishop)* [2003] 2 Cr.App.R.(S.) 95 (p.563), *Attorney General's Reference No.32 of 1994 (Dawson)* (1995) 16 Cr.App.R.(S.) 710, *Attorney General's Reference No.19 of 1994 (Arnold)* (1995) 16 Cr.App.R.(S.) 541, *Davies* (1986) 8 Cr.App.R.(S.) 97, *Mannion* [1999] 2 Cr.App.R.(S.) 240, *Attorney General's Reference No.68 of 2002 (Catterall)* [2003] 1 Cr.App.R.(S.) 94 (p.498)

H6   **References:** wounding with intent to cause grievous bodily harm, *Current Sentencing Practice* B 2-2

H7   *Miss S. Whitehouse* for the Attorney General.
      S. Reid for the offender.

JUDGMENT

1   **ROSE L.J.:**   The Attorney General seeks the leave of the Court, under s.36 of the Criminal Justice Act 1988, to refer a sentence said to be unduly lenient. We grant leave. The offender is 52 years of age having been born in December 1951. On January 12, 2004 he pleaded guilty to an offence of causing grievous bodily harm with intent, contrary to s.18 of the Offences Against the Person Act 1861. He was sentenced, on that occasion, by H.H. Judge Hughes Q.C. at Snaresbrook Crown Court to three years' imprisonment.

2   In summary, the offender attacked his wife with a hammer, so that she suffered two depressed and commutated fractures of the skull. The attack was witnessed by the couple's 13-year-old son, who intervened, with a knife, in order to stop the attack.

3   In a little more detail, the offender and his wife had known each other for 14 years and had been married for about eight. They had three sons, aged 13, six and four. When Mrs Weekes was pregnant with her second son instability developed in the marriage because the offender became abusive towards her and jealous and possessive. About three years before the attack Mrs Weekes told the offender that she wanted to leave. He thereafter threatened to hit her and threatened other forms of violence to her on several occasions.

4   On April 24, 2003 she was in bed at about 11 o'clock in the evening. The three sons were asleep elsewhere in the house. The offender came in and asked about her work and there was a brief conversation between them, in the course of which the offender became irritated. At that stage Mrs Weekes' mobile telephone rang. This caused the offender to be even more angry. He took the telephone from her, pulled out the land line telephone from its socket and left the room. She followed. She began to run down the stairs, but she fell and, at the foot of the stairs, skidded along the corridor on her knees. She was not seriously hurt but she asked the offender to call for an ambulance because she was frightened of him. He refused

but brought a duvet for her and her bag and then fetched a bottle of beer for himself. He told her that if she could not walk she could crawl into the sitting room. He then went back into the kitchen. She lay on the floor for about 20 minutes and then she tried to sit up. As she did so, the offender attacked her with a hammer which had been lying in the hall. The first blow caused her to urinate. The offender hit her again twice as she tried to get up. The 13-year-old son, who had been awakened by the noise, saw his father hitting his mother with the hammer and he, with a knife, intervened, challenging his father to stop. Mrs Weekes was able to escape while the offender was distracted by their son and she sought help from a neighbour.

5   The consequences to the victim were two multiple uneven lacerations of the scalp, mainly on the top and back of the head and two depressed and comminuted compound skull fractures, in connection with which there were pieces of broken bone which could be felt. She underwent surgery. The wounds were stitched and cleaned and she was discharged from hospital after about four or five days. In the meantime, the offender had presented himself at a police station, at 1.30 in the morning, claiming to the police that his wife had hit him and he had hit her. When formally interviewed, he declined to answer any questions.

6   On behalf of the Attorney General Miss Whitehouse draws attention to seven aggravating features. First, the attack was in the victim's own home. Secondly, the children were asleep at the time. Thirdly, the attack was unprovoked. Fourthly, it took place when the victim was lying defenceless on the floor. Fifthly, a hammer was deliberately used on the head. Sixthly, the 13-year-old son witnessed the attack, and seventhly, the attack only ceased when the child intervened.

7   Miss Whitehouse draws attention to the mitigation to be found, first, in the fact that the offender was a hard-working man of good character. Secondly, he pleaded guilty, in relation to which, although the plea came fairly late, he was given full credit by the sentencing judge. Thirdly, the offender's conduct on this occasion was out of character and took place against a background of depression and morbid jealousy, in the context of the consumption of three or four cans of beer that evening.

8   The Court's attention has been drawn to a number of authorities by Miss Whitehouse. In *Hudson* [2003] 2 Cr.App.R.(S.) 52 (p.327), a sentence of six years was upheld by this Court, following a plea of guilty; in *Attorney General's Reference No.98 of 2002 (Bishop)* [2003] 2 Cr.App.R.(S.) 95 (p.563), Kay L.J., giving the judgment of the Court (which included an indication that the appropriate sentence in that case should have been three and a half years in the court below), pointed out that violence in the domestic context is no less serious than other contexts and, in some cases, can be even more serious. With that observation we agree. In *Attorney General's Reference No.32 of 1994 (Dawson)* (1995) 16 Cr.App.R.(S.) 710, following a guilty plea, a sentence of 30 months was increased by this Court to five years. The offender in that case had a previous conviction for attempted murder. In the course of giving the judgment of the Court Lord Taylor C.J. said, at p.713 of the report, that the results of an attack of this kind are important but the conduct of the offender is of even more importance. In *Attorney General's Reference No.19 of 1994 (Arnold)* (1995) 16 Cr.App.R.(S.)

541, following a trial, a sentence of two years was increased to five years, and in *Davies* (1986) 8 Cr.App.R.(S.) 97, following a plea of guilty, in a case in which the violence had even graver consequences than in the present case, a sentence of seven years was upheld in relation to a man of good character. Miss Whitehouse's submission is that the sentence of three years imposed by the sentencing judge failed to reflect the aggravating features to which attention is drawn.

9   On behalf of the offender, Mr Reid invited our attention to other authorities: in particular, *Mannion* [1999] 2 Cr.App.R.(S.) 240, where a sentence of four years' imprisonment was reduced to three years following a guilty plea, and *Attorney General's Reference No.68 of 2002 (Catterall)* [2003] 1 Cr.App.R.(S.) 94 (p.498), where a sentence of two and a half years was increased to four years following a trial. In the course of the judgment given in that case, it was indicated that, in the light of the facts of that case, a sentence in the court below of the order of five years' imprisonment was to have been expected.

10   Mr Reid accepts that the sentence passed by the learned sentencing judge was a lenient one towards the bottom of whatever range is appropriate following a guilty plea in relation to s.18 offences. He stressed the indication of remorse given by the offender in addition to the guilty plea.

11   He invites the Court, in the light of all the circumstances, not to interfere with the sentence which was passed by the learned trial judge. That is not a submission to which we are able to accede.

12   In our judgment, a sentence in the court below of the order of five and a half to six years ought to have been imposed. It follows that the sentence passed was unduly lenient. Taking into account double jeopardy, that is to say that the offender is being sentenced a second time, the sentence which we pass, in the light of all the circumstances of this matter to which we have drawn attention, in substitution for the sentence of three years imposed by the Crown Court judge, is one of four and a half years' imprisonment.

ATTORNEY GENERAL'S REFERENCE NO.99 OF 2003 (KEVIN VIDLER)

Court of Appeal (Lord Justice Rose (Vice President, Court of Appeal Criminal Division), Mr Justice Grigson and Mr Justice Andrew Smith): May 20, 2004

[2004] EWCA Crim 1622; [2005] 1 Cr.App.R.(S.) 33

Aggravating features; Assault on constables; Grievous bodily harm; Resisting arrest; Undue leniency

H1   *Causing grievous bodily harm with intent to resist or prevent arrest—attack on police officer involving kicks to the head—length of sentence*

H2   Thirty months' imprisonment for causing grievous bodily harm with intent to resist or prevent arrest, where the offender attacked a police officer and kicked him to the head, varied to three years and 11 months' imprisonment.

H3   The offender was convicted of causing grievous bodily harm with intent to resist or prevent lawful apprehension, and of affray. Two police officers were called to a club where there had been a disturbance. The manager of the club was attacked by a youth, and a police officer intervened. While the officer was struggling with the man, the offender seized him by the neck and squeezed his throat, and then pushed him to his knees, punched his head and stamped on his face. The offender then kicked the officer in the head until the officer became unconscious. The officer sustained various cuts and swellings, and persistent double vision. He was off duty for about 18 months. Sentenced to 30 months' imprisonment for causing grievous bodily harm, and 12 months concurrent for affray. The Attorney General asked the Court to review the sentence on the ground that it was unduly lenient.

H4   **Held:** (considering *Attorney General's Reference No.35 of 1995 (Russell Hartley)* [1996] 1 Cr.App.R.(S.) 413, *Attorney General's Reference No.47 of 1994 (Robert John Smith)* [1995] 16 Cr.App.R.(S.) 865, *Attorney General's Reference No.76 of 1998 (Gary Kirkham)* [1999] 2 Cr.App.R.(S.) 361) for the Attorney General it was submitted that the offence was aggravated by the fact that the victim was a uniformed police officer; the attack was serious and sustained; feet were used as a weapon, and the offender had a record for offences of violence. The Court had no doubt that the sentence was unduly lenient. The Court would have expected a sentence of at least five years' imprisonment on a trial. Having regard to the element of double jeopardy and the offender's progress in prison, the Court would substitute a sentence of three years and 11 months' imprisonment.

H5   **Cases cited:** *Attorney General's Reference No.35 of 1995 (Russell Hartley)* [1996] 1 Cr.App.R.(S.) 413, *Attorney General's Reference No.47 of 1994 (Robert John Smith)* (1995) 16 Cr.App.R.(S.) 865, *Attorney General's Reference No.76 of 1998 (Gary Kirkham)* [1999] 2 Cr.App.R.(S.) 361

H6   **References:** causing grievous bodily harm, *Current Sentencing Practice* B2-2

H7   *M. Khamisa* for the Attorney General.
      R. Colover for the offender.

JUDGMENT

1   **ROSE L.J.:**   The Attorney-General seeks the leave of the Court, under s.36 of the Criminal Justice Act 1988, to refer a sentence said to be unduly lenient. We grant leave.

2   The offender was born in March 1966 and so is 38 years of age. On October 23, 2003 he was convicted by the jury, before H.H. Judge Neligan, at Maidstone Crown Court, of causing grievous bodily harm with intent to resist or prevent the lawful apprehension or detainer of himself and another, contrary to s.18 of the Offences Against the Person Act 1861. He was also convicted of affray, contrary to s.3(1) of the Public Order Act 1986. On December 1, 2003 he was sentenced by Judge Neligan to 30 months' imprisonment for the s.18 offence and to 12 months concurrently for the affray.

3   The facts were these. On New Year's Eve 2002 Constable Langley, who became the victim in this case and who was a serving police officer, was, together with another officer, Police Constable Malcolm, on uniformed patrol. They were called to Southborough Working Men's club, where there had been a disturbance. They were speaking outside the club to the manager, Mr Deacon, in relation to that disturbance, which had involved members of the offender's family. During that earlier incident the offender's brother, Neil, had assaulted Mr Deacon.

4   Constable Langley tried to speak to the offender who was the worse for drink and who told the officer to "fuck off". At that stage the officer noticed another male, younger than the offender, attacking Mr Deacon. The officer went to aid Mr Deacon and seized the younger man. While he was struggling with that man, the offender seized him by the neck and squeezed his throat, so the officer was unable to speak. The offender then pushed the officer backwards, onto his knees and punched him in the head, knocking him to the ground. Thereupon the offender stamped on the right side of the officer's face, with considerable force, causing the officer to cry out in pain and his right eye to close. The offender then repeatedly kicked Constable Langley in the head, with such violence as to cause his head to go backwards and forwards. The officer, unsurprisingly, began to lose consciousness. As he raised his arms to cover his face he felt another kick to his upper chest near his throat. Thereupon, he lost consciousness. The offender then attacked the other officer. The offender was ultimately disabled by police officers using CS spray and he was arrested.

5   In interview, he denied the offence. He claimed that it was his brother, Neil, who had carried out the attack and that was the defence which he ran at trial.

6   The officer, in the meanwhile, had been, immediately following this attack, spitting blood on the floor and he was taken to hospital by ambulance. He was discharged later that night. Thereafter, his head was painful to touch. He had a small cut to the hairline on the left, above the ear and the right side of his face was swollen, including a black eye. He also had a 2 inch by 1.5 inch cut to the left temple and forehead and a wound to the upper lip that split the lip inside out and required four stitches. He also had a swelling under his right jaw.

7   In a medical report, eight months after the attack, it was recorded that the officer had continued to visit the orthoptic department for persistent double vision. In addition he suffered from continual headaches and a persistent click from his jaw. Today, an operation for the double vision, which persists, is still a possibility. He has just returned to light duties in the police force, almost 18 months after these events.

8   The offender has previous convictions for offences involving drugs, dishonesty and violence, spanning the period between 1985 and 1999. In particular, in 1986, he was placed on probation by the magistrates for assault occasioning actual bodily harm. In February 1993, he was conditionally discharged for 12 months, for assault on the police. His most recent offence, in early 1999, was, again, for assault occasioning actual bodily harm, for which he was fined £500 and ordered to pay compensation and costs. The offender has never previously experienced a loss of liberty and for the most part has been dealt with by the magistrates.

9   On behalf of the Attorney General, Mr Khamisa draws attention to five aggravating features. First, the victim was a uniformed police officer on duty. Secondly, the attack was serious and sustained and continued even though the officer was defenceless on the ground. Thirdly, feet were used as a weapon. Fourthly, the offender contested the matter, so the officer had to give evidence. Fifthly, offences of violence, including violence against the police appear, as we have indicated, in the offender's record.

10   Mr Khamisa draws attention to three mitigating features. First, the offender has, since these events, sought to address his alcohol and anger management problems. Secondly, at the time of these events the offender's wife was mentally unwell. Thirdly, as is apparent from what we have already said, the offender is presently enduring his first period of incarceration. But the submission is made by Mr Khamisa that, in the light of all the circumstances of this offence, the 30-month sentence failed adequately to reflect the aggravating features and the seriousness of the offence.

11   Mr Khamisa drew attention to three authorities. In *Attorney General's Reference No.35 of 1995 (Russell Hartley)* [1996] 1 Cr.App.R.(S.) 413, this Court increased from three years to four years the sentence passed for an offence of causing grievous bodily harm with intent by kicking a police officer, the plea having been one of guilty. The defendant in that case had four previous convictions for assault. In the course of giving judgment, Lord Taylor C.J. indicated that

the sentence in that case ought to have been of the order of five years. At p.415 of the report, Lord Taylor, in the last paragraph said this:

"To kick somebody on the ground, and in particular to kick a police officer who was merely acting in the exercise of his duty, to kick him in the face, and to kick him repeatedly is a very grave offence indeed. This Court wishes to make it clear that anyone committing offences of that kind must expect a substantial sentence."

In *Attorney General's Reference No.47 of 1994 (Robert John Smith)* (1995) 16 Cr.App.R.(S.) 865,following a trial, a sentence of two and a half years was increased to four years and, in the course of giving the judgment on that occasion, Lord Taylor C.J. said at 867:

"An attacker who uses his shod feet, or who bites somebody with his teeth is just as much using a weapon as someone who wields an object in his hand."

12   In *Attorney General's Reference No.76 of 1998 (Gary Kirkham)* [1999] 2 Cr.App.R.(S.) 361, this Court, following a plea of guilty, increased a sentence from three to five years, the offender having stamped on the head of the victim, and having four previous convictions for violence.

13   On behalf of the offender, Mr Colover accepts that the sentence passed by the learned judge was a lenient one. But he poses the question: was it unduly lenient? He relies on the principle of double jeopardy, that is to say the fact that the offender is being, by this Court, sentenced a second time and he submits that, if the sentence has to be increased, consideration should be given to not making the offender a long-term prisoner. In particular, Mr Colover points out that, although the victim's injuries were severe, they were not of the utmost severity. That is undoubtedly so. But, as has been said by this Court on earlier occasions, although the consequences of violent conduct are important, the nature of the offender's conduct is even more important.

14   Mr Colover further relies upon a number of documents placed before the Court. They include a letter from the offender himself, expressing remorse, and a letter from the prison where the offender is serving his sentence, which indicates that he has achieved enhanced prisoner status and is being trained by the Samaritans as a listener. Mr Colover also puts before the Court a medical report on the offender's wife and a report on their son. He submits that the offender, albeit at rather a late age, is now maturing.

15   We have regard to all of these matters. There is no doubt that the sentence passed in this case was unduly lenient. We would have expected, following a trial, a sentence in the court below, on this offender, for this offence, of at least five years' imprisonment.

16   We take into account, however, double jeopardy. We also take into account the significant progress which the offender is making in prison. Having regard to that matter in particular, we take the view that it is not necessary to make the offender a long-term prisoner. Accordingly, the sentence which we pass in substitution for the 30 months passed by the learned Crown Court judge is one of three years and 11 months.

R. v JONATHAN RICHARD COLLARD

Court of Appeal (Lord Justice Rose (Vice President, Court of Appeal Criminal Division), Mr Justice Grigson and Mr Justice Andrew Smith): May 20, 2004

[2004] EWCA Crim 1664; [2005] 1 Cr.App.R.(S.) 34

(LT) Duration; Indecent photographs of children; Internet; Restraining orders; Sentencing powers

H1 *Restraining order—Sex Offenders Act 1997 s.5A—downloading images of children—whether restraining order appropriate*

H2 General observations on the propriety of making restraining orders under the Sex Offenders Act 1997, s.5A, in relation to offences of downloading indecent images of children contrary to the Protection of Children Act 1978.

H3 The appellant pleaded guilty to seven counts of making indecent photographs or pseudo-photographs of children, and 16 counts of possession of indecent photographs or pseudo-photographs of children. 5,284 similar offences were taken into consideration. The appellant had been employed as a school teacher for 26 years. His computer was seized and numerous indecent images of children were found. Counts 1 to 7 related to legitimately taken photographs of female pupils which the appellant had altered. Counts 8 to 24 related to images which he had downloaded from the internet. Counts 8 to 24 related to images at levels 4 and 5; the offences taken into consideration included 278 images at the same levels. The offences had been committed over a period of 18 years starting in 1984. Sentenced to a total of two years' imprisonment, disqualified from working with children under the Criminal Justice and Court Services Act 2000, s.28, and subjected to a restraining order under the Sex Offenders Act 1997, s.5A, in terms which prohibited him indefinitely from owning, possessing or having any access to any computer or other equipment capable of downloading any material from the internet otherwise for the purpose of any lawful employment and only at a place of lawful employment. The appeal was limited to the restraining order.

I4 **Held:** the Sex Offenders Act 1997, s.5A, came into force on May 2, 2001, and therefore did not apply to the offences charged in counts 1 to 7. Section 5A applied where the Crown Court or Court of Appeal imposed a sentence of imprisonment, or a hospital order or guardianship order in respect of a person convicted of a sexual offence to which the Act applied, or a youth court made a detention and training order for a term of 12 months or made a hospital order or guardianship order in respect of a person convicted of such an offence. The court was permitted to make an order in respect of the offender if it was satisfied that it was necessary to do so in order to protect the public in general or any particular members of the public from serious harm from him. The order might prohibit the offender from doing anything described in the order. If the offender did anything that he was prohibited from doing by the order he was guilty of an either way offence punishable on conviction on indictment with five years' imprisonment. The effect of an order under s.5A was to make the requirement to register as a sex offender coterminous with the period of the order, if the period of the order was longer than the statutory period of notification. There was provision for the offender to make an application for the order to be varied or discharged. The section had been analysed by the Court in *Halloren* [2004] 2 Cr.App.R.(S.) 57 (p.301). The Court there held that the sentencing court had a discretion whether to exercise the power to make a restraining order, and that before it could exercise its discretion it must be satisfied that it was necessary to do so in order to protect the public in general or any particular members of the public from serious harm from the offender. The Court explained that "necessary" was a higher qualifying test than for example "desirable". The Court added that there must be material upon which the sentencing judge could reach the conclusion that such an order was necessary in order to protect the public from serious harm. "Serious harm" had the same meaning as in the Powers of Criminal Courts (Sentencing) Act 2000, s.161. The position in effect was that the court might make a restraining order if there was material which satisfied it that it was necessary to make the order in the terms that it was made for the protection of the public or particular members of the public from death for serious personal injury, whether physical or psychological, caused by further offences committed by the offender. The Court had added that where the Crown invited a judge to make a restraining order, it was incumbent on the Crown to be familiar with the necessary statutory provisions and to be in a position to put before the judge the material which showed the statutory provisions to have been met. The Court entirely agreed with the sentiments expressed in *Halloren*. In *Halloren* the Court had considered that there was no material which could have satisfied the trial judge that it was necessary to make a restraining order. In *Beaney* [2004] 2 Cr.App.R.(S.) 82 (p.441) the Court was referred to *Halloren*. The Court did not dissent from the basic propositions advanced in that case, but analysed the evidence in a different way. The Court found that in cases of this kind the members of the public at risk of serious psychological harm were the children who were forced to pose or to submit to sexual conduct for the purpose of making the images to be produced and disseminated. Such children were subjected to risk from people who downloaded the images and viewed them. The psychological harm from which the children would suffer would be increased by their awareness that there were people who would get a perverted thrill from watching them being forced to pose and behave in this way. If the logic of the Court in *Beaney* was correct, potentially every person convicted of this sort of offence qualified for a restraining order under s.5A. The Court had no doubt that the reasoning was correct. The reasoning behind both the legislation and the sentencing policy was that participation in indecent or pornographic activity damaged children and that those who downloaded such material from the internet contributed to such damage. However it did not follow that the court would be satisfied that it was necessary to make a restraining order in every case. That was only part of the test the court should consider. The court should consider the number of offences, their duration, the nature of the material, the extent of publication and the use to which the material was put. The court should also consider the offender's antecedents, his personal circumstances and the risk of reoffending. Where the court was satisfied that there was a real risk of the offender committing further offences and that the further offences would cause serious harm to children, it would be necessary to make a restraining order. The terms of the restraining order must be tailored to meet the danger presented by the offender. It must be proportionate, and not oppressive. The court was aware of the ever-increasing legitimate use of the internet. Increasing numbers of people used the internet as a source of news, information and entertainment. Many products were advertised online and could be purchased online. Employment might require the use of the internet at home as well as in the workplace. A wide prohibition on an offender might have the effect of depriving his wife and children of the benefit of legitimate use of the internet. The Court was satisfied that the sentencing judge was entitled to reach the conclusion that the appellant qualified for a restraining order on looking at the nature and extent of the material, the duration of the offences and the occupation of the appellant. The Court bore in mind that the appellant could apply to discharge the order at any time. With that in mind, the Court was satisfied that it was appropriate for the order to be indefinite. However, the terms of the order were too wide and should be curtailed. It would have been sufficient if the order had been in terms prohibiting the offender from downloading any material from the internet, other than that required for the purpose of any lawful employment or lawful study. The restraining orders on counts 1 to 7 would be quashed and the orders on counts 8 to 24 would be varied accordingly.

15   **Cases cited:** *Halloren* [2004] 2 Cr.App.R.(S.) 57 (p.301), *Beaney* [2004] 2 Cr.App.R.(S.) 82 (p.441)

16   **References:** sexual offence prevention orders, *Current Sentencing Practice* H 11, *Archbold* 20-323

17   **Commentary:** [2004] Crim.L.R. 757

18   *Miss S. Thorne* for the appellant.
       R. Cherrill for the Crown.

JUDGMENT

1 **GRIGSON J.:** On October 10, 2003 at the Crown Court at Lewes this appellant pleaded guilty to seven counts of making indecent photographs or pseudo-photographs of children (1–7) and to 16 counts of possession of indecent photographs or pseudo-photographs of children (8–24).

2 On November 4 at the same Court H.H. Judge Brown sentenced the applicant on counts 1–7 to one years' imprisonment on each count, and on counts 8–24 two years' imprisonment on each count. All sentences to be served concurrently.

3 5,284 similar offences were taken into consideration.

4 No appeal is made against those sentences.

5 The judge also made a restraining order under s.5A of the Sex Offenders Act 1997. The appellant was ordered to register under the Sex Offenders Act 1997 and disqualified from working with children under s.28 of the Criminal Justice and Court Services Act 2000.

6 It is against the restraining order that leave to appeal was granted. The appeal came before the Full Court on February 27, 2004 and the hearing was adjourned as there was an apparent conflict between two decisions in this Court: *Halloren* [2004] 2 Cr.App.R.(S.) 57 (p.301) and *Beaney* [2004] 2 Cr.App.R.(S.) 82 (p.441).

7 The terms of the restraining order imposed by H.H. Judge Brown were as follows:

> "that you be prohibited from owning, using, possessing or having any access to any personal computer, laptop computer or any other equipment capable of downloading any material from the Internet. That prohibition does not apply to any such equipment which you have and use for the purpose of any lawful employment at and only at a place of such employment."

8 The judge ordered that the appellant register under the Sex Offenders Act 1997 for a period of 10 years and that the disqualification from working with children last indefinitely.

9 These orders were made in respect of each offence. In fact s.5A only came into force on May 2, 2001 and so was only available on counts 8–24. The order made on counts 1–7 must therefore be quashed.

10 Section 5A of the Sex Offenders Act 1997 reads:

> "(i) This section applies when —
> a) the Crown Court or Court of Appeal imposes a sentence of imprisonment or makes a hospital or guardianship order, in respect of a person convicted of a sexual offence to which this Part applies.
> b) The Crown Court or the Court of Appeal orders that a person who has been found not guilty of such an offence by reason of insanity, or to be under a disability and to have done the act charged against him in respect of such an offence, be admitted to hospital or make a guardianship order in respect of him.

    c) a Youth Court makes a Detention and Training Order for a term of twelve months or more or a hospital or guardianship order in respect of a person convicted of such an offence.

    d. a Youth Court makes a hospital or guardianship order in respect of a person who has been found not guilty of such an offence by reason of insanity, or to be under a disability and to have done the act charged against him in respect of such offences.

2) The court may make an order under this section in respect of the person ('the offender') if it is satisfied that it is necessary to do so in order to protect the public in general or any particular members of the public, from serious harm from him.

3) The order may prohibit the offender from doing anything described in the order.

4) The order shall have effect for the period specified in it or until further order; and the offender shall not cease to be subject to the notification requirements of this Part while the order has effect.

8) If without reasonable excuse the offender does anything which he is prohibited from doing by an order under this section, he is guilty of an offence.

9) A person guilty of an offence under this section is liable —

    a) On conviction an indictment to imprisonment for a term not exceeding five years or a fine or both.

    b) on summary conviction to imprisonment for a term not exceeding six months, or a fine not exceeding the statutory maximum, or both."

11   The effect of s.5A(4) is to make the requirement to register co-terminous with the period of prohibition when the period of prohibition is longer than the requirement to register. It also provides that the court can specify the length of the period of prohibition. If the court does not specify the period, then the order continues indefinitely unless and until the court orders otherwise under subs.(7).

> "On the application, the court may, after hearing the applicant and the other persons mentioned in subsection (6) above (if they so wish) make any order under this section varying or discharging the previous order which the court considers appropriate."

2   Subsection 6 sets out who may make the application to the court. In this case, no period was specified for the prohibition so that it continues unless discharged on application. The requirement to register would continue indefinitely unless the court discharged the order of prohibition within the 10-year period. It can be seen immediately that this section gives the court very wide powers indeed, and that breach of the order may result in substantial punishment.

3   In *Halloren* [2004] 2 Cr.App.R.(S.) 57 (p.301) H.H. Judge Broderick, giving the judgment of the Court, analysed the section in this way:

1) that the court had a discretion as to whether to exercise its power to make a restraining order.

2) that before the court can exercise its discretion it must be satisfied that it is necessary to do so in order to protect the public in general or any particular members of the public, from serious harm from him (the offender). The Court explained that "necessary" was a higher qualifying test than, for example, "desirable".

3) that there must be material upon which the judge can reach the conclusion that such an order is necessary in order to protect the public from serious harm.

4): that "serious harm" had the same meaning as appears in subs.(4) of s.161 of the Powers of Criminal Courts (Sentencing) Act 2000, namely

"In this Act any reference, in relation to an offender convicted of a violent or sexual offence, to protecting the public from serious harm from him . . . shall be construed as a reference to protecting members of the public from death or serious personal injury, whether physical or psychological, occasioned by further such offences committed by him."

14   To summarise the position: the court may make a restraining order if there is material which satisfies the court that it is necessary to make the order (in the terms that it was made) for the protection of the public or particular members of the public from death or serious personal injury, whether physical or psychological, caused by further offences committed by the offender.

15   H.H. Judge Broderick added:

". . . where the Crown invite a judge to make an order of this nature, it seems to us that it is incumbent upon them to be familiar with the necessary statutory provisions and to be in a position to put before the judge the material which shows that those statutory provisions have been met."

With those sentiments we entirely agree.

16   The Court in *Halloren*'s case having considered the evidence concluded that there was no material which could have satisfied the trial judge that it was necessary to make a prohibition order.

17   In *Beaney* the Court was referred to the judgment in *Halloren* and did not dissent from the basic propositions advanced in that case. But they analysed the evidence before the sentencing judge in this way:

a) that in cases of this sort the members of the public at risk of serious psychological harm were the children who "are forced to pose or worse to participate in sexual conduct, for the purpose of enabling these images to be produced and disseminated".

b) that such children were subjected to risk from "people like the applicant who simply downloaded the images and viewed them".

18   Keith J., giving the judgement of the Court, said:

"If people like the applicant continue to download and view images of this kind, even when they have not had to pay for the images downloaded, the offences which they commit can properly be said to contribute to the psychological harm which the children in those images would suffer by the children's awareness that there were people out there getting a perverted thrill from watching them forced to pose and behave in this way."

19   If the logic of the Court in *Beaney* is correct then potentially every person convicted of this sort of offence qualifies for a restraining order under s.5A.

20   We have no doubt that the reasoning is correct. The reasoning behind both the legislation and sentencing policy is that participation in indecent or pornographic activities damages children and that by downloading such material from the internet offenders contribute to such damage.

21   However, it does not follow that the court will be satisfied that it is necessary to make a restraining order in every case. That is only one part of the test the court must apply.

22   The court should consider:

    a) the offences: the number of offences, their duration, the nature of the material, the extent of publication and the use to which the material was put.

    b) the offender: his antecedents, his personal circumstances and the risk of re-offending.

23   Where the court is satisfied that i) there is a real risk of the offender committing further offences and ii) the further offences will cause serious harm to children, then it will be necessary to make a restraining order.

24   Where the court makes a restraining order, its terms must be tailored to meet the danger that the offender presents. It must not be oppressive, it must be proportionate. The Court is well aware of the ever increasing legitimate use of the internet. More and more people use the internet as a source of news, information and entertainment. All sorts of products are advertised online, and can be purchased online. Employment may require use of the internet at home as well as in the workplace. The internet is used as a legitimate tool by both adults and children. A wide prohibition on an offender might have the effect of depriving his wife and children of the benefit of legitimate use of the internet.

25   This appellant was employed as a teacher and had been for 26 years. He was arrested on December 17, 2002 and a search warrant executed at his house. His computer was seized and numerous indecent images of children were found. Counts 1–7 related to legitimately taken photographs of female pupils which the appellant had altered. Counts 8–24 related to images at Levels 4 and 5 which he had downloaded from the internet. The offences taken into consideration related mainly to images at Level 1 but there were 261 images at Level 4 and 17 at Level 5. In interview, the appellant admitted all his offences. The offences started in 1984 and continued until his arrest.

26   Miss Thorne, counsel for the appellant, makes three submissions. The first is that there was no material before the judge upon which he could decide that this appellant qualified for a restraining order. Mr Cherrill, who appears on behalf of the Crown, submits that the court was entitled to reach that conclusion simply by

looking at the nature of the material, the extent and duration of the offending and the occupation of the appellant. Mr Cherrill submits that the Court is entitled to look at the facts in relation to the first seven counts in making the judgment as to whether a restraining order should be imposed.

27   We are satisfied that Mr Cherrill's submission is correct. The nature and extent of the material, the period of the offences and his occupation clearly qualified this appellant for a restraining order. Miss Thorne goes on to submit that the period of the restraining order, that is that it was made indefinitely, was manifestly excessive. Again, Mr Cherrill points to the nature of the material itself, the depth of what he describes as the appellant's addiction or obsession and the fact that there was no material before the court indicating when this particular appellant's proclivities might cease.

28   We bear in mid that the appellant can apply to discharge this order at any time. Keeping that in mind, we are satisfied that Mr Cherrill's submission as to the appropriateness of the order being indefinite is correct and that the proper order as to duration was made.

29   Miss Thorne's last submission is that the terms of the order are too wide. Again, Mr Cherrill argues otherwise. But we are satisfied that the terms of the order here are in fact too wide and must be curtailed. The prohibition in the order was draconian. In our view, it would have been sufficient if the order had been in these terms:

> "that you be prohibited from downloading any material from the internet, that prohibition not applying to downloading for the purpose of any lawful employment or lawful study."

30   The appeal is allowed to this extent: the restraining order on counts 1–7 be quashed. The restraining order on counts 8–24 be varied as above.

ATTORNEY GENERAL'S REFERENCE NO.28 OF 2004 (GEORGE MCLUSKIE)

COURT OF APPEAL (Lord Justice Rose (Vice President, Court of Appeal Criminal Division), Mr Justice Grigson and Mr Justice Andrew Smith): May 20, 2004

[2004] EWCA Crim 1440; [2005] 1 Cr.App.R.(S.) 35

⟨LT⟩ Detention; Glassing; Grievous bodily harm; Undue leniency; Young offenders

H1   *Long term detention of juvenile—wounding with intent to cause grievous bodily harm—attack with broken bottle—length of term of detention*

H2   A detention and training order for 18 months imposed on a youth aged 17 for wounding with intent to cause grievous bodily harm by striking a man repeatedly with a broken bottle varied to three years' detention under the Powers of Criminal Courts (Sentencing) Act 2000, s.91.

H3   The offender, aged 17 at the time of the offence, pleaded guilty to wounding with intent to do grievous bodily harm. The offender and another youth approached three people standing outside a nightclub in the early hours of the morning. There was an exchange of words and the offender's behaviour frightened one of the other party. The victim of the offence intervened to calm the situation down, but the offender produced a bottle and hit the victim. The bottle broke. The offender then held the victim's arm down while he brought the broken bottle down on the victim's face at least six times. The offender then ran off but was arrested shortly afterwards. The victim had lacerations to the face and was referred for plastic surgery. Subsequently he had visible scars to the head and his hair had not grown back over the scar. Sentenced to a detention and training order of 18 months. The Attorney General asked the Court to review the sentence on the ground that it was unduly lenient.

I4   **Held:** (considering *Attorney General's Reference Nos 59, 60 and 63 of 1998 (Goodwin and Others)* [1999] 2 Cr.App.R.(S.) 128, *Attorney General's Reference No.121 of 2002* [2003] EWCA Crim 684) for the Attorney General it was submitted that the offence was aggravated by the use of a bottle as a weapon, and the fact that the attack was unprovoked and on a stranger who had intervened to try to stop violence; the offender was acting with another man and inflicted deliberate and repeated blows with a broken bottle. It seemed to the Court that the sentencing judge was unduly influenced by the personal circumstances of the offender and paid too little regard to the gravity of the offender's conduct in repeatedly using a broken bottle to the face of an entirely innocent victim in the street at night. The Court would have expected, even on a plea of guilty, a sentence of four years' detention under the Powers of Criminal Courts (Sentencing) Act 2000, s.91. Having regard to the element of double jeopardy, the Court would substitute a sentence of three years' detention.

H5   **Cases cited:** *Attorney General's Reference Nos 59, 60 and 63 of 1998 (Goodwin and Others)* [1999] 2 Cr.App.R.(S.) 128, *Attorney General's Reference No.121 of 2002* [2003] EWCA Crim. 684

H6   **References:** long term detention—wounding with intent to cause grievous bodily harm, *Current Sentencing Practice* E4

H7   *Miss B. Cheema* for the Attorney General.
      K. Talbot for the offender.

JUDGMENT

1   **ROSE L.J.:**   The Attorney General seeks the leave of the Court, under s.36 of the Criminal Justice Act 1988, to refer a sentence said to be unduly lenient. We grant leave.

2   The offender was born in May 1986 and will be 18 years of age next week. On December 17, 2003, notice of additional evidence having been served on the day before, in relation to glass fragments, the offender pleaded guilty to wounding with intent to do grievous bodily harm, contrary to s.18 of the Offences Against the Person Act 1861. He was sentenced on February 11, 2004 by H.H. Judge Badley, at Preston Crown Court, to an 18-month detention and training order.

3   In summary, the offence occurred late at night, in the street, outside a night-club, the offender being very drunk. He and another man approached a friend of the victim, the offender being in an agitated condition. The victim tried to intervene in an argument between the offender and the victim's friend. The offender thereupon produced a bottle with which he hit the victim on the head and the bottle then broke. Thereupon, holding the victim's arm, the offender brought the now broken bottle down in the victim's face, six or seven times. Permanent and disfiguring scarring resulted.

4   In a little more detail, on September 6, 2003 the victim, a 23-year-old man called Gareth Turner, was socialising that evening with his female cousin and a male friend called Liam Johnson. By a little before 2 o'clock in the early hours of the morning of September 7, Johnson, in particular, was the worse for wear and the three of them were standing outside a nightclub. The two youths, of whom the then 17-year-old offender was one, approached. There was an exchange of words. The offender, in drink and agitation, frightened, in particular, the female in the victim's party. She screamed and ran back to the club for help. From about 10 metres away she saw part of the incident which followed.

5   The victim tried to position himself between his friend Johnson and the offender in order to calm the situation down. But, as we have said, the offender produced a bottle and struck the victim. The bottle broke. The offender then took

hold of the victim's arm, which he was holding out to keep the offender away, and held it while he brought the broken bottle down into the victim's face at least six times. The other youth who was with the offender punched Johnson in addition.

6   Police officers arrived. The offender ran off. He was chased and caught. His clothing was heavily bloodstained. He said on arrest: "It was not my fault, I've done fuck all. That man tried to grab me." In interview he maintained that he had not started the fight and he denied using the bottle.

7   The victim was bleeding heavily. He was taken to hospital. He had lacerations to the left temporal area, left eyebrow, left ear, chin, right arm and hand. Glass had been left in the wound to his eyebrow. The wounds required 20 stitches and gluing, and he came back to hospital two days later with post concussion syndrome, having been suffering from headaches and vomiting. Part of the wound to his scalp did not heal well and an area of skin measuring about five by two and a half centimetres died. He was referred for plastic surgery.

8   In the victim impact statement which was before the sentencing judge, the victim set out the lasting effects of the attack. He has visible scars to his head and face. His hair has not grown back over the wound. On the scalp he has a lump on the site of the injury to his hand and he is very self-conscious about his scarring. He has lost social confidence and is nervous going out on his own. He does not sleep properly and wonders why he was targeted.

9   The offender has a substantial record of appearances before the courts on previous occasions; a total of 15 appearances, for over 30 offences, since June 1998. His first appearance was for theft, committed on bail. Thereafter he acquired convictions for common assault, cruelty to animals, arson being reckless life would be endangered, theft, handling, possession of an offensive weapon, assault occasioning actual bodily harm, offences contrary to ss.4 and 6 of the Public Order Act 1986, affray, criminal damage, theft of motor vehicles and driving offences. He has variously been dealt with by discharges, fine, being placed on supervision, attendance centre orders, a detention and training order for six months and a community punishment and rehabilitation order.

10   On behalf of the Attorney General Miss Cheema draws attention to a number of aggravating features. First, a bottle was used as a weapon. Secondly, the attack was unprovoked and on a stranger, in the street, late at night. Thirdly, the victim had intervened to try to stop violence. Fourthly, the offender was acting with another man. Fifthly, there were deliberate and repeated blows with a broken bottle, to the face and head. Next, there was little remorse or acknowledgment of guilt until the overwhelming evidence was served. Next, such offences, in town centres, late at night are prevalent and, finally, the offender's bad record.

11   Miss Cheema draws attention to five mitigating features: first, the plea of guilty for which the sentencing judge allowed full credit; secondly, the youth of the offender, he being, as we have said, only 17 at the time of the offence; thirdly, no serious permanent physical disability resulted to the victim; fourthly, some remorse was ultimately demonstrated; and, fifthly, the difficult personal history and background which the offender has, having lost, first, his father at the age of 3 and then his mother to a psychiatric hospital, so he was, for a time, brought up by an aunt.

12   Miss Cheema referred to two authorities: *Attorney General's Reference Nos 59, 60 and 63 of 1998 (Goodwin and Others)* [1999] 2 Cr.App.R.(S.) 128. In that case this Court, in which the then Lord Chief Justice, Lord Bingham, presided dealt with three young offenders, the first of whom had no violence in his record, the second of whom had a single previous conviction for robbery some years previously, and the third of whom had a previous record of only minor offences.

13   In the course of giving judgment, Lord Bingham at 131 said this:

"When an offender, however young, deliberately inflicts serious injury on another there is a legitimate public expectation that such offender will be severely punished to bring home to him the gravity of the offence and to warn others of the risk of behaving in the same way. If such punishment does not follow, public confidence in the administration of the criminal law is weakened and the temptation arises to give offenders extra- judicially the punishment that the formal processes of law have not given. When we speak of the public we do not forget the victim, the party who has actually suffered the injury, and those close to him."

Miss Cheema also drew attention to *Attorney General's Reference No.121 of 2002* [2003] EWCA Crim 684, in which Mantell L.J. gave the judgment of the Court in relation to a 16-year-old who, having pleaded guilty to wounding with intent, was placed on probation. He was a young man of good character. The Court indicated, in para.[15] of the judgment, that a sentence of the order of four years' detention in the court below would not have been appealable and the least proper appropriate sentence would have been three years' detention. The Court went on to impose a detention and training order of 18 months because, among other reasons, that offender was being sent to custody after a non-custodial sentence had been passed upon him. It is to be noted from the description of the injuries in para.[5] of that judgment that the target area for the offender had not been the face or head of the victim.

14   The submission which Miss Cheema makes is that the sentence passed by the learned judge in this case failed adequately to mark the gravity of this offence. She gave too much credit for the mitigating features arising, in particular, from the offender's difficult background. But the sentence she passed would fail to act as a deterrent to others and adequately to reflect the public's proper concern about offences of this kind.

15   On behalf of the offender, Mr Talbot conceded, at the outset of submissions, that the sentence passed by the learned judge was unduly lenient. But he sought by his submissions to persuade the Court either not to interfere with the sentence passed, or to make such short additional order by way of sentence that s.91 of the Powers of Criminal Courts (Sentencing) Act 2000 would not be invoked. Mr Talbot dealt, at some length, with the circumstances in which the offender came to plead guilty after the additional evidence had been served upon him. He submitted that a discount for that plea of at least 25 per cent ought to have been given. Mr Talbot described this young man's unfortunate and unhappy upbringing. Mr Talbot stressed that, since he has been in custody, the offender has acquitted himself

well; in particular he has completed one course and is about to attend an anger management course. Mr Talbot stresses that the consequences for the victim could have been a good deal worse. He points out, in relation to the offender's antecedents, that prior to the present sentence, the offender had not been deprived of his liberty for longer than six months. Mr Talbot also stressed that, as and when the offender emerges from custody, he can anticipate support from his family.

16   Mr Talbot relies on the element of double jeopardy which is a feature of the second sentencing process in all Attorney General's References. He made the submission that, following a trial for this offence, the sentence in the court below might properly have been four years. On a plea it might properly have been three years or somewhat less.

17   To all of those matters we have regard. It seems to us that the learned sentencing judge was unduly influenced by the personal circumstances of the offender and paid too little regard to the gravity of the offender's conduct in repeatedly using a broken bottle to the face of an entirely innocent victim in the street, at night.

18   We would have expected, in the court below, even on a plea of guilty, taking into account all the other circumstances of this case, to which we have referred, including the youth of this offender and his record, a sentence of four years' detention under s.91.

19   Having regard to the element of double jeopardy, the sentence which we pass in substitution for the 18-month detention and training order passed by the learned judge is one of three years' detention under s.91.

R. v CURTIS BRAXTON

COURT OF APPEAL (Lord Justice Hooper, Mr Justice Leveson and Judge Mettyear): May 21, 2004

[2004] EWCA Crim 1374; [2005] 1 Cr.App.R.(S.) 36

(LT) Anti social behaviour orders; Breach; Imprisonment; Public protection

H1   *Breach of antisocial behaviour order—length of sentence*

H2   Three and a half years' imprisonment upheld for repeated breaches of an anti-social behaviour order.

H3   The applicant was convicted by a magistrates court of two offences of breach of an anti-social behaviour order, and one of assault. He was committed to the Crown Court for sentence. The applicant was the subject of an anti-social behaviour order made by a magistrates' court under the Crime and Disorder Act 1998, s.1, on the complaint of a local authority. The order prohibited the appellant from entering a city centre for five years or using threatening abusive or similar behaviour towards any person or property in a city centre. Two months after the order was made the applicant twice broke the terms of the order. He was convicted in the Crown Court and sentenced to four years' imprisonment. The sentence was later reduced on appeal to two years' imprisonment. The applicant was released from that sentence and within a few weeks was seen behaving in an aggressive manner in the area to which the order related. The following day he was seen again in the same area. He was arrested. At the police station he spat into the face of a police officer. The appellant had 37 previous appearances. He had been convicted on nine occasions of the offences contrary to the Public Order Act 1986 and on nine occasions, of assault. Sentenced to three and a half years' imprisonment for each of the breaches of the order, concurrent, and three months consecutive for the assault (total sentence, three years and nine months' imprisonment).

H4 **Held:** the applicant did not understand the nature or effect of the order made against him. The order was specifically designed to protect the public from frequent and distressing behaviour of the type which was the subject of the order. He had acted in breach of the order, on four different occasions. The Court agreed that the public were entitled to be protected from the applicant. His application for leave to appeal would be refused.

H5 **References:** breach of antisocial behaviour order, *Current Sentencing Practice* B 3-7

No counsel appeared.

JUDGMENT

1   **LEVESON J.:** On October 24, 2003 this applicant appeared before H.H. Judge McCreath in the Crown Court at Birmingham, having been committed for sentence by the Birmingham City magistrates following his conviction for two offences of breaching an antisocial behaviour order and one offence of assaulting a constable in the execution of his duty. He was sentenced to terms of three-and-a-half years' imprisonment on each of the breaches and three months' imprisonment consecutive for the assault, making three years and nine months in all. He now renews his application for leave to appeal against that sentence following refusal by the single judge.

2   The background is important. On October 31, 2001, upon the complaint of the Housing Department of Birmingham City Council, an antisocial behaviour order was made by Birmingham magistrates under s.1 of the Crime and Disorder Act 1998. This order prohibited the applicant, for a period of five years, from entering Birmingham City Centre, using or engaging in any threatening, abusive, offensive, intimidating, insulting language or behaviour or threatening or engaging in violence or damage against any person or property within the city centre.

3   It is undeniable that this represents a serious infringement upon the liberty of the applicant, not only because it represents a restriction on his right of free movement, but also because breach constitutes a criminal offence punishable with a

term of up to five years' imprisonment, which is greater than the maximum penalty which could be imposed for offences which might otherwise be reflected within the terms of the order. It is, however, a response by Parliament to the increasing concern about the impact on the public of antisocial behaviour in its many constituent forms. It follows that this concern must be reflected in the sentences which the court imposes for breach of the order.

4   I go back to the history. Within two months of the order being made, the applicant twice breached its terms. He was prosecuted and, in June 2002, tried in the Crown Court at Birmingham before H.H. Judge Stanley and a jury. He represented himself, as he was entitled to do, but during the course of the prosecution case he fell out with the judge and was not in fact present thereafter. He was convicted and sentenced to terms of four years' imprisonment on each count concurrent.

5   His appeal against conviction was dismissed, but in relation to sentence, Keith J., giving the judgment of the Court (Tuckey L.J., Keith J. and Sir Brian Smedley) said:

> "9. We have every sympathy with the judge's determination to protect the public for as long as possible from a man whom he regarded as posing a danger to the public. But, as the judge himself recognised, the sentence which he passed was close to the maximum for a single offence of acting in breach of an antisocial behaviour order and it made the applicant a long term prisoner. We think that a sentence close to the maximum should really be reserved for cases in which the antisocial behaviour order had itself been the subject of persistent and prolonged breaches, or where the breaches of the antisocial behaviour order had consisted of conduct more serious than abusive, offensive and insulting language or conduct, in other words, in which the behaviour was truly intimidating.
>
> 10. It is possible that what the judge was doing in the present case was sentencing the applicant for the behaviour which had caused the antisocial behaviour order to be sought in the first place, rather than for the subsequent breaches of the antisocial behaviour order, though we recognise, of course, that the applicant's behaviour following the antisocial behaviour order had to be seen in the context of everything which had gone before. In our judgment, it was not appropriate for sentences as long as these to be passed for the first breaches of an antisocial behaviour order, especially where the behaviour which constituted the breaches was not of the worst kind. In our opinion, sentences totalling two years' imprisonment would have been appropriate."

6   So it was that on April 3, 2003 the applicant was released from prison on licence, which lasted until December 2. Unfortunately, very quickly, he was arrested for breaching the antisocial behaviour order in these circumstances.

7   On July 8, 2003 a police officer was working as a CCTV operator, watching cameras trained on Broad Street in the City of Birmingham. At around 10 o'clock the applicant was seen to approach people. He was trying to stop them, bar their way, and he appeared to be begging. His behaviour was described by

the operator as aggressive and he looked as if he was asking for money. As soon as people refused he acted in an aggressive manner and then simply went about his way and started blocking other people, again asking for money and again being aggressive in manner.

8   The following day, also in Broad Street, the applicant was again seen by the operator of the CCTV. On this occasion a young lady was seen to refuse the applicant's advances for money, and as she walked past him he slapped her on the bottom. The police arrived and the applicant was arrested.

9   Upon his arrest he was totally compliant. He was cuffed and placed in a police car and taken to the police station. When walking down a corridor from one custody suite to another, however, the applicant happened to cross a police officer whom he knew. He said "Fuck you, Stuart" and then spat in the constable's face. The officer described the spit going into his eyes and mouth. He recoiled and tried to wipe the spittle from his face. When arrested for that offence, the applicant replied in a nonsensical manner.

10   The applicant appeared before Birmingham City magistrates on July 9. The court's memorandum of conviction records that, on that day, in relation to two allegations of breach of the antisocial behaviour order, he intimated before venue pleas of not guilty. The matter was considered suitable for summary trial, and it is also recorded that he consented to summary trial and pleaded not guilty. He also pleaded not guilty to the allegation of assaulting the police officer. He was remanded in custody for trial on 15th August, on which occasion he was convicted of each and committed for sentence.

11   We have recorded that history because one of the complaints which the applicant now makes is that he had dispensed with the services of his legal adviser and that his right of summary trial was waived in his absence without his consent, or alternatively not offered. The difficulty with that assertion is that, as we understand his lengthy grounds of appeal, he only dispensed with the services of his solicitor after he was refused bail, that is at the end of the process.

12   In any event, this complaint goes to the conviction recorded by the magistrates on August 15, 2003. Even if made out, it could only be the subject of challenge either in the Crown Court or, in some circumstances, by way of judicial review. Each of these routes is now well out of time and, if the services of the solicitor were dispensed with only following the remand in custody, appear to be devoid of merit. It could not, in any event, be the subject of a ground of appeal to the Court of Appeal Criminal Division.

13   When a lawyer within the Criminal Appeal Office sought to assist the applicant by pointing out that he could not appeal his conviction in this Court, the applicant made a formal complaint about the lawyer to the effect that his private papers should not have been considered by such a person but only by the judges of the Court of Appeal. That complaint is entirely misconceived. This Court is only concerned with convictions imposed following trial in the Crown Court or sentences imposed by the Crown Court, and the attempts by the Criminal Appeal Office to assist the applicant in that regard were both entirely appropriate and proper. We have explained the position only so that the applicant can under-

stand what has happened and why. Whatever other complaints he might have, he has no legitimate grievance with the Criminal Appeal Office.

14   We turn now to the appeal against sentence and summarise, first, the position of the applicant himself. Now 39 years of age, he has appeared before the courts on 37 previous occasions. On no fewer than nine occasions in the eight years prior to his release from prison in April 2003 he had been convicted of using threatening, abusive, insulting words or behaviour contrary to ss.4(1)(a) or 5(1)(a) of the Public Order Act 1986. On nine occasions he had also been convicted of an offence of violence, albeit usually assault or battery. While in custody for these matters he sent a letter to the husband of a prison officer, saying that he intended to kill her. This led to a term of four months' imprisonment, and although obviously not relevant to the appropriate sentence in this case, provides an indication of the applicant's volatility, which is also reflected in comparatively old psychiatric and pre-sentence reports which raise question marks over his psychological health. There was also a pre-sentence report dated October 20, 2003, but it was compiled after the applicant had refused to see the probation officer. The report concluded:

> "Mr Braxton can present not only as an intelligent man, but also as someone who has a variety of social difficulties. His ability to engage with a range of agencies to resolve such difficulties is questionable and I have grave doubts whether his full co-operation will ever be forthcoming. Because of this he will continue to pose problems for anyone involved in the management or monitoring of his chosen lifestyle."

15   This case thus posed a difficult sentencing decision. Judge McCreath noted the observations of the Court of Appeal on the previous occasion, observing in particular that he had regard to the extent to which behaviour of the kind in which the applicant indulged was menacing to members of the public, disquieting and disturbing. He took the view that he would not re-impose the sentence originally passed by Judge Stanley; neither would he specifically impose the unexpired portion of his previous sentence, amounting to just short of three months. Rather, he had regard to the total sentence commensurate with the gravity of his offending, including the fact that he was in breach of his licence and the fact that this was his second appearance for breach of the antisocial behaviour order, and in that regard to the need to protect the public.

16   In his very lengthy grounds of appeal, the applicant challenges the basis on which he was convicted, but takes the more general point that his behaviour must be considered at the lower end of nuisance activity. He observes that begging, if that is what he was doing, is not an imprisonable offence and that for an officer to say that what he was doing was obviously intimidating, aggressive or likely to cause alarm and distress is no more than the expression of his opinion, at best subjective and wholly devoid of objective deduction. As for slapping the bottom of the woman, this was no more than good natured, boisterous exuberance, and again led to no complaint. Turning to the offence of common assault, he argued that this was committed only in response to nine years of physical and psychological abuse from this officer.

17   Unfortunately, the applicant still does not appear to understand the nature or effect of the order made against him. The antisocial behaviour order is specifically designed to protect the public from frequent and distressing repeated misbehaviour of the type which is the subject of this order, and the applicant was indeed committing a serious criminal offence, even entering the City of Birmingham within the confines set out within the map served upon him when the order was made. He acted in deliberate breach of that order not once but twice (which led to the four-year term,reduced to two years) and yet again twice more within weeks of his release from that prison sentence. He must understand that what he might consider as trivial in his case, because of the persistence of his conduct, is now treated seriously, specifically to protect the public. It is thus vital that he address this issue and his behaviour in public if he is to avoid further conflict with the law.

18   When refusing leave to appeal, Silber J.observed that when reducing the first sentence, the Court of Appeal had considered the applicant "a menace . . . and a serious danger to members of the public", and went on to say that the judge was entitled to impose the sentence which he did. We agree that the public are entitled to be protected from this applicant. We have endeavoured to explain why the courts have approached his behaviour in the way in which they have so that he might understand the consequences of what he does and seek some help to deal with his difficulties. For that reason, we direct that a copy of the transcript of this judgment should be sent to him. Having said that, however, this application is refused.

ATTORNEY GENERAL'S REFERENCE NO.34 OF 2004 (MICHAEL JOHN WEBB)

COURT OF APPEAL (Lord Justice Hooper, Mr Justice Leveson and Mr Justice Roderick Evans): May 26, 2004

[2004] EWCA Crim 1470; [2005] 1 Cr.App.R.(S.) 37

Abuse of position of trust; Extended sentences; Indecent assault; Undue leniency; Young persons

H1   *Indecent assault on boy aged 14 by man aged 47—offence committed in breach of trust—length of sentence*

H2   An extended sentence with a custodial term of six months and an extension period of two and a half years for indecent assault on a boy aged 14 by a man aged 47 varied to an extended sentence with a custodial term of two years and an extension period of two years.

H3   The offender, aged 47, pleaded guilty to indecent assault on a male. The offender met a boy aged 14 at a course for football referees. They occasionally met in similar circumstances and the offender telephoned the boy at home. It was arranged that the boy would stay at the offender's home for two nights so that he could attend a football match. When the boy arrived, it was arranged that he would sleep in a folding bed in the offender's bedroom. While the boy was in the bed, the offender took the boy's hand and placed it on the offender's penis, and then touched the boy's penis. He then inserted something into the boy's anus. The boy left the house in the early hours of the morning and called the police. The offender was arrested later that morning and denied any indecent conduct. Sentenced to an extended sentence, consisting of a custodial term of six months and an extension period of two and a half years. The Attorney General asked the Court to review the sentence on the ground that it was unduly lenient.

H4   **Held:** (considering *Attorney General's Reference Nos 37, 38, 44, 51, 53, 35, 40, 43, 45, 41 and 42 of 2003* [2004] 1 Cr.App.R.(S.) 84 (p.499), *Attorney General's Reference No.5 of 2001 (Terence Culshaw)* [2001] 2 Cr.App.R.(S.) 106 (p.473), *Attorney General's Reference No.41 of 2000 (David Harrison)* [2001] 1 Cr.App.R.(S.) 107 (p.372)) for the Attorney General it was submitted that the offender had abused his position of trust and exploited the vulnerability of the victim. The Court did not accept the submission on the offender's behalf that psychological harm was less important than physical harm. Having regard to the authorities, the Court took the view that the appropriate sentence was in the region of two and a half to three years' imprisonment. Recognising the element of double jeopardy, the Court would substitute a sentence with a custodial term of two years' imprisonment and an extension period of two years, together with a disqualification order under the Criminal Justice and Court Services Act 2000, s.28.

H5   **Cases cited:** *Attorney General's Reference Nos 37, 38, 44, 51, 53, 35, 40, 43, 45, 41 and 42 of 2003* [2004] 1 Cr.App.R.(S.) 84 (p.499), *Attorney General's Reference No.5 of 2001 (Terence Culshaw)* [2001] 2 Cr.App.R.(S.) 106 (p.473), *Attorney General's Reference No.41 of 2000 (David Harrison)* [2001] 1 Cr.App.R.(S.) 107 (p.372)

H6   **References:** indecent assault, *Current Sentencing Practice* B 4-8

H7   *M. Ellison* for the Attorney General.
       Miss R. Butler for the offender.

JUDGMENT

1   **HOOPER L.J.:**   Her Majesty's Attorney General applies for leave to refer a sentence as being unduly lenient. We grant that leave.
2   The offender's name is Michael John W. He is 47 years old.
3   On March 5, 2004 he pleaded guilty to indecent assault on a male person under the age of 16, contrary to s.15(1) of the Sexual Offences Act 1956. He was sen-

tenced by H.H. Judge Hall on the same day to six months' imprisonment, with an extended licence period of two and a half years.

4   The agreed facts are as follows. The victim of the offence, BS, aged 14 years, first met the offender when they both attended a football referees' course at Wycombe Wanderers Football Club in November 2002. Thereafter they occasionally met in similar circumstances. They also spoke quite often on the telephone. The offender would telephone BS at home, sometimes several times a week, which resulted in BS trusting him and looking up to him.

5   BS wanted to attend an adult football match that the offender was due to referee on Saturday March 15, 2003, but it was difficult for BS to travel there. The offender had spoken to, but had never met, members of BS's family. BS's parents had come to understand from the offender that he was caring alone for two sons. It was agreed with the mother of BS that he would spend two nights (March 14 and 15) at the offender's home so that he could attend the match.

6   The offender collected BS from his mother's place of work in the early evening of Friday March 14, 2003. On the way to his home the offender told BS that he would sleep on the settee downstairs. However, later in the evening he said that he would put up a Z-bed for BS in his bedroom. On behalf of the Attorney General, Mr Ellison suggests, and we agree, that this shows a degree of pre-planning on the part of the offender. The offender's sons, aged 16 and 19 years, were both present during the evening and overnight. They each had their own bedroom.

7   Before they went to bed the offender questioned BS at some length concerning his relationship with his parents, during which BS became upset and tearful. It seemed to BS as if the offender was trying to identify a "soft spot" capable of upsetting him, and it did. Mr Ellison comments that this demonstrates exploitation on the part of the offender. We agree. Once BS became upset, the offender put his arm around BS and cuddled him for some time. When they went to bed they both undressed to their underpants and BS got into the Z-bed. That bed had been placed close enough to the offender's bed to enable him, whilst lying in his bed, to touch BS. BS tried to go to sleep, but the offender began to question him about his family life and again BS became upset. The offender invited BS to sit on his bed and he again put him arm around him. Then he asked BS to lie down on the bed with him and he put his arm around him. Before BS went to sleep the offender had his front against BS's back. Later:

> "The offender took BS's hand and placed it over his crotch area under his boxer shorts and onto his penis. BS pretended not to be awake. The offender then placed his hand under BS's boxer shorts and touched his penis for a while. BS turned over onto his front and took his hand away from the offender's crotch. The offender again put his hand on BS's penis and he then pulled BS's boxer shorts down to his knees. The offender started to rub BS's bottom, opening and closing his buttocks with his hands. BS could then feel that something was inserted into his bottom, but he had no idea what it was, it went in quite far and was then removed. The offender then touched BS's penis again, making it erect, before he pressed his own

buttocks against BS's penis for some time. When the offender moved his position BS got up saying he needed a drink".

He left the room and looked for his clothes but could not find them. He then returned to the bedroom and told the offender he was going to sleep on the Z-bed. The offender then reached out and took hold of BS's hands, saying that he loved him. After a while the offender pulled his hand away. The offender told BS to get back onto his bed, so he did, being able to think of no excuse for not doing so. A little later BS said he was too hot as an excuse to get off the offender's bed. He went downstairs, found a fleece top (that was not his) and left the house, wearing only his boxer shorts and a fleece. It was just after 0400 hours and he made a 999 emergency call to the police. That, in our view, is significant in that it shows the traumatic effect on BS of the offender's behaviour.

8   Police officers met BS at 0405 and found him to be apparently shocked and a little confused. There were reports before the court which indicated that BS subsequently developed difficulties sleeping and some behavioural problems that affected his family life and school work. In September 2003 BS was diagnosed as having post-traumatic stress disorder and thereafter received a protracted period of counselling. We have read the victim impact statement dated February 9, 2004.

9   The offender was arrested at 0555 on the morning of March 15. He accepted that when he and BS had discussed BS's home life, BS had become upset and that he, the offender, had put his arm around him, but he denied any indecent conduct with him and denied inviting him to lie on his bed. He said that BS's allegations were probably just an attempt to "draw attention to himself".

10   The offender has no previous convictions.

11   The basis upon which the offender pleaded guilty was that he disputed the prosecution facts only insofar as he did not hide BS's clothes from him and that he did not masturbate when he touched BS.

12   The mitigation advanced by the offender included reference to the fact that if he was given a custodial sentence of more than six months, he would lose his home, because of problems with the mortgage, and that his younger teenage son, C, would have no home to go to and no means whatsoever by which to support himself.

13   In mitigation Miss Butler said:

> "The problem is with the younger boy [C]. [C] is still at home, [C] being the contact with [BS] in the first place. [C] lives at home full-time. The relationship with their mother is not such that they can go and live with her in any event. She runs a bed and breakfast and has a fairly full clientele list at any given time so there is not space for [C] to go and live with his mother. He sleeps in a store-room as and when he does go and visit her but there certainly is not permanent accommodation for [C]. He is still at college . . ."

14   Miss Butler went on to say that there was no means whatsoever by which C could support himself and that there was no way that money could be mobilised in order to support C were the father to be sent away for a period longer than six

months. The judge was asked to bear those factors in mind "very, very highly" when considering the period of custody.

15   There is then further reference to the severe problems faced by the offender's parents, one aged 74 and the other aged 85, and the role that the offender played in their care.

16   In concluding her submissions on mitigation, Miss Butler said:

> ". . . any period of custody that you impose today will wreak havoc in the lives certainly of [C], to a slightly lesser extent [J] [another brother] and then the parents, so the risk is that there will be more victims to what has already been a most unfortunate incident, and it would be very regrettable that [C's] career could not progress to fruition . . ."

17   In passing sentence, the learned judge said:

> "Miss Butler has eloquently told me about the effect that any sentence of imprisonment of any length would have on your sons, and on your father in particular, and I have read their heartrending letters to me and they reveal the good side of you."

Clearly, that mitigation was an important factor in the decision of the trial judge to pass a sentence of only six months.

18   We turn now to a statement by C's mother which has been prepared for these proceedings and submitted by the Attorney General:

> "I understand that it was suggested to the Court that I have refused to house my son [C].
>
> I would like to make it clear that this is not the case. [C] who is now 16 years has always had a room at my home which he occupies for most of the week. As previously stated he does still stay at his father's address in Thame at weekends and occasionally during the week.
>
> [C] attends [the name of the college]. I pay for all his college costs including transportation. I take him from my home most mornings to Thame where he gets the college minibus and in the evening I collect him from his father's house and bring him home.
>
> I should add that I receive all the child benefit and Child Tax Credit relating to [C]."

19   It is, to say the least, most unfortunate that the sentencing judge was misled in the way that he was about this matter. We are not suggesting, of course, that either Miss Butler or her solicitor knew about this apparent deception.

20   We turn to the pre-sentence report. The author of the report said that he regarded the risk of non-sexual offending as low and went on to say:

> "As regards sexual offending there may be a higher risk, although Mr W is adamant that he will never allow himself to be in a situation where such behaviour could occur. He does however still struggle with self awareness, understanding why he offended, and has a limited acceptance and under-

standing of the victim's perspective. Self knowledge and victim awareness
are key areas which impact on behaviour change."

There is then a reference to a proposal that the offender take part in sex offender
treatment, such as that offered by the Thames Valley Project.

21   Mr Ellison, on behalf of the Attorney General, submits that the following
aggravating features are present. We agree. The offender abused his position
of trust to commit the offence and exploit the vulnerability of his victim. The victim was away from home, the offender learnt about his home problems and took
advantage of that to indecently assault the victim.

22   In the skeleton argument prepared for this hearing by Miss Butler, she said that
grooming was of limited duration over the evening of March 14, 2003. That is
right. Mr Ellison has not suggested that there was any grooming before the evening in question. Nonetheless, we take the view that when the decision was made
by the offender to put the Z-bed up in his room and to invite BS to come into his
bedroom, the offender was planning for what was to happen thereafter.

23   It is submitted on behalf of the Attorney General that the assault was prolonged, probably about half an hour. Mr Ellison also submits that it involved
both masturbating the victim and the insertion of something into his anus, making
this a serious indecent assault. Mr Ellison then refers to the long-term effects that
this has had upon the victim.

24   As the Attorney General accepts, there were mitigating factors. First of all, the
offender had pleaded guilty. However, he did not plead guilty until after the plea
and directions hearing, albeit before the trial. He is not, therefore, entitled to full
credit. Secondly, this was a single offence—this is not one of those cases where
the Court is concerned with a series of indecent assaults over a period of time.
Thirdly, Mr Ellison points out that the offender has no previous convictions.

25   Mr Ellison drew our attention to three cases. In *Attorney General's Reference
Nos 37, 38, 44, 51, 53, 35, 40, 43, 45, 41 and 42 of 2003* [2004] 1 Cr.App.R.(S.) 84
(p.499) this Court, presided over by Kay L.J., re-affirmed that sentencers should
consider the following when passing a sentence for an offence of this kind, the
degree of harm to the victim, the level of culpability of the offender, the level
of risk posed by the offender to society and the need to deter others from acting
in a similar fashion. The Court re-affirmed the proposition that good character
does not justify a substantial reduction.

26   In para.[6] Kay L.J. summarised the submissions of the Attorney General in
those 12 cases to the effect that far too great regard had been paid to the interests
of the defendant and insufficient account had been taken of the seriousness of the
offending. He repeated the Attorney General's submissions to the effect that the
courts have failed to recognise the seriousness of the harm caused to the victim
and the proper interests of the public at large, both in protecting others from
serious harm from the individual offenders and also in deterring others from committing like offences. The Court continued at [8]:

    "However, it is clearly undesirable for many reasons that courts should pass
    sentences that are out of line with proper sentencing practice. To do so can
    only cause public concern and affect the confidence of the public in the sys-

tem. It runs the risk that people may feel that sexual offenders have not received proper punishment thereby increasing the danger that extra-judicial punishment may be meted out. An inadequate sentence frequently adds to the anguish of the victim, who feels that society has not recognised his or her suffering, particularly when they have had to steel themselves to speak of offending against them that they might have chosen not to rehearse publicly. Nor is such a sentence any kindness to an offender, who will in all probability be subjected to a reference to this Court with the unnecessary anguish of having to start the sentencing process all over again."

27   In para.[9] Kay L.J. said that the Court ventured to suggest that in some of the cases considered, if the sentencer had stood back and looked at the matter, he or she might well have recognised that too great a weight had been attached to the interests of the offender and insufficient weight to the victim's proper interests and the interests of the public at large. In our view, that also applies to this case.

28   Two further authorities were drawn to our attention by Mr Ellison. The first is *Attorney General's Reference No.5 of 2001 (Terence Culshaw)* [2001] 2 Cr.App.R.(S.) 106 (p.473). The case involved three offences committed some considerable time before over a period of some four years, starting when the victim was seven–eight years old. During visits to the offender's home, the offender performed sexual acts with the victim. The offender was convicted. In reaching the conclusion that the sentence of six months' imprisonment was unduly lenient, Lord Woolf C.J., giving the judgment of the Court, said that it had reached the conclusion that if these matters were to come before the court today, having been committed fairly recently, an appropriate sentence would be not less than four years' imprisonment.

29   The other case to which Mr Ellison referred is *Attorney General's Reference No.41 of 2000 (David Harrison)* [2001] 1 Cr.App.R.(S.) 107 (p.372). In that case the offender had met a 13-year-old boy, who attended a school for children with special needs. The offender took the boy to a restaurant and then to a swimming pool, later they met in a cafe, and subsequently went to the offender's flat, where the offender gave the boy a karate suit and a mobile telephone. They met again the following week when they again went swimming. The offender asked the boy to model for him and the boy agreed to do so. Subsequently the offender took a variety of photographs of the boy naked. The boy was given £20 and vouchers for the mobile telephone. Police officers found photographs in the offender's possession showing the boy and other children naked. Some photographs showed the offender and another boy apparently engaged in simulated sexual intercourse. He was sentenced to a probation order for three years and the Attorney General asked this Court to review that sentence. In para.[20], Rose L.J., Vice President of the Court of Appeal Criminal Division, said:

"In our judgment, the circumstances of these offences were of a gravity which required the imposition of a prison sentence in the court below of at least threeyears' imprisonment in total. The gravity lay not so much in the nature of the sexual activity in itself but in the grooming of this vulnerable and handicapped boy, over a period of time and the giving of money and other gifts."

In that case the offender had pleaded guilty.

30   We turn to the mitigation advanced on behalf of the offender by Miss Butler. She submits, first of all, that the sentence should reflect the fact that the offence was not of a violent nature or confrontational. Thus, so she submits, it did not have the damaging physical effects that such violence might have caused. She accepted that there was harm of a psychological nature, although she asked us to treat the victim impact statement with some care because the offender is not able to challenge it.

31   The thrust of her submissions, it seems to us, was that harm of a psychological nature is somehow less important than physical harm. It is not, at least in this case. As the victim impact statement makes clear, BS has lost confidence in, and the ability to trust, other people and now suffers from post-traumatic stress disorder.

32   She submitted that the assault was at the lower end of seriousness. We do not accept that. This was an offence planned over a short period of time, but nonetheless it was a serious indecent assault involving masturbation and penetration.

33   Miss Butler submits that the sentence is not unduly lenient. We disagree.

34   Having regard to the authorities to which we have already referred, we take the view that the appropriate sentence was a sentence in the region of two and a half to three years' imprisonment.

35   Recognising the element of double jeopardy, the sentence which we now impose is one of two years' imprisonment.

36   We turn to the consequential orders that follow from that. The judge, under s.85, made an order extending the licence period for two and a half years. In the light of the alteration that we have made to the sentence, we take the view that the extended licence period should be one of two years.

37   Given that we have now increased the sentence, we are required to make the appropriate order under s.28 of the Criminal Justice and Court Services Act 2000, disqualifying the offender from working with children. Finally, we note that the provisions regarding the Sex Offenders Register will apply also to this offender.

R. v GARY MILLS

Court of Appeal (Lord Justice Hooper, Mr Justice Leveson and
Mr Justice Field): May 28, 2004

[2004] EWCA Crim 1466; [2005] 1 Cr.App.R.(S.) 38

Possession with intent to supply; Prison officers; Sentence length

H1   *Possessing heroin with intent to supply—prison officer smuggling heroin into
prison for inmate—length of sentence*

H2   Seven years' imprisonment imposed on a prison officer for attempting to
smuggle heroin into a prison for an inmate reduced to six years, on the ground
that he had cooperated fully with the authorities.

H3   The appellant pleaded guilty to possessing a class A controlled drug, heroin,
with intent to supply. The appellant was a prison officer. He arrived for work
and was searched. A package containing two knotted corners from a plastic
bag was discovered on his person; the knotted corners contained 9.35g of heroin
at 20 per cent purity. The appellant admitted that he had tried to smuggle drugs
into the prison for an inmate, whom he named. He was to be paid £400. He
later admitted that he had smuggled a package into the prison on an earlier
occasion. Sentenced to seven years' imprisonment.

H4   **Held:** (considering *Prince* [1996] 1 Cr.App.R.(S.) 335 and *Whenman* [2001] 2
Cr.App.R.(S.) 87 (p.395)) the offender's difficult personal circumstances were of
limited value in deciding the appropriate length of the sentence. The fact that the
appellant was a prison officer increased the seriousness of the offence as he knew
well the problems caused by drugs in prison. The Court had decided to reduce the
sentence only because the appellant had co-operated by naming his co-defendant
and the inmate for whom the drugs were intended. Recognising that factor, the
Court would substitute a sentence of six years' imprisonment.

H5   **Cases cited:**   *Prince* [1996] 1 Cr.App.R.(S.) 335, *Whenman* [2001] 2
Cr.App.R.(S.) 87 (p.395)

H6   **References:** supplying heroin, *Current Sentencing Practice* B 11-2

H7   *P.A. O'Shea* for the appellant.
A. Nimmo for the Crown.

JUDGMENT

1   **HOOPER L.J.:**   On May 6, 2003 at the Crown Court at Doncaster, Gary Mills, now aged 44, pleaded guilty to possessing a class A controlled drug with intent to supply, namely heroin. We have today granted him leave to appeal against sentence.

2   On October 10, 2003, he was sentenced to seven years' imprisonment. Other orders were made which are not the subject matter of this appeal.

3   There was a co-defendant, Susan Mankin. She ultimately pleaded guilty to one offence of supplying a class A controlled drug; one offence of possessing a class A controlled drug with intent to supply, and was sentenced to a total sentence of three years and nine months' imprisonment.

4   At the time of the offence, the appellant was a prison officer based at Moorlands Prison. He had been a prison officer for some three years and had served some part of an early period as a prison officer away from his family at Feltham.

5   On October 25, 2002, he arrived for work at the prison and was searched. During that search a package containing two knotted corners from a plastic bag was discovered in his underwear. Those knotted corners contained 9.35 grams of heroin of 20 per cent purity. The appellant immediately admitted to one of the searching officers that he was carrying heroin and he was then and there arrested. In interview he immediately admitted that he had tried to smuggle the drugs into prison and that they were intended for an inmate, whose name he gave. He also stated that the package had been given to him the previous evening by the co-defendant at the Doncaster Railway Station car park. He was to be paid £400 by the inmate for delivering the drugs.

6   In interview he made a further admission of a fact unknown to the prosecution, namely that he had smuggled a package into the prison two weeks earlier for the same inmate.

7   He pleaded guilty, as we have said, on May 6. There then was a significant delay until he was sentenced on October 10. It is accepted by Mr Nimmo, who appears today for the respondent, that the appellant pleaded guilty at the earliest opportunity. Secondly, it is accepted that the delay between May 6 and October 10, when he was sentenced, was not the responsibility of the appellant.

8   On May 6, an issue arose about the plea of the co-defendant. The prosecution were not content with what the co-defendant was saying, and the appellant then, as Mr Nimmo accepts, offered to give evidence for the prosecution against the co-defendant. It follows therefore that the appellant co-operated fully, suffered a delay which was not his responsibility, and, most importantly, offered to give evidence for the prosecution.

9   He had no previous convictions. The pre-sentence report sets out the background to the offending, which involved both financial and considerable emotional stress for the appellant. The appellant and his family were suffering financial hardship because of his wife's lengthy illness and an industrial accident suffered by his son. He had incurred additional expenses for a variety of reasons. One of the prisoners used information about his financial position to apply pressure to him. Ultimately, his wife separated from him.

10   Although we set that out, and Mr O'Shea has relied upon those matters as part
of his mitigation, we take the view that that is of very limited value indeed in
deciding what is the appropriate length of the sentence. It may explain why he
committed the offence, but offers little or no mitigation when considering the
length of the sentence. The learned judge in passing sentence noted the co-operation in interview and noted the information which led to the arrest of the co-
defendant. The judge gave credit for the early guilty plea, but pointed out, rightly,
that a custodial sentence had to be imposed to act as a deterrent. The fact that the
defendant was a prison officer, so she said, rightly, increased the seriousness of
the offence as he knew full well the problems caused by drugs in prison.

11   Two authorities have been drawn to our attention. The first is *Prince* [1996] 1
Cr.App.R.(S.) 335. In that case the appellant was a father who took into prison
some 10 wraps of heroin for his son. The appellant was not a prison officer. He
was sentenced to five years' imprisonment. Curtis J., giving the judgment of
the Court, presided over by Rose L.J., not only dismissed the appeal, but also
said that the sentence was right.

12   We were also referred to *Whenman* [2001] 2 Cr.App.R.(S.) 87 (p.395), where a
sentence of seven years' imprisonment was upheld in a case of a serving prison
officer who brought heroin into a prison on some 15 to 20 occasions. The sentence was described by the Court as being not excessive or wrong in principle.

13   We have reached the conclusion that, for one reason and one reason only, there
should be a reduction in the appellant's sentence. That reason relates not just to
his co-operation, the naming of the co-defendant and of the inmate, but also the
fact that he offered to give evidence against the co-defendant. It is difficult to
think that anyone could have co-operated more than this man has co-operated
with the authorities.

14   We take the view that, in recognition of this factor, the sentence should be one
of six years' imprisonment and not seven years' imprisonment. To that extent this
appeal is allowed. We make a representation order for you, Mr O'Shea.

R. v JAMES STEPHEN KELLY

Court of Appeal (Lord Justice Hooper, Mr Justice Leveson and Mr Justice Field): May 28, 2004

[2004] EWCA Crim 1629; [2005] 1 Cr.App.R.(S.) 39

LT Aggravating features; Causing death by dangerous driving; Detention; Speeding; Young offenders

H1 *Detention in a young offender institution—causing death by dangerous driving— unqualified driver causing deaths of two people by driving at high speed while uninsured—length of sentence*

H2   Four years' detention in a young offender institution upheld for causing death by dangerous driving where an unqualified driver caused the deaths of two people by driving at high speed while uninsured.

H3   The appellant, aged 17 at the time of the offence, pleaded guilty to two counts of causing death by dangerous driving. The appellant purchased a powerful car, although he had not yet passed the driving test. He subsequently failed the driving test. He drove the car on a couple of occasions although he was uninsured. His mother put a lock on the gate of the drive where the car was parked to stop him from taking the car onto the road. The appellant and a friend sawed through the lock and took the car away. They picked up another youth who sat in the back of the car as a passenger. The car overtook another car at extremely high speed. The appellant lost control of the car at the bottom of a hill and the car hit a tree. The two passengers died as a result of their injuries. Sentenced to four years' detention in a young offender institution and disqualified from driving for 10 years and until an extended driving test had been passed.

H4   **Held:** (considering *Cooksley* [2004] 1 Cr.App.R.(S.) 1 (p.1), *Attorney General's References Nos 14 and 24 of 1993* (1994) 15 Cr.App.R.(S.) 640, *Howell* [1999] 1 Cr.App.R.(S.) 449, and *Boswell* (1984) 6 Cr.App.R.(S.) 257) the sentencing judge identified various aggravating features, including driving at excessive speed, deliberate bad driving, the facts that the appellant was unlicensed and was driving without insurance, and that two passengers were killed. He found that the facts of the case came within the third category, "higher culpability", identified in *Cooksley*. The sentence of four years' detention was a severe sentence for a young man of 18 of otherwise good character, but the judge's weighing of the aggravating and mitigating features was not to be criticised, in view of the very serious aggravating features of the case. It was important for all courts to make drivers appreciate the gravity of the consequences that could flow from not maintaining proper standards of driving. This applied as much to young and inexperienced drivers as to mature drivers with considerable driving experience. The sentence of four years' detention in a young offender institution would stand, but the period of disqualification would be reduced to five years.

H5 **Cases cited:** *Cooksley* [2004] 1 Cr.App.R.(S.) 1 (p.1), *Attorney General's References Nos 14 and 24 of 1993* (1994) 15 Cr.App.R.(S.) 640, *Howell* [1999] 1 Cr.App.R.(S.) 449, *Boswell* (1984) 6 Cr.App.R.(S.) 257

H6 **References:** detention in a young offender institution—causing death by dangerous driving, *Current Sentencing Practice* E 2-4

H7 *R. Shellard* for the appellant.

JUDGMENT

1   **FIELD J.:**   On December 17, 2003 at the Crown Court at Cardiff, the appellant, James Stephen Kelly, pleaded guilty to two counts of causing death by dangerous driving. On each count he was sentenced by H.H. Judge Wyn Morgan to concurrent terms of four years' detention in a young offender institution. He was also disqualified from driving for 10 years and required to pass an extended driving test before he could resume driving at the end of the disqualification period. The appellant appeals against those sentences with leave of the single judge.

2   The relevant facts can be shortly stated. On June 6, 2003, the appellant purchased a 1600cc Ford Escort RS Turbo for £2,000. The appellant was then aged 17 and had not yet taken his driving test. He took the test on July 8, 2003 but failed. He was told that it would cost him £4,000 to be insured for the vehicle. Although he had not passed his test and was uninsured, the appellant drove the car on a couple of occasions unsupervised around the estate on which he lived. When his mother heard of this she put a lock on the gate to the drive where the car was parked to stop anyone, including the appellant, from taking the car out onto the road.

3   On July 11, 2003, the appellant and his friend, Michael Stickler, who was also aged 17, sawed through the lock and drove the car away. The appellant was the driver. Michael sat in the front passenger seat. Some time later they picked up another boy, Christopher Breakspeare, aged 14, who sat in the back. Not only was the appellant not licensed or insured to drive the car, the car did not have a current valid MOT certificate.

4   The appellant drove the car down the A48 in the direction of Bridgend. He overtook an American stretch limousine which had tinted windows. The stretch limousine was a taxi carrying a group of six off-duty police officers, who were travelling from Cardiff Wales Airport to the Bridgend area. On the straight section of the A48 before Crack Hill, the appellant drove up alongside the stretch limousine for a short period, hooting his horn. His two passengers looked into the limousine smiling and one of them waved. The appellant then accelerated away at high speed down Crack Hill. The speed limit was 60 miles per hour. A

witness described the appellant's speed as being at least 100 miles per hour as he drove into the bend at the bottom of the hill. At this point the appellant lost control of the car, which collided with a tree. Christopher Breakspeare died at the scene of the accident. Michael Stickler died of his injuries in hospital three days later. The appellant was conscious and only slightly injured.

5   The learned sentencing judge prefaced his sentencing remarks with the oft-quoted words of Lord Taylor C.J. in *Attorney General's References Nos 14 and 24 of 1993* (1994) 15 Cr.App.R.(S.) 640 at 644, which we too desire to cite, having read the victim impact statements of the mothers of Michael and Christopher.

> ". . . we wish to stress that human life cannot be restored, nor can its loss be measured by the length of a prison sentence. We recognise that no term of months or years imposed on the offender can reconcile the family of the deceased victim to their loss, nor will it cure their anguish."

6   The learned judge sentenced the appellant on the basis of the guidelines laid down by Lord Woolf C.J. in this Court in *Cooksley* [2004] 1 Cr.App.R.(S.) 1 (p.1). He found that the facts of the case came within Lord Woolf's third category, namely that of "higher culpability". In his view, the following aggravating features were present: the appellant drove at excessive speed and was showing off; there was evidence that he had driven deliberately badly for a distance behind the stretch limousine and alongside; the way in which the appellant accelerated down Crack Hill; the appellant was unlicensed to drive, having failed his test just days before the accident; he was driving without insurance; he put at risk the lives of his passengers; those passengers were killed; this was the first time he had driven any distance unsupervised and with passengers; he should not have allowed either of the two boys to enter the car, particularly Christopher Breakspeare, to whom he showed a complete lack of responsibility.

7   The learned judge found the following mitigating factors: the appellant had no previous convictions and there was positive evidence about his contribution to society; he had achieved six grade A passes at GCSE and was studying for A levels whilst working part-time in a useful job with the Post Office; he had pleaded guilty; he was still only 18 years of age and he felt genuine remorse; both of the boys who died had been his friends, particularly Michael.

8   The appellant's counsel, Mr Shellard, does not challenge the judge's finding that the case came within the category of higher culpability. In *Cooksley*, this Court said that the starting point for this category was four to five years' custody. Mr Shellard draws attention to the fact that the sentence of four years means that the appellant is a long-term prisoner, and submits that, given the mitigation available to his client, the judge must have erroneously used a starting point of in excess of five years. Another way of putting the submission is to contend that the judge gave insufficient weight to the mitigating factors.

9   Mr Shellard refers to *Howell* [1999] 1 Cr.App.R.(S.) 449. There, the appellant, who was 24 and of good character, had borrowed his mother's high-performance car and raced another driver, causing the death of the other driver and one of his (the appellant's) passengers. The appellant was sentenced to four years, which

was reduced to three and a half years on appeal. We do not, however, gain any real assistance from this authority since it was decided under the old guidelines handed down in *Boswell* (1984) 6 Cr.App.R.(S.) 257, and also very much turned on its own facts, which included the fact that the deceased driver was as much responsible for the accident as was the appellant.

10   It is plain from his clear and detailed sentencing remarks that the learned judge approached the task of sentencing the appellant with commendable care. A sentence of four years is a severe sentence for a young man of 18 of otherwise good character with a promising future. However, in our judgment, the judge's weighing of the aggravating and mitigating features is not to be criticised, and the length of the sentence does not imply that he applied a starting point that was too high. The aggravating features in this case were very serious, particularly the appellant's putting at risk the lives of the two passengers who died by allowing them to accompany him when he was an unqualified driver, and then by driving in such a dangerous and foolhardy manner that led to the deaths of both of those boys.

11   As Lord Woolf observed in *Cooksley*, it is important for the courts to make drivers appreciate the gravity of the consequences that could flow from not maintaining proper standards of driving. It need hardly be said that this applies as much to young and inexperienced drivers as it does to mature drivers who have considerable driving experience.

12   In our judgment, therefore, the sentence of four years' detention should stand. We are, however, persuaded that the 10-year period of disqualification imposed by the judge was too long. Disqualification is designed to protect road users in the future from an offender who has shown himself to be a risk on the roads. Although there was a high level of culpability in this case, in our judgment account had to be taken of the appellant's young age and the strong likelihood that he has learnt his lesson. We have little doubt that, after a few years, his approach to the care that needs to be taken when driving will be a responsible one, and he will not pose a risk to the public.

13   Accordingly, we propose to set aside the period of disqualification imposed by the judge, and substitute for it disqualification for a period of five years, at the end of which the appellant must take an extended driving test. To that extent only, this appeal is allowed.

R. v IAN ROBERTS

Court of Appeal (Lord Justice Clarke, Mr Justice Jack and Judge Fabyan Evans): May 28, 2004

[2004] EWCA Crim 1445; [2005] 1 Cr.App.R.(S.) 40

LT Aggravating features; Causing death by dangerous driving; Sentence length; Speeding

H1 *Causing death by dangerous driving—causing deaths of two persons by aggressive driving at high speed—length of sentence*

H2   Five years' imprisonment upheld for causing the deaths of two persons by aggressive driving at high speed.

H3   The appellant pleaded guilty to two counts of causing death by dangerous driving. The appellant was a passenger in his mother's car with two young women. The appellant's mother wished to visit a shop, and asked the appellant to drive the car around the block while she did so. The appellant drove the car to a bypass with a single carriageway in each direction which was subject to a speed limit of 60mph. The appellant drove the car at high speeds, reaching at least 120mph. The appellant overtook other vehicles and forced oncoming vehicles to pull over. Both of the passengers requested him to slow down. Other drivers saw the car being driven at speeds estimated to be at least 100mph. The car eventually collided with a car coming in the opposite direction. The driver of the other car and one of the passengers in the car driven by the appellant were killed. The appellant pleaded guilty, on the basis that he was driving at approximately 100mph but that he was not under the influence of any substance that would have been impaired his ability to drive. Sentenced to five years' imprisonment and disqualified from driving for five years and until he had taken an extended driving test.

I4   **Held:** (considering *Cooksley* [2004] 1 Cr.App.R.(S.) 1 (p.1)) the sentencing judge accepted that the case fell within the range of higher culpability identified in *Cooksley* for which a starting point of four to five years was appropriate. The case involved a number of aggravating features including driving at greatly excessive speed, showing off, disregard of warnings from passengers, a prolonged persistent course of bad driving, aggressive driving, previous convictions for motoring offences and the deaths of more than one person. The Court was satisfied that the case fell within the "most serious" category identified in *Cooksley*. After taking into account the aggravating features and mitigating features the sentence of five years was appropriate.

H5   **Cases cited:**   *Cooksley* [2004] 1 Cr.App.R.(S.) 1 (p.1)

H6   **References:** causing death by dangerous driving, *Current Sentencing Practice* B
1-7

H7   *M.S. Brogan* for the appellant.
M. Wall for the Crown.

JUDGMENT

[Paragraph 1 has been omitted.]

2   **JACK J.:**   On September 30, 2003 in the Crown Court at Shrewsbury the
appellant, Ian Roberts, changed his plea on two counts of causing death by
dangerous driving to guilty. On November 12 he was sentenced to five years'
imprisonment on each count with disqualification of five years and until he
had taken an extended re-test. He was also required to serve three months of a
suspended sentence of 12 months passed on September 2, 2001. He now appeals
against the sentence of five years by leave of the single judge. His earlier pleas of
not guilty had been entered at the plea and direction hearing. The hearing on
September 30 was a pre-trial review for a trial in December.

3   The charges of causing death by dangerous driving related to September 30,
2002. About 2 o'clock in the afternoon of that day the appellant's mother collected the appellant's fiancee, Laura Reynolds, and another young woman,
Lynette Caughey, in her BMW 330 coupé. The appellant was also a passenger.
They drove into Whitchurch in Shropshire, where Mrs Roberts wanted to get a
key cut. As parking was not easy she suggested that the appellant drive around
the block.

4   He drove off with the two young women in the rear. After a little while the
appellant stated that "the by-pass was calling". It is apparent from what followed
that this meant that he was going to put the car through its paces on the Whitchurch bypass. On the bypass he told his passengers to watch the car reach 140mph.
The bypass is a carriageway with one lane in each direction and is subject to a
speed limit of 60mph. Miss Caughey was aware of the car reaching at least
120mph. The appellant was overtaking other vehicles driving in the middle of
the road, forcing on-coming vehicles to pull over. He was, in effect, treating a
two-lane road as if it was three. Both the appellant's passengers warned him
that he was going too fast and requested him to slow. He did not.

5   One driver he overtook, Guvdial Singh, described his car as travelling in the
middle of the road, forcing its way through the traffic and giving no thought to
anyone else on it. The driver estimated his speed as a minimum of 100mph.
Another driver, Nyree Clarke, an advanced driving instructor, was coming in
the opposite direction to the appellant. As she came out of the bend she saw
the appellant coming towards her. She said in her statement:

"When I first saw it, the BMW was no more than 150 yards ahead of me. It was already straddling the centre line but came across on to my carriageway. My initial reaction was that due to the speed the car was coming towards me at, it must have been stolen. As it started to come across the road towards me, due to the speed, the BMW was tilting dramatically to the offside and the rear nearside wheel was raised. I then realised it was coming straight at me and I thought it was going to hit full on. I applied my brakes which brought my speed down to about 40 mph. I was already moving to the left and I had to go over the white line onto the outer boundary of the road and felt the rumble as my vehicle went over the warning edging."

She looked at the driver and saw that he was smiling. The two cars continued on a collision course. She saw the appellant turn the steering wheel and brake hard, which caused a huge cloud of smoke from the rear wheels. As he passed her she said that she knew he had lost control.

6   Teresa Oakes was in a car close behind, also approaching the appellant and coming round the bend. She saw the appellant coming straight at her. His wheels, she said in her statement, were screeching and smoking. She saw the BMW over-take three cars and she turned as hard as she could. They missed by two feet. She thought that if she had not completed driving courses in the police and the army there would have been a collision. Her nearside wheel subsequently went off the carriageway and onto the stones at the side of the road.

7   Louise Marie Evans, driving her Peugeot 309, was also coming round the bend towards the appellant. She was behind Teresa Oakes. Because she herself may have been intending to overtake she was marginally on the wrong side of the road at the moment of the collision which occurred between her car and the appel-lant's BMW. Her front wheels were on the correct side of that point but not her rear offside wheel. The front offside of the BMW struck the side of her car. She was killed as a result of the impact. So also was Laura Reynolds. The appel-lant was seriously injured and now walks with a limp and has a deformation to his arm. Lynette Caughey escaped with lacerations to her head.

8   The appellant pleaded guilty on a written basis which was as follows. He accepted he must have been driving at approximately 100mph. Speed was the only basis for his acceptance that he was driving dangerously. He was not under the influence of any substance that would have impaired his ability to drive. It was important to note that the car driven by Louise Marie Evans was overtaking and all the evidence shows that on impact his car was on the correct side of the carriageway. The evidence shows that her car had started to brake when partially on the incorrect side of the road. However, the appellant accepted that at the speed he was travelling she did not have sufficient time to correct this. It was asserted that this fact (established on the facts of the Crown's case) was a contributory factor. The appellant only accepted that his dangerous driving was a cause, and not the only cause, of the two deaths. Another factor was that Laura Reynolds was not wearing her seatbelt, whereas Lynette Caughey and the appel-lant were.

9   The Crown Prosecution Service responded to that plea by a letter of November
7, 2003 and agreed with some points and not with others. But there was no hearing
before the judge to decide any points that were in dispute and the appellant therefore fell to be sentenced on the written basis of his plea.

10   We simply record that the finding of the officers who had investigated the accident was that at the moment of the impact the appellant's car was a few
centimetres over the centre line of the road.

11   At the time of the accident the appellant was 23. He had at one time been a successful auto cross driver and it is clear prided himself on being able to drive at
high speeds. Apart from speeding offences he has been before the court on five
previous occasions, which included on November 6, 2002 an offence of failing
to provide a specimen of breath, and on May 20, 2003 taking a vehicle without
consent. He had never served a custodial sentence. He had also been disqualified
from driving for having accumulated four speeding convictions.

12   The sentencing judge had a pre-sentence report before him which was in some
respects unfavourable to the appellant. It stated that the appellant did not take full
responsibility for the offences and was bitter that he was to blame for them.
Although he expressed regret he implied that he would act in the same way
again. He was assessed as being vulnerable to reoffending unless his attitudes
changed. He gave no indication that he would change his style of driving and
therefore the risk of harm to the public was assessed as being high. He was
also assessed as being of some risk of self-harm due to depression.

13   There was also before the court at the time of sentence a medical report and a
psychological report. The sentencing judge also had victim impact statements
which spoke of the losses that the deaths had caused to the two families. We
have in addition today a prison report which describes the appellant as being
well behaved and co-operative.

14   In mitigation it was submitted to the judge that the appellant's pleas had been
the subject of a difficult decision and showed that he now accepted his culpability. It was said that the appellant was deeply affected not only by his own injuries
but by the death of his fiancee, and that he was also suffering from post-traumatic
stress impounded by bereavement and grief.

15   In passing sentence the judge in summary referred to the following. He said
that the appellant was not entitled to full credit for his guilty plea as it was
late. The appellant was only on the bypass at that time to drive fast and show
off. He deliberately drove at grossly excessive speed down the centre of the
road even though he knew it was dangerous to overtake on that road. After the
accident the appellant tried to blame the driver of the vehicle he had killed and
his attempt to shift the blame was shameful. His belief in his own prowess and
driving speed showed he had not learnt his lesson from a previous disqualification for speeding. The appellant's deliberate excessive speed, his reckless
overtaking at a place he knew was unsafe, his previous history of speeding and
the fact that he left two people dead were all aggravating features.

16   Before us today Mr Michael Brogan in his pointed and succinct submissions
has suggested to us that the judge's sentence was too long. He begins, as one
must, with the guideline case of *Cooksley* [2004] 1 Cr.App.R.(S.) 1 (p.1),

which considered the appropriate levels of sentencing in cases of causing death by dangerous driving. By the Road Traffic Offences Act 1988 the maximum sentence for that offence is ten years' imprisonment. In *Cooksley* the Court set four starting points with appropriate sentences as follows: no aggravating circumstances—12–18 months; intermediate culpability—2–3 years; higher culpability—4–5 years; most serious culpability—6 years or over. Those are sentences following a trial.

17   When he was mitigating before the judge Mr Brogan made a momentary slip and referred to the intermediate culpability range. The judge disagreed and Mr Brogan corrected himself and accepted that the case fell within the range of higher culpability, though not the most severe range. The judge made no further comment. Mr Brogan submits that a sentence of five years following a plea, even without a full one-third remission for plea, must be equivalent to a sentence of six and a half years after trial, and so the judge must have put the case into the category of the most severe culpability. We agree. We are also satisfied that the judge must have been well aware that he was doing so. It is clear that he gave the case particularly careful attention. The question is whether he was right.

18   In *Cooksley* the Court adopted the Sentencing Panel's comments as to offences of higher culpability, save that it put the starting point at four–five years for a contested case.

19   The Panel had stated, in para.32 of its advice, quoted at para.[25] of *Cooksley*:

> "When the standard of the offender's driving is more highly dangerous as would be indicated, for example, by the presence of one or two of factors (a) to (i) the Panel suggests that the appropriate starting point would be a custodial sentence within the range from two to five years. The exact level of sentence would be determined by the dangerousness of the driving and by the presence or absence of other aggravating or mitigating factors."

20   As to the most serious category, the Panel had stated in para.34, quoted at para.[28] in *Cooksley*:

> "The Panel suggests that custodial sentences over five years should be reserved for cases involving an extremely high level of culpability on the offender's part. This might be indicated by the presence of three or more aggravating factors (a) to (i), although an exceptionally bad example of a single aggravating feature could be sufficient to place an offence in this category. A sentence close to the maximum would be appropriate in a case displaying a large number of these features, or where there were other aggravating factors."

The Court in *Cooksley* adopted this and gave a starting point of six years for a contested case.

The aggravating features identified by the Sentencing Panel were also adopted by *Cooksley*. The following among them are present in this case: (b) greatly excessive speed; "showing off"; (c) disregard of warning from fellow passengers; (d) a prolonged, persistent and deliberate course of very bad driving; (e) aggressive driving; (k) previous convictions for motoring offences; (l) more than one person killed (especially if the offender knowingly put more than one person at risk or the occurrence of multiple deaths was foreseeable).

22   While we have set out all of these, we appreciate that on the facts of this case there is some overlap between (b), (d) and (e), in that the appellant's conduct can be described as forcing his way up the centre of a two-lane road at speeds up to, and in excess, of 100mph. We must also have in mind that the previous motoring offences were minor, but they show that the appellant was someone who habitually drove too fast. That is also borne out by his interview by the police where his love of speed and his pride in his ability to control a car at speed were apparent.

23   The Court in *Cooksley* also identified mitigating features. Here we should refer among them to these: a timely plea of guilty; genuine shock or remorse (which may be greater if the victim was a close relation or a friend); and serious injury to the offender. There is also the point that Miss Evans was slightly on the wrong side of the road, which contributed to the collision. That is a factor that we must take into account.

24   The decision in *Cooksley* is also helpful because there were four cases whose facts were examined by the Court before reaching conclusions on the appropriate sentences. Among them, the case of *Cooke* was found to be in the most severe category and a sentence of seven years was reduced to six, following a plea. Also, there had been two deaths. Cooke was 20 years old, but had a bad driving record including three previous offences of disqualified driving. Other passengers had been severely injured.

25   We have to consider the various factors in this case. We are satisfied that it does fall within the most serious category and that the sentence is to be assessed accordingly. We have concluded that the judge was right to pass the sentence he did. After taking into account the aggravating features which we have mentioned and the mitigating features, we consider that the sentence of five years was appropriate. The appeal is dismissed.

R. v ROY MITCHELL

Court of Appeal (Lord Justice Hooper, Mr Justice Leveson and Mr Justice Field): May 28, 2004

[2004] EWCA Crim 1516; [2005] 1 Cr.App.R.(S.) 41

(LT) Bigamy; Making false statements; Sentence length

H1 *Bigamy—defendant deceiving woman as to marital status—defendant subsequently divorced by first wife and lawfully marrying second wife—length of sentence*

H2 Nine months' imprisonment for bigamy and perjury upheld in the case of a man who deceived a woman as to his marital status and went through a bigamous ceremony of marriage with her, and subsequently remarried her after being divorced by his first wife.

H3 The appellant pleaded guilty to bigamy and perjury. The appellant married, but separated from his wife after a few months. About two years later the appellant met another woman. His wife petitioned for divorce although the petition was not served on him for some time. The appellant told the other woman that he was not married and in due course went through a ceremony of marriage with the other woman, having signed a certificate which contained a declaration that there was no impediment to his marrying. The second woman discovered that the appellant was already married and the police were informed. Eventually the appellant was divorced by his first wife a few months after the second marriage ceremony. He later married the second wife. Sentenced to nine months' imprisonment on each count concurrent.

H4 **Held:** perjury in normal circumstances required an immediate custodial sentence, and where a person with a record for persistent dishonesty committed that offence, exceptional circumstances which might justify a non-custodial sentence could not be found to exist. The appeal would be dismissed.

H5 **References:** bigamy, *Current Sentencing Practice* B 9-4

H6 *T.H. Stead* for the appellant.

JUDGMENT

LEVESON J.:   On March 19, 2004 at the Crown Court at Bradford, before H.H. Judge Gullick, this appellant was sentenced to terms of nine months' imprisonment concurrent for bigamy and perjury, having previously pleaded guilty on re-arraignment to those offences. He now appeals by leave of the single judge.

2   The facts can be summarised briefly. On June 14, 2000, the appellant married. That marriage was disastrous and within one week his wife moved out of the matrimonial home. The parties tried to keep the relationship going for some three months but then they separated permanently. In September 2002, the appellant met another woman. Shortly after that, his existing wife petitioned him for divorce, although it took many months before the petition was served upon him. During that time the appellant had gone to the other woman in the Philippines, and in April 2003 they agreed to marry. He told her that he was not married.

3   In order to marry he went to a register office, and after speaking to the registrar, signed a notice of marriage which was a certificate that there was no impediment to his marrying, and contained a declaration that he had been married before but that this marriage had been dissolved in 1994. He signed a further declaration that he had not been since married.

4   A certificate of no impediment to marriage was issued, and on April 21, 2003 he took part in a ceremony of marriage. Meanwhile, he did not sign or acknowledge a petition for divorce from his existing wife until May 14, 2003. Subsequently his new wife answered a telephone call from his existing wife and found that he was still in fact married. The police were informed. He was finally divorced from his existing wife on August 20, 2003, having on July 8, 2003 been arrested. When interviewed he said that he believed that he was divorced from his existing wife when he married his new wife because he had signed some papers in relation to it. He has since remarried his second wife.

5   At the time of these offences the appellant was 47 years of age. Unfortunately he has a not insubstantial record for offences of dishonesty. Indeed, he has twice been sentenced to terms of imprisonment for dishonesty, the most recent being in April 1999 when he received a total sentence of six months' imprisonment for two offences of theft.

6   When passing sentence, the learned judge observed that the lady whom the appellant had sought to marry came from a highly religious family who had been appalled to find out what had happened. He had clearly deceived her in a most material way, although he recognised that she had now forgiven him and married him a second time.

7   The judge observed that the most serious aspect of this case was the offence of perjury because he told the registrar "a pack of lies". He went on that such offences were treated with the utmost seriousness and that custody was inevitable unless there were the most exceptional of circumstances.

8   Before this Court, Mr Stead advanced the submission that, although serious, this offence was not one which required an immediate loss of liberty, and he prayed in aid the recommendation in the pre-sentence report. Had this appellant been a man of prior good character, we could have seen considerable force in that submission. However, the offence of perjury is extremely serious and does, in the normal circumstances, require an immediate custodial sentence. Where a person commits that offence with a prior record for persistent dishonesty, those exceptional circumstances could not possibly be found to exist. This appeal is dismissed.

R. v JOHN DICKETTS MIDDLETON

Court of Appeal (Lord Justice Tuckey, Mr Justice Treacy and Sir Richard Tucker): June 9, 2004

[2004] EWCA Crim 1487; [2005] 1 Cr.App.R.(S.) 42

Living on prostitution; Mitigation; Sentence length

H1   *Living on the earnings of prostitution—owner of shop where sexual services were provided—no evidence of coercion or corruption—length of sentence*

H2   Sentences totalling 12 months imposed on the owner of a shop where sexual services were provided for payment reduced to nine months where there was no evidence of coercion or corruption.

H3   The appellant pleaded guilty to two offences of living on the earnings of prostitution. The appellant owned a shop selling lingerie and sex toys. Upstairs there were two rooms which were used as a massage parlour. Police officers who visited the premises were offered various sexual services for payment. An undercover police officer visited the premises and the appellant explained the range of services which could be offered. The appellant was arrested and released on bail; the activities continued after his release on bail. Sentenced to nine months' imprisonment for the earlier offences, with three months' consecutive for the offence committed while on bail (total sentence, 12 months' imprisonment).

H4   **Held:** the appellant was a man of effectively good character. It was accepted that there were no aggravating features, such as the use of threats of force, coercion or corruption. The women involved were of full age and acted voluntarily. There was no evidence of offence or disruption being caused to neighbours. The offence was aggravated by the appellant's continuing to offend while on bail. The Court was satisfied, from a consideration of the authorities, including *Rousseau* [2003] 1 Cr.App.R.(S.) 15 (p.60), that a custodial sentence was justified for the activities revealed in the case, but that the sentence of nine months imposed on the first count was too long. The Court would reduce that sentence to six months, but would not interfere with the sentence of three months consecutive on the second count. The sentence would be reduced to a total of nine months' imprisonment.

Case cited: *Rousseau* [2003] 1 Cr.App.R.(S.) 15 (p.60)

References: living on the earnings of prostitution, *Current Sentencing Practice* B5

C.Q. Morrison for the appellant.

JUDGMENT

1   **TREACY J.:**   This appellant, John Dicketts Middleton, is aged 61. On January 6, 2004 in the Crown Court at Teesside he pleaded guilty to two offences of living on the earnings of prostitution. He was sentenced on February 27, 2004 to a term of 12 months' imprisonment. That term was made up as follows: in relation to count 1, he was sentenced to nine months' imprisonment and in relation to count 5 he was sentenced to three months' imprisonment to run consecutively, making a total of 12 months in all. Other counts on the indictment were left to lie on the file on the usual terms. The charge in relation to count 5 represented offending on bail after the appellant's initial arrest in relation to count 1. The single judge has granted leave to appeal.

2   The circumstances can be briefly put. The appellant owned a shop selling lingerie and sex toys in Darlington, but upstairs there were two rooms that were used as a massage parlour. On various dates in November 2002 undercover police officers visited the premises and went to the massage parlour. They were offered sexual services as well as massages. The sexual services included masturbation, oral sex and full intercourse. The girls who worked there charged different prices for the different services they offered. Girls indicated that sometimes they earned as much as £1,000 a week. They also disclosed that the appellant had recruited them by placing adverts for masseuses.

3   At the end of November 2002 a police officer in undercover guise attended at the premises, having made an appointment with the appellant. The appellant explained to the officer the range of services which the girls upstairs could offer.

4   He was arrested in February 2003. He declined to comment when interviewed. The charge in count 1 therefore represented activities taking place between November 2002 and February 19, 2003. The appellant was released on bail and the activity at the premises continued, as is reflected in count 5. That was for a period for the first two weeks of March 2003, when the police intervened again.

5   The appellant has no relevant previous criminal conviction. He appeals on the basis that a sentence of nine months' imprisonment in relation to count 1 is excessive and is out of line with other cases which have been before this Court.

6   In this case the judge was dealing with a man of effective good character. He had pleaded guilty, albeit not at the earliest opportunity. It was accepted that potential aggravating features, such as the use or threat of force, coercion or corruption were absent from this case. The females involved were of full age and acted voluntarily. There was no evidence of offence or disruption being caused to neighbouring tradesmen. On the other hand, these were well organised offences, involving a number of young women—perhaps up to 20. The appellant must have been aware that what he was doing was illegal and he chose to benefit in a significant way from this deliberate law-breaking. His position is aggravated by his continuing offending whilst on bail.

7   We are satisfied, from a consideration of the authorities which are collated in Vol.4 of *Current Sentencing Practice*, that a custodial sentence was justified for the activity revealed in this case. The most recent citation is that of *Rousseau* [2003] 1 Cr.App.R.(S.) 15 (p.60), where a sentence of nine months' imprisonment was said to be out of line with authorities there cited.

8   Applying those decisions to this case, we consider that there is force in the argument that nine months imposed on count 1 was too long. We reduce it to a term of six months. We have asked ourselves whether or not this amounts to tinkering with the sentence imposed at the Crown Court. We conclude that it does not, as it represents a reduction of one-third. There is, however, no good reason why the sentence on count 2, that is one of three months' imprisonment consecutive, representing an identical offence committed on bail, should not have been passed. We consider that it was correctly imposed.

9   Accordingly, this appeal is allowed to the extent of reducing the sentence on count 1 to six months, and thus the total term to be served is now one of nine months' imprisonment.

R. v CHARAN VERDI

COURT OF APPEAL (Lord Justice Tuckey, Mr Justice Treacy and Sir Richard Tucker): June 9, 2004

[2004] EWCA Crim 1485; [2005] 1 Cr.App.R.(S.) 43

ᴸᵀ Criminal damage; Detention; Deterrence; Trains; Young offenders

H1   *Criminal damage—spraying graffiti onto Underground trains—length of sentence*

H2   Two years' detention in a young offender institution for criminal damage in the form of spraying graffiti onto Underground trains reduced to 18 months.

H3   The appellant pleaded guilty in a magistrates' court to nine offences of criminal damage. He was committed to the Crown Court for sentence. The offences involved spraying graffiti on public service transport vehicles, mainly London Underground trains. The appellant with others used cans of spray paint to paint designs or slogans mainly on the outsides of trains as they were kept in sidings overnight. There was evidence that the annual cost of removing such paint from London Underground trains amounted to £10 million. Sentenced to two years' detention in a young offender institution, with an anti-social behaviour order under the Crime and Disorder Act 1998 s.1C for 10 years.

H4   **Held:** the sentencing judge described graffiti as an unpleasant nuisance, sometimes offensive, which frequently resulted in destruction, delay and expense to the transport authority and the travelling public. The Court endorsed those observations. Those who carried out these activities did so for their own gratification and self-advertisement, without regard for anyone else. The activities were widespread and a deterrent sentence was called for. The only question was whether a sentence as long as two years was necessary. The Court would substitute a sentence of 18 months' detention.

H5   **References:** criminal damage, *Current Sentencing Practice* B 7-2

H6   *Miss F. Chinner* for the appellant.

JUDGMENT

1   **SIR RICHARD TUCKER:**   The appellant is named Charan Verdi. He is aged 18. On November 28, 2003 in the magistrates' court he pleaded guilty to nine offences of criminal damage. He was committed to the Crown Court for sentence. There, in the Crown Court at Middlesex Guildhall on January 2, 2004, he was sentenced to two years' detention in a young offender institution on each of nine counts concurrent. In addition, a 10-year anti-social behaviour order was imposed. He now appeals against sentence by leave of the single judge. There is no appeal against the imposition of the anti-social behaviour order.

2   These offences represent examples of behaviour which have become a prevalent scourge of modern urban society and of the public transport system. They concern the activity of spraying graffiti or, in the vernacular, "tagging" on public service transport vehicles and their surroundings.

3   The offences were committed during an eight-month period between March and November 2003, during which time this appellant was aged 17 or 18. They occurred at various sidings or works where London Underground trains are kept overnight. The appellant, with others, used various cans or sprays to mark those vehicles with his tag—he adopted the name "Case". As we have said, he sometimes worked alone and sometimes with others. Sometimes he just used his tag "Case" and sometimes it was embellished inside, but mostly outside, the trains in black. On some occasions the design covered the whole side of the carriage, and we have seen photographs showing the damage that was caused: because it is *damage*. In addition, the appellant sometimes used phrases such as "Drop the bomb", "I drop bombs like Bin" or "Kill that officer", and on one occasion he inscribed the message "Case caught London sleeping".

4   The court had evidence of the damage which this activity causes. London Transport does not clean graffiti on a piecemeal basis, otherwise, we assume, the trains would be out of action all the time. They are taken out of service to be cleaned only when the damage reaches a certain level. The evidence before the court to support the making of the anti-social behaviour order was this:

> "The effects of graffiti affect communities countrywide. In terms of damage
> caused to London Underground property, graffiti has a lasting negative
> impact. It can increase the fear of crime for those using the railway system
> and therefore damage caused by graffiti is taken seriously.

When a train is vandalised by graffiti it is withdrawn from service. Each day out of service costs £23,000. . . . Where a train is repeatedly subject to graffiti, the life service can be reduced by five years at a cost of £4 million to the company. London Underground currently spend £10 million removing graffiti.

Cleaning up the capital incurs an annual bill of £100 million."

5   It is against that background that we note Miss Chinner's submission that these are offences which merely make life unpleasant though not unstable. Miss Chinner submits that these offences were of an anti-social and economic nature. We bear in mind that they did not directly threaten physical violence or physical injury. Miss Chinner goes so far as to submit that a custodial sentence was not necessary, and points to the fact that the appellant has now in fact served five and a half months' detention and submits that that would be sufficient.

6   We return to the circumstances of the offences. On one occasion, at an early stage of the activity, on March 15, the appellant was almost caught at a certain underground station, but he ran off with others along the tunnel. It should be borne in mind that those who run through tunnels and the people who have to chase them themselves run a serious risk of injury from electrified lines. He was eventually seen on video by closed circuit television cameras and identified by officers and this led to his arrest on November 10. It is to be observed that during the course of this activity, some time during June 2003, he was arrested for causing graffiti on a bus and was subsequently convicted of that offence.

7   Eventually his home was searched. Police officers found examples of graffiti art. There were wire cutters and equipment used to cause the criminal damage, such as pens, a dye and spray cans. When he was interviewed it is to his credit that the appellant admitted the offences.

8   When the learned judge sentenced him he said this:

". . . These persistent graffiti are, at best, an unpleasant nuisance, sometimes offensive and also frequently resultant in disruption, delay and expense to the transport authority and, indirectly, the travelling public.

They have no better purpose than, it seems, your own satisfaction, and people who insist, night after night, in going round with spray cans and so forth and making all this mess on public trains will have to be shown that there comes a time when it can no longer be put up with, and in your case, taking into account your age and the fact that you have admitted all this, that time has come now."

This court endorses those observations.

9   Those who carry out these activities do so for their own self-indulgent gratification and self-advertisement, without regard for anyone else. As all travellers on public transport are aware, the activities are widespread. A deterrent sentence was called for and is appropriate. The only question is whether, recognising that a deterrent sentence should be imposed, it was necessary to impose a sentence as high as this.

10   We have had regard to reports on the appellant. They are good reports. There is
a pre-sentence report, which of course was before the learned sentencing judge,
and there is a prison report, which in the nature of things was not before him. The
prison report speaks well of the appellant's conduct while in detention and he has
become apparently an enhanced prisoner. His overall behaviour whilst in custody, it is said, has been excellent. We take all those matters into account.

11   Having said what we have about the necessity for a deterrent sentence we are
prepared to accept that a sentence of two years was perhaps unnecessarily long. It
would represent a sentence in the region of three years' detention or imprisonment had this been a contested case. So we are prepared to make some
reduction. The sentence we reduce it to will be one of 18 months. We intend
that sentence to be noted as a deterrent sentence, in the hope that the courts by
their attitude to these offences will make some contribution to stamping them
out. To that extent the appeal succeeds.

R. v THOMAS JOSEPH CASSIDY

COURT OF APPEAL (Lord Justice Hooper, Mr Justice Keith and
Judge Patience Q.C.): June 10, 2004

[2004] EWCA Crim 1480; [2005] 1 Cr.App.R.(S.) 44

(LT) Controlled drugs; Illegal importation; Sentence length

H1   *Importing cocaine—assisting in the importation of cocaine by collecting
packages from mail boxes—length of sentence*

H2   Sixteen years' imprisonment for assisting in the importation of cocaine by collecting packages from mail boxes reduced to 11 years.

H3   The appellant pleaded guilty to being knowingly concerned in the fraudulent
evasion of the prohibition on the importation of cocaine. The appellant opened
two mail boxes in a false name, giving a false address and using forged documents to support the application. Six deliveries were made to the mail boxes.
The final delivery was intercepted by the police and contained a total of
5.95kg of cocaine, equivalent to 4.27kg at 100 per cent purity. The appellant collected the package and was immediately arrested. The appellant admitted
collecting packages on behalf of another person to whom he owed money. He
was promised a modest payment for each package he collected and was threatened with violence if he failed to make the collections. He made a total of six
collections before being arrested. He claimed not to know the amount of cocaine
in each consignment. Sentenced to 16 years' imprisonment.

H4   **Held:** (considering *Aroyewumi and others* (1995) 16 Cr.App.R.(S.) 211) the
sentencing judge did not state what his starting point was, but he did indicate

that he had given the appellant credit for an early plea of guilty and his candour with the police. The sentence had to reflect the five occasions on which the appellant collected packages which he knew contained cocaine, as the charge related to the evasion of the prohibition on importation over a period of almost one year. In the Court's judgment, an appropriate starting point would have been in the region of 16 years' imprisonment, and an appropriate discount to reflect the appellant's early plea of guilty and frankness with the police would have justified reducing the sentence to 11 years' imprisonment. The Court would substitute a sentence of 11 years' imprisonment.

H5   **Cases cited:** *Aroyewumi and others* (1995) 16 Cr.App.R.(S.) 211

H6   **References:** importing cocaine, *Current Sentencing Practice* B 11-2

H7   *C. Chadwick* for the appellant.

JUDGMENT

1   **KEITH J.:**   On November 21, 2003 at Blackfriars Crown Court the appellant was sentenced by Judge Marr-Johnson to 16 years' imprisonment for being knowingly concerned in the fraudulent evasion of the prohibition on the importation of cocaine. He had pleaded guilty to the charge. He now appeals against his sentence with the leave of the single judge.

2   The facts were these. On August 31, 2002 the appellant opened two mail boxes, one in Notting Hill Gate and the other in the Kings Road, in a name which was not his own, Brian King. He gave a false address in Ilford, and used a forged driving licence and a forged gas bill in the name of King to do so. Between March 17 and July 17 2003 six deliveries were made to the mail boxes. The last delivery was intercepted by the police. It had come from the West Indies. It contained engine parts, but inside those parts were ten packages which were found on analysis to contain a total of 5.95 kilograms of cocaine, which was equivalent to 4.27 kilograms at 100 per cent purity. The police removed the cocaine and replaced it with rock salt. The appellant collected the package on July 28 and was immediately arrested.

3   He claims that he became involved in the importation of cocaine through a friend of his called Ray, whom he had known since early 2002. They used to gamble together, and Ray would frequently cover the appellant's losses. Ray told the appellant that he ran a number of photographic studios in East London and Essex with his business partner, Brian King, and that they wanted to expand into the lucrative West London market. He therefore asked the appellant, who lived near Notting Hill Gate, to collect photographic and framing equipment for him as and when it was delivered. That is how the appellant came to open the two mail boxes in the name of Brian King. Presumably the appellant says that Ray provided him with the forged documents, and that he did not appreciate that they had been forged.

4   When the appellant collected the first consignment, he became suspicious as the package came from the West Indies. He confronted Ray about his suspicions, and Ray told him that the package had contained cannabis. When the appellant pressed Ray further about it, Ray admitted that the package had contained cocaine. The appellant claims that he told Ray that he did not want to have anything more to do with it, but Ray reminded him that he owed Ray sums amounting to several thousand pounds. He was told that he could work off his debt by continuing to collect packages as and when he was required to do so. In return for each collection, he would be paid £150 and his debt would be reduced by £250. He was threatened with violence to himself and his family if he refused to go along with Ray's demands. He made five further collections before being arrested. He was shocked when he discovered the amount of the cocaine in the last consignment. He had not known the amounts in the consignments, but he had assumed that they had been about half a kilogram each.

5   That was consistent with the account which he gave to the police when he was interviewed following his arrest. Since he was caught in possession of the cocaine, and in the light of his confession, he had little option but to plead guilty. The judge sentenced him on the basis that his plea of guilty had been tendered at the earliest opportunity. The judge purported to give him credit for that and for revealing his own involvement to the police. There was nothing to contradict his account of the extent of his involvement and, although there were features of his account which one might be sceptical about, his account was the basis on which he had to be sentenced. The judge did not disbelieve the threats to which the appellant claimed he had been subjected. The judge simply thought that those threats were not a significant mitigating factor. The appellant's duty had been to report the matter to the police and not to continue with the importation over a substantial period.

6   The appellant is 38 years old. He has a number of previous convictions, almost all of which are for offences of dishonesty. He has been to prison a number of times. He gambles habitually, and he claims that his present offences were committed to fund his gambling habit. He told the author of the pre-sentence report on him that at the time of his arrest he was running his own building firm from which he was making about £30,000 a year.

7   The judge did not state what his starting point was, but since he purported to give the appellant credit for his plea of guilty at the earliest opportunity, and his candour with the police, and since the judge said that he was "largely" ignoring the appellant's previous convictions, the judge must have taken as his starting point a sentence of 20 years' imprisonment or more. It is true that the sentence had to reflect the five occasions on which the appellant had collected consignments of cocaine (when he knew that the consignments contained cocaine), first because of his own confession, and secondly because the charge to which he pleaded guilty was not limited to the consignment which he had just collected on the day of his arrest. The charge was that he had been concerned in the fraudulent evasion of the prohibition on the importation of cocaine on "days between" August 1, 2002 and July 28, 2003. But was a starting point of at least 20 years'

imprisonment nevertheless too long, bearing in mind that the appellant's role was not significantly different from that of a courier?

8   The guideline case is *Aranguren* (1994) 99 Cr.App.R. 347 (sub nom. *Aroyewumi and others* (1995) 16 Cr.App.R.(S.) 211). It dealt with the importation of class A drugs, such as heroin and cocaine, and established the principle that the sentence should be related to the weight of the drugs rather than the estimated street value of the consignment, and to take the notional weight of the drugs at 100 per cent purity for that purpose. When the weight of the drugs at 100 per cent purity was of the order of 500 grams or more, sentences of 10 years' imprisonment and upwards would be appropriate. When the weight of the drugs at 100 per cent purity was of the order of 5 kilograms or more, sentences of 14 years' imprisonment and upwards would be appropriate. Those were the sentences to be imposed after a contested trial.

9   The weight of the cocaine to which the last consignment related suggested a starting point close to 14 years' imprisonment, but to be factored into the equation were the facts that (a) there had been four previous consignments, which the appellant knew had contained cocaine, which could have weighed more or less than the final consignment, and (b) the relatively mundane level of the appellant's involvement akin to that of a courier. In our judgment, a starting point in the region of 16 years' imprisonment would have been appropriate. An appropriate discount to reflect the appellant's early pleas of guilty and his frankness with the police would have justified reducing the sentence to 11 years' imprisonment.

10   Accordingly, we have concluded that the sentence which the judge imposed was too long. We therefore allow the appeal, we set aside the sentence of 16 years' imprisonment, and we substitute for it one of 11 years' imprisonment. This is not an appropriate case for a recovery of defence costs order to be made.

R. v ROY VINCENT PRIME

COURT OF APPEAL (Lord Justice Judge, Mrs Justice Hallett and Mr Justice Treacy): June 16, 2004

[2004] EWCA Crim 2009; [2005] 1 Cr.App.R.(S.) 45

(LT) Assault; Child abduction; Disqualification from working with children; Guilty pleas; Sentence length; Unlawful sentences

11   *Child abduction—abducting child by stranger for no apparent reason—length of sentence*

12   Four years' imprisonment for the abduction of a nine-year-old boy (and assault on him) by a stranger, for no apparent reason, reduced to three years.

13   The appellant pleaded guilty to abducting a child, contrary to the Child Abduction Act 1984, s.2. The appellant arrived at a house where a children's party was

taking place. The appellant was a friend or acquaintance of the boyfriend of the mother of one of the children attending the party. The appellant asked a nine year old boy to go with him to a supermarket to buy cigarettes. He took the boy away from the party to a piece of ground and asked him whether he wanted any money. The appellant then grabbed the boy by the arm and pulled him to the ground. The boy got up but the appellant again pulled him to the ground, hit him in the face and kicked him on the head. The boy suffered some injuries, resulting in a swollen left eye. A pre-sentence report assessed the appellant as presenting a direct risk of harm to the public, particularly children. References asserted that the offence was out of character. Sentenced to four years' imprisonment, with a disqualification order under the Criminal Justice and Court Services Act 2000, s.28.

H4   **Held:** the offence under the Child Abduction Act 1984, s.2 was not an offence listed in Schedule 4 of the Criminal Justice and Court Services Act 2000 as an offence against a child, and accordingly the court had no power to make a disqualification order for that offence. The Court was surprised at this omission, and would invite the Secretary of State to consider amending the schedule by Order in Council. The sentencing judge stated that a lengthy sentence was necessary for the offence, as there was no real explanation for what happened. There was nothing in the appellant's past to suggest that he was a danger to children. The maximum sentence for the offence was seven years' imprisonment. In the Court's judgment the sentence of four years was too long, particularly in view of the guilty plea, and a sentence of three years would be substituted. The disqualification order would be quashed.

H5   **References:** child abduction, *Current Sentencing Practice* B 3-4

H6   *H. Wallace* for the appellant.

JUDGMENT

[Paragraph 1 has been omitted.]

2   **TREACY J.:**   This appellant, who has been granted leave by the single judge, pleaded guilty on February 2, 2004 in the Crown Court at Cardiff and was sentenced on February 16 by H.H. Judge Denyer Q.C. to a term of four years' imprisonment. That term was imposed for an offence of abducting a child contrary to s.2 of the Child Abduction Act 1984. There was on the indictment a second count alleging assault occasioning actual bodily harm. That was left on the file on the usual terms but the parties in the court below and counsel before us today have treated the undoubted assault which took place as part and parcel of the offence of abduction.

3   In addition to imposing a term of four years' imprisonment for the offence of abduction the learned judge also disqualified the appellant from working with children under the provisions of s.28 of the Criminal Justice and Court Services Act 2000. Counsel has helpfully drawn our attention to Sch.4 to that Act which

sets out qualifying offences which enable the court to make such an order. In para.1 there is a reference to an offence committed under the Child Abduction Act 1984 but that relates to an offence committed under s.1—that is an offence committed by a parent in relation to the abduction a child. There is no reference in para.1 to the offence for which this appellant faced a charge, namely an offence under s.2 of the Act. It appears, therefore, that the Crown Court had no power to impose an order of disqualification under s.28, having regard to the provisions of para.1 of Sch.4.

4   We have considered the matter and we express our surprise at this omission from the list of qualifying offences, and we invite the Secretary of State to consider exercising the power which he has under s.26(2) of the Act to amend Sch.4 by Order. In the interim we observe, for the benefit of prosecutors, that under para.2 of Sch.4 the offence of kidnapping is a qualifying offence and there may be circumstances where prosecution authorities consider it appropriate to prefer such a charge rather than a charge under s.2 of the 1984 Act so as to enable the courts to have power to consider an order under s.28.

5   The circumstances of the offence are these. On November 5, 2003 a fireworks party was held at a private house. A Mrs D took her three children to the party. The victim of this offence was her nine-year-old son, A, who accompanied her. Mrs D describes A as being not the brightest child in his school. He did not have special needs and does not require any additional help, but his intelligence level was low; however he knew right from wrong and he knew that he should not go with strangers. Mrs D's boyfriend also attended that party. He appears to have been a friend or acquaintance of this appellant. They had met on the way to the party and the appellant had followed the boyfriend to the party. Two men arrived at the party at about 7.15pm. The householder had not invited the appellant but she did not object to him being there since she had known him for a number of years as he was a neighbour of hers. In fact he had taken her 13-year-old son fishing in the past.

6   About 20 minutes after he arrived at the party the appellant asked young A to go with him to a nearby Tesco supermarket to buy some cigarettes. He then took A away from the party and to a piece of ground near the supermarket. He asked A whether he wanted any money. A said "Go on then", but the appellant did not produce any money. The appellant instead grabbed A by the arm and pulled him to the ground. A fell on his back. It appears that the appellant then stumbled, enabling A to get up. Unfortunately that was not the end of the incident. The appellant again pulled A to the ground. He now hit him in the face and kicked him on the leg and scratched his neck before running off leaving A alone.

7   At about 8.30pm a police officer was approached by two girls who had found A, and A told the police officer what had happened. At that stage the officer could see that A had suffered some injuries. His left eye was swollen, there was reddening in that area of his face and his eye was slightly closed. In the meantime A's mother had realised that he was missing and in her alarm had herself contacted the police. Eventually mother and son were reunited.

8   The appellant was arrested and was interviewed the following day. He gave an account which tended to indicate that he understood that A had told others where

he was going with the appellant, which effectively asserted that any physical force used or occurring between himself and A was entirely accidental. On entering his plea of guilty and today before us the appellant has accepted the Crown's case in relation to the factual elements of this case, rather than the non-incriminatory version which he proffered in interview.

9   The appellant is 36 years of age. He has a single previous conviction recorded in 1992. He was sent to prison for an offence of violent disorder for a period of 18 months; but apart from that no other matter appears on his record. The sentencing court had before it a psychiatric report. It referred to a partial alcohol dependency syndrome which it was said this appellant was suffering from. The sentencer also had available to him a pre-sentence report which referred to the appellant's heavy drinking since his mother's recent death in August 2003. It is said that the appellant had demonstrated motivation to change and would accept professional assistance. The author of that report also observed that in his opinion there was a concern about the circumstances of the offence and what appeared to be an assault on a child in an unprovoked manner. The author of the report assessed this appellant as appearing to present a direct risk of harm to the public, particularly children. There were references before the court which were favourable to the appellant and which asserted that this offence was out of character and spoke of him as a hard-working person. The appellant himself wrote to the court and expressed his regret and remorse for what has happened.

10   The grounds of appeal advanced before us assert that the judge treated the case more seriously than the facts warranted and that the judge failed to give sufficient credit for the guilty plea which was entered, or alternatively took too high a starting point before making a discount. When the judge passed sentence he said that this was a deeply troubling offence, which involved the appellant in abducting a boy and then physically assaulting him by putting him to the ground twice, hitting him to the face and kicking him. The judge was concerned that there was no real explanation for what had happened and in those circumstances felt that a lengthy sentence was necessary.

11   We can understand the judge's concern. There was nothing in this man's past or background to suggest that he was a danger to children, but the circumstances of the offence are disquieting. Even today the appellant's counsel (who has raised the issue with the appellant in conference) is unable to provide any clear explanation for what happened. We are perturbed by unexplained conduct which points towards an apparent intention to do violence or to assault this child sexually.

12   On the other hand this appellant pleaded guilty. He acknowledged his regret in the letter to the court and he had the benefit of favourable references. His heavy drinking and the recent effect upon him of his mother's death provide relevant background which may help to explain his actions. Those factors can assist the appellant, but they cannot save him from a significant custodial sentence. We remind ourselves that the maximum sentence available under the Act is one of seven years. It follows that on a trial the sentencing judge must have been contemplating the sentence of around six years for this offence. This seems to us to be too high a starting point for what was involved here.

13   We bear in mind that the period involved was relatively short, somewhat under an hour, and that nothing in the form of sexual touching actually occurred. What did occur does not appear to have been substantially premeditated and the child was not taken away from the area where he lived in a vehicle or anything of that sort.

14   In our judgment, the sentence of four years was too long in the circumstances, particularly the guilty plea which was tendered, and we consider that a sentence of three years would represent a proper sentence in this case. We substitute that sentence for the four years which was imposed. We quash the order under s.28 of the Criminal Justice and Court Services Act 2000 for the reasons expressed earlier in this judgment. To that extent the appeal is allowed.

R. v NAUSHAD YOONUS

COURT OF APPEAL (Lord Justice Kennedy, Mr Justice Astill and Mr Justice Gross): June 16, 2004

[2004] EWCA Crim 1734; [2005] 1 Cr.App.R.(S.) 46

(LT) Commercial activities; Foreign currencies; Money laundering; Sentence length

H1   *Money laundering—assisting in the conversion of the proceeds of unspecified crimes—defendant playing minor role—length of sentence*

H2   Six years' imprisonment imposed on a defendant who played a minor role in converting the proceeds of unspecified crimes into foreign currencies reduced to four years.

H3   The appellant pleaded guilty to two offences of conspiring to convert the proceeds of drug trafficking or other criminal conduct. The appellant was concerned in converting sterling into large denominations of currencies such as dollars or euros. The appellant received bags of sterling in a hotel room from a number of persons. The money was then converted into other currencies, which were handed back to the other persons. One person leaving the hotel was found to have $300,000 and others had larger amounts. The appellant pleaded guilty on the basis that on some of the occasions on which he was observed he had been carrying on a legitimate business, and that not all of the money recovered could be attributed to money laundering. The appellant denied that the money was the proceeds of drug trafficking or other serious crime, and claimed that he had played a minor role in the scheme. Sentenced to six years' imprisonment on one count and three years' imprisonment concurrent on the other (total sentence, six years' imprisonment).

H4   **Held:** (considering *Everson* [2002] 1 Cr.App.R.(S.) 132 (p.553) and *Basra* [2002] 2 Cr.App.R.(S.) 100 (p.469)) the Court agreed that the sentence was too long on the basis that the appellant fell to be sentenced. It was not shown that the money came from serious crime; and the dishonesty was part of a legitimate commercial operation. The Court would substitute a sentence of four years for the sentence of six years (total sentence, four years).

H5   **References:** money laundering, *Current Sentencing Practice* B 13-8.3E

H6   *R. Sones* for the appellant.

JUDGMENT

1   **ASTILL J.:**   The appellant, Naushad Yoonus, is 31 years of age. He was of previous good character. He pleaded guilty on re-arraignment at the Crown Court at Kingston-upon-Thames before H.H. Judge William Thomas to two offences of conspiracy to convert the proceeds of drug trafficking and/or other criminal conduct. On July 11, 2003, he was sentenced to terms of six years' and three years' imprisonment to run concurrently. He now appeals against sentence by leave of the single judge.

2   The appellant was charged with conspiring with others to convert sterling, which was the proceeds of crime and called "street money", into large denomination currencies such as dollars or euros. A co-defendant, Lathiff, had a number of businesses in West London, including hotels, which incorporated bureaux de change. The Radnor Hotel in Bayswater was the one most frequently used. A room would be made available to the appellant, where he would receive bags of sterling. There were a number of defendants who brought money to the hotel. They would collect money from various venues, where it would be handed over and exchanged into a suitable currency.

3   Officers of Her Majesty's Customs and Excise kept observation on the operation. On June 28, 2002, the co-defendant, Lathiff, was seen to enter the home of a man and leave with a rucksack. That was count 1.

4   On July 9, 2002, the appellant was seen to go into the Radnor Hotel with a rucksack. Two of the co-defendants were present. One was arrested as he came out of the hotel. He was found to have on him US$300,000. Count 1 included all who were arrested at the hotel and another occasion in Portsmouth when the appellant had been seen dealing with various co-defendants, including one who had in his possession over US$580,000. At the homes of two of the co-defendants were found US$566,000 and $600,000.

5   Count 2 related to the appellant's dealings with co-defendants on two separate dates in 2002. The first was an exchange at the Radnor Hotel, and the second an exchange in a motor car.

6   The appellant pleaded guilty on the basis that on some of the occasions he was observed he had been carrying on legitimate business. Not all of the money recovered could be attributed to the money laundering. In relation to count 2

he pleaded guilty on the basis of two transactions with a co-defendant when he knew that the money came from crime.

7   Before the sentencing judge there were a number of documents: letters, references and a prison report. We have read them. Mr Sones, on behalf of the appellant, submits, in short, that the total sentence of six years was too long, given the extent of the money laundering that was involved; that the appellant was of previous good character; and that a sentence of imprisonment would have a considerable effect upon his family. We have read today a letter written by the appellant to this Court which specifically deals with the effect of the prison sentence upon his family. In addition, Mr Sones adopts the written submissions of Mr Rees Q.C., that there was no certainty as to the source of the laundered money. The appellant denied that it was the proceeds of drug trafficking or other serious crime, and that was accepted by the sentencing judge. The appellant's case was that he was not the main player behind the money-laundering scheme. It was the prosecution's case against him that he allowed himself to be used to facilitate the conversion of sterling to US dollars. He did that at a respectable bureau de change. It was not a sophisticated scheme and he was in effect the labourer for others. He received very little financial benefit, compared with the amount of money involved—probably as little as £5,000.

8   Mr Sones again adopting the written submissions of Mr Rees, has referred this Court to *Everson* [2002] 1 Cr.App.R.(S.) 132 (p.553) and *Basra* [2002] 2 Cr.App.R.(S.) 100 (p.469), in which appellants who played a similar role to that of this appellant were sentenced to three and a half years' imprisonment. Relying on all of those matters Mr Sones submits that the sentence of six years' imprisonment was too long.

9   On the basis upon which the appellant fell to be sentenced we agree. It was not shown that the money came from serious crime. The dishonesty was part only of a legitimate commercial operation. They were the bases upon which the appellant was expressly sentenced by the learned sentencing judge. Nevertheless, the sums involved were significant.

10   Taking all of those matters into account, we have come to the conclusion that the sentence of six years' imprisonment was too long, particularly following a plea of guilty. One of the matters stressed by Mr Sones is that he received insufficient credit for that plea. We quash the sentence of six years' imprisonment and substitute for it one of four years. The sentences remain concurrent, making a total sentence of four years' imprisonment. To that extent this appeal is allowed.

R. v O. (TINA DONNA)

COURT OF APPEAL (Lord Justice Kennedy, Mr Justice Astill and Mr Justice Gross): June 16, 2004

[2004] EWCA Crim 1750; [2005] 1 Cr.App.R.(S.) 47

(LT) Child cruelty; Failure to act; Guilty pleas; Sentence length; Third party acts

H1 *Cruelty to child—mother of six-year-old failing to prevent beating of six-year-old by mother's boyfriend—length of sentence*

H2 Two years' imprisonment for cruelty to a child imposed on the mother of a six-year-old girl for failing to prevent the beating of the child by the mother's boyfriend reduced to 18 months on account of her early plea.

H3 The appellant pleaded guilty to cruelty to a child. The appellant's six-year-old daughter was found to be suffering from extensive bruises. The child said that her mother's boyfriend had hit her with a stick on a number of occasions and that the appellant knew what was happening, but did nothing to prevent it. Sentenced to two years' imprisonment.

H4 **Held:** it was submitted that the sentence did not fully take account of the appellant's early plea and the fact that the injuries to the child were not of the gravest nature, and that the appellant had not inflicted them. The Court could see nothing wrong with the sentence for the offence, but would allow a greater discount for the appellant's early plea, particularly as there had been a prolonged period between the entering of the plea and the imposition of the sentence. The Court would substitute a sentence of 18 months' imprisonment.

H5 **References:** cruelty to child, *Current Sentencing Practice* B 2-7

H6 *M. Orsulik* for the appellant.

JUDGMENT

1 **KENNEDY L.J.:** On July 31, 2003, in the Magistrates' Court at Ealing, this 26-year-old appellant pleaded guilty to the offence of cruelty to a child. She was committed to the Crown Court for sentence. On March 10, 2004, in the Crown Court at Isleworth, she was sentenced to two years' imprisonment. She is a lady with no previous convictions. She appeals against sentence by leave of the single judge.

2 On June 20, 2003, Child Protection Officers and representatives of Social Services attended at her home after they had received an anonymous tip-off that her six-year-old daughter was limping and had facial bruises. When the house was

searched, they found the appellant's then boyfriend and that child hiding in a cupboard. The child was taken to a doctor and was found to be extensively bruised. We have photographs which show that the bruises covered every part of her body. The bruises to the face, which had attracted the attention of the neighbours, were in some respects the least serious of the injuries. But it is rightly said on behalf of the appellant by Mr Orsulik this morning that at least the injuries did not involve broken bones or internal injuries.

3   The child said that her mother's boyfriend had hit her with a substantial stick which he kept on top of the cupboard, and that had happened on a number of occasions. Her mother knew what was happening, but did nothing effective to prevent it. In time the child was beaten in front of the mother. Mr Orsulik submitted that the appellant made some sort of protest and attempted to intervene. If so, her efforts were, it seems, wholly in vain.

4   The appellant was found to be a woman of average intelligence who was not mentally ill, but had very little support in the life that she led. She tended to drift from one abusive relationship to another.

5   On her behalf this morning, Mr Orsulik submits that in passing sentence the learned judge failed to take into account fully the appellant's early plea of guilty tendered in the magistrates' court. That is a matter which this court has indicated more than once should attract a substantial discount from the penalty otherwise to be imposed. Secondly, he submits that although these were very serious injuries they were not, as we have already indicated, of the very gravest. Nor was it she who inflicted the injuries; there has never been any suggestion of that. Thirdly, he invites us to have regard to her good character, her age, and the fact that her good character is of a positive kind. There is no suggestion that she had been abusive towards the child. Fourthly, we are invited to have regard to her personality. She was found by a psychologist to be a woman suffering from a dependent personality disorder—a situation which made it very difficult for her to extricate herself from an abusive relationship. The appellant has been the victim of violence, in particular violence at the hands of the man who was violent to her child. The police having visited, as we have already indicated, in June 2003, in early 2004 she had to seek refuge in a hostel because of the violence which had been inflicted upon her.

6   As a result of the intervention of the Child Protection Officers and the Social Services in June 2003, the appellant has not seen her daughter for a period of a year now. She has written a letter, which we have all read, setting out the extent to which she is suffering from the sentence which has been imposed upon her.

7   In all those circumstances it is said to us that the sentence which was imposed was too long. In our judgment, for the offence,there was nothing wrong with this sentence and we would uphold it. However, we have regard to one particular feature in this case to which Mr Orsulik has drawn attention and that is the early plea followed by the prolonged period before she was sentenced in the Crown Court. That arose because it was hoped that the man with whom she had been living and who was said to be the person who had been violent to the child could be tried before sentence was passed upon the appellant. In the event that did not happen

because he disappeared. Thus a period of about seven or eight months elapsed before the appellant was sentenced.

8   In those circumstances, and having regard to the fact that she pleaded guilty in the magistrates' court at the first opportunity, we have come to the conclusion that she was entitled to a somewhat greater discount than that given to her by the sentencing judge. Accordingly, we set aside the sentence of two years' imprisonment. We substitute for it a sentence of 18 months' imprisonment. To that extent only this appeal is allowed.

ATTORNEY GENERAL'S REFERENCE NO.30 OF 2004 (ROSS PAUL TARONI)

Court of Appeal (Lord Justice Kay, Mr Justice Curtis and Mr Justice Newman): June 16, 2004

[2004] EWCA Crim 1754; [2005] 1 Cr.App.R.(S.) 48

(ʟᴛ) Grievous bodily harm; Undue leniency; Weapons; Wounding with intent

H1   *Wounding with intent to cause grievous bodily harm—unprovoked attack with hammer causing grave injuries—length of sentence*

H2   Three years' imprisonment for wounding with intent to cause grievous bodily harm by an unprovoked attack with a hammer which caused grave injuries increased to four and a half years.

H3   The offender pleaded guilty on the day on which his trial was due to begin to wounding with intent to do grievous bodily harm. The offender was present at a public house when a dispute arose concerning credits left in a juke box. Some time later, the offender approached the victim and struck him from behind on the side of the head with a hammer. Two further blows were struck. The victim was found to have a depressed skull fracture which required surgery. He later experienced headaches and other symptoms including a cranial depression at the site of the main injury. He had undergone a personality change. Sentenced to three years' imprisonment. The Attorney General asked the Court to review the sentence on the ground that it was unduly lenient.

H4   **Held:** (considering *Attorney General's Reference No.18 of 2002 (Christopher Simon Hughes)* [2003] 1 Cr.App.R.(S.) 9 (p.35), *Attorney General's Reference No.36 of 1996 (Jason Leon Johnson)* [1997] 1 Cr.App.R.(S.) 363, *Attorney General's Reference No.68 of 2002 (Stephen Catterill)* [2003] 1 Cr.App.R.(S.) 94 (p.498), *Attorney General's Reference No.12 of 2004 (Alfred Washington Weekes)* [2005] 1 Cr.App.R.(S.) 32, *Attorney General's Reference No.11 of 1992 (Robert Charles Howes)* (1993) 14 Cr.App.R.(S.) 136) it was submitted for the Attorney General that the case was aggravated by the use of the hammer as a weapon, the fact that the attack was an unprovoked attack on a stranger in public, involving repeated deliberate and forceful blows, and causing a significant injury which had lasting consequences. The offence was mitigated by the plea of guilty, the offender's remorse and the fact that the offence was out of character. The Court agreed that the sentence was unduly lenient for a savage attack on an innocent person. The proper sentence following a guilty plea entered at a late stage would have been of the order of five and a half to six years. Allowing for the element of double jeopardy, the court would substitute a sentence of four and a half years' imprisonment.

H5   **Cases cited:** *Attorney General's Reference No.18 of 2002 (Christopher Simon Hughes)* [2003] 1 Cr.App.R.(S.) 9 (p.35), *Attorney General's Reference No.36 of 1996 (Jason Leon Johnson)* [1997] 1 Cr.App.R.(S.) 363, *Attorney General's Reference No.68 of 2002 (Stephen Catterill)* [2003] 1 Cr.App.R.(S.) 94 (p.498), *Attorney General's Reference No.12 of 2004 (Alfred Washington Weekes)* [2005] 1 Cr.App.R.(S.) 32, *Attorney General's Reference No.11 of 1992 (Robert Charles Howes)* (1993) 14 Cr.App.R.(S.) 136

H6   **References:** wounding with intent to cause grievous bodily harm, *Current Sentencing Practice* B 2-2

H7   *Miss B. Cheema* for the Attorney General.
    L. Wilcox for the offender.

JUDGMENT

1   **KAY L.J.:**   Her Majesty's Attorney General seeks the leave of the Court to refer to it a sentence that he considers to be unduly lenient pursuant to s.36 of the Criminal Justice Act 1988. We grant leave.

2   The offender is now 30 years of age, 29 at the time when he was sentenced.

3   On September 5, 2003 he pleaded not guilty to a count of wounding with intent. Following two further hearings the matter was listed for trial.

4   On January 20, 2004, the day on which the trial was due to begin and when all the prosecution witnesses had attended, the offender was re-arraigned and entered a guilty plea on a written basis. The basis of the plea was not disputed by the Crown. Sentence was adjourned for the preparation of a pre-sentence report.

5   On February 13, 2004 H.H. Judge O'Malley, sitting at the Taunton Crown Court, sentenced him to three years' imprisonment.

6   The facts are these. On June 6, 2003 the victim, a 36-year-old man, called Scott Hunter, was spending the evening with a friend in a local public house and then the bar of an hotel, where they were both known. At about 9.30pm the victim went to put some money into the jukebox which had gone quiet. Whilst there the offender came up to him and said that he had three credits left in the jukebox. Without looking at him, the victim said that they might have been lost, but if

they were still there after his selection had been played the offender could have them. The offender left and the victim went and sat down with his friend.

7   About 10 minutes later, without any sort of warning, the offender approached him and struck him from behind with a hard blow to the right side of his head, which knocked him over to the left. Hunter described it as a dull sensation. As he looked up, Hunter saw the blur of a hammer coming towards him again. He was struck again, and as he moved away he was struck for a third time, the blow landing on his shoulder when he put his hand up to protect himself. The barmaid who was present described the offender holding the victim down with one hand as he swung the hammer down.

8   The blows were in quick succession and left the victim bleeding onto his face, neck and clothing. When he came to his senses he saw the offender being restrained by other men, while he shouted words to the effect, "That'll teach you to take my free credit". The offender was then seen to pick up a glass ashtray and throw it at the victim, although, fortunately, it missed.

9   The offender was removed from the bar and the hammer was taken from him. When he was leaving the premises the victim came across the offender, who continued to abuse him about the jukebox. The hammer was taken behind the bar by the barmaid and later given to the police.

10   The following day the victim felt slow, as he described it "dopey", but went to work. Once there his colleagues realised he was unwell and took him to hospital. He was X-rayed and it was discovered from a CT scan that he had a depressed skull fracture and damage to the dura (the membrane lining the brain). An operation was carried out under general anaesthetic so that the depressed skull could be elevated. It was clear at the operation that a blow of considerable force had been struck as it was sufficient to drive a disc-shaped wedge of bone deep into the skull surface. Hair and skin fragments had been driven through the skull and were found amongst the bone fragments lying over the dura which had been breached by the blow. The wound was cleaned and the skull was re-secured with titanium plates. Fourteen clips were then used to close the site. He also had a cut to his right ear and a numb shoulder that lasted a few days. He had to spend three days in hospital.

11   There have been after-effects from the assault. The victim experienced headaches every day for about a month, then intermittent pain in the area of the scar. He has experienced a constant high-pitched noise in the head, more noticeable at night in the quiet, which has interfered with his sleep. He has a five-inch scar and a cranoid depression at the site of the main injury. There was, as a result of the injury, a risk of epileptic seizures, although none, fortunately, had been suffered by the time of the sentencing hearing. He was not allowed to drive for six months or play football. He himself was aware of a personality change in that he had become quiet and shy and reluctant to socialise, whereas before the assault he was confident and outgoing. He found it harder to concentrate for long periods and carried out tasks at a slower pace. In January 2004 the victim was still receiving treatment and was due to see a hearing specialist in respect of the constant noise in his head.

12   Mr Hunter has since felt compelled to avoid two nearby towns because he has been afraid that he might come across the offender or his friends. He has lost his employment as a result of the attack and now earns less than he did before.

13   On the night of the incident the police were called but the offender had by then left. He subsequently surrendered voluntarily to the police on June 23. In interview, he admitted owning the hammer. He explained that it was a work tool. He also admitted that he was responsible for the assault, but claimed to have been too drunk to remember the incident, apart from the argument at the jukebox with a young man whom he did not know. After the argument the offender claimed to have left the public house, only returning because he had forgotten to take his bag of tools with him. He had taken 14 pints of a mixture of lager and bitter and had been extremely drunk. The next thing he recalled was being dragged out and told he had hit someone with a hammer. He did not at that stage accept three blows as he could not remember them and he thought that the victim was exaggerating. He expressed remorse at the end of the interview for using the hammer. He said: "Just about the business with the hammer. It was a very stupid move and I'm sorry for it. I was drunk with beer. That's all I can say". He had also told a mutual friend that he was sorry for the injuries.

14   The basis of plea, as it was put forward when he entered his plea of guilty, was as follows:

15   First, the offender had been working all day in hot weather without food or drink. When he subsequently took alcohol the effect was more marked.

16   Secondly, the offender did not recall the assault but admitted forming a drunken attempt to cause the victim grievous bodily harm.

17   Thirdly, the offender bitterly regretted the incident and injuries. As soon as he realised what had happened he contacted his solicitor and surrendered to the police.

18   Finally, he had always maintained a plea to causing the injuries but contested the element of specific intent due to his drunken state. Upon service of medical evidence confirming that three blows were struck, he accepted that he must have formed the drunken intention that was required.

19   The offender has previous convictions, and over the eight years between 1992 and 2000 he was convicted of over 40 offences, ranging from criminal damage and driving offences to assault occasioning actual bodily harm, robbery, burglary, possession of cannabis, handling and public order matters. Significantly, the offences of violence were 10 years old and there were no details available as to exactly what they were. They had resulted in short terms of imprisonment. He had been dealt with in a variety of ways including imprisonment, fines and community service.

20   On behalf of the Attorney General it is submitted that this case had a number of aggravating features: first, the use of the hammer as a weapon; secondly, this was an unprovoked attack on a stranger in public; thirdly, the victim was struck repeatedly and the offender only desisted when others intervened; fourthly, the deliberate and forceful striking to the head of the victim, which caused a significant injury in that the section of the skull was driven into the dura together with surrounding skin and hair; fifthly, it was a case with serious and lasting conse-

quences from the injuries, including the insertion of metal plates and the consistent ringing in the ears which was still unresolved; finally, there was his past history of offending.

21   It is recognised, on the other side, that there were a number of mitigating features. First, there was the plea of guilty. The judge, in dealing with the plea of guilty, made it clear that he viewed it as a significant plea, bearing in mind that he accepted that the offender had no actual recollection of what he had done. Next, it was recognised that there was genuine remorse, demonstrated particularly by contact with a prosecution witness and what he had said then, and also by the very act of surrendering to the police. Next, the judge viewed the matter as being one which was out of character. Bearing in mind his earlier violent history, it must be that the judge meant by that, first, that this was far more serious than anything he had ever done before, and, in particular was outside his recent character in that he had not behaved violently for a significant number of years. Finally in terms of mitigating features, it is recognised that this is an offender with a difficult personal history; in particular, he had a history of drug abuse, and that he had made a significant effort to try and reform, assisted by his father, and that there had been a significant improvement in his behaviour as a result of his efforts.

22   The Attorney General submits that the sentence was unduly lenient and, in particular, contends that the sentence failed to mark adequately the gravity of the offence and the aggravating features present. It is submitted that the learned judge gave too little heed to the high degree of force used in the assault and too great credit for the mitigating features in the case, including the late guilty plea. It is also submitted that this is a sentence which will fail to act as a deterrent to others considering committing similar offences and one which failed to heed the proper concern in society in respect of violent offences of this kind which cause harm to a wholly innocent victim.

23   In support of those contentions, we have had our attention drawn to a number of authorities: *Attorney General's Reference No.18 of 2002 (Christopher Simon Hughes)* [2003] 1 Cr.App.R.(S.) 9 (p.35); *Attorney General's Reference No.36 of 1996 (Jason Leon Johnson)* [1997] 1 Cr.App.R.(S.) 363; and *Attorney General's Reference No.68 of 2002 (Stephen Catterill)* [2003] 1 Cr.App.R.(S.) 94 (p.498). Further, our attention was drawn to a very recent decision of this Court, in respect of which there is no full transcript, *Attorney General's Reference No.12 of 2004 (Alfred Washington Weekes)* [2005] 1 Cr.App.R.(S.) 32, which was heard by this Court on May 19, 2004. We have a short report in relation to that but no further information over and above the short report.

24   In addition, whilst we are referring to the authorities that we have considered, Mr Wilcox, on behalf of the offender, also drew our attention to the case of *Attorney General's Reference No.11 of 1992 (Robert Charles Howes)* (1993) 14 Cr.App.R.(S.) 136.

25   Many of those authorities have similar features to the offences in this case, although one can never find two cases that are exactly the same and they can do no more than provide general guidance as to the appropriate level of sentencing.

26 On behalf of the offender, Mr Wilcox submits that whilst he accepts that the sentence was a lenient sentence, it cannot properly be characterised as being unduly lenient. He submits in those circumstances that the Court ought not to interfere with the existing sentence, and if it feels compelled to do so should raise it by no more than the minimum that is consistent with the Court's duty.

27 We have carefully considered all the submissions in this case and we find ourselves agreeing with the Attorney General that the sentence was unduly lenient. This was a very savage attack on a wholly innocent person. There was not even the sort of background that one often finds in cases of this kind where there had been some quarrel and somebody simply took the quarrel out of the league in which it ought to have been. The victim here was a person going about his ordinary business, legitimately behaving in a public house, who, for no sort of reason at all, was attacked in this savage way. It is further significant, in our judgment, that the offender had left the public house after the minor episode with the victim and actually returned to the public house in order to collect his tools and then, and only then, well removed from any contact which he had with the victim, he attacked him at that stage. Further, there were a number of separate blows, and even when he was taken hold of by others, he was still attempting to throw the ashtray at the victim. Those are serious features.

28 The other critically important feature, in our judgment, is the extent of the injuries suffered by the unfortunate victim. There is no doubt that the blow to the head has caused him serious long-term consequences. Just how those will resolve in the future is impossible to tell, but this is a case where there has been serious injury leading to consequences that will go on reminding the victim of this very unpleasant attack for a substantial length of time.

29 In our judgment, facts of that kind, even on a guilty plea, merit a longer sentence than the one imposed by the judge. Our conclusion in this case, and one we believe in line with the authorities to which we have been referred, is that the proper sentence in respect of this matter, following a guilty plea, which was entered at the door of the court, would have been a sentence of the order of five and a half to six years.

30 We have, as is always the practice of the Court in a case of a referral of this kind, to make an allowance for what has become known as double jeopardy; that is, the fact that, through no fault of his own, the offender has had to go through the sentencing process twice. We make that allowance.

31 We think the justice of this case would be met if we reduced the sentence from that which we have indicated to one of four and a half years' imprisonment. Accordingly, we quash the sentence of three years' imprisonment and substitute for it one of four and a half years' imprisonment.

R. v PATRICK M

COURT OF APPEAL (Lord Justice Kennedy, Mr Justice Astill and Mr
Justice Gross): June 16, 2004

[2004] EWCA Crim 1679; [2005] 1 Cr.App.R.(S.) 49

LT Aggravating features; Detention; Kidnapping; Knives; Rape; Young
offenders

H1   *Long-term detention of juvenile—rape and kidnapping—rape with aggravating
     features—length of term of detention*

H2   Six years' detention under the Powers of Criminal Courts (Sentencing) Act
     2000, s.91 upheld for a rape with aggravating features committed by a youth
     aged 16 at the time.

H3   The appellant, aged 16 at the time of the offences, pleaded guilty to kidnapping
     and rape. The appellant approached a young woman who was walking home from
     a shop at night. When she told him she did not wish to talk to him any more, he
     pulled her arm and produced a knife which he held towards her neck. He forced
     her to walk to a children's playground, threatening to kill her with the knife. At
     the playground he made her kneel down, forced her to perform oral sex on him by
     threatening to kill her and then pulled her clothing down and raped her. He then
     dragged her across the play area and raped her again. The appellant denied the
     allegations at interview but pleaded guilty on re-arraignment, in the light of
     DNA evidence. Sentenced to six years' detention under the Powers of Criminal
     Courts (Sentencing) Act 2000, s.91, for rape, with three years' detention concur-
     rent for kidnapping.

H4   **Held:** (considering *Millberry* [2003] 2 Cr.App.R.(S.) 31 (p.142)) the appellant
     although young, had a bad record. The rape clearly attracted the higher starting
     point of eight years, as discussed in *Millberry*. The victim was abducted and
     raped twice and there were other significant aggravating features, forced oral
     sex and the use of a knife. This was a grave and deeply disturbing case. The dis-
     count for the appellant's age and plea was ample, bearing in mind that the plea
     followed the appellant having been traced through DNA. There was nothing
     wrong with the sentence passed by the judge. The appeal would be dismissed.

H5   **Case cited:**   *Millberry* [2003] 2 Cr.App.R.(S.) 31 (p.142)

H6   **References:** long term detention—rape, *Current Sentencing Practice* E 4

H7   *F. Tizzano* for the appellant.

JUDGMENT

1   **GROSS J.:**   On January 19, 2004, at the Crown Court at Wood Green, the appellant, who is now 18 (17 at the time of sentence and 16 at the time of the offences), pleaded guilty on re-arraignment and was sentenced as follows. For kidnapping, three years' detention under s.91 of the Powers of Criminal Courts (Sentencing) Act 2000, and for rape, a concurrent term of six years' detention under the same s.91. Other counts were left on the file on the usual terms. The total sentence was therefore six years' detention under s.91. The appellant appeals against sentence by leave of the single judge.

2   The facts may be summarised as follows. Shortly before 11pm on April 14, 2003, the 21-year-old victim left her home to purchase some cigarettes from her local shop. As she was making her way home afterwards, she entered an alley-way, where the appellant approached her from behind and engaged her in conversation. After a while, she told him she did not want to talk to him any more and was going home. At that point, he pulled her arm and as she turned towards him he produced a knife, which he held towards her neck. He told her to accompany him and to pretend she was his girlfriend. He threatened that if she made any noise or screamed, he would kill her. He linked his arm through hers and started to walk with her. He put the knife away and asked her if she knew any parks in the area. There was a further conversation about parks and her boyfriend and so on. The detail does not matter. Ultimately, she broke down, started crying and pleaded with him to release her. She began to struggle against him, at which point he produced the knife again, held it to the small of her back and forced her to walk with him. At one point, the victim saw a pedestrian, with whom she desperately tried to make eye contact, but the appellant again warned her not to scream or raise the alarm or he would kill her. To emphasise his point, he repeatedly poked her with the knife. The victim offered him her mobile telephone and money and asked him if he intended to hurt her, to which he replied he did not know. It depended on her giving some information.

3   Eventually, they arrived at a children's playground. He told her that she must have known about the park there and that she had lied to him earlier. Once in the park he made his way to a bench. He ordered her to kneel in front of him. He held the knife to her chest and undid his trousers. He moved the knife underneath her chin, forced her to tilt her head back and commanded her to perform oral sex on him. She refused. He threatened to kill her again. He grabbed hold of her head and compelled her to perform oral sex on him.

4   Finally, he stopped. As she got up and bent over to retrieve her handbag, he told her to remain in that position whist he took out a condom. He told her to take her trousers down. She resisted. There was a brief struggle. He pulled her trousers and underwear down and he raped her as she was leaning over the bench. He then dragged her across the play area, told her to lie on her back and raped her again. Subsequently it would seem that he took some money from her handbag, but that is neither here nor there in the context of these offences.

5 The victim ran out of the park in the opposite direction. Almost immediately she came across a couple standing outside their home. She told them what had happened. The police were contacted. It was by now about 11.34pm.

6 In interview the appellant initially denied all the allegations, but in a subsequent interview, after DNA samples had been taken from him, he declined to comment. Eventually, as already recorded, he pleaded guilty on re-arraignment.

7 When sentencing, the judge observed that the appellant had been traced through his DNA at the scene. The appellant was by then in custody for other matters. There had been no immediate "frank admission" in interview. That said, ultimately, there had been a plea of guilty which we underline, the judge remarked that he took into account and which saved the complainant the ordeal of giving evidence. The appellant was "a danger to young females". Notwithstanding his age, the appellant had a number of previous convictions and had not responded to community punishments.

8 The appellant's antecedents show that, despite his young age, he had accumulated between May 2000 and August 2003 eight convictions comprising 16 offences. These included having an article with a blade with a sharp point, assault occasioning actual bodily harm, and possession of an offensive weapon in a public place.

9 The judge took into account the appellant's plea and his age, given that he was still only 16 at the time of committing the offence, and also the principle of totality. The judge remarked that the sentence passed was less than it would have been for an older person.

10 Before us today Mr Tizzano's submissions proceeded as follows. First, the judge had taken too high a starting point. Secondly, the judge had given insufficient credit for the plea and the appellant's age. Thirdly, Mr Tizzano asks us to have regard to the guidelines and the individual cases in *Millberry* [2003] 2 Cr.App.R.(S.) 31 (p.142). Fourthly, Mr Tizzano said that the appellant had shown remorse and that he had made substantial efforts to improve himself whilst in custody.

11 With respect, and despite Mr Tizzano's forceful submissions, we are wholly unable to accept them. This appellant had a bad record, even at his young age. He had the chance of responding to community punishments, but he chose not to. The rape here plainly attracted the higher starting point of eight years, as discussed in *Millberry*. The complainant was abducted and was raped twice. Moreover, there were significant aggravating features: the forced oral sex, and the use of a knife. Sentence is *not* a mechanistic arithmetical exercise. *Millberry* at para.[34] sets out the true role of guidance as follows:

> "Before concluding our general guidance with regard to sentencing on rape, and turning to the cases of the individual offenders, we would emphasise that the guidelines such as we have set out above can produce sentences which are inappropriately high or inappropriately low if sentencers merely adopt a mechanistic approach to the guidelines. It is essential that, having taken the guidelines into account, sentencers stand back and look at the circumstances as a whole and impose a sentence which is appropriate, having

regard to all the circumstances. Double accounting must be avoided and can be as a result of guidelines if they are applied indiscriminately. Guideline judgments are intended to assist the judge arrive at the correct sentence. They do not purport to identify the correct sentence. Doing so is the task of the trial judge."

12   This was a grave and deeply disturbing case. The discount given by the judge for age and plea, bearing in mind too that the plea followed the appellant having been traced through DNA, was both ample and substantial. Discounts are not set in stone. In a case of this nature progress in custody, while always welcome and of course in the appellant's own interests, does not persuade us to reduce the sentence further. Nor does the fact that the appellant spent time on remand for other matters, which will not reduce his sentence. The reality is that for this appalling case there is nothing whatever wrong with the sentence passed by the judge. Even at 16, the appellant knew full well that what he did was very wrong indeed. This appeal is dismissed.

R. v DAVID ANDREW PARFITT

COURT OF APPEAL (Lord Justice Kay, Mr Justice Curtis and Mr Justice Newman): June 16, 2004

[2004] EWCA Crim 1755; [2005] 1 Cr.App.R.(S.) 50

_LT_ Aggravating features; Consecutive sentences; Manslaughter; Police officers; Sentence length; TWOC

I1   _Manslaughter—manslaughter of police officer attempting to prevent driver of vehicle escaping—driver driving vehicle away with officer hanging on to window—officer falling and receiving fatal injuries—length of sentence_

I2   Twelve years' imprisonment upheld for manslaughter where the appellant drove away in a vehicle while a police officer was attempting to prevent him from escape by holding on to the window, causing the officer to fall and suffer fatal injuries.

3   The appellant was convicted of manslaughter on an indictment charging murder. He pleaded guilty to burglary, theft, driving while disqualified, and taking a conveyance. The appellant, who was a disqualified driver, stole a car and continued to use it for some time. He was seen by police officers driving the vehicle and made off on foot. He hid in the garage of the house and was able to persuade the occupant of the house to call a taxi. When the taxi arrived, the appellant ran to the taxi and got into the driver's seat. A police officer went to the driver's door in an attempt to detain the appellant, and got an arm inside the window. The vehicle drove off, at increasing speed and the officer was dragged along. The appellant caused the car to swerve from side to side while the taxi-

driver in the passenger seat attempted to reach the ignition key. After about 100 yards, the officer was dislodged from the vehicle and fell, hitting his head on a bollard and then on the kerb. The officer died two days later. The taxi-driver was able to stop the car and the appellant ran away. He was arrested the following day after a struggle. Sentenced to 12 years' imprisonment for manslaughter, with sentences totalling 12 months' imprisonment consecutive for the other offences (total sentence, 13 years' imprisonment).

H4   **Held:** (considering *Rule* [2003] 1 Cr.App.R.(S.) 47 (p.224), *Pimm* (1993) 14 Cr.App.R.(S.) 730, *Wright* [2004] 1 Cr.App.R.(S.) 4 (p.40)) it was submitted that the case should be approached as if the appellant had pleaded guilty to manslaughter throughout. The Court had considered other decisions. In those decisions the Court did not indicate that any sentence longer than the sentence passed would have been inappropriate; the Court was simply considering whether the sentences imposed were manifestly excessive. Looking at the facts of the present case, the case was worse than any of the others. The appellant was a man who had been recently released from prison and caused the death of a police officer doing his duty. These circumstances made it a particularly aggravated form of manslaughter. The Court had reached the conclusion that the sentence was not manifestly excessive. It was within the appropriate range, bearing in mind the aggravating features. There was nothing wrong in making the other sentences consecutive. The appeal would be dismissed.

H5   **Cases cited:** *Rule* [2003] 1 Cr.App.R.(S.) 47 (p.224), *Pimm* (1993) 14 Cr.App.R.(S.) (p.730), *Wright* [2004] 1 Cr.App.R.(S.) 4 (p.40)

H6   *I. Way* for the appellant.
        P. Joyce Q.C. for the Crown.

JUDGMENT

1   **KAY L.J.:**   On December 2, 2003, in the Crown Court at Nottingham, the appellant pleaded guilty on re-arraignment to a number of counts. On December 11, 2003, at the same court before Tracey J. and a jury, he was found not guilty of a further count of murder but guilty of the alternative of manslaughter. The counts to which he pleaded guilty were theft, driving whilst disqualified, burglary and taking a conveyance. The judge imposed sentences that totalled 13 years. The bulk of those sentences represented a sentence of 12 years' imprisonment for the manslaughter offence and the other matters were concurrent sentences totalling 12 months for the various other offences, the 12 months being imposed for an offence of theft. He appeals against sentence with leave of the single judge.

2   In May 2001 the appellant was sentenced to two years' imprisonment for an offence of robbery. In due course he was released on licence subject to tagging and to regular drug testing. He breached his licence conditions by taking drugs and failing to attend probation appointments, and in November 2002 his licence was revoked.

3   On December 31, 2002, in Derby, he stole a Vauxhall Astra motorcar and drove it to his home address in Nottingham and, although a disqualified driver, continued to use it for the next week.

4   In the early afternoon of January 7, 2003 police officers in Nottingham saw him driving the Astra. He abandoned the vehicle and made off on foot, followed by the officers. He managed to hide in the garage of a house, where he was found by the lone female occupant. He told her that he had been attacked over a drug debt and asked to use the telephone to call a taxi.

5   The taxi, driven by Mr Camm, attended. As the appellant left the premises he was seen by a police officer, Constable Walker, a dog handler, who was involved in the search. The appellant ran to the driver's door of the taxi and jumped in, while the taxi driver ran after him and got into the front passenger seat.

6   At the same time Constable Walker went to the driver's door in an attempt to detain the appellant, and managed to get his arm or arms inside the window and thereby to hang on. He remained initially running alongside the vehicle as it drove off, and then as its speed increased he was dragged along, still attached to his dog. The appellant accelerated off in first gear. He was swerving from side to side in an attempt to dislodge Constable Walker. Mr Camm, the taxi driver, meanwhile shouted to the appellant to stop and tried to hold the steering wheel to control the vehicle and reach the ignition key. Mr Camm also heard Constable Walker clearly frightened, shouting, "Stop it, you'll kill me, stop it". After a distance of about 100 yards the officer appears to have been dislodged from the vehicle and fell, hit his head on a central reservation bollard and then on the kerb. Constable Walker died from his injuries two days later.

7   The appellant continued in the vehicle until Mr Camm was able to grab the ignition key, which broke, and the vehicle came to a halt. The appellant then ran from the vehicle. He later broke into an outhouse and stole painting materials and took a motor van.

8   The following day the appellant was traced to his mother's address and found to be hiding in the loft area. He tried to escape the officers by breaking through the roof, but was restrained after a violent struggle.

9   In interview the appellant said he had been aware of the officer shouting for him to stop and that the officer appeared to be running alongside the vehicle. He said he believed the officer was trying to seize the ignition key. As he accelerated the officer disappeared from view. He said that he had not wished to harm the officer.

0   The appellant did not contest the other counts apart from the murder charge. So far as that was concerned, he had from an early stage indicated that he accepted he was guilty of manslaughter. That fact was made known verbally and in writing to the Crown, and the Crown rejected that plea and he went to trial on the single count of murder. The case was conducted in such a way that the jury were made aware that he conceded his guilt of manslaughter, of which they subsequently convicted him.

      In passing sentence, the trial judge said this:

"Although you have been acquitted of the crime of murder, I nonetheless regard this as an extremely serious case of manslaughter. Your conduct was aggravated by the following factors: you, plainly, disregarded warnings given to you by your reluctant passenger, Mr Camm, and his pleas to you to stop. You, plainly, disregarded what you acknowledge were the cries from the police officer to stop, whether or not you heard remarks he made that you were going to kill him. You, plainly, disregarded his cries to stop. You persisted in a course of driving, despite those warnings and pleas, and you persisted despite the attempt of Mr Camm to stop you driving the vehicle by turning the wheel and by attempting to get the ignition key.

It must have been obvious to you, as we have seen from the photographs of St Albans Road, that there were obstacles ahead, various sets of bollards, a parked vehicle. You were driving daytime when there were likely to be vehicles coming the other way in a built-up area. Nonetheless, drive on you did. You, again, as you appreciated and acknowledged in the evidence which you gave, were aware that the officer was at the side of your car.

You were offending at a time when you were on licence from prison. Your record in relation to motoring and in relation to your regard to other road users is dreadful and, plainly, those are all severely aggravating features.

But the gravest of the aggravating features of this case is the causing of death to a police officer who was doing his duty in the course of your attempt to escape from justice and to escape from being brought, rightly, to custody as you should have been."

12   On behalf of the appellant it is submitted that the sentence of 12 years was manifestly excessive for this offence of manslaughter. It is further submitted that whilst, in principle, it may have been right to impose a consecutive sentence of 12 months in relation to the theft and other matters, having regard to totality the sentences ought in any event to have been made concurrent with one another.

13   So far as the sentence in respect of manslaughter is concerned, our attention has been drawn to two cases by Mr Way. The first of those cases is the case of *Rule* [2003] 1 Cr.App.R.(S.) 47 (p.224). That was a case in which, again, a police officer was killed by a motorist. The circumstances were somewhat different. In that case the police officer was conducting radar checking of motor vehicles' speed, and as the appellant approached, at 52mph in a 30mph limit, the officer stepped out in order to use his radar gun. The appellant in that case's response was to swerve towards him in an attempt to frighten the officer so that he would jump backwards. The officer did not do so. The appellant misjudged the extent of his swerve and collided with the officer, killing him. The sentence imposed on that occasion was one of nine years' imprisonment. The single judge in relation to that matter had refused leave, and the full court, when it came to consider the matter, concluded that he was right to do so since it was not even arguable that the sentence was manifestly excessive.

14   The other case drawn to our attention by Mr Way is an older case, *Pimm* (1993) 14 Cr.App.R.(S.) (p.730). There again the Court of Appeal upheld a sentence of nine years, it being nine years' detention in a young offender institution, in

relation to a driver who had carried a person who was trying to stop him from taking a vehicle on the bonnet of his car until he fell off and so suffered fatal injuries. Again, the Court's view was that nine years could not be seen to be manifestly excessive.

15   Apart from those two authorities, we have also looked at the case of *Wright* [2004] 1 Cr.App.R.(S.) 4 (p.40). That again was a case in which the Court upheld a long sentence for manslaughter involving the use of a motor vehicle, the sentence on that occasion being one of eight years' imprisonment. Again, on that occasion it was the carrying of somebody on the bonnet until they fell off sustaining fatal injuries.

16   Mr Way submits to us that those cases demonstrate that the appropriate level of sentencing in this case was less than 12 years.

17   He submits, with justification, that the proper approach to this case is to deal with it as if it had been a plea of guilty to manslaughter throughout since, but for the prosecution wishing the jury to determine whether it was murder or not, that is what it would have been. We certainly accept that part of his argument and approach the case in that way.

18   He submits that when one looks at the facts, particularly of *Rule* and of *Pimm*, this case is not as serious as those cases, or at the very least is no more serious. Hence, he submits that since in each of those cases sentences of nine years were deemed to be appropriate, something of the same order would have been appropriate in this case.

19   We have carefully considered those submissions. The first point that we would wish to make is that in neither of those cases was the Court of Appeal saying that any longer sentence would have been inappropriate; the Court was simply considering sentences of nine years and determining whether or not they were manifestly excessive. In the one case they concluded it was not; in the other case they thought it was so clear a case that they would not even grant leave to appeal. It seems to us that one cannot draw the inference that Mr Way suggests, that the appropriate level of sentencing, even in those cases of the highest proper level of sentencing, is one of nine years' imprisonment.

20   We, therefore, have to look at the facts of this case. In our judgment, this case was worse than each of those other cases in any event. This was a case where a man, who was in breach of his licence anyway, having been released from prison, was committing offences and was approached by a police officer doing his duty. As the learned judge made clear, the fact that the killing was in those circumstances makes it a particularly aggravated form of manslaughter.

21   The other factors are that there was no doubt at all that two people were making clear to this appellant that he should stop—one was the police officer, who, we are satisfied, the judge concluded was telling him that he would be killed if he continued. The judge was not sure that the appellant necessarily heard that part of it, but it is clear from his sentencing remarks that he was quite sure that the appellant knew that he was shouting for him to stop. Common sense would have dictated to anyone that to continue in the circumstances in which he was driving was as dangerous an act as one could possibly imagine, and the sort of danger involved, of necessity, either very serious injury or death to the person concerned.

22   We are aware and take into account that the jury were not satisfied that this was a case of murder. It is perhaps right to observe that if the jury had thought it was murder, the least sentence that we see that could have been determined as being the appropriate sentence in respect of him would have been one that would have led to him remaining in custody for 14 years before such time as he was considered for parole, the equivalent of a minimum of a 28-year sentence. Thus, this sentence of 12 years has to be seen in that context, and it is clear that the judge was making a very significant allowance for the fact that the jury were not satisfied that this was a case of murder. Nonetheless, as he rightly observed, it was right up at the top of the bracket of cases of this kind.

23   We have to ask ourselves whether in those circumstances we could properly conclude that this was a sentence that was manifestly excessive. We have come to the conclusion that it was not. It was within the range that was appropriate to a judge bearing in mind the aggravating features which he so clearly set out in the passage to which we have already referred.

24   The second issue is whether or not a sentence of 12 months should have been made to run consecutively, or whether, as is submitted, it should have been concurrent.

25   Generally speaking, in our judgment, where a person has committed offences and causes injury to another in his attempt to escape, particularly a police officer, that should attract, as a matter of principle, a consecutive sentence so that offenders know full well that if they aggravate the offences that they have committed by harming others they will get additional penalties and the two will not be merged in the way that happens with concurrent sentences.

26   We see no reason to think that the judge could not properly reach the conclusion that he did that it was right to impose the sentence of 12 months and make the 12 years consecutive. We have no doubt he had regard to the totality of the matter in fixing the sentence that he did, and it follows that we can see nothing wrong at all with the sentences that he passed. For those reasons, this appeal is dismissed.

R. v ANTHONY HAMPSON, DAVID JAMES HAMPSON

COURT OF APPEAL (Mrs Justice Hallett and Mr Justice Treacy):
June 18, 2004

[2004] EWCA Crim 2011; [2005] 1 Cr.App.R.(S.) 51

⟨LT⟩ Conspiracy; Conversion of firearms; Guilty pleas; Sentence length

H1 *Firearms offences—converting imitation firearms to fire live ammunition—length of sentence*

H2 Six years' imprisonment upheld for conspiring to convert imitation firearms to fire live ammunition.

H3 The appellants pleaded guilty to conspiring to convert an imitation firearm into a firearm. Searches of the homes of the appellants led to the discovery of a number of imitation firearms which had been converted to firearms. Examination established that the imitation firearms had been converted by sawing off the barrels and inserting steel tubes to create new barrels. The converted weapons were then able to fire live ammunition. Sentenced to six years' imprisonment and five and a half years' imprisonment respectively.

H4 **Held:** the sentencing judge observed that the appellants were engaged in converting imitation firearms into functioning lethal weapons which would have found their way to criminals. The methods used were sophisticated and the operation had lasted for a considerable time. The maximum sentence for the offence was seven years' imprisonment. The Court was entirely satisfied that the sentences adequately reflected the credit to which the appellants were entitled by reason of their pleas. The appeals would be dismissed.

5 **References:** firearms offences, *Current Sentencing Practice* B 3-3

6 *A. Carney* for the appellants.

JUDGMENT

1 **HALLETT J.:** On November 11, 2003 at the Liverpool Crown Court before H.H. Judge Boulton the appellants, Anthony John Hampson and David James Hampson, who are brothers, changed their pleas to guilty to conspiracy to convert an imitation firearm into a firearm. H.H. Judge Boulton sentenced Anthony Hampson to six years' imprisonment and David Hampson to five years and six months' imprisonment. A count of conspiracy to sell firearms and ammunition was ordered to remain on the file in the usual terms.

2   They appeal against sentence by leave of the single judge.

3   The background to the offence is as follows. On September 25, 2002 police officers searched the home of David Hampson in Liverpool. They discovered £12,000 in cash, and removed a number of items related to firearms. There were prohibited firearms which had been converted from blank firing parts. There were parts of prohibited firearms, improvised ammunition, a modified blank firing gun, parts removed from a blank firing gun and debris from dismantled ammunition. On forensic examination experts established that imitation firearms had been converted by sawing off the barrels and inserting lengths of steel tubing to create new barrels. The converted pistols were then able to fire live ammunition. The examination also showed that blank cartridges had been converted by drilling out the cartridge and inserting a missile.

4   David Hampson was arrested. He made no comment in interview.

5   On December 6, 2002 the police searched the home of his brother Anthony. This was also in Liverpool. Anthony Hampson was arrested and removed from the flat. During the search police officers discovered a rifle and a self-loading pistol that had to be made safe by the armed response unit. They also recovered eight prohibited firearms converted from blank firing guns, prohibited ammunition, improvised bulleted ammunition, debris and dismantled ammunition and ammunition components associated with reloading. Fingerprint evidence established a link between the premises of both the brothers.

6   Anthony Hampson, too, gave a no comment interview.

7   In sentencing the appellants H.H. Judge Boulton observed that they were engaged in converting imitation firearms into fully functioning lethal firearms. These weapons would have found their way to criminals in or around Merseyside. This, it seems, had been accepted by the appellants. The premises and methods used, said the learned judge, were sophisticated and the operation had lasted for a considerable time. They had been making genuine firearms, and, although no use was made of the firearms found, the fact that they were going to find themselves in the hands of serious criminals was taken into account.

8   Both the appellants had bad records. Anthony Hampson had two previous convictions for firearms offences. David Hampson did not and the judge was prepared to make a "tiny distinction" between them. The learned judge said that there was no more serious way of committing this particular offence, and had the appellants been convicted on the more serious count they would have been facing eight years' imprisonment each. A minor discount was given for the guilty pleas, but to some extent they had already benefited from that as the Crown did not proceed with count 2.

9   As far as Anthony Hampson, who is 48 years of age, is concerned, his previous convictions go back many years. He has 35 previous court appearances for over 77 offences. These offences include offences of theft, offences associated with motor vehicles, supplying class A drugs and assault. The firearms offences to which the learned judge referred occurred in 1999, when he was sentenced to six months' imprisonment. David Hampson has 12 previous court appearances for 23 offences going back to 1980. These included numerous offences of dishonesty.

10   On behalf of Anthony Hampson it was argued that the sentence was excessive in that the learned judge had failed to give him proper credit for his plea of guilty. Secondly, it was argued that the learned judge wrongly indicated he was discounting the credit for the plea of guilty on the basis that the Crown had chosen not to proceed with the more serious count on the indictment. In any event, this was not the most serious case of its kind, because the weapons converted were crude and the tools used were simple.

11   Similar arguments were advanced on behalf of David Hampson. We were reminded that the maximum sentence for a substantive offence of this kind is seven years, and that, it was said, was the wrong starting point. Again, it was argued that inappropriate credit had been given for the guilty plea and the judge should not have reflected the fact that the Crown had not proceeded with count 2 in the sentence he imposed.

12   The learned single judge in granting leave observed that the judge was wrong to suggest that he was discounting the credit that he would give in the light of the Crown's attitude to count 2. On that basis he recommended that the sentence be reconsidered by this Court.

13   We respectfully agree with the single judge that it was appropriate to reconsider these sentences in the light of the learned judge's unfortunate remark about count 2. It was not appropriate, in our judgment, to make such a comment. We wonder, however, if that remark had not been made, whether anybody would have advised either of these two appellants that these sentences were fit for appeal. These converted guns and the associated equipment may well have been crude, the tools used may have been simple, but they were, nonetheless, potentially lethal. It was inevitable that they would end up, as the learned judge pointed out, in the hands of serious criminals in the Merseyside area. This was plainly a well organised and continuing conspiracy to convert these firearms. Whether or not the tools used were simple or the weapons themselves crude, would, we suspect, be of little comfort to the innocent member of the public at the receiving end of a gun being pointed at them.

14   Given the armoury of weapons converted by these two brothers and the potential effect of their conversion of them, we entirely agree with the sentencing judge that this was a very serious offence of its kind. It is right to say that the maximum sentence for one substantive offence is seven years, but this case was, of course, a conspiracy involving a large number of weapons and ammunition equipped to make those weapons lethal.

5   Having put to one side the unfortunate remark of the learned judge, as we have indicated, and having looked afresh at the circumstances of this offence, and the circumstances of these offenders, we are entirely satisfied that a sentence of this length adequately reflects the credit to which these two appellants were entitled. In our judgment, men who involve themselves in converting firearms to be used on the streets of this country deserve little or no sympathy from these courts. Accordingly, they cannot complain when they receive sentences of this length, albeit on pleas of guilty. Accordingly, the appeals must be dismissed.

ATTORNEY GENERAL'S REFERENCE NO.3 OF 2004 (ANDREW FRANK AKUFFO)

COURT OF APPEAL (Lord Justice Hooper, Mr Justice Bell and Mr Justice Keith): June 18, 2004

[2004] EWCA Crim 1532; [2005] 1 Cr.App.R.(S.) 52

(LT) Associated offences; Automatic life imprisonment; Double jeopardy; Minimum term; Parole; Seriousness of offence; Totality of sentence; Undue leniency

H1   *Automatic life sentence—offender convicted of other offences not subject to life imprisonment—calculation of specified period*

H2   Where an offender is sentenced to life imprisonment for one or more offences, and to concurrent determinate sentences for other associated offences, the specified period should take account of the combination of all the offences for which the offender is to be sentenced. The specified part of the sentence should relate to the total determinate sentence appropriate for the totality of the offender's offending in respect of the primary offence and the other associated offences.

H3   The offender was convicted of two counts of possessing a firearm with intent to endanger life, three counts of possessing Class A controlled drugs with intent to supply, and one count of handling stolen property. The offender was seen by police officers driving a borrowed car. He failed to stop when required to do so and was chased for some distance before getting out of the vehicle and running away. He was eventually detained. A loaded hand gun with live ammunition was found along the route which he had taken. The gun and the ammunition were both prohibited weapons for the purposes of the Firearms Act 1968 s.5. The offender was released on bail. Some months later the offender was kept under observation on suspicion of dealing in drugs. He was eventually approached by armed officers and a semi-automatic hand gun was found in a pocket of a vehicle from which he was removed. The hand gun contained live ammunition. A search of premises occupied by the offender's girlfriend disclosed a substantial sum in cash. Various quantities of drugs were found in the car. The offender had numerous previous convictions going back to 1988. He had been convicted of robbery, burglary, escape from custody and theft. As a result of these offences he had a accumulated a total sentence of 17.5 years' imprisonment, consisting of an aggregate of various terms, the first of which was imposed in July 1991. It was accepted that by virtue of his previous convictions, he was liable to an automatic life sentence under the Powers of Criminal Courts (Sentencing) Act 2000, s.109. Sentenced to life imprisonment on each count of possessing a firearm with intent to endanger life, with a minimum term of four and a half years (derived from a notional determinate sentence of

12 years), with sentences of eight years and two years all concurrent for three other offences. The Attorney General asked the Court to review the sentence on the ground that it was unduly lenient.

H4   **Held:** the Attorney General submitted that the offences were aggravated by the fact that the offences were committed while the offender was on licence from the earlier sentences, the second firearms offence was committed while he was on police bail for the first, the firearms which were loaded were being carried in public places, and were prohibited weapons. The second firearms offence was committed while the offender was actively supplying Class A drugs. It was submitted for the Attorney General that the sentencing judge's notional determinate sentence for the firearms offences of 12 years' imprisonment failed to reflect the gravity of each of the offences in the indictment, in view of the aggravating features. The Court began by asking itself what would be the appropriate sentence if a sentence of life imprisonment had not been passed. It was accepted that because the aggregate sentence of 17.5 years included a term which had been imposed before October 1, 1992, the power to order the offender to return to prison in respect of the earlier sentences under the Powers of Criminal Courts (Sentencing) Act 2000, s.116, did not apply and the sentencing judge would have had no power to order the offender to return to prison to serve the balance of that sentence. The Court took the view that an appropriate sentence for the totality of offending for which the offender had to be sentenced was at least 16 years, taking into account all the aggravating features including the fact that the offences were committed while he was on licence from the earlier sentence. The Court then considered the Powers of Criminal Courts (Sentencing) Act 2000, s.82A, which required the court to specify a period which it considered appropriate taking into account "the seriousness of the offence, or of the combination of the offence and one or more offences associated with it". Section 161(1) of the Act, provided that an offence was associated with another if the offender was convicted of it in the proceedings in which he was convicted of the other offence. It followed that all the offences other than the firearms offences for which the offender fell to be sentenced were associated offences for the purposes of s.82A. The Court had held in *Lundberg* (1995) 16 Cr.App.R.(S.) 948 that in fixing the minimum period to be served in conjunction with a discretionary life sentence, the court should take into account the combination of all the offences for which the offender was to be sentenced. The specified part of the sentence must relate to the total determinate sentence appropriate for the totality of the offender's offending in respect of the primary offence and the other associated offences. In *Hann* [1996] 1 Cr.App.R.(S.) 267 the Court had reached a decision to similar effect. In the Court's view, if this approach were not adopted, a person sentenced to life imprisonment for a number of different offences would be given an opportunity to apply for parole at a time earlier than he would be able to do so if he had not been sentenced to life imprisonment. A defendant should not be in a better position because he had been given a life sentence. The principle was demonstrated again in *Haywood* [2000] 2 Cr.App.R.(S.) 418. Applying the principle in *Lundberg*, the Court had reached the conclusion that the sentencing judge should have set a period of at least 16 years as the appropriate notional determinate sentence. It was contended for the Attorney General that the specific period should have been higher than one half of the notional determinate sentence. The Court had considered this question in *Szczerba* [2002] 2 Cr.App.R.(S.) 86 (p.387), where it was said that more than half of the notional determinate sentence might be specified if the offender was liable to an order for return to custody in relation to an earlier sentence under the Powers of Criminal Courts (Sentencing) Act 2000, s.116. As the offender was not liable to be returned to custody under s.116, the Court agreed that the sentencing judge was right to take half of the notional determinate sentence as the basis of the specified period. The Court would halve the notional determinate sentence of 16 years, so as to produce a provisional period of eight years. It was not argued on the Attorney General's behalf that the sentencing judge was wrong to deduct from half of the notional determinate sentence a period equal to the period spent in custody on remand. It followed that the provisional specified period of eight years was reduced to six and a half years. The final question was the element of double jeopardy. It had now been established in *Attorney General's Reference No.6 of 2000 (Simon Goldsmith)* [2001] 1 Cr.App.R.(S.) 20 (p.72) that where the Attorney General argued successfully that a s.82A period was unduly lenient, the Court would give some discount but not as much as was normally given. The Court would accordingly deduct a period of six months from the six and a half years so as to produce a final specified minimum period of six years instead of the four and a half years specified by the sentencing judge.

H5   **Cases cited:** *Lundberg* (1995) 16 Cr.App.R.(S.) 948, *Hann* [1996] 1 Cr.App.R.(S.) 267, *Haywood* [2000] 2 Cr.App.R.(S.) 418, *Szczerba* [2002] 2 Cr.App.R.(S.) 86 (p.387), *Attorney General's Reference No.6 of 2000 (Simon Goldsmith)* [2001] 1 Cr.App.R.(S.) 20 (p.72)

H6   **Commentary:** [2004] Crim.L.R. 956

H7   **References:** life imprisonment, specified period, *Current Sentencing Practice* F 3-4

H8   *R. Horwell* for the Attorney General.
       K. Metzger for the offender.

JUDGMENT

1   **HOOPER L.J.:**   We grant the Attorney Capital General leave to make a reference in this case.

2   The offender is Andrew Frank Akuffo. He is 36 years of age having been born on July 20, 1967.

3   The offender was charged on an indictment containing eight counts. He pleaded not guilty to each count. On December 5, 2003 he was convicted before H.H. Judge Hawkins Q.C. and a jury after a trial at the Central Criminal Court of

the following six offences: possessing a firearm with intent to endanger life (Count 1); possessing a firearm with intent to endanger life (Count 3); three offences of possessing a controlled drug of class A with intent to supply it to another (Counts 5 to 7) and handling stolen goods (Count 8). No verdicts were taken on Counts 2 and 4 which were lesser alternatives to Counts 1 and 3.

4   By virtue of a previous serious qualifying offence under s.109 of the Powers of Criminal Courts (Sentencing) Act 2000, ("the 2000 Act") the offender was liable to an automatic life sentence. It being conceded that there were no exceptional circumstances, the offender was sentenced to imprisonment for life for the offences in Counts 1 and 3. The sentence in respect of each drugs offence was eight years' imprisonment concurrent and for the handling offence two years' imprisonment concurrent.

5   The judge went on to set the specified minimum period after which the offender could make an application to have his case considered by the Parole Board. He indicated that were the automatic life sentence not required he would have passed determinate sentences of 12 years' imprisonment on each of the firearms offences; eight years concurrent for each drugs offence; and two years' concurrent for the handling.

6   He then took account of the period the offender had served in custody on remand awaiting his trial which was 18 months and (after a temporary miscalculation), gave the specified period as four and a half years. He had thus used a proportion of one half of the notional determinate sentence of 12 years.

7   The agreed facts in the Reference are as follows, as slightly amended during the hearing:

> "(i) In summary, the offender, a persistent robber and burglar who had used an imitation firearm in the past and who had been given early release by the Parole Board from a total sentence of $17\frac{1}{2}$ years' imprisonment, was arrested twice by police officers with a loaded firearm in his possession. On the second occasion he also had a quantity of three different class A drugs, some split into small saleable packages, and was using a stolen high value car with false number plates. The two firearms offences were committed four months apart, the second one together with the drugs and handling offences, whilst he was on bail for the first.
>
> (ii) The facts in more detail were: at about 11.30pm on Saturday 16th February 2002 the offender was alone, driving a borrowed car in south London. Police officers in a marked patrol car noticed that the front offside headlight was defective and followed the offender intending to stop the vehicle. They used their blue lights and flashing headlights but the offender did not stop. He appeared to be following another car ahead of him. In spite of the continued flashing and use of the blue lights, and, eventually, the two tone siren, the offender ignored the attempts to stop him. Instead he accelerated away and in due course turned sharply down a road in contravention of a 'No Entry' sign. The chase continued until the offender abruptly got out

of his vehicle at a busy junction. He left the engine running and ran away chased by police. The offender's car ran into a stationary vehicle.

(iii) The offender was eventually detained in Almeric Road SW11, having climbed over several fences and in and out of various private gardens. When asked why he had failed to stop for police he replied that it was because he did not have a licence.

(iv) Just before midnight a member of the public found a loaded hand-gun which had been discarded into the road along the route the offender had taken.

(v) The firearm was examined and found to be a 'Mauser' self-loading pistol with a housed magazine containing 6 rounds of .32mm live ammunition and one round in the breech. It was a prohibited weapon under section 5 (1) (aba) of the Firearms Act 1968 as amended, due to its dimensions.

(vi) The ammunition was live and 'hollow point', designed to expand on impact. It was similarly prohibited under section 5 (1A) (f) of the Firearms Act 1968 as amended.

(vii) During subsequent examination of his clothes a single particle of firearms residue was found in the left inside pocket of the jacket the offender was wearing at the time of his arrest. Firearms residue containing similar chemical components was also found in a sample from the bore of the hand-gun.

(viii) When interviewed on 17th February 2002 the offender denied knowledge of the firearm and said the money belonged to his girlfriend. He claimed to have been unaware that the police were trying to stop his vehicle and did not recall contravening 'No Entry' signs or that he had left the car while it was still in motion. The car belonged to his friend and he was driving to his girlfriend's home in Almeric Road.

(ix) The offender was released on bail.

(x) On Monday 10th and Tuesday 11th June 2002 the offender was kept under observation by the police as it was suspected that he was dealing in cocaine. He was seen in the South, West and East London area driving a black Golf registration S854 GGP. His girlfriend Sasha Beckford was seen driving a silver BMW carrying the number plate 'Y488 WKE'.

(xi) During the period of observation the offender was seen to meet with a number of unknown males in various locations. At 2.10pm on 11th June 2002 he was seen arriving in Almeric Road in the Black Golf, walking to the next street, going to the boot of the unattended silver BMW which was parked there and taking out an orange/red plastic carrier bag. He handed the bag to an unknown man who had come out of 26, Almeric Road and both of them went back into that property.

(xii) After further comings and goings during which the offender left and returned to the address in Almeric Road, the offender re-emerged from No. 26 at 3.58pm. He was carrying the red/orange bag but it was now rolled up. He went to the silver BMW and left the bag in that car. He then drove away in the black Golf with the other man who had originally taken the bag from him earlier that afternoon. At 4.57pm the offender was approached by armed police officers while he was in the black Golf in Wandsworth Road SW8 together with another man, Leon Ennis. As the offender was removed from the vehicle by the police a black semi-automatic hand-gun could be seen in a pocket of the driver's door. The offender was arrested on suspicion of being concerned in the supply of class A controlled drugs.

(xiii) After the arrests searches were carried out on the black Golf, the silver BMW and 26, Almeric Road.

(xiv) From the black Golf, the firearm found in the driver's door pocket was examined. It was a Valtro 9mm self-loading pistol and the magazine contained 5 rounds of 9mm live ammunition. Also in the car was a single car key on a BMW fob.

(vx) The flat at 26B Almeric Road was occupied by the offender's girlfriend Sasha Beckford. Keys to the flat were found on the offender. During the search £6,770 in cash was found in a blue plastic carrier bag in the bedroom. The money was not in paper seals of £1,000 each but in bundles of £100 in various denominations with one of the notes folded over the others in each £100. In the same carrier bag was found the offender's passport.

(xvi) A quantity of empty bank money bags was found on the left hand side of the chimney breast in the living room together with a clear self seal bag containing a quantity of elastic bands.

(xvii) The silver BMW was searched, it was entered using the key found in the black Golf. In the glove compartment on the front passenger side were found two plastic bags, one of them red, containing a number of other bags within which was found powder which appeared to be cocaine and crystals which appeared to be crack cocaine. The red bag also contained a set of electronic scales. The car itself was stolen and was bearing false number plates.

(xviii) The drugs were analysed and found to consist of 131g of powder cocaine in one bag, 176.323g of crack cocaine in 8 separate cling film packages and 14.496g of heroin in 2 plastic packages. The estimated street value of the drugs was £28,000.

(xix) The offender's fingerprints were found on the bags in which the drugs were contained.

(xx) The banknotes were analysed for contamination by controlled drugs. The frequency of contamination from heroin on the notes was higher than would be expected on banknotes taken from general circulation although the frequency of contamination from cocaine was typical of that found on notes in general circulation.

(xxi) The firearm was further examined and found to be a modified firearm and a prohibited weapon. It had been produced as a blank cartridge firing pistol but had been adapted by the removal of the original obstructed barrel and its replacement by an unobstructed barrel which would allow the discharge of projectiles. It was a prohibited weapon under section 5 (1) of the Firearms Act 1968 as amended.

(xxii) The ammunition consisted of modified blank cartridges which had had the original plastic closures removed and replaced with metal projectiles. The ammunition was live and capable of causing lethal injury.

(xxiii) Swabs were taken from the firearm and ammunition. A DNA profile matching that of the offender was found on the lower back of the handle.

(xxiv) When interviewed on 12th June 2002 the offender claimed to have been in the process of buying the silver BMW car from an acquaintance who had temporarily left the country. The car had been left with him and while he was checking the boot to see if it had a spare tyre he found hidden a bag in which there were drugs and the gun. He said that he had spent a couple of days deciding what to do and had shown the items to various people. He said that he had been advised to hand the gun into the police but was concerned that he would be implicated. He said that he had almost made up his mind to do as he had been advised but was arrested.

(xxv) The offender was charged in respect of the firearm found in the black Golf, the drugs found in the silver BMW and handling the stolen BMW itself on 12th June 2002. No one else was charged with any offences arising from these facts.

(xxvi) The offender was interviewed again on 10th September 2002 in respect of the 17th February 2002 arrest. On this occasion he made no comment to all questions he was asked. He was charged with this earlier offence on 10th September 2002."

8   The offender had been in custody from his arrest on June 12, 2002.

9   The offender has a number of previous convictions going back to 1988. In the years between 1988 and 1996 the offender was convicted of three robberies, one of them armed, six burglaries or attempted burglaries and also offences of affray, escape from custody and theft. In 1988 the offender was sentenced to a term of nine months' youth custody (on each count concurrently) in respect of three offences of domestic burglary. In 1989 he was sentenced to 12 months' imprisonment in respect of two offences (six months on each consecutively). The first was an offence of robbery and the second a non-dwellinghouse burglary. In 1989 the offender was sentenced to 15 months' imprisonment for one offence of domestic burglary but the sentence was suspended for two years.

10   On July 4, 1991 during the currency of the suspended sentence, the offender was convicted at Doncaster Crown Court of robbery, attempted burglary and theft. He was sentenced to 10 years' imprisonment for the robbery, six months concurrent for the attempted burglary, six months concurrent for the theft and the suspended sentence was activated to the extent that 12 months' imprisonment was imposed and ordered to be served consecutively. The total term was therefore 11 years' imprisonment. The facts of the robbery were: it was committed with an

imitation firearm and during the course of the offence the offender hit the victim with the imitation firearm causing injury.

11   On December 12, 1995 the offender was convicted at Northampton Crown Court of escaping from custody, being carried in a motor vehicle taken without consent and affray. He was sentenced to four and a half years' imprisonment for escape, one and a half years' imprisonment consecutive for being carried and two years' imprisonment concurrent for affray, those sentences being ordered to be served consecutively to the sentence of 11 years passed on July 4, 1991. The facts were: in July 1993 whilst being transferred from one of Her Majesty's prisons to another the offender used a craft knife to threaten a prison warder, head-butted and bit him and made good his escape from the prison vehicle. Thereafter he, and others, took by force a motor car driven by an elderly female motorist, causing her to be injured as the car was driven away.

12   On May 13, 1996 at Bradford Crown Court the offender was convicted of robbery and sentenced to six months' imprisonment, also consecutive to the sentences he was then serving. The facts were: whilst unlawfully at large from having escaped from custody in July 1993, the offender committed a street robbery. It follows that by 1996 he was serving a total sentence of 17 and a half years' imprisonment.

13   In August 2000 the offender was granted early release on licence by the Parole Board. The expiry date for the last total term of imprisonment is April 30, 2008.

14   The Attorney General submits that the following aggravating features appear to be present. We agree.

> "(i) Each of the offences was committed while the offender was on early release on licence with a significant part of the licence period remaining;
> (ii) the second firearms offence was committed while on police bail for the first;
> (iii) the firearms were being carried in public places and the first was abandoned in a street;
> (iv) the firearms were loaded on both occasions; 6 rounds in the magazine and 1 in the breech in the first case and 5 rounds in the magazine in the second case;
> (v) both firearms were prohibited weapons;
> (vi) the ammunition for the first firearm was prohibited;
> (vii) the second firearms offence was committed whilst the offender was actively supplying class A drugs;
> (viii) the stolen car had been provided with false number plates;
> (ix) the offender's antecedent history."

5   There were no mitigating features.

6   It is submitted by the Attorney General that the notional determinate sentence of 12 years' imprisonment for the firearms offences failed adequately to reflect the gravity of each of the offences in the indictment. In particular the sentence failed to have due regard to the aggravating features present in the case, in par-

ticular, the commission of firearms offences while on licence and on bail, and public concern about the carrying of loaded firearms.

17   Mr Metzger submits that the determinate term of 12 years was neither lenient nor unduly lenient and properly reflected the seriousness of the offences.

18   We start with asking ourselves what would be the appropriate sentence if, hypothetically, a sentence of life imprisonment had not been passed.

19   It is accepted that, by virtue of the complicated provisions of ss.116 and 117 of the 2000 Act and because he had begun serving the sentence of 17 and a half years prior to October 1, 1992, the judge would have had no power to order the offender to be returned to prison to serve a period reflecting the fact that he had committed the instant offence at a time when he had a period of some six years to serve of that sentence. During the course of mitigation the learned judge accepted that proposition. Although the Secretary of State could have revoked the licence, he had not done so and, it is agreed, cannot now do so.

20   We take the view that an appropriate sentence for the totality of offending for which the offender had to be sentenced was at least 16 years' imprisonment, taking into account all the aggravating features listed by the Attorney General and including the fact that the offences were committed whilst on licence and also taking into account the principle of totality.

21   We turn to s.82A of the 2000 Act, as inserted by the Criminal Justice and Court Services Act 2000. By virtue of subs.(3) if the court sets a period at the expiry of which the defendant is eligible for parole, it shall be:

"such as the court considers appropriate taking into account—

    (a) the seriousness of the offence, or of the combination of the offence and one or more offences associated with it".

    (b) the effect of any direction which it would have given under section 87 below (crediting periods of remand in custody) if it had sentenced him to a term of imprisonment; and

    (c) ...".

22   By virtue of s.161(1), an offence is associated with another if, amongst other things,

"(a) the offender is convicted of it in the proceedings in which he is convicted of the other offence, or (although convicted of it in earlier proceedings) is sentenced for it at the same time as he is sentenced for that offence".

23   It follows that all the offences other than the firearms offences for which the offender fell to be sentenced were associated offences for the purposes of s.82A.

24   *Lundberg* (1995) 16 Cr.App.R.(S.) 948 provides important guidance as to how to interpret what is now s.82A(3)(a). The appellant pleaded guilty to manslaughter by reason of diminished responsibility, two counts of unlawful wounding and one of destroying property, being reckless as to whether life was endangered. The trial judge had passed a sentence of life imprisonment for the manslaughter which was upheld on appeal. The Court then turned to the second ground of appeal which related to the decision of the trial judge to

set the period at the expiry of which the defendant would be eligible for parole at seven years. Roch L.J., giving the judgment of the Court, summarised the appellant's submission that the judge must have arrived at the period of seven years on the basis that the appropriate determinate sentence for the offence of manslaughter was one of between 10 and a half and 14 years. Counsel submitted that a sentence of 12 years would have been a manifestly excessive sentence for the manslaughter on its own. The Court accepted that submission. The Court, however, went on to consider the effect of what is now s.82A. In the light of the wording of what is now subs.(3)(a), Roch L.J. said:

> "This wording allows, if it does not require, the sentencing court in determining the part of the sentence to be specified under section [82A] to take into account the combination of the offence, in this case the manslaughter . . . and the other offences associated with it . . .. Inevitably, because of the life sentence, Tucker J ordered that all the terms of imprisonment were to run concurrently. However, arriving at the part of the sentence to be specified under section [82A], Tucker J was entitled to look at the appellant's offending that night . . . In our judgment determinate sentences totalling between 10 and a half and 14 years for the whole course of the appellant's criminal conduct that evening could not have been said to be manifestly excessive, had the four offences been punished by determinate prison sentences. In summary, when it is borne in mind that the specified part of the sentence must relate to the total determinate sentence appropriate for the totality of the offender's offending in respect of the primary offence and other offences associated with it, taking account of the elements of punishment and deterrence, then the period specified by Tucker J in the present case cannot be criticised."

25   The Court dismissed the appeal. The decision of this Court in *Hann* [1996] 1 Cr.App.R.(S.) 267 is to a similar effect.

26   In our view if this approach were not adopted, a person sentenced to life imprisonment in circumstances such as these would be given an opportunity to apply for parole at a time earlier than he would have been able to do if he had not been sentenced to a period of life imprisonment. Although Mr Metzger submitted to the contrary, we take the view that a defendant in these circumstances should not be in a better position because he has been given a life sentence.

27   This principle is demonstrated in the case of *Haywood* [2000] 2 Cr.App.R.(S.) 418. In that case the appellant had been sentenced to a total of eight years' imprisonment for offences of robbery and related offences. Two days after being sentenced he attacked a prison officer with a makeshift knife made from razor blades. He subsequently pleaded guilty to an offence against s.18 of the Offences Against the Person Act 1861. He was sentenced to an automatic life sentence by the Recorder of Liverpool who took as a starting point a notional total sentence of 15 years' imprisonment, subsequently reducing it by half and allowing for time spent in custody. The Recorder indicated that on its own he would have passed a sentence of seven years imprisonment for the offence against s.18 which he would have ordered to be served consecutively to the sentence which the appel-

lant was serving at the time. The Recorder added those two terms together to reach the 15-year notional sentence. Lord Bingham said that the course which the Recorder had adopted promoted "the public policy underlying the Act". If the Recorder had chosen seven years as the notional determinate sentence "that would have the effect of adding virtually nothing to the existing sentence which the appellant was serving" (at 422). That, Lord Bingham said, was "obviously absurd".

28   Given that the offences of robbery were not associated offences for the purposes of what is now s.82A, it followed that in determining the "seriousness of the offence" with which the sentence is concerned, the sentencing judge may take into account offences committed earlier and may do so in the mathematical way in which it was done in *Haywood*.

29   Applying *Lundberg*, we have reached the conclusion that the judge should have set a period of at least 16 years as the appropriate notional determinate sentence.

30   We now turn to the setting of the appropriate period before the offender is eligible to make an application for parole. The Attorney General submits that:

> "on the particular facts of this case, the proportion of the notional determinate sentence to be served as the specified minimum period should have been higher than the half that was set."

31   The Attorney General referred us to *Szczerba* [2002] 2 Cr.App.R.(S.) 86 (p.387). In that case Rose L.J., Vice President of the Court of Appeal Criminal Division, said:

> "31 Finally, Mr Fitzgerald submits that there was no reason for the recorder to take, as the specified period to be served, a higher proportion of the determinate term than one half, which the recent authorities show should be the norm in the absence of exceptional circumstances (see *Marklew and Lambert* [1999] 1 Cr.App.R.(S.) 6 at 12, *Adams and Harding* [2000] 2 Cr.App.R.(S.) 274 and *McQuade* [2002] 1 Cr.App.R.(S.) 128 (at 540). Indeed, Mr Fitzgerald goes further and submits that one-half of the notional determinate sentence should be the invariable rule.
>
> 32 In our judgment, as *Marklew and Lambert* makes plain, whether the specified period should be half or two-thirds of the determinate term, or somewhere between the two, is essentially a matter for the exercise of the sentencing judge's discretion. But that discretion must be exercised in accordance with principle. We accept that half should normally be taken. Some of the decisions in this Court, in which the Court has taken a higher proportion, are not, as it seems to us, obviously explicable, save on the basis that the relevant principles were not always argued or addressed.
>
> 33 There are, however, circumstances in which more than half may well be appropriate. Dr Thomas identified two examples. In *Haywood* [2000] 2 Cr.App.R.(S.) 418 a life sentence was imposed on a serving prisoner for an offence committed in prison. In such a case the term specified can appropriately be fixed to end at a date after that on which the defendant would have

been eligible for release on licence from his original sentence. This may involve identifying a proportion of the notional determinate term up to two- thirds. Another example is where a life sentence is imposed on a defendant for an offence committed during licensed release from an earlier sentence, who is therefore susceptible to return to custody under section 116 of the Powers of Criminal Courts (Sentencing) Act 2000. In such a case the specified period could properly be increased above one-half, to reflect the fact that a specified period cannot be ordered to run consecutively to any other sentence.

34 There may well be other cases, apart from these two examples, in which it is appropriate to specify a period greater than one-half. It would not, in our judgment, be helpful to seek to list all the circumstances in which the sentencing judge's discretion can properly be so exercised.

35 But, as we have said, unless there are exceptional circumstances, half the notional determinate sentence should be taken (less, of course, time spent in custody) as the period specified to be served. If a judge specifies a higher proportion than one-half, he should always state his reasons for so doing.

36 In the present case, there was no good reason to take a proportion greater than one-half." (Underlining added)

32   Given that the offender was not "susceptible to return to custody under s.116 of the 2000 Act" we agree that the trial judge was right in this case to halve the period. We halve the period of 16 years to one of eight years. We should add that Mr Horwell was content, on the facts of this case, that the fact that the offences were committed while the offender was on early release on licence with a significant part of the licence period remaining, should be recognised either when setting the notional determinate sentence (which we have done) or at this second stage.

33   H.H. Judge Hawkins then deducted the period spent on remand in custody. Mr Horwell does not argue that this was wrong. We note that, if the Secretary of State had revoked the licence, then the period spent in custody following that and prior to sentencing would not have been deducted. The period of eight years is therefore reduced to six and a half years.

34   We turn finally to double jeopardy. It is now established that in cases where the Attorney General successfully argues that the s.82A period is unduly lenient, this Court will give some discount but not as much as is normally given. In *Attorney General's Reference No.6 of 2000 (Simon Goldsmith)* [2001] 1 Cr.App.R.(S.) 20 (p.72), Rose L.J. said:

"17 In our judgment, so far as the double jeopardy aspect is concerned, in a case of this kind, this Court should give some discount for the element of double jeopardy, but not as much as would be appropriate where the overall total sentence is affected by the decision of this Court."

35   We reflect that by deducting a period of six months from the six and a half years.

36   In conclusion the specified minimum period after which the offender could make an application to have his case considered by the Parole Board set by H.H. Judge Hawkins was unduly lenient and we increase the period, taking into account double jeopardy, to one of six years.

R. v STEPHEN MICHAEL O'ROURKE

COURT OF APPEAL (Lord Justice Hooper, Mr Justice McCombe and Sir John Alliott): June 25, 2004

[2004] EWCA Crim 1808; [2005] 1 Cr.App.R.(S.) 53

(LT) Aggravating features; Causing death by dangerous driving; Driving while over the limit; Roadworthiness; Sentence length; Speeding

H1   *Causing death by dangerous driving—multiple aggravating factors—length of sentence*

H2   Six and a half years' imprisonment for causing death by dangerous driving, where an unqualified driver drove a motorcycle with an excess blood alcohol level, at excessive speeds and in a dangerous manner, and caused the death of his pillion passenger, reduced to five and a half years.

H3   The appellant pleaded guilty to causing death by dangerous driving. The appellant spent an afternoon drinking in a club and had consumed at least three and a half pints of lager. He left the club on a motorcycle, with his girlfriend as a pillion passenger. They travelled along a road subject to a speed limit of 60mph, overtaking other vehicles at speeds between 80 and 100mph. The appellant crossed to the opposite carriageway in contravention of double white lines and hatch markings on the road. The appellant came up behind a car and moved out to overtake it. He clipped the offside of the car and as a result the car spun round in the road. The appellant and his girlfriend were thrown from the motorcycle. The girlfriend received injuries from which she died almost immediately. The appellant was taken to hospital where a blood sample taken two and a half hours later revealed an alcohol content of 116mg in 100ml of blood. The appellant did not have a licence or insurance to ride a motorcycle. The rear brake pads of the motorcycle were not working correctly. The appellant suffered some injuries in the accident. Sentenced to six and a half years' imprisonment, consecutive to an order under the Powers of Criminal Courts (Sentencing) Act 2000, s.116, requiring him to serve one year, seven months and 12 days in respect of an earlier sentence for robbery.

H4   **Held:** (considering *Cooksley* [2004] 1 Cr.App.R.(S.) 1 (p.1)) it was submitted that the sentence of six and a half years' imprisonment following a plea was equivalent to a sentence of between nine and 10 years after a contested trial.

As the Court had pointed out in *Cooksley*, the dominant factor in assessing where the particular offence came within the level of serious crimes was culpability. It was accepted that the appellant's driving fell within the "highly culpable" standard of driving, in view of the consumption of alcohol, excessive speed, aggressive driving and the poor standard of maintenance of his motorcycle. The Court agreed with the submission that an appropriate sentence following a trial would have been eight years and would substitute a sentence or five and a half years' imprisonment, consecutive to the period ordered to be served under the Powers of Criminal Courts (Sentencing) Act 2000, s.116.

H5   **Case cited:**   *Cooksley* [2004] 1 Cr.App.R.(S.) 1 (p.1)

H6   **References:** causing death by dangerous driving, *Current Sentencing Practice* B 1-7

H7   *F.G. Burrell Q.C.* for the appellant.

JUDGMENT

1   **HOOPER L.J.:**   On February 13, 2004 at the Crown Court at Sheffield before H.H. Judge Murphy Q.C., the appellant (now aged 25) pleaded guilty and was sentenced for one offence of causing death by dangerous driving to six-and-a-half years' imprisonment. On June 24, 1999 at the Crown Court at Nottingham he had been sentenced to six-and-a-half years' detention in a young offender institution for two offences of robbery. He had been released on licence on January 2, 2002 and the sentence expiry date was March 24, 2005. Exercising the powers under s.116 of the Powers of Criminal Courts (Sentencing) Act 2000, H.H. Judge Murphy required the appellant to serve one year, seven months and 12 days' imprisonment outstanding of the six and a half years' detention with the six and a half years' imprisonment to follow, making a total of eight years, one month and 12 days' imprisonment. He was also disqualified from driving for 10 years. There is no appeal from that.

2   Leave to appeal against sentence was granted by Morland J.

3   At about 5.20pm on August 14, 2003 the appellant was riding his motorcycle on an A road in South Yorkshire when he was in collision with a car. At the time he was driving it was at an excess speed, and he was over the legal limit for alcohol and had traces of cannabinoids in his blood. The victim was a 19-year-old girlfriend, who was a pillion passenger on the motorcycle. The motorcycle was a 600cc Suzuki and had worn front and rear brake pads. The appellant knew about this, a friend having examined the motorcycle a couple of days beforehand and having told the appellant he needed to replace the pads. The appellant had purchased new pads but had not fitted them.

4   On the afternoon of August 14 the appellant had spent at least two and a half hours in a club and consumed at least three and a half pints of lager with his girlfriend. They left the premises at about 4pm and set off to his girlfriend's home on the motor cycle. As they travelled along the A road, which had a speed limit of 60

miles an hour, the appellant overtook other vehicles at speeds at between 80 and 100 miles per hour. He overtook long streams of traffic and in doing so crossed over to the opposite carriageway in contravention of both double white lines and hatch markings on the road.

5   The appellant came up behind a Ford Focus motor car and moved out to over-take it. In doing he clipped the rear offside of the car with such force that it spun round in the road and went across the carriageway before striking a lamp post and coming to a rest. The impact meant that the appellant and his girlfriend were flung from the motor cycle. The motor cycle somersaulted in the air and both the appel-lant and his girlfriend landed in grass at the side of the road some distance apart. It was immediately apparent that his girlfriend was seriously injured and she died almost straight away from head injuries she had received. He suffered injuries to his leg and wrist. He was taken to hospital where some two and a half hours later a blood sample was taken from him. When it was analysed it was found to contain 116 milligrams of alcohol in 100 millilitres of blood, the legal limit being 80.

6   The appellant was subsequently interviewed. He said he did not think that he was over the legal limit to drive. He said that he had smoked some cannabis the previous evening. He accepted he did not have a licence or insurance, but stated he had been riding motorcycles for many years. He agreed there was some diffi-culty with the brake pads and said that he had moderated his driving because his girlfriend was on the rear. He made it perfectly clear that he was very upset that his girlfriend had lost her life.

7   There was one previous relevant conviction, namely for driving with excess alcohol.

8   A medical report, dated January 28, 2004, stated he had sustained nasty injur-ies in the accident which resulted in the loss of his right testicle and a serious compound fracture to his left tibia and fibula which was taking some time to heal. He would also have long-term problems with stiffness of movement in his right wrist. There was a character reference.

9   In passing sentence H.H. Judge Murphy said:

> "The defendant can remain seated for the time being. Stephen Michael O'Rourke, you are 25 years of age and I have taken into consideration in your favour your plea of guilty, although, in the face of such evidence that exists in this case, it is difficult to see how you could have denied your guilt.
>
> I am aware that the victim of this crime was your girlfriend and that you do feel considerable remorse at her death, although I note in the pre-sentence report at paragraph 2.4 it is stated: 'Whilst the defendant accepts he was over the legal limit for alcohol, he does not believe that he was culpable for his actions.' I am aware that you have suffered some injuries yourself in this collision and I have these factors in mind when passing sentence.
>
> But, I have in mind also the enormous tragedy that you have caused to the family of Joanne Lisa Cleary, this unfortunate 19 year old girl whose young life was cut short by your wild and dreadful driving that day, and also, I am

afraid, by your breathtaking arrogance in the way you conducted yourself on that road.

I have considered the Court of Appeal guidelines in *Cooksley* for sentencing on this kind. In my judgment it easily falls into the category of offence the Lord Chief Justice describes as higher culpability.

There are aggravating features to your conduct and it is difficult to know where to begin. Anybody who knows this area of Sheffield, the Stocksbridge bypass, know it is a road that demands particular care from drivers. Even if you were unaware of the history of this road in terms of the number of fatal accidents, and even if you were unaware of it being a dangerous road, you must have realised as you drove along it that it is not a dual carriageway, and, at the best of times, it requires careful driving.

This offence occurred at about 5.20 in the evening. It is a busy time and a particularly dangerous time. You chose to drive along it after you had been drinking for several hours and when you had taken cannabis the night before. The drink that you took put you well above the prescribed limit and you have a conviction for that very offence in December 1998.

You have never passed a driving test in your life. You were uninsured, you were driving a 600 cc motorcycle with brakes that were barely adequate and such was your arrogance that you considered yourself a good driver. I do not consider you a good driver. I consider you a menace and danger on the road. That is a view shared by other road-users that day.

The witness, Mr Grey, at page 15 says you came near to hitting his car as you passed him. He put your speed as in excess of 90 miles an hour. He said: 'It would not have surprised me if he had been going into three figure numbers'. As he came across the accident he felt this is what he would have expected from the way in which he saw you driving. His reaction at the news that your passenger had been killed was anger at what he described as a complete waste of human life. As you sped past the witness Mr Sharp, his reaction was 'mad bastard'. He put your speed in excess of 100 miles an hour. Mr Cooper, the consultant surgeon who happened to be driving along that road said to himself 'stupid idiot' and put your speed at between 80 and 100 miles an hour.

All of the witnesses who speak of your speed put it as greatly in excess of the speed limit and describe your driving as dangerous and frightening. But not only are there many of the aggravating features identified in the case of *Cooksley* in this case, but if matters could be made worse you made them worse by driving like this when on licence for a six and a half year sentence for armed robbery. You will be disqualified from driving for a period of ten years. You will have to take and pass an extended driving test before you drive on the road again.

Stand up, please. For the offence of causing death by dangerous driving the sentence is six and a half years' imprisonment. There will be no further sentence on other matters. You will begin your present sentence only after you have served the entirety of your licence period of 586 days. You may go down. Thank you very much."

10   We make one small point about those sentencing remarks. The learned judge
said that the matters were made "worse by driving like this" whilst on licence.
We express some concern about the risks of "double counting" if the sentence
for the causing death by dangerous driving is increased and because the defendant
was on licence the whole period outstanding on that licence is then implemented.

11   This Court has been provided with a prison report, which shows that the appellant has caused no problems and has had no health problems.

12   We have had a letter from him expressing his deep remorse for what had
occurred.

13   The submissions of Mr Burrell Q.C. can be simply stated. The learned judge
took too high a starting point before giving credit for the mitigating features. A
sentence of some six and a half years' imprisonment would mean a sentence of
between nine and just under 10 years, depending on the extent to which the mitigating feature, and in particular the plea of guilty, reduced the sentence. He drew
our attention to the case of *Cooksley* [2004] 1 Cr.App.R.(S.) 1 (p.1).

14   This was a case, in our judgment, where it must have been obvious to the
offender that the driving was dangerous and, additionally, he knew that the
work needed to be done to the brake pads of the vehicle. We stress, as has been
stressed on many occasions, that no term of months or years imposed on a defendant can reconcile the family of a deceased victim to their loss, nor will it cure their
anguish.

15   As was pointed out in *Cooksley*, culpability is the dominant factor when assessing where, in the level of serious crimes, the particular offence comes. Mr
Burrell rightly accepted that this driving fell within the highly culpable standard
of driving at the time of the offence. There were the aggravating features of the
consumption of alcohol, excessive speed, aggressive driving and driving a poorly
maintained vehicle to his knowledge. Additionally, the offence was committed
against a background of never having had a licence, thus driving without a licence
and thus no insurance.

16   There were the mitigating factors of a plea of guilty at the earliest opportunity,
genuine remorse, which may be greater if the victim, as here, is a close friend.
There is the additional mitigating factor of the injuries suffered to the offender,
but as the Court pointed out in *Cooksley*, such injuries will only have a significant
effect on the sentence if they are very serious or life changing. They are not in this
case.

17   We invited Mr Burrell to tell us what, in his submission, was the appropriate
starting point following a trial. He submitted that the appropriate sentence,
given the guidelines set out in *Cooksley*, was a sentence of some eight years.

18   We agree with that submission. In the light of the plea and the other mitigating
factor to which we have referred, we take the view that the proper sentence in this
case was one of five and a half years' imprisonment. Mr Burrell rightly did not
seek to argue that the judge was wrong to order that the one year, seven months
and 12 days' imprisonment should be served followed by the sentence for this
offence. So this appellant's appeal is allowed to the limited extent that for the
causing death by dangerous driving the sentence will be one of five and a half
years' imprisonment and not six and a half years.

R. v ANTHONY UNDERWOOD

Court of Appeal (Lord Justice Hooper, Mr Justice McCombe and Sir John Alliott): June 25, 2004

[2004] EWCA Crim 1816; [2005] 1 Cr.App.R.(S.) 54

(LT) Criminal record; Dangerous driving; Disqualification; Previous convictions; Speeding

H1   *Dangerous driving—driving at 137mph—offender with previous conviction for driving in excess of 100mph—whether three years' disqualification excessive*

H2   Three years' disqualification upheld for dangerous driving by driving at 137mph on a dual carriageway road.

H3   The appellant pleaded guilty to dangerous driving. The appellant was observed by police officers driving a motor car along a dual carriageway road at a speed of 137mph. The appellant had a previous conviction for a speeding offence relating to driving at a speed in excess of 100mph. Sentenced to a fine of £400, disqualified from driving for three years and until after passing an extended driving test, and ordered to pay £600 towards the costs of the prosecution.

H4   **Held:** the sentencing judge thought that the appellant took the view that because his car was a high performance car he was entitled to drive fast. In this case there was grossly excessive speed and the slightest incident could have had the most serious consequences. The Court did not consider that the period of disqualification was excessive. The appeal would be dismissed.

H5   **Case cited:**
Cooksley [2004] 1 Cr.App.R.(S.) 1 (p.1)

H6   **References:** dangerous driving, *Current Sentencing Practice* B 12

H7   *M. Sylvester* for the appellant.

JUDGMENT

1   **McCombe J.:** On January 19, 2004 at the Crown Court at Taunton the appellant pleaded guilty to an offence of dangerous driving, and on February 13 before H.H. Judge Hume-Jones he was fined £400 (with 14 days' imprisonment in default of payment) and was disqualified from driving for three years and until after passing an extended driving test. He was also ordered to pay £600 towards the prosecution costs. The plea of guilty was entered on rearraignment on the day of trial.

2   He now appeals against such sentence by leave of the single judge, the only element of the appeal being against the period of disqualification imposed, which, it is argued, was excessive.

3   The facts were these. On Thursday April 24, 2003 police officers set up a camera observation on a bridge over the A303 at South Cadbury in Somerset, viewing west bound traffic on the dual carriage way below. Other officers were in patrol cars on a nearby slip road in order to stop vehicles identified by officers on the bridge as having potentially committed offences.

4   At 7.10pm the officers on the bridge observed the appellant driving a Ford Focus motor car at high speed in the outside lane, overtaking cars in the inside lane. An officer used the camera to obtain a speed reading for the appellant. This was recorded at 137 miles per hour at a range of 565 metres. The appellant had been sighted approximately 800 metres from the bridge as he had come round the sweeping left hand curve. The road then straightened and levelled up. The officers on the slip road were contacted. The appellant was stopped, and informed of the speed which had been recorded, his reply was "you're joking". He was cautioned and required to produce his documents at a later date. The weather was fine and dry, the road was dry, the traffic was light to moderate and visibility was good. The other traffic was thought to be driving at speeds approaching 70 miles per hour.

5   On Thursday May 1, 2003 the appellant was interviewed. He did not dispute the speed, and stated that on the day he had driven a fair distance and was in a bit of a hurry home. His car, he said, was a high-performance one and he was used to driving at high speeds on motorways in Germany.

6   The appellant was born on March 17, 1972 and he is therefore now aged32. He has two convictions for offences which were not driving related. He has, however, one other conviction for a speeding offence relating to driving at in excess of 100 miles an hour, on that occasion thought to be some 102 miles per hour, in respect of which he was disqualified for a period of 50 days. That was in May 1999.

7   The pre-sentence report of February 3 of this year noted the appellant's personal circumstances were stable. It assessed his potential risk to the public as low. It was found that the appellant's motivation and ability to change were good and that the offence was based on a thrill-seeking experience. The author of the report recommended a substantial financial penalty, coupled with a disqualification from driving, which, it was hoped, would remind the appellant of the foolishness of his behaviour and deter him from the recurrence of such driving.

8   In passing sentence H.H. Judge Hume-Jones said that he found the appellant's arrogance a concern. The appellant had been travelling at the speed which we have already mentioned. The judge acknowledged that this may have been a large wide road and the appellant may have regarded himself as an expert driver. However, the learned judge noted the previous conviction for speeding in excess of 100 miles per hour and he had been dealt with by way of disqualification on that occasion. The judge, in his assessment, thought that the appellant took the view that, because his car was of a high-performance nature and because he

had driven fast in other countries, he was entitled to behave in that way in this country. The judge noted that the appellant had contested the matter up to the door of the court, although it seems that there may have been some legal advice which led to that course. The learned judge concluded that a lesson was necessary to be taught to the appellant and consequently he said he would take him off the roads for rather longer than was perhaps normal for an offence of this nature. The learned judge indicated that he would reduce the financial penalty accordingly because of the effect of the disqualification on the appellant's business.

On the present appeal Mr Sylvester in short submissions, but none the worse for that, argued that the sentence of three years' disqualification from driving was manifestly excessive. He submits that the level of culpability did not support the length of disqualification being more than three times the minimum disqualification with only one aggravating feature. That feature was, of course, an important one, namely the previous conviction for a not dissimilar offence. It was urged that the only aggravating feature in this case was the conviction. The high speed constitutes the offence in this case. He points out that there were no other aggravating features that are some times present in cases of this type, such an alcohol or drug consumption, disregard of passengers' warnings, bad or aggressive driving, using mobile phones and many other which we do not need to recite. It is argued that in the view of legal advice the plea of guilty was timely and, further, it is pointed out that the road conditions were good, the traffic was light and was travelling at the speeds we have mentioned.

Counsel has referred us to the well-known guideline case of *Cooksley* [2004] 1 Cr.App.R.(S.)1 (p.1), which, of course, deals primarily with cases of causing death by dangerous driving. Counsel has recited to us the passage from the judgment of the Court given by the Lord Chief Justice dealing with his disqualification of drivers for offences of that character. It is to be noted that for that offence the minimum disqualification is a mandatory one of two years. In the present case it is accepted that by statute the minimum disqualification was one of one year.

In giving the judgment of this Court in *Cooksley* the Lord Chief Justice said this:

> "The main purpose of disqualification is as the Panel [Sentencing Advisory Panel] advised, 'forward looking and preventative rather than backward looking and punitive'. It is designed to protect road users in the future from an offender who had shown himself to be a real risk on the roads. We do, however, accept that for the offender being disqualified is a real punishment. The Panel suggests the risk represented by the offender is reflected in the level of culpability which attaches to his driving so that matters relevant to fixing the length of the driving disqualification for the offence of causing death by dangerous will be much the same as those factors we have already listed."

In the case of offences of causing death by dangerous driving this Court endorsed the advice of the Panel in the following passage of his report to the following effect:

"Short bans of two years or so will be appropriate where the offender has a good driving record before the offence and where the offence resulted from a momentary error of judgment. Longer bans, between three and five years, will be appropriate where, having regard to the circumstances of the offence and the offender's record, it is clear that the offender tends to disregard the rules of the road, or to drive carelessly or inappropriately. Bans between five and ten years may be used where the offence itself, and the offender's record, show that he represents a real and continuing danger to other road users. Disqualification for life is a highly exceptional course . . ."

13   Those passages, we remind ourselves, are stated in the context of a minimum disqualification period of two years; that is twice the minimum period in the present case.

14   In this case there was quite clearly grossly excessive speed employed by this appellant. As my Lord, Hooper L.J., pointed out in the course of argument, the slightest incident could have had the most serious consequences. It is difficult to exaggerate the appalling speeding that was demonstrated in this case, which constituted a second speeding offence for driving in excess of 100 miles an hour.

15   Having regard to those features and to the passages which we have quoted, we do not think that there was any other alternative to the learned judge but to impose a very substantial period of disqualification indeed. In the circumstances we cannot find that the period he chose was in any way excessive. Therefore, this appeal is dismissed.

R. v JUNE ELIZABETH SZLUKOVINYI

Court of Appeal (Lord Justice Keene, Mr Justice Mitting and Sir John Alliott): June 28, 2004

[2004] EWCA Crim 1788; [2005] 1 Cr.App.R.(S.) 55

(LT) Careless driving; Causing death when under the influence; Denial; Sentence length

H1   *Causing death by careless driving with an excess alcohol level—length of sentence*

H2   Four years' imprisonment for causing death by driving without due care and attention, while unfit to drive through drink or drugs, reduced to three years.

H3   The appellant was convicted of causing death by driving without due care and attention, while unfit to drive through drink or drugs. The appellant was driving a car late at night along a single carriageway road subject to a 60mph limit. The appellant lost control of the car as she negotiated a bend. The vehicle rotated, left the carriageway and collided with a tree. One passenger died from his injuries at the scene and a second passenger received serious injuries. The appellant was taken to hospital. A blood specimen showed that at the time of the accident the appellant had between 76 and 136mg of alcohol in 100ml of blood. An accident investigator concluded that the most likely cause of the accident was the appellant's misjudgement of a bend and the fact that the car was travelling at a marginally excessive speed. The appellant denied that she had been the driver at the time. Sentenced to four years' imprisonment, disqualified from driving for three years and thereafter until she had passed an extended driving test.

H4   **Held:** the Court had reached the conclusion that the sentence was unnecessarily long. A sentence of three years would be substituted.

H5   **References:** causing death by careless driving with an excess alcohol level, *Current Sentencing Practice* B 1-7.3

H6   *J. Dale* for the appellant.

JUDGMENT

1   **Sir John Alliott:**   On August 8, 2003 at the Crown Court at Lewes the appellant was convicted of causing death by driving without due care and attention whilst unfit to drive through drink or drugs. Sentence was adjourned for reports. On September 8, 2003 the appellant failed to appear for sentence and a bench warrant was issued. On February 10, 2004 at the same court H.H. Judge Kemp sentenced the appellant to four years' imprisonment. She was also disqualified for three years and ordered to take an extended test.

2   She appeals against sentence by leave of the single judge.

3   The facts of the matter are these. At about 22.45 on Sunday February 3, 2002 the appellant was driving a Mercedes motor car between Hailsham and Stone Cross. It was dark, the weather was dry, but there was a blustery wind blowing. The road has one carriageway for traffic travelling in each direction. The road was windy, with many sharp bends, and for that reason there were frequent warning signs. The majority of the road is in open countryside, bounded by trees and hedges. The road is subject to a 60 mile an hour limit.

4   As the appellant travelled towards Stone Cross she lost control of the Mercedes as she negotiated a right hand bend. The right hand bend is quite severe and has warning chevron boards positioned at its apex. The nearside wheels left the road and went onto a grass verge. The vehicle then rotated, probably as the appellant attempted to regain control, and then completely left the carriageway. Having turned through 180 degrees, the centre nearside of the vehicle collided with a tree, causing the vehicle to rotate back in the opposite direction.

5   26-year-old Richard Wilson was in the rear nearside passenger seat. He died from his injuries at the scene. Nicholas Hoggins was in the front passenger seat. He did not believe he was wearing a seat belt. At hospital he was found to have suffered punctured lungs, all the ribs on the left hand side of his body were broken, his pelvis was broken and his spleen had to be removed.

6   The appellant was found on the bonnet of the car. She remained in hospital for 11 days. A blood specimen was taken at hospital. A count back showed that at the time of the accident the appellant had between 76 and 136 milligrammes of

alcohol in 100 millilitres of blood, the most likely value being 108 milligrammes. The legal limit was 80 milligrammes.

7   Mr Dale, in a comment upon the summary, contends that the appellant *may* have been over the legal limit, but the Crown case was that her skills were impaired by alcohol.

8   An accident investigator later concluded that excessive speed in isolation was unlikely to have been the primary factor. It was more likely that the appellant misjudged the bend, being inattentive on the approach, or had been travelling at a marginally excessive speed to negotiate the bend. The Mercedes had no faults or defects that would have contributed to the accident.

9   When interviewed on March 6, 2002 the appellant gave a prepared statement in which she said she had been drinking that evening. She was sure that she would not have been driving as she never drove after drinking. When interviewed on October 22 the appellant made no comment.

10   The appellant was born on June 7, 1979. She was of previous good character with a young child.

11   A pre-sentence report, dated September 3, indicated that the appellant had no memory of the accident or several hours prior to it. Her continued denial of responsibility was a matter of concern.

12   A prison report, dated April 8, 2004, indicated that the appellant was gainfully employed and had access to health care, education and physical activities.

13   A letter from the appellant indicated that she now accepted the facts of her conviction and felt deeply sorry she had put witnesses through the anguish of giving evidence. She apologised for absconding.

14   When the learned judge came to sentence he said this:

> "You drove that car that night having consumed a quantity of beer and vodka in circumstances which in my view, and it was obvious to others around you who gave evidence at the trial, that you should not be driving; it should have been obvious to yourself. Shortly after leaving that house in Hailsham you lost control of the car on a sequence of notoriously hazardous bends and the car crashed with tragic consequence. Richard Wilson, your passenger, a young man of 26 and in the prime of his life, died of his injuries. You, and the only other passenger in that car, Nicholas Hoggins, also received serious injuries.
>
> You fought the case, and that is your undoubted right, but you sought to suggest to the jury that you were not the driver, that perhaps Hoggins was. Even after the jury's verdict, you could not bring yourself to accept that you indeed had been the driver. Certainly, on the date when I would have sentenced you in September 2003 that was your stance adopted towards the reporting probation officer, and that was a very great shame, certainly so far as the family of Mr Wilson was concerned and Mr Hoggins himself.

I have read today a letter which you have written and addressed to me in which you explain your reasoning, and you say that you now accept the jury's verdict and wished that you had pleaded guilty; I join you in that. You also explain in that letter your reasons for absconding to Hungary for avoiding the sentence hearing in September.

. . .

I have considered your case very carefully. I have looked at it again in the light of the guidelines set out by the Court of Appeal in the case of *Cooksley* . . .. I take the view that notwithstanding that it is an ingredient of your offence, the fact that you consumed alcohol to that degree, it indeed aggravates the facts of the events of that night.

Balanced against that, I am conscious of your good driving record and absence of any previous convictions at all, and indeed the fact that you yourself received serious injuries. . . . I must reflect the public's abhorrence of drink/driving and also to attempt, at least, to seek to deter persons who might be minded to take the risk that you took that night.

You are 24 years old and a single mother. Frankly, it is a tragedy that your little boy will be deprived of your care for some time; you will have to explain to him one day the reason for that. The offence is so serious, in my view, that only a custodial sentence can be justified, and you will go to prison for four years."

15   This Court has come to the conclusion that, whereas the judge took all the relevant factors into account, he imposed an unnecessarily long sentence. We therefore quash the sentence of four years and impose instead a sentence of three years' imprisonment. To that extent this appeal is allowed.

R. v ANTHONY ROGER CHARLES

Court of Appeal (Mr Justice Henriques and Mr Justice Gross): June 28, 2004

[2004] EWCA Crim 1977; [2005] 1 Cr.App.R.(S.) 56

(LT) Airports; Criminal intent; Custodial sentences; Possession of offensive weapons

1   *Possession of offensive weapon—possession of cosh, CS gas canister and lock knife at airport—objects unintentionally included in luggage—whether custodial sentence appropriate*

2   Two months' imprisonment upheld in the case of man whose luggage was found at an airport to contain a cosh, a CS gas canister and a lock knife.

3   The appellant was convicted of possessing a prohibited weapon, a CS gas canister, and an offensive weapon. The appellant was stopped at an airport as he

passed through an x-ray machine. A cosh and a lock knife were detected in his luggage. When police officers searched his bag they found a CS gas canister. When interviewed, the appellant admitted that the items were in his luggage. He said that he had packed the bag in haste and forgotten they were there. He had carried the cosh for his own protection for several years, and had confiscated the CS gas canister at the door of a club where he was employed as a doorman. He used the lock knife in the course of his main employment as a cheese dispatcher. Sentenced to a total of two months' imprisonment.

H4   **Held:** the sentencing judge was entirely right to treat seriously both the unlawful possession of the gas canister and the importance of safety and security at airports. The Court had emphasised the aggravating feature of possessing such weapons in sensitive localities. Notwithstanding the considerable mitigation available in the case, the combination of weapons in the appellant's bag and the importance of security in the air meant that a short custodial sentence could not be described as either wrong in principle or manifestly excessive. The appeal would be dismissed.

H5   **Cases cited:**
Celaire and Poulton [2003] 2 Cr.App.R.(S.) 116 (p.610)

H6   **References:** offensive weapons, *Current Sentencing Practice* B 3-5

H7   A. *Montgomery* for the appellant.

JUDGMENT

1   **Gross J.:**   On May 21, 2004 in the Crown Court at Chelmsford, before Mrs Recorder Bradley, the appellant was convicted and on June 14, 2004 was sentenced as follows: for a count of possessing a prohibited weapon, two months' imprisonment, the weapon being a CS gas canister; on a count of possessing an offensive weapon, in the event a cosh, one month's imprisonment concurrent, and on a count of possessing a bladed article, in the event a lock-knife, one month's imprisonment concurrent. The total sentence was thus two months' imprisonment in all. The appellant appeals against sentence by leave of the single judge. Expedition was ordered.

2   The facts are these. On October 15, 2003 the appellant was stopped at Stansted Airport as he passed through an X-ray machine on his way to board a flight to Ireland. A cosh and a lock-knife were detected in his luggage. When police officers searched his bag they found a CS gas canister as well. He was arrested.

3   When interviewed the appellant admitted that the items were in his luggage. He said he had packed the bag in haste and forgotten the weapons were there. He added that he had carried the cosh for several years for his own protection and that he had confiscated the CS gas canister at the door of the club, where he was employed as a doorman. He used the lock-knife for his main employment as a cheese dispatcher.

4   By way of further elaboration, the purpose of the appellant's trip to Ireland was
to accompany a family group to attend a kick boxing tournament in which his
partner's niece was competing. In his holdall were the weapons. The bag had
been packed in haste and he had not realised they were there. For that matter
the cosh had been buried at the bottom of the bag, the gas canister had been
obtained many years before and kept at home with a view to being used by the
appellant's partner in an emergency, if there was a burglary while she was at
home and he at work. It had been transferred to the bag on the occasion of moving
premises and had never been removed.

5   In her sentencing observations, the recorder accepted a number of matters, all
favourable to the appellant. He had packed his bag in haste; he had forgotten the
items were in his bag and throughout the investigation he had been exceptionally
polite and courteous and helpful. The recorder recounted the details as explained
by the appellant as to why he had those weapons and why they were in the bag.

6   The appellant was a man of good character, in a stable relationship. He was
hard working and sober, and the convictions had clearly had a devastating effect
on him and his family. There was undoubtedly genuine remorse. Nonetheless the
recorder said that a custodial sentence could not be avoided. The essence of the
recorder's reasoning was this. She said that the offence had taken place at an airport; that in these troubled times airport security was a matter of the very first
importance and that the offence, or offences in question could have triggered a
very major alert. Notwithstanding all the matters in the appellant's favour, nonetheless a custodial sentence could not be avoided.

7   The grounds of appeal were shortly stated in writing as follows: the imposition
of a custodial sentence was manifestly excessive, given the nature of offences and
the quality of the mitigation. The recommendation for a community punishment
order ought to have been adopted. Alternatively, the sentence should have been
appreciably shorter.

8   Developing his submissions today, Mr Montgomery stressed the matters of
personal mitigation and also underlined two points at the outset of his submissions, which he said were of particular importance. The first was that the
appellant had not realised that he had the weapons on him. The second that, certainly on the facts as accepted by the recorder, there was no sinister intent.

9   These are worrying matters. Moreover there was no plea of guilty for which
credit could be given. The recorder was entirely right to treat seriously both
the unlawful possession of the gas canister and the importance of safety and
security at places such as airports. We need not belabour that last point. Only
very recently this Court has given guidance for offences of this nature, in the
decision of *Celaire and Poulton* [2003] 2 Cr.App.R.(S.) 116 (p.610). In that
decision the Court emphasised the aggravating feature of possessing such
weapons in sensitive localities. While it is true that the Court did not expressly
make mention of an airport or an airport check in, we have no doubt at all that
possession of such weapons at such a locality would have been viewed with considerable gravity. The Court said that, even in relation to an adult offender of
previous good character, the custody threshold would invariably be passed
where there was a combination of dangerous circumstances and the actual use

of the weapon to threaten or cause fear. Custody may still be appropriate, depending on the circumstances, where no threatening use was made of the weapon.

10   Notwithstanding the considerable mitigation available in this case, the combination of weapons in the appellant's bag and the importance of security in the air which, again, we say we need not stress, meant, in our judgment, that a short custodial sentence of the length passed by the recorder could not be described as either wrong in principle or as manifestly excessive. Not least too, there is the absence of credit which would have been available on a plea of guilty.

11   The recorder had well in mind the points properly made by counsel in favour of the appellant and by way of mitigation. In our judgment, the recorder allowed for those matters by keeping the sentence passed as short as she did. The sad fact of the matter is that the appellant should never have retained the CS gas canister and on no view carried any of these items in his hand language. In the circumstances, after anxious consideration, this appeal must be dismissed.

R. v ANDREW TATAM

COURT OF APPEAL (Lord Justice Maurice Kay, Mr Justice Bell and Judge Goldsack Q.C.): June 29, 2004

[2004] EWCA Crim 1856; [2005] 1 Cr.App.R.(S.) 57

(LT) Extended sentences; Indecent photographs of children; Internet; Sexual intercourse with animals

H1   *Indecent images of children—large numbers of images at levels 4 and 5—length of sentence*

H2   An extended sentence with a custodial term of five years upheld for downloading large numbers of indecent images of children from the internet, including images at levels 4 and 5.

H3   The appellant pleaded guilty to 18 counts of making indecent photographs of a child, one count of possession of indecent photographs, and one count of attempted buggery with an animal. An investigation of a website in the United States led to a search of the appellant's home. The appellant's computer and other equipment were seized. The computer equipment contained 495,524 indecent photographs and images of children, of which 3,140 were at level 4, showing penetrative sexual activity involving children, and 336 showed sadism and other activities. The appellant had made all the images by downloading them from the worldwide web. The images were stored on computer hard drives under specific category headings. One of the videos showed the appellant attempting to encourage a dog to commit buggery with his girlfriend. Sentenced to an extended sentence consisting of a custodial term of five years and an extension period of one year for offences committed after February 2001, with concurrent sentences for the earlier offences.

H4   **Held:** (considering *Oliver* [2003] 2 Cr.App.R.(S.) 15 (p.64)) in the Court's view this was a case of exceptional gravity. The manner in which the images were organised demonstrated the appellant's level of interest in the material. The sentences imposed were not excessive individually or in totality.

H5   **Case cited:**
Oliver [2003] 2 Cr.App.R.(S.) 15 (p.64)

H6   **References:** indecent images, *Current Sentencing Practice* B 10-1

H7   *H. Milne* for the appellant.
J. Kirk for the Crown.

JUDGMENT

1   **Bell J.:**   On December 12, 2003, in the Crown Court at Lincoln, the appellant, Andrew Tatam, aged 35, pleaded guilty to 18 counts of making indecent photographs of a child, one count of possession of indecent photographs and one count of attempted buggery with an animal. On March 2, 2004, in respect of three counts of making indecent photographs of a child in December 1997 and March and April 1999 he was sentenced to two years' imprisonment on each count concurrent. On 15 counts of making an indecent photograph of a child from February 2001 onwards (by which time the maximum sentence had been increased by Parliament), he was sentenced to an extended sentence of a total of six years pursuant to s.85 of the Powers of Criminal Courts (Sentencing) Act 2000, comprising a custodial sentence of five years and an extension period of one year. That sentence was concurrent on all 15 of those counts. For one count of possessing indecent photograph of a child on September 27, 2002, he was sentenced to four years' imprisonment again concurrent. For one count of attempted buggery on September 28, 2002, he was sentenced to three months' imprisonment concurrent. Orders were made for forfeiture and destruction of the relevant computer equipment. He was disqualified from working with children and the statutory notification provisions took effect. He now appeals against the five-year custodial element of the extended sentences and against the concurrent four-year sentence by leave of the single judge.

2   The prosecution of the appellant arose from the use of his credit card to access child pornography on the Landslide web site based in Texas. In the summer of 1999 the US authorities investigated the web site and as a result of those investigations they recovered a database which held records of credit card transactions. Details of transactions from the United Kingdom were passed to the relevant police forces in this country. Information recovered from the database led the police to the appellant's home and work address on September 27, 2002 as part of "Operation Ore", a nationwide inquiry carried out in co-operation with the US authorities. The officers seized computer equipment, video tapes and compact and optical discs. They also recovered a red folder next to the appellant's

bed which contained 350 pornographic pictures of children. Material was also removed from his work address.

3   The computer equipment and file contained 495,524 indecent photographs and video images of children among other photograph images. Using the categories from *Oliver* [2003] 2 Cr.App.R.(S.) 15 (p.64), 472,000 were at Level 1 showing nudity and no sexual activity; 9,149 were at Level 2 showing sexual activity between children and solo masturbation; 10,966 were Level 3, depicting non-penetrative sexual activity between children and adults, but including oral sex; 3,140 were Level 4 showing penetrative sexual activity between children and adults; there were 336 Level 5 images of sadism involving adults and children and bestiality. This was the biggest seizure of child pornography as part of Operation Ore in the United Kingdom.

4   The appellant made all the indecent photographs by downloading them from the worldwide web. The vast majority of them was stored on computer hard drives. He then stored those images under specific category headings, for instance: scatology, bondage, extreme, rape, burning, torture and vomiting. However, many of the images were of adult pornography. The appellant also subscribed to several child pornography news groups.

5   When opening the facts to the sentencing judge, prosecuting counsel, Mr Kirk, referred to four examples. One of the images was of a female child approximately three to six years old, fully naked, hanging upside down. She was bound by rope around her waist and left leg. Both arms were secured behind her head by restraints and she was gagged with a scarf. Her legs were spread open and an object was being inserted into her vagina. Another image showed a female child between nine and 12 years old lying naked on her back, exposing her genitalia. She was secured by arm restraints and a spike neck collar and chains. A further image involved a five- to eight-year-old girl leaning back on a sofa. Her legs were spread open exposing her genitalia. A dog lay in front of her with its snout against the girl's vagina. There was an image involving a baby whose age was put at three to six months (though Mr Milne suggests up to 12 months of age), with an adult male placing his erect penis in the baby's mouth.

6   One of the videos seized from the appellant's home showed the appellant attempting to encourage a dog to commit buggery with his girlfriend. That was the count of attempted buggery.

7   The appellant was arrested on the same day as the search of his home and work place. In interview he made admissions about material in the red file and admitted that he had downloaded images of child pornography from the internet. He also admitted that he had instigated the attempted buggery, but denied that penetration had taken place. That was accepted by the Crown.

8   After analysing the material, the police re-arrested the appellant on August 18, 2003 when he admitted downloading indecent images of children. He said that the collection of the images had become an obsession.

9   It was agreed that the appellant would plead guilty at the plea and directions hearing to 20 counts, mainly samples of individual images. The one count of possession of images for which he was sentenced to four years' imprisonment

represented the totality of the material seized. There was no evidence that the appellant distributed the images to any other person.

10   It was the appellant's case in mitigation, and reported in the pre-sentence report and a psychological assessment, that the appellant had no sexual interest in children but that his harvesting of pornographic images of adults inevitably led to the gathering of images of children. The judge rejected that, rightly in our view.

11   Nevertheless, Mr Milne argues that the custodial sentences of five years and four years concurrent were excessive. His submission relies upon the guidance given in *Oliver*, and in particular para.[17] of the judgment of the Court as follows:

> "In relation to more serious offences a custodial sentence of between 12 months and 3 years will generally be appropriate for (a) possessing a large quantity of material at Levels 4 or 5, even if there was no showing or distribution of it to others; or (b) showing or distributing a large number of images at Level 2; or (c) producing or trading in material at Levels 1–3. Sentences longer than three years should be reserved for cases where (a) images at Levels 4 or 5 have been shown or distributed; or (b) the offender was actively involved in the production of images at Levels 4 or 5, especially where that involvement included a breach of trust and whether or not there was an element of commercial gain; or (c) the offender has commissioned or encouraged the production of such images."

12   Mr Milne says that this case falls firmly within those guidelines and that in his sentencing exercise the judge should have started at a maximum of three years. He makes the point that there was no question of any distribution by the appellant or involvement in the taking of the original photographs or films. It would have been quite impossible for the appellant to look at more than a modest proportion of the images which were stored. The guidance given in *Oliver* is given on the basis of a contested trial, and here the appellant pleaded guilty at an early stage having co-operated with the police from an early stage. In addition, as Mr Milne notes in his skeleton argument, there is the personal mitigation that the appellant is of previous good character, although the mitigating effect of good character is limited in this kind of case.

3   However, we note also para.[13] of the judgment in *Oliver*, where the Court said:

> "We stress that the proposals we make are guidelines intended to help sentencers. They are not to be construed as providing sentencers with a straitjacket from which they cannot escape."

There must, in our view, always be cases of exceptional gravity, even within their broad type. This was such a case. It had certain of the aggravating features set out in para.[20] of *Oliver* to an exceptional degree, most notably the vast number of images, including the exceptionally high number of images at Levels 4 and 5. The way in which the appellant's collection of images was organised demonstrated to our mind a high level of interest in the material. There were a significant number of particularly young children who had been abused for the purposes of the original making of the images.

14   It is clear to us that the sentencing judge had all the material factors well in mind. We cannot fault his assessment of the gravity of the case; nor can we fault the sentences or the total sentence which was imposed. Mr Milne conceded that he could not have criticised the judge had the judge imposed a consecutive sentence for the offence of attempted buggery. Regardless of that, the sentences imposed were not excessive individually or in their totality. This appeal is accordingly dismissed.

R. v KEITH SMITHERINGALE

COURT OF APPEAL (Lord Justice Maurice Kay, Mr Justice Bell and Judge Goldsack Q.C.): June 29, 2004

[2004] EWCA Crim 1974; [2005] 1 Cr.App.R.(S.) 58

Possession with intent to supply; Sentence length

H1   *Possession of cocaine with intent—courier transporting 618g of cocaine for payment—length of sentence*

H2   Seven years' imprisonment upheld for possession of cocaine with intent by a courier transporting 618g of cocaine for payment.

H3   The appellant pleaded guilty to possessing cocaine with intent to supply. The appellant was seen to leave his shop carrying a bag which had just been delivered to the shop by another person. He drove off in his car which was stopped by police. The package was found to contain 981g of cocaine at 63 per cent purity, equivalent to 618g of cocaine at 100 per cent purity. The appellant said that he had agreed to act as a courier for the package in return for payments of between £500 and £1,000. Sentenced to seven years' imprisonment.

H4   **Held:** (considering *Attorney General's Reference No.64 of 1997* [1999] 1 Cr.App.R.(S.) 237, *Aroyewumi* (1995) 16 Cr.App.R.(S.) 211) it was submitted that the appellant fell to be sentenced as a courier carrying the drugs on a single occasion. Moving the drugs from one place to another, for however short a period, was an important step towards the final distribution. A person such as the appellant would act as courier because someone of more importance in the supply chain knew that he could be trusted. The Court considered that the sentence was stern, but not outside the legitimate range of sentences for the particular offence. The appeal would be dismissed.

H5   **Cases cited:**
Attorney General's Reference No.64 of 1997 [1999] 1 Cr.App.R.(S.) 237, *Aroyewumi* (1995) 16 Cr.App.R.(S.) 211

H6   **References:** possessing cocaine with intent, *Current Sentencing Practice* B
          11-2.

H7   *N. Johnson* for the appellant.

JUDGMENT

1   **Bell J.:**   On January 26, 2004, at the Crown Court at Teesside, the appellant,
          Keith Smitheringale, now aged 39, pleaded guilty on re-arraignment to pos-
          session of a class A drug (cocaine) with intent to supply: count 2. On March
          12, 2004, he was sentenced to seven years' imprisonment. A not guilty verdict
          was entered under s.17 of the Criminal Justice Act 1967 in respect of count 1,
          an allegation of conspiracy to supply the drug. He now appeals against sentence
          by leave of the single judge.

2   A co-accused, Andrew Pickering, was found not guilty of both counts at a trial
          which took place between the appellant's plea of guilty and his sentence.

3   The facts of the appellant's offence were that on December 18, 2002 Pickering
          was seen to enter the appellant's shop in Middlesbrough carrying a package in a
          bag. Within a minute the appellant left the shop with the same bag, which he put in
          the boot of a BMW before driving off with his wife and children. The police stop-
          ped the car and a package containing 981 grammes of cocaine was found. The
          cocaine was of 63 per cent purity, the equivalent of 618 grammes of cocaine at
          100 per cent purity. The appellant said that he had been approached and agreed
          to act as a courier for the package in return for payment of between £500 and
          £1,000. He said that he was effectively, although not precisely, aware of what
          was in the package.

4   The appellant had previous convictions for dishonesty between 1981 and
          1987. In 1991 he was fined for two offences of possessing controlled drugs
          with intent to supply. We assume that those were class B drugs in the light of
          the sentence. He had not been convicted of any offence since 1991. The judge
          said that credit would be given to the appellant for his plea and admissions to
          the police, but they had to be looked at in the light of him being caught red-han-
          ded. He would be sentenced on the basis that he was a courier, but he was a key
          player in an efficiently run organisation.

5   The basis of Mr Johnson's submissions to us today is that the sentence imposed
          was excessive when compared with the sentence which this Court thought appro-
          priate in *Attorney General's References Nos 64 and 65 of 1997* [1999] 1
          Cr.App.R.(S.) 237. In that case sentences of 30 months were imposed on two
          men found in possession of 1,485 grammes of 100 per cent heroin who were trea-
          ted as minders for the purpose of sentence and who had pleaded guilty to
          conspiracy to supply heroin. Their sentences were varied to six years. The report
          of this Court's proceedings does not say what sentence the court thought appro-
          priate but for the double jeopardy involved in the Reference, but the judgment
          records that the offenders had been in custody for some time before the Refer-
          ence. One of the offenders could see the end of his sentence and the other had
          suffered a depressive illness while in prison. Mr Johnson compares this appel-

lant's case with the cases of the offenders in that matter. He submits that the key factor in this case was that the appellant was a courier of 618 grammes of cocaine at 100 per cent purity, rather less than half the heroin involved in the reference. As in the case of the Reference this was a single occasion of carrying the drug for a short duration. He reminds us that the observation of the appellant on the occasion in question was followed by six months' covert surveillance during which no further illegal activity by the appellant was observed. The allegation in count 1 of conspiracy failed in the light of that surveillance. The plea was tendered after investigations which followed the plea and directions hearing. There was 16 months between the original admissions made by the appellant and the sentence imposed on him. The judge accepted that no significant account could be taken of his previous convictions and he had remained in work while on bail pending his sentence. In *Attorney General's References Nos 64 and 65 of 1997* the Court paid heed to the guidelines in respect of importing class A drugs as revised in *Aranguren* (1994) 99 Cr.App.R. 347 (also reported as *Aroyewumi* (1995) 16 Cr.App.R.(S.) 211), which indicate that for 500 grammes or more at 100 per cent purity sentences of 10 years or more are appropriate after a contested trial. Most Crown Court judges are guided by that importation case when the offender is a courier as in this case, rightly in our view.

6   Moving drugs from one place to another, for however short a period, is an important step towards their final distribution. Presumably a person such as the appellant is the courier because someone of more importance in the supply knows that he can be trusted. It appears to us that in the *Attorney General's Reference* to which we have referred, this Court probably had in mind a sentence of something like eight years, but for the particular circumstances involved in re-hearing the matter of sentence.

7   Looking at all the points which have been made, and Mr Johnson's submissions, shortly and clearly put as they were, we consider that this was a stern sentence, but in our view it was not outside the legitimate range of sentences for the circumstances of this particular offence. It was not, in our view, manifestly excessive. This appeal is therefore dismissed.

ATTORNEY GENERAL'S REFERENCE NO.44 OF 2004 (KEITH E)

COURT OF APPEAL (Lord Justice Kennedy, Mr Justice Henriques and Mr Justice Gross): June 30, 2004

[2004] EWCA Crim 2038; [2005] 1 Cr.App.R.(S.) 59

Intoxication; Rape; Relationships; Undue leniency; Violence

H1   *Rape—rape of sexual partner—length of sentence*

H2   Three years' imprisonment for the rape by a man of a woman with whom he had an existing sexual relationship considered lenient but not unduly lenient.

H3   The appellant was convicted of rape. The victim of the offence was the daughter of a woman with whom the offender had previously had a relationship for a number of years. The victim fell out with her mother and the offender allowed her to move into his spare bedroom. A sexual relationship developed between the victim and the offender and they had sexual intercourse regularly. On the day before the offence the victim went to bed earlier than the offender who eventually followed her. The victim refused sexual intercourse and the offender began to use force, but desisted. The following evening the victim and the offender had both been drinking. The offender made advances to the victim but the victim indicated that she did not wish for sexual intercourse. The offender then pinned her arms to the bed and raped her. The offender then apologised for the incident. The victim reported the incident to a supervisor at work the following day. The offender admitted that intercourse had taken place but said that the victim had consented. Sentenced to three years' imprisonment. The Attorney General asked the Court to review the sentence on the ground that it was unduly lenient.

H4   **Held:** the Court agreed that the sentence was lenient and that a sentence of four years' imprisonment might have been passed , but the sentence was not unduly lenient and the Court would not interfere with it.

H5   **Cases cited:**
Millberry [2003] 2 Cr.App.R.(S.) 31 (p.142), *M* (1995) 16 Cr.App.R.(S.) 770, *Price* [2003] 2 Cr.App.R.(S.) 73 (p.440)

H6   **References:** rape, *Current Sentencing Practice* B 4-1

H7   *Miss B. Cheema* for the Attorney General.
B. Cox for the offender.

JUDGMENT

1   **Kennedy L.J.:**   Her Majesty's Solicitor-General, on behalf of the Attorney General, seeks leave of this Court to refer to the Court, under s.36 of the Criminal Justice Act 1988, a sentence which she considers to be unduly lenient. We grant that leave.

2   The offender is Keith E, who is 43 years of age. On March 24, 2004 he was convicted of rape, the offence itself being committed on March 20, 2003. He was then sentenced to three years' imprisonment. The sentencing judge being H.H. Judge Wolstenholme sitting at Leeds Crown Court.

3   The victim, whom we will refer to only as ASB, is 33 years of age. She was the adult daughter of the woman with whom the offender had previously had a relationship for a number of years. At the end of 2002 the offender allowed the victim to move into his spare bedroom after she had fallen out with her mother, with whom his relationship had come to an end.

4   Between January 2003 and the date of the offence in March a sexual relationship developed between the victim and the offender. The offender found the victim work with his employer and he agreed that she should use his bank account for her wages and initially she used the spare bedroom. But they drank together after work and one night, apparently in January, she let him have sexual intercourse with her. She said that she immediately regretted it and returned to her own bedroom thereafter but he continued his suit and eventually she agreed to share his bed. Thereafter sexual intercourse took place regularly and, she accepted, when she refused his approach he respected her decision and they simply slept together in the same bed.

5   One of the problems undoubtedly was that they were both abusing alcohol. No doubt that fuelled arguments between them. On March 18, 2003 she went to bed earlier and the offender eventually followed her. He had been drinking; he wanted to have sexual intercourse and was persistent but she refused. On that occasion he began to use a certain amount of force, grabbing her and trying to prise her legs open. She resisted. She ran downstairs. She had a cigarette and then went upstairs and told him that she did not want to have intercourse that night and he accepted her decision.

6   The next day he refused to give her any more money and after work she slept on the sofa. Then the two of them spent the evening in the house eating and drinking. The offender, it seems, was drunk by the end of the night. She claims to have been somewhat less so. They argued. He retired first. When she went upstairs he put his arm round her and tried to kiss her. She resisted him and told him she did not want that to happen. He then became violent. He pulled her by her arms but she got free and ran to the far corner of the room. She was by this stage crying. He got out of bed, and she saw that he was naked. He went towards her with his fist raised and told her: "I could fucking do you" and pulled her to the bed by her hair. He then forced her pyjama bottoms off and when she put her hand between her legs he pulled them out, pinned her arms to the bed by pressing his hands on her upper arms. He then used his knees to prise her legs open and to insert his penis into her vagina. He then continued to commit the offence of rape.

7   She was saying to him not to do it, but in fact he did. Then after he had completed the act of intercourse and ceased to have contact with her he apologised, saying: "I'm sorry chuck. You won't tell anyone at work about this, will you?" She said: "About what?" He said: "I raped you". She commenting "thank you for admitting it". He apologised again the following morning before leaving for work. When she went to work she found that she was unable to concentrate and she reported the rape to her supervisor, who took her home. She then went to the doctor's surgery and spoke to a practice nurse who arranged for the police to be called. Both of those people gave evidence at the trial of her appearance of distress.

8   She was medically examined. There were fingertip bruising to her upper arms, bruising to her shoulders and some bruising to her inner thighs. We have seen the photographs of that bruising and, compared with many other regrettable cases, in this case the bruising is relatively slight.

9   The offender was arrested later that day. He accepted that intercourse had taken place but said, at that stage, the victim had consented. He said that she had been drunk at the time and really, as he put it, lost it.

10   In November 2003, some eight months after this incident in March, the victim provided an impact statement, which set out a number of matters: that she had been through five jobs in six months; that initially after March she had indulged in binge drinking; she had been on antidepressants and tried to avoid leaving home at all and that she was having difficulty in a then existing relationship because she could not trust her boyfriend. She also said that she was concerned about her personal safety. She was very subdued and unable to socialise as she had previously. She had become afraid of the dark and had to sleep with the light on. All of this, or at any rate some of it, was explored in cross-examination on the basis that really she was exaggerating the effect of the incident upon her.

11   On behalf of the Attorney General Miss Cheema admits that the previous convictions of the offender are, in this case, of relatively little relevance and with that we agree. Many years ago he did have some convictions, but for present purposes we have no doubt that he should be regarded as a man of no relevant previous convictions.

12   But it is submitted that there are features to which any sentencing judge should have regard. Miss Cheema was careful to point out that they are not aggravating features as envisaged by the leading case of *Millberry* [2003] 2 Cr.App.R.(S.) 31 (p.142). She submits that the force and threats which were used went beyond what was necessary for the commission of the offence and she points out that the victim had to re-live her ordeal and subject herself to cross-examination about her medical history, drinking habits and her psychiatric state. That point has to be approached with some care.

13   It is the right of a defendant, in a criminal case, to contest his or her guilt. If he or she puts forward the defence in a proper way, as was unquestionably done in this case, it is not the place of the prosecution, in a Reference, to start being critical of the fact that the case was contested.

14   There is here, in our judgment, no element of breach of trust beyond that to be found in every case of rape by a cohabitee, and, although there is clearly evidence

that the impact on this victim was of significance, it may be, as was put to her in cross-examination, that there is some degree of exaggeration in the victim impact statement.

15   As we have indicated, this was a man who was, for all practical purposes, of good character. He had no history of sexual offending and, on his behalf, a number of things are put forward by Mr Cox. Mr Cox accepts that the sentence of the learned judge was lenient but he submits that it was not unduly lenient.

16   In relation to the leading case of *Millberry*, Mr Cox accepts that it was appropriate for the sentencing judge to start by thinking in terms, after a contested case, of a sentence of five years' imprisonment. But he emphasises that that decision did not seek to do more than suggest guidelines and that any sentencing judge should have a degree of latitude. He seeks to draw some support from a case which was referred to during the decision of the Court in *Millberry*, namely the case of *M* (1995) 16 Cr.App.R.(S.) 770. Suffice it to say that we do not regard that case as being of particular assistance after the decision in *Millberry* itself.

17   However, we do accept Mr Cox's further submission that, in the present case, although there was during the actual course of the rape a degree of violence, there was not the sort of violence which is normally an aggravating feature when one is talking in those terms. This was a very dreadful incident so long as it lasted. But it did not, for example, lead to very significant bruising and the way in which the victim conducted herself for the rest of that night is perhaps some indication of the immediate impact of the force upon her.

18   There was also, as Mr Cox has rightly pointed out, the complicating factor here of the effect of drink, something which affected both of the parties and which the sentencing judge was able to evaluate during the course of the trial. We accept that after the decision in *Millberry* it is inappropriate to have any particular regard to the relationship which exists between an offender and a victim. The fact that such a relationship does exist cannot, of itself, be regarded as a mitigating factor. That, for example, is made clear in the case of *Price* [2003] 2 Cr.App.R.(S.) 73 (p.440), to which our attention has been helpfully invited (see in particular para.[10]). But having said that, any case of this kind does have to be approached with a degree of common sense. The learned sentencing judge here had advantages which we do not enjoy.

19   In delivering the judgment of this Court in *Millberry*, the Lord Chief Justice, at [26], said this:

> "There can be situations where the offender and victim are sharing the same bed on a regular basis and prior to retiring to bed both had been out drinking and because of the drink that the offender consumed he failed to show the restraint he should have. It would be contrary to common sense to treat such a category of rape as equivalent to stranger rape as on one interpretation of the research material the panel would appear to be suggesting."

With that we respectfully agree. It seems to us that that must have been a matter to which the sentencing judge had regard when he was sentencing in the present case.

20   We agree with the concession made by Mr Cox, that this sentence was lenient. If we had been passing sentence in this case, we would have passed a sentence of four years' imprisonment. However, in our judgment, the sentence which was imposed was not unduly lenient and, furthermore, if we were to approach this matter in the way which we normally approach a reference before us by the Attorney General, we would inevitably have to bear in mind, now, in passing sentence the element of double jeopardy. Accordingly, we do not interfere with the sentence which was imposed.

ATTORNEY GENERAL'S REFERENCE NOS 38 AND 39 OF 2004 (AARON RANDALL, TROY DONAGHUE)

COURT OF APPEAL (Lord Justice Keene, Mr Justice Mitting and Sir John Alliott): July 1, 2004

[2004] EWCA Crim 1820; [2005] 1 Cr.App.R.(S.) 60

(LT) Aggravating features; Deterrence; Robbery; Undue leniency; Violence

H1   *Robbery—robbery of vulnerable man in his own home—length of sentence*

H2   Sentences of three years' imprisonment for the robbery of a vulnerable man with gratuitous violence in his own home increased to five and a half years.

H3   The offenders pleaded guilty to robbery. The offenders and a third man went to the home of a man aged 57, who was known to be vulnerable and to have learning difficulties. The victim opened a door of his house and was confronted by the men who pushed him into the hallway where he was restrained and punched. The men demanded money and took about £100 in cash, which represented the victim's savings. The victim suffered fractures of the right cheek bone and eye socket. Sentenced to three years' imprisonment in each case, with four months consecutive in the case of one of the offenders for a bail offence. The Attorney General asked the Court to review the sentence on the ground that it was unduly lenient.

H4   **Held:** (considering *Attorney General's References Nos 32 and 33 of 1996 (Shane Robin Pegg and Mark Anthony Martin)* [1996] 2 Cr.App.R.(S.) 346, *Attorney General's Reference No.89 of 1999 (Neil Jack Farrow)* [2000] 2 Cr.App.R.(S.) 382, *Attorney General's Reference No.48 of 2000 (Martin Clive Johnson)* [2001] 1 Cr.App.R.(S.) 123 (p.423)) for the Attorney General it was submitted that the offence involved the targeting of a man who was known to be vulnerable and frail in his own home, and the use of gratuitous violence by a group of men. The offence was committed at night time and involved serious injury to the victim. The Court had spelt out on many occasions the gravity with which attacks in the home on the elderly or otherwise vulnerable people would be viewed. The Court accepted that deterrent sentences were required in such cases. The sentences of three years were unduly lenient. The appropriate sentence at first instance allowing for the pleas of guilty would have been in the range of six and a half to seven years' imprisonment. Allowing for the element of double jeopardy, the Court would substitute a sentence of five and a half years' imprisonment in each case for robbery.

H5   **Cases cited:**
Attorney General's References Nos 32 and 33 of 1996 (Shane Robin Pegg and Mark Anthony Martin) [1996] 2 Cr.App.R.(S.) 346, *Attorney General's Reference No.89 of 1999 (Neil Jack Farrow)* [2000] 2 Cr.App.R (S.) 382, *Attorney General's Reference No.48 of 2000 (Martin Clive Johnson)* [2001] 1 Cr.App.R.(S.) 123 (p.423)

H6   **References:** robbery, *Current Sentencing Practice* B 6-2

H7   *Miss B. Cheema* for the Attorney General.
D. Maunder for the offender Randall.
G. Nelson for the offender Donaghue.

JUDGMENT

1   **Keene L.J.:**   These are applications under s.36 of the Criminal Justice Act 1988 by Her Majesty's Attorney General for leave to refer two sentences to this Court because they appear to him to be unduly lenient. We grant leave and treat this as being the hearing of the references.

2   On March 5, 2004 Aaron Randall and Troy Donaghue were each sentenced at the Crown Court at Gloucester by H.H. Judge Tabor Q.C. to three years' imprisonment for robbery. Randall was also sentenced to four months consecutive for failing to surrender to bail. Both offenders had previously pleaded guilty to the robbery charge; Donaghue on November 20, 2003 and Randall on February 13, 2004.

3   The robbery, in which both offenders and a third man were involved, took place at night time at about 1.00am on July 17, 2003. The three men went to the home of the victim, a 57-year-old frail man, whom they knew to have learning difficulties and to be vulnerable. He was someone who needed help in carrying out such basic activities as washing and shaving. He had been the target of local children pestering him for money, and on occasions he had complied with those requests. One of the children to whom the victim had given money was Randall's stepson, aged 10, who was apparently given £10 by the victim the day before this offence.

4   The men called at the house, the victim was woken and he opened the door. The three men confronted him and he was pushed backwards into the hallway. The men entered and the victim was restrained by Donaghue and punched in the face. At least one of the men demanded money and the victim was asked where it was. He replied that he had money in an envelope upstairs. There was approximately £100 in cash in one of the upstairs rooms. The money was the

totality of the victim's savings from his benefits. Randall at least went upstairs and took the money. All three men then left. A neighbour heard the noise and the police were called. In due course the men were found hiding in a hedge. The victim suffered fractures to the right cheek bone and the eye socket.

5   At interview all three men made no comment. The victim was incapable of being a witness on an identification parade and his evidence was video-taped. The victim's blood was found on clothing attributed to both offenders. Randall's finger-prints were also found on the inside of the envelope upstairs in the victim's house which had contained the money.

6   At a further interview Randall said that he had been to the victim's house previously because he wanted to know why the victim had given his stepson money. There was a suggestion in the interview that the offender was concerned lest the victim be intent on sexually abusing the boy. This suggestion was subsequently withdrawn because both offenders recognised that there was no basis for it. Both offenders were released on bail.

7   During the time in which the case was making its way to the Crown Court, Randall breached his bail. He was at large between September 8, 2003 and February 3, 2004. Both offenders subsequently pleaded guilty at their respective preliminary hearings at the Crown Court. They both claimed to have been heavily drunk at the time of the offence.

8   Randall is aged 21. He has a number of previous convictions, mainly for burglary, theft and motoring offences. He has been made the subject of supervision orders, fined and sentenced to youth custody. His longest previous sentence was nine months imposed in November 1999 for a burglary committed on bail. Donaghue is aged 39. He has a substantial criminal record with over 100 previous convictions, mostly for burglary and theft and a number of minor offences. He has received several custodial sentences, the longest being a term of three years' imprisonment passed in 1995.

9   In sentencing both offenders, the learned judge said:

> "You confronted a man at his own doorstep who was especially vulnerable and frail and you both knew that. You had another man with you. You used gratuitous and quite unnecessary violence between you and then went into his house and rifled through his possessions and stole his money, and then produced an excuse that it was something to do with passing £10 to a child."

The judge went on to stress the pleas of guilty before passing the three-year sentences of imprisonment for robbery.

0   Some of those matters mentioned by the judge are among the aggravating features to which the Attorney General now refers: the targeting of a vulnerable and frail man known to the offenders to be such; the fact that the attack took place in his own home; the use of gratuitous violence; the fact that three men were involved in a group; and the rifling through of the victim's possessions, although there is some dispute as the to accuracy of that last item. In our view it makes no difference to the outcome of the case.

1   Ms Cheema, who appears on behalf of the Attorney General, emphasises certain aggravating matters not mentioned in the court below in the passage to which

I have referred. Thus, the offence was committed at night time; serious injury was caused to the victim; and an element of vigilante behaviour attached to the offence in that both these offenders accepted that at the time of the offence they attributed unsavoury motives to the victim's actions towards children. Moreover, both men had considerable previous convictions. Our attention is drawn also to the pre-sentence reports which indicate that both offenders sought to minimise their blameworthiness and revealed no sense of remorse.

12   This Court has been referred on behalf of the Attorney General to a number of authorities. The earliest in time is the *Attorney General's References Nos 32 and 33 of 1995 (Pegg and Martin)* [1996] 2 Cr.App.R.(S.) 346. In that case the then Lord Chief Justice, Lord Taylor, giving the judgment of the Court said at 350:

> "We have had drawn to our attention a number of cases where attacks have been made on elderly victims. Counsel have sought to compare and minimise the injuries that were inflicted as against those in other cases. However, the general effect of the decisions to which we were referred is to show that where an elderly victim, living alone, is violently attacked by intruders within the home and is injured the likely sentence will be in double figures. We wish to stress that attacks on elderly people in their own homes are particularly despicable and will be regarded by the court as deserving of severe punishment. Elderly victims living alone are vulnerable, not only because of the lack of assistance but also because of their own weakness and isolation. Any attack on such a person is cowardly and can only be expected to be visited with a very severe punishment indeed."

13   The attack in that case was more serious, involving the use of a knife, and the injuries suffered were grave. Sentences of between 7 and 10 years were passed reflecting the element of double jeopardy. Higher sentences would have been passed at first instance.

14   The next authority relied on by the Attorney General is the *Attorney General's Reference No.89 of 1999 (Farrow)* [2000] 2 Cr.App.R.(S.) 382. That case involved a robbery in the home by a single offender. The victim was aged 69 and lived alone. The offender forced his way into the house, threatened the victim with a knife and demanded money. He then punched the victim to the floor, applied pressure to his neck and then pulled some cable around the neck until the victim lost consciousness. £120 and a souvenir coin were taken. There was no plea of guilty. This Court took the view that the sentence for this offence at first instance should have been one of 10 years' imprisonment. That was reduced to allow for double jeopardy to a term of eight years' imprisonment.

15   Finally Ms Cheema refers us to the *Attorney General's Reference No.48 of 2000 (Johnson)* [2001] 1 Cr.App.R.(S.) 123 (p.423). In that case there was a plea of guilty to robbery. It was an offence committed by a single offender who went to a flat occupied by man of 79 who suffered from arthritis. The victim was pushed to the floor and punched in the mouth and to the nose. His pockets were searched, as was the flat, and in all £24 was taken. The offender had many previous convictions. This Court said that the bracket for such offences on a plea of guilty was between four and seven years' imprisonment. No signifi-

cant injury had been caused and no facial bruising was found. It seems to this Court that the bracket of four to seven years on a plea, referred to in that case, must have reflected that particular factor that the Court had in mind of the absence of any significant injury. Given that absence in that case, the plea of guilty and the indications of remorse, the Court declined to interfere with the four-year sentence.

16   In the light of those authorities, it is submitted on behalf of the Attorney General that the sentence in this case on each offender failed to mark adequately the gravity of the offence and aggravating features present. It is said that the judge gave too much credit for the guilty plea in spite of the fact that it was entered in the face of overwhelming evidence, particularly forensic evidence, and was accompanied by little remorse. It is also contended that the learned judge should have passed a deterrent sentence which reflected the need to protect vulnerable members of society from attack in their own homes. For those reasons, the submission by the Attorney General is that the sentence of three years' imprisonment in both these cases fell outside the proper bracket of sentencing and was unduly lenient in the circumstances of this case.

17   On behalf of the appellant, Randall, Mr Maunder acknowledges that the sentence was a lenient one. But he points out that the judge attached considerable weight to the guilty pleas, which avoided this frail victim having to give evidence at a trial. Reference is also made to the fact that Randall is only 21 and that the initial impetus behind the three men going to the house may not have been to rob. Moreover, no surgical intervention or treatment was needed for the injuries, even though there were fractures. It is suggested that the case is no worse than that of *Johnson* and that the sentence of three years' imprisonment cannot be regarded as unduly lenient.

18   On behalf of Donaghue, Mr Nelson adopts much of what was said by Mr Maunder on behalf of Randall. In particular he emphasises the point about the early guilty plea. He, too, compares this case to that of *Johnson* and emphasises that, in that case, the offender had previous convictions for robbery, quite unlike Donaghue.

19   We accept that the aggravating features in this case were, principally, the fact that a vulnerable and frail man was targeted; that the offence involved an invasion of his home at night time; that gratuitous violence was used; that significant injury resulted; and that a group of men were involved. We do not attach weight to the fact that surgical intervention or other treatment was not required. Two fractures of the face, in the judgment of this Court, do amount to significant injury.

20   We would also emphasise that the real test in these cases is that of vulnerability. The precise age of the victim is of less relevance. It is simply a factor which, along with other factors, may contribute to the victim being a vulnerable person living alone. This Court has spelt out on many occasions the gravity with which such attacks in the home on elderly or otherwise vulnerable people will be viewed. Such offences cause widespread anxiety amongst the elderly or vulnerable. We entirely accept the point made by the Attorney General that deterrent sentences in such cases are required.

21   We are in no doubt that the sentences of three years imposed in these two cases were lenient and unduly so. There was no allowance to be made here for good character. We are not impressed by the argument that there may not initially have been an intent to rob. If there was some other intent, which took the three men to the house of this frail and vulnerable man, it seems to this Court itself to have been equally reprehensible, of the kind referred to by Ms Cheema in her submissions.

22   Taking into account the authorities to which we have referred, the appropriate sentence at first sentence for this robbery, allowing for the pleas of guilty, would have been in the range of six and a half to seven years' imprisonment. That reflects the injury caused and the number of men involved, which is a relevant factor. Allowing for double jeopardy, we set aside the sentences for three years on the robbery count, and in each case we shall substitute a sentence of five and a half years' imprisonment. In the case of Randall, that will still have four months' imprisonment for failing to surrender to be added to run consecutively to it. The total, therefore, will be five and a half years' imprisonment in the case of Donaghue and five years 10 months in the case of Randall.

ATTORNEY GENERAL'S REFERENCE NO.53 OF 2004 (ALLAN LOWE)

COURT OF APPEAL (Lord Justice Keene, Mr Justice Mitting and Sir John Alliott): July 1, 2004

[2004] EWCA Crim 1831; [2005] 1 Cr.App.R.(S.) 61

(LT) Abuse of position of trust; Children; Indecent assault; Undue leniency

H1   *Indecent assault on male—indecent assaults over long periods of time on boys aged between eight and 13 by man trusted by their parents—length of sentence*

H2   Sentences totalling five years' imprisonment with an extended licence order for a large number of indecent assaults committed over 20 years previously on boys aged between eight and 13 by a man trusted by their parents increased to six years.

H3   The offender pleaded guilty to 45 counts of indecent assault on a male person. The offences were committed against three boys, aged between eight and 13 years at the time, over a period of seven years between the mid-1970s and the early 1980s. The offences involved incidents of masturbation and oral sex. The offender, aged between 36 and 43 at the time of the offences and now aged 65, was trusted by the parents of the boys and was allowed to take them on holiday. The boys were rewarded with presents and treats and threatened with punishment such as taking back the presents. The first victim estimated that he had been subject to at least 300 separate instances of abuse. The abuse began when the victims were aged eight and continued for a period of five years. It had had serious effects on each of the victims. Sentenced to five years' imprisonment on each count, with an order under the Powers of Criminal Courts (Sentencing) Act 2000, s.86, extending the licence. The Attorney General asked the Court to review the sentence on the ground that it was unduly lenient.

H4   **Held:** (considering *Millberry* [2003] 2 Cr.App.R.(S.) 31 (p.142), *Cubitt* (1989) 11 Cr.App.R.(S.) 380, *Attorney General's Reference No.12 of 1994 (Philip Dyke)* (1995) 16 Cr.App.R.(S.) 559, *Sweeney* [1998] 2 Cr.App.R.(S.) 43, *Burton-Barri* [1999] 2 Cr.App.R.(S.) 253, *Attorney General's References Nos 91, 119 and 120 of 2002* [2003] 2 Cr.App.R.(S.) 5 (p.338), *Attorney General's References Nos 37, 38, 44, 54, 51,53, 35, 40, 43, 45, 41, and 42 of 2003* [2004] 1 Cr.App.R.(S.) 84 (p.499)): it was submitted that the sentencing judge had correctly identified the aggravating features of the case, but had adopted too low a starting point. The judge had referred to the fact that the offender was trusted by the boys' parents and had clearly abused that trust; there were three victims; the abuse began when the boys were aged eight and took place over a protracted period; the abuse occurred frequently and had a marked and profound effect on the lives of the boys and their families. There was deliberate grooming of each boy and a systematic use of presents. It seemed to the Court that such abuse of children had come to be treated more severely in recent times. Despite the mitigating factors, and the offender's age, it seemed to the Court that the sentence at first instance should not have been less than seven years' imprisonment. Allowing for the element of double jeopardy, the Court would substitute sentences of six years' imprisonment concurrent.

H5   **Cases cited:**
Millberry [2003] 2 Cr.App.R.(S.) 31 (p.142), *Cubitt* (1989) 11 Cr.App.R.(S.) 380, *Attorney General's Reference No.12 of 1994 (Philip Dyke)* (1995) 16 Cr.App.R.(S.) 559, *Sweeney* [1998] 2 Cr.App.R.(S.) 43, *Burton-Barri* [1999] 2 Cr.App.R.(S.) 253, *Attorney General's References Nos 91, 119 and 120 of 2002* [2003] 2 Cr.App.R.(S.) 5 (p.338), *Attorney General's References Nos 37, 38, 44, 54, 51,53, 35, 40, 43, 45, 41, and 42 of 2003* [2004] 1 Cr.App.R.(S.) 84 (p.499)

H6   **References:** indecent assault on males, *Current Sentencing Practice* B 4-8

H7   *J. Lewis* for the Attorney General.
G. Hoare for the offender.

JUDGMENT

1   **Keene L.J.:**   This is an application under s.36 of the Criminal Justice Act 1998 by Her Majesty's Attorney General for leave to refer a sentence to this court because it appears to him to be unduly lenient. We grant leave and treat this as being the hearing of the reference.

2   On April 13, 2004 at Carlisle Crown Court the offender pleaded guilty to 45 counts of indecent assault on a male person contrary to s.15(1) of the Sexual

Offences Act 1956. He was sentenced on the same day by H.H. Judge Phillips to five years' imprisonment on each count to run concurrently. It was ordered under s.86 of the Powers of Criminal Courts (Sentencing) Act 2000 that he should remain on licence to the end of that sentence after his release. In addition he was disqualified from working with children indefinitely and ordered to register as a sex offender indefinitely. The total term of imprisonment imposed, therefore, was five years.

3   The offences involved the sexual abuse of three boys, each over a five period. In each case the victim was aged between 8 and 13 years. The offences took place between the mid 1970s and early 1980s over a period of seven years in all, but they only came to light more recently. In the case of each victim there were numerous incidents of masturbation of the boy by the offender and of oral sex both on the boy and on the offender. In the case of one of the victims there were incidents of masturbation where the offender inserted his penis between the boy's legs with the boy lying face downwards. We note that there were no offences to be dealt with by the judge of buggery or of anal penetration of any kind.

4   The offences arose out of a relationship between the offender and the families of the boys who are themselves related. There were regular family holidays together, which in time developed into the boys being allowed to travel for holidays on their own with the offender without any parental supervision. That was when the abuse began. There can be no doubt that the offender was trusted by the parents of the boys.

5   The sentencing judge rightly noted that the offences were aggravated by the buying of presents for, and the giving of treats to, the boys as inducements. In one case he promised the boy that he would receive £500 in the offender's will when he died. The offender also used a system of threats and punishments to induce the boys to comply with his wishes, on one occasion locking the victim out of their hotel room for three hours because the boy had refused to perform oral sex on him. There were threats to take back presents already given if the boy did not do as the offender wanted. By these processes he groomed each of the victims for the sexual abuse.

6   The first victim estimated that he had been subjected to at least 300 separate instances of abuse over the period of about five years. In the case of the second victim, the assaults occurred on almost every occasion when the offender was alone with him; those occasions being numerous. Those on the third victim were of a similar frequency.

7   In each case, we emphasise, the sexual abuse began when the offender was aged eight. Its continuation, in each case over a period of five years, has had a profound effect on each of the three victims. One boy, in his impact statement, speaks of not a day passing without thinking of the abuse he suffered and the fear he had of anybody finding out what had occurred to him. He described being unable to allow anyone to get too close or to know anything about him.

8   The second victim has suffered from severe depression and suicidal feelings. The third has found that the memories of the abuse have seriously affected his

relationship with his wife and children to the extent that he could not stand physical contact with children.

9   This abuse occurred when the offender was between the ages of 36 and 43. He is now aged 65. He is a man without previous convictions. At interview he admitted the offences and, as indicated, he pleaded guilty in court.

10   In his sentencing remarks the judge noted a number of aggravating features possessed by these offences. First, the offender was in a position of trust in respect of each boy, being trusted by the parents. He clearly abused that trust. Secondly, there were three victims. Thirdly, the abuse began when each victim was young, only eight years old. Fourthly, the abuse took place over a protracted period, some five years or so, in each case. Fifthly, it occurred frequently during that time. Sixthly, it had a marked and profound effect on the lives of these boys and their families. Seventhly, there was deliberate grooming of each of them with a systematic use of presents and threats to achieve compliance.

11   The Attorney General draws attention to that accumulation of aggravating features, but he adds the fact that the offender clearly had, and continues to have, a complete lack of awareness as to the impact of his behaviour and the damage he has done. There is some issue as to that taken on behalf of the offender by Mr Hoare, but it is to be noted that the pre-sentence reports states that Mr Lowe ". . . does not now want to consider the harm he has created", and that he continues to see the boys as complicit in the offences.

12   The Attorney General recognises that there were some mitigating features present, namely the offender's previous good character and his pleas of guilty. Nonetheless, it is submitted on his behalf by Mr Lewis, that the total sentence of five years' imprisonment failed properly to reflect the seriousness of this offending and the aggravating features present; in particular, that there were three very young victims who were subject to many serious assaults committed over a prolonged period. In addition, it is contended that the sentences failed to punish the offender adequately and deter others from committing similar offences, as well as not reflecting the degree of public concern about this kind of abuse.

13   Consequently Mr Lewis submits that the sentences passed were unduly lenient. He argues that the judge adopted too low a starting point even though he identified most of the aggravating features. Reliance for that submission is placed on a number of authorities: *Millberry* [2003] 1 Cr.App.R. 25, *Cubitt* (1989) 11 Cr.App.R.(S.) 380; *Attorney General's Reference No.12 of 1994* (1995) 16 Cr.App.R.(S.) 559, *Sweeney* [1998] 2 Cr.App.R.(S.) 43, *Victor Burton-Barri* [1999] 2 Cr.App.R.(S.) 253, *Attorney General's References Nos 91, 119 and 120 of 2002* [2003] 2 Cr.App.R.(S.) 5 (p.338), and the group of Attorney General's References from 2003 beginning with 37, which are reported collectively in [2004] 1 Cr.App.R.(S.) 84 (p.499).

4   On behalf of the offender, Mr Hoare acknowledges the aggravating features to which we have referred, but he emphasises not merely the early cooperation by the offender with the police but also his present age and relative poor health. It is recognised that these have only a limited effect these days upon the length of sentence as the authorities indicate but, nonetheless, it is emphasised that they are

matters which should still be taken into account. It is argued that the five-year sentence was one which properly reflected the great credit which has to be given for the mitigation of a prompt plea in cases of this kind. Had there been a trial, Mr Hoare submits that sentences in the region of about eight years would have been apt.

15   Some of the authorities referred to, it is stressed, reflect significantly longer periods of abuse than occurred in the present case. Mr Hoare accepts that there could have been no complaint if the sentence in total had been one or two years longer, but he submits that, even if lenient, the sentence imposed cannot be said to be so far below the expected level as to render it unduly lenient.

16   It seems to this court that the aggravating and mitigating factors in this case have been fully identified by the parties to this reference. We do not need to rehearse them individually again. The only additional matter which has some relevance, only we stress to a limited degree, is that these offences occurred between 22 and 30 years ago. The issue essentially concerns the appropriate length of custodial sentence in such a case on those acknowledged facts.

17   As was said in *Burton-Barri*, the relevant factors of cases such as this will include the ages of the victims, their number, the nature of the sexual misconduct, the frequency with which it occurred and whether it involved a breach of trust. We would add to that that the impact upon the victims will be of importance, as will whether or not there was systematic grooming of the victims. These matters are of course capable of almost infinite variety.

18   Moreover, on looking at the authorities, it seems to this Court that, as the Attorney General submits, such sexual abuse of children has come to be treated more severely in terms of sentencing in recent years than would at one time have seemed appropriate. That is brought out in the group of cases beginning with *Attorney General's Reference No.37 of 2003* which indicates that less weight these days is to be attached than in the past to such factors as the age of the offender, the staleness of the offences and the previous good character of the offender.

19   We do not intend to refer in any detail to the earlier authorities which have been cited to us. Guidance can be obtained from more recent decisions of this Court, particularly those where there has been deliberate grooming of the victims and where several children were involved. We refer briefly to those which seem to us to be most relevant. In *Sweeney* the appellant had pleaded guilty to a series of sexual assaults on young girls aged between 6 and 14. There were seven victims in all and the assaults took place over periods of years, in some cases five, eight or even nine years. The assaults consisted mostly of digital penetration of the vagina. There was no oral sex involved and no threats or bribes or other forms of grooming. However, the impact on the victims was significant. The appellant had been in a position of trust and he was aged 65 at the time of sentence. Reflecting his pleas of guilty, this Court reduced his total sentence to seven years' imprisonment.

20   In *Burton-Barri*, to which we have already referred, there were five victims, boys and girls, who were aged between 8 and 16 at the time of the offences. Again, there was a plea of guilty; again the appellant had been in a position of

trust and he was aged 63 at the time of sentence. The assaults involved masturbation, oral sex and anal penetration either digitally or by an object. This took place in individual cases over four and six years and the appellant had given the children presents in order to achieve compliance. This Court reduced the total sentence to one of 10 years' imprisonment. The case was, in certain respects, worse than the present one in that there were more victims, the abuse went on for longer in total and included anal penetration as well as oral sex.

21   One of the group of Attorney General's References 2003, which began with number 37, seems to us to have particular relevance to the present case. It concerns an offender known as RD who was 63 and who had pleaded guilty to eight counts of indecent assault on a total of five boys. He had groomed them for his abuse, which consisted of masturbation, oral sex and stimulated intercourse. The boys were aged 9, 10, 11 and 13. In four at least of the cases the abuse was frequent and took place over something like two to four years. The offender had been in a position of trust and the abuse had had a serious effect on the lives of the victims. This Court indicated that the appropriate sentence at first instance, had the offender not served already a sentence in Spain, would have been seven years.

22   Finally, we were referred to the *Attorney General's Reference No.112 of 2002 (Wood)* [2002] 2 Cr.App.R.(S.) 57 (p.249) where the offender had been convicted after a trial of indecent assaults on four boys between the ages of 9 and 13 and one girl aged 13. The assaults consisted of masturbation, some digital penetration, simulated anal intercourse but no oral sex. The offender had been in a position of trust and had groomed and threatened his victims. Unlike many of these cases the offender had a record of previous offences of a similar kind in respect of children. He was aged 50. Allowing for double jeopardy the Court increased the sentence to one of eight years custodial with an extended licence period of two years. Eight years was a longer than commensurate one to protect the public from serious harm.

23   In the light of those authorities, we turn to the present case. Here we have three victims whom the offender deliberately groomed for abuse over about five years in each case. The effect on his victims' lives has been grave. He was undoubtedly in a position of trust. His pleas of guilty are important in a case such as this because they avoid the need for the victims to give evidence, but we also note the offender's failure to appreciate the harm which he has caused and the absence of real remorse.

24   Despite the mitigating factors, including his age, it seems to this Court that at first instance there could not have been a total sentence of less than seven years' imprisonment. It follows that the sentences of five years' imprisonment were lenient. In this Court's judgment they were unduly lenient. We shall quash them and in their place, having made allowance for double jeopardy because this is a Reference, we shall in each case substitute a sentence of six years' imprisonment, those sentences to run concurrently. The total term, therefore, will be six years' imprisonment. As before, this offender must remain on licence for the whole of that period. The other orders made below will stand.

R. v JARNEIL SINGH SAINI AND OTHERS

Court of Appeal (Lord Justice Maurice Kay, Mr Justice Bell and
Judge Goldsack Q.C.): July 1, 2004

[2004] EWCA Crim 1900; [2005] 1 Cr.App.R.(S.) 62

(LT) Assisting illegal entry; Commercial activities; Consecutive sentences;
Conspiracy; Disparity of sentence; Guilty pleas

H1   *Facilitating illegal entry—organising large-scale illegal entry—no cruelty or
exploitation—length of sentence*

H2   Seven and a half years' imprisonment upheld on the principal participant in a
conspiracy to organise large-scale illegal entry into the United Kingdom.

H3   The appellants pleaded guilty to conspiring to facilitate the entry into the
United Kingdom of illegal immigrants. The prosecution alleged that the appellants were members of an organised group who facilitated the illegal entry of
foreign nationals into the United Kingdom over a period of about nine months.
The group provided forged passports and visas and arranged passage for foreign
nationals, primarily from the Indian subcontinent. The group provided coaching
in personal details and sufficient teaching in English to board a ferry. Free legal
representation was arranged for all those who were caught. Clients paid fees of
between £3,000 and £8,000 each. The prosecution asserted that the entry of
large numbers of persons had been facilitated in this way. Sentenced to seven
and a half years' imprisonment in the case of the principal offender and five
years and four years respectively in the case of the other appellants.

H4   **Held:** (considering *Le and Stark* [1999] 1 Cr.App.R.(S.) 422) it was submitted
for the principal offender that the sentence of seven and a half years' imprisonment on a plea of guilty was manifestly excessive, as the offence would not
have justified the maximum sentence of 10 years after a trial. The Court did
not consider that there need be actual cruelty, danger or exploitation to place a
conspiracy on this scale at or close to the maximum sentence were the charge
to be contested. In the Court's view, the principal offender would have deserved
the maximum or near the maximum sentence if the charge had been disputed. He
had been given real credit for his plea and the sentence of seven and a half years
was not excessive. The sentences on the other appellants were equally not manifestly excessive.

H5   **Case cited:**
Le and Stark [1999] 1 Cr.App.R.(S.) 422

H6   **References:** immigration offences, *Current Sentencing Practice* B 9-5

H7   *S. Sandhu, J. Barratt* and *Balbir Singh* for the appellants respectively.
       P. Clement for the Crown.

JUDGMENT

1   **Bell J.:**   On June 27, 2003 in the Crown Court at Harrow, the applicant,
       Sohan Lai Kalyan, pleaded guilty to count 1: conspiracy to facilitate the entry
       into the United Kingdom of persons whom he knew to be illegal immigrants.

2   On October 10, 2003, the appellants, Jarnail Singh Saini and Sarwan Singh
       Deo also pleaded guilty to that count. On November 19, 2003, they were sen-
       tenced as follows: Deo, seven and a half years' imprisonment; Saini, five
       years' imprisonment; Kalyan, four years' imprisonment.

3   A co-defendant, Sucha Singh Deol, pleaded guilty to the same count 1 and to a
       second count of conspiracy to handle stolen passports and identification docu-
       ments, which was really part of the conspiracy reflected by count 1. He
       pleaded guilty on June 27, the same day as Kalyan. He was sentenced to three
       years' imprisonment on each count concurrent. A further co-defendant, Povytar
       Singh Rai, pleaded guilty to count 1 on October 17, 2003 and was sentenced to
       three and a half years' imprisonment. His application for leave to appeal against
       sentence was refused and has now lapsed.

4   Deo and Saini now appeal against sentence with the leave of the single judge.
       Kalyan renews his application for leave to appeal against sentence after refusal
       by the single judge.

5   The dates of the conspiracy alleged in the indictment are between January 1,
       2001 and October 2, 2001, although the events which led to the indictment, sub-
       stantially, if not completely, occurred from January or February 2002 onwards. It
       was the prosecution case that Deo, Saini and Kalyan were members of a pro-
       fessional and organised group involved in facilitating the illegal entry of
       foreign nationals principally from the Indian sub-continent into the United
       Kingdom.

6   They were arrested on October 1, 2002, together with the co-defendants to
       whom we have referred, following an operation by the National Crime Squad's
       Immigration Team which had lasted several months. The investigation, invol-
       ving extensive video, photographic and audio surveillance, revealed a
       sophisticated criminal operation headed by Deo, an Indian national who was resi-
       dent in the Handworth area of Birmingham and had been for some years.

7   His and the group's business in illegal immigrants spread across continents
       from India to the Middle East and to Africa, and then into Europe and into the
       United Kingdom. It has been said on behalf of Mr Deo that he was only concerned
       with the European end but, of course, the European end was part of the exercise as
       a whole. The group provided a complete illegal entry service, which ranged from
       the forging of passports and visas to arranging passage, whether by sea, land or
       air. It provided coaching in personal details to be given in English and teaching
       sufficient English to board a ferry. If any of the would-be immigrants was caught,
       free legal representation was arranged. The motivation behind the activities of

the group as a whole was financial, with "clients" paying a fee of between £3,000 and £8,000 per person per passage.

8   The prosecution estimated that, while only 34 immigrants had been caught or stopped, the venture facilitated the illegal entry of many, many more. It is impossible for this Court to put a precise number upon the number of illegal immigrants. For the purposes of sentencing, it has to be accepted, in our view, that there were a significant number, certainly not a small number. The group profits must have been significant.

9   It was common ground that the group did not indulge in inherently dangerous methods of smuggling people in vehicles. There was no need for that because, as we have already indicated, the group organised passports, tickets, instructions and identity documents.

10   The flow of illegal immigrants was comparatively steady. If any were caught then the fall-back position was to claim asylum with the legal representation to which we have referred. Inevitably the immigrants, or a proportion of them, would be placed in a hostel or a hotel and then disappear. There was one example which was not commercial in the sense that it involved a relative of a conspirator. The criminal enterprise clearly demanded a team effort to ensure success. Mr Clement, for the Crown, has told us that the Crown did not attempt, nor did the sentencing judge, to put the defendants in a formal hierarchy, save to put Deo at the top as the organiser or an organiser. But it was possible to identify the roles of the defendants, each contributing to the conspiracy as a whole.

11   Deo was the principal. Audio surveillance revealed him directing and talking about the enterprise extensively and discussing the services to be provided, the cost to a client, clothing that entrants should wear and routes and methods of transport to the United Kingdom. He travelled extensively through Europe and to India and North Africa for no apparent legitimate purpose. On one occasion he was recorded talking about how he had tutored an illegal entrant from Ethiopia for two weeks before putting him on a flight to London. Trafficking in illegal immigrants was his principal if not sole business. The success of the scheme depended upon some unorthodox practices within the Indian Consulate General in Birmingham, in which it appears that Deo was involved. There is some issue as to the exact extent of those practices and whether they might have affected Italy more than this country. Investigators were unable to get to the bottom of that because, when the conspiracy came to light, the officials in question were moved to other missions. In interview, Deo denied his involvement in any illegal activity but said that he had unofficially helped Indian nationals already in the United Kingdom to obtain visas to remain there.

12   Saini was an Indian national residing in Leipzig, who was arrested at Deo's address in Handworth. He had been recorded on several occasions discussing the supply of forged travel documents and the facilitation of illegal entrants to the United Kingdom. He was very much an international traveller and his role in the conspiracy was described as more in the nature of a "foot soldier", but giving assistance and advice.

13   In interview, he admitted being involved in the organisation run by Deo. He provided details of addresses used by the group as safe houses for clients. The

basis of his plea, accepted by the Crown, was that he wanted to help his sister get back to India, or to the United States, but did not have the finances to pay for that. He was introduced to Deo and Kalyan in Germany, who said they could assist. He agreed to assist them in return for their assistance in respect of his sister. He was not a planner or organiser, but was told what was needed to be done and duly carried out the tasks.

14   He did not receive any money for his help, nevertheless the judge found, as she was entitled to, that when he did enter the ongoing conspiracy in May 2002, he pursued it with gusto as evidenced by recorded conversations.

15   Saini took responsibility for facilitating his sister's illegal travel, which was done out of the loyalty, it was accepted, that led to his involvement in the commercial venture.

16   Kalyan was Deo's lieutenant. His principal role was to meet the illegal entrants in Europe, hand over forged travel documents as necessary, and escort them to the United Kingdom. He was seen fulfilling that role on several occasions and had been recorded discussing the gang's trade in human trafficking. He admitted to some 20 to 25 expeditions. He too was treated as a foot soldier with the role of escort. In interview, he admitted that he personally facilitated the illegal entry of the entrants to whom we have referred, acting on the instructions of Deo and Deol. His admissions came relatively early during his interviews. His basis of plea was the 20 to 25 immigrants to whom we have referred, but with no involvement in the production or provision of false documentation. He accepted that he had received about £2,500–£3,000 payment for his services.

7   We must mention Deol and Rai, as comparison has been made with them and their sentences in the grounds of appeal. Deol was Deo's brother. Surveillance revealed him discussing the facilitation of illegal entrants into the United Kingdom. He had been observed collecting illegal entrants at the United Kingdom ports and taking them to addresses around the country. False passports were served and seized from his address. Despite the evidence of fuller involvement against him, he pleaded guilty on the specific and limited basis that he had assisted his brother on about five occasions by picking illegal immigrants up from their ports of entry and taking them to addresses in the United Kingdom, and on the basis that he had received no financial reward and had no part in the organisation.

Rai was involved in the forgery of passports, but the basis of his plea was specifically limited to the alteration of four passports by the substitution of photographs over a period of six months in 2002.

The judge found a number of the aggravating features identified in the case of *Le and Stark* [1999] 1 Cr.App.R.(S.) 422, namely a conspiracy over a period, an ongoing enterprise involving the repeated entry of large numbers of illegal immigrants, carried out for financial profit, with a high degree of planning and organisation.

We turn to the individual offenders. Deo is now aged 44 with previous convictions but not related to illegal immigration. He is a family man whose family will suffer from his prolonged imprisonment, but that is often the case with those who commit serious offences which are bound to attract substantial sentences.

21   Mr Balbir Singh has referred us to the transcript of mitigation at the sentencing hearing, and we take full account of that. But he has highlighted the following points. He submits that although this was a serious case, it was far from the worst of its kind, and it might assist us to consider where the court should start after a contested trial. Even after a contested trial, what Deo did could not justify the maximum sentence of 10 years, it is said. Mr Balbir Singh speculated about respects in which there might be more serious cases: hundreds of thousands of illegal immigrants over many years; treated in inhumane ways and brought into this country for purposes such as prostitution or cheap labour; or indiscriminately bringing in people who might be criminals or associated with terrorist organisations. He points out that the conspiracy established against Deo was restricted to some nine months, and that although his plea came relatively late in the day, the indication of it was given before the deadline which the judge specified for full credit for plea. His plea saved a long trial which would have involved the need for expensive translation of recorded conversations. He did not involve himself in a rich lifestyle and spoke of being in debt.

22   The second limb of Mr Balbir Singh's submissions is to suggest that his sentence of seven and a half years was unfairly disparate from that of three years imposed on his brother, Deol.

23   All that said, Deo was a prime mover in a conspiracy which, in our view, had a full hand of the aggravating features mentioned in *Le and Stark*. Mr Balbir Singh was unable to refer us to any report of a worse case, especially bearing in mind the scale and breadth of organisation of this conspiracy. We do not consider that there need be any actual cruelty or danger or exploitation so far as immigrants are concerned to put a conspiracy such as this at, or very close to, deserving the maximum sentence of 10 years were the charge to be contested.

24   Features such as cruelty, danger or exploitation might mean that other offences would be committed which would attract their own consecutive sentences. The plea was given before the deadline for full credit for plea, but Deo could not claim any additional credit for an earlier admission of his involvement. Although the extent of his profit may be difficult to ascertain, he clearly worked consistently in the conspiracy with profit in mind. There is no disparity with the sentence of Deol, in our view, once one bears in mind the basis of Deol's plea. The appellant Deo must appreciate that the judge had to sentence Deol on the basis of his plea, and any reasonable observer judging the sentencing exercise must come to the same conclusion.

25   One can always speculate about what case might be worse than the one before the Court, but in our view the judge in this case was right to assess Deo's guilt as deserving the maximum or near the maximum sentence had the charge been disputed. On that basis, she clearly gave him real credit for his plea. We do not consider the sentence of seven and a half years to be excessive, taking account of all the information either spoken in this Court or in the papers before us.

26   Turning to Saini. He is 38. He is of previous good character, although that can have limited effect in a case such as this, save in the respect that it means that he had not been involved in illegal immigration before. He has behaved well in prison as one would expect.

27   Mr Sandhu's main submission was that an unfair distinction was made between Saini and Kalyan when it came to sentence because Saini was sentenced to a year more than Kalyan in circumstances where Kalyan was part of the conspiracy from January and February 2002, and did escort a significant number of immigrants and received significant payment.

28   He also contended that there was an unfair disparity between Saini's sentence and the sentence on Deol. We have already referred to the basis upon which the judge was bound to sentence Deol. So far as comparison with Kalyan is concerned, he did receive money whereas Saini did not, but the judge was entitled to find that Saini's actual involvement once he did become involved in May 2002 was enthusiastic.

29   He did deserve credit for his plea of guilty, but not to the extent of Kalyan who, as we have said, made early admissions and the earliest of all the pleas, which may have had some beneficial effect so far as later pleas from co-defendants were concerned.

30   We bear in mind Mr Sandhu's other points, including the fact that Saini must serve his sentence in England while his family are in Germany, unable to visit him for financial reasons. But bearing all those points in mind, we do not consider that his sentence of five years was excessive. Nor is he entitled to feel unfairly sentenced in comparison with any of his co-defendants.

31   Kalyan is 50. So far as he is concerned, Mr Barratt agreed that, to some extent, the fate of his application depended upon the result of the appeals of Deo and Saini. But he also claimed that there was an unfair disparity with the sentences of Saini, Rai and Deol. We cannot accept that. He was clearly given greater credit than Saini for his prompt admissions and earlier plea. He played a more significant part in the conspiracy than Deol and Rai, on the bases of their pleas. We do not consider that the sentence of four years imposed on Kalyan in this case was manifestly excessive, nor is he entitled to feel any sense of grievance with regard to the lesser sentences imposed on two of his co-defendants.

32   It follows from what we have said that the appeals of Deo and Saini must be dismissed, and the renewed application on behalf of Kalyan refused.

R. v J (PATRICIA), M (CHRISTOPHER MICHAEL)

COURT OF APPEAL (Lord Justice Maurice Kay, Mr Justice Henriques and Judge Goldsack Q.C.): July 2, 2004

[2004] EWCA Crim 2002; [2005] 1 Cr.App.R.(S.) 63

ᴌᴛ Basis of plea; Child cruelty; Codefendants; Community rehabilitation orders; Custodial sentences; Ill treatment; Newton hearings

H1 *Neglect of children—difference between neglect and ill-treatment—treatment of offenders each blaming the other*

H2 In cases of child cruelty there is an important distinction between cases of wilful ill-treatment and cases of neglect. Where a defendant pleads guilty on the basis of neglect, the judge must not sentence on the basis of wilful ill-treatment, without following the procedures set out in *Newton* (1982) 4 Cr.App.R.(S.) 388 and *Tolera* [1999] 1 Cr.App.R. 29. Where two defendants blame each other, the sentencing judge must resolve the conflict by hearing evidence, or accept the mitigation, sentencing each defendant on the basis of his or her plea, notwithstanding the fact that one was inconsistent with the other.

H3 The appellants each pleaded guilty to five counts of cruelty to a child. The first appellant also pleaded guilty to escape. The appellants had five children between the ages of three and nine. Health visitors had expressed concerns over a long period of time. The house was dirty and the children did not attend medical appointments. The family had been involved with the Social Services since 1999. In 2003 Social Services found the house was filthy, with rubbish piled behind doors. The beds had no bedding and were ridden with fleas. The children attended school spasmodically. The first appellant pleaded guilty on the basis that she had done her best in the circumstances. The second appellant pleaded guilty on the basis that the first appellant was primarily responsible for the offences. Sentenced to eight months' imprisonment in the case of the first appellant and 18 months' imprisonment in the case of the second appellant.

H4 **Held:** (considering *McIntyre and McIntyre* (1993) 14 Cr.App.R.(S.) 308, *Cammile and Partridge* (1993) 14 Cr.App.R.(S.) 296, *Crank* [1996] 2 Cr.App.R.(S.) 363, *Yasmin L and Alvin L* [2004] 1 Cr.App.R.(S.) 3 (p.34)) the Court was satisfied that in the case of both the appellants the offence was so serious that only a custodial sentence could be justified. In cases of child cruelty there was an important distinction between cases of wilful ill-treatment and cases of neglect. Where a defendant pleaded guilty on the basis of neglect, the judge must not sentence on the basis of wilful ill-treatment, without following the procedures set out in *Newton* (1982) 4 Cr.App.R.(S.) 388 and *Tolera* [1999] 1 Cr.App.R. 29. Where two defendants blamed each other, the sentencing judge must resolve the conflict by hearing evidence, or accept the mitigation, sentencing each defendant on the basis of his or her plea, notwithstanding the fact that one was inconsistent with the other. The Court could see no significant basis for the distinction between the appellants. The Court considered that for the second appellant the appropriate sentence would be nine months' imprisonment and in the case of the first appellant a term of six months; however as the first appellant would shortly be released from custody and would welcome the assistance of the probation service, the Court would substitute a community rehabilitation order.

H5   **Cases cited:**
McIntyre and McIntyre (1993) 14 Cr.App.R.(S.) 308, *Camille and Partridge* (1993) 14 Cr.App.R.(S.) 296, *Crank* [1996] 2 Cr.App.R.(S.) 363, *Yasmin L and Alvin L* [2004] 1 Cr.App.R.(S.) 3 (p.34), *Newton* (1982) 4 Cr.App.R.(S.) 388, *Tolera* [1999] 1 Cr.App.R. 29

H6   **References:** neglect of child, *Current Sentencing Practice* B 2-7.3C

H7   *G. Purcell* for the first appellant.
E. Ballentyne for the second appellant.

JUDGMENT

1   **Henriques J.:**   These are appeals with the leave of the single judge against sentences passed on April 30 in the Crown Court at Nottingham. The appellant, J, having pleaded guilty to escape for which she was sentenced to one month's imprisonment, and five counts of child cruelty for which she was sentenced to eight months' imprisonment concurrent. The appellant, M, pleaded guilty to five counts of child cruelty and was sentenced to 18 months' imprisonment, with a community punishment order and community rehabilitation order for handling stolen goods, damaging property, failing to surrender to bail, common assault and theft being revoked. Pleas in both cases were tendered at an earlier hearing on April 5 before Judge Pert.

2   The facts are very sad. The appellants have five children aged between three and nine. Since 1994 visiting health visitors had regular concerns. The house was dirty. The children did not attend medical examinations, nor appointments. The health visitor's advice was ignored. After December 2001 no visitor was allowed over the doorstep. Social Services became involved in 1999 and concluded that the children had been exposed to an extremely unhealthy environment which was filthy. There were mounds of clothes, broken toys and there was reference to fleas.

3   In February 2001 the premises were damp with no heating. A week later, J would not allow the social worker to see the children's bedrooms although it is right that the children at the time were clean.

4   Although the file was closed in March 2000 it was reopened in May 2001. Up to the end of 2002 there were a number of referrals to other agencies. Social Services concluded that the appellants were not creating an appropriate environment and were uncooperative with those trying to help them.

5   On April 8, 2003 Social Services found the house to be filthy. Rubbish was piled behind doors. Beds had no bedding and were smelly and were ridden with fleas. The children had attended school spasmodically and on one occasion one child had to be collected from school because of "an intolerable odour about him". The appellants were aggressive towards school staff when their shortcomings were pointed out. Arrangements were made to remove the children to live with other family members.

6   On November 14, 2003 J was arrested and en route to the police station leapt out of the police vehicle and made to escape. She was arrested nearby and fought on re-arrest.

7   In interview she denied all the allegations and blamed her partner for the state of the children, saying he would not let her look after them and that he would be violent if she tried to get assistance from Social Services. She tendered a basis of plea when pleading guilty in these terms:

> "I have decided, following legal advice, to plead guilty to each offence. I do so on the basis of my answers given in two interviews. I accept that although I tried my best, I struggled to cope with five children in my domestic circumstances and that accordingly they were neglected. This was made worse for me when I lost my baby."

8   M, in interview, admitted that the children had been exposed to dangers and had not been looked after properly. He strongly implicated his partner in the offences. He pleaded guilty on that basis and expressly denied that the children had at any time been exposed to the drug habit of either parent either directly or indirectly.

9   M denied coercing his co-accused into neglecting the children. He maintained that J was just as much to blame as he was in their neglect. He asserted it was his wife who resisted help from the Social Services. By wife he was referring to J.

10   There was no trial of any issue and it is manifest from the nature of the pleas and mitigation that the pleas tendered were very much on the limited and specific basis referred to.

11   Complaint is made on behalf of each appellant that having heard no evidence, the judge passed sentence on both appellants on the basis which was inconsistent with the limited basis of the plea in each case. It is noteworthy that no reference was made in the sentencing remarks to the fact that either appellant had pleaded guilty and was receiving specific credit for those pleas of guilty.

12   In J's case the judge commented that this was not simply inadequacy but an active disregard. In particular, when passing sentence the judge observed:

"They were exposed to the effects of drug abuse not only of your own drug abuse but those of other adults who visited the house."

She also said:

"Neither of you are able to face up to your own responsibility, each of you has sought to blame the other."

13 It is important to note that each count was widely drawn alleging that each defendant wilfully ill-treated, neglected or exposed the said child in a manner likely to cause unnecessary suffering or injury to health. Each defendant was asserting that he or she was guilty of neglect through inadequacy and not through wilful ill-treatment. The sentencing remarks tend to indicate that this was not accepted by the judge.

14 It is also important to note that J, through Mr Purcell, who represented her, specifically blamed M for violence towards her and made specific reference to a conviction in November 2003 for common assault, an offence committed albeit after the children had been removed from the home but an offence which Mr Purcell indicated characterised the relationship between them over a number of years.

5 There was also an offence of criminal damage before the court on August 3, 2003. That offence being committed on June 11, 2003, when M had smashed a window during an argument with J by throwing a piece of wood.

6 It was contended on behalf of J that those convictions supported her allegations against M sufficiently to allow the judge to draw the positive inference that M was substantially far more to blame for the commission of these offences than she, J, was.

7 In sentencing M to 18 months this was clearly the starting point adopted by the judge. We have considered the relevant authorities beginning with *McIntyre & McIntyre* (1993) 14 Cr.App.R.(S.) 308. In that case 18 months' imprisonment was upheld for wilfully neglecting a child aged two over a period of 12 months. It was held not to be a case of wilful violence or wilful cruelty. It was a case of grossly inadequate parents. The child was not properly fed, lost weight and showed signs of severe emotional abuse.

3 Whilst the children in the present case were properly nourished, it can be said that in the present case there was neglect over three and a half years to five different children. The consequences, however, in *McIntyre & McIntyre* were far worse. Indeed in the case of *Crank*, Auld L.J. referred to *McIntyre & McIntyre*, stating the facts were far worse, indeed they were worse than in the present case.

In *Camille & Partridge* (1993) 14 Cr.App.R.(S.) 296, sentences of six months' and four months' imprisonment were upheld on a woman and man for neglecting three children over a period of about 18 months. There the conduct was pure neglect with no wilful ill-treatment. Particular reliance is placed by Mr Cassell on the case of *Crank* [1996] 2 Cr.App.R.(S.) 363, a case in which 18 months' imprisonment, imposed on a heroin addict for neglecting her four children, over a period of seven months was reduced to nine months.

20   The appellant and her husband were both heroin addicts and over a period of six months they wilfully neglected the children. The children were not properly fed, their teeth were badly damaged and they were frequently dirty and were eventually taken into care. The appellant in that case had a number of previous convictions for dishonesty and drug related offences but had not previously lost liberty. Auld L.J. said this:

> "In our view, a proper balance of need to mark the seriousness of the offences with the general living circumstances and hopeless inadequacy of the appellant, passed offences and other offences to which he was committed for sentence, indicate a sentence of no more than 9 months' imprisonment as appropriate."

21   Finally, most recently, *Yasmin L and Alvin L* [2004] 1 Cr.App.R.(S.) 3 (p.34). A sentence of two years' imprisonment, on each of two parents for neglect of a child aged between 9 months and 18 months by leaving him at home alone on various occasions for periods of several hours varied to six months' imprisonment suspended for two years in each case in view of exceptional personal circumstances and the interests of the child. The facts were very different to the present. Both parents went out to work. On a number of occasions they left the child alone for between three and six hours, without food and water. On one occasion with heaters at a position close to him. He was said to have been found in circumstances that the judge described as shocking neglect. Giving judgment Laws L.J. said:

> "No one should suppose that in quashing these prison sentences we do so out of any sense that these were not serious offences, they were. It is disgraceful that a child so young should be left alone in those circumstances and it was at least potentially dangerous. We do not say that these parents did not deserve to be sent to prison but this is surely a case in which the punitive considerations of retribution and deterrence should give way to the interests of the child."

22   In the present case, we are satisfied that these offences in the case of both appellants are so serious that only a custodial sentence can be justified. However, we would make the following observations.

1. In cases of child cruelty there is an important distinction between cases of wilful ill-treatment and cases of neglect. Where a defendant pleads guilty on the basis of neglect, a judge must not sentence on the basis of wilful ill-treatment, without following the clear procedures set out in *Newton* and subsequent cases, particularly *Tolera* [1999] 1 Cr.App.R. 29 in which Lord Bingham said the court should make it clear that it did not accept the defence account and why. There is an obvious risk of injustice if the defendant did not learn until sentence was passed that his version of the facts was rejected, because he could not then seek to persuade the court to adopt a different view. The court should therefore make its

view known, and failing any other resolution, a hearing could be held and evidence called to resolve the matter. That would usually involve calling the defendant.

2. Where two defendants blame one another, the sentencing judge must either resolve the conflict by hearing evidence, or accept the mitigation, sentencing each defendant on the basis of his or her plea, notwithstanding the fact that one is inconsistent with the other.

23   We can see no significant basis for the distinction in this case between the appellants, save and except for their antecedent history. J has no previous convictions, M has some 18 previous convictions, almost all for dishonesty, with two convictions for common assault.

24   Taking *Crank* as an appropriate sentencing authority, on the facts remarkably similar to the present, we conclude that nine months is the appropriate sentence in M's case. To that extent his appeal is allowed by substituting the term of nine months.

25   We were minded to reduce the sentence in J's case to a sentence of six months' imprisonment. That we believe to be the correct and appropriate sentence having regard to the facts of the case. However, she is due to be released at any date. Mr Purcell states she would very much welcome the assistance of the probation service on a continuing basis. We bear in mind the many difficulties that she has faced, including, of course, the comparatively recent loss of a child, wholly unconnected with any allegation made against her.

26   In those circumstances, we are minded to substitute for the sentence imposed in her case a community rehabilitation order which will be for the duration of two years.

[Paragraphs 27–28 have been omitted.]

R. v IAN WILSON, CRAIG MAINPRIZE

COURT OF APPEAL (Lord Justice Thomas, Mr Justice Gage and Sir
Richard Rougier): July 2, 2004

[2004] EWCA Crim 2086; [2005] 1 Cr.App.R.(S.) 64

(LT) Causation; Death; Divers; Health and safety offences; Prosecution costs

H1   *Health and Safety offences—proprietors of diving training centre failing to comply with regulations through ignorance—trainee diver dying—death not caused
by fault of appellants—amount of fine*

H2   Fines of £3,000 imposed on each of the proprietors of a diving training centre
where a trainee diver was drowned reduced to £1,500 in each case, on the ground
that although there was a failure to comply with regulations through ignorance,
this did not cause or contribute to the death.

H3   The appellants each pleaded guilty to failing to conduct an undertaking in such
a way as to ensure the safety of persons involved. The appellants were concerned
in providing a recreational diving course at an inland diving site. The appellants
were both qualified divers who operated a shop and provided diving courses on a
part-time basis. A lady who was planning a holiday with her family enrolled in a
course in order to learn scuba diving. The course involved preparatory lectures,
followed by diving first at low level and then later in deeper water in a disused
quarry. The lady successfully completed two of four planned dives in the quarry
and was placed with others in a group under an instructor. The lady got into difficulties in her first dive to a depth of 10 metres, and it was decided that she should
be paired with a trained rescue diver. During a lower dive, they became separated
from the rest of the group and the lady panicked and lost her mouth piece. The
trained rescue diver attempted to restore the situation but the lady was found
to be dead when she was brought to the surface. It was alleged that the death
of the lady had been caused by the failure of the appellants to comply with the
Diving at Work Regulations 1997, and the Code of Practice. Sentenced to a
fine of £3,000 in each case and ordered to pay the prosecution costs in a total
amount of £7,500 in each case.

H4   **Held:** although the case had been presented to the sentencing judge as one of
total and flagrant disregard of all safety regulations, only three aspects were mentioned by the sentencing judge. These were that the appellants were ignorant of
the existence of the Diving Regulations and Code of Practice; there was no written diving project plan as required by the Regulations and the diving supervisor
had not been formally appointed. The sentencer stressed that the prosecution had
failed to satisfy him that the death of the lady was in any way caused or contributed to by any failures of the appellants operating on the day in question.
This was not a flagrant or cavalier breach by men who did not care. The sen-

tencing judge accepted that each appellant was highly conscientious in matters of safety but was unaware of the existence of regulations. The Court had considered the amount of the fines in relation to the actual findings of the sentencing judge. Once it was accepted that there was no connection between the shortcomings of the appellants and the death of the deceased, attention was focused on the extent to which the breaches jeopardised the general safety aspects of the operation. The Court considered that the fines were excessive. They would be reduced to £1,500 in each case. The orders for the payment of prosecution costs would be reduced to £4,000 in each case.

H5   **References:** public safety offences, *Current Sentencing Practice* B 13-2

H6   *J. Matthews* for the appellants.
      S. Killalea for the Crown.

JUDGMENT

1   **Sir Richard Rougier:**   The appellants, Ian Wilson, 44 years old, and Craig Mainprize, 38, at October 6, 2004 at the Crown Court at Luton, on rearraignment, pleaded guilty to an offence under s.3(1) of the Health and Safety at Work Act 1974, as particularised in the indictment that they "failed to conduct their undertaking, namely the provisional of a recreational diving course at Stoney Cove inland diving site, in such a way as to ensure, so far as was reasonably practicable, that persons involved in the recreational diving course, including one Janet Reed, were not exposed to risks to their health and safety". They were each fined a sum of £3,000 and ordered to pay what were said to be the prosecution costs at that time of £15,000, thereby paying £7,500 each. They appeal against not only the sentence but the order in relation to costs by leave of the learned single judge, who at the same time pointed out that the grounds of appeal were not particularly helpful in identifying the issues and called upon the prosecution to provide the court with assistance on two matters: (1) what was in issue between the experts called on behalf of each side, and (2) how the total costs of £40,000 were incurred.

2   The facts arose from a most tragic death of the lady mentioned whilst undergoing basic training for scuba diving. The appellants are both highly qualified divers with the appropriate certificates and they ran a small private business, called Hydroactive Outdoor Pursuits, which operated as a sort of dive shop and provided diving courses for trainees, not only those who wanted to be amateur scuba divers but also those who wished to qualify. It was very much a part-time affair, with voluntary help. But it should be stated that, unlike certain other concerns which have been prosecuted, this was in no sense a cowboy operation and, as the learned sentencing judge pointed out, was conducted responsibly and with a good deal of care, apart from certain lapses to which we will come.

3   Mr and Mrs Reed, a couple in their 30s, who had two small children, were about to go on holiday in the Seychelles and thought it would be a good idea to learn how to scuba dive. Accordingly in February 2001 they enrolled with the appellants on one of their basic training courses. This started with a series of lectures and then diving in a local pool at very low level. Then it moved on

to open water dives in deeper water, the deeper water being a disused quarry with a lot of debris at the bottom, including a sunken helicopter.

4   On March 17, 2001, under the instruction of the appellant Mainprize and another instructor, a group including the Reeds successfully completed two of four planned dives at the quarry, going to a depth of 6 metres and then performing various exercises and routines as part of the basic training. The next day the group reformed in a somewhat different configuration and the Reeds were placed with three others under an instructor called Simister. Mainprize was not at the quarry and the appellant Wilson took himself off to be instructor for another group. Simister too was a highly qualified instructor, and he and Wilson discussed the depths and dives of the routine which was to be done.

5   During the course of the first dive, Mrs Reed got into some difficulties with her hearing at the 10-metre level. Simister thereupon decided that she should be what is known as "buddied" by a trained rescue diver, a Mrs Morrell. So the two of them, as it were, were paired. During the course of the lower dive, down to some 18 metres, as always happens, of course, visibility became much more enclosed and the two of them were separated from the rest of the group. Tragically, Mrs Reed began to panic and lost her mouthpiece—in fact it is thought that she probably pulled it off in an attempt to swim back to the surface. Mrs Morrell vainly tried to restore the situation but was unsuccessful, and effectively by the time she was ultimately brought to the surface it was discovered that Mrs Reed was dead.

6   The prosecution from an early stage seem to have taken the view that their duties required them to present a case on the basis that the death of Mrs Reed had been caused by the failures of the appellants to abide by the Diving at Work Regulations 1997 and the Code of Practice which was attached thereto. As can be seen from a document entitled "Points of aggravation", with references to the report of their expert, a Mr Scammell (which we have not seen), it made a great number of criticisms of the appellants' diving procedures, many of which, it must be said, demonstrate the bureaucratic love of form in preference to that of substance. For instance, it seems that neither appellant had formally registered as a diving contractor, although each of them was perfectly qualified to do so; in other words, the correct document was not in existence. Similarly, they were criticised for the fact that Mr Simister was not appointed in writing as a diving supervisor, although again he was perfectly qualified to be so.

7   As a result of the fusillade of criticisms which were made against them, the defence, reasonably enough, instructed a Mr Bevan to consider the criticisms made by Mr Scammell (over whose total objectivity there might some queries since he turns out to have been a competitor of the appellants, operating in the same quarry). As a result of Mr Bevan's researches and comments, ultimately a case which had been presented to the learned judge as one of a total and flagrant disregard by the appellants of all safety regulations ultimately was shrivelled into a mere three aspects which were set out by the learned sentencing judge.

8   They were as follows. First, and possibly most important of all, there was revealed the fact that the two appellants had an alarming ignorance of the existence of the Diving Regulations and the Code of Practice and of the fact that they

were supposed to operate in accordance with those Regulations. This in turn led to the fact that there was at no time any written diving project plan, as the Regulations demand, dealing with such things as the route to be taken, the depth to be achieved, what emergencies or trainee errors were to be anticipated, and what emergency procedures were to be followed and so forth. This, as the learned judge correctly described, was a serious matter, in that the preparation of a written plan, adverting to all possible contingencies, is something that is bound to concentrate the mind and lead to a much more thorough preparation for a dive than instructions merely given by word of mouth.

9   The learned judge also said that he regarded as serious the fact that there was no formal appointment of a diving contractor or supervisor. With all due respect to him, that does seem to this Court to be rather more a matter of form than of substance, since there is no doubt that the persons in charge of this operation were in fact perfectly qualified to act in those capacities.

10   The learned judge went on to stress that the prosecution had failed to satisfy him and had accepted that they failed to satisfy him that the death of Mrs Reed, tragic though it was, was in any way either caused or contributed to by any failures of the appellants operating on the day in question. It is extremely important to bear that fact in mind when considering the extent of the fine and the costs which were consequently imposed.

11   The learned judge added that this was not a flagrant, cavalier breach by men who simply did not care. He said he had no doubt that each appellant was, and is, normally highly conscientious in matters of safety, but it is undeniable that they did not adhere to the Regulations for the simple reason that, regrettably and culpably, they were unaware of their existence.

12   The grounds of appeal against the level of the fine imposed are that the learned judge erred in failing to give adequate weight to the evidence of Mr Bevan, the defence expert, and did not make it clear when passing sentence the extent to which he had accepted that expert's conclusions, in particular that the diving instructors were aware of all the relevant risk factors involved. We cannot think that that particular ground is very well founded because the very fact that dozens of allegations had been reduced to a mere three effective ones, in our opinion, shows all too clearly that the learned judge, though he may not have read Mr Bevan's report in its entirety, accepted what indeed the prosecution accepted, namely that it had effectively torpedoed most of their criticisms.

13   It is maintained that insufficient account was taken of the fact that had there been no suggestion of a causal link and the matter could have been disposed of by the magistrates. That, in our judgment, is indeed a valid criticism.

14   It is said that insufficient credit was given for the guilty pleas, even on rearraignment. On that aspect we are urged by Mr Matthews that it was perfectly reasonable for the appellants, faced as they were with so many allegations which reflected upon their competence generally, to argue the case from top to bottom. That, in our judgment, is only partly sustainable. The appellants elected, ultimately, to argue the very application of the Regulations themselves, which was, in our view, a matter which could not possibly have succeeded.

15   We have considered the amount of the fines imposed in relation to the actual findings of the learned judge as to the extent of the breaches. Once it is accepted that there is no connection between Mrs Reed's death and the shortcomings of these appellants, the attention focuses on the extent to which the breaches by the appellants jeopardised what one might describe as the general safety aspects of what is in any event a hazardous occupation.

16   We also have paid attention to previous cases where diving operations have fallen foul of the authorities. We are particularly struck by the fact that far lesser fines have been imposed upon persons whose conduct has drawn very strong remarks from the Bench, such as being a "cavalier outfit" and being conducted "in total disregard of safety", and that is not the case here. Taking a rather broader approach than the very detailed submissions which have been made to us by Mr Matthews, we think that the fines were, in all the circumstances, excessive. We propose in each case to halve them by substituting a figure of £1,500.

17   We now turn to the question of costs, where the position is even less satisfactory. In no particular critical sense we have to say that, despite the request from the learned single judge, the prosecution have been unable to explain to us in any comprehensible form just how the various costs were made out. On the one hand, the argument is that a prosecution was launched which almost entirely failed. On the other hand, it is undoubtedly right that the Health and Safety Executive were under a duty to investigate the matter. Again, despite the very detailed submissions that have been made to us, in the unsatisfactory nature of the whole position in relation to costs, we think there is no option but again to take a somewhat broad brush stroke. We think that in view of the fact that much of what the prosecution were alleging ultimately failed to pass the winning post as it were, the costs payable by the appellants were placed too high and we would reduce the total to £8,000, thereby imposing £4,000 on each. To that extent this appeal has succeeded. The period in default will be reduced to 45 days.

ATTORNEY GENERAL'S REFERENCE NO.37 OF 2004 (JAMES ANTHONY DAWSON)

COURT OF APPEAL (Lord Justice Latham, Mr Justice Stanley Burnton and Mr Justice Mitting): July 6, 2004

[2004] EWCA Crim 1854; [2005] 1 Cr.App.R.(S.) 65

⟨LT⟩ Attempts; Community rehabilitation orders; Depression; Possession of firearms; Robbery; Undue leniency

H1   *Robbery—attempted robbery at sub-post office by offender armed with air pistol—offender suffering from depression at time of offence—whether community rehabilitation order unduly lenient*

H2   A community rehabilitation order with psychiatric requirements held not to be unduly lenient for an attempted robbery at a sub-post office by an offender armed with an air pistol on the ground that the offender, aged 20, was suffering from depression at the time of the offence.

H3   The offender, aged 20, pleaded guilty to attempted robbery and possessing a firearm at the time of committing an indictable offence. The offender, aged 20, left his mother's house following an argument. He went to a sub-post office close to his mother's house, waited until a customer had left and approached the post master. He produced a gun with a six-inch barrel from the waist band of his trousers and pushed a plastic carrier bag through the hatch of the screen. The post master dived below the level of the counter and pressed an alarm. The offender fled without stealing anything. He was arrested about two hours later and eventually accepted responsibility. The firearm was found to be a repeating air pistol in working order which looked like a large self-loading gun. It was capable of causing a fatal wound. The sentencing judge was told that at the time of the offence the offender was suffering from a depressive illness which would have clouded his judgement. Sentenced to a community rehabilitation order with a condition that the offender work with a psychiatric counsellor. The Attorney General asked the Court to review the sentence on the ground that it was unduly lenient.

H4   **Held:** (considering *Attorney General's Reference No.2 of 1989 (Darren Major)* (1989) 11 Cr.App.R.(S.) 481, *Attorney General's Reference No.9 of 1989 (Stephen Lacey)* (1990) 12 Cr.App.R.(S.) 7, *Attorney General's References Nos 3, 4, 8, 9, 10 and 11 of 1990 (Dixon and others)* (1990) 12 Cr.App.R.(S.) 479, *Attorney General's Reference No.83 of 2001 (Stephen David Fidler)* [2002] 1 Cr.App.R.(S.) 139 (p.588), *Attorney General's Reference No.4 of 1989* (1989) 11 Cr.App.R.(S.) 517) the sentencing judge was fully aware that the Court of Appeal had repeatedly stated that such offences would normally call for a deterrent custodial sentence for the protection of those running small businesses. He referred to the fact that a substantial period of imprisonment would normally result. He took account of the offender's abnormal mental condition, and the fact that he had taken no steps to conceal his identity. He indicated that the fact that the offender was depressed at the time of the offence enabled him to take a wholly exceptional course. For the Attorney General, it was submitted that the circumstances did not fall into the category of wholly exceptional cases in which the ordinary consequences should not follow. The Court had repeatedly said that sentencing was not always a mechanical exercise. There must be room for a sentencer in an appropriate case to exercise individual judgment in relation to the particular facts before him in order to do justice to the offender and to provide more protection for the public. In the present case an experienced judge took the view after careful thought that the interests of the offender and of the public generally would best be served by making the order which he did. Dealing with the case on the basis of the position before the sentencing judge, the Court would refuse leave to make the reference.

H5   **Cases cited:**
Attorney General's Reference No.2 of 1989 (Darren Major) (1989) 11 Cr.App.R.(S.) 481, *Attorney General's Reference No.9 of 1989 (Stephen Lacey)* (1990) 12 Cr.App.R.(S.) 7, *Attorney General's References Nos 3, 4, 8, 9, 10 and 11 of 1990 (Dixon and others)* (1990) 12 Cr.App.R.(S.) 479, *Attorney General's Reference No.83 of 2001 (Stephen David Fidler)* [2002] 1 Cr.App.R.(S.) 139 (p.588), *Attorney General's Reference No.4 of 1989* (1989) 11 Cr.App.R.(S.) 517

H6   **References:** robbery, *Current Sentencing Practice* B 6-2

H7   *E. Brown* for the Attorney General.
Miss A. Nicholson for the offender.

JUDGMENT

1   **Latham L.J.:**   In this case the Attorney General seeks leave to refer to this Court a sentence which was imposed on March 8, 2004 on the offender for an offence of attempted robbery and an offence of possession of a firearm at the time of committing an indictable offence. The sentence imposed by H.H. Judge Lyon on that occasion was a three-year community rehabilitation order with a condition that the offender work with a psychiatric counsellor from the young offender team.

2   The facts of the offence for which he was sentenced were that on the afternoon of August 15, 2003 the offender then 20 years old left his mother's house having had an argument with her and having been told not to come back. He was in possession of an air pistol. He went to the Burnsall Walk sub-post office in Wythenshawe, Manchester, which was close to his mother's home. The sub-postmaster, Howard Meadowcroft, was working alone in the post office serving a customer from behind the counter. Once that customer had finished and had

left the shop, the offender approached and pushed a plastic carrier bag through the hatch of the screen. He pulled the gun from the waistband of his trousers. This was described as a black Luger-type handgun with a six-inch barrel. The offender told Mr Meadowcroft to fill the bag with money and not to press any alarms. Fearing that he would be shot, Mr Meadowcroft dived below the level of the counter and pressed the panic alarms. This sounded an alarm not only at the alarm company but also inside and outside the shop. The offender fled. Nothing had been stolen.

3   The offender was arrested about two hours or so later in the Woodhouse area of Wythenshawe, his description having been circulated. When first stopped he denied knowledge of the offence but once he was told that there had been closed circuit television coverage of the shop he accepted that he had been responsible. He took the police officers to where he had discarded the gun in some nearby bushes. He also said that he had changed his clothing after the offence. He was picked out at an identification parade on August 20, 2003.

4   The gun was examined by a firearms expert and was found to be a .177 repeating air pistol in working order and had the appearance of a large self-loading handgun. Although it fell into the low to medium power range it was capable of causing a fatal wound and therefore fulfilled the criteria for a lethal barrelled weapon for the purposes of the Firearms Act 1968.

5   The offender had no previous convictions but had been cautioned once for threatening behaviour and once for criminal damage.

6   The sentencing judge had before him a pre-sentence report setting out the fact that his upbringing had been an unhappy one, culminating in his leaving home when he was 16. He thereafter began drinking heavily and had discovered matters relating to the family history which had clearly caused him real distress. The report concluded that the offender could benefit from a community rehabilitation order and considered that the risks of future offending were low.

7   Also before the sentencing judge was a report from a Dr Strickland, a consultant psychiatrist, which stated that at the time of the offence the offender was suffering from a depressive illness which was complicated by his alcohol dependency. The psychiatrist recorded that at the time of the alleged offence the offender was in a state of crisis and concluded that in many ways the offender would appear to have both expected and wanted to be caught as a result of this incident. It is in that context appropriate to comment that he was clearly likely to have been recognised at the time that he committed this offence because of the fact that the post office was the local post office to his mother's home. The conclusion of the psychiatrist was that at the time of the offence the appellant was suffering from a depressive illness which would have clouded his judgment.

8   The judge, who is an extremely experienced judge, was clearly concerned about the right disposal in this case being fully aware, as his sentencing remarks make clear, that this Court has repeatedly stated that offences such as these will ordinarily carry not only a custodial sentence but a custodial sentence which is intended both to deter others from committing such offences and to provide protection for those running small businesses such as the one in question. He expressly referred in his sentencing remarks to the fact that a substantial period of imprisonment would normally result and said as follows:

"Frankly, when I first looked at this case that was my intention. I have considered very carefully the following facts; you went into a post office that you were known at. You took no steps to conceal your identity. You were undoubtedly at the time in an abnormal mental condition. Whilst it is clear that you are depressed today, as I am told, and that is a depression I have no doubt consequent from your appearance before my court. It is also clear that you were depressed at the time of the offence. It seems to me that that enables this court to take a wholly exceptional course."

It was in those circumstances that the learned judge sentenced the offender in the way that he did.

9   On behalf of the Attorney General, Mr Brown submits that he fell into error, that the circumstances of this case did not fall into the category of the type of wholly exceptional case in which the ordinary consequences should not follow. He has reminded us of the consistent line of authority which we have already referred to, which essentially starts with the decision of this Court in *Attorney General's Reference No 2 of 1989 (Darren Major)* (1989) 11 Cr.App.R.(S.) 481 in which this Court indicated that a sentence of substantial length had to be imposed particularly where a firearm was involved, as it had been in that case, and imposed a sentence of seven years' imprisonment. That case has formed the basis for the Court's decisions in *Attorney General's Reference No.9 of 1989 (Lacey)* (1990) 12 Cr.App.R.(S.) 7, and *Attorney General's References Nos 3, 4, 8, 9, 10 and 11 of 1990 (Dixon and others)* (1990) 12 Cr.App.R.(S.) 479, with particular reference to *Reference No.11* which is the case of *Duffy*. That was a case involving a 20-year-old who entered a post office wearing a mask and carrying a gun which in fact fired blanks. He in fact was successful in obtaining some money and used the gun when he was arrested. It is pointed out by Mr Brown that in the case of Duffy there was a medical report indicating that he (that is the offender) did suffer from some mental abnormality at the time. However, it is clear that when one reads the reports in question that is not a mental illness such as the illness with which we are concerned in the present case, but was a tendency to over-dramatise situations and behave in somewhat bizarre ways. In that case the lower court had imposed the sentence of 18 months for the robbery and 12 months for the firearms offence and those were increased by this Court to five years' imprisonment in respect of the robbery and two years' imprisonment to run consecutively in respect of the firearms offence, making seven years' imprisonment in total.

10   Mr Brown has pointed out that the only case which can be found in the authorities in which this Court has upheld a non-custodial sentence for an offence of robbery is the *Attorney General's Reference No.83 of 2001 (Stephen David Fidler)* [2002] 1 Cr.App.R.(S.) 139 (p.588). In that case the offender was a man who suffered from schizophrenia and it was whilst he was being treated for his schizophrenia that he confessed to the psychiatrist by whom he was being treated that he had committed the robbery in question. That was the robbery of a small shop. The offender had held an object which was intended to look like a weapon, had demanded money, some brandy and some cigarettes. The manager-

ess in fact opened the till. He took a handful of coins from it, some cigarettes and a bottle of brandy and left the shop. The psychiatrist was given permission by the offender to report that offence to the authorities and it was in those circumstances that the offender was charged with the offence and then sentenced ultimately to a community rehabilitation order with a requirement to undergo psychiatric treatment. Mr Brown submits that that case can properly be described as one in which there were wholly exceptional circumstances justifying the course that was taken and those characteristics are not met in the present case.

11   It seems to us, however, that that case reinforces that which this Court has repeatedly said, that sentencing is not always a mechanical exercise. There must be room for a sentencer in an appropriate case to exercise individual judgment in relation to the particular facts before him in order to do justice not only to the offender but also in seeking to provide ultimately more protection for the public. As Lord Lane said in *Attorney General's Reference No.4 of 1989* (1990) 90 Cr.App.R. 366:

> "However it must always be remembered that sentencing is an art rather than a science; that the trial judge is particularly well placed to assess the weight to be given to various competing considerations; and that leniency is not in itself a vice. That mercy should season justice is a proposition as soundly based in law as it is in literature."

12   In the present case this experienced judge took the view clearly after careful thought that the interests both of this offender and of the public generally would be best served by making the order that he did. He considered that the extent of the offender's mental condition at the time was such as to justify that course being taken.

13   We have a report before us as to how the offender has progressed since the making of that order. The conclusion of the probation officer is that he has been most impressed with the offender's ability to solve his problems despite his emotional difficulties and his past alcohol misuse. He concluded that the offender was using the community sentence in a positive way which could result in long term change. The only matter which has caused this Court concern arising out of that report is the fact that not long after he was sentenced, a matter of days, he committed an offence of burglary for which he was given a conditional discharge by the magistrates' court. But it is clear that the circumstances of that burglary were extraordinary. When he was sentenced by H.H. Judge Lyon his mother was not willing to have him back. He was accordingly homeless at the time. The offence was committed when he broke into his mother's house by the back door a few days later. He in fact took some personal items from the premises, hence the offence of burglary, but it can be seen that it was an offence of a very individual nature.

4   Mr Brown has indicated to us that another division of this Court is shortly to give a judgment which may deal with the question of principle as to whether we should take into account a post-sentence report such as this. It seems to us that we can satisfactorily deal with this case, as we have indicated, by reference simply and solely to the position before the judge and that, in our view, justifies

the conclusion that we should refuse leave to make this reference. However, it is of some comfort to this Court to find that the probation report which has been provided to this Court is positive and we can accordingly hope that that progress is continued in a way which justifies the exceptional course taken by H.H. Judge Lyon in this case with which we do not consider that this Court should interfere.

ATTORNEY GENERAL'S REFERENCES NOS 13, 14, 15, 16, 17 AND 18 OF 2004 (SHARON ANN MCKEOWN AND OTHERS)

COURT OF APPEAL (Lord Justice Hooper, Mr Justice Gage and Judge Richard Brown): July 7, 2004

[2004] EWCA Crim 1885; [2005] 1 Cr.App.R.(S.) 66

(LT) Children; Conspiracy; Supply of drugs; Undue leniency

H1   *Dealing in heroin—retail dealing on significant scale—length of sentence*

H2   Five years' imprisonment imposed on two principals in a conspiracy to deal in heroin on a significant scale increased to eight years.

H3   The six offenders either pleaded guilty or were convicted of conspiracy to supply heroin over a period of about four months. The conspiracy operated from two houses in succession. The entrance to the first house was fortified by steel inserted into the door frame and a steel gate outside the front door. When the local authority instituted eviction proceedings, the supply base was moved a short distance away to another flat. Heroin was sold in small deals weighing 0.15 grams at about 50 per cent purity. Purchasers contacted the conspirators' mobile telephone from a public telephone kiosk in view of the premises from which the heroin was supplied. Purchasers were given instructions where to go and were supplied with heroin at various locations. On some occasions stolen goods were received in payment. During a 40-day period, approximately 600 calls were made from the telephone kiosk to the conspirators' mobile telephone, and some of the purchasers made contact using their own mobile telephones. It was estimated that about 30 to 40 transactions were conducted on any given day. Sentenced to terms of five years in the case of the principal offenders, with lesser terms for the other offenders. The Attorney General asked the Court to review the sentences on the grounds that they were unduly lenient.

H4   **Held:** for the Attorney General it was submitted that the scale of the dealing in heroin was significant, the conspiracy was well organised and involved a large number of people; some of those involved as dealers and purchasers were relatively young and the acceptance of stolen goods in payment promoted further criminal activity. In the Court's view, the trial judge was in the best position to decide on the relative culpability of the offenders. Cases such as *Djahit* [1999]

2 Cr.App.R.(S.) 142 and *Twisse* [2001] 2 Cr.App.R.(S.) 9. (p.37), and *Attorney General's Reference No.84 of 2000 (Ollrick Mark Francis)* [2001] 2 Cr.App.R.(S.) 71 (p.336), dealing with low-level dealing by addicts to support their habits, demonstrated that sentences of five years' imprisonment for the two principal offenders were unduly lenient indeed. The cases of *Davis and Chung* (1995) 16 Cr.App.R.(S.) 970 and *Attorney General's Reference No.16 of 1991(William Peter Clark)* (1992) 13 Cr.App.R.(S.) 653 gave some indication of the normal upper limit for a conspiracy of this kind. In the light of the aggravating features, the Court considered that a sentence at the top end of the bracket for retail distribution of heroin was justified. The Court noted that this kind of retail supply made things unpleasant and dangerous for law abiding citizens who lived nearby. In the Court's view, the proper sentence for the principal offenders following a trial was in the region of 10 years. The sentences of five years' imprisonment imposed on the principal offenders would be increased to eight years, allowing for double jeopardy, and the sentences on the other offenders would be adjusted accordingly.

H5   **Cases cited:**
Djahit [1999] 2 Cr.App.R.(S.) 142, *Twisse* [2001] 2 Cr.App.R.(S.) 9 (p.37), *Attorney General's Reference No.84 of 2000 (Ollrick Mark Francis)* [2001] 2 Cr.App.R.(S.) 71 (p.336), *Davis and Chung* (1995) 16 Cr.App.R.(S.) 970, *Attorney General's Reference No.16 of 1991 (William Peter Clark)* (1992) 13 Cr.App.R.(S.) 653

H6   **References:** dealing in heroin, *Current Sentencing Practice* B 11-2

H7   *R. Horwell* for the Attorney General.
M. Wolkind Q.C., A. Smith, A. Barker Q.C., J. Hayes, R. Thomas Q.C. and *J. Hankin* for the respective offenders.

JUDGMENT

1   **Hooper L.J.:**   Her Majesty's Attorney General applies for leave to refer to this Court the sentences passed on six offenders on January 13, 2004 by H.H. Judge Fisher sitting in the Crown Court at Birmingham. The six offenders are: Sharon Ann McKeown, Adam Victor Parsons, Nigel Christopher McKeown, Jason Michael McKeown, Peter Singh Baria and Leon Jones. All six offenders either pleaded guilty or were found guilty of a conspiracy to supply heroin during the period August 6, 2002 to November 21, 2002. All had one or more previous convictions recorded against them, but those convictions were not such as to constitute aggravating features. There was no evidence of extravagant living by any of the offenders.

2   During the hearing we granted leave and announced that we had quashed all the sentences and substituted new and higher sentences.

3   Additionally there were two applications for leave to appeal sentence in respect of two co-defendants. Those applications were sensibly abandoned.

4   The facts as set out in the consolidated reference and approved by prosecuting counsel are as follows:

"(i) The West Midlands police mounted an operation to target the activities of drug dealers in the Northfield area of Birmingham. This particular conspiracy to supply heroin covered a period in excess of three months from August to November 2002. Although there was no evidence of large profits or high living, this was a significant and organised retail enterprise to distribute heroin in exchange for either cash or stolen goods.

(ii) The evidence came primarily from police observations and video tapes compiled during parts of 39 days within the indictment period. Two customers to the conspiracy also gave evidence for the prosecution: James Harrison and Terence Coffey.

(iii) The conspirators used two premises as their base. [The first address] was the home of Sharon McKeown and Peter Baria where they lived with their five children. The entrance to their home was heavily fortified by steel inserts inside the doorframe and a large steel gate outside the front door. [The first address] was a large block of council owned flats in which they were the site occupants. All of the other tenants had left in anticipation of the block being demolished.

(iv) On 4 September 2002 there was a hearing at Birmingham County Court to evict Sharon McKeown from [the first address]. Counsel for the housing authority suggested that drug dealing was being conducted at the flat. This was the first warning that the conspirators had been given that the authorities might be aware of what was happening. There had to be a change of premises.

(v) The supply base was moved a short distance away to [the second address], the home of Nigel Christopher McKeown, Sharon McKeown's brother, and Christine Hutton, where they lived with their two children.

(vi) Throughout, heroin was sold in £10 deals which weighed 0.15 gms. The purity was relatively high at about 50%.

(vii) Purchasers contacted the conspirators by calling a dedicated mobile telephone which was always in the possession of one of the dealers. Telephonic contact was frequently made from a public telephone kiosk which was in view from each set of premises. Purchasers, therefore, were able to be scrutinised and, once approved, were then given instructions as to where to go to be supplied with heroin. The heroin was distributed at a number of different locations, for example, the entrance to the [the first address]; in the road outside; in a nearby car park; outside an adjacent school; and in a local recreation ground. Some of the dealers were of a young age, namely C 14 and P 15. Video evidence showed persons of a similar age to them appear to buy drugs from the conspirators. If payment was to be made by stolen goods they were taken to [the first address] and heroin was supplied from a cache on the landing outside the flat. On occasions specific goods were stolen to order and were traded at one-third of their retail value.

(vii) In assessing the scale of the distribution there was the following evidence. A listening device was placed in the public telephone kiosk outside [the first address] and the billing details were obtained. During a 40 day period there were approximately 600 calls to the dedicated mobile telephone. Not all purchasers made contact through the public telephone kiosk, about half of the buyers used their own mobile telephones. Over the 39 days of police observations each observation lasted, on average, about four-and-a-half hours only. On the busiest day, a total of 28 separate incidents of apparent drug dealing were observed. Not all transactions could be seen from the observation post. As another example of the scale of this enterprise, on 25 October 2002, Terence Coffey, who gave evidence for the prosecution, stole 30 deals of heroin from outside [the second address]. Notwithstanding this loss, dealing in heroin continued on that day and on the days immediately thereafter, such was the extent of the stock in trade. It is estimated that about 30 to 40 separate transactions were conducted by the conspirators on any given day."

5   During the course of argument counsel for Peter Baria, Mr Thomas Q.C. made a few observations about these facts. As to para.(iii) he submitted that the heavy fortifications had been installed for general security purposes and not to protect the trade in drugs. We shall proceed on that assumption. As to para.(vii) he objected to the words "outside a local school". He also questioned the proposition that "persons of a similar age" to C aged 14 and P aged 15 had bought drugs. He later accepted that that may well have happened on a few occasions.

6   In passing sentence the learned judge said this:

"One of the aggravating features of this particular case is that the adults involved caused juveniles and much younger people to participate in this conspiracy to supply Class A drugs.

One only has to see the observation logs and the video to realise that drug dealing took place in the presence of young children, in some cases very young children. The drug dealing took place very often in public areas near, for example, to shops, outside a public house; near to a school and in the vicinity of a medical centre. Those of course are aggravating features."

7   This passage confirms the accuracy of the reference, if one substitutes for the words "outside the school" the words "near the school". The passage in the sentencing remarks also makes it clear that the dealing took place in the presence of young children and in some cases very young children. Mr Thomas submits that there was no evidence of actually targeting young children to become purchasers of heroin. We shall assume that that is right.

8   The Attorney General relies upon the following aggravating features in all six cases:

1. The scale of the dealing in heroin was significant.
2. The conspiracy was well organised.
3. A large number of persons were involved in the distribution of heroin.
4. The young ages of some of the dealers and purchasers. Some of the dealers were of a young age, namely C 14 and P 15. Video evidence showed persons of similar age to them appear to buy drugs from the conspirators. Drugs were sold close to schools and on a local recreation ground.
5. On occasions transactions were conducted relatively openly within the local community.
6. Children lived at [the premises concerned].
7. The receipt of stolen goods as payment for heroin promoted and encouraged further criminal activity.

To that list of aggravating features with which we agree, we add the aggravating feature identified by the judge, namely the presence of young and in some cases very young children whilst supplies of heroin were being made.

9   It is submitted on behalf of the Attorney General that the sentences were unduly lenient. They failed to reflect properly the gravity of the offence, the aggravating features present, the need for deterrence and public concern about the supply of heroin and the obvious personal and social consequences which follow from the use of this dangerous drug.

10   We start with the references relating to the two offenders, Sharon McKeown, aged 35, and Peter Baria, aged 35. Both pleaded not guilty and were found guilty after a trial lasting some six weeks. Both were sentenced to five years' imprisonment. The learned judge found that Sharon McKeown and Peter Baria were at the forefront of the conspiracy. They lived together at [the first address] with their five children. The reference sets out their involvement:

11   **"Sharon Ann McKeown**
The judge sentenced this offender on the basis that she and her partner, Peter Baria, were at the forefront of the conspiracy and that the offender had very little concern or empathy for the effects of heroin on those whom she supplied. The offender and Peter Baria lived together at [the first address] with their five children. On the evidence of Terence Coffey, the offender dealt with stolen goods when these were offered in exchange for heroin and such role continued after the base for this conspiracy had moved from [the first address] to [the second address]. She had a leading role within the conspiracy when it was based at [the first address]; she was responsible for the change in premises to [the second address]; thereafter, supplies of heroin continued to be held at [the first address]; dealers regularly visited [the first address]; the offender organised the appropriate response when one of the dealers within the conspiracy was arrested; and the main Street dealers within the conspiracy were her brother Jason McKeown and Nigel McKeown.

Peter Singh Baria

As already indicated, the judge sentenced this offender on the basis that he and his partner, Sharon McKeown, were at the forefront of the conspiracy. The offender assisted Sharon McKeown in the exchange of drugs for stolen goods; on at least four occasions he was identified as being involved in the supply of drugs and was concerned in the storing of drugs at [the first address] for distribution therefrom."

12   Mr Wolkind Q.C. for Sharon McKeown did not dissent from those comments. Mr Thomas Q.C. argued that Peter Baria was not in the forefront of the conspiracy, particularly after the dealing moved to [the second address]. He relied on the comparative absence of video evidence showing his involvement thereafter.

13   In our view the judge, after a trial lasting some six weeks, was in the best position to decide on the relative culpability of the various defendants. We see no reason to disturb her finding, endorsed by the Attorney General that Peter Baria, like Sharon McKeown, was in the forefront of the conspiracy. There was nothing to suggest that he had left the conspiracy after the actual dealing had moved to [the second address].

14   It was agreed that there are apparently no cases directly comparable. Cases such as *Djahit* [1999] 2 Cr.App.R.(S.) 142 and *Twisse* [2001] 2 Cr.App.R.(S.) 9 (p.37), dealing with low level dealing by an addict to support his habit (five to seven years' imprisonment after a trial) and *Attorney General's Reference No.84 of 2000* [2001] 2 Cr.App.R.(S.) 71, dealing with a few sales of Class A drugs to undercover officers (four to five years on a plea) demonstrate that a sentence of five years' imprisonment for this conspiracy for these two offenders is unduly lenient.

15   *Davis and Chung* (1995) 16 Cr.App.R.(S.) 970, and *Attorney General's Reference No.16 of 1991* (1992) 13 Cr.App.R.(S.) 653, give some help as to the normal upper limit for a conspiracy of this kind following a trial. In our judgment the present case had almost all the aggravating features of a retail supply of heroin, except, we shall assume, the targeting of children to buy heroin.

16   In the light of the aggravating features identified by the Attorney General and in particular the young ages of some of the dealers and purchasers, the involvement of children, the fact that transactions were conducted openly within the community in the presence of children and that stolen goods were received in exchange for heroin, a sentence which is at the top end for the retail and distribution of heroin is justified. We note in particular the impact that this kind of retail supply of heroin has on the community. It is difficult to imagine how unpleasant and dangerous it must be for law-abiding citizens to live on an estate of this kind where heroin is being sold so publicly and in recreation and open areas used by the community.

17   In our view the proper sentence for these two offenders following a trial was in the region of 10 years, making it equivalent to the sentence which importations of some 500g of Class A drugs attract (see *Aramah* (1982) 4 Cr.App.R.(S.) 407, as

subsequently amended). We quash the sentences of five years' imprisonment and substitute sentences of eight years, taking into account double jeopardy.

18   We turn to the other four offenders. Nigel McKeown is aged 23. He is an addict and he received a sentence of three years' imprisonment. Jason McKeown, his brother, is aged 36 and he received a sentence of three-and-a-half years' imprisonment. They both pleaded guilty on the first day of trial, having indicated their proposed pleas only the week before. Counsel for Jason McKeown sought to persuade us that they were entitled to more credit than a plea at such a late stage would normally attract because they had to see the many hours of video evidence before pleading. We find that an unattractive submission. In effect, the defendant is saying that he will not plead guilty until he is satisfied that the video evidence shows that he is guilty. That hardly reflects the kind of remorse which one is seeking to reward when giving a discount for plea.

19   Adam Parsons and Leon Jones both contested the case. Adam Parsons is aged 19 and received a sentence of three and a half years' detention, and Leon Jones, aged 24, also received a sentence of three and a half years, but in his case, imprisonment. Leon Jones was also an addict, but it is to his credit that it appears that he is no longer one.

20   Paragraph 6 of the reference sets out the involvement of these four. We set it out here:

> ### "Nigel Christopher McKeown
> The judge sentenced this offender on the basis that his involvement was limited in time. He is the brother of Sharon McKeown and Jason McKeown and he lived at [the second address]. His involvement began when the operation moved from [the first address] to his home address. Thereafter, however, the offender became a significant contributor. During nine days of police observations from late September to late October 2002 he was concerned in a large number of transactions or apparent transactions most of which occurred inside his home. On 29 October 2003 the offender was arrested in the street and was in possession of twelve deals of heroin, £80 in cash and the dedicated mobile telephone. In mitigation, this offender pleaded guilty, albeit at a late stage. He pleaded guilty on the day the trial was due to proceed but had indicated the change of plea in the previous week.
>
> ### Jason Michael McKeown
> The judge sentenced this offender on the basis that he had a substantial role in the conspiracy. He was the most prolific street dealer and was involved in the majority of the transactions. He was seen regularly on the police observation videos concerned in the operation of the conspiracy and was the usual holder of the dedicated mobile telephone. In almost all of the calls recorded by the listening device located in the public telephone kiosk, the prospective purchasers spoke to this offender. He was involved both at [the first address] and [the second address]. In mitigation, this offender pleaded guilty, albeit at a late stage. He pleaded guilty on the day the trial was due to proceed but had indicated the change of plea in the previous week.

Adam Victor Parsons

The judge sentenced this 19-year-old offender on the basis that he was less involved than some of the other conspirators. This offender's role, as shown by the police observation videos and from the evidence of purchasers, was to drive the 'duty dealer' around the locality when heroin was being supplied to customers in the street. On three particular occasions he supplied customers directly when they had gone to [the first address] and were waiting outside for the supply of heroin. The offender did not play any overt part in the conspiracy after the middle of October 2002.

Leon Jones

The judge sentenced this offender on the basis that his involvement was limited in time. The offender had been in [the first address] on occasions when apparent drug dealing had taken place. On two occasions in August 2002, on 16th and 28th, the offender was concerned in the supply of drugs directly to purchasers in the area of [the second address] and [the first address]."

21   In so far as Nigel McKeown is concerned, Mr Barker Q.C. on his behalf explained the circumstances in which he had become an addict. Mr Barker stressed the offender's more limited involvement and pointed out that the bulk of the calls were taken by another defendant. Nonetheless he was, as the reference describes him, "a significant contributor" and the scale of his involvement is demonstrated by the circumstances of arrest. Also—and this is important—he permitted his premises to be used for the substantial supply of heroin.

22   We take the view that after a trial he could have expected a sentence in the region of about eight years. In our judgment three years' imprisonment after a plea is unduly lenient. Taking into account his late plea and double jeopardy we quash that sentence and substitute a sentence of five years' imprisonment.

23   We turn to Jason McKeown. Mr Hayes on his behalf explained the circumstances in which he started dealing in heroin, namely to pay off a debt. He said that there was no evidence of targeting or introducing addicts. He compared Jason McKeown's involvement with that of the appellant Chung in the case of *Davis and Chung*. Chung was described as the manager of a "classic crack dealing house", selling, over 13 days, from the house half a gram of cocaine for £50, making some 160–200 supplies on a good day, and 30–40 on a bad day. He received a sentence of 10 years' imprisonment following a plea, which was reduced to seven years, equivalent to some nine to 10 years after a trial. Without in any way diminishing the seriousness of dealing from a crack house, such dealing does not have many of the aggravating features in this case. It is clear to us that Jason McKeown was the most prolific of the dealers in the conspiracy. H.H. Judge Fisher distinguished between the two brothers, and so do we. After a trial he could have expected a sentence in excess of eight years' imprisonment. The sentence that was passed was unduly lenient. Taking into account his late plea and double jeopardy, we quash the sentence and substitute a sentence of five and a half years' imprisonment.

24   As to Adam Victor Parsons, he is, as we have already said, aged 19. Mr Smith on his behalf stressed his age, his lesser role and the fact that a longer sentence

would convert him into a long-term offender. We take the view that given his age and role the sentence should have been in the region of seven years. The sentence which was passed was unduly lenient and we substitute a sentence of five years' detention taking into account double jeopardy.

25   Finally we turn to Leon Jones. Mr Hankin referred us to para.4.1 of the pre-sentence report. That reads:

> "4.1. I feel that Mr Jones is a young man who is yet to fulfil his true potential and like many black young men, the educational system failed him and he left school early. He is, however, well motivated to study and acquire qualifications which will enable him to secure employment and live a law-abiding life. If sent to prison Mr Jones intends to avail himself of every opportunity open to him to acquire qualifications, he feels that custody will be harder upon his family than upon him, as the burden of child care will lie with his partner. Mr Jones was adamant that the court would be imposing a custodial sentence upon him, but if consideration is being given to a non-custodial sentence then a referral has been made to the Drug Treatment and Testing Order Team who requested a short adjournment to assess Mr Jones's suitability."

26   There has clearly been an improvement in prison. He is the least involved. We take the view that after a trial he could have expected a sentence in the region of six years. The sentence that was passed was unduly lenient, and we substitute for it a sentence of four and a half years taking into account double jeopardy.

R. v MELVIN TERRENCE SULLIVAN, MARTIN GOODWIN GIBBS, BARRY ELENER, DEREK ELENER

COURT OF APPEAL (The Lord Chief Justice, Lord Justice Judge, Mr Justice Holland, Mr Justice Astill and Mr Justice Gross): July 8, 2004

[2004] EWCA Crim 1762; [2005] 1 Cr.App.R.(S.) 67

(LT) Mandatory life imprisonment; Minimum term; Murder; Practice statements; Sentence length; Transitional provisions

H1   *Murder—minimum term—general considerations—transitional provisions*

H2   Guidance on the application of the Criminal Justice Act 2003, Schs 21 and 22, in cases of murder.

H3   The Court dealt with four appeals by offenders convicted of murder and sentenced to life imprisonment, with minimum terms fixed by the sentencing judge in accordance with the Criminal Justice Act 2003, s.269.

H4   **Held:** the judgment was intended to provide general assistance as to the approach that courts should adopt when applying those provisions. The catalyst for the need to include the provisions in the 2003 Act was the decision of the House of Lords in *R. (on the application of Anderson) v Secretary of State* [2003] 1 A.C. 837. Before that decision, the minimum period in the case of those sentenced to a mandatory life sentence was determined by the Secretary of State after considering recommendations made privately by the trial judge and the Lord Chief Justice. Following a series of decisions of the European Court of Human Rights, the House of Lords in *Anderson* made it clear that the involvement of the Secretary of State contravened Art.6 of the European Convention on Human Rights. The task of determining a minimum period should be performed by the judge. The decision in *Anderson* did not affect the fact that the mandatory sentence for murder remained life imprisonment. Although an offender might be released on licence, and the minimum period affected the date on which this might happen, the offender remained at risk of being returned to prison for the rest of his life. The sentence of life imprisonment in effect contained two periods: the initial period, known as the minimum term, was a period to be served by an offender as a punishment and a deterrent, and the subsequent period during which the offender could, but might not be, released on licence by the Parole Board if the Board decided that the safety of the public did not require the offender to remain in prison. The 2003 Act transferred the role of the Secretary of State in determining the minimum term to the trial judge. The Act included guidance in s.269(5) and Sch.21 in the form of general principles. The general principles applied to determinations made after December 18, 2003, the date on which s.269 came into force, even if the offence was committed before that date. The Act therefore contained transitional provisions that were intended to ensure that an offender was not made subject to a determination which contravened Arts 5 or 7(1) of the European Convention. Article 7(1) prohibited the imposition of a heavier penalty "than the one that was applicable at the time the criminal offence was committed."

I5   Before considering the provisions of the Act in detail, it was desirable to observe that while all murders were grave crimes, the offence covered a broad spectrum of gravity. Murder might be committed without the offender having an intention to kill, an intention to inflict grievous bodily harm being sufficient. The definition covered sadistic killings and mercy killings by a caring member of the deceased's family. Minimum terms could range from a whole life term to less than eight years. The second observation was that in order to compare a minimum term with a determinate sentence, it was necessary approximately to double the determinate sentence. This was because an offender sentenced to a determinate sentence was released or became eligible for parole at the halfway stage. A mandatory life prisoner became eligible for release only after serving the whole of the minimum term. Part 12 of the 2003 Act contained many provisions which were not yet in force. Section 142 set out the purposes of sentences. It did not apply to the sentence for murder, which was fixed by law and excluded from s.142 by subs.(2)(b). That subsection underlined the difference in the task performed by a judge when deciding the length of the minimum term, having imposed a life sentence, from the task that he performed when he decided what should be the length of a determinate sentence. In the case of the minimum term he was only directly concerned with seriousness, the protection of the public being provided by the imposition of a life sentence. After the minimum term had been served, the protection of the public became the responsibility of the Parole Board, who then decided when it was safe to release the offender on licence. Further sections provided for the determination of the seriousness of an offence and the reduction in sentences for guilty pleas. The appropriate credit for a plea of guilty should be deducted from the minimum term which the judge would have determined if there had been no plea of guilty.

H6   The provisions of the Act dealing with the calculation of the minimum term began with s.269. It was important to note that the judge retained a discretion under subs.(3) to determine the appropriate period. Subsection (3) provided that the part of the sentence which the judge was to specify as the minimum term should be such term "as the court considers appropriate". The Court emphasised that the principal task of the sentencing court was to determine the period which the court considered appropriate. Notwithstanding the statutory guidance, the decision remained one for the judge. In certain circumstances, the court might order that the early release provisions should not apply to the offender; this would result in the offender serving a whole life term. Section 269(5) required the court to "have regard to" the general principles set out in Sch.21. It was important to note that the judge complied with the section if he had "regard" to the principles set out in Sch.21. As long as he bore them in mind, he was not bound to follow them. If he did not follow the principles, he should explain why he had not done so. Schedule 21 to the Act set out the new statutory guidance. For adults, the Schedule had three starting points. If the seriousness of the offence was exceptionally high, the appropriate starting point was a whole life order. If the seriousness of the offence was particularly high, the starting point was a minimum term of 30 years. In other cases the appropriate starting point was a minimum term of 15 years. Different starting points were suggested for offenders under 21 and under 18. Paragraphs 8 and 9 indicated that having chosen the starting point, the court should take into account any aggravating or mitigating factors, and doing so might result in a minimum term of any length, whatever the starting point. The Schedule set out a well established approach to sentence. Paragraph 9 in particular made clear that despite the provision of starting points, the judge had a discretion to determine a term of any length as being appropriate because of the particular aggravating and mitigating circumstances that existed in that case. This discretion must be exercised lawfully, and this required the judge to have regard to the guidance set out in the Schedule, though he was free not to follow the guidance if in his opinion this would not result in an appropriate term for the reasons he identified. His decision was subject to an appeal either by the offender or on an Attorney General's Reference. Paragraphs 10 and 11 listed a number of aggravating and mitigating factors, but it was plain that the listed factors were not exhaustive. Paragraph 12 referred to the relevance of the offender's guilty plea.

H7 Schedule 22 set out transitional provisions. The greater part of the Schedule provided for offenders sentenced to life imprisonment before December 18, 2003, but para.10 applied to the case of an offender sentenced after December 18, 2003 for an offence committed before that date. It provided that the order made under s.269(2) must not specify a part of the sentence which in the opinion of the court was greater than that which the Secretary of State would have been likely to notify under the practice followed by him before December 2002. It was clear that the judge was intended to follow a two-stage approach in determining the minimum term for this category of offender. The judge had initially to assess what would have been the appropriate period, having regard to Sch.21. Having ascertained that period, he would then reduce the period so far as was necessary in order to avoid specifying a minimum period greater than would have been specified by the Secretary of State under the former practice. In the great majority of cases the determination of the period having regard to Sch.21 should not be materially different from that which would have been chosen under the practice previously followed by the Secretary of State. Under the former practice, the Secretary of State in the great majority of cases fixed the minimum period in accordance with the recommendation of the trial judge and the Chief Justice or either of them. The statutory guidance given in Sch.21 only significantly affected the minimum term in the case of the first two starting points; that was when the seriousness of the offence was either "exceptionally" or "particularly" high. The difference was not in the length of the terms but the breadth of the cases to which they applied because of the examples included in Sch.21. The great majority of murders would not fall into these categories. The general starting point of 15 years would apply to a broad range of offences, and left the judge free to determine for this category of offender an appropriate figure very much in the same way as would be the case prior to the 2003 Act. At that time the figure selected by the Secretary of State was on average 14 to 15 years.

H8 The difference in practice was likely to be confined to the minority of cases where the higher starting points applied. In these cases it was critically important to have the provisions of Sch.22, para.10 in mind. The language of para.10 created a difficulty by establishing a ceiling for the minimum term based on the practice of the Secretary of State prior to December 2002. Neither the recommendations made by the judiciary nor the determinations of the Secretary of State were normally made public. In order to assist the Court in the hearing of the appeals, the Secretary of State had provided the Court with considerable information, which made it clear that the best guide as to what would have been the practice of the Secretary of State was the Practice Directions published respectively by the present Lord Chief Justice and his predecessor Lord Bingham C.J. It could reasonably be assumed that the judiciary and in particular the Lord Chief Justice would have applied the relevant Practice Direction while it was in force and in a high percentage of the cases it was their recommendations that the Secretary of State followed. There remained two more complications. First, in the most serious cases the Secretary of State might select a higher figure than that indicated by the two Practice Statements. Secondly, by the date of the decision in *Anderson*, the Secretary of State had not yet made a determination in any case where the offender was sentenced after the date of the later Practice Direction. In February 1997, Lord Bingham C.J. had sent to judges a letter containing detailed guidance on the making of recommendations in murder cases. He identified two periods: a higher period of 30 years which would be recommended only in very rare cases and the normal period of 14 years. It appeared that the 14-year period was intended to cover the more serious murders, as absence of an intention to kill and lack of premeditation were listed as mitigating factors. The statement was followed by a statement made by Lord Woolf C.J. in 2000, which related to juveniles sentenced to be detained during Her Majesty's pleasure. In March 2002, the Sentencing Advisory Panel published its advice on the fixing of the minimum term in murder cases, and that advice was implemented by a Practice Statement in May 2002. The 2002 Practice Statement suggested a starting point of 12 years for the killing of an adult victim arising from a quarrel or loss of temper. It provided for the period to be varied from the starting point upwards or downwards to take account of aggravating or mitigating factors. In the most serious cases the appropriate minimum term might be 30 years.

H9   On examination of the relevant passages it appeared that the 2002 Practice Direction proposed a starting point of eight or nine years for cases with reduced responsibility, a normal starting point of 12 years, higher starting points of 15 or 16 years, 20 years in an especially grave case and 30 years in extremely serious cases. A whole life term might be appropriate in cases of exceptional gravity. When the relevant passages were compared with the earlier statement of Lord Bingham C.J., it appeared that the proposed normal starting point of 12 years in the latest Practice Statement was dealing with categories of cases less grave than those included in the earlier Practice Statement with a suggested minimum of 14 years. The difference between the two Statements was a consequence of the fact that the later guidance was more specific than the earlier guidance. Both Practice Statements gave the sentencing judge a considerable degree of discretion. Comparing the position under the statutory and non-statutory guidance, and giving due weight to what had been described in a helpful article in *Archbold News* as the "legitimate and extensive discretion in its operation" given to the judge making the determination by the statutory guidance, the Court was of the opinion that if there were any differences between the earlier and the later Practice Statements, it was not as great as had been supposed. The differences in the figures were largely explained by their different structures.

H10   Where there were differences, they were at the top of the range for the most serious crimes. This was the area in which the Secretary of State could differ significantly from the figure recommended by the judiciary. However this was still a category of case where it was most likely for the judge to have to consider reducing the figure reached in applying the approach suggested in Sch.21, relying on Sch.22, para.10. The judge would also have to be on guard against determining a higher figure merely because the starting figure that was taken was greater, particularly where the 15 year figure was the starting point selected. In the Court's judgment it would be wrong to assume that Parliament had intended to raise minimum terms over those recommended by the Sentencing Advisory Panel by merely applying the 15-year starting point to all murders other than those whose seriousness was exceptionally or particularly high. The statutory guidance, unlike the non-statutory guidance, focused on the more serious cases and described them in more detail than it did with respect to the very wide range of offences to which the 15-year period applied. The non-statutory guidance of 2002, while covering the whole range of murders, provided three different starting points for murders covered by the 15-year period in the statutory guidance and the 14-year starting point in the earlier guidance given by Lord Bingham C.J. It was more specific and amplified the considerations that were relevant. The wider the range of gravity to which a starting point applied, the more important became the discretion of the judges to determine the appropriate minimum term within that range.

11   In December 2003, guidance was given to the judiciary by a letter from Lord Woolf C.J. The letter suggested that in applying Sch.22, para.10, judges should have regard to the earlier guidance rather than to the Practice Statement of May 2002. This letter was criticised by counsel, but the material provided by the Secretary of State confirmed that he had not dealt by December 2002 with any cases in which the judges would have based their recommendations on the later Practice Direction. Therefore, as a matter of fact, the later Practice Direction could not have been evidence of the practice followed by the Secretary of State before December 2002. It was argued that the later Practice Statement should be used in respect of offences committed after May 2002. The Court had indicated that on a close examination of the relevant Schedule and Practice Statement, a judge was entitled to come to the same conclusion irrespective of which Practice Direction was used. It was therefore questionable whether it would be possible to establish any contravention of the Convention as a consequence of the Practice Direction that was followed by the sentencing judge. The Court considered that Sch.21 and the Practice Statement, properly applied, should produce broadly similar results except possibly in regard to the higher statutory categories. As to the higher categories any difference was of no significance because it could be corrected by the application of either Practice Direction since they dealt with them in the same way. In addition the application of the Practice Direction could in fact be unduly generous to the offender since the Secretary of State contended that he did on a number of occasions increase the recommendations in the case of the most grave offences. However the Court had decided that to avoid any prejudice to the offender, the letter of December 16, 2003 should no longer be followed in the case of an offender if his offence was committed after May 2002. In such a case a court in determining the minimum term should apply the later Practice Direction. By doing so, any danger of the judge coming to a conclusion adverse to the offender would be avoided. This would be needed because otherwise Sch.22, para.10 would not have achieved its objective since in the absence of the 2003 Act a lower minimum term would be likely to be imposed for the offence when it was committed. A further advantage of using the latest guidelines when appropriate was that it would not deprive judges of the more refined guidance which the later Practice Direction provided. In addition, the judge's task would be simplified further, since the Practice Direction itself would

produce the result required by Sch.22, para.10. This was because when the minimum term was calculated applying the later Practice Direction, the period of the minimum term would either be the same as or shorter than the minimum term calculated by applying Sch.21.

H12   **Case cited:**
       R. (on the application of Anderson) v Secretary of State [2003] 1 A.C. 837

H13   **Commentary:** [2004] Crim.L.R. 853

H14   *Ms P. Lynch Q.C.* and *Ms K. Moore* for the appellant Sullivan.
       R. Tedd Q.C. and *Ms S. Hobson* for the Crown.
       E. Fitzgerald Q.C. and *P. Taylor* for the appellant Gibbs.
       N. Hilliard for the Crown.
       B. Nolan Q.C. and *O. Jarvis* for the appellant B. Elener.
       G. Evans Q.C. and *R. Gioserano* for the appellant D. Elener.
       R. Smith Q.C. for the Crown.

JUDGMENT

The Lord Chief Justice:

Introduction

1   The Criminal Justice Act 2003 (the "2003 Act") contains provisions of great significance to the sentencing of offenders. This judgment deals with the provisions dealing with offenders sentenced to life imprisonment for murder. It provides what is intended to be general assistance as to the approach that courts should adopt when applying those provisions. It does this in the context of four appeals (that we have heard together) against the minimum periods that the appellants had been ordered to serve before they could be considered for release on licence by the Parole Board under the early release provisions contained in Ch.7 of the 2003 Act.

2   The catalyst for the need to include the early release provisions in the 2003 Act was the decision of the House of Lords in *R. (on the application of Anderson) v Secretary of State* [2003] 1 A.C. 837, November 25, 2002. Before the decision in *Anderson* the minimum period in the case of those sentenced to a mandatory life sentence was determined by the Secretary of State after considering recommendations made privately by the trial judge and the Lord Chief Justice. Following a series of decisions of the European Court of Human Rights (the ECtHR), in *Anderson* the House of Lords made it clear that this involvement of the Secretary of State was unacceptable and contravened Art.6 of the European Convention on Human Rights. This was because the process of determining a minimum period is considered to be indistinguishable from that of determining a sentence. Both tasks should be performed by a judge and not by a member of the executive. The Secretary of State after that decision ceased to determine minimum periods

though trial judges continued to make recommendations until the new provisions came into force.

3   The decision in *Anderson* does not affect the fact that the mandatory sentence for murder remains life imprisonment. Although an offender may be released on licence, and the minimum period affects the date on which this may happen, the offender remains at risk of being returned to prison for the rest of his life. The sentence of life imprisonment has been treated, both as a matter of reality and for many legal purposes, as containing two periods. The initial period, known as the minimum term, that is a period to be served by the offender as a punishment and a deterrent, and a subsequent period during which the offender can, but may not, be released on licence by the Parole Board if the Board decides that the safety of the public does not require the offender to remain in prison. (This is very much a simplification of a position that developed by stages over many years chronicled in a number of judgments. There is a brief history set out in *Anderson* (at 842/5).)

4   The 2003 Act transferred the role of the Secretary of State in determining the minimum term to the trial judge. The relevant statutory provisions came into force on December 18, 2003.

5   To assist trial judges to make their recommendations under the pre- *Anderson* practice and to encourage greater consistency, the present and previous Lord Chief Justices had provided general guidance to sentencing judges as to the approach to be adopted. The 2003 Act, for the first time, includes the guidance in an Act of Parliament in s.269(5) and Sch.21 in the form of "general principles".

6   The general principles in Schedule 21 apply to determinations made after December 18, 2003 even if the offence was committed before that date. The 2003 Act therefore contains transitional provisions that are intended to ensure that an offender is not made subject to a determination which contravenes Arts 5 and 7.1 of the ECHR. Under Art.5 every one has the right of liberty and security of person and Art.7.1 prohibits the imposition of a heavier penalty "than the one that was applicable at the time the criminal offence was committed".

7   We now turn to consider the relevant provisions of the 2003 Act. Before considering these in detail, it is desirable to make two general points. The first is that, while all murders are grave crimes, because murder can be committed without the offender having an intention to kill, an intention to inflict grievous bodily harm being sufficient, the offence covers a particularly broad spectrum of gravity. For example, besides the sadistic killer, it covers mercy killing by a caring member of the deceased's family responding to a plea to bring terminal suffering to a more rapid conclusion. Minimum terms can range from whole life to even less than eight years. The second is that in order to compare a minimum term with a determinate sentence it is necessary approximately to double the determinate sentence. This is because in the case of a sentence of a fixed duration the offender is either released or eligible for parole at the half way stage. This is the position of a life prisoner only after the whole of the minimum term has been served.

The statutory provisions

8   For present purposes we shall start with the general provisions of Ch.1 of Pt 12 of the 2003 Act, which although not yet in force provides valuable insight into the overall intention of Parliament. The heading is "General Provisions About Sentencing", and under "Matters to be taken into account in sentencing", continues as follows:

"142 **Purposes of sentencing**

(1) Any court dealing with an offender in respect of his offence must have regard to the following purposes of sentencing—

(a) the punishment of offenders,

(b) the reduction of crime (including its reduction by deterrence),

(c) the reform and rehabilitation of offenders,

(d) the protection of the public, and

(e) the making of reparation by offenders to persons affected by their offences.

(2) Subsection (1) does not apply—

(a) in relation to an offender who is aged under 18 at the time of conviction,

(b) to an offence the sentence for which is fixed by law."

9   The sentence for murder is, of course, fixed by law so s.142 does not apply to the determination of the minimum period in the case of a life sentence. However, the section is still important. This is because it underlines the very different task that a judge performs when deciding the length of a minimum term, having imposed a life sentence, from the task that he performs when he decides what should be the length of a determinate sentence. In the case of the minimum term he is only directly concerned with "seriousness", the protection of the public being provided by the imposition of the life sentence. After the minimum term has been served, protection of the public becomes the responsibility of the Parole Board, who then decide when it is safe to release the offender on licence. As to seriousness, s.143 is relevant. It provides:

Determining the seriousness of an offence

"143 (1) In considering the seriousness of any offence, the court must consider the offender's culpability in committing the offence and any harm which the offence caused, was intended to cause or might forseeably have caused.

(2) In considering the seriousness of an offence ('the current offence') committed by an offender who has one or more previous convictions, the court must treat each previous conviction as an aggravating factor if (in the case of that con-

viction) the court considers that it can reasonably be so treated having regard, in particular, to—

  (a) the nature of the offence to which the conviction
      relates and its relevance to the current offence, and
  (b) the time that has elapsed since the conviction.

(3) In considering the seriousness of any offence committed
    while the offender was on bail, the court must treat the fact
    that it was committed in those circumstances as an aggravat-
    ing factor.

(4) Any reference in subsection (2) to a previous conviction is to
    be read as a reference to—

  (a) a previous conviction by a court in the United
      Kingdom, or
  (b) a previous finding of guilt in service disciplinary pro-
      ceedings.

(5) Subsections (2) and (4) do not prevent the court from treating
    a previous conviction by a court outside the United Kingdom
    as an aggravating factor in any case where the court considers
    it appropriate to do so."

10   Section 144 deals with the effect of guilty pleas and also applies to setting the
minimum term. It provides as follows:

Reduction in sentences for guilty pleas
    "144 (1) In determining what sentence to pass on an offender who has
             pleaded guilty to an offence in proceedings before that or
             another court, a court must take into account—

       (a) the stage in the proceedings for the offence at which
           the offender indicated his intention to plead guilty, and
       (b) the circumstances in which this indication was
           given."

The appropriate credit for a plea of guilty should be deducted from the period of
the minimum term which the judge would have determined if there had been no
plea of guilty.

1   The provisions of the 2003 Act dealing with the calculation of the minimum
term commence with s.269. What is important to note about that section is that
the judge retains a discretion under subs.(3) to determine the appropriate period.
The relevant terms of s.269 are as follows:

Determination of minimum term in relation to mandatory life sentence
    "269 (1) This section applies where after the commencement of this
             section a court passes a life sentence in circumstances
             where the sentence is fixed by law. [That is after December
             18, 2003]

(2) The court must, unless it makes an order under subsection (4), order that the provisions of section 28(5) to (8) of the Crime (Sentences) Act 1997 (referred to in this Chapter as 'the early release provisions') are to apply to the offender as soon as he has served the part of his sentence which is specified in the order.

(3) The part of his sentence is to be such <u>as the court considers appropriate</u> taking into account—

    (a) the seriousness of the offence, or of the combination of the offence and any one or more offences associated with it, and

    (b) the effect of any direction which it would have given under section 240 (crediting periods of remand in custody) if it had sentenced him to a term of imprisonment."

We have emphasised the words underlined because they make it clear what is the principal task of the court. It is to determine the period *the court considers appropriate*. Thus notwithstanding the statutory guidance, the decision remains one for the judge. While the provision requiring credit to be given for periods on remand is new, in practice it will not make any practical difference to the result so far as the offender is concerned since credit would have been given administratively under the previous practice.

"(4) If the offender was 21 or over when he committed the offence and the <u>court is of the opinion</u> that, because of the seriousness of the offence, or of the combination of the offence and one or more offences associated with it, no order should be made under subsection (2), the court must order that the early release provisions are not to apply to the offender."

[If the judge decides that subs.(4) applies then no minimum term should be identified and the early release provisions do not apply to the offender. This results in the offender serving a whole life term.]

"(5) In considering under subsection (3) or (4) the seriousness of an offence (or of the combination of an offence and one or more offences associated with it), the court must have regard to—

    (a) the general principles set out in Schedule 21, and

    (b) any guidelines relating to offences in general which are relevant to the case and are not incompatible with the provisions of Schedule 21."

12 It is important to note that the judge complies with the section if he has "*regard*" to the principles set out in the Schedule. As long as he bears them in mind he is not bound to follow them. However if he does not follow the principles he should explain why he has not done so.

13 The duty to give reasons is set out in s.270 that provides:

Duty to give reasons

"Section 270 (1) Any court making an order under subsection (2) or
(4) of section 269 must state in open court, in ordinary language, its reasons for deciding on the order
made.

(2) In stating its reasons the court must, in particular—

(a) state which of the starting points in Schedule 21 it has chosen and its reasons for
doing so, and

(b) state its reasons for any departure from that
starting point."

4   Section 275 of the Act makes the necessary amendments to the duty to release
certain life prisoners that is contained in s.28 of the Crime (Sentences) Act 1997.

Schedule 21

5   Schedule 21 of the Act sets out the new statutory guidance. So far as adults are
concerned the Schedule has three starting points. We have identified these points
by using bold type in setting out the terms of the Schedule as follows:

**"Determination Of Minimum Term In Relation To Mandatory Life
Sentence**

Interpretation

1. In this Schedule—
'child' means a person under 18 years;
'mandatory life sentence' means a life sentence passed in circumstances where the sentence is fixed by law;
'minimum term', in relation to a mandatory life sentence, means the
part of the sentence to be specified in an order under section 269(2);
'whole life order' means an order under subsection (4) of section 269.

2. Section 28 of the Crime and Disorder Act 1998 (c. 37) (meaning of
'racially or religiously aggravated') applies for the purposes of this
Schedule as it applies for the purposes of sections 29 to 32 of that Act.
3. For the purposes of this Schedule an offence is aggravated by sexual
orientation if it is committed in circumstances falling within subsection
(2)(a)(i) or (b)(i) of section 146.
Starting points

4. (1) If—
(a) the court considers that the seriousness of the offence (or
the combination of the offence and one or more offences
associated with it) is **exceptionally high**, and
(b) the offender was aged 21 or over when he committed the
offence,
the appropriate starting point is a **whole life** order.

(2) Cases that would normally fall within sub-paragraph (1)(a)
include—

    (a) the murder of two or more persons, where each murder
involves any of the following—

        (i) a substantial degree of premeditation or planning,

        (ii) the abduction of the victim, or

        (iii) sexual or sadistic conduct,

    (b) the murder of a child if involving the abduction of the
child or sexual or sadistic motivation,

    (c) a murder done for the purpose of advancing a political,
religious or ideological cause, or

    (d) a murder by an offender previously convicted of murder.

5. (1) If—

    (a) the case does not fall within paragraph 4(1) but the court
considers that the seriousness of the offence (or the combination of the offence and one or more offences
associated with it) is **particularly high**, and

    (b) the offender was aged 18 or over when he committed the
offence, the appropriate starting point, in determining **the
minimum term, is 30 years**.

(2) Cases that (if not falling within paragraph 4(1)) would normally
fall within sub-paragraph (1)(a) include—

    (a) the murder of a police officer or prison officer in the
course of his duty,

    (b) a murder involving the use of a firearm or explosive,

    (c) a murder done for gain (such as a murder done in the
course or furtherance of robbery or burglary, done for
payment or done in the expectation of gain as a result
of the death),

    (d) a murder intended to obstruct or interfere with the course
of justice,

    (e) a murder involving sexual or sadistic conduct,

    (f) the murder of two or more persons,

    (g) a murder that is racially or religiously aggravated or
aggravated by sexual orientation, or

    (h) a murder falling within paragraph 4(2) committed by an
offender who was aged under 21 when he committed
the offence.

6. If the offender was aged 18 or over when he committed the offence and
the case does not fall within paragraph 4(1) or 5(1), the appropriate
starting point, in determining **the minimum term, is 15 years**.

7. If the offender was aged under 18 when he committed the offence, the
appropriate starting point, in determining **the minimum term, is 12
years**.

Aggravating and mitigating factors

8. Having chosen a starting point, the court should take into account any aggravating or mitigating factors, to the extent that it has not allowed for them in its choice of starting point.

9. Detailed consideration of aggravating or mitigating factors may result in a minimum term of any length (whatever the starting point), or in the making of a whole life order."

6 The Schedule sets out a well established approach to sentencing. It makes clear (in para.9) that despite the starting points, the judge still has a discretion to determine any term of any length as being appropriate because of the particular aggravating and mitigating circumstances that exist in that case. This discretion must, however, be exercised lawfully and this requires the judge to have regard to the guidance set out in Sch.21, though he is free not to follow the guidance if in his opinion this will not result in an *appropriate* term for reasons he identifies. His decision is subject to appeal either by the offender or on Attorney General's Reference in accordance with ss.270 and 271.

"10. Aggravating factors (additional to those mentioned in paragraph 4(2) and 5(2)) that may be relevant to the offence of murder include—
  (a) a significant degree of planning or premeditation,
  (b) the fact that the victim was particularly vulnerable because of age or disability,
  (c) mental or physical suffering inflicted on the victim before death,
  (d) the abuse of a position of trust,
  (e) the use of duress or threats against another person to facilitate the commission of the offence,
  (f) the fact that the victim was providing a public service or performing a public duty, and
  (g) concealment, destruction or dismemberment of the body.

11. Mitigating factors that may be relevant to the offence of murder include—
  (a) an intention to cause serious bodily harm rather than to kill,
  (b) lack of premeditation,
  (c) the fact that the offender suffered from any mental disorder or mental disability which (although not falling within section 2(1) of the Homicide Act 1957 (c. 11)), lowered his degree of culpability,
  (d) the fact that the offender was provoked (for example, by prolonged stress) in a way not amounting to a defence of provocation,
  (e) the fact that the offender acted to any extent in self-defence,
  (f) a belief by the offender that the murder was an act of mercy, and
  (g) the age of the offender."

It is clear from the presence of the word "include" in paras 10 and 11 that the listed factors are not exhaustive of what can be mitigating and aggravating factors. Finally, para.12 provides as follows.

"12. Nothing in this Schedule restricts the application of—
(a) section 143(2) (previous convictions),
(b) section 143(3) (bail), or
(c) section 144 (guilty plea)."

17   The transitional provisions are set out in Sch.22. Schedule 22 deals with three different situations:

(i) existing prisoners who in respect of a life sentence had prior to December 18, 2003 been notified by the Secretary of State of the minimum period they were to serve.

(ii) existing prisoners on that date not so notified by the Secretary of State; and

(iii) offenders sentenced to life imprisonment after December 18, 2003.

18   The first two categories of offenders may have been sentenced to life imprisonment at any date prior to December 18, 2003. They do not have an immediate right of appeal. Instead, in the case of category (i) they are "existing prisoners", as defined in Sch.22 to the 2003 Act and may apply to the High Court for a review of the minimum period which has been notified by the Secretary of State or of his determination that they should never be released (Sch.22, paras 2 to 4). In the case of category (ii), the Secretary of State must refer the case to the High Court for an order to be made under subs.(2) or (4) of s.269 of the 2003 Act (Sch.22, paras 5 to 8). In the case of categories (i) and (ii), para.14 of Sch.22 provides for a right of appeal to the Court of Appeal Criminal Division from the High Court judge's decision.

19   Section 269 (1) provides that that section only applies where the life sentence is imposed after the commencement of that section (December 18, 2003). In the case of the first two categories of cases to which the transitional provisions apply the sentences will have been passed prior to that date. However, in the case of both categories the judge is required to have regard to the general principles set out in Sch.21 (Sch.22, paras 4(1) and 7) and in respect of category (ii) there is a cap placed on the minimum term that can be determined in similar terms to that contained in para.10 to which we refer later.

20   In the case of category (iii), s.9 (1) of the Criminal Appeal Act 1968 provides that:

"A person who has been convicted of an offence on indictment may appeal to the Court of Appeal against any sentence (not being a sentence fixed by law) passed on him for the offence . . .".

21   Section 271 of the 2003 Act amends s.9 of the Criminal Appeal Act 1968 to insert s.1(A), which provides that:

"In subsection (1) of this section, the reference to a sentence fixed by law does not include a reference to an order made under subsection (2) or (4) of section 269 of the Criminal Justice Act 2003 in relation to a life sentence . . . that is fixed by law."

The effect of the amendment is that a person who is sentenced to mandatory life imprisonment <u>after</u> the commencement date of December 18, 2003 may apply to the Court of Appeal for leave to appeal against the minimum term set by the trial Judge (or against an order under Section 269 (4) that the early release provisions are not to apply).

22   These appeals deal with the third category and the transitional provisions relevant to their situations are as follows:

> "SCHEDULE 22
> **Mandatory Life Sentences: Transitional Cases**
> Sentences passed on or after commencement date in respect of offences committed before that date
> 9. Paragraph 10 applies where—
>   (a) on or after the commencement date a court passes a life sentence in circumstances where the sentence is fixed by law, and
>   (b) the offence to which the sentence relates was committed before the commencement date.
>
> 10. The court—
>   (a) may not make an order under subsection (2) of section 269 specifying a part of the sentence which in the opinion of the court is greater than that which, under the practice followed by the Secretary of State before December 2002, the Secretary of State would have been likely to notify as mentioned in paragraph 2(a), and
>   (b) may not make an order under subsection (4) of section 269 unless the court is of the opinion that, under the practice followed by the Secretary of State before December 2002, the Secretary of State would have been likely to give the prisoner a notification falling within paragraph 2(b)."

The difficulties created by the transitional provisions in paragraph 10 of Schedule 22

3   Paragraph 10 only applies to the third category of offender with which these appeals deal. Its purpose is plain. It is to avoid the offender having a minimum term determined that offends the requirements of Arts 5 and 7.1 of the ECHR to which we referred at the beginning of this judgment. It prohibits a heavier penalty being imposed than could be imposed at the time the offence was committed. As the jurisprudence of the European Court of Human Rights makes clear, a minimum term is a "penalty" for this purpose. So the minimum term calculated in accordance with the guidance contained in Sch.21 must not exceed that which would have been capable of being imposed at the time the offence was committed.

It is also clear that the approach a judge is intended to adopt in determining the minimum term for this category of offender under the 2003 Act falls into two stages. The judge has to initially assess what would be the appropriate period applying Sch.21. Having ascertained that period he then reduces the period so far as is necessary in order to comply with the requirements of para.10 of Sch.22. This is intended to avoid any question of a breach of Arts 5 and 7.1.

25   As to the first stage, the judge should have no particular difficulty in applying Sch.21. Indeed the result in the majority of cases of the determination should not be materially different under Sch.21 from that which used to be adopted by the Secretary of State in reaching his decision prior to the *Anderson* decision. This is for the following reasons:

(a) In the great majority of cases, under the former practice the Secretary of State fixed the minimum period in accordance with the recommendation of the trial judge and the Lord Chief Justice or either of them (in the few cases where their recommendations differed).

(b) The statutory guidance only significantly affects the minimum term in the case of the first two starting points; that is when the seriousness of the offence is either *exceptionally* or *particularly* high. The difference is not in the length of the term but the breadth of the cases to which they apply because of the examples included in Sch.21. These are statistically the minority of murders, the great majority (two thirds) being murders where the perpetrators know each other and usually involve a quarrel, revenge, or loss of temper (see the advice of the Sentencing Advisory Panel, ("the Panel") of March 15, 2002).

(c) The statutory guidance applies the third starting point of 15 years to all other murders apart from those to which the first two starting points apply. This means 15 years applies to a broad range of offences and it leaves the judge free, for reasons we will explain, to determine for this category of offender an appropriate figure very much in the same way, as would have been the case prior to 2003. At that time the figure selected by the Secretary of State, on the information available to the Court was, on average, 14/15 years.

26   The difference in practice is likely therefore to be confined to the minority of cases where the higher starting points apply. It is in these cases that it will be particularly important to have the provisions of para.10 of Sch.22 in mind. When para.10 has to be applied, its language creates difficulties on which the appellants rely. It establishes a ceiling for the minimum terms based on the *practice* of the Secretary of State prior to December 2002. But what was the *practice* of Home Secretaries prior to that date? Neither the recommendations made by the judiciary nor the determination of the Secretary of State were usually made public. The Secretary of State took into account information that was not available to the public or the judiciary. In order to assist the Court after the main hearing of these appeals, the Secretary of State provided the Court and the parties with considerable information in the form of statistics and records and correspondence between the Lord Chief Justice and the Home Office. This information makes it clear that the best guide to what would have been the *practice* of the Secretary of State is the Practice Directions issued, respectively, by the present Lord Chief Justice and his predecessor, Lord Bingham of Cornhill. This is because it can

reasonably be assumed that the judiciary and in particular the Lord Chief Justice will have applied the relevant Practice Direction while it was in force and in a high percentage of the cases it was their recommendations that the Secretary of State followed.

27   There remain at least two more complications. First, as has been made clear by the Secretary of State, in the most serious cases he tended to select a higher figure than that indicated by the judiciary. Secondly, by the date of the decision in *Anderson*, the Secretary of State had not yet made a determination in a case where the offender was sentenced after the date of the latest Practice Direction (May 31, 2002).

The contents of the relevant Practice Directions

28   A letter was sent by Lord Bingham C.J. on February 10, 1997 to the judges who had to make recommendations as to minimum terms. We should refer to that letter.

> "As all recipients of this letter are very well aware, the imposition of a mandatory life sentence for murder is under current arrangements followed by a three-stage procedure to fix the term to be served by the convicted defendant".

[Lord Bingham then makes general remarks describing the role of the trial judge and the Lord Chief Justice and then continues]

> "While I would not, therefore, wish to seek to bind trial judges in any way, I think it may be helpful to outline my personal approach. My current practice is to take 14 years as the period actually to be served for the 'average', 'normal' or 'unexceptional' murder. This is longer than the period (12 years) which Lord Lane took as his norm 10 years ago. I take this higher norm because I think the level of sentence may in the past, with some reason, have been considered too low; I think the recommended level has risen over the last decade; it is necessary to keep an eye, for purposes of comparison, on sentences for other offences (such as the worst drug offences); and I think the deliberate taking of human life must continue to carry a very heavy penalty.
>
> I regard a number of factors as <u>capable</u>, in appropriate cases, of mitigating the normal penalty. Without seeking to be comprehensive I would list the following factors:
>
> 1. Youth.
> 2. Age (where relevant to physical capacity on release or the likelihood of the defendant dying in prison).
> 3. Sub-normality or mental abnormality.
> 4. Provocation (in a non-technical sense), or an excessive response to a personal threat.
> 5. The absence of an intention to kill.

6. Spontaneity and lack of premeditation (beyond that necessary to constitute the offence: e.g. a sudden response to family pressure or to prolonged and eventually insupportable stress).

7. Mercy killing.

8. A plea of guilty, or hard evidence of remorse or contrition.

Without again seeking to be comprehensive, I would list the following factors as likely to call for a sentence more severe than the norm:

1. Evidence of a planned, professional, revenge or contract killing.

2. The killing of a child or a very old or otherwise vulnerable victim.

3. Evidence of sadism, gratuitous violence, or sexual maltreatment, humiliation, or degradation before the killing.

4. Killing for gain (in the course of burglary, robbery, blackmail, insurance fraud, etc).

5. Multiple killings.

6. The killing of a witness or potential witness to defeat the ends of justice.

7. The killing of those doing their public duty (policemen, prison officers, postmasters, firemen, judges, etc).

8. Terrorist or politically motivated killings.

9. The use of firearms or other dangerous weapons, whether carried for defensive or offensive reasons.

10. A substantial record of serious violence.

11. Macabre attempts to dismember or conceal the body.

The fact that a defendant was under the influence of drink or drugs at the time of the killing is so common that I am inclined to treat it as neutral. But in the not unfamiliar case in which a married couple, or two derelicts, or two homosexuals, inflamed by drink, indulge in a violent quarrel in which one dies, often against a background of longstanding drunken violence, I tend to recommend a term somewhat below the norm.

. . . .

While a recommendation of a punitive term longer than, say, 30 years will be very rare indeed, I do not think one should set any upper limit. Some crimes will certainly call for terms very well in excess of the norm.

The third stage is, of course, the final fixing of the punitive or tariff term by the responsible Home Office minister in the light of the judicial recommendations. I do not think we should concern ourselves with this stage at all. If it emerged that the term fixed was fairly consistently higher or lower than the judicial recommendations, that should not in my view cause us to alter our practice unless on further reflection it seemed to us right to do so. I think it important that our input into the procedure should, so far as possible, be independent of what may prove to be transient phases of penal fashion or popular opinion".

29   Lord Bingham only identified two periods, a higher period than 30 years which would only be recommended in very rare cases and the 14 years "norm". He did not, in relation to the 14 years, explain what was an "average" or "normal" or

"unexceptional murder", but an indication of what he was including in those terms is provided by his description of the factors he identified as being capable of mitigating and aggravating the normal period. In particular the reference included in mitigating factor (5) to the absence of an intention to kill and in mitigating factor (6) to lack of premeditation suggest that the 14 year period was intended to cover more serious murders, since if intentional and premeditated murders were not included (5) and (6) would be inappropriate mitigating factors.

30   The next statement to which it is necessary to refer primarily relates to juveniles and the conducting of the same process when they are sentenced to be detained during Her Majesty's pleasure. It is in the form of a *Practice Statement—Life Sentence for Murder* (Lord Woolf C.J., of July 27, 2000 reported at [2000] 4 All E.R. 831). Its only significance is that it stated that the amount of time actually to be served by an adult convicted of murder in order to meet the requirements of retribution and general deterrence was to continue to be a period of 14 years before the possibility of release arises.

31   The next event was the Advice of the Sentencing Advisory Panel of March 15, 2002. The Advice noted that minimum terms recommended varied "widely above and below the 14-year 'norm'" for an adult. It therefore suggested that it would be helpful for there to be three starting points, a higher, middle and lower *starting point.* The middle figure suggested was 12 years; the higher figure indicated was to be 15 or 16 years; for a lower figure it suggested eight or nine years. The middle figure is a different figure from Lord Bingham's 14 years for a murder of "normal" gravity. However, the middle figure was to cover the case that "arises from a quarrel or loss of temper between two people known to each other" (para.17). The lower figure was for "cases where the offender's culpability is significantly reduced. Such cases which in any event come close to the borderline between murder and manslaughter, includes . . ." (para.18). From their respective descriptions of the murders for which Lord Bingham was suggesting 14 years and the Panel was suggesting 12 years, it does appear that the Panel was applying 12 years to a less grave category of murder than that to which Lord Bingham was applying his norm of 14 years. Instead of altering Lord Bingham's view of what level of punishment was necessary, the Panel was analysing, supplementing and refining his 14-year period to tackle the fluctuations which the Panel had identified were occurring in practice.

32   The Panel's Advice was implemented by a *Practice Statement (Crime, Life Sentences)* [2002] 3 All E.R. 412; [2002] 1 W.L.R. 1789; [2002] 2 Cr.App.R. 18, handed down on May 31, 2002, by Lord Woolf C.J., which was subsequently incorporated as part of the *Consolidated Practice Direction* [2002] 3 All E.R. 938; [2002] 1 W.L.R. 2870, paras 49.2 to 28. This was to be applied by judges in cases in which they made recommendations after May 31, 2002. As the statement is reported it is not necessary to set out all of its terms but, because they are important, we do set out three sections of the Practice Statement.

"49.10 Cases falling within this starting point [12 years] will normally involve the killing of an adult victim, arising from a quarrel or loss of temper between two people known to each other. It will not have the characteristics referred to in para 49.13. Exceptionally, the starting point may be reduced because of the sort of circumstances described in the next paragraph. [We have emphasised the use of the word exceptionally. Its presence following the Advice of the Panel provides some support for the view that the 12 year starting point is meant to deal with less serious cases than Lord Bingham's 14 years. The word is there to avoid an offender receiving credit twice for the same mitigating factors which could happen with the selection of a 12 year starting point and then again in the form of a further mitigating factor.]

49.14 Whichever starting point is selected in a particular case, it may be appropriate for the trial judge to vary the starting point upwards or downwards, to take account of aggravating or mitigating factors, which relate to either the offence or the offender, in the particular case.

49.19 A substantial upward adjustment may be appropriate in the most serious cases, for example, those involving a substantial number of murders, or if there are several factors identified as attracting the higher starting point present. In suitable cases, the result might even be a minimum term of 30 years (equivalent to 60 years) which would offer little or no hope of the offender's eventual release. In cases of exceptional gravity, the judge, rather than setting a whole life minimum term, can state that there is no minimum period which could properly be set in that particular case.

49.20 Among the categories of case referred to in para 49.13, some offences may be especially grave. These include cases in which the victim was performing his duties as a prison officer at the time of the crime or the offence was a terrorist or sexual or sadistic murder or involved a young child. In such a case, a term of 20 years and upwards could be appropriate."

33   On examination of these passages it can be seen that there are a series of starting points in this Practice Direction: a reduced starting point of eight/nine years for a case with reduced responsibility (para.49.11); a normal starting point of 12 years (para.49.10); a higher starting point of 15/16 years (para.49.13); 20 years and over in an especially grave case (para.49.20); and in an extremely serious case, 30 years can be appropriate; and finally in cases of such exceptional gravity (for which there is to be no minimum term) that there is in effect a whole life term (para.49.19).

34   When the passages we have cited are compared with Lord Bingham's statement it appears that the normal starting point of 12 years in the later Statement, as in the advice of the Panel, is dealing with a category of cases less grave than those included by Lord Bingham in his 14 years. The difference between the two is a consequence of the fact that the later guidance is more specific than the earlier guidance. The approach to the very serious cases also accords with Lord Bingham's guidance. While Lord Bingham does not identify as many starting points, it is open to the judge to come to exactly the same decision irrespective of which guidance was followed. In general it is our con-

clusion, therefore, that while a judge might be helped to be consistent by the more specific guidance contained in the 2002 directions, their general effect is the same. Both give the judge a considerable degree of discretion.

35   Comparing the position under the statutory and non-statutory guidance and giving due weight to the ample discretion (described in a helpful article by Dr Thomas Q.C. in *Archbold News*, Issue 3, April 3, p.9 as a "legitimate and extensive discretion in its operation") given to the judge making the determination by the statutory guidance, we are of the opinion that if there is any difference between them it is not as great as has been supposed. The differences in figures are largely explained by their different structures. Where there are differences they are at the top of the range for the most serious crimes. This, interestingly, is the area in which the records show the Secretary of State could differ significantly from the figure recommended by the judiciary. However, this is still the category of case where it is most likely for the judge to have to consider reducing the figure reached in applying the approach suggested in Sch.21, relying on para.10 of Sch.22. The judge would also have to be on his guard against determining a higher figure merely because the starting figure that is taken is greater. This is particularly true where the 15-year figure is the starting point selected. In our judgment it would be wrong to assume that Parliament had intended to raise minimum terms over those recommended by the expert Sentencing Advisory Panel by merely applying the 15-year starting point to all murders other than those whose seriousness is exceptionally or particularly high.

36   The statutory guidance, unlike the non statutory guidance, first and foremost focuses on the most serious cases and describes them in more detail than it does with respect to the very wide range of offences to which the 15-year period applies. The non-statutory guidance of 2002 on the other hand, while covering the whole range of murders, provides three different starting points for murders covered by the 15-year period in the statutory guidance and the 14-year starting point in Lord Bingham's guidance. It is more specific and amplifies the considerations that are relevant.

37   The wider the range of gravity to which a starting point applies, the more important becomes the discretion of the judge to determine the appropriate minimum term within that range. We recognise that the very fact that judges adopt a lower starting point (12 rather than 14 or 14 rather than 15 years) could have the tendency to influence the minimum term decided upon and even though this tendency should be avoided in practice, it may not be.

38   We turn to the final guidance given to the judiciary which was in the form of a letter sent initially to the judiciary dated December 16, 2003 but later published as a Practice Direction on May 18, 2004.

> "On 18 December 2003, the transitional provisions contained in Schedule 22 of the Criminal Justice Act 2003 come into force. This is very short notice, so I felt it important to provide guidance as to the practice judges should follow, after that date, when sentencing someone to a mandatory life sentence in respect of an offence committed before that date.

[The letter then refers to the relevant provisions of the Act which the judge has to apply and continues:]

"The problem created for those sentencing offenders subject to these transitional arrangements, is to know what was the practice followed by the Secretary of State before December 2002.

The most recent guidance to judges on minimum terms is set out in my Practice Statement of 31 May 2002. However, it seems that, by December 2002, judicial recommendations made in accordance with that Practice Statement had not yet been acted upon by the Secretary of State. This being the position, judges dealing with these transitional cases should not use the May 2002 Practice Statement as a guide to the Secretary of State's practice, but should refer to Lord Bingham's letter of 10 February 1997 and my Practice Statement of 27 July 2000. Since, in the majority of cases, the Secretary of State set minimum terms in line with one or both of the judicial recommendations, these two documents provide the best available evidence of the practice followed by the Secretary of State before December 2002.

The only area where the Secretary of State tended to differ from the guidance set out in Lord Bingham's letter and the Practice Statement of 27 July 2000 was in relation to the gravest murders. In cases involving multiple or serial murder, where there are aggravating circumstances and no compelling mitigating factors, the Secretary of State has set minimum terms at a level considerably higher than judicial recommendations. In such cases, the minimum terms have generally fallen between 30 years and whole life."

[The letter then continues by referring to other statutory provisions to which we have referred already and then adds:]

"Having determined the period which should be served for the purposes of retribution, judges should remember to deduct the period which has already been spent in custody in order to arrive at the specified part of the sentence for the purposes of section 269(2). Accordingly, there should also be announced the total period and the period deducted as having been spent in custody.

The Secretary of State is aware that I am intending to give this guidance and agrees that I should do so.

I enclose Lord Bingham's letter, my Practice Statement and a copy of the relevant statutory provisions. In due course, I will communicate with you further as to the review of minimum terms in relation to existing prisoners already notified by the Secretary of State (paragraphs 2 to 4 of Schedule 22) and the setting of minimum terms in relation to existing prisoners not yet notified by the Secretary of State (paragraphs 5 to 8 of Schedule 22)."

39   The appellants have criticised this letter for its suggestion that judges should not use the later Practice Direction of May 31, 2002. However, the material provided to this Court by the Secretary of State confirms that he has not dealt with any cases on which the judiciary would have based their recommendations on that Practice Direction. Therefore, as a matter of fact it cannot be evidence of

the practice that had been "followed by the Secretary of State before December 2002" and so it is rightly disregarded.

40   However, a more sophisticated argument is advanced on behalf of the appellants led by Miss Patricia Lynch Q.C. She with justification contends that the combined effect of Arts 5 and 7 of the ECHR is to require the criminal law to be sufficiently accessible and certain and to enable an individual to know in advance whether his conduct is criminal and to foresee the consequences of such conduct. She accepts, as to the first requirement of the conduct being criminal, there is no possible problem. As to the second part of the requirement, she submits the position is made less clear by the letter of December 16, 2003 in that it excludes reference to the later Practice Direction. This is subject to two requirements. First, the offence was committed after the May 2002 Practice Direction was in force, and secondly, there is a difference in the minimum period that would be determined by a judge first, in using the statutory guidance instead of the practice statements and secondly, in using the earlier instead of the later Practice Direction.

41   As to this argument, we have already indicated that on a close examination of the relevant Schedule and the practice statements, a judge is entitled to come to the same conclusion irrespective of which Practice Direction is used. It is therefore questionable whether it would be possible to establish any contravention of either Art.5 or 7.1 as a consequence of the Practice Direction that was followed by the sentencing judge. In addition we consider that Sch.21 and the practice statements, properly applied, should produce the broadly similar results except possibly in regard to the two higher statutory categories. As to these higher categories, any difference is of no significance because it would be corrected by the application of either Practice Direction since they deal with them in the same way. In addition the application of the Practice Directions could in fact be unduly generous to the offender since the Secretary of State contends, and there is evidence to support him, that he did on a number of occasions increase the recommendations in the case of the most grave offences.

42   However, this is an area where the offender's rights must be seen to be protected and so, although we doubt whether Miss Lynch's argument will produce any different result on the facts of a particular case as to what should be the *appropriate* term, we have decided that to avoid any prejudice to an offender the letter of December 16 should no longer be followed in the case of an offender whose offence was committed after May 2002. In such a case the judge in determining the minimum term should apply the Practice Direction of that date. By doing this any danger will be avoided of a judge coming to a conclusion that is adverse to the offender because of the adoption of a higher starting point (14 years) resulting in a longer minimum term than that which would have been determined if a lower starting point (12 years) had been adopted. This would be needed because otherwise para.10 of Sch.22 would not have achieved its objective since absent the 2003 Act a lower minimum term would have been likely to be imposed for the offence when it was committed. In this situation s.3 of the Human Rights Act would come into play and it would be necessary to interpret Art.10 in a manner that enabled the May 2002 Practice Direction to be used as being the best evi-

dence of the Secretary of State's practice in relation to those offences committed during the time it was in force.

43   A further advantage of the judge using the later guidelines when appropriate is that it will not deprive judges of the more refined guidance the later Practice Direction provides. In addition, the judge's task can be simplified further, since the Practice Direction itself will produce the result required by para.10 of Sch.22. This is because when the minimum term is calculated applying the later Practice Direction the period of the minimum term will either be the same or shorter than the minimum term calculated applying Sch.21.

44   A different argument is advanced by Mr Ben Nolan Q.C. on behalf of the appellant Barry Elener whose minimum term is 27 years. In his case it is rightly conceded in the light of the evidence from the Home Secretary that the non-use of the May 2002 Practice Direction can no longer be relied on. It was, however, argued that a generous discount should be given because of the difficulty of saying with reasonable certainty what the practice of the Home Secretary would have been likely to be prior to December 2002. Accordingly, his client should be given the benefit of the doubt. In addition, the cases where, on the evidence, more than 25 years was taken as being the minimum term have been of a different character from his clients case. As to giving the benefit of the doubt, that is what we have done by proposing the use of the May 2002 direction in future. Especially in serious cases there can be no need for any further protection because there is absolutely no evidence to suggest that the Home Secretary's practice was ever more lenient than that set out in the May 2002 Practice Direction.

45   Although we have modified the guidance contained in the letter dated December 16, 2003, as to the use of the May 2002 Practice Direction, it would be wrong to assume that because it has already been applied in its unmodified form this means that the wrong minimum term has been determined in those cases in which it was applied.

The individual appeals

46   Because of the conclusions to which we have come as to the effect of the different practice statements our task in determining the appeals is made less complicated. We will deal with the appeals in turn using the May 2002 direction where appropriate. They have all been given leave to appeal. Before this Court, for an appeal against the length of a minimum term to succeed it has to be shown, as is the case with any other appeal against sentence, that the minimum term is manifestly excessive.

Melvin Terrence Sullivan

47   On March 9, 2004, at the Crown Court at Norwich before Aikens J., the appellant was convicted by a majority of 10:2 of murder and sentenced to life imprisonment with a minimum term of 13 years and 88 days, pursuant to s.269 of the Criminal Justice Act 2003. His application for leave to appeal against conviction was dismissed at the commencement of the hearing for reasons that were then announced.

The facts

48   In the early hours of the morning of June 7, 2003, the appellant became involved in an altercation with his neighbour, Michael Bailey, who had returned home with his fiancée and two friends after a night out. The appellant objected to the noise made as they went into the house and he or his wife banged on the internal wall between the two houses. Bailey went outside, followed by his fiancée Amy Cottrill, and they shouted abuse towards the appellant's home. The appellant went out with a long thin sword-like weapon. During the course of the ensuing argument the appellant stabbed Bailey once with the weapon so that the weapon entered Bailey's body at one side and emerged from the other, puncturing his heart and lungs. Bailey died shortly afterwards from the wound, which was 33cm deep.

49   The prosecution case was that during their argument, Bailey had told the appellant that the best thing would be for him to go inside. He had stepped forward, lifted his right arm and pointed at the road. The appellant had then deliberately thrust the weapon into the left side of Bailey's chest with at least moderate force. An intention to kill or at least to do Bailey really serious harm could be inferred from the appellant's actions.

50   The defendant's case was that Bailey had been abusive outside and had banged on the window of the appellant's downstairs bedroom. The appellant had been afraid for his safety and had taken the weapon out as protection, not knowing how many people were outside and being aware that Cottrill was connected to a family of some notoriety. He saw four people outside and saw that Cottrill was armed with a knife. As Bailey stepped towards him with his arm raised, the appellant lifted the weapon and realised he had caught Bailey. He had acted in self-defence and had no intention to kill or cause really serious harm. The issues for the jury were whether the appellant had acted in self-defence, whether he had acted with the necessary intent and whether he had been provoked. The verdict means that the jury rejected these defences.

51   Cottrill gave evidence that she had returned home with Bailey in the early hours of the morning with two others and that she heard banging lasting about a minute after the door had shut. Bailey said, "What the fuck are they banging about?" and went outside in his socks. He did not have his top on, had nothing in his hands and did not have a weapon. She followed him out. Bailey was shouting, as was she. She said to the appellant, "You may be bullying everyone else down the street but you are not bullying us." The other two came outside. She did not have a weapon in her hand.

52   The appellant was at arm's length from Bailey. She was standing behind Bailey and slightly to his left. She saw what she thought was a metal bar in the appellant's hand and asked him why he had it. He replied, "I do not know how many of you there is." She told Bailey to "leave it", but he stepped forward and said to the appellant, "the best thing for you to do is to fuck off back into your house as we have not done anything wrong." He pointed with his right arm towards the road as he said it. The appellant stepped backwards then thrust forward towards Bailey. The appellant then went back into his home. In cross-examination she

confirmed that Bailey shouted and that there was shouting from next door in response. Bailey had invited the appellant to come out if he had anything to say. She did shout, "get Walter", but she could not remember why. It was dark but there was a streetlight. The appellant had not waved the bayonet at all. It all happened in a split second when Bailey moved forward and the appellant stepped back. The appellant kept a collection of knives and bayonets. There was evidence that a large degree of movement was needed to cause the blade to move 33cm. The wound tracked slightly upwards from left to right. The pathologist considered that it would have been necessary to grip the handle of the weapon firmly and would need some force to pull it out.

53   The appellant gave evidence. He lived with his wife. He said he was watching television (with headphones) late on June 6 and his wife was working on her computer. He was disturbed at 2.45 by a loud bang from the street next door. It was not the first time. His wife banged on the wall, but he did not. He then heard a loud bang from what he thought was the bedroom window. He heard shouting and swearing outside and believed it to be directed to his wife who was on the bed, crying. He could see the silhouette of Bailey through the window. He dressed and left the bedroom, being fearful that something might be thrown through the window. He knew that one of the neighbours was related to a family with a reputation as people who did not take kindly to those who upset them and could be violent. He knew that from his son, who had worked for one of the Cottrills.

54   His wife had become hysterical and inconsolable. He went to the front door and picked up the bayonet or sword from behind the curtain. He kept it there with the coshes for protection. He had been collecting weapons since he was a lad, but the coshes were his wife's. The machete was something he used in the garden but he kept it under the settee to stop it getting rusty. The weapon he took was the first thing that came to hand. He thought there would just be a verbal argument. There were four people outside when he went out. Bailey was swearing and shouting and squared up to him with a clenched fist. When he was within three feet of Bailey he saw that Amy Cottrill had a knife in her right hand, which she was moving up and down. He stopped at about arm's length from Bailey, who suddenly stepped forwards and raised his hands. He accepted that he was also shouting and that he swore. Bailey threatened to "do him" and he then remembered Bailey stepping forward and raising his right hand towards his (the appellant's) chest. He stepped back and raised his right hand with the weapon. He did so because he thought Bailey was armed and because he had seen Amy was armed. He did not have time to think and was scared of being harmed. He stepped back and brought the weapon up and round. Bailey staggered back whereupon he backed away and said "get the police", or words to that effect. He went back inside and put the weapon back behind the door. He asked his wife to call the police. She was hysterical and thought they would come round and force their way into the house. The defence pathologist confirmed that it was possible that having pushed a bayonet 13 inches into someone and then pulled it out, a man might not be aware of having done so.

The trial judge's sentencing remarks

55   In sentencing the appellant the judge said that he was satisfied on the evidence that the deceased had come out of his house, followed by his fiancée, and had been noisy and abusive. The appellant had confronted him and, as the deceased stepped forward, lifted his right arm and pointed to the road, the appellant had deliberately thrust the bayonet into his left side with moderate force or a little more. The appropriate starting point for sentence was 15 years, bearing in mind the provisions of para.4 of Sch.21 of the 2003 Act. An aggravating feature of the case was the appellant's decision to go outside the house armed with a bayonet, a weapon designed to kill or seriously wound. So far as mitigating factors were concerned, the court did not accept that he had only intended to cause serious harm to the deceased; his deliberate thrusting of the weapon indicated an intention to kill. There was, however, no premeditation. He had not been goaded into the killing by the argument with the deceased, nor had he lost his self-control. There was no question of a long-term dispute with the neighbours. He had not acted to any extent in self-defence. The deceased was unarmed and bare-chested and had made no attempt to physically attack him. The court did not accept that Amy Cottrill was armed before the deceased was stabbed.

56   If there were no other factors to consider, on the above basis the appropriate minimum term would be 15 years. However, as the offence pre-dated the commencement of the Act, Sch.22 of the Act applied. The minimum term was not therefore permitted to exceed the minimum term which would have been notified by the Secretary of State under the practice which he followed before December 2002. There was no guidance before the court and nothing in the Act to directly indicate what period would have been notified by the Secretary of State before December 2002. There had been no publication of the practice. Such guidance as there was came from the Practice Directions. Under the earlier practice note the appropriate term in a case such as the present would have been 14 years. The later practice statement stipulated the starting point as 12 years. Counsel for the appellant had submitted that the later Practice Direction was the relevant one for determining what the Secretary of State's practice would have been before December 2002. The court was not satisfied that such was the correct approach though, as the practice appeared to have been to act in accordance with the earlier Practice Direction. The best evidence of the practice of the Secretary of State at the relevant time came from the letter of the Lord Chief Justice dated 16 December 2003, which counsel had seen. Accordingly the minimum term (subject to time spent in custody) had to be fixed at 14 years.

Antecedents

57   The appellant was 45 and had 12 previous convictions from 1975 onwards, mostly spent and mostly for dishonesty offences. He had two convictions for violence: for assault occasioning actual bodily harm in 1982, for which he was fined, and his most recent conviction, for common assault in 1990, for which he was sentenced to three months' imprisonment, suspended.

Grounds of appeal

58   The judge erred in his approach to setting the tariff and acted contrary to Art.6 in his reliance on the contents of the letter of December 16, 2003 (from the Lord Chief Justice) and the documents referred to therein, in place of the relevant published and accessible Practice Statement indicating a starting point of 12 years. In addition the minimum period of 13 years and 88 days was manifestly excessive and/or wrong in principle.

Decision

59   We say this appeal provides support for the reasoning set out already for saying that the outcome should be the same irrespective of which Practice Direction is used by the trial judge. We also consider (contrary to Aikens J.) that it would be the same in this case applying Sch.21 even though the starting points are different. The appropriate minimum term would be about 14 years whichever guidelines were used. Under Sch.21 the 15-year starting point would stand to be reduced because there are mitigating circumstances that the Schedule identifies. In particular there is the lack of premeditation. This would justify the reduction to 14 years. On the other hand if 12 years were taken as the starting point, an increase to 14 years would be required. This is because of the aggravating feature that would then have to be taken into account because Aikens J. found (which on the evidence he was entitled to do) that in this case there was an intention to kill. We appreciate that there was a degree of provocation in this case which is a factor that can justify a reduction in a normal starting point. However, because the intention to kill was found by the judge, provocation could not provide any excuse for the appellant's offence on the facts of this case. Miss Lynch was right in her argument to concentrate on her submissions based on the Human Rights Act. Those submissions having already been considered and the correct deduction having been made for the appellant's period in custody, we dismiss this appeal.

Martin Godwin Gibbs

The facts

60   On December 22, 2003 at the Central Criminal Court before H.H. Judge Morris Q.C. the appellant was convicted of murder (count 1) following a re-trial and was sentenced to life imprisonment with a minimum term of 17 years, pursuant to s.269 of the Criminal Justice Act 2003. He had earlier pleaded guilty to an alternative count of manslaughter (count 2). The appellant was originally convicted on March 15, 1999. On May 7, 2003 the Full Court quashed the conviction and ordered a re-trial.

61   In the early afternoon of July 15, 1998, the appellant and the deceased, Wilbourne Williams, were both passengers on a London bus travelling from Victoria to Lewisham. The appellant was sitting at the back of the bus on the lower deck and Williams was sitting in front of him, on a seat facing the side of the bus. At some point the appellant threw a bottle out of the bus window,

whereupon Williams told him off. Other passengers heard the appellant tell Williams to mind his own business and to leave him alone. Williams said again he should not have done it and the appellant threatened to "stab him" or "cut him". Williams was calm and quiet in tone.

62   As the bus crossed Vauxhall Bridge Williams stood up and rang the bell for the bus to stop. The appellant stood up to follow him and was shouting aggressively and asking him if he wanted to fight. Both men got off the bus, together with another passenger. She saw that the appellant had a knife in his hand and was pushing Williams. He then stabbed him once in the chest. A witness, watching from the bus, saw the appellant take a long kitchen knife from his pocket and try several times to stab Williams who was throwing punches to protect himself. Other passengers saw Williams punch the appellant, or described the two men fighting.

63   The appellant then ran off and was pursued by a witness. The appellant managed to evade him. The emergency services were called and attempts made to resuscitate Williams but he was pronounced dead at 1.55pm. He had died from a single stab wound to the right upper chest, angled downwards to a depth of 9.4cm. According to the pathologist, no more than moderate force would have been required to inflict the injury.

Sentence

64   The judge in sentencing said the victim was a gentle, peaceful man who was loved by his family, his friends and the members of his church. He was 56 at the time of his death and was killed for no other reason than he had told the appellant off for throwing a bottle out of a bus window. The appellant was an extremely dangerous and manipulative man, who was prone to violence and aggression and who sought out confrontation so that he could use violence against others.

65   For many years he had been prone to carry knives and to use them when the opportunity arose. He had a record for wounding his girlfriend with a knife in 1993 when she required 26 stitches as a result. In 1993 and 1996 he had been convicted of possessing a knife in a public place. On at least two occasions after the murder he became involved in further incidents where he threatened to stab people and on at least one of those occasions the court was satisfied that he was carrying a knife.

66   On the day of the offence he had taken a 12-inch-long knife with him when he left home. His version that he stole a knife to cut up fruit was rejected. He had threatened to stab the victim and did not do so on the bus because he realised it would be difficult to make good his escape. Having waited until the victim got off the bus he tried several times to stab him. It was accepted that he may not have intended to kill him. He had a paranoid and antisocial personality disorder which may have lowered his culpability. He was, however, a very clever man and had managed to deceive a number of psychiatrists by lying about his symptoms, so that they thought he was suffering from schizophrenia. He had been fully able to control himself on July 15, 1998 but had chosen not to do so because he enjoyed using violence against others.

67   The appropriate starting point for his sentence to meet the requirements of retribution and deterrence was one of 15 years, as counsel had agreed. Taking into account his previous record, his habit of carrying knives and the premeditated nature of the offence, balanced against the mitigating features identified, the starting point would be increased to 17 years.

Antecedents

68   He was 51 and had convictions (some spent) between 1969 and 1998, mostly for dishonesty offences (theft, burglary, handling). He also had a conviction for unlawful wounding from 1993 for which he was imprisoned for nine months. The same year he had been imprisoned for one day for possession of an offensive weapon and in 1996 had been fined for possession of a bladed article.

Grounds of appeal

69   The 17-year term was manifestly excessive in that:

A) The judge erred in taking into account incidents two months after the offence when the appellant was alleged to have threatened to stab other people. They were wholly separate matters; the appellant denied having a knife on either occasion and he had not been warned about the right not to incriminate himself in respect of those matters which could have formed the basis of other offences.

B) The judge failed to take adequate account of the mitigating factor; namely substantial mental disability and a history of mental illness, deprivation as a child (including being hit by his mother with a machete) and the fact that he had only one previous conviction for violence.

C) Mr Edward Fitzgerald Q.C. who appeared for Mr Gibbs relied at the hearing on the arguments advanced so effectively by Miss Lynch on behalf of Mr Sullivan based on the Human Rights Act and the 2002 Practice Direction. He submitted that if the latest Practice Direction was used, the starting point would have been 12 years and from this starting point the calculation would have resulted in a figure of less than 17 years.

Decision

70   If 17 years is the appropriate period then that figure could have been determined as being the minimum term regardless of which starting point was adopted. So we would reject Mr Fitzgerald's reliance on Miss Lynch's argument for the reasons already given. As the trial judge indicated, this was a case of an individual attacking a perfectly innocent member of the public without any justification at all. The crime itself was especially serious because Mr Gibbs was a person who was in the habit of carrying a knife and would not hesitate in using it.

71   It is also, however, a case in which it is very important to distinguish the two aspects of a life sentence. The reference to the later incidents would not be justifiable if the judge was referring to them to illustrate the risk that Mr Gibbs

constitutes, as this is a matter for the Parole Board. In addition, Mr Gibbs' mental condition undoubtedly played a part in this offence. This is capable of being a mitigating factor which would justify reducing the minimum term, although it will be a matter to which the Parole Board will have to pay particular attention in the future in deciding whether the risk is sufficiently reduced to justify releasing Mr Gibbs on licence.

72   Looking at the picture as a whole it is our view that 17 years does not pay sufficient attention to Mr Gibbs' mental disability and a more appropriate figure is 14 years. Whether 12 or 14 years is adopted as the starting point, the going armed with a knife and the unprovoked nature of the attack on a perfectly innocent person could justify a figure of 17 years; however, there then would have to be a substantial discount for the offender's mental state which would reduce the appropriate term to 14 years. We accordingly allow the appeal and substitute a minimum term of 14 years, in relation to which there will need to be credit for any period spent on remand.

Barry Elener and Derek Elener

The facts

73   On February 3, 2004 at the Crown Court at Leeds before Wakerley J. Derek Elener, who is the father of Barry Elener, pleaded guilty on re-arraignment. On March 2, 2004 the son was convicted and on March 12, 2004 they were sentenced as follows:

B. Elener

Count 25—Robbery—15 years' imprisonment concurrent to count 27
Count 26—Possession of firearm when committing Sch.1 offence—Three years' imprisonment concurrent to count 29
Count 27—Robbery—17 years' imprisonment concurrent to count 28
Count 28—Murder—Life imprisonment
Count 29—Possession of firearm with intent to endanger life—Five years' imprisonment consecutive to count 27
TOTAL SENTENCE: Life imprisonment with a recommendation he serve 27 years' imprisonment.

D. Elener

Pleaded guilty to: counts 1, 4, 7, 9, 11, 14, 16, 18, 20, 23, 25 and 27–12 counts of robbery. Sentenced to 15 years' imprisonment on each count concurrent and concurrent to count 28
Counts 2, 5, 12, 2 2 and 29—Possession of firearm with intent to endanger life × 5. Sentenced to five years' imprisonment on each concurrent but consecutive to count 1
Counts 3, 31 and 32—Causing grievous bodily harm with intent × 3. Sentenced to 20 years' imprisonment on each concurrent and concurrent to count 28

Counts 8, 10, 15, 17, 19, 24 and 26—Possession of firearm or imitation firearm when committing Sch.1 offence × 7. Sentenced to three years' imprisonment on each concurrent and concurrent to count 2.

Count 28—Murder. Sentenced to life imprisonment.

TOTAL SENTENCE: Life imprisonment with a recommendation he serve 25 years' imprisonment.

74   These offences involved 12 armed attacks on security guards undertaking high-value cash collections and deliveries in the Bradford area. On five occasions, a firearm was used, on the last occasion with fatal consequences. The total amount of money stolen was £192,626. The father, who is 65, was involved in all the offences and his son, who is 42, on the last two occasions.

75   Between December 1985 and April 1995, the father was employed by Securicor and, following his departure, Securicor received an intelligence report that he had been spotted watching one of their vehicles making a delivery and the police were informed.

76   The first 26 counts are connected to a series of similar robberies that took place between November 1994 and November 2002. In each case a man holding a handgun frightened a security man into handing over or dropping a money container which the robber ran off with to a waiting car that drove off making an escape. On one occasion the gun was fired into the security guard's abdomen although the robber had already taken possession of the cash. On another occasion the gun was fired into the back of the security guard who was trying to obtain safety in his security van. On a third occasion the gun was fired but missed.

77   At about 5.10pm on January 27, 2003, a security guard was collecting cash from travel agents. As he made his way back to the van with a box containing £40,000 in cash, he was confronted by an armed man who demanded the box and threatened to shoot him. The guard released the box and the man made off in a Nissan motorcar with his accomplice.

78   As the robbers drove off in the Nissan, the occupants of a BMW motorcar followed them, since they had witnessed the robbery. The Nissan came to a halt and the BMW pulled up alongside it. A passenger in the BMW alighted from the car and was challenged by one of the men in the Nissan. The passenger in the Nissan then shot the man in the chest. The shot was fatal. The Nissan was driven off (counts 27, 28 and 29).

79   On February 7, 2003, the applicants were arrested. When interviewed, they both denied any involvement in the final robbery or murder.

Sentence

80   The judge in sentencing said that the father had instigated and inspired this campaign of 12 serious robberies of cash in transit over an eight-year period. He had used his knowledge of the system gained through his employment in the planning and execution of the robberies. His role was generally as the driver of the getaway car. He would be dealt with on the basis that he was not the gunman but that he continued the campaign in the knowledge that his accomplice had a

gun, which had been used, and in the realisation that this accomplice would shoot to kill, which is what his son had done.

81   The robberies and associated offences were aggravated by the use of a firearm, which was discharged on five occasions to dreadful effect. The fact he had no relevant convictions was of minimal relevance. He was 65 but had played for high stakes over several years and had eventually lost. In view of the consequences of his conviction for murder, the sentence could not be significantly discounted because of his age. The starting point for the robberies and associated offences was one of 25 years. He was entitled to some credit for his plea.

82   The sentences for the firearms offences would run consecutively to the sentences for the robberies. The sentence for murder was fixed by law but the period he would have to serve had to be specified. This was a grave offence, committed during the course of the robbery. The specified period would be 25 years, less the period he had spent on remand.

83   As to the son, he had shot and killed a man who had bravely sought to intervene. He had not shown one jot of remorse. The sentences for the firearms offences would run consecutively to the sentence for the robberies. As far as the murder was concerned, he had deliberately shot at the man, intending to kill him. The specified period in his case would be 27 years, less the period he had spent on remand.

Antecedents

84   The son was born on July 10, 1961 and was of previous good character. The father who was born on November 15, 1938 had no previous convictions of any relevance.

Grounds of appeal

85   The son's grounds of appeal were that the recommendation that he serve 27 years was manifestly excessive in all the circumstances of the case. Insufficient account was taken of the principle of parity with his father, who had been committing extremely violent offences over a 10-year period, whereas the appellant was involved over two months. He had a good character and insufficient account had been taken of the fact that the appellant's decision to discharge the firearm although not spontaneous, was a course of action decided on in a moment during the escape from the robbery.

86   The father's grounds of appeal were that the minimum term he must serve was manifestly excessive in all the circumstances of the case. Insufficient account was taken of his age; his guilty pleas, which were courageous, and good character; his contrition; the fact he had not pulled the trigger; and the principle of parity with his son, who did not plead guilty and was directly responsible for the death of the victim.

Decision

Derek Elener

87   We regard these crimes as very serious indeed and as certainly justifying starting points of 30 years. This would be the figure under Sch.21 and under both
practice statements. They display a total disregard for human life and it is fortunate that there is only one person who has been killed. The father was more than a
"get-away" driver. He continued to act as a driver even after he must have known
that guns had been used and knowing the nature of the offences he recruited his
son. His age means he could never leave prison. However, for professional crime
of this nature, whatever your age, you must still be severely punished. The
reduction to 25 years is justified by the plea and his age. These mitigating factors
are of reduced significance because the plea was not made at the outset and his
age had not deterred him from playing his active role in the crimes.

Barry Elener

88   The son was involved after a pattern had been established of how the crimes
were to be committed and the son acted in accordance with that pattern. Thirty
years is the appropriate starting point and the judge recognised what mitigation
there was fully in reaching the minimum terms he considered appropriate.

89   Due credit must be allowed for the period spent on remand. Both appeals are
dismissed.

R. v HASSAN LAHBIB

COURT OF APPEAL (Lord Justice Maurice Kay, Mr Justice Simon
and Judge Goldsack Q.C.): July 8, 2004

[2004] EWCA Crim 1877; [2005] 1 Cr.App.R.(S.) 68

(LT) Knives; Manslaughter; Provocation; Sentence length

H1   *Manslaughter—manslaughter by reason of provocation—stabbing after attacks*
by deceased—length of sentence

H2   Ten years' imprisonment imposed for manslaughter apparently by reason of
provocation, where the appellant stabbed the deceased with a knife the appellant
carried for protection after the deceased had attacked him three times, reduced to
eight years.

H3   The appellant was convicted of manslaughter on an indictment charging murder. The appellant had been attacked on two occasions while travelling home
from work late at night. As a result, he carried a lock knife in his pocket when
out at night, for the purpose of scaring off potential assailants. The appellant visited a public house where the deceased was a regular drinker. The deceased

attacked the appellant without provocation, punching him to the face so as to knock him to the ground, and then kicked him while he lay on the ground. The manager of the public house arrived and insisted that the appellant and the deceased should leave the public house. Outside the public house, the deceased attacked the appellant for a second time, and the appellant ran away. The appellant returned home but discovered that his wrist watch was missing. He returned to the public house to look for it. The deceased had also returned to the public house to look for keys and a mobile telephone. Outside the public house there was a further confrontation and the deceased attacked the appellant again. The appellant eventually took out his knife, opened it and shouted to the deceased to leave him alone. There was then a scuffle in which the deceased received four blows from the knife, including a stab wound to the heart which was fatal. The appellant's defence at the trial was self-defence and lack of intent to cause serious injury. The trial judge left the question of manslaughter to the jury on the bases of lack of intent to cause serious harm and provocation. The jury returned a verdict of manslaughter. No inquiry was made as to the basis of the verdict. Sentenced to 10 years' imprisonment.

Held: (considering *Attorney General's Reference No.33 of 1996 (Daniel Latham)* [1997] 2 Cr.App.R.(S.) 10, and *Attorney General's Reference No.19 of 1999 (Marvin Wayne Kitchener)* [2000] 1 Cr.App.R.(S.) 287) the sentencing judge accepted that the appellant had been provoked but said that the jury had rejected the appellant's claim that he was acting in necessary or reasonable self-defence. The sentencing judge referred to the fact that the appellant had carried a lock knife regularly for nearly a year. It was submitted for the appellant that the sentencing judge had taken too high a starting point in view of the nature and extent of the provocation and the fact that the final confrontation was not planned. The Court had concluded that the sentence of 10 years was too long and a sentence of eight years would be substituted.

Cases cited:
Attorney General's Reference No.33 of 1996 (Daniel Latham) [1997] 2 Cr.App.R.(S.) 10, *Attorney General's Reference No.19 of 1999 (Marvin Wayne Kitchener)* [2000] 1 Cr.App.R.(S.) 287

References: manslaughter, *Current Sentencing Practice* B 1-2

D.E. Waters Q.C. for the appellant.
T. Kark for the Crown.

JUDGMENT

1   **Simon J.:**   On February 2, 2004, at the Central Criminal Court before H.H. Judge Paget Q.C. and a jury, the appellant, who faced a single count of murder, was convicted of manslaughter. On February 3 he was sentenced to 10 years' imprisonment. He appeals against that sentence with the leave of the single judge.

2   The defendant is a 27-year-old Moroccan who came to this country about four years ago, having met and married an English schoolteacher. In Morocco he worked as a tour guide. Since coming to England he has worked in various restaurants. In 2002 his first child was born. Financial difficulties followed and his marriage was at a low ebb in May 2003. He was working as a kitchen porter in Central London. On a few occasions he visited The Victoria Public House, Hoe Street, E17 for a drink and a game of snooker. He was a man of good character and was described by two character witnesses as gentle and kind.

3   In the year before April 2003 he had been attacked on two occasions while travelling home from work late at night. From this time he carried a lock knife in his trouser pocket when he was out at night. The purpose of doing so was, he said, to scare off any potential assailants.

4   The deceased was Anthony O'Keefe, a man in his mid-40s who was a regular drinker at The Victoria Public House. He was known by all the staff and other regulars and had been known to be violent in drink on previous occasions.

5   On May 31, 2003 the appellant visited The Victoria Public House. He was alone and began to play snooker. There were a number of regulars playing and the appellant had two games during the course of the evening. Although he drank some beer, he was not described by anyone as being intoxicated. At about 9.00pm the deceased walked up to the appellant and punched him on the face sufficiently hard that he fell on the ground. Other people present intervened. Everyone agreed that it was entirely unprovoked. Some of the witnesses described the deceased kicking the appellant whilst on the ground once; others, two or three times.

6   The appellant got to his feet and asked why he had been attacked. He wanted to call the police. One of the women present was a special constable. She told the appellant that they had been called. She tried to calm the situation. The deceased was aggressive and drunk during this time. Someone summoned the manager, who was on his evening off. In due course the manager arrived and appeared to take against the appellant, who was not a regular customer of the pub. One of the barmaids tried to explain to the manager that the appellant had done nothing wrong. However, the manager insisted he leave, as well as the deceased, and escorted them both from the premises.

7   While outside a witness saw the three men while collecting a fare from the premises. He saw the deceased attack the appellant a second time, lashing out and shouting. The appellant did not retaliate, he put his hands up and ran away. The manager went back into the public house. At no point during this time had the appellant removed his knife. We will return to this point later in the judgment.

8   When the appellant spoke to some girls he saw in the street he appeared friendly and calm, but when he reached home his wife's sister and husband

were present. He began to feel uncomfortable at the tense atmosphere there. At this point he realised that his watch was missing and returned to the public house to see if it had fallen off during the earlier incident.

9   When he returned to the pub he was seen looking around the floor by the snooker table. Unfortunately, and unknown to him, the deceased too had returned, looking for his keys and his mobile telephone. As the appellant walked out he said something to the deceased, who walked out behind him. There is an issue as to what was said. Once outside there was a further confrontation, the deceased shouting and again in drink. The appellant again told him to leave him alone. There was an attack. The appellant told the deceased he had a knife but this did not deter him. The appellant took the knife out, opened it and shouted to the deceased to leave him alone. There was then a scuffle in which the knife was to make contact four times with the deceased: a glancing blow to the head, a defensive type injury on the arm, a superficial cut to the neck and a stab wound to the very edge of the heart. It was the fourth wound which was fatal.

10   The appellant was arrested on June 6, 2003 at his place of work. In interview he made no comment to questions asked of him.

11   The defence at trial was self-defence and lack of intent to cause serious harm. In summing up, the judge left the manslaughter issue to the jury on two bases: lack of intent to cause serious harm and provocation. In returning their verdicts, the jury found the appellant not guilty of murder but guilty of manslaughter. No inquiry was made as to the basis of the verdict. It is accepted on the appellant's behalf that this was a matter for the discretion of the judge and no criticism is made of that.

2   In his sentencing remarks the judge accepted that there had been provocation. The deceased was quite prepared to fight and had knocked the appellant down an hour earlier. On the other hand, as the judge observed, the jury had rejected his case that he was acting in necessary or reasonable self-defence. The appellant was younger than the deceased and he could have escaped. Instead he pulled a knife. The judge referred to the lock knife which was carried regularly for nearly a year, according to his own evidence:

> "You claimed in evidence that you were unaware that it was against the law to carry such a weapon. I find that impossible to believe. On your own admission you never told anybody that you had that knife and you were careful only to carry it at night which suggests at least some knowledge on your part that you should not have had it, but whether you knew it was against the law to carry a knife or not, it is against the law precisely because knives are so dangerous and so often lead to unnecessary killings such as this one."

In conclusion, the judge observed:

> "The Courts must do what they can to prevent the use of knives and the unnecessary loss of life that they cause. I have considered the guidance of the Court of Appeal in *Attorney General's Reference No.33 of 1996 (Latham)* and I have considered a number of cases collected together on the general topic of manslaughter involving knives when there is a lack of intent."

He then passed the sentence of 10 years' imprisonment.

13   In his submissions today, Mr Waters Q.C. has made three points in support of the appeal. First, the nature and the extent of the provocation which the appellant endured. Secondly, this was not a case in which the appellant had deliberately gone out with a knife. Thirdly, he submitted that the judge gave insufficient weight to the appellant's good character and the circumstances of the offence.

14   It is convenient to take the first two points together because, Mr Waters submits, it resulted in the judge starting at too high a point in the sentencing exercise. We have been referred to two cases, the first that to which the judge himself referred, *Attorney General's Reference No.33 of 1996 (Latham)* [1997] 2 Cr.App.R.(S.) 10. In that case Kennedy L.J., giving the judgment of the Court, said this at para.[8]:

> "Even when a particular type of manslaughter is isolated from the rest it has to be recognised that it covers a wide field, and if justice is to be done sentencers must not be put in straitjackets, but for the reasons identified in this judgment it seems to us that where an offender deliberately goes out with a knife, carrying it as a weapon, and uses it to cause death, even if there is provocation he should expect to receive on conviction in a contested case a sentence in the region of 10 to 12 years."

15   The second case is *Attorney General's Reference No.19 of 1999 (Marvin Wayne Kitchener)* [2000] 1 Cr.App.R.(S.) 287. In that case the Court of Appeal, describing a sentence of five years on conviction as a lenient but not unduly lenient sentence, distinguished the *Latham* type of case from a case in which the offender did not deliberately go out with a knife, carrying it as a weapon and using it to cause death.

16   Mr Waters submitted that the facts of the present case also have factual features that take it out of the *Latham* bracket. He relies primarily on the nature and the extent of the provocation: the deceased's attack in the pub, the unjustifiable manhandling of the appellant from the pub by the licensee and the second unprovoked attack by the deceased outside the pub before the appellant went home. Mr Waters submits that this was extreme provocation relevant to the sentence to be imposed; but he also submits that, since on none of these occasions did the appellant draw his knife, these facts demonstrate that the appellant was not a man who deliberately carried his knife intending to use it as a weapon of offence. It seems to us that there is considerable force in this point.

17   Taking into account this point and the other points urged upon us by Mr Waters, including the fact that the final confrontation was not planned and the appellant's good character, we have concluded that the sentence of 10 years was too long and that the sentence should have been one of eight years. Accordingly, we quash the sentence of 10 years and substitute a sentence of eight years. To that extent the appeal is allowed.

R. v JAMES TERRANCE ALGER

Court of Appeal (Lord Justice Hooper, Mr Justice Gage and Judge Richard Brown): July 9, 2004

[2004] EWCA Crim 1868; [2005] 1 Cr.App.R.(S.) 69

(LT) Attempts; Deterrence; Possession with intent to supply; Prisoners; Sentence length

H1 *Possessing cannabis resin with intent to supply—attempting to supply 12.3 grams of cannabis resin to a prisoner—length of sentence*

H2   Twenty one months' imprisonment upheld for an attempt to supply 12.3 grams of cannabis resin to a prisoner by a man with a previous conviction for supplying drugs.

H3   The appellant pleaded guilty to possessing cannabis resin with intent to supply. The appellant visited an inmate at a prison. The behaviour of the appellant was observed and he was found to be in possession of a total of 12.3 grams of cannabis resin. Sentenced to 21 months' imprisonment.

H4   **Held:** (considering *Freeman* [1997] 2 Cr.App.R.(S.) 224) the dangers caused by the availability of drugs to prisoners were well known, and those caught passing drugs to prisoners or attempting to do so must expect deterrent sentences. The appellant had a previous conviction for supplying drugs. The sentence was not manifestly excessive.

H5   **Case cited:**
Freeman [1997] 2 Cr.App.R.(S.) 224

H6   **References:** supplying cannabis, *Current Sentencing Practice* B 11-1

H7   *A. Bell* for the appellant.

JUDGMENT

1   **Gage J.:**   This appellant, James Terrance Alger, is 36. On February 27, 2004 at the Crown Court at Stafford on rearraignment he pleaded guilty to an offence of possessing cannabis resin, a Class B drug, with intent to supply. The recorder sentenced him to 21 months' imprisonment. He now appeals that sentence with the leave of the single judge, who also granted him an extension of time.

2   The facts of the matter are these. On August 8, 2003 the appellant visited an inmate at Dovegate Prison. Visits took place in a room which included a canteen counter. The room is watched by prison staff and is covered by CCTV cameras. The appellant bought crisps and a drink, and shared them with an inmate and

others visiting that inmate. The appellant then went to buy some more drinks and a packet of prawn cocktail crisps. The officer at the canteen counter noted that the appellant appeared hesitant and jumpy. The appellant then asked for a further two packets of crisps. As the officer went to get them he saw the appellant open the first packet, put something inside and eat a few crisps. He then held the top of the packet closed. After the appellant had paid for the items and returned to the table the officer alerted colleagues, who arrested the appellant and seized the packet of crisps. The appellant gave a false name of Fred Bloggs. When asked what was in the bag of crisps he said it was cannabis. Two wraps were found to contain a total of 12.3g of cannabis resin. When interviewed the appellant made no comment.

3   In sentencing him the recorder stressed the dangers of bringing drugs to prison. He said this:

> "The danger of drugs going into prison largely comes down to this. Firstly of course there is the danger to the prison discipline system of having inmates under the influence of drugs. But also there is another danger, and that is those who are serving sentences who are present in prison awaiting sentence may be tempted, where otherwise they would not, to resume the use of drugs inside prisons. So it is capable of defeating what could be one of the better elements that arises from people being away from drugs, and that is the real danger and menace of it."

He then referred to a previous conviction, to which we will come, of this appellant and sentenced him to 21 months' imprisonment.

4   The appellant is aged 36. He has a number, previous convictions for burglary and other offences of dishonesty and in our judgment, importantly, a conviction on December 6, 2001 at the Crown Court at Exeter. For one count of possessing amphetamine and one of supplying heroin he was sentenced to a two-year community rehabilitation order and a 12-month drug treatment and testing order. However, on July 5, 2002, notwithstanding what might be considered a lenient sentence, the orders were breached and the appellant was resentenced to a term of eight months' imprisonment. On September 27, 2002 at Exeter magistrates' court he was sentenced for one offence of possessing cannabis. He was on that occasion given a conditional discharge.

5   The short point in this appeal is that the sentence of 21 months was too long and out of line with decided cases. It is argued on behalf of this appellant that the sentence did not accord with sentences passed and appealed in decisions of other divisions of this Court.

6   Counsel in his advice has helpfully referred the Court to a number of decisions, of which perhaps the most significant is *Freeman* [1997] 2 Cr.App.R.(S.) 224. That was also a case where the appellant had supplied drugs in prison. They were supplied by a man to a friend in prison and the sentence of 21 months was reduced to 15 months. The appellant had no previous convictions and was under a serious disability.

7   The difference between that case and this one is that it did not contain what we regard as an aggravating feature, namely the previous conviction for supply. That

makes, in our judgment, the case before this Court different from the case of *Freeman* and distinguishable.

8   Anyone who has had anything to do with prisons knows the dangers caused by drugs being freely available to prisoners. As we have already indicated, the recorder in this case referred to those dangers. It also is extremely difficult for the authorities to stamp out the trade in and use of drugs in prisons. That is why, in our judgment, those caught passing drugs to prisoners or attempting to do so must expect sentences designed to deter others.

9   Bearing in mind all the factors and everything that has been submitted to us on behalf of this appellant by counsel we nevertheless conclude that the sentence, whilst severe, was not manifestly excessive and this appeal must be dismissed.

R. v PAUL HAMMOND HOLLIDAY, PAUL LEBOUTILLIER

COURT OF APPEAL (Lord Justice Clarke, Mr Justice Henriques and Mr Justice Beatson): July 9, 2004

[2004] EWCA Crim 1847; [2005] 1 Cr.App.R.(S.) 70

LT Harassment; Malicious communications; Public nuisance; Sentence length; Telephones; Threats; Vivisection

1   *Public nuisance—making large numbers of phone calls to companies, shareholders and employees—some calls including threats—length of sentence*

2   Five years' imprisonment for public nuisance imposed on a man who made large numbers of phone calls to companies, their shareholders and employees, some of which included threats, reduced to 30 months.

3   The appellants pleaded guilty to public nuisance. The appellants were involved in making numerous telephone calls to employees and shareholders of companies. The second appellant's mobile telephone bills showed that he had made over 1,000 calls to one company in particular. The calls to the company were nuisance calls designed to jam telephone lines, but calls made to individuals and their homes had involved threats, including death threats. The first appellant made over 1,000 nuisance calls in the course of a year. None of his calls included threats. The first appellant pleaded guilty on the basis that he had made no threats or references to letter bombs. The calls were not in an aggressive tone of voice; they were of a nuisance nature. The first appellant did not engage in direct conversation with the person called, but left telephone messages. The majority of his calls were made to a company with a view to jamming the company's switchboard and preventing access to potential or existing customers. Sentenced to 18 months' imprisonment in the case of the first appellant and five years' imprisonment on the case of the second appellant.

H4   **Held:** (considering *Schilling* [2003] 2 Cr.App.R.(S.) 45 (p.295) and *Harley* [2003] 2 Cr.App.R.(S.) 3 (p.16)) the Court had been persuaded that the appropriate sentence for the first appellant was nine months' imprisonment and in the case of the second appellant 30 months' imprisonment.

H5   **Cases cited:**
Schilling [2003] 2 Cr.App.R.(S.) 45 (p.295), *Harley* [2003] 2 Cr.App.R.(S.) 3 (p.16)

H6   **References:** public nuisance, *Current Sentencing Practice* B 13-4

H7   *P. Cosgrove Q.C.* for the appellant Holliday.
M. George for the appellant Leboutillier.

JUDGMENT

1   **Henriques J.:**   These are renewed applications by Paul Hammond Holliday, aged 38, and Paul Leboutillier, aged 44, for permission to appeal against sentences of 18 months' imprisonment and five years' imprisonment passed by Judge Hoffman at the Crown Court at York on February 26, 2004, both appellants, albeit indicted separately, having pleaded guilty to causing a public nuisance. It is significant in the case of the appellant Holliday that he pleaded guilty on May 2, 2003 but was not sentenced until February 26, 2004 by reason of the fact that Leboutillier had earlier pleaded not guilty and had only changed his plea on December 8, 2003 shortly before a jury was to be empanelled. The appellants were separately indicted but for obvious reasons it was appropriate to sentence in both cases at the same hearing and it is equally appropriate to deal with the two applications concurrently today.

2   Between December 2000 and February 2001 letter bombs were sent to a number of people in the agricultural, pet and fish industries. It is important to state immediately that neither appellant had anything whatsoever to do with the sending of such bombs.

3   Some of those targeted in that campaign thereafter received malicious telephone calls. A number of other people also received annoying calls either at work or at home. The appellants were particularly involved telephoning employees and shareholders connected with Covance and Huntingdon Life Sciences. A number of calls were traced to Leboutillier's mobile phone. Itemised billing showed over 1,000 calls to Covance Laboratories, Huntingdon Life Sciences and a variety of individuals' home phones. When his home was searched large numbers of documents relating to animal liberation were found. The documents detailed not only the names and addresses of those contacted but also their phone numbers. He had a list of the internal telephone numbers of Covance Laboratories and a shareholder list for Huntingdon Life Sciences. His calls to employees at Covance were plainly nuisance calls designed to jam the telephone lines, but many of the calls to individuals at their homes were more threatening in nature. Some of the threats during the phone calls referred to the fact that letter bombs

had been sent and included references such as "Watch your mail" or "Watch yourself". The calls were abusive and intimidatory. Some included death threats and a reference was also made to where the individuals lived. The calls were made between November 2000 and April 6, 2001 when Leboutillier was arrested. When interviewed he denied making any calls of any harassing or threatening nature and only pleaded guilty at the last moment.

4   Holliday for his part made over 1,000 nuisance calls between August 8, 2000 and August 9, 2001. None of the calls he made contained any reference to letter bombs or any threat in relation to them, although many of them took place during the course of the letter bomb campaign. The vast majority of calls he made were intended to jam switchboards. When arrested he denied making any of the calls.

5   It is convenient to deal with Holliday's case first. A lengthy document entitled "Basis of plea" was placed before Judge Hoffman. Holliday accepted that he had made the nuisance telephone calls. He pleaded guilty on the basis that whilst some complainants received junk mail and threatening letters, he played no part in that. Most of the nuisance telephone calls that the complainants received were not from the appellant's telephones. The appellant played no part in leaving any message that contained any direct or indirect reference to bombs being used. There was no evidence of any link with bombs. None of the calls from the appellant's telephone made any reference to the Animal Liberation Front. The calls were not in an aggressive tone or voice. The calls were of a nuisance nature but not of a threatening type. The appellant never engaged in direct conversations with the complainants. Where a home phone was called the appellant left telephone messages. His home was searched, no telephone numbers were found or were ex-directory and therefore not accessible to the public. No directors' home addresses were found. There were no lists of telephone numbers to anyone associated with animal experimentation. The majority of nuisance calls were made to Covance Laboratories. The appellant was jamming the switchboard thus preventing access for potential or existing customers. He used no words when jamming the switchboard, no names addresses or telephone numbers of potential targets were found at Holliday's home. Whilst there were references to other matters in the basis of plea, we have mentioned the critical matters.

    That basis of plea was given to the prosecution on 4th April 2003 for their consideration. When the case was relisted on May 2, 2003 the basis was entirely acceptable to the prosecution and a guilty plea was entered on that date.

    Holliday had originally been indicted together with Leboutillier. However, the latter was charged with a separate count of public nuisance which involved nuisance telephone calls. The Crown did not allege any conspiracy between the two appellants but asserted, and this was accepted by Holliday, that they both offended at the same time as part of a wider campaign by those who felt strongly about animal rights.

    On behalf of Holliday it was indicated that an application would be made as to the indictment being wrongly joined as the links between the two appellants was not sufficient to amount to a nexus in law. Accordingly, the prosecution agreed to prefer two new indictments, one for each appellant. Since Leboutillier maintained his not guilty plea, this meant that sentence was not possible until February 26, 2004.

9   The mitigation covered the following factors, on Holliday's behalf: the plea of guilty, tendered almost a year earlier; the contents of three supportive letters, two short letters from Mr Holliday's general practitioner, a psychiatric report from Dr Mendelson and a pre-sentence report. The features of the basis of plea already referred to, the nature of the appellant himself, namely he had cut links with all organisations and persons involved in these campaigns, he was already disillusioned and had turned his undoubted but vulnerable and previously misguided good intentions to helping people through the Citizens Advice Bureau. He was a vulnerable individual with mental health weaknesses, having suffered depression and anxiety. Dr Mendelson described him as a passive, retiring person greatly lacking in social or assertive skills. He was diagnosed as having a dependent personality disorder and was all too easily overwhelmed by stress and intimidated by others. He had fallen under the influence of the more militant members of the animal rights movement. He greatly regretted the offences and rued his involvement. This was a submission accepted by the learned judge. Further, he was a low risk of reoffending. Given his vulnerability he would be at risk of deterioration in his mental health position if sent to prison again according to Dr Mendelson.

10   It is to be noted that in his sentencing remarks the judge observed that there was no evidence that Holliday was depressed at the material time of offending. Reference should however be made to Dr Turner's letter of April 8, 2003 in which it is said:

"In the past he has suffered from mental health problems, typified by depression and anxiety."

Dr Mendelson referred to longstanding depression. He also stated that he suffers from depression and is under treatment from his doctor. He informs me that he suffers from anxiety and panic attacks as well as agoraphobia. His court case has, I understand, exaggerated these symptoms.

11   Turning to the case of Leboutillier, it is submitted in his case that in arriving at the sentence of five years the judge must have taken a figure of about seven years as appropriate in the event of conviction after a trial. Such a starting point, it is submitted, is far too high. Whilst the judge noted that the phone calls were threatening and intimidating, it is submitted he failed to give proper weight to the absence of other aggravating features. The phone calls were not repeated to any particular victim. No actual violence was offered to anyone. No property was damaged and no one was the object of demonstrations outside their homes.

12   The aggravating features referred to in the case of *Schilling* [2002] EWCA Crim 3198 were absent, namely the appellant never followed up threats by taking any action, no one who received a phone call was subject to any other harassment, there were no demonstrations outside their homes and no criminal damage was caused to any of their property. It is said the judge failed to give adequate credit for the appellant's previous good character and hardworking life and the fact that he had previously conducted himself appropriately in over 10 years of campaign-

ing on the issue of animal rights. There was insufficient credit if any for the plea of guilty, albeit tendered on the first day of the trial. The judge, it is said, found himself being influenced by what he thought was a connection between the appellant and the person responsible for the campaign of letter bombs when in fact there was no such connection. The Crown in fact indicated that they accepted that there was no such link. For his part the judge did make it clear in these terms:

> "I further accept, and the Crown have made clear, that there is no suggestion that you were an associate of the bomber, but, if I may borrow the words of your learned counsel, you were riding on the coat tails of the bomber or his activities. There was a confluence of timing, as counsel has put it, and you took advantage of it happening."

3   We have been referred not only to the case of *Schilling* but also to the case of *Harley* [2002] EWCA Crim 2650 in which the appellant had made some 4,845 nuisance telephone calls to over 1,000 people. Some were silent, some were explicitly and unpleasantly sexual, and to that extent the facts cannot properly be compared. The great majority of those telephoned were women, the conduct lasted for three months, two months later the appellant was arrested, he was of good character, psychiatric report indicated he had sustained a moderate depressive episode after sustaining multiple jaw fractures and in his depressed state he took to telephoning. He pleaded guilty to public nuisance and was sentenced to 21 months' imprisonment, which was reduced on appeal to this Court to nine months' imprisonment. In *Schilling*, the appellant had pleaded guilty to three offences, contrary to s.4 of the Protection from Harassment Act 1997. She was sentenced to four and a half years' imprisonment reduced on appeal to this Court to three and a half years' imprisonment.

Had the prosecution brought proceedings under the Protection from Harassment Act the case against Holliday would necessarily have been pursuant to s.2, there having been no threats of violence. Such an offence is triable summarily only and thus carries a maximum sentence of six months' imprisonment. It is to be noted in Holliday's case that in September 1998 for an offence of violent disorder and criminal damage, committed at a business operating at a farm which had attracted considerable attention from animal rights campaigners, he was sentenced to a term of 12 months' imprisonment. He had no other relevant or significant convictions.

We do not suggest that the Crown Court was restricted to the maximum sentence for harassment. We do however consider that the court should have had that factor well in mind. We also in appropriate cases commend that form of prosecution rather than prosecution for public nuisance since there is power to make a restraining order to protect any victim from further conduct pursuant to s.5 of that Act.

Taking all matters into consideration, we have concluded that the appropriate sentence in Holliday's case would have been one of nine months' imprisonment.

In Leboutillier's case the submission that a starting point of seven years would be manifestly excessive is well made. He is also a man of good character and was not in a conspiracy with the bomber. Of course this was a serious matter. Many members of the community had been put in fear. There was no actual violence nor criminal damage sustained. The facts are less grave than the facts in *Schilling's* case. We bear in mind that under s.4 of the Protection from Harassment Act 1997 the maximum sentence would have been five years. In Leboutillier's case we have concluded that the appropriate sentence is one of 30 months' imprisonment. Accordingly, the sentences of nine months and 30 months' imprisonment will be substituted in the absence of any representation to the contrary to this Court within the next seven days.

[Paragraphs 18–23 have been omitted.]

R. v PAAVO TOPIAS KUOSMANEN

Court of Appeal (Lord Justice Auld, Mr Justice Henriques and Mr Justice Beatson): July 12, 2004

[2004] EWCA Crim 1861; [2005] 1 Cr.App.R.(S.) 71

(LT) Commercial activities; Counterfeits; Criminal intent; Good character; Guilty pleas; Passports; Possession; Sentence length

H1   *Passport offences—possessing 250 counterfeit passports with intent—length of sentence*

H2   Five years' imprisonment upheld for possessing 250 counterfeit passports with intent.

H3   The applicant pleaded guilty to three counts of having a false instrument with intent. The applicant was stopped by a Customs officer after arriving by train from Brussels. He was found to be in possession of 250 forged French, Italian and Belgian passports together with other counterfeit identity documents. The applicant claimed that he had met two men in a bar in Bangkok and had agreed to take documents for them on his next trip to Europe. He was to receive £200 for taking the package. Sentenced to five years' imprisonment.

H4   **Held:** (considering *Cheema* [2002] 2 Cr.App.R.(S.) 79 (p.356)) the offending in the present case was on a totally different scale to that in *Cheema*. Here, 250 forged passports were imported in a professional operation. In those circumstances, the sentence of five years did give appropriate credit for the applicant's guilty plea.

H5   **Case cited:**
Cheema [2002] 2 Cr.App.R.(S.) 79 (p.356)

H6   **References:** passport offences, *Current Sentencing Practice* B 13-8.3B

H7   *R. Newcombe* for the applicant.

JUDGMENT

1   **Beatson J.:**   The applicant pleaded guilty on January 8, 2004 to three counts
of having a false instrument with intent. On January 28 he was sentenced at the
same court, Middlesex Guildhall Crown Court, by H.H. Judge Blacksell Q.C. to a
total of five years' imprisonment.

2   The offence consisted of three counts: count 1, having 50 French passports;
count 3, 100 Italian passports; and count 4, 100 Belgian passports. Similar counts
in relation to identity cards were left on the file. He renews his application for
leave to appeal against sentence after refusal by the single judge.

3   The facts of the case are as follows. The applicant arrived at the Eurostar Terminal at Waterloo on September 19, 2003 travelling on his own Finnish passport.
He was stopped by a Customs officer and questioned. The train had come from
Brussels. He stated that the baggage was his, everything inside it belonged to
him, and he had packed it himself. The applicant stated, in response to a question,
that no one had given him anything, such as packages or presents, to bring into the
United Kingdom. He stated that he had started his journey in Thailand, flying
from Bangkok to Copenhagen and from there to Brussels, and then taking the
Eurostar to London. He stated this was cheaper than a direct flight. He showed
the officer his flight ticket. On searching his baggage, the officer found five
envelopes with brown tape wrapped around the seals. She asked what was in
it, and the applicant replied that he did not know but he thought it had documents
inside. He was going to go to a hotel to pass them to someone whose name was in
his phone. On examination, the contents contained the 250 passports, other identity documents, and loose pieces of paper with the appearance of fiscal stamps.
Another immigration officer examined the documents and stated they appeared
to be counterfeit, which was later confirmed by a specialist document examiner.

4   In interview, the applicant stated that he lived in Thailand and was working by
importing and exporting jewellery to and from Europe. He stated that he met two
men in a bar in Bangkok when drunk and agreed to take the documents for them
on his next trip to Europe. A week or two later, he was contacted by telephone and
agreed to meet the men in a cafe. He did so and was handed the envelopes and told
there was nothing illegal in them, merely documents and notebooks. He stated
that he felt around the packages in order to ascertain whether or not this was correct and it did not feel like drugs or powder. He was given a SIM card and was
asked to contact a person called "Phil" when he got to London. He stated he
was to receive £200 for taking the packages and that the person to whom he delivered them would pay him.

     Throughout the interview he berated himself for having been naïve in agreeing
to deliver the packages, but he did also say that he realised that it was likely that
there were passports in the envelopes.

     The learned judge had before him a pre-sentence report, various testimonials
and a letter from the applicant. He stated in his sentencing remarks:

"You have pleaded guilty to three counts on the indictment . . . ."

He states that the passports were sophisticated forgeries and he had no doubt at all that they were to be used by sophisticated criminal gangs who realised that trafficking in people can be more lucrative than trafficking in serious drugs. He noted that the applicant had realised that it was likely that the contents of the envelope were passports, and did not accept that the applicant was naïve for a moment. He then stated:

"People smuggling is a nasty offence and the provision of passports to people by use of couriers like you, I again remind myself, in the case of *Cheema*, the Court of Appeal have said the same approach is required as that for people smuggling drugs."

The learned judge then stated that he took into account everything that was said and passed the sentence.

7   The grounds of appeal are first, that in view of the case of *Cheema*, to which we will return, a sentence of five years' imprisonment is too long, and the learned judge erred in failing to apply the correct starting point, which Mr Newcombe submits should have been five years or below on the basis of the decision in *Cheema*. He also submits that the learned judge failed to give sufficient or any weight to the mitigation, in particular for the plea, but also for his good character, both in this country and in Finland, and his genuine remorse. At the centre of his submissions on this second matter was that the judge did not explicitly articulate in his sentencing remarks that he was giving credit for the guilty plea.

8   The case of *Cheema* on which reliance is placed was one in which the appellant was convicted of having custody or control of twelve false passports. It appears from the report of the case that he had a further 32 passports in his possession. He was, however, convicted of knowingly having 12 counterfeit passports. He was convicted as a courier, who had visited Amsterdam solely to obtain those passports, and who had previous convictions for offences of the same kind. The appellant in that case was 65 years old at the time his case came before this Court. This Court reduced a sentence of four years' imprisonment to one of three years. The Court stated that:

"While it is not an exact analogy, a person acting as a courier for those trading in illegal drugs is not treated less seriously than a person carrying drugs for his own use. Indeed, the contrary is usually the case. Sentences on couriers for illegal drugs are substantial in order to deter. The same approach is required in the illegal trade in false passports."

9   Mr Newcombe submits that, since in *Cheema* the appellant was convicted following a trial and was not of good character, the starting point in this case was too high.

10   We do not agree. As the single judge observed in refusing leave, the offending in the present case is on a totally different scale to that in *Cheema*. Here 250 passports, forged in a sophisticated way, were imported in what was a professional operation. The applicant was given a phone to enable him to contact the people

who were to receive the passports, without the possibility of tracing him. Although, as the Court stated in *Cheema*, there is no exact analogy with drug offending, we have concluded in the present case the sheer scale of this operation means that it would not have been inappropriate for the starting point to have been seven years. In those circumstances a sentence of five years does accord the appropriate credit for the early guilty plea.

11   Mr Newcombe submits that, having regard to the provisions of s.152 of the Powers of Criminal Courts (Sentencing) Act 2000, the judge should have stated that he took into account the plea when pronouncing sentence.

12   It is of course the case that a sentencing judge should always make it clear that a reduction for a guilty plea has been made in sentencing remarks. This Court has emphasised this in the case of *Fearon* [1996] 2 Cr.App.R.(S.) 25. It is, however, not inevitable that a reduction in sentence follows a failure so to do. In *Bishop* [2000] 1 Cr.App.R.(S.) 432, this Court stated that:

> ". . . the nature of the sentence, when measured against the facts of the crime and the mitigation other than plea, may provide a strong indication that the sentencing court must have given . . . credit for the plea."

In that case sentences for assaults occasioning actual bodily harm were held to be more consistent with due credit having been given to the plea in view of the seriousness of the assaults and the aggravating factors.

13   In the present case, given the scale of the importation and what we have said in relation to the starting point, it is similarly clear that this experienced judge, who referred to the plea at the outset of his sentencing remarks, did take it into account. For these reasons we refuse this application.

ATTORNEY GENERAL'S REFERENCE NO.49 OF 2004 (KIERAN JAMES QUINN)

COURT OF APPEAL (Lord Justice Keene, Mr Justice Moses and Mr Justice Mitting): July 12, 2004

[2004] EWCA Crim 1952; [2005] 1 Cr.App.R.(S.) 72

LT Criminal record; Extended sentences; Guilty pleas; Manslaughter; Public protection; Undue leniency; Violence

H1   *Manslaughter—man causing death of woman by compressing her chest during fight—whether longer than commensurate sentence appropriate*

H2   Six years' imprisonment for the manslaughter of a woman by the compression of her chest in a fight by a man with a long record of violence varied to a longer than commensurate sentence of nine years' imprisonment.

H3   The offender pleaded guilty to manslaughter on an indictment charging him with murder. The offender had a relationship with a younger woman. They attended a barbecue together and afterwards went to a public house, were they were seen arguing. Both appeared to be drunk. They left separately and the women went to her sister's. Eventually the victim went home where there was a fight in the course of which the offender punched her in the face before applying pressure to her chest from which she died. A post mortem examination disclosed bruising and a laceration to the eye, further areas of bruising to the nose and other parts. Death was caused by a blunt trauma to the chest, most likely the result of compression. There was evidence that an object had been introduced into the anus with considerable force. The offender pleaded guilty on the basis that he did not intend to kill or cause grievous bodily harm. He tendered a written basis of plea which was not accepted by the Crown. Following a *Newton* hearing, the judge found that the injury to the chest was as a result of compression, and that the non-consensual injuries to the anus had been inflicted by the offender. Sentenced to six years' imprisonment. The Attorney General asked the Court to review the sentence on the ground that it was unduly lenient.

H4   **Held:** the Attorney General drew attention to the offender's record, which included various offences of violence. For the Attorney General it was submitted that the sentence, considered as a commensurate sentence, was unduly lenient in that it failed to reflect adequately the aggravating features of the case, and that a longer than commensurate sentence of imprisonment was necessary to protect the public from serious harm from the offender. A term of five years' imprisonment might seem surprisingly low, but reflected two factors. The first was that where a plea was accepted to manslaughter, the sentencing judge had to proceed on the footing that there was no intent to kill or to cause serious injury to the victim. This was a very important consideration which should always be borne in mind by prosecutors and judges before such a plea was accepted on an indictment charging murder. Secondly, the sentence had to reflect the credit to be given for a plea of guilty. However, aggravating circumstances could and would normally lead to a longer sentence than five years. Where important factual matters were put in issue by the defence, the credit for a plea of guilty might well be reduced. Approaching the matter as a commensurate sentence, it seemed that on a straightforward plea of guilty, with no *Newton* hearing, a term of around five years' imprisonment could have been appropriate as a starting point. The offender had contested the manner of the victim's death and committed a violent sexual assault on the victim. Any sentence should take account of the extent of the violence including that which was not causally connected to her death. The penetration of the victim's anus was not adequately reflected in the sentence imposed in the court below. The case called for a commensurate sentence of between seven and eight years. However, the offender's record indicated that he was a man who could not control his violent instincts. He had regular convictions for offences of violence. The Powers of Criminal Courts (Sentencing) Act 2000, s.80(2)(b) required the court, where the offence was a violent or sexual offence, to impose a longer than commensurate sentence if that was necessary to protect the public from serious harm from the offender. The offence of manslaughter qualified as a violent offence. The Court asked itself whether a longer than commensurate sentence was necessary to protect the public from serious harm from the offender. In the Court's opinion, such a sentence was indicated and was necessary to protect the public from such harm. Such a sentence should have been imposed in the first instance and should have been of the order of 10 years. Allowing for the element of double jeopardy, the Court would substitute a sentence of nine years' imprisonment.

Cases cited:
Silver (1994) 15 Cr.App.R.(S.) 836, *Tzambazles* [1997] 1 Cr.App.R.(S.) 87, *Attorney General's References Nos 74, 95 and 115 of 2002 (Darren Anthony Suratan, Leslie Humes, Mark Paul Wilkinson)* [2003] 2 Cr.App.R.(S.) 42 (p.273)

References: manslaughter, *Current Sentencing Practice* B 3

J. Laidlaw for the Attorney General.
J. Smith for the offender.

JUDGMENT

1   **Keene L.J.:**   This is an application under s.36 of the Criminal Justice Act 1988 by HM Attorney General for leave to refer a sentence to this Court because it appears to him to be unduly lenient. We grant leave and we treat this as being the hearing of the reference.

2   On December 12, 2003 at Liverpool Crown Court this offender pleaded guilty to manslaughter on an indictment charging him with murder. That plea was accepted on the basis that he did not intend to kill or to cause grievous bodily

harm. On April 7, 2004 he was sentenced by H.H. Judge Roberts to six years' imprisonment. The offence had been committed during the unexpired part of an earlier custodial sentence and the offender was ordered to serve the outstanding part of that sentence, 137 days, to which the above term was consecutive.

3   The offender had provided a written basis of plea which was not accepted by the Crown. There consequently had to be a *Newton* hearing to resolve a number of factual matters which were in dispute. We set out the facts of the case as determined after that *Newton* hearing.

4   The victim, Kelly Reid, was 22 years old at the time. She began a relationship with the offender late in 2002 and shortly afterwards he moved into her home. On July 6, 2003 the two of them attended a barbecue and then went on in the evening to a public house. They were seen there arguing. Both of them were evidently drunk. They left separately with the victim going to her sister's for a time. There was evidence that she was upset and crying. Her sister suggested to her that she left the offender, but the victim said that she could not end the relationship because he would kill her.

5   Eventually the victim left and went home. There, it seems, there was a drunken fight in which the offender lost his temper and punched her in the face before applying considerable pressure to her chest from which she died. She was found lying almost naked in the living room with nothing but socks below the waist and a bra and T-shirt above the waist, the T-shirt having been pulled up so as to expose the bra.

6   Paramedics, who eventually came, saw that she was bleeding from the nose and there was bruising to the eyes. They also saw faeces and blood on the floor and around the patient. The house was in disarray with broken pieces of furniture scattered over the room. Kelly Reid was not breathing and it proved impossible to resuscitate her.

7   During the post-mortem examination the pathologist found bruising and a laceration to the left eye, further areas of bruising to the nose, to the muscles deep to the right shoulder blade, to the right side of the vertebral column and to the tissues above and below the heart. Death had occurred as a result of blunt trauma to the chest, most likely the result of compression such as might occur in a forceful bear hug. There were also fresh tears to the skin around the anus, oozing blood. The rectal lining was reddened and there was damage to the underlining muscle fibres of the anus. There was evidence at the *Newton* hearing that the cause of those injuries was the introduction with considerable force of an object such as a penis, a finger, a hand, or an inanimate object, tearing the sphincter muscle.

8   In interview the offender spoke of an argument during which he had punched the victim in the face and she had slumped to the ground. He said that he had sought to resuscitate her by pressing on her chest and had then noticed she had defecated. He said he had tried to clear that up.

9   In court he provided a written basis of plea in which he claimed that the fatal injury had been as a result of a single blow to the chest because he could not hear her breathing. He denied responsibility for the anal injuries suffered by the vic-

tim. His case on that was that she must have had anal sex with someone else before arriving home.

10   Having heard evidence at the *Newton* hearing from the paramedic who attended the scene, two pathologists and the offender, the judge found that the trauma to the chest was as a result of compression and that non-consensual injuries to the anus had been inflicted by the offender. The judge also observed that the victim had been a young woman of 22 and that the offender was a much heavier man.

11   The Attorney General draws attention to the record of the offender for violence. The offender is now aged 38 and he has a total of 27 previous convictions. Those include repeated offences of violence. He was convicted of s.20 wounding in 1985 and again of the same offence in 1988, together with an assault occasioning actual bodily harm. The following year he was convicted of grievous bodily harm under s.20, of which offence he was again convicted in 1991. In 1992 he was convicted of a further offence of assault occasioning actual bodily harm. In 1992 he was also sentenced to 30 months' imprisonment for aggravated burglary. There was another conviction for occasioning actual bodily harm in 1997, as there was in 1998 along with one for common assault. In 2002 he was again convicted of assault occasioning actual bodily harm, as well as a public order offence. We add for completeness that he also has convictions for criminal damage.

12   In those circumstances the Attorney General makes two submissions. First, it is contended that, as a commensurate sentence, six years' imprisonment was unduly lenient for this offence. It failed, it is said, to reflect adequately the aggravating features present in this case and, in particular, the sexual aspect of the attack and the offender's appalling criminal record for committing offences of violence. It is also said on behalf of the Attorney General that that sentence fails adequately to punish this offender sufficiently, or to deter others from committing similar offences, or to reflect public concern about such cases.

13   On behalf of the Attorney General Mr Laidlaw argues that the sentence here imposed would be appropriate for an ordinary case of no intent manslaughter, but simply does not properly take account of the very serious sexual assault, the very bad record of this offender for violence and the fact that this offence occurred soon after his release from prison for an offence of violence.

14   Secondly, the Attorney General submits that the judge should have passed here a longer than commensurate term of imprisonment pursuant to the provisions of s.80(2)(b) of the Powers of Criminal Courts (Sentencing) Act 2000 ("the 2000 Act") in order to protect the public from serious harm from this offender. Mr Laidlaw particularly emphasises the fact that this manslaughter was the latest in a long series of violent offences, and it is contended that this was clearly an appropriate case where the need to protect the public required a longer sentence than a commensurate one.

15   As aggravating features Mr Laidlaw relies upon the following matters. First, the fact that this was a deliberate and drunken attack carried out by a physically superior offender upon a victim who would have been unable to defend herself. Secondly, that whilst the offender's plea of guilty was on the basis that he had not

intended to cause really serious harm, the nature of the act that led to the victim's death demonstrates the offender to have been indifferent to the consequences of what was obviously a very dangerous act. Thirdly, emphasis is placed upon the subjecting of the victim to a gratuitous extremely serious and degrading sexual attack, so that she suffered the indignity and pain of penetration and damage to anus and rectum. Fourthly, reference is, of course, made to this offender's bad record and his record, in particular, for violent offending. Finally, emphasis is placed on the fact that this offence occurred after his release from prison in respect of an offence of violence while there was still an unexpired part of that term.

16   The Attorney accepts that some discount had to be given for the plea of guilty, but it is argued that the degree of credit had to be reduced by the disputing by the offender of some of the factual features of the offence. Reliance is placed by the Attorney General on three authorities, *Silver* (1994) 15 Cr.App.R.(S.) 836, *Tzambazles* [1997] 1 Cr.App.R.(S.) 87, and *Attorney General's References Nos 74, 95 and 115 of 2002 (Darren Anthony Suratan, Leslie Humes, Mark Paul Wilkinson)* [2003] 2 Cr.App.R.(S.) 42 (p.273).

17   For the offender Mr Smith emphasises that this was not a case of premeditated violence. It was violence occurring in the course of a short fight which seems to have been initiated by the victim. He also stresses the fact that the offender here showed remorse immediately after the killing and did indeed seek to obtain an ambulance through a neighbour. The point is made that there was a plea here at the earliest opportunity. Mr Smith draws attention also to the fact that the offender has no record for domestic violence, or for violence against women. His offences in the past of violence have all been ones against men, either through his work as a doorman, or taking place in public houses. In the light of those factors, it is argued that this was not a lenient sentence imposed by the judge below, or, if it was, it was not unduly so.

18   Mr Smith submits that a sentence of five years is one which should have been the starting point as indicated in *Silver* as an appropriate sentence unless there are aggravating circumstances present. It is accepted that the sexual assault on the victim is an aggravating feature of the present case which had to be reflected in the sentence. But it is argued that the judge below did properly reflect that by increasing what otherwise would have been the appropriate term of imprisonment to one of six years. That, it is said, reflects all the aggravating circumstances pointed to on behalf of the Attorney General. Mr Smith accepts that s.80(2)(b) could apply here, but he contends that that provision does not need to be applied. In essence his argument is that the public would be adequately protected by the sentence imposed by the judge below.

19   We bear in mind that the authorities relied on by the Attorney General are inevitably of limited assistance because the facts of manslaughter cases vary so much and the range of sentences has to reflect that. Cases like *Silver* do indicate that on a plea of guilty to manslaughter because of the absence of the intent necessary for murder, even where great violence was used on the victim, a sentence of five years will often be appropriate where there is no weapon employed. That is, in our view, consistent with the decision in *Tzambazles*, where six years'

imprisonment was upheld by this Court. There, there was no plea of guilty and it seems to us that that is consistent with the decision in *Silver*.

20   A term of five years' imprisonment may seem surprisingly low to some observers in cases such as this, but it reflects two factors. First, where a plea is accepted on such a basis to manslaughter the sentencing judge has to proceed on the footing that there was no intent to kill, or even to cause serious injury to the victim. That is a very important consideration and it is something always to be borne in mind by prosecutors and judges before such a plea on a murder indictment is accepted in the first place.

21   Secondly, a sentence of the order we have indicated also reflects the credit to be given for a plea of guilty on the normal principles. However, it is to be noted that, as was said in *Silver*, aggravating circumstances can and normally should lead to a longer sentence than five years. In addition, where important factual matters are put in issue by the defence, the credit for a plea of guilty may well have to be reduced and normally will be reduced.

22   Approaching this matter, first, as a commensurate sentence, it seems to us that with no *Newton* hearing, but simply a straightforward plea of guilty demonstrating remorse, a term of around five years' imprisonment could have been appropriate as a starting point, despite the offender's record. But the offender here did contest the manner of the victim's death, seeking to reduce his blameworthiness. Of even greater significance is the violent sexual assault by the offender on this victim. Any sentence in this case had to take into account the extent of the violence used by the offender, including that which was not causally connected to her death. The forceful penetration of her anus by some object, which must have caused her great pain and humiliation, is an aggravating feature which needed to be reflected in the length of the term of imprisonment. In our judgment, it was not adequately reflected in the term imposed in the court below. This was a case, which, at first instance, called for a sentence as a commensurate sentence of between seven and eight years.

23   But the matter does not stop there. All the evidence from his record of previous convictions indicates that this offender is a man who cannot control his violent instincts, especially when he has been drinking. There have been regular convictions for offences of violence against the person as we have already pointed out: four under s.20 of the Offences Against the Person Act for wounding or grievous bodily harm, five of assault occasioning actual bodily harm, plus a common assault and an aggravated burglary. Section 80(2)(b) of the Act of 2001 requires the court as a duty, where the offence is a violent or sexual offence, to impose a longer than commensurate term where that is necessary to protect the public from serious harm from the offender. The term is to be of a length as is, in the court's opinion, necessary to protect the public from such harm. The present offence of manslaughter qualifies as a violent offence under the Act.

24   We have asked ourselves whether a longer than commensurate term was necessary in this case to protect the public from serious harm from this offender. We are not impressed by the argument that his victims in the past have all been male, sometimes injured in public houses when the offender has been drinking, whereas the present victim was female. They are, all of them, members of the

public put at risk of violent attack by this man, who, it seems to us, readily resorts to violence. In our opinion a longer sentence than the commensurate one earlier indicated was and is necessary to protect the public from such harm. Such a sentence should have been imposed here and at first instance it should have been of the order of 10 years.

25   We have to allow for double jeopardy, because this is a reference by the Attorney General and this man is now being sentenced for a second time. Making such allowance, we quash the sentence of six years and in its place we put one of nine years' imprisonment. As that is passed as being of an appropriate length to protect the public, we quash the order under s.116 of the Act of 2000 ordering his return to prison for 137 days. That means that the total sentence we have substituted is one of nine years' imprisonment.

R. v LISA JAYNE PEARCE

COURT OF APPEAL (Lord Justice Thomas, Mr Justice Gage and Judge Richard Brown): July 13, 2004

[2004] EWCA Crim 2029; [2005] 1 Cr.App.R.(S.) 73

LT Criminal record; Fixed sentences; Justice; Minimum term; Possession with intent to supply

H1   *Powers of Criminal Courts (Sentencing) Act 2000, s.110—minimum sentence on third conviction for Class A drug trafficking offence—circumstances making minimum sentence unjust*

H2   The imposition of a minimum sentence under the Powers of Criminal Courts (Sentencing) Act 2000, s.110, for possessing a small amount of cocaine with intent to supply, held not to be unjust on the ground that the appellant had been convicted of class A drug trafficking offences on three previous occasions and had not been sentenced to a mandatory sentence on her previous appearance.

H3   The appellant was convicted of possessing a Class A drug, cocaine, with intent to supply. Paramedics were summoned to the appellant's house and found the appellant lying unconscious. A bag containing 10.3 grams of cocaine, at a purity of about 28 per cent, was found in her left hand. The appellant was taken to hospital and subsequently arrested. In interview, the appellant claimed that she had taken the drugs from a friend and intended to dispose of them down a lavatory; she thought that the drugs were amphetamines. She did not intend to take any of them and had not done so. The prosecution case was that the appellant intended to return the drugs to a man to whom they belonged because she was frightened of the man. The jury, by its verdict, rejected her defence. The sentencing judge passed sentence on the basis that the appellant was minding the cocaine for a man who was the father of the appellant's child, and who had previous convictions for offences of violence and drugs offences. The sentencing judge accepted that the appellant might well have been looking after the cocaine for the man. The appellant had various previous convictions, including a conviction in 1998 for supplying a class A drug, a further conviction in July 2000 for being in possession of heroin with intent to supply and a conviction in August 2002 for supplying heroin. In 1999 (the offence of which she was convicted in 2000), a quantity of heroin was found at the appellant's home address. In 2002, the appellant supplied a single wrap of heroin to an undercover police officer. Sentenced to seven years' imprisonment, in accordance with the Powers of Criminal Courts (Sentencing) Act 2000, s.110.

Held: the case centred on the Powers of Criminal Courts (Sentencing) Act 2000, s.110, which provided that, where a person was convicted of a class A drug trafficking offence and had two convictions for similar offences, the court was required to impose a custodial sentence of at least seven years except where the court was of the opinion that there were particular circumstances which related to any of the offences or to the offender, and which would make it unjust do so in all circumstances. For the appellant it was submitted that in the circumstances of the case, taking account of her history and her history of offending, it was unjust for the judge to have imposed a mandatory minimum sentence of seven years. In relation to the latest offence, the appellant had held the drugs for no longer than one day and was proposing, as the judge found, to pass them on to her partner. She was acting under stress from looking after her child, and there was no suggestion of commercial supply. The sentencing judge did not take into account her evidence to the effect that she thought the drug was amphetamine. The previous offences all related to offences of supply at the very lowest end of the scale in relation to such offences. The Court had been referred to *McInerney* [2003] 2 Cr.App.R.(S.) 39 (p.240) and to *Harvey* [2000] 1 Cr.App.R.(S.) 368. In *Harvey*, the Court had said that the object of the section was to oblige the court to impose the prescribed custodial sentence in a case where, but for the section, the court would or might not do so. In *Harvey* the offence had been at the lower end of the scale. Once the principles had been set out in *Harvey* and *McInerney*, other cases were no more than examples of the application of s.110 based on their own particular facts. The Court had to decide whether the judge in this case was right to conclude that it was not unjust to pass the minimum sentence. The judge conceded that there were features which might have been persuasive in other circumstances, but considered that in the light of *Harvey* it was not open to him to say that if the statutory scheme did not apply, the appellant would receive less than seven years, therefore it would be unjust to pass the sentence. In the sentencing judge's view, the appellant was caught four square within the statutory scheme and he had no alternative but to impose a minimum sentence. In the Court's judgment, the facts of the previous convictions could not in this case amount to such circumstances as to make it unjust to pass a sentence of seven years. The Court accepted that the basis on which the judge sentenced for the latest offence could be capable of amounting to circumstances which would make it unjust to apply the full rigour of the section. The difficulty for the appellant was that this was not the third offence of supplying a class A drug, but the fourth such offence. The Court was not aware why, on the previous occasion in 2002, when she qualified for a sentence of seven years, she was sentenced only to 33 months. Assuming that it was on the basis that it would be unjust to sentence her to seven years on that occasion, the appellant must have been well aware of the peril she was in if she committed yet another such offence. At the time of the latest offence, the appellant was liable to be returned to custody in respect of the earlier sentence, but the judge rightly did not order her to serve the seven-year sentence consecutive to the unexpired portion of the previous sentence. In the Court's judgment, the sentencing judge correctly concluded in the circumstances that he had no option but to impose a minimum term of seven years in accordance with the Powers of Criminal Courts (Sentencing) Act 2000, s.110.

H5 **Cases cited:**
McInerney [2003] 2 Cr.App.R.(S.) 39 (p.240), *Harvey* [2000] 1 Cr.App.R.(S.) 368

H6   **Commentary:** [2004] Crim.L.R. 961

H7 *J. Lindsay* for the appellant.

JUDGMENT

1   **Gage J.:** Lisa Jayne Pearce is aged 35. On March 24, 2004, at the Crown Court at Great Grimsby, she was convicted of an offence of possessing a Class A drug, namely cocaine, with intent to supply. In accordance with the provisions of s.110 of the Powers of Criminal Courts (Sentencing) Act 2000, she was sentenced to a mandatory term of imprisonment of seven years. She now appeals against that sentence with the leave of the single judge.

2   The facts are as follows. On the evening of August 26, 2003 paramedics were summoned to the appellant's home. After they had gained entry, they found the appellant lying unconscious in the bathroom. She was quite blue and was not breathing. One of the paramedics recovered a bag containing 10.3gms of cocaine from her left hand. The cocaine was found to have a purity of about 28 per cent and had a street value of £618. The appellant was eventually roused and taken to hospital. She was subsequently arrested.

3   Following her arrest, she was interviewed on October 21, 2003. She said that the drugs were not hers, but that she had taken them from a friend and intended to dispose of them down the lavatory. She said that she had injected herself with a strong pain killer and that was why she had passed out. She maintained that she thought that the drugs were amphetamine and that she had not taken any of them, nor did she intend to take any of them. That was her defence at trial. The Crown's case was that she did not intend to dispose of the drugs; rather she intended to return them to the friend because she was too scared to do otherwise. By its verdict the jury rejected her defence and convicted her.

4   In sentencing her the learned judge said this:

"The prosecution, in pursuing this case against you, had been prepared to accept that it may well have been that you were simply minding this drug for a man by the name of Terry Geraghty, the father of your child, who, it is right, had previous convictions for offences of violence and dangerous drugs and who had been arrested and charged with an offence of possession of cocaine in June before this incident occurred involving you in August and in sentencing you I deal with you upon that basis.

I accept that there is no evidence of any drug paraphernalia, such as scales or bags, being found at your address, and I repeat that it may very well have been that you were simply looking after this cocaine for Terry Geraghty."

5   The appellant has a number of previous convictions, including convictions for supplying drugs. She also has offences of dishonesty. Relevant to this appeal are three previous convictions: the first in August 1998, when for six offences of supplying controlled drugs she was sentenced to a term of imprisonment for 12 months. The sixth of the six charges was for supplying a Class A drug. On July 28, 2000, at the Great Grimsby Crown Court, she was sentenced to a term of imprisonment of 18 months on each of two counts concurrently, the first being for possession of a controlled drug with intent to supply, that being a Class A drug, heroin, and the other of possessing a controlled drug of Class B. Finally of relevance is a sentence of 33 months' imprisonment imposed at the Grimsby Crown Court in August 2002, also for an offence of supplying a controlled drug of Class A, heroin.

6   Attached to the previous convictions is a conviction summary. So far as the second of those three offences to which we have referred, the facts are shortly stated as being:

"At 2 pm on 11th November 1999 at Hamilton Street, Grimsby, a drugs warrant was executed at her home address and a quantity of heroin in individual wraps."

That description of that offence is disputed by the appellant. Her case is that on that occasion she was simply handing drugs out of the window to someone on the other side when she was attending her own supplier.

7   So far as the third offence is concerned, the facts are shortly stated and as we understand it are not disputed. On March 29, 2002 at Grimsby the appellant supplied a single wrap of heroin to an undercover police officer. As we have indicated, she was sentenced on that occasion to a sentence of 33 months' imprisonment.

8   Before the court was a pre-sentence report. Having set out a number of facts about her history the author of the report, under the heading "Assessment of the risk of harm to the public and the likelihood of reoffending" stated:

"20. It is difficult to assess risk given Ms Pearce's denial of the offence. She does however admit to being foolish and impulsive in her involvement with Mr Geraghty and on this evidence alone there would be concerns about her ability to stay out of trouble in the future. Unless she changes this element of her behaviour then there remains a risk of reoffending.

21. Though this would not necessarily involve drugs her convictions over the last years suggest that this is a continuing pattern. Ms Pearce denied this."

9   Before this Court there is a report from the prison which reflects well on her behaviour, save for the failure of a mandatory drug test which occurred, it is said, on April 24, 2004. That was, as counsel has pointed out, on a date two days before her sentence for these offences, when the appellant was no doubt understandably anxious and concerned about the likely sentence that might be passed upon her.

10   The grounds of appeal in this case centre on s.110 of the Powers of Criminal Courts (Sentencing) Act 2000. Section 110 so far as is material for this appeal reads:

"110 — (1) This section applies where —
    (a) A person is convicted of a class A drug trafficking offence committed after 30th September 1997;
    (b) . . .
    (c) . . .
(2) The court shall impose an appropriate custodial sentence for a terms of at least seven years except where the court is of the opinion that there are particular circumstances which —
    (a) Relate to any of the offences or to the offender; and
    (b) Would make it unjust to do so in all the circumstances."

It is submitted that in the circumstances of this case and in the circumstances which apply to the appellant, her history and her history of offending, it was unjust for the judge to have imposed the mandatory sentence of seven years. Counsel relies on the fact that in relation to this particular offence the appellant held the drugs for no longer than one day and was proposing, as the judge found, to pass them on to her partner. She was holding them at a time when she was under stress from looking after her child and there was no suggestion of commercial supply. It is also submitted that the judge did not take, but ought to have taken, into account her evidence, which was that she thought that it was amphetamine and not heroin. Counsel relies on the facts that lie behind the three previous convictions for possessing Class A drugs with intent to supply. He submits that in each case they were at the very lowest end of the scale in relation to such offences and that fact, coupled with the peculiar and unusual facts lying behind this offence, make it unjust for the full rigour of s.110 to be applied.

11   We have also been referred to a number of decisions of this Court differently constituted. Perhaps the most important is the case of *McInerney* [2002] EWCA Crim 3003. As is pointed out by counsel, this is a judgment in relation to burglary

offences but it has some application to the matter with which we are concerned. The Lord Chief Justice, giving the judgment of the Court, at para.[15] referred to the case of *Harvey*. That was a decision of the Court presided over by Lord Bingham, when he was considering a precisely similar provision to s.110, which was contained in the Crime (Sentences) Act 1997—s.3 in fact. Lord Bingham said this, in a passage cited by Lord Woolf:

> "The purpose of the section is, in the absence of specific or particular circumstances which would render it unjust to do so, to oblige the court to impose the prescribed custodial sentence. This means that Parliament has chosen a term of seven years as the standard penalty on a third drug trafficking conviction meeting the conditions in subsection (1). The object of the section quite plainly is to require the courts to impose a sentence of at least seven years in circumstances where, but for the section, they would not or might not do so. If that were not the intention of the section it is in our judgment very difficult to see what the intention of the section was."

We pause there to note that the facts in the case of *Harvey* were that the appellant had been in a public house and was found in possession of two wraps of Class A drugs—again an offence at the lower end of the scale. Commenting on that passage from *Harvey*, Lord Woolf said in *McInerney* at p.16, in a passage to which we have regard:

> "We respectfully agree with the sentiments expressed in that paragraph and recognise that they apply equally to section 111. However, that does not preclude situations arising where it would be unjust to impose a sentence of three years, even where the offender qualifies. It may be helpful to give examples of the type of situation where a three-year sentence may be unjust. The sentence could be unjust if two of the offences were committed many years earlier than the third offence, or if the offender has made real efforts to reform or conquer his drug or alcohol addiction, but some personal tragedy triggers the third offence or if the first two offences were committed when the offender was not yet 16."

Counsel on behalf of this appellant submits that those comments have application in this case.

12   We were also referred to another decision of this Court, the case of *Stenhouse*. But in our judgment it is not necessary to refer to that decision. Once the principles have been set out, as they were in *Harvey* and *McInerney*, other cases are no more than examples of the application of s.110 based on their own particular facts. What we have to decide in this case is whether the judge was right to conclude that it was not unjust to pass this sentence.

13   What he said, after referring to the various mitigating factors that had been put before him and all the other features of the offence, was this:

> ". . . all of those features might have been persuasive in other circumstances that the sentence that you ought to receive at the end of the day would be less than seven years, but the decided case of *Harvey* has been canvassed

between counsel and myself, and it seems clear to me from that case that I should not lapse into an approach of saying that if the statutory scheme did not apply you would get less than seven years, therefore it would be unjust to pass that sentence upon you. I am afraid that as I see the situation you are caught foursquare within the statutory scheme and I am driven by that scheme to impose the minimum sentence of seven years upon you."

14   In the judgment of this Court the facts of the previous convictions in this case cannot amount to such circumstances as to make it unjust to pass a sentence of seven years. *Harvey* shows that to be the position. However, we accept that the basis on which the judge sentenced for this offence are or could be capable of amounting to circumstances which would make it unjust to apply the full rigour of the section. But the difficulty for this appellant is that this was not the third offence of supplying a Class A drug, but the fourth such offence. We do not know why on the previous occasion when she did qualify for a sentence of seven years she was only sentenced to 33 months. Assuming that it was on the basis that it would be unjust to do so, the appellant must have been well aware of the peril she was in if she committed yet another such offence. It is also noteworthy that at the time she committed this offence there was still an unexpired portion of the licence period in respect of the previous conviction outstanding. The judge, rightly no doubt, did not order her to serve the seven years consecutive to the unexpired portion.

15   In the circumstances, in our judgment, the sentencing judge correctly concluded that he had no option but to impose the minimum term of seven years pursuant to s.110 of the Powers of Criminal Courts (Sentencing) Act 2000 and this appeal must be dismissed.

R. v DAVID PAUL PACE

COURT OF APPEAL (Lord Justice Keene, Mr Justice Moses and Mr Justice Mitting): July 14, 2004

[2004] EWCA Crim 2018; [2005] 1 Cr.App.R.(S.) 74

LT Aggravating features; Breach; Custodial sentences; Harassment; Mitigation; Restraining orders; Sentencing guidelines

H1   *Protection from harassment—breach of restraining order—length of sentence*

H2   Two years' imprisonment for breach of a restraining order made under the Protection from Harassment Act 1997 reduced to 18 months.

H3   The appellant was convicted by a magistrates' court of breach of a restraining order made under the Protection from Harassment Act 1997. He was committed to the Crown Court for sentence. A restraining order was made in April 2003, requiring the appellant not to contact or harass a particular woman. The appellant accosted the woman just over six months later when she was walking her dog. The appellant grabbed her chin when she refused to hug him, followed her as she walked away and said "I have got a blade. Come here." The woman called the police and the appellant was arrested. Sentenced to two years' imprisonment.

H4   **Held:** (considering *Kasoar* [2002] 2 Cr.App.R.(S.) 60 (p.260), *Lumley* [2001] 2 Cr.App.R.(S.) 21 (p.110), *Goble* [2004] 2 Cr.App.R.(S.) 4 (p.12)) there was no guideline case on the sentence which should be imposed for breach of a restraining order. Relevant factors which went to determining the length of sentence would include the nature of the act giving rise to the breach; the use of actual violence and the threat of serious violence would be aggravating features; secondly, the effect on the victim; thirdly, whether or not the offence was the first breach or the last in a series of breaches; fourthly, the offender's record and his response to previous community penalties; fifthly, the need to protect the person named in the order. This offence was the first breach of the restraining order; it arose out of a chance meeting. There were aggravating features-the persistence in the offending, the implied threat of serious violence, and the effect on the victim. In the Court's view, inadequate weight had been given to the fact that the offence was spontaneous and that the appellant had not breached the order during the first six months of its existence. The Court would substitute a sentence of 18 months' imprisonment.

I5   **Cases cited:**
Kasoar [2002] 2 Cr.App.R.(S.) 60 (p.260), *Lumley* [2001] 2 Cr.App.R.(S.) 21 (p.110), *Goble* [2004] 2 Cr.App.R.(S.) 4 (p.12)

I6   **References:** breach of restraining order, *Current Sentencing Practice* B 3-6

I7   *A. Orchard* for the appellant.

JUDGMENT

1   **Mitting J.:**   This appellant is 39. On December 16, 2003 he was convicted in his absence by South Worcester magistrates of breaching a restraining order imposed by Worcester magistrates on April 14, 2003. On December 17, 2003 he was committed to the Crown Court for sentence under s.3 of the Powers of Criminal Courts (Sentencing) Act 2000. He appealed against his conviction to the Crown Court. On January 16, 2004 his appeal against conviction was dismissed and he was sentenced to two years' imprisonment for the breach. He appeals with leave of the single judge.

2   The facts are as follows. An order was made on April 14, 2003 by which he was required not to contact or harass Donna McDonald. On October 24, 2003 she was walking her dog in Worcester when the appellant, who was then the worse for drink, accosted her, by holding out his hands and saying he wanted to hug her. She told him to go away, but he would not. He grabbed him under the chin. She pushed him away and walked away, but he kept following her. Then he said, "I have got a blade. Come here", and put his hand in his pocket. She then ran

to a telephone box and called the police. The whole incident lasted about 10 minutes in all.

3   The appellant was arrested. At interview he denied the offence and said that Miss McDonald was lying.

4   Since 1978 he has been convicted on 27 separate occasions of 75 different offences, and had served custodial sentences for offences of dishonesty and violence as a young man. Since 2001 he had been sentenced to community penalties and fined for a variety of offences, including damage to property, assault on a police officer, disorderly behaviour and possession of an offensive weapon. The offence for which he was sentenced put him in breach of a community rehabilitation order imposed on April 14, 2003 by the same court that made the restraint order. He had not complied with that order. He had completed, by the time of his sentencing in January, 38 and three quarter hours of 100 hours of a community punishment order imposed on August 29, 2003 for shoplifting and handling. He was about to be the subject of breach proceedings for failing to attend to work on two occasions.

5   The author of the pre-sentence report noted that the root of his offending is drink and drug misuse. She assessed the likelihood of his reoffending as high.

6   He had been committed to the Crown Court in custody. That has had a beneficial effect upon him. He had, whilst in custody, been detoxified.

7   The judge when passing sentence said that, considering the nature of the offence and the fear caused to the victim, the proper sentence was two years' imprisonment. He revoked the community orders.

8   There is no guideline case on the sentence which should be imposed for breach of a restraining order. Sentences of between 12 months and two years have been upheld. In *Kasoar* [2002] 2 Cr.App.R.(S.) 60 (p.260) a sentence of 12 months was upheld, in *Lumley* [2001] 2 Cr.App.R.(S.) 21 a sentence of two and a half years was reduced to 18 months, in *Goble*, an unusual case, [2004] 2 Cr.App.R.(S.) 4 (p.12) a sentence of two years was upheld. Relevant factors which go to determining the length of the sentence and, on occasion, its nature must include the following: first, the nature of the act giving rise to the breach. The use of actual violence and the threat of serious violence would clearly be aggravating features. Secondly, the effect on the victim. Thirdly, whether or not the offence was the first breach, or the last in a series of breaches. Fourthly, the offender's record and, in particular, how he had responded to community penalties in the past and whether or not he was subject to community penalties at the time of the breach. Fifthly, the need to protect the person named in the restraining order. Doubtless there are other factors which would apply in particular cases.

9   This offence, it is to be noted, was the first breach of the restraining order. It did not come at the end, as sometimes in these cases, of a series of escalating acts of harassment against the person protected by the order. It was not premeditated; it was a chance meeting in Worcester centre. The appellant's conduct was, as we have noted, undoubtedly influenced by the amount he had had to drink. There were aggravating features it is true. The offending on the day was persistent. It lasted for 10 minutes. It involved the implied threat of serious violence by reference to "the blade". The victim was terrified. The appellant had, as we have

recited, showed a persistent disregard of community sentences in the recent past. The victim undoubtedly required protection to be afforded to her by the imposition of a prison sentence.

10   We have asked ourselves whether it was necessary to impose a prison sentence of the length imposed by the judge. The factors last mentioned suggest that his sentence was not excessive and was appropriate to the offending. But, in our view, he gave inadequate weight to the fact that this offence was spontaneous, that it was the first time that he had breached the order and that he had managed to go without breaching it, despite committing other offences, for six months.

11   For those reasons, in our view, the appropriate sentence should have been, even after he contested the case, a sentence that lies in the middle of the bracket identified, and should have been a sentence of 18 months' imprisonment. We therefore quash the sentence of two years' imprisonment and substitute a sentence of 18 months' imprisonment. To that extent this appeal is allowed.

R. v NICHOLAS THOMAS DUFFY

COURT OF APPEAL (Lord Justice Auld, Mr Justice Henriques and Mr Justice Beatson): July 15, 2004

[2004] EWCA Crim 2054; [2005] 1 Cr.App.R.(S.) 75

(LT) Imitation firearms; Police officers; Possession of firearms with intent; Resisting arrest; Sentence length; Threatening to kill

I1   *Possessing firearm with intent to resist arrest and cause fear of violence—threatening police officers with imitation firearm—length of sentence*

I2   Five years' imprisonment upheld for possessing a firearm with intent to resist arrest and cause fear of violence in a case where police officers were threatened with an imitation firearm.

I3   The appellant pleaded guilty to having a firearm or imitation firearm with intent to resist arrest, possessing an imitation firearm with intent to cause fear of violence, and making a threat to kill. Police officers were called in the early hours of the morning to an address where the appellant was causing a disturbance. The appellant ran into a house and later he emerged from an upstairs window. He produced a hand gun and pointed it at a police officer saying "I am going to shoot you". The appellant did not put the gun down when requested to do so by the officer but pointed the gun at three other officers threatening to shoot them. When the appellant's girlfriend was arrested, the appellant pointed the gun at the arresting officer and threatened to shoot him. Armed police officers arrived. They believed that the weapon was a replica. The officers agreed that if the appellant put his gun down, the appellant's girlfriend would be released. The appellant later produced a petrol can and threatened to burn the place down, and came out with a plastic toy weapon. The siege continued for eight hours until police officers decided to enter the property. The weapons were found to be a toy hand gun and an ornamental musket. Sentenced to a total of five years' imprisonment.

H4   **Held:** (considering *Costen* (1989) 11 Cr.App.R.(S.) 182, and *Attorney General's Reference No.26 of 2001 (Richard Spahn)* [2002] 1 Cr.App.R.(S.) 2 (p.3)) the sentencing judge observed that the incident was very frightening for the police officers even if they believed that the gun was an imitation. It was well established that, in appropriate circumstances, the court might withhold the discount for a plea of guilty, or substantially reduce the credit, where a man had pleaded guilty in the face of overwhelming evidence. In the present case, the sentencing judge was correct to reduce the discount. The Court had considered whether the sentence of five years was excessive. The sentencing judge had deliberately passed a sentence which expressed grave disapproval. The Court considered that he was correct to do so and that the sentence was entirely appropriate.

H5   **Cases cited:**
Costen (1989) 11 Cr.App.R.(S.) 182, *Attorney General's Reference No.26 of 2001 (Richard Spahn)* [2002] 1 Cr.App.R.(S.) 2 (p.3)

H6   **References:** firearms offences, *Current Sentencing Practice* B 3-3

H7   *C. Beyts* for the appellant.

JUDGMENT

1   **Henriques J.:** On March 3 of this year the appellant, aged 21, pleaded guilty to having a firearm, or imitation firearm, with intent to resist arrest, possessing an imitation firearm with intent to cause fear and violence, and making a threat to kill, and was sentenced by Judge Bing at Snaresbrook Crown Court to five years' imprisonment, three years' imprisonment and three years' imprisonment all to run concurrently.

2   Police officers were called to an address in London E17 at 3.00am. The appellant was causing a disturbance. He ran into a house. A name enquiry revealed that the appellant was sought on a warrant not backed for bail. He emerged from an upstairs window, giving his brother's name, and claiming that the police were harassing him. Other police units arrived.

3   He produced a black handgun and pointed it at a police officer saying, "I am going to shoot you." The officer feared for his safety and told the appellant to put the gun down. The appellant did not do so. He pointed the gun at three other officers threatening to shoot them.

4   At one stage the appellant's girlfriend was taken away under arrest. The appellant pointed the gun at the arresting officer and shouted, "Let her go or I will shoot her." Armed officers were called, and the first group of officers were led away to safety. The firearms officers believed the weapon was a replica owing to the ease of movement. The appellant was demanding that his girlfriend be released. The police in due course agreed that if he put his gun down she would be released.

When he did put his gun down on a window sill it fell to the floor. The appellant then produced a petrol can and threatened to burn the place down. He then retreated from view and came out shortly afterwards with another weapon which the police correctly believed to be a plastic toy which he waved around.

5   The siege continued with the local area being cordoned off. At 11.30 that morning, eight and a half hours after the police were first called, a decision was made to enter the property, and the appellant was located in an upstairs bedroom. One weapon proved to be a toy, the other was an ornamental flintlock musket. The actual siege had lasted for eight hours. The appellant made no comment when interviewed.

6   In sentencing, the judge expressed the view that this was a disgraceful incident and very frightening for the officers involved. He accepted that they believed the weapons were imitation, but belief was not the same as certainty. It was an aggravating factor that the appellant was wanted on warrant at the time. The appellant had a bad record for violent behaviour, including affray and assault occasioning actual bodily harm. The court passed a sentence which expressed grave disapproval and sent out a message that this sort of behaviour cannot be tolerated.

7   The first ground of appeal is that the judge erred in considering that little credit should be given for the guilty plea in respect of ground 1. It is well established that in appropriate circumstances the court may withhold discount for a plea of guilty, or substantially reduce the credit where the offender pleads guilty in the face of overwhelming evidence. As Lord Lane C.J. said in *Costen* [1989] 11 Cr.App.R.(S.) 182:

"... where the man has been caught red-handed and a plea of guilty is practically speaking inevitable ... any discount may be reduced or indeed lost."

8   In the present case the judge merely sought to reduce the discount rather than extinguish it, and in our judgment he was correct to do so. The evidence of numerous police officers would have rendered a trial a foregone conclusion.

9   The second ground of appeal is that the sentence on count 1, namely the five-year sentence, was excessive. The single judge has drawn our attention to the case of the *Attorney General's reference No.26 of 2001*, reported as *Richard Spahn* [2002] 1 Cr.App.R.(S.) 2 (p.3), in which five years, after a partial trial in a case involving a real weapon and ammunition, was described as the very lowest sentence thought to be appropriate. In fact the Lord Chief Justice said that five years would have been a merciful sentence in that case, and that offender had no convictions in the United Kingdom and no relevant convictions overseas.

10   We have given careful thought as to whether the sentence of five years was indeed excessive. We bear in mind, in particular, that the learned judge quite deliberately passed a sentence which expressed grave disapproval and sent out a message that this sort of behaviour cannot be tolerated.

11   He was, in making those remarks, indicating that this was a severe sentence. We think that he was correct to do so and that the sentence was entirely appropriate in the very grave circumstances of this case. Very many hours of police time were wasted; the police officers were subjected to a very frightening experience. For those reasons this appeal is dismissed.

[Paragraphs 12–13 have been omitted.]

ATTORNEY GENERAL'S REFERENCES NOS 31, 45, 43, 42, 50 AND 51 OF 2004

COURT OF APPEAL (The Lord Chief Justice, Mr Justice Forbes and Mr Justice Bell): July 16, 2004

[2004] EWCA Crim 1934; [2005] 1 Cr.App.R.(S.) 76

(LT) Community sentences; Criminal procedure; Jurisdiction; Public interest; Undue leniency

H1 *Unduly lenient sentence—reference by the Attorney General—circumstances in which Court of Appeal, Criminal Division will vary sentence on a reference by the Attorney General*

H2   Observations on the circumstances in which the Court of Appeal, Criminal Division will vary a sentence which has been referred to the Court by the Attorney General on the ground that it appears to the Attorney General to be unduly lenient.

H3   The Court dealt with six cases in which the Attorney General had invited the Court to review the sentences on the ground that they were unduly lenient.

H4   **Held:** the Criminal Justice Act 1988, s.36, provided that the Attorney General might refer a case to the Court of Appeal, with leave of the Court, if he considered that the sentencing of a person in a proceeding in the Crown Court for an offence to which the section applied had been unduly lenient. On such a reference, the Court of Appeal might quash any sentence passed on the offender in the proceedings, and in place of it pass such sentence as they thought appropriate for the case and which the court below had power to pass when dealing with him. An application by the Attorney General could be made only if it appeared to the Attorney General that the sentencing of the offender was unduly lenient. The statute did not identify what should be the approach of the Court of Appeal when a case was referred. The section indicated that the Court had power, if it decided to intervene, to substitute a sentence which the court thought was "appropriate". The Court was given an extremely wide discretion. Assistance was given by *Attorney General's Reference No.4 of 1989* (1989) 11 Cr.App.R.(S.) 517 (and *Attorney General's Reference No.5 of 1989 (Hill-Trevor)* (1989) 11 Cr.App.R.(S.) 489) which indicated that the Court should not intervene unless it was shown that there was some error of principle in the judge's sentence, so that public confidence would be damaged if the sentence were not altered. It was most important that the Court should adhere to this test in deciding whether to interfere with a sentence after having reviewed it. The Court did not interfere with a sentence which was said to be too severe unless it was manifestly excessive. Similarly, the Court would not interfere with a sentence on an Attorney General's reference unless it was manifestly not sufficiently severe. The power of the

Attorney General to refer cases to the Court was not intended to interfere with the proper exercise of discretion by the trial judge as to what sentence was the appropriate sentence to apply. The trial judge was required to have regard to guidelines issued by the Court and in future would also have to take into account guidelines issued by the Sentencing Guidelines Council. However, guidelines remained guidelines and it was perfectly appropriate for a judge not to follow the guidelines or not follow an earlier authority of the Court on similar facts if in the circumstances he concluded that doing so would not result in the appropriate sentence. The judge should, however, explain, when passing sentence, why the guidelines or the authority were not being followed. Sentencing was an art and not a science. It was part of the task of the sentencing judge to identify a case where the interests of the public would be best served by taking an exceptional course. The position was different when the Court was considering whether to grant the Attorney General's application to refer the case. The decision to apply was made by the Attorney General or Solicitor General personally after considering advice from the Crown Prosecution Service, trial counsel and treasury counsel. The role of the Attorney General was separate from the role of the Court. It was appropriate for the Attorney General to take into account considerations when deciding to make an application which it would not be appropriate to the Court to take into account when deciding the outcome of the application. In the normal way, the Court would usually grant leave for an application to be made by the Attorney General. The Court did not consider it necessary to provide any advice as to how the jurisdiction should be exercised in the future. Where the Attorney General was contending on a reference that the trial judge had wrongly imposed a community sentence rather than custody, it was important that the Court and the Attorney General were provided with up-to-date information about the progress which the offender had made since the sentence was passed. This was important because, even if the sentence was not an appropriate sentence at the time it was passed, the offender's response to the community sentence could affect the outcome of the reference. Reports should be obtained not later than seven days before the hearing of the application and made available to the Attorney General. The Attorney General could then consider whether it was desirable to withdraw the applications.

The Court then dealt with the individual cases.

H5   **Cases cited:**
Attorney General's Reference No.4 of 1989 (1989) 11 Cr.App.R.(S.) 517, *Attorney General's Reference No.5 of 1989 (Hill-Trevor)* (1989) 11 Cr.App.R.(S.) 489

H6   **References:** reference by the Attorney General, Archbold, 7–366

H7   *R. Horwell* and *M. Haywood* for the Attorney General.
M. Aspinall-Miles, A. Downie, M. Benson, Ms M. Holt, Miss A. Byrnes and *J. O'Higgins* for the respective offenders.

JUDGMENT

The Lord Chief Justice:

Introduction

1   This judgment relates to the review by this Court of six sentences passed on offenders. The power of this Court to review sentences arises under ss.35 and 36 of the Criminal Justice Act 1988. Section 35 identifies the cases to which the Act applies. Section 36 sets out the conditions which have to be fulfilled before this Court can interfere with a sentence. The relevant provisions of s.36 are as follows:

> "36 (1) If it appears to the Attorney General —
>   (a) that the sentencing of a person in a proceeding in the Crown Court has been unduly lenient; and
>   (b) that the case is one to which this Part of this Act applies, he may, with the leave of the Court of Appeal, refer the case to them for them to review the sentencing of that person; and on such a reference the Court of Appeal may —
>   (i) quash any sentence passed on him in the proceeding; and
>   (ii) in place of it pass such sentence as they think appropriate for the case and as the court below had power to pass when dealing with him.
>   (2) Without prejudice to the generality of subsection (1) above, the condition specified in paragraph (a) of that subsection may be satisfied if it appears to the Attorney General that the judge erred in law as to his powers of sentencing or failed to impose a sentence required by section 109(2), 110(2) or 111(2) of the Powers of Criminal Courts (Sentencing) Act 2000.
>   [These sections refer to automatic life sentences and minimum fixed term sentences.]
>   (3) For the purposes of this Part of this Act any two or more sentences are to be treated as passed in the same proceeding if they would be so treated for the purposes of section 10 of the Criminal Appeal Act 1968."

2   The application of Her Majesty's Attorney General can only be made (as is stated in s.36(1)) if it "appears" to him that the sentence is unduly lenient. The section does not identify what should be the approach of this Court when a case is referred. Instead the section indicates that the Court's power, if it decides to intervene, is to substitute a sentence that the Court thinks is "appropriate". The discretion of the Court is, therefore, extremely wide. Assistance is, however, given as to when the Court should intervene in *Attorney General's Reference (No.4 of 1989)* (1990) 90 Cr.App.R. 366 and *Attorney General's Reference No.5 of 1989 (Hill-Trevor)* (1990) 90 Cr.App.R. 358. In those cases it was indi-

cated that this Court should not intervene unless it was shown that there was some error of principle in the judge's sentence, so that public confidence would be damaged if the sentence were not altered.

3   It is most important that this Court should adhere to this test in deciding whether to interfere with a sentence after having reviewed it under s.36. This Court does not interfere with a sentence which is said to be too severe unless it is manifestly excessive. Similarly, this Court will not interfere with a sentence on an Attorney General's reference unless it is manifestly not sufficiently severe.

4   The power of the Attorney General to refer cases to this Court is not intended to interfere with the proper exercise of discretion of the trial judge as to what sentence is the appropriate sentence to apply. The trial judge is required to have regard to the guidelines issued by this Court. In the future the trial judge will also have to take into account the guidelines issued by the new Sentencing Guidelines Council established under s.167 of the Criminal Justice Act 2003 ("the 2003 Act") as required by s.172. However, guidelines remain guidelines and it is perfectly appropriate for a judge not to follow the guidelines or not to follow an earlier authority of this Court on similar facts if in the circumstances he concludes that doing so will not result in the appropriate sentence. The judge should, however, explain when passing sentence, why the guidelines or the authority are not being followed. (Even in relation to the statutory guideline contained in Sch.21 of the Criminal Justice Act 2003 in respect of minimum terms for those sentenced to a mandatory life sentence, the Schedule makes it clear that the judge retains a wide discretion.) As has been said on many occasions previously sentencing is an art and not a science, it is part of the task of the sentencing judge to identify a case where the interests of the public will be best served by taking an exceptional course.

5   The position is different when this Court is considering whether to grant the Attorney General's application to refer the case. For the purposes of the present appeals, in a letter dated June 22, 2004 (which was made available at the hearing), the Attorney General provided the Court with an account of the steps which are taken to ensure that, so far as possible, a reference is made only when it is justified. The decision to apply is made by the Attorney General or Solicitor General personally. In addition to the advice of the Crown Prosecution Service they are also advised by trial counsel for the prosecution and Treasury counsel. The defendant's counsel is also involved in the process. It is clear great care is being exercised.

6   However, the role of the Attorney General is separate from that of this Court and it is appropriate for the Attorney General to take into account considerations when deciding to make an application to this Court which it would not be appropriate for this Court to take into account when deciding the outcome of the application. Nonetheless, in the normal way, when an application is made by the Attorney General this Court will usually grant leave for the application to be made.

7   Having heard these six references we do not find it necessary to provide any advice to the Attorney General as to how this jurisdiction should be exercised in the future. The references did, however, reveal that where the Attorney Gen-

eral is contending on a reference that the trial judge has wrongly imposed a community sentence rather than custody, it is important that this Court and the Attorney General are provided with up-to-date information as to the progress which the offender has made since the sentence was passed by the trial judge. This is important because even if the sentence at the time it was passed was not an appropriate sentence, if the offender is responding to the community sentence then that could affect the outcome of the Attorney General's reference.

8   In some cases the progress made by the offender after sentence will undermine the whole purpose of the application and because of this, not later than seven days before the hearing, this Court should not only obtain the reports that are relevant in this category of case but it should make the reports available to the Attorney General. The Attorney General can then consider whether it is desirable to withdraw the application.

9   At the conclusion of the hearing of the applications, so as not to prolong the uncertainty of the outcome of the applications, which the Court appreciates will be worrying for the offenders, the Court announced its decision in respect of each of the applications and indicated that the reasons for the decision would be given in this judgment later. We have given leave for all the applications which are before us to be made and now give reasons for our decisions.

10   We turn now to consider each of the applications in turn.

R. v Thomas McInerny

11   Thomas McInerny is 16 years of age, having been born on October 20, 1987. On February 2, 2004 he was convicted of one offence of robbery contrary to s.8(1) of the Theft Act 1968 and one offence of intimidation contrary to s.51(1) of the Criminal Justice and Public Order Act 1994. On February 20, 2004, when he was aged 16, he was sentenced in respect of each offence to 24 months of supervision with a requirement to attend 90 days at a specified activities intensive supervision and surveillance programme. A curfew order with a tagging provision for six months was also made.

The facts

12   The offence took place during the evening of September 25, 2003 when the offender was 15. The victim (to whom we will refer as SW) was a young man acquainted with the offender who was walking in a street in Fulham when the offender approached and asked for money for cigarettes. SW refused. Some play fighting commenced but then events took a turn for the worse after the offender's jacket had been ripped. The offender became abusive and violent, beating the victim about the body and manhandling him until the victim had parted with his mobile phone worth £280. SW, who had been bruised on his chest and back, made his way home to his parents with whom he was living. Subsequently, the offender made a threatening telephone call warning SW not to contact the police. He threatened violence to SW and his parents in the event of non-compliance. It was common ground that when SW handed over his telephone, he removed the SIM card. This provides some confirmation of what the offender

told the police when interviewed, namely that the victim had left his mobile telephone with the offender until he could raise the money for the damage to the
offender's jacket.

13   The offender had previous convictions during 2002 and 2003. He had previously been subject to supervision and attendance centre orders for indecent
assault, taking a motor vehicle without consent and criminal damage.

14   Between the date of these offences and the date on which he was sentenced, in
relation to an earlier matter, the offender was made the subject of a supervision
order for handling stolen goods and was conditionally discharged for possession
of cannabis. He was also found to be in breach of curfew conditions attached to
his bail. On February 26, 2004 he was sentenced to a four-month detention and
training order for driving offences.

15   A pre-sentence report, prepared by a social worker from the Youth Offending
Team dated March 2, 2004, was before the sentencing judge (Mr Recorder
Shanks). The report indicated that the offender was minimising his role in the
robbery and appeared reluctant to accept the impact of or the responsibility for
what he had done. He did, however, recognise to some extent the impact upon
the victim caused by the offence of intimidation. The report stated that the writer
had been informed that the victim did not want the defendant to receive a custodial sentence and felt that the court process had been sufficient. The telephone
had been returned. The writer of the report was of the view that the offender
was lacking in social skills and this led him to respond in an aggressive or an inappropriate way. She was of the opinion that this could be linked to the difficulties
he had at school and his resistance to any group work. He was then casually working with his brother-in-law earning £50 per day. She considered that he was at a
high risk of reoffending. She recommended a curfew order together with a supervision order which would provide a higher level of supervision than the existing
order in his case. She considered there should also be rigorous reporting requirements.

16   The recorder also had available to him the assessment of his suitability for the
intensive supervision and surveillance program. It was considered that the
offender had shown the necessary commitment, attitude and motivation required
to undertake "this rigorous and demanding programme".

17   For the hearing of the reference, this Court had requested up-to-date reports
indicating how the offender had responded to the order made by the recorder.
Unfortunately, the report was only available immediately before the hearing
and so it was not seen by Mr Richard Horwell and Mr Mark Heywood, who
appeared on behalf of the Attorney General, until immediately prior to the hearing.

18   Among the authorities relied upon by the Attorney General was the *Attorney
General's References Nos 4 and 7 of 2002* [2002] 2 Cr.App.R.(S.) 77 (p.345).
In the course of giving the judgment of the Court in that case, Lord Woolf C.J.
referred to the prevalence of the offence of robberies in relation to mobile phones.
He added, that ". . . those who did so must understand they would be punished
severely. Custodial sentences would be the only option available to the courts
where these offences were committed, unless there were exceptional circum-

stances. That would apply irrespective of the age of the offender and irrespective of whether the offender had previous convictions. However, both these factors were very important when a judge came to decide on the length of sentence." Although the Court was careful to indicate in that case it was not giving new guidelines, it certainly supports the suggestion that the usual disposal in a case of this sort will be a custodial one. However, the reference to "exceptional circumstances" should be noted. Exceptional circumstances can include the real possibility that greater protection to the public would be provided by a meaningful sentence in the community rather than a custodial sentence.

19   The offender was a young man who had real problems. The indications were that unless his underlying offending behaviour was tackled, he would be likely progressively to commit more serious crimes. If the Court could divert him from this prospect, that would certainly be constructive from the offender's and the public's point of view. The most recent report does suggest that the offender is responding positively to the order which the recorder made. The order was an example of the more constructive sentencing options which are becoming increasingly available. The availability of tagging also provides a valuable safeguard for the public.

Our conclusion

0   Having considered the facts of this particular case, it is our view that it cannot be said that the order made by the recorder was one which was inappropriate. That it was appropriate was substantiated by subsequent events. Of course, this Court accepts that there is still a significant risk that despite the progress which is at present being made by this offender he could "go off the rails" again. If he does, then the court will have ample powers to make sure that the appropriate punishment is passed. It is fortunate that orders of this nature are being more satisfactorily "policed" now than was the case in the past. This means that this type of order can achieve better long-term protection for the public than can be achieved by a relatively short custodial sentence.

1   Whilst we remain concerned about the risk of Thomas McInerny's reoffending, it is our opinion that this is reduced by the fact that he has attended all youth offending team appointments, his conforming to the requirements of his curfew order and his positive attitude towards employment. Thomas McInerny has a close family who are concerned about his offending and are supporting him in meeting the requirements of the order and his wish to work. The reporting officer's opinion was that the most effective way of reducing the residual risks of his reoffending is for him to continue to attend his youth offending team appointments which focus on a cognitive behavioural approach in relation to his thinking skills. She also thought the acquisition of employment would engage him in a positive way within the community and help him to develop a sense of responsibility.

    This Court therefore decided not to interfere with the sentence of the recorder. It would, however, stress that if the offender does not comply with the present order, he cannot expect the present opportunity he has been given to be repeated.

R. v Adele Mclean

23   Adele McLean is 20 years of age, having been born on January 31, 1984. On March 4, 2004, at the Crown Court at Liverpool before H.H. Judge Crompton, she pleaded guilty to robbery. The case was then adjourned for the preparation of pre-sentence reports. On March 26, 2004 she was sentenced to eight months' detention.

The facts

24   On May 10, 2003 the victim was sitting in a car making a telephone call. It was about 4.30pm. The offender approached the car from the front, looked into the car and then passed around the back of the car and opened the driver's door. She asked the victim to call the police because her boyfriend had taken her child. The victim was suspicious but nonetheless agreed to call the police. The offender then changed her mind and said that would not be possible. The victim then offered to drive the offender to wherever the child was. The victim made the offer because she felt intimidated by the offender's presence. The offender then tried to grab the car keys. There was a struggle and the offender slapped the victim across the face. Part of the bunch of keys broke off and the offender ran away with this section of keys and the victim's mobile telephone.

25   The victim attempted to follow the offender but was unable to do so and she returned to the place where the robbery had taken place. She then saw the offender again and the offender again tried to open the door of the car, so the victim drove off. She then returned with a friend and once again the offender tried to open the car door but when she was challenged she ran away pursued by the victim's friend and another man. A few minutes later she was arrested and the victim's property was returned to her.

26   When the offender pleaded guilty, she was unaware that it was thought at that time that the victim was unwilling to give evidence. Her solicitors were subsequently apprised of the difficulty of which the judge was also aware, but the offender stood by her plea. Without the victim's evidence there could have been difficulties in securing a conviction.

27   The Attorney General relies on the fact that the attack was pre-meditated on a lone female and that the offender returned to the scene as aggravating factors. The Attorney General treats as mitigating factors: the fact that the offender had no previous convictions for robbery; the fact that the violence was limited to a single slap; and the offender's plea which was maintained, despite the fact that the victim might not attend court. He submits that the sentence was unduly lenient.

28   In addition to *Attorney General's References Nos 4 and 7 of 2002*, which we have already cited, the Attorney General relied upon the case of Attorney General's Reference No. 76 of 2003 (sub nom *Attorney General's Reference No.76 of 2003 (Carson)* [2004] EWCA Crim 886). In that case the offender was 26 years of age and pleaded guilty to one count of robbery. She was originally sentenced to an 80-hour community punishment order and a two-year community rehabilitation order. The violence was greater than that in this case. Two people were involved and, in addition to a mobile phone, £170, £4 of milk tokens and a

Child Benefit book was stolen. The victim's protests that it would leave her and her child with nothing at all went unheeded. The offender also threatened more violence if she contacted the police. The victim had a black eye, a cut behind the ear and a lump on her head. The offender in *Carson* had, as in this reference, a bad record when she was dealt with by this Court. But she had completed 80 hours of the community punishment, and in addition, she had made progress on the community rehabilitation order, although there were some earlier breaches of the order. In giving the judgment of this Court, Kay L.J. said that this was a case which demanded a custodial sentence. He also rejected the suggestion that it was not necessary to impose a custodial sentence because of the progress that the offender had made. The Court quashed the sentence which was passed and substituted for it a sentence of 12 months' imprisonment.

9   Judge Crompton, when sentencing on this reference, had a pre-sentence report which indicated that the offence was motivated by the offender's need to finance her use of heroin. She was ashamed of her actions, but at the time when she committed the offence her only thoughts were for herself. She had previously received a 12-month community rehabilitation order with a condition to attend an "addressing substance related offending" programme in June 2003 but her response had been poor. She had a child when she was 15 and that child was then living with one of the offender's aunts. The probation officer's conclusions were that the offender's life "had escalated out of control; she is behaving in reckless way which she says has shocked her. She was tearful in interview and appeared genuine in her regret." Whilst she was the sole defendant, the probation officer thought she was under the influence of other male offenders. The offender also wrote to the judge expressing her regrets.

0   In sentencing the offender, Judge Crompton indicated, "in the ordinary run of events I may well have sentenced you to something like two-and-a-half years imprisonment", he then went on to say that there were "fairly unusual circumstances" and because of them he intended to impose "an exceptionally lenient sentence of eight months". It appears probable that part of the unusual circumstances the judge was referring to was the fact that the offender had not sought to go back on her plea notwithstanding that she would have had reason to think that a prosecution might have difficulty in proving its case.

The judge also referred to the fact that the offender was now drug-free and this could make it possible for consideration to be given to her being reunited with her child.

Although the offender was entitled to full credit for her frankness, the fact that she did not seek to change her plea is not a matter to which we would attach great weight. She knew she had committed the offence and if, as she suggested, she was repentant about what she had done, her proper course was to plead guilty.

Even if the matters had remained as they were when this case was before the trial judge, we would have regarded the sentence as being low but we would probably not have interfered with it. If we had done so, we would have to make an allowance for double jeopardy and, bearing in mind the early release arrangements, which are now in place, we would have doubted that any advantage would be achieved by sending this offender back into prison, because she would inevitably been released before this Court could intervene. The trial judge, as he made clear, knew what would be the normal sentence and that he was taking an exceptional course and had made it clear in his sentencing remarks that he was taking an unusual course. There was no point of principle therefore involved.

34   However, there was before us an additional report from a different probation officer indicating that the offender had been released on April 16, 2004, that while her initial response to supervision had been unsatisfactory, she was in the process of regaining custody of her daughter and as part of the process was undertaking drug tests to determine whether she was capable of taking full parental responsibility. With the support of her supervising officer she was now taking necessary steps to address her drug use. A referral was being made to a supported housing project that provided rehabilitation to families recovering from drug dependency. It offered a range of therapeutic services, family support, parenting skills and advice. The officer concludes by saying, "the offender had shown commitment to trying to regain custody of her daughter and in taking her life in a more positive direction which process would be adversely affected by her being returned to prison". The officer considered that to return her would "in fact, damage her motivation and her willingness to move her life in a more productive manner".

Our Conclusion

35   We can understand why the officer came to this conclusion and we have decided it would not be in the public interest to return her to prison. *Attorney General's Reference No.76 of 2003 (Carson)* is a more serious case than this and the eight months' detention in this case is comparable with the 12 months' custody imposed by Kay L.J. in that case. Accordingly, we make no order on the Attorney General's application.

Daniel Lee Burgess

36   We turn next to the offender Daniel Lee Burgess. He is now aged 21, having been born on April 6, 1983. On December 12, 2003, following a trial at the Manchester Crown Court before Mr Recorder Osbourne and a jury, the offender was convicted of wounding with intent to do grievous bodily harm, contrary to s.18 of the Offences Against the Person Act 1861 (the "1861 Act"). After a pre-sentence report had been obtained, on March 12, 2004 the offender was sentenced to a two-year community rehabilitation order, with a condition that he should attend an "addressing substance related offending" programme. He was also ordered to pay £500 compensation to the victim.

The facts

37   The circumstances of the offence were as follows. At about 9.00pm on Friday April 18, 2003, the victim W.O., who was then aged 16, and a friend were walking along Wolsey Street in Radcliffe towards the town centre. They were going to a snooker club. They passed a group of about four or five young men, including the

offender, who were standing outside the Lord Raglan public house. One of the group was heard to say, "Are you going to bottle him?" The offender, who was holding a glass bottle, then began to walk across the road towards the victim. The victim's friend shouted at him to run and at the same time the offender began to run towards the victim. The victim ran along the pavement and took refuge in a chip shop, closing the door behind him. However, the offender followed the victim into the shop. He pushed the victim against the counter and hit him a number of times on the head, shoulders and upper body with the bottle. Some of the blows also landed on the victim's hands as he sought to protect himself. The offender then made off, leaving behind the bottle which was still intact.

The proprietor of the shop gave the victim some paper towels for his injuries, some of which were bleeding. The victim then went to the Accident and Emergency Department of Fairfield Hospital, where he was found to have a two-centimetre laceration to the top of his head and a one and a half centimetre laceration to the right side of his head. The wounds were stapled. The victim also had pain in the right shoulder and hand. He was given medication and a support bandage for his right wrist. The victim recovered physically from his injuries, but remains wary of the offender or any of his associates. He has subsequently moved away from his home and the Radcliffe area for fear of reprisals from the offender.

Three months after the incident in question, the offender approached the victim on the street and asked, "Are you the one that got bottled a couple of months ago in the chippy?" When the victim confirmed that he was, the offender said "Well I got the wrong person". The offender entered his name and number into the victim's mobile telephone and said "My name's Danny Burgess, if you're ever in trouble, phone me".

When subsequently arrested and interviewed, the offender said that he had entered the chip shop to buy food. He said that he thought that the victim was someone else, a person who owed money to his sister's friend. He claimed that he threw a punch at the victim, not realising that he still had a bottle in his hand. At trial, he pleaded guilty to the alternative lesser offence of wounding, contrary to s.20 of the 1861 Act. However, that plea of guilty was not acceptable to the prosecution.

The offender had previous convictions for driving offences in 2001 and 2003. In March 2003, the offender was sentenced to a community rehabilitation order for 18 months for offences of aggravated vehicle taking and driving with excess alcohol. Between the date of the index offence and the date on which he was sentenced, the offender pleaded guilty at the Bury magistrates' court to a further separate offence of wounding, contrary to s.20 of the 1861 Act. That matter was committed to the Manchester Crown Court for sentence on the same day as the index offence and was dealt with by the same judge, who imposed no separate penalty in respect of that particular offence.

In passing sentence for the index offence, the recorder expressed the view that the offender's criminality was "more adequately dealt with by section 20 of the Act, to which you were willing to plead guilty". So far as concerns the separate s.20 offence, the recorder observed that "it would be futile to impose any particular penalty or to impose a concurrent penalty", because the two years' community rehabilitation order would be sufficient to make the offender see the error of his ways.

43   The Attorney General relied upon the following features as aggravating the index offence: first, the offender singled out his victim and then pursued him and cornered him; secondly, the offender carried out an unprovoked, sustained and violent attack upon the victim, striking his head and body and causing significant injury; thirdly, the offender had used a weapon, namely a glass bottle. On the other hand, the Attorney General recognised that there were mitigating features, namely that the offender readily admitted that he had carried out the attack on the victim and that he had purported to explain his actions as a case of mistaken identity.

44   On behalf of the offender, Mr Benson frankly acknowledged that this Court was very likely to come to the conclusion that the sentence passed by the recorder for this offence of wounding with intent was unduly lenient. In our view, Mr Benson's approach was both realistic and entirely right in the circumstances of this case. Mr Benson then referred to and relied upon the information provided and views expressed by the probation officer in her supplementary report dated May 4, 2004. It was Mr Benson's core submission that, in the light of the undoubted progress made by the offender whilst complying with the terms of the community rehabilitation order and the fact that he is now in proper, full-time employment, this Court should exercise its discretion not to interfere with the sentence passed by the recorder.

45   We say at once that we entirely agree with the Attorney General's submission that the recorder's community sentence for the index offence was unduly lenient. As the Attorney General pointed out, the sentence wholly failed to mark the gravity of the offence, which consisted of an unprovoked attack upon an innocent victim who suffered head injuries as a result, and the aggravating features present during the commission of the offence, namely the chasing and cornering of the victim, the use of a bottle as a weapon and the repeated blows to the head and upper body of the victim with that weapon.

46   As Lord Taylor C.J. pointed out, when giving the judgment of the Court in *Attorney General's Reference No.41 of 1994 (Michael James O'Boyle)* (1995) 16 Cr.App.R.(S.) 792 at 794, the level of sentencing for this sort of s.18 offence is "somewhere between two-and-a-half years' to five years' imprisonment, depending on the individual circumstances". In this case, it is apparent from his sentencing remarks that the recorder considered that s.20 of the 1861 Act more properly reflected the offender's actual criminality with regard to the index offence and he appears to have approached the question of sentence on that basis. Having regard to the circumstances of the offence and the verdict of the jury, we consider that approach to have been wholly inappropriate and wrong. The result was a sentence that was not only unduly lenient but also one that was manifestly so.

47   We have come to the conclusion that the sentence actually passed was so unduly lenient that it would not be a proper exercise of our discretion to take the course urged upon us by Mr Benson. In our judgment, bearing in mind the

offender's age and his previous convictions, the appropriate sentence for this offence of wounding with intent would have been three and a half years' imprisonment. To take account of double jeopardy, we reduce that sentence to one of two and a half years' imprisonment. We therefore discharge the community rehabilitation order made by the recorder and substitute for it a term of two and a half years' imprisonment.

48   We conclude our judgment in this particular reference by observing that, in our view, the recorder also fell into significant error in his treatment of the s.20 offence. We have been made fully aware of the factual circumstances of that particular offence, but do not feel that is necessary to set them out in this judgment. Suffice it to say that we are satisfied that the offence was a further and entirely separate offence of significant violence, the seriousness of which required that it be dealt with by a separate and appropriate sentence. In our view, the way in which the recorder actually dealt with the matter was wrong in principle and, once more, the result was a wholly inappropriate sentence. However, having regard to the conclusion that we have reached with regard to the index offence, we have come to the conclusion that it is not necessary to go on and consider whether it would be either possible or appropriate in this reference for us to interfere with the order made by the recorder in respect of the separate s.20 offence. In our view, it is sufficient that we make abundantly clear our disapproval of the course actually taken by the recorder.

AC

9   We now deal with the case of AC. We describe him by initials to avoid the victim being identified.

0   On March 12, 2004, at Derby Crown Court, AC pleaded guilty to 14 counts of indecent assault. On each of counts 1 to 10 he was sentenced to nine months' imprisonment. On each of counts 11 to 14, which were committed after s.85 of the Powers of Criminal Courts (Sentencing) Act 2000 took effect from September 30, 1998, he was sentenced to concurrent extended sentences of two years and nine months, consisting of a custodial sentence of nine months and an extended licence of two years. All the sentences were concurrent. The judge purported to make it a condition of the extended licence that the offender should participate in a community sex offender group work programme.

The facts

1   The victim of the indecent assaults was the offender's stepdaughter, J. He moved in to live with her mother, Mrs C, and her elder brother in 1995 when she was five years of age. Mrs C suffered from physical and mental health problems including depression. She was dependent on the offender's care and support.

2   The offender and J appeared to get on well, but in 2000 when she was 11 she told her mother that the offender had been touching her in an indecent way. Mrs C confronted the offender who denied any improper conduct. No report was made to the authorities and the family continued to live together.

53   However, in the early summer of 2003 Mrs C discussed the matter with her GP who reported the matter to a social worker who spoke to J, then 14. J alleged that the offender had touched her between her legs between the ages of five and 11. She did not wish to complain to the police. Nevertheless her allegations were reported to the police who put them to the offender at the end of July 2003. He admitted indecently assaulting J. He believed that J was six or seven when the abuse began. It occurred about once a week in a bedroom at home or in his lock-up garage when Mrs C was out. He said that he had touched J's genital area both over and under her pants. He denied any digital penetration. He said that neither he nor J had removed their clothes and he had never required her to touch him.

54   The offender told the police that when J had told her mother he had realised that his actions were wrong and he had wanted to get matters back on an even keel. He said that no indecent conduct had occurred since then, three years ago. He was willing to undertake counselling to help prevent him committing similar offences.

55   J was seen by the police. She did not wish to be interviewed on video or attend court to give evidence. She also indicated, and confirmed in a formal statement dated February 1, 2004, that although she thought the offender deserved to go to prison she did not want him to go to prison because if he did her mother would live with her and her elder brother. If he did not go to prison her mother would live with him. She did not want to live with her mother, as they did not get on.

56   By the time of the court hearing the offender was still largely looking after Mrs C although her 18 year old son was her registered carer because the offender was in work. Since the offender's imprisonment the son has cared for her.

57   The aggravating features of the offences were that the victim was young, the offender was in a position of trust towards her, and the conduct was repeated regularly over a period of about six years.

58   The mitigating features were that the offender made full admissions and pleas were entered at the first opportunity. But for his admissions the Crown would have been unable to prosecute him. The offender, who is 44, was of previous good character. He had shown genuine remorse.

59   The judge was aware of previous decisions of this Court, in particular *Attorney General's References Nos 37, 38, 44, 54, 51, 53, 35, 40, 43, 45, 41 and 42 of 2003* [2004] 1 Cr.App. R.(S) 83 (p.499), at that time only available to him in short form in the *Times Law Report*. That case confirmed that in all sexual offences sentencers should consider the degree of harm to the victim, the level of culpability of the offender, the level of risk posed by the offender to society, and the need to deter others from acting in a similar fashion.

60   The judge told the offender that in the normal course of events the proper sentence would be in the order of three years' imprisonment, bearing in mind the length of time of offending. But in what he saw as the exceptional circumstances of the case he was reducing that sentence to a period of nine months. He said: "I am moved to take that lenient course by your plea of guilty, by the fact that you have by yourself provided the evidence in this case, by the appeal made by the victim . . . that you are not sent to prison, by the desperate condition of your

wife . . . the burden will now fall on her children to . . . assist her, and by the fact which I consider of particular relevance that this course of conduct . . . was over, finished, three years ago and there has been no repetition or reiteration since." The judge then proceeded to deal with the need for an extended period of licence with a condition of participation in a community sex offender work programme after release from prison.

61   By the time of the hearing before us, J, now 15, had made a further statement dated June 18, 2004, saying that she would like the offender to receive a lengthier prison sentence. She thought his abuse had affected her life. It had made her suspicious of meeting men and forming new relationships with men.

62   Mr Holt, for the offender, did not take issue with the extended licence, but he argued that the circumstances of the offender's case were wholly exceptional and that the judge did not fall into error at all. He stressed the features which appealed to the sentencing judge. He submitted that the care provided by Mrs C's 18-year-old son could only be a short, temporary measure, and that the victim's views were neither clear nor consistent.

Our conclusion

63   In our view, as Mr Horwell submitted for the Attorney General, sentencers should exercise caution in attaching weight to particular elements of victim impact statements in this kind of case where the victim was still of immature years and a member of a family of which the offender was still part. In the present case, in our view, the judge attached too much weight to the victim's statement that she did not want the offender to go to prison. Her wishes in that respect were not based on any feeling that he did not deserve imprisonment but on her antipathy to the prospect of having to live with her mother if the victim did go to prison. The judge also attached too much weight to the fact that the offender had not assaulted the victim for some three years before he was prosecuted. He desisted only when the victim showed herself to be old enough to tell her mother, his wife, what had happened, and he must have appreciated the risks he would take if he attempted further indecency. It is the nature and special vice of sexual offences committed within the family that they, and the sentences which follow, bring suffering not only to the victim but to other members of the family, particularly if they are vulnerable as Mrs C was, and although the judge could not ignore the effect of the offender's imprisonment on his wife, it was, in our view, no justification for the judge reducing the proper sentence as he did.

64   We agree with the Attorney General's submissions that the sentence imposed in this case was unduly lenient. He referred to *Millberry* [2003] 2 Cr.App.R.(S.) 31 (p.142) 25 and to the *Attorney General References Nos 91, 119 and 120 of 2002* [2003] 2 Cr.App.R.(S) 55 (p.328). In our view, taking all the mitigating factors into account, the custodial sentence should still have been of the order of three years, bearing in mind particularly the age of the victim, her relationship to the offender and the multiplicity and duration of offending.

65   The extension period of two years further licence was amply justified, but it was accepted in *Attorney General's References Nos 37, 38, 44, 54, 51, 53, 35,*

40, 43, 45, 41 and 42 of 2003, to which we have already referred, that there is no power in the Powers of Criminal Courts (Sentencing) Act 2000 for the judge to impose a condition of participation in a course or programme. The decision as to conditions to be imposed during the licence period is one to be made prior to release on licence and not, therefore, for the Court.

66   We must take account of the double jeopardy caused by the offender facing sentence for a second time. So we quash the sentences imposed by the judge and substitute sentences of two years' imprisonment on counts 1 to 10. On counts 11 to 14 there will be extended sentences of four years consisting of custodial sentences of two years and extension periods of two years during which the offender will be subject to licence. Those sentences will run concurrently.

67   The increase of the custodial sentence to a total of two years will not affect the duration of the notification requirements under the Sex Offenders Act 1997, which will remain 10 years. The increase in sentence does, however, means that the provisions of s.28 of the Criminal Justice and Court Services Act 2000 apply. Unless the offender gives notice within 14 days that he wishes to be heard on the matter, there will be an order that the offender be disqualified from working with children, that is with persons under the age of 18.

Surinder Lehal and Bhupinder Lehal

68   Finally, we turn to the case of Mr and Mrs Lehal. Surinder Lehal is 40 years of age having been born on February 7, 1964. His wife is Bhupinder Lehal. She is 37 years of age, having been born on October 20, 1966. Hereafter, we refer to them as "the first offender" and "the second offender".

69   On March 12, 2004 the first and second offenders pleaded guilty to doing acts tending and intended to pervert the course of public justice. This was at the Maidstone Crown Court before H.H. Judge McKinnon. They were each sentenced to 12 months' imprisonment suspended for two years.

The facts

70   The offences were committed following the stabbing to death of Kamaljit Singh "Bobby" Kalon on July 10, 2003 between 8 and 8.15pm. As a result of the stabbing Kalon died. One of those suspected of being responsible for the death was Jinder Kooner who is the brother of the second offender and the other was Guljinder Singh Grewal, the cousin of the second offender.

71   Kalon had worked in the same factory as the second offender and the two became friends. He married in April 2001 but his friendship with the second offender continued. It was a volatile friendship and the deceased constantly pestered the second offender and used or threatened violence towards her and her property. He was often drunk. Two days before his death Kalon confronted the second offender in the street and bullied her to get into his car. He then assaulted her and refused to let her get out of the car. He threatened to kill her and took her purse away and the chip from her mobile telephone. Eventually, at the request of the second offender he took her to hospital. In the hospital he told the second offender that he loved her and wanted to marry her.

72   The first offender found out that the second offender was at the hospital and he came to collect her with her brother, Jinder. They all then returned to the first and second offender's home at 94 Edwin Street. The following morning when the second offender was alone at 94 Edwin Street Kalon came to the house and banged and kicked the door repeatedly. The second offender was sufficiently disturbed to call the police. Kalon then telephoned her several times and later pushed the purse and telephone chip which he had taken through the letterbox. That evening the first offender returned to his home with Guljinder. He was told that Kalon had caused injuries to the second offender. Guljinder then telephoned Kalon's wife and said he was going to kill Kalon.

73   On July 10, 2003 Kalon telephoned the second offender three times. She told the police that Kalon said he was coming to get her and that nobody could save her. After the final telephone call the second offender telephoned Guljinder twice and he in turn telephoned the first offender.

74   The first offender came home from work at about 8pm and Kalon was stabbed between 8pm and 8.15pm that same evening. Kalon had armed himself with a knife but was disarmed and was stabbed to death by Guljinder while Jinder held him down. Later Guljinder and Jinder ran into the basement of 94 Edwin Street which was unlocked. The second offender was leaning out of the window when they arrived. They were covered in blood and sweating. They changed into clean clothes which they took from the washing line and asked the second offender to call a taxi. She refused. The first offender told them to leave and they did so at between 8.30pm and 9.30pm in a car belonging to a close friend of the offender. They subsequently travelled through the Blackwall Tunnel and round the North Circular Road. The police arrived at the scene and hearing that two blood-stained men had run into the basement of 94 Edwin Street they called at the house but found no relevant clothing or blood. The offenders denied they had seen the man.

75   It was the prosecution's case that if the offenders had told the truth at the outset it would have been possible to apprehend the suspects before they crossed the river at the Blackwall Tunnel. In the case of the first offender, on July 10 and 11, 2003, and in the case of the second offender on July 24, 2003, the offenders continued to deny or omitted to mention the presence of the two men.

76   The first offender was arrested on suspicion of murder and the second offender was arrested on suspicion of conspiracy to murder on August 6, 2003. It was then that the second offender admitted that the two men had run into her house blood-stained and sweating and told her they had had a fight with Kalon. She gave the police the names of the men. The first offender was also interviewed on August 6. It was suggested to him, by the police, that he was in fact one of the men who had run into the basement of 94 Edwin Street. Initially, he persisted in his denial, but when the second offender's account was put to him he admitted that he had seen them and had told them to get out.

7   Both offenders were remanded in custody. The first offender was charged with murder based on identification evidence that proved to be unreliable and on December 10, 2003 no evidence was offered against him. He was, however, granted conditional bail on December 15, 2003 after he had been charged with

perverting the course of justice. After the second offender was charged with conspiracy to murder she was remanded in custody from August 6, 2003 until the charge was withdrawn on September 19, 2003. She was then released from custody but immediately re-arrested and charged with perverting the course of justice. She was released on bail on December 24, 2003.

78   The prosecution accepted that the defendants did not know what happened to Kalon that night and did not know, when the suspects ran into the basement, that Kalon had been murdered. They knew, however, that a violent incident had taken place. This was obvious from the bloody condition of the two men.

79   The Attorney General contended that the offences were aggravated because the denials were maintained until August 6, 2003. In addition, there was the fact that the offenders' conduct may have assisted the murder suspects to evade justice. There were a number of mitigating features referred to by the Attorney General. There was their plea of guilty at the plea and directions hearing; their good character in the case of the second offender and the fact that the first offender was treated as having a good character and the fact that they had each spent approximately four months in custody charged with serious offences which were later withdrawn. There was also the fact that the second offender had spent four and a half months in custody from August 6, 2003 to December 24, 2003 (of which six weeks was in relation to the offence which was later withdrawn). The time that both offenders spent in custody, on charges which were withdrawn, would not fall to be subtracted from any term of imprisonment imposed in relation to the instant offence.

80   The offenders were separated from their children and family and community by the remand in custody and thereafter by the restrictive bail conditions. It was also treated as a mitigating fact by the Attorney General that the offenders were motivated by a desire to distance themselves from a violent offence rather than by a wish to assist the suspects escape.

81   The Attorney General submits that there are no exceptional circumstances that justify the suspension of the sentence.

82   It is submitted by Mr Horwell, on behalf of the Attorney General, that the fact that the sentences were suspended in itself makes them unduly lenient. He also submitted to us that in any event the sentences were unduly lenient.

83   Miss Byrnes, on behalf of the first offender, and Mr O'Higgins, on behalf of the second offender, both contend that there were exceptional circumstances which justified the sentence being suspended. No submissions to the contrary were made on behalf of the prosecution before the judge.

84   In his sentencing remarks the judge indicated he regarded the case as difficult a sentencing exercise as any judge could face. He referred to the cases that he had considered, some of which were the same cases as are now relied upon by the Attorney General. He said that the offenders had no time to think and they made the wrong decision, not with the intention of thwarting the police enquiries, but with a view to them being distanced from the offence. He then concluded that the right sentence in each case was 12 months' imprisonment and that there were exceptional circumstances that allowed him to suspend the sentence. He stressed

that a judge must be ready to be merciful when justice requires this and he considered that this case required mercy.

85   He referred to the problem created by the fact that the offenders had been in custody for the offences which were no longer being pursued and in relation to which the offenders would not obtain credit. He then passed the sentence which he clearly regarded as appropriate.

Our conclusion

86   Having considered the authorities on which the Attorney relies, we do not consider that 12 months' imprisonment, if it had been an immediate sentence, would have been an unduly lenient sentence or one which could be regarded as inappropriate from the public's point of view. As Stanley Burnton J. said in *Paul Michael Rayworth* [2004] 1 Cr.App.R.(S.) 75 (p.440) in relation to a sentence in a case involving perverting the course of justice, "cases such as the present must depend on their own facts". If the sentence would not have been unduly lenient or one which should have affronted the public, does the fact that the sentence was suspended alter the position? We do not think it does, at least, if it was lawful to suspend the sentence. It is still a sentence involving two years imprisonment and the sentence, if activated, will be activated in full unless it is unjust to do so (s.119(2) of the Powers of Criminal Court (Sentencing) Act 2000).

87   This is, however, not the end of the story because the Attorney General contends that the sentence was inappropriate in this case because a court is prohibited from dealing with an offender by means of a suspended sentence, "unless it is of the opinion . . . that the exercise of that part can be justified by the exceptional circumstances of the case" (s.118(4)(b) of the Powers of Criminal Courts (Sentencing) Act 2000).

88   The purpose of this prohibition is to deter courts from passing a suspended sentence of imprisonment in circumstances where, if the sentence were not suspended, the court would not have passed a sentence of imprisonment. This purpose colours what is meant by exceptional circumstances. We agree with the statement of Lord Taylor of Gosforth C.J. in *Okinikan* [1993] 1 W.L.R. 173 where he says: "Parliament has given statutory force to the principle that a suspended sentence should not be regarded as a soft option, but should only be imposed in exceptional circumstances. This court cannot lay down a definition of "exceptional circumstances". They will inevitably depend on the facts of each individual case. However, taken on their own, or in combination, good character, youth and an early plea are not exceptional circumstances justifying a suspended sentence. They are common features of many cases. They may amount to mitigation sufficient to persuade the court that a custodial sentence should not be passed or to reduce its length. The statutory language is clear and unequivocal. In the present case exceptional circumstances were not shown."

9   The position is similar to that in relation to mandatory and minimum custodial sentences reconsidered in *Offen* [2001] 1 W.L.R. 253. Approaching the issue of what can be exceptional circumstances, taking into account the purpose of the

section, the conclusion that we have come to, is that the judge was entitled to form the opinion that exceptional circumstances existed here. The exceptional circumstances would be the fact that the offenders have already spent time in custody in relation to even more serious offences for which they would not be entitled to credit if the sentence were either not suspended or suspended and activated.

90   The points with which we have dealt with so far are technical. Reviewing the sentence, ignoring the technicalities, we have come to the conclusion that the sentence which was imposed on each of the offenders can be justified as being within the limits of his discretion. Accordingly, in these cases we also make no order.

91   Regard has also to be paid to the judgment of Tomlinson J. in *Sara Jane Smith* [2002] 1 Cr.App.R.(S.) 61 (p.258).

R. v RAMOSA LTD

COURT OF APPEAL (Lord Justice Maurice Kay, Mr Justice Simon and Judge Goldsack): July 16, 2004

[2004] EWCA Crim 2170; [2005] 1 Cr.App.R.(S.) 77

LT Common fisheries policy; Deterrence; False records; Fines; Fisheries offences; Strict liability

H1   *Fisheries offences—underdeclaration of catches—amount of fines*

H2   Fines totalling £500,000 for underdeclaring fish catches reduced to £250,000.
H3   The appellant company pleaded guilty to 11 counts of failing to comply with European Union provisions relating to fisheries. The offences concerned failure to record quantities of fish taken and the operation of log books. Sentenced to fines totalling £500,000 and ordered to pay £17,819 towards the costs of the prosecution.

H4   **Held:** (considering *Anglo-Spanish Fisheries Ltd* [2001] 1 Cr.App.R.(S.) 73 (p.252)) the Court would proceed on the basis that it was agreed by the appellant company that the 11 counts to which pleas had been entered were representative of a longer and more detailed course of conduct over a period of 16 months. In the Court's judgment, it was clear that it was understood and accepted by the prosecution, defence and the judge that the 11 counts were the minimum acceptable to the prosecution and that they were admitted by the company to be representative of the strict liability offences spanning a longer period. The Court considered that in circumstances where there was any scope for misunderstanding, it would be preferable if such pleas were expressed in writing and explained as such. It was submitted that the sentencing judge erred by sentencing on the basis that the company knew of the offences and had a commercial motive for committing them. That submission was rejected by the sentencing judge. The Court did not accept the submission that the fact that the company had not pleaded guilty to offences charged to have been committed "knowingly or recklessly" prevented the judge from sentencing for the strict liability offences on the basis that there were aggravating features of knowledge and a commercial motive. The third submission for the appellant company was that the company disputed knowledge and could not be sentenced on that basis unless there was a trial of an issue which was resolved against it. The difficulty was that the sentencing judge was assured by counsel for the appellant company that a *Newton* hearing would not be necessary. It was further submitted that in fixing the amount of the fines, the judge considered that they must bear some relation to the value of the underdeclaration. The Court rejected the submission that the offences were technical and regulatory. Although they arose in the context of regulations, they were serious offences. The regulations were a vital part of the structure by which the member states of the European Union endeavoured to control the activities of the fishing industry. Breaches, particularly persistent breaches, called for fines which were real deterrents. The Court had been referred to *Anglo-Spanish Fisheries Ltd* [2001] 1 Cr.App.R.(S.) 73 (p.252). The Court agreed with the general approach taken by the Court in that case and would apply it to the different facts of person case. This was a more prolonged course of conduct pursued with a commercial motive. The question was whether the fines were manifestly excessive. Notwithstanding the persistence of the offence, the Court had concluded that they were. The fines would be reduced in total to £250,000.

5   Case cited:
Anglo-Spanish Fisheries Ltd [2001] 1 Cr.App.R.(S.) 73 (p.252)

6   References: *Current Sentencing Practice*, B13–8

**7   *M. Ryder* for the appellant company.
G. Walters for the Crown.

JUDGMENT

1   **Maurice Kay L.J.:**   On February 10, 2003, in the Crown Court at Swansea, Ramosa Limited, the appellant company, pleaded guilty to 11 counts concerning failure to comply with European Union provisions relating to fisheries. In essence, the offences concerned failing to record quantities of fish and the alteration of log books. Those 11 counts formed part of an indictment which extended to 101 counts. 45 of the remaining counts lay against Ramosa. No pleas were taken on them. The further remaining counts lay against the masters of the vessels in question. They were not before the courts on February 10, 2003. We understand them to have been at large at the time. They have been dealt with subsequently.

2   On April 3, 2003 Ramosa was sentenced for its offences by the imposition of fines totalling £500,000 and ordered to pay £17,819 towards the costs of the prosecution. It now appeals against sentence by leave of the single judge.

3   The first ground of appeal is somewhat technical. The judge clearly sentenced on the basis of a course of conduct which included, but was not limited to, the occasions referred to in the 11 counts to which Ramosa had entered guilty pleas. Relying on *Canavan and Kidd* [1998] 1 Cr.App.R.(S.) 243, Mr Ryder submits that the judge was wrong to go beyond the parameters of those eleven counts: a defendant is only to be sentenced for what has been proved against him by the verdict of a jury, a plea of guilty, a request to take further offences into consideration, or an unequivocal acceptance that the offences of which he has been found guilty, or to which he has pleaded guilty, are representative of a wider course of conduct which is suitably particularised, preferably in writing.

4   Mr Ryder did not appear for Ramosa in the Crown Court at Swansea. The company was then represented by experienced local counsel. We have read Mr Walters's account of how the pleas were negotiated, but we do not need to rely upon it. The position is clear from the transcripts.

5   When the matter was before the court on February 10, 2003, the presiding judge was H.H. Judge Gerald Price Q.C. The transcript discloses how counsel instructed on behalf of Ramosa had been able to have a conference that day with a director of Ramosa so as to discuss the question of pleas. Although the director and everyone concerned with Ramosa is Spanish, the director's English was said to be perfect. Counsel said this:

> ". . . I was always empowered on behalf of the company to enter pleas on their behalf and I can do that today. I can indicate . . . that in relation to the indictment the company pleads guilty to the following charges: counts 3, 8, 55, 60 and 64, 66 and 73, 86 and 91, and lastly 95 and 100 — 11 charges in effect . . . it is quite clear as between my learned friend and myself that these charges represent in effect a course of conduct over that time by various different masters — in effect the three who have not appeared today. And on a strict liability the company has no defence, and therefore we enter the pleas on that basis."

6   The reference to "strict liability" arises in this way. The charges in the indictment as a whole referred to two different offences, one of which has been referred to before us as the strict liability offence; the other is a similar offence but which has the alternative *mens rea* of knowingly or recklessly. The maximum punishment under the regulations is the same in both cases, namely an unlimited fine upon conviction on indictment. What defence counsel had said then led to Mr Walters, on behalf of the prosecution, saying this to the judge:

> "What DEFRA needed was in fact pleas to certain counts, and an agreement as to what they represent in the overall and wider picture. We have reached that now, and the number of pleas entered are satisfactory, and the basis . . . likewise satisfactory."

7   The matter was not disposed of that day. Arrangements were made for a further hearing, and that is what occurred on April 3, 2003 before H.H. Judge Morton, who has considerable experience of dealing with cases of this kind in West Wales.

8   It is again instructive to refer to the transcript. Mr Walters told the judge about the guilty pleas to 11 offences having been entered, saying that they were "representative of a course of conduct that spanned the period January 2000 through until April 2001, a period of some 15 months . . . the company accepted that the offences were representative of a course of conduct spanning the period I have identified". A little later he said:

> "So in effect on the indictment there were five trips that attracted guilty pleas, as representative examples of the course of conduct alleged to have spanned the period of 15 months, involving, as I say, both vessels operated by Ramosa and involving each of the three masters being responsible in effect for the same kind of scam when it came to alterations."

When defence counsel rose to his feet, he said:

> ". . . although this is a course of conduct over 15 months, this company — and I am obviously speaking from the company point of view — . . . there had been no prior warning as such, and one of the concerns the company does have is that had it been alerted to the mismanagement and alterations, they could have stepped in and done something at a much earlier stage."

9   It seems to us that what was plainly being put before the judge, without contradiction or inconsistency, was an agreement that the 11 counts to which guilty pleas had been entered were representative of a longer and more detailed course of conduct. When the learned judge came to pass sentence, he said this:

> "I have to sentence the company . . . in respect of 11 counts arising out of five shipping trips spread over a 16-month period from January 2000 to April 2001 inclusive . . . It pleaded guilty to the offences on the basis that it accepted that the counts and the five trips represented a whole course of conduct over the 16-month period, a course of conduct which included almost identical offending on a number of other occasions."

There was no dissent from counsel then representing the company then or at any later stage that has manifested itself to this Court.

10   In our judgment, it is abundantly clear that it was understood and accepted by the prosecution, the defence and the judge that the 11 counts were the minimum acceptable to the prosecution as regards the number of pleas and the reference to the two vessels and the three masters, but that those 11 counts were accepted and admitted by the company to be representative of the other strict liability offences spanning the entire period of the indictment. We therefore reject this ground of appeal.

11   We do take the view that, in circumstances where there is any scope for misunderstanding, it would be preferable if representative pleas were expressed in writing and explained as such. In the present case, however, we do not find any room for misunderstanding and are content that all knew and accepted the basis on which the pleas were entered and in respect of which the fines were imposed.

12   Mr Ryder next submits that the judge erred by sentencing on the basis that Ramosa knew of the offences and had a commercial motive for committing them. Counsel had sought to urge on the judge that Ramosa had no such knowledge or motive and that the offences were therefore the brainchildren and execution of the masters. The judge rejected that submission. He observed that he had heard no evidence from any director of Ramosa and added:

> "I infer knowledge (at the very least) of offences continuing, and I infer that on the criminal standard of proof from these matters: the duration of the offending, and the fact that no less than three masters offended in precisely the same way. The log books were seized in April 2000. On 13th October 2000 the Department wrote to the company saying they were investigating irregularities, and making it quite clear that the present prosecution was contemplated; and on 7th November 2000 a director of the company was interviewed under caution. The offending continued to April 2001. It follows that these were not technical breaches, nor were they ones of which the company was ignorant.
> The only possible motive is commercial."

13   It is suggested that these were impermissible findings when Ramosa had pleaded to the strict liability offences and not to the "knowingly or recklessly" offences.

14   We do not accept this submission. We can understand why Ramosa was anxious to avoid convictions for offences with a *mens rea*. However, that does not necessarily inhibit the judge from sentencing for the strict liability offences on the basis that there were aggravating features of knowledge and a commercial motive.

15   Mr Ryder's third submission is that Ramosa disputed knowledge and a commercial motive and was entitled to be sentenced on the basis of what it accepted, unless there was a trial of an issue which was resolved against it.

16   The difficulty with this submission is that the transcript discloses that the judge was alert to the possible need for a *Newton* hearing, but was assured by Ramosa's counsel that that would not be necessary. We can well understand why Ramosa was unenthusiastic about such a hearing. We find nothing in this ground of appeal.

17   Mr Ryder begins to enter stronger ground with his fourth submission. It is clear that, in fixing the amount of the fines, the judge considered that "they must bear some relation to the value in money of the underdeclaration"; in other words, the value of the underdeclared fish. He based that observation on something that had been said in the appeal of *Anglo-Spanish Fisheries Ltd* [2001] 1 Cr.App.R.(S.) 73 (p.252), which had been an earlier appeal from fines imposed by the same judge. The appeal in that case was dismissed.

18   Although this was in dispute at the time of the hearing and remained so until very recently, Ramosa's case is that it could have purchased sufficient additional quota entitlements on the open market for about £50,000, and its gain from the offences was therefore no more than that figure. Although the prosecution previously disputed that there is such a lawful market, it now accepts that one

exists and does not dispute the availability or the price asserted by Ramosa. We regard this as a potentially material consideration, but we do not accept that the judge was bound to link the fines to the cost of purchasing additional quota entitlements on the open market.

19   This brings us to the crux of this case. We reject Mr Ryder's submission that these were merely technical or regulatory offences. Although they arise in the context of regulations, they are serious offences. The regulations are a vital part of the structure through which the member states of the European Union endeavour to control the activities of the fishing industry. In the *Anglo-Spanish* case Wright J., giving the judgment of this Court, referred to:

> ". . . the paramount necessity to protect and maintain the fish stocks in the waters of the European Community and the need to deal fairly with and to give the best chance of survival to the fishing industries of the various member states".

That is why breaches, particularly persistent breaches, call for fines which are "very real deterrents". We agree. This is the reason why we reject the simplistic suggestion that the fines should reflect the deemed cost of buying additional quota entitlements on the open market.

20   In the *Anglo-Spanish* case the Court dismissed appeals against fines totalling £115,000, and in particular a fine of £80,000 on one count, expressing the view that the sentencing judge would have been justified in imposing substantially larger fines in relation to the other counts, for most of which the fine was £10,000 per count. The total value of the underdeclared fish in that case was £12,400. In the present case it is said to be approaching half a million pounds. The count in the *Anglo-Spanish* case which attracted the £80,000 fine was charged as a strict liability offence, but had the aggravating feature of deliberate concealment by physical adaptation. Also, the appellant company there had been convicted on four previous occasions.

21   We agree with the general approach taken by this Court in the *Anglo-Spanish* case. Our task is to apply it to the different facts of the present case. This appellant had no previous convictions and there is no suggestion of physical adaptation. On the other hand, this was a more prolonged course of conduct. As in the *Anglo-Spanish* case, it was pursued with a commercial motive. Whilst we take notice of the availability of additional quota on the open market, there are severe limits to that mitigation. If everyone intended to resort to supplementing their quotas in that way, the open market would not be able to satisfy the demand. In our view, the point is, to a considerable extent, a hypothetical excuse. It does not overcome the reality that these are serious offences in an important regulatory context which call for deterrent sentences. Ramosa was entitled to credit for its guilty pleas and lack of previous convictions, but for nothing else. The judge proceeded on that basis.

22   It has not been suggested to us that the company is unable to pay the fines as imposed by the judge. The question now is whether those fines were manifestly excessive. Notwithstanding the seriousness of the offences and the duration of the course of conduct, we have concluded that they were. In reaching this con-

clusion we have not forgotten that the persistence of the offending was aggravated by the fact that it continued even after the initial intervention of the
enforcement authorities in April 2000. Nevertheless, we shall allow the appeal,
quash the fines of £50,000 and substitute fines of £25,000. The lesser fines of
£40,000 and £20,000 will be replaced with fines of £20,000 and £10,000. This
will produce a total financial penalty in terms of fines of £250,000. To that extent
the appeal is allowed.

[Paragraphs [23]–[43] have been omitted.]

ATTORNEY GENERAL'S REFERENCE NOS 54, 55 AND 56 OF 2004 (S, W, G)

COURT OF APPEAL (Lord Justice Rose (Vice President, Court of
Appeal Criminal Division), Mr Justice Nelson and Mr Justice
McCombe): July 20, 2004

[2004] EWCA Crim 2062; [2005] 1 Cr.App.R.(S.) 78

LT Community punishment and rehabilitation orders; Detention and training
orders; Greivous bodily harm; Undue leniency; Young offenders

H1   *Young offenders—causing grievous bodily harm with intent—attack by boys aged
15 and 16 on boy aged 14, involving kicking, threats to kill, and throwing boy into
canal—whether community order unduly lenient*

H2   Community orders imposed on three youths aged 15 and 16 at the time of the
offence for causing grievous bodily harm with intent by attacking a boy aged 14
who was kicked, threatened with death and thrown into a canal varied to detention and training orders.

H3   The offenders, aged 15 and 16 respectively at the time of the offence, pleaded
guilty to causing grievous bodily harm with intent. The offenders approached a
14-year-old boy late one evening. One of the offenders took the boy's bicycle and
rode it away, while the other two walked alongside him. When the boy tried to
retrieve his bicycle, one of the offenders rammed the bicycle into the boy's
leg, causing him to fall back against a wall. All of the offenders then began punching and kicking him about the body and head. They threatened to kill the boy, and
dragged him to some spiked railings and threatened to force his head on to the
spikes. They then dragged him to a canal and threw him into the canal. The
boy was able to swim to the other side of the canal. It was later found that his
elbow was broken in three places and that he had bruises and abrasions to his
face, the back of his head and other parts of the body. Sentenced in the case of
the first and third offenders to a community punishment and rehabilitation
order, and in the case of the second offender to a community rehabilitation

order. The Attorney General asked the Court to review the sentences on the ground that they were unduly lenient.

H4   **Held:** (considering *Attorney General's Reference No.59 of 1996 (Terence Grainger)* [1997] 2 Cr.App.R.(S.) 250, *Attorney General's References Nos 30 and 31 of 1998 (Keith John Copping and Gary Justin Collins)* [1999] 1 Cr.App.R.(S.) 200, *Attorney General's Reference No.121 of 2002* [2003] EWCA Crim 684, *Attorney General's References Nos 59, 60 and 63 of 1998 (Goodwin)* [1999] 2 Cr.App.R.(S.) 128) for the Attorney General it was submitted that a community order wholly failed to reflect the gravity of the offence, and that a custodial penalty was required. In the Court's view, this was a terrible offence in its persistence, in the variety of violence, in the numbers involved, and in its culmination in the victim being cast into the canal. The victim suffered serious physical and mental injuries. Notwithstanding the pleas of guilty and the youth of the offenders, the Court would have expected a sentence in the court below of three years' detention under the Powers of Criminal Courts (Sentencing) Act 2000, s.91. Having regard to the element of double jeopardy, the Court would substitute detention and training orders of two years in the case of two offenders; an order for 12 months would be substituted in the case of one offender on account of time spent in custody prior to sentence which would not count towards the detention and training order.

H5   **Cases cited:**
Attorney General's Reference No.59 of 1996 (Terence Grainger) [1997] 2 Cr.App.R.(S.) 250, *Attorney General's References Nos 30 and 31 of 1998 (Keith John Copping and Gary Justin Collins)* [1999] 1 Cr.App.R.(S.) 200, *Attorney General's Reference No.121 of 2002* [2003] EWCA Crim 684, *Attorney General's Reference Nos 59, 60 and 63 of 1998 (Goodwin)* [1999] 2 Cr.App.R.(S.) 128

H6   **References:** long term detention, *Current Sentencing Practice* E4

H7   *Miss S. Whitehouse* for the Attorney General.
Miss J. Hayne for the offender Stechman.
Miss C. Hadfield for the offender Walton.
Miss K. Bex for the offender Griffin.

JUDGMENT

1   **Rose L.J.:**   The Attorney General seeks the leave of the Court under s.36 of the Criminal Justice Act 1988 to refer sentences on these three offenders to this Court on the ground that they were unduly lenient. We grant leave.

2   The offender Stechman is 16, having been born in January 1988. The offender Griffin is 17, having been born in October 1986, and the offender Walton is 16, having been born in March 1988.

3   On November 7, 2003, Griffin pleaded guilty to causing grievous bodily harm with intent, contrary to s.18 of the Offences against the Person Act 1861. On

February 23, 2004, the two other offenders, Walton and Stechman, pleaded guilty to the same offence. On April 16, 2004, they were sentenced at Inner London Crown Court by Mr Recorder Conlin. Stechman and Griffin were sentenced to a community punishment and rehabilitation order consisting of 100 hours' community punishment and 24 months' rehabilitation, and both were also subjected to an electronically monitored curfew for six months from 8.00pm to 8.00am. In relation to Walton, a community rehabilitation order for two years was made, together with a similar curfew order.

4   In summary, the three offenders approached the 14-year-old male victim at about 11 o'clock on the evening of August 22, 2003. They took his bicycle, pushed it into his leg, kicked and punched him about the face and body, threatened to kill him, broke his arm and threw him into a nearby canal.

5   In a little more detail, the victim was sitting on a kerb in Dame Street, London N1 on this summer evening. His bicycle was propped behind him. The three offenders approached. The victim recognised the offender, Stechman. Walton took the bicycle and rode it away. Stechman and Griffin walked alongside Walton, laughing and joking. The victim followed, trying to retrieve his bicycle. Walton rammed the bicycle into the boy's right leg, causing him to fall back against a wall. All three offenders then began punching and kicking him about the head and body. The boy pleaded with them to stop. They continued, saying he had better not tell the police or he would get more.

6   Stechman suggested they kill the victim by "popping" his head on the spikes of some railings nearby. The kicking and punching continued. The boy tried to protect his face with his arm, but Walton pulled his right arm away and said he was going to break it. Thereupon the boy's face became unprotected and Stechman and Griffin punched him repeatedly in the face. All three said they were going to kill him.

7   They dragged him to the spiked railings and the earlier threat was repeated. Walton suggested that, instead, they should throw him into the canal. That was agreed. They dragged him, still beating him, to the canal. They took off his jacket. They swung him backwards and forwards twice, before throwing him into the canal. He surfaced about halfway across and was able to swim to the other side. As he did so, he heard the offenders say, "Let's throw some rocks at him". They did not in fact throw rocks.

8   Later, at hospital, it was found that his left elbow was broken in three places. He had bruising around his left eye and right cheek, and abrasions to his forehead, the back of his head, his left arm and knees.

9   On behalf of the Attorney General, Miss Whitehouse draws attention to the following aggravating features: first, the attack was unprovoked; secondly, it was carried out by three against one; thirdly, the victim was only 14; fourthly, he was kicked with shod feet as he lay on the floor; finally, he was thrown into a canal, with his arm by that stage broken whether the offenders knew it or not, so that he had to swim to survive.

10   Miss Whitehouse draws attention to the mitigation to be found in the fact that Stechman and Walton were only 15 and Griffin only 16 at the time. Griffin pleaded guilty at the earliest opportunity and had no previous convictions of rel-

evance. It is right to say that none of these offenders has any previous conviction for violence. Walton has a poor record for dishonesty.

11   Miss Whitehouse drew attention to a number of authorities, including *Attorney General's Reference No.59 of 1996* [1997] 2 Cr.App.R.(S.) 250, *Attorney General's Reference Nos 30 and 31 of 1998* [1999] 1 Cr.App.R.(S.) 200 and *Attorney General's Reference No.121 of 2002* [2003] EWCA Crim 684. In *Attorney General's Reference Nos 59, 60 and 63 of 1998* [1999] 2 Cr.App.R.(S.) 128 at 131, Lord Bingham C.J., giving the judgment of the Court, said this:

> "When an offender, however young, deliberately inflicts serious injury on another there is a legitimate public expectation that such offender will be severely punished to bring home to him the gravity of the offence and to warn others of the risk of behaving in the same way. If such punishment does not follow, public confidence in the administration of the criminal law is weakened and the temptation arises to give offenders extra-judicially the punishment that the formal processes of law have not given. When we speak of the public we do not forget the victim, the party who has actually suffered the injury, and those close to him. If punishment of the offender does little to heal the victim's wounds, there can be little doubt that inadequate punishment adds insult to injury."

12   The submission which is made by Miss Whitehouse in the light of those authorities and the circumstances of this case is that a community punishment wholly failed to reflect the gravity of the offence and a custodial penalty was required. In consequence, she submits, the sentences passed by the learned recorder were unduly lenient.

13   On behalf of Stechman, Miss Hayne concedes that the sentence was lenient and that the authorities show that custody is ordinarily appropriate. But, she submits, there are, in the present case, personal circumstances of mitigation so far as Stechman is concerned which justify a non-custodial penalty. She points out, as we have already said, that he was only 15 and he has no previous convictions. This offence was entirely out of character. He had been drinking heavily, not looking for violence. He accepts that what he did was appalling and despicable. But, she submits, he has shown genuine remorse and has made progress in the months which have passed since he was sentenced in April. He has not breached his order. He has, it is true, difficulty in talking about the offence, but he is only 16, even now.

4   There are indications in one of the pre-sentence reports upon him that he is experiencing difficulty in expressing sympathy with the victim. Miss Hayne points out that the nature of the area where he lives is such that he is being taunted by some for his part in this attack and taunted by others for having pleaded guilty to the offence. Sadly, as Miss Hayne points out, his grandfather died soon after the offence was committed, but before Stechman was sentenced. She submits that he has taken such opportunity as was presented by the recorder's sentence to show signs of improvement for the future, and she asserts he will not be before the courts again. He spent a week in custody before he was sentenced by the recorder.

15   Miss Hadfield, on behalf of Walton, accepts that the sentence was an unusually lenient one, but he spent some seven months in custody before he was sentenced, and during that period, had to endure the death of a baby born prematurely to his girlfriend of which he was the father.

16   Miss Hadfield's second submission is that, even if the sentence was unduly lenient, the Court should not exercise its discretion to interfere with it. She stresses the plea of guilty, the absence of premeditation and the lack of any sign of violence in the offender, Walton's, previous record. She said that it was not obvious why in Walton's case the recorder had imposed a different sentence to that imposed on the other two offenders. But it may be that he had in mind the fact that Walton had already spent seven months in custody.

17   Miss Hadfield drew attention to the contents of the reports upon Walton, indicating that he has taken responsibility for doing that which he did, and has written a letter of apology and expressed his remorse. He has an unhappy youthful background, having been in and out of care, in particular during the currency of previous supervision orders.

18   He has apparently been in breach of the curfew order which the recorder imposed, and that is due to be dealt with later this week. That came about because he left his mother's address and he is now apparently living in sheltered accommodation. It is apparent that the evidence which his mother gave before the recorder, indicating an apparent increase in maturity following the death of his baby, had a significant influence upon the recorder.

19   Miss Hadfield submits that, in view of Walton's age, the balance in his case tips in favour of rehabilitation rather than punishment. He has responded to the order which was made and has engaged fully, apart from the breach of curfew to which we have referred.

20   Miss Hadfield refers to double jeopardy, that is the second sentencing process, which is involved in all Attorney General's References, and she submits that the offender, Walton, is being rehabilitated by the sentence which the recorder passed.

21   On behalf of Griffin, Miss Bex stresses that he displayed courage in that he was the first to plead guilty: by reason of that, he is entitled to maximum credit. He has been on bail throughout and for a short period worked. Indeed his then employer gave evidence before the recorder as to how well he was doing after some two weeks, and the recorder was clearly impressed by that. The present position is that the offender is not living with his mother. He has been sleeping at her garden gate and breach proceedings in relation to the curfew are to be considered by the youth court next week. She accepts that he has, as is apparent from the reports, failed to comply with the punishment part of the order, and he has, according to the report, been verbally abusive to staff. She submits that his present position, as we have briefly described it, is cruel so far as he is concerned.

22   There are clearly particular circumstances of mitigation affecting each of these three offenders in different ways: in relation to Stechman, the sad death of his grandfather; in relation to Walton, the sad death of his baby; in relation to Griffin, his early plea of guilty. Looking at the picture in the round, we are satisfied that no distinction should be drawn in the way in which the three offenders are dealt with.

23   This was a terrible offence—in its persistence, in the variety of violence, in the numbers involved, and in its culmination in the victim being cast into the canal. The physical injuries were serious and included the multiple fractures of the elbow, to which we have referred. There were mental injuries as well. The victim has required psychological treatment. That being so, notwithstanding the pleas of guilty and the youth of all these three offenders, we would have expected a sentence in the court below in relation to each of them of three years' detention under the Powers of Criminal Courts (Sentencing) Act 2000, s.91. That is not a sentence which this Court should now impose, having regard both to double jeopardy and the fact that, if they are incarcerated now, having previously been at liberty since they were sentenced, a further discount is called for from the sentence which would be appropriate. Taking those matters into account, subject to one matter in relation to Walton, which we will deal with, the sentence which would here be appropriate in relation to all three offenders is a detention and training order of two years.

24   So far as Walton is concerned, because, as we have said, he has spent seven months in custody prior to sentence which period would not count towards his sentence, the sentence which we impose on him is a detention and training order of 12 months. In relation to Stechman and Griffin, the sentence is a 24-month detention and training order. Those sentences will start to run when the offenders respectively surrender to custody.

[Paragraphs [25]–[28] have been omitted.]

ATTORNEY GENERAL'S REFERENCE NO.3 OF 2003 (HASNAIN MOHAMMED SUCHEDINA)

COURT OF APPEAL (Lord Justice Latham, Mr Justice Astill and Mr Justice Gray): July 21, 2004

[2004] EWCA Crim 1944; [2005] 1 Cr.App.R.(S.) 79

⟨LT⟩ Confiscation orders; Conspiracy; Drug trafficking; Jurisdiction; Money laundering; Proceeds of crime

1   *Conspiracy to commit money laundering offences—count charging conspiracy to launder proceeds of drug trafficking and other offences—whether conspiracy a "drug trafficking offence" for the purposes of the Drug Trafficking Act 1994*

2   An offender convicted of conspiring to launder the proceeds of drug trafficking and other offences has been convicted of a drug trafficking offence within the meaning of the Drug Trafficking Act 1994, s.1.

3   The offender was convicted of conspiring to convert or transfer the proceeds of drug trafficking or other criminal conduct, contrary to the Criminal Law Act 1977, s.1. An investigation was carried out into suspected money laundering at a bureau de change of which the offender was the director and chief executive.

The evidence suggested that a total of £7 million was laundered through the bureau in a period of about six months. The offender was tried on an indictment containing three counts. Count 1 charged conspiracy to convert or transfer of the proceeds of drug trafficking, count 2 charged conspiracy to convert or transfer of the proceeds of criminal conduct, and count 3 alleged conspiracy to convert or transfer the proceeds of drug trafficking or of criminal conduct. The offender was acquitted on counts 1 and 2 and was convicted on count 3. Sentenced to five years' imprisonment. The sentencing judge subsequently concluded that he had no jurisdiction to make a confiscation order in the offender's case, on the ground that the offence of which the offender had been convicted was neither a "drug trafficking offence" within the meaning of the Drug Trafficking Act 1994, s.1, nor an "offence of a relevant description" within the meaning of the Criminal Justice Act 1988. The Attorney General asked the Court to review the sentence on the ground that the judge had erred in law as to his powers of sentence.

H4   **Held:** the particulars of the offence charged in count 3 were that the offender conspired with others to convert, transfer or remove from the jurisdiction bank notes, knowing or having reasonable grounds for suspecting that they represented another person's proceeds either of drug trafficking or of an offence to which Pt VI of the Criminal Justice Act 1988 applied. The prosecution sought a confiscation order under the Drug Trafficking Act 1994, on the ground that the offence of which the offender had been convicted was a drug trafficking offence within s.1(3) of the Drug Trafficking Act 1994. Section 1(3) provided that an offence under the Criminal Law Act 1977, s.1, of conspiring to commit any of the offences listed in the Drug Trafficking Act as drug trafficking offences was itself a drug trafficking offence. The sentencing judge concluded that this definition did not include the offence of which the offender was convicted as it was charged as a conspiracy to commit an offence under either s.49 of the Drug Trafficking Act, or s.93 of the Criminal Justice Act 1988. The alternative formulation did not in the judge's judgment entitle him to conclude that the conspiracy was a relevant conspiracy. The provisions of the Criminal Justice Act 1988, s.71 were to the effect that drug trafficking offences were excluded from the scope of that Act. The difficulties which arose when the prosecution had clear evidence of money laundering, but was unable to identify the precise provenance of the money laundered, had been considered in *El-Kurd* [2001] Crim.L.R. 234 and *Hussain* [2002] 2 Cr.App.R. 26. In those cases the Court held that a count charging conspiracy to commit such offences in the alternative was not bad for duplicity. For the offender it was argued that, as he had been acquitted of the count which unequivocally related to a drug trafficking offence, the count of which he had been convicted did not enable the sentencing judge to say that there had been a conviction which was a necessary pre-condition for a confiscation order under the Drug Trafficking Act 1994. It would follow that the court was unable to say whether the jury's verdict enabled the court to exercise the jurisdiction to make a confiscation order. In the Court's view, counsel for the Attorney General was correct in his submission that this approach misunderstood the nature of the offence of conspiracy. The Criminal Law Act 1977, s.1, provided that if a person agreed with another person that a course of conduct would be carried out, which if the agreement was carried out in accordance with their intentions, would necessarily amount to or involve the commission of "any offence or offences", he was guilty of conspiracy to commit "the offence or offences in question". It was submitted that this section made clear that the conspiracy could amount to an agreement to commit one or more offences. The offence of conspiracy was completed by the agreement and not by the way in which the agreement was to be implemented. An agreement to commit a number of different offences remained an offence under s.1 of 1977 Act even if only one or none of those offences was in fact committed. It was the agreement which constituted the offence. In the Court's judgment, it followed that the offender's conviction on count 3 of the indictment meant that he was guilty of conspiracy to commit offences under both the Drug Trafficking Act 1994, and the Criminal Justice Act 1988. The precondition for confiscation proceedings under the 1994 Act was met. This was right both in principle and practice. It would be an affront to justice if a judge was unable to sentence conspirators who had entered into an agreement of the kind alleged in count 3 in the present case. The effect of the jury's verdict was that they did not consider that the conspiracy was limited to the proceeds of drug offences on one hand or the proceeds of crime on the other; it was an agreement to launder money whatever its provenance. This necessarily involved the offender's guilt of conspiracy to commit an offence under the 1994 Act, and the sentencing judge was wrong to hold that he had no jurisdiction to entertain confiscation proceedings.

Cases cited:
El-Kurd [2001] Crim.L.R. 234, *Hussain* [2002] 2 Cr.App.R. 26

References: confiscation order, *Current Sentencing Practice* J7, *Archbold* 5-

Commentary: [2004] Crim.L.R. 954

D. Perry and *D. Connolly* for the Attorney General.
T. Owen Q.C. and *A. Bodnar* for the offender.

JUDGMENT

Latham L.J.: On March 22, 2002, in the Crown Court at Inner London, the offender was convicted of an offence of conspiracy to convert or transfer the proceeds of drug trafficking or of criminal conduct, contrary to s.1 of the Criminal Law Act 1977. On that day he was sentenced to five years' imprisonment. A confiscation hearing was postponed until December 16, 2002. On December 16, 2002, H.H. Judge Philpot declined to make a confiscation order in the offender's case. The judge did not consider that he had jurisdiction to do so, as the offence of which the offender had been convicted was neither a "drug trafficking offence" within the meaning of s.1 of the Drug Trafficking Act 1994, nor an offence of a relevant description within the meaning of the Criminal Justice Act 1988. On July

12, 2004, we gave leave to the Attorney General to refer the judge's refusal to make a confiscation order pursuant to his powers under s.36 of the Criminal Justice Act 1988, on the grounds that the judge had erred in law as to his powers of sentencing. Mr Owen on behalf of the offender accepted that on the authority of *Flowers* [2003] EWCA Crim 3374, a confiscation order is a sentence for the purposes of s.36. Having given leave, we quashed the judge's decision, and ordered that confiscation proceedings should take place, for which we gave appropriate directions. We now give our reasons.

2   The factual background leading to the offender's conviction can be relatively shortly stated. In March 2001 an investigation began into suspected money laundering being carried on at a Bureau de Change called Multi Currency Foreign Exchange Ltd of which the offender was the directior and chief executive. A man known as Hussain Hafedh transferred substantial amounts of money to the offender and other representatives of Multi Currency Foreign Exchange Ltd, which were then added to money in various currencies which had been air freighted to Multi Currency Foreign Exchange Ltd from a company in Dubai. This money was then converted to United States dollars and transferred via an account held at the Royal Bank of Scotland by Multi Currency Foreign Exchange Ltd to an account held by the company with the Middle East Bank in Dubai. The evidence suggested that the amount of money laundered during the period January 2001 to June 2001, when the offender and six others were arrested, was as much as £7 million.

3   The offender was tried on an indictment containing three counts. Count 1 alleged a conspiracy to convert or transfer the proceeds of drug trafficking, contrary to s.1 of the Criminal Law Act 1977; count 2 alleged a conspiracy to convert or transfer the proceeds of criminal conduct, contrary to s.1 of the Criminal Law Act 1977; count 3 alleged a conspiracy to convert or transfer the proceeds of drug trafficking or of criminal conduct, contrary to s.1 of the Criminal Law Act 1977. The offender pleaded not guilty to all three counts. He was found not guilty on counts 1 and 2, but guilty on count 3.

4   Count 3 was in the following terms:

> **"Statement of Offence**
> Conspiracy to convert or transfer the proceeds of drug trafficking or of criminal conduct, contrary to Section 1 of the Criminal Law Act 1977.
> **Particulars of Offence**
> [The offender and others] between 1st January 2001 and 5th June 2001, at Maida Vale, London and elsewhere conspired together and with others to convert, transfer or remove from the jurisdiction property, namely bank notes knowing or having reasonable grounds to suspect that, in whole or in part, directly or indirectly, that property represented another person's proceeds either of drug trafficking or of an offence to which Part VI of the Criminal Justice Act 1988 applies, for the purpose of assisting any person to avoid prosecution for such an offence or the making of or enforcement

of a confiscation order in contravention of Section 49(2)(b) of the Drug Trafficking Act 1994 or Section 93C(2)(b) of the Criminal Justice Act 1988."

5   The prosecution sought a confiscation order against the offender under s.2 of the Drug Trafficking Act 1994 ("the 1994 Act") on the grounds that he was a defendant appearing before the Crown Court to be sentenced "in respect of one or more drug trafficking offences" which is the pre-condition for the making of such an order. By s.1(3) of the 1994 Act, a "drug trafficking offence" includes the following:

"(f) an offence under Section 49 . . . of this Act . . ..
(g) an offence under Section 1 of the Criminal Law Act 1977 of Conspiracy to Commit any of the offences in paragraphs (a) to (f) above."

6   The judge concluded that this definition did not include the offence of which the offender had been convicted, because the conspiracy which was charged was not a conspiracy to commit an offence under s.49 of the 1994 Act, but a conspiracy to commit an offence under s.49 of the Drug Trafficking Act 1994, or s.93C of the Criminal Justice Act 1988. That alternative formulation did not, in his judgment, entitle him to conclude that the conspiracy of which the offender had been convicted was, therefore, a relevant conspiracy.

7   The dichotomy reflected in the wording of the count was the result of the statutory distinction between the proceeds of drug trafficking on the one hand, and the proceeds of crime on the other which was the result of the wording of the provisions of the Criminal Justice Act 1988 ("the 1988 Act"). By s.71 of that Act, provision is made for a confiscation order if an offender is convicted "of an offence of a relevant description"; such an offence is described by s.71(1E) as "an offence to which this Part of this Act applies". By s.71(9) such an offence includes "an indictable offence, other than a drug trafficking offence". It also excludes offences under the Terrorism Act 2000.

8   The difficulties created by these provisions have been the subject-matter of two decisions of this Court, *El-Kurd* [2001] Crim.L.R. 234, and *Hussain* [2002] 2 Cr.App.R. 26. Those difficulties have now been addressed by the Proceeds of Crime Act 2002. But they remain difficulties in relation to cases involving proceeds of drug trafficking offences or proceeds of crime which pre-date the coming into effect of that Act. The particular difficulties with which we are concerned, as was this Court in *El-Kurd* and *Hussain*, arise when the prosecution has clear evidence of money laundering, but is unable to identify the precise provenance of the money laundered.

9   In *El-Kurd* the appellant was indicted on four counts, two counts of conspiracy in relation to the proceeds of criminal conduct, and two counts of conspiracy in relation to the proceeds of drug trafficking. He was convicted of the counts relating to the proceeds of criminal conduct, and acquitted of the counts relating to the proceeds of drug trafficking. On appeal it was argued that the two regimes required the prosecution to establish that the property in question was wholly or in part, directly or indirectly, the proceeds of criminal conduct on the one

hand, or of drug trafficking on the other. In other words the submission was that without proof that the property was in fact the proceeds of drug trafficking or criminal conduct, none of the counts in the indictment were made out.

10   In dismissing the appeal on the facts, this Court said:

> "Before we leave this appeal we would express some concern that the mat-
> ter proceeded before the jury on an indictment which, perhaps
> understandably, reflected the dichotomy that we have referred to, when it
> seems to this Court that the appropriate course to take, when confronted
> with problems in relation to the provenance of the proceeds in relation to
> which it is said that the defendant has carried out the activity of money laun-
> dering, is by way of a compendious count of conspiracy which would avoid
> the necessity for any choice to have to be made so that in a case such as the
> present if the jury were satisfied, as they would have been bound to have
> been, that the proceeds were the proceeds of illicit activity, the jury should
> be provided with the opportunity to conclude that the conspiracy was a con-
> spiracy by the conspirators to launder money illicitly obtained, whether it be
> by way of drug trafficking or other criminal activity. That seems to us to
> have been the reality in the present case and, would, therefore, perhaps
> have been more appropriately reflected by a count drawn in such terms."

11   That suggestion, which was not part of the ratio of the decision, was adopted by the prosecution in *Hussain*. In that appeal, as in the present, the appellants were indicted on three alternative counts of conspiracy; a conspiracy to contravene the provisions of the 1994 Act, a conspiracy to contravene the 1988 Act, and a con-spiracy to contravene either the 1994 Act or the 1988 Act. But at a preparatory hearing, it was argued that the count relating to both the 1994 Act and the 1988 Act was bad for duplicity. This Court held that it was not, because what was alleged was a single agreement, constituting a single offence of conspiracy, to commit one or more offences, the essence of the conspiracy offence being the making of the agreement and not its implementation. This Court accordingly confirmed that the course suggested in *El-Kurd* was an appropriate course to take where the conspiracy could properly be described in such terms. The issue of the effect of a conviction on such a count on confiscation proceedings was expressly reserved by the Court which said: "The Crown might or might not get into difficulties" if defendants were convicted on such a count. That is the issue with which we are now confronted.

12   There is a superficial attraction in the judge's approach which Mr Owen Q.C. has skilfully sought to support. The fact is that the offender was acquitted of the count which unequivocally related to the offence under the 1994 Act. The count of which he was convicted does not, he submits, enable the Court to say that there has been such a conviction which is the necessary pre-condition for the relevant confiscation order. The Court is, accordingly, not able to say whether the jury's verdict entitles the Court to exercise the jurisdiction which the prosecution seeks. There is accordingly an uncertainty as to the basis upon which the court should proceed which offends against the principle of legal policy that a person

should not be penalised except under clear law as described in F.A.R. Bennion, *Statutory Interpretation* (2002 ed.), p.705.

13   But in our view, Mr Perry on behalf of the Attorney General is right in his submission that this approach misunderstands the nature of the offence of conspiracy and the effect of s.1 of the Criminal Law Act 1977 ("the 1977 Act"). This provides as follows:

> "(1) Subject to the following provisions of this Part of this Act, if a person agrees with any other person or persons that a course of conduct shall be pursued which, if the agreement is carried out in accordance with their intentions, . . .
>
> > (a) will necessarily amount to or involve the commission of any offence or offences by one or more of the parties to the agreement, . . .
> >
> > . . .
> >
> > he is guilty of conspiracy to commit the offence or offences in question."

14   His submission is that this provision makes it clear that a conspiracy can amount to an agreement to commit one or more offences. The offence of conspiracy itself is completed by the agreement and not by the way in which the agreement is to be implemented. Thus an agreement to commit a number of different offences remains an offence under s.1 of the 1977 Act even if only one, or even none, of those offences is in fact committed. It is the agreement which constitutes the offence. Equally, if the agreement is to commit either of two offences, that is also an indictable conspiracy. For example, if conspirators agree that they will steal a particular item and that they will, if necessary, either commit burglary or commit robbery in order to obtain that item, that will amount to an agreement to commit the offences of theft, burglary and robbery. That submission was accepted by this Court in *Hussain* at [27] and is, in our view, correct. The fact that the agreement to burgle or rob is contingent on the particular circumstances, does not affect the nature of the conspiracy.

5   In our judgment, it follows that the offender's conviction on count 3 in the indictment with which we are concerned means that the offender was guilty of a conspiracy to commit offences under both the 1994 Act and the 1988 Act. The result is that the pre-condition for confiscation proceedings under the 1994 Act has been met. This is, in our view, both right in principle and in practice. If the judge is correct, the court would not be able to sentence conspirators who have entered into an agreement of the kind alleged in count 3, or in the circumstances we have envisaged in the previous paragraph upon a basis which reflects the conspirators', true criminality. That would be an affront to justice. It would not reflect the true nature of the agreement. In the present case, the effect of the jury's verdicts was that they did not consider that the conspiracy was restricted to either the proceeds of drugs offences on the one hand or the proceeds of crime on the other, but was an agreement to launder the money whatever its provenance. In our view, that necessarily, as we have explained, involved the offender's guilt of conspiracy to commit the offence under the 1994 Act. The

judge was accordingly wrong to hold that he had no jurisdiction to entertain the confiscation proceedings.

16   Mr Owen Q.C. on behalf of the offender has submitted, however, that we should nonetheless refuse leave to the Attorney General to refer the ruling on the basis that the court would be in no position to make the appropriate allowance for "double jeopardy" which is a factor which this Court has consistently taken into account when determining what order to make under s.36 of the 1988 Act. We accept that the mere fact that we consider that the judge was wrong does not require us to give leave, or indeed to quash the decision. Section 36(2) makes it plain that it remains a matter of discretion. The fact that the judge erred in law as to his powers of sentencing does not, of itself, require the court to give leave. It merely provides a yardstick for determining whether or not the sentence was "unduly lenient" for the purposes of s.36(1)(a). But where, as here, the effect is that the court did not proceed to carry out a statutory requirement (s.2 of the 1994 Act says that where the necessary pre-conditions apply, the court "shall act as follows") this Court is unlikely to conclude that it should refuse leave to the Attorney General to refer the matter, or to make the order required by statute.

R. v TERRENCE ALAN HORROCKS

COURT OF APPEAL (Lord Justice May, Mr Justice Gray and Mrs Justice Hallett): July 22, 2004

[2004] EWCA Crim 2129; [2005] 1 Cr.App.R.(S.) 80

(LT) Aggravating features; Grievous bodily harm; Guilty pleas; Sentence length; Wounding with intent

H1   *Causing grievous bodily harm with intent—attack involving blows with hammer to the head, causing grave injuries—length of sentence*

H2   Twelve years' imprisonment upheld for causing grievous bodily harm with intent in the form of an attack involving blows with a hammer to the victim's head, which caused grave injuries.

H3   The appellant pleaded guilty to causing grievous bodily harm with intent on an indictment charging attempted murder. The appellant had been drinking in a public house. He left the public house and went to his van. A man who had also been drinking in the public house asked him for a lift and the appellant agreed to give him a lift. During the journey the man picked up a hammer which was in the van and began to wave it about. The appellant stopped the van and tried to retrieve the hammer. Eventually the appellant lost his temper; he got hold of the hammer and hit the man on the head with it. He then pushed the man out of the van and began to leave. Seeing the man get up, the appellant climbed out of the van and hit him two or three more times on the head with the hammer. The appellant returned home and told his partner that he had killed a man. The appellant's partner eventually found the man and called an ambulance. The appellant attempted to destroy evidence of the attack by washing the hammer and getting rid of the blood stained clothing. The victim was found to have a depressed skull fracture and other injuries which required major surgery. A victim impact statement indicated that the victim would never be able to work again and that he would require constant attention. Sentenced to 12 years' imprisonment.

14   **Held:** (considering *Hailes* (1992) 13 Cr.App.R.(S.) 540) the appellant had several previous convictions for offences of violence. A psychiatric report indicated that the appellant was prone to lose his temper when drunk. The sole question for the Court was whether the appellant received sufficient credit for his plea. So far as the appellant was concerned, he believed his victim was dead and left him for dead. He tried to cover his tracks. Given the facts of the offence, the background of the offender and the aggravating features, this was one of the most serious offences of its kind. The sentence of 12 years' imprisonment was justifiably severe.

15   **Case cited:**
Hailes (1992) 13 Cr.App.R.(S.) 540

16   **References:** causing grievous bodily harm with intent, *Current Sentencing Practice* B 2-2

7   *W. Harbage Q.C.* for the appellant.
S. Lowne for the Crown.

JUDGMENT

1   **Hallett J.:**   On November 21, 2003 in the Crown Court at Hull the appellant, Terrence Horrocks, pleaded guilty to causing grievous bodily harm with intent. He pleaded not guilty to an offence of attempted murder and no verdict was entered on that alternative count. On December 12, 2003 H.H. Judge Mettyear sentenced him to 12 years' imprisonment. He appeals against sentence by leave of the single judge.

2   The facts of the offence are as follows. On July 10, 2003 the victim, Mr Batty, had been drinking in a public house and his behaviour had become irritating to some of the other patrons. The appellant had also been out drinking that evening. He left the public house and went to his van near his home in order to get it ready for work the following day. Mr Batty approached him and asked for a lift. According to the appellant, Mr Batty being unable to assist as to what had occurred thereafter, he agreed to give Mr Batty a lift and the pair set off in the appellant's van.

3   During the journey the appellant said that Mr Batty picked up a hammer, which was lying in the van, and started waving it around in a drunken manner. The appellant said he stopped the van and tried to retrieve the hammer. A tug of war developed and the appellant lost his temper. The appellant finally got hold

of the hammer and he hit the victim on the head with it. He then pushed him out of the van and began to leave. Seeing the victim get up, the appellant turned the vehicle around. He climbed out of the van and hit the victim two or three more times on the head with the hammer.

4   The appellant then returned home. His partner saw that he was covered in blood and he was holding the hammer behind his back. She asked him what he had done. He said that he had killed a man. When asked why, he said:

> "Some idiot in the pub kept cheesing me off. Go and have a look, I bet he's not moving."

5   She went off to try and find Mr Batty. Eventually the appellant directed her to where Mr Batty was lying unconscious and she discovered that he had a very serious head injury. She called an ambulance by using her mobile.

6   Meanwhile the appellant was doing his best to cover his tracks. His partner had seen him washing the hammer of Mr Batty's blood. He bleached work surfaces. He had removed his blood stained clothing, and taken that clothing together with a towel he had used to get rid of the blood and dumped them in a rubbish bin from which they were later found.

7   Mr Batty was taken to Leeds General Infirmary. His injuries consisted of a right temporal depressed skull fracture pressing against the brain, right temporal contusion, namely bruising on the brain, a right temporal Zygoma, namely bruising under the eye above the cheek, multiple scalp lacerations, soft tissue damage to the right ear, which in fact was only hanging on by fragments of skin, and a fracture to the middle finger of his left hand. Mr Batty required major reconstructive surgery. His head injuries were so severe that he will have to attend a rehabilitation centre if he is to have any kind of life outside a hospital setting. The prognosis, according to Mr Harbage Q.C. who appears on behalf of the appellant, is uncertain.

8   In a victim impact statement dated November 7, 2003, Mr Batty said he was now deaf in his right ear and would require a hearing aid. He suffered from epileptic fits and memory loss. He would never be able to work again because of his injuries. He also felt that he would never be able to leave the hospital because he required someone with him at all times. As he put it, this assault had destroyed his life. There are photographs included in our papers which illustrate the nature of his appalling injuries. According to the doctors a significant amount of force must have been used to cause these appalling injuries from repeated blows to the head.

9   When the appellant was arrested his first comment was to the effect "I take it the bloke is still alive". Thereafter he made no comment in interview to relevant questions.

10   The appellant is now aged 29. He has a number of previous court appearances, including several offences of violence. He has been convicted of offences of assault occasioning actual bodily harm, affray, wounding, possession of an offensive weapon, using threatening behaviour, knife point robbery, criminal damage and threats to kill. Penalties have varied from community penalties to several custodial sentences. On February 14, 2003 he was made subject to a community punishment order and community rehabilitation order which were current at

the time of this offence. These orders were imposed for offences of affray and possession of an offensive weapon. Following the still birth of the appellant's child, he had gone to the hospital and produced a knife and claw hammer, demanding an explanation as to his son's death.

11   A psychiatric report was before the lower court and this Court. By the time the appellant was seen by the doctor, Dr Hayes, who prepared the report, he expressed remorse and contrition for his actions. He did not seek to minimise the serious harm he had caused. He was described as a binge drinker of alcohol which made him more irritable and violence more likely. Dr Hayes set out the tragic circumstances of the death of the appellant's son and indicated that in his opinion the appellant was suffering from a degree of depression. This was as the result of not only the grief at the loss of his son, who had been still born, but the fact that he had been unable to bury his son. There had been a dreadful mix-up at the hospital and his child's body had been incinerated. The doctor said that the main problem, as far as the appellant was concerned, was in controlling his temper.

2   Mr Harbage Q.C. in his helpful submissions has argued that the sentence imposed on a plea of guilty to an offence of grievous bodily harm with intent leaves no room for the courts to draw the necessary distinction between this offence and the more serious offence of attempted murder. He submitted that the learned judge took too high a starting point for an offence of causing grievous bodily harm with intent, notwithstanding the very serious nature of this offence. He reminded the Court that the appellant's conduct was not premeditated and submitted that the learned judge had given the appellant too little credit for his plea of guilty and his genuine remorse. He also submitted that the learned judge had failed adequately to reflect the appellant's personal mitigation, particularly the very sad circumstances of his son's still birth.

3   He also submitted that the psychiatrist had not given as his opinion that the appellant posed a danger to society. It is right to say that he did not express such an opinion. He does not seem to have addressed the issue. What he did say was, as we have indicated, that this appellant, when drunk, is prone to lose his temper, and plainly does, in our judgment, then pose a danger to those who cross him. We are glad to hear that he is taking steps within the prison system to address the problems of alcohol abuse and anger management.

4   Mr Harbage has drawn our attention to a number of authorities, including *Hailes* (1992) 13 Cr.App.R.(S.) 540. In *Hailes* a man pleaded guilty to a s.18 wounding and a robbery of a woman in a multi-storey car park. He had struck the woman over the head with a blunt instrument, possibly a hammer. She suffered brain injuries, including severe and permanent brain damage. The Court addressed the very issue put before us by Mr Harbage, namely the distinction to be drawn between offences of attempted murder and those of causing grievous bodily harm with intent to do so. Having considered the distinction that had to be drawn, the Court reduced the sentence of 15 years to one of 12 years. Mr Harbage argues that that was a worse case than the present, there being the aggravating feature of robbery.

15   As far as this appellant is concerned, there are, however, other significant aggravating features. We note that, despite his conviction in February 2003, the appellant was still driving around in his van with a hammer, the very same kind of implement with which he had threatened members of the hospital staff. That hammer was accessible to all, including, of course, himself.

16   Mr Batty's conduct amounted at most, it seems, to irritation, yet this appellant took the hammer from Mr Batty, hit Mr Batty repeatedly about the head with it and then pushed him out of the van. But a significant aggravating feature, in our judgment, is that that was not sufficient for this appellant. When he realised that Mr Batty was still moving, he turned round, returned to the scene and continued his awful attack upon Mr Batty. Had it not been for the appellant's partner, whom we commend for her actions, Mr Batty would no doubt have died. We have seen, as we have indicated, the photographs of Mr Batty's injuries. They are truly horrifying. It is a miracle that he survived.

17   It is not clear to this Court, and may not have been clear to H.H. Judge Mettyear, why exactly the Crown accepted the plea of not guilty to attempted murder, but this Court and the learned judge must proceed on the basis that this was an offence of causing grievous bodily harm with intent.

18   We turn to the sole question that has caused this Court any concern; that is whether or not this appellant received sufficient credit for his plea of guilty. As Mr Harbage accepted, it was a plea that was not entered at the first opportunity, but it was entered, it is right to say, on the first occasion the prosecution indicated a willingness to accept it. The trial was not due to take place until some weeks later. No witnesses had been brought to court.

19   We remind ourselves, however, that, as far as the appellant was concerned, he believed his victim was dead. He essentially left him for dead. He tried to cover his tracks. He failed to express any remorse in his no comment interview. Had Mr Batty died, and had this appellant faced a charge of murder to which he would have had no defence, he would, of course, have served a considerably longer sentence than that actually imposed. Having considered all the material before us about his background, we are satisfied the appellant has shown himself to be a man who, despite knowing his own capacity for terrible violence when drunk, has continued to abuse alcohol. The attack upon Mr Batty was yet another example of the kind of drunken rages in which this appellant indulges.

20   The maximum sentence for an offence of causing grievous bodily harm with intent is life imprisonment. Given the facts of this offence, the background of the offender and the aggravating features to which we have referred, in our judgment this is one of the most serious offences of its kind. The sentence of 12 years was a severe one, but, in our judgment, justifiably so. Accordingly, this appeal must be dismissed.

R. v GARY DEAN LONGWORTH

Court of Appeal (Lord Justice Potter, Mr Justice Gibbs and Sir Michael Wright): July 23, 2004

[2004] EWCA Crim 2145; [2005] 1 Cr.App.R.(S.) 81

(LT/ Conditional discharge; Convictions; Indecent photographs of children; Sex Offenders Register;

H1 *Sex Offenders Act 1997—obligation to notify—whether obligation to notify applicable where offender discharged conditionally*

H2   An offender who has been conditionally discharged for an offence falling within the scope of the Sex Offenders Act 1997 is obliged to comply with the notification requirements of that Act as a "person of any other description".

H3   The appellant pleaded guilty before the Crown Court to two counts of making an indecent photograph or pseudo-photograph of children. The appellant took a computer to be repaired at a shop. Staff at the shop found indecent images on the computer. The images consisted largely of adult pornography, which was not the subject of any charge, but there were also indecent images of children. All of the images were in Level One of the categories set out in *Oliver* [2003] 2 Cr.App.R.(S.) 15 (p.64)), the least serious of the categories applicable. Sentenced to a conditional discharge for 12 months. The question arose whether the appellant was required to comply with the notification requirements of the Sex Offenders Act 1997 Pt 1. The sentencing judge gave a considered ruling that the notification requirements did apply.

H4   **Held:** there had been contradictory decisions on the matter. In *Malone* [2001] 2 Cr.App.R.(S.) 43 (p.203) it was held that the notification requirements did apply but in *Oliver* it was held that they did not. The Sex Offenders Act 1997, s.1, provided that a person became subject to the notification requirements of the Act if he was "convicted" of a sexual offence to which the Act applied. Section 1(4) set out a table in which different periods of notification were related to particular sentences. The last category was "a person of any other description". The other relevant statutory provision was the Powers of Criminal Courts (Sentencing) Act 2000, s.14, which provided that a conviction for an offence for which a conditional or absolute discharge was made "shall be deemed not to be a conviction for any purpose other than the purposes of the proceedings in which the order is made and of any subsequent proceedings which may be taken against the offender under section 13 above". Section 14(3) provided that the conviction of an offender who was discharged absolutely or conditionally "shall in any event be disregarded" for the purposes of any enactment which imposed any disqualification or disability on convicted persons. For the appellant it was submitted that once the proceedings in which the offender had been discharged were concluded, the conviction ceased to be a conviction. The 1997 Act did not contain any provision expressly disapplying s.14(1). It was conceded that the notification requirements did apply in the case of a defendant who received a caution rather than being charged or convicted and that this produced an anomaly. It was submitted that this was a matter for Parliament to deal with. For the Crown it was submitted that by s.1(4) of the 1997 Act, by referring to "a person of other description", it was intended to include a person who had been sentenced by means of a discharge. It was submitted that the notification requirements were preventive in nature and not punitive. The Court had concluded that but for the provisions of s.14 of the 2000 Act, the appellant would be liable to the notification requirements of the 1997 Act. For the appellant, it had been rightly conceded that the notification requirements could not be said to impose any disqualification or disability on the appellant. The statutory requirements were preventive in nature; a person subject to an order was not disqualified or disabled. Section 14(1) contained an exception to the general proposition that the discharge was not deemed to be a conviction save in certain circumstances. The effect of the exception was that a discharge was to be regarded as a conviction for the purposes of the proceedings in which the order was made. The notification requirement did fall within the ambit of the "purposes of the proceedings in which the order is made". The requirement followed inevitably under the 1997 Act from the fact of conviction, being an ancillary condition attached by virtue of that statute to the orders of the judge made in those proceedings. The Court concluded, applying the ordinary meaning of the language of s.14(1) of the 2000 Act, that the notification requirements fell within the exception. It followed that the appellant's conviction, notwithstanding the conditional discharge, did constitute a conviction for the purposes of the registration requirements. It followed that the appellant was a person of the description referred to in s.1(4) of the 1997 Act, as a person "of any other description". It was appropriate to note, first, that the notification requirements took effect independently of the judge's order. They did not depend on anything decided or spoken by the judge. However it was desirable in the light of the conflicting views expressed on the topic that the issue should be determined and this the Court had sought to achieve. Secondly, the Sexual Offences Act 2003 had changed the notification requirements. The Court did not find the new provisions of assistance in interpreting the legislation in effect at the relevant time to the appeal before the Court.

H5 **Cases cited:**
Malone [2001] 2 Cr.App.R.(S.) 43 (p.203), *Oliver* [2003] 2 Cr.App.R.(S.) 15 (p.64)

H6 **References:** *Conditional discharge, Current Sentencing Practice* D11, *Archbold* 5–113

H7 **Commentary:** [2004] Crim.L.R. 1047

H8 *M.I. Davies* for the appellant.

S. Medland for the Crown.

JUDGMENT

1   **Gibbs J.:**   This matter comes before the Court by way of an appeal against sentence with the leave of the sentencing judge, who issued a certificate under s.11(1)(a) of the Criminal Appeal Act 1968. On December 2, 2003 the appellant, Gary Dean Longworth, pleaded guilty before the Crown Court at Warrington to two offences of making an indecent photograph or pseudophotograph of children. H.H. Judge Hale, who presided over the court, sentenced the appellant to concurrent 12-month conditional discharges. An issue arose as to whether, in the light of the sentences of conditional discharge, Pt I of the Sex Offenders Act 1997 applied to the appellant so that he was required to comply with the provisions of s.2 of the Act to notify certain prescribed information to the police (to be referred to in this judgment as "notification requirements"). The issue was adjourned for argument. This took place on January 12, 2004, and the judge gave a considered ruling to the effect that the notification requirements did apply.

2   The facts can be extremely briefly stated. The appellant had delivered a computer belonging to him to be repaired at a shop. Staff at the shop found indecent images on the computer. The police were called. The images consisted largely of adult pornography (which are not the subject of any charges), but there were also indecent images of children. All those images were within level 1 as set out in the case of *Oliver* [2003] 2 Cr.App.R.(S) 15. Level 1 is the least serious of the categories applicable. The appellant was arrested and gave an explanation, with which we need not trouble, for the presence of the child pornography images on his computer.

3   On issue in this case, there have been contradictory decisions and opinions of different courts and, indeed, different learned writers. In the case of *Malone* [2001] 2 Cr.App.R.(S) 43, it was held that the notification requirements did apply in the case of a conditional discharge. In the case of *Oliver*, to which we have already referred, it was held that they did not. It is right to say that in neither case was the matter argued. The editors of *Archbold* 2005 at ch.20–271c, prefer the view in *Oliver*, as does a commentary on the case of *Malone* to be found in *Criminal Law Week* 2001/26/42.

4   The applicable statutory provisions to which we need to refer for resolution of this issue are as follows. The Sex Offenders Act 1997, s.1:

"**Sex offenders subject to notification requirements**
    1.— (1) A person becomes subject to the notification requirements of this Part if, after the commencement of this Part—
            (a) he is convicted of a sexual offence to which this Part applies;
            (b) he is found not guilty of such an offence by reason of insanity, or to be under a disability and to have done the act charged against him in respect of such an offence; or

(c) in England and Wales or Northern Ireland, he is cautioned
by a constable in respect of such offence which, at the
time when the caution is given, he has admitted."

Subsection (4), so far as material, provides as follows:

"(4) A person falling within subsections (1) to (3) above shall continue to
be subject to those requirements for the period set out opposite a person of his description in the second column of the following table."

There then is set out the table. This recites a series of categories of person who
have either been sentenced to imprisonment for the relevant offence or have
been admitted to hospital under a hospital order. However, the last category is
"a person of any other description", and the applicable period provided in the
table for such a person is a period of five years beginning with the date of the conviction.

5   The other relevant statutory provisions are to be found in the Powers of Criminal Courts (Sentencing) Act 2000, in particular at s.14:

"Effect of discharge
14.— (1) Subject to subsection (2) below, a conviction of an offence for
which an order is made under section 12 above discharging the
offender absolutely or conditionally shall be deemed not to be a
conviction for any purpose other than the purposes of the proceedings in which the order is made and of any subsequent
proceedings which may be taken against the offender under
section 13 above."

. . .

(3) Without prejudice to subsections (1) and (2) above, the conviction of an offender who is discharged absolutely or
conditionally under section 12 above shall in any event be disregarded for the purposes of any enactment or instrument
which—
(a) imposes any disqualification or disability upon convicted persons; or
(b) authorises or requires the imposition of any such disqualification or disability."

6   On behalf of the appellant, Mr Davies relies upon s.14(1) of the 2000 Act. He
does not maintain the argument (if indeed it was ever advanced on behalf of the
appellant) that the notification requirements constituted any disqualification or
disability upon the appellant, and therefore subs.(3), he accepts, can be disregarded for the purposes of this appellant. He relies in particular upon the proposition
that unless an offence is committed within the period of discharge the 2000 Act
provides that the conviction is not a conviction for any purpose other than the purposes of the proceedings. He points out that the requirement to notify under the
1997 Act must be complied with within three days of the conviction. He says that
once the proceedings in which the offender has been discharged are concluded

the conviction ceases to be a conviction. He submits, therefore, that any requirement which arose immediately following the appellant's plea of guilty must thereby cease, and consequently a failure to notify in those circumstances cannot give rise to an offence under the Act. He submits that the notification requirement does not constitute a matter within the purposes of the proceedings in which the order is made. He says that the notification requirement is a *consequence* of the proceedings and not "for the purposes of the proceedings". He relies further on the fact that the 1997 Act does not contain any provision expressly disapplying s.14(1) of the 2000 Act. This, he points out, is in contrast to s.121 of the Social Security Administration Act 1992, for example, in which s.14(1) was specifically disapplied.

7   He addresses a point made on behalf of the respondent to this appeal, namely that if the appellant's argument is right then a discrepancy arises. The discrepancy derives from the fact that the notification requirements undoubtedly do apply in the case of an appellant who receives a caution rather than being charged or convicted at all. He concedes that it is arguable that this does produce an anomaly. But if there is an anomaly, he contends that that is a matter for Parliament to deal with and not for the courts. In any event he submits that, if one views the situation broadly, no real anomaly exists. A caution is administered in circumstances in which an offender expressly admits his offence to the police, whereas Mr Davies contends that a conditional discharge or indeed an absolute discharge involves a judicial assessment of the degree of guilt. Thus if a judge, having heard the facts of the case, assesses that the level of criminality is so low as to merit no more than a discharge, there is no anomaly if the registration requirement does not apply.

8   In answer on behalf of the respondent, Mr Medland invites us to take a straightforward common-sense view of the 1997 Act, s.1(4), and to find that Parliament clearly intended the words "a person of other description" at the conclusion of the table to that section to include a person who had been sentenced by means of a discharge for the offence. He accepts, and indeed relies upon the fact, that notification requirements are preventive in nature and not punitive, and that they follow inexorably from the fact of a conviction. This principle was established in the European case of *Ibbotson v United Kingdom* [1999] Crim.L.R. 153. He submits that there is nothing in the wording of the 2000 Act which alters the obvious statutory intention which Parliament had evinced in the 1997 Act. Importantly, he submits that the notification requirements cannot be described as anything other than for the "purposes of the proceedings in which the order was made". He points out that the proceedings for this purpose include, for example, the process of requiring attendance at court, the plea of guilty or the verdict, the sentence that follows, and also, by implication, as indeed Mr Davies conceded, orders for costs and other orders ancillary to the proceedings. Accordingly, Mr Medland invites us to uphold the decision of the sentencing judge.

9   We have the benefit of the detailed and careful ruling of the sentencing judge. It is not out of any disrespect to him that we do not rehearse his ruling. Our conclusions are as follows. But for the provisions of the 2000 Act, it is agreed that the appellant would be liable to the notification requirements under the 1997

Act. With regard to the 2000 Act, we have already referred to the provisions of s.14(3). We think that Mr Davies has rightly conceded that the notification requirements cannot be said to impose any "disqualification or disability" on the appellant. We are reinforced in that view by the decision in *Ibbotson*. The statutory requirements are preventative in nature. A person subject to an order is not disqualified or disabled by it.

10   That being our conclusion on subs.(3), the effect of subs.(1) falls to be considered. It contains an exception to the general proposition that a discharge is not deemed to be a conviction save in certain circumstances. The material effect of the exception in our judgment is that a discharge is to be regarded as a conviction for the purposes of the proceedings in which the order is made. The notification requirement does fall within the ambit of the "purposes of the proceedings in which the order is made". The requirement follows inevitably under the 1997 Act from the fact of conviction, being an ancillary condition attached by virtue of that statute to the orders of the judge made in those very proceedings. We also attach weight to the fact that the proceedings themselves are brought under the Sex Offenders Act and that when Parliament enacted that statute it thought it right, in the case of certain offences, to attach the notification requirements. Thus we conclude that, applying the ordinary meaning of the language of s.14(1) of the 1997 Act, the notification requirements undoubtedly fall within the exception. It follows that the appellant's conviction, notwithstanding the conditional discharge, does constitute a conviction for the purposes of the registration requirements. Under those circumstances it follows that the appellant is a person of the description referred to in s.1(4) in the 1997 Act. In the table attached to that subsection he is "a person of any other description". It follows that the judge reached the right decision.

11   It is appropriate to make two further observations. First, the notification requirements take effect independently of the judge's order. Technically they therefore do not depend on anything decided or spoken by the judge. However, it is clearly desirable, in the light of the conflicting views expressed on the topic, that the issue arising in these proceedings should be determined, and this we have sought to achieve. And, secondly, our attention has been drawn to the fact that, by virtue of the Sexual Offences Act 2003, the notification requirements have now been changed in respects which are undoubtedly material to the issue which has arisen in this case. Whether those changes will lead to clarification or further argument remains to be seen, but we do not find ourselves assisted in interpreting the legislation current at the time relevant to this appeal by considering those new provisions.

12   In all the circumstances, therefore, this appeal will be dismissed.

R. v DAVID GEORGE WHEATON

COURT OF APPEAL (Lord Justice Rose (Vice President, Court of Appeal Criminal Division), Mr Justice Treacy and Sir Edwin Jowitt): July 26, 2004

[2004] EWCA Crim 2270; [2005] 1 Cr.App.R.(S.) 82

(LT) Deterrence; Discretionary life imprisonment; Double punishment; Minimum term; Public protection; Rape

H1   *Life imprisonment—specified period—notional determinate sentence incorporating element reflecting danger to public—avoidance of "double counting" in determining notional determinate sentence*

H2   **Editor's note:** where a court has passed a life sentence on a defendant and is deciding on the notional determinate sentence from which to calculate the specified period of the sentence for the purposes of the Powers of Criminal Courts (Sentencing) Act 2000, s.82A, the need to protect the public from the danger posed by the defendant should not be taken into account.

H3   The appellant was convicted of two counts of rape. On the first occasion, the appellant approached a young woman as she was crossing a road, pushed her to the ground and raped her. A few weeks later, the appellant followed a 14-year-old girl as she was walking home. He caught up with her, grabbed her from behind and brought her to the ground. He then punched the girl, dragged her into some bushes and raped her. On each occasion the appellant kept the victim's underwear. The appellant was arrested later that day. He claimed that in each case the intercourse was consensual. A psychiatric report which was before the Crown Court for the purpose of sentencing concluded that the appellant represented a grave and unpredictable risk of further sexual offending. Sentenced to life imprisonment with a minimum period of eight years.

H4   **Held:** the appellant did not challenge the discretionary life sentence, but argued that the minimum period of eight years was manifestly excessive because it was based on the "15 years plus" category identified in *Millberry* [2003] 2 Cr.App.R.(S.) 31 (p.142). That category was said to include an extension of normal sentencing due to the inherent dangerousness of someone convicted of more than one offence, and it was accordingly submitted that there was an element of double sentencing when the life sentence was imposed. It was further submitted that the sentencing judge failed to take account of the fact that the appellant had spent 304 days in custody on remand which did not count towards the specified period. In specifying the minimum term in accordance the Powers of Criminal Courts (Sentencing) Act 2000, s.82A, the sentencing judge did not perform the exercise laid down in *Marklew and Lambert* [1999] 1 Cr.App.R.(S.) 6, of fixing what would otherwise have been an appropriate determinate term and then specifying the proportion, between a half and two-thirds, and giving credit for remand time . It had been confirmed in *Szczerba* [2002] 2 Cr.App.R.(S.) 86 (p.387) that the normal proportion should be one half, and that if a greater proportion were to be served, reasons must be given. Looking backwards from the eight-year period specified by the sentencing judge, it appeared that the judge had a determinate sentence of about 17 years and nine months in mind. For the appellant it was conceded that if a life sentence had not been appropriate, the sentence to be passed would have come within the "15 year plus" category in *Millberry* and that a sentence of 17 years and nine months would not necessarily have been excessive as a straightforward determinate sentence. It was argued that such a sentence, taken as a starting point in fixing a minimum term, involved an element of double sentencing and reflected the elements of dangerousness and risk to the public, which were covered by the passing of a discretionary life sentence, as opposed to the punitive element of the sentence. The Court accepted the argument that in fixing a notional determinate term, the element of sentence reflecting the need to protect the public from the danger posed by the defendant should not be taken into account when a discretionary life sentence was being passed. However, judges should not overlook the need to reflect an element of deterrence, which might properly feature in fixing a notional determinate term. In *Millberry* it was plain that a factor in the fixing of the 15-year starting point was the level of risk posed by the offender to society, and so potentially the observations in *Campbell* [1997] 1 Cr.App.R.(S.) 119 and *Marklew and Lambert* would apply to it. However the Court had to consider the circumstances of the two offences. The appellant was convicted after a trial in which both victims had to give evidence, so that he lost any available mitigation that would have resulted from the guilty plea. Both offences were committed by night and involved some element of deliberation and stalking. Both offences involved a fetishistic element and the second victim was subjected to additional degradations. She was only 14. Both victims had been seriously damaged as a result of their ordeal. Even ignoring the element of danger or risk posed to society, these were grave offences, and the second offence represented an escalation of gravity and exacerbation of the first offence. The problem was that the sentencing judge did not indicate what factors were in his mind in fixing the specified period. The Court had concluded that, setting aside the risk aspect, a term in the region of 16 years would have been appropriate and the term of 17 years and nine months could not be justified. The Court had reached the figure of 16 years by concluding that consecutive sentences were appropriate in relation to the two offences. The first offence would have attracted a sentence of five years, with 11 years consecutive for the second offence. In making a discount in fixing a notional determinate sentence, a precise mathematical exercise was not required. The judge should be alive to the risk of double counting and he should perform a mental balancing exercise in arriving at an appropriate discount. He should ensure that the public risk element was not reflected in fixing the notional determine sentence. Applying the appropriate practice to the notional term of 16 years, the Court would divide the figure by two to arrive at eight years, and deduct the period of 304 days spent in custody on remand. The minimum term would be fixed at eight years less 304 days, in place of the eight years specified by the judge.

H5   **Cases cited:**
Millberry [2003] 2 Cr.App.R.(S.) 31 (p.142), *Marklew and Lambert* [1999] 1 Cr.App.R.(S.) 6, *Szczerba* [2002] 2 Cr.App.R.(S.) 86 (p.387), *Campbell* [1997] 1 Cr.App.R.(S.) 119

H6   **References:** life imprisonment—specified period, *Current Sentencing Practice* F 3–4, *Archbold* 5–310

H7   **Commentary:** [2005] Crim.L.R. 68

H8   *P. Weatherby* for the appellant.
R. Hill for the Crown.

JUDGMENT

1   **Treacy J.:**   We would like to express our gratitude to both counsel for their clear submissions and the helpful written submissions supplied in advance of this hearing.

2   This appellant, David George Wheaton, has been granted leave and an extension of time to pursue his appeal by the full court.

3   On May 22, 2000, in the Crown Court at Winchester, he was convicted after a trial, and on June 30, 2000 H.H. Judge Hooton sentenced him as follows. There were two counts of rape and he received a sentence of life imprisonment in relation to each count to run concurrently. The judge recommended that a minimum period of eight years be served before release.

4   The circumstances of the offences are these. Count 1 related to a 21-year-old victim. On August 11, 1999 she went to a public house in Swindon with her boyfriend and other friends. A little later they went to the home of the victim's boyfriend. There was an argument and the victim left his flat in order to buy some cigarettes from a nearby petrol station. Having bought the cigarettes, she began to walk home. As she crossed a road the appellant grabbed her from behind and told her to shut up and do as she was told. Initially she thought that the assailant was her boyfriend, but then the victim realised that it was not and she started to scream. The appellant threatened the victim, "Do that again and I'll cut your throat". The victim was frightened but she managed to telephone her boyfriend and to shout to him that she was in trouble. The appellant thereupon took her mobile phone from her, removed the battery and pushed his victim to the ground. He then removed her trousers and ripped off her knickers. He knelt between her legs and put his finger into her vagina, and then he raped her.

5   Afterwards the victim attempted to get the appellant to walk back towards the garage, hoping that he would be recorded by the CCTV cameras. As they approached the garage the appellant gave the victim £5 and told her to go and

buy a drink. She in fact used her mobile phone to telephone 999 and the appellant ran off.

6   The appellant was not immediately caught, and so some three weeks later he was free to commit the second offence of rape. This time the victim was a 14-year-old girl. She was walking home on the evening of September 2, 1999. She became aware of the appellant following her. She increased her pace, but he continued to follow her and matched her increased pace. She ran across a roundabout and up an embankment. By now she was close to her home, but the appellant caught her and grabbed hold of her from behind. He brought her to the ground and landed on top of her. The victim was screaming for her mother. She could see her home in the distance and nearby residents could hear the screams, but no-one came to help her.

7   The appellant repeatedly punched the girl to the kidneys as he told her to shut up, and he tried to drag her into some bushes. He made her get on her hands and knees and began to undress her. He pulled off her trousers and then ripped off her knickers, put his finger into her vagina and then removed her upper clothing, leaving her only wearing her socks. His victim pleaded with him not to kill her. He said "I just want what I want and then I'm going". He then grabbed her by the hair, pulled back her head and raped her.

8   During the rape he asked how old his victim was. She told him and he said, "You're the youngest girl I've ever raped".

9   When he had completed the act, he then spanked her bottom with his hand and removed a belt from his trousers and whipped her across her lower back. He told her not to scream and he threatened to bite off her nipple if she did. He had ejaculated inside his victim.

10   After the rape was complete the appellant gave the victim her clothes, with the exception of her knickers which he kept. She ran home in a naked and distressed condition. She had a number of scratches, grazes and bruising to various parts of her body.

11   The rape was reported to the police and later that evening, at about 10.15pm, the appellant was seen running into some undergrowth. He was apprehended by police officers.

12   When interviewed the following day in relation to count 2, he claimed that the victim had said that she was 17 years of age, that she had offered to have sex with him having met him in the street, and that consensual intercourse had taken place.

13   He was interviewed also in relation to the rape the subject of count 1. Again, he told the story that there had been consensual intercourse between himself and his victim. Indeed, in this instance he claimed that his victim had suggested that sexual intercourse take place and was willing to accept £30 as the price of that.

14   In the course of these interviews he agreed that he had torn off and kept the girls' knickers as some sort of fetish. In each case there was DNA evidence confirming that intercourse had taken place.

15   The appellant is 34 years of age. He has no relevant previous convictions. There are two minor matters on his record in the early 1990s, but neither involves sex or violence.

16   The sentencing judge had available to him a psychiatric report. By the time the report was prepared the appellant had been convicted by the jury. He admitted to the psychiatrist that he had committed the offences of rape. However, he very much played down or denied the aggravating details of each of the two cases. The psychiatrist found that there was no mental disorder of a degree or nature which would warrant a hospital order, but he found that the appellant had a deviant sexual arousal to rape and sexual violence. He found that the appellant was a person who was unable to make full disclosure of the extent of his sexual fantasies and drive, and he concluded that the appellant represented a continuing grave and unpredictable risk of further sexual offending.

17   In the light of that report and the circumstances of the sexual attacks, it is hardly surprising that a discretionary life sentence was passed, and no complaint is made about that element of the sentence before us.

18   Counsel's grounds of appeal assert that the specified period of eight years is manifestly excessive because it appeared to have been based upon the 15-year plus category identified in *Millberry* [2003] 1 Cr.App.R. 25 (p.425). That category is said to include an extension of normal sentencing due to the inherent dangerousness of someone convicted of more than one offence, and therefore it is submitted there is an element of double sentencing when a life sentence is imposed.

19   Further, it is submitted to us that the judge failed to take account of the fact that this appellant had spent some 304 days on remand prior to sentencing which did not count towards the period specified by the judge.

20   When the judge passed sentence, he concluded his remarks in this way:

> "The sentences on you for the two counts of rape for which you were convicted by the jury are ones of life imprisonment and the minimum at which you would be considered for release by the parole board will be no less than eight years."

Defence counsel then queried whether that took account of the 304 days spent in custody on remand, to which the judge replied in the affirmative.

21   In specifying the minimum term pursuant to what is now s.82A of the Powers of Criminal Courts (Sentencing) Act 2000, the judge did not perform the exercise laid down in *M* (Discretionary Life Sentences) [1999] 1 Cr.App.R.(S) 6, of fixing what would otherwise have been an appropriate determinate term and then specifying the proportion, between a half and two-thirds, and giving credit for remand time. The later case of *Szczerba* [2002] 2 Cr.App.R.(S) 86 (p.387) confirmed that the normal proportion should be one half and, if a greater proportion was to be served, reasons must be given.

22   Working backwards from the 8-year term specified by the judge, it would appear that the judge had a determinate sentence of around 17 years and 9 months in mind.

23   Counsel for the appellant concedes that, if a life sentence had not been appropriate, the sentence passed in this case would have come within the 15-year plus category indicated in *R. v Millberry*. He further acknowledges that a sentence of 17 years and 9 months would not necessarily have been excessive as a straight-

forward determinate sentence. However, he urges that such a sentence, as a starting point in fixing a minimum term, involves an element of double sentencing. He
submits that such a starting point reflects elements of dangerousness and risk to
the public as opposed to the punitive element of the sentence, and goes on to argue
that the former element is covered by the passing of a discretionary life sentence
and so should not feature in fixing the starting point for the minimum term calculation.

24   We have been referred to *Campbell* [1997] 1 Cr.App.R.(S) 119. This was a case
where the court was considering what is now s.80(2)(b) of the Powers of the
Criminal Courts (Sentencing) Act 2000, that is longer than commensurate sentences, but the point seems to us to be analogous. At p.123 of the report,
Longmore L.J. says:

> "It seems to us that the right approach is this. If a court thinks that it is appro-
> priate to pass a section 2(2)(b) sentence [that was the precursor to section
> 80(2)(b)], the judge should make up his mind as to the appropriate sentence,
> leaving out of account, in the first instance, any element of enhancement to
> protect the public. Thus in a *Turner* or *Billam* case he may start with a lower
> sentence than he would have imposed if he did not intend also to impose a
> section 2(2)(b) sentence. After the sentencer has arrived at his starting point,
> he will then add the greater element needed for protection of the public from
> serious harm under section 2(2)(b). In this way the danger of imposing an
> element for the sentence of imprisonment twice over . . . can successfully
> be avoided."

25   We have also been referred to the case of *Marklew and Lambert* [1999] 1
Cr.App.R.(S.) 6, to which we have referred earlier in this judgment. It appears
to us that the remarks made by Thomas J. in the course of the Court's judgment
have a particular relevance in the context of this case. At p.12 of the report he says
this:

> "In the case of a young person who is to be sentenced to a period of detention
> for life under the provisions of section 53(2) or an adult who is to be sen-
> tenced to a discretionary life sentence, the general approach is to decide
> first the determinate part of the sentence that the judge would have imposed
> if the need to protect the public and the potential danger of the offender had
> not required him to pass a life sentence. It is the imposition of the life sen-
> tence that protects the public and is necessitated by the risk that the defend
> poses. That element is therefore not to be reflected in the determinate part of
> the sentence that the court would have imposed; the determinate part is
> therefore that part that would have been necessary to reflect punishment,
> retribution and the need for deterrence. It is we consider important that
> the judge should, when passing sentence, make clear to the defendant
> what that determinate period would have been."

26   We accept the argument of counsel that, in the fixing of a notional determinate
term, the element of the sentence reflecting the need to protect the public from
danger posed by the defendant should not be taken into account where a dis-

cretionary life sentence is being passed. However, judges should not overlook the need to reflect an element of deterrence, which may properly feature in fixing a notional determinate term. That much is made clear by the passage which we have cited from the case of *Marklew and Lambert*.

27   In the case of *Millberry* it is plain from a reading of paras [5] and [8] that a factor in the fixing of the 15-year starting point is the level of risk posed by the offender to society, and so, potentially in this case, the observations we have cited from *Campbell* and from *Marklew and Lambert* apply. However, we have to consider the circumstances of the two offences involved.

28   The appellant was convicted after a trial in which his victims had to give evidence, and so he lost any available mitigation which would result from a guilty plea. Both offences were committed by night and involved some element of deliberation and stalking. Both offences involved a fetishistic element in relation to the underwear, and the second girl was spanked and whipped and thus subjected to additional degradation. The second girl was only 14 and her youth was apparent to the appellant. The appellant used force over and above that necessary to commit the offence against the second girl. The judge, who had seen both victims, spoke of the seriously damaging effects on both of their lives as a result of their ordeal. The element of repetition is itself an aggravating feature. Previous good character in relation to violence and sexual offending can only be of limited value in the present circumstances.

29   That analysis leaves this Court to consider that these were grave offences, even ignoring the element of danger or risk posed to society. The second offence represents an escalation of gravity and an exacerbation of the picture depicted by the first offence.

30   The problem with this case, however, is that the judge did not indicate what factors were in his mind in fixing the specified period.

31   Our conclusion is that, even setting aside the risk aspect, a term in the region of 16 years would have been appropriate and that a term of 17 years and 9 months could not be justified in the circumstances. We have reached the figure of 16 years by concluding that consecutive sentences were appropriate in relation to the two offences. In our judgment, the first offence would have attracted a sentence of 5 years, with 11 years consecutive for the second offence.

32   It is important, in our judgment, to point out that, in making some discount in the fixing of a notional determinate sentence, a precise mathematical exercise is not required. What is required is that the judge should be alive to the risk of double counting and that he should perform a mental balancing exercise in arriving at an appropriate discount. What he must do is to make an allowance in relation to the public risk element of the term and ensure that it is not reflected in fixing the notional determinate sentence.

33   Applying what we consider to be the appropriate practice to the notional term of 16 years which we have arrived at, we divide that figure by two, arriving at 8 years, and from that it is appropriate to deduct the period of 304 days spent in custody on remand. Thus, we fix the minimum term to be served prior to release by the Parole Board at 8 years less 304 days. It is that term which we fix in place of

the eightyears specified by the judge, and to that extent only this appeal is allowed.

R. v DANIEL KENT LAWRENCE

COURT OF APPEAL (Lord Justice Mance, Mr Justice Gibbs and Judge Openshaw Q.C.): July 26, 2004

[2004] EWCA Crim 2219; [2005] 1 Cr.App.R.(S.) 83

(LT) Guilty pleas; Intimidation of witnesses; Intoxication; Sentence length; Threatening to kill

H1   *Threatening revenge on witness—defendant threatening father following dispute while drunk—length of sentence*

H2   Sixteen months' imprisonment for threatening revenge on a witness, imposed on a man who threatened his father who had called the police after a dispute, varied to eight months.

H3   The appellant pleaded guilty to threatening to take revenge on a witness. The appellant had been living with his father in his father's flat, but the relationship was difficult. The appellant and his father went out drinking. In the early hours of the morning the appellant pushed his father and took £160 from him. The appellant's father called the police but the appellant refused to allow them into the flat. He left the flat when police officers forced an entry. The appellant's father was advised to lock himself inside the flat while the police looked for the appellant. The appellant's father locked himself inside the flat but found the appellant was there. The appellant began to abuse his father, threatening to kill him. The appellant was subsequently found by police officers hiding in a cupboard. Sentenced to 16 months' imprisonment.

H4   **Held:** the sentencing judge observed that the appellant had made a serious threat by way of revenge against his father for having gone to the police, and had repeated the threats in the presence of police officers. The appellant had previous convictions for threatening behaviour, assault and wounding. The Court considered that as the offence was committed when the appellant was in drink and in part when he was in police custody, the sentence was more severe than was necessary. Despite the seriousness of any offence involving a threat to kill, an appropriate starting point would have been 12 months, and giving a discount for the appellant's plea of guilty would result in a sentence of eight months' imprisonment. That sentence would be substituted.

H5   **References:** intimidating a witness, *Current Sentencing Practice* B 8-2.3AA

H6   *Miss L. Whittle-Martin* for the appellant.

JUDGMENT

1   **Mance L.J.:**   On April 26, 2004 at the Crown Court at Portsmouth the appellant pleaded guilty on rearraignment and was sentenced by H.H. Judge Milligan to 16 months' imprisonment for an offence of threatening to take revenge, the particulars of which were that on December 12, 2003, knowing or believing that John Cyril Lawrence (that is his father) had assisted in the investigation of an offence, and because of what he knew or believed threatened to do an act, namely to kill him, which was intended to cause John Cyril Lawrence to fear harm. The appeal against that sentence is brought by leave of the single judge.

2   The circumstances of the offence need explaining because they put a slightly different aspect on what, from the particulars, would seem a very serious charge. At the time of the offence the appellant had been living with his father at his father's flat for about six months, but the relationship was fraught and the father was not really content that the appellant continue to stay. However, the father felt under some pressure from the appellant in that regard.

3   On the evening of December 11, 2003 the two of them had been out at bingo and drinking. At about 4.30am on December 12 they argued about money. The appellant had won some money on bets he had placed on football, apparently at Ladbrokes. John Lawrence maintained that he had won money playing bingo the night before. It was alleged that the appellant punched John Lawrence to the chest and took £160 from him. That gave rise to two counts which were, at the end of the day, left on the file on the usual terms: that was a count of assault occasioning actual bodily harm and a second count of robbery.

4   As a result, however, of this altercation John Lawrence left the flat and telephoned the police. He then returned with the police, but the appellant refused to let them into the flat. Officers forced entry, when it appeared that the appellant had left the premises through a balcony door. John Lawrence was advised to lock himself inside the premises whilst the police looked for the appellant. John Lawrence went back inside the flat and locked the door of the balcony, but turned round and then saw the appellant behind him. The appellant began verbally to abuse him, saying, "I'm gonna kill you. You're dead. You can't do nothing. I'll tell everyone around that you are a sex offender" and "You'll be dead".

5   John Lawrence left the flat again and locked the appellant inside. He telephoned the police and then returned to the flat with officers. The flat was again searched. The appellant could again not be found. But as the officers were about to leave, they opened a cupboard door and found the appellant inside. The appellant was then arrested, and as he was in police custody and being led to the police van he shouted the words: "You paedophile. I'm gonna tell all the mums you're a paedophile. I'll get bail and kill you" and "I'm gonna write to all the mums and tell them you're a paedophile".

6   The judge in sentencing the appellant said that he had made very serious threats by way of revenge against his father for having gone to the police and he had repeated those threats in the presence of the police officers. The threats were thoroughly offensive, intimidating and unpleasant by anyone's standards. Being drunk was no excuse for an offence as serious as this. The appellant had

been offending since 1985. At the age of 35 he seemed to have committed every offence in the book. He seemed to have had every sentence available and seemed to have learned nothing. The pre-sentence report was taken into account. It indicated that he had little, if any, idea of the effect of the threats and he did not seem to care very much what the effect might have been. He did not see the need to change anything about the way he behaved, drunk or sober. The judge concluded that there was no alternative to a custodial sentence. He took account of the factors raised on his behalf by counsel, particularly, of course, the plea of guilty; but said that anybody who is prepared to get involved in threatening witnesses, taking revenge on complainants and acting in any way that is calculated to undermine the proper processes of law in a free society must recognise that there is no alternative in their case but a prison sentence. He concluded that the appropriate sentence would be two years but gave one-third remission for the plea.

7   The previous convictions of this appellant, who was born on February 21, 1968, include five prior offences of threatening behaviour, six in respect of assault on an officer, four of damaging property, two of assault occasioning actual bodily harm, one of wounding contrary to s.20, and one of common assault.

8   The pre-sentence report referred to a history of offending underpinned by difficulty in controlling anger, especially when drinking, and a high risk of reoffending with a medium risk of harm. It reflected what the judge had said: that, until he developed a greater appreciation of these factors and began to consider others, the risks would remain. He did not seem well motivated to develop insight into his behaviour.

9   The grounds of appeal are straightforward: the sentence of imprisonment was manifestly excessive; and that found some sympathy on the part of the single judge.

10   We too think that, bearing in mind the circumstances of this offence, the fact that what was said was said in drink, and the fact that the latter part of the threats were made from police custody at a time when clearly he could not fulfil them, the sentence passed was more severe than was necessary, even against the background of the record.

11   As regards the first part of the threats, they were not executed in any way, although the police were not at that point there—indeed John Lawrence, the father, was able to leave the flat and to lock the appellant inside and telephone the police again and return with officers. Looking at the matter in the round, we consider that the judge's starting point of two years on a guilty plea was considerably too high and that an appropriate starting point, despite the seriousness of any offence involving a threat to kill, and despite the seriousness of the context, namely the investigation of the offence, would have been one year. Giving the one-third discount for the plea of guilty which the judge gave, the resulting sentence which we consider would be appropriate in the circumstances is one of eight months' imprisonment. To that extent this appeal succeeds. We therefore quash the sentence of 16 months' imprisonment passed and substitute it by a sentence of 8 months' imprisonment.

[Paragraph [12] has been omitted]

R. v THOMAS MAGUIRE

COURT OF APPEAL (Lord Justice Scott Baker, Mr Justice Richards
and Dame Heather Steel): July 26, 2004

[2004] EWCA Crim 2220; [2005] 1 Cr.App.R.(S.) 84

(LT) Automatic life imprisonment; Extended sentences; Grievous bodily harm;
Minimum term; Public protection; Wounding with intent

H1 *Life imprisonment—automatic life sentence—specified period for the purposes
of the Powers of Criminal Courts (Sentencing) Act 2000, s.82A—whether appropriate to calculate specified period on the basis that the notional determinate
sentence would have been a longer than commensurate sentence passed in
accordance with the Powers of Criminal Courts (Sentencing) Act 2000,
s.80(2)(b)*

H2 **Editor's note:** a court fixing the specified period of life sentence for the purposes of the Powers of Criminal Courts (Sentencing) Act 2000, s.82A, should not
calculate the period on the basis that the appropriate notional determinate sentence would have been a longer than commensurate sentence passed in
accordance with the Powers of Criminal Courts (Sentencing) Act 2000,
s.80(2)(b).

H3 The appellant was convicted of wounding with intent to cause grievous bodily
harm, and of doing an act tending and intended to pervert the course of justice. A
dispute arose between the appellant's family and a man who owed them money in
connection with the supply of cannabis. The appellant stabbed the man around
the groin and thigh, cutting his left femoral artery and causing him to suffer severe
blood loss. The victim was taken to hospital where he required surgery. The
appellant had been convicted in 1994 of manslaughter and was liable to an automatic life sentence under the Powers of Criminal Courts (Sentencing) Act 2000,
s.109. Sentenced to an automatic life sentence with a specified period of six years
and 20 weeks, derived from a notional determinate sentence of 14 years' imprisonment, and allowing for a period of 32 weeks spent in custody on remand.

H4 **Held:** (considering *Marklew and Lambert* [1999] 1 Cr.App.R.(S.) 6 and *Pollin*
[1997] 2 Cr.App.R.(S.) 356) the sentencing judge observed that the appellant
posed a risk of serious harm to the public and that the notional determinate sentence would have been a longer than commensurate sentence of 14 years'
imprisonment. It was submitted that the sentencing judge erred in principle by
fixing the notional determinate sentence by reference to a longer than commensurate sentence. The effect of the relevant legislation had been considered in
Marklew and Lambert [1999] 1 Cr.App.R.(S.) 6, where the Court made clear
that in determining the notional determinate sentence, the sentencer should
leave out of account the additional element of the need to protect the public,

since that need was being met by the imposition of a life sentence in the first place. Against that background, the Court's conclusion was that the sentencing judge did err in setting the notional determinate sentence as a longer than commensurate sentence. The setting of a notional determine sentence where an automatic life sentence had been passed was part of the process of specifying the minimum period to be served before the offender's release could be considered by the Parole Board. In the Court's judgment, the correct approach to the setting of that notional determinate sentence was to leave out of account the need to protect the public, which was catered for by the imposition of a life sentence, and to focus on the other elements of sentencing. Where a longer than commensurate sentence was imposed as a determinate sentence, it was because of the need to protect the public from serious harm from the offender. Accordingly it was inappropriate to apply the concept of a longer than commensurate sentence in setting the notional determinate sentence for the purposes of s.82A. It followed that it was necessary for the Court to consider what an appropriate notional determinate sentence would have been, leaving aside the additional consideration of the need to protect the public from serious harm. This was a very serious offence of violence involving a knife attack which the victim survived only because of prompt medical attention. In the Court's judgment, an appropriate notional determinate sentence would have been 12 years' imprisonment. Applying the principles in *Marklew and Lambert*, and allowing for the time spent in custody on remand produced a specified period of 5 years and 20 weeks, which would be specified for the purposes of the Powers of Criminal Courts (Sentencing) Act 2000, s.82A. The concurrent sentence of 5 years' imprisonment for perverting the course of justicei would be reduced to 18 months.

H5   **Cases cited:**
Marklew and Lambert [1999] 1 Cr.App.R.(S.) 6, *Pollin* [1997] 2 Cr.App.R.(S.) 356

H6   **References:** life imprisonment, specified period, *Current Sentencing Practice* F 3–4, *Archbold*

H7   *R. Thorn Q.C.* for the appellant.

JUDGMENT

1   **Richards J.:**   On March 25, 2003 in the Crown Court at Newcastle-upon-Tyne, the appellant, Thomas Maguire, was convicted on count 2 of wounding with intent to cause grievous bodily harm and on count 3 of doing an act tending and intended to pervert the course of justice. He was acquitted on count 1 of attempted murder. On April 16, 2003 he was sentenced by H.H. Judge Hodson to life imprisonment on count 2 and five years' imprisonment concurrently on count 3. The sentence upon count 2 was expressed to be an automatic life sen-

tence under s.109 of the Powers of Criminal Courts (Sentencing) Act 2000. The notional determinate sentence was said to be 14 years' imprisonment and the specified period, allowing for a period of some 32 weeks in custody on remand, was 6 years and 20 weeks. An appeal is now brought against sentence with leave of the single judge.

2   The victim of the offence of wounding with intent was a man called Kevin Millar who had known the appellant, the appellant's nephew Michael Maguire and the appellant's mother for many years. It was said that the Maguires were involved in the supply of cannabis in their area and that Millar had worked for them. During 2001 he gradually withdrew from dealing to spend more time with a girlfriend. But he had become indebted to the Maguires in the sum of about £300 and was in financial difficulties. He tried to remedy the situation by cheating the Maguires, a strategy which did not work. His debt increased to over £1,000. Eventually he told them that he had lost a nine-ounce bar of cannabis from a hiding place.

3   On August 21, 2002 Millar called on the appellant's mother to run some errands for her. The appellant and his nephew Michael were in the house. Michael began shouting at Millar about his debt. The sentencing judge accepted that what followed may have sprung up spontaneously. The appellant came towards Millar with a knife and shouted at him: "You little shit, you've ripped me off, I know about it, You'd better watch out cos I'm going to kill you". With this he put the point of the knife in the centre of Millar's chest and ran the blade down, producing a shallow laceration. He then said words to the effect of: "I'm gonna put you six feet under" and stabbed Millar around the groin and thigh, cutting his left femoral artery and causing him to suffer severe blood loss. Millar fell to the floor. He heard Michael Maguire say words to the effect of: "I think you went too far Tommy, I'll take him to hospital". The appellant responded with: "Na, just let him bleed to fucking death". Michael, however, tied something around Millar's thigh to lessen the bleeding and did take him to hospital.

4   At hospital Millar needed resuscitation and a massive blood transfusion. He spent some time in surgery. His injuries were found to consist of the chest laceration, a one-inch laceration to the front of his right thigh requiring four stitches, and two stab wounds within what appears as a surgical scar to the inside of his theft thigh. It was the wound to the left thigh which resulted in the blood loss. The wound was initially left exposed to prevent infection, but was subsequently dealt with by skin grafts. A home office pathologist gave as his opinion that had skilled medical assistance not been immediately available it was likely that Millar would have died. Those were the events that were the subject of count 2.

5   The day after that incident, the appellant met up with a Mr Newton, another man who had been involved in the sale of drugs for the Maguires. Mr Newton was aware of the injuries to Millar. Referring to Millar as "Jock", the appellant said to Mr Newton words to the effect of: "Tell Jock, whisper in his lug, that there is five to ten 'G' when he's all sweet and back on his feet." Taken in the context of an earlier conversation which we need not recite, those words were in effect an attempt to silence Millar by offering him money. Mr Newton later went to Millar's home, spoke to Millar's partner and asked her to pass the message on to

Millar, which she did. Far from silencing Millar, however, the offer led to count 3, the charge of perverting the course of justice.

6   When arrested and interviewed in early September the appellant denied involvement in the stabbing and gave an alibi. A week or so later his nephew Michael made a statement to the police claiming that he, Michael, had been responsible for the stabbing and that the appellant had not been present at the time. The appellant and Michael adhered to that line in their evidence at trial. The underlying reality of the matter was that Michael agreed to take the blame because the appellant would be subject to an automatic life sentence if he were found guilty. In any event the appellant was convicted and Michael thereafter pleaded guilty on rearraignment to assisting an offender by supplying false information.

7   The appellant is a man aged 35 and has a bad record of violent offending. In 1994 he was sentenced to five years' imprisonment for manslaughter. That arose out of an incident in which he had forced entry into a house and had assaulted one of the occupants by hitting him about the head with an iron bar. The following day the father and brother of the injured man confronted the appellant who then stabbed the father in the leg, severing an artery and causing fatal injuries, and also stabbed the brother. He was convicted of the manslaughter of the father and of wounding the brother with intent. It is not in dispute that by reason of those earlier convictions the automatic life sentence provisions of s.109 of the 2000 Act were triggered in this case. Apart from those offences the appellant had five or six convictions for assaulting police officers and six or seven for assault occasioning actual bodily harm. There had, however, been no further convictions between 1994 and the events giving rise to the present case.

8   The pre-sentence report said that since his release from prison in late 1996 the appellant had curbed his previous pattern of excess consumption of alcohol and had acquired settled accommodation and a settled relationship. He had a fiancee and responsibility for looking after a young child. The report also referred to the fact that his previous record of behaviour in prison was good. To this we can add what is said in a prison report of April 2003 which states that during his period in prison since he was first remanded in custody for the present offences, the appellant had conducted himself in an exemplary fashion, which is a credit to him. We are told that that good conduct has continued. We take those matters into account, though they are of limited relevance to the decision we need to make.

9   In passing sentence the judge said that he had absolutely no doubt that the appellant posed a risk of causing serious harm to the public. He referred to the appellant's record and to the similarity of the present offence to the circumstances of the 1994 manslaughter. It was his view that the appellant had attacked Millar to teach him a lesson for cheating him. In relation to the notional determinate sentence on count 2, he then said this:

> "Bearing in mind your previous convictions, bearing in mind the risk that you pose to the public of causing serious harm to the public, I take the view that for the protection of the public a determinate sentence would

have required a longer than commensurate sentence and the determinate sentence which I would have had in mind would have been one of 14 years' imprisonment."

10 The main ground of appeal as advanced on the appellant's behalf by Mr Thorn Q.C., is that the judge erred in setting the notional determinate sentence by reference to a longer than commensurate sentence. It is submitted that a longer than commensurate sentence is excluded or is wrong in principle when setting the notional determinate sentence in the case of an automatic life sentence under s.109.

11 General provisions concerning the length of discretionary custodial sentences are laid down in s.80 of the 2000 Act:

"(1) This section applies where a court passes a custodial sentence other than one fixed by law or falling to be imposed under section 109(2) below.

(2) Subject to sections 110(2) and 111(2) below, the custodial sentence shall be—

(a) for such term (not exceeding the permitted maximum) as in the opinion of the court is commensurate with the seriousness of the offence, or the combination of the offence and one or more offences associated with it; or

(b) where the offence is a violent or sexual offence, for such term (not exceeding that maximum) as in the opinion of the court is necessary to protect the public from serious harm from the offender."

Section 109 reads:

"(1) This section applies where—

(a) a person is convicted of a serious offence committed after 30th September 1997; and

(b) at the time when that offence was committed, he was 18 or over and had been convicted in any part of the United Kingdom of another serious offence.

(2) The court shall impose a life sentence, that is to say—

(a) where the offender is 21 or over when convicted of the offence mentioned in subsection (1)(a) above, a sentence of imprisonment for life . . .

(4) An offence the sentence for which is imposed under subsection (2) above shall not be regarded as an offence the sentence for which is fixed by law."

2 Where a life sentence is passed the sentencer is required to specify a period to be served before the offender can be considered for release on licence by the Parole Board.

This is dealt with by s.82A of the 2000 Act, which provides:

This section applies if a court passes a life sentence in circumstances where—

    (a) the sentence is not fixed by law; . . .

(2) The court shall, unless it makes an order under subsection (4) below, order that the provisions of section 28(5) to (8) of the Crime (Sentences) Act 1997 (referred to in this section as the 'early release provisions') shall apply to the offender as soon as he has served the part of his sentence which is specified in the order.

(3) The part of his sentence shall be such as the court considers appropriate taking into account—

    (a) the seriousness of the offence, or the combination of the offence and one or more offences associated with it;

    (b) the effect of any direction which it would have given under section 87 below (crediting periods of remand in custody) if it had sentenced him to a term of imprisonment; and

    (c) the early release provisions as compared with sections 33(2) and 35(1) of the Criminal Justice Act 1991."

13   The effect of the corresponding provisions of earlier legislation, including the reference across to s.28 of the Crime (Sentences) Act 1997 and the effect of the relevant Practice Direction, now in para.47 of the Consolidated Practice Direction for Criminal Proceedings, was considered in *Marklew and Lambert* [1999] 1 Cr.App.R.(S) 6, albeit the specific context was that of discretionary life sentences rather than automatic life sentences. It is unnecessary to repeat the detail of the guidance there given. In the course of the judgment, however, the Court made clear that in determining the notional determinate sentence the sentencer should leave out of account the additional element of the need to protect the public, since that need was being met by the imposition of a life sentence in the first place. Thus it was said at 12:

"In the case of . . . an adult who is to be sentenced to a discretionary life sentence the general approach is to decide first the determinate part of the sentence that the judge would have imposed if the need to protect the public and the potential danger of the offender had not required him to pass a life sentence. It is the imposition of the life sentence that protects the public and is necessitated by the risk that the defendant poses. That element is therefore not to be reflected in the determinate part of the sentence that the court would have imposed; the determinate part is therefore that part that would have been necessary to reflect punishment, retribution, and the need for deterrence."

On the following page the Court stated that the judge should spell out not only the period specified under s.28(3) of the Crime (Sentences) Act but also the determinate sentence he would have passed "but for the need to protect the public."

14   Against that background our conclusion in relation to the main ground of appeal is that the judge in this case did err in setting the notional determinate sentence as a longer than commensurate sentence. This is not however, as Mr Thorn

put forward as his primary submission, simply because s.80(1) excludes a sentence passed under s.109(2). That exclusion reflects the obvious point that an automatic life sentence under s.109(2) is not governed directly by the general provisions relating to discretionary custodial sentences in s.80. The setting of a notional determinate sentence where an automatic life sentence has been passed is a separate exercise. It is part of the process of specifying, as required by s.82A, the minimum period to be served before the offender's release can be considered by the Parole Board. In our judgment, for the reasons given in *Marklew and Lambert*, the correct approach to the setting of that notional determinate sentence is to leave out of account the need to protect the public, which is catered for by the very imposition of a life sentence, and to focus on the other elements of sentencing. Where a longer than commensurate sentence is imposed as a determinate sentence under s.80(2)(b) it is because of the need to protect the public from serious harm from the offender. Accordingly it is inappropriate to apply the concept of a longer than commensurate sentence in setting the notional determinate sentence in accordance with s.82A.

5   Since, in our judgment, the sentencing judge was wrong to approach the matter in terms of a longer than commensurate sentence, it is necessary for us to consider what an appropriate determinate sentence would have been, leaving aside the additional consideration of the need to protect the public from serious harm. As to that, this was on any view a very serious offence of violence involving a vicious knife attack which the victim survived only because of prompt medical intervention.

6   Mr Thorn has referred us to *Pollin* [1997] 2 Cr.App.R.(S.) 356, a case involving a premeditated, vicious, repeated and near fatal knife attack, in which a sentence of nine years' imprisonment on a plea of guilty was upheld on appeal, with the Court stressing the public concern about the use of such weapons. We do not suggest that the present case is on all fours with *Pollin*, but *Pollin* does give a measure of the seriousness with which offences of this kind are viewed.

7   As to the present case, we have borne in mind the various aggravating and mitigating features to which we have already referred. In our judgment an appropriate notional determinate sentence in the circumstances of the case would have been one of 12 years' imprisonment. Applying the same approach as the judge, and again in line with the principles started in *Marklew and Lambert*, we will halve that sentence and deduct the time spent in custody on remand in order to reach the specified period for the purposes of s.82A. The resulting figure is one of five years and 20 weeks. Accordingly, we will quash the judge's specified period of 6 years and 20 weeks and substitute one of 5 years and 20 weeks. We stress that release after that time will of course depend on the Parole Board assessing that the appellant no longer poses a danger to the public.

8   Mr Thorn raises in addition the sentence on count 3 which is to some extent academic. Perverting the course of justice is itself a serious offence and, as the judge observed, would have called for a consecutive sentence had it not been for the imposition of a life sentence on count 2. On the other hand, account must be taken of the fact that the offence in question did not involve threats or

intimidation, but an attempt to bribe the victim into silence, and although the offer was communicated to the victim it was conspicuously unsuccessful.

19   In our view, a sentence of five years' imprisonment was manifestly excessive given the circumstances of that offence. We will quash that sentence and substitute one of 18 months' imprisonment on count 3, still of course concurrent with the life sentence on count 2. To that extent, for the reasons we have given, the appeal is allowed.

R. v SEAN HUNTROYD

Court of Appeal (Lord Justice May, Mr Justice Gray and Mrs Justice Hallett): July 27, 2004

[2004] EWCA Crim 2182; [2005] 1 Cr.App.R.(S.) 85

Attempts; Dangerous driving; Grievous bodily harm; Motor vehicles; Police officers; Sentence length

H1   *Attempting to cause grievous bodily harm with intent—driver of car driving at police officer, then driving off at speed with officer on roof of car—length of sentence*

H2   Nine years' imprisonment upheld for attempting to cause grievous bodily harm with intent, where the driver of a car drove at a police officer, then drove off at speed with the officer on the roof of the car and swerved so as to throw the officer off the car.

H3   The appellant was convicted of attempting to cause grievous bodily harm with intent. A police officer on foot patrol noticed a person in a car in a service area holding a can of lager and asked for a CCTV operator to alert him when the vehicle left the service area. The officer was later informed that the vehicle had left the service area. The officer approached the area on foot, moved into the middle of the road and signalled to the appellant, who was driving the car, to stop. The appellant appeared to begin to stop the car, but then appeared to drive directly at the officer. The officer managed to turn his body before the vehicle hit him at knee height at a speed of between 15 and 20 miles an hour. The officer ended up on the roof of the car, and the appellant drove off with the officer hanging on to the sun roof. The appellant accelerated, reaching a speed of about 36 miles an hour, went the wrong way around a roundabout and continued to try to throw the officer off the car by swerving from side to side, accelerating and braking. The speedometer reading was seen to reach 60mph. The officer repeatedly asked the appellant to stop but the appellant took no notice and attempted to close the sun roof in order to force the officer to let go. The officer was eventually thrown into the road. The officer suffered various injuries including a fracture. Sentenced to nine years' imprisonment, with one year and nine months' imprisonment concurrent for dangerous driving.

H4   **Held:** (considering *Cooper* [1996] 1 Cr.App.R.(S.) 303, *Boulter* [1996] 2 Cr.App.R.(S.) 428, *Hall* [1997] 1 Cr.App.R.(S.) 62, *Attorney General's Reference No.78 of 2000 (Jason Jones)* [2002] 1 Cr.App.R.(S.) 116 (p.500)) the sentencing judge proceeded on the basis that the appellant did everything he could to throw the officer off the car. The Court accepted that the injuries suffered by the officer were less serious than might have been anticipated. His injuries might well have been fatal, given the speed at which the appellant was driving. The gravity of the offence lay in the appellant's intent. The victim was a police officer doing his duty; even if the appellant did not drive at the officer, his manner of driving after the initial impact demonstrated that his intent was to cause really serious harm. His motivation was to escape the prison sentence which he knew he would face if apprehended. This was a grave offence. The sentence of nine years was wholly appropriate.

I5   **Cases cited:**
Cooper [1996] 1 Cr.App.R.(S.) 303, *Boulter* [1996] 2 Cr.App.R.(S.) 428, *Hall* [1997] 1 Cr.App.R.(S.) 62, *Attorney General's Reference No.78 of 2000 (Jason Jones)* [2002] 1 Cr.App.R.(S.) 116 (p.500)

I6   **References:** causing grievous bodily harm with intent, *Current Sentencing Practice* B 2-2

I7   *S. Montrose* for the appellant.
Miss N. Merrick for the Crown.

JUDGMENT

1   **Gray J.:**   This is an appeal against sentence brought with the leave of the single judge.

2   The appellant, Sean Huntroyd, was convicted by a jury at the Central Criminal Court on February 19, 2004 of attempting to cause grievous bodily harm with intent contrary to s.18 of the Offences Against the Person Act. This was an alternative verdict, the appellant having been indicted for the full offence of causing grievous bodily harm with intent. The appellant had pleaded guilty to two other offences on the indictment, namely assault occasioning actual bodily harm and dangerous driving. The sentences which were imposed by the trial judge, H.H. Judge Paget, on the day of conviction were these: for attempting to cause grievous bodily harm with intent, nine years' imprisonment, for assault occasioning actual bodily harm, no separate penalty, for dangerous driving one year and nine months' imprisonment concurrent. The appellant was, in addition, disqualified from driving for 10 years and was ordered to take an extended driving test. There were five other summary offences. No separate penalty was imposed in respect of them. The total custodial sentence was, therefore, one of nine years' imprisonment.

3   The offences took place in the following circumstances. On July 19, 2003 PC Teague was on duty on foot patrol in Camberley, Surrey. At around lunch-time he

went to the Main Square security control room and noticed, via CCTV, a blue car in the service area at the rear of some shops. The passenger in the car was holding a can of lager and the officer asked the CCTV operator to alert him when the vehicle left the service area as he wished to discover whether the driver, who was the appellant, had also been drinking.

4   PC Teague resumed his foot patrol in the town centre until he was informed that the vehicle, driven by the appellant, was leaving the service station. The officer then approached the service area on foot. As he did so, the appellant drove towards the officer who moved into the middle of the road, which was a one way street, and signalled to the appellant to stop. The appellant appeared to acknowledge the officer and started to pull the car over as if to stop. However, he then put the car into gear and appeared to some witnesses present to drive directly at the officer. The officer tried to move towards the opposite side of the road to get out of the way, but knew there was no chance of avoiding the vehicle. He managed to turn his face, body and backside away at which point the car struck him on the back of his legs. The impact was at knee height and was just like a massive smack. He estimated that the car was being driven at between 15 and 20 miles per hour.

5   The windscreen of the car was smashed and the police officer ended up on the roof of the car. The appellant then drove off with the officer hanging onto the sunroof. At one point the officer heard the appellant say, "That takes care of that fucking cunt." He could smell alcohol coming up from the middle of the car. The passenger in the vehicle then said, "What have you done, you idiot, you've fucking killed him, you're crazy." We should record the fact that the appellant denied saying what was attributed to him.

6   The appellant's reaction was to accelerate, reaching, according to some of the evidence, a speed of 36 miles an hour down a busy high street crowded with shoppers on a Saturday afternoon. He went the wrong way round a roundabout and continued to try to throw the officer off the car by swerving from side to side, accelerating and putting the brakes on. The victim saw the speedometer reach 60 miles an hour. He repeatedly asked the appellant to stop. The appellant took no notice and at one point tried to close the sunroof onto the officer's fingers in order to force him to let go. When he reached the end of that road, he turned left at such speed that the car lurched across to the wrong side of the road and the officer was thrown into the road. The appellant sped off and later abandoned the vehicle. It turned out that he had taken his partner's car without consent and was a disqualified driver.

7   The officer was shaking uncontrollably after his experiences. He was taken to hospital. He complained of pain in his head and over his left arm. He had two large superficial abrasions at the level of the shoulder blades and had multiple abrasions to both hands and fingers. There was a large superficial wound to the left elbow and he was also tender over the carpal bones and unable to flex his left wrist joint. The wounds were cleansed and dressed and he was allowed to go home. It was later found that he had sustained a fracture of the scaphoid bone. By the time of the trial, some six months after the incident, the fracture

was starting to mend. By that stage the officer was still unable to return to normal duties and was experiencing difficulty sleeping.

8 The appellant is now a 31-year-old man. He and his partner have three young children. We are told this morning that there is reason to suppose that one of them is highly disturbed at what has happened to his father.

9 No pre-sentence report was obtained before sentence. There is, however, before this Court a medical report which describes an extensive drug and alcohol history which the appellant has apparently being trying to bring to an end. He has a bad criminal record with many offences of both dishonesty and violence. Amongst other driving offences, the appellant has three convictions for driving whilst disqualified.

10 The principal ground on which Mr Montrose, on behalf of the appellant, contends that this sentence was manifestly excessive is that the injuries suffered by the officer were happily less serious than they might have been. It was the doubt on the part of the jury as to whether the injuries were really serious that apparently caused them to bring in the alternative verdict of attempting to cause grievous bodily harm with intent. Mr Montrose submits that what happened was that, when he saw the police constable standing in the middle of the road, the appellant panicked and was trying to get away from the officer in order to avoid being sent back to prison. He argues that evidence of the accident investigators tends to show that the appellant was trying to drive around the officer rather than driving at him. Mr Montrose is critical of the judge for accepting the evidence of the eye witnesses who thought that the appellant had driven at the officer.

11 The judge had heard all of the evidence and was entitled to form his view. Be that as it may, there can be no disputing the fact that the appellant did everything he could afterwards to throw the officer off the car which would have given rise to the obvious risk of his being seriously injured.

2 The appellant is said to be remorseful. We accept that he pleaded guilty to the subsidiary counts of actual bodily harm and dangerous driving at the first opportunity and that thereby he accepted responsibility for some of the injuries and, of course, for the quality of his driving.

3 Mr Montrose has referred this Court to a number of authorities: *Cooper* [1996] 1 Cr.App.R.(S.) 303, *Boulter* [1996] 2 Cr.App.R.(S.) 428, *Hall* [1997] 1 Cr.App.R.(S.) 62 and, finally, *Attorney General's Reference No.78 of 2000* [2001] 1 Cr.App.R.(S.) 116. The sentences imposed in those cases, which all involved defendants causing really serious injuries to police officers by the dangerous use of cars, is within a range from $7\frac{1}{2}$ years to 12 years. We accept that in each of those cases the injuries sustained by the officers were more serious than in the present case. In *Boulter*, for example, the injuries were far worse, but the intent charged on the indictment against that appellant was a lesser one than in the present case. That appellant had his sentence reduced to seven-and-a-half years' imprisonment. In *Hall* again the injuries were worse, but that case lacked the aggravating feature present in this case, namely the prolonged and persistent attempt by the appellant to throw the police officer off the car. In *Cooper* the sentence was one of $7\frac{1}{2}$ years, but the appellant in that case was aged only $18\frac{1}{2}$.

14   We accept that the injuries suffered by this police officer were remarkably, in the circumstances, much less serious than might have been anticipated. If he had been thrown off the roof, however, his injuries might well have been fatal given the speed at which the appellant was driving. As it was, the experience for the officer was plainly traumatic and the effects of what he had undergone were by no means short lived. Whilst we accept that the comparatively minor nature of the injuries is a factor to be taken into account, it is the intent which in terms of the appellant's criminality weighs more heavily with us. This was a police officer doing his duty. Even if the appellant did not drive at the officer, his manner of driving after the initial impact demonstrates with crystal clarity his intent, as the jury found, to cause that officer really serious harm. The motivation of the appellant was to escape the prison sentence which he knew, in the light of his record, he would face if he was apprehended.

15   This was, in our judgment, a grave s.18 offence. The appellant contested the case, albeit offering guilty pleas to the subsidiary counts. There is no real personal mitigation. We take the view that the sentence of nine years which was imposed was a wholly appropriate sentence and in no way out of line with the guidance to be provided from the authorities to which we have referred. In these circumstances, the appeal must be dismissed.

R. v BASSAM OMAR

COURT OF APPEAL (Lord Justice Scott Baker, Mr Justice Richards and Dame Heather Steel): July 27, 2004

[2004] EWCA Crim 2320; [2005] 1 Cr.App.R.(S.) 86

LT Cheating the Revenue; Confiscation orders; Corporate personality; Justice; Proprietory rights

H1   *Confiscation order—company used as vehicle for fraud—whether appropriate to treat benefits received by company as benefits received by defendant—"lifting corporate veil"*

H2   **Editor's note:** where the appellant's company was used as the vehicle for a fraud on the Revenue, and the appellant was in sole charge of the company which was his alter ego, it was appropriate to "lift the corporate veil" and treat benefits received by the company as benefits received by the appellant, and property owned by the company as property owned by the appellant.

H3   The appellant was convicted of cheating the Public Revenue. The appellant was involved in a scheme by which computer parts were imported into the United Kingdom by a company with invoices which undervalued the goods, so that import duty and VAT were paid on the reduced value. The goods were then sold on and the purchasers were charged the full retail value. False invoices were provided to the company purporting to show that the goods had been purchased at their true value and that that appropriate VAT had been paid, which was then offset against the VAT collected by the company. The appellant's company was used as a vehicle for the fraud for more than a year. Sentenced to 18 months' imprisonment with a confiscation order under the Criminal Justice Act 1988 in the amount of £790,649. The appeal was limited to the confiscation order.

Held: the appellant submitted that the benefit which accrued to him was in fact a benefit which accrued to the company and could not be attributed to him personally. The sentencing judge rejected that submission, holding that the appellant had allowed the company to be used as the vehicle for committing the fraud and that it was therefore appropriate to lift the corporate veil. The matter had been considered in *Dimsey and Allen* [2000] 1 Cr.App.R.(S.) 497, where it was held that the corporate veil might be lifted when companies were used as a vehicle for fraud and the companies in question were the alter ego of the defendant. The appellant submitted that in this case the company acted as a conduit and that any monies unlawfully obtained were passed to and dissipated by the other defendants. It was not shown what monies were received by the appellant personally and it would be unfair for the corporate veil to be lifted and for the company's benefit to be attributed to the appellant. It was further submitted that various properties which had been treated as realisable property were the property of the company and not of the appellant. The Court rejected these submissions. In the Court's judgment, it could make no difference whether a company was set up as a sham in the first place or was an existing legitimate company which was then deployed for the purpose of fraud. The important point was that the company was used by the appellant for the purposes of fraud and was the appellant's alter ego, with the appellant running it and making all the decisions. The judge's findings were properly open to him on the evidence, and meant that the judge was fully entitled to lift the corporate veil and to treat the benefit accruing during the period of the company's involvement in the fraud as a benefit of the appellant. The judge's order was not unfair and did not create a risk of serious injustice. The fact that the appellant was ordered to pay more than his co-defendants, whose benefit was greater than his, did not affect the position. He paid more because he had the assets. The appeal would be dismissed.

Cases cited:
Dimsey and Allen [2000] 1 Cr.App.R.(S.) 497, *Benjafield* [2003] 1 A.C. 1099 *Re H* [1996] 2 All E.R. 391

References: confiscation order, *Current Sentencing Practice* J11–1A, *Archbold* 5–527

M. Kelly for the appellant.
S. Draycott Q.C. and *Miss J. Goldring* for the Crown.

JUDGMENT

1   **Richards J.:**   On March 11, 2002 at the Crown Court at Birmingham, this
appellant was convicted of an offence of cheating the Public Revenue. The effect
of further orders made that day and on July 4, 2002 is that he was sentenced to 18
months' imprisonment and a confiscation order was made against him under s.71
of the Criminal Justice Act 1988 in the sum of £790,649 to be paid within 12
months, with a period of 3 years' imprisonment consecutive in default. He
appeals by leave of the single judge against the confiscation order alone.

2   There were three co-defendants. Nicholas Skidmore pleaded guilty to four
counts of cheating the Public Revenue. He was sentenced to seven years' imprisonment and a confiscation order in the sum of £643,783 was made against him.
David Withers was convicted on two counts of cheating the Public Revenue. He
was sentenced to six years' imprisonment and a confiscation order in the sum of
£205,723 was made against him. Paul Burke pleaded guilty to two counts of
cheating the Public Revenue. He was sentenced to three years' imprisonment
and a confiscation order in the sum of £439,760 was made against him.

3   Skidmore and Withers had been involved in a company, Computerwise, which
imported computer memory parts from the USA and the Far East. Their suppliers
would dispatch the goods with invoices that gave a false description of goods and
a deliberate undervalue of them. Import duty and VAT were paid on that under-
stated value, though Computerwise would pay the suppliers the true value of the
goods. Computerwise would then sell the goods on at a true value, in the main to a
company called GSI, and the purchaser would be charged VAT on that true value.

4   In order to avoid accounting to the Commissioners of Customs and Excise for
the difference between the low VAT paid on importation and the higher VAT
charged on resale, Skidmore and Withers created false purchase invoices purporting to show that Computerwise had acquired the goods from a UK
company at true value and had paid the requisite VAT. The VAT showed on
those false invoices was then offset against the VAT owed to the Commissioners
in respect of the resale of the imported parts. That was the origin of the fraud.

5   In 1997, Skidmore and Withers fell out and Skidmore could no longer use
Computerwise to continue the fraud. He required a company through which
the memory parts could be imported and supplied to GSI. It was under those circumstances that he approached the appellant. The appellant was a college
lecturer teaching computer science. In 1996 he had set up a limited company
called Cambridge Computer Supplies Limited ("CCSL"). He and his wife
each held one share. Initially his wife was the director and he was the company
secretary. The company was registered for VAT in April 1996. It had retail premises and also supplied parts and fully assembled computers by mail order. The
judge accepted that CCSL had grown out of a legitimate business enterprise started by the appellant and that the company itself had been trading legitimately. But
in about August 1997, as a result of Skidmore's approach to the appellant, CCSL
took over the role formerly played by Computerwise in the fraud. Subject to that
change, the fraud continued in essentially the same way as before. At some point
Burke became involved in the fraud. It was decided that Burke would set up his

own business to be used specifically and solely as a vehicle for the fraud. In 1998 once Burke's business was established, that business took over the role played by CCSL, and CCSL's involvement came to an end.

6   The appellant was arrested in 1999, following which a restraining order was made against him. Eventually he faced one count in the indictment on which he was convicted, which related to the period of CCSL's involvement in the fraud. Skidmore and Burke pleaded guilty to the same count, as well as pleading guilty to one or more counts relating to other periods of time. At the confiscation hearing before the judge (H.H. Judge Stanley) it was agreed that, subject to his ruling on certain contested matters, the benefit figure relating to the relevant count was a sum of £2,008,715.40.

7   In his ruling, the judge considered three issues that had been raised before him. The first concerned the benefit. The appellant's case was that the benefit alleged to have accrued to him was in fact a benefit that accrued to the company, CCSL, and as such could not be attributed to him personally. The judge rejected that submission, holding that the appellant had allowed the company to be used as the vehicle for committing fraud and it was therefore appropriate to lift the company veil. On that point, he said this:

> ". . . having heard all the evidence in the case, particularly from Mr Omar himself, I am perfectly satisfied that CCSL was his alter ego. He ran the company, he made all the decisions, he decided what properties were going to be bought, how the business was to be run, who was to be employed and how all the principal decisions were made. True it is that his wife was brought into the company, I think as the company secretary at one stage and certainly as shareholder. But again on all the evidence that is available to me, particularly from what I heard in the trial, she played absolutely no part in the day-to-day running of the company and made none of the important decisions about it. It is quite plain that she had nothing to do with the actual operation of the fraud. It has never been suggested that she did. But she does not feature in the running of the company at all."

He thus concluded that the benefit was that of the appellant and not the company, though the appellant was of course responsible together with Skidmore and Burke in relation to that benefit.

The second issue was the need to guard against injustice. The judge cited passages in *Benjafield* [2003] 1 A.C. 1099. He cited passages both from Lord Woolf C.J. in the Court of Appeal and Lord Steyn in the House of Lords, to the effect that a judge must not make a confiscation order if there is, or might be, a serious or real risk of unfairness or injustice. The judge observed that those principles were relevant to the question of double recovery. Although the matter was complicated by his having to deal with confiscation orders piecemeal so that he did not have final figures in relation to the co-defendants, he concluded that the amount recoverable by way of confiscation orders against Skidmore and Burke in respect of the relevant count would be no more than £700,000 and £400,000 respectively, that is a total of £1.1 million. That would leave £900,000 out of the total benefit unsatisfied. The assets of the appellant taken at their highest would not exceed that figure. He therefore considered that there was no potential problem of double recovery, and the court did not need to moderate its order to avoid the risk of double recovery.

10   The third issue is what assets were available to the appellant himself. The question concerned a number of properties that had been bought out of the profits made by CCSL prior to the operation of the fraud. The properties had been registered in the appellant's sole name or the joint names of himself and his wife, though it appears that in the case of those in the joint names of himself and his wife only 50 per cent of the value of the property was being taken into account, thus leaving out of account the 50 per cent that might be attributable to his wife.

11   The submission for the appellant was that none of the value of those properties should be taken into account. It had always been the intention to treat them all as company assets. The judge heard from a chartered accountant, Mr Williams, who said that he had been instructed that the properties had been bought for company trading premises or as investments, and that after various enquiries he had satisfied the Inland Revenue that they were company assets. The judge said that he did not feel bound by the decision reached by the Inland Revenue about that. He also referred to certain correspondence and declarations of trust in 1999 and 2001 which treated the properties as company assets, though it is fair to say that he expressed a degree of scepticism about those documents, having regard to their timing.

12   Having examined the evidence, the judge accepted the prosecution approach, which was expressed in these terms:

> ". . . look at the reality of the matter and conclude that these properties, however they are treated for the purposes of accounting and revenue, were in reality the assets available to and controlled by Mr Omar . . .
>
> Mr Omar plainly treated these properties as under his control. There were various manoeuvrings of the properties for accounting and revenue purpose which obviously made sense from his point of view, but I reject the submission of the defence that they should be treated as company assets."

13   Accordingly, he concluded that their value was to be taken into account for the purposes of setting the amount of the confiscation order against the appellant. It was upon that basis that he concluded that the confiscation order should be in the sum of £790,649, a figure that had been agreed subject to his ruling on the contested issues to which we have referred.

14   Mr Kelly, appearing before us today on behalf of the appellant, raises a number of grounds of challenge to the judge's decision. He submits, first, that the judge was wrong to lift the corporate veil and to treat the benefit as attributable to the appellant rather than to the company, CCSL. A similar point arose in *Dimsey and Allen* [2000] 1 Cr.App.R.(S.) 497, also a case on cheating the Public Revenue and involving a confiscation order under s.71 of the 1988 Act. It was argued in that case that any pecuniary advantage that had arisen was that of certain offshore companies and not of the appellant. The Court of Appeal dismissed that argument in robust terms, stating:

"It is plain from authorities cited by the Crown that the corporate veil may fall to be lifted where companies are used as a vehicle for fraud. Here the companies in question were the appellant's alter ego . . .
On this part of the case it seems to us that the Crown's position is simply incontestable."

15　　Earlier, in *Re H* [1996] 2 All E.R. 391, a case involving the making of a restraint order and the appointment of a receiver under the provisions of the 1988 Act, the court carried out a somewhat more detailed review of the authorities and concluded that as a matter of law the corporate veil could clearly be lifted in appropriate cases. In that case, the evidence was said to provide a prima facie case that the defendants controlled the companies in question, that the companies had been used for fraud, in particular the evasion of excise duty on a large scale, that the defendants regarded the companies as carrying on a family business and that company cash had benefited the defendants in substantial amounts. In all the circumstances it was considered appropriate to lift the corporate veil and to treat the company's assets as property held by the defendants.

6　　Mr Kelly understandably concedes that a corporate veil can be lifted in appropriate circumstances. He submits that the present circumstances were not appropriate and he seeks to distinguish the two cases to which we have referred. He says that the company acted in the present case as a conduit. The monies unlawfully obtained were in fact passed through to, and dissipated by, the other defendants. It is not shown what, if any, monies were received by the appellant personally as a result of the fraud, and it would be unfair for the corporate veil to be lifted and the company's benefit to be attributed to him in those circumstances. The benefit, to the extent that it was derived by either the company or the appellant, was derived by the company.

7　　Further, it is submitted that the properties that had been purchased were the property of the company, which was a legitimate company set up for a legitimate purpose. The evidence demonstrated that it was always the intention that there should be a separation between CCSL and the appellant in relation to the properties which were regarded as properties of the company long before the appellant's arrest and the making of a restraint order against him. Although legal title in the properties was in the appellant's name or joint names of himself and his wife, they were all purchased with company funds and were either occupied by the company or purchased as an investment for the company. The profits from one of them, a hotel, were included in the company's accounts. The properties were shown on the company's balance sheet. The accountant, Mr Williams, produced a calculation that shareholders' funds would be in deficit to the sum of almost £200,000 if the net book value of the properties were excluded. Mr Williams had also, when instructed in about 1998, produced accounts which, because they showed a much higher profit than hitherto, triggered an Inland Revenue investigation, but during that investigation, the Revenue accepted that the properties had been paid for by and belonged to the company. So one sees in all of that, it is said, the operation of a legitimate business, acquiring property with the profits of that business. The company was plainly not a mere facade; it was not a sham. Prior to the participation in the fraud, it was trading properly and the properties were purchased before that participation in the fraud. In all those circumstances, it is submitted the lifting of the corporate veil was not appropriate.

18　　　We have no hesitation in rejecting those submissions. In our judgment, it can make no difference whether the company was set up as a sham in the first place or is an existing legitimate company that is then deployed for the purposes of fraud. The important point in the present case is that the company was used by the appellant for the purposes of fraud and that, as the judge found, it was the appellant's alter ego, with the appellant running it and making all the decisions, including decisions on the purchase of the properties. The judge's findings on those matters were all properly open to him on the evidence. They meant that he was fully entitled to lift the corporate veil and to treat the benefit accruing during the period of the company's involvement in the fraud as a benefit of the appellant. Once the corporate veil was lifted, subject to the arguments that we will consider in a moment as to unfairness, he was entitled on the facts to treat the properties as assets of the appellant, even though they had been purchased with company money.

19　　　The second broad ground advanced by Mr Kelly is one of unfairness, that is to say that it was unfair in the circumstances for the judge to make the confiscation order in the terms he did. There are really two aspects to that argument. The first concerns the position of the appellant's wife. It is said that it was wrong, if the corporate veil was to be lifted, to attribute to the appellant the whole of the value of the company's properties. The mere fact that the company's properties were realisable assets did not mean that they should be attributed to him. The judge should have considered whether there were any other incumbrances or interests, as Mr Kelly put it, in respect of the property. It seems to us from the rest of his submissions that he was not there talking about incumbrances or interests over the properties themselves, but the broader point that the appellant's wife was an equal shareholder in the company. It is submitted that, in those circumstances, she should have had attributed to her half the value of the company's assets rather than that the entirety, or nearly the entirety, be attributed to the appellant. In support of that submission, reference is made to the fact that the Crown had accepted in relation to the individual properties in joint ownership that only 50 per cent of the value should be taken into account.

20　　　It is submitted by reference to *Benjafield* that what was done by the judge created injustice or a risk of serious injustice. Again, that is a submission that we reject. It seems to us that, once the corporate veil was lifted as it properly was, then, having regard to the judge's findings of fact, there was no unfairness in his treating the properties as assets of the appellant to the extent that he did. It is plain that the wife's involvement in the company was simply nominal. She had no active part in it and no part in the decision making. Although she was a shareholder apparently from the start, all the relevant decisions, including the decisions to purchase the relevant properties, were made by the appellant. It is difficult to see on what basis it could be said to have given rise to an unfairness or a risk of serious injustice for the properties in question to be treated as assets of the appellant to the extent that they were.

21   The second element of the case on unfairness concerns the relative positions of the appellant and the co-defendants. What is said is that the certified benefit for the other defendants far exceeded that for the appellant. The total benefit in the case of Skidmore was in the sum of £34 million or thereabouts, and in the case of Burke, in the sum of some £7 million. That is a figure that takes account of their involvement in the fraud in respect of other periods beyond those when the appellant and CCSL got involved.

22   It is submitted that, although the judge considered the principles of fairness referred to in *Benjafield*, he treated them as relevant only to the question of double recovery, that is to say whether the total amount to be confiscated from the appellant, Skidmore and Burke would exceed the amount of benefit relating to the relevant account, namely just over £2 million. It is submitted that the principle has a wider application and that where a number of defendants have been convicted of an offence of this nature, the total benefit should be divided in equal shares in the absence of evidence to the contrary. In this case, there was no evidence to the contrary because there was nothing to show how the total benefit had been divided between the individual defendants. To divide it in equal shares would have meant that the amount of the confiscation order in the case of the appellant would have been no more than one third of the total benefit, a sum of approximately £670,000. To order this rather than the higher sum of £790,000 or so actually ordered, would have gone some way to avoid or reduce the risk of injustice. In support of that submission, reference is made to *Gibbons* [2002] EWCA Crim 3161, in the course of which the Court was considering the way in which to deal with benefit where there were a number of conspirators and it had not been shown how much total benefit had been enjoyed by each of the individual conspirators. In para.[62], it was stated:

> "In our judgment, where there is clear evidence of movement of money to conspirators as in this case and in the absence of any evidence as to how the benefit of the conspiracy has been divided between individuals, dividing the total amount between those identified is as good a starting point as any."

3   In that way the Court upheld the approach that had been adopted towards the calculation of benefit by the judge in that particular case. It is submitted that the same approach should have been adopted here.

4   These various arguments on unfairness now advanced before us by Mr Kelly were not those which were advanced before the judge. The appellant's reply to the prosecution statement under the 1998 Act simply put the prosecution to strict proof that the same benefit was not being claimed from each of the appellant, Skidmore and Burke on the basis that the Crown cannot recover the same total benefit for more than one person. That is also how it was argued on the appellant's behalf at the confiscation hearing; the example being given was that if there were a £1 million fraud and four people were involved, it would be unfair to order confiscation of £4 million and to recover £1 million from each of them. It would also be contrary to the purpose of the Act, which is to remove ill-gotten gains and not to punish. That is the point that the judge dealt with in the course of his ruling when checking that the confiscation orders would not lead to double recovery.

In our judgment, he dealt with it properly and he cannot be criticised, and we think is not actually criticised by Mr Kelly for having concentrated on the particular point canvassed when dealing with the issue of fairness. Nor, we would stress, could it be inferred that he regarded that as the only aspect of fairness that fell to be considered in accordance with *Benjafield* principles. It is plain from his ruling that he had those principles very clearly in mind. Given that and the evident care with which the judge approached the whole matter, the reasonable inference is that he was satisfied that to make the orders he did would not give rise to a serious risk of unfairness or injustice. It seems to us that that view was one reasonably open to him on the evidence.

25   The particular suggestion that the total benefit of just over £2 million should have been divided equally between the appellant, Skidmore and Burke is again not a suggestion that was advanced before the judge. Mr Kelly does not seek to suggest that it is in any way a rule that must be adopted in cases of this kind. In the case of *McKechnie and Gibbon*, it was adopted as a good starting point by the judge below, a view with which this Court agreed. It was not suggested that this is the only way of going about it.

26   In the circumstances of this case, given that the matter was not ventilated below and that one has to look generally at whether the result achieved by the judge was one that offended the principles of fairness stated in *Benjafield*, it suffices to say that, in our judgment, the order made by the judge was one that was neither unfair nor created a risk of serious injustice.

27   We should also stress that the fact that the appellant ended up paying more than his co-defendants does not affect the position. He paid more because he had more assets. It is plainly not the intention of the draconian regime under the 1988 Act that if one co-defendant has few assets then another co-defendant with large assets may have the confiscation order against him reduced in order to reflect the lack of assets of his co-defendant. A so-called proportionality exercise of that kind would not be an appropriate approach under the Act.

28   In the result, we are satisfied that the order that was made by the judge in this case was well within his discretion, and this appeal is dismissed.

R. v ANDREW MARK DADLEY

Court of Appeal (Lord Justice Mance, Mr Justice Gibbs and Sir Michael Wright): July 29, 2004

[2004] EWCA Crim. 2216; [2005] 1 Cr.App.R.(S.) 87

LT Breach; Custodial sentences; Guilty pleas; Harassment; Restraining orders

H1 *Protection from Harassment Act 1997—breach of restraining order—persistent breaches—length of sentence*

H2   Thirty months' imprisonment for breach of a restraining order under the Protection from Harassment Act 1997, where the appellant had persistently breached previous orders in respect of the same person, reduced to 20 months.

H3   The appellant pleaded guilty to breach of a restraining order made under the Protection from Harassment Act 1997, assault with intent to resist arrest and driving while disqualified. The appellant was sentenced in 2001 to a community punishment order for an offence of harassment against a woman with whom he had had a relationship which had broken down. A restraining order was made, preventing the appellant from contacting the woman. In October 2002 the appellant was in breach of the restraining order and received a community rehabilitation order and a second restraining order was made preventing him from contacting the woman. The appellant was subsequently in breach of that restraining order and was sentenced to four months' imprisonment in November 2002. On that occasion for a further restraining order was made. In May 2003 the appellant was in breach of that restraining order and was sentenced to a further four months' imprisonment. A further restraining order was made. A few days after this restraining order had been made, the woman received a number of telephone calls on her mobile telephone. She answered one of them and found that it was from the appellant. The woman told the appellant to stop calling her. Some months later a police officer saw the appellant driving his car and attempted to arrest him for breach of the restraining order. The appellant resisted arrest and there was a struggle, in the course of which the appellant and the officer fell to the floor. Sentenced to 30 months' imprisonment for breach of the restraining order, with three months consecutive for assault with intent to resist arrest.

H4   **Held:** (considering *Liddle and Hayes* [2000] 1 Cr.App.R.(S.) 131) it was submitted that the sentence imposed for breach of the restraining order was manifestly excessive, in that the sentencing judge had failed to take account of the guilty plea. The appellant had pleaded guilty on the basis that no threat had been made in the course of the telephone call. Guidance on determining the appropriate length of sentence in cases of breach of restraining orders had been given in *Liddle and Hayes*. The present case was not an offence under s.4 of the Act, but there was a history of breaches of orders under the Act on many occasions. The seriousness of the offence was high by reason of the persistence of the offending and associated offences of criminal damage. The victim had been frightened by the appellant, and required protection. The level of risk remained high. There was only one act of harassment to which the appellant had pleaded guilty. There had been no repetition of the harassment for several months between the date of the latest offence and the time of the appellant's arrest. In the Court's judgment the sentencing judge was right to form the view that a sentence in excess of 15 months was appropriate, but the Court considered that the sentence of 30 months was excessive. Bearing all the relevant factors in mind, a sentence of 20 months would have sufficed. Such a sentence would be substituted, with the three months consecutive.

H5   **Case cited:**
Liddle and Hayes [2000] 1 Cr.App.R.(S.) 131

H6   **References:** restraining order, *Current Sentencing Practice* B 3–6

H7   *J. Macnamara* for the appellant.

JUDGMENT

1   **Gibbs J.:** This is an appeal against sentence with the leave of the single judge by Andrew Mark Dadley, a 42-year-old appellant, the sentence having been passed on December 9, 2003 at the Crown Court at Nottingham. The appellant pleaded guilty and was sentenced by H.H. Judge Teare on January 6, 2004 in the following way: on count 1, for breach of a restraining order which had been made under s.5 of the Protection from Harassment Act 1997, 30 months' imprisonment; for an offence of assault with intent to resist arrest, a sentence of three months' imprisonment consecutively was imposed; on a further count of driving while disqualified, a sentence of one month's imprisonment was imposed to run concurrently; The appellant was disqualified from driving for a period of a year; no separate penalty was imposed for using a vehicle without insurance. The resulting sentence was one of 33 months' imprisonment in total. In addition, a further restraining order was made under s.5 of the 1997 Act. This appeal focuses on, and is restricted to, the sentence of 30 months' imprisonment on count 1 ·. ⁻ʰe indictment. Reference is also made to the scope of the further restraining order. The appeal grounds originally drafted included a challenge to the scope of the further restraining order made by the sentencing judge. However, subsequent to the drafting of the grounds, the scope of the restraining order has been substantially reduced and is therefore no longer challenged in this appeal.

2   The facts upon which the prosecution was based are these. In August 2001 the appellant was sentenced to a community punishment order for an offence of harassment against a woman called Carol Holland following the breakdown of her relationship with the appellant. A restraining order was made preventing the appellant from contacting Miss Holland. In October 2002, the appellant was in breach of the restraining order and received a community rehabilitation order.

He was also made the subject of a second restraining order preventing him from contacting Miss H. The appellant was in breach of that restraining order and was sentenced for that to four months' imprisonment on November 20, 2002. This was accordingly the second breach. On this occasion a further restraining order was made in the same terms until November 20, 2004. On May 12, 2003 the appellant was in breach of that restraining order and was sentenced to a further four months' imprisonment. This was the third breach. He was made subject to a fourth restraining order for a period of three years. That brings us to count 1 of the current indictment.

3   Shortly after 11pm on May 29, 2003, Miss H. received a series of calls to her mobile telephone. The phone display indicated that they were being made from a private number, so she did not answer them. She contacted the police, as she thought that the appellant was making the calls, and was advised to switch the phone off. She did not do so, for reasons which she gave in her statement and which seem to us to be understandable. At about 11.30pm she received a further call which she answered. She immediately recognised the voice as that of the appellant and she asked him whether he did not understand the terms of the restraining order. She told him to stop calling her otherwise she would involve the police. The call lasted for about 15 minutes and was terminated by Miss H. It is clear from her statement that she was in fear of the appellant.

4   The circumstances surrounding the phone call increased her fear, since it was plain that somebody was causing an extremely disturbing nuisance in the vicinity in the house, although it is right to say that that could not be proved to have been the appellant. In addition to that, her account of the telephone call involves the appellant making a frightening threat. But again it is right to say that the basis on which the appellant pleaded to this offence was that he did not issue such a threat and the matter proceeded upon his basis of plea.

5   During the morning of September 2, 2003 (some three months later) Police Constable Beaton saw the appellant with his son driving a car. The police officer stopped the appellant and arrested him for having been in breach of the restraining order. As the officer tried to handcuff the appellant, he began to struggle and called to his son, "Come on lad, don't let him arrest me". The officer called for assistance. However, the appellant took his radio extension from his shirt and prevented him from finishing the call. As the struggle continued, the appellant and the officer fell to the floor. At this point, a 16-year-old boy came to the officer's assistance and the appellant was restrained. Other officers came to the scene and the appellant was taken to the police station. The officer sustained abrasions and bruising to the left shoulder, finger and right knee.

6   The appellant was interviewed and admitted resisting arrest, saying that he had struggled as he did not want to be handcuffed in the presence of his son. He denied driving, but conceded that he was disqualified from driving, having been disqualified for four years in March 2001. At that stage, he denied having been in contact with Miss H. Subsequently, as we have mentioned, he pleaded guilty on the basis that he accepted having made the phone call but denied any threat of violence.

7   The appellant was born on February 6, 1962. He has been convicted on 6 occasions of a total of 16 offences, 3 of which were for a course of conduct which
amounted to harassment on August 8, 2001, October 18, 2002 and November
20, 2002. There were, as mentioned, also breaches of restraining orders, in
addition to which there were other offences, including criminal damage, which
were apparently associated with the offences of harassment which we have mentioned.

8   The pre-sentence report before the court noted that the appellant's previous
offending derived from his alcohol dependency, albeit that the appellant denied
that alcohol was a factor in the current offence.

9   The probation officer formed the view that the repeated breach of the restraining orders suggested a high risk of reoffending, although he pointed out an intent
expressed by the appellant to avoid a further custodial sentence. The probation
officer was persuaded that the motivation somewhat reduced the risk of reoffending. He was of low risk of causing serious harm to the public. However, the more
he used alcohol the more the risk would be, previous or subsequent partners being
the people who stood to suffer most from the appellant's activities. The appellant
expressed shame about his behaviour and regret for his offending.

10   A prison report has been obtained since the sentence from a probation officer.
This shows that the appellant has had no problems with his health and no psychiatric problems since being in prison. He has behaved well and has caused no
difficulties with staff. The appellant told the probation officer about his plans
for the future, and described the appellant as apparently having moved on emotionally, being chastened and respectful.

11   However, there is also in the prison report an indication that the appellant still
continues to minimise the seriousness of his offending. The following passage
occurs:

> "He says he was sober and it was a reasonable conversation, which was not
> terminated by his ex-partner. He states he did not understand the seriousness
> of making such contact."

This Court hopes that he has by now grasped the seriousness of such conduct and
the fact that repetition in the future will inevitably result in substantial prison sentences.

12   In sentencing the appellant the judge said that he took into account that there
were no previous convictions up to the year 2000. His conduct since, however,
had demonstrated that he refused to obey any order of the court and refused to
leave the complainant alone. Although he had given assurances that there
would be no repetition of the conduct, that had been when he was sober and/or
in prison. Upon his release and upon taking drink, reoffending had occurred.
The judge referred to the fact that the appellant had sought mercy because of
his son, but the judge felt constrained to point out that his son had been a passenger in the car in connection with the offence of assault and had witnessed it. The
fact of the matter was that, on the last occasion, immediate release had been
allowed and the appellant had reoffended within 17 days. He had assaulted a

police officer when arrested, who did not deserve to be injured and assaulted, and that should attract a consecutive sentence.

13   The grounds of appeal are that the sentence imposed in respect of count 1 was manifestly excessive, in that the judge had failed to take any or sufficient account of the guilty plea or of the fact that the offence constituted a single incident, not a persistent course of conduct. The absence of violence was mentioned in the grounds of appeal, although this Court notes that the previous harassment had been accompanied on occasions by the causing of criminal damage.

14   The basis of plea was relied upon, in that it is submitted that there was no threat made in the course of the telephone call. It was also submitted that eight months had passed since the act of harassment by the date of the sentence. The grounds also relied on remorse and the reduced risk of reoffending.

15   We are guided in determining the appropriate length of sentence in cases of this kind by the decision of this Court in the case of *Liddle and Hayes* [2001] Cr.App.R.(S.) 131. In the judgment of the Court, at 134, a series of considerations are set out which affect the length of sentence. These include: first, whether the offence is a s.2 or s.4 offence. Secondly, whether there is a history of disobedience to court orders in the past and whether those orders are under the Act or whether they are civil orders. Thirdly, the seriousness of the defendant's conduct, particularly the degree of violence, if any. Fourthly, is there persistent misconduct by the defendant or a solitary instance of misbehaviour. Fifthly, the effect upon the victim, physical or psychological, and (associated with that) what level of risk is posed by the defendant, either to that victim or the children and family of the victim. Sixthly, the mental health of the victim. Seventhly, what is the offender's reaction to the court proceedings, including whether or not there is a plea of guilty or an expression of remorse or a recognition of the need for help. The judgment goes on to consider the appropriate length of sentences for this offence. It expresses the view that for a first offence a short, sharp sentence may be appropriate. It observes that the facts of each case vary and the facts of any particular case may require a longer sentence. It then, pertinently, says this:

> "For a second offence longer sentences of about 15 months on a plea of guilty would, in our view, be an appropriate starting point, and from then on it is possible to see from the maximum of five years fixed by the statute for this offence where each case fits into the statutory framework working from the figure of 15 months, which may be appropriate on a plea of guilty."

6   Bearing those factors in mind, we take into consideration that this offence is not a s.4 offence. However, there is an extremely serious history of breach. There have been breaches of the order under the Act on many occasions. The degree of seriousness is high by reason not only of the persistence of this offending but also the associated offences of criminal damage. The victim has been frightened by the conduct and she requires protection. The level of risk, in our view, remains high, whatever the sentence imposed upon this appellant. He has no mental health problems.

7   On the other hand, it is right to say that on this occasion there was only one act of harassment proved. He pleaded guilty to that. We are dubious about the gen-

uineness of any signs of remorse on his part. The comments that he has made about this offence have been mainly exculpatory. However, we also take into consideration that there was no repetition of the harassment for several months between the date of the offence and the time of the appellant's arrest.

18   In our judgment the judge was right to form the view that a sentence in excess of the 15-month guideline was appropriate in this case. However, having regard to the matters set out in the grounds of appeal and the mitigating circumstances to which we have just referred, we consider that the sentence of 30 months was in the circumstances excessive. We think that, bearing all the relevant factors in mind, a sentence of 20 months' imprisonment would have sufficed in this case. The sentence for the remaining offences is not criticised, nor is the fact that that sentence was made consecutive to the sentence on count 1. Accordingly, we quash the sentence of 30 months on count 1 and substitute a sentence of 20 months. The three months' imprisonment imposed consecutively will remain in place. The total sentence will therefore be 23 months' imprisonment. To that extent this appeal is allowed.

[Paragraph [19] has been omitted.]

R. v ALAN JOHN GOODENOUGH

COURT OF APPEAL (Lord Justice May, Mr Justice Gray and Mrs Justice Hallett): July 29, 2004

[2004] EWCA Crim 2260; [2005] 1 Cr.App.R.(S.) 88

(LT) Compensation orders; Confiscation orders; Double punishment; Matrimonial home; Protection of property; Right to fair trial; Right to respect for home

H1   *Confiscation order—confiscation order made on the basis that defendant's equity in his matrimonial home was realisable property—whether violation of Art.8 of the European Convention on Human Rights*

H2   **Editor's note:** a confiscation order made under the Criminal Justice Act 1988 on the basis that the defendant's realisable property included his share of the equity in his matrimonial home did not violate his rights under Art.8 of European Convention on Human Rights.

H3   The appellant admitted two offences of theft before a magistrates' court and was committed to the Crown Court for sentence. He asked for 11 other offences to be taken into consideration. The appellant was employed at a travel company. One of his duties was to order foreign currency for customers of the company. Over a period of almost two years, the appellant ordered currency for himself and misappropriated it. The total amount came to £14,822. The money was spent on gambling. Sentenced to nine months' imprisonment on each count, currently, with a confiscation in order in the amount of £14,822. The appeal was limited to the confiscation order.

Held, before the appellant was sentenced in the Crown Court, the Crown served a notice in accordance with the Criminal Justice Act 1988, s.71, initiating confiscation proceedings. Some time later, the company wrote to the appellant's solicitors confirming that the company did not wish the confiscation proceedings to take place, and that the company would seek repayment from the appellant on a voluntary basis without the assistance of the court. The appellant's solicitors later confirmed that the company would not be instituting civil proceedings. When the confiscation proceedings started, counsel for the appellant accepted that he had obtained the sum of £14,822 and that no payment had been made to the company. The appellant and his wife owned a house with a joint equity of about £79,000, and the appellant's interest in the property was £39,000. This was a realisable asset so far as appellant was concerned. It was submitted for the appellant that the making of a confiscation order would contravene the appellant's rights under Arts 6 and 8 of the European Convention on Human Rights, and under Art.1 of the First Protocol. The sentencing judge rejected the submission. Article 8 of the Convention protected the right to respect for private and family life, home and correspondence, and provided that there should be no interference by a public authority with the exercise of this right except such as was in accordance with the law and necessary in a democratic society in the interests of national security, public safety or the economic well-being of the country, for protection of disorder or crime, for the protection of health or morals or for the protection of the rights and freedoms of others. Article 1 of the First Protocol provided that every natural or legal person was entitled to the peaceful enjoyment of his possessions, and that no one should be deprived of these possessions except in the interest of the public and subject to the conditions provided for by law and by the general principles of international law. These provisions did not impair the right of the State to enforce laws for various purposes, including to secure the payment of penalties. It was argued that the order of the Crown Court requiring the appellant to pay the sum of £14,822 or in default go to prison for 12 months interfered with his right to peaceful enjoyment of his possessions and was disproportionate to the aim of the domestic legislation, because the court was already invested with the power to make a compensation order in favour of the victim of crime. It was also submitted that given that the only realisable asset of the appellant was the matrimonial home, the effect of making the confiscation order amounted to an interference with the Art.8 rights of the appellant and his wife, which was not necessary in a democratic society. It was further argued that, alternatively, the court should impose a compensation order, in place of the existing confiscation order. For the Crown it was argued that as the company had not instituted civil proceedings against the appellant, or had indicated an intention to do so, the sentencing judge was under a duty to make the confiscation order. A confiscation order was simply an order for the payment of a sum of money, and could not infringe the Art.8 rights of the appellant, even if in order to pay he would have to sell the matrimonial home. Alternatively, it was submitted that the confiscation provisions were justified by Art.8 (2) of the Convention and the second sentence of Art.1 of the First Protocol. It appeared to the Court to be clear on authority that the confiscation regime introduced by the Criminal Justice Act 1988 was compatible with the Convention, in the light of *Rezvi* [2002] 2 Cr.App.R.(S.) 70 (p.300). Although no reliance had been placed in those cases on Art.8, it seemed plain that if the confiscation regime did not contravene either Art.6 or Art.1 of the First Protocol, it could not be said to contravene Art.8 either. The Court could not accept that the Convention rights of the appellant were infringed or interfered with by the making of the confiscation order. The rights of the appellant's wife might be infringed if the home were to be sold in order to raise money to pay the amount of the confiscation order, but on the material available, the Court was not persuaded that such a sale would be necessary. It would be open to the appellant's wife to oppose any application to appoint a receiver to enforce the confiscation order. On the information before the Court, it was not apparent that the appellant was suffering a double penalty, and there was no justification for replacing the confiscation order with a compensation order. The appeals would be dismissed.

H5   **Case cited:**
Rezvi [2002] 2 Cr.App.R.(S.) 70 (p.300)

H6   **References:** confiscation order, *Current Sentencing Practice* J9
H7   **Commentary:** [2005] Crim. L.R. 72

H8   *R. Burke-Gaffney* for the appellant.
D.A. Bartlett for the Crown.

JUDGMENT

1   **Gray J.:**   On July 8, 2002 at the East Dorset magistrates' court the appellant, Mr Alan Goodenough, admitted two offences of theft and was committed for sentence to the Crown Court at Bournemouth. On 2nd August he was sentenced by H.H. Judge Beashel to nine months' imprisonment on each count to be served concurrently. Eleven other offences were taken into consideration. On December 10, 2003 at the same court the Crown instituted confiscation proceedings and an order was made under s.71 of the Criminal Justice Act 1988 ("the Act") in the sum of £14,822.97 to be paid within 12 months. A 12-month sentence of imprisonment was imposed in default.

2   The present appeal, brought with the leave of the Full Court, relates, and relates only, to the confiscation order made by the learned judge. The appellant has already served his sentence.

3   Before coming to the grounds of appeal we should summarise briefly the facts giving rise to the criminal proceedings. The appellant was, at the material time, employed by a company named Bath Travel as an operations and technical executive at their Bournemouth branch. One of his duties in that capacity was to order foreign currency for customers at the travel company. Between February 2000 and January 2002 he ordered currency for himself rather than for customers and misappropriated it. As is accepted by the appellant, the total amount con-

cerned came to £14,822.97, that being the amount of the confiscation order. It appears that the appellant spent the money on gambling.

4   As we have indicated, before the appellant was sentenced on August 2, 2002 the Crown had by a notice, dated July 24, 2002, pursuant to s.71 of the Act, initiated confiscation proceedings against the appellant. Thereafter correspondence took place between the Crown Prosecution Service, the appellant's solicitors and Bath Travel, the former employer of the appellant and the losers as a result of his stealing.

5   On September 13, 2002 Bath Travel wrote to the solicitors in terms which included the following:

> "It was not until my company received your letter that we were aware of the proposed application, and after discussion with my fellow directors I write to confirm that it is not the wish of the company for the application for confiscation order to proceed against our former employee. This company will make its own arrangements to seek repayment on a voluntary basis and do not require the assistance of the court to recover those monies."

6   That letter was followed by a letter from Miss Branford-Wood of the Crown Prosecution Service to the appellant's solicitor dated November 6, 2002. That letter concluded with the following:

> "Mr Bath confirms that Bath Travel will not be instituting civil proceedings against Mr Goodenough, although he intends to speak to Mr Goodenough in an effort to arrange for the voluntary repayment of the money."

7   The confiscation proceedings came before H.H. Judge Beashel on October 25, 2002. In the course of that hearing Mr Burke-Gaffney, who then appeared for the appellant as he does before us today, told the judge that, whilst making no formal admission that the appellant had benefited from relevant criminal conduct as defined by s.70(1)(iv) of the Act, he accepted that the sum of £14,822.97 had been obtained by his client. At that date no payment had been made, voluntarily or otherwise, by the appellant to his former employers. The court then had to determine, in accordance with s.71(6) of the Act, whether the amount that might be realised at the time of the order was less than the amount of the benefit.

8   As to that, the judge summarised the position as follows. He said:

> "I think about 10 years or so ago the defendant, together with his wife, purchased a freehold property at Horndean in Hampshire, and the approximate valuation of such property in the sum of £150,000 is not challenged. There is a mortgage with Lloyds TSB and the mortgage debt is about £71,000. The joint equity is thus of the order of £79,000. Half of that represents the defendant's interest in the property, say £39,000, and that, plainly, is a realisable asset as far as he is concerned."

9   We are told today by Mr Burke-Gaffney that the appellant and his wife have now parted company, but that would not appear to affect the availability of a sufficient sum by way of realisable asset.

10   The judge then dealt with a submission by Mr Burke-Gaffney that the making of a confiscation order in the circumstances of the case would contravene the rights of the appellant under the European Convention on Human Rights, in particular his rights under Arts 6 and 8 and Art.1 of the First Protocol.

11   The learned judge rejected that submission. He said that the Human Rights Act did not assist the appellant. There was no breach of Art.6, and Art.8 did not assist him. He was satisfied that the appellant's wife would oppose any application to appoint a receiver in the High Court proceedings. The judge, therefore, felt it was perfectly proper to make a confiscation order in the amount of what he had found to be the benefit from the appellant's criminal conduct.

12   To complete the history, we are told today that the position as between the appellant and Bath Travel, his former employers, is that discussions have taken place and that some sort of accommodation is or may have been arrived at. We were furnished by Mr Burke-Gaffney with a letter from the managing director of Bath Travel, dated April 8, 2004, which includes the following:

> "As early as our meeting of 05 June 2002 when he first confessed to theft, he [the appellant] was adamant that he would repay the money in full over a period of time and that is still my understanding."

13   Before addressing the arguments advanced on behalf of the appellant and the Crown on this appeal, we will set out the relevant sections of the Act, together with the material parts of the Convention. The Act of 1988 provides for the recovery of proceeds of relevant criminal conduct and specifies how the amount recoverable should be determined. The provisions which are relevant to this appeal are mainly to be found in s.71. That section is, so far as material, in the following terms:

> "(1) Where an offender is convicted, in any proceedings before the Crown Court or a magistrates' court, of an offence of a relevant description, it shall be the duty of the court—
>> (a) if the prosecutor has given written notice to the court that he considers that it would be appropriate under this section, or.
>> (b) if the court considers, even though it has not been given such notice, that it would be appropriate for it so to proceed.
>
> to act as follows before sentencing or otherwise dealing with the offender in respect of that offence or any other relevant criminal conduct.
>
> (1A) The court shall first determine whether the offender has benefited from any relevant criminal conduct.
>
> (1B) Subject to subsection (1C) below, if the court determines that the offender has benefited from any relevant criminal conduct, it shall then—
>> (a) determine in accordance with subsection (6) below the amount to be recovered in his case by virtue of this section, and
>> (b) make an order under this section ordering the offender to pay that amount.

(1C) If, in a case falling within subsection (1B) above, the court is satisfied that a victim of any relevant criminal conduct has instituted, or intends to institute, civil proceedings against the defendant in respect of loss, injury or damage sustained in connection with that conduct—

    (a) the court shall have a power, instead of a duty, to make an order under this section;

    (b) subsection (6) below shall not apply for determining the amount to be recovered in that case by virtue of this section; and

    (c) where the court makes an order in exercise of that power, the sum required to be paid under that order shall be of such amount, not exceeding the amount which (but for paragraph (b) above) would apply by virtue of subsection (6) below, as the court thinks fit.

(1D) In this Part of this Act 'relevant criminal conduct', in relation to a person convicted of an offence in any proceedings before a court, means (subject to section 72AA(6) below) that offence taken together with any other offences of a relevant description which are either—

    (a) offences of which he is convicted in the same proceedings, or

    (b) offences which the court will be taking into consideration in determining his sentence for the offence in question."

14   We do not need to read any of the other subsections of s.71, save for subs.(6) which reads:

"Subject to subsection (1C) above the sum which an order made by a court under this section requires an offender to pay shall be equal to—

    (a) the benefit in respect of which it is made; or

    (b) the amount appearing to the court to be the amount that might be realised at the time the order is made,

whichever is the less."

15   We should also recite s.72(7) which reads:

"Where—

    (a) the court makes both a confiscation order and an order for the payment of compensation under section 130 of the Powers of Criminal Courts (Sentencing) Act 2000 against the same person in the same proceedings; and

    (b) it appears to the court that he will not have sufficient means to satisfy both the orders in full,

it shall direct that so much of the compensation as will not in its opinion be recoverable because of the insufficiency of his means shall be paid out of any sums recovered under the confiscation order."

16   Section 72AA contains several assumptions which the court may make. Those assumptions are not directly material on this appeal.

17   We pass to the provisions of the European Convention on Human Rights which are relied on. First, there is Art.6 which guarantees the right to a fair trial. It is in

familiar terms so we need not quote it. Amongst other things it includes an entitlement to the presumption of innocence.

18   Article 8 is in the following not unfamiliar terms:

"(1) Everyone has the right to respect for his private and family life, his home and his correspondence.

(2) There shall no interference by a public authority with the exercise of this right except such as is in accordance with the law and is necessary in a democratic society in the interests of national security, public safety or the economic well-being of the.country, for the prevention of disorder or crime, for the protection of health or morals, or for the protection of the rights and freedoms of others."

19   Reliance placed is also on behalf of the appellant on Art.1 of the First Protocol which reads:

"Every natural or legal person is entitled to the peaceful enjoyment of his possessions. No one shall be deprived of his possessions except in the interest public and subject to the conditions provided for by law and by the general principles of international law.

The preceding provisions shall not, however, in any way impair the right of a State to enforce such laws as it deems necessary to control the use or property in accordance with the general interest or to secure the payment of taxes or other contributions or penalties."

20   Section 3 of the Human Rights Act 1998 provides where, so far as it is possible to do so, primary legislation must be read and given effect to in a way which is compatible with Convention rights, including those rights relied upon by the appellant here. Section 6 of the Act provides that it is unlawful for a public authority, which includes the court, to act in a way which is incompatible with a Convention right.

21   The argument of Mr Burke-Gaffney on this appeal is that the order that the appellant pay the sum which we have identified, or in default go to prison for 12 months, interferes with his right under Art.1 of the First Protocol to the peaceful enjoyment of his possessions and is disproportionate to the aim of the domestic legislation, because the court is already invested with the power to make a compensation order in favour of the victim of the crime. Further, or in the alternative, Mr Burke-Gaffney submits that given that the only realisable asset is the matrimonial home, the effect of the making of the confiscation order amounts to an interference with the Art.8 rights of the appellant and of his wife. He contends that such interference is not necessary in a democratic society within the meaning of Art.8(2). He argues that the appellant's rights under Art.6 were interfered with.

22   Mr Burke-Gaffney further argues in the alternative that if the Court is against him on his Convention arguments, this Court should, in place of the existing confiscation order, impose a compensation order. In support of that contention reliance is placed on the case of *Mitchell* [2001] 2 Cr.App.R.(S.) 29 (p.468), to which we will come in due course.

23   Mr Bartlett, on behalf of the Crown, points out that since, as we have indicated, Bath Travel has not instituted civil proceedings against the appellant, or indicated an intention to do so, s.70(1)(1C) of the Act has no application with the consequence that the judge had a duty under the Act to make a confiscation order. In reliance on *Phillips v United Kingdom* 11 B.H.R.C. 280 and *Rezvi* [2002] 2 Cr.App.R.(S.) 71 (p.300), Mr Bartlett contends in his skeleton argument that the confiscation order against this appellant does not interfere with his rights under Art.1 of the First Protocol of the Convention, or under Art.6.

24   As to Art.8, Mr Bartlett argues that the confiscation order is, on the authority of *Norris* [2001] 1 W.L.R. 1388, simply an order for the payment of a sum of money, and as such cannot be said to infringe the Art.8 rights of the appellant even if in order to pay that sum of money the appellant will have to sell the matrimonial home. He submits, in the alternative, that the confiscation provisions of the Act are justified by Art.8(2) of the Convention and by the second sentence of Art.1 of the First Protocol.

25   It appears to us to be clear on authority that the confiscation regime introduced by the Act is compatible with the Convention. In support of that conclusion we refer, first, to *Phillips*, in which case the European Court held that the imposition of a confiscation order in criminal proceedings was analogous to the determination of the amount of a fine. It was therefore held in that case that Art.6 was not engaged because it does not apply to sentencing proceedings.

26   In *Rezvi* a confiscation order had been made against the appellant. He contended that the making of the order interfered with his rights under Art.6 and/or Art.1 of the First Protocol. In support of that contention he relied, in particular, on the statutory assumption introduced by s.72AA of the Act. The certified question before the House of Lords was:

> "Are the provisions of section 72AA of the Criminal Justice Act 1988, as amended, and section 4 of Drug Trafficking Act 1994 incompatible with Article 6 of the European Convention on Human Right and/or Article 1 of the First Protocol?"

That question was answered in the negative.

27   Lord Steyn, with whom the other Law Lords agreed, said of Art.6:

> "In agreement with the unanimous view of the Court of Human Rights in *Phillips v United Kingdom* I would hold that Part VI of the 1988 Act is a proportionate response to the problem which it addresses."

28   In regard to the reliance which was placed in that case on Art.1 of the First Protocol, having quoted that Article, Lord Steyn continued:

> "Counsel argued that Article 1 of the First Protocol required a different conclusion on proportionality. That cannot be right. The legislation is a precise, fair and proportionate response to the important need to protect the public. In agreement with the European Court of Human rights and *Phillips* I would hold that the interference with Article 1 of the First Protocol is justified."

29   In neither *Phillips* nor *Rezvi* was reliance placed, as it is in this case, on Art.8, but it seems to us to be plain that, if the confiscation regime under the Act does not contravene either Art.6 or Art.1 of the First Protocol, it cannot be said to contravene Art.8 either. The terms of Art.8(2) are, in their material respects, just as wide as the qualifying second sentence of the Art.1 of the First Protocol. It may be that is the reason why no reliance was placed on Art.8 in *Rezvi*.

30   In the light of the authorities we cannot accept that the Convention rights of the appellant are infringed or interfered with by the making of the confiscation order.

31   As to the appellant's wife, who is the joint owner of the matrimonial home, her Convention rights will be capable of being said to be infringed if, and only if, the home was to be sold in order to raise the money to pay the amount of the confiscation order. On the material available to this Court, we are not persuaded that such a sale will, in the event, prove to be necessary. In any case, as the learned judge below pointed out, it will be open to the appellant's wife to oppose any application to appoint a receiver.

32   It is perfectly true that neither this Court nor the House of Lords in *Rezvi* considered the particular problem, which, on Mr Burke-Gaffney's argument, arises in this case. What Mr Burke-Gaffney says, and he can put it no higher than this, is that if the appellant does enter into a binding agreement with Bath Travel and in due course he pays back by way of compensation the full amount misappropriated, then the appellant will be able to say that he was being doubly penalised by the combination of the confiscation order and the compensation order. In order to avoid that outcome Mr Burke-Gaffney invites us to adopt the solution which this Court felt able to adopt in the case of *Mitchell*, namely to quash the confiscation order and substitute in its place a compensation order.

33   The facts in *Mitchell* can be summarised as follows. The judge at the confiscation hearing made, as he was under a duty to do, a confiscation order in the amount of the benefit obtained by the two offenders. He declined to make a compensation order on the ground that to do so would be oppressive. The victims, or losers, from the offenders' criminal conduct subsequently commenced civil proceedings to recover their loss. They obtained judgment and had, before the matter came before this Court, obtained charging orders against the offenders. It was in these circumstances that this Court felt able in the light of the changed circumstances to discharge the confiscation order that had been made and to substitute for it a compensation order.

34   Mr Bartlett correctly points out that there is an important distinction between *Mitchell* and the present case. In *Mitchell* the victims had not only commenced proceedings, they had obtained judgments, which, by virtue of the charging order, they were likely to be able to enforce. In the present case, by contrast, the appellant has not, as we understand it, paid anything by way of compensation. Indeed, as we have said, it does not appear that he has bound himself to do so. The arrangement which has come into existence between the appellant and his former employers, such as it is, appears to us to be thoroughly nebulous. There is the further curious feature that, whereas the Full Court was informed in October 2003 that a voluntary agreement had been entered into in April 2003, the letter put before the Court today, which we have quoted, is dated April 2004 and its

terms suggest that no binding agreement has yet been concluded between the appellant and Bath Travel. In those circumstances, we conclude that Mr Bartlett is right when he says that on the information before the Court the appellant is not suffering a double penalty and, indeed, may never do so. That being so, there is, in our judgment, no justification for following the course taken in *Mitchell* by this Court of replacing the confiscation order with a compensation order.

35   It follows that this appeal must be dismissed.

R. v MICHAEL GEORGE CRONSHAW

COURT OF APPEAL (Lord Justice Rix, Mr Justice Nelson and Judge Barker Q.C.): July 29, 2004

[2004] EWCA Crim 2057; [2005] 1 Cr.App.R.(S.) 89

⟨LT⟩ Indecent assault; Indictments; Justice; Maximum sentences; Sexual activity with children; Time limits

11   *Unlawful sexual intercourse with girl between 13 and 16—indecent assaults accompanying act of sexual intercourse—defendant acquitted of rape—whether sentence for indecent assaults could exceed the maximum sentence for unlawful sexual intercourse*

12   **Editor's note:** where an offender is convicted of indecently assaulting a girl under 16 on the basis of an act of consensual sexual intercourse which could not be prosecuted as an offence of unlawful sexual intercourse for procedural reasons, the settled practice of sentencing on the assumption that the maximum sentence was two years' imprisonment should be followed, unless the indecent assaults were separate and distinct from the intercourse, as where a girl was "groomed" by an older man.

13   The appellant was convicted of one offence of unlawful sexual intercourse with a girl under the age of 16, and two offences of indecent assault. He was acquitted of rape. The victim of the offence was a 14-year-old girl who ran away from home. She met the appellant by chance at a bus station and the appellant asked her if she was homeless. The girl confirmed that she was homeless, and the appellant invited her to his home. The girl declined the appellant's invitation to contact her family. The appellant made sexual advances to the girl. Having removed some of her clothing he penetrated her digitally and had oral intercourse with her before having sexual intercourse with her. The girl spent the night at the appellant's flat and left after two days. There was no further sexual contact between them. Police officers called at the appellant's flat after a disturbance outside and eventually the appellant was arrested. The appellant maintained that all the sexual contact had been consensual and that he believed that the girl was over 16. The appellant was 24 at the time of the offences and had no previous convictions for sexual offences or violence. Sentenced to 15 months' imprisonment for

unlawful sexual intercourse and three and a half years' imprisonment on each count of indecent assault, all concurrent (total sentence three and a half years' imprisonment.)

H4   **Held:** (considering *Quayle* (1993) 14 Cr.App.R.(S.) 726, *Hinton* (1995) 16 Cr.App.R.(S.) 523, *Blair* [1996] 1 Cr.App.R.(S.) 336, *Brough* [1997] 2 Cr.App.R.(S.) 202, *Iles* [1998] 2 Cr.App.R.(S.) 63, *Martley* [2000] 1 Cr.App.R.(S.) 416, *Jones* [2003] 2 Cr.App.R. 134, and *Figg* [2004] 1 Cr.App.R.(S.) 68 (p.409)) the appellant contended that the sentences for indecent assault should not have exceeded the maximum sentence of two years for unlawful sexual intercourse with a girl under 16, as the offences of indecent assault were the prelude or foreplay to the act of sexual intercourse and should not therefore be treated more seriously than the act of unlawful intercourse itself. It was submitted that as the appellant had been acquitted of rape, the sentencing judge was not justified in finding that the appellant must have realised that the complainant did not wish to be involved in the sexual activities constituting the indecent assaults. It was submitted that the only proper basis for sentence was that the appellant was aware that the complainant was under 16, but he believed that she was consenting to the activities which constituted the indecent assaults. The increase in the maximum sentence for indecent assault on a female over the age of 13 undoubtedly created an anomaly in relation to sexual offences with consenting girls over 13 but under 16. The problem was discussed in a commentary on the case of *Figg* [2004] 1 Cr.App.R. (S.) 68 (p.409). If a defendant was charged with indecent assault, the maximum sentence was 10 years' imprisonment; if he was charged with unlawful sexual intercourse, the maximum sentence was limited to two years. Defendants whose actions amounted to the offence of unlawful sexual intercourse could find themselves charged with indecent assault where, for example, they were indicted for rape but acquitted on the basis that the jury was not satisfied that the act had occurred without the consent of the victim. Where in such circumstances the time-limit for a prosecution for unlawful sexual intercourse had expired, such a defendant might be charged with indecent assault rather than unlawful sexual intercourse. These anomalies led to a line of cases in which the Court of Appeal had accepted that where in truth the indecent assaults charged were no more than unlawful sexual intercourse, the maximum sentence should be two years (the maximum for unlawful sexual intercourse) rather than 10 years, the maximum sentence for indecent assault. In *Jones* the Court had observed that nothing the Court said in that case should detract from the settled practice of the Court of treating two years' imprisonment as the maximum sentence appropriate to a charge of indecent assault brought in circumstances where but for the expiry of the 12-month time-limit, the charge would have been laid as unlawful sexual intercourse. In *Figg* the Court concluded that where a justifiable choice to prosecute for indecent assault was made, that offence did not carry with it the limitation imposed in *Hinton*. In the Court's judgment in *Figg*, the Court made it clear that a prosecution for indecent assault was justified on the facts of that case, bearing in mind the background of a middle-aged man grooming a 14-year-old child and persuading her to consent to the act of sexual intercourse. That would not necessarily be the case if the facts were different, for example revealing adolescent experimentation. The case of *Jones* was not cited in *Figg*; it was not suggested in *Jones* that the Court had consistently failed to identify some limitation on the principle stated in *Hinton*. The Court was satisfied that, as the Court said in its review of the cases in *Jones*, that there was a settled practice of the Court of Appeal in treating two years' imprisonment as a maximum sentence appropriate to a charge of indecent assault brought in circumstances where a charge of unlawful sexual intercourse would have been brought, but for the expiry of the 12-month time-limit relating to that offence. Whether or not the settled practice applied would depend on the facts of any given case, but the principle lying behind the practice was that where the offence of indecent assault was, in truth, no more than the unlawful sexual intercourse, it would not be fair or appropriate to impose a greater sentence than that which would have been available had unlawful sexual intercourse been the offence charged. In some cases it would be clear that the only offence which would be charged had it been available but for the time limit would have been unlawful sexual intercourse, and hence the appropriate maximum sentence for indecent assault, where charged instead of unlawful sexual intercourse, would be two years. The same might also apply where unlawful sexual intercourse was charged as well as indecent assault but where the indecent assaults might be regarded as part of the foreplay leading to the unlawful sexual intercourse and should not be regarded properly as separate or distinct offences. In other cases the practice might not apply. If the acts of indecent assault were separate and distinct, for example where they occurred on different days to the sexual intercourse, or where the indecent assaults could be regarded, as they were in *Figg*, as acts of grooming by a man who was considerably older, they could not be regarded as part of or no more than the unlawful sexual intercourse. The Court did not regard the case of *Figg* as either overruling or seeking to overrule the line of cases starting with *Quayle* and *Hinton*. The Court in *Figg* was distinguishing those cases and setting out the reasons why the convention or practice did not apply to the facts of the case being considered by the Court on that occasion. The maximum permissible sentence for indecent assault remained 10 years, even in cases where the convention or practice applied so as to make the effective maximum one of two years. The conventional practice was based on the concept of unfairness and did not alter the maximum sentence. For the purposes of the Powers of Criminal Courts (Sentencing) Act 2000, s.85(5), the maximum term permitted for the offence of indecent assault, even where the conventional practice applied, was 10 years, not two years. It was therefore within the powers of the court to order an extended sentence consisting of a custodial term and an extension period. When considering the facts of the present appeal, the Court was satisfied that the indecent assaults could properly be regarded as being part of the prelude or foreplay to the act of intercourse. The complainant's evidence raised the issue of consent in relation to all the activities which took place, including the indecent assaults. The jury's verdict must be taken to indicate that they were not sure either whether consent had been disproved by the Crown or whether it was the appellant's belief that the complainant had consented in relation to all sexual activities. It was difficult on the facts to separate the acts of indecent assault from the act of sexual intercourse. As the jury had acquitted on the offence of rape, the Court considered that this was a case where the indecent assaults could not properly be regarded as separate or distinct, but were so closely related to the act of intercourse itself that their criminality should not be regarded as separate or different from the act of intercourse. In such circumstances the convention or practice was applicable. A custodial term of no more than two years should have been passed in respect of the offences of indecent assault. It was open to the judge to accept the view that the appellant was a risk to young women and to form the opinion that the normal licence period would not be adequate for the purpose of preventing the commission by him of further offences or securing his rehabilitation. The Court concluded that the sentence which would meet the justice of the case was an extended sentence of three and a half years, consisting of a custodial term of two years and an extension period of 18 months.

H5   **Cases cited:**
Quayle (1993) 14 Cr.App.R.(S.) 726, Hinton (1995) 16 Cr.App.R.(S.) 523, Blair [1996] 1 Cr.App.R.(S.) 336, Brough [1997] 2 Cr.App.R.(S.) 202, Iles [1998] 2 Cr.App.R.(S.) 63, Martley [2000] 1 Cr.App.R.(S.) 416, Jones [2003] 2 Cr.App.R. 134, and Figg [2004] 1 Cr.App.R.(S.) 68 (p.409)

H6   **References:** unlawful sexual intercourse, Current Sentencing Practice B 4-3
H7   **Commentary:** [2004] Crim.L.R. 1044

H8   M. Scholes for the appellant.
S. Medlanc' for the Crown.

JUDGMENT

1   **Nelson J.:**   On November 7, 2003, at the Crown Court at Warrington, the appellant was convicted of one offence of unlawful sexual intercourse with a girl under the age of 16 and two offences of indecent assault. On November 28, 2003 he was sentenced to 3½ years imprisonment on each of the indecent assault offences concurrent, and 15 months' imprisonment in respect of the offence of sexual intercourse with a girl under 16, also concurrent. The total sentence was therefore three-and-a-half years imprisonment. The appellant was found not guilty of rape.

2   He appeals against sentence by leave of the single judge. He contends that the sentence for the offences of indecent assault should not have exceeded the two-year maximum for unlawful sexual intercourse with a girl under 16, as although the statutory maximum for indecent assault on a female is 10 years, the offences of indecent assault were the prelude or foreplay to the act of sexual intercourse and should not therefore be treated more seriously than the act of unlawful intercourse itself. The jury had acquitted the appellant of rape either on the basis that they were not sure that the victim had not consented to sexual intercourse or that the appellant may have believed that she had consented. It would be wholly artificial to find that the jury were sure that the complainant did not consent to the

acts of indecent assault when they were clearly unsure in relation to the issue of consent to intercourse. In such circumstances, where the acts amounting to indecent assault were a prelude to the act of intercourse and could not properly be treated in a different manner, the judge should have sentenced the appellant to no more than the two-year statutory maximum for unlawful sexual intercourse with a girl under 16.

3   The facts are that the victim was a 14-year-old girl, who was vulnerable with the mental age of a 12-year-old. On the afternoon of June 3, 2003 she ran away from home, and by chance happened to meet the appellant and his cousin at a bus station in Warrington. She asked for a cigarette and the appellant asked her if she was homeless. She confirmed that she was and he invited her home with him and his cousin. Having arrived at his flat, she was given food, had a bath, and smoked some cannabis with him. He invited her to contact her family but she declined. He began to make advances towards her. He kissed her and eventually removed her trousers and underwear before digitally penetrating her and having oral intercourse with her. He then had full intercourse with her wearing a condom.

4   She spent the night in his flat. The following morning, a friend of the appellant's arrived at the flat and asked how old the victim was. She replied that she was 15. The victim remained in the flat for a further two days until the evening of June 6, 2003, despite the appellant's efforts to persuade her to contact her family. There was no further sexual contact after the conversation with the friend about her age. On the evening of June 6 police officers called at the appellant's flat after a disturbance outside. They asked the victim how old she was and she gave false details. The appellant initially supported her story but ultimately told the police that she was a runaway and was under 16. He was subsequently arrested, and when interviewed maintained all the sexual contact had been consensual and that he believed she was over 16 at the time. The appellant was 24 at the time of the offences and is now 25. He has various previous convictions for dishonesty, driving offences and possession of cannabis. He has no previous convictions for sexual offences or for violence.

5   A pre-sentence report dated November 25, 2003 recommended a lengthy community rehabilitation order with a condition that the appellant attend a Sex Offender Programme. His understanding of the impact of his behaviour was minimal and until he undertook offence focused work he presented a significant risk of harm, especially to young females. He expressed no remorse.

6   When he was sentenced the judge noted that he had been acquitted of the most serious charge. The victim however was only 14 with a mental functioning age of 12 and had been a virgin. She was a vulnerable child, with a stammer and some learning difficulties. He had known very well that she was under 16 and had repeatedly asked her if she wanted to go home. He had realised she should have contacted her parents, and it must have been obvious to him that her parents would be distraught with worry. He did nothing to encourage her to go home after he had taken her back to his flat. He could easily have contacted the police, and although he had shown some kindness to her, his conduct was more to keep her available for him to have sex with rather than look after her best interests. It was an aggravating feature of the case that when he took her to his flat he assumed

responsibility for her. She put her trust in him and he flagrantly betrayed that trust by having sex with her and also by indecently assaulting her by licking and fingering her vagina, activities which the judge said he was satisfied she did not want be involved in with him and that he must have realised that.

7   In his submissions to this Court on behalf of the appellant Mr Michael Scholes accepted that, in the light of the case of *Figg* [2004] 1 Cr.App.R.(S.) 68 (p.409), the judge was not bound to follow any convention or practice of imposing a sentence limited to the maximum of two years for unlawful sexual intercourse. Nevertheless, he submitted, that is the course the judge should have taken on the facts of this case. The judge took insufficient account of the jury's verdict on the rape charge and was not justified in finding that the appellant must have realised that the complainant did not wish to be involved with him in the sexual activities constituting the indecent assaults. Such a finding was inconsistent with the jury's verdict in relation to the intercourse itself. The only proper basis upon which the judge could pass sentence was that the appellant was aware that the complainant was under 16 but not on the basis that she had neither consented to nor acquiesced in the activities reflected in the indecent assault counts.

8   The contents of the pre-sentence report relied upon by the judge are also challenged. The report was based upon one meeting with a probation officer who had no prior knowledge of the appellant, and who apparently had not contacted any other probation officer who may have supervised the appellant in the past. The report was hostile to the appellant and contrary to his interests and there was no proper basis for the view that the appellant constituted a risk to young women. Even if the judge was entitled to rely upon the report the appropriate way to deal with the aspect of risk was by means of an extended period of licence. Both counsel accepted that as the statutory maximum for indecent assault was 10 years an extended licence period beyond any conventional maximum of 2 years, which the authorities might support, was permissible and appropriate.

9   Nor was it appropriate for the judge to find that the appellant had only provided food and a bath for the complainant in order to make her available for sex with him. As soon as she had disclosed, in front of another person, that she was under 16, he had no further sex with her for some two nights and sought to persuade her to contact her parents. The judge should have taken more account of the fact that the appellant was only 24 at the time of the offence, with no previous conviction for sexual offences.

10   Mr Simon Medland submitted on behalf of the respondent that the victim's evidence was opaque as to whether the defendant knew that she was not consenting. The proper interpretation of the jury's verdict was that the defendant might not have known that she was not consenting. The video interview of the victim and her evidence made it clear that she found the indecent assaults distasteful. She said that they were painful and "disgusting". The judge's view that she did not want to be involved in the activities amounting to indecent assault was justified upon the evidence and not gainsaid by the jury's verdict. She was and remained a young and highly vulnerable girl and the Appellant was guilty of a serious breach of trust.

11   It is to be noted that the video interview indicates that the victim was saying that she did not consent to anything but repeatedly said no. Mr Scholes contends that it follows in these circumstances that the issue of consent was raised in relation to all the activities, both the sexual intercourse and the indecent assaults immediately preceding it and the jury must therefore be taken to have been unsure on the issue of consent throughout. The only proper basis for sentencing the appellant was therefore that whilst he may have believed that she was consenting to all the activities, he knew that she was under 16.

12   The increase in the maximum sentence for indecent assault on a female over the age of 13 undoubtedly created an anomaly in relation to sexual offences with consenting girls over 13 but under 16. The problem is helpfully discussed in the commentary on the case of *Figg*. If a defendant is charged with indecent assault, the maximum sentence is 10 years' imprisonment; if he is charged with unlawful sexual intercourse the maximum sentence is limited to 2 years. Defendants whose actions amounted to the offence of unlawful sexual intercourse could find themselves charged with indecent assault where, for example, they were indicted for rape but acquitted on the basis that the jury was not satisfied that the act had occurred without the consent of the victim. Where, in such circumstances the time limit for a prosecution for unlawful sexual intercourse of one year had expired, such a defendant might be charged with indecent assault rather than unlawful sexual intercourse.

13   These anomalies led to a line of cases in which the Court of Appeal has accepted the argument that where, in truth, the indecent assaults charged are no more than unlawful sexual intercourse the maximum penalty should be two years, *i.e.* the sentence for unlawful sexual intercourse rather than 10 years, *i.e.* the maximum sentence for indecent assault. *Quayle* [1993] 14 Cr.App.R.(S.) 726, *Hinton* [1995] 16 Cr.App.R.(S.) 523, *Blair* [1996] 1 Cr.App.R.(S.) 336, *Brough* [1997] 2 Cr.App.R.(S.) 202, *Iles* [1998] 2 Cr.App.R.(S.) 63, *Martley* [2000] 1 Cr.App.R.(S.) 416 and *R. v Jones* [2003] 2 Cr.App.R. 8 (p.134).

14   In the case of *Jones*, an abuse of process case, the authorities are reviewed. Having found that it was not an abuse of process to bring charges of indecent assault where the time limit for a prosecution for unlawful sexual intercourse had expired, the Court of Appeal continued:

> "Equally, nothing we have said should detract from the now settled practice of this Court in treating two years imprisonment as the maximum sentence appropriate to a charge of indecent assault brought in circumstances where, but for the expiry of the twelve month time limit, the charge would appropriately have been laid under section 6."

        In the case of *Figg* the Court concluded that where a justifiable choice to prosecute for indecent assault is made, that offence does not carry with it the limitation imposed by *Hinton*. In the full transcript of the hearing Leveson J., giving the judgment of the Court, made it clear that a prosecution for indecent assault was justifiable on the facts of that case "bearing in mind the background of a middle-aged man grooming a 13 year old child and persuading her to consent to the act of sexual intercourse. That would not necessarily be the case if the facts were different, for example, revealing adolescent experimentation."

16   The Court also noted that a significant feature in the case of *Hinton* was that the Crown had been prepared to accept a plea of guilty to unlawful sexual intercourse and would have proceeded with that offence had it not been time barred. The substitution of the offence of indecent assault for that of unlawful sexual intercourse produced, in the circumstances an unfair result as, had it not been for the time bar, the appellant could not have been sentenced to more than two years imprisonment.

17   The case of *Jones* was not cited in *Figg*, a situation described in the commentary upon that case as unfortunate as the cases reviewed in *Jones* and *Jones* itself had not suggested that the Court had consistently failed to identify some limitation on the principle stated in *Hinton*. Nor did the Court in *Figg* consider the implications for possible abuse of process applications of rejecting the principle in *Hinton* ([2004] Crim.L.R. 390).

18   We for our part are satisfied that, as this Court said in its review of the cases in *Jones*, there is a settled practice of the Court of Appeal in treating two years' imprisonment as the maximum sentence appropriate to a charge of indecent assault brought in circumstances where a charge of unlawful sexual intercourse would have been properly brought, but for the expiry of the 12-month time limit relating to that offence. Whether or not the settled practice applies will depend upon the facts of any given case, but the principle lying behind the practice is that where the offence of indecent assault is, in truth, no more than the unlawful sexual intercourse, it would not be fair or appropriate to impose a greater sentence than that available to the Court had unlawful sexual intercourse been the offence charged. (See *Quayle per* Schiemann J., as he then was, and Lord Taylor C.J. in *Hinton*.) In some cases it will be clear that the only offence which would have been charged had it been available, but for the time bar, would have been unlawful sexual intercourse, and hence the appropriate maximum sentence for indecent assault, where charged instead of unlawful sexual intercourse, would be two years. (*Quayle, Hinton* and *Brough*.) The same may also apply where unlawful sexual intercourse is charged as well as indecent assault but where the indecent assaults may be regarded as part of the foreplay leading to the unlawful sexual intercourse and should not be regarded properly as separate or distinct offences.

19   In other cases however, such as in the case of *Figg*, where rape and indecent assault were before the court but unlawful sexual intercourse was not, and was not likely to be charged, the practice may not apply. If the acts of indecent assault are separate and distinct, for example where they occur on different days to the sexual intercourse, or where the indecent assaults can be, as they were in *Figg*, regarded as acts of grooming by a man who was considerably older, they could not be regarded as part of or, as Schiemann J. said in *Quayle*, "in truth, no more than unlawful sexual intercourse." We do not regard the case of *Figg* as either overruling or seeking to overrule the line of cases starting with *Quayle* and *Hinton*. We reject Mr Medland's submission to this effect. The Court in *Figg* was distinguishing those cases and setting out the reasons why the convention or practice did not apply to the facts of the case being considered by them.

20   The maximum permissible sentence for indecent assault remains one of 10 years even in cases where, as set out above, the convention or practice applies so as to make the effective maximum one of 2 years. The convention or practice is based upon the concept of unfairness and does not alter the lawful maximum sentence of 10 years. (See Lord Taylor C.J. in *Hinton*). For the purposes of s.85(5) of the Powers of Criminal Courts (Sentencing) Act 2000 the maximum term permitted for the offence of indecent assault, even where the convention or practice is applied, is 10 years not 2 years. It is therefore within the powers of this Court to order an extended sentence consisting of a custodial term and an extension period, provided, as Mr Medland on behalf the Crown submitted, the appellant is not more severely dealt with on appeal than he was dealt with by the court below under s.11(3) of the Criminal Appeal Act 1968.

21   When considering the facts of the present appeal we are satisfied that the indecent assaults, albeit separately charged, could properly be regarded as being part of the prelude or foreplay to the act of intercourse. The complainant's evidence raised the issue of consent in relation to all the activities which took place including the indecent assaults which preceded the intercourse. The jury's verdict must therefore have been taken to indicate that they were not sure either as to whether consent had been disproved by the Crown or whether it was the appellant's belief that the complainant had consented in relation to all sexual activities. It was difficult on the facts to separate the acts of indecent assault from the act of sexual intercourse. As the jury had acquitted of the offence of rape and convicted of unlawful sexual intercourse, we consider that this is one of those cases where the indecent assaults could not properly be regarded as separate or distinct, but as so closely related to the act of intercourse itself that their criminality should not be regarded as separate or different from the act of intercourse. In such circumstances the convention or practice is applicable and a custodial term of no more than two years should have been passed in respect of the offences of indecent assault.

2   We do not however accept that the judge was wrong in accepting the opinion of the writer of the pre-sentence report even though that report was somewhat less well researched than the Court might have wished. It was proper for the judge to accept the view that the appellant was a risk to young women. In such circumstances it would have been open to the judge to have formed the opinion that the normal licence period would not be adequate for the purpose of preventing the commission by the appellant of further offences or securing his rehabilitation. The Court clearly needed to look to the future risk of re-offending.

3   We conclude that the sentence which would fairly meet the justice of this case is an extended sentence of $3\frac{1}{2}$ years consisting of a custodial term of 2 years and an extension period of 18 months. Accordingly the sentence of $3\frac{1}{2}$ years imprisonment is quashed and an extended sentence of $3\frac{1}{2}$ years is substituted for it, with a custodial term of 2 years and the extension period of 18 months. The appeal is allowed to this extent.

R. v KEVIN JOHN UNDERWOOD AND OTHERS

Court of Appeal (Lord Justice Judge, Deputy Chief Justice, Mr Justice Douglas Brown and Mr Justice Bean): July 30, 2004

[2004] EWCA Crim. 2256; [2005] 1 Cr.App.R.(S.) 90

(LT) Basis of plea; Facts; Gulty pleas; Justice; Newton hearings; Sentencing guidelines; Supply of drugs

H1   *Factual basis for sentence—defendant pleading guilty, but disputing relevant facts—procedure*

H2   General guidance on determining the factual basis for sentence in cases where the defendant pleads guilty on an agreed "basis of plea".

H3   The Court dealt with four unrelated appeals in which questions concerned with *Newton* hearings arose.

H4   **Held:** although the principles relating to *Newton* hearings were clear they were not always fully understood or applied. The appeals had been listed to enable the Court to repeat and emphasise general guidance about the procedure to be adopted where the defendant pleaded guilty on a factual basis different from that which appeared from the Crown's case, or a study of the papers. The Court was concerned with the process which would achieve a sentence appropriate to reflect the justice of the case where there was a plea of guilty, but some important fact or facts relating to the offence which the defendant was admitting, of potential significance to the sentencing decision, were in dispute. The essential principle was that the sentencing judge must do justice. So far as possible offenders should be sentenced on a basis which accurately reflected the facts of the individual case. The principle of the *Newton* hearing was recognised in *Newton* (1982) 4 Cr.App.R.(S.) 388. The relevant procedures had developed in subsequent decisions. Unfortunately they were not being applied consistently. The starting point had to be the defendant's instructions. His advocate would appreciate whether any significant facts about the prosecution evidence were disputed, and the factual basis on which the defendant intended to plead guilty. If the resolution of the facts in dispute might matter to the sentencing decision, the responsibility of taking any initiative and alerting the prosecutor to the areas of dispute rested with the defence. The Crown should not be taken by surprise, and if it was suddenly faced with a proposed basis of plea of guilty where important facts were disputed, it should if necessary take time for proper reflection and consultation to consider its position and the interests of justice. In any event, whatever view might be formed by the Crown on any proposed basis of plea, it was deemed to be conditional on the judge's acceptance of it. The Crown might accept and agree the defendant's account of the disputed facts. If so the agreement should be reduced into writing and signed by both advocates. It should then be made available to the judge before the start of the Crown's opening and if possible before the judge was invited to approve the acceptance of any plea or pleas. If pleas had already been accepted and approved, it should be available before the sentencing hearing began. If the agreed basis of plea was not signed by the advocates for both sides, the judge was entitled to ignore it; similarly if the document was not legible. The Crown might reject the defence version. If so, the areas of dispute should be identified in writing and the document should focus the court's attention on the precise fact or facts which were in dispute. The third and most difficult situation arose where the Crown might lack the evidence positively to dispute the defendant's account. In many cases an issue raised by the defence was outside the knowledge of the prosecution. The prosecution might have no evidence to contradict the defence assertions. That did not mean that the truth of matters outside their knowledge should be agreed. In those circumstances, particularly if the facts relied on by the defendant arose from his personal knowledge and depended on his own account of the facts, the Crown should not normally agree the defendant's account unless it was supported by other material. There was an important distinction between assertions about the facts which the Crown was prepared to agree and its possible agreement to facts about which the prosecution was ignorant. Neither the prosecution nor the judge was bound to agree facts merely because the prosecution could not "gainsay" the defendant's account. The court should be notified at the outset in writing on all points in issue and the Crown's responses. After submissions from the advocates, the judge should decide how to proceed. If not already decided, he would address the question whether he should approve the Crown's acceptance of pleas. Then he would address the proposed basis of plea. The court would emphasise that whether or not the basis of plea was agreed, the judge was not bound by any such agreement and was entitled of his own motion to insist that any evidence relevant to the facts in dispute should be called before him. The judge was responsible for the sentencing decision and might therefore order a *Newton* hearing to ascertain the truth about disputed facts. The prosecuting advocate should assist the judge by calling any appropriate evidence and testing the evidence advanced by the defendant. The defence advocate should similarly call any relevant evidence and in particular where the issue arose from facts which were within the exclusive knowledge of the defendant and the defendant was willing to give evidence in support of his case, to call him. If the defendant was not willing to give evidence, and subject to any explanation which might be put forward, the judge might draw such inferences as he thought fit from the fact. Unless it were impractical, for some exceptional reason, the hearing should proceed immediately. The judge must then make up his mind about the facts in dispute. He might reject evidence called by the prosecution and might reject assertions advanced by the defendant or his witnesses, even if the Crown did not offer a positive contradictory evidence. The judge must of course direct himself in accordance with ordinary principles in relation to the burden and standard of proof. Having reached his conclusions, the judge should explain them in a judgment. There would be occasions when a *Newton* hearing would be inappropriate. Some issues required a verdict from the jury. For example where there was a dispute whether the defendant was carrying a firearm to commit a robbery; if the defendant was denying that a specific criminal offence had been committed, the tribunal for deciding whether the offence had been proved was the jury. At the end of the *Newton* hearing the judge could not make findings of fact and sentence on a basis which was inconsistent with the pleas to counts which had already been accepted and approved by the Court. Particular care was needed in relation to a multi-count indictment and indictments involving a number of defendants, and circumstances in which the Crown accepted and the court approved a guilty plea to a reduced charge. Where there were a number of defendants to a joint enterprise, the judge should bear in mind the relative seriousness of the joint enterprise on which the defendants were involved. He should take care not to regard a written basis of plea offered by one defendant as evidence justifying an adverse conclusion against another defendant. Generally speaking, matters of mitigation would not normally be dealt with by way of a *Newton* hearing. It was always open to the court to allow a defendant to give evidence of matters of mitigation which were within his own knowledge. For example, defendants in drug cases would assert that they were acting under some form of duress, not amounting in law to a defence. If there was nothing to support such a contention, the judge was entitled to invite the advocate for the defendant to call his client rather than depend on the unsupported assertion of the advocate. Where the impact of the dispute on the eventual sentencing decision was minimal, a *Newton* hearing was unnecessary. The judge was entitled to decline to hear evidence about disputed facts if the case advanced on the defence behalf was for good reason to be regarded as absurd or obviously untenable. The judge should explain why he had reached that conclusion. The final question was whether the defendant should lose the mitigation available to him for a guilty plea if, having contested facts alleged by the prosecution, the issues were resolved against him. The principles were clear. If the issues at the *Newton* hearing were resolved in the defendant's favour, the credit due to him should not be reduced. If the defendant was disbelieved, or if he obliged the prosecution to call evidence from the victim who was then subjected to cross-examination, or if the defendant conveyed to the judge that he had no insight into the consequences of his offence and no genuine remorse for it, these were all matters which might lead the judge to reduce the discount which the defendant would otherwise have received for his plea of guilty, particularly if that was tendered at a very late stage. Accordingly there might be exceptional cases in which the normal entitlement to credit for a guilty plea was wholly dissipated by the *Newton* hearing. In such cases the judge should explain his reasons.

H5   **Case cited:**
      Newton (1982) 4 Cr.App.R.(S.) 388

H6   **References:** factual basis for sentence, *Current Sentencing Practice* L2, *Archbold* 5–64

H7   **Commentary:** [2004] Crim. L.R. 1049

18   *M. Duffy* for the appellant Underwood.
     J. Elliott for the Crown.
     D. Barlow for the appellant Arobieke.
     G. Cook for the appellant Khan.
     D. Jackson for the Crown.
     D. Taylor for the appellant Connors.

JUDGMENT

1   **Judge L.J.:**   In these appeals, which we heard and decided earlier this week,
     we are concerned with what can compendiously be described as *Newton* hear-
     ings. Although the principles are clear, they are not always fully understood or
     applied. These appeals have therefore been listed together to enable this Court
     to repeat and emphasise general guidance about the procedure to be adopted
     where the defendant pleads guilty on a factual basis different from that which
     appears from the Crown's case, or, indeed, a study of the papers. In short, we
     are concerned with the process which will achieve the sentence appropriate to
     reflect the justice of the case where there is a plea of guilty, but some important
     fact or facts relating to the offence which the defendant is admitting, of potential
     significance to the sentencing decision, are in dispute.

2   The essential principle is that the sentencing judge must do justice. So far as
     possible the offender should be sentenced on the basis which accurately reflects
     the facts of the individual case. In *Newton* (1983) 77 Cr.App.R. 13 itself, Newton
     was charged with, and pleaded guilty to, very serious sexual offences involving
     his wife. As the law then stood, her consent provided no defence. It hardly needs
     saying that for sentencing purposes the difference between forced and consensual
     sexual activity was huge. It was therefore a classic example of an imperative need
     to establish the facts. To proceed to sentence without doing so, would have been
     productive of injustice. Lord Lane C.J. identified one method of approach where
     there was a sharp divergence between the differing accounts of the offence:

> "the second method which could be adopted by the judge in these circum-
> stances is himself to hear the evidence on one side and another, and come to
> his own conclusion, acting so to speak as his own jury on the issue which is
> the root of the problem."

This is the *Newton* hearing. Inevitably, the relevant procedures have developed
through subsequent decisions. We do not propose to cite any of them. They are
fully summarised in Blackstone, *Criminal Practice*, 2004 edition at D18.2–
D18.13, Archbold, *Criminal Pleading Evidence and Practice*, 2004 edition at
5–18 to 5–222, and Morrish and McLean, *Crown Court Index 2004*, under the
chapter heading "Newton Hearings". Our judgment is confined to well-estab-
lished principles, which, unfortunately, are not consistently being applied.

     The starting point has to be the defendant's instructions. His advocate will
appreciate whether any significant facts about the prosecution evidence are disputed and the factual basis on which the defendant intends to plead guilty. If the
resolution of the facts in dispute may matter to the sentencing decision, the

responsibility for taking any initiative and alerting the prosecutor to the areas of dispute rest with the defence. The Crown should not be taken by surprise, and if it is suddenly faced with a proposed basis of plea of guilty where important facts are disputed, it should, if necessary, take time for proper reflection and consultation to consider its position and the interests of justice. In any event, whatever view may be formed by the Crown on any proposed basis of plea, it is deemed to be conditional on the judge's acceptance of it.

4   The Crown may accept and agree the defendant's account of the disputed facts. If so, the agreement should be reduced into writing and signed by both advocates. It should then be made available to the judge before the start of the Crown's opening, and, if possible, before he is invited to approve the acceptance of any plea or pleas. If, however, pleas have already been accepted and approved, then it should be available before the sentencing hearing begins. If the agreed basis of plea is not signed by the advocates for both sides, the judge is entitled to ignore it; similarly, if the document is not legible. The Crown may reject the defendant's version. If so, the areas of dispute should be identified in writing and the document should focus the court's attention on the precise fact or facts which are in dispute.

5   The third, and most difficult, situation arises when the Crown may lack the evidence positively to dispute the defendant's account. In many cases an issue raised by the defence is outside the knowledge of the prosecution. The prosecution's position may well be that they had no evidence to contradict the defence assertions. That does not mean that the truth of matters outside their own knowledge should be agreed. In these circumstances, particularly if the facts relied on by defendant arise from his personal knowledge and depend on his own account of the facts, the Crown should not normally agreed the defendant's account unless it is supported by other material. There is, therefore, an important distinction between assertions about the facts which the Crown is prepared to agree, and its possible agreement to facts about which, in truth, the prosecution is ignorant. Neither the prosecution nor the judge is bound to agree facts merely because, in the word currently in vogue, the prosecution cannot "gainsay" the defendant's account. Again, the court should be notified at the outset in writing of the points in issue and the Crown's responses. We need not address those cases where the Crown occupies a position which straddles two, or even all three, of these alternatives.

6   After submissions from the advocates the judge should decide how to proceed. If not already decided, he will address the question whether he should approve the Crown's acceptance of pleas. Then he will address the proposed basis of plea. We emphasise that whether or not the basis of plea is "agreed", the judge is not bound by any such agreement and is entitled of his own motion to insist that any evidence relevant to the facts in dispute should be called before him. No doubt, before doing so, he will examine any agreement reached by the advocates, paying appropriate regard to it, and any reasons which the Crown, in particular, may advance to justify him proceeding immediately to sentence. At the risk of stating the obvious, the judge is responsible for the sentencing decision and he may therefore order a *Newton* hearing and to ascertain the truth about disputed facts.

7   The prosecuting advocate should assist him by calling any appropriate evidence and testing the evidence advanced by the defence. The defence advocate should similarly call any relevant evidence and, in particular, where the issue arises from facts which are within the exclusive knowledge of the defendant and the defendant is willing to give evidence in support of his case, be prepared to call him. If he is not, and subject to any explanation which may be proffered, the judge may draw such inferences he thinks fit from that fact. An adjournment for these purposes is often unnecessary. If the plea is tendered late when the case is due to be tried the relevant witnesses for the Crown are likely to be available. The *Newton* hearing should proceed immediately. In every case, or virtually so, the defendant will be present. It may be sufficient for the judge's purpose to hear the defendant. If so, again, unless it is impracticable for some exceptional reason, the hearing should proceed immediately.

8   The judge must then make up his mind about the facts in dispute. He may, of course, reject evidence called by the prosecution. It is sometimes overlooked that he may equally reject assertions advanced by the defendant, or his witnesses, even if the Crown does not offer positive contradictory evidence.

9   The judge must, of course, direct himself in accordance with ordinary principles, such as, for example, the burden and standard of proof. In short, his self-directions should reflect the relevant directions he would have given to the jury. Having reached his conclusions, he should explain them in a judgment.

0   Again, by way of reminder, we must explain some of the limitations on the *Newton* hearing procedure.

(a) There will be occasions when the *Newton* hearing will be inappropriate. Some issues require a verdict from the jury. To take an obvious example, a dispute whether the necessary intent under s.18 of the Offences against the Person Act 1861 has been proved should be decided by the jury. Where the factual issue is not encapsulated in a distinct count in the indictment when it should be, then, again, the indictment should be amended and the issue resolved by the jury. We have in mind, again for example, cases where there is a dispute whether the defendant was carrying a firearm to commit a robbery. In essence, if the defendant is denying that a specific criminal offence has been committed, the tribunal for deciding whether the offence has been proved is the jury.

(b) At the end of the *Newton* hearing the judge cannot make findings of fact and sentence on a basis which is inconsistent with the pleas to counts which have already been accepted by the Crown and approved by the court. Particular care is needed in relation to a multi-count indictment involving one defendant, or an indictment involving a number of defendants, and to circumstances in which the Crown accepts, and the court approves, a guilty plea to a reduced charge.

(c) Where there are a number of defendants to a joint enterprise, the judge, while reflecting on the individual basis of pleas, should bear in mind the relative seriousness of the joint enterprise on which the defendants were involved. In short, the context is always relevant. He should also take care not to regard a written basis of plea offered by one defendant, without more, as evidence justifying an adverse conclusion against another defendant.

(d) Generally speaking, matters of mitigation are not normally dealt with by way of a *Newton* hearing. It is, of course, always open to the court to allow a defendant to give evidence of matters of mitigation which are within his own knowledge. From time to time, for example, defendants involved in drug cases will assert that they were acting under some form of duress, not amounting in law to a defence. If there is nothing to support such a contention, the judge is entitled to invite the advocate for the defendant to call his client rather than depend on the unsupported assertions of the advocate.

(e) Where the impact of the dispute on the eventual sentencing decision is minimal, the *Newton* hearing is unnecessary. The judge is rarely likely to be concerned with minute differences about events on the periphery.

(f) The judge is entitled to decline to hear evidence about disputed facts if the case advanced on the defendant's behalf is, for good reason, to be regarded as absurd or obviously untenable. If so, however, he should explain why he has reached this conclusion.

11   The final matter for guidance is whether the defendant should lose the mitigation available to him for his guilty plea if, having contested facts alleged by the prosecution, the issues are resolved against him. The principles are clear. If the issues at the *Newton* hearing are wholly resolved in the defendant's favour, the credit due to him should not be reduced. If for example, however, the defendant is disbelieved, or obliges the prosecution to call evidence from the victim, who is then subjected to cross-examination, which, because it is entirely unfounded, causes unnecessary and inappropriate distress, or if the defendant conveys to the judge that he has no insight into the consequences of his offence and no genuine remorse for it, these are all matters which may lead the judge to reduce the discount which the defendant would otherwise have received for his guilty plea, particularly if that plea is tendered at a very late stage. Accordingly, there may even be exceptional cases in which the normal entitlement to credit for a plea of guilty is wholly dissipated by the *Newton* hearing. In such cases, again, the judge should explain his reasons.

12   We shall now address the individual appeals.

13   Kevin Underwood is now 55 years old. He was born in 1949. He had many court appearances, starting in 1973. The longest custodial sentence he had previously received was three and a half years' imprisonment some 20 years ago in January 1983. His most recent custodial sentence, before the matters with which we are concerned, was one month's imprisonment for possession of a controlled drug of class A. That sentence was imposed in December 2002.

14   On August 15, 2003 in the Crown Court at Peterborough before H.H. Judge Jacobs, the appellant pleaded guilty to two counts in an indictment containing a total, after amendment, of 24 counts. He pleaded guilty to count 23, offering

to supply a controlled drug of class A, cocaine, and count 24, which was an amendment of the original count 17, and, again, was offering to supply a controlled drug of class A, diamorphine.

5   After a *Newton* hearing on October 8 before H.H. Judge Coleman, he was sentenced on November 4, 2003 to five years' imprisonment on each of these two counts to run concurrently. In the course of the proceedings an order had been made that count 11, another count alleging an offer to supply a controlled drug of class A, should remain on the file in the usual terms, and on count 22, an offence of being concerned in supplying a class A drug, the Crown offered no evidence. That decision is of importance to the outcome of this appeal.

6   There were three co-accused. Christopher John Penhall pleaded guilty to three counts of supplying a class A controlled drug and one count of being concerned in the supply of a class A controlled drug. He was sentenced to three years and six months' imprisonment on each count to run concurrently. Peter Travanti pleaded guilty to three counts of supplying a class A controlled drug and one count of offering to supply a class A controlled drug. He was sentenced to four years' imprisonment on each count to run concurrent. Jacqueline Hateley pleaded guilty to two counts of permitting her premises to be used for supplying a class A controlled drug, one count of being concerned in supplying a class A controlled drug and one count of supplying a class A controlled drug. She was sentenced to three-and-a-half years' imprisonment on each count to run concurrently.

7   This appellant appeals against sentence with leave of the single judge.

8   It is unnecessary to examine the facts in any great detail. The prosecution of these four defendants arose from a police operation, known as "Operation Laker", which began in Huntingdon in March 2003. The object of the operation was to target the sale and supply of class A drugs in and around Huntingdon at street level. The evidence was generated by the deployment of police officers working undercover and posing as drug users. Those officers were known as Kate, Jim and Holly. The operation took place between March 20 and May 6 2003.

9   The four defendants were linked to each other. According to the Crown's case, they shared a common interest in illicit class A drugs. The Crown's case in opening included these important words "There is no principal offender". The text continues to record that criminal behaviour was centred on the home address of the defendant Hateley, who moved into the address with her three children in December 2002. This appellant became her lodger. She had had a relationship with her co-defendant Travanti which came to an end by March 2003. The defendant Penhall was known by all of the three other defendants, and, on occasion, he was observed visiting Hateley's home address.

0   We can now come, very briefly, to the facts of the two counts in the indictment which affect this appellant. First we deal with count 17, which became count 24. On April 8 the undercover officer Jim telephoned the appellant. He arranged a £50 heroin deal; that was five wraps in £10 deals. The officer was told to go to Hateley's home address. As he, together with the female officer Holly, approached the address Underwood and Penhall left the house together and

joined up with them. Penhall walked ahead of Jim, saying "Here", or something like that, before passing the drugs to him. Holly gave money to Underwood.

21   So far as count 23 was concerned, on April 23 Holly telephoned Underwood asking about crack cocaine. He told her to telephone back in about 10 minutes' time. She did so. He then invited her to Hateley's home address and gave her directions. Hateley answered the door and invited her in. She took the officer upstairs to Underwood's room, where Underwood was found kneeling on the floor chipping pieces off a rock of crack cocaine. He crashed the chip into little pieces before putting ash on the end of a pipe and placing crack cocaine on top. He then offered the officer the pipe to smoke. She refused, saying, "It's not for me, it's for my boyfriend". Hateley and Underwood both then smoked several pipes between them.

22   Then came a matter in dispute. The Crown's case was that during this period Underwood was dialling numbers for the officer in order to get some rocks of crack cocaine and he dialled the numbers, indicating that he was getting an answer phone, and then, when he spoke to another person, he was told that he would have to wait for 45 minutes. The officer waited with the appellant for about an hour, but left before any supply could be arranged or took place.

23   All four defendants were arrested on June 16. In interview this appellant made no comment.

24   Returning to the indictment: on 4 counts in the 23 count indictment, guilty pleas were offered by him to two counts. The basis of plea was put verbally to counsel for the prosecution with an undertaking from counsel for the defence to put it into writing. In due course count 17 was replaced by count 24. The written basis of plea, signed by counsel for the appellant, reads:

> "The basis of the defendant's plea to counts 17 and 23 of the Indictment herein is as follows:—Count 17 [then in handwriting beneath it 'count 24']—the defendant has entered a plea of guilty to offering to supply dia-morphine to a test purchase officer, 'Jim', in consequence and within the context of the evidence of the telephone conversation recited by 'Jim' at page 97, lines 7 to 10 of the prosecution bundle. The offer to supply was made by one user of the heroin to help a fellow user and/or addict and not on a commercial basis. In consequence of his conduct, the defendant prof-ited not at all, either in cash or in kind."

25   Pausing there, that basis of plea is entirely uncontentious. There is no dispute of fact whatever. The text makes clear that the conversation recited by the under-cover police officer is accepted, and the purpose of this basis of plea was simply to assert matters of mitigation.

26   As to count 23, the basis of plea reads:

> "The defendant has again entered a plea of guilty to offering to supply, on this occasion 'crack cocaine'. The offer was made to a test purchase officer, 'Holly', within the circumstances described by her at page 144 of the pros-ecution bundle, lines 4 to 10, and rejected. Thus the context of the offer is a user of 'crack' offering a perceived fellow user a pipe containing (inter alia)

the drug to smoke within a purely social setting with only one other user present, who later made an identical offer, similarly rejected. Again, the offer to supply was not upon a commercial basis and being part of purely social intercourse as described by 'Holly', again profited the defendant not at all, save perhaps simply in social terms."

27   The Crown did not accept the basis of plea insofar as it related to count 23 and sensibly asked for time to consider whether a *Newton* hearing would be needed. The judge expressed some reservations about the proposal, but the pleas to the four counts involving this appellant were approved. When the basis of plea was eventually reduced to writing, counsel for the Crown required a *Newton* hearing in relation to count 23. The issue which concerned the Crown was whether the appellant simply offered the investigating police officer a pipe to smoke, or whether his activity extended more widely to telephone calls which demonstrated, as the undercover woman police officer indicated, that he was close enough to the sources of supply to obtain crack cocaine if he needed or wished to do so.

28   If that was the single difference of view, we doubt the value of a *Newton* hearing at all. The dealings between the undercover police officer and the appellant sufficiently demonstrated that he was close to a source of supply. The reasons advanced in support of this *Newton* hearing overlooked the stark fact that the Crown had already decided not to pursue the two further counts alleged against the appellant, and, in particular, had offered no evidence on the count of being concerned in supplying a class A drug. So, although like his co-accused committed for trial on a charge of conspiracy to supply class A drugs, the appellant was not convicted of conspiracy to supply drugs, nor being concerned in the supply of drugs over an identified period, nor even with the actual supply of drugs. There were offers to supply on two distinct occasions. The pleas accepted by the Crown may well have been unrealistic and the Crown may well have been unwise to accept them. Nevertheless, they were accepted and the appellant was to be sentenced on the basis of the counts to which he had pleaded guilty; in the result, therefore, two counts of offering to supply class A drugs.

29   On September 12 H.H. Judge Coleman sentenced Hateley, Travanti and Penhall. He had before him written bases of plea from each of those three defendants. In relation to Hateley the written basis read:

> **"Count 1**
> I accept that I suffered Kevin Underwood to supply heroin from my premises although I informed him on numerous occasions that I did not want him to do so. I was using heroin at the time and was dependent upon him for my drugs."

30   Then in relation to count 2:

> "I accept that on two occasions I was involved in the supply of crack cocaine at my premises."

31   In relation to counts 12 and 16:

"I accept my involvement in these offences on the basis that I was made aware by the undercover officers that they required crack cocaine and I became involved in count 12 and count 16 to enable them to receive the drugs they had requested. Had I not been approached by them I would not have offered to assist. I did not receive any financial gain from these trans- actions."

32   So far as Penhall was concerned, his written basis of plea read:

"I plead guilty to count 17 on the following basis only."

Pausing there, it will be remembered that count 17 was the count in which Under- wood was jointly involved with Penhall. We return to the basis of plea:

"The deal had been arranged by Kevin Underwood alone without my knowledge. I accept however what once officer Jim arrived, Kevin Under- wood asked me to pass the package to Jim, which I did and said something like 'here'. This was my part of the supply and I plead guilty on that basis."

33   The judge passed sentence on Hateley, saying that he had taken into account the basis of her plea, and in sentencing Penhall he said that he would give effect to the basis of his plea.

34   The *Newton* hearing took place on October 8. At the end of the *Newton* hearing the judge made findings which, as he said, were limited to the events set out in count 23 of the indictment, and, it will also be remembered, related, so far as the Crown was concerned, to a relatively narrow issue. The judge set out the facts and he came to the conclusion that the undercover police officer went to the address in question to obtain crack cocaine. He noted that when she had first telephoned the defendant he said he did not have anything. The judge made the remark that there was no evidence to gainsay this. When she said, "What about white?", a reference to crack cocaine, she was asked to phone back in 10 minutes. She did so and she went to the house to find crack cocaine.

35   The judge concluded that she was offered a pipe. He then recorded:

"Hence the plea to count 23. It seems that the basis of plea is perfectly proper in that respect. There is nothing to gainsay that. She refused the offer. It was a social offer, and it was done by one addict (as he perceived) to another."

So that was the finding.

36   The judge also found that, during the course of these transactions, the defend- ant was seeking to obtain crack cocaine from people he knew could supply in the same way, as the judge put it:

". . . as he would have tried to find a tyre from a supplier or distributor, and if he had got it, no doubt, although of course history does not relate, then it would have been supplied."

In other words, therefore, he went on to conclude that the Crown's case in relation to the telephone calls reported by the woman police officer was accurate. So far, so good.

37   The judge then recorded:

> "The prosecution have of course addressed me about the role this defendant played in the drugs scene in Huntingdon. When I say the drug scene, it is of course the supply of class A drugs which Operation Laker was designed to detect and root out, and they were investigating (I quote) 'the supply of class A drugs' on what might be described rather colloquially as the drugs scene. This defendant is said to be a user dealer. There is no dispute about that. It is conceded by the prosecution that there is no evidence that he profited from his dealings."

Then going to the end of his judgment:

> "The defendant of course will be sentenced on count 23 in the way that the basis of plea has been tendered, but it is clear in my judgment his role overall goes further than that which is set out in count 23."

38   On November 4 the appellant came back before Judge Coleman for sentence. The judge said that he had to deal with the defendants individually, noting that he had to consider each case separately, that the context was that the appellant was one of several people who were arrested as part of the major operation in Huntingdon. The judge said:

> "That said, of course, given what I know about the nature of the operation and the extent of dealing in that city/town deterrent sentences are, in my judgment, called for."

Those observations, of course, would have applied with equal force to the three co-defendants who had been sentenced earlier by the same judge.

39   The judge went on:

> "It is clear from what I know about you, and from the *Newton* hearing which was conducted in my presence, that you are a user/dealer that you were, as might be described, a 'facilitator'."

Then these important words:

> "You were clearly deeply immersed in the drugs scene in that city and you were closely connected with the ready supply of heroin and crack cocaine."

He then recorded that he had sentenced Hateley and Penhall on the basis of what he described as:

> ". . . their connections with you. I heard much about them. What I heard about them and what I have heard about you, puts you, in my judgment, more deeply in this than they were, thus any sentence must be more severe."

In the result, therefore, the appellant was sentenced to five years' imprisonment, a year-and-a-half longer than two of his co-accused and one year longer than the third of them.

40   In our judgment, in agreement with counsel for the appellant, this produced an unfortunate result. It is difficult to avoid the conclusion that the appellant was sentenced on a basis which went beyond the counts to which he had pleaded guilty. The judge's analysis may well have been right in fact. Nevertheless, he was not entitled to sentence the appellant on a basis which was not properly reflected in the outcome of the four counts on the indictment which affected the appellant himself. If the appellant was more deeply involved, the pleas should not have been accepted, and possibly, also, counts in the indictment should have been more specific. The Crown should not have invited the judge to conduct a *Newton* hearing. On the basis on which he was asked to do so, a *Newton* hearing was unnecessary. But the Crown should also have borne in mind, and perhaps drawn to the judge's attention, and if they had drawn to the judge's attention the judge should not have overlooked, that the Crown's case was that as between the four of these defendants there was no principal offender.

41   Moreover, the judge seems to have treated the written basis of pleas of two of the co-defendants, who had not given any evidence before him, as relevant to support the conclusions he reached adverse to the appellant. We do not think that any of this material was put to the appellant in the course of the *Newton* hearing, but, in any event, the documents themselves were not admissible in evidence against him.

42   In effect, therefore, our conclusion is that the defendant was sentenced for offences with which he was not in truth charged and which was inconsistent with the way in which the pleas were tendered and accepted. Accordingly, we conclude that the sentence on the appellant was excessive after his plea of guilty. Even allowing for the dispute of fact resolved by the judge against him in relation to the telephone calls, given the finding that he had made no profit and no commercial gain from his activities and reflecting broad justice without being constrained by the judge's sentences on the co-accused, we concluded that this sentence should be reduced to three-and-a-half years' imprisonment.

Akinwale Arobieke

43   He was born in July 1961. He has a very long record for criminal offences. His last significant conviction before the matters with which we are concerned occurred in August 2001 when he was sentenced to 30 months' imprisonment for threats to kill. On January 15, 2003 in the Crown Court at Preston before H.H. Judge Slinger he pleaded guilty on rearraignment to 15 counts of harassment contrary to s.4 of the Protection from Harassment Act 1997, together with one count of intimidating a witness. The pleas were accepted. Forty-two counts of indecent assault on males and additional counts of harassment and witness intimidation were ordered to lie on the file. Because he was on trial for other matters, of which he was eventually acquitted, he was not sentenced for these offences until September 15, 2003. On that date Judge Slinger sentenced him

to a total of six years' imprisonment and made appropriate restraining orders in each case.

44   Arobieke now renews his application for leave to appeal against sentence after refusal by the single judge.

45   The essential facts can be briefly summarised. In September 2000 a complaint was made to the police about the applicant's relationship with youths in the area of St Helens. As a result 18 young men made complaints of harassment against him. His guilty pleas related to offences in respect of 16 of these youths. The pleas were acceptable to the Crown, which did not proceed with the counts of indecent assault. A written basis of plea was entered. The Crown's position was that they did not endorse the plea, but did not seek a *Newton* hearing.

46   The offences took place over a period of approximately three-and-a-half years, from June 1997 to January 2001. The ages of the victims ranged from 14 to 17 years and the majority of the offences involved boys aged 15 and 16 years. In some cases the same boys were pursued over several years, although the harassment in a number of others lasted for much shorter periods.

47   They followed a similar pattern. The applicant would begin by approaching and some times appearing to befriend the complainants. He made them flex their biceps and felt their arms, chests and legs. He would ask them to lean over and perform squatting exercises while he rested his weight against their back or buttocks. He met the complainants when they were walking to and from school or work, or just out socially. They might be approached at any time of the day or night and would often by taken by the applicant to his car and required to perform these activities either in the car, or at some lonely area. Five of the complainants were harassed for a period exceeding three years, several of them somewhere in the region of two years and four of them from four months up to one year. Some saw the applicant daily, some saw him two or three times a week, but the common feature was that contact would resume after a break. No direct violence was used, but the applicant was a large and commanding figure who undoubtedly intimidated these young men. His conduct had an adverse effect on all of them and some suffered from depressive illness as well as fear. One gave up his job and tried to run away from home to escape the applicant's attentions.

48   One example of the applicant's activities in relation to a young man, we will describe as M, will suffice. M was harassed by the applicant for approximately two years. He would be stopped on his way to and from the gym. He was scared that the applicant would make enquiries about him after discovering whether he used a specific gym. He was subjected to what was described as "measuring" and made to carry out squatting exercises, together with "scarecrowing", for which he would be made to stand with his arms out stretched. When he did so, the applicant would lift him from behind. He was made to carry out these squatting exercises on over 15 separate occasions. The applicant developed a control over him which left this young man frightened, helpless, sick and dirty. As a result, although he had greatly enjoyed it, he stopped going to the gym and kept his head down; by which he meant he kept out of the applicant's way.

49   M was also the victim of the count alleging witness intimidation. In November 2000 the applicant came across him by accident and asked whether the police had spoken to him. He said to M, "I want you out of this. I don't want you involved any more. Better for you if you were not involved." He then asked M if M had signed a statement. He told him that if he had, he would get a copy of it and find out what M had said. He repeated that he did not want M involved. The context, and this is important, was that M had, of course, already been a victim of the prolonged harassment at the applicant's hands which we have already described.

50   The basis of plea in relation to the offence of harassment read:

> "He accepts that his behaviour of touching and measuring muscles, together with the squat exercises, and his behaviour towards the complainants involve a course of conduct.
>
> By his guilty pleas he accepts that this course of conduct as viewed by a reasonable person would amount to harassment.
>
> He acknowledges that with hindsight this course of conduct does amount to harassment and that each complainant would be distressed and fear that violence would be used. At no stage did he intentionally go out to cause such distress or fear to the complainants or their families. He now accepts that a reasonable person would think that his conduct would cause the complainants to fear that violence would be used.
>
> This behaviour stems from a genuine friendship and interest with these young men, sport and muscle development. Since the age of 18, this defendant has been engaged in such behaviour with other males. He now understands that such behaviour could be viewed as being strange. At no stage did he receive any overt sexual gratification from this course of conduct. It was genuine interest in muscle development but he now accepts that this obsessive and strange behaviour did cause distress.
>
> The defendant does not accept any of the specific allegations that he verbally threatened violence against any of the complainants."

51   In relation to witness intimidation the written basis of plea was:

> "The incident on 8th November 2000 where the defendant met M in St Helen's town centre was not premeditated by the defendant. It was a chance meeting. This complainant knew the other two males. They spoke for about 20 minutes. He accepts the thrust of what he is alleged to have said but denies any direct or indirect threat against the complainant B. By his guilty plea he now accepts that M would have felt intimidated at the time when the defendant said he did not want him involved in the investigation. This stemmed from the defendant's deep mistrust of the police and their motives. This belief should be viewed in light of the basis of pleas entered above. Further given the statutory provisions contained within section 51(7) of the Criminal Justice and Public Order Act 1994 the statutory presumption would operate thereby establishing the required intent under these provisions given the admissions made by the defence."

There is in the written basis of plea a good deal of unnecessary material, which is simply mitigation and does not contest facts alleged by the Crown.

52   This applicant has a lengthy criminal record. There are 23 previous court appearances recorded for some 38 offences, principally for offences of violence, offences relating to the police and offences of dishonesty. We have already recorded that his most recent conviction, before the matters with which we are concerned, occurred at Chester Crown Court on August 3, 2001 when he was sentenced to 30 months' imprisonment for threatening to kill.

53   During his time on remand he was seen by a psychiatrist, but he declined to make the psychiatric report available either to the probation service or the court.

54   When the judge came to deal with the case he referred to the basis of plea, in particular, in view of the way in which the counts of indecent assault were accepted, that there had been no sexual element in what had occurred. He then said:

> "As I have said, you claim not to have verbally threatened violence, but there is a clear pattern from youth after youth that any attempt to put a stop to your behaviour either attempts by themselves or by their families was followed by conduct—and I ignore anything for which there is no evidence that you were responsible—which put them at fear. What is beyond dispute is that fear—the effect upon them—forms a consistent pattern in what they said. Attempts altering their daily lives to try to avoid you."

55   In our view, the judge was fully justified in the comments which he made. They were entirely consistent with the pleas of guilty. When he came to sentence, the judge meticulously summarised the offences and the effect on the respective victims. He decided that he should place the offences into three different categories: first, and most serious, those where harassment had continued for 3 years or more; secondly, medium length cases, up to 2 years, over 2 years and towards 3 years; and the third category, where the conduct had persisted between 4 and 12 months. He decided on the relevant levels of sentence and by means of consecutive and concurrent sentences arrived at a total of five years' imprisonment in relation to the harassment cases and one further year in relation to witness intimidation.

56   The judge expressed the view, in agreement with the author of the pre-sentence report, that the applicant represented a danger to young men. That was an entirely justified conclusion based on the circumstances of the offences, the applicant's previous record and, as we hold, by his refusal to allow psychiatric evidence obtained about him to be presented to the court. In our judgment, therefore, the judge's approach to the basis of plea was entirely correct.

7   The first matter we address is the consecutive sentence for witness intimidation. That is consecutive to the total sentence of five years for offences of harassment. That sentence was entirely justified. It is true that no direct violence was threatened and if that offence were to be reviewed in total isolation the sentence might well have been lower than 12 months. However, the context is that the witness was a young man who had already been victimised by the applicant and was already in fear of him. In those circumstances, the 12 month sentence

was appropriate. We also conclude that the total sentence for harassment, although lengthy, is not arguably manifestly excessive, given the course of conduct and the large number of victims and the fear with which the applicant's intimidation instilled in them. In his careful approach to this sentencing exercise, the judge arrived at a total sentence which, in our judgment, cannot be challenged. This renewed application was, therefore, refused.

Mohammed Khan

58   He was born in October 1980. In July 2000 for offences of kidnapping and blackmail mail he was sentenced to four years' detention in a young offender institution. On March 2, 2004, in the Crown Court at Birmingham before H.H. Judge Faber, he changed his plea to guilty of robbery and admitted breach of a licence relating to that sentence. On the same occasion his co-accused, Winifred Hall, also changed her plea to guilty of robbery. On April 7, before H.H. Judge Faber, the appellant was sentenced to six years' imprisonment for robbery and one month's imprisonment consecutive for breach of licence. His co-accused was sentenced to four years' imprisonment.

59   This application for leave to appeal against sentence was referred to the Full Court by the Registrar. We granted him leave to appeal.

60   The essential facts were very simple. At around 1.30am on October 13, 2003 Hall was working as a prostitute in Hagley Road Edgbaston. She was picked up by the complainant. As he thought, he drove her to her home. In fact she took him back to the appellant's home. She asked the complainant to take his bags in, but he refused. He locked his car and went into the flat. The door was unlocked.

61   After entering, the complainant removed his clothing. Something about the atmosphere disturbed him and he changed his mind, but just as he was going to put his clothes back on the appellant burst out of the kitchen, according to the complainant, holding a machete and extendable truncheon. The complainant was ordered to lie on the side of the bed. He refused to do so. The appellant struck on the left side of his face. Winifred Hall then took the complainant's car keys. His briefcase was removed from his car and his possessions, which included his credit and debit cards, were stolen. He was forced to give up his PIN number. His watch and necklace were also stolen. The complainant was then tied up loosely and the appellant and Hall left the flat, taking his clothes with them and leaving him naked.

62   The complainant managed to untie himself and tried to make his escape. He found that he was locked in. He broke a window with his foot and climbed out of it, hoping in that way to be able to descend to a lower ledge. He was unable to reach the lower ledge and for a time, and disconcertingly, was hanging out of a window some three storeys high. Fortunately he managed to get back into the room from which he had escaped. Eventually he managed to prise open the front door. He found some of his clothes by the car, put them on and alerted the police. He had had a deeply distressing experience. He required hospital treatment for swelling and bruising to his face and cuts to his hands and feet. Quite

apart from any injuries, he lost a number of very valuable papers, including his passport and birth certificate.

63 Hall was arrested on October 21. The appellant was arrested on October 22. In interview he denied the offence. When the case was first listed neither the appellant nor Hall pleaded guilty. However, on March 2, he advanced a written basis of plea. The document was signed by the appellant at the hearing. It reads as follows:

> "The defendant pleads guilty on the following basis.
> The defendant had formed an association with the co-defendant and considered themselves to have moved beyond being merely a customer and prostitute. He had been waiting for the co-defendant at the flat. He did not anticipate his co-defendant returning with a client and was angry and upset when he saw the injured party. In anger he picked up the broomstick and struck the injured party with it once. This was not a premeditated robbery. They both then took the possessions of the injured party and left the flat."

64 The document was not signed by counsel for the Crown. There is, however, a note, initialled by Judge Taylor, which is added at the end of it:

> "Prosecution submit it doesn't matter materially whether there was long term planning or not. They also submit a trial of the issue as to what the weapon was is not necessary bearing in mind the actual injuries caused in the attack and the fact that the cuts to the victim were caused when he was attempting to escape from the incident."

65 In Hall's case the basis of plea document had comments by prosecution counsel inserted on it. The comments were illegible and had to be interpreted for us by counsel. It read as follows:

> "(a) . . . I do not accept any premeditation in this offence. I had met with the injured party and we returned to the flat for sex as agreed.
> [in script] Prosecution cannot gainsay.
> (b) once at the flat I saw that Mr Khan was already there and he was upset that I had brought a client to the flat and he picked up a broomstick and assaulted the injured party.
> [in script] Pros wit says machete/baton, but *Newton* hearing unnecessary as only injury was by one blow . . .; cuts caused by glass when escaping.
> (c) we both took the possessions of the injured party and left the flat."

This document was signed by Hall and her counsel countersigned. Counsel for the prosecution did not sign that document.

66 There is, in the text we have read out, no reference to a factor to which reference was made in the course of the opening on behalf of the Crown before Judge Taylor when he dealt with the appellant's case on April 7. Counsel for the Crown then said to him that she understood that on the earlier occasion the Crown had not sought to litigate the issue of the weapons carried by the appellant, bearing in mind that this particular victim was very worried about publicity.

67   There were important, but distinct factual issues disclosed by the written basis of plea by both defendants. First, whether the weapons carried by the appellant were a broomstick, as he asserted, or a machete and baton as alleged by the complainant. Given the natural reluctance of the victim to give evidence in a public court, the Crown's decision to let the sentencing decision proceed on the basis that the appellant undoubtedly was carrying a serious weapon, even if less terrifying than the weapons which he was alleged to be carrying, was entirely understandable.

68   Nevertheless, it is surprising that the issue of premeditation, or long term planning, was significantly diminished so that, as Judge Taylor recorded, the prosecution concluded that it did not "materially" matter. And, more important, that the prosecution could not "gainsay" the appellant's contention about premeditation, supported as it was by the co-accused.

69   The obvious inference to be drawn from the evidence, as we have narrated it, was that the prostitute took her customer back to the appellant's home so that he would be robbed; a plan which was then carried out. Such offences are commonplace. There is a significant difference in the sentencing decision between what we may describe as a standard prostitute/customer robbery and an incident which occurred because the assailant was driven wild with fury at the presence of a customer with his girlfriend.

70   Either Judge Faber or Judge Taylor, the sentencing judge, would have been entitled to decline to accept this part of the basis of plea, even if apparently agreed but not fully supported by the Crown. The Crown would not have had to call the complainant to give evidence in relation to that issue. The appellant and his co-accused could have given evidence before the judge which he could have accepted or rejected. Equally, this was a case in which the judge would, in our view, have been entitled to start from the proposition that this basis of plea was obviously untenable. If so inclined, of course, he would no doubt have told counsel for the appellant and the co-accused of the preliminary view he had formed and invited them to address him.

71   Unfortunately we do not know how Judge Taylor approached the problem. His sentencing remarks did not address the basis of plea at all, so we do not know whether he accepted the basis of plea in relation to premeditation, or rejected it. He said, rightly, that this was a particularly nasty offence involving injury and humiliation to someone who was expecting to have consensual sex, adding:

> "This matter was very serious indeed and there is no need for me to say any more about it, other than to make you realise how appalling the courts regard this kind of behaviour."

72   We agree with all those observations. This was a particularly nasty offence. However, as we have noted, there is a significant difference between the nature of the offence as derived from the papers and the offence limited in the way that it was by the basis of plea. We think it probable that Judge Taylor passed sentence on the basis that the written basis of plea in relation to premeditation was nonsense. Unfortunately, he did not say so. There is, therefore, a distinct possibility that the appellant was sentenced on the basis that this was indeed a pre-

meditated offence without the judge either giving appellant the opportunity to give evidence in support of his basis of plea, or, through his counsel, the chance to persuade the judge that it represented a tenable view of the facts.

73   We decided in these circumstances that the appellant should be sentenced on the basis of his plea. We think he is fortunate, but our reluctant conclusion is unavoidable. To reflect what for the victim, on any view, was a dreadful experience a substantial sentence was appropriate. However the sentence should be reduced from six years to four years' imprisonment. The sentence in relation to the licence period is unaffected.

James Connors

74   He was born in February 1984. He had been before the court previously on minor matters. He had never served a custodial sentence and, effectively, he was a young man of good character. On October 7, 2003 in the Crown Court at Leeds before H.H. Judge Benson he pleaded guilty on rearraignment to conspiracy to burgle and rob. The conspiracy alleged that he, together with Alfred Adams, between October and the end of November 2002, conspired to burgle dwelling houses and rob their occupants. A third member of the conspiracy was a man called Hanrahan. Adams failed to answer to his bail and a bench warrant was issued. Adams has not been arrested. Hanrahan was indicted for the same conspiracy, but he was sentenced in relation to substantive counts in separate proceedings a few months after the appellant. Both Hanrahan and Adams were much older than the appellant and, we were told, men with very substantial criminal records.

75   The appellant was sentenced to eight years' detention in a young offender institution. A document described as "basis of plea" was produced to the court and signed by him. This was a helpful document, indicating the very large number of substantive offences in which the appellant was involved in the conspiracy to burgle and rob. Beyond that, the written basis of plea, in our view rightly, made no assertions about matters of personal mitigation. These were reserved for and developed in the course of counsel's plea in mitigation. We commend counsel's approach. There was no dispute about any of the essential facts relating to this crime. Therefore, nothing in the form of a *Newton* hearing was required.

76   When Hanrahan pleaded guilty on the later date, he pleaded to a number of specific offences of robbery and burglary and was sentenced to nine years' imprisonment.

77   This was a very serious conspiracy in which elderly people were targeted by the conspirators, who entered their homes by tricking them, or by forcing their way into them. Having gained access, the main objective was cash savings. The average age of the victims was 80 years old, but one was 96 years old. The method was very simple. The conspirators would steal a car and change the number plate. On every occasion, save one, the role of the appellant was to drive the car. The target would be chosen and one or other of Adams or Hanrahan would pose as an official, for example from the water board, or as some contractor having some coverable excuse for knocking on the door. Whichever of them it

was would seek to enter on the basis that they were working nearby and had some reason to enter the house.

78   The first of these robberies occurred on November 5, 2002. A lady aged 84 years old was alone at home. At lunch time she heard a knock. She opened the door and spoke to a man who posed as an installer of washing machines who was working at a nearby property. This man gained entry by pushing the lady aside. She gradually became aware of the fact that someone else was present in her house. She was asked for her pension book. She said that her son had that. After an untidy search upstairs, the two men left, saying they would be back. During that day seven further burglaries and an attempted burglary took place. All, as we have already narrated, involved elderly victims. The total amount of cash stolen was just under £3,000, but in the case of one victim, an elderly lady, she lost her wedding ring and some jewellery. This pattern of events continued on a number of days in November. Eventually the conspirators were arrested after a police chase on November 25.

79   We must record two specific offences as part of this pattern. In one, on November 16, the victim was a gentleman of 76 years of age who was already suffering from acute angina. While he was being robbed, he tried to stand up at one point and he was threatened with a fist by, as the Crown would say, Adams and forced to sit down again. His life savings of £1,300 were stolen, and when the police eventually arrived he had a severe attack of angina. He died some two months afterwards. On the same day a couple, aged 76 and 75, were threatened with knives which were taken from their kitchen after the conspirators had tricked their way into the home.

80   These were, as the judge said, very serious offences which had, again using the judge's word, "blighted" the lives of the victims. The judge accepted that none of the victims was directly injured during the commission of any of the offences, but recorded that force, trickery and intimidation had been used to gain entry into their homes. The team had deliberately targeted elderly and vulnerable people. The judge rightly recorded that, irrespective of whether the sums of money stolen were substantial, these particular victims would have suffered a serious sense of loss.

81   The position of the appellant needs a little closer analysis. At the time when the offences were committed he was still a very young man, it is to be said, of small build. The judge treated him effectively as a man of good character whose co-conspirators were much older and whose records suggested that they were indeed serious criminals. In mitigation on his behalf it was argued that this much younger man had been subjected to levels of intimidation and pressure by his older and more experienced co-conspirators who had prevailed on him to act as the driver. He himself had caused no injury or fear personally. He had taken no direct share of any of the proceeds. He was offered £50 or so on each of the days when he drove the car.

82   It was suggested that something of the level of intimidation exercised over him was illustrated by an incident which was said to have taken place in prison after he had pleaded guilty. He was coming under some pressure not to assist the police in their investigations and indeed not to attend court. We were told by counsel on his

instructions that the appellant had suffered a fractured wrist when he was attacked, as he believed, by associates of Adams. For completeness, we have to record that this assertion was not supported by any references in the pre-sentence report and the writer did not record that any such complaint had been made to her.

83 It was further pointed out that this appellant was the first of the conspirators to plead guilty and he had done so on the basis that it would save the attendance of elderly complainants for whose distress he had begun to have some appreciation, not least because among his own community he was being ostracised for having committed offences against the elderly.

84 We have already recorded that we entirely agree with the judge's view that these were very serious offences and he was right to be deeply concerned about the level of misery which had been created among the elderly victims of these crimes. The judge concluded that the main mitigation available to the appellant was the fact that he had pleaded guilty and, of course, his age and comparative youth at the time when the offences were committed. The judge, of course, was not then in a position to set the culpability of Adams into context, nor indeed the direct culpability of Hanrahan.

85 We agree, therefore, that substantial sentences were called for. We were persuaded, however, that, given the appellant's youth, his lack of criminal sophistication, the actual role he played in those offences and the involvement of much older, hardened criminals in the conspiracy, as well as taking account of the nine year sentence of imprisonment imposed on Hanrahan, should lead to the conclusion that the eight year sentence should be reduced by two years to one of six years' detention. Accordingly, to that extent, we allowed the appeal.

R. (ON THE APPLICATION OF UTTLEY) v SECRETARY OF STATE FOR THE HOME DEPARTMENT

House of Lords (Lord Steyn, Lord Phillips of Worth Matravers, Lord Rodger of Earlsferry, Baroness Hale of Richmond, Lord Carswell): July 30, 2004

[2004] UKHL 38; [2005] 1 Cr.App.R.(S.) 91

(LT) Date of offence; No punishment without law; Rape; Release on licence; Sentencing powers

H1   *Release on licence—offender sentenced for offence committed before changes in parole scheme resulting in longer period on licence—whether violation of Art.7(1) of European Convention on Human Rights*

H2   The respondent was convicted in 1995 of a number of offences, including rapes, committed before 1983. He was sentenced to a total of 12 years' imprisonment. The practical consequences of that sentence were different from those which would have followed had he been sentenced to 12 years' imprisonment in 1983, as a result of the change in the release regime implemented by the Criminal Justice Act 1991. If the respondent had been sentenced to 12 years' imprisonment under the pre-1991 release regime, he would have been released on remission after serving two-thirds of the sentence. Under the new regime introduced by the 1991 Act, the appellant was released after serving two-thirds of his sentence on a licence which would remain in force until he had served three-quarters of the sentence, that is for one year. While subject to the conditions of the licence, the respondent was at risk of recall to serve the balance of the sentence, and if he committed a further imprisonable offence before the 12-year term of his sentence had expired, the court dealing with the offence would be entitled to order all or part of the outstanding period of the 12-year sentence to be added to any new sentence imposed. The respondent applied for judicial review, seeking a declaration that the provisions of the 1991 Act were incompatible with Art.7(1) of the European Convention on Human Rights. The Court of Appeal (Civil Division) had held that the changes in the release regime made by the 1991 Act meant that the 12-year sentence imposed on the respondent was a "heavier penalty" than a 12-year sentence imposed under the old regime would have been. The Court granted a declaration of incompatibility.

H3   **Held:** (Lord Phillips) Article 7(1) prohibited the imposition of a penalty which was heavier than the one which was "applicable" at the time the offence was committed. No one in the courts below appeared to have focused on the meaning of the word "applicable". There appeared to have been an assumption that this meant "that which would have been applied" and that the sentence "that would have been applied" was one of 12 years' imprisonment. The question had recently been considered by the Privy Council in *Flynn v HM Advocate* [2004] UKPC D1, and by the European Court of Human Rights in *Coeme v Belgium* App.No.32492/96. The European Court of Human Rights said that in relation to Art.7 the court should verify that at the time when an accused person performed the act which led to his being prosecuted and convicted there was in force a legal prohibition which made the act punishable, and that the punishment imposed did not exceed the limits fixed by that provision. Article 7(1) would only be infringed if a sentence was imposed on the defendant which constituted a heavier penalty from that which could have been imposed on the defendant under the law in force at the time his offence was committed. The maximum sentence which could be imposed for rape at the time that the respondent committed the rapes for which he was convicted was life imprisonment. That was the "applicable" penalty for the purposes of Art.7(1). The sentence of 12 years' imprisonment on the respondent was manifestly a less heavy penalty than life imprisonment. It was accepted that a penalty was an autonomous concept and that the addition of a new constituent to a sentence could have the effect of making the sentence a heavier penalty. The decision in *Welch v United Kingdom* did require the House to consider that the conditions of the respondent's licence were a discrete penalty from the sentence of imprisonment. The part of a sentence which would be spent released on licence could not be considered in isolation. The remission regime was an integral feature of a sentence of imprisonment. When considering how heavy a penalty had been imposed by the sentence, it was necessary to consider the overall effect of the sentence. The release of a prisoner on licence, albeit subject to onerous conditions, mitigated rather than augmented the severity of the sentence of imprisonment which would otherwise be served. A sentence of 12 years' imprisonment with release on licence after serving two-thirds was a less heavy penalty than a sentence of 12 years' imprisonment, all of which had to be served. A sentence of 12 years' imprisonment, with release on licence after serving eight years, imposed on the respondent under the new regime, was a less heavy penalty than a sentence of 15 years, with unconditional release after 10 years, which could have been imposed on him under the old regime, and manifestly less severe than a sentence of life imprisonment which could have been imposed under the old regime.

4   **Cases cited:**
Flynn v HM Advocate [2004] UKPC D1, *Coeme v Belgium* App.No.32492/96, *Welch v United Kingdom* (1995) 20 E.H.R.R. 247

5   **Commentary:** [2004] Crim. L.R. 1056
6
D. Pannick Q.C. for the appellant.
A. Scrivener Q.C. for the respondent.

7   Lord Rodger, Baroness Hale and Lord Carswell gave opinions to similar effect; Lord Steyn agreed with Lord Phillips, Lord Rodger and Lord Carswell.

JUDGMENT

Lord Steyn:
My Lords,

1   I have read the opinions of my noble and learned friends Lord Phillips of Worth Matravers, Lord Rodger of Earlsferry and Lord Carswell. I agree with those opinions. I would also allow the appeal.

Lord Phillips of Worth Matravers:
My Lords,

2   Over a period prior to 1983 the respondent Mr Uttley committed a number of sexual offences, including three rapes. My noble and learned friend Lord Rodger of Earlsferry has described these in detail, together with the maximum sentence which, in 1983 could have been imposed for each offence. It suffices to note that rape carried a maximum sentence of life imprisonment.

3   The respondent was not prosecuted for these offences until 1995. He pleaded guilty to some of the offences, was convicted of the others and was sentenced to a total of 12 years' imprisonment. The practical consequences of that sentence differed significantly from those that would have followed had the respondent been sentenced to 12 years' imprisonment in 1983, which has been treated for the purposes of this case as the date upon which he committed the offences in question. This was because the release regime applicable to prisoners had been changed by the Criminal Justice Act 1991 ("the 1991 Act") which had come into effect on October 1, 1992. I shall describe the post-October 1992 regime as "the new regime" and the regime that applied in 1983 as "the old regime".

4   Had the respondent been sentenced to 12 years' imprisonment under the old regime he would, subject to good behaviour, have been released on remission after serving two-thirds of his sentence, which would then have expired. That would have been the effect of s.25(1) of the Prison Act 1952 and r.5 of the Prison Rules 1964 (SI 1964/388), which remained applicable up to the introduction of the 1991 Act. In accordance with the provisions of the 1991 Act the respondent was released on October 24, 2003 after serving two-thirds of his sentence, but he was released on licence, the terms of which will remain in force until he has served three-quarters of his sentence, that is for a year. Those terms place the respondent under supervision and impose certain restrictions on his freedom.

5   While subject to the conditions of the licence the respondent is at risk of recall to serve the balance of his sentence, should he fail to comply with those conditions. Furthermore, should he commit a further imprisonable offence before the 12-year term of his sentence has expired, the court dealing with that offence will be entitled to add all or part of the outstanding period of his 12-year sentence to any new sentence imposed.

6   In December 2002 the respondent made an application for judicial review. The remedy that he sought was a declaration that the provisions of the 1991 Act which would make his release subject to licence were incompatible with Art.7 (1) of the European Convention on Human Rights.

7   Article 7 (1) provides:

"No punishment without law

1. No one shall be held guilty of any criminal offence on account of any act or omission which did not constitute a criminal offence under national or international law at the time when it was committed. Nor shall a heavier penalty be imposed than the one that was applicable at the time the criminal offence was committed."

8   The respondent's case has never, so far as I can see, been fully formulated. On analysis it necessarily involves the following propositions:

    i) The 1991 Act had the effect that the 12-year sentence imposed on the respondent under the new regime was a heavier penalty than a 12-year sentence would have been had it been imposed under the old regime;

    ii) From this, it follows that Art.7 (1) was infringed;

    iii) From this, it follows that the 1991 Act is incompatible with Art.7 (1).

9   It appears to have been accepted by all before this case reached Your Lordships' House that, if proposition i) was established, propositions ii) and iii) followed as a matter of course. Thus the sole issue canvassed in the courts below was whether a 12-year sentence imposed under the new regime constituted a heavier penalty than a 12-year sentence imposed under the old regime.

0   As to this issue, the argument before Moses J., who on April 8, 2003 gave judgment on the application for judicial review, appears to have concentrated exclusively on the restrictions imposed by the licence: [2003] EWHC 950 (Admin). It was argued that these constituted an additional penalty, imposed during the one year period between release after two-thirds of the sentence had been served and the expiry of the licence after three-quarters of the sentence had been served. Under the old regime the respondent would not have been exposed to these restrictions.

1   Moses J. rejected the application for judicial review on the ground that the imposition of the licence restrictions did not constitute a penalty. He concluded that a sentence of 12 years' imprisonment under the new regime was no heavier a penalty than a sentence of 12 years' imprisonment under the old regime.

2   Before the Court of Appeal the respondent took a further point. Not only did the licence impose restrictions on his freedom, while on licence he was subject to the risk of recall to serve the balance of his sentence. During that period his sentence had not expired but was, in effect, suspended. It followed that the sentence was a heavier penalty than a 12-year sentence under the old regime, which would have expired after service of two-thirds of the term.

3   The Court of Appeal reversed the decision of Moses J: [2004] Cr.App.R.(S.) 61 (p.362). They concluded that the changes to the release regime affected by the 1991 Act had the effect that the 12-year sentence imposed on the respondent was a heavier penalty than a 12-year sentence imposed under the old regime would have been. As Longmore L.J. put it, at 2600:

    "Any prisoner would regard the penalty of 12 years as harsher after 1992 than before. So, in my view, would the ordinary informed observer"

The Court allowed the appeal and granted the respondent the declaration of incompatibility that he sought.

14   Before this House Mr Pannick Q.C. for the Secretary of State argued that the reasoning of the Moses J. was correct and that of the Court of Appeal erroneous. He contended that the imposition of the licence conditions was designed to protect the public and to prevent further offending. It followed that the licence conditions did not constitute a "penalty" within the meaning of Art.7 (1). He went on to advance two novel points, the latter of which was not even presaged in the Secretary of State's written case. I have found these new arguments conclusive. They render it unnecessary to decide whether a sentence of 12 years' imprisonment under the new regime constitutes a heavier penalty than a 12-year sentence under the old regime. I do not propose to attempt to resolve that issue. To do so would be to encroach on issues raised in at least one other appeal that is pending before your Lordship's House.

15   Argument in the lower courts proceeded on the premise that the sentence of 12 years imposed on the respondent was a sentence of the same term of years that would have been imposed on the respondent under the old regime. Before this House Mr Pannick challenged that premise. He drew attention to a *Practice Note (Crime: Sentencing)* [1992] 1 W.L.R. 948, issued by Lord Taylor of Gosforth C.J. on the day that the 1991 Act came into force. This provided as follows:

> "1. Sections 32 to 40 of the Criminal Justice Act 1991 come into force on 1 October 1992. They make radical changes with regard to sentences.
>
> 2. Remission is abolished.
>
> 3. Parole will affect only those sentenced to four years' imprisonment and above.
>
> 4. Where the sentence of the court is less than four years the Secretary of State will be under a duty to release the prisoner after he has served one half of his sentence. Thus, where the sentence is three years, 18 months will be served. This is significantly longer than would normally have been served before the new provisions came into force. Furthermore, on release the prisoner will in effect be subject to a continuing suspended sentence. If between his release and the end of the period covered by the original sentence, he commits any offence punishable by imprisonment, he will be liable to serve the balance of the original sentence outstanding at the date of the fresh offence.
>
> 5. For determinate sentences of four years or longer the Secretary of State will have a continuing but reduced element of discretion on release. Prisoners will be released on licence after serving two thirds of the sentence. Whereas hitherto they became eligible for parole after serving one third of the sentence, they will not now become eligible until they have served half. The 'at risk' provisions following release will be the same for long term as for short term prisoners.
>
> 6. It is therefore vital for all sentencers in the Crown Court to realise that sentences on the 'old' scale would under the 'new' Act result in many prisoners actually serving longer in custody than hitherto.

7. It has been an axiomatic principle of sentencing policy until now that the court should decide the appropriate sentence in each case without reference to questions of remission or parole.

8. I have consulted the Lords Justices presiding in the Court of Appeal (Criminal Division) and we have decided that a new approach is essential.

9. Accordingly, from 1 October 1992, it will be necessary, when passing a custodial sentence in the Crown Court, to have regard to the actually period likely to be served, and as far as practicable to the risk of offenders serving substantially longer under the new regime than would have been normal under the old.

10. Existing guideline judgments should be applied with these considerations in mind.

11. I stress however that, having taken the above considerations into account, sentencers must, of course, exercise their individual judgment as to the appropriate sentence to be passed and nothing in this statement is intended to restrict that independence."

6   Mr Pannick submitted that, in accordance with this direction, the respondent's sentence must have been appropriately reduced from the term of years that would have been imposed under the old regime in order to reflect the fact that the conditions of release under the new regime were more onerous. Mr Scrivener Q.C., for the respondent, challenged this contention. He submitted that the thrust of the Practice Direction was directed at short-term sentences where, under the new regime, defendants would serve "significantly longer" than under the old regime. It was certainly not aimed at the punitive effect of the licence conditions themselves. In any event it was not possible to adjust the sentence so as precisely to compensate for the new release regime. In support of this last contention Mr Scrivener drew attention to the following passage from the judgment of Lord Taylor of Gosforth C.J. in *Cunningham* [1993] 1 W.L.R. 183 at 186:

"The Practice Statement does not require an arithmetically precise calculation to be made. Its object was to give general guidance by alerting sentencers to the changed regime of early release and requiring them to have regard to the possible effects of passing sentences after October 1992 of the same length as those they would have passed before. Precise and calculated comparisons are not possible."

I am persuaded that it is at least possible that the sentence imposed on the respondent was shorter, in terms of years, than the sentence that would have been imposed on him in 1983. It does not, however, seem to me that it is material to the issue before your Lordships, namely the compatibility of the 1991 Act with Art.7 (1), whether or not the trial judge in fact reduced the sentence that he imposed on the respondent in order to reflect the extent to which the release conditions were more onerous under the new regime. The important question is whether it was open to him to do so. If it was necessary for him to do so in order to avoid infringing Art.7 (1) and the 1991 Act left him free to do so, it cannot be said that the 1991 Act is incompatible with Art.7(1). At first blush it would seem evident that, by reducing the term of years imposed, it was possible for the trial judge to compensate, or certainly to over compensate, for the more onerous release conditions under the new regime. If so, then that in itself is reason to allow this appeal. Mr Scrivener argued, however, that because release under licence, introduced by the 1991 Act, was a novel constituent of any sentence of imprisonment imposed under the new regime, Art.7(1) was necessarily infringed where such a sentence was imposed in respect of offences committed before October 1992. This brings me to the point that in my opinion is determinative of this appeal.

18   Article 7 (1) prohibits the imposition of a penalty which is heavier than the one that was "applicable" at the time that the offence was committed. No one in the hearings below appears to have focussed on the meaning of the word "applicable". There appears to have been an assumption that this meant "that which would have been applied" and that the sentence that "would have been applied" was one of 12 years' imprisonment. I have already stated my conclusion that the latter assumption may have been unfounded. I now turn to consider the meaning of "applicable" in Art.7 (1).

19   This question was recently considered by the Judicial Committee of the Privy Council in *Flynn v Her Majesty's Advocate* [2004] UKPC D1. The issue in that case was whether changes made by Scottish legislation to the release regime applicable in the case of mandatory life sentences infringed Art.7(1). My noble and learned friend Lord Carswell, who was a member of the Committee, will in his speech, which I have had the privilege of reading in draft, describe the difference of opinion as to the meaning of "applicable" expressed by members of the Committee.

20   Had the Committee had cited to them, as we have had cited to us, the decision of the European Court of Human Rights in *Coeme v Belgium*, June 22, 2000 their task might have been made the easier. Ours certainly is, for at para.145 the court said this in relation to Art.7:

> "The Court must therefore verify that at the time when an accused person performed the act which led to his being prosecuted and convicted there was in force a legal provision which made that punishable, and that the punishment imposed did not exceed the limits fixed by that provision."

21   This passage lends strong support to the opinions as to the meaning of "applicable" expressed by my noble and learned friends Lord Rodger of Earlsferry and Lord Carswell in *Flynn*. I am persuaded that those opinions correctly state the law. It follows that Art.7(1) will only be infringed if a sentence is imposed on a defendant which constitutes a heavier penalty than that which could have been imposed on the defendant under the law in force at the time that his offence was committed. I observe, in passing, that if statutory changes are made to the release regime of those serving mandatory life sentences those changes may affect the severity of the sentence that the law requires. That is not this case.

22   The maximum sentence which could be imposed for rape at the time that the respondent committed the rapes for which he was convicted was life imprisonment. That was the "applicable" penalty for the purposes of Art.7(1). The

sentence of 12 years' imprisonment imposed on the respondent would seem, manifestly, a less heavy penalty than life imprisonment. Mr Scrivener sought to challenge this conclusion. He submitted that, for the purposes of Art.7(1) a "penalty" was an autonomous concept. He further submitted that the fact that a sentence of imprisonment under the new regime included a new constituent, namely release on licence, it was a heavier penalty than one which could be imposed under the old regime.

23   I accept that, for the purposes of Art.7(1), a penalty is an autonomous concept. I also accept that the addition of a new constituent to a sentence can have the effect of making the sentence a heavier penalty. It may be that had the trial judge imposed on the respondent a sentence of life imprisonment, this would have constituted a heavier penalty than life imprisonment under the old regime. This was not a matter that was explored before your Lordships. The suggestion, however, that a sentence of 12 years' imprisonment under the new regime was a heavier penalty than life imprisonment under the old regime would seem manifestly unsound. Before dismissing it, however, it is necessary to consider the effect of the decision of the European Court of Human Rights in *Welch v United Kingdom* (1995) 20 E.H.R.R. 247.

24   On January 12, 1987 the Drug Trafficking Offences Act 1986 came into force in the United Kingdom. This Act, for the first time, gave the court power, when a defendant was convicted of drug trafficking offences, to make, when sentencing him, a confiscation order. A confiscation order required the defendant to pay such sum as the court determined constituted the proceeds of drug trafficking received by the defendant, whether received before or after the 1986 Act came into force. The applicant Welch was convicted in August 1988 of drug trafficking offences committed in 1986. He was given an overall sentence of 22 years' imprisonment. In addition the judge imposed a confiscation order pursuant to the 1986 Act in the sum of £66,914 in respect of the proceeds of drug trafficking received before the 1986 Act came into force. In default of payment of this sum he would be liable to serve a further two years' imprisonment.

25   The applicant claimed that the imposition of the confiscation order violated Art.7(1) as it could not have been imposed at the time that he committed the offences for which he was convicted. The Court agreed. The Court observed at para.26 that:

> ". . . the retrospective imposition of the confiscation order is not in dispute in the present case. The order was made following a conviction in respect of drugs offences which had been committed before the 1986 Act came into force. The only question to be determined therefore is whether the order constitutes a penalty within the meaning of Article 7(1), second sentence."

The Court went on to conclude that the confiscation order did constitute a penalty and that, in consequence, Art.7(1) had been infringed.

26   In *Welch* the United Kingdom did not argue that the sentence of 22 years' imprisonment, coupled with the confiscation order, was a less heavy penalty than that which could have been imposed for the offences for which Welch was convicted, namely life imprisonment. Nor does this point appear to have

been considered by the Commission or by the Court. The confiscation order was considered in isolation as a discrete penalty.

27   I do not believe that the decision in *Welch* requires your Lordships' House to consider the conditions of the respondent's licence as a discrete penalty, divorced from his sentence of imprisonment. One cannot properly consider in isolation that part of a sentence of imprisonment which will be spent released on licence. The remission regime is an integral feature of the sentence of imprisonment. When considering how heavy a penalty has been imposed by the sentence it is necessary to consider the overall effect of the sentence. That, indeed, has been the respondent's case throughout.

28   The release of a prisoner on licence, albeit subject to onerous conditions, mitigates rather than augments the severity of the sentence of imprisonment which would otherwise be served. A sentence of 12 years' imprisonment, with release on licence after serving two thirds, is a less heavy penalty than a sentence of 12 years' imprisonment, all of which has to be served. The sentence of 12 years' imprisonment, with release on licence after serving eight years, imposed on the respondent under the new regime, was a less heavy penalty than a sentence of 15 years, with unconditional release after 10 years, which could have been imposed on him under the old regime, and manifestly less severe than the sentence of life imprisonment which could have been imposed on him under that regime.

29   For these reasons I conclude that there has been no infringement of Art.7(1) and I would allow the appeal.

Lord Rodger of Earlsferry
My Lords,

30   I have had the privilege of reading in draft the speeches of my noble and learned friends, Lord Phillips of Worth Matravers and Lord Carswell. I agree with them and for the reasons they give I too would allow the appeal. Since your Lordships are differing from the Court of Appeal, however, I add some observations of my own on the first argument presented by Mr Pannick Q.C., which is dispositive of the appeal.

31   Before 1983 the respondent, Mr Uttley, committed a large number of sexual offences: three rapes; six indecent assaults on a woman, contrary to s.14(1) of the Sexual Offences Act 1956; one act of sexual intercourse with a girl under 16, contrary to s.6(1) of the same Act; and four acts of gross indecency with a child, contrary to s.1(1) of the Indecency with Children Act 1960. On one occasion he took an indecent photograph or pseudo-photograph of a child, contrary to s.1(1)(a) of the Protection of Children Act 1978 ("the 1978 Act") and on two occasions he distributed a photograph or pseudo-photograph of a child, contrary to s.1(1)(b) of the same Act. Although all the offences are said to have been committed before 1983, both counsel argued the appeal on the basis of the penalties that applied in 1983.

32   The respondent was not caught and tried for the offences until 1995. In October of that year, at the Crown Court at Leeds, the respondent either pleaded guilty to, or was convicted of, counts relating to all of these acts. On October 24, 1995 he

was sentenced for the offences. In respect of the three rapes, he was sentenced to 11 years' imprisonment on one count and to two periods of nine years, concurrently, on the two other counts. On each of the six counts of indecent assault on a woman, he was sentenced to two years' imprisonment, to run concurrently with one another and with the other sentences. On the count of sexual intercourse with a girl under 16, he was sentenced to one year's imprisonment, again concurrently with the other sentences. On three of the counts of committing gross indecency with a child, the respondent was sentenced to 18 months' imprisonment, and on the other to 12 months' imprisonment, all to run concurrently with the other sentences. On the count relating to the taking of the indecent photograph or pseudo-photograph of the child, he was sentenced to one year's imprisonment to run concurrently. On one of the two counts relating to distributing such a photograph or pseudo-photograph, he was sentenced to one year's imprisonment to run consecutively, on the other to one year's imprisonment to run concurrently. The overall practical effect was, accordingly, that the respondent was sentenced to a period of 11 years' imprisonment on one of the rapes plus a further one year's imprisonment consecutively in respect of one of the counts of distributing an indecent photograph. This made a total of 12 years' imprisonment. The respondent did not appeal against the sentences.

33   At the time when he committed the acts, they all constituted offences under the various statutory provisions to which I have referred. Similarly, at that time, in terms of the relevant legislation, a court was entitled to impose periods of imprisonment for the offences which exceeded the periods actually imposed by the court for them in 1995. In particular, by reason of s.34(3) of, and para 1(a) of Schedule 2 to, the 1956 Act, the maximum sentence for rape was life imprisonment at the time of the offences. In 1995 rape remained punishable with life imprisonment under the same provisions of the 1956 Act. When the respondent distributed the indecent photograph or pseudo-photograph of the child, under s.6(2) of the 1978 Act the maximum penalty for that offence was a sentence of three years' imprisonment. That remained the position in October 1995.

4   The respondent complains that his rights under Art.7(1) of the European Convention on Human Rights have been violated. Article 7 is headed "No punishment without law" and Art.7(1) provides:

> "No one shall be held guilty of any criminal offence on account of any act or omission which did not constitute a criminal offence under national or international law at the time when it was committed. Nor shall a heavier penalty be imposed than the one that was applicable at the time the criminal offence was committed."

As I have just explained, the provisions criminalising the offences in question and prescribing the punishments that could be imposed for them did not change in any relevant respect between 1983 and 1995. The only authority for the court's sentence of 11 years' imprisonment for rape was to be found in s.34(3) of, and para.1(a) of Sch.2 to, the 1956 Act, while the court's only authority for imprisoning him for the offence of taking an indecent photograph or pseudo-photograph was to be found in s.6 of the 1978 Act. The provisions of these two Acts were not only the basis in law for the court imposing the total sentence which it did: they would have allowed the court to impose a heavier sentence. The provisions of the 1956 Act alone would have given the court power, in 1983 as in 1995, to impose any sentence of imprisonment for the rapes up to, and including, life imprisonment. Similarly, s.6(2) of the 1978 Act would have authorised the court to impose a consecutive sentence of up to three years' imprisonment for taking the indecent photograph or pseudo-photograph. None of these provisions prescribes a minimum sentence and the case therefore raises no issue of the kind considered by the Court of Appeal in *Sullivan* [2004] EWCA Crim 1762.

35   The respondent does not base his complaint on the provisions that I have just narrated, however. Which is presumably why the courts below make no mention of them. He says, rather, that there has been a violation of Art.7(1) because, by virtue of the relevant provisions of the Criminal Justice Act 1991 ("the 1991 Act") which came into force in 1992, a heavier penalty was imposed on him than the one that was applicable at the time when the criminal offences in question were committed. The argument is based on a comparison of the effect of these provisions on the 12-year sentence imposed by the court in 1995 and the effect which s.25(1) of the Prison Act 1952, r.5 of the Prison Rules 1964 and s.60 of the Criminal Justice Act 1967 would have had on any equivalent sentence imposed by a court in 1983.

36   It is agreed that, if the pre-1991 Act provisions had remained in force, then, provided he had been of good behaviour, the respondent would have been entitled to be released when he had completed two thirds of his sentence, on October 24, 2003. Thereupon his sentence would have expired under s.25(1) of the Prison Act 1952. Instead, by virtue of s.33 of the 1991 Act the respondent was released on the same day, October 24, 2003, when he had completed two thirds of his 12-year sentence—but his release was on licence. The licence contains a number of conditions and remains in force until October 24, 2004. During that period, under s.39 of the 1991 Act, the respondent is liable to be recalled to prison if he fails to comply with the conditions. Even after the end of the licence period, if the respondent is convicted of an imprisonable offence, under s.40 the court dealing with the new offence has the power to require him to serve the whole, or part, of the remainder of his 12 year sentence. The argument for the respondent, which the Court of Appeal accepted, is that, because he remains subject to the licence period and liable to be required to serve the remainder of his 12-year sentence, in terms of Art.7(1) the sentence of 12 years imposed on him in 1995 is "heavier" than a sentence of 12 years would have been if it had been imposed on him in 1983, before the 1991 Act came into force.

37   Since the alleged violation of the respondent's rights under Art.7(1) would not have materialised until he was released in October 2003, Mr Pannick accepted that, if there was a violation, the Human Rights Act 1998 would apply even though the sentence had been imposed before October 2, 2000.

38   The respondent's argument is misconceived. For the purposes of Art.7(1) the proper comparison is between the penalties which the court imposed for the offences in 1995 and the penalties which the legislature prescribed for those offences when they were committed around 1983. As I have explained, the cumu-

lative penalty of 12 years' imprisonment that the court imposed for all the offences in 1995 was not heavier than the maximum sentence which the law would have permitted it to pass for the same offences at the time they were committed in 1983. There is accordingly no breach of Art.7(1).

In applying Art.7(1) in this way, I interpret the word "applicable" as referring to the penalties which the law authorised a court to impose at the time of the offences. Section 20(1) of the Constitution of India expresses the same idea when it says that no person is to be subjected to a penalty "greater than that which might have been inflicted under the law in force" at the time of the commission of the offence. These and similar provisions embody a principle of comparatively modern origin: there can be no room for it in legal systems which do not use statutes to prescribe a particular punishment or range of punishments for individual offences, but rely instead on the court to choose the appropriate punishment for any given offender. That was once the case with most legal systems. Therefore, although traces of the doctrine can be found in the writings of Bartolus de Saxoferrato in the 14th century (*Commentaria ad digestum vetus, de iustitia et iure*, 1.9.49–51), it really came to prominence only towards the end of the 18th century when developments in constitutional thinking led to the idea that crimes and their punishments should be regulated by statutes passed by the legislature. Article 8 of the French Declaration of the Rights of Man 1791 famously proclaimed that "nul ne peut être puni qu'en vertu d'une loi établie et promulguée antérieurement au délit et légalement appliquée." Ten years later, in his *Lehrbuch des gemeinen in Deutschland geltenden peinlichen Rechts*, p.20, para.24, von Feuerbach gave the principle its familiar and enduring Latin form, *nulla poena sine lege*. From these beginnings the principle came to be generally recognised and eventually to take its place in many constitutions, as well as, for example, in Art.7(1) of the European Convention on Human Rights and Art.15 of the International Covenant on Civil and Political Rights. There is some discussion of the limits to the principle in English law in Glanville Williams, *Criminal Law: The General Part* (2nd ed., 1961), pp.606–608.

The idea that one should not be punished for doing an act that was lawful at the time meets with ready acceptance. Leaving aside the general argument against retroactive legislation, it is perhaps less obvious why, if his conduct was criminal, a court should not be able to impose on the offender a sentence that is authorised by law and otherwise appropriate, simply because it is heavier than the sentence which the law authorised for that offence at the time when it was committed. Even if the perpetrator was aware of the penalty that the law prescribed for the offence at the time he committed it, in the case of a crime such as rape, at least, it will scarcely lie in his mouth to claim that he would not have carried out the rape if he had known that the new heavier penalty would be applied to him and that it is, accordingly, unfair to impose it. In practice, however, changes in the law which are designed to allow a heavier punishment for an offence that has already been committed may tend to be made for the purpose of unfairly penalising the past acts of particular individuals, for political or other reasons. Art.7(1) eliminates that risk.

41   The wording of Art.7(1) is indeed well adapted to counteract such dangers. The European Court of Human Rights has therefore been able to give proper effect to the article while interpreting its wording in a straightforward fashion. In *Coëme v Belgium* ECtHR 2000-VII 75 the Court held, at para.145:

> "The Court must therefore verify that at the time when an accused person performed the act which led to his being prosecuted and convicted there was in force a legal provision which made that act punishable, and that the punishment imposed did not exceed the limits fixed by that provision . . .."

One has to identify the legal provision which made the act punishable at the time it was committed and make sure that the punishment which the court imposes does not exceed the limits fixed by that provision. Although the decision of the European Court was not cited to the Privy Council in *Flynn v HM Advocate* [2004] UKPC D1; 2004 S.C.C.R. 281, Lord Carswell encapsulated the same interpretation when he said, at 314G–315A, [109]:

> "It seems to me difficult to escape the conclusion that the meaning of the provision is that the penalty which was 'applicable' at the time the criminal offence was committed is that which a sentencer could have imposed at that time, ie the maximum sentence then prescribed by law for the particular offence . . .. The object of the provision appears to have been to prevent a sentence being imposed which could not have been imposed at the time of the offence, because the maximum was then lower."

Putting the matter within the specific context of the Scottish system for mandatory life sentence prisoners, I adopted the same construction, at 310D–F, [85].

42   Mr Scrivener Q.C. reminded your Lordships that under s.2 of the Human Rights Act decisions of the European Court of Human Rights are not binding. It respectfully appears to me, however, that not only is no other interpretation required in order to give effect to Art.7(1), but indeed no other interpretation is feasible in the present case. Mr Scrivener could not begin to paraphrase Art.7(1) so as to specify which penalties were "applicable" at the time of the offences if they were not the penalties or range of penalties that the law permitted a court to impose at that time. As Lord Carswell shows, there are obvious difficulties in any attempt to interpret "applicable" as referring to the penalty that the court could in practice have been expected to impose for an offence at the time it was committed. The decision of the European Court demonstrates, however, that Art.7(1) does not envisage such speculative excursions into the realm of the counter-factual. Its purpose is not to ensure that the offender is punished in exactly the same way as he would have been punished at the time of the offence, but to ensure that he is not punished more heavily than the relevant law passed by the legislature would have permitted at that time. So long as the court keeps within the range laid down by the legislature at the time of the offence, it can choose the sentence which it considers most appropriate. The principle of legality is respected.

43 Here there was no change in the relevant penalties which the law permitted a court to impose. What changed between 1983 and 1995 were the arrangements that were to apply on the prisoner's early release from any sentence of imprisonment imposed by the court. In particular, since 1992 a prisoner such as the respondent has remained subject to his sentence for its entire duration of 12 years, whereas before 1992 an equivalent sentence would have expired when he was released after serving eight years. The respondent says that, for this reason, the sentence of 12 years imposed on him in 1995 was "heavier" than a sentence of 12 years imposed at the time of the offences in 1983. Leaving aside all the other possible objections, this argument simply involves a misinterpretation of Art.7(1). Of course, if legislation passed after the offences were to say, for instance, that a sentence of imprisonment was to become a sentence of imprisonment with hard labour, then issues would arise as to whether the article was engaged, even where the maximum sentence had been life imprisonment at the time of the offences. But in this case there is no suggestion that the actual conditions of the respondent's imprisonment changed. The very worst that could have happened to him under the 1991 Act was that he would have required to serve the whole of his 12-year sentence in gaol. Happily for him, that has not in fact happened. But, even if it had, he would still have spent only 12 years in prison—which is well within the limits of the penalty that was allowed by law for the three rapes and many other offences at the time when he committed them. There is no violation of Art.7(1).

Baroness Hale of Richmond

My Lords,

 I too have reached the conclusion that the change from the remission and parole system to the licence system for early release of prisoners was not a "heavier penalty . . . than the one that was applicable at the time" when these offences were committed. I believe that this conclusion is not incompatible with the views I expressed in *Flynn v Her Majesty's Advocate* [2004] UKPC D1 at [99] to [100], but I certainly owe the respondent an explanation.

 It is quite clear that the words "penalty . . . applicable" in Art.7(1) refer to the penalty or penalties prescribed by law for the offence in question at the time when it was committed. It does not refer to the actual penalty which would probably have been imposed upon the individual offender had he been caught and convicted shortly after he had committed the offence. The court does not have to make a comparison between the sentence he would have received then and the sentence which the court is minded to impose now. In *Flynn*, I did not accept the argument that it did. As I said at [100], "[My] conclusion does not cast doubt upon the validity of sentencing guidelines which may indicate that the existing applicable sentence is to be applied in a more severe way than had been the previous practice". As the European Court of Human Rights said in *Coeme v Belgium*, App.nos 32492/96, 32547/96, 32548/96, 33209/96 and 33210/96, at para.145,

"The court must therefore verify that at the time when an accused person performed the act which led to his being prosecuted and convicted there was in force a legal provision which made that act punishable, and that the punishment imposed *did not exceed the limits fixed* by that provision." (emphasis added)

46   However, it is clear from the Court's decision in *Welch v United Kingdom* (1995) 20 E.H.R.R. 247 that Art.7 is not limited to the sentences prescribed by the law which creates the offence. It can also apply to additional penalties applied to that offence by other legislation. The concept of a penalty is an autonomous Convention concept. When considering what are the "limits fixed" by the law, the maximum duration of any permitted sentence of imprisonment (or the maximum fine which may be payable) may not be the only relevant factor. There may be changes in the essential quality or character of such a sentence which make it unquestionably more severe than any sentence which might have been imposed at the time of the offence. Examples might be the reintroduction of hard labour with every sentence of imprisonment or the automatic conversion of a sentence of imprisonment into a sentence of transportation. These may seem fanciful today. Less fanciful might be the replacement, for certain juvenile offenders, of committal to the care of a local authority with determinate sentences of detention in prison department establishments. The care order was ostensibly a welfare disposal, rather than a penalty, although of indefinite duration up to the age of 18. The detention order was unquestionably punitive in intent and effect, although of definite duration. There must, at the very least, be an argument that Art.7 is engaged by such a change.

47   *Flynn* concerned a radical change in the legal effect of a mandatory life sentence, through the introduction of a fixed "punishment part" into what had previously been in reality an indeterminate sentence. The nature of the sentence begged the question of what it was that the law prescribed, notional imprisonment for life or imprisonment for a term to be fixed. As there was only one penalty for murderers, it mattered what it meant. I readily acknowledge that, as with the care order example, there is room for argument about whether this change made that penalty in itself more severe than it had previously been. Some might think that it did and some might think that it did not. It was, after all, introduced to protect the human rights of offenders. Nevertheless, the equivalent legislation for England and Wales took the precaution of protecting those sentenced to life imprisonment for offences committed before the change from a longer tariff than that already fixed or likely to have been fixed under the previous regime: see Criminal Justice Act 2003, Sch.22. Without that protection, some offenders might do better than they might previously have done whereas others might do worse. But for the reasons given earlier, that is not the question. The question, as I believe all your Lordships agree, is whether the penalty now legally applicable (and applied) to the offence is heavier than (or exceeds the limits of) the penalty which was legally applicable at the time it was committed.

48   In this case we are concerned with a sentence of imprisonment which could have been of any duration up to life imprisonment. I am persuaded that a change

in the arrangements for determining how much of that time is actually spent in prison and how much in the community does not make the penalty heavier than it previously was. A longer term of imprisonment was always available. It can be distinguished from a mandatory life sentence, which is the only penalty available, where the consequences prescribed by law might become heavier than those which previously obtained. (Whether I was right to consider that they had done is another matter.) Just as there might once have been some forms of death penalty which were heavier than others, there may be forms of incarceration which are heavier than others. But in this case the complaint is essentially about duration and a longer duration has always been available. I therefore agree Art.7(1) is not breached.

49   It follows that I too would allow this appeal.

Lord Carswell

My Lords,

50   The respondent Brian Uttley was on October 24, 1995 sentenced to an effective total of 12 years' imprisonment for a series of sexual offences committed over a period prior to 1983. He had pleaded guilty to several counts of sexual assault and was convicted on three counts of rape and also on charges of taking indecent photographs.

51   Upon sentence the respondent became subject to the provisions of the Criminal Justice Act 1991 (the 1991 Act), whereby he was entitled to release on licence after serving two thirds of his term of imprisonment (having been eligible for consideration for parole after serving half of the term) and was then subject to a number of restrictions under the licence until the expiry of three quarters of the term.

2   In accordance with these statutory provisions he was released on licence on October 24, 2003, the date of expiry of two thirds of his term of imprisonment, and will remain on licence until October 24, 2004, when three quarters of the term will have expired. The conditions of the licence (with which he must comply, as provided by s.37(4) of the 1991 Act) impose a number of significant restrictions on his freedom and require him to place himself under the supervision of a probation officer, keep in touch with him and receive visits from him. Under s.39 of the 1991 Act where a prisoner is released on licence the Secretary of State may revoke his licence and recall him to prison, if so recommended by the Parole Board. By virtue of s.40 of the 1991 Act (now replaced by s.116 of the Powers of Criminal Courts (Sentencing) Act 2000), if he is convicted of a new offence during the currency of the licence the sentencing court may, in addition to passing any other sentence, order him to be returned to prison to serve out the whole or any part of the original sentence unexpired at the date of commission of that offence.

The respondent points to the fact that if he had been convicted and sentenced before the 1991 Act came into operation on October 1, 1992 he would, subject to good behaviour, have been unconditionally discharged after serving two thirds of his sentence, which would then have expired by virtue of s.25(1) of the Prison Act 1952. He would have been eligible for parole after serving one third of his sentence. It is not necessary for present purposes to delve into the refinements of remission and prisoners' legitimate expectations, for it was not in dispute that the release provisions would have operated as I have outlined.

54   The respondent maintains that the effect of subjecting him to the regime of the 1991 Act was to violate the provisions of Art.7(1) of the Convention for the Protection of Human Rights and Fundamental Freedoms (the Convention), the material part of which reads:

"Nor shall a heavier penalty be imposed than the one that was applicable at the time the criminal offence was committed."

He brought an application for judicial review of the decision to release him on licence on October 24, 1993, claiming declarations that Sch.12 to the Criminal Justice Act 1991 is incompatible with Art.7 of the Convention and that the imposition of a period of licence and/or the imposition of conditions of licence under the provisions of the 1991 Act are incompatible with Art.7. Moses J. in the Administrative Court rejected the respondent's arguments and dismissed the application ([2003] EWHC 950 (Admin)) , but the Court of Appeal (Pill and Longmore L.JJ. and Maurice Kay J.) allowed his appeal: [2003] 1 W.L.R. 2590. The Secretary of State has appealed to your Lordships' House against the decision of the Court of Appeal.

55   The decisions of the Administrative Court and the Court of Appeal centred round the issue whether the licence provisions constituted a heavier penalty for the purposes of Art.7(1). Moses J. held that they did not, concluding in para.[15] of his judgment that

"the nature and purpose of the licence are such that they dominate the factors which go to the conclusion as to whether the imposition of the licence is a penalty or not. The imposition of the licence is designed to protect the public once a prisoner is released, and assist in preventing the prisoner from committing further offences."

The Court of Appeal differed from Moses J. in their classification of the licence provisions. They held that, whatever the purpose of those provisions, their effect was onerous as a part of the sentence imposed. Viewing the matter as a matter of substance rather than form, the sentence was thereby increased and the penalty imposed was heavier. The transitional provisions in the 1991 Act for release on licence of prisoners whose offences had been committed at a time before the introduction of such licences were accordingly incompatible with Art.7(1) of the Convention. They made a declaration in the following terms:

"A declaration pursuant to section 4(2) of the Human Rights Act 1998 that section 33(2), section 37(4A) and section 39 of the Criminal Justice Act 1991 are incompatible with the applicant's rights under article 7 of the European Convention for the Protection of Human Rights and Fundamental Freedoms in so far as they provide that he will be released at the two-thirds point of his sentence on licence with conditions and be liable to be recalled to prison (he having committed the index offences before the Criminal Justice Act 1991 came into force), and at a time when he would have expected (subject to good behaviour) to be released at the two-thirds point of any sentence unconditionally, pursuant to the practice that had developed in implementing rule 5 of the Prison Rules 1964)."

56   Mr Pannick Q.C. on behalf of the Secretary of State advanced a new argument before your Lordships' House, based on the construction of the word "applicable" in Art.7(1), in addition to those relied on in the courts below. He marshalled his arguments into four main contentions:

(i) The penalty imposed was well within the maximum allowed by law in 1983 and therefore did not violate the terms of Art.7(1) of the Convention, when properly construed.

(ii) The respondent's complaints are about early release provisions, which concern the administration of sentences and are not covered by Art.7.

(iii) The trial judge was required by the Practice Statement to take the changes in early release provisions into account when sentencing.

(iv) Licensing provisions are not a penalty, but are designed to assist the offender in his rehabilitation and protect the public against the risk of his re-offending.

57   In the course of developing his first contention Mr Pannick argued that the word "applicable" in Art.7(1) means the sentence which could have been imposed on the offender at the time when he committed the offence, ie the maximum sentence then fixed by law for that offence. The object of Art.7(1) was to prevent persons from being subjected to penalties heavier than those which could have been imposed at the time of commission of the crime. An obvious example is the increase in the maximum sentence for indecent assault on a woman from two years to ten years by the Sexual Offences Act 1985: persons convicted after the date on which that Act came into operation of indecent assaults committed before that date could not be sentenced to a term of imprisonment longer than two years.

58   The wording of Art.7(1) of the Convention has its origins in the early constitutional documents of the human rights movement. It was purposely framed so as to follow closely the terms of Art.11(2) of the Universal Declaration of Human Rights, approved by the General Assembly of the United Nations in 1948, save that in the English version of the Convention the phrase "penal offence" became "criminal offence". In the International Covenant on Civil and Political Rights (1966) the first two sentences of Art.15.1 are identical in wording to Art.7(1) of the Convention. A third sentence, however, was added which is of significance for present purposes:

"If, subsequent to the commission of the offence, provision is made by law for the imposition of a lighter penalty, the offender shall benefit thereby."

This sentence gives support to the interpretation propounded on behalf of the appellant, that in the previous sentence in Art.15.1 of the ICCPR, like the second sentence of Art.7(1) of the Convention, the word "applicable" was intended to refer to the maximum sentence which could be imposed by law. That interpretation is also borne out by the references in the travaux préparatoires to a penalty "authorised by the law" and the "maximum penalty under the law in force at the time".

59   Further support for the appellant's proposition may be derived from the decision of the European Court of Human Rights in *Coëme v Belgium* (App. nos 32492/96 *et al.*), which was cited on behalf of the appellant. The major issue with which the case was concerned was whether the defendants could properly have been tried in the Cour de Cassation. Two of the applicants claimed that the extension of the limitation period for trial of criminal offences under Belgian law which was brought in after the commission of the offences with which they were charged was in breach of Art.7(1) of the Convention. In para.145 of its judgment the Court observed that offences and the relevant penalties must be clearly defined by law and went on:

> "The Court must therefore verify that at the time when an accused person performed the act which led to his being prosecuted and convicted there was in force a legal provision which made that act punishable, *and that the punishment imposed did not exceed the limits fixed by that provision* . . ." (my emphasis).

60   This issue was considered by the Judicial Committee of the Privy Council in a devolution appeal from Scotland, *Flynn v Her Majesty's Advocate* [2004] UKPC D1. The appeal concerned complaints from prisoners sentenced to imprisonment for life in Scotland prior to the passing of the Convention Rights (Compliance) (Scotland) Act 2001 that under the regime brought into operation by that Act—their complaint being directed specifically to para.13 of the Schedule to the Act, which dealt with transitional provisions—they would serve a longer period in prison than they would have expected to serve under the arrangements in force at the time when they were originally sentenced. It is not necessary for present purposes to go into details of the issues in the appeal and it is sufficient to say that the Judicial Committee rejected the appellants' claim. They were able to give an interpretation to para.13 whereby the reviewing court would be entitled to avoid the necessity to impose a higher "sentence". It followed that no breach of Art.7(1) could be involved and para.13 was within the competence of the Scottish Parliament. It had been argued on behalf of the appellants that the "applicable" sentence in Art.7(1) of the Convention is that which would have been imposed by a court if it had passed sentence under the law in force at the time of the commission of the offence. It followed from this reasoning that if the length of the punishment part of the life sentence (previously known in common parlance as the "tariff") exceeded that which they could realistically have expected under the previous arrangements for fixing that part, Art.7(1) could be engaged.

61   In the course of reaching our conclusions my noble and learned friend Lord Rodger of Earlsferry and I specifically rejected this construction of Art.7(1). Lord Rodger of Earlsferry stated in his judgment at [85] that he was not persuaded that Art.7(1) was engaged in the circumstances of the appeals. Adopting the con-

struction propounded on behalf of the appellant in the present appeal he said in
that paragraph:

> "Under paragraph 13 the appellants are liable to be required to serve a
> longer period than would have been likely, but not a longer period than
> would have been competent, before the first review under the previous sys-
> tem. That is not incompatible with article 7(1)."

62   I adopted the same construction of Art.7(1) as did Lord Rodger of Earlsferry. I
stated in a passage in para.[109] of my judgment which I venture to repeat:

> "I am unable, however, to accept the construction of article 7(1) propoun-
> ded by the appellants. It seems to me difficult to escape the conclusion that
> the meaning of the provision is that the penalty which was 'applicable' at the
> time the criminal offence was committed is that which a sentencer could
> have imposed at that time, ie the maximum sentence then prescribed by
> law for the particular offence. I may observe in passing that resort to the
> French text of article 7 is of little avail, since the word used is 'applicable',
> which does not throw any further light on the draftsman's intention. The
> object of the provision appears to have been to prevent a sentence being
> imposed which could not have been imposed at the time of the offence,
> because the maximum was then lower."

63   Mr Scrivener Q.C. for the respondent supported the construction of Art.7(1)
which had been advanced on behalf of the appellants in *Flynn v HM Advocate*.
He argued that the licensing provisions introduced a new component into the system, which did not exist at the time when the respondent committed the offences.
This was in reality, as Longmore L.J. indicated at para.[36] of his judgment in the
Court of Appeal, a lengthening of the sentence which would have been imposed
before 1992. It accordingly violated the terms of Art.7(1).

64   Mr Scrivener reminded the House that Art.7, like all provisions of the Convention, must be construed autonomously, purposively and giving primacy to
substance. I have borne this in mind, but I still believe that the construction of
Art.7(1) which Lord Rodger of Earlsferry and I adopted in *Flynn v HM Advocate*
is correct and I adhere to the views which I expressed in that case. As I there
stated, in my opinion other interpretations fail to give due effect to the fact that
Art.7(1) refers to the time when the offence was committed, not the time when
the sentence was passed. If the interpretation propounded on behalf of the respondent were correct, it would frequently be necessary to attempt to divine what
sentence a court would have passed if sentencing at the time of commission of
the offence, a quest fraught with obvious difficulties. For example, the guidelines
for length of sentences appropriate for the offence may have changed and the general level of sentence may have been increased, as may be seen to have occurred
in the case of such offences as dangerous driving causing death.

65   When one applies this conclusion of law to the facts of the present case, the
answer is entirely clear. The maximum sentence for rape, the most serious of
the offences committed by the respondent, was imprisonment for life both before
and after 1983 and so remains. A court sentencing the respondent before 1983

could if it thought fit have imposed imprisonment for life or for a term very much longer than 12 years. It is in my opinion impossible to regard a sentence of 12 years, even with the new element of a licence, as a heavier penalty than that which could have been imposed at the time when the offence was committed. Accordingly on this ground alone I consider that the judge was right to dismiss the application for judicial review.

66   I do not find it necessary to express an opinion on the issue whether the effect of the 1991 Act was to impose a heavier penalty on the respondent, as the Court of Appeal held, and I should prefer not to do so.

67   For the reasons which I have given I would allow the appeal and affirm the judge's dismissal of the respondent's application for judicial review.

R. v MICHAEL GEORGE CAMPBELL

COURT OF APPEAL (Lord Justice Rose (Vice President, Court of Appeal Criminal Division), Mrs Justice Rafferty and Mr Justice Pitchers): August 5, 2004

[2004] EWCA Crim 2333; [2005] 1 Cr.App.R.(S.) 92

(LT Criminal record; Drug trafficking; Risk of reoffending; Sentence length; Travel restriction orders

H1   *Travel restriction order—evasion of the prohibition of importation of cannabis— offender with previous convictions—length of travel restriction order*

H2   A travel restriction order for 10 years made under the Criminal Justice and Police Act 2001 in the case of a man convicted of being knowingly concerned in the fraudulent evasion of the prohibition on the importation of a class B drug, cannabis, reduced to five years.

H3   Theappellant was convicted of being knowingly concerned in the fraudulent evasion of the prohibition on the importation of a class B drug, cannabis. The appellant, who was resident in the United Kingdom, arrived at Gatwick airport. A search of his luggage resulted in the discovery of a total of 17 kilograms of cannabis resin. The appellant had previous convictions for importing controlled drugs. Sentenced to seven years' imprisonment, with a travel restriction order under the Criminal Justice and Police Act 2001 for 10 years.

H4   **Held:** the sentence of seven years' imprisonment would be reduced to six years. The travel restriction order made under the Criminal Justice and Police Act 2001, s.33, would run from the date on which the appellant was released. The Court in *Mee* [2004] 2 Cr.App.R.(S.) 81 (p.434) had considered a similar order. Against that background, the appellant's record showed that he posed a real risk for future importations. An order longer than the minimum was appropriate. However an order of the length of 10 years was not justified. In the Court's judgment, the appropriate length of the order would be five years.

H5   **Cases cited:**
Aramah (1982) 4 Cr.App.R.(S.) 407, *Ronchetti* [1998] 2 Cr.App.R.(S.) 100, *Mee*
[2004] 2 Cr.App.R.(S.) 81 (p.434)

H6   **References:** travel restriction order, *Current Sentencing Practice* H9

H7   *G. Cockings* for the appellant.

JUDGMENT

1   **Pitchers J.:**   On March 23, 2004 at the Crown Court at Croydon in front of
Miss Recorder Wickham, this appellant was convicted of being knowingly concerned in the fraudulent evasion on the prohibition or restriction on importation
of a class B drug, namely cannabis, and sentenced to seven years' imprisonment.
The learned recorder also imposed a travel restriction order under s.33 of the
Criminal Justice and Police Act 2001 for a period of 10 years, expressed by
her to run from the date of sentence.

2   He appeals against sentence with leave of the single judge.

3   On April 26, 2003 the appellant came back to this country from Kingston,
Jamaica, and went through the green channel at Gatwick Airport. He was stopped
and questioned. He told the Customs officer that he had been to Jamaica to attend
an aunt's funeral. He was asked to open his suitcase. As the Customs officer
opened it, the appellant stated that the suitcase was not his. She then took his
shoulder bag, which he confirmed belonged to him. Another of her colleagues
went to the conveyer belt and found an identical suitcase with a luggage label
which had his details on it. The first suitcase was examined and found to contain
13 packages of cannabis resin, weighing in total just under 17 kilogrammes with a
street value of £51,000. They were packed amongst some ladies' clothing. The
luggage label had another person's address on it which was later found to be false.

4   He was arrested. In interview he denied knowledge of the suitcase, insisting he
had only checked in one bag at Kingston Airport. His documents revealed that he
had checked in with two bags. It was the Crown's case that he ripped off the
sticker from one bag on the outward bound journey in order to demonstrate, as
he had hoped, that he had only taken the one bag from Gatwick to Kingston.

5   He is 47 years old. He has the following extremely relevant previous convictions. In the 1980s he had two convictions for drug offences in Jamaica, the exact
nature of which is not clear from the record. He was also imprisoned for 20 weeks
in 1984 for fraudulent evasion of chargeable duty or prohibition under the Customs and Excise Management Act. More recently, on December 15, 1993, for
importing a controlled drug he was fined £120. On February 22, 1995, for importing a controlled drug, he was made subject to a community service order. Then on
January 11, 2001 for being knowingly concerned in fraudulently evading duty
chargeable on goods, again class B drugs, he was sent to prison for 27 months.
It follows, therefore, that the present offence was committed shortly after the
expiry of his last sentence. It was those facts that led the recorder to say, correctly

in our judgment, that the appellant was prepared to go on and on importing drugs and nothing would stop him.

6　　The grounds of appeal drafted by counsel, and supported by Mr Cockings this morning in admirably succinct and relevant arguments, were two-fold: first, that the sentence of seven years was manifestly excessive; and, secondly, that the travel restriction was too long in itself and, in any event, was wrongly ordered to run from the date of sentence.

7　　Dealing, firstly, with the sentence of imprisonment. There is no doubt that if this was the appellant's only drug offence the sentence of seven years was above the normal level of sentence for importing this amount of cannabis: see the well-known cases of *Aramah* (1983) 76 Cr.App.R. 190 and *Ronchetti* [1998] 2 Cr.App.R.(S.) 100. In the latter case this Court made clear that that sort of level of sentencing was appropriate for amounts of about 100 kilogrammes. However, neither of those cases considered the situation where a defendant has demonstrated that he will continue to import drugs whatever the courts may do. In our judgment, defendants of that sort, who may believe that the risk they run is outweighed by the rewards that they hope for, must expect significantly longer sentences than would be imposed for a single importation. However, the question remains whether this sentence takes that principle too far.

8　　In our judgment, it does, but not by much. In our judgment, the appropriate sentence here, bearing in mind this appellant's record, would have been a sentence of six years' imprisonment. The appeal will be allowed to the extent of reducing the sentence of seven years to one of six years.

9　　Turning now to the travel restriction order. That is an order made under s.33 of the Criminal Justice and Police Act 2001. So far as it is relevant s.33 is as follows:

"(1)

     (a)　[where] a person ('the offender') has been convicted by any court of a post-commencement drug trafficking offence;

     (b)　the court has determined that it would be appropriate to impose a sentence of imprisonment for that offence; and

     (c)　the term of imprisonment which the court considers appropriate is a term of four years or more."

then the court is bound to impose a travel restriction order with a minimum period of two years."

10　　So far as the time from which it runs is concerned, that is contained in s.33(3), where, under subs.(a), any order begins from the offender's release from custody. It is that subsection which also deals with the minimum period.

11　　It is clear, therefore, that this was a case which called for a travel restriction order. It is clear, also, that that order must run from the date of release. Therefore the expression of intention by the recorder that it should run from the date of sentence was incorrect.

12　　Thirdly, so far as the length is concerned, we have been helpfully referred to the recent case of *Mee* [2004] EWCA Crim 629, where this Court had to consider a similar order. In giving the judgment of the Court, Newman J. said this at [14]:

"Having regard to the impact of the restrictions, the length of an order should be measured to the defendant. Some factors can be enumerated by way of example; his age, his previous convictions, the risk of reoffending, which can be assessed generally, and of course, as we have mentioned, family contacts, employment considerations and so forth. The length should be that which is required to protect the public in the light of the assessment of the degree of risk which is presented by the facts. But, as we have said, it should be tailored to the defendant to such a degree as the court feels able when balanced against the risk."

We agree with those words of that Court of Appeal.

3   Against that background, we consider what the appropriate length of sentence of order should be in this case. The appellant's record shows that he poses a real risk for future importations. Therefore an order longer than the minimum required was appropriate. However, an order of the length of 10 years was not justified in this case, nor indeed an order which would have the same effect, since it will run from his date of release. In our judgment, the appropriate length of order here would have one of five years. We substitute that term for the 10 years imposed by the learned recorder.

4   To that extent, in those two respects, this appeal is allowed.

R. v REMUS TENISTOCLE CHIRILA AND OTHERS

COURT OF APPEAL (Lord Justice Latham, Mr Justice Grigson and Sir Edwin Jowitt): August 10, 2004

[2004] EWCA Crim 2200; [2005] 1 Cr.App.R.(S.) 93

ᴌᴛ Cash cards; Conspiracy; Deterrence; Fraud; Good character; Guilty pleas

1   *Conspiracy to defraud—arranging to obtain details of cash cards used by bank customers and then using the details to obtain cash from their bank accounts— length of sentence*

2   Six years' imprisonment upheld for conspiracy to defraud by arranging to obtain details of cash cards used by bank customers and then using the details to obtain cash from their bank accounts.

3   Three appellants pleaded guilty to conspiracy to defraud. The appellants installed a device in a bank which took the details of customer cards as they were used by the card holder to gain access to the lobby of the banks concerned. The details from these cards were then transferred to other cards capable of carrying magnetic data. The appellants installed a small wireless camera above the keyboard of the cash machine so as to acquire the PIN numbers from the cards. Approximately 60 customers who had used the branches of the bank had their

cards read and the details taken. 55 of the customers had money taken from their accounts, to a total of £24,460. Sentenced to six years' imprisonment in each case.

H4   **Held,** it was submitted the sentences failed to give sufficient credit for the guilty pleas and good character of the appellants. The offences were very prevalent and it seemed to the Court that a strong deterrent element must be incorporated into the sentences. The Court had reached the view that given the sophistication of the fraud and the need for a strong deterrent element in sentencing, the sentences were not manifestly excessive.

H5   **Cases cited:**
Taj, Gardner and Samuel [2003] EWCA Crim 2633, *Attorney General's Reference No.73 of 2003 (Rangathan)* [2004] EWCA Crim 183

H6   **References:** conspiracy to defraud, *Current Sentencing Practice* B 6-3

H7   *M. Upson* and *K. Jones* for the respective appellants.

JUDGMENT

1   **Grigson J.:**   On January 23, 2004 at the Crown Court at Sheffield each appellant pleaded guilty to conspiracy to defraud. Each was sentenced to six years' imprisonment. They appeal by leave of the single judge.

2   The conspiracy was to defraud banks by the use of cloned debit and credit cards. Stating the facts shortly, on Sunday September 28, 2003 staff at the HSBC Bank were monitoring cash withdrawals, having been alerted to the possibility of fraud. They noted unusual activity at the Abbey National Bank at Fargate, Sheffield. At 3.15am on the Monday morning they noted further such activity. The police were informed. They attended the bank and found the appellant Monteanu and Remus Chirila at the scene. Both men were arrested and searched. Monteanu had on him 23 Orange top-up phone cards and Remus Chirila £9,600 in cash, together with 19 Orange and 12 Vodafone top-up cards. He also had a handwritten note on which was written PIN numbers.

3   The appellants gave false names on arrest, but enquiries led to the Travel Inn at Sheffield. When the police attended rooms there, Adina Chirila was arrested. In those rooms officers found a large quantity of sophisticated high-tech equipment. They also found £18,200 in cash.

4   The fraud was highly sophisticated. The appellants installed a device which took the details of genuine customer cards as they were used by the card holder to gain access to the lobby of two particular banks. They were able to transfer the details from those cards on to other cards which had magnetic data carrying strips, for example, the Orange top-up cards. To acquire the relevant PIN numbers they had installed an incredibly small wireless camera above the keyboard of the cash machine. Approximately 60 customers who used these two branches of the bank had their cards read and their details taken. 55 of those customers had money taken from their accounts, a total of £24,460.

5   The appellants had also targeted two banks in the region of Liverpool and had obtained some £3,340 from four separate bank accounts. Since May of 2003 they had transferred over £130,000 to Romania. But the conspiracy which they admitted ran from August through to the end of September and in that period £22,500 was transferred.

6   It was the prosecution case that each appellant had been trained in Romania in the skills necessary to perpetrate this fraud. Each was a Romanian national, each an illegal immigrant and each in possession of false documentation as to their identity.

7   Monteanu is 28 years old, Remus Chirila 25 years old and Adina Chirila 24 years old. Each is of previous good character.

8   The sentence is criticised as failing to give sufficient credit for the guilty pleas which were entered at the first opportunity and insufficient credit for their previous good character. Counsel points out that the maximum sentence for these offences is one of 10 years and they argue that the judge must have started at too high a point. It is to be noted that the evidence against each was overwhelming and that consequently the credit to be given is necessarily limited.

9   In fact the learned judge had asked if there was any assistance to be gained by way of guideline cases on sentencing and was told that there was there was none. The single judge drew the attention of the Court to two particular cases, *R. v Taj, Gardner and Samuel* [2003] EWCA Crim 2633, and *Ranganathan*, which is in fact *Attorney General's Reference No 73 of 2003* [2004] EWCA Crim 183. Counsel referred to the fact that the starting point on a guilty plea, indicated in those sentences, would appear to be one of four years. It is argued that the fraud in *Ranganathan* lasted longer and that more money was actually obtained. That may be true, but this fraud is of a more sophisticated nature than the Court was considering in those cases.

10   The additional point is that these offences are now prevalent. It seems to this Court that, whatever happened before, a strong deterrent element must be incorporated into these sentences in the same way that a strong deterrent element is employed against those who are used to bring drugs into this country.

11   Mr Upton, on behalf of Adina Chirila, seeks to make a distinction on her part. He points out that she was at the hotel and not at the scene where the other two appellants were arrested. He uses this to base his argument that she was a reluctant conspirator. We are unable to accept that that argument can be sustained on the basis of her absence from the scene of the crime. It seems to us that each of these appellants must be dealt with on the same basis. And the fact is that they were part of a team determined on operating a sophisticated fraud and intending to benefit from it. This is the sort of fraud which has the effect of undermining the confidence of the public in the electronic banking system.

12   We have had to consider carefully whether this sentence in respect of each of them is manifestly excessive. We take the view that, although it comes at the top end of the scale, granted the sophistication of the fraud, need for a strong deterrent element in the sentencing and the limited credit available for their pleas of guilty, that it does not come within that definition. In those circumstances, the appeals are dismissed.

R. v JOHN HAMILTON DUNN RIDLEY

Court of Appeal (Lord Justice Latham, Mr Justice Grigson and Sir Edwin Jowitt): August 12, 2004

[2004] EWCA Crim 2275; [2005] 1 Cr.App.R.(S.) 94

(LT) Automatic life imprisonment; Grievous bodily harm; Guilty pleas; Minimum term; Racially aggravated offences

H1   *Automatic life sentence—specified period—causing grievous bodily harm with intent—racial aggravation—length of specified period*

H2   A period of four years and three months specified as the minimum term in connection with an automatic life sentence imposed for causing grievous bodily harm with intent which was found to be racially aggravated reduced to three years.

H3   The appellant pleaded guilty to causing grievous bodily harm with intent. The appellant and two other youths were in a market square when two youths of different ethnic origin drove into the market square. One of these youths went off to purchase food. The appellant and his companions began staring at the car and eventually offered to fight the youth who remained in the car. The youth picked up some pliers and told the appellant to go away. The appellant seized the pliers and began to rain blows on the youth's head. He then pulled him out of the car and kicked and punched him as he lay on the ground. The youth suffered bruising to the head, neck and body and damage to his right eye which caused him to lose the sight of the eye. The appellant had been convicted on a previous occasion of causing grievous bodily harm with intent and was therefore liable to an automatic life sentence under the Powers of Criminal Courts (Sentencing) Act 2000, s.109. Sentenced to life imprisonment with a specified period of four years and three months, derived from a notional determinate of 10 years, on the assumption that the appropriate sentence after a contested trial would have been 13 years.

H4   **Held,** it was submitted that the starting point for calculating the notional determinate sentence was too high. The sentencing judge had taken 11 years as a starting point on a contested trial in the absence of racial aggravation; he then found that the offence was racially aggravated and added two years for the racial aggravation and then reduced the figure by three years to reflect the appellant's plea, so as to produce the notional determinate sentence of 10 years. The Court accepted the submission that the starting point for determining the notional determinate sentence was too high and should have been eight years. The sentencing judge was right to add two years to this to reflect the fact that the offence was racially aggravated. The Court would adopt a term of 10 years as the basis for the notional determinate sentence, reduce that term by two and a half years to reflect the guilty plea and take half of the resulting figure of seven and a half years to produce a term of three years and nine months, from which nine months would be deducted on account of the time spent in custody on remand giving a specified period of three years.

H5   **Cases cited:**
Meredith and Craven [2000] 1 Cr.App.R.(S.) 508, *Morrison* [2001] 1 Cr.App.R.(S.) 5 (p.12), *Kelly and Donnelly* [2001] 2 Cr.App.R.(S.) 73 (p.341)

H6   **References:** life imprisonment—specified period, *Current Sentencing Practice* F 3–4

H7   *J. Farmer* for the appellant.

JUDGMENT

1   **Grigson J.:**   On November 3, 2000 this appellant was convicted of causing grievous bodily harm with intent contrary to s.18 of the Offences Against the Person Act 1861. He was sentenced to three years' detention in a young offender institution. On November 20, 2003 at the Crown Court at Luton on rearraignment the appellant pleaded guilty to an offence of causing grievous bodily harm with intent contrary to the same section. Section 109 of the Powers of Criminal Courts (Sentencing) Act applied. He had committed a second serious offence and consequently qualified for a life sentence. There were no exceptional circumstances and no appeal is made against the imposition of a life sentence by the learned judge. However, as he is required to do, the judge went on to specify a minimum period to be served before the appellant could be released on licence. The period he specified was four years and three months.

2   The mechanics of the sentencing process were these. The judge took as his starting point the sentence he would have imposed upon the appellant on conviction after trial as 11 years. He added to that a period of two years to reflect the fact that the offence was racially aggravated, taking the total to 13 years. He then reduced the total by three years to reflect the guilty plea. The consequent 10-year period he halved and deducted from it the time that the appellant had spent in custody which was nine months. Thus he reached the specified period of four years and three months. It is that period, four years and three months, which is the subject of this appeal.

3   Mr Farmer of counsel argues that the period of 11 years was manifestly excessive and also that the uplift of two years for the racial aggravation was manifestly excessive.

4   The appellant was 21 when the offence was committed and 22 at the point of sentence. He had been previously convicted. We deal only with the offences involving violence. In July 1998 when 16 he was convicted of assault occasioning actual bodily harm. A supervision order was made for 12 months which he breached and in June of the next year a probation order was substituted. On the same day he was convicted of possession of an offensive weapon. Two months later, in the August, he pleaded guilty to wounding contrary to s.20 of the

Offences Against the Person Act and was sentenced to six months in a young offender institution. He was then 17. In January of 2000 he was fined for threatening and abusive behaviour. In July of the same year he was convicted of a similar offence. In November he admitted an offence of assault occasioning actual bodily harm and was sentenced to nine months' youth custody. On the same occasion he was convicted of an offence against s.18 of the Offences Against the Person Act and a concurrent period of three years was then imposed. He was 17. He is a persistent violent offender. The last conviction involved attacking a man with a hammer.

5   Turning to the facts of this offence. The incident occurred on May 1, 2003. The victim was Mohan Rahman, then 16 years old. He with a friend, Ibrar Ahmed, and two young white girls drove into the Market Square at Luton. Ibrar Ahmed went off to purchase food. The appellant was in the square with two other white youths and they began staring at the car. The appellant was heard to say something to his friends which included the word "Paki". He then approached the car and said to Mohan Rahman, "What are you looking at?" The reply was, "Nothing". He then offered to fight Mohan Ahmed and started to kick the car. Ahmed picked up some pliers from the footwell and told the appellant to get away. The appellant then seized the pliers and began raining blows on Mohan Ahmed's head. He then opened the door and pulled him out of the car. Ahmed went to the ground and there the appellant kicked and punched him. The appellant was pulled away by a member of the public and left the scene. As a result of the assault Mohan Ahmed suffered bruising to his head, neck and body, but there was damage to his right eye which has caused him to be blind in that eye. The attack was not prolonged, but plainly its consequences were very serious.

6   The appellant was arrested and interviewed. He denied involvement. He eventually pleaded guilty before trial, but not at the first opportunity. We are told by Mr Farmer, his counsel, that his initial denial resulted from his mistaken belief that life imprisonment meant exactly that. The basis of the plea tendered was this: that the assault involved two men, that the injury to the eye could not be attributed to him, and that the injury was not inflicted with a weapon. The Crown accepted that.

7   They did not accept the appellant's contention that the attack was not racially aggravated. The judge held a *Newton* hearing and found that it was. In the course of that hearing the appellant gave evidence and evidence was called on his behalf. He gave evidence that the attack was not racially aggravated and in re-examination advanced the suggestion that it arose from a dispute over drugs. The judge nonetheless held that the attack was racially aggravated. He accepted the evidence called on the appellant's behalf that normally he is not racist. He belongs to no racist organisations and indeed lives in harmony within a multiracial family. The appellant does not seek to challenge that ruling and consequently s.153 of the Powers of Criminal Courts (Sentencing) Act comes into force. That section requires the court to regard the fact that an offence was racially aggravated as an aggravating factor. That is a factor which makes the offence the more serious.

8   The first and principal submission is that the sentencing point at which the judge started, namely 11 years, was too high. We have been referred to the case of *Meredith and Craven* [2000] 1 Cr.App.R.(S.) 508, where a determinate sentence of 12 years was upheld, but described as being at the top end of the bracket. The defendant there was older, the attack was prolonged and the injuries the more serious. Taking the matter shortly, we agree with Mr Farmer's submission that that starting point was too high. We accept his submission that the starting point for this offence should have been eight years.

9   In *Morrison* [2001] 1 Cr.App.R.(S.) 5 (p.12), the Court of Appeal stated that where an offence is racially aggravated the judge should determine, first, the appropriate sentence for the offence had it not been racially aggravated and then specify the appropriate increase. The extent of the increase depends upon all the circumstances of the offence. In *Kelly and Donnelly* [2001] EWCA Crim 170 the Vice President, Rose L.J., listed some of the factors to be considered when deciding what that uplift should be. He referred to the offender's intention and the consequences. Also, he referred to other factors which are wholly absent here. This was a spontaneous offence, it was not planned, the offender is not part of a racist group. Indeed, as Mr Farmer observes, he lives within a multicultural family. However, this offence was very plainly solely motivated by racism. The effect on the victim is extremely serious. The attack was entirely unprovoked. The consequences are not only that the victim has lost the sight of an eye, but he has been severely traumatised and has suffered from post-traumatic stress syndrome and depression, and it has affected his academic progress also. In the circumstances, we take the view that the uplift of two years is wholly appropriate and cannot be described as manifestly excessive.

10   The consequences are these. We substitute for the period of 11 years one of eight years. We add to that the two-year uplift to reflect the racially aggravated nature of the offence which takes us to 10 years. We think in the circumstances here that the appropriate reduction to reflect the guilty plea is one of two and a half years which takes the total down to seven and a half years, half of which takes us to three years and nine months. From that we have to deduct the nine months that the appellant spent in custody, giving a specified period of three years. To the extent that that order is effective, we allow the appeal.

R. v ROBIN JASON LOWRIE

Court of Appeal (Lord Justice Latham, Mr Justice Grigson and Sir Edwin Jowitt): August 12, 2004

[2004] EWCA Crim 2325; [2005] 1 Cr.App.R.(S.) 95

(LT) Emergency services; Improper use of telecommunications; Psychopathic disorder; Public nuisance; Public protection; Sentence length

H1   *Public nuisance—persistently making false calls to emergency services—repeated offences over long period of time—length of sentence*

H2   Eight years' imprisonment upheld for public nuisance in the form of persistently making false calls to the emergency services by an offender who repeated similar offences over a long period of time.

H3   The appellant pleaded guilty to 12 offences of public nuisance. The appellant, aged 24, had a history of making hoax phone calls asking for the attendance of the emergency services. This conduct began when the appellant was seven years old. He had been convicted on a number of previous occasions and sentenced to various sentences, culminating in a sentence of five years' detention for public nuisance. Two months after his release from than sentence he made further hoax calls. Sentenced to eight years' imprisonment.

H4   **Held,** psychiatric reports indicated that the appellant was suffering from a psychopathic disorder, in the form of either anti-social or emotionally unstable personality disorder. A hospital order was not indicated. It was submitted that the sentencing judge had selected too high a starting point. The Court accepted that the sentence was long and the situation faced by the judge was one of despair. There was no reason to think that once the appellant was at liberty there would be any change in his behaviour. The Court had to bear in mind the impact of the appellant's behaviour on innocent people and the likelihood that someone in real peril would not receive the attention that was required. The appeal would be dismissed.

H5   **References:** public nuisance, *Current Sentencing Practice* B 13-4

H6   *M.P. Styles* for the appellant.

JUDGMENT

1   **Sir Edwin Jowitt:**   This appellant is 24 years old. He has a history of irrational behaviour which has taken the form of hoax calls asking for the attendance of the emergency services. This conduct began when the appellant was only seven years old. It was not until 1996, when he was 16, that it first brought him before a criminal court when, for a series of such offences and an offence of using threatening behaviour, he was prosecuted under the Telecommunications Act 1984. He was made the subject of a supervision order to continue until he reached the age of 18 which would take him to the end of May 1998. Sadly supervision was not successful in restraining the appellant.

2   In October 1997 he was again before the court, when for a further series of hoax phone calls to the emergency services he was sentenced to two months' detention in a young offender institution. Also on this occasion offences of affray, common assault and threatening behaviour were dealt with. In total the detention period was four months.

3   Then in January 1998 the appellant was put on probation for six months for making further hoax calls. In November of that year for more such offences, an offence of arson and an offence of deception he was made the subject of a two-year probation order and required to attend an anger management course. The hoax calls had begun within days of making the earlier probation order.

4   In February 1999 for more such offences the appellant was sentenced to be detained for three months in a young offender institution. For the next series of offences the prosecution decided to prosecute the appellant for the common law offence of committing a public nuisance and at Newcastle upon Tyne Crown Court he was sentenced to five years' detention. The appellant was released from that sentence on March 21 last year. Two months later the hoax calls began again and on February 17 this year at the same Crown Court for 12 offences of public nuisance the appellant was sentenced to concurrent sentences of eight years' imprisonment.

5   He appeals against these sentences by leave of the single judge.

6   It would not be helpful if we were to prolong this judgment by rehearsing the facts of every one of these 12 offences, but we refer to a few of them to give a picture of their variety. On May 20 the appellant called the fire brigade from his mobile phone claiming that his house was on fire. Two fire engines were dispatched. On May 22 he made four calls. He twice called for an ambulance, falsely claiming he had been assaulted. He called for the coastguard, claiming that he was suicidal after a family row. He called the police, saying he was going to jump into the water at Blyth docks. On May 28 the appellant called the ambulance service, giving a false name, claiming that a friend had taken an overdose. Finally, on June 14, the appellant called the fire service claiming there was a fire in a public house in Blyth. Two fire engines attended. It was discovered that they had been called as a result of a hoax call. Later that day the appellant made another hoax call to the coastguard which resulted in a search and rescue operation being launched. Using a false name, he said that his friend had threatened to throw him-

self into Blyth docks. The search and rescue operation lasted for 45 minutes. It even included the use of a police helicopter.

7   The appellant was arrested on that same day. In interview he admitted making the hoax calls. He said that he felt suicidal and needed help.

8   The pre-sentence report makes the point that the calls for help were made on the pretext that the appellant's suicidal thoughts were genuine. A more obvious body for him to approach would have been the Samaritans. The writer of the report says that, although the appellant accepts that his hoax calls had caused constant disruption, he seems to have only a superficial appreciation of the potential harm involved. He appears to have no real understanding of the risk to genuine victims in genuine life and death situations to whom help may be delayed because his hoax calls are being attended to. The writer speaks of the attempts which have been made to help the appellant, all without avail. When under supervision in the community the appellant has failed to respond each time to any attempt made to help him. This includes also the period when the appellant was on licence after he was released from his five-year sentence.

9   The writer of the report accepts that prison has not acted as a deterrent, but she concludes:

> "Until he makes some prolonged and consistent attempt to find an alternative way of coping with personal crises, then the danger is that he will revert to making phone calls. The risk of reoffending is therefore high."

10   In the parole assessment report, made while the appellant was serving the five-year sentence, the writer recorded that, prior to that sentence being imposed, the appellant had been seen by five different psychiatrists. He writes:

> "The general consensus by all was that he was neither significantly mentally impaired nor presenting symptoms of mental illness."

11   It was noted, however, that he has a history of conduct disorder and a personality disorder. He had been offered voluntary out-patient counselling at the Kolvin Unit of the Department of Forensic Psychiatry at Newcastle General Hospital, but failed to keep appointments.

12   The writer adds:

> "On the recent visit Mr Lowrie told me that he was now very sorry for what he has done and fully understands the consequences of his action. However, his main motivation for not reoffending appears to be to avoid further custodial sentences. The persistence and nature of these his offending would indicate that Mr Lowrie does not understand the seriousness of and potential dangers of his actions."

13   We point out that, despite the appellant's protestations to the writer of this report, the appellant's telephone calls began, as we have said, only two months after his release from a substantial period of imprisonment.

14   We have before us today two psychiatric reports written since the period the appellant received that earlier sentence of five years. The first is from Professor

Grubin, Professor of Forensic Psychiatry, and is dated January 2000. He concludes:

> ". . . there can be little doubt that Robin Lowrie meets the criteria for psychopathic disorder as defined in the Mental Health Act. Clinically he could be diagnosed as suffering from either antisocial or emotionally unstable (impulsive type) personality disorder. His behaviour and his interactions with others are clearly inflexible, maladaptive, and persistent. He is impulsive and deceitful, he has little regard for social norms or for the safety of others, and he displays little in the way of remorse. There is also evidence of emotional instability."

15   Professor Grubin concludes by referring to the views of other psychiatrists, one of them being Professor Graham, that at the time of writing the report a hospital order was not indicated.

16   The second report is dated August 31, 2003, before the sentence under appeal was imposed. Its author is Dr Turkington. He says at para.25:

> "Mental state examination: This revealed that he was able to talk about all his problems in tremendous detail but showed almost nothing in the way of emotional resonance with any of the distressing matters discussed. He was not depressed when seen and showed no evidence of anxiety. There was no evidence to indicate a psychosis."

17   Then at para.30, continuing through to para.33, Dr Turkington says:

> "There is clear psychiatric mitigation. . ... Unfortunately the problem in this case is that he has a severe personality disorder with antisocial and alexythmic traits which will respond only minimally despite the best efforts of psychological support as delivered by the community psychiatric nursing served from North Tyneside District General Hospital.
> As such there must be a high risk of repetition and a strong likelihood of further abuse of illegal substances and alcohol. Though he currently appears very highly motivated to engage in treatment, it is unfortunately the opinion of all medical health professionals involved that his personality disorder is such that it would be very unlikely to respond to any degree that might allow the level of risk to diminish of repetition."

18   Speaking of provision if the appellant were to retain his liberty, Dr Turkington said:

> "There would be no advantage to be received by having this young man attending the psychiatric out-patient clinic as he would not benefit from any form of psychiatric medication of any kind. The supportive psychotherapy by nursing staff would have to be ongoing over a very long period of time and would help to a small degree but not enough to diminish risk of repetition."

19   This is the factual and psychiatric context in which we have to consider this appeal.

20   Mr Styles for the appellant says that, bearing in mind the plea of guilty, the judge at first instance must have selected too high a starting point to impose the sentence that he did. We accept this was a long sentence and that the situation faced by the judge was one of despair. All things have been tried to prevent this man behaving as he so persistently does behave. There is simply no reason at the present time to think once he regains his liberty there will be any change. Everything seems to indicate to the contrary.

21   What we have to bear in mind, despite the psychiatric mitigation, which plainly there is, is the impact of this appellant's behaviour on innocent people. The more often this type of offence occurs, the greater the likelihood that one day, for example, an ambulance will be on its way to deal with some call and in response to a hoax call by the appellant some person in desperate peril will not receive the prompt attention that is required and will lose his or her life. The Court takes the view that society is entitled to expect the courts to provide protection against that eventuality.

22   Regrettable though it is, nothing can be done to help this appellant. This appeal has to be dismissed.

R. v JAHMARL

Court of Appeal (Lord Justice Hooper, Mr Justice Holland and Sir Charles Mantell): August 17, 2004

[2004] EWCA Crim 2199; [2005] 1 Cr.App.R.(S.) 96

Age; Attempts; Detention and training orders; Robbery; Sentencing powers; Young offenders

H1   *Young offender—offender convicted at age 15 of attempted robbery committed at age 14—whether Crown Court may impose custodial sentence of less than two years—whether Crown Court may impose detention and training order*

H2   **Editor's note:** when an offender under the age of 18 is committed to the Crown Court for trial for an offence to which the Powers of Criminal Courts (Sentencing) Act 2000, s. 91 applies, on the assumption that a sentence of two years' detention or more may be appropriate if he should be convicted, the Crown Court is not restricted in the exercise of its sentencing powers and may impose a term of detention of less than two years.

H3   The appellant, aged 14 at the time of the offence, was convicted at the age of 15 of attempted robbery. Together with two other youths of similar age he approached two young brothers who were travelling on the top deck of a bus. The appellant asked one of the brothers if they had mobile telephones. When he said that they had not, the appellant demanded cash. The appellant then punched one of the boys, and produced a small knife which he held to the boy's neck. One of the appellant's accomplices said that the appellant would "switch" the boy. The appellant then gave the knife to an accomplice who held the other brother by the neck and held the knife to his neck. The appellant and his accomplices then left the bus. No property had been taken. They were arrested shortly afterwards. Sentenced to two years' detention under the Powers of Criminal Courts (Sentencing) Act 2000, s.91.

14   **Held,** the appellant was of previous good character; according to the pre-sentence report he was aware of the seriousness of the offence and expressed remorse. There was positive support available to him and there was a low risk of re- offending. A supervision order was recommended. The sentencing judge concluded that the appellant was probably the first person to demand money and the mobile telephones and that he was the one who had produced and opened the knife which was put to the victim's throat. The sentencing judge observed, having been referred to the relevant legislation and authorities, that the court was faced with a 15-year-old of good character convicted of offences committed at the age of 14. It followed that he had the choice between a non-custodial penalty or a sentence of at least two years' detention under the Powers of Criminal Courts (Sentencing) Act, s.91. The Court had no doubt that a custodial sentence was required, or that the seriousness of the offence was such that the sentencing judge was entitled to invoke s.91. The Court did not agree that the sentencing judge was faced with the stark choice between a non-custodial sentence and a custodial sentence of at least two years' detention under s.91. The Court did not agree that the appellant did not qualify for a detention and training order. The Court's view was that the proper sentence in the light of all the circumstances, unless prevented either by legislation or the authorities, was a sentence of one year in custody. The Magistrates' Courts Act 1980, s.24(1) provided that if a person under the age of 18 appeared in a magistrates' court charged with an indictable offence other than homicide, he should be tried summarily unless the court considered that if the offender was found guilty it ought to be possible to sentence him under s.91 of the Powers of Criminal Courts (Sentencing) Act, s.91. Section 91 provided that where a person under 18 was convicted of certain offences, which included robbery, the court might sentence the person to be detained for such a period, not exceeding the maximum term of imprisonment, as might be specified. The Court had to consider three lines of authorities. In *S-J.R and DG* [2001] 1 Cr.App.R.(S.) 109 (p.377) two youths aged 14 had used a knife to rob a 14-year-old boy. Each was sentenced to a term of detention under s.91; the terms were reduced from 20 months to 15 months, and from three years to 30 months respectively. The Court rejected the submission that an offender under the age of 15 could not be sentenced to a custodial sentence of less than two years if he was not a "persistent offender" and therefore not eligible for a detention and training order. The Court observed that the power under s.91 to award detention to a young person for whatever period had been expressly preserved. If that case remained good law, the sentencing judge was not prevented from passing a sentence of less than two years' detention under s.91. The second line of authority (*R. (on the application of W) v Southampton Youth Court and R. (on the application of K) v Wirral Borough Magistrates' Court* [2003] 1 Cr.App.R.(S.) 87 (p.455), *R. (on the*

application of D) v Manchester City Youth Court [2002] 1 Cr.App.R.(S.) 135 (p.573), *R. (on the application of W) v Thetford Youth Court and R. (on the application of M) v Waltham Forest Youth Court* [2003] 1 Cr.App.R.(S.) 67 (p.323)) gave guidance to youth courts on the circumstances in which they should commit for trial a defendant under the age of 15 with a view to a sentence under s.91. It was held that a youth court which was unable to pass a short detention and training order because the defendant was under the age of 15 and not a persistent offender should only rarely commit to the Crown Court. The fact that the detention and training order was not available indicated that Parliament intended that generally a non-custodial sentence should be passed. Those cases set out the approach to be taken by a youth court when faced with the decision whether to commit a defendant under the age of 15 with a view to a possible sentence of detention under s.91. They did not restrict the power of the Crown Court when it had to sentence a defendant who had been convicted before it. A third line of authority (*Ghafoor* [2003] 1 Cr.App.R.(S.) 84 (p.428), *L.M.* [2003] 2 Cr.App.R.(S.) 26 (p.124)) dealt with the treatment of a defendant convicted at the age of 15 of offences committed at the age of 14, who would not have been eligible for a detention and training order if convicted at the age of 14. The Court had indicated that in such a case the sentence which would have been passed at the date of the commission of the offence was a "powerful factor" in the sentencing court's considerations, but other factors might have to be considered. There had to be a good reason for departing from the starting point. The present case was different from those cases. The offence of robbery was one in respect of which the sentencing judge was right to invoke s.91. The Court had decided that the appropriate length of the sentence was one year's detention, should the sentence be a sentence of detention under s.91 or could it be a sentence of one year's detention: and training order? The Court had been advised that a one-year detention and training order was more appropriate for a 15-year-old than a sentence of detention under s.91. In those circumstances it seemed to the Court to be right to pass a detention and training order for a period of one year. Section 100 gave the court power to sentence a young person aged 15 at the time of conviction to a detention and training order even though he was 14 at the time of the offence. It followed that the sentencing judge was wrong in concluding that the appellant did not qualify for a detention and training order. The Court would stress that it was passing a sentence of one year's detention and training order in rather unusual circumstances which included the exceptional personal mitigation available to the appellant and the fact that an accomplice who had pleaded guilty had been dealt with by means of a supervision order.

H5 **Cases cited:**
S-J.R and DG [2001] 1 Cr.App.R.(S.) 109 (p.377), *R. (on the application of W) v Southampton Youth Court and R. (on the application of K) v Wirral Borough Magistrates' Court* [2003] 1 Cr.App.R.(S.) 87 (p.455), *R. (on the application of D) v Manchester City Youth Court* [2002] 1 Cr.App.R.(S.) 135 (p.573), *R. (on the application of W) v Thetford Youth Court and R. (on the application of M) v Waltham Forest Youth Court* [2003] 1 Cr.App.R.(S0.) 67 (p.323)), *Ghafoor*

[2003] 1 Cr.App.R.(S.) 84 (p.428), *L.M.* [2003] 2 Cr.App.R.(S.) 26 (p.124) *Danga* (1992) 13 Cr.App.R.(S.) 408.

16   **References:** detention of juveniles, *Current Sentencing Practice* E4, *Archbold* 5–538

17   **Commentary:** [2004] Crim.L.R. 1052

18   *M. Pinfold* for the appellant.
Miss J. Hacking for the Crown.

JUDGMENT

1   **Hooper L.J.:**   On March 19, 2004 at the Crown Court at Isleworth before Mr Recorder Topolski Q.C. and a jury the appellant was convicted of an offence of attempted robbery. On April 16, 2004 he was sentenced to two years' detention under s.91 of the Powers of Criminal Courts (Sentencing) Act 2000 ("the 2000 Act"). The appellant was born on November 24, 1988 and was aged 14 at the time of the offence. He was 15 by the time he came to be convicted.

2   There were two co-defendants. The first was Ashley Foster who pleaded guilty on re-arraignment on February 5, 2004. He was subsequently sentenced to a three-year supervision order, with a 90-day special action plan as well as a three months curfew order. Foster was also aged 14 at the time of the offence and, it appears, just 15 at the time of sentence (there is some confusion in the papers about his date of birth).

3   The second co-defendant was Frederick Osei, born on January 3, 1989. He was also convicted on March 19 on one count of attempted robbery. He absconded. We were informed by Mr Pinfold after the hearing that he had now learnt that Osei was, at some point, given a two-year detention and training order ("DTO"). We have no further details.

4   At about 8.10pm on September 17, 2003, 14-year-old Jamie Pearcy and his 12-year-old brother Jordan boarded a bus at Harrow-on-the-Hill travelling to Ruislip. They went to the top deck and sat at the front of the bus. After a short while they became aware of the appellant, Foster and Osei. The appellant stood in front of Jamie and Jordan. Osei sat behind Jordan and Foster remained at the rear.

The appellant asked Jamie and Jordan if they had mobile telephones and they said no. The appellant then asked Jamie whether he had any cash. When Jamie said he had one pound the appellant demanded it. When Jamie refused Foster said something like, "you shouldn't take that". The appellant punched Jamie to the stomach, produced a small knife, went behind Jamie and held the knife to his neck. Jamie pushed the appellant's hand away and refused to give up the money. Foster said, "Just give him the money or he will switch on you".

The appellant then handed the knife to Osei, who was sitting behind Jordan. Osei grabbed Jordan around the neck and held the knife to his neck. Jordan began to cry. When it was discovered that Jordan was Jamie's brother, Osei released Jordan. Foster said something about taking Jamie off the bus to "switch" on him and knife him for letting his brother suffer.

7   The appellant and the co-accused left the bus at Ruislip Manor. No property had been taken. Jamie or Jordan told the driver what had happened. The police were contacted and Jamie and Jordan were driven around the area. They pointed out the appellant and the co-accused who were then arrested.

8   The offence lasted for seven to eight minutes. As a result of the offences Jamie and Jordan's family moved to a different part of the country.

9   When interviewed the appellant initially denied being on the bus. He later admitted being present and talking to the two boys, but denied that he threatened them, assaulted them or demanded property from them. Osei said he tried to stop the appellant and Foster from committing the offence. Foster made no comment.

10   The appellant was of previous good character. According to the pre-sentence report the appellant was fully aware of the seriousness of the offence and expressed remorse. He had no history of getting into trouble. There were no concerns about alcohol or drug use. He had not associated with the co-defendants and had not re-offended since the date of the offence. The author of the report said that the court process had had a salutary effect. There was positive educational, sporting and family support available to him. In all these circumstances there was a low risk of re-offending. A supervision order coupled with ancillary orders was recommended. Six references were provided to the court, the effect of which were that the appellant was an honest and decent boy who was polite and well mannered. His commitment to his football team was exemplary. He had not kept good company since he had moved from Shrewsbury to Harrow. He had been overwhelmed by the whole way of life in Harrow compared to that in Shrewsbury.

11   The recorder in passing sentence concluded that the appellant was probably the first person to demand money and the mobile, that he had not acted playfully when he had punched the victim in the stomach and that he was the one who had probably produced and opened the knife, putting it to the victim's throat. As far as Foster was concerned the recorder said that although he was probably not the holder or user of the knife, he was "part of the general threat and intimidation" and played his part in a terrifying attack. He said that Foster's role was "probably less actually violent than the others" and he said to Foster that "distinguishes you from them". He went on to point out that what further and importantly distinguished Foster from the others was that he had the courage to plead guilty and to admit what he had done. He was told that he would receive considerable credit for the plea of guilty. Foster also had no convictions prior to the commission of the offence.

12   The recorder said that the two victims had suffered trauma as a result of having to come to court.

13   Prior to the sentencing there had been a lengthy argument about the sentencing options. Subsequently the case was called back on April 23, 2004 to make a minor adjustment to one part of the order that concerned only Foster. The recorder then referred to the legislation and the authorities and said this in further explanation of the sentence which he had earlier passed on the appellant:

"The court was faced with a convicted 15 year old of good character who was 14 at the time of committing the offence which in my view clearly passed the custody threshold and was sufficiently serious to merit consideration of a sentence of at least two years following conviction by the jury. The defendant did not qualify for a detention and training order.

In my view, the position on the state of the law, sentencing, practice and principle, was that the stark choice before the court was to impose either a non-custodial penalty or a custodial one of at least two years in length under Section 91 as amended. That proposition was accepted by all parties."

14   Before us Mr Pinfold went further and said that the choice was between a non-custodial penalty and a sentence in excess of two years' detention. He submitted therefore that the sentence should have been a non-custodial sentence.

15   We have no doubt that a custodial sentence was required. We also have no doubt that the seriousness of the offence was such that the recorder was entitled to invoke the provisions of s.91.

16   We do not agree however that he was faced with the stark choice of, on the one hand, a non-custodial sentence and, on the other hand, a custodial sentence of at least two years' detention under s.91. Nor do we agree that the appellant did not qualify for a DTO.

17   It may well be that if the recorder had not felt constrained to pass a sentence of two years' detention, he would have passed a lower custodial sentence.

18   Unless prevented from so doing by either the legislation or the authorities we reach the conclusion that the proper sentence for this appellant in the light of all the circumstances and, in particular, in the light of the sentence passed on Foster, was a sentence of one year in custody.

19   By virtue of s.100 of the 2000 Act, courts are given the power to pass a DTO. Subsection (2) provides, however, that a court shall not make such an order:

"(a) In the case of an offender under the age of 15 at the time of the conviction, unless it is of the opinion that he is a persistent offender."

20   Section 24(1) of the Magistrates Courts' Act 1980 provides that a person under the age of 18 charged in a magistrates' court with an indictable offence other than homicide shall be tried summarily unless the offence is one that falls within s.91 "and the court considers that if he is found guilty of the offence it ought to be possible to sentence him" under that section.

21   Section 91 provides that where a person aged under 18 is convicted on indictment of certain specified offences, including robbery:

"(3) If the court is of the opinion that none of the other methods in which the case may legally be dealt with is suitable, the court may sentence the offender to be detained for such period, not exceeding the maximum term of imprisonment with which the offence is punishable in the case of a person aged 21 or over, as may be specified in the sentence."

22   There are three lines of authorities which need to be considered. We start with *S-J.R and DG* [2001] 1 Cr.App.R.(S.) 109 (p.377). The two appellants were aged

14 when one pleaded guilty to robbery and the other was convicted of robbery. In company with another youth and using a knife they robbed a 14-year-old boy walking home from school. The appellant who pleaded guilty was sentenced to 20 months' detention under what is now s.91. The appellant who had been convicted was sentenced to three years' detention also under what is now s.91. The two terms of detention were reduced from 20 months to 15 months and from three years to 30 months respectively. Counsel had submitted that the combined effect of what is now s.91 and of the decision in *Ganley* [2001] 1 Cr.App.R.(S.) 17 (p.60) was that no offender under the age of 15 could be sentenced to a custodial sentence of less than two years if, not being a persistent offender, he is not eligible for a DTO. As Hallett J. said (at [11]):

> "The power to order the detention of a young person under [section 91], for whatever period, has been expressly preserved and in appropriate cases, provided the conditions are met, may be imposed."

23 If this case remains good law then the recorder was not prevented from passing a sentence of under two years' detention pursuant to s.91.

24 We turn to the second line of authorities upon which the recorder relied for his conclusion, namely those cases in the Divisional Court in which guidance has been given to youth courts as to the circumstances in which they should commit a defendant under the age of 15 for trial with a view to a sentence under s.91. In *R. (on the application of W) v Southampton Youth Court* and *R. (on the application of K) v Wirral Borough Magistrates Court* [2002] EWHC 1640 (Admin); [2003] 1 Cr.App.R.(S.) 87(p.455) Lord Woolf C.J. and Kay L.J. considered and approved the earlier decisions in *R. (on the application of D) v Manchester City Youth Court* [2002] 1 Cr.App.R.(S.) 135 (p.573) and *R. (on the application of W) v Thetford Youth Court* and *R. (on the application of M) v Waltham Forest Youth Court* [2003] 1 Cr.App.R.(S.) 67 (p.323).

25 Lord Woolf agreed, as did Kay L.J., with the approach of Gage J. in the *Thetford* and *Waltham Forest* cases. Gage J. said at [27]:

> "Finally I must refer to *R (on the application of D) v Manchester City Youth Court* [2002] 1 Cr.App.R.(S.) 135 (p.573). That was a decision of mine on an application precisely similar to the applications made in these cases. The facts of the offence are however slightly different. In that case I said (paras 22 and 23 page 578):
>
> '22. In my judgment, the effect of s.24 is that a magistrates' court should not decline jurisdiction unless the offence and the circumstances surrounding it and the offender are such as to make it more than a vague or theoretical possibility that a sentence of detention for a long period may be passed. Although, under s.91 and pursuant to recent authority, it is no longer necessary for a court to pass a sentence of at least three years, in my judgment s.91 is primarily applicable to cases of such gravity that the court is or may be considering a sentence of at least two years. Anything less, it seems to me, falls primarily to be dealt with as a detention and training order.

23. There is no statutory restriction on a court, using its powers under s.91, passing a sentence of less than two years. But it seems to me that it will only be in very exceptional and restricted circumstances that it will be appropriate to do so, rather than making a detention and training order. The fact that an offender, as here, does not qualify for a detention and training order because he is not a persistent offender does not seem to me such an exceptional circumstance as to justify the passing of a period of detention of less than two years under s.91 of the Act of 2000.'"

26   Gage J. went on to say:

"29 My conclusion is that the authorities cited to this Court do not undermine or alter my conclusions already expressed on the relationship between ss.91 and 100. I adhere to my view that in respect of offenders under 15 a custodial sentence will ordinarily only be available in the form of a detention and training order. If the court is prohibited from making such an order in general an order under s.91 will not be appropriate. Having considered the submissions made in this Court , on a rather fuller basis than those before me in *D v Manchester City Youth Court*, I see no reason to change to any great extent the views which I expressed in that case. I remain of the opinion that where an offence or offences are likely to attract a sentence of less than two years custody the appropriate sentence will be a detention and training order. In the case of an offender under 15, who is not a persistent offender or a child under 12, the most likely sentence will be a non-custodial sentence. It follows that in most cases the appropriate place of trial will be the youth court.

30. However, I accept that there may be cases where, despite the fact that the offender is under 15 and no detention and training order can be made, the only appropriate sentence is a custodial sentence pursuant to s.91 and possibly for a period of less than two years. But I remain of the opinion that the circumstances of the offence and offender will only rarely call for a sentence pursuant to s.91, particularly if the Court is dealing with an offender under the age of 12. In expressing my views, as I did, in *D v Manchester City Youth Court*, my use of the expression 'very exceptional' may be more restrictive than was strictly necessary or justified. But, I remain of the view that the mere fact that a youth court, unable to make a short detention and training order, considers that the option to pass a short custodial sentence should be available, does not mean that it should decline jurisdiction. It seems to me that in such circumstances the fact that a detention and training order is not available indicates that Parliament intended that generally a non-custodial sentence should be passed. Perhaps it would be better to say that cases involving offenders under 15 for whom a detention and training order is not available will only rarely attract a period of detention under s.91; the more rarely if the offender is under 12."

7   In this latter paragraph Gage J. is modifying what he had said in para.[23] of the *Manchester City Youth Court* case. A youth court unable to make a short detention

and training order because the defendant is under the age of 15 and not a persistent offender should only rarely commit to the Crown Court. The fact that a
detention and training order is not available, as Gage J. states, indicates that Parliament intended that generally a non-custodial sentence should be passed.

28   These extracts, approved by Lord Woolf C.J. and Kay L.J., set out the approach
to be taken by a youth court when faced with a decision whether to commit a
defendant under the age of 15 for possible sentence pursuant to the provisions
of s.91. What, in our view, this line of cases does not do is to restrict the powers
of the Crown Court when it has to sentence a defendant once committed to it. We
take the view that nothing in this line of authorities affects the decision of this
Court in *S-J.R and DG*.

29   We turn now to the third line of authorities. In *L.M.* [2002] EWCA Crim 3047;
[2003] 2 Cr.App.R.(S.) 26 (p.124) the then 14-year-old appellant had been committed to the Crown Court for an offence against s.18 of the Offences against the
Person Act 1861. At the Crown Court, the appellant, by now 15, was convicted of
an offence against s.20. He was not a persistent offender. In the light of the provisions of s.100(2)(a) of the 2000 Act, the court had the power, the appellant now
being 15, to sentence him to a DTO. Having been convicted of an offence against
s.20, s.91 had no application. The judge passed a DTO for a period of 18 months.
Had the appellant originally been charged only with the offence against s.20 he
would have been dealt with by a youth court and would probably have been convicted before he reached the age of 15. Giving the judgment of this Court, H.H.
Judge Gordon said:

> "5. The learned judge, in sentencing, recognised that the court was placed
> in a dilemma and expressed herself as the 'troubled being by the way in
> which the court's powers are limited in a case such as this.' She went on
> to express the view that it would be wrong in principle not to impose a cus-
> todial sentence in view of the appellant's behaviour and its dreadful
> effects."

30   H.H. Judge Gordon went on to say:

> "7. Section 100(2)(a) is not the only provision to make a court's sentencing
> powers dependant upon the date of conviction rather than the date of the
> offence. Section 93 (6) of the same Act is another example. There is a
> clear logic in such provisions, for instance, where offences committed as
> a teenager are not discovered for many years but the provisions are also, a
> cause of difficulties that have troubled the Courts in a series of cases start-
> ing, for these purposes, with the case of *Danga* (1992) 13 Cr.App.R.(S.) 408.
> That case, and subsequent authorities, were all reviewed in a judgment of a
> division of this Court, given by Dyson LJ, in the case of *Ghafoor* on 19th
> July 2002. The appellant, in that case, had committed an offence of riot
> when he was 17. Had he been 17 at the date of conviction the maximum sen-
> tence would have been one of 2 years. As it was, by then he was 18, he

pleaded guilty and he was sentenced to a term of four-and-a-half years in a young offender institution. Having completed his review of the authorities, Dyson LJ said, at paragraph 30:

'For reasons that we shall explain, we are quite satisfied . . . that the sentence passed by the judge was wrong in principle. If he had applied the guidance given in the line of cases to which we have referred, he could not properly have passed a sentence in excess of 18 months on facts of this case.'

Then at paragraph 31:

'The approach to be adopted where a defendant crosses a relevant age threshold between the date of the commission of the offence and the date of conviction should now be clear. The starting point is the sentence that the defendant would have been likely to receive if he had been sentenced at the date of the commission of the offence. It has been described as 'a powerful factor'. That is for the obvious reason that, as Mr Emmerson points out, the philosophy of restricting sentencing powers in relation to young persons reflects both (a) society's acceptance that young offenders are less responsible for their actions and therefore less culpable than adults, and (b) the recognition that, in consequence, sentencing them should place greater emphasise on rehabilitation, and less on retribution and deterrence than in the case of adults. It should be noted that the 'starting point' is not the maximum sentence that could lawfully have been imposed, but the sentence that the offender would have been likely to receive.

32. So the sentence that would have been passed at the date of the commission of the offence is a 'power factor'. It is the starting point, and other factors may have to be considered. But in our judgment, there have to be good reasons for departing from the starting point. An examination of the authorities to which we have been referred shows that, although the court has looked at other factors to see whether there should be a departure from the starting point, it is not obvious that there has in fact been a departure in any of them. This serves to demonstrate how powerful a factor the starting point is. That is because justice requires for there to be a good reason to pass a sentence higher than would have been passed at the date of the commission of the offence.

33. That is not to say that the starting point may not be tempered somewhat in certain cases. We have in mind in particular cases where there is a long interval between the date of commission of the offence and the date of conviction. By the date of conviction, circumstances may have changed significantly. The offender may now have been revealed as a dangerous criminal, whereas at the date of the offence that was not so. By the date of conviction, the tariff for the offence in question may have increased. These are factors that can be taken into account, and can, in an appropriate

case properly lead to the passing of a sentence somewhat higher than the sentence that would have been passed at the date of the commission of the offence.

34. But in a case such as the present where the date of conviction is only a few months after the date of the offence, we think that it would rarely be appropriate to pass a longer sentence than that which would have been passed at the date of the offence.'"

31   The Court in *L.M.* went on to hold that the same principles applied in the appellant's case, adding:

"Indeed, the sequence of events that caused the conviction to be recorded after the appellant's 15th birthday rather than before, none of which were within his control, provide a strong argument for following the usual course."

32   The Court held that a custodial sentence was not therefore appropriate. The sentence was quashed and for it was substituted a supervision order.

33   In *L.M.*, it was to the appellant's advantage to sentence him as if he had been convicted at the age of 14.

34   The present case is quite different. As we have said, the offence of robbery of which the appellant was convicted was such that the recorder was right to invoke the provisions of s.91. This Court now having decided that the appropriate length of the sentence is one of one year's detention, must that be a sentence of detention in a young offender institution ("YOI") under s.91 or can it be a sentence of one year DTO?

35   During the course of the hearing we asked the liaison probation officer, Mr Gardner, to help us as to the difference between the two regimes for a 15-year-old. He said a one-year DTO was more appropriate for a 15-year-old than a sentence of detention in a YOI. It would more likely achieve the rehabilitation of the appellant and the period of post-release supervision following a DTO is longer. In the light of that response, Mr Pinfold did not argue that the appellant would be "better off" if he received a sentence of detention in a YOI.

36   In those circumstances it seems to us right to pass a DTO for a period of one year. Section 100 gives the power to sentence a young person aged 15 at the time of conviction to a DTO even though he was 14 at the time of the offence. It follows that the recorder was wrong to conclude that the appellant did not qualify for a detention and training order (albeit understandably wrong in the light of the arguments presented to him).

37   In conclusion we stress that we are passing a sentence of a DTO for one year in rather unusual circumstances. But for the sentence passed on the co-defendant and, to a lesser extent, the exceptional personal mitigation enjoyed by the appellant, a longer sentence would have been inevitable.

R. v KC

Court of Appeal (Lord Justice Hooper, Mr Justice Grigson and Mr Justice Stanley Burnton): August 20, 2004

[2004] EWCA Crim 2361; [2005] 1 Cr.App.R.(S.) 97

Arson; Detention; Extended sentences; Manslaughter; Sentence length; Young offenders

1   *Long-term detention—manslaughter—manslaughter by boy aged 15—setting fire to contents of container while friend inside—friend unable to escape—length of term of detention*

2   Four years' detention under the Powers of Criminal Courts (Sentencing) Act 2000, s.91, imposed on a boy aged 15 for the manslaughter of his friend by setting fire to the contents of a container while his friend was inside, reduced to three years.

3   The appellant, aged 15 at the time of the offence, was convicted of manslaughter. The appellant and two other boys of the same age were playing on bicycles. They removed pallets and pieces of wood from a waste container in order to construct ramps on which to cycle. In the course of the play the second boy put the third boy's bicycle into the steel container; when the boy went into the container to retrieve his bicycle the appellant and second boy closed the door of the container and secured it with a chain. The two boys went to the top of the container and dropped narrow pieces of wood through a gap at the top of the door. The pieces of wood became wedged in the gap between the door and the frame of the container causing the chain to become taut. A short while later the appellant lit a piece of paper and posted the paper into the container through the narrow gap. A small fire started inside the container. The appellant shouted to the victim to put it out and the boys attempted to release the door of the container. They were unable to do so. The contents of the container caught fire and the appellant summoned the fire brigade. The fire brigade were able to release the third boy using bolt croppers but by that time he had suffered extensive burns and died the following morning. Sentenced to four years' detention under the Powers of Criminal Courts (Sentencing) Act 2000, s.91.

Held, the verdict of manslaughter had been returned on the basis of manslaughter by an unlawful act, the unlawful act being arson, being reckless as to life. It followed that the jury was satisfied that the appellant realised there was a risk to the life of the deceased when he dropped the lit paper into the container. He did not think that the risk would materialise because he believed that the container could easily be opened. It was submitted that the sentence was manifestly excessive and did not take account of the mitigating factors, including the fact that the appellant thought that he could open the door of the container. The

Court had given anxious consideration to the case and had reached the conclusion that the sentence ought to have been three years' detention.

H5   **References:** long term detention—manslaughter, *Current Sentencing Practice* E4

H6   *P. Lodder Q.C.* for the appellant.
B. Foster Q.C. for the Crown.

JUDGMENT

1   **Hooper L.J.:**   KC was born on June 10, 1988. He is now 16 years old and has no previous convictions. On April 1, 2004, following a trial, he was sentenced by Henriques J. to four years' detention under s.91 of the Powers of Criminal Courts (Sentencing) Act 2000 for an offence of manslaughter. He was found by the jury not guilty on a second count of false imprisonment. There was a co-defendant, LG, born on March 30, 1987. He was also found not guilty on that count, the only count which he faced.

2   On the evening of July 15, 2003 the appellant, then aged just 15, and LG, were playing with the 15-year-old deceased, Michael Temperley, on their bicycles at the rear of a retail park. They were friends and attended school together. They had removed pallets and pieces of wood from a waste container in order to construct ramps to cycle over. That container was a large metal box which was about two-thirds full of paper, wood and cardboard. Access to the container was gained through a large steel door at one end of the container. That door had a small chain attached to it. By dropping a pin through a lug mounted on the side, the door could be secured shut. However, when secured in this way there remained a narrow gap between the door and the frame of the container.

3   As part of their game the boys had hit the deceased over the head with bits of polystyrene and were luring each other into the container and then locking the door. At some point LG put the deceased's bicycle in the container whilst the appellant restrained the deceased. When he was released the deceased went into the container to retrieve his bicycle and they then closed the door on him and secured it with the chain. The two boys went on top of the container and dropped pieces of wood through the narrow gap at the top of the door in an attempt to hit the victim's feet. Unbeknown to them those pieces of wood became wedged in the gap between the door and the frame of the container, causing that chain to become too taut to be capable of release. The count of false imprisonment upon which both the appellant and LG were found not guilty related to that part of the events.

4   A short while later the appellant lit a piece of paper and despite being told "no" or "don't know" when he asked two other boys and LG whether he should put the lit paper into the container, he "posted" the lit paper into the container through the narrow gap. A small fire started inside the container. The appellant shouted to the victim to put it out and he and LG immediately made frantic efforts to release the chain. Those efforts were unsuccessful because, as we have said, the door had, unknown to them, now become jammed as a result of the dropping of the pieces of

wood. Very quickly the contents of the container were ablaze. They stopped passers-by to assist them. The appellant summoned the fire brigade. The victim was making frantic pleas to be freed, but by the time the fire brigade arrived he was silent and smoke was pouring from the top and side of the container. The firemen cut the chain with bolt croppers and brought the deceased out. By now he had suffered 30 per cent burns and although efforts were made to resuscitate him, he was certified dead in the early hours of the morning. In the words of the mother of the deceased: "Our whole family has been completely devastated by the loss of our son."

The appellant was arrested at the scene. When interviewed he confirmed that they had been playing near the container and said that at one point he had been locked in the skip himself. He added that after the victim had been locked in the skip he had appeared unconcerned and had smoked a cigarette. He stated he had then lit a piece of paper and dropped it on the ground outside the skip next to the gap where a piece of cardboard was sticking out. He gave an explanation as to how the contents caught fire and said that the victim had tried to stamp the flames out. He said he could see smoke coming from the skip and thought it came from where the victim had flicked his cigarette. He added as the fire spread the victim was shouting and he and others had tried to release the chain to no avail. He stressed he did not put the lighted paper in the skip but dropped it on the ground next to the skip. It is clear that the jury did not accept much of the appellant's account of how the fire started.

We asked both Mr Lodder Q.C. and Mr Foster Q.C., who appeared at the trial and who appeared before us, to explain the nature of the manslaughter charge. We were told that it was manslaughter by an unlawful act, the unlawful act being arson reckless as to life. It follows that by the jury's verdict they were satisfied that the appellant realised there was a risk to the life of the deceased as a result of what he did when he dropped the lit piece of paper into the container. Nonetheless, it is right to add that he did not think that that risk would materialise because he believed that the door would easily be opened, as it had before.

We turn to the pre-sentence report which was before Henriques J. In para.3.1 the author states that the appellant "has an unblemished record and therefore has no pattern of his offending behaviour." The appellant lived with his parents and two younger brothers. According to the appellant's parents, K grew up with little problems, he attended school regularly, had appropriate peers who lived nearby and seemed happy and content. In the words of the author of the report:

"They told me that he had has continued in this pattern without any major problems".

In para.3.3 we find the following:

"K and his family have enormous compassion for the victim's family who are well-known to them, particularly as K and Michael were good friends."

The appellant was attending a comprehensive school. There was a report of struggling academically but no reports of truancy and reports that his behaviour within school was appropriate. He was due to sit his GCSEs at the time of sentencing and according to a subsequent report he completed those GCSEs whilst in detention following conviction. Paragraph 3.5 reads:

"Prior to this offence K told me that when he is not at school he spends his time with his family and friends. He has constructive activity and his peers appear to be pro-social and of his own age . . . Mrs C told me that she is always aware of K's whereabouts and he abides by rules such as the time to return home and restricted areas."

There was, according to the author of the report, no question of substance misuse and neither Mr or Mrs C had any concerns about that. Indeed, the appellant was tested for substance abuse on the night of this offence and the tests proved negative. That confirmed the denials by the appellant of any usage of drugs. Paragraphs 4.1 and 4.2 of that report read as follows:

"4.1. KC has no previous convictions and therefore no pattern of offending behaviour is identified. Given the circumstances surrounding this offence and the many protective factors within K's life I assess the risk of him offending in a similar vein as low. The only risk factor identifiable at present that may contribute to future offending is his reckless behaviour and failure to think through the consequences of his actions. Positive factors include his supportive family network and friends that live close by and his good level of remorse and regret for being involved in this offence. Also he has appropriate education and attends school regularly and he has inspirations for the future.

4.2. Given that K has no antecedents, has a high level of remorse and has a good understanding of the seriousness of this offence and the terrible and tragic consequences of such behaviour, it is my assessment that he is at a low risk of serious harm to the public."

9   We turn to the sentencing remarks. Henriques J. in passing sentence said:

"KC, you are 15 years of age and you stand convicted by a jury, on the clearest and most compelling evidence, of the very serious crime of manslaughter.

You lit a piece of paper, and by way of showing off to two other boys, strangers, and to your friend, LG, you asked this question, 'Shall I hoy it in?', meaning, shall I throw it into that container. The two strangers both said 'No', L either said 'No', or, 'I don't know'.

You decided to hoy the lighted paper into the secured metal container, which was some two-thirds full of paper, wood and cardboard, in which your friend, Michael Temperley was then imprisoned. You knew exactly what was in the skip, and you are quite old enough, and bright enough, to have appreciated the risk to which you were exposing Michael.

Your mother described you as, 'Not the brightest button', but you were due to sit six GCSE examinations. I recognise, of course, that you believed you could very swiftly open the skip door and release Michael.

At the same time, having observed the evidence during a trial that lasted for some eight days, I have concluded that you were showing off to those three boys, and in relation to Michael there was a clear element of bullying.

In his absence, and before he had arrived, you were shut in the container by LG for a short time. You saw what was in the container, and you did not enjoy yourself being in the container. When Michael arrived both you and L took up pieces of polystyrene, and you hit him over the head. Then, after L threw Michael's hat into the container, both of you tried to shut him in. He struggled, and he prevented you at that stage from closing the door.

Later, L took Michael's bike to the skip, whilst you held Michael back by the shoulders. Once L had placed the bike in the skip you released Michael, and when he went to recover his bike you attempted to close the door on him. He used part of a chair to prevent the door being closed, but two onto one you removed the chair back and were able to fasten the door.

You were found not guilty of false imprisonment, and I accept that at this point you believed that you were playing a game, and you believed that in reality, notwithstanding his reaction, that Michael consented to being in the skip. I will be faithful to the jury's verdict.

Thereafter, you started to throw wood into the skip, through the gap between the door. You told the police that you did that just to scare him.

If that bordered on bullying, what you did when you hoyed the flaming paper into the skip was unqualified bullying. I unhesitatingly accept that you thought you could open the door, and that you had good reason for thinking that. I equally accept that you did everything in your power to open the door. I also accept that you were exposed to the most traumatic and terrifying ordeal, which you will never put out of your mind. I bear in mind the distress that you have caused every member of your own family. I accept that you yourself are now grief ridden, and I accept that you are most unlikely ever to offend.

It is, however, a tragedy that in this court you have been unable to accept responsibility for what you did. Your accusations of G, C and L were shameful. You accused them of barefaced lies, and then you asserted that it was Michael who was the author of his own death. The sentence will not be increased by reason of your defence, but you have forfeited the real opportunity of earning for yourself a very meaningful discount from the sentence which I must pass.

I have considered all sentencing options, including the intensive supervision and surveillance programme that has been so well and graphically described to me by Julie Turner, who gave evidence.

A boy of 15 has lost his life; a loving family have lost Michael. This offence is so serious that no method of dealing with you other than detention is appropriate.

In passing sentence I have regard to your welfare, as I must. You are receiving credit for your youth, and for your positive good character. I have in mind the evidence given by three witnesses during your trial, I have in mind the burdensome period whilst you have been on bail, the fact that you believed you could open the door, your attempts to open the door and the trauma of the experience.

The sentence I pass is shorter than it would have been had you been convicted of false imprisonment. You will be detained, pursuant to s.91 of the Powers of Criminal Courts (Sentencing) Act, for a period of four years."

10   For the purposes of this appeal and in accordance with the order made by the single judge who granted permission, we have been provided with a report by Aycliffe Secure Services dated August 16. That report describes how the appellant was admitted from Newcastle Crown Court to Heron House, a ten-bedded mixed sex unit which holds predominantly persistent young offenders sent via the criminal courts—in other words it holds young offenders who are very different from this appellant.

11   The report describes how the appellant would tend to gravitate towards the staff for conversation, feeling that he was out of place and had nothing in common with those who were detained with him. In the words of the report:

> ". . . he stands out from the group as he has no experience of offending behaviour and has no experiences with any of the individual group members."

The report continues:

> "K has coped well with the occasional taunting he receives from the other young people for his continued good behaviour towards members of staff. It is fair to say that whilst K does complete all programmed group work he finds it a struggle to stay motivated as he has little to identify with the subject of the work on the other individuals within the group. Whilst this may be a source of frustration for K, he is always impeccably behaved within all of the intervention group work sessions.
> **Conclusion**
> Whilst K has settled more into the secure environment, it is fair to say that he stands out from his peers and living in a frantic group with whom he has nothing in common has an effect on his emotional well being. He is locked up at a crucial stage of his adolescent development having been separated from a close knit network of family and friends both within the home and educational settings. This separation is compounded by the other young people he is forced to reside with, with whom he has little in common and the time spent in his room to reflect upon his difficulties (all young people are locked in their rooms at 9.30 pm until 7.00 am the next day).
> K has coped due to a number of factors namely;
> • A supportive network of friends and family.
> • By keeping himself occupied through much of the day ie education work and Duke of Edinburgh Award Scheme.
> • Whilst K has suffered through the cessation of mainstream schooling, he continued to study for his GCSEs which proved a positive distraction.

● The positive relationships built with the members of staff within Heron House.

Despite the above obstacles K presents as a mature, well adjusted individual who is still coming to terms with living away from home in a communal, secure environment. He has yet to really face the difficult issue of the bereavement of his best friend but does not seem emotionally/mentally ready to address this currently.

K is fully complying with all that is required of him but still presents as a very vulnerable young person, at times overwhelmed by a sense of hopelessness for the future, given the separation those he loves and the perception that pre-arranged educational/vocational plans are indefinitely on hold. It is important not to lose sight of the fact K is adapting to major change in an important stage of his young life arising from a tragic set of circumstances in which he also lost a close friend."

12   We turn now to the grounds of appeal. It is submitted that the sentence was manifestly excessive and that insufficient account was taken of the following mitigating factors: the fact that the appellant believed he could open the door to the container and that it was in his power to do so, the trauma suffered by the appellant himself, the fact that he was grief-ridden and was, as the author of the pre-sentence report said, most unlikely to re-offend. It is further submitted that the judge gave insufficient weight to the fact that what happened was all part of a game and that the appellant was not guilty of false imprisonment.

13   In particular it is said that the learned judge erred in describing what happened when the paper was lit as "unqualified bullying". We asked Mr Foster whether he had used the word "bullying" and he told us that he had not. It is right to say that there was no evidence in the pre-sentence report that this appellant had been a bully. It is also right to say that his conduct whilst in detention shows no indication that he is a bully. If anything it shows the risks that he may be bullied. Henriques J. heard the trial and we would be unwilling to dissent from those words, although it is right to say that we have some concern about them. However, we do not see that the use of those words, whether rightly or wrongly, affect the outcome of this appeal.

14   Neither counsel put any authority before us. That is understandable. The learned judge was faced with a particularly difficult case. There is no doubt that the appellant had available to him all the mitigation that he could possibly have had, other than, and importantly, the fact that he chose to contest the case by pleading not guilty.

15   Sentencing a young man for causing the death of a much-loved son is extremely difficult. We have given very anxious consideration to the case and we have reached the conclusion, as we said at the end of the hearing, that the sentence ought to have been one of three years' detention. The jury found that the appellant committed the offence of arson being reckless as to whether the life of Michael Temperley would be endangered. In our view that finding and the fact that Michael died required a custodial sentence of substantial length, albeit

for someone as young as this appellant. Nonetheless, we take the view that a sentence of three years' detention is sufficient.

R. v TONY JASON LAZARUS

COURT OF APPEAL (Lord Justice May, Mr Justice Eady and Mr Justice Hughes): August 24, 2004

[2004] EWCA Crim 2297; [2005] 1 Cr.App.R.(S.) 98

Assets; Confiscation orders; Consecutive sentences; Drug trafficking; Justice; Proceeds of crime

H1   *Confiscation order—Drug Trafficking Act 1994—basis of plea accepted by Crown—whether there would be a serious risk of injustice if statutory assumptions were made in confiscation proceedings*

H2   **Editor's note:** where a basis of plea is put forward by the defendant and accepted by the Crown, there is no serious risk of injustice in making the assumptions required by the Drug Trafficking Act 1994, s.4, if the assumptions are not inconsistent with the basis of plea.

H3   The appellant pleaded guilty to one count of being concerned in the supply of cocaine between December 2002 and May 2003, and six additional counts of possession of drugs found on particular dates. A search warrant was executed at the appellant's house and police found five or six packages containing either heroin or cocaine, and £13,880 in cash. He was released on bail and was later seen driving a car although disqualified. When he was seen by police officers, he ran off, and a further small quantity of cocaine was found in the car. A further search of his house led to the discovery of six grammes of cocaine and crack cocaine and £600 in cash in a safe. The appellant pleaded guilty on the basis that for about six months before his first arrest he had offered his home as a place of safe storage for money generated by drug dealing by somebody else, and that the £13,880 found on the first occasion was money being kept there by him for the dealer. He asserted that the drugs found were for his own use. Sentenced to a total of four-and-a-quarter years' imprisonment, with a confiscation order under the Proceeds of Crime Act 2002 in the amount of £20,802.

H4   **Held,** there was nothing wrong with the total sentence of four-and-a-quarter years. The confiscation order was made under the Proceeds of Crime Act 2002. It had now been realised that as the period specified in the first count on the indictment began on December 1, 2002, the Proceeds of Crime Act 2002 did not apply. At the relevant time, there were in force the very similar provisions of the Drug Trafficking Act 1994. Had it been appreciated that the 1994 Act applied, the procedure which followed and the steps of reasoning required of the judge would have been substantially the same. The Court had power under the Criminal Appeal Act 1968, s.11(3), to substitute for the order made under the Proceeds of Crime Act 2002 such order as the court below had power to make under the under the Drug Trafficking Act 1994, so long as the appellant was as a result not dealt with more severely than he was in the court below. It was accepted on behalf of the appellant that this course was open to the court, subject to any argument on the merits. The argument on the merits was that the statutory assumptions arising under the Drug Trafficking Act 1994, s.4, could not be made, given the basis of plea, without serious risk of injustice to the appellant. Under the Drug Trafficking Act 1994, s.4(3), and the Proceeds of Crime Act 2002, s.10, when the court was assessing the defendant's benefit, it was required to make a statutory assumption that any property in his hands at any time during the period of six years before the commencement of the proceedings represented the proceeds of drug trafficking or crime as the case might be. Under both Acts, the court was required not to make that assumption if either it was shown to be incorrect, or there would be a serious risk of injustice if the assumption was made. In the Crown Court, the issue in the confiscation proceedings was whether substantial sums passing through the defendant's bank account over the six-year period were or were not on the balance of probabilities other than the proceeds of drug trafficking. The defendant gave evidence, which the judge disbelieved. Over the six-year period, the relevant sums amounted to £51,345. It was agreed that only the £11,591 passed through the account during the period covered by count one of the indictment. For the appellant, it was submitted that because his basis of plea was accepted, it followed that there must be a serious risk of injustice if the statutory assumption was made in relation to any money passing through his hands other than during the six-month period when he admitted he was involved in the supply of cocaine by storing the money for the dealer. A similar point was addressed in *Lunnon* [2005] 1 Cr.App.R.(S.) 24 (p.111). In *Lunnon* the appellant pleaded guilty on the basis that he had played a limited part in handling the drug and that he had derived no financial benefit from the transaction, and that prior to the particular incident of importation with which the appellant was charged, he had had no previous involvement in drug trafficking at all. The Crown accepted the basis of plea without qualification. Accordingly, in that case the Court held that there was a serious risk of injustice if the statutory assumptions were made against the appellant, to the reverse effect of the basis of plea which the Crown had accepted. In the present case, however, the appellant admitted being involved in the supply of cocaine for a period of six months prior to his arrest. The admission left wholly open the question whether there had been any benefit from drug trafficking before that period. The Court was unable to agree that the Crown's acceptance of that basis of plea carried with it the further assertion that the appellant had never done it before. The Crown had not been invited to address that point. There was no concession by the Crown that the defendant had never previously been involved with drugs. A defendant would normally be charged on an indictment with a specific offence. It might be charged as having been committed on a single day, or as having been committed over a defined period, but in the latter case, the period would normally be a great deal less than six years. The confiscation order was not limited to the proceeds of the offence which was charged on the indictment. The effect of the Act was that any conviction for a drug trafficking offence opened the confiscation inquiry into property which had passed through the defendant's hands, not simply during the period of the offence, but for six years prior to the commencement of the proceedings. It was then for the defendant to show on the balance of probabilities that such property was not the proceeds of crime or drug trafficking as the case might be. It was also the duty of the court to consider whether there was a serious risk of injustice if the statutory assumption was made. The scheme of the Drug Trafficking Act 1994 made clear that such risk of injustice did not and could not rise simply because the assets in question were unrelated to the charge on the indictment. The confiscation scheme was subject to rules quite different from those which governed the laying of charges on an indictment. When laying a charge on an indictment, the Crown could charge only what it could prove to the criminal standard. In the case of confiscation proceedings, the onus was on the defendant to the civil standard. The defendant could be ordered to provide information, which he could not be required to do when the offence itself was in question. It followed that it would often be the case that offending which could not be proved to the criminal standard in support of a count on the indictment fell to be considered when it came to confiscation. It would often happen that a defendant fell to be sentenced on information and evidence which was quite different from that which was relevant to subsequent confiscation proceedings. *Lunnon* and the present case were salutary reminders that care needed to be taken by the Crown when considering a proffered basis of plea. In some cases the Crown might be in a position to make the kind of express acknowledgement that was made in *Lunnon*, that the indicted offence was the defendant's first involvement in relevant crime, knowing that that acknowledgment would be carried forward into confiscation proceedings. In other cases, the Crown might be able to say no more than that for the purposes of sentence it did not dispute a particular assertion made by a defendant, but that it could not say what information might arise in any subsequent confiscation proceedings. That was likely to be true when at the time of the consideration of the basis of plea, the financial inquiry had not yet been undertaken. The Crown ought , as a matter of good practice when responding to a basis of plea which was advanced in a case where confiscation proceedings might follow, to bear in mind the question whether any concession now made would apply to the confiscation inquiry. *Lunnon* showed that an admission made by the Crown might be withdrawn subsequently, but it was generally undesirable that a defendant should not know from the outset how far the Crown was prepared to go. In both the Drug Trafficking Act 1994 and the Proceeds of Crime Act 2002 there was always the possibility that the court might of its own motion decide that a confiscation enquiry should be made. In the present case the appellant knew perfectly well from shortly after the acceptance of his plea that the Crown was seeking to rely on the statutory assumptions and he had ample opportunity to rebut them. It followed that there was no injustice to him and that the judge was right to hold there was no unfairness in making the statutory assumptions. The order made under the Proceeds of Crime Act 2002 would be quashed and an order in the same amount would be substituted under the Drug Trafficking Act 1994.

15   **Case cited:**
Lunnon [2005] 1 Cr.App.R.(S.) 24 (p.111)

16   **References:** confiscation orders, *Current Sentencing Practice* J7, *Archbold* 5–
52

17   **Commentary:** [2005] Crim.L.R. 63

18   *M. Tregilgas-Davey* for the appellant.
C. Quinlan for the Crown.

JUDGMENT

1   **Hughes J.:**   This applicant pleaded guilty at Swindon Crown Court to offences associated with dealing in and possession of drugs. He renews his application for leave to appeal against, first, sentences totalling four-and-a-quarter years' imprisonment, and secondly, a confiscation order in the sum of £20,802.04.

2   The defendant was twice arrested. First, on May 7, 2003 a search warrant was executed at his house. In the house were found five or six packages containing either heroin or cocaine in batches which were worth between £100 to £200 apiece. He also had a safe in his house and in it was £13,880 in cash.

3   When he was interviewed the defendant said that the drugs were for his own use and that the money had been paid to him by way of advance instalments on the sale by him of a BMW motorcar. He did not at that stage say who the suggested purchaser was. He was granted bail.

4   On June 27 of the same year, about seven weeks later, he was seen driving a motorcar, although disqualified. Seeing the police he ran off, but in the car which he abandoned the police found a further small quantity of cocaine. That generated a second search of his house and there just under six grammes of cocaine and crack cocaine was found, worth about £700, together with a small quantity of cannabis. There was another £600 in the safe and some electronic scales.

5   In interview he repeated the story about the intended sale of the motorcar and this time named the anticipated purchaser. The story about the sale of the car, however, proved to be a false one which fell apart and by the time of the plea and directions hearing in the Crown Court the defendant was accepting that the £13,880 found in the safe on the first occasion was the proceeds of drug trafficking, although he said it was drug trafficking which had not personally been carried out by him.

6   At that plea and directions hearing, and therefore at an early opportunity, the indictment was modified to take account of the admissions the defendant was now making and he pleaded guilty to seven counts. The first was one of being concerned in the supply of cocaine between December 1, 2002 and May 7, 2003, that is the date of the first arrest. The others were counts of simple possession of the drugs found on the occasion of each of the arrests. The

defendant entered those pleas and they were accepted by the Crown prosecutor then appearing for the Crown on a written basis. That was that for a period of about six months prior to the first arrest he had offered his home as a place of safe storage for money generated by drug dealing by somebody else and that the £13,880 found on the first occasion was such money being kept there by him for the man who was the dealer. The drugs found, he asserted, were for his own use and had been provided to him by the dealer, together with some money, as consideration for the storage of the dealer's funds.

7   The first question for us accordingly is whether sentences totalling four-and-a-quarter years were arguably either wrong in principle or manifestly excessive for those offences. The judge passed sentences of three-and-a-half years for the principal offence of being concerned in the supply of cocaine in the manner which the defendant admitted, and he passed shorter sentences amounting to nine months consecutive for the various offences of possession of the drugs.

8   We accept that it will often, although not necessarily always, be appropriate to distinguish in sentencing between a man who is a dealer on his own account and one who gives assistance in one of a number of ways, whether by storing the drugs or moving them about or otherwise. That said, the banker (such as this defendant was) is providing a significant service to a drug dealer. He is protecting him against the attentions both of the police and of others who might steal his ill-gotten gains. He is making it easier and safer for the drug dealer to deal. This drug dealer, whoever he was, was operating on a more than minimal scale if he had approximately £14,000 capital to keep at one time. His sentence, if he had been caught, would have been, we suspect, something in the general region of seven to eight years if he had been tried, perhaps four-and-a-half years or five years on a plea of guilty. In that context it is plain that there is nothing arguably wrong with three-and-a-half years for the banker.

9   Mr Tregilgas-Davey submits that consecutive sentences were wrong in principle for the possession of the drugs because, he says, those drugs were payment for the storage of the money and thus the possession was part and parcel of the supplying offence. We do not necessarily agree. The defendant was himself in possession of drugs, itself a criminal offence. But whether or not there is force in that submission in relation to the drugs which were found on the occasion of the first arrest, it cannot begin to apply to those found seven weeks later. The first count, being concerned in supply, covered only the period up to May 7, the first arrest. The events of June 27 showed that independently of any arrangement with the supplier, the drug dealer, this defendant was in possession of class A drugs in by no means minimal quantities seven weeks later. Moreover that was an offence which he committed when on bail. A consecutive sentence was fully justified for it, if not inevitable. Overall, standing back, we see nothing wrong with four-and-a-quarter years. It was a sentence within the bracket available to the sentencing judge and in relation to that sentence the application for leave to appeal is refused.

10   The confiscation order was ostensibly made under the Proceeds of Crime Act 2002. Everybody in the court below proceeded on the basis that that was the right statute. We should say that we are very grateful to Mr Quinlan, who did not appear

for the Crown below, for drawing attention to the fact that because the drug trafficking count (count 1) spanned a period which began on December 1, 2002, the
Proceeds of Crime Act did not apply. It applies only to offences committed on or
after March 24, 2003. Plainly nobody appreciated this in the court below, including the Crown which prepared detailed financial submissions couched in terms of
the Proceeds of Crime Act. It follows that the order under that Act cannot stand
and for that reason we grant leave to appeal that order.

11   There were, however, in force the very similar provisions of the Drug Trafficking Act 1994. In this case, had it been appreciated that it was the 1994 Act which
applied, the procedure which followed and the steps of reasoning required of the
judge would, it is accepted, have been substantially the same. We have power
under s.11(3) of the Criminal Appeal Act 1968 to substitute for the order under
the Proceeds of Crime Act such order which the court below had power to
make under the 1994 Act, so long as the appellant is not as a result dealt with
more severely than he was below. Sensibly and realistically it is accepted on
behalf of the appellant that, subject to the submission which is made on his behalf
as to the merits of the confiscation order, that is a course which we ought to take.

2   The argument on the merits is that the statutory assumptions arising under s.4
of the Drug Trafficking Act cannot be made given the accepted basis of plea without serious risk of injustice to the appellant. Under both the 1994 Act and the 2002
Act, ss.4(3) and s.10 respectively, when the court is assessing the defendant's
benefit it is required to make a statutory assumption that any property in his
hands at any time during the period of six years before the commencement of proceedings represented the proceeds of drug trafficking or crime, as the case may
be. However under both Acts the court is required not to implement that assumption if either it is shown to be incorrect, the burden falling upon the defendant
upon the balance of probabilities, or there would be a serious risk of injustice
if the assumption were made.

3   In the court below the issue of fact in the confiscation hearing was whether
quite substantial sums passing over the six year period through the defendant's
bank account were or were not shown on the balance of probabilities to be
other than drug related. The defendant gave evidence about it. The learned
judge heard his evidence and he disbelieved the explanations for these sums
which he advanced. Over the six year period those sums amounted to £51,345
and some pence. The judge's conclusion was supported by the fact that within
a day or so of his first arrest the defendant had effectively emptied his bank
account by transferring £11,000 to his father, who in turn moved it on to two different accounts. There can be and there is no suggestion that that determination
by the judge could be successfully appealed. However, of that £51000-odd it is
agreed that only the sum of £11,591 (and some pence) passed through the account
during the six month period of the charge which formed count 1 in the indictment.
What Mr Tregilgas-Davey here does is to renew the submission which he made to
the judge, which is that because the basis of the defendant's plea was accepted it
follows that there must be a serious risk of injustice if the statutory assumption is
made in relation to any money passing through the defendant's hands other than

during the six month period when he admitted that he was involved in the supply of cocaine by storing the money for the dealer.

14   In *Lunnon* [2004] EWCA Crim 1125, a similar point was addressed. We are, we should say, very grateful to Mr Quinlan for the Crown for drawing that decision to our attention. In that case the defendant pleaded guilty to a conspiracy to supply cannabis, which count arose out of an importation of nearly two tonnes of that drug. There were a number of defendants. Lunnon was a minor member of the conspiracy and had played a limited part in the handling of the drug. The part which he had played was set out when his plea was tendered and accepted by the Crown. More, the Crown accepted the proposition that he had derived no financial benefit from the transaction, and critically, and further, the Crown made a further explicit concession: it explicitly accepted that prior to that single incident of importation charged on the indictment that the appellant (Lunnon) had had no previous involvement in drug trafficking at all. That admission by the Crown was not qualified in any way, nor was it limited to saying that he fell to be dealt with as a man with no previous convictions and nor was it ever withdrawn, though this Court recognised that it could have been. Accordingly, when it came to confiscation proceedings, this Court held in that case that the Crown's admission stood and created a serious risk of injustice if the statutory assumptions to reverse effect were then made against that appellant.

15   That however is not this case. In this case the defendant's written basis of plea began with this paragraph:

> "For a period of about six months prior to his arrest on 7th May 2003, Tony Lazarus had been involved in the supply of cocaine to others in the way detailed below."

It then went on to explain the manner in which he had been thus involved, namely by looking after money for the dealer.

16   That admission of an offence committed over a period of six months leaves wholly open the question whether there had been any benefit from drug trafficking before that period. Despite Mr Tregilgas-Davey's submissions, we are unable to agree that the Crown's acceptance of that basis of plea carried with it the further assertion "and we agree he had never done it before". That is not what the Crown was being invited to address. There was in this case no concession by the Crown that the defendant had never previously been involved in drugs.

17   It will, we observe, normally be the case that what is charged on the indictment is a specific offence. It may be charged as having been committed on a single day, or it may be charged as having been committed over a defined period, but it will nearly always, if the latter, be a period a great deal less than six years.

18   A confiscation order is not limited to the proceeds of the offence which is charged on the indictment. The effect of the Act is that any conviction for a relevant drug trafficking offence opens the confiscation enquiry into property which has passed through the defendant's hands, not simply during the period of the offence but for six years prior to the commencement of proceedings. It is then for the defendant to show on the balance of probabilities that such property was not the proceeds of crime or drug trafficking as the case may be. It is also

for the court to keep a careful eye on whether there is a serious risk of injustice if the statutory assumption is made. This obligation on the court is a critical part of the scheme of the Act and is essential if injustice is to be avoided—see *Benjafield* [2002] 2 Cr.App.R.(S.) 71 (p.313). But what the scheme of the Drug Trafficking Act makes clear is that such risk of injustice does not and cannot arise simply because the assets in question were unrelated to the charge on the indictment. The confiscation scheme is subject to rules quite different from those which govern the laying of charges upon an indictment. When laying a charge on an indictment the Crown can charge only what it can prove to the criminal standard of proof. In the case, however, of confiscation proceedings the onus is not on the Crown but on the defendant (to the civil standard). Moreover the defendant can be ordered to provide information, which is something which he cannot be required to do when proof of the offence is in question.

19   It follows that it will often be the case that offending which could not be proved to the criminal standard in support of counts on the indictment does fall to be considered when it comes to confiscation. It therefore follows also that although confiscation proceedings are a part, if a discrete part, of the sentencing process, it will often happen that a defendant falls to be sentenced upon information and evidence which is quite different from that which is relevant to subsequent confiscation proceedings. The justification for that position, as contained in the scheme of the Act, is that it only arises when first the defendant has been convicted to the criminal standard of a relevant offence.

20   *Lunnon* and this case are perhaps salutary reminders that some care needs to be taken by the Crown when considering proffered bases of plea. In some cases the Crown may be in a position to make the kind of express acknowledgment that was made in *Lunnon*, that the indicted offence is the defendant's first involvement in relecant crime, and to do so knowing that that acknowledgment will be carried forward into confiscation proceedings. In other cases, and we suspect in the majority, the Crown may be able to say no more than that for the purposes of sentence it does not and cannot dispute a particular assertion made by a defendant, but that it cannot say what information may arise in any subsequent confiscation proceedings. That, as it seems to us, is likely especially to be true if, as not infrequently happens, at the time of consideration of the basis of plea the financial enquiry has not yet been undertaken. We have no doubt that the Crown ought, as a matter of good practice, when responding to a basis of plea which is advanced in a case where confiscation proceedings might follow, to bear in mind the question whether it will be asking for a confiscation enquiry to be made and, if so, what if any admission is now being made which will apply to that enquiry. *Lunnon* shows that an admission made by the Crown at the sentencing stage might be withdrawn subsequently, but we would suggest that it is generally undesirable that a defendant should not know from the outset how far the Crown is prepared to go. In addition, of course, both Crown and defendants need to remember that under both the Drug Trafficking Act (s.2(1)) and the Proceeds of Crime Act (s.6(3)) there is always the possibility that the court of its own motion may decide that a confiscation enquiry should be made.

21   We should add this. In the present case the detailed financial reports put forward by the Crown shortly after the acceptance of plea make it abundantly clear that the Crown was seeking to rely on all the unexplained credits to the defendant's bank statements over the full six year period. The second of those financial statements followed a skeleton argument tendered on behalf of the defendant and responded to the submission which is made here. It follows that, unlike the defendant in *Lunnon*, this defendant knew perfectly well that the Crown was seeking to rely on the statutory assumptions, and he had ample opportunity to rebut them on the balance of probabilities by evidence if the truth was that the money was other than the proceeds of drugs.

22   There is accordingly no unfairness to him and it was not unjust to make against him the statutory assumptions required by the Drug Trafficking Act. If, contrary to our view, the Crown had ever made any concessions as to drug trafficking before the period covered by the indictment, those financial statements effectively and fairly withdrew it. The judge accordingly was right to hold that there was no unfairness to the defendant in making the statutory assumptions.

23   It follows that this appeal succeeds to this extent only. We quash the order made under the Proceeds of Crime Act and we substitute for it this order: pursuant to the Drug Trafficking Act 1994 the defendant's benefit from drug trafficking is determined at £51,345.12 and the amount recoverable is determined at £20,802.04.

[Paragraphs [24]–[39] have been omitted.]

R. v AMERICO PRACTICIO AFONSO, MOHAMMED SAJID, DOUGLAS ANDREWS

COURT OF APPEAL (Lord Justice Rose (Vice President, Court of Appeal Criminal Division), Mr Justice Owen and Mr Justice Mitting): September 9, 2004

[2004] EWCA Crim 2342; [2005] 1 Cr.App.R.(S.) 99

Drug addiction; Motive; Sentence length; Sentencing guidelines; Supply of drugs; Unemployment

H1   *Supplying Class A drugs—length of sentence for supply of small quantities by unemployed addicts*

H2   Guidance on sentencing certain categories of suppliers of Class A drugs.

H3   The Court heard three appeals together, to take the opportunity to give guidance in relation to the sentencing of a particular group of offenders within the category of retail suppliers of class A drugs identified in *Dhajit* [1999] 2 Cr.App.R.(S.) 142 and *Twisse* [2001] 2 Cr.App.R.(S.) 9 (p.37). The Court took account of the guidance given in relation to the making of drug treatment and testing orders in *Attorney General's Reference No.64 of 2003* [2004] 2 Cr.App.R.(S.)

22 (p.106). Nothing which the Court said was intended to affect the level of sentence indicated for offenders, whether or not themselves addicts, who for largely commercial motives, stocked and repeatedly supplied small quantities of Class A drugs to drug users. As was pointed out in those authorities, the scale and nature of dealing was important when deciding the level of sentence. Nor did anything the Court said call into question the propriety of the levels of sentence for the supply of drugs in the circumstances dealt with in *Attorney General's References Nos 13 to 18 of 2004* [2004] EWCA Crim 1885. There was a group of offenders who supplied Class A drugs, for whom the Court believed that the level of sentence indicated in *Djahit* and *Twisse*, mainly in the region of six years following a trial, was disproportionately high. The Court considered that some review was called for. These were offenders who were out-of-work drug addicts, whose motive was solely to finance the feeding of their own addiction, who held no stocks of drugs and who were shown to have made a few retail supplies of the drug to which they were addicted to undercover police officers. An unemployed addict had in practical terms, three means of financing his or her addiction—prostitution, theft or supplying others. Sentencers should recognise that in consequence, his or her culpability was likely to be less than that of many other suppliers. If they were shown only to have supplied undercover police officers and held no stock for supplying others, the harm caused by the conduct was comparatively slight. There would be some such adult and young offenders for whom drug treatment and testing orders would be appropriate. Where such an order was not appropriate, generally speaking adult offenders in the category which had been identified, if it was their first drugs supply offence, should following a trial be short-term prisoners, and following a plea of guilty at the first reasonable opportunity should be sentenced to a term of the order of two to two and a half years' imprisonment. For young offenders the custodial term was likely to be less. It had long been recognised that the Court had power to review existing tariffs upwards or downwards. It accordingly would not be appropriate, for the reasons explained in *Graham* [1999] 2 Cr.App.R.(S.) 312 at 315, for the Court's judgment to be regarded as a basis either for applications for leave to appeal against sentence out of time, or for references to the Court by the Criminal Cases Review Commission.

14 **Cases cited:**
Dhajit [1999] 2 Cr.App.R.(S.) 142, *Twisse* [2001] 2 Cr.App.R.(S.) 9 (p.37), *Attorney General's Reference No.64 of 2003* [2004] 2 Cr.App.R.(S.) 22 (p.106), *Graham* [1999] 2 Cr.App.R.(S.) 312 at 315
Attorney General's References Nos 13 to 18 of 2004 (Sharon Ann McKeown and others) [2005] Cr.App.R.(S.) 66 (p.300), *Iqbal* [2000] 2 Cr.App.R.(S.) 119, *Beevor* [2001] 2 Cr.App.R.(S.) 77 (p.362), *Day* [2000] 2 Cr.App.R.(S.) 312, *Barnett* [2003] 1 Cr.App.R.(S.) 24 (p.102), *Cargill* [1999] 2 Cr.App.R.(S.) 72, *Devaney* [2002] 1 Cr.App.R.(S.) 109 (p.438)

15 **Commentary:** [2005] Crim.L.R. 72

H6　　*Miss G. Gibbs* for the appellant Afonso.
　　　M. Magee for the Crown.
　　　A. Smith for the appellant Sajid.
　　　D. Munro for the Crown.
　　　J. Goodman for the appellant Andrews.
　　　Miss M. Dineen for the Crown.

JUDGMENT

1　　**Rose L.J.:**　We have heard three appeals together. There was to have been a fourth case, an Attorney General's application under s.36 of the Criminal Justice Act 1988, seeking to challenge as unduly lenient a deferment of sentence, but yesterday afternoon the Attorney General, wisely, withdrew that application. These appeals provide an opportunity for this Court to give guidance in relation to the sentencing of a particular group of offenders within the category of retail suppliers of Class A drugs identified in *Dhajit* [1999] 2 Cr.App.R.(S.) 142 and *Twisse* [2001] 2 Cr.App.R.(S.) 9 (p.37). We take into account the guidance given in relation to the making of drug treatment and testing orders in *Attorney General's Reference No.64 of 2003* [2004] 2 Cr.App.R.(S.) 22 (p.106).

2　　Nothing which we say is intended to affect the level of sentence indicated by *Djahit* and *Twisse* for offenders, whether or not themselves addicts, who, for largely commercial motives, stock and repeatedly supply to drug users small quantities of Class A drugs: and, as was pointed out in those authorities, as well as other authorities, the scale and nature of the dealing are important when deciding the level of sentence. Nor does anything we say call into question the propriety of the levels of sentence for the supply of drugs in the circumstances dealt with in *McKeown (Attorney General's References 13 to 18 of 2004)* [2004] EWCA Crim 1885; [2005] 1 Cr.App.R.(S.) 66 (p.300).

3　　But there is a group of offenders who supply Class A drugs for whom we believe that the level of sentence indicated by *Djahit* and *Twisse*, namely in the region of six years following a trial, is disproportionately high and we think some review is called for. These are the offenders who are out-of-work drug addicts, whose motive is solely to finance the feeding of their own addiction, who hold no stock of drugs and who are shown to have made a few retail supplies of the drug to which they are addicted to undercover police officers only. An unemployed addict has, in practical terms, three means of financing his or her addiction—prostitution, theft or supplying others; and sentencers should recognise that, in consequence, his or her culpability is likely to be less than that of many other suppliers. Furthermore, if they are shown only to have supplied undercover police officers and hold no stock for supplying others, the harm caused by their conduct is comparatively slight.

4　　There will be some such adult and young offenders for whom a drug treatment and testing order will be appropriate in the circumstances indicated in *Attorney General's Reference No.64 of 2003*, to which we have already referred. Where such an order is not appropriate, generally speaking, adult offenders in the category we have identified, if it is their first drugs supply offence, should, following a trial, be short-term prisoners, and, following a plea of guilty at the first reasonable opportunity, should be sentenced to a term of the order of two to two-and-a-half years' imprisonment. For young offenders, the custodial term is likely to be less.

5   It has long been recognised that this Court has power to review existing tariffs upwards or downwards: see, for example, *Avis* [1998] 2 Cr.App.R.(S.) 178, *Ollerenshaw* [1999] 1 Cr.App.R.(S.) 65; *Attorney General's Reference No.3 of 1996 (Latham)* [1997] 2 Cr.App.R.(S.) 10, and *Kefford* [2002] 2 Cr.App.R.(S.) 106 (p.495). It accordingly would not be appropriate, for the reasons explained in *Graham* [1999] 2 Cr.App.R.(S.) 312 at 315, for this judgment to be regarded as a basis either for applications for leave to appeal against sentence out of time or for references to this Court by the Criminal Cases Review Commission.

6   We turn to the three appeals before us. As will appear, none of these appellants falls entirely within the group which we have identified. All of them supplied undercover officers, were addicted to a Class A drug and had no previous drug convictions, but Andrews had stock, Afonso and Sajid supplied more than one Class A drug, and Sajid's appeal depends primarily on disparity with his co-accused.

7   Afonso, who is now 37, pleaded guilty at Peterborough Crown Court on January 16, 2004 to a number of offences for which he was sentenced by H.H. Judge Coleman. There were four counts of supplying heroin, for which he was sentenced to five years' imprisonment on each concurrently, two counts of supplying crack cocaine, for which he was likewise sentenced to five years' imprisonment concurrently and concurrently to the sentences for heroin offences, and there was a further offence of being concerned in supplying heroin, for which he was sentenced to three years' imprisonment concurrently. His total sentence was therefore five years' imprisonment, and orders were made for forfeiture and disposal of the drugs under s.27 of the Misuse of Drugs Act 1971. He appeals against sentence by leave of the single judge.

8   The facts were these. In September 2003, police officers mounted an undercover operation targeting drug dealers in Peterborough. On September 15, 2003, an undercover officer entered a centre for the homeless asking for someone called Lucy and he met the appellant. They left together. In the ensuing conversation, the appellant asked if the officer was looking for heroin. In consequence, two telephone calls were made, a third male was met, and the appellant, who on this occasion had drugs in his possession, handed the officer a wrap of heroin in exchange for £10.

9   Three days later, on the 18th, the appellant supplied the officer with £20 worth of cocaine, which he obtained for another man, and he also arranged for another man to supply the officer with heroin. The next day, the 19th, the appellant supplied the officer with crack obtained from another man; on the 23rd he supplied the officer with £10 worth of heroin obtained from another man, and he did precisely the same again on September 25.

10   In passing sentence, the learned judge said that there was an issue as to what the precise role of the appellant was. His offending had been brought about by his

£150-a-day addiction to crack cocaine, but he was trying to rid himself of that addiction, which was to his credit.

11   The operation in the course of which the appellant had been arrested was directed at a further drug-dealing operation which had sprung up as a consequence of the closing down of an earlier operation in Peterborough. The judge described what the appellant and others were doing as "filling the vacuum" that the closing down of the earlier operation had caused.

12   The learned judge referred to the appellant's record. He has no previous convictions in relation to drugs, but he has a substantial record over a four-year period from late 1999, particularly of offences of shoplifting, for which he has been dealt with by the magistrates in a variety of ways, including, in 2001, the making of a drug treatment and testing order—an order which was revoked a few months later when a one-month sentence of imprisonment was imposed. Thereafter, he continued to shoplift. During 2002 and early 2003, a community punishment order, a community rehabilitation order and then sentences of imprisonment, the longest of which was three months, were imposed. In the autumn of 2003, he continued to shoplift, having a knife with him on one occasion, and sentences of seven days' imprisonment and by way of a deferred sentence were passed. It was against that background that these offences were committed in September 2003.

13   A pre-sentence report obtained for magistrates in relation to offences of theft in September 2003 assessed the risk of him reoffending as high and continuing to remain high unless he addressed his drug addiction. An addendum to that report in January 2004 said that there was a high risk of reoffending if the defendant, who at that time had stopped taking drugs, reverted to his old ways when back in the community.

14   On Afonso's behalf, Miss Gibbs stresses the plea of guilty at the earliest opportunity, the absence of drugs convictions from the appellant's record and the continuing drug-free state of the appellant in prison. She says that the appellant made no profit from these dealings, which were prompted by his addiction, though she accepts, of course, that he dealt with two different kinds of Class A drugs. She points out that, because the appellant had himself been an addict for some three years, that is to say addicted to crack cocaine, he knew a number of suppliers and therefore it is unsurprising that he sought, for others in the supplies which he made to these officers, a number of different sources of the drugs. She points out the relatively short period over which these drugs were supplied; though it is to be observed that they were supplied on virtually a daily basis. It is also apparent, both from Miss Gibbs's submissions and from the evidence in relation to the appellant's dealings with a man in a Mitsubishi motorcar, that the appellant was close to at least one source of supply.

15   Miss Gibbs contrasts the present case *Djahit*, on the basis that there was no money in the appellant's possession, nor did he have any drug-dealing paraphernalia. She referred the court to *Beevor* [2001] 2 Cr.App.R.(S.) 77 (p.362), where a sentence of five years was reduced to four in relation to an appellant who had pleaded guilty to supplying heroin. He was an addict who had supplied two dif-

ferent drugs—heroin and cocaine—and he had stocks of both. His supplies were not limited to undercover police officers.

16   With the assistance of Mr Magee on behalf of the prosecution, Miss Gibbs referred the Court to the sentences passed on others with whom the appellant was involved. They were sentenced by a different judge. They were Abdezade, who received four years, having pleaded guilty on the day of trial; Pinto, who received four and a half years after a trial in relation to the supply of heroin; and Thomas, who had a crack house in relation to the activities from which he pleaded guilty and was sentenced to a term of five and a half years' imprisonment. Mr Magee accepts that all those three were higher in the chain than this appellant.

17   Mr Magee, in a written skeleton argument, helpfully referred the Court to a number of pertinent authorities about which we shall pass a few observations.

18   *Djahit*, to which reference has already been made, was an addict who had a stock of drugs, both at his flat and on his person, and he was in possession of a list of names and addresses, running to some 10 pages.

19   *Twisse* was dealing from home in Class A drugs, both heroin and cocaine, and did so for a period of months; and it is implicit, if not express, that he held stocks of drugs. He was addicted to heroin. He had a previous conviction for supplying drugs and he was subject to a conditional discharge in relation to a drugs offence at the time when he came to be sentenced.

20   *Iqbal* [2000] 2 Cr.App.R.(S.) 119, had a stock of cocaine and he was not an addict. Four-and-a-half years was said to be the upper limit of what could be described as the existing tariff in relation to him.

21   *Day* [2000] 2 Cr.App.R.(S.) 312, supplied cocaine, but he was also in possession of cannabis and ecstasy, and he was not an addict.

22   *Barnett* [2003] 1 Cr.App.R.(S.) 24 (p.102), was not an addict. He had previous convictions in relation to Class A drugs. He was on licence at the time of the offences and he did not make his plea at the first available opportunity.

23   *Cargill*, [1999] 2 Cr.App.R.(S.) 72, had a stock of crack and was "trying to make a living". He was not an addict and he behaved dangerously on arrest.

24   *Devaney* [2002] 1 Cr.App.R.(S.) 109 (p.478), supplied others in addition to police officers. He received orders on his mobile telephone. He had no previous convictions in relation to drugs but was described as a "career criminal". He was not addicted. He was on licence for other matters at the time of the relevant offences.

25   The submission which is made by Miss Gibbs, from which Mr Magee rightly does not dissent, is that, particularly in the light of the sentences passed on the other related defendants to which we have referred, a sentence of five years passed on this appellant was too long. We agree. That sentence is quashed and the appeal allowed in relation to all the five-year sentences of imprisonment in relation to heroin and crack cocaine. In substitution for those periods of five years the sentence will be one of three-and-a-half years' imprisonment concurrently in each case and concurrently also with the three-year sentence imposed for the offence of being concerned in supplying heroin. To that extent, his appeal is allowed.

26   We turn to Sajid. He was born in December 1979 and so is not quite 25. On February 27, 2004, at Warwick Crown Court, he pleaded guilty to a number of offences, for which he was sentenced by H.H. Judge Coles Q.C. on April 7, 2004. They were four offences of supplying heroin and three of supplying cocaine. The sentence passed on each count concurrently was one of three years three months' imprisonment. Orders were also made under s.27 of the Misuse of Drugs Act 1971. He appeals against sentence by leave of the single judge.

27   A co-accused called Jamil, who pleaded guilty to counts of supplying heroin and cocaine—the same counts to which the appellant had pleaded guilty—was sentenced to four years' imprisonment on each, that four years to run consecutively to a period of two months imposed for breach of licence.

28   The facts were that, in the autumn of 2003, an undercover operation was mounted in Leamington Spa targeting drug dealers. The appellant and Jamil at that time lived in Birmingham and went daily to Leamington Spa for the purpose of dealing in drugs.

29   On September 17, the officers telephoned a mobile number used by the appellant and Jamil and were told to go to a field, where they met Jamil, the appellant and another man. In consequence, Jamil supplied the officers with £20 worth of heroin and was seen to have six or seven more wraps in his possession.

30   The next day, the 18th, the officers met the men again at the same place and this time the appellant supplied £20 worth of heroin and crack.

31   On September 20, by arrangement, the officers went again to the same place and again met the same people. This time the appellant supplied them with £10 worth of crack and Jamil supplied £10 worth of heroin.

32   On October 2, the officers met the men again in a car park. Jamil supplied them with crack and another unknown man supplied them with heroin. The officers paid Jamil £20 and again on this occasion saw that he had further wraps in his possession.

33   On December 17, the appellant was arrested. He admitted in interview handing packages to the officers on September 18 and 20, but at that time claimed not to know what was in them.

34   In passing sentence, the learned judge said that the appellant and his co-accused were fully aware of what they were doing, namely supplying Class A drugs on a commercial basis. The learned judge drew attention to the fact that it was not the first time that Jamil had been before the court for drug offences, that he had a poor record and, indeed, was in breach of licence at the time these offences were committed. The appellant, the judge accepted, had become addicted to drugs when at a particularly low period in his life. He did not, as the judge said, have as bad a record as Jamil and had no previous history of drug-related offending. He was now drug free and there was an impressive letter in support of him from a prison officer. In all the circumstances, the judge said, he should receive a lesser sentence than Jamil. To the records of the appellant and Jamil we shall in a moment return.

35   There was a pre-sentence report on the appellant indicating that the offences were committed whilst he was abusing drugs, but as he had, apparently, by the

time of the report in March 2004 ceased drug use, there was only a medium risk of him reoffending.

36   The submission which is made by Mr Smith on behalf of Sajid is directed primarily to the disparity of the sentence passed upon this appellant when compared with the four-year sentence passed upon Jamil. The appellant is still, it appears, drug free in prison. Mr Smith stresses that this was not a case of the appellant making any commercial gain.

37   Mr Munro, on behalf of the prosecution, accepted that the Crown had always regarded Jamil as playing the greater role in these activities when compared with the appellant.

38   Bearing in mind that two Class A drugs were supplied and that Jamil on at least one occasion had a stock of drugs in his possession, the sentence of four years in relation to him may well have been a lenient one. But, in our judgment, the argument based on disparity is well founded. There are several reasons why the sentencing judge ought, in our judgment, to have drawn a greater distinction than he did between this appellant and Jamil. They include the fact that the appellant had only one previous conviction, for which he had been conditionally discharged, and he had no previous convictions in relation to drugs. Jamil, on the other hand, had on five occasions been convicted of possessing drugs, which included, in October 2002, heroin. Also, over a seven-year period, Jamil had many other convictions for dishonesty, violence and the possession of weapons. He had lost his liberty on several occasions, the longest sentence being for a total of three years, from which he had been recently released and was on licence at the time of the present offences. Furthermore, as we have said and as the prosecution accept, the appellant's role in these activities was subsidiary to that of Jamil.

39   Taking into account also that the only people shown to have been supplied by the appellant were police officers, that he is now drug free, and all the other circumstances of the case, we allow his appeal by quashing the sentences of three years and three months' imprisonment imposed concurrently by the learned judge and substituting for them sentences of two-and-a-half years' imprisonment concurrently in relation to each count.

40   We turn to Andrews. He was born in July 1978, is therefore 26 years of age, and he was of previous good character. On March 3, 2004, at Bury St Edmunds Crown Court, he pleaded guilty on rearraignment and, on May 14, 2004, he was sentenced by H.H. Judge Holt to five years' imprisonment concurrently on each of five counts of supplying cocaine. Orders again were made under s.27 of the Misuse of Drugs Act 1971. He appeals against sentence by leave of the single judge.

41   The facts were that, in July 2003, an undercover operation was mounted by police officers targeting drug dealers, particularly those dealing with crack cocaine, in Ipswich. Two officers made contact with the appellant, and on five separate occasions, between July 22 and July 29, he supplied a total of 2.8 gms in exchange for £240.

42   On the first occasion, the appellant asked the officers to follow him slowly, and, eventually, he retrieved a bag from its hiding place in some weeds. From

it he took two wraps, which he sold to the officers for £40. The officers noted that there were a number of other similar cellophane wraps in the bag. The officer asked the appellant for his mobile telephone number, which he gave, and he also told the officers that he was known as "Doggy". Other purchases were made following contact by the officers over the mobile telephone.

43   On July 31, he was arrested at his home address and a mobile telephone was recovered. He said in interview that he was from Sierra Leone and had lived in Ipswich for about two years. He confirmed that the telephone was his, but at that stage denied supplying drugs. He claimed as part of his basis of plea that he had not supplied anyone other than the undercover police officers; but, as we have already said, the stock which he had demonstrated his ability to supply others. He was a user of crack cocaine.

44   There had been a telephone call on July 23 (which it will be recalled is, between the dates of the 22nd and 29th, when dealing took place) when he had told the officers he did not want to deal. But, as we have said, he did in fact supply the officers thereafter. The prosecution did not accept, for obvious reasons, that he only supplied drugs to undercover officers.

45   In passing sentence, the judge said that there had been five supplies over a seven-day period; these were examples of his criminality and it was clear that he was a commercial trader with access to considerable stock. He had not pleaded guilty at the earliest opportunity, but his good character was in his favour and regard was paid to a pre-sentence report in March 2004, which assessed the risk of him reoffending as low. The judge said that the number of offences and their clear commercial nature could not be overlooked.

46   On Andrews' behalf, Mr Goodman seeks to explain the plea of guilty on rearraignment by reference to difficulties in relation to disclosure and the audibility of certain tapes which had to be examined.

47   As was pointed out to counsel in the course of his submission, a defendant who defers admitting his guilt until such time as he has been able to investigate the strength of the prosecution case, when he has had the opportunity at an earlier stage of showing his remorse by pleading guilty in the knowledge of what he has done, cannot expect the same discount for a plea of guilty as one who pleads guilty at the earliest opportunity.

48   Mr Goodman draws attention to the industry which, in the period between his incarceration in May and the middle of August, the appellant has shown by achieving a variety of certificates in prison in relation to self-help and substance and alcohol awareness. He has also been awarded a certificate in relation to desktop publishing.

49   Mr Goodman stresses that no drug paraphernalia was found when Andrews' home was searched; that the total sale price of the drugs supplied to these officers was the comparatively modest figure which we earlier identified; and that the appellant is now drug free and is of previous good character. He is also, apparently, HIV positive.

50   On behalf of the Crown, Miss Dineen pointed out that, when interviewed, the appellant was shown a photograph which depicted the appellant, among others, but he at that stage denied that he was "Doggy" and made no comment. She also

draws attention to the circumstances of the first supply, indicating, as we have already said, that the appellant had a stock of drugs for supply to persons other than the police officers who made statements about these matters.

51 Taking all the circumstances which we have identified into account, we take the view that the sentence of five years imposed by the learned judge did not sufficiently reflect the appellant's plea of guilty, albeit late, his good character and the aspect of his addiction to which we have referred. Accordingly, Andrews' appeal is allowed. The sentence of five years imposed concurrently on each of the five counts of supplying cocaine is quashed. There is substituted for it a sentence of four years concurrently on each count.

R. v DANIEL WALTERS

COURT OF APPEAL (Lord Justice Scott Baker, Mr Justice Bean and Judge Barker): September 17, 2004

[2004] EWCA Crim 2587; [2005] 1 Cr.App.R.(S.) 100

(LT) Arson; Detention; Manslaughter by gross negligence; Sentence length; Young offenders

1 *Detention in a young offender institution—manslaughter by gross negligence—setting fire to mattress on which intoxicated man was asleep—length of term of detention*

2 Six years' detention in a young offender institution upheld for manslaughter by gross negligence where a youth set fire to a mattress on which an intoxicated man was sleeping and left the scene.

3 The appellant pleaded guilty to manslaughter by gross negligence and to a separate offence of assault occasioning actual bodily harm. The victim of the manslaughter was a man aged 37 who was addicted to alcohol and prone to drinking large quantities of cider. The victim was abused from time to time while he was drunk and incapable of looking after himself by people including the appellant. On the evening of the offence the victim was drunk. He set off with the appellant to an outbuilding where he was accustomed to sleep on a mattress. During the evening some horseplay took place involving a lighted article of clothing, which landed on the mattress causing it to catch fire. The appellant ran off but did not raise the alarm. The victim died as a result of extensive burns. Sentenced to six years' detention in a young offender institution for manslaughter and 15 months concurrent for assault occasioning actual bodily harm.

Held, the sentencing judge indicated that there was a history of bullying and violence towards a man who made himself vulnerable by drinking. The sentencing judge said that the appellant was playing a dangerous game with a lighted article which caused the deceased's mattress to catch fire. The appellant did not put the fire out or get the deceased out of the building. It was submitted

that the sentence failed to take account of the appellant's youth, his early plea and
the disadvantages which he suffered as a result of his psychological background.
The fact was that by his criminal conduct the appellant took an innocent life. In
the Court's judgment, the total sentence of six years could not be described as
manifestly excessive.

H5   **References:** detention in a young offender institution—manslaughter, *Current Sentencing Practice* E 2–4

H6   *P. Joyce Q.C.* for the appellant.
S. Coupland for the Crown.

JUDGMENT

1   **Scott Baker L.J.:**   On October 30, 2003, in the Crown Court at Nottingham,
this appellant pleaded guilty to manslaughter on the basis of gross negligence. On
January 30, 2004 he pleaded guilty to a quite separate offence of assault occasioning actual bodily harm. On March 9, 2004 he was sentenced by Pitchers J. to six
years' detention for the manslaughter and 15 months concurrent for the assault
occasioning actual bodily harm. The sentence was detention in a young offender
institution. The appellant was 18 at the time of sentence. He appeals against sentence by leave of the single judge.

2   The facts of the case were in summary as follows. The first offence in time was
the assault occasioning actual bodily harm. On April 30, 2003 the victim and his
male companion visited an address in Nottingham, the home of Rebecca Olds-
worth, who was present in the house. The victim was confronted at the door by
a co-defendant called Powell, who had locked the door to the house and
demanded something of value from the victim. Powell then pushed the victim
through to the kitchen of the house and threatened him with an adjustable spanner
and then with a wrench. At about that time the appellant arrived at the house along
with another person whose identity is unknown. The victim's companion mentioned that the victim had a mobile telephone. The unknown person asked to
have it. When the victim refused, violence broke out amongst all the people in
the house directed at the victim. There was a good deal of punching and the appellant kicked the victim on the nose which immediately started to bleed. Several
people, including the appellant, demanded the victim's telephone and it was
eventually taken from him before he was ejected from the house. The victim
went to a neighbouring house where he raised the alarm. He was taken to hospital
for treatment to his bruised swollen nose. He also had swelling and cuts around
his face and to his arms and back, as a result of the punches from all those concerned.

3   The appellant was arrested in May 2003 and when interviewed responded "no
comment". He was identified during an video identification procedure.

4   Turning then to the manslaughter. This occurred on July 22, 2003. The victim,
37-year-old Robert Owen, had for some time a serious problem with alcohol
addiction and was prone to drinking very large quantities of cider. The appellant's
mother was a close friend of the victim's partner with whom he shared a home.

The victim was somewhat frail and pathetic and was treated as a punch bag by many of his supposed friends, including the appellant. There were times when he was punched, his hair and clothes set alight or inflammable liquid put on his hands and feet and set alight. He was often so drunk that he was incapable of looking after himself and was therefore an easy target. At times he would sleep in a small brick outbuilding of a disused petrol station in Nottingham. He had a mattress on the floor and it was a squalid place. Nevertheless, the appellant and the victim had a reasonably close attachment.

5   On the evening in question, July 22, 2003, the victim was so drunk that his partner would not allow him to remain at her home. During the afternoon he set off for a walk accompanied by the appellant and eventually they made their way to that outbuilding where the victim lay on the mattress in a drunken state. During that early evening some horseplay took place, involving a lighted article of clothing, which landed on the mattress, causing it to catch fire. The appellant ran off but did not raise the alarm. He disappeared for a while before returning home to his mother where he remained until his arrest at 9.40pm. Sadly, the victim died as a result of extensive burns.

6   In interview the appellant denied responsibility for the outbreak of the fire.

7   The appellant has convictions for various relatively minor offences. He had, on several occasions, been made the subject of a supervision order. Indeed, he was the subject of such an order at the time that he committed the first assault. The judge had before him a pre-sentence report. The report made the point that the appellant was susceptible to peer pressure and prone to use violence as a means to gain the acceptance of his peers. He was identified as mixing with the wrong people. Alcohol was a problem for him.

8   The probation officer described a demonstrable pattern of offending which has at its roots low self-esteem, a desire to be accepted by his peers, underlying anger and aggression which had alcohol and drug misuse as triggers. He assessed the risk of further offending by the appellant as high in the light of his previous history, in particular his tendency towards becoming progressively violent under the influence of alcohol. He said: "I assess his risk of causing harm to the public as high."

9   The judge also had the advantage of a detailed psychological report, which had been prepared by a Mr Prebble. Mr Prebble described the appellant as a young person of low intelligence, saying that fewer than three per cent of the population would have a lower level of general conceptual ability. He said that by his own admission he would have appeared to have used both alcohol and drugs as a quick solution to his difficulties. He said this in his opinion: the appellant is a particularly disturbed and disturbing young individual who is particularly vulnerable and frequently isolated and may in general feel estranged from wider society. There is much which is good about him. But this is not generally revealed to significant others. On the contrary, he is likely to maintain a tough approach to others in non-family and non-familiar surroundings. He said that he believed the appellant was in need of a heavy level of counselling, probably using cognitive behavioural methods with additional level psychiatric interven-

tion, if he is to move on and eventually be restored to the accepted standards of the wider society. He concluded by saying:

> "He is, by anybody's standards, a highly marginalised member of society and it is particularly clear to me that without appropriate levels of support or guidance that he is likely to provoke others by whom he feels rejected or is frustrated and every effort should be made to break down his cycle of self-protection and aggressiveness using whatever methods may be seen by other professionals as being most appropriate."

10   The judge in passing sentence made it clear that he was going to pass a concurrent sentence for the assault occasioning actual bodily harm, notwithstanding that it was a quite separate offence and would ordinarily have justified a consecutive sentence. We can well understand why he did this. Had he passed consecutive sentences he would have been obliged to pass a lesser sentence for the manslaughter than the offence warranted on its own because of the principle of totality. The judge said this about the basis of the manslaughter sentence:

> "I reject the version set out in the Pre-Sentence Report that you gave to the probation officer as inconsistent with the various versions you gave after the event and it is quite clear that the background to this was a history of bullying and violence towards a man whom you regarded as more vulnerable than yourself because of the state he got himself into with drinking. In my judgment, the safest approach to the factual basis for sentence is to put together the accounts that you gave immediately afterwards to various witnesses, Steven Walters, Rebecca Oldsworth, Rachel Oldsworth, Peter Wardle and Robert and Angela D'Argue. Clearly you were saying to them that you were playing a very dangerous game with a lighted article of clothing in that shed, that lighted article of clothing caused the deceased man's mattress to catch fire. You then did not put the fire out, you did not get him out, although I accept that if he was reluctant in his drunk state to leave you might have found that difficult and you then ran off and here I do think your difficulties as set out in the psychological report are relevant because I suspect it was partly in panic that you ran off, but the fact remains that you did not take such steps as you could have done to try and prevent the catastrophe that occurred. The result of all that is that a man who, whatever his problems, had harmed nobody, suffered a dreadful death over the hours that followed."

The judge took into account the material in the psychiatric report but pointed out that the appellant was well able to make choices about whether he bullied the deceased and the victim of the assault. He also took into account the plea of guilty and the appellant's youth.

11   Mr Joyce Q.C., who has appeared for the appellant and has advanced his case with his customary skill and succinctness, submits that this is, first of all, an unusual case being manslaughter by gross negligence. Secondly, that sentences for manslaughter vary almost infinitely, according to the facts of the particular case and that, in the circumstances, there was no purpose or advantage in relying

on any authority. Then, he submitted that the judge passed too high a sentence for the manslaughter, having failed to take into account adequately, first, the appellant's youth, second, his early plea of guilty, and thirdly and perhaps most importantly, all the disadvantages that he suffered as a result of his psychological background as set out in the report to which we have referred. Mr Joyce submitted that the total sentence should have been one of in the region of four-and-a-half years rather than in the region of six years.

12   We have read moving letters from the deceased's mother and sister. They believe it would be an injustice were the sentence to be reduced. We have, however, to form our own view of the appropriate sentence in the context of the Court's experience of dealing with manslaughter cases.

13   The fact is that by his criminal conduct the appellant took an innocent life and that this followed an earlier offence of unprovoked violence on another man some months before. There could have been no possible complaint, in our judgment, if the judge had passed consecutive sentences of 15 months for the assault occasioning actual bodily harm and four-and-three-quarter years for the manslaughter. But, for the reasons that we have explained, the judge did not pass consecutive sentences, and he was plainly right not to do so.

14   In our judgment, the total sentence of six years cannot be described as manifestly excessive. Indeed, that is what the offence of manslaughter deserved. In these circumstances, the appeal will be dismissed.

R. v ANDREW NEISH MOORE

Court of Appeal (Mr Justice Moses and Mr Justice Royce):
October 4, 2004

[2004] EWCA Crim 2574; [2005] 1 Cr.App.R.(S.) 101

(LT) Breach; Public protection; Sentence length; Sex offender orders

1 *Sex offender order—breach of sex offender order—length of sentence*

2 Sentences totalling six years' imprisonment for four breaches of a sex offender order, reduced to three years.

3 The appellant pleaded guilty to four counts of breach of a sex offender order made under the Crime and Disorder Act 1998. The appellant had a record of serious offences of sexual abuse of young boys and had served a number of sentences of imprisonment. In 2001 a magistrates' court made a sex offender order on complaint, which prohibited the appellant from unsupervised access to or control of any child under the age of 16, and prohibited him from inviting into or allowing access to his home any child under 16 unless that child was accompanied by his parents. The appellant was released from a sentence of imprisonment for offences of burglary in October 2003, and frequently visited his brother's house, where his nephew aged 11 was living. The appellant engaged in friendship with friends of the nephew. On one occasion the appellant was decorating the house when a friend of the nephew knocked on the door and the appellant allowed the boy to enter the house and help with the work. No sexual impropriety took place. On a later occasion in the course of a family outing the appellant manipulated the situation so as to leave with two young boys in his car. He had also played on a video game at an arcade with those boys. The following day the appellant was seen walking a dog and inviting a nine-year-old boy to accompany him. Sentenced to a total of six years' imprisonment.

4 **Held:** (considering *Brown* [2002] 1 Cr.App.R.(S.) 1 (p.1) , *Beech* [2002] 1 Cr.App.R.(S.) 3 (p.7), *Clark* [2003] 1 Cr.App.R.(S.) 2 (p.6), *Wilcox* [2003] 1 Cr.App.R.(S.) 43 (p.199), *Munday* [2003] 2 Cr.App.R.(S.) 23 (p.112)) the sentencing judge observed that the appellant had deliberately breached the sex offender order. In the Court's view, the sentencing judge was entitled to take the view that the appellant was a danger to young boys and had deliberately and flagrantly breached the order in circumstances which clearly posed a risk to young boys. It was submitted that the sentencing judge took too high a starting point and failed to take into account the appellant's plea of guilty. The Court took the view that the sentences totalling six years were manifestly excessive and out of line with the authorities to which the Court had been referred. In the Court's judgment, having regard to the fact that the order was breached on four occasions, the appropriate total sentence was three years' imprisonment.

H5   **Cases cited:**
Brown [2002] 1 Cr.App.R.(S.) 1 (p.1) , *Beech* [2002] 1 Cr.App.R.(S.) 3 (p.7),
Clark [2003] 1 Cr.App.R.(S.) 2 (p.6), *Wilcox* [2003] 1 Cr.App.R.(S.) 43
(p.199), *Munday* [2003] 2 Cr.App.R.(S.) 23 (p.112).

H6   **References:** breach of sex offender order, *Current Sentencing Practice* B 3–
7.3E

H7   *R. M. Barradell* for the appellant.

1   **Moses J.:**   This is an appeal by leave of the single judge against a sentence of
six years' imprisonment passed by H.H. Judge Keen Q.C. at Sheffield Crown
Court. The sentences were passed in May 2004 in respect of four counts of
breaching a sex offender order contrary to s.2(8) of the Crime and Disorder
Act 1998.

2   The appellant is aged 36. He has a bad record of serious offences of sexual
abuse against young boys. It is unnecessary to detail the facts of those offences,
but between 1995 and 2001 serious sexual offences were committed which led to
prison sentences. In April 2001 the appellant was made the subject of a sex
offender order at Sheffield Magistrates' Court following a complaint by the
police. This order prohibited the appellant from unsupervised access to or control
of any child under 16, and further prohibited him from inviting into or allowing
access to his home of any child under 16 unless that child was accompanied by his
parent.

3   In October 2003 the appellant was released from custody for burglary offences
and became a frequent visitor to his brother's house. There lived his 11-year-old
nephew, his brother's son. The appellant said that he visited that house because it
was somewhere where there were cooking facilities that were not otherwise
available to him.

4   The offences were committed when the appellant took the opportunity of
engaging in friendship with friends of his nephew. The first occasion was
when a young boy knocked on the door of the house to visit his nephew. The
appellant was decorating. He allowed that boy to enter the house and help with
the work. No suggestion of sexual impropriety is alleged to have taken place,
but it requires no imagination to appreciate the dangers to which that young
boy was exposed or the signal failure of the appellant to use any risk avoidance
strategy to keep himself away from temptation.

5   Matters became exacerbated when in November 2003 there was a plan in the
family to go ice-skating with two teenagers. When the family came round to go
skating they discovered that the appellant had taken advantage in a manipulative
way of the situation to leave earlier with two of the younger brothers of the family
(both under 16), whom he persuaded to travel alone in a car to the ice rink. At the
ice rink he had played on a video game in an arcade with those two young boys.

6   One day later the appellant's sister-in-law saw him walking the family dog and
inviting a nine-year-old, who was with a friend to accompany him. She also saw

him in the company of that boy alone. When challenged he denied that he had gone off with that boy. Subsequently he was arrested.

7   In his sentencing remarks the judge, rightly in our view, noted that the effect of the order must have been perfectly plain to the appellant and that he had deliberately breached it. He remarked that his behaviour demonstrated "his true danger". In our view, whatever the terminology he used, the judge was entitled to take the view that the appellant was a danger to young boys and had deliberately and flagrantly breached the order, and, moreover, that he had done so in circumstances which clearly posed a risk to those young boys and would have been of concern to any court determined, by means of enforcing the sex offender order, to protect the public. That that is part of the purpose of the order which a sentencing court is entitled to take into account is clear from the authorities to which we have been helpfully referred by Mr Barradell. His submissions in reliance upon those authorities are essentially that the starting point of the judge was far too high, and that, whatever the circumstances of these offences, particularly bearing in mind that no sexual offence took place, a starting point in the region of nine years was wholly wrong.

8   His next submission follows from that: that the judge clearly failed to take into account the appellant's plea of guilty. Whether it was made at the earliest opportunity, he says, is beside the point. Even if it was not, it was made well before the trial and saved those young boys from having to give evidence. He supports those submissions by reference to the authorities to which we have already referred. In *Brown* [2002] 1 Cr.App.R.(S.) 1 (p.1), the Court upheld a sentence of three years following a contest. That was a case where sexual remarks had been made by the subject of such an order to a young boy. The case is of importance in that it demonstrated and identified the purposes of such an order, namely the protection of the public and the fact that a sentencing court can take that purpose into account when sentencing. The other authorities demonstrate that far shorter sentences have been applied than the sentence in the instant case. In *Beech* [2002] 1 Cr.App.R.(S.) 3 (p.7), the appellant was sentenced to a period of 12 months' imprisonment in respect of a breach of a sex offender order when the appellant in that case had visited a number of public houses with the police and made sexual and violent remarks to a woman police sergeant. In *Clark* [2003] 1 Cr.App.R.(S.) 2 (p.6), where an appellant had moved into a house where there were two young children, a sentence of 3 years' imprisonment was reduced to 18 months. In *Wilcox* [2003] 1 Cr.App.R.(S.) 43 (p.199), a sentence of 2 years' imprisonment was reduced to one of 12 months where, in flagrant breach of an order that had been varied to allow an appellant to conduct a part-time business of providing equipment for children's parties, he had actually attended those parties. Finally, in *Munday* [2003] 2 Cr.App.R.(S.) 118 (p.623), a sentence of 2 years' imprisonment was reduced to one of 12 months where an appellant regularly visited a house where there were young children.

We take the view that, whilst it is important not mechanically to compare one set of facts with another, and although these were serious offences calculated to cause anxiety in the mind of any court who had to deal with such a breach, they were out of line with the authorities to which we have referred. Six years' imprisonment was manifestly excessive. However, there were four occasions of breach. Whether they should have been consecutive or concurrent in one sense is immaterial, so long as the total was appropriate and not out of line with previous authorities. In our judgment this sentence was out of line with those authorities. But having regard to the fact that the order was breached on four occasions, the appropriate sentence, in our judgment, as a matter of totality was one of three years' imprisonment.

10   In those circumstances we propose to vary the orders of the judge by imposing a sentence of two years' imprisonment in respect of counts 1, 3 and 4; and on count 2 to substitute a sentence of three years' imprisonment to run concurrently, making a total of three years' imprisonment in all. To that extent this appeal is allowed.

R. v IP

Court of Appeal (Lord Justice Rose (Vice President, Court of Appeal Criminal Division), Mr Justice Richards and Mr Justice Bean): October 5, 2004

[2004] EWCA Crim 2646; [2005] 1 Cr.App.R.(S.) 102

(LT) Community rehabilitation orders; Custodial sentences; Video recordings; Voyeurism

H1   *Voyeurism— Sexual Offences Act 2003, s.67—arranging video camera so as to watch adult step daughter taking shower—whether custodial sentence justified*

H2   Eight months' imprisonment for voyeurism in the form of arranging a video camera so as to watch an adult step-daughter taking a shower varied to a community rehabilitation order.

H3   The appellant indicated an intention before a magistrates' court to plead guilty to voyeurism, contrary to the Sexual Offences Act 2003, s.67. He was committed to the Crown Court for sentence. The appellant installed a video camera in the loft above the bathroom in his home so that he could view his step-daughter, aged 24, in the shower. The step-daughter became suspicious and while he was out of the house, she searched the house, in company with her mother and sister, and found the camera which was connected to a screen in the bedroom. The shower could be seen on the screen. The appellant admitted installing the camera with a view to watching the step-daughter in the shower and that he also installed a cable so that he could view the images on the screen in his bedroom. He had done it on a number of occasions, at least one of which took place after May 1, 2004, the date on which the Act came into force. Sentenced to eight months' imprisonment.

H4   **Held:** the fact that the appellant made recordings of the complainant having a shower made the case somewhat worse than if he had simply spied on her; however there was no feature of showing the recording to other people, circulating copies, posting pictures on the internet or selling the recordings for gain. The appellant was of previous good character and had made earlier admissions followed by an early plea of guilty. He had moved out of the family home. In the Court's view, the case did not justify a custodial sentence. The Court would follow the recommendation for a community rehabilitation order, with a condition that the appellant participate in a sex offender group programme.

H5   **References:** voyeurism, *Current Sentencing Practice* B 4A-14

H6   **Commentary**: [2005] Crim.L.R. 152

H7   *D. McDowell* for the appellant.
   C. Sutton for the Crown.

1   **Bean J.:**   The Sexual Offences Act 2003 came into force on May 1, 2004. Section 67 of the Act creates the offence of voyeurism. Section 67(1) provides as follows:

> "A person commits an offence if—
>> (a) for the purposes of sexual gratification, he observes another person doing a private act, and
>> (b) he knows that the other person does not consent to being observed for his sexual gratification."

Section 67(4) provides:

> "(4) A person commits an offence if he instals equipment, constructs or adapts a structure or part of a structure, with the intention of enabling himself or another person to commit an offence under subsection (1)."

This application by the applicant for leave to appeal against sentence is, so far as the Criminal Appeal Office are aware, the first case under the Act and certainly under s.67 to come before this Court. We grant leave to appeal and refer to the applicant as the appellant.

2   The facts are that the appellant installed a video camera in a loft above the bathroom in his home so that he could view his 24-year-old stepdaughter in the shower. She became suspicious of him. On May 15, 2004, while he was out of the house, she, her mother and sister searched the house and found that he had connected a camera from the loft to a screen in the bedroom and the shower could be seen on the screen.

3   The appellant was subsequently arrested. When interviewed he admitted installing the camera with a view to watching the complainant in the shower and that he had also installed a cable so that he could view the images on the screen in his bedroom. He said he had done it three or four times. It is implicit in his plea of guilty that at least one of these observations by him took place after the Act came into force.

4   On July 6, 2004, in the magistrates' court, he indicated a plea of guilty to both charges and was committed to the Crown Court for sentence. On August 6, in the Crown Court at Northampton, he came before Mr Recorder Redgrave Q.C. who

sentenced him to eight months' imprisonment concurrent on each count. We have some sympathy with the learned recorder in having to pass sentence on what may have been the first occasion under a new statute.

5   What the appellant did was, in the complainant's own words, "disgusting". The fact that he made recordings of the complainant having a shower makes the case somewhat worse than if he had simply spied on her. On the other hand, the case did not have the aggravating feature of the voyeur showing the recordings to other people, still less circulating copies, posting pictures on the internet or selling the recordings for gain. Moreover, the victim was not a child.

6   The appellant was of previous good character and he is entitled to credit for his early admissions followed by early pleas of guilty. We should add that he moved out of the family home after the offences were revealed and his wife has made it clear that she does not wish him to return.

7   In our view, the facts of this case did not justify a custodial sentence. The appellant is plainly in need of therapy and our view is that the recommendation of the probation service for a community rehabilitation order should have been followed. We shall follow it.

8   We allow the appeal. We set aside the sentences of imprisonment and substitute on each count, concurrently, a community rehabilitation order for one year, with a condition under Sch.2 to the Powers of Criminal Courts (Sentencing) Act 2000 that the appellant must participate in a Community Sex Offender Group Work Programme as directed by the supervising officer of the Probation Service throughout the one year period in so far as the officer so directs. The requirement of notification under the Sex Offenders Act 1997 registration provisions is reduced consequentially on our principal order to one of fiveyears from the date of sentencing by the learned judge.

R. v PAUL ERIC FLEMING

COURT OF APPEAL (Lord Justice Auld, Mr Justice Owen and Mr Justice Hedley): October 5, 2004

[2004] EWCA Crim 2471; [2005] 1 Cr.App.R.(S.) 103

LT Aggravating features; Causing death when under the influence; Failing to provide specimen; Sentence length

H1   *Causing death by careless driving having consumed excess alcohol, and failing to provide a specimen—length of sentence*

H2   Five years' imprisonment for causing death by careless driving having consumed excess alcohol, and failing to provide a specimen, reduced to four.

H3   The appellant pleaded guilty to causing death by careless driving having consumed excess alcohol, and failing to provide a specimen, contrary to the Road Traffic Act 1988, s.3A(1)(c). The appellant was driving a motor car in the early hours of the morning when he made a right turn into a side road. His passenger called "stop" and the appellant stopped his car directly in the path of a motorcycle. The motorcycle collided with the car and the motorcyclist suffered a fatal injury. The appellant left the scene of the accident and walked home. He was later arrested and taken to a police station where a doctor believed that he was under the influence of drink or drugs. Sentenced to 5 years' imprisonment and disqualified from driving for 10 years, and until he had taken an extended driving test.

4   **Held:** (considering *Cooksley* [2004] 1 Cr.App.R.(S.) 1 (p.1)) the sentencing judge commented that the appellant left the scene of the accident because he was aware that he had alcohol in his bloodstream and he wished to avoid the process of measuring the alcohol level. The appellant had no driving licence or insurance; he had a previous conviction for dangerous driving and a blood alcohol offence for which he had been disqualified. The sentencing judge was entitled to conclude that this was a bad case of its type. The Court had come to the conclusion that the sentence was longer than was needed in the circumstances, and a sentence of four years' imprisonment would be substituted.

5   **Case cited:**
Cooksley [2004] 1 Cr.App.R.(S.) 1 (p.1)

6   **References:** causing death by careless driving with an excess alcohol level, *Current Sentencing Practice* B 1–7.3K

7   *J. Gibson* for the appellant.

1   **Hedley J.:**   This is an appeal with leave of the single judge against a sentence of five years' imprisonment, imposed by H.H. Judge Denis Clark in the Crown Court at Liverpool, following the appellant's plea of guilty to an offence of causing death by careless driving having consumed excess alcohol and failing to provide a specimen contrary to s.3A(1)(c) of the Road Traffic Act 1988 as amended. He was also disqualified from driving for a period of 10 years and thereafter until he had taken an extended driving test.

2   The facts of this accident are tragically stark. At about four o'clock in the morning on Christmas Eve the appellant was travelling in a Rover motor car on a main road known as Crosby Road South. He had been to an all night petrol station and was returning home. It was his intention to turn right into Kinross Road. Mr Michael Morrin was travelling on his motor cycle in the opposite direction on Crosby Road South, going to his place of work in Sandhills, Liverpool where he was an HGV driver. The appellant turned right across Mr Morrin's path, and, when his passenger cried "stop", did so directly in the path of the motor bike. There was a collision in which Mr Morrin suffered fatal injury. After the accident the appellant remained briefly at the scene before walking off home. In fairness it must be added that a passing ambulance had stopped at the scene and Mr Morrin was receiving attention before the appellant left.

3   He was traced to his home, arrested and taken to the police station. The doctor believed that he was under the influence of drink or drugs. The appellant was at every stage deliberately obstructive of that enquiry.

4   It is not surprising that the learned judge in passing sentence said this:

> "I am convinced that [this] careless driving was brought about by the amount of alcohol in your bloodstream. I am also of the opinion that you did not flee the scene out of panic or anxiety, you fled it out of callous self-ishness because you wanted to obviate, to circumvent, to frustrate the blood alcohol process. That is why the police found you as they did when eventually they arrested you.
>
> I also accept the evidence of an experienced doctor, that you had all the indications of a man noticeably affected by alcohol. The fact that we will never know the reading is because of your obstructive attitude to the doctor when he wanted to take a sample from you. You knew, you know, you knew why you scarpered and you knew why you should not have been behind the wheel of a car."

Those were views the learned judge was fully entitled to take.

5   Judge Clark identified a number of aggravating features. The appellant had no driving licence or insurance policy; his behaviour, as has already been described; a previous conviction for dangerous driving and a blood alcohol offence resulting in a disqualification period of two-and-a-half years; and repeated convictions for being drunk and disorderly. They were all factors that he was entitled to take into account. He also had a victim impact statement from Mrs Morrin which is rendered the more powerful by the very moderation of its expression. The learned judge also correctly reminded himself that this was not a case of dangerous driving, though he was entitled to conclude that drink or drugs were causative of the careless driving. Again he recognised the guilty plea and was careful to make it clear that the loss of Mr Morrin was irreplaceable and could never be reflected in any sentence of the court. In our view, the judge correctly identified the aggravating and mitigating features in the case.

6   We have, of course, carefully considered the case of *Cooksley and Others* [2004] 1 Cr.App.R.(S.) 1 (p.1), but noted Mr Gibson's observation that it did not deal explicitly, or at length, with this particular offence, as opposed to the much more usual dangerous driving offence.

7   The essence of Mr Gibson's helpful submission to this Court, and a point identified by the single judge as of potential merit, is that the judge must have taken a starting point at about seven and a half years, which, having regard to the statutory maximum of 10 and the features of the case already identified, is much too high. That is said even though a guilty plea was probably almost inevitable in this case. It is that question of length, and the implications of what the appellant may have received had he contested the matter, that provides the real point in the case.

8   The learned judge clearly thought that this was a bad case of its type and he was entitled so to conclude. He was entitled to look for as severe a sentence as the features of the case would justify. The issue that has troubled us is whether, in all the

circumstances, this sentence really is too long having regard to the matters correctly identified by the learned judge.

9   Having given this matter careful attention, we have come to the conclusion that the sentence was longer than it needed to have been in all the circumstances, particularly having regard to the actual driving, notwithstanding all the aggravating features that surrounded it.

10   In the circumstances, we think that a sentence of four years' imprisonment is a substantial and effective marker of the culpability of this appellant in all the circumstances, reminding ourselves, as the judge so rightly reminded himself, that no sentence could begin to measure the loss that had been sustained by those who that night were cruelly deprived of husband and father. To that limited extent this appeal is allowed.

R. v RAMON GANTZ

COURT OF APPEAL (Lord Justice Scott Baker, Mr Justice Forbes and Judge Roberts Q.C.): October 7, 2004

[2004] EWCA Crim 2862; [2005] 1 Cr.App.R.(S.) 104

LT Administering poison; Aircraft; Controlled drugs; Criminal intent; Sentence length

H1   *Causing noxious thing to be administered or taken with intent to injure, aggrieve or annoy—placing ecstasy tablet in woman's drink—offence committed on aeroplane in flight—length of sentence*

H2   Three years' imprisonment upheld for causing a noxious thing to be administered or taken with intent to injure, aggrieve or annoy by placing an ecstasy tablet in a woman's drink in the course of a flight.

H3   The appellant was convicted of causing a noxious thing to be administered or taken with intent to injure, aggrieve or annoy, contrary to the Offences against the Person Act 1861, s.24. The appellant and a friend flew from Israel to Gatwick. While waiting to check in at the airport they found themselves in front of a woman and her grandmother. The appellant was seen by cabin crew after the plane had taken off to be drinking from a bottle of schnapps. He refused to stop doing so and a bottle was confiscated. The appellant fell into conversation with the woman and invited her to a party. She declined the invitation. The appellant made a cup of coffee for the complainant which she tasted but did not drink. The appellant subsequently went to the galley area of the aeroplane and obtained two cans of orange juice. He was seen to take the cans into a lavatory and emerged carrying two glasses of orange juice. He handed one glass to the women which she started to drink. She noticed some residue at the bottom of the glass, and complained to the cabin crew that something had been put into her drink. The glass was seized and later analysis of the contents of the glass revealed traces of ecstasy. The women later felt unwell. When the plane landed the woman was taken to hospital for observation. Samples of blood and urine revealed traces of ecstasy. A search of the aeroplane resulted in the discovery of three ecstasy tablets near where the appellant had been sitting. The prosecution case was that the appellant had put ecstasy into the woman's drink to relax her inhibitions and make her more susceptible to the appellant's advances. The defence case was that the appellant had no recollection of putting ecstasy into the woman's drink and that he did not have the intention to injure, aggrieve or annoy her. Sentenced to three years' imprisonment.

H4   **Held:** (considering *Liles* [2000] 1 Cr.App.R.(S.) 31) it was submitted that the sentencing judge had erred in equating the offence to an aggravated form of supply of a Class A drug and had selected too high a starting point. The Court found little guidance in previous decisions of the Court. The sentencing judge was right to regard the fact that the noxious substance was a Class A drug as a seriously aggravating feature of the case. The victim was a wholly innocent woman who had not encouraged the appellant's attentions in any way, and thought that she was pregnant at the time of the offence. She was distressed to discover that something had been administered to her and suffered significant adverse effects. The incident occurred on an aeroplane which had limited medical facilities and the victim was some time away from proper medical attention. The offence was a significant and serious one of its type. The sentence was at the upper end of the range that was appropriate in a case such as this, but could not be stigmatised as being manifestly excessive. The appeal would be dismissed.

H5   **Case cited:**
Liles [2000] 1 Cr.App.R.(S.) 31

H6   **References:** administering noxious substance, *Current Sentencing Practice* B 2–2.3C

H7   *M. Vere-Hode Q.C.* for the appellant.
W. Hornsby for the Crown.

1   **Forbes J.:** On October 24, 2003 at the Lewes Crown Court, this appellant was convicted of causing a noxious thing to be administered or taken with intent to injure, aggrieve or annoy, contrary to s.24 of the Offences Against the Person Act 1861 and was sentenced to three years' imprisonment. The court adjourned making a recovery of defence costs order pending enquiries from the special investigations unit. However, on March 22, 2004 an order was made in the sum of £12,000. That order has been appealed and the matter stayed pending the determination of this appeal. The appellant now appeals against conviction by leave of the single judge who also referred the application for leave to appeal against sentence to the full court. The appeal against conviction is limited to grounds 1 and 2 of the perfected grounds of appeal. It has been made clear to us this morning that ground 3 is no longer pursued.

2   The facts of this matter are as follows. The appellant is a 31-year-old Israeli national who makes regular trips to the United Kingdom to visit his family. Apparently he runs a successful gym in Tel Aviv. At some time prior to April 25, 2003 the appellant invited his friend Shai Finkelstein to come over to England with him. They had decided to catch the early morning flight from Tel Aviv to Gatwick on April 25, 2003. It appears that the night before the flight the appellant went to an all-night party where he had taken an ecstasy tablet and smoked some cannabis, as well as consuming alcohol. At some stage he had also taken cocaine, although he claimed not to have been aware of that fact.

3   On the Friday morning, April 25, 2003, the appellant met up with Finkelstein and they went to the airport. Whilst they were waiting in the queue to check in, the appellant and Finkelstein found themselves in front of Mrs Z, the complainant, and the complainant's grandmother, Mrs H. The complainant was travelling to London for work purposes and her grandmother was going to see a friend in Sussex. The appellant and the two women had not met before.

4   According to Mrs H's evidence, the appellant offered to buy her and the complainant some coffee at the airport before boarding. However, the invitation came to nothing because there was insufficient time available.

5   Before boarding the plane, the appellant and Finkelstein went to the Duty Free shop and bought a litre bottle of Goldschlager schnapps, approximately 40 per cent proof. They then got the bus to the plane and, according to the appellant, it was probably at that stage in the journey that Finkelstein had given him a sleeping pill, Diazepam, to help him to sleep after he had boarded the aircraft.

6   Once the plane had taken off, the appellant was seen by cabin crew to be drinking the Goldschlager schnapps. He was asked to stop doing so. However, he ignored the request and carried on drinking. The result was that the bottle was eventually confiscated.

7   The appellant's and the complainant's seats were one row apart. The appellant and his companion, Finkelstein, were sitting in seats 34E and 34D. The complainant was in seat 35C and seated next to her grandmother. The cabin crew gave evidence as to how they saw the appellant and the complainant having a conversation at some stage during the journey, whilst they were still seated. It appeared that the conversation was friendly. The appellant and the complainant then left their seats and stood at the back of the plane. The reason for doing that apparently was to avoid disturbing Mrs H who was asleep. At the rear of the plane the complainant and the appellant chatted about a number of different topics of no particular consequence, such as music and their knowledge of a mutual acquaintance. The appellant asked the complainant if she wanted to go with him to a party in London that weekend, but she declined. Her perception was that the appellant would not take "No" for an answer although the complainant told the appellant that she was married. In due course they returned to their seats.

8   At some stage during the flight the appellant made a cup of coffee for the complainant which Finkelstein handed over to her. The complainant took a small sip but left the rest because she did not like the taste of it. Eventually the complainant took off her shoes and went to sleep.

9   According to his evidence, the appellant took what he thought was another Diazepam tablet, but he still could not get to sleep. He said that the "big cocktail" of the sleeping pills, the cannabis, the alcohol and not having had any sleep the night before, made him feel dizzy and tired. As he could not sleep, he decided to get some orange juice. According to his evidence, he tapped the complainant on her leg to see if she wanted a drink as well. According to the complainant she was woken up by the appellant stroking her foot and thigh. However, she agreed that he offered to go and get her an orange juice. She accepted the offer. The appellant went to the galley area saying as he went, according to the complainant, that she should really relax or loosen up a bit. The appellant was gone for quite a while. The cabin crew gave him two cans of Britvic orange juice and two glasses. The appellant was then seen to take the two containers of orange juice plus the two glasses into a lavatory. Shortly afterwards he was seen to come out with two poured glasses of orange juice. Two orange juice cans were later found in the lavatory.

10   The appellant returned to his seat. He handed a glass of juice to the complainant which she then started to drink. When she had nearly finished, she noticed some "bits" at the bottom of her glass. She went to the back of the plane and complained to the cabin crew that someone had put something in her drink. The glass was seized and later analysis of the contents of the glass revealed traces of ecstasy. The complainant became alarmed because she thought she had taken something but it was not clear what it was. Her anxiety was increased because she also thought that she might be pregnant at the time. She was reassured by the staff. However, a little while later, she felt unwell with a rapid pulse, her vision was affected and she thought she was having a panic attack. On several occasions during this period the appellant came to the back of the plane, enquiring how the complainant was. In evidence, the appellant said that he was not conscious of having put a pill in the complainant's orange juice, although anything could have happened as he had been "blurry and not 100 per cent." He denied that he had been trying to pick up the complainant.

11   The plane landed some time later and the complainant was taken to hospital for observation and for samples to be taken. She was released after three to four hours without treatment. However, her samples of blood and urine revealed traces of ecstasy.

12   The plane was searched shortly after landing. In the seat pocket in front of row 34B an empty Diazepam pill packet was found. Three ecstasy tablets were found a few rows in front, under seat 31.

13   In short it was the prosecution case that the appellant had put ecstasy into the complainant's orange juice to "loosen her up" and thus make her more susceptible to the appellant's advances. The defence case was that the appellant had no recollection of putting ecstasy into the complainant's drink and that, in any event, he did not have the requisite intention to injure, aggrieve or annoy.

[Paragraphs [14]–[26] have been omitted.]

27   We now turn to the application for permission to appeal against sentence. As indicated earlier, we have given leave for an appeal against sentence in this case.

28   The appellant is now aged 31. He has one minor conviction for theft committed in 1998 for which he was fined.

29   Mr Vere Hodge submitted that the sentence passed was manifestly excessive and in support of that submission, Mr Vere Hodge made three main points. First, he submitted that the judge had erred in equating the index offence to an aggravated form of supply of a Class A drug. This, it was submitted, had resulted in the judge selecting a starting point that was too high. What the judge said was this at p.2:

> ". . . what you did then, in ordinary speech, was you have drugged her. She was an entirely innocent woman. She believed that she was pregnant at the time; you did not know that, but I am afraid that when you give somebody class A drugs you take your victim as you find them. What you did to her, plainly, was done in an attempt to make her more amenable to your will.
> As Mr Vere Hodge has said, and he must be right, it is highly unlikely that anything would have come of it, but I still regard this as an aggravated form of supplying a class A drug, because you are not supplying it to someone who wants to receive it, you are supplying it to someone who does not even know that you are doing that to them."

30   The second matter upon which Mr Vere Hodge relied was that the judge failed to give sufficient weight to his factual finding that nothing would have come of the appellant's actions. Mr Vere Hodge also submitted that the adverse side effects which the complainant did experience were unforeseen by the appellant, were short-lived and required no medical attention.

31   The third matter advanced by Mr Vere Hodge was that the judge failed to attach sufficient weight to the appellant's age, good character, likely deportation and his intoxicated state that had led to such irresponsible behaviour.

32   There is very little in the way of guidance to be found in previous decisions of this Court in this particular field. The only case to which we have been referred and which we consider does provide some assistance, is the case of *Liles*, April 19, 1999. In that case the appellant pleaded guilty to two offences under s.24. The victims were two brothers aged five and six. The appellant gave isobutyl nitrate to both boys orally and by way of sniffing and they both felt dizzy and unwell. When the appellant was arrested he explained that he had been buying isobutyl nitrate for some years and used it with alcohol to give him a high. In that case a sentence of three years' imprisonment was reduced to two years. However, we remind ourselves that, unlike the appellant in *Liles*, this appellant was not entitled to any credit for a plea of guilty.

33   We have given careful consideration to Mr Vere Hodge's submissions but we find that we are not persuaded. This was a case in which the appellant administered a Class A drug to the complainant without her knowledge. It is unfortunate that, in his sentencing remarks, the judge appears to have equated the offence with an aggravated form of supplying a class A drug in the passage in his sentencing remarks to which we have already referred. The appellant was not charged with supplying a Class A drug and therefore he was not being sentenced for an aggravated form of that form of supply. However, in our view, the judge

was quite right to regard the fact that the noxious substance in question was a Class A drug as a seriously aggravating feature of the case. There were also other aggravating features which made this a serious case. The complainant was a wholly innocent woman. She had not encouraged the appellant's attentions in any way. At the time she thought that she was pregnant. When she discovered that she had had something administered to her, understandably she panicked and was very distressed. She suffered various significant adverse effects of the drug. Furthermore, the incident occurred on an aeroplane which had limited medical facilities. The complainant was some time away from proper medical attention. That will have undoubtedly increased the distress and fear that she was already experiencing. In our view, all these matters make the offence a significant and serious one of its type. Further, the appellant has never at any stage shown any remorse for what he did. In our view these aggravating features mark this down as a serious case. Although we are inclined to the view that the sentence passed was at the upper end of the range of sentence that was appropriate in a case such as this, having regard to the aggravating features that we have identified, we are satisfied that it would be wrong to stigmatise the sentence as being manifestly excessive. At most this sentence was at the upper end of the appropriate bracket of sentence, but it was not manifestly excessive. In those circumstances therefore and for those reasons this appeal against sentence is dismissed.

R. v ALAN DAVID COX

COURT OF APPEAL (Mr Justice Richards and Mr Justice Bean): October 8, 2004

[2004] EWCA Crim 2552; [2005] 1 Cr.App.R.(S.) 105

(LT) Breach; Compassionate grounds; Sex offender orders; Sentence length

H1   *Breach of sex offender order—length of sentence*

H2   Four years' imprisonment for breach of a sex offender order under the Crime and Disorder Act 1998, reduced to two-and-a-half years' imprisonment.

H3   The appellant pleaded guilty before a magistrates' court to breach of a sex offender order made under the Crime and Disorder Act 1998. He was committed to the Crown Court for sentence. The appellant, aged 66, had a history of sexual offences going back many years. In 1999, the appellant indecently assaulted a 14-year-old boy and was sentenced to an extended sentence. Following his release, a 14-year-old boy was found in the appellant's home and children complained that the appellant had made suggestive comments to them. A sex offender order was made in December 2003, prohibiting the appellant having any contact with any child under the age of 16 and having any child under the age of 16 in any accommodation occupied by him. Within a few weeks the appellant was seen speaking to five children under age 16. The appellant was alleged to have asked one of the boys to come back to see him later in the day. Sentenced to four years' imprisonment.

14   **Held:** (considering *Brown* [2002] 1 Cr.App.R.(S.) 1 (p.1)) it was clear that the protection of the public was an important consideration in sentencing for breach of a sex offender. Nevertheless the maximum sentence for breach of an order was five years' imprisonment, and credit had to be given for a plea of guilty. The circumstances of the present offence gave rise to cause for concern, but did not place the breach at the very highest level of seriousness. Taking into account the appellant's plea of guilty and failing health, the sentence was manifestly excessive and a sentence of two and a half years imprisonment would be substituted.

15   **Case cited:**
Brown [2002] 1 Cr.App.R.(S.) 1 (p.1)

16   **References:** breach of sex offender order, *Current Sentencing Practice* B 3–7.3E

17   *C. Gabb* for the appellant.

1   **Richards J.:**   On January 15, 2004 at Southampton Magistrates' Court, this appellant pleaded guilty to one offence of breach of a sex offender order made under s.2 of the Crime and Disorder Act 1998. He was committed to the Crown Court for sentence. On February 12, 2004 he was sentenced in the Crown Court at Southampton by H.H. Judge Leigh Q.C. to four years' imprisonment. He now appeals against that sentence by leave of the single judge.

2   The appellant is 66 years of age and has a history of sex offending going back to 1961. His record includes six offences of indecent assault on a male, six of gross indecency, three of indecent exposure, two of soliciting, two of attempting to procure acts of gross indecency, one of buggery and one of attempted buggery. The victims were often young boys.

3   We can take the history up in 1999, following a gap in the appellant's offending since 1990. On July 24, 1999 the appellant called to a 14-year-old Asian lad from his garden. The lad had mild learning difficulties. The appellant cupped the lad's face and kissed him, putting his tongue in the lad's mouth. He rubbed the lad's scrotum and groin and removed his own erect penis from his trousers. The lad became alarmed, however, and returned home. That incident led to the appellant being charged with an offence of indecent assault on a male under 16. On November 26, 1999, in the Crown Court at Southampton, the appellant was sentenced in respect of that offence to an extended sentence of three years pursuant to s.85 of the Powers of Criminal Courts (Sentencing) Act 2000, made up of a custodial term of 18 months' imprisonment and an extension period of 18 months. In May 2000 the appellant was released on licence. In July of the same year he was charged with a further offence of indecent assault. He was later found not guilty of that further offence but his behaviour was considered to have amounted to a

breach of licence and he remained in prison until the end of his previous sentence. He was released in July 2002. During his time in prison he attended a sex offender treatment programme but this was considered to have resulted in little significant movement towards positive change. Following his release there were continued concerns about allegations that children were being invited into the appellant's flat. A resident warden at the sheltered accommodation where he lived was asked to keep a log of incidents. The police felt it necessary to arrest and caution the appellant on several occasions.

4   On September 4, 2000 a 14-year-old boy was found within the appellant's flat. On September 22, a report by the warden indicated that five children had complained that the appellant had made suggestive comments to them, such as: "I could shag your ass but you're too skinny for me". The children said that the appellant spoke to them outside a local shop where he purchased cigarettes and alcohol which he then offered to the boys along with a place to go to. As a result of that incident the appellant was moved to alternative accommodation. This was fairly close to schools and his flat faced a footpath regularly used by school children.

5   On December 4, 2003, at the Aldershot Magistrates' Court, a sex offender order was made under s.2 of the 1998 Act. The order prohibited the appellant having any contact with any child under the age of 16 and from having any child under the age of 16 in any accommodation occupied by him. The order was to last for 10 years.

6   On December 31, 2003, at about 9.45am, a neighbour saw the appellant speaking to five children—four of them boys, the fifth a girl. All of them were aged under 16. The police were informed. The five children were traced. They said that the appellant had spoken to them. They described him as having done a little dance and winked at them. He had claimed to be Hulk Hogan. At one point he had invited one of them to feel his muscles and had opened his shirt to show his chest. He had asked one boy to come back at 2pm when he said he would have something for the boy. The appellant was arrested later the same day.

7   In sentencing him the judge referred to his terrible record of sex offending and to various reports on him. A psychiatric assessment, in 1999, found unsurprisingly that he had strong paedophile tendencies. A recent pre-sentence report referred to a very high risk of re-offending and expressed grave concerns regarding the risk he posed to children and young people. The judge agreed with that assessment and stressed that a sentence of four years was being imposed for the protection of those children.

8   It is clear from the very nature of an order under s.2 of the 1998 Act, and from the reported cases on it, that the protection of the public is a very important consideration in sentencing for breach of an order (see, for example *Brown* [2002] 1 Cr.App.R.(S.) 1 (p.1)). Nevertheless, it has to be borne in mind that the maximum sentence for breach of an order is five years and that credit has to be given for a plea of guilty, where such a plea is entered. It is also necessary to look carefully at the particular circumstances of the specific breach.

9   The circumstances of the present offence plainly give rise to real cause for concern, especially since they occurred only a few weeks after the order was

imposed. On the other hand, what happened was limited to one occasion and, as counsel has submitted on the appellant's behalf, took place outside the appellant's flat and not inside it. It seems to us that the actual conduct of the appellant on the occasion in question, although giving rise to the concerns to which we have expressed, does not place this breach at the very highest level of seriousness.

10   Taking into account those considerations, the fact that the appellant pleaded guilty at the first opportunity and also his age and failing health, we take the view that the sentence imposed was manifestly excessive. In our judgment, an appropriate sentence, on the facts of this case, would have been one of two and a half years' imprisonment. For those reasons, we allow this appeal by quashing the sentence of four years' imprisonment and substituting a sentence of two and a half years' imprisonment.

R. v MOHAMMED MAZAR FAZAL

COURT OF APPEAL (Lord Justice Mance, Mr Justice Newman and Mr Justice Fulford): October 12, 2004

[2004] EWCA Crim 2811; [2005] 1 Cr.App.R.(S.) 106

⟨LT⟩ Grievous bodily harm; Motor vehicles; Provocation; Racial harassment; Sentence length

H1   *Causing grievous bodily harm with intent—driving taxi at pedestrian after repeated racial abuse by pedestrian—vehicle striking another person, causing grave injuries—length of sentence*

H2   Four years' imprisonment for causing grievous bodily harm with intent reduced to three, where the appellant drove his taxi at a pedestrian after repeated racial abuse by the pedestrian, but collided with another person, causing grave injuries.

H3   The appellant pleaded guilty to causing grievous bodily harm with intent. The appellant, a minibus taxi driver, was flagged down by a group of 12 people and agreed to take them to their destination. During the course of the journey some members of the group subjected the appellant to sustained racial abuse. When the taxi arrived at the destination there was an argument about the fare. One of the passengers made more racist comments and tried to dissuade his companions from paying the fare. This passenger challenged the appellant to a fight. As the group began to move away, the appellant reversed his vehicle and then accelerated forwards, aiming the car at the passenger who had abused him. The passenger got out of the way but another member of the group, who was crossing the road on a zebra crossing, was hit instead. The appellant did not realise that he had struck the victim and continued to drive for some distance, dragging the victim under the vehicle. Eventually the appellant was alerted to what he had done and stopped the vehicle. The victim was released from underneath the vehicle. The appellant telephoned the police and returned to the scene of the incident. The victim was found to have fractures at the base of the skull and other injuries. He was in intensive care for seven days and was unable to return to work for almost a year. He had continuing problems with his eyesight and was unable to continue as a boxer at which he had been a youth champion. He could no longer hope to rejoin the army. The appellant was sentenced to four years' imprisonment.

H4   **Held:** by his plea the appellant accepted that he drove the minibus intending to hit the man who had abused him. He accepted that his behaviour was excessive and disproportionate. Since the incident he had suffered depression and post-traumatic stress disorder. It was argued that the sentencing judge had taken too high a starting point. The Court had been referred to *Attorney General's Reference No.13 of 2001 (John Ivor Cole)* [2001] 2 Cr.App.R.(S.) 112 (p.497). This case presented a difficult sentencing exercise. Given the exceptional mitigation available to the appellant and as an act of mercy, the Court was persuaded that the sentence was unnecessarily long, and would substitute a sentence of three years' imprisonment.

H5   **Case cited:**
Attorney General's Reference No.13 of 2001 (John Ivor Cole) [2001] 2 Cr.App.R.(S.) 112 (p.497).

H6   **References:** causing grievous bodily harm with intent, *Current Sentencing Practice* B 2-2

H7   *N. Guest* for the appellant.

1   **Fulford J.:** On December 15, 2003 at the Wolverhampton Crown Court, on rearraignment, the appellant pleaded guilty to causing grievous bodily harm with intent. Thereafter on February 27, 2004 he was sentenced by H.H. Judge Challinor to four years' imprisonment. He appeals to this Court against that sentence with the leave of the single judge. We observe at the outset that the appellant pleaded guilty in circumstances where it appears he was entitled exceptionally to full credit for his plea, given that legal representation changed late in the day and there appears to have been a problem that had arisen over advice he had been given by his previous legal advisers. Secondly, the Court notes at the outset that this case demonstrates three things in particular: first, the sometimes unexpected but often significant effects of racism; secondly, the ease with which motorcars can be used as lethal or near-lethal weapons; and thirdly, the difficulties presented in sentencing when both the injuries inflicted by the defendant are grave and the defendant has powerful mitigation both as to the reasons for the offence and as regards his personal circumstances.

2   The underlying facts can be summarised shortly. In the early hours of the morning of May 5, 2002, the appellant, whilst driving his minibus taxi, was flagged

down by a group of 12 people who included the victim in this case, Matthew Tobin. The appellant agreed to take them to Wednesbury for £15. On the pretext, so it appears, that they were worried about his driving, some of the group subjected the appellant to sustained racial abuse of an unpleasant kind and in particular one of the passengers, Craig Foster, was persistent in his racially based insults.

3   On arrival an argument developed about the fare that was due to be paid. Foster offered more racist comments and tried to make his companions refrain from paying the appellant. The victim's girlfriend, Louise Osbourne, who was sitting in the front seat, collected at least part of the fare. In the meantime, Foster, who had got out of the van with other members of the group, removed his jacket and effectively challenged the appellant to a fight. At this the appellant shouted back.

4   Instead of leaving matters there, as the group began to move off the appellant reversed back some 30 feet, hitting some railings, and then he accelerated forwards effectively aiming his car at Foster. The latter got out of the way, but the victim, who was on a zebra crossing, was hit instead. The appellant, who had been concentrating on Foster, did not realise that Mr Tobin had been struck. He continued to drive for a distance and thereby dragged Mr Tobin, who was caught under the minibus, for the length of the adjacent Islamic Centre.

5   Miss Osbourne shouted out and alerted the appellant to what he had done and he stopped. He drove a little further away after Mr Tobin had been released from the undercarriage of the minibus. He pushed Miss Osbourne out of the vehicle and 10 minutes later he telephoned the police and returned to the scene, at which point he was arrested. We wish to stress that there is no suggestion in this case that any of the provocative remarks were made by the victim in this case, Mr Tobin, who was seriously injured. He had fractures at the base of his skull, the left temple and his jaw, and air got into the base of his skull. There was external injury to his left temple and grazing to his shoulders, hands and knees, as well as what was described as a major wound to the hip. In terms of lasting harm there was damage to the nerves in Mr Tobin's face and since this event he has had significant problems with his eyesight.

6   This case demonstrates the value of victim impact statements. The extent of the consequences for Mr Tobin are revealed in the statement provided in this case to have been grave. He was in intensive care for seven days and was unable to work for six-and-a-half months. He could not return to his old job for nearly a year and he has had continuing problems, as we have just observed, as regards his eyesight, and although there may yet be some further recovery a permanent defect will remain in this regard. At the age of 14 to 15 he was the Midland Youth Champion Boxer but this incident has ended his ability to follow that sport. Further, he had hoped to rejoin the army but that career move is now no longer possible.

7   For the appellant, significant and diverse mitigation was advanced. He is a relatively young man, now aged 23. He has one wholly unrelated previous conviction of theft from an employer for which he received an attendance centre order in 1998. He was working as a taxi driver at the time of this offence to help pay for his law course at university, an LLB, and his first child was born

at the beginning of this year. That latter matter is of some importance because this sentence inevitably means that the appellant will not be available to help financially, or in any other way, during this significant period in both his child's and his wife's lives. At the time of sentence he was working for N Power and was considered a good employee and was in line for promotion.

8   By pleading guilty the appellant accepted that he drove the minibus intending to hit Mr Foster. He has, as is clear from his record, no history of violence and it appears therefore that he acted as he did on this occasion because of the racially provocative statements that were made. Having said that, the appellant accepts that this behaviour on his part was wholly excessive and disproportionate. This incident has had a truly significant effect on him. Two psychiatrists submitted reports that were available to the lower court that indicated that he has suffered from chronic or clinical depression following these events. He has experienced panic attacks and the condition known as post traumatic stress disorder, and he is assessed by one of the doctors as posing a risk of self- harm and indeed at one point that same doctor considered that he was unfit to stand trial.

9   Looking at all of the material before us, there is no doubt that this event has at least in part shattered this appellant's life and he feels profound remorse for what he did. Before the court below, as before us, there were some impressive testimonials to which we have paid careful attention, as well as a helpful and favourable prison report.

10   In passing sentence the judge reflected all of the relevant matters set out above in his remarks to the appellant.

11   In consequence this appeal is argued not on the basis that the judge overlooked or ignored any relevant factor, but that he took too high a starting point given the facts of this case and the appellant's mitigation. It is accepted that a custodial sentence was appropriate, but it is submitted that this sentence on these facts was too long. In particular we have been directed to *Attorney General's Reference No.13 of 2001 (John Ivor Cole)* [2001] 2 Cr.App.R (S) 112 (p.497) [2001] EWCA Crim 721. That was a bad case of road rage where over an extended period of time the offender tailgated a number of other cars by driving up close behind them and then braking hard. When a driver pulled over to let the offender past, he was driven at and hit by the offender, after their cars had come to a halt and the other driver had got out in order to speak with the offender. The victim was thrown onto the bonnet of the offender's car with such force as to shatter the windscreen. He suffered a broken wrist and had other injuries. The offender, who had bad convictions, attempted to avoid prosecution by falsely alleging that he had sold the car he had been driving at the time. That he had some personal mitigation, including an absence of offences of violence, a guilty plea, albeit entered late, and a young family. This court in quashing the sentence of community service said that had it not been for the element of double jeopardy the offender could have expected a sentence of 4 years' imprisonment for the offence of causing grievous bodily harm with intent and 12 months' imprisonment for the offence of perverting the course of justice.

12   Comparing that authority with the instant case, on the one hand in the matter before us the injuries were significantly worse, whilst the underlying cause of the

offence on the other provides the present appellant with a significantly greater degree of mitigation. We do not underestimate the significance of the racist taunting in this case. Moreover, this appellant did not try to hide and gave himself up to the police, and he has not only shown significant remorse but, as we have already observed, his life has been seriously affected by what occurred. This was on any view a difficult sentencing exercise which the judge approached as regards his sentencing remarks faultlessly.

13   Given the exceptional mitigation available to this appellant and as no more than an act of mercy on the particular facts of this case, we are persuaded by a narrow margin that notwithstanding the appalling injuries this sentence on a plea was unnecessarily long. We are fully aware of the grave and permanent consequences for the victim of what occurred, but the exceptional mitigation, presented to us forcefully and succinctly by Mr Guest, leads us to conclude that a shorter sentence would have met the justice of this case. The mitigation bears short repetition. This appellant was provoked by sustained racist remarks into acting in a way that was wholly out of character. He has suffered significantly, both personally and professionally as a result. His sense of remorse and regret is real and substantial. Accordingly, we quash the sentence of four years' imprisonment and substitute a sentence of three years. To that extent this appeal is allowed.

ATTORNEY GENERAL'S REFERENCE NO.64 OF 2004 (BARBARA BOWER)

COURT OF APPEAL (Lord Justice Rose (Vice President, Court of Appeal Criminal Division), Mr Justice Richards and Mr Justice Bean): October 12, 2004

[2004] EWCA Crim 2618; [2005] 1 Cr.App.R.(S.) 107

(LT) Criminal intent; Seriousness of offence; Undue leniency; Unlawful act of manslaughter

1   *Manslaughter—death caused by striking man with piece of wood, causing wounds to abdomen—length of sentence*

2   Two-and-a-half years' imprisonment for manslaughter, where a woman attacked a vulnerable man with a piece of wood, inflicting injuries to the abdomen in particular, but without intending to cause grievous bodily harm, increased to three-and-a-half years.

3   The offender pleaded guilty to manslaughter on an indictment charging murder. The victim, an alcoholic aged 68, was attacked in his home by two men, who attempted to steal money from him. Police officers and the ambulance service attended but the man refused to accept medical help. An hour or two later the

offender arrived at the man's flat looking for her daughter. She was said to be drunk. The offender alleged that the victim had sexually interfered with her children. She threw a television set at the victim and then hit him a number of times with a piece of wood. She then threw various objects at the victim. The police were called the following morning when the deceased was found to be dead. A post-mortem examination revealed various injuries, including large lacerations in the small bowel which resulted in blood entering the abdominal cavity. In interview the offender admitted visiting the victim but denied assaulting him. She eventually pleaded guilty on the basis that she did not intend to kill or cause serious bodily harm. Sentenced to two and a half years' imprisonment. The Attorney General asked the Court to review the sentence on the grounds that it was unduly lenient.

H4   **Held:** for the Attorney General was submitted that the offence involved a sustained attack with considerable force and the use of a weapon on a vulnerable man aged 68. The attack was unprovoked and the victim was left without medical help. In the Court's judgment, taking into account the mitigating circumstances relating to the offender, a sentence of the order of four and a half years' imprisonment would have been expected on a plea of guilty. It followed that the sentence of two and a half years was unduly lenient. Taking into account the element of double jeopardy and progress which the offender had made while in prison, the Court would substitute a sentence of three and a half years' imprisonment.

H5   **Case cited:**
Attorney General's References Nos 19, 20 and 21 of 2001 (Alan Edward Byrne and others) [2002] 1 Cr.App.R.(S.) 33 (p.136)

H6   **References:** manslaughter, *Current Sentencing Practice* B 1–3

H7   *R. Horwell* for the appellant.
P. Wright Q.C. for the offender.

1   **Rose L.J.:**   The Solicitor General for the Attorney General seeks leave of the Court, under s.36 of the Criminal Justice Act 1988, to refer a sentence said to be unduly lenient. We grant leave. The offender was born in April 1963 so is 41 years of age.

2   Her trial was due to commence on March 16, 2004. She faced an indictment for murder. In relation to that she had pleaded not guilty at the plea and directions hearing. On March 16 she pleaded guilty to manslaughter on the ground of lack of intent and a written basis of plea was accepted. She had indicated, about a month before the trial, that she was prepared to plead guilty to manslaughter. On April 23, at Liverpool Crown Court, she was sentenced by Morland J. to two-and-a-half years' imprisonment.

3   In summary the offender, when she was drunk, attacked a 68-year-old man in his home. She threw a television set and other objects at him and she repeatedly hit him with a piece of wood in the area of the abdomen. The deceased had mul-

tiple injuries, not all of which were caused by the offender, but it seems highly likely that she caused the abdominal injuries from which he died.

4   The victim, Mr Hyde, was an alcoholic. For several years he had lived at a flat in Preston New Road, Blackburn. There were other flats in the same building and most of the occupants had a serious drink problem.

5   On June 11, 2003 there were two separate incidents in his flat. The first took place before 10.15pm, when the police and ambulance service attended in response to a report that a man had been assaulted. They went into Mr Hyde's flat and found him lying across a mattress which was half on the floor and half on the bed. He was semiconscious and very drunk. An officer tried to speak to him but he gave an abusive reply. He had signs of dried blood around his nostrils and his nose appeared somewhat swollen. He did not seem to have any other injury but there was no thorough examination carried out because of his general attitude and his refusal to accept medical help.

6   It was the case for the Crown that, by this time, Mr Hyde had been assaulted by two men called Hartley and Burns, who had attempted to steal money from him. That assault was seen by two witnesses, a Mr McNally, who described Mr Hyde being shaken and stamped on the thigh (without any great force), and a Mr Whittle, who described Mr Hyde as being shaken violently and thrown on the bed over a period of 10 to 20 minutes. Both Hartley and Burns had slapped Mr Hyde on the face but neither of the witnesses saw any punches or kicks. In due course, both Hartley and Burns pleaded guilty to assault with intent to rob and were sentenced respectively to three and two years' imprisonment.

7   Within an hour or two of that first incident the offender arrived at Mr Hyde's flat looking for her daughter, who she thought might be with Hartley. The only witness as to what then occurred was Mr McNally. The Crown invited the court to approach his evidence with caution because he, together with others, had consumed three bottles of sherry in the course of the evening. Mr McNally described the offender as being "steaming drunk". The moment she came into the flat she said to Mr Hyde: "You, you little bastard, you mess with kids. I don't like people like that. My kids have been messed about with." Many years previously Mr Hyde had been convicted of offences of unlawful sexual intercourse and attempted sexual intercourse and, also, some 15 or more years earlier, he had been convicted of indecent assault on a 10-year-old girl, for which he was sentenced to a short period of imprisonment.

8   The offender was in a rage. She picked up the television and threw it at Mr Hyde and it hit him on the lower part of the face and the upper chest. He looked as though that had hurt him. He fell backwards to the floor and Mr McNally thought he may have been unconscious. The offender then picked up a piece of wood (used as a door prop) and brought it down, jagged end lowermost, in a stabbing motion into Mr Hyde's stomach as he lay on the floor. According to Mr McNally, she did that five or six times, with considerable force, looking mad with rage. She then pulled an electrical clock and clock radio from their sockets and threw them at Mr Hyde: the first hit him on the head, the second on the chest. The offender also hit Mr Hyde on the back with the piece of wood. She then took a mirror and a clock and walked off. She later showed

these to a friend and said that they had come from what she described as "a paedophile's house".

9   Soon afterwards, Mr McNally fell asleep. The police were not called until the
following morning. They arrived just after eight o'clock. Mr Hyde by that time
was dead. His body was on the floor of the flat. There were various pieces of
broken wood and splinters near the body and some of them were bloodstained.

10   A postmortem examination revealed multiple lacerations to the left arm, some
of which contained splinters of wood, consistent with an assault by the piece of
wood found at the scene, bruises to the knuckles which could have been offensive
or defensive, and abrasions on the front of the left hipbone which were typical of
injuries caused by blows from a shod foot. There was extensive bruising on the
lower abdomen. Internal examination revealed three large lacerations in the
small bowel mesentery which had resulted in more than a litre of blood entering
the abdominal cavity. It would have needed a significant degree of force to cause
those lacerations, which are injuries of a kind usually found in road traffic accidents or falls from a height. There were also fractures of the deceased's hyoid
bone at the front of the neck. The conclusion reached was that the deceased
had been subjected to a sustained and forceful assault causing the injuries
which we have described, the most severe of which were to the abdomen. It is
also of significance that those lacerations would have bled swiftly and would
have caused very severe abdominal pain. In consequence, it was the pathologist's
view that it was highly unlikely that those abdominal injuries had been caused
during the first of the two incidents. It will be recalled that there was a substantial
time lag between these two incidents.

11   The offender was arrested on June 12. She denied being in Preston New Road
the previous day. In interview, however, she admitted visiting Mr Hyde's flat but
claimed to have found him on the floor and to have done no more than make him
comfortable by placing a cushion under his head. She denied assaulting him.

12   On behalf of the Solicitor General, Mr Horwell draws attention to what he submits are five aggravating features: first, the attack was sustained and involved the
use of considerable force; secondly, a weapon was used; thirdly, the victim was
68 years of age, vulnerable and defenceless; fourthly, the attack was unprovoked;
and fifthly, the offender had left the victim without seeking any medical help.

13   Mr Horwell draws attention to four mitigating features: first, the plea of guilty;
secondly, effectively the offender is of good character, having one spent previous
conviction of assaulting the police for which she was fined some years ago;
thirdly, she is responsible for the care of three children who are aged 16, 8 and
4, and fourthly, that she has shown genuine remorse.

14   There are a number of authorities referred to in the written reference. It suffices, having regard to a concession made by Mr Wright Q.C., to which in a
moment we shall come, to refer only to one of these, *Attorney General's References Nos 19, 20 and 21 of 2001* [2002] 1 Cr.App.R.(S.) 33 (p.136) where, in
the course of giving the judgment of the Court, Kay L.J. at p.145, para.[42] said:

"As in the other settings in which death may result to which we have referred, this public concern and the need for deterrence must be reflected in sentences passed by the court. This inevitably will mean longer sentences than might have been considered appropriate some years ago in a different climate of opinion and concern."

15   The submission that is made by Mr Horwell is that the sentence was unduly lenient. It failed to mark the gravity of the offence, the aggravating features, the need for punishment and public concern about the needless loss of life.

16   On behalf of the offender Mr Wright Q.C. accepts that the sentence was lenient but he submits that it was not unduly lenient and, even if it were, he invites the Court to exercise its discretion not to interfere with the sentence which was passed. He stresses that the judge was highly experienced and he had, Mr Wright submits, regard to all the facts, including the initial earlier incident of violence, the remorse shown by the offender and the other circumstances to which we have referred. This, he points out, is the first custodial sentence which the offender has endured and it has, understandably, had a significant effect both upon her and upon her family.

17   So far as the offender herself is concerned, her present earliest date of release is July 10, 2005. The possibility of her offending again in a similar fashion is very small indeed. She has, during her time in prison, achieved the highest status and the most privileges which can be achieved. She has engaged in a variety of courses, including thinking skills, anger management, alcohol control and computer skills.

8   Mr Wright draws attention to the unhappy history of the offender, as set out in the psychiatrist report which was before the learned sentencing judge, to which it is unnecessary to refer in detail. At the time of these events he had what Mr Wright described as a fragile current relationship with a man in loco parentis to her children and it was contemplated that he would look after the children with assistance from the social services.

9   Mr Wright accepted, properly, the proposition which was put to him in the course of his submissions that, if the offender had not been a woman, with the mitigation in her favour arising, in particular, from her family circumstances, the least sentence that could properly have been passed in the court below would have been five years and it would probably have been six years' imprisonment.

0   In our judgment, taking into account the particular circumstances of mitigation in relation to the offender, we would have expected, on a plea of guilty in the court below, a sentence of the order of four and a half years' imprisonment. It follows that the sentence of two-and-a-half years was unduly lenient. It is necessary for this Court, if it interferes with the sentence which was passed, to take into account double jeopardy, that is to say that the offender is being sentenced a second time. It is also appropriate to take into account in the present case the obvious progress which the offender has sought to make while she has been in prison.

We bear in mind, above all, in relation to this offender, the investigation arising from the family circumstances. That said, the learned judge, as it seems to us, was unduly influenced by the mitigation in relation to this offender and paid too little regard to the gravity of this offence.

22   In the light of all those circumstances, we quash the sentence of two and a half years which was imposed by the learned judge and we impose in its place a sentence of three-and-a-half years' imprisonment.

R. v JONATHAN GRIFFITHS

COURT OF APPEAL (Lord Justice Mance, Mr Justice Newman and Mr Justice Fulford): October 13, 2004

[2004] EWCA Crim 2656; [2005] 1 Cr.App.R.(S.) 108

(LT) Compassionate grounds; Letter bombs; Possession of explosives with intent; Sentence length

H1   *Explosives offences—possessing explosive substance with intent—attempting to make letter bombs for unknown purpose—offender seriously injured by premature explosion—length of sentence*

H2   Fifteen years' imprisonment upheld for possessing an explosive substance with intent, where the offender attempted to make two letter bombs using military high explosives but was seriously injured when the explosive detonated prematurely.

H3   The applicant pleaded guilty to having an explosive substance. He was convicted of having an explosive substance with intent, and doing an act with intent to cause an explosion. The applicant went to the house of his co-accused where he set about making two letter bombs using military high explosive and detonators. While the applicant was making the bombs, the explosives detonated, causing injuries to the applicant and damage to the house. The applicant had both hands amputated and suffered other serious injuries. A further quantity of explosive was found in the applicant's home. The applicant repeatedly declined to comment on being interviewed. The applicant claimed that he had prepared the explosive device to frighten two people into paying off a debt. Sentenced to 15 years' imprisonment.

H4   **Held:** the sentencing judge said that the motive and intentions of the applicant and his accomplice were unclear, but that his explanations for having the explosive were untrue. The sentencing judge found that the applicants had plotted together to make bombs with the intention of endangering the lives of recipients. It was submitted for the applicant that the sentencing judge did not have sufficient regard to the applicant's disability. The Court considered that the sentence of 15 years' imprisonment could not be considered manifestly excessive. The only question was whether the applicant's disability merited a further discount. The sentencing judge might have imposed a consecutive sentence for the possession of a further quantity of explosives found at the applicant's house. He had taken into account the applicant's disability in not doing so. The application would be refused.

15 **References:** explosives offences, *Current Sentencing Practice* B 7-3

16 No counsel appeared.

1   **Mance L.J.:**   On July 31, 2002 in the Crown Court at Cardiff before McKinnon J., the applicant was convicted of having an explosive substance with intent (count one) and doing an act with intent to cause an explosion (count two). He had previously pleaded guilty on January 30, 2002 to having an explosive substance (count three). On the same day he was sentenced in respect of the first two offences to 15 years' imprisonment and in respect of the third offence to 3 years' imprisonment, all those sentences being ordered to run concurrently, making therefore a total of 15 years' imprisonment. His co-accused, Geoffrey Howard Wildy, was convicted of having an explosive substance with intent (count one) and doing an act with intent to cause an explosion (count two) and was sentenced to 15 years' imprisonment on each count concurrent. His appeal against that sentence was determined by this Court on May 12, 2003 [2003] EWCA Crim 1571, [2004] 1 Cr.App.R (S) 11(p.99).

2   The facts in outline are that on October 4, 2001 the applicant travelled from Wisbech in Cambridgeshire to South Wales where he met up with his co-accused, Wildy. They went to the co-accused's house in Bridgend. In the kitchen of the house the applicant set about making two letter bombs using British military high explosive known as PE4 and detonators. The co-accused Wildy was evidently in the lounge. While in the process of being made into bombs by the applicant, the explosives on which he was working detonated prematurely and caused extensive injuries to the applicant, to which we will return, as well as £7,000 worth of damage to the house. Wildy was sitting in an area in the lounge where pieces of equipment associated with bomb making were also found. He sought to explain those on the basis that they must have been blown through into the lounge from the kitchen.

3   The applicant's injuries were so severe that both of his hands had to be amputated and he also suffered injuries to his thighs, genitalia, anterior trunk, neck and face, as well as perforated ear drums. Wildy was uninjured. The applicant was detained in hospital and not fit to be interviewed until November 5, 2001, after which he was interviewed nine times in all and each time gave a "no comment" interview.

4   At trial he ran the defence that the explosives had been forced on him by people whom he had picked up in his minicab earlier in the year. Belatedly during the course of the trial he also stated that he had prepared the device in order to deliver them by hand to and so frighten two other Cardiff residents, the intention being to frighten them to pay off a debt of £5,000 that had been owed to him. Counsel for the applicant, in an advice on appeal, comments that this explanation too was clearly rejected by the jury, although we note that it is repeated in an undated letter which we have seen which goes into the asserted background in some detail

with regard to a Libyan transaction, but does not in any way explain the origin of the explosives or indeed other equipment which was being worked on.

5   The prosecution relied on the fact that among the contents of the house were two jiffy bags, addressed to the two people whom the applicant had identified, with first class postage stamps attached. They suggested that that was inconsistent with the applicant's explanation that he was going to hand deliver the envelopes. However, his answer, as we understand it, was that it was to lend verisimilitude to the idea that the envelopes had come through the post. The prosecution was however also able to point to the fact that when they searched the applicant's house in Wisbech they recovered further substantially greater quantities of explosive, 349g of PE4, and three letters addressed to the South Wales police which put the blame anonymously for the "explosions in Cardiff" on the same two gentlemen to whom the applicant asserted that the explosives were to be delivered. The whole position and the applicant's intentions therefore remained a matter of some obscurity.

6   In sentencing, the judge said that the applicant and co-accused had been convicted of very serious offences. The explosive concerned was PE4, British military plastic explosive. What their real motive and intentions were was unclear. However, the applicant's explanation for having the explosive—that it had been forced upon him by complete strangers—had been a "cock and bull" story. It was clear that both the applicant and his co-accused had lied. It was also clear that they had plotted together to make bombs, probably to be delivered through the post, with the intention of endangering the lives of the recipients. It was obvious, the judge said, that the applicant knew very much more about bomb making than he was prepared to say. It was not known how much PE4 was used in making the bombs or how it was distributed between the bombs if there was more than one. What was clear was that he had attached to a detonator, or perhaps two detonators, sufficient PE4 to cause these very serious injuries to himself and serious structural damage to Wildy's kitchen. It was not known where the electric detonators or indeed the PE4 came from. It was not known who made the pressure switches, the bomb's triggering device, or who assembled all the various bits and pieces of explosive paraphernalia, including batteries, connectors, wires and so on. It was, however, a scheme to endanger by explosions the lives of two people who could well have been killed. It was unclear whether there was a much more sinister case with the further explosive being kept in reserve for the making of further explosions, but the judge said that he would not sentence on the basis that this was but the beginning of a campaign of letter bombs. He took into account the fact that the applicant had suffered severe injuries and so ordered the three years' imprisonment in respect of count three to run concurrently.

7   He also referred to the antecedents of the applicant and Wildy. Wildy was without previous convictions, aged 58. The applicant was aged 42 with some previous convictions but nothing approaching the seriousness of the present offences. Indeed, the convictions were old and dated from between 1975 and 1997, in July of which he had been sentenced to six months in a detention centre for possessing an offensive weapon, that being the longest custodial sentence he ever received.

8   There were psychiatric and medical reports. According to the first the applicant appeared to be coming to terms with his injuries and showed adaptive coping mechanisms and there were no psychotic features or suicidal issues. According to the second, after identifying the injuries suffered, the author expressed concern that while in custody the applicant was not receiving the care he required and made recommendations including daily bathing, regular cleaning and dressing of wounds and the regular issue of prescribed medication.

9   The grounds of appeal are that the sentence was manifestly excessive because the judge in imposing a term of 15 years' imprisonment did not have sufficient regard to the applicant's disability. A letter dated June 9, 2004 also sets out the applicant's own submissions relating to the sentence passed. He refers there to the two grounds and submits in support of the first that the trial judge should have sought further expert advice about his injuries before deciding how much to allow for such injuries, pointing out the suffering which a double amputee has to endure, while in support of the second ground he submits that it was wrong for him not to be represented or granted representation by a Q.C. and that a Q.C. would have developed certain further matters, in particular would have drawn the attention of the judge to the fact that his occupation had been that of lift engineer, electrical and mechanical. He argues that that contravened the European Convention on Human Rights.

10   In refusing leave to appeal, the single judge observed:

> "It is not arguable that a sentence of 15 years' imprisonment for having an explosive substance with intent and doing an act with intent to cause an explosion is manifestly excessive."

He then referred to the decision in *Wildy* which supports that proposition. He continued:

> "As to the argument that the judge did not adequately take the extensive disability you sustained in the explosion into account, he took this into account in deciding not to make the sentence for count 3 a consecutive sentence which he might otherwise have done. It is not arguable that his approach in this displayed error."

We have considered the reasoning in *Wildy* and it supports what the single judge said. The applicant, although this is a minor matter, was in fact somewhat younger and had a less good character than Wildy, but in reality it would have been impossible to distinguish between them, and the Court in *Wildy* saw no criticism in the fact that there was no distinction made between the two.

1   The only substantial point, therefore, is whether the disability suffered merited a further discount. In our view the single judge's comments on that were entirely correct. The judge made an allowance for it by making the sentence for the further very substantial quantity of explosive, which this applicant alone had elsewhere, concurrent. There is also in our view nothing in the suggestion that there was unfairness or breach of the Human Rights Convention in refusal of representation by a Q.C. The applicant had representation by counsel. The applicant says that the judge would have looked at his position very differently if he had known the

applicant was a lift engineer and he refers to words which he suggests the judge used, namely, "I think you have done this many times before". Those words do not appear in the judge's sentencing remarks and, as we have pointed out, he expressly sentenced on the basis that he was dealing with this bomb making. He was correct, however, to point out that the background to the bomb making and the origin of the explosives and indeed of other equipment were still wholly uncertain, as they remain. Whether or not counsel informed the judge of the applicant's former occupation, as to which we have no confirmation, although we suspect that this would have come out during trial or been referred to by counsel, we cannot see how it could bear on the proper length of sentence. It certainly would not account for this applicant's ability to obtain explosives or probably some of the other equipment, and it was obvious from what the applicant was doing at the time of the explosion and from the wealth of electrical equipment and parts around him, of which we have seen photographs, that he was someone with considerable electrical skills.

12   In all these circumstances this renewed application is, in our view, without merit and fails.

R. v JASON LEE PALMER

Court of Appeal (Lord Justice Auld, Mr Justice Owen and Mr Justice Hedley): October 15, 2004

[2004] EWCA Crim 2631; [2005] 1 Cr.App.R.(S.) 109

⟨LT⟩ Attempts; Family relationships; Good character; Murder

H1   *Attempted murder—attack with knife on former partner—length of sentence*

H2   Twelve years' imprisonment for an attack with a knife on a former partner by a man of previous good character reduced to 10 years.

H3   The appellant was convicted of attempted murder. The appellant formed a relationship with a woman and they had a daughter. They separated after about three years, and there were difficulties over access to the child. The woman became concerned about the appellant's attitude and the possibility of a confrontation, and arrangements were made for her to be escorted to her car by a security officer when she left work at the end of the day. Instead it was suggested that she should leave work half an hour early in the hope of avoiding any confrontation with the appellant. The woman left work early accompanied by a colleague. As she reached her car she saw the appellant walking towards her. She got into the car to lock herself in, but the appellant prevented her from doing so. The women felt two blows to her head and was then subjected to a frenzied attack with a knife. The woman's colleague ran towards the car and the appellant ran off. The woman sustained 16 lacerations, including one to the side of her neck which was a potentially life threatening injury. Sentenced to 12 years' imprisonment.

H4   **Held:** this was a vicious and sustained attack on an unarmed defenceless girl. The most potent mitigation was the appellant's positive good character. The Court accepted that the appellant did not present a risk to others. The Court was persuaded that the sentence was too high, and that the appropriate sentence was 10 years' imprisonment.

H5   **Case cited:**
Davis [2001] 1 Cr.App.R.(S.) 53 (p.186)

H6   **References:** attempted murder, *Current Sentencing Practice* B 2-1

H7   *F.G. Burrell Q.C.* for the appellant.
A. Semple for the Crown.

1   **Owen J.:**   On February 17, 2004 the appellant was convicted of attempted murder at the Crown Court at Hull and was sentenced to 12 years' imprisonment. He appeals against that sentence with the leave of the Full Court.

2   The appellant was born in March 1976 and is therefore now 28 years of age. His victim, Rebecca W, was his former partner and the mother of their two-year-old daughter. Their relationship began in about 2000 when she was 18. It appears to have been stormy and they finally separated in July of 2003, four or five weeks before the attack which gave rise to his conviction. There were difficulties over access to the child, and Miss W was sufficiently concerned about the appellant's attitude to her and the risk of confrontation with him that she spoke both to her parents and to her colleagues at work. On the day before the attack she was threatened by a female as she left work, who shouted at her that she was "going to get it" and that she should "watch her back".

3   Miss W was employed as a clerical officer at Scunthorpe Hospital. On the following day, August 13, 2003, arrangements were made for her to be escorted to her car in the car park by a security officer when she left work at the end of the day, but instead her manager suggested that she leave work half an hour earlier in the hope of avoiding any confrontation with the appellant.

4   She duly left work at 4pm accompanied by a colleague. They walked to the car park together and her colleague then left her a short distance from her car. As she reached her car, she looked up and saw the appellant walking towards her. She got into the car and was about to close the door and lock herself in, but the appellant prevented her from doing so. She started the engine, but he said something to her which she could not hear. She told him that she did not want to see him there and then she felt two blows to her head. She fell to her left, towards the gear lever, and then realised that she was bleeding. The appellant then climbed into the car and subjected her to what can properly be described as a frenzied attack with a knife.

5   At one point she managed to get the knife out of his hand and he slumped in the passenger seat saying he was sorry and did not know what he was doing. She mis-

takenly thought that the attack was over and released her grip on the knife. But he grabbed it from her and started attacking her again, saying "die, you bitch". She managed to sound the car horn which alerted her colleague who ran across to the car. When the appellant saw her, he ran off.

6   In the course of her evidence Miss W said that Mrs Sanderson, her colleague, had saved her life. The judge observed in passing sentence that that was only partially true and that her life had been saved by a combination of Mrs Sanderson's actions and by her own courage in putting up such a valiant defence to the attack. He added that he had no doubt that but for those factors she would now be dead.

7   The police arrived at the scene; by that time the appellant had returned. He made the first officer there aware of where he had dropped the knife. He was arrested. When interviewed, he gave details of his relationship with Miss W, complaining that he had been denied access to their child and that in consequence he had become increasingly frustrated and depressed. He denied any knowledge of the incident on the previous day. He admitted taking the knife from his mother's home, but said that he had had no intention of using it. He had waited in the car park, wanting to talk to her.

8   As a result of the attack Miss W sustained 16 lacerations to her neck, head, shoulders, arms, legs and hand, the most serious of which was a very deep laceration, about four inches long, to the right side of her neck, below her ear. This was a potentially life threatening injury and required a number of operations to close the wound and to stem the blood loss.

9   The learned judge in passing sentence summarised the impact of those injuries in the following terms:

> ". . . she suffered badly as a result of what you did. She was hospitalised; she was off work for two months, and she went through what must have been agony for her when her daughter seemed to react against her because of the injuries that she had suffered and the surprise to her, so her mother had to take over for a time the job of primary carer for Leah. She suffered headaches, nervousness at all sorts of things. She has been left with scars, nightmares and anxiety. She has been forced to change her job."

10   This appeal is advanced on five grounds; first, that the appellant is a man of good character and that this offence is completely out of character; secondly, that the relationship between the appellant and Miss W had been volatile and that she had in the past cut up his clothing and damaged his CD collection; thirdly, Mr Burrell Q.C. submits that there was no evidence that he was a future risk to anyone; fourthly, that Miss W was left with no permanent serious injury, save some scarring largely to the back of the neck; finally, that the appellant was entitled to be sentenced on the basis that the intent was formed in the course of the struggle.

11   As to the first, it is correct that the appellant was a man of good character. In passing sentence the learned judge made express reference to that and to the letters written to the court on his behalf, copies of which are before us. But having said that he accepted without reservation that there was a good side to the appellant, the learned judge said this:

". . . we have seen a different side to you in this court. Your defences of accident and self-defence were, in the light of the evidence, simply ludicrous.
Yet, watching you, as I have done for the last week, it seemed to me that
you had convinced yourself that they were true. This demonstrates a distor-
tion of thinking that is very worrying for the future."

2   Notwithstanding that observation, we accept that on the current evidence the
appellant does not present a future risk.

3   As to the remaining grounds of appeal, the fact that the relationship between
the appellant and Miss Willey was highly volatile provides a background to
the offence, but little by way of mitigation. The fact that she has been left with
no permanent serious injury is more due to luck than to anything that can be
attributed to the appellant. As to the last argument advanced by Mr Burrell,
namely that he was entitled to be sentenced on the basis that the intent was formed
during the course of the struggle, while we accept that that was a matter left to the
jury, and it was not possible to determine the basis upon which the jury convicted
him, it has to be borne in mind that he went to the car park having forearmed himself with a knife.

4   In support of this appeal Mr Burrell has most helpfully drawn our attention to a
large number of decisions in which this Court has had to consider the appropriate
sentence for cases of attempted murder. We were greatly assisted by his analysis
of those authorities, but it is not necessary for us to deal with them in detail. We
were particularly assisted by the decision of this Court in *Davis* [2001] 1
Cr.App.R.(S.) 53 (p.186). It was a case in which the appellant had an established
relationship with his victim, a woman aged 36. Following a domestic argument,
she told him to leave, but he immediately reacted by chasing her and stabbing her
in the back and stomach with a kitchen knife and by slashing her face. She was
permanently scared in a disfiguring manner. The appellant was sentenced to 12
years' imprisonment.

5   In giving the judgment of the Court Burton J. emphasised, as is plainly the case,
that no case can be decisive of another, because all depend on their own facts, but
he continued:

"In *Wooton*, in a decision of the Court presided over by Swinton Thomas LJ,
there was an attack on the defendant's wife's father with a knife, stabbing
him in the stomach and the chest. Steel J, giving the judgment of the
Court, concluded that a starting point of 12 years for a conviction on an
offence of that kind was normal, and on a plea, and in relation to specific
evidence of a serious medical condition in the case of the defendant, reduced
the sentence of 11 years given by the judge in that case to eight years. The
defendant pleaded guilty, so the starting point was 12 years."

The Court came to the conclusion that the sentence that had been imposed was
entirely appropriate in the light of the authorities and the appeal was dismissed.

This was a vicious and sustained attack on an unarmed and defenceless girl, the
appellant having lain in wait for her with a knife. She was lucky to escape with her
life. The most powerful mitigation that can be urged on behalf of the appellant is

that he is a man of positive good character, as demonstrated by the number of people who spoke well of him and came to court to give evidence on his behalf. We also take account of the fact that this incident has to be viewed against the background of a volatile and at times violent relationship between these two people. We accept that the appellant does not present a risk to others and we have in mind that in the case of *Davis* the injuries that were sustained by the victim were substantially more serious than those suffered by Miss W.

18   It is because of those factors that we have been persuaded that the sentence that was imposed upon the appellant was too high. In our judgment, the appropriate sentence is one of 10years' imprisonment. This appeal will be allowed to that limited extent.

R. v JOSEPH GRAHAM, LEE PAUL MARSHALL, ROBERT JAMES WATSON

COURT OF APPEAL (Lord Justice Mance, Mr Justice Mackay and Mr Justice Fulford): October 18, 2004

[2004] EWCA Crim 2762; [2005] 1 Cr.App.R.(S.) 110

⟨LT⟩ Actual bodily harm; Guilty pleas; Racially aggravated offences; Sentence length

H1   *Racially aggravated assault occasioning actual bodily harm—attack by group of youths accompanied by racial abuse but not apparently motivated by racial hostility—length of sentence*

H2   Six years' imprisonment for racially aggravated assault occasioning actual bodily harm, where a group of youths attacked a man who was racially abused but the attack was not apparently motivated by racial hostility, reduced to five years and six months.

H3   The appellants pleaded guilty to racially aggravated assault occasioning actual bodily harm. The appellants became involved in an incident in a public house when one of the appellants kicked a woman as she was playing pool. The woman complained to a man who was a Rastafarian of Afro-Caribbean descent. The man asked the appellant if he was responsible. The appellant then challenged the man to a fight. The second appellant then punched the man in the eye, causing it to bleed. The first appellant then repeatedly punched the man and a third appellant struck him across the top of the back with a pool cue. The fourth defendant then joined in the attack. After a lull in the fighting, the third appellant again attacked the victim with a pool cue and later attempted to stab him with the pool cue. Towards the end of the episode, racial abuse was addressed to the victim and a dreadlock was pulled from his head. The victim was taken to hospital where he was found to have various injuries, including a fractured rib. Sentenced to six years' imprisonment in the case of one appellant and five years and eight months' in the case of each of two other appellants. The fourth defendant was sentenced to two years and six months' imprisonment.

Held: the sentencing judge indicated that without the element of racial aggravation, the sentences would have been four years, and three years and eight months respectively. It followed that he had imposed an additional two years' imprisonment on each appellant for the racial aggravation. It followed that he had departed from the usual approach of allowing some reduction for a guilty plea. In considering the aggravating features, it was to be observed that the offence was not planned and did not in any real sense form part of a pattern of racist offending. The forcible ripping of a dreadlock from the head of a Rastafarian was a further significant aggravating feature. Although the incident had been recorded on CCTV, the racially aggravated circumstances, which consisted primarily of the racial abuse, were not caught by the recording. The Court considered that this was a very bad assault; it was wholly unprovoked and involved extensive and prolonged violence in an attack by more than three people on one defenceless man. The Court considered that the sentencing judge was justified in taking the starting points he did with reference to the underlying offence of assault occasioning actual bodily harm. Although the Court did not accept the appellants' arguments, it considered that the additional period in respect of the racial aggravation was somewhat excessive, bearing in mind that there was a plea in relation to both the assault and the racially aggravating circumstances. In the circumstances, the sentences would be reduced to five and a half years' imprisonment and five years and two months' imprisonment respectively.

A. Reynolds for the appellant Watson.
Miss N. Shant for the appellants Marshall and Graham.
M. Auty for the Crown.

Cases cited:
Kelly and Donnelly [2001] 2 Cr.App.R.(S.) 73 (p.341)
Saunders [2000] 2 Cr.App.R.(S.) 71.

References: racially aggravated assault occasioning actual bodily harm, *Current Sentencing Practice* B 2–4.3H

JUDGMENT

Fulford J.:   On March 22, 2004 in the Crown Court at Nottingham the appellants pleaded guilty, on re-arraignment and on the day fixed for trial, to one offence of racially aggravated assault occasioning actual bodily harm. On May 14, 2004, Judge Teare sentenced Watson to six years' imprisonment and Marshall and Graham to five years eight months' imprisonment each. They all now appeal to this court against those sentences with the leave of the single judge. A co-accused, John McNee, received a sentence of two years, six months' for the same offence, to be served consecutively to a sentence of three months' imprisonment for an unrelated offence of common assault.

2   The circumstances of this racially-aggravated assault were as follows. At about 10pm on September 9, 2003 the complainant, Mr Senior, who is Afro-Caribbean by descent and a Rastafarian by religion, went to a public house in Nottingham with a friend, Ms Robertson, who is a social worker; they were hoping to meet the manager, a friend of Mr Senior. They started to play pool in the public house while they waited. Watson passed Ms Robertson as she was playing a shot and he kicked her on the backside for no apparent reason. She complained to Mr Senior about this, who approached Watson merely to ask if he was responsible. Watson, who was celebrating his birthday, immediately challenged Mr Senior to a fight outside and refused to apologise. Mr Senior, in the light of Watson's reaction, simply made to leave the public house, but then Graham punched him hard in his right eye causing it to bleed. Notwithstanding this behaviour, Mr Senior remained calm and persisted in his attempt to leave. He was unable to do so, not least because Graham and Watson repeatedly punched him. Marshall then joined in the attack, in that whilst Graham and Watson continued to assault Mr Senior, who did not at any stage attempt to hit his assailants, Marshall raised a pool cue to shoulder height and struck Mr Senior across the top of his back, the first of a number of such blows delivered by that appellant.

3   By this stage, Graham had delivered at least three full-blooded punches to Mr Senior. Marshall's second blow with the pool cue caused it to shatter. Graham then pushed Mr Senior over the pool table enabling Marshall to deliver a further blow with the shattered pool cue. It was at this moment that McNee joined in the general melee. During a lull in this attack Watson and Mr Senior spoke to each other, but this was brought to an end by Marshall, now armed with a fresh pool cue, who hit Mr Senior for what was by then the sixth time with a weapon of this kind. Throughout this continuing attack, Ms Robertson, showing conspicuous courage, tried to help her friend. We observe that no-one else in the public house lifted a finger to assist the victim, even when Graham in particular tried to hit her. Thereafter, there were further punches. Marshall tried to stab Mr Senior with the pool cue and the other appellants and McNee all took at different times the role of lead attacker and generally in that way this assault continued for some time.

4   We will not deal with each and every episode of this attack. Suffice it to say that, in addition to the matters set out above, it was prolonged and involved repeated punching with many of the blows clearly being delivered with considerable force. Towards the end of the attack one of the appellants tore one of the victim's dreadlocks from his head and Mr Senior, in his statement, described the excruciating pain he felt when this happened. At this point in the attack, whilst Mr Senior was being dragged across the floor by his hair, one of the group said, "Get the fucking nigger" and, "Get the wog". Moreover, before they left, Ms Robertson heard one of the men say "Don't fucking come back here you niggers".

5   After Mr Senior and Ms Robertson escaped, the group celebrated their attack laughing and joking, and they danced around the public house holding up Mr Senior's hat and dreadlock as if they were trophies. These events were filmed by a CCTV camera and all the members of this Court have had an opportunity

of viewing the relevant footage. Suffice it to say that what we have seen reveals, as we have described, a cowardly and very serious attack on a man who offered no resistance at any stage. Mr Senior was taken to hospital bleeding profusely, his right eye was stitched and he was treated for swelling, bruising, a laceration to the back of his head, and he had a fractured rib which was very painful and he experienced pain to his left elbow. In the Victim Impact statement, Mr Senior stated:

> "I have been more deeply affected by what happened to me on that evening than I could possibly have imagined. The physical scars and injuries have slowly healed albeit they alone were bad enough. However, the mental scars have not healed, nor are they ever likely to totally do so."

6 He went on to explain how deeply he had felt the insult to his religion that was caused by the forcible tearing out of one of his dreadlocks and the subsequent use of it, as he was informed afterwards, as a trophy.

7 The appellants said nothing when interviewed after arrest and the indications were, when the case first came before the Crown Court, that they disputed having been involved and were seeking to put the prosecution to proof as regards identification. However the CCTV film footage was enhanced, proving beyond doubt that each of these appellants participated in this attack in the way we have set out above, save that the racist statements were not picked up by the CCTV recording. In those circumstances, the credit they were entitled to for their pleas—certainly as regards the assault element of the offence—was diminished or extinguished, both because of the delay on their part in admitting their guilt, and on account of the fact that they did so only when confronted with what was effectively incontrovertible evidence.

8 All of the appellants have bad criminal records. Watson, who is aged 26, has 29 previous convictions in which dishonesty features most prominently, but he has three convictions for affray, three for assault and three for public order offences. His last conviction for affray, on July 18, 2003 at Lincoln Crown Court, resulted in an eight-month prison sentence. The incidents of violence he has been involved in hitherto have included attacking someone with a CS gas spray while they were sitting in a car, throwing plastic boxes in a supermarket in order to steal, assaulting and injuring police officers with a screwdriver and kicking someone outside a public house thereby fracturing their cheek bone.

9 Marshall, who is aged 24, has 50 previous convictions of which four are either offences of assault or wounding. In addition to many road traffic offences he has, amongst other crimes, a conviction for robbery and a conviction for intimidating a witness. Graham, who is aged 23, has 17 previous convictions, including one for assault, one for wounding, and, perhaps most worryingly, one for racially aggravated criminal damage. The latter conviction resulted in a prison sentence of 18 months in September 2002. In brief, Graham shouted racial abuse at the victim of that offence. He then produced a knife that he pointed at the victim and he jumped on and substantially damaged the victim's car.

10 The authors of the pre-sentence reports had little to offer by way of encouragement. Watson was assessed as being a dangerous man who poses a high risk of re-

offending. The probation officer considered the attack on Watson's part (and this applies to all of the appellants) to have been a sadistic one in which gratification was gained. Marshall was also assessed as posing a high risk of re-offending, not least given his resort to binge drinking, and Graham has had a hopeless life in terms of education and work, and his past offending has been linked to the misuse of cocaine, ecstasy and alcohol.

11   In passing sentence the judge summarised the circumstances of the assault consistently with the summary set out above and he added the following:

> "The [additional] racial element . . . is what you did with his dreadlocks afterwards. It was like tearing the turban from a Sikh or a crucifix from a Christian. That is the severe element in this case and something that I take on board very strongly."

12   As regards Watson, the judge considered on all the material before him that he had started the violence and thereafter was the main perpetrator. Absent the racial element, the judge indicated that the sentence on Watson would have been one of four years and on Graham and Marshall three years eight months. It follows that the judge imposed the maximum period available (two years' imprisonment) on each appellant for the racially aggravating circumstances, notwithstanding their guilty pleas, and he thereby departed from the usual approach to sentencing that some reduction in sentence will accompany a guilty plea; indeed by s.152 of the Powers of Criminal Courts (Sentencing) Act 2000, the judge is bound to take into account the stage in the proceedings at which the offender indicated his intention to plead guilty, together with the circumstances in which this indication was given when determining what sentence to pass on an offender who has pleaded guilty. The circumstances when it is appropriate to withhold all discount for a guilty plea are relatively rare, but they importantly include the situation when an offender pleads guilty in the face of overwhelming evidence: *Davis* (1980) 2 Cr.App.R.(S.) 168.

13   The submissions made in support of this appeal can be summarised as follows. For all of the appellants it is submitted first the judge approached the sentencing exercise from an excessively high starting point, given that the maximum sentence for the offence of assault occasioning actual bodily harm is five years' imprisonment, and the maximum sentence for racially aggravated assault occasioning actual bodily harm is seven years. Although it is accepted that the judge was wholly correct to identify what the appropriate sentence would have been without the racial aggravation, it is submitted that for both elements of the offence the judge arrived at terms of imprisonment that were excessive. In particular, it is submitted that it was wrong to impose the maximum element for the racially aggravating circumstances (two years' imprisonment).

14   Secondly, we have been taken to the guidelines laid down in *Kelly and Donnelly* [2001] 2 Cr.App.R.(S.) 73, [2001] EWCA Crim 170 and *Saunders* [2000] 1 Cr.App.R.(S.) 71. On the basis of those authorities, it is submitted that this case did not involve the more serious aggravating features identified by this Court.

15   In considering those aggravating features it is correct to observe that this offence did not involve any planning by the offenders. The offence was not in any real sense part of a pattern of racist offending. None of the appellants are members of racist groups, and the victim was not set up for the purposes of this humiliating attack.

16   As far as the victim is concerned, the prolonged nature of this attack and the abuse he was subjected to are, in our view, aggravating features which should be taken into account, as the judge did. We also agree with the judge that the forcible ripping of a dreadlock from the head of a Rastafarian, followed by its use as a trophy, was a further significant aggravating feature. We consider that the judge's remarks in relation to this aspect of the case were wholly appropriate.

17   Thirdly, each of the appellants has sought to diminish, or indeed wholly avoid, the racially aggravated circumstances of this offence. In the written grounds of appeal on behalf of Watson, it was suggested that the attack was really alcohol related and the victim had himself sparked it off or inflamed events by standing up to the bullying, and on behalf of Marshall and Graham it was suggested that the pulling off of the dreadlock was not racially motivated.

18   We immediately indicate that this Court unhesitatingly rejects that third submission. These appellants pleaded guilty to the racially aggravated version of this offence and there was no suggestion that there should be a *Newton* hearing. Accordingly, the proper basis of sentence was that, whilst Mr Senior was being dragged along the floor and one of his dreadlocks was being pulled out, one of the group said, "Get the fucking nigger" and, "Get the wog". Thereafter, that dreadlock was treated as if it was a trophy, and in those circumstances, it does not assist the appellants in the course of this appeal to attempt to play down the racially aggravated circumstances of this offence.

19   However, we do give regard to the fact that none of the appellants in the event sought to contest this element of the offence, when perhaps it was open to them to do so, given these remarks were not caught by the CCTV recording. In consequence, as regards that part of the allegation—the racially aggravating circumstances—the evidence, although strong, could not be described as overwhelming. Accordingly, applying the principle set out above as regards discount, the appellants' pleas for that part of the offence alone merited some, though not necessarily substantial, credit.

20   Fourthly, the personal mitigation of each appellant is relied on. They are each the father of young children and individually they submit that, now in their early 20s, they have good reason to stop what is for each of them a cycle of offending. For Watson it was additionally argued that there was no proper basis for passing a longer sentence on him than on his two co-accused. In that regard, it is particularly brought to our attention that, in opening the case to the judge, Mr Auty for the Crown incorrectly suggested that Watson had delivered the first punch.

21   In considering each of those submissions, we immediately observe that this was a very bad assault. It was wholly unprovoked. The violence was extensive and prolonged and involved an attack of more than three people onto one defenceless man, and the injuries were at the top end of the bracket for an offence of actual bodily harm. It would not have taken a great deal more to have made the

appropriate charge one of s.20 of the Offences Against a Person Act 1861. Not only were the guilty pleas entered very late, but as regards the assault element of the offence the evidence against the appellants was overwhelming, thereby meriting little or no discount for the pleas. In all the circumstances, bearing in mind the background of each appellant, we do not consider that the judge took too high a starting point as regards the part of the offence that involved the assault occasioning actual bodily harm. This offence merited a sentence towards the maximum available.

22   For the part of the offence that reflected the racially aggravating circumstances, although we consider that the appellants' arguments are largely misconceived, the additional period was, in all the circumstances, somewhat excessive, particularly given the offence did not involve the worst of the aggravating factors this court highlighted in *Kelly and Donnelly* and *Saunders*, and bearing in mind that there was a plea in relation to both elements of the offence: the assault and the racially aggravating circumstances. As we have indicated, the evidence as regards this part of the offence, although strong, could not be described as overwhelming, given that the racist statements (which were the main foundation for this part of the charge) were not caught by the CCTV recording. In the premises, we are of the view that imposing the maximum sentence available for this part of the offence was wrong in principle.

23   That conclusion is not meant to undermine in any way the impact this attack will have had on Mr Senior. For him this must have been an excruciating ordeal, involving lasting consequences, but it is the highly regrettable experience of this Court that there are even worse cases of racially aggravated attacks than the instant appeal.

24   Finally, we indicate we reject the argument advanced by Watson as regards disparity. The judge's reasons for imposing a slightly longer sentence on him was that he started the violence, which he undoubtedly did by kicking Ms Robinson, and he then played, in the judge's view, the role of main perpetrator. Having watched the CCTV footage, we consider the judge was entitled to determine that Watson did play that role, regardless of who delivered the first main punch.

25   In all the circumstances, in order to reflect our decision in relation to the racially aggravated element of this sentence, we propose to reduce the sentence on Watson to five and a half years' imprisonment and the sentences on Marshall and Graham to five years and twomonths' imprisonment. To that limited extent these appeals are allowed.

[Paragraph [26] has been omitted.]

ATTORNEY GENERAL'S REFERENCE NO.20 OF 2004 (DANIEL BARKER)

Court of Appeal (Lord Justice Rose (Vice President, Court of Appeal Criminal Division), Mr Justice Richards and Mr Justice Bean): October 18, 2004

[2004] EWCA Crim 2723; [2005] 1 Cr.App.R.(S.) 111

LT Aggravating features; Seriousness of offence; Undue leniency; Wounding with intent

H1   *Wounding with intent to cause grievous bodily harm—sustained attack with weapons causing grave injuries—adequacy of sentence*

H2   Five years' imprisonment for wounding with intent to cause grievous bodily harm in the form of a sustained attack with weapons causing grave injuries, increased to nine years.

H3   The offender was convicted of one count of wounding with intent to cause grievous bodily harm. A group of men went to a petrol station to buy food; as they were giving their order, the offender drove onto the petrol station and attempted to obtain petrol from the pump, but was unable to do so as advance payment was required. The offender pushed in front of the group of men, and the victim protested. There was an argument, and the offender returned to his car and took a steering wheel lock from the boot. He then advanced towards the group of men together with his passengers, one of whom was armed with a knife. The passenger with the knife stabbed the victim and the offender hit him over the head and shoulders with the steering wheel lock a number of times. The victim twice fell to the floor and managed to get up before being hit again. Eventually he collapsed. He was taken to hospital where he was found to have three stab wounds. The consequential loss of blood had caused severe brain injury. The victim was effectively blind and was subject to a dense spastic tetraplegia. He had no useful movement and required constant attention. The offender was eventually arrested as he was about to leave the country. Sentenced to five years' imprisonment. The Attorney General asked the Court to review the sentence on the ground that it was unduly lenient.

H4   **Held:** (considering *Palma* (1989) 11 Cr.App.R.(S.) 329, *Hailes* (1992) 13 Cr.App.R.(S.) 540, *Moseley* [1999] 1 Cr.App.R.(S.) 452, *Roberston* [2003] 1 Cr.App.R.(S.) 31 (p.143.)) for the Attorney General it was submitted that the offence was aggravated because the offender instigated the attack and enlisted the assistance of two others, weapons were used against an unarmed victim; the attack was unprovoked and premeditated, and the injuries were permanent. The Court would have expected for this grave offence of wounding with intent to cause grievous bodily harm a sentence of at least 12 years' imprisonment. It followed that the sentence was unduly lenient. Taking into account the element of double jeopardy the Court would substitute a sentence of nine years' imprisonment.

H5   *R. Horwell* for the Attorney General.
J. Doyle for the offender.

H6   **Cases cited:**
Palma (1989) 11 Cr.App.R.(S.) 329, *Hailes* (1992) 13 Cr.App.R.(S.) 540, *Moseley* [1999] 1 Cr.App.R.(S.) 452, *Roberston* [2003] 1 Cr.App.R.(S.) 31 (p.143.)

H7   **References:** wounding with intent to cause grievous bodily harm, *Current Sentencing Practice* B 2-2

JUDGMENT

1   **Rose L.J.:**   The Attorney General seeks the leave of the Court, under s.36 of the Criminal Justice Act 1988, to refer a sentence said to be unduly lenient. We grant leave.

2   The offender is 29 years of age, having been born in June 1975. He was indicted on two counts, each of wounding with intent, contrary to s.18 of the Offences Against the Person Act. The victim in count 1 was a Mr Kanata and in count 2, a Mr Kavira. The offender pleaded not guilty to both counts. He was, following a trial between November 4 and 14, 2003, convicted on count 1 but acquitted on count 2. Sentence was adjourned for reports and, on January 26, 2004, he was sentenced by H.H. Judge Bathurst-Norman, at Southwark Crown Court, to five years' imprisonment.

3   In summary, he had armed himself with a steering lock and, together with another man, armed with a knife, assaulted Mr Kanata in a vicious and wholly unprovoked attack. The consequence was that Mr Kanata suffered very severe brain injuries and remains and will remain profoundly disabled for the rest of his life.

4   Mr Kanata was, at the time of the attack, 24 years of age. He was born in Morocco in February 1980 and is a Spanish national. He came to work in the United Kingdom in 1998. Pausing there, it is not suggested that this attack, terrible though it was, was in any way racially motivated or aggravated.

5   On the evening of Friday May 4, 2001 Mr Kanata was with three other friends in a house in Hackney Road, E2. At about 3.30 in the morning of Saturday, the following day, a number of those present set off to buy food from a nearby Texaco petrol station. The group consisted of Mr Kanata, Mr Kavira, Mr Beoladj and a Mr Duncan. As they were giving their order to the cashier at the petrol station, a car, driven by the offender, pulled up at the petrol pump nearest to them. There were two passengers in addition to the driver. The offender attempted to obtain petrol from the pump but, at that time in the morning, the pumps would not operate unless payment was made in advance. In consequence, the offender went to

the cashier's window, pushing to the front of the group of men of whom Mr Kanata was a member. Mr Kanata protested. There was an argument between him and the offender. At that stage, the offender returned to his car and signalled to his two passengers to get out. The offender took from the boot of the car a steering lock. Together with the other two he advanced towards the group at the cashier's window. The group buying the food were, of course, unarmed. The offender, as we say, had the steering lock. One of his two passengers had a knife.

6   The passenger armed with the knife stabbed Mr Kavira and that offence was the basis of count 2 of which, as we have said, the offender was acquitted. The same knife-armed passenger and the offender then confronted Mr Kanata. The passenger stabbed Mr Kanata and the offender hit him over the head and shoulders with the steering lock which he was holding in both hands. Mr Kanata tried to get away. He was chased by the offender, who continued to hit him about the head and shoulders with the steering lock. Mr Kanata collapsed to the floor. He got up. The offender chased him and hit him again with the steering lock. Again Mr Kanata fell to the floor and again he managed to get up. Again he was hit by the steering lock. The offender used, according to more than one witness, a swinging motion, with the steering lock held in both hands above his shoulder. There was however one witness, as Mr Doyle on behalf of the offender pointed out, who suggested that the offender was striking blows in a rather half-hearted manner. That is not the picture created by the other witnesses. Mr Kanata collapsed yet again. This time he did not get up. The offender returned to his car and drove away.

7   Mr Kanata was admitted to hospital unconscious. He had three stab wounds in the chest and abdomen, one of which penetrated the pericardium. The consequential loss of blood caused severe hypoxic brain injury. The prognosis, which remains as effective today as when given three years ago, was and is that Mr Kanata is deeply disabled by the brain injury caused by the stab wounds to the heart and chest. He is effectively blind. He is immobilised by a dense spastic tetraplegia complicated by flexion dystonia and contractions in the upper limbs, especially the right. He has no useful movement of any limb and is confined to a wheelchair. He is doubly incontinent and totally dependent on 24hr specialist nursing. No significant change is to be expected. The consequences, not just for Mr Kanata but for the other members of his family, have been devastating.

8   Following these events there was an extensive public appeal. Information was received. Suspicion fell on the offender, although the other two involved in this incident have not been traced. A search warrant was executed in September 2001 at the offender's home, but he was not present. He was arrested on December 3, 2002 at Stansted Airport, about to leave the country on a one-way ticket to Malaga with a sum in excess of £1,300 in cash in his possession. When he was interviewed, he made just one reply to the questions which he was asked: "I'd just like to say I never stabbed anybody, that's all I'd like to say." At the trial, the offender's defence was alibi.

9   On behalf of the Attorney General Mr Horwell draws attention to what he rightly submits are six aggravating features. First, the offender instigated the attack and enlisted the assistance of the two others. Secondly, both the steering

lock and the knife were used as weapons. Thirdly, the victim was unarmed. Fourthly, the attack was unprovoked. Fifthly, the attack was planned. Sixthly, the injuries were extremely severe and permanent.

10   Mr Horwell draws attention to the mitigation to be found in the fact that the offender is of previous good character.

11   Mr Horwell draws attention to four authorities, *Palma* (1989) 11 Cr.App.R.(S.) 329, *Hailes* (1992) 13 Cr App R(S) 540, *Moseley* [1999] 1 Cr.App.R.(S.) 452 and *Robertson* [2003] 1 Cr.App.R.(S.) 31 (p.143). The submission which he makes is that, in the light of those authorities, the sentence passed by the learned judge was inadequate to mark the gravity of this offence and its aggravating features, the need to deter others who might be minded to act in this way and public concern over the gratuitous use of violence, especially involving the use of weapons.

12   On behalf of the offender, Mr Doyle submits to the Court a letter written by the chaplain at the prison where the offender is detained. He speaks of the offender being hard working and determined to live a life beyond prison, when able to do so, and to contribute to society in a positive and constructive manner. He is not the sort of streetwise prisoner sometimes encountered. He is a simple, likeable character, though he does not appear to be vulnerable to manipulation. The chaplain had hoped to attend Court today but, by reason of short staffing, is unable to do so. We have regard to all that he says in that letter. Mr Doyle has also placed before us a letter from the mother of one of the offender's children, which speaks in graphic terms of the impact upon the children of the offender's incarceration. Mr Doyle refers to the psychiatric evidence before the Court which indicates that the offender has suffered from depression and claustrophobia, the latter of those conditions bearing on the effect on him of imprisonment.

13   Mr Doyle submits that, although this incident was planned, it took place in a very short space of time. He also comments, in passing, that the sole issue at trial was one of identification and the issue of joint enterprise may not have been investigated as fully as it might have been. We observe in relation to this that the jury acquitted on count 2 and only convicted the offender on count 1 which suggests a careful assessment by them of joint enterprise.

14   All of these matters we take into account. So far as this very grave offence of wounding with intent is concerned, we would have expected in the court below, following a trial, a sentence of at least 12 years' imprisonment. It follows that the sentence passed upon the offender was unduly lenient.

15   We take into account double jeopardy, that is to say that the offender is being sentenced a second time. We also take into account, to the limited extent which it is permissible to do so, the circumstances of personal mitigation which are advanced on behalf of this offender. Having regard to those matters, we quash the sentence of five years which was passed in the court below and substitute for it a sentence of nineyears' imprisonment

ATTORNEY GENERAL'S REFERENCE NO.79 OF 2004 (SYED HUSSAIN)

COURT OF APPEAL (Lord Justice Rose (Vice President, Court of Appeal Criminal Division), Mr Justice Richards and Mr Justice Bean): October 18, 2004

[2004] EWCA Crim 2722; [2005] 1 Cr.App.R.(S.) 112

LT Abuse of position of trust; Extended sentences; General practitioners; Indecent assault; Indecent photographs of children; Patients; Undue leniency

H1 *Indecent assault—indecent assaults by medical practitioner on female patients—length of sentence*

H2   An extended sentence of five-and-a-half years, with a custodial term of three-and-a-half years, imposed on a medical practitioner for indecent assaults on female patients, varied to an extended sentence of eight years with a custodial term of four-and-a-half years.

H3   The offender pleaded guilty to 5 counts of indecent assault on a female, 10 counts of making an indecent photograph of a child, and 8 counts of possessing an indecent photograph of a child. The offender was a general medical practitioner. Over a period of seven months he indecently assaulted five female patients by conducting vaginal examinations which were either unnecessary or inappropriate. Some of these were recorded by the offender using a concealed camera. A search of the contents of his computer resulted in the retrieval of large numbers of indecent images of children, and recordings of examinations of his patients. Two of the patients were girls aged 9 and 7, and a third was 15. Sentenced to an extended sentence of five-and-a-half years with a custodial term of three-and-a-half years. The Attorney General asked the Court to review the sentence on the ground that it was unduly lenient.

H4   **Held:** (considering *Millberry* [2003] 2 Cr.App.R.(S.) 31 (p.142), *Attorney General's References Nos 91, 119 and 120 of 2002* [2003] 2 Cr.App.R.(S.) 55 (p.338), *Attorney General's References Nos 37 and 38 and others of 2003* [2004] 1 Cr.App.R.(S.) 84 (p.499), *Prokop* (1995) 16 Cr.App.R.(S.) 598, *Pike* [1996] 1 Cr.App.R.(S.) 4, *Attorney General's Reference No.6 of 1999* [2000] 2 Cr.App.R.(S.) 286, *Green* [2002] EWCA Crim 1501, *Healy* [2003] 2 Cr.App.R.(S.) 87 (p.520), *Attorney General's Reference No.3 of 2002 (Christopher John Allison)* [2004] 1 Cr.App.R.(S.) 60 (p.357), *Oliver* [2003] 2 Cr.App.R.(S.) 15 (p.64)) for the Attorney General it was submitted that the offences involved a gross breach of trust, they were repeated and involved different patients. Some of the assaults involved penetration and some of the victims were particularly vulnerable. The offences had a considerable impact on some of the victims. In the Court's judgment, it was pertinent that at least three of the victims had experienced serious consequences. There was a high degree of culpability because of the grave breach of trust occurring in the doctor and patient relationship. This was a clear case where a deterrent element in relation to doctors or those professing to be doctors must be incorporated into the sentence process. The Court considered that the extended sentence was unduly lenient. The Court would have expected an extended sentence of eight years, even on a plea of guilty, with a custodial term of at least five and a half years' imprisonment. The Court would impose an extended sentence of eight years, but to reflect the element of double jeopardy, the custodial term would be four-and-a- half years' imprisonment.

H5   *R. Horwell* for the Attorney General.
       T. Robert Q.C. for the offender.

H6   **Cases cited:**
       Millberry [2003] 2 Cr.App.R.(S.) 31 (p.142), *Attorney General's References Nos 91, 119 and 120 of 2002* [2003] 2 Cr.App.R.(S.) 55 (p.338), *Attorney General's References Nos 37 and 38 and others of 2003* [2004] 1 Cr.App.R.(S.) 84 (p.499), *Prokop* (1995) 16 Cr.App.R.(S.) 598, *Pike* [1996] 1 Cr.App.R.(S.) 4, *Attorney General's Reference No.6 of 1999* [2000] 2 Cr.App.R.(S.) 286, *Green* [2002] EWCA Crim 1501, *Healy* [2003] 2 Cr.App.R.(S.) 87 (p.520), *Attorney General's Reference No.3 of 2002 (Christopher John Allison)* [2004] 1 Cr.App.R.(S.) 60 (p.357), *Oliver* [2003] 2 Cr.App.R.(S.) 15 (p.64).

H7   **References:** indecent assault, *Current Sentencing Practice* B 4–6

JUDGMENT

1   **Rose L.J.:**   The Attorney-General seeks the leave of the Court, under s.36 of the Criminal Justice Act 1988, to refer sentences said to be unduly lenient. We grant leave.

2   The offender is 30 years of age, having been born in December 1973. He was indicted on a total of 26 counts. At the plea and directions hearing at Durham Crown Court in November 2003, he pleaded not guilty to each count. On May 17, 2004, at Leeds Crown Court, he pleaded guilty to 23 of the 26 counts and the remaining three counts were left on the file. Witnesses did not attend because an indication of those pleas had been given, in writing, in March 2004.

3   The 23 counts to which he pleaded guilty comprised five counts of indecent assault on a female, contrary to s.14 of the Sexual Offences Act 1956, 10 counts of making an indecent photograph of a child, contrary to s.1(1)(a) of the Protection of Children Act 1978 and eight counts of possession of an indecent photograph of a child, contrary to s.160 of the Criminal Justice Act 1988. On May 17 he was sentenced by the Recorder of Leeds, H.H. Judge Norman Jones Q.C., to an extended sentence of five-and-a-half years, the custodial part of which was three-and-a-half years' imprisonment. The offender was also disquali-

fied from working with children. As to the custodial element of that sentence the learned Recorder, in relation to counts 1, 2, 5, 7 and 9, which were all of indecent assault, imposed a sentence of two-and-a-half years' imprisonment, concurrently on each. As to counts 4 and 6, which were both of making an indecent photo-graph, he imposed a sentence of one years' imprisonment on each concurrently to each other but consecutively to the two-and-a-half year sentence imposed in relation to the offences of indecent assault. Thereby the total custodial term of three-and-a-half years to which we have referred was reached.

4   In relation to all the other counts in the indictment, he imposed concurrent sen-tences of three months in relation to counts 11 to 18, which were of making an indecent photograph and in relation to counts 19, 20 and 22, which were of pos-sessing an indecent photograph. Likewise, he imposed a sentence of eight months on each concurrently, in relation to counts 21, 23, 24, 25 and 26, each of which alleged possession of an indecent photograph: the level of the indecency in the photographs was 3 or 4.

5   In summary, the offender was a general practitioner working in Darlington. Over a period of seven months, he indecently assaulted five of his female patients by, in particular, conducting vaginal examinations which were either unnecess-ary or inappropriate. On occasions, those examinations were recorded by the offender using a covert digital camera. From the computer at his home police retrieved just under 1600 indecent images of children. The officers also retrieved 36,000 individual J peg images which comprised recordings of the medical examinations of four female patients, three of which had been conducted in the surgery and one in a private bedroom. Each of the recordings lasted several minutes. During one such recorded examination the offender's penis was seen to be exposed.

6   In a little more detail, the practice of which the offender was a part consisted of 5 doctors, 2 nurses and 10 other members of staff. The offender started working there on a salaried basis at the beginning of October 2001, having qualified as a doctor in 1997. One of the other doctors and both of the nurses were female and approximately 95 per cent of vaginal examinations and smear tests of patients were carried out by the female practitioners, wearing gloves. On those occasions where a male doctor carried out such an examination, it was usual for there to be a chaperone.

7   The first count in the indictment, the first of the five counts of indecent assault, related to a 32-year-old married lady whom we shall call Mrs A. She went to the surgery in July 2003 complaining of a feeling of sickness after eating. She was seen by the offender, who examined her abdomen and provided a bottle for a urine sample. Just under a week later, on July 22, she returned to the surgery and was told by the offender that he needed to take some vaginal smears. Mrs A had her young daughter with her and thought it inappropriate for that to take place in the child's presence. The offender insisted that she come back as soon as possible and he gave her an appointment for the following day. It was usual for receptionists to make such appointments.

8   She returned on July 23. The offender asked her if she needed a chaperone. She declined because she trusted the offender. She lay down on the examination

couch. The offender did not wear gloves. He inserted a speculum and took internal swabs and then said he wanted an outer swab and told Mrs A to part her labia and hold it open. At that point she noticed a tissue box positioned between her legs, about a foot away from her private parts. It had a circular hole cut in one side, behind which she saw a lens. Unsurprisingly, she felt frightened and humiliated but, not knowing quite what to do, she remained silent. The offender then rubbed something on her clitoris and conducted another internal examination, positioning his hand high inside her, so that she felt as though the entire hand was there. At this stage the offender was wearing a glove, but this supposed examination lasted for about five minutes, and was painful. Mrs A, unsurprisingly, thought she was being sexually abused. After that, the appellant placed another object inside her and made her force it out. The examination lasted about 20 minutes and, at its conclusion, the offender removed the tissue box and prescribed antibiotics.

9   Having left the surgery, Mrs A eventually told her mother and a complaint was made to the nurse in the surgery. In consequence, on July 28, a partner in the practice found in the offender's room a tissue box with a circular hole cut in it, covered by a piece of Blu Tac on the side. The partner called for the offender and put these matters to him. He denied the allegation made by Mrs A and claimed that the hole in the tissue box was to facilitate the removal of issues. Thereafter, access was gained to a programme on the offender's home computer. The following day the offender was suspended from practice and the police were informed.

10   In the course of their investigation, they examined the offender's computer at the surgery and the one at his home. The home computer contained recordings of the offender examining undressed female patients and child pornography downloaded from the internet, which gave rise to many of the counts to which earlier we referred.

11   Count 2, also of indecent assault, related to a 74-year-old patient, called Mrs J. She is extremely vulnerable: she has cognitive impairment as well as physical disabilities. One of the sequences on the offender's home computer showed him examining her at her home. He did not wear gloves. He fondled her breasts. He helped her to remove her pants and to expose her private parts. He rubbed her clitoris and digitally penetrated her and there were times when he deliberately played to the camera. He massaged her buttocks against which he placed his penis. He made her kneel down on the bed and, having exposed her vaginal area, filmed her from behind.

12   The complainant in count 4 was a nine-year-old girl, E. She was shown in a sequence from the home computer removing her tights. The camera then recorded a view of her perineum. That girl had been taken by her father to see the offender at the end of February 2003. The offender said that he had to take a vaginal swab to check for infection.

13   Count 5, of indecent assault, and count 6, of making an indecent photograph, referred to a seven-year-old girl, K. Again, there was a sequence in the home computer where the offender's ungloved hand was seen repeatedly massaging the girl's clitoris and parting the labia. Her mother had taken that girl to the offender's surgery in January 2003 because she had stomach cramps and was

wetting herself. The offender said he would have to take a vaginal swab and conduct an internal examination. The girl's mother had been present throughout the examination but she had been sitting a little distance away. The offender had his back to her and she was quite unaware of what the offender was doing to the girl.

14   Count 7, also indecent assault, related to an unknown adult female, depicted in a sequence from the home computer. The offender was stimulating her clitoris without any medical justification. She has not been identified.

15   Count 9, the last of the counts of indecent assault, related to a 15-year old girl called L, who was taken to the offender with a vaginal discharge. She went a second time with her mother who, again, was present throughout the examination but she saw very little of what happened because the offender had his back to her. The mother was aware of the offender persisting in a rubbing motion. He spent some two minutes with his hand under a sheet rubbing the girl's vagina and, when the mother asked what he was doing, he said he was checking for bacteria. It was only on a later visit, when a swab was taken by a nurse, that the mother realised that the examination conducted by the offender was not what it should have been.

16   Counts 11 to 26 arose from images on the offender's home computer. None of them depicted patients of the offender. Just under 1600 indecent images were retrieved. Just over 1500 had been deleted but were retrieved by an expert and there were some 86 which had never been deleted. The vast majority of those images were at level 1, but there were 23 images at level 2, 35 at level 3 and 18 at level 4 and one (which did not give rise to a count in the indictment) at level 5.

17   Counts 11 to 26 were sample counts. The images in counts 11 to 18 had not been deleted and it was apparent had been downloaded between July 7 and 10, 2003, usually in the early hours of the morning.

18   The offender was arrested on July 29, 2003 and on two subsequent occasions in August. Two boxes of issues, each with a hole cut out at the side, were recovered, one from the surgery and one from the offender's home.

19   When he was interviewed, the offender initially denied any sexual impropriety and said that the pornography had been downloaded by accident. When he was confronted with the recordings of the examination of four of his patients, he claimed that they had been made to enable him to review his techniques and treatment to see whether they could be improved. When shown the recordings, the offender admitted having committed certain acts of indecency and having voyeuristic tendencies.

20   We turn to the impact of the offender's conduct on four of the victims. Mrs A lost her confidence in the medical profession and her relationship with her partner also broke down. The girl K, in view of her age, has not been made known of the sexual nature of the conduct against her but she knows that the offender did something wrong and took photographs of her. The consequence is that she does not trust doctors and needs to be encouraged when it is necessary for her to see one. She becomes distressed and worried when an appointment is due. She had been a confident child but she now needs to be chaperoned and does not like to

be away from her family. The victim's mother clearly was also distressed by what had taken place in her presence.

21   The girl, L, who is now 16, has shown a significant change in her personality and attitude to men. She has become withdrawn and is unable to forget what happened to her. Her studies have suffered and she has lost interest in the career which she had planned as a beauty therapist. She does not trust men and does not want to get physically close to a man. Her relationship with her male relations and male friends has been adversely affected. Mrs J, the 74-year-old lady, has, fortunately for her, no knowledge of the offences which were committed against her.

22   On behalf of the Attorney General Mr Horwell draws attention to what he rightly submits are eight aggravating features. First, the offences were committed against patients in a gross breach of trust. Secondly, they were repeated and six patients were the victims of his misbehaviour. Thirdly, at least four of the patients had their medical examinations recorded. Fourthly, some of the indecent assaults involved penetration of the victims. Fifthly, some of the victims, as we have indicated were particularly vulnerable by reason of youth or age and, in addition, the elderly patient had a degree of mental impairment. Sixthly, she suffered indignities and was treated in a particularly degrading and humiliating fashion. Seventhly, the offences have had a considerable impact on the lives of some of the victims. Eighthly, there was a very large number of indecent images of children found.

23   Mr Horwell draws attention to three mitigating features: first, the plea of guilty, albeit not at the earliest stage; secondly, the fact that the offender was of positive previous good character; and thirdly, that the offender has demonstrated genuine remorse.

24   A number of authorities were cited in the written reference and it is desirable to identify many of them, *Millberry* [2003] 2 Cr.App.R.(S.) 31 (p.142), *Attorney General's References Nos 91, 119 and 120 of 2002* [2003] 2 Cr.App.R.(S.) 55 (p.338), *Attorney General's References Nos 37, 38, 44, 54, 51, 53, 35, 40, 43, 45, 41 and 42 of 2003* [2004] 1 Cr App R(S) 84 (p.499), *Prokop* (1995) 16 Cr.App.R.(S.) 598, *Pike* [1996] 1 Cr.App.R.(S.) 4, *Attorney General's Reference No.6 of 1999* [2000] 2 Cr.App.R.(S.) 67, *Attorney General's Reference No.60 of 1998* [1999] 2 Cr.App.R.(S.) 128, *Green* [2002] EWCA Crim 1501, *Healy* [2003] 2 Cr.App.R.(S.) 520 and *Attorney General's Reference No.3 of 2002* [2004] 1 Cr.App.R.(S.) 60 (p.357). Mr Horwell also referred, in relation to the pornographic images, to *Oliver* [2003] 2 Cr.App.R.(S.) 15 (p.463).

25   The submission which is made is that the sentences imposed in total by the learned judge were unduly lenient in that they failed to mark the aggravating features of these grave offences, particularly the gross breach of trust, the particular vulnerability of some of the patients and the impact which such offences have not only on the victims, but also on public confidence in the medical profession.

26   Mr Horwell, by reference to the authorities, correctly identified the four matters which have to be taken into account when approaching sentence in cases of this kind: first, the degree of harm done to the victims; secondly, the level of culp-

ability of the offender; thirdly, the level of risk which the offender poses; and fourthly, the need for deterring others.

27   Mr Horwell also drew attention to the observations made by Kay L.J., giving the judgment of the Court in *Attorney General's Reference No.37 and Others* [2004] 1 Cr App R(S) 84 (p.499), at 505, where, at [14], he dealt with the question of good character:

> "In Millberry at para. [29], the Court considered the weight to be attached in rape cases to an offender's good character. It concluded that whilst it could not be ignored, it could not justify a substantial reduction of what otherwise would be the appropriate sentence. Again that proposition seems equally applicable to other serious forms of sexual offending and it is perhaps important to observe that where an offender has taken advantage of the standing that he enjoys in the community to breach the trust placed in him by others, especially parents, it is difficult to see how the positive attributes that were the very circumstance of his offending can benefit him very much when it comes to sentence. Those who enjoy much standing in the community, be they teachers, priests, doctors or anyone else, have to recognise that the benefits that they enjoy from their position are necessarily balanced by the responsibilities that arise as a result. If they offend in breach of trust and of those responsibilities, they can hardly expect to enjoy the further benefit of a substantial reduction in their sentence."

28   On behalf of the offender Mr Roberts Q.C. submits that the sentence passed by the learned judge was a merciful one but not unduly lenient. He was, as Mr Roberts rightly stresses, a highly experienced judge and he had dealt with this matter throughout its time at the Crown Court. Mr Roberts drew attention to a number of features which distinguish the authorities to which we have referred from the circumstances of the present case. He pointed out that, save in the case of *Healy*, all had been defendants who were tried and convicted and therefore did not exhibit any remorse. He points out that in none of the authorities was an extended sentence passed, though of course the power to pass an extended sentence did not exist at the time when some of the decisions were reached.

29   There are, submits Mr Roberts, a number of aggravating features to be found in the authorities, looked at in the round, which are not to be found in the present case. These can be identified as follows: the defendants were generally mature practitioners in their forties and fifties compared with this recently qualified practitioner in his thirties. There were, in some cases, lengthy periods of offending, whereas, in the present case, the period of offending was of the order of 12 months. Some of the defendants in the authorities continued, even after they had been suspended from practice, or indeed prosecuted. Some of the defendants had made overt sexual approaches to their victims. Some had merely bogus rather than genuine medical qualifications. Some had administered stupefying drugs. Some had not had a genuine reason for carrying out the examinations which they did, and some had carried out repeated examinations, on a false basis, of patients who were required by the offender to return for treatment time and time again.

30   So far as this offender is concerned, Mr Roberts stresses the pleas of guilty,
notified some two months prior to the date fixed for trial. He submits that
there was genuine remorse in this case and a low risk of reoffending, borne out
by the fact that the offender had only been practising for some 18 months at
the time of these offences.

31   He is a shy and introverted Muslim with a skin disorder. He has written a substantial letter to the Court, which the sentencing judge read and which we have
read, setting out the background, (including the fact that no marriage had been
arranged for him by his parents), which gave rise to the commission of these
offences. Mr Robert points out that the recorder clearly had in mind all the relevant statutory provisions with regard to his sentencing powers. He accepted
that witnesses had been spared from giving evidence, that there was considerable
remorse and that the offender was unlikely to behave in this way again. Furthermore, which is plainly the case, the recorder's approach was to determine the
appropriate overall sentence. That is an approach with which we entirely agree.

32   We take all these matters into account. It is, in our judgment, pertinent that
there were serious consequences to three, at least, of the offender's victims.
There was clearly a high degree of culpability on the offender's part because
of the grave breach of trust occurring in the doctor and patient relationship. So
far as the reports upon the offender are concerned, they show a medium risk of
re-offending, which will rise if he has access to children or vulnerable adults
in the future. This is clearly a case where a deterrent element in relation to doctors
or those professing to be doctors must be incorporated into the sentencing process.

33   In our judgment, in the light of all these circumstances, we take the view that
the extended sentence of five-and-a-half years passed in the court below and the
custodial term of three-and-a-half years' imprisonment were both unduly lenient.
We would have expected, in the court below, in all the circumstances of this case,
an extended sentence of eight years and, even on a plea of guilty, a custodial term
of at least five-and-a-half years' imprisonment. The course which we propose to
follow is to impose an extended sentence of eight years, but the custodial part of
that sentence will reflect the element of double jeopardy, that is to say, that the
offender is being sentenced a second time. The custodial part of that eight-year
sentence will therefore be four-and-a-half years' imprisonment. That will be
made up in the following way: in relation to counts 1, 2 and 5, the most serious
counts of indecent assault, we shall quash the sentence of two-and-a-half years
imposed by the learned recorder and substitute for it a sentence of three-and-a-
half years' imprisonment. That sentence will run concurrently with the two-
and-a-half years imposed by the learned recorder on counts 7 and 9. Just as the
recorder did, so we order that there shall run, consecutively to that three-and-
a-half year term, a period of one year, made up of a one-year sentence in relation
to each of counts 4 and 6, which were of making an indecent photograph of,
respectively, a nine-year old and a seven-year old. The total custodial term, therefore, is one of four-and-a-half years' imprisonment. All the other sentences on the
remaining counts for making an indecent photograph and possession of an indecent photograph will be the same as the three- and eight-month terms imposed by

the learned recorder. They will all run concurrently with each other and concurrently with the total period of four-and-a-half years which we have already identified.

R. v BRIAN PHILLIPS

Court of Appeal (Lord Justice Mance, Mr Justice Mackay and Mr Justice Fulford): October 19, 2004

[2004] EWCA Crim 2651; [2005] 1 Cr.App.R.(S.) 113

(LT) Consecutive sentences; Criminal record; Dangerous driving; Driving while disqualified

H1   *Dangerous driving—disqualified driver driving dangerously to avoid apprehension—length of sentence*

H2   Eighteen months' imprisonment for dangerous driving, with six months consecutive for driving while disqualified, upheld in the case of a persistent disqualified driver who drove dangerously to avoid apprehension.

H3   The appellant pleaded guilty to dangerous driving and driving while disqualified. The appellant was seen driving a motor car by police officers who pursued him in a marked police vehicle. The appellant drove off to avoid apprehension, driving through built up streets in the wrong direction and at speeds in excess of the speed limit. Eventually he skidded to a halt and ran off on foot before being detained. The appellant was a disqualified driver. The appellant had numerous previous convictions, including 17 for driving while disqualified. He had been convicted of driving while disqualified three times in the previous year. Sentenced to 18 months' imprisonment for dangerous driving, with six months consecutive for driving while disqualified.

H4   **Held:** while it was the general practice that courts should impose concurrent terms for offences committed on the same occasion, it was not an inflexible rule of law applied in every case. In the present case the offence of driving while disqualified was complete and had been committed in full before the course of dangerous driving began. The reason for the dangerous driving was the fact that the appellant had been detected as having committed the offence of driving while disqualified. This, taken together with the appellant's record for driving while disqualified, justified the sentencer in imposing the maximum sentence for driving while disqualified and making it consecutive to the sentence for dangerous driving. So far as the offence of dangerous driving was concerned, a sterner view was taken, since the 1990s, of those who drove dangerously, whether or not death was caused. There were four aggravating factors—the appellant's previous record of driving while disqualified and uninsured, the culpability of the offence itself, the relatively prolonged course of dangerous driving and most significantly the fact that the offence was an attempt to outrun justice and avoid yet another conviction for the offence. The sentence was neither excessive nor wrong in principle.

H5 **Cases cited:**
Skinner (1986) 8 Cr.App.R.(S.) 166, *Khan* (1990) 12 Cr.App.R.(S.) 352, *Chalmers* (1990) 12 Cr.App.R.(S.) 446, *Moriarty* (1993) 14 Cr.App.R.(S.) 575, *Templeton* [1996] 1 Cr.App.R.(S.) 380

H6 **References:** dangerous driving, *Current Sentencing Practice*, B 12-1.3

H7 *A. Rafati* for the appellant.

JUDGMENT

1 **Mackay J.:** On March 26, 2004, in the Crown Court at Plymouth, this appellant pleaded guilty to count 1 (dangerous driving) for which he received a sentence of 18 months' imprisonment on April 23, 2004, and driving whilst disqualified (count 2) for which on the same date he was sentenced to six months' imprisonment, ordered to run consecutively, making a sentence of two years' imprisonment in all. In addition he was disqualified for a period of 12 months, the minimum period of disqualification for the offence of dangerous driving, and ordered to take an extended retest. He has the leave of the single judge to appeal against that sentence.

2 The facts were that on January 24, 2004 this appellant drove a motorcar dangerously in the Mutley area of Plymouth. Police officers noticed him and pursued him in a marked police vehicle. The appellant took off to avoid apprehension and drove through some of this area's built-up streets in the wrong direction, on occasions at 60mph which was twice the legal limit. He had during this pursuit to brake hard on more than one occasion to avoid collisions. He eventually skidded to a halt and ran off on foot before being detained by the police. The total distance, we are told by counsel, of this pursuit was just over a mile. He was a disqualified driver and therefore had no insurance at the relevant time.

3 His relevant previous convictions are extremely extensive. In addition to convictions for offences of dishonesty, drug-related offending and other motoring matters, he has 17 convictions prior to this for driving whilst disqualified and 28 for driving with no insurance. His recent history of relevant offending included a conviction on June 13, 2003 at Plymouth Magistrates Court for driving while disqualified where he received a community rehabilitation order. On June 20, 2003, again for driving while disqualified, he received five months' imprisonment. On November 28, 2003, again for driving while disqualified, he received four months' imprisonment, and on the same date for a further offence of driving while disqualified he received six months' imprisonment concurrent. He therefore could not have been long out of prison for those offences when he committed the instant offences.

4   His pre-sentence report showed that he did not consider he had driven dangerously. He was described as a longstanding drug addict who had used heroin and amphetamine but was in regular employment as a motor mechanic earning about £250 per week. His risk of reoffending was assessed as high, an assessment with which the appellant himself did not disagree.

5   The grounds of this appeal are that the sentences passed were manifestly excessive, that they should not have been made to run consecutively and that he received insufficient credit for his guilty pleas.

6   Although the recorder reflected the guilty plea on count 1 by reducing the sentence from the maximum of 24 months to one of 18 months, he passed the maximum sentence for driving while disqualified and it is argued that in respect of that second sentence some discount, however slight, should have been given to mark the fact that he had pleaded guilty. It is also argued on his behalf by Mr Rafati that these sentences should not have been ordered to run consecutively as essentially the two offences arose out of the same facts. On this last point, reference has been made to the case of *Skinner* (1986) 8 Cr.App.R.(S.) 166 which cited earlier authorities in favour of the proposition that where one act of driving was both, as in that case, reckless and gave rise to an offence of driving whilst disqualified, as a general matter of practice the court should impose concurrent terms. While that is plainly so, this is not an inflexible rule of law to be applied in every case. In the present case the offence of driving whilst disqualified was complete and had been committed in full before ever the course of dangerous driving was embarked upon. Indeed, the very reason for the dangerous driving was the fact that he had both committed and been detected as having committed the offence of driving while disqualified. The appellant himself addressed this subject in interview and one cannot improve upon his account "Yeah, I meant to do it . . . I didn't want to stop because those bastards would [have] sent me back to prison." This feature, in the judgment of this Court, taken with the appellant's appalling record for driving while disqualified, in our judgment justified the course of action taken by the sentencer to impose both the maximum sentence for driving while disqualified, as to which there was not the merest shadow of a defence, and to make it run consecutively to whatever was the appropriate sentence on count 1.

7   Turning to count 1, reliance is placed on a number of authorities: *Khan* (1990) 12 Cr.App.R (S) 352; *Charters* (1990) 12 Cr.App.R (S) 446; *Moriarty* (1992) 14 Cr.App.R (S) 575; *Templeton* [1996] 1 Cr.App.R (S) 280. That last authority underlines the dangers in this area of sentencing in citing authority which is of such relative antiquity. Hirst L.J., if he may be paraphrased for these purposes, pointed out that over the 1990s the courts have been responding to urgings from the public and from this Court to take a sterner view in sentencing terms with those who drive vehicles dangerously, even when death does not follow. Nothing which has happened in the eight years since *Templeton* has done anything other than reinforce this point. The public's intolerance of dangerous driving has caused the courts and Parliament to respond by increasing sentences passed, and sentences available as maxima where death follows.

8   In a case of dangerous driving such as this, it is purely a matter of chance and good fortune whether serious injury or death is caused. One can readily here identify the following aggravating features. First, the appellant's previous record of driving whilst disqualified and uninsured. Secondly, the culpability of the offence itself involving the circumstances described at the outset of this judgment. Thirdly, the relatively prolonged course of dangerous driving and the fact that it was not momentary or brief. Fourthly, and perhaps most significantly the reason for it, namely an attempt to outrun justice and avoid yet another conviction for the offence from which he had but shortly been released from prison.

9   His counsel fairly points out that there are aggravating features which are not present, principally that there is no suggestion of drink or drugs having been taken, and that indeed is right and avoids placing this act of dangerous driving at the very top of the scale of seriousness. But the factors which we have outlined take the overall culpability well towards the top end of the scale. The learned recorder did give some credit for the plea of guilty to count 1. He also tempered the disqualification which he might have imposed so as to keep it to the minimum period. In the judgment of this Court the recorder sentenced within the range of sentencing which was available to him and the overall sentence cannot be called either wrong in principle or manifestly excessive. This appeal is therefore dismissed.

R. v RASHEED DEKSON

COURT OF APPEAL (Lord Justice Mance, Mr Justice Mackay and Mr Justice Fulford): October 19, 2004

[2004] EWCA Crim 3205; [2005] 1 Cr.App.R.(S.) 114

(LT Bank accounts; Conspiracy; Fraud; Obtaining services by deception; Totality of sentence

H1   *Conspiracy to defraud—advanced fee fraud—obtaining £1.7 million by means of advance fee fraud—length of sentence*

H2   Six years' imprisonment upheld for obtaining £1.7 million by means of an advanced fee fraud.

H3   The appellant was convicted of conspiracy to defraud, obtaining services by deception and having a false instrument. The appellant was concerned in an advanced fee fraud. Potential victims were contacted by letter and told that a large sum of money was to be removed from Nigeria. The victim was invited to make his bank account available for the purpose and was promised a significant proportion of the sum as a fee. One intended victim was asked to collect a draft for $55 million. The second was promised 25 per cent of $71 million. The total amount obtained by fraud from the victims was £1.7 million, although £950,000 had been frozen and might be recovered by the victims. The sentencing judge found that the appellant was the principal behind the fraud and had received a large proportion of the money. One victim used all his own money and that of his family and friends. The other had borrowed heavily. Sentenced to 6 years' imprisonment for conspiracy to defraud with 18 months consecutive for possessing a false instrument, and 18 months consecutive for obtaining services by deception: 9 years' imprisonment in all.

14   **Held:** (considering *Singh* [1999] 1 Cr.App.R.(S.) 490, *Balasubramanian* [2002] 2 Cr.App.R.(S.) 17 (p.57), *Attorney General's Reference Nos 48 to 52 of 2002 (Paulssen and others)* [2003] 2 Cr.App.R.(S.) 192, *Palmer* [2003] 2 Cr.App.R.(S.) 2 (p.5), *Iwuji* [2001] 1 Cr.App.R.(S.) 131 (p.456)) the sentence of 18 months for obtaining services by deception in connection with opening a bank account was not challenged. So far as the offence of possessing a false passport was concerned, the sentence of 18 months was higher than was necessary, and would be reduced to 12 months. So far as the conspiracy to defraud was concerned, the case was in a special category by reason of its prevalence. The offence involved a high degree of skill, insight and organisation, using a number of people over a considerable period of time. The amounts obtained were substantial. The sentence of six years for conspiracy to defraud could not be considered to be wrong in principle or manifestly excessive. The total sentence would be reduced to eight-and-a-half years.

15   **Cases cited:**
Singh [1999] 1 Cr.App.R.(S.) 490, *Balasubramanian* [2002] 2 Cr.App.R.(S.) 57, *Attorney General's Reference Nos 48 to 52 of 2002 (Paulssen and others)* [2003] 2 Cr.App.R.(S.) 192, *Palmer* [2003] 2 Cr.App.R.(S.) 2 (p.5), *Iwuji* [2001] 1 Cr.App.R.(S.) 131 (p.456).

6   **References:** obtaining by deception, *Current Sentencing Practice* B 6-3

7   *R. Banks* for the appellant.

JUDGMENT

1   **Mance L.J.:**   On July 23, 2003, in the Crown Court at Harrow, before H.H. Judge Mole Q.C., the appellant was convicted of six offences and on July 25, 2003 was sentenced as follows: in respect of count 25 (which became at trial count 1), conspiracy to defraud, 6 years' imprisonment; in respect of count 9 (trial count 3), obtaining services by deception, to 18 months consecutive; in respect of counts 27, 31 and 32 (trial counts 4, 5 and 6), obtaining services by deception, to 1 year concurrent on each; and in respect of count 33 (trial count 7) having a false instrument, to 18 months consecutive to counts 25 and 9. The sentences on counts 25, 9 and 33 (trial counts 1, 3 and 7) were therefore consecutive, making a total of 9 years' imprisonment. The sentences on counts 27, 31 and 32 (trial counts 4, 5 and 6) were concurrent with each other and with the other sentences, in particular the six years on count 25. The appellant was given by the single judge, in February 2004, limited leave to appeal against conviction

and representation for counsel in respect of the single ground to which such limited leave related. In respect of two other grounds on which the appellant sought leave, the single judge refused him leave. No application was notified to the Registrar of Criminal Appeals to renew his request for leave in respect of those other grounds. We are told today, however, that he wishes to do this now.

[Paragraphs [2]–[16] have been omitted.]

17   We come now to sentence in this matter and we have before us a renewed application for leave to appeal. In dealing with conviction we have described the offences. To clarify the numbering, the position is that the advance fee fraud in respect of which this appellant was charged with conspiracy to defraud was originally count 25 but that was renumbered at trial so as to become trial count 1. Count 9 (obtaining services by deception) became trial count 3. Counts 27, 31 and 32 became trial counts 4, 5 and 6, and count 33 became trial count 7.

18   The subject matter of trial count 1, the advance fee fraud, was this. Between May 1999 and January 2002 the appellant conspired with a number of other persons to carry out a series of such frauds. A potential victim or "mark" was contacted by letter which purported to come from an official in the Nigerian Petroleum Company seeking to remove a considerable amount of over-invoiced money from Nigeria. The victim was invited to make a bank account available for this purpose and he was promised a significant proportion of the sum concerned as a fee.

19   Two victims gave evidence, one from the US, Alan Parkes, and another from Hong Kong, Stephen Chan. They described how, following a flurry of (bogus) documents they were invited to London where a conspirator played the role of a friend and they were persuaded, in the belief that all was genuine, that arrangements to collect bank drafts from various banks were going well. The victim was taken to a bank and there seated—however away from the sight of any cashier. A conspirator supposedly collected a draft in the bank and handed it to another playing the role of delighted recipient. The victim was shown a draft briefly long enough to convince him it was real, but he was informed that although this was his draft it could not be released until a percentage fee was paid. The friend pretended to protest and then to negotiate the fee down by offering to shoulder some of it himself. Once the friend had in this way convinced the victim that all was still well, there was then another percentage handling charge to be paid. A bribe to a Nigerian official was also paid, intended to make the victim feel less inclined to complain. If it was paid then the bribe fee was increased, each time luring the victim to make just one more payment to receive the money.

20   The evidence of Stephen Chan, who was requested to fly to London to collect a bank draft for $55 million and met at least six people involved in the charade, was summed up by the judge in detail. He was a self-employed accountant. He was cross-examined about his motivation and the degree to which as an accountant he appreciated that this was a "dodgy" deal. The position regarding Alan Parkes, who was first contacted in September 1999 and was promised 25 per cent of $71 million, was also the subject of a detailed summing up. It is of relevance to read some passages in view of counsel's submissions before us that this sort of offending should be viewed in the light that the victims themselves were involved in

criminal activities. That does not appear to us to be a fair representation of the picture. It seems to us that the judge summarised the position correctly. He said, for example, at 65:

> "You will remember that Stephen Chan was cross-examined, very properly, about his motivation and the degree to which he perhaps must have appreciated that this was dodgy, and you will have to reach your own view about that. Was he greedy? Very probably you will think. Was he at least too uncritical? Again, you will think probably, it's a matter entirely for you, but you may well think almost certainly too uncritical. Was he comprehensively fooled, anxious to be fooled despite being increasingly desperate, or perhaps because of being increasingly desperate? Well, members of the jury, you may think he was. When he was cross-examined did you think that perhaps he was embarrassed, at best, a bit defensive, even evasive. maybe you will think not wholly frank, about shutting his eyes to the increasingly obvious, although he did admit, of course, he did acknowledge that he knew at one stage that he was paying bribes and of course that was completely contrary to his professional ethics as an accountant. It may be that as a result of that you may think that he's brought some of it on himself, and perhaps you're less inclined to be sympathetic than you otherwise might have been.
>
> But you will consider this, I'm sure, that those who practice frauds choose their victims carefully. They prey most easily on those who are weak, the naive, the unworldly, sometimes the old and the confused, not in this case, they're not very bright sometimes. In this case more the greedy and the not very scrupulous. But it doesn't, you may think, make it any the less unlawful. If the case is proved against those involved in the fraud it's no less unlawful because the victim contributed to his own troubles. You may think, and again this is a matter entirely for your impression, that the whole subtlety of the original letters is that they do, from a fairly early start, hint at something not being quite right, so that the letters select people who are either very naive or not too scrupulous. Because those who read them carefully and think about them and are reasonably scrupulous aren't going to go ahead. Only the ones who read them, and either they don't read them very carefully or aren't terribly scrupulous may go ahead."

Then he turned to the other victim and said this:

> "Perhaps we make one slight exception for Alan Parkes, because Alan Parkes . . . is unusual in that he actually asked his financial adviser about the letter and got some, you may think, rather astounding advice."

Then the judge turned to that, a little later after a break, at 69 and said this:

> "It starts with this rather familiar letter . . .
> Alan Parkes said that obviously he had never heard of these characters, the reference to the Nigerian Chamber of Commerce rang no bells with him. But he had a financial adviser who was called Stephen Lander, and he gave the

letter to him and asked him. Stephen Lander said: 'Well if it was legal you could make a good profit from it. Give the guys a call and why not set up a meeting'. You'll remember that that's effectively what happened . . ."

The judge, further down at 70, referred to a confirmation of legality which was sent. He said:

"Again, you might think it's a slightly bizarre letter in some ways. It says a number of things that might be designed to raise one's suspicions, you might think, but it's a matter for you to read this. Then it does say in paragraph 5, last sentence: 'We will obtain from the Federal Ministry of Justice a vetting approval to authenticate that this transaction is genuine and is not contradicting any local or international laws and also to guide against any suspicion from your bankers in your country or your government'. Well there we are, that's what it says, and that Alan Parkes and his adviser, Stephen Lander, took as sufficient reassurance."

In our view, that is a more accurate characterisation of the background. The advance fee frauds in relation to these two victims extracted a total of £1.7 million. We are told that some £950,000 has been frozen and is likely to be recovered by the victims, though no doubt they may have incurred legal fees and loss of interest. The appellant was in the judge's view, after hearing the evidence and after conviction, the guiding spirit behind the accounts, and a large proportion of the £1.7 million went to him. As to the offences of obtaining by false deception, he either opened the bank accounts fraudulently or at some stage used them fraudulently in a manner from which a representation of intention to discharge the ostensible holder of the bank account's obligations could be inferred.

21   From February 2000 the applicant, using his own name, had hired a self storage box, No.4400 at Safe Store in Goodmayes, Essex. That was searched by the police on January 29, 2002 and, amid some 8,000 pages of documents found, the police found links to names including those used in relation to the accounts the subject of trial counts 3, 5 and 6. There were also forged drafts for millions of pounds and dollars, and there was a fourth passport which formed the basis of trial count 7.

22   In sentencing, the judge said that the evidence was overwhelming and the appellant had attempted to answer it by making unsupported allegations of fabrication and planting of documents against the police which the jury rejected. The offences were executed, he said, with care, planning and professionalism. One victim not only used all his own money but also that of his family and friends. The other had borrowed very heavily. The last drop was squeezed out of each by ingenuity and psychological insight. The appellant played an absolutely central role and a large proportion of the money had gone to him in one way or another. Significant incriminating documents were found in the storage box. Some indicated that another fraud was planned, for example a Citibank draft issued for £16.50 had been altered to show £16.5 million—no doubt potentially for use in the course of another advance fee fraud. The box also contained lost, stolen or forged passports, birth certificates, driving licenses and employment

records. However, he was to be sentenced on the basis of the offences for which he was convicted.

23   The judge considered a number of authorities including *Palmer* [2003] 2 Cr.App.R.(S.) 2 (p.5) and *Iwuji* [2001] 1 Cr.App.R (S) 131 (p.456). He considered that there were factors in the appellant's case which made the offences more serious than *Iwuji*, for example the amount involved and the greater degree of sophistication with further offences planned. He mentioned that the appellant had a previous conviction for obtaining and going equipped, although the facts postdated the conspiracy to defraud. That was the Kent conviction, which, although a relatively minor conviction in July 2001, appears to have had no effect on the appellant's enthusiasm for continuing on the path of fraud. There was no credit for any plea and his defence showed he lacked any remorse. His attitude in trial was one of amused contempt. The appellant had involved his wife, had exposed her and had done nothing to soften the blow when it fell on her. Account was taken of the delay between arrest and conviction but there was nothing to persuade the judge that he should reduce the sentence below the six years he would have considered was an appropriate sentence for conspiracy to defraud.

24   The judge, turning to trial counts 3 to 5, considered that abusing Barclays Bank justified a consecutive sentence of, as we have said, 18 months' imprisonment (count 3). As to counts 4, 5 and 6 (that is the Abbey National account, the Henry Nsakala Citibank bank account, and the passport) in respect of the first two the judge passed a sentence of one year concurrent, also concurrent with the advanced fee fraud sentence. In respect of the passport he passed a sentence of 18 months' imprisonment, on the basis that this was a serious example of the offence, and made it consecutive. He said in relation to the passport that he took into account the fact that a number of other passports were found, some of which had been reported as lost in the post and stolen, whilst other passports found in the box were forged.

25   Counsel now submits that the total sentence was excessive and the individual components in some respects excessive and that the judge's approach to the authorities drew distinctions which they do not justify. He also submits that the appellant should have received some discount for previous good character because the previous conviction in respect of the Kent fraud on John Lewis was a matter relied on to prove count 4—that is obtaining services by deception from Abbey National. He submits that the passport offence was treated too severely and in his written grounds suggests that a more appropriate sentence would have been a community penalty or a short custodial sentence and that it should not in any event have been a consecutive sentence.

26   In his oral submissions before us counsel really focused on only two matters— the sentence of 18 months passed consecutively in respect of the offence relating to the passport and the sentence of six years in respect of the advanced fee fraud. He took no other points. He accepted the length of the sentence of 18 months for the offence of obtaining services by deception relating to the Barclays account and he accepted that that could legitimately be made consecutive to the advanced fee fraud sentence, and he also took no issue with the sentences of one year con-

current passed in respect of the other two offences of obtaining services by deception.

Turning therefore to the sentence of 18 months in respect of the possession of a
forged passport, the maximum for this offence is two years. Counsel points out
that it was an offence evidently committed in order to enable the wife to have
such a passport. He says, no doubt rightly, that she did not need one since she
had her own passport. It seems to us that that does not really mitigate the matter.
Rather it suggests there is more to it than meets the eye, as the judge evidently
thought. Counsel is correct in saying there is no positive information as to why
the passport was necessary. On the other hand, it is right to say that it was used
to book some tickets although no travel followed (apparently, according to the
appellant, because of illness of his son). Counsel takes issue with the judge's reliance on the general background of fraud pervading this matter and also takes
issue with the judge's reference to and reliance on the existence of other stolen
passports in the safe box. Counsel points out that they were not the subject of
any charge and that this was not a specimen count. In the absence of any other
sensible explanation why a passport was created for the appellant's wife, who
already had one, we think that, against the general background of fraud in this
case, the judge was entitled to conclude that this passport was held for some
fraudulent purpose over and above a mere wish to have a further document on
which the wife might travel to the United States. But we think that there is
force in counsel's criticisms of the judge, in so far as the judge appears to have
placed some significance on the existence of other stolen and forged passports
which were not the subject of any charges.

We have looked at the authorities, particularly *Singh* [1999] 1 Cr.App.R.(S.) 490,
which points to the appropriateness of a six to nine month sentence in respect of
an attempt to use a false passport to board a flight to Canada even on a guilty plea.
In *Singh* a sentence of eight months was upheld on a guilty plea for attempting to
use a false passport to board that flight. In the present case, of course, this appellant does not have any benefit of a plea. We have also considered
Balasubramanian [2002] 2 Cr.App.R (S) 17 (p.57) where a sentence of 12
months was reduced to six months on a plea of guilty in circumstances where
the appellant had the most compassionate reason for wanting to travel temporarily to Canada—his mother was very ill there. The Court explained the
distinction between that type of exceptional situation and situations of, for
example, use for financial gain or use to subvert the entry requirements as an
end in itself, or use to seek employment in a country which would not otherwise
grant admission. Here, it seems to us, that the inference of use for a fraudulent
financial purpose was drawn by the judge legitimately, and this is not a case
where there is any compassionate reason for wanting to have and to use or try
to use a false passport. There is no credit for a plea and in those circumstances
the actual sentence in that case offers no useful parallel to the present case.
The general reasoning does however give some assistance.

We have come to the conclusion that the sentence of 18 months was, viewing the
facts as they ought to be viewed, higher than was strictly necessary, but we cannot
accede to the submission that this case falls within the six to nine months bracket.

On conviction we think that the appropriate sentence would have been one of 12 months. We see nothing wrong with making that sentence consecutive, although considerations of totality must, at the end of the day, also be taken into account. We turn now to the advance fee fraud. We have already dealt with counsel's first point relating to the fact that these are offences which in his submission involved victims who were not themselves innocent. We think that is considerably over-stated. Further, as we have pointed out, others were also drawn in, albeit indirectly—in one case the family and friends who are on any view entitled to be viewed as innocent and were no doubt doing their best to help someone who they genuinely believed to need temporary financial help; in the other case lenders were drawn in and one does not know what prospect they have of being repaid in full. It seems to us the likely consequence of this type of offending that the victim will in desperation in one way or another lay hands on or borrow the money of others who may indirectly suffer.

This brings us to the second point. We think that this category of case is a special category of case made so by its very prevalence. It involved, as the judge said also, a high degree of skill, psychological insight and organisation using, as the present instances show, numbers of other people over quite considerable periods of time. We think that a deterrent element has some role to play in sen-tencing in relation to this type of offence.

Thirdly, the amounts involved were very substantial, although recoveries were made.

Fourthly, we turn to the authorities. We were referred to the case of *Attorney General's Reference Nos 48 to 52 of 2002 (Paulssen and others)* [2003] 2 Cr.App.R (S) 36 (p.192). That case involved an investment fraud causing to the public a loss of some $7 million. The charge was, as here, conspiracy to defraud carrying a maximum of 10 years' imprisonment and there were convictions at trial. In relation to *Paulssen* himself, a German residing in Zurich, the Court drew from an earlier authority, the authority of *Clark* [1998] 2 Cr.App.R (S) 95, where Rose L.J. said that contested cases involving between £250,000 and £1 million would merit between five and nine years, whereas cases involving £1 mil-lion or more would merit 10 years or more. That was in a context of theft by employees where there was, at least at that time, no 10-year maximum. Neverthe-less, in *Paulssen* there was a maximum sentence available of 10 years and the Court drew on that as giving some general assistance. In the particular case, how-ever, it relied on three factors as reducing the starting point: the amount of money involved, although high, could have been even higher and the conspiracy, although lengthy, did not last overlong; there was no deliberate targeting of small investors; and thirdly, although in part attributable to the activities of one or more of the offenders themselves, there was a substantial delay between 1996 when all except Paulssen were arrested for this offence and October 2001 when the trial began. That was a longer delay than any in the present case and in the present case there is an element of deliberate targeting, not perhaps of the public at large, but certainly of members of the public, selected no doubt in the hope that they would be vulnerable or weak. These types of advance fee fraud do however commonly seem to involve almost indiscriminate attempts to target people by correspondence. But, be that as it may, we think that there are those two differences from *Paulssen*. On the other hand, as in *Paulssen*, so in this case it is true that the amount could have been higher and the time span of the present advance fee fraud appears to have extended over some eight months or so. In *Paulssen* the actual sentence passed on him was further reduced to take account of his good character and the special feature that he was a German living in Zurich who would be serving a prison sentence in this country far from his home and unable in the circumstances to see or be visited by his disabled daughter in Zurich, whom he used to see regularly. Those two factors led to a reduction in the sentence to six years. Here the appellant has his character slightly qualified by the Kent offence, committed however after the commission of this advance fee fraud—committed in fact on July 11, 2001. He was sentenced for that on the next day to a fine with one day's imprisonment in default for two offences of obtaining property by deception twice and going equipped to steal. Those were, as we have said, very minor matters, although they fit into the overall context of his fraudulent activity in so far as they involved the use of the Abbey National account, the subject of trial count 4. He does not, however, have any special feature, such as *Paulssen* did because he would have to serve his sentence abroad away from his family and daughter.

Making allowances for the differences between the offending in this case and the offending in *Paulssen*, and taking account of the prevalence of the present type of offence and its character, we do not think that *Paulssen* suggests that the judge's sentence of six years was in any way out of line with an appropriate sentence.

The next case counsel referred us to was *Palmer* which was considered by the judge [2003] 2 Cr.App.R (S) 2 (p.5). In that case there were two counts of conspiracy to defraud, again each carrying a maximum of 10 years. There were two counts because essentially the same conspiracy had come to an end but had been revived and developed and therefore it was thought appropriate to have separate counts for the two periods of its existence. The conspiracy was a timeshare fraud. The court sentenced on the basis, if one looks at para.[15], that the losses involved were somewhat in excess of £2 million; compensation orders were made in favour of approximately 400 named losers in that total. The court disregarded the amount of the much larger confiscation order which had been quashed by the court. Not all the customers of Palmer's timeshare frauds were dissatisfied. The frauds took place over a longer period of time and were on a somewhat greater scale, it may be said. But Palmer received on the major count a seven-year sentence and a one-year sentence consecutive on the second count added to deal with the revived conspiracy. Palmer was, like the present appellant, convicted on a trial by the jury. Attempting, as best we can, to compare that case with this, again we conclude that, bearing in mind the character and prevalence of the present type of offence, it cannot be said that a six-year sentence was manifestly excessive.

Finally we turn to evaluate that conclusion in the light of the case of *Iwuji* [2001] 1 Cr.App.R (S) 131 (p.456) where a three-and-a-half year sentence was passed on a plea of guilty for attempting to obtain some $305,500 by an advance fee fraud. The Court's decision amounts to no more than this: that that was not manifestly excessive—so it does not necessarily represent the highest sentence that could be passed. But even so it suggests that five years on a conviction for that much lesser advance fee fraud, involving only one person and involving an attempt not a completed transaction, would not have been excessive. That seems to us consistent with a conclusion that six or even a little over six years would have been appropriate for the present completed offences against two persons involving much larger sums. The judge drew precisely that distinction in his sentencing remarks at p.7 and also pointed out that the evidence made it plain that the present appellant was at the very least planning for more frauds and that the present frauds were, so far as he could judge, on a higher degree of sophistication and planning and certainly of subtlety, persistence and pressure. Finally, he pointed out that in *Iwuji*, although the Court did not accept the suggestion of the appellant that he had a peripheral role, it was not clear that he was at the heart of the conspiracy, whereas the present appellant clearly was. It is correct that the court in *Iwuji* spoke of the applicant as a determined fraudster (see para.[14] in its remarks) because he had a prior sentence of 30 months for possessing false instruments (cloned credit cards) with intent to use them. It is true that there is nothing of precisely that nature in this case, although the judge, when discussing *Iwuji*, did mention this appellant's conviction. However, it is clear that the judge had in mind the nature of the present conviction and that the facts giving rise to it post-dated the advance fee fraud. It seems to us that the other distinctions he drew in any event justify the view that six years was an appropriate prison sentence, although the position relating to prior record differs from that of the appellant in *Iwuji*.

In those circumstances, we have come to the conclusion that the single judge was correct in concluding that the sentence on trial count 1 of six years was not arguably wrong in principle or manifestly excessive. As we have pointed out, a consecutive sentence of 18 months for obtaining services by deception (trial count 9) is not challenged. We have concluded that permission should be granted and that the appeal in respect of trial count 7 (that is the passport offence) should be allowed to the extent that the further consecutive sentence of 18 months' imprisonment should be quashed and substituted by a further consecutive sentence of 12 months' imprisonment. To that limited extent this appeal will be allowed. The total sentence resulting in lieu of the previous total of nine years is a sentence of eight-and-a-half years' imprisonment. We have considered that sentence in its totality and have concluded that there is nothing wrong with it, bearing in mind the severity of offending and its persistence and variety in the present case. In those circumstances this appeal will be allowed to that limited extent but no further.

[Paragraphs [27] and [28] have been omitted.]

R. v CHERYL ANGELA GRAHAM, ALBERT JOHN WHATLEY

COURT OF APPEAL (Lord Justice Auld, Mr Justice Owen and Mr Justice Hedley): October 22, 2004

[2004] EWCA Crim 2755; [2005] 1 Cr.App.R.(S.) 115

Benefits fraud; Deterrence; Inflation; Sentence length; Sentencing guidelines

H1   *Obtaining by deception—benefit fraud—revised sentencing guidance*

H2   Observations of the need to revise the sentencing guidance in cases of benefit fraud, as laid down in *Stewart* (1987) 9 Cr.App.R.(S.) 135, in the light of inflation.

H3   The Court dealt with two unrelated appeals in order to consider the proper approach to sentencing in cases of benefit fraud.

H4   *Graham.* The appellant pleaded guilty before a magistrates court to 10 offences of benefit fraud, and asked the court to take a further 471 offences into consideration. She was committed to the Crown Court for sentence. The appellant, a woman aged 36, began to receive benefits in 1992 on the basis that she was separated from her partner and was not earning. She continued to receive benefits until 2002, when she applied to change from income support to incapacity benefit. Investigations then revealed that she had been in employment since June 1992 before she began to receive benefits. During the period in question she received income support amounting to £34,500 and housing benefit amounting to £16,000. The appellant made a full admission when arrested. Sentenced to two years and six months' imprisonment concurrently for each offence.

H5   *Whatley.* The appellant, aged 64, was convicted on 13 counts of benefit fraud after a contested trial. The prosecution case was that over a lengthy period the appellant claimed sickness benefit while working as a street trader. The appellant made a claim for sickness benefit in 1994, and in 1997 completed a review form in which he declared that he was not working either full-time or part-time and that he had no other income. Between May 1997 and July 2001, the appellant received benefits totalling in excess of £90,000. From 1992 the appellant held a casual traders licence and in 1997 applied successfully for it to be upgraded to a permanent street licence. The appellant was convicted on one count charging false accounting in relation to the review form completed in 1997, 10 counts relating to the falsification of documents in the form of a payable order and two counts alleging dishonestly obtaining money transfer orders. Sentenced to a total of 30 months' imprisonment.

H6   **Held:** the appeals gave rise to the issue of the appropriate sentence in cases of benefit fraud, and in particular of the continued applicability of the sentencing guidelines set by the Court in *Stewart* (1987) 9 Cr.App.R.(S.) 135. Observations had been made in cases such as *Bendris* [2000] 2 Cr.App.R.(S.) 183 that the guidelines in *Stewart* might be reconsidered. The judgment of the Court in *Stewart* was given by Lord Lane C.J., who pointed out that there had been a sharp drop in the number of prosecutions for social security offences between 1980 and 1981, and 1983 and 1984. He explained that this was the result of a change in prosecution policy, in which cases involving small amounts were not normally prosecuted. Lord Lane C.J. observed that only a small proportion of offences were dealt with in the Crown Court and that the deterrent effect of any Crown Court sentence was unlikely to be great. The Court then gave indications of the appropriate level of sentences. At the top of the range, sentences of two-and-a-half years and upwards were appropriate for carefully organised frauds on a large scale in which considerable sums of money were obtained. These cases bore little relation to the average offenders who formed the great majority of those appearing in the Crown Court. Factors which would influence sentence in such cases included a guilty plea, the amount involved and the length of time over which the fraud took place, the circumstances in which the events began, the use to which the money was put, the previous character of the offender, mitigating factors particular to the offender, and any voluntary repayment of the amounts overpaid. The courts were encouraged to consider whether a custodial sentence really was necessary or whether a community service order or suspended sentence was appropriate. If immediate imprisonment was necessary, a term of between 9 and 12 months would usually be sufficient in a contested case where the overpayment was less than £10,000. The observations in *Stewart* as to the aggravating and mitigating features did not require any modification, but it was a question whether the figure of £10,000 as a guide to the appropriate level of sentence should be updated, whether deterrence remained a factor of limited application in such cases, and whether the guidelines in *Stewart* reflected current sentencing practice.

There had been a substantial fall in the value of money since 1987. It had been said in *Clark* [1998] 2 Cr.App.R.(S.) 95 that the effect of inflation since *Barrick* (1985) 7 Cr.App.R.(S.) 142 meant that £17,000 was the present day equivalent of £10,000. The guidelines for theft in breach of trust were adjusted accordingly. The decision in *Clark* indicated that sentencers should be aware of the effects of inflation on sentencing guidelines, and it was also relevant to the relationship of sentences for benefit frauds to sentences for other types of fraud.

The second question was whether deterrence continued to be a factor of limited application in sentencing offenders for benefit fraud. It had been said in *Bendris* that social security fraud was increasingly prevalent. In the Court's judgment, there would be cases in which courts would be justified in taking the view that the sentence should contain a deterrent element.

As to whether the guidelines reflected current sentencing practice, the Court had considered a number of decisions in cases of benefit fraud since the decision in *Stewart* (in particular, *Bolarin* (1990) 12 Cr.App.R.(S.) 543, *Browne* (1993) 14 Cr.App.R.(S.) 491, *Tucker* (1994) 15 Cr.App.R.(S.) 349, *Weild* (1994) 15 Cr.App.R.(S.) 685, *Adewuyi* [1997] 1 Cr.App.R.(S.) 254, *Nowoya* [1997] 2 Cr.App.R.(S.) 1, *Oyediran* [1997] 2 Cr.App.R.(S.) 277 , *Armour and Sherlock*

[1997] 2 Cr.App.R.(S.) 240, *Ellison* [1998] 2 Cr.App.R.(S.) 382, *Rosenburg* [1999] 1 Cr.App.R.(S.) 365, *Bendris* [2000] 2 Cr.App.R.(S.) 183 and *Evans* [2000] 1 Cr.App.R.(S.) 144. The Court had been referred to the cases of evading duty on tobacco and alcohol including *Czyzewski* [2004] 1 Cr.App.R.(S.) 49 (p.289), and to the decisions in *Kefford* [2002] 2 Cr.App.R.(S.) 106 (p.495) and *Mills* [2002] 2 Cr.App.R.(S.) 52 (p.229), in which the Court had commented on the need to avoid unnecessary imprisonment.

H10   The Court drew the following conclusion: (1) if *Stewart* was to continue to apply, the figure of £10,000 should be updated for inflation; (2) there would be cases in which a sentence should properly reflect an element of deterrence; (3) the decisions to which the Court had been referred were broadly consistent with *Stewart*; (4) in the light of the Court's conclusions, and taking account of the guidelines for comparable offences and the decisions of the Court in *Kefford* and in *Mills*, the Court did not consider that the guidelines in *Stewart* required revision, save in relation to the effect of inflation. Accordingly, the Court considered that where imprisonment was necessary, short terms of up to about 9 to 12 months would usually be sufficient in contested cases where the overpayment was less than £20,000. As the Court had indicated, the aggravating and mitigating features identified in *Stewart* did not require modification or amplification. Sentences would depend on an almost infinite variety of factors. Serious aggravating factors, such as the obtaining of large sums, frauds persisted in over lengthy periods, claims for benefit that were fraudulent from the inception, sophisticated fraud involving the use of false and or multiple identities, and the maintenance of an extravagant lifestyle over the period in question, would be likely to result in substantial periods of imprisonment.

H11   The case of *Whatley* gave rise to a further question. The appellant had been convicted on the number of sample counts. The Crown adduced evidence that the total amount of the benefits received by the appellant was in excess of £90,000, but the sums involved in the counts in the indictment amounted to £3,100. The sentencing judge approached the sentencing exercise on the basis that the whole sum of £90,000 could be traced back to the fraudulent review form completed in 1997. This he treated as an incepting claim, and the subsequent counts were treated as stepping stones demonstrating the period over which the fraud was perpetrated. It was submitted that this approach was wrong in principle and contrary to the decisions in *Canavan, Kidd and Shaw* [1998] 1 Cr.App.R.(S.) 243 and *Clark* [1996] 2 Cr.App.R.(S.) 351. *Clark* and *Canavan* had been followed in cases involving benefit fraud including *Rosenburg* [1999] 1 Cr.App.R.(S.) 365 and *Evans* [2000] 1 Cr.App.R.(S.) 144, where the Court expressed sympathy with the trial judge and observed that the consequence of the principle in *Canavan* might well be that a defendant who had pleaded guilty and confessed the full extent of his fraud might be treated more harshly than a defendant who had contested the matter and had been convicted only in respect of so-called specimen counts. The Court agreed with those observations. The problem presented by *Canavan* was graphically illustrated by the two cases before the Court. The appellant in *Whatley* stood to be sentenced for dishonestly obtaining £3,100, when the Crown's case was that he had received in excess of £90,000, while in *Graham* the appellant pleaded to an indictment containing 10 counts, and asked for 471 offences to be taken into consideration. The matter had been considered by the Law Commission. In *Whatley* the sentencing judge sought to distinguish *Canavan* and *Evans* on the basis that the whole sum could be traced back to the fraudulent review form. In the Court's judgment that attempt was misconceived for two reasons. First, it was not conceded that the total sum in excess of £90,000 had been received by way of benefits during the relevant period because the defence case was that he had not been working. The highest that the Crown case could be put was that the appellant had not been entitled to receive benefit on the dates specified in the individual counts in the indictment. The review form was a declaration that at the date of the review form the appellant was not working. It was not and could not be a declaration as to the future. It followed that in the Court's judgment a valiant attempt by the sentencing judge to circumvent the decisions in *Clark* and *Canavan* was misconceived and that he erred in imposing a sentence on the first count intended to reflect the receipt of £90,000 by dishonest means. The appellant stood to be sentenced for offences of fraud involving a total of £3,100. In the light of the guidance afforded by *Stewart*, as updated, the total sentence of 30 months' imprisonment was plainly manifestly excessive in the case of *Whatley* and the Court would substitute sentences of 12 months' imprisonment on each count concurrently. In the case of *Graham* there were various mitigating factors and the Court would substitute sentences totalling 18 months' imprisonment.

L.P. Moll for the appellant Graham.
R. Cifonelli for the Crown.
Miss C. Davenport for the appellant Whatley.
S. Earnshaw for the Crown.

Cases cited:
Stewart (1987) 9 Cr.App.R.(S.) 135, *Bolarin* (1990) 12 Cr.App.R.(S.) 543, *Browne* (1993) 14 Cr.App.R.(S.) 491, *Tucker* (1994) 15 Cr.App.R.(S.) 349, *Weild* (1994) 15 Cr.App.R.(S.) 685, *Adewuyi* [1997] 1 Cr.App.R.(S.) 254, *Nowoya* [1997] 2 Cr.App.R.(S.) 1, *Oyediran* [1997] 2 Cr.App.R.(S.) 277, *Armour and Sherlock* [1997] 2 Cr.App.R.(S.) 240, *Ellison* [1998] 2 Cr.App.R.(S.) 382, *Rosenburg* [1999] 1 Cr.App.R.(S.) 365, *Bendris* [2000] 2 Cr.App.R.(S.) 183, *Evans* [2000] 1 Cr.App.R.(S.) 144, *Czyzewski* [2004] 1 Cr.App.R.(S.) 49 (p.289), *Kefford* [2002] 2 Cr.App.R.(S.) 106 (p.495), *Mills* [2002] 2 Cr.App.R.(S.) 52 (p.229), *Canavan, Kidd and Shaw* [1998] 1 Cr.App.R.(S.) 243, *Clark* [1996] 2 Cr.App.R.(S.) 351, *Rosenburg* [1999] 1 Cr.App.R.(S.) 365.

References: benefit fraud, *Current Sentencing Practice* B 6-3.3F
Commentary: [2005] Crim. L.R. 247

JUDGMENT

1   **Owen J.:**   These appeals raise the issue of the appropriate sentence in cases of benefits fraud and, in particular, of the continued applicability of the sentencing guidelines set by this Court in *Stewart* (1987) Cr.App.R.(S.) 135. In granting leave in *Whatley* the single judge commented that:

> " *Stewart* is generally regarded by sentencers as somewhat dated in the current climate of pervasive benefit fraud."

echoing the observation of Rose L.J. in *Bendris* [2000] 2 Cr App R(S) 183 at 184:

> "It may be that, in the not very distant future it will be necessary for this Court to reconsider the level of sentences indicated in *Stewart* in the light of the continuing and increasing prevalence of social security fraud during the 13 years since that case was decided."

2   The appeal of Whatley also raises again the question of the proper approach to sentence in a case in which a defendant has been convicted on a number of specimen or sample counts, a situation which will often arise in cases of benefits fraud.

The *Stewart* Guidelines

3   In *Stewart* the judgment of the Court was given by Lord Lane C.J. He pointed out that there had been a sharp drop in the number of prosecutions for social security offences between 1980 and 1981 and 1983/1984, and explained that this was attributable to a change of policy, adding that:

> "Nowadays the policy is for cases involving small amounts not to be prosecuted except where there are special features such as repeated fraud, or the necessity to provide a deterrent to a particular type of fraud prevalent in a particular locality."

4   Secondly he observed that it was only a small proportion of offences of this nature that were dealt with in the Crown Court and that the deterrent effect of any Crown Court sentence was unlikely to be great. Lord Lane then indicated the appropriate level of sentence in such cases in the following terms:

> "In some cases immediate unsuspended imprisonment (or youth custody) is unavoidable. At the top of the range, requiring substantial sentences, perhaps of two and a half years imprisonment and upwards, are the carefully organised frauds on a large scale in which considerable sums of money are obtained, often by means of frequent changes of names or address or of forged or stolen documents. Examples are *Adams* (1985) 7 Cr App R(S) 411, to which we have referred in the course of the appeals and applications today, and *Dennehy* which is a case in our list today.
> These offenders are in effect professional fraudsters, as is often apparent from their previous records. They have selected the welfare departments as an easy target for their depredations and have made a profitable business out of defrauding the public in this way. The length of the custodial sentence

will depend in the first instance on the scope of the fraud. Of course, as in all fraud cases, there may be a variety of mitigating circumstances and in particular a proper discount for a plea of guilty should always be given. These cases bear little relation to the average offender in this area.

As to the remainder, who form the great majority of those appearing in the Crown Court, the sentence will depend on an almost infinite variety of factors, only some of which it is possible to forecast . . . Other considerations which may affect the decision of the Court are: (i) a guilty plea;

(ii) the amount involved and the length of time over which the defalcations were persisted in (bearing in mind that a large total may in fact represent a very small amount weekly;

(iii) the circumstances in which the offence began (e.g. there is a plain difference between a legitimate claim which becomes false owing to a change of situation and on the other hand a claim which is false from the very beginning);

(iv) the use to which the money is put (the provision of household necessities is more venial than spending the money on unnecessary luxury;

(v) previous character;

(vi) matters special to the offender, such as illness, disability, family difficulties et cetera;

(vii) any voluntary repayment of the amounts overpaid.

Before sentencing the offender the court should consider the following questions which were set out in *Clarke* (1982) 4 Cr App R(S) 197 at 200: (i) is a custodial sentence really necessary? The fraud cases dealt with in the Crown Court (as already indicated) are likely to be relatively serious and a non-custodial sentence will often be appropriate; (ii) if a custodial sentence is necessary, can the court make a community service order as an equivalent to imprisonment, or can it suspend the whole sentence? It seems to us that a suspended sentence or (especially) a community service order may be an ideal form of punishment in many of these cases; (iii) if not, what is the shortest sentence the court can properly impose? If immediate imprisonment is necessary, a short term of up to about nine or 12 months will usually be sufficient in a contested case where the overpayment is less than, say, £10,000.''

5   Lord Lane's observations as to the aggravating and mitigation features of such offences do not require any modification. But there are three issues that have been raised for our consideration: first, whether the figure of £10,000 suggested by Lord Lane as a guide to the appropriate level of sentence should be updated; secondly, whether it remains the case that deterrence is a factor of limited application in such cases; and, thirdly, whether the guidelines reflect current sentencing practice.

The effect of inflation

6   As to the first there has been a substantial fall in the value of money since 1987. In *Clark* [1998] 2 Cr.App.R.(S.) 95, a case involving a theft and breach of trust, this Court adjusted the figures by reference to which guidelines were set in *Bar-*

rick (1985) 7 Cr.App.R.(S.) 142, to take account of inflation. In *Barrick* Lord Lane C.J. advanced guidelines defined by reference to the figures of £10,000, £50,000 and £100,000. In giving the judgment of the Court in *Clark*, Rose L.J. said that:

> "The effect of inflation since *Barrick* means that approximately £17,000, £85,000 and £170,000 are the present day equivalents of respectively £10,000, £50,000 and £100,000."

7   The Court went on to adjust the guidelines by reference not only to the effect of inflation on the guidelines in *Barrick*, but also to other considerations, such as the increase in the scale of white collar crime and the changes in the law with regard to remission and parole in the following terms:

> "Where the amount is not small, but is less than £17,500, terms of imprison-ment from the very short up to 21 months will be appropriate; cases involving sums of between £17,500 and £100,000, will merit two to three years; cases involving sums between £100,000 and £250,000, will merit three to four years; cases involving between £250,000 and £1 million will merit between five and nine years; cases involving £1 million or more, will merit ten years or more."

8   The decision in *Clark* is not only relevant to the need for sentencers to be aware of the effect of inflation on sentencing guidelines, but is also relevant to the relationship of sentences for benefit frauds to sentences for other types of fraud, a point to which we shall return. As to the effect of inflation, the inflation table in *Kent and Kent* Vol.10–1189 indicates that the current value of £1.00 in January 1987 is approximately £1.80. If the *Stewart* guidelines are to continue to apply, then plainly the figure of £10,000 should be revised.

The deterrent element

9   The second issue is whether it remains the case that deterrence is a factor of limited application in sentencing such offenders. In *Stewart*, and having con-sidered the statistics as to such offences, and the policy adopted by prosecuting authorities, Lord Lane said:

> "We have ventured to go into matters at some length to show that it is only a small proportion of offences of this nature which are dealt with in the Crown Court and to demonstrate that the deterrent effect of any Crown Court sen-tence is unlikely to be great. This is because any one minded to embark upon this sort of fraud, unless he had a large scale operation in mind, or the fraud is blatant, is unlikely to find himself in the Crown Court. If prosecuted at all, the run of the mill offence is almost certain to be before the Magistrates."

10   He continued at 140:

> "For the reasons we have mentioned earlier in this judgment, we do not think that the element of deterrence should play a large part in the sentencing of this sort of case in the Crown Court."

11　　As Lord Lane said in *Stewart*, such offences are easy to commit and difficult and expensive to detect, as is illustrated by the facts of both the appeals before us. Furthermore, and as Rose L.J. observed in *Bendris*, social security fraud is increasingly prevalent. In our judgment, there will be cases in which courts will be justified in taking the view that a sentence should contain a deterrent element.

Relevant decisions since *Stewart*

12　　The third issue is whether the guidelines reflect current sentencing practice. As to that, it is first necessary to consider a number of decisions of this Court in cases of benefit fraud since the decision in *Stewart*. *Current Sentencing Practice* B6–33F22 provides a helpful selection of such decisions, but there are a number of other decisions that are of assistance.

13　　In *Bolarin* the appellant pleaded guilty to 11 counts of obtaining money by deception, having made fraudulent claims for income support and unemployment benefit over a period of 21 months obtaining a total of £18,500. The claims were fraudulent from the outset. He was sentenced to two years' imprisonment, but on appeal the sentence was reduced to 15 months in the light of *Stewart*.

14　　Jowitt J., who gave the judgment of the Court, indicated that the case plainly went some considerable way beyond the 9 to 12 month bracket in *Stewart* falling:

"Somewhere between the worst kind of case and that kind of case near the worst kind of case."

15　　In *Browne* the appellant pleaded guilty to 15 counts of obtaining by deception and false accounting, and asked for 68 offences to be taken into consideration. He had obtained a total of £5,208 over a period of 18 months by making fraudulent claims for benefit in the names of his brother and another man. He was sentenced to a total of 18 months' imprisonment. Guided by the decision in *Bolarin* the Court reduced the sentence to a total of one year.

16　　In *Tucker* (1994) 15 Cr.App.R.(S.) 349, the appellant pleaded guilty to four counts of obtaining by deception, and asked for 43 similar offences to be taken into consideration. The appellant claimed supplementary benefit when her husband left her. Five years later she became employed, but continued to obtain benefit order books by representing that her circumstances had not changed. She drew benefit to which she was not entitled for about 18 months. The sum involved was approximately £1,500. She was sentenced to six months' imprisonment. The appellant was a woman of mature years of previous good character with responsibilities for her family. She had pleaded guilty and had started, to the best of her ability, to repay what she had dishonestly obtained. In giving the judgment of the Court Judge J., as he then was, said that the sentencing judge had fairly balanced such mitigating features against the aggravating features of the case, namely:

". . . deliberate, persistent, and, it must be said, systematic fraud which involved dishonest acquisition of thousands of pounds of public money."

Her appeal was dismissed.

17   In *Weild* the appellant pleaded guilty to eight counts of obtaining by deception and asked for 283 offences to be taken into consideration. She claimed benefit in various forms over a period of three years by failing to disclose that she was co-habiting, that she was working during part of the relevant period, and that she had capital assets, receiving a total of just under £15,000. She was sentenced to 15 months' imprisonment, a sentence that was upheld on appeal.

18   In *Adewuyi* [1997] 1 Cr.App.R.(S.) 254, the appellant was convicted of 10 offences of theft and 5 of obtaining services by deception. She had made false claims for child benefit, income support and housing benefit over a period of four years. The claims had been made both in her own name and in other names. The total sum involved was in excess of £100,000. She was sentenced to four years' imprisonment, a sentence that was upheld on appeal.

19   *Nwoya* [1997] 2 Cr.App.R.(S.) 1, was a case of conspiracy to defraud the DSS by making false claims for benefit. A total of 59 claims were made over a period of 21 months. Payments in excess of £300,000 were obtained. The fraud was facilitated by means of information obtained from a DSS computer by one of the appellants, an employee of the department. Two of the appellants, including the employee of the department, were sentenced to six years' imprisonment, a third to four years. In giving the judgment of this Court, McKinnon J. indicated that by reference to the level of sentences for mortgage fraud:

> "It does seem to us that the appropriate sentence on a plea of guilty in cases of this kind is one of three and a half years to four years imprisonment which would mean, after a contested trial, a proper sentence would be of the order of six years imprisonment."

20   In *Oyediran* [1997] 2 Cr.App.R.(S.) 277 the claimant made false applications for benefit over a period of three years, stating that he had no other source of income when he was at one stage in receipt of a student grant and subsequently employed on a part time basis. He obtained £18,105 and was sentenced to 18 months' imprisonment. His appeal was dismissed. In giving the judgment of the Court Lord Bingham C.J. said:

> "In our judgment the sentence which the judge imposed was severe but not manifestly excessive. Were it to be reduced at all, it would be reduced by so small an amount as to lay the Court open to justified reproach. In our judgment the sentence is not one with which this Court should interfere."

21   In *Armour and Sherlock* [1997] 2 Cr.App.R.(S.) 240, the appellants conspired to obtain money from the DSS by obtaining and using stolen benefit books. One admitted obtaining a total of £1,300, the other £809. Both were sentenced to 18 months' imprisonment. The sentences were upheld on appeal, the Court expressly taking account of the increased prevalence of this type of offence and of the degree of organisation and sophistication involved.

22   In *Ellison* [1998] 2 Cr.App.R.(S.) 382, the appellant pleaded guilty to five counts of obtaining by deception and asked for 88 other offences to be taken into consideration. He had claimed income support over a period of years on

the basis that neither he nor his wife were working, when in fact his wife had worked throughout the period. Benefits fraudulently obtained amounted to £10,948. He was sentenced to a total of 15 months' imprisonment. The principal ground of appeal was that the total sentence was outside the guidelines set in *Stewart*. It was also argued that the Court should take account of the effect of inflation. The Court came to the conclusion that the sentence was too high in the light of *Stewart* and should be reduced to a total of 10 months' imprisonment.

23 In *Rosenburg* [1999] 1 Cr.App.R.(S.) 365, the appellant was convicted on nine counts of obtaining by deception. The total sum involved in the counts was approximately £2,000 paid by way of income support, when in fact the appellant had been operating a business known as the UK Glamour Models and Entertainment Limited by which he acted as agent for aspiring dancers throughout the relevant period. The evidence adduced at trial also demonstrated that during the relevant period he was living an extravagant lifestyle, driving a Porsche motor car and acquiring two properties which were let to tenants. He was sentenced to 30 months' imprisonment. On appeal this Court concluded that, given the sums involved in the counts upon which the appellant was convicted, the sentences imposed upon him were manifestly excessive. They were reduced to sentences totalling two years' imprisonment.

24 In *Bendris* [2000] 2 Cr.App.R.(S.) 183, the appellant pleaded guilty to conspiracy and to obtaining by deception. He had conspired fraudulently to claim income support and job seekers allowance for a period of over four years. The claim had been made on the basis of a fictitious unemployed person, a false passport bearing the appellant's photograph being used to support the claim. He was sentenced on the basis that £10,000 had been paid in benefits as a result of his activities. In giving the judgment of the Court, Rose L.J. indicated that the Court was approaching the matter in accordance with *Ellison*, and on that basis reduced the sentence to 10 months' imprisonment.

25 Finally, in *Cheryl Eleanor Evans* [2000] 1 Cr.App.R.(S.) 144, the appellant pleaded guilty to 4 counts on an indictment containing 24 counts and was convicted on the remaining counts. The offences related to involvement in a housing benefit fraud. She had claimed housing benefit in respect of premises where she lived, when in fact the house was the property of the local council. Claims were also made in false names, supported by false details of a fictitious landlord, in respect of several further addresses. She was sentenced to three years' imprisonment on each count concurrently. As Mantell L.J. observed in giving the judgment of the Court:

"... this was a persistent and sophisticated fraud which displayed considerable guile on the appellant's part."

But the sums involved in the offences for which she was convicted totalled only £2,807. With the decisions of *Stewart* and *Adewuyi* in mind, the Court allowed the appeal, albeit with some misgivings, and reduced the sentence to two years' imprisonment concurrently on each count.

26 Mr Earnshaw, who appeared for the Crown in Whatley, helpfully provided us with some statistics as to the incidence of such fraud derived from the 31st report

of the Public Accounts Committee published in 2002. The Department of Works and Pensions then estimated that more than £2 billion *per annum* is lost in benefit fraud. Secondly, he informed us that last year between 12,000 and 14,000 cases of benefit fraud were prosecuted by the Department with 80 per cent being dealt with in the magistrates' court. Less than 150 defendants were sent to prison, the average sentence in such cases being in the bracket of six to nine months. Those figures suggest that the overwhelming majority of such offences are committed by omission, that is to say where the defendant has been lawfully in receipt of benefit but fails to inform the Department of changes of circumstances affecting their entitlement, and by those who are able to pray in aid substantial mitigation, persons of good character, often with dependent children for whom the conviction has had a devastating effect.

Sentencing guidelines for comparable offences

27   We have already referred to *Barrick* in the context of the effect of inflation on sentencing guidelines. But it is noteworthy that in *Olusoji* (1994) 15 Cr.App.R.(S.) 356, a case of benefit fraud, a court presided over by Lord Taylor C.J. indicated that the *Barrick* guidelines were relevant when considering deliberately persistent frauds involving public money. All will depend on the circumstances of the individual case, but as a general proposition benefit frauds will be less serious an offence than frauds committed in breach of trust, the subject of the *Barrick* guidelines.

28   In this context Miss Davenport, who appeared for the appellant Whatley, also referred us to the guidelines involving the evasion of duty on tobacco and alcohol recently set in *Czyzewski* [2004] 1 Cr.App.R.(S.) 49 (p.289). The Court indicated that following trial for a defendant with no relevant previous convictions and disregarding any personal mitigation, the following starting points were appropriate:

> "(i)   where the duty evaded was less than £1,000, and the level of personal profit was small, a moderate fine, if there is particularly strong mitigation, and provided that there had been no earlier warning, a conditional discharge might be appropriate;
>
> (ii)   where the duty evaded by a first time offender is not more than £10,000 . . . or the defendant's offending is at a low level . . . a community sentence or curfew order enforced by tagging, or a higher level of fine; the custody threshold is likely to be passed if any of the aggravating features . . . is present.
>
> (iii)   where the duty evaded is between £10,000 and £100,000, whether the defendant is operating individually or at a low level within an organisation, up to nine months custody . . .
>
> (iv)   when the duty evaded is in excess of £100,000, the length of the custodial sentence will be determined, principally, by the degree of professionalism of the defendant and the presence or absence of other aggravating features; subject to this, the duty evaded will indicate starting points as follows: £100,000 to £500,000, nine months to three

years; £500,000 to £1 million, three to five years; in excess of £1 million . . . five to seven years."

29   Excise duty cases are very different in nature from benefit fraud, but help to set the context within which to consider the *Stewart* guidelines.

The decision in *Kefford*

30   In *Kefford* Lord Woolf C.J., who sat with Rose L.J. and Judge L.J., considered the problem presented by the overcrowding of the prison system. In giving the judgment of the Court, Lord Woolf observed that in the present situation it is of greatest importance to the criminal justice system as a whole that only those who need to be sent to prison are sent to prison, and that they are not sent to prison for any longer than is necessary.

31   In the course of his judgment he also drew attention to the recent decision in *Mills* [2002] 2 Cr.App.R.(S.) 52 (p.229), in which similar guidance had been given in the context of the dramatic rise in the female prison population. At p.498 he addressed the approach to economic crimes in the following terms:

"In the case of economic crimes, for example obtaining undue credit by fraud, prison is not necessarily the only appropriate form of punishment. Particularly in the case of those who have no record of previous offending . . . Certainly, having to perform a form of community punishment can be a very salutary way of making it clear that crime does not pay . . ."

Conclusions

32   We draw the following conclusions from that analysis.

1. If *Stewart* is to continue to apply, the figure of £10,000 should be updated for inflation.
2. There will be cases in which a sentence should properly reflect an element of deterrence.
3. The decisions to which we have been referred are broadly consistent with *Stewart*. In *Armour and Sherlock* Newman J. suggested that the increasing prevalence of such offences had led to a more serious view of such offences being taken by the courts, but the heavier sentences that have been imposed in some cases are readily explicable by reference to aggravating features and to an element of deterrence.
4. In the light of our conclusion at 3 and taking account of the guidelines for comparable offences and of the decisions of the Court in *Kefford* and *Mills*, we do not consider that the *Stewart* guidelines require a revision, save in relation to the effect of inflation.
5. Accordingly, we consider that where imprisonment is necessary, short terms of up to about nine to 12 months will usually be sufficient in a contested case where the over payment is less than £20,000.

33   As we have already indicated, the aggravating and mitigating features identified in *Stewart* do not require modification or amplification. As Lord Lane

observed, sentences will depend upon an almost infinite variety of factors. Serious aggravating factors, such as the obtaining of large sums, frauds persisted in over length periods, claims for benefit that are fraudulent from their inception, sophisticated fraud involving the use of false and/or multiple identities, the maintenance of an extravagant lifestyle over the periods in question, will be likely to result in substantial periods of imprisonment.

34   We turn then to consider the two appeals before us.

Whatley

35   On March 25, 2004 the appellant, Albert John Whatley, who is now 64 years of age, was convicted on an indictment containing 13 counts of benefit fraud and on March 14 was sentenced to a total of two-and-a-half years' imprisonment. He appeals against that sentence with the leave of the learned single judge.

36   The Crown's case in essence is that for a considerable period the appellant claimed sickness benefit to which he was not entitled. He was working as a street trader at East Street Market, Southwark. The story begins in September 1994 when the appellant first made a claim for sickness benefit, claiming that he was unable to work because of degenerative osteoarthritis. In May 1997 the appellant completed an A2 Review Form, by which, as its name suggests, his claim for income support was reviewed, and in which he declared that he was not working either full-time or part-time and that he had no other income. Between May 1997 and the end of the period covered by offences in the indictment, July 2001, the appellant received benefits, both income support and mortgage interest repayments, totalling in excess of £90,000. But from 1992 the appellant held a casual trader's licence for the East Street Market issued by Southwark Council. In April 1997 he applied successfully for it to be upgraded to a permanent street licence.

37   It was the Crown's case that the appellant had worked as a street trader for the period covered by the indictment, namely from May 1997 to July 2001, and as a casual street trader since 1992, but had not declared such work and the income that it generated to the Department of Works and Pensions, in other words that he was guilty of benefit fraud. The Crown adduced evidence that the appellant was seen by trading inspectors at his pitch serving people and paying over his rent. At other times there were what were described as 'assistants' working the pitch or providing temporary cover. Evidence was also adduced as to approximately 16 trips made by the appellant to France between February and September 2001. On three of those trips he was stopped by Customs and Excise, and found to have alcohol and cigarettes in his car. The Crown argued that such evidence proved he was well enough to drive a car to a ferry, take a day trip and load his car with goods, and that it also showed that he could afford the goods.

38   There was also evidence that during the relevant period the appellant had made an agreement with his bank to pay monthly instalments of approximately £700 off his mortgage. The appellant began to make such payments from September 1998. The amounts varied, and in some months nothing was paid at all, but the payments totalled £21,600.

39   In a number of voluntary statements, not made under caution, the appellant maintained that he had never worked at the market. He said that others ran his stall and that he had not received any financial benefit from it. He denied taking trips to France, except one in 2001 when he had been apprehended by Customs and Excise.

40   As we have already indicated, the indictment contained 13 counts. The first count was a charge of false accounting contrary to s.17(1)(a) of the 1968 Theft Act which related to Form A2 completed by the appellant in May 1997. Counts 2 to 11 inclusive also alleged offences contrary to s.17(1)(a). Each related to the falsification of a document required for an accounting purpose, namely a paid order in the name of Albert John Whatley. They covered the period August 2000 to July 2001. Count 12 alleged that the appellant dishonestly obtained a money transfer in the sum of £1,048.74 on or about April 28, 1997 by deception, namely by falsely representing that he was entitled to claim income support and thereby still entitled to receive mortgage interest benefit, an offence contrary to s.15(1)(a) of the Theft Act. Count 13 was an identical offence committed on June 14, 2001. On count 1 the appellant was sentenced to 30 months' imprisonment; on counts 2, 3 and 4, 9 months' imprisonment on each concurrent and concurrent with count 1; on counts 5, 10, 11, 12 months' imprisonment on each count concurrent with count 1; on count 12, 9 months' concurrent; and on count 13, 18 months' concurrent, giving a total sentence of 30 months' imprisonment.

41   In passing sentence the learned judge referred to the decision in *Stewart* and continued:

> "Put simply, blatant fraudsters such as you are devoid of any conscience about the fact that you are not only helping yourself to honest tax payers' money, but also taking the bread out of the mouths of those who genuinely need it. I am quite satisfied, and it is conceded, that these offences are so serious that only a custodial sentence is justified. In my judgment the only issue is length."

42   The learned judge then went on to address the proper approach to sentence in a case where a defendant has been convicted on a number of sample counts. As we have already indicated, the Crown adduced evidence that the total of the benefits received by the appellant during the period in issue was in excess of £90,000. But sums involved in the counts in the indictment totalled approximately £3,100. The learned judge approached the sentencing exercise on the basis that there was no dispute that the sum in excess of £90,000 received by way of benefits could all be traced back, as he put it, to the fraudulent A2 Review Form. He continued:

> "That enables me to say, whilst keeping faith with the case of Cheryl Evans, that here one has on the indictment very much what their Lordships had in mind, an incepting claim. Count 1, the review form, subsequent counts being stepping stones, each in themselves all relatively small amounts, but demonstrating the period over which the fraud was perpetrated and thus going to prove period rather than amount, amount being accepted in the bundle and accepted in the course of the mitigation."

43   It is submitted on behalf of the appellant that the judge's approach was wrong in principle and contrary to authority. Miss Davenport took as her starting point the decision the decision of this Court in *Canavan, Kidd and Shaw* [1998] 1 Cr.App.R.(S.) 79 at 243, in which the judgment of the Court was given by Lord Bingham, then Lord Chief Justice. Lord Bingham began his judgment in the following terms:

> "These three appeals raise a common issue of principle concerning specimen or sample counts in an indictment. The issue may be expressed as follows:
>
> 'If a defendant is indicted and convicted on a count charging him with criminal conduct of a specified kind on single specified occasion or on a single occasion within a specified period, and such conduct is said by the prosecution to be representative of other criminal conduct of the same kind on other occasions not the subject of any other count in the indictment, may the court take account of such other conduct so as to increase the sentence it imposes if the defendant does not admit the commission of other offences and does not ask the court to take them into consideration when passing sentence?'."

44   The question was of great practical importance to those responsible for preparing indictments, differing answers to it having been given by this Court in *Clark* [1996] 2 Cr.App.R.(S.) 351 and in *Bradshaw* [1997] 2 Cr.App.R.(S.) 128.

45   At 84E Lord Bingham concluded that the Court reached the correct conclusion in *Clark*:

> ". . . and to the extent that that decision is at variance with other authority it is in our judgment to be preferred."

46   *Clark* was a case of indecent assault on a male person in which the indictment contained a single specimen count. In giving the judgment of the Court, Henry L.J. said at 357:

> "When you have specimen counts in (say) thefts or benefit frauds, then on conviction in the specimen counts there is reasonable chance that the defendant will admit the others—first the prosecution should have no difficulty in proving them, and second, the slate will be wiped clean only if the defendant does admit them. Those pressures are less likely to apply with specimen counts in sexual cases. First, offenders of this kind are often in denial at this stage. Secondly, they will be well aware that the prosecution will be unwilling to make the victim give evidence again.
>
> So what is to be done? We regret that we can do no better than to suggest that prosecutors charge sufficient offences fairly to reflect the criminality of the offending."

47   *Clark* and *Canavan* have been followed in a number of cases involving benefit fraud. In *Rosenburg*, to which we have already made reference, the appellant was convicted on nine counts of obtaining income support by deception. He had

claimed income support on the basis of incapacity to work in 1992, and he was paid continuously until March 1996. The prosecution limited the counts to a period from the beginning of 1994 to mid-1996, because that was when the business was most profitable. The total amount obtained in that period was £30,000, whereas the sums specified in the counts of the indictment totalled only £2,500. In passing sentence on the basis of the total amount received by the appellant, the sentencing judge said:

> "It is wrong for a judge to usurp the function of the jury where there is a genuine possibility that they could have acquitted the defendant of an offence or offences which have not been charged. However, I cannot believe that the decision in *Clark* was intended to restrict me to the sentence upon the basis of simply nine offences in this case. The nine representative charges cover the whole two and a half year period. The facts remain the same throughout the period. The defendant was drawing the same benefit each week while working in the same way. It is inconceivable to me that the jury would not have convicted him of all the other charges that could have been placed on the indictment for the periods in between, I notice the jury are nodding their heads."

48   Those observations are understandable given what Lord Bingham C.J. acknowledged in *Canavan* to have been the long standing practice of prosecuting authorities to frame indictments said to be representative of other criminal offences of like kind committed by a defendant, and the practice of the courts to pass sentences that took account not simply of the isolated instances specified in the counts, but also of the conduct of which, on the evidence adduced by the prosecution, those counts were representative. But this Court held that the sentencing judge fell into error in not following *Canavan*, and that the appellant ought to have been sentenced on the basis of the sum involved in the counts on the indictment and not on the basis of the sums received over the whole of the period in issue.

49   Similarly, in *Evans* the appellant was charged with housing benefit fraud over a period of four-and-a-half years. She pleaded guilty to four counts and was convicted on a further 20 counts. The sums involved in the counts to which she either pleaded or was found guilty amounted to £2,807, whereas the prosecution contended that she was involved in a sophisticated fraud involving a sum in excess of £25,000 over the period in question. In passing sentence the judge specifically stated that he was sentencing her for a fraud involving £25,000.

50   After reviewing the decisions in *Clark* and *Canavan* and referring to the decision in *Rosenburg* Mantell L.J. said:

> "In the case of this appellant we have some sympathy with the trial judge when he came to pass sentence. The prosecution had presented their case against her in 24 counts. We are told that, had every cheque which had been procured been included in this indictment as a separate offence, there would have been 200 counts or more. We cannot see any judge embarking upon a trial with a jury in those circumstances with any degree

of enthusiasm and without firmly insisting that the number of counts be substantially reduced. Likewise, it might well be considered unacceptable to
proceed on a number of separate indictments. Also we regard it as unrealistic to expect any defendant who has contested a case of this nature, upon
being convicted to ask, for offences to be taken into consideration which
she has hitherto denied. The consequence may well be that a defendant
who has pleaded guilty and confessed the full extent of his fraud may be
treated more harshly than a defendant who has contested the matter but
has been only convicted in respect of so-called specimen counts. We have
no doubt that the anomaly will be exploited by those who otherwise have
no answer to a multitude of charges, a tactic of which this case is an acute
illustration. Also it may be that some will attempt to apply the undoubted
logic of *Clark* and *Canavan* to other situations, perhaps in connection
with *Newton* hearings, or other occasions on which hitherto the judge has
been able to form his own view of the facts as to the basis of the jury's verdict. However, it is not within the province of this Court and certainly not on
this occasion to suggest any solution. It may be it is something which can be
overcome by the ingenuity of those who frame indictments. For the time
being, however, we simply remark that the position is far from satisfactory."

51   Those are observations with which we wholeheartedly agree. In so doing we
respectfully part company with Lord Bingham, who, in *Canavan*, had suggested
that prosecuting authorities would wish in the light of the decision in *Clark* to
include more counts in some indictments saying:

> "We do not think this may be unduly burdensome or render the trial unman-
> ageable."

52   The problem presented by *Canavan* is graphically illustrated by the two cases
before us: Whatley in which the appellant stands to be sentenced for dishonestly
obtaining £3,000, when it was the Crown's case that he had received in excess of
£90,000 by fraud, and Graham in which the appellant pleaded to an indictment
containing ten counts, but asked for 471 counts to be taken into consideration,
has been addressed by the Law Commission in its paper No.277, "The Effective
Prosecution of Multiple Offending". We are grateful to Mr Earnshaw for drawing
it to our attention.

53   The executive summary contains the following paragraphs:

> "3. The logic and correctness in principle of this decision [the decision of
> *Canavan*] cannot be faulted and we do not seek to do so. The decision does,
> however, pose an intractable dilemma for prosecutors and the courts in cases
> such as multiple theft and multiple fraud. In essence it counterposes the
> inability of a court to deal with an indictment with hundreds of separate
> counts with the inability to sentence for the totality of offending in the
> absence of a decision on each instance of offending. The problem is an
> important one because the consequence of the impracticability of pros-
> ecuting the full extent of dishonest offending in such cases is that the vast
> majority of such offending will not be prosecuted and the offenders will

escape appropriate sanction. We have been told that the practice of fraud squads faced with this problem is to charge merely a handful of offences, making no attempt to reflect the full criminality in any given case. Clearly this is not a desirable solution. From the judiciary, we have heard that the present law is found to be "pedantic and unworkable', and the senior judges whom we have consulted recognise that 'very real inherent difficulties' exists.

4. Under the present system (where there is a limit to the number of separate counts, each containing a single offence, that can be managed within a jury trial) it is not possible to give full respect to each of the following two fundamental principles. To some degree, one is bound to yield to the other. The principles are:

(1) defendants should only be sentenced for that which they have admitted, or which has been proved following a trial in which both sides can be examined on the evidence.

(2) It should be possible to sentence for the totality of an individual's offending. Defendants should not escape just punishment because the procedure cannot accommodate this.

5. The legal system should operate so as to reflect in full each of these fundamental principles. The constraints that prevent full recognition being given to both of these principles are threefold:

(1) the requirement of all issues that go to guilt must, if not admitted, be proved to a jury/magistrates;

(2) the strict limitations to the inclusion of more than one offence in any single charge/count;

(3) the limit to the number of separate counts or charges that can be managed within a trial."

54   The Law Commission proposed a number of possible solutions. All would require primary legislation. Unless and until there is such legislation prosecutors and judges will continue to be faced with an intractable problem.

55   In the case of *Whatley* the learned judge sought to distinguish *Canavan* and *Evans* on the basis that in *Evans* there were no concessions, whereas in this case there was no dispute, as he put it, that the whole of the sum of approximately £90,000 could be traced back to the fraudulent A2 Review Form. In our judgment, that attempt was misconceived for two reasons. First, although it was not conceded that a total sum in excess of £90,000 had been received by way of benefits during the relevant period, it was conceded that the appellant had not been entitled to benefits throughout that period. On the contrary, it was the defence case that he had not been working. The highest that it could be put was that the Crown was able to satisfy the jury that the appellant had not been entitled to receive benefit on the dates specified in the counts in the indictment. Secondly, the A2 Review Form was a declaration that at that date the appellant was not working. It was not, and could not be, a declaration as to the future. That is no doubt why the system for claiming benefit requires the recipient to

sign a declaration in a benefit book on each occasion that he or she receives benefit; hence counts 2 to 11 of the indictment.

56   It follows that, in our judgment, the valiant attempt by the learned judge to circumvent the decisions in *Clark* and *Canavan* was misconceived and that he erred in imposing a sentence on count 1 intended to reflect the receipt of over £90,000 by dishonest means. The appellant stood to be sentenced for offences of fraud involving a total of approximately £3,100.

57   The second limb of the appeal in *Whatley* is that the learned judge gave insufficient weight to the personal mitigation available to the appellant. It is submitted that it was accepted by the judge that this was not a sophisticated fraud and that the appellant had not sought to conceal his identity. Secondly Miss Davenport prayed in aid that the appellant is a family man with two daughters and grand children. At the date upon which he was sentenced his 90-year-old father, to whom he was very close, was dying of cancer. Sadly, his father has since died.

58   According to the appellant's general practitioner, who gave evidence at the trial, the appellant has suffered from chronic degenerative osteoarthritis for many years, and has undergone numerous operations to his knee and shoulder. He is not able to sit or stand for long periods, or walk unaided further than 50 metres. As a result of his disabilities he has been clinically depressed. We are satisfied that in those circumstances life in prison will inevitably be very hard. We were also informed that since being sentenced to imprisonment the appellant has twice undergone surgery and currently has to use crutches. As a result, he cannot be moved to an open prison.

59   We are satisfied that the learned judge was right to conclude that the offences crossed the custody threshold. These were deliberate and persistent offences, committed over a considerable period. As Miss Davenport conceded in the course of argument, the claims were fraudulent from their inception. We also take account of the fact that during the period in which the offences were committed, the appellant made a number of trips to France to buy alcohol and cigarettes, and was able to pay some £21,600 off his mortgage.

60   But constrained, as we are, by the decision in *Canavan* and in the light of the guidance afforded by *Stewart*, as updated, the total sentence of 30 months' imprisonment was plainly manifestly excessive. In our judgment, the appropriate sentence would have been one of 12 months' imprisonment on each count concurrently. The appeal is therefore allowed, and we substitute sentences of 12 months' imprisonment on each count concurrently.

Graham

61   On March 25, 2004 Cheryl Graham pleaded guilty to 10 offences of benefit fraud at Stratford Magistrates' Court. She asked the court to take a further 471 offences into consideration and was committed to the Crown Court at Snaresbrook for sentence. On April 20, 2004 she was sentenced to two years and six months' imprisonment concurrently on each offence.

62   The appellant is 36 years of age. She lives with a dependent child, her son, who was aged 17 at the time of her appearance at the Crown Court. She was a woman

of good character. In December 1992 she started receiving benefits, both income support and housing benefit, on the basis that she was separated from her partner and was not earning. She continued to receive such benefits until 2002, when she applied to change from income support to incapacity benefit. Investigations then revealed that she had been in employment since June 1992 before she began to receive benefits. During the period in question she received income support amounting to £34,500 and housing benefit of £16,000, a total in excess of £50,000. Of the 10 charges to which she pleaded guilty, 5 related to the housing benefit and were based on the annual declarations as to her financial circumstances made in the years 1998 to 2002. The remaining five charges related to income support. They were sample charges, but the 471 offences that she asked to be taken into consideration related to income support paid on a weekly basis from September 6, 1993 and February 3, 2003. When arrested and interviewed, the appellant made a full admission.

53   It was submitted on her behalf that the sentencing judge failed to have regard to the mitigation available to her. She was of good character, pleaded guilty at the first opportunity, showed genuine remorse for her actions and was deeply distressed by her contact with the police and the courts, of itself a substantial punishment. It was further submitted that the offences were committed against a background of very modest earnings on which she had been unable to cope. The offences were not committed to support an extravagant lifestyle. On the contrary, in September 2002, a year before her arrest, she had submitted to an administration order in the county court. Finally, the appellant is a woman who had suffered from abusive relationships in the past, which had had a detrimental effect upon her son, who had been repeatedly excluded from school, and upon the appellant herself. The medical records show that she had suffered from severe depression, and on two occasions had attempted to commit suicide. It is also submitted that the sentencing judge failed to pay sufficient regard to the decisions of this Court in *Kefford* and *Mills*, decisions to which we have already made reference.

54   In passing sentence the learned judge said:

> ". . . these offences show, in my judgment, a prolonged and deliberate course of fraud. You knew at all times that you were not entitled to these benefits, they are a fraud on all other tax payers, it is a very serious matter.
> The tax system relies, essentially, upon people's honesty, it would rapidly deteriorate into chaos if it could not rely on people's honesty.
> You were thoroughly dishonest and dishonest on a prolonged scale and on a large scale."

55   Those are observations that we strongly endorse. In our judgment, the learned judge was fully justified in forming the view that, taken together, the offences were so serious that only a custodial sentence was warranted.

56   Against the substantial personal mitigation available to the appellant, there were a number of serious aggravating features. The appellant persisted in her fraud on the state over a period of 10 years. She received a total of approximately £59,000. Her claims to benefit were fraudulent from the outset.

67   Taking full account of her pleas of guilty and of the mitigating factors that we
have summarised, we have come to the conclusion that the appropriate sentence
in her case was one of 18 months' imprisonment. Accordingly, we are satisfied
that the sentences imposed upon her were manifestly excessive. Her appeal is
allowed and we substitute sentences of 18 months' imprisonment on each
count in the indictment to be served concurrently.

R. v MOHAMMED ASLAM

COURT OF APPEAL (Lord Justice Rose (Vice President, Court of
Appeal Criminal Division), Mr Justice Richards and Mr Justice
Bean): October 22, 2004

[2004] EWCA Crim 2801; [2005] 1 Cr.App.R.(S.) 116

(LT) Acts of Parliament; Commencement; Confiscation orders; Criminal
charges; Date of offence; Jurisdiction

H1   *Confiscation orders— Criminal Justice Act 1988—defendant convicted of
offences committed both before and after November 1, 1995—whether prosecution entitled not to rely on earlier offences—whether court entitled to
proceed in accordance with the Criminal Justice Act 1988 as amended by the
Proceeds of Crime Act 1995—interpretation of the Proceeds of Crime Act
1995, s.16(5)*

H2   **Editor's note:** where a defendant is convicted of a number of offences, some
committed before November 1, 1995 and some after that date, confiscation proceedings may be conducted in accordance with the Criminal Justice Act 1988
("the 1988 Act") as amended by the Proceeds of Crime Act 1995 ("the 1995
Act"), provided that the prosecution do not rely on the offences committed
before November 1, 1995 for the purposes of confiscation.

H3   The appellant pleaded guilty before a magistrates' court to 24 offences of dishonesty and asked for a further 14 offences to be taken into consideration. He was
committed to the Crown Court for sentence. Sentenced to 18 months' imprisonment, with a confiscation order in the amount of £25,000. The defendant did not
appeal against the sentence of 18 months' imprisonment. In relation to the confiscation order, one of the offences to which he pleaded guilty was committed
before November 1, 1995 and one of the offences taken into consideration
occurred before that date. November 1, 1995 was the date on which the relevant
provisions of the 1995 Act came into effect. Before the confiscation order was
made, the defence argued that because the confiscation schedule included one
offence to which the offender had pleaded guilty and one offence which he
asked to be taken into consideration, each of which pre-dated November 1,
1995, the court had no jurisdiction to continue with confiscation proceedings
brought under the Criminal Justice Act 1988, as amended by the 1995 Act.

The prosecution accordingly abandoned reliance on the offences which occurred before November 1, 1995. The defence submitted that this manoeuvre failed to achieve its purpose and that the confiscation proceedings remained fatally flawed. The sentencing judge rejected the defence submission and made a confiscation order in accordance with s.72AA of the 1988 Act, as amended by the 1995 Act.

H4 **Held:** the 1995 Act, s.1, amended the law relating to confiscation orders in a number of respects. Section 16(5) of the Act provided that s.1 should not apply in the case of any proceedings against any person where that person was convicted in those proceedings of an offence committed before the commencement of that section. If s.1 of the 1995 Act did not apply in the present case, it would follow that the confiscation proceedings could only have been brought under the original version of the 1988 Act. The meaning of s.16(5) was considered by the Court in *Simpson* [2004] 1 Cr.App.R.(S.) 24 (p.158) where one offence to which the appellant pleaded guilty concerned facts which took place before November 1, 1995. The Court held that s.16(5) was to be interpreted as though it read " Section 1 above shall not apply in the case of any proceedings against any person where that person is convicted in those proceedings of an offence *in respect of which a confiscation order is or could be sought*, which was committed before the commencement of that section." The additional words were suggested by counsel for the prosecution in his skeleton argument. No confiscation order was sought in *Simpson* in respect of the offence committed before November 1, 1995, but it appeared that a confiscation order could have been sought in respect of that count. The latent purpose of s.16(5) was to prevent the Crown from dividing convictions against the defendant in one set of proceedings into pre- and post-November 1, 1995 matters and then taking confiscation proceedings under both statutes. If at the time the judge was asked to make the confiscation order under the 1995 Act in respect of a number of counts there remained a pre-commencement count on which the Crown sought or could still seek a confiscation order under the earlier version of the 1988 Act, there was no jurisdiction to make an order under the 1995 Act . If the pre-commencement count was one which could not be the basis of confiscation proceedings there was no obstacle to using the 1995 Act regime. Similarly if the Crown had expressly abandoned any reliance on the pre-commencement count for the purposes of a confiscation order, the fact that it could have sought such an order in respect of that count seemed to be entirely immaterial. In such a case in the Court's judgment there was no obstacle to using in the 1995 Act regime in respect of the post-commencement counts. In the present case, the Crown had sought a confiscation order in respect of the pre-November 1, 1995 Act offence until the issue was raised before the sentencing judge, at which point reliance on that count was abandoned by the Crown. The Court interpreted the phrase "in respect of which a confiscation order was sought" as referring to a case where the prosecution maintained their reliance on the offence in question at a substantial hearing of the application for the confiscation order. The Court agreed with the sentencing judge that the abandonment of confiscation proceedings in respect of one count at that stage was analogous to the Crown offering no evidence on one count of an indictment at the beginning of the trial. The Court could not agree that this abandonment was an abuse of process. The Court accepted the submission that it was for the Crown to decide on the counts in respect of which it wished to pursue and maintain confiscation proceedings. The appeal would be dismissed.

H5 **Case cited:**
Simpson [2004] 1 Cr.App.R.(S.) 24 (p.158)

H6 **References:** confiscation order, *Current Sentencing Practice* J9
H7 **Commentary:** [2005] Crim. L.R. 145

H8 *D. Cox* for the appellant.
R. D'Cruz for the Crown.

JUDGMENT

1   **Bean J.:**   This is an appeal against a confiscation order by leave of the single judge. On April 29, 2003 at Stratford Magistrates' Court the appellant pleaded guilty to 24 offences of dishonesty and asked for a further 14 offences to be taken into consideration. On May 30, 2003, in the Crown Court at Snaresbrook, he was sentenced by Mr Recorder Lowe Q.C. to a total of 18 months' imprisonment. There is no appeal against that decision.

2   The Crown initiated confiscation proceedings which, after some delay, came before H.H. Judge Birtles on January 7, 2004. The Crown had, in the usual way, served a schedule detailing the matters in respect of which they sought confiscation. One of these, count 1 on the indictment, related to an offence committed which had been committed prior to November 1, 1995. Similarly, one of the offences taken into consideration occurred before that date. November 1, 1995 is of significance since it was the date on which the relevant provisions of the Proceeds of Crime Act 1995 came into force. The Crown were seeking to proceed under that Act. The previous legislation was the Criminal Justice Act 1988 as amended by the Criminal Justice Act 1993.

3   On January 7, 2004 the defence took the point which is the subject of this appeal, namely that because the confiscation schedule included one count and one offence to be taken into consideration, each of which pre-dated the commencement of the 1995 Act, the court had no jurisdiction to continue with the confiscation proceedings brought under that Act. The response of the Crown, after reflecting on the matter, was to abandon reliance on the count and the offence taken into consideration which occurred before November 1, 1995.

4   The defence submitted that this manoeuvre failed to achieve its purpose and that the confiscation proceedings remained fatally flawed. Judge Birtles reserved judgment and in a careful written decision, to which we would pay tribute, he rejected the defence submissions. He accordingly made a confiscation order under the 1995 Act in the sum of £25,000 with a term of imprisonment of nine months, consecutive to the earlier sentences, in default of payment.

5   It should be noted that if the offending count 1 had remained in play, the benefit allegedly received by the defendant, would, on the Crown's case, have been increased by £35,000; on the other hand, under the pre- 1995 legislation some £7,000 would have had to be deducted from the amount of the confiscation order since it related to a "course of conduct" covered neither by the convictions nor by the offences taken into consideration. The "course of conduct" confiscation provisions were first introduced by s.2 of the 1995 Act, creating a new s.72AA of the Criminal Justice Act 1988.

6   It is possible to summarise the facts of the offences quite briefly, since they do not affect the jurisdiction point which is before us. The appellant produced two forged documents, one a death certificate purporting to show his father was dead, and one a letter purportedly from a doctor saying he was ill, in response to queries from people who ran the medical course he was attending. He stole a quantity of stationery and cleaning products from a hospital where he worked, and also stole a computer from the same hospital. He used his computer at work to disguise the origin of orders he was making for goods with stolen credit card details to arrange for goods to be delivered at a number of addresses. He was also falsely claiming certain social security benefits.

7   Section 1 of the 1995 Act amended the law relating to confiscation orders in a number of respects, for example by imposing a duty on the court to conduct confiscation proceedings where it considered that to be appropriate even though the prosecution had not served written notice of their intention to do so. Section 16(5) of the 1995 is as follows:

> "Section 1 above shall not apply in the case of any proceedings against any person where that person is convicted in those proceedings of an offence which was committed before the commencement of that Section."

If s.1 of the 1995 Act did not apply in the present case, it would follow that confiscation proceedings could only have been brought under the earlier statute.

8   The meaning of s.16(5) was considered by this Court, specially constituted with five judges, in *Simpson* [2004] 1 Cr.App.R.(S.) 24 (p.158), upon which Mr Cox, appearing for the appellant, strongly relies. Simpson pleaded guilty to six offences arising from a value added tax fraud. He was sentenced to 30 months' imprisonment and a confiscation order was made against him. The Crown failed to serve a properly constituted notice complying with s.72 of the 1988 Act as amended in 1993. That did not matter if the 1995 Act applied, since under s.1(2) of that Act the court could proceed of its own motion.

9   It was argued on Simpson's behalf that one count (count 6) to which he had pleaded guilty concerned facts which took place a fortnight before November 1, 1995. Accordingly, it was argued that s.16(5) had the effect that the 1995 amendments did not apply and the failure to serve a proper notice was fatal to the confiscation order, even though "count 6 was not a count on which the confiscation order was based" (para.[15] of the judgment).

0   The court rejected that submission. It noted that the submission, if correct, would have the curious result that an acquittal on count 6 would have left the Crown free to seek a confiscation order under the 1995 Act in respect of the

remaining counts, whereas the conviction on count 6, even though irrelevant to the confiscation order, would have rendered the confiscation proceedings under the 1995 Act a nullity. The court held that s.16(5) was to be interpreted as though it read:

> "Section 1 above shall not apply in the case of any proceedings against any person where that person is convicted in those proceedings of an offence *in respect of which a confiscation order is or could be sought*, which was committed before the commencement of that section."

The words "in respect of which a confiscation order is or could be sought" were apparently suggested by Mr David Barnard, counsel for the prosecution, in his skeleton argument. No confiscation order *was* apparently sought, or at least made, in respect of count 6. But so far as we can see a confiscation order *could* have been sought in respect of that count since that was simply one of a number of VAT offences before the court (see para.[2] of the judgment).

11   The legislative purpose of s.16(5), as it seem to us, was to prevent the Crown from dividing convictions against a defendant in one set of proceedings into pre- and post-November 1, 1995 matters and then taking confiscation proceedings (concurrently or consecutively) under both statutes. So if at the time the judge is asked to make a confiscation order under the 1995 Act on a number of counts there remains a pre-commencement count on which the Crown is seeking, or *could still* seek, a confiscation order under the 1988 Act as amended in 1993, there is no jurisdiction to make an order under the 1995 Act. However, if the pre-commencement count is one which could not be the basis of confiscation proceedings, there is no obstacle to using the 1995 Act regime. Similarly if (as in this case) the Crown has expressly abandoned any reliance on the pre-commencement count for the purposes of a confiscation order, the fact that it *could have* sought such an order in respect of that count seems to us entirely immaterial. In such a case also, in our judgment, there is no obstacle to using in the 1995 Act regime in respect of the post- commencement counts. We do not understand *Simpson* to require a contrary conclusion.

12   We agree with the observations of this Court in *Sekhon* [2003] 2 Cr.App.R.(S.) 38:

> "28 . . . we suggest that it would not have been the intention of Parliament to exclude the jurisdiction of the court in relation to the making of confiscation orders because of procedural defects of a technical nature that caused no injustice to the defendant. In this context it is interesting to note that certainly this is not Parliament's intention now. The most recent legislation in this area is the Proceeds of Crime Act 2002. Section 14(11) of that Act provides: 'A confiscation order must not be quashed only on the ground that there was a defect or omission in the procedure connected with the application for or the granting of a postponement.'

29 We would expect a procedural failure only to result in a lack of jurisdiction if this was necessary to ensure that the criminal justice system served the interests of justice and thus the public or where there was at least a real possibility of the defendant suffering prejudice as a consequence of the procedural failure."

13 The other aspect of s.16(5) of the 1995 Act as interpreted in *Simpson* is that a confiscation order cannot be made under that Act if the defendant is convicted in those proceedings of a pre-commencement offence in respect of which a confiscation order *is sought*. Here, as Mr Cox points out in his able argument on behalf of the appellant, a confiscation order *was* sought in respect of the offending count until he raised the s.16(5) issue at the outset of the confiscation hearing before Judge Birtles, at which point reliance on that count was abandoned by the Crown.

14 As to that, we interpret the phrase "in respect of which a confiscation order is sought" from the judgment in *Simpson* as referring to a case where the prosecution maintain their reliance on the count in question at the substantive hearing of the application for a confiscation order. We agree with the learned judge that the abandonment of confiscation proceedings in respect of one count at that stage is analogous to the Crown offering no evidence on one count of an indictment at the beginning of a trial. We cannot agree with Mr Cox that this abandonment was an abuse of process. Conversely, we accept the submission of Mr D'Cruz that it is for the Crown to decide on the counts in respect of which it wishes to institute and maintain confiscation proceedings.

15 For the sake of completeness we should mention the one offence taken into consideration which antedated November 1, 1995. Given that s.16(5) refers to convictions, we doubt whether an offence taken into consideration brings it into play at all. However, it is unnecessary to decide the point in this case, since if s.16(5) does apply to the offence taken into consideration our decision as to the proper interpretation of that section in relation to count 1 plainly applies to the matter taken into consideration as well.

16 Accordingly, in our judgment, the learned judge was right to permit the prosecution to proceed under the 1995 Act.

17 Mr Cox submitted, as a fall back position, even if the Crown was so entitled, it would be wrong to permit a confiscation order in respect of the "course of conduct" which represents £6997.75 of the total of £25,000. But we consider that his argument on jurisdiction is, as he submitted to the learned judge, an "all or nothing" argument. If the Crown was entitled to proceed under the 1995 Act, it was entitled to rely on the appellant's course of conduct in so far as it occurred after November 1, 1995, and thus the amount of the order was properly fixed at £25,000.

18 For these reasons we dismiss the appeal.

[Paragraphs [19]–[24] have been omitted.]

ATTORNEY GENERAL'S REFERENCE NO.104 OF 2004 (WAYNE GARVEY)

COURT OF APPEAL (Lord Justice Rose (Vice President, Court of Appeal Criminal Division), Mr. Justice Henriques and Mrs Justice Dobbs): October 25, 2004

[2004] EWCA Crim 2672; [2005] 1 Cr.App.R.(S.) 117

Assault by penetration; Sentencing guidelines; Undue leniency

H1   *Sexual Offences Act 2003—assault by penetration—sentencing guidance*

H2   Sentencing guidance for offences of assault by penetration contrary to the Sexual Offences Act 2003, s.2.

H3   The offender pleaded guilty to assault by penetration, contrary to the Sexual Offences Act 2003, s.2. The offender went to the home of an adult female, knowing that the door of the premises would not be locked and that she would be likely to be asleep and on her own. He went into the bedroom, removed his lower clothing, got into her bed and digitally penetrated her vagina for several minutes. The woman awoke to find the offender in her bed. The offender was arrested later the same morning. Sentenced to 18 months' imprisonment. The Attorney General asked the Court to review the sentence on the ground that it was unduly lenient.

H4   **Held:** (considering *Millberry* [2003] 2 Cr.App.R.(S.) 31 (p.142), *Attorney General's Reference No.51 of 1999 (DH)* [2000] 1 Cr.App.R.(S.) 407, and *Brown* [2002] EWCA Crim 2050) for the Attorney General it was submitted that the effect of the Sexual Offences Act 2003, which stipulated that the maximum sentence for assault by penetration should be life imprisonment, whereas previously such an offence would have been categorised as indecent assault with a maximum sentence of 10 years, was inevitably to increase the sort of sentence which was appropriate for this kind of conduct. It was submitted that the aggravating and mitigating features identified in *Millberry* as being relevant to rape must apply to offences of assault by penetration. In the Court's judgment, the re-definition of the offence of rape and the introduction of the new offence of assault by penetration with a maximum sentence of life imprisonment in relation to both offences must mean that sentences to be passed by the court in relation to digital penetration were at a higher level than would have been appropriate had they been dealt with as offences of indecent assault subject to the lesser maximum. The courts had always regarded digital penetration as a particularly serious feature of indecent assault. The Court accepted that the offender's entry into the victim's home was an aggravating feature as was the victim's vulnerabilty which resulted from the fact that her condition was affected by drink. The Court had regard to the suggestions made by the Sentencing Advisory

Panel which might or might not become guidelines drafted by the Sentencing Guidelines Council which might be, in due course, issued as definitive guidelines. In the meantime, the Court offered the following guidance for sentencers:

> "the starting point for an adult for rape, as now defined in the Sexual Offences Act 2003, section 1(1), should be five years, whether the penetration was of the vagina, anus or mouth, and whether the victim was male or female. It should be varied by upwards or downwards in accordance with the aggravating and mitigating features and higher starting points identified in *Millberry*.
>
> In the case of an adult victim, whether male or female, bearing in mind the absence of the risk of pregnancy or infection inherent in rape, the starting point for assault by penetration, as defined in s.2 of the Act, should generally be somewhat lower than that for rape, in the region or four years. If non-penile penetration was by an object of such size or character, whether by reference to the age of the victim or otherwise, that there was a significant risk of physical injury, the starting point should be five years. The aggravating and mitigating features and higher starting points identified in *Millberry* should also assault by penetration.
>
> If, in assault by penetration, the degree of penetration or time which the penetration lasted was minimal, a lower starting point than four or five years was likely to be appropriate.
>
> For young offenders, the sentence for rape and assault by penetration should be significantly shorter than that for an adult.
>
> A plea of guilty should be taken into account."

15   In the light of these observations, the Court regarded the sentence passed on the offender as being unduly lenient. Having regard to the aggravating features of intrusion into the victim's home when she was asleep and vulnerable, the Court would have expected a sentence in the court below, had there been a trial, of six years' imprisonment. In the light of the guilty plea, the Court would have expected a sentence of four years' imprisonment. Taking into account the element of double jeopardy, the sentence of 18 months' imprisonment imposed by the Crown Court would be quashed and a sentence of 3 years and 3 months' imprisonment substituted.

16   **Cases cited:**
Millberry [2003] 2 Cr.App.R.(S.) 31 (p.142); *Attorney General's Reference No.51 of 1999 (DH)* [2000] 1 Cr.App.R.(S.) 407; *Brown* [2002] EWCA Crim 2050

17   **Commentary:** [2005] Crim.L.R. 150

18   *R.Horwell* for the Attorney General.
R.Clews for the offender.

JUDGMENT

1   **Rose L.J.:**   The Attorney General seeks the leave of the Court under s.36 of the Criminal Justice Act 1988 to refer a sentence said to be unduly lenient. We grant leave.

2   The offender was born in December 1972, so is now 31. He was indicted with a single count of assault by penetration, contrary to s.2 of the Sexual Offences Act 2003. On May 28, 2004, at the s.51 preliminary hearing, he pleaded guilty and sentence was adjourned for reports. On July 22, 2004 he was sentenced to 18 months' imprisonment and reminded of the notification requirements under the Sex Offenders Act 1997.

3   The judge who passed sentence was Mr Recorder Heaton, sitting at Leeds Crown Court. We comment in passing that we find it surprising that such a case was listed before this recorder. We would have expected it to be listed either before a circuit judge or a recorder especially authorised to deal with serious sex cases, which this recorder was not.

4   In summary, what happened was that, in the early hours of the morning, the offender went to the home of an adult female. He knew, for reasons which we shall come to, that the door at her premises would not be locked. He also knew that she would be on her own and that it was likely that she would be asleep. He went into her bedroom, removed his lower clothing, got into her bed, and, while she was asleep, digitally penetrated her vagina for between five and ten minutes. The lady awoke to find the offender in her bed with his arm around her. Eventually, in interview, he admitted the offence.

5   In a little more detail, the victim was a 23-year-old married lady living with her husband in West Yorkshire. On April 30, 2004 she went with her husband to a neighbour's home for a drink. The offender, his partner and their children were also there. During the course of the evening, when the victim was dancing, she became uncomfortable because the offender was trying to push himself against her.

6   Soon after midnight, she was very much the worse for drink and decided to go home. Her husband decided to stay. They only had one key, and so she announced (and the offender, no doubt, heard) that she would leave the door open. She left the party. She crossed the road to her home and went to bed.

7   She awakened about 5.45am. There was an arm around her waist, which she knew was not that of her husband. She was frightened. She jumped out of bed. She saw it was the offender. He was awake and naked from the waist down. He put his trousers on and said that he loved the victim as a friend. She told him to leave. He attempted to cuddle her and say that he had meant nothing by what he had done. The lady was, understandably, frightened and felt threatened. The moment he left, she locked the door and telephoned her husband. He came back and found his wife in shock. The police were called.

8   The victim felt sore in her vagina. She noticed that two buttons on her pyjama top had been undone and she had an aching pain in her left arm.

9   Not very long after, about 7am the same morning, the offender was arrested. It was May 1, 2004 and the new Act had come into force.

10   At first, he denied doing anything to the victim, but later admitted having gone to her home and found her asleep. He said that he had digitally penetrated her for between five and ten minutes, and also touched one of her breasts. He said that he had taken alcohol, cannabis and amphetamine.

11   He has appeared before the criminal courts on eight previous occasions, for nine offences of violence or dishonesty. But he has no previous convictions for sexual offences and he had not previously been sentenced to custody.

12   There is a psychiatrist's report upon the offender, which shows that, after the offence, the offender developed a major depressive disorder. He was assessed as having the potential to pose serious harm to females if his cognitive skills and awareness did not improve, and there remains a moderate risk that he will reoffend.

13   On behalf of the Attorney General, Mr Horwell draws attention to what he submits, rightly, are two aggravating features: first, the offence was committed in the victim's home; secondly, the victim was very vulnerable, in that she was asleep in bed and had consumed a large quantity of alcohol.

14   Mr Horwell draws attention to the mitigation to be found in the plea of guilty at the earliest opportunity and the development of a depressive disorder of mild to moderate intensity since the offence.

15   Mr Horwell referred to three authorities: *Millberry* [2003] 2 Cr.App.R.(S.) 31 (p.142); *Attorney-General's Reference No.51 of 1999* [2000] 1 Cr.App.R.(S.) 407; and *B (Stuart Scott)* [2002] EWCA Crim 2050.

16   Mr Horwell submits that the effect of the Sexual Offences Act 2003, in stipulating imprisonment for life as the maximum sentence for assault by penetration, whereas previously such an offence would have been categorised as indecent assault, with a maximum sentence of 10 years, is, inevitably, to increase the sort of sentence which is appropriate for this kind of conduct. Mr Horwell also submits that the aggravating and mitigating features identified in *Milberry* as being relevant to rape must likewise apply to offences of assault by penetration.

17   Mr Clews, on the other hand, on behalf of the offender, submits that the increased maximum does not necessarily mean that there should always be a higher starting point for this sort of conduct.

18   In our judgment the re-definition of the offence of rape in s.1 of the Act and the introduction of the new offence of assault by penetration in s.2, with a maximum sentence of life imprisonment in relation to both of these offences, must mean that the sentences to be passed by the court in relation to digital penetration are at a higher level than would have been appropriate had they been dealt with as offences of indecent assault, subject to the lesser maximum. We comment, in passing, that digital penetration was always regarded by the courts as a particularly serious feature of indecent assault.

19   Mr Horwell draws attention, in the judgment in *Milberry*, to para.32(vi) in support of his submission that the offender's entry into this victim's home is an aggravating feature. With that we agree.

20   It is also, as we have indicated, an aggravating feature that, because of her condition, the victim was vulnerable. But we also bear in mind that the length of

conduct admitted by the offender was not something of which the victim was aware, because she was asleep.

21   Mr Clews drew attention to one of the suggestions made by the Sentencing Advisory Panel in their Consultation Paper of February 12, 2004 as to two years being an appropriate starting point for brief digital penetration. This was not such a case.

22   Mr Clews submits that there was not, in the present case, the element of pre-planning which is to be found in some of the authorities. We entertain some doubt about that submission, bearing in mind that it was some little time before he entered the victim's house that the offender was aware of the opportunity to do so, because of what had been said about the door key.

23   Mr Clews stresses that the only evidence in relation to the time which this penetration lasted comes from the offender. That, of course, is an inevitable consequence of his victim being asleep at the time.

24   Mr Clews rightly stresses that the offender made admissions at an early stage and pleaded guilty at the first opportunity. Mr Clews also refers to the offender's mild to moderate depression.

25   So far as the authority of B (Stuart Scott) is concerned, not only was the offence there charged differently, the circumstances were also very different from the present case, and we derive no assistance from it.

26   So far as the Attorney-General's Reference No.51 of 1999 is concerned, as Mr Horwell accepts, that involved the rape of a sleeping woman, whereas the court here is concerned with assault by penetration.

27   We have regard to the suggestions made by the Sentencing Advisory Panel in paragraphs 38 to 43 of their Consultation Paper which we have identified. We bear in mind that, following consultation, those suggestions may or may not become proposals to the Sentencing Guidelines Council under s.71(2) of the Criminal Justice Act 2003 and that the Council, thereafter, may frame draft guidelines which, having been the subject of consultation in accordance with s.70(8)(b) of the Act, may, in due course, be issued as definitive guidelines to which the courts must have regard by virtue of s.72 of the Act.

28   In the meantime, for the benefit of sentencers who have been dealing with these offences since May 2004, while deploring too rigid or formulaic an approach (compare Millberry at [34]), we proffer the following guidance:

   (a) The starting point for an adult for rape, as now defined by s.(1) of the Sexual Offences Act 2003, should be five years, whether penetration is of the vagina, anus or mouth, and whether the victim is male or female, and should be varied upwards or downwards in accordance with the aggravating and mitigating features and higher starting points identified in Millberry. The court must also take into account a guilty plea (s.152 of the Powers of Criminal Courts (Sentencing) Act 2000).

   (b) In the case of an adult victim, whether male or female, bearing in mind the absence of the risk of pregnancy or infection inherent in rape, the starting point for assault by penetration, as defined in s.2 of the Act, should, generally, be somewhat lower than that for rape—that is, in the region of four years. If non-penile penetration is by an object of such size or character that, whether by reference to the age of the victim or otherwise, there is a significant risk of physical injury, the starting point should be five years. The aggravating and mitigating features and higher starting points identified in *Millberry* should also apply to assault by penetration, and a plea of guilty must also be taken into account.

(c) If, in assault by penetration, the degree of penetration or the time which penetration lasts is minimal, a lower starting point than four or five years is likely to be appropriate.

(d) For young offenders, the sentence for rape and assault by penetration should be significantly shorter than that for an adult (see para.[30] of *Millberry*).

9   In the light of those observations, we would regard the sentence passed on this offender as being not merely lenient, as Mr Clews submits, but as being unduly lenient. We would have expected, having regard to the aggravating features of intrusion into the victim's home and bed when she was asleep and vulnerable, a sentence in the court below, had there been a trial, of six years' imprisonment. In the light of the guilty plea, we would have expected a sentence of four years' imprisonment. Taking into account double jeopardy, that is to say that the offender is being sentenced for a second time in this Court, we quash the sentence of 18 months which was imposed upon him and substitute for it a sentence of 3 years and 3months' imprisonment.

0   Registration under the Sex Offenders Act will now be for life.

R. v BILLY PAUL HALL

COURT OF APPEAL (Mr.Justice Hunt and Mr.Justice Tugendhat):
October 25, 2004

[2004] EWCA Crim 2671; [2005] 1 Cr.App.R.(S.) 118

(LT) Anti social behaviour orders; Duration; Public protection; Road traffic offences

1   *Anti social behaviour order— Crime and Disorder Act 1998 s.1C—order prohibiting offender from driving while not in possession of valid licence or insurance—offender persistent driving offender—whether order appropriate in principle*

2   An order under the Crime and Disorder Act 1998 s.1C prohibiting the appellant, a persistent dangerous and disqualified driver, from driving when not the holder of a valid licence, upheld.

H3   The appellant pleaded guilty before a magistrates' court to dangerous driving, driving while disqualified, using a vehicle without insurance and failing to stop on a signal of a police officer. He was committed to the Crown Court for sentence. Sentenced to a total of 12 months' imprisonment, disqualified from driving for 2 years, with an indefinite anti-social behaviour order made under the Crime and Disorder Act 1998, s.1C, prohibiting the appellant from driving any mechanically propelled vehicle on a public road in the United Kingdom without being the holder of a valid driving licence and certificate of insurance.

H4   **Held:** the sentence of imprisonment was not challenged. It was submitted that the anti-social behaviour order was unnecessary. The appellant, aged 30, had an appalling history of driving offences as well as other serious offences. He had 10 previous convictions for driving while disqualified, 3 for taking vehicles without consent, 1 for dangerous driving, 1 for reckless driving and other road traffic offences. The sentencing judge observed that the regularity of the appellant's offending demonstrated his total disregard for the law. The Court had considered previous decisions, including in particular *P* [2004] 2 Cr.App.R.(S.) 63 (p.343). The point made before the Court was that the effect of the order was that if the appellant offended again, he would be liable to imprisonment for up to five years for breach of the anti-social behaviour order, instead of six months' imprisonment for driving while disqualified. The terms of the order were precise and capable of being understood by the appellant, and their practical effect had been set out by the sentencing judge. In the Court's view, the order was not wrong in principle, except in its indefinite nature. The Court would specify the length of the anti-social behaviour order as two years.

H5   **Case cited:**
P [2004] 2 Cr.App.R.(S.) 63 (p.343)

H6   **Reference:** order under the Crime and Disorder Act 1998, *Current Sentencing Practice* H 10

H7   *A.Selby* for the appellant.

JUDGMENT

1   **Hunt J.:**   On June 22, 2004 at the Central Sussex Magistrates' Court the appellant pleaded guilty and was committed to the Crown Court for sentence. On June 30 at the Crown Court he was sentenced as follows: on the first offence of driving whilst disqualified 5 months' imprisonment concurrent to 12 months' imprisonment for dangerous driving, offence 3; no separate penalty for using a vehicle without insurance and no separate penalty for failing to stop on the signal of a constable. The total sentence was 12 months' imprisonment. That is not a matter which has been contested in this Court. What has been contested is the

anti social behaviour order which was also made prohibiting the appellant from driving any mechanically propelled vehicle on a public road in the United Kingdom without being the holder of a valid driving licence and certificate of insurance. That ASBO, as they are known, was ordered to run indefinitely. Indeed, indefinitely was the word used by the judge in sentencing.

2   Today before us Mr Selby argues, and argues powerfully, that the ASBO was unnecessary for this offending. As we have observed, an anti social behaviour order is not made just for this offending and Mr Selby has that point well in mind. But this appellant is 30 and he has the most appalling history of driving convictions, as well as other serious offending. Indeed, he began offending at the age of 10. He has 10 previous convictions for driving while disqualified and without insurance, three of taking vehicles without consent, one of attempting, one of dangerous driving, one of reckless driving, one of failing to provide a specimen, one of failing to stop, one of failing to report, one of having no test certificate. It is, bearing in mind all of that offending and the regularity of it, that the judge made the anti social behaviour order, saying that the appellant had repeatedly demonstrated a total disregard for the law.

3   We have had our attention drawn to other cases, including, particularly, the case of *P* heard in February of this year by the Lord Chief Justice, Richards J. and Henriques J., where the orders were considered and the following principles emerged. The test for making an order is one of the necessity to protect the public from further anti social acts by the offender. There is nothing wrong in principle in making such an order when they are driving offences of such a regularity and type and in such an area that they do constitute anti social behaviour. It is said that the terms of the order must be precise and capable of being understood by the offender. The findings of fact giving rise to the making of the order must be recorded and the order must be explained to the offender. The exact terms of the order must be pronounced in open court and the written order must accurately reflect the order as pronounced. It was noted that the making of such an order is strictly not part of the sentencing process.

4   The point that is made before us is that it is said that the judge only made this order in order that, in the event of this appellant's offending again, he would not just be liable to six months' imprisonment for driving whilst disqualified, but he would be liable to imprisonment for up to five years for breach of the anti social behaviour order.

5   In fact, when we look at it, this is what the judge said in sentencing, in spelling out to this appellant what the practical effect of the order was. He said:

> "The practical effect of this is as follows: the two years' disqualification [which was passed] runs from today, but it continues until you pass a driving test. If you drive a motor car in this country on a public road without getting through a test and getting a licence after your period of disqualification, you will be in breach of this order and you will not then be liable merely to six months' imprisonment for driving whilst disqualified, you will liable to imprisonment of up to five years. Do you understand?"

6   The appellant said that he did understand. Of course, the judge is obliged to
spell out the consequences of the order. As was said in the case of *P*, the terms
of the order must be precise and capable of being understood by the offender.
The practical effect was, and is, as the judge set it out. In our view, as we say,
it was not wrong in principle for the judge to make this order and the order followed the principles set out in *P*, save for one particular which we are going to
come to in a moment.

7   We should, perhaps, add that this offending, though the details are not crucial,
occurred in May 2004. The appellant was in the driver's seat of a Ford Granada
Scorpio motor car parked in a lay-by at 11 o'clock in the morning on the A27. He
was recognised as a disqualified driver. He drove on to the A27. The police,
having seen him, followed him. He turned off. He became aware that he was
being followed, but when police lights were activated he accelerated away, driving at speed through a junction with a giveway sign. There were various other
features of driving, speeds in excess of 80 miles an hour, even when he had
gone off into a very limited speed limit area. He was weaving in and out of traffic
with black smoke from the exhaust. He came to a stop when he collided with
some traffic lights and street furniture. People working at that point had to leap
out of their way, having come, as they described it, close to death. He was trapped
inside the vehicle, but managed to get out and then was caught by the police. He
made no comment in interview.

8   The matter which has concerned us, and which we have discussed today with
Mr Selby, is the indefinite nature of this order. Just as it is not advisable to make
long periods of disqualification, because it only makes it much more difficult for
somebody to comply, in our view the specific terms of the anti social behaviour
order should have been set out, rather than an indefinite order. We agree with Mr
Selby's submissions on this part of the appeal and we shall specify the length of
the anti social behaviour order as two years. That is two years from July when the
order was made. To that limited extent, and that extent only, this appeal is
allowed.

R. v JASON DOCKING AND OTHERS

Court of Appeal (Lord Justice Rose (Vice President, Court of Appeal Criminal Division), Mr Justice Henriques and Mrs Justice Dobbs): October 25, 2004

[2004] EWCA Crim 2675; [2005] 1 Cr.App.R.(S.) 119

Attempts; Murder; Possession of firearms with intent; Sentence length; Shotguns; Vigilantes

H1 *Attempted murder—firing shot gun during car chase in revenge attack—length of sentence*

H2   Sentences totalling 20 years' imprisonment for attempted murder by firing a sawn-off shot gun during a car chase in the course of a revenge attack reduced to a total of 16 years.

H3   The first appellant was convicted of attempted murder, possessing a shotgun with intent to endanger life, dangerous driving and driving while disqualified. He was concerned in an incident in which a car containing two other persons was chased by a car driven by the first appellant. The appellant fired a sawn-off shotgun at the driver of the pursued car from a distance of about two metres. He then pursued the other car at speeds of up to 100mph through city streets. Eventually the first appellant rammed the other car so that it stopped. The first appellant was heard to shout threats to kill and fired the sawn-off shotgun again. The occupants of the pursued car then ran off and the first appellant ran away. The car in which he had been driving was later found burnt out. Sentenced to 18 years' imprisonment for attempted murder, 15 years concurrent for possessing a shotgun with intent to endanger life, 2 years consecutive for dangerous driving, and 6 months concurrent for driving while disqualified (total sentence, 20 years' imprisonment and 5 years' disqualification from driving.)

H4   **Held:** the sentencing judge observed that the appellant had set out to avenge an earlier attack on a friend; the verdict of the jury established that he intended to kill the victim—the victim had avoided death only because he had seen the gun in time and ducked. The judge observed that the use of guns on the streets was a comparatively recent feature of life in the city and it was necessary to send a clear message to those who might contemplate being involved in the use of guns that they would be taken out of circulation for a very long time to punish them, protect the public and deter others. It was submitted that the sentence for attempted murder was excessive in the light of *White* (1991) 13 Cr.App.R.(S.) 108. Since *White* was decided, there had been increasing concern on the part of the public and the courts. Sentences longer than 14 years had been upheld for attempted murder in a number of cases for example: *Evans and Stroud* (1995) 16 Cr.App.R.(S.) 508, *Ellis* (1995) 16 Cr.App.R.(S.) 773, *Suckley*

[2001] 2 Cr.App.R.(S.) 66 (p.313) and *Gouldthorpe* [2004] 1 Cr.App.R.(S.) 38 (p.248). The offence of attempted murder was a serious one and the sentencing judge was entitled to impose a deterrent sentence. However, the Court took the view that the total sentence was excessive. The sentence would be adjusted by reducing the sentence of 18 years for attempted murder to 16 years and ordering the sentence for dangerous driving to run concurrently. The total sentence would therefore be reduced from 20 years' imprisonment to 16. The applications of the other applicants for leave to appeal against sentence would be refused.

H5   **Cases cited:**
White (1991) 13 Cr.App.R.(S.) 108, *Evans and Stroud* (1995) 16 Cr.App.R.(S.) 508, *Ellis* (1995) 16 Cr.App.R.(S.) 773, *Suckley* [2001] 2 Cr.App.R.(S.) 66 (p.313), *Gouldthorpe* [2004] 1 Cr.App.R.(S.) 38 (p.248.)

H6   **References:** attempted murder, *Current Sentencing Practice* B 2-1

H7   *F. Gilbert* for the appellant Docking.
Miss L. Brickman for the applicants Wild and Lewis.
R. Barradell for the applicant Cook.

JUDGMENT

1   **Rose L.J.:**   On July 8, 2003, at Sheffield Crown Court, before H.H. Judge Goldsack Q.C., the applicants Wild, Lewis and Cook pleaded not guilty to count 4 in the indictment against them, which alleged conspiracy to commit criminal damage, and on July 22, they were convicted both on that count and on count 2, which alleged conspiracy to commit grievous bodily harm. Cook was also convicted on count 1, which was of unlawful wounding. They were put back for sentence.

2   On August 1, before the same court, the appellant Docking was convicted on a separate indictment containing four relevant counts, and he too was put back for sentence.

3   On August 8 they were all sentenced by Judge Goldsack. In the case of Docking, his sentence on count 1, which was attempted murder, was 18 years' imprisonment; on count 3, which was possessing a shotgun with intent to endanger life, 15 years concurrently; on count 4, dangerous driving, 2 years consecutively; and on count 5, driving while disqualified, 6 months concurrently. His total sentence was therefore 20 years' imprisonment and he was also disqualified from driving for 5 years.

4   Wild was sentenced to eight years' detention in a young offender institution for conspiracy to commit grievous bodily harm, and no separate penalty was imposed for conspiracy to commit criminal damage.

5   Lewis was sentenced to 14 years' detention in a young offender institution for conspiracy to commit grievous bodily harm, and again no separate penalty was imposed for the criminal damage count.

6   Cook was sentenced to 12 years' detention in a young offender institution for
conspiracy to cause grievous bodily harm, consecutively to 2 years' detention for
unlawful wounding on count 1. No separate penalty was imposed for the criminal
damage offence. His total sentence was, therefore, as in the case of Lewis, 14
years' detention in a young offender institution.

7   There were two co-accused: a man called Grantham, who was convicted on the
same indictment as the three applicants of the same conspiracies, namely to cause
grievous bodily harm and to commit criminal damage, was sentenced in relation
to the first of those offences to five years' detention in a young offender institution. His application for leave to appeal was refused by the single judge and
has not been renewed. A woman called Rebecca Reeve pleaded guilty to making
a false statement, and she was made the subject of a 150-hour community punishment order.

8   Before us, Docking appeals against sentence by leave of the single judge. Wild,
Lewis and Cook renew their applications for leave to appeal against sentence, following refusal by the single judge. Lewis also sought leave to appeal against his
conviction. That was refused by the single judge and has not been renewed.

9   In relation to the indictment involving the three applicants, count 1, the offence
of unlawful wounding, occurred on July 20, 2002. The applicant Cook went with
another man to the home of a man called Fletcher and inflicted wounds on him
with a weapon. Fletcher has a number of convictions. He declined to report the
matter to the police. It appears that the reason for the incident was his earlier
relationship, in the spring of 2002, with a 16-year-old girl who later became
involved with Cook.

10   So far as the second and fourth counts in that indictment are concerned, they
took place on August 30/31, 2002.

11   On August 30, the applicants Cook and Wild, together with another man called
Allen, followed Fletcher about during the evening and the early hours of the following morning.

12   So far as Allen is concerned, although he was initially charged in the same
indictment as these applicants, the prosecution were obliged to offer no evidence
against him because none of the witnesses who might have implicated him came
to court in order to do so. Thereafter, it appears that he attended the trial of the
applicants and sat in court while that trial proceeded.

13   Allen, Cook and Wild having followed Fletcher about during the evening of
August 30, and in the early hours of the following morning, August 31, were
seen about 10am, together with the applicant Lewis, preparing for some sort of
disturbance. They had between them three weapons: a cosh, a baseball bat
and, as transpired in view of what followed, a loaded gun.

14   Wild drove the three men to Fletcher's house, and those three who had the
weapons which we have described put on balaclavas. They left the car. They
kicked in a side door at Fletcher's premises and, according to the evidence
(although for the reasons implicit in what we have already said in relation to
Allen, that evidence tended to change from time to time) Cook and Allen entered
Fletcher's house. He had with him his son and three other people. Wild stayed in
the car. Lewis remained outside smashing car windows.

15   There was damage done to two vehicles belonging to Fletcher and to his house. One of the three men (said to have been, in the evidence given at trial, Cook, who was acquitted of attempted murder) went upstairs and shot Fletcher at point blank range, causing wounds to his head at which the firearm was aimed. He managed to get his arm in front of his head and a bullet lodged in his wrist, causing a fracture which required plating. The gun then jammed and could be fired no more, but it was used to beat Fletcher about the head. After that, those who had been in the house and Lewis fled back to the car where Wild was.

16   Later, police officers stopped a different car driven by Grantham, to whom we referred earlier, and in the car were Cook and Wild.

17   On interview, Wild and Grantham made no comment. Cook claimed there had only been an intention, at least on his part, to damage Fletcher's cars.

18   Lewis was arrested on September 4, 2002 and initially denied involvement.

19   Allen was arrested two days later, denied involvement, and, as we have already said, had the good fortune in due course for no evidence to be offered against him.

20   Turning to the separate indictment which involved the appellant Docking, that reflected the reprisal expedition which took place in order to avenge what had happened to Fletcher.

21   On September 12 police officers saw Fletcher, Docking and a girl called Cherie Land in a motorcar. The next day they saw Docking in another motorcar with a woman. It was parked next to a car in which Fletcher was.

22   On September 22, Cherie Land was given a lift shortly before 11pm. She and a girlfriend were picked up by Docking. About 11pm Docking and Miss Land encountered Lewis and a man called Sully. They were in a vehicle being driven by a man called Wigley. Docking pulled his car in front of Wigley's car to block it, but Wigley managed to drive past. He was followed by Docking. Miss Land then passed a sawn-off shotgun to Docking and, from a distance of about two metres, aiming at Lewis's head, he fired through the window of the car in which Lewis was travelling, and pellets from the gun struck Lewis and Wigley. Wigley drove off and was chased at speed through the streets of Sheffield, the speeds being up to 100mph. Docking, as we have said, was driving the pursuing car.

23   Eventually he rammed the other car so that it spun into bollards and stopped. Docking was heard to shout, "I'm going to shoot you, you fucking bastards. You're dead, you're dead." He fired again, again breaking a window in the other car. He then got out of his car, carrying a gun and a baseball bat, and, after a brief confrontation with the three men in the other car, they, unsurprisingly, ran off fearing for their lives. The wadding of a 12-bore shotgun cartridge was found inside their recently vacated car. Docking drove off with the two girls and dropped them off. The car which he had been driving was later found burnt out in Rotherham.

24   Docking was arrested on September 24. He denied being in the car or being involved in the incident. He claimed to have been with a girlfriend, who was Rebecca Reeve to whom we referred earlier. She provided him with a false alibi which she later retracted, and that gave rise to her prosecution for the offence to which we referred.

25   In passing sentence, the learned judge commented that Cook, Lewis, Grantham and Wild were young Sheffield men without any convictions other than relatively minor convictions, although each of them had, to some, albeit limited, extent, been involved with drugs. The judge said that, in the light of the evidence which he had heard, he was satisfied that Cook and Lewis were the prime movers and that both of them were aware that a loaded gun was being carried when the visit was paid to Fletcher. He accepted, for the purpose of sentencing, that their intention was not to kill but to cause grievous bodily harm.

26   Wild he described as an essential part of the plan in providing transport to and from the scene. The judge pointed out that Wild had seen the weaponry and the disguises, but he, the judge, was not sure that Wild knew of the loaded gun. That lack of knowledge would be reflected in the sentence passed upon him.

27   Grantham had provided a second getaway car. The judge said that he had doubts about the extent of Grantham's awareness of the violence contemplated in this enterprise: his sentence would reflect this.

28   Docking was a man with a substantial criminal record as a car thief and burglar. The judge described him as a career criminal, indifferent to whether innocent people were injured or killed, and very dangerous. He pointed out that Docking still had some months of a licence period still to run when he set out on the avenging expedition in relation to Fletcher. He had been convicted by the jury of attempted murder because it was his intention to kill Lewis. The only reason Lewis had not died was that he had seen the gun in time and ducked. The fact that no serious injury had occurred could not disguise that this was an offence of great gravity. The judge also commented on the extremely dangerous manner of driving following the discharge of the firearm.

29   The judge went on to observe that each of the defendants appeared to be relying on a criminal code of silence and the fact that ordinary witnesses would be too frightened to give evidence. They were, as the judge said, "nearly right". Witnesses had been assaulted, threatened and terrified and, although there was no evidence that any of those in the dock was responsible for this, it did show the level of seriousness of the crime which they were involved in.

30   The judge also commented, as he was particularly well placed to do, that use of guns on the streets of Sheffield was a comparatively recent feature of life in that city. It was serious and it was necessary to send out a clear message to those who were involved and who might contemplate being involved in the use of guns that, if they did, they would be taken out of circulation for a very long time to punish them, protect the public and deter others.

31   Docking's last sentence had been four-and-a-half years' detention in a young offender institute, imposed in June 1999 for burglary and other matters; he was on licence in relation to that sentence at the time of his commission of these offences. He is 24 years of age.

32   Wild and Cook are both 21. Lewis is just 22. Each of those three has four previous convictions, including offences for drug possession. None has previously served a custodial sentence.

33   On behalf of Docking, the written grounds of appeal, supported by oral submission from Mr Gilbert, are, first, that 18 years for attempted murder was

excessive and that the appropriate level of sentencing for attempted murder is shown by the decision of this Court in *White* (1991) 13 Cr.App.R.(S.) 108, where, following a trial, a sentence of 14 years was deemed appropriate. It is to be noted that the defendant in that case was not, as Docking was, on licence at the time of the offence; and, in any event, we expressly reject the proposition that, 12 years after *White* was decided, it provides appropriate guidance in relation to the use of firearms when the offence is attempted murder.

34   We say that because, since *White* was decided, there has been increasing concern on the part of the public and on the part of the courts about the use of firearms. That concern can be illustrated, for example, by this Court's decision in *Avis* [1998] 2 Cr.App.R.(S.) 178 and the observations by Lord Bingham of Cornhill C.J. at the foot of p.185 in the report of that case. The tariff in relation to the carrying and use of firearms has, by virtue of the authority of *Avis* and otherwise, increased since *White* was decided.

35   Furthermore, it is worth commenting that there are a number of cases of attempted murder to be found in the decisions of this Court where a sentence in excess of 14 years has been regarded as appropriate: for example, *Evans and Stroud* (1995) 16 Cr.App.R.(S.) 508; *Ellis* (1995) 16 Cr.App.R.(S.) 773; *Suckley* [2001] 2 Cr.App.R.(S.) 66(p.313); and *Gouldthorpe* [2004] 1 Cr.App.R.(S.) 38(p.248).

36   It follows from what we have said that the offence of attempted murder of which Docking was convicted was a serious one. It follows also that the learned judge was entitled to impose a deterrent sentence, particularly having regard to the position in relation to the use of firearms in Sheffield. Docking's position was not made any happier by the fact that, as we have already said, he was on licence for the earlier offence at the time when these offences were committed. That said, we take the view that a total sentence of 20 years in relation to his conduct was excessive.

37   What we propose to do is adjust the sentence of 20 years first by quashing the 18 years which was passed by the learned judge and substituting for it a sentence of 16 years in relation to attempted murder. This was not a case, as it seems to us, where, in addition to that very long sentence, a consecutive sentence ought to have been imposed for the offence of dangerous driving. Consequently, the two-year sentence imposed for that offence by the learned judge will be ordered to run concurrently with the sentence for attempted murder, rather than consecutively to it. We think it unnecessary to alter the sentence in relation to possession of the shotgun with intent to endanger life. But the consequence of our judgment is that the total sentence to be served by Docking will be one of 16 years' imprisonment rather than 20.

38   We turn to Wild. On his behalf, Miss Brickman submits that the sentence of eight years was excessive and not commensurate with an offence of conspiracy to cause grievous bodily harm. She points out that the learned judge accepted, for the purposes of sentencing, that the applicant Wild did not know of the carrying of the loaded shotgun. It is submitted in the written grounds that there was some disparity between Wild's sentence and the five years passed upon Grantham. That can be readily be disposed of because, for reasons given by the judge when he

sentenced Grantham, his knowledge of what was going to take place was significantly less than even Wild's.

39   It is also said in the written grounds that this attack was not drug related. Whether it was or was not seems to us entirely irrelevant.

40   We agree with the observation made by the single judge that, although a sentence of eight years on Wild was a severe one, it was not even arguably manifestly excessive. Accordingly, Wild's renewed application is refused.

41   On behalf of Lewis, Miss Brickman submits that the sentence of 14 years passed on him demonstrates that the judge had started at a wrong and too high starting point. The applicant Lewis's age, just 22, and his lack of significant convictions were such that he ought to have been treated as being effectively as good character. Miss Brickman points out, correctly, that the victim Fletcher did not name Lewis as having been inside the house.

42   It is submitted that he was not the prime mover in the conspiracy and that, in consequence, the sentence which was passed upon him was longer than it should have been. She accepted, however, that there was evidence which would have supported the judge's conclusion that Lewis was aware that a loaded gun was being carried. The judge, as is apparent from his remarks, also took the view that Lewis, as well as Cook, were prime movers in the conspiracy. There was no evidence that Lewis went into Fletcher's house. As against that the judge was entitled to conclude that Lewis knew that a loaded firearm was being carried.

43   It is to be observed that Miss Brickman in the court below was, as she told this Court, expressly instructed not to advance mitigation on Lewis's behalf. That, as it seems to us, puts counsel in an extremely difficult position in this Court if he or she is required to advance by way of mitigation matters which, for whatever reason, it was not thought appropriate should be ventilated before the trial judge. This court's role is to address the propriety or otherwise of a sentence passed by the sentencing judge in the light of the information before him. In consequence, there are great difficulties in the way of an applicant who seeks to advance in this Court matters which he expressly did not seek to advance in the court below.

44   In our judgment, despite Miss Brickman's valiant attempts, there is no reason to regard the sentence passed upon Lewis in relation to his role in these very grave offences as being, even arguably, excessive. Accordingly, his renewed application is refused.

45   So far as Cook is concerned, Mr Barradell advances a number of reasons why, he submits, the sentence totalling 14 years passed upon Cook was excessive. He sought to submit that there was no basis for the judge's conclusion that Cook was aware that a loaded gun was being carried. Mr Barradell was constrained to accept that it was the evidence of Mr Fletcher that Cook was the one who fired the gun.

46   It is true that that evidence differed from the section 9 statement which Fletcher had originally made in which he had apparently identified both Cook and Allen as coming into his house at the time when he was shot. We have already referred to the figure cut by Allen in connection with these events and this trial. It may very well be that the whole of the evidence given by Fletcher was not accepted by the

jury. It may very well be that, for whatever reason, some of the evidence which he gave was by no means truthful. The question which arises, however, in relation to Cook, is whether the learned judge, bearing in mind the evidence that Cook went into the house and was there when the shooting was carried out and the other evidence in relation to the carrying of three weapons by three men, all of whom wore balaclavas, was entitled to conclude that Cook knew that a loaded gun was being carried. In our judgment, there was material before the judge which justified that conclusion, although it would have been preferable had he, in the course of his sentencing remarks, spelt out, in a way which he did not, the evidence which supported that conclusion.

47   It is also submitted on Cook's behalf by Mr Barradell that a sentence of 2years imposed consecutively for the unlawful wounding offence was excessive in conjunction with the 12-year sentence in relation to the conspiracy to cause grievous bodily harm.

48   It is apparent from the history which we have rehearsed that the events giving rise to the first count in the indictment constituted a wholly separate incident. A consecutive sentence was appropriate. As it seems to us, there is no sustainable complaint against the totality of the sentence imposed upon Cook, nor that a consecutive element in relation to unlawful wounding formed part of it. Accordingly, the renewed application on behalf of Cook is likewise refused.

ATTORNEY GENERAL'S REFERENCE NO.106 OF 2004 (SHAHAJAN KABIR)

COURT OF APPEAL (The Lord Chief Justice, Mr Justice McCombe and Mr Justice David Clarke): October 27, 2004

[2004] EWCA Crim 2751; [2005] 1 Cr.App.R.(S.) 120

(LT) Aggravating features; Children; Mandatory life imprisonment; Minimum term; Murder; Transitional provisions; Undue leniency

H1   *Murder—minimum term— Criminal Justice Act 2003 s.269 and Sch.21*

H2   A minimum term imposed under the Criminal Justice Act 2003, s.269, for the murder of a child aged 10 months by his father, increased from 12 years and 3 months to 15 years and 3 months.

H3   The offender was convicted of the murder of his son, aged 10 months. The offender, a native of Bangladesh, entered the United Kingdom illegally. He met a young woman who was about 17 at the time and a relationship developed between them. Their son was born in December 2002. While the young woman was pregnant, the offender was detained as an illegal immigrant, but was later released on bail. The relationship between himself and the young woman deteriorated and the offender was told to leave the young woman's home. There were disputes over access which led to an incident when a window in the young woman's house was broken. In October 2003, the young woman, her mother and son were in the town centre when the offender appeared. He demanded access but this was declined. A week later, the young woman, together with her mother and son, was again in the town centre. The child was strapped into a pushchair. They went to a number of shops and went in to a bakery. The offender followed them into the bakery and demanded to have access to the child. He was told that the matter would be resolved by solicitors. He then pulled out a knife and a struggle took place. Eventually the offender took hold of the child, who was still strapped in the pushchair, and deliberately cut his throat. The young woman sustained a deep wound to the left arm and her mother received a wound to the finger. The offender was restrained until police arrived at the scene. The child was found to be dead soon after arrival at hospital with a 17 centimetre wound which had cut the main carotid arteries and jugular veins. At the trial the defences were accident, self-defence and diminished responsibility, based on psychiatric evidence that the offender was suffering from depression. Sentenced to life imprisonment with a minimum term specified in accordance with the Criminal Justice Act 2003, s.269 of 12 years and 3 months, based on a term of 13 years and reducing it by 9 months to take account of time spent in custody on remand. The Attorney General asked the Court to review the sentence on the ground that it was unduly lenient.

14   **Held:** the Attorney General submitted that the offence was aggravated by the fact that the offender had armed himself with a knife prior to the offence, there was a real degree of planning in that the offender had deliberately gone in search of his son, carrying a knife, and that he intended to kill his son so that nobody else could enjoy his company and that the mother would suffer the loss of the son. The victim was young and vulnerable. The sentencing judge accepted that the offender had gone deliberately in search of the son. He indicated that in accordance with Sch.21 he would not have found any of the aggravating features set out in para.10, although there was a real degree of planning. The only mitigating feature was the fact that the offender suffered from a mental disorder not amounting to diminished responsibility. He concluded that the appropriate term was 13 years, from which 9 months should be deducted to reflect time spent in custody on remand, and that the same period would have resulted from the scheme which was an effect before the Criminal Justice Act 2003 came into force. In the Court's view the sentencing judge was in error in finding no statutory aggravating features in the case. Schedule 21 indicated a general starting point of 15 years for cases which did not fall within the higher category of seriousness. It was agreed by both counsel that the appropriate starting point was 15 years. Although 15 years was a starting point, it was important to note that Sch.21 set out aggravating and mitigating features. One aggravating factor mentioned in para.10(a) was a "significant degree" of planning or premeditation. It was accepted for the Attorney General that although there was planning and premeditation, there was not a "significant degree" of planning or premeditation. However, para.10(b) referred to the fact that the victim was particularly vulnerable because of age or disability. It was important to note that the list of aggravating features was not exhaustive; they were only examples. The Schedule went on to identify mitigating features. Paragraph 11(c) provided for an offender who suffered from

a degree of mental disorder or mental disability which lowered his degree of culpability. Having regard to those provisions, it was clear that the judge was right to regard the offender's depression as a mitigating factor but was wrong not to have included among the matters he had to consider as aggravating factors the vulnerability of the victim. Offences of murder involving a young child could vary considerably. A young child might be abducted and killed without the murderer having any connection at all with the child. On the other hand, there might be a case where it was reasonably clear that, but for the fact that the offender's relationship with the mother had broken down and he was unable to see the child, the offender would not have committed an offence of violence. In applying the statutory provisions, this was a case where the starting point of 15 years would have to be increased to take account of the aggravating features and then amended to take into account the mitigating features. A substantial increase on the starting point of 15 years was called for, then there had to be appropriate reduction. It was difficult to determine the precise position within the bracket which the court should identify as being the appropriate term for an offence of this nature. It was to be treated as a "normal murder" in that it did not call for either of the higher periods in the Act. The offence was very serious, because of the effect on the family of the deceased and its effect on members of the public who witnessed the commission of the crime. The Court had come with some hesitation to the conclusion that the minimum term should be increased to 16 years, from which 9 months would be deducted to produce a minimum term of 15 years and 3 months. This was a transitional case, but the Court was satisfied that under the earlier practice, based on the Practice Direction of 2002, the minimum term might have been longer.

H5   **Commentary:** [2005] Crim.L.R. 156

H6   **References:** murder, *Current Sentencing Practice*, B 0–1

H7   *R. Horwell* for the Attorney General.
     J. R. Jones Q.C. for the offender.

JUDGMENT

1   **Lord Woolf C.J.:**   The Attorney General applies for leave under s.36 of the Criminal Justice Act 1988 to refer to this Court for review a sentence which he considers to be unduly lenient.

2   The statutory provisions dealing with the power of this Court to increase a sentence which is unduly lenient also apply to the minimum term set by a judge after a person has been convicted of murder and sentenced to life imprisonment. The statute has that effect, although the minimum term does not—and this is very important to have in mind—determine when an offender is released. All that it does is determine the period that has to elapse before an offender can be considered for release. If the offender would remain a danger to the public after the period which is fixed as the minimum term, then he is not released. Furthermore, if he is released he can be recalled to prison for the rest of his life if circumstances arise where that is necessary.

3   The offender in this case is 40 years of age, having been born on February 28, 1964. He comes originally from Bangladesh. He entered this country illegally. He was indicted on three counts. On count 1 he was charged with murder. The victim was Hassan Martin, his son, who was 10 months of age at the time. On counts 2 and 3 he was charged with wounding with intent to do grievous bodily harm, contrary to s.18 of the Offences against the Person Act 1861. The victim on count 2 was Lorna Martin, the mother of his son, Hassan Martin. The victim on count 3 was Pauline Martin, who was Lorna Martin's mother. The offender pleaded not guilty to each offence. He was found guilty of murder. In respect of each of counts 2 and 3 he was found not guilty, but was convicted of the alternative and lesser offence of wounding, contrary to s.20 of the 1861 Act.

4   On July 28, 2004, in addition to passing a sentence of life imprisonment, the trial judge determined that the minimum term should be 13 years. The minimum term was then reduced, as it was required to be by statute, by 9 months to 12 years and 3 months to take account of the time that the offender had spent in custody. In respect of counts 2 and 3, he was sentenced to concurrent terms of two years' imprisonment.

5   The facts are of some importance. We take them from the Attorney General's document headed "Final Reference". In late 1999 or 2000, the offender met Miss Lorna Martin, who is now 21 years of age having been born on January 19, 1983. It will be observed that, having regard to the date on which she was born, she was at that time a young woman of probably 17. A relationship developed between them. At the end of 2001 the offender began to live with Miss Martin and her mother at their home. Following a miscarriage, Miss Martin became pregnant again. Her son Hassan was born on December 6, 2002.

6   During the pregnancy the offender was arrested as an illegal immigrant. He was detained in custody and later given bail. Initially he showed no particular interest in his son, but after a while he did do so. However, the relationship deteriorated between himself and Miss Martin. In about August 2003 he was told to leave Miss Martin's home.

7   Thereafter, the offender sought access to his son. There were difficulties over access. As a result, the offender was involved in an incident when a window at Miss Martin's home was broken. He was arrested for this and was later fined. Access then ceased. Each side sought professional advice from solicitors. Throughout this period, because of his immigration status, the offender was liable to be deported.

8   So far as is known, the offender had no criminal convictions of any sort. He had led an honest life in this country until the breaking of the window associated with the domestic stress to which he was undoubtedly subject.

9   On October 14, 2003 Miss Martin, her mother and son were in the town centre. On that occasion the offender suddenly appeared. He grabbed the pushchair containing his son and demanded to have access. He did not obtain access. Miss Martin and her mother walked away with the son. They consulted a solicitor, went to the police station and made a complaint.

10   A week later, on October 21, 2003, Miss Martin, together with her mother and son, were in the town centre. Hassan was strapped into his pushchair. They visited

a number of shops and eventually went into a bakery to make an enquiry about a cake for the baby's forthcoming birthday. The Crown's allegation was that the offender must have been waiting in the shopping centre for his son to arrive. There is no dispute that the offender followed them into the bakery. He was armed with a large kitchen knife which he had taken from the restaurant at which he then worked. The knife was concealed between newspapers which he carried inside his jacket.

11   Having entered the bakery, the offender pulled the pushchair towards him and demanded to have access to his son. Miss Martin said that he could not and that solicitors were seeking to resolve the issue. The offender opened his jacket and pulled out the knife. A struggle ensued. Eventually the offender took hold of Hassan, who was still strapped in the pushchair, and deliberately cut his throat. According to the mother, the offender looked proud and smug as he did so. During these events Miss Martin sustained a deep laceration to her left arm and minor cuts to two fingers. An X-ray revealed a fracture to the distal radius of the left wrist. Mrs Martin received a wound to one finger.

12   Others who were present in the bakery disarmed the offender and restrained him until the police arrived. The scene of the offence was hugely distressing, particularly to the mother and grandmother of the baby, but also to those members of the public who were present.

13   The baby was taken to an infirmary but was found to be dead soon after arrival. A post-mortem examination confirmed that the cause of death was an incised wound to the neck. The wound measured 17 centimetres in length. It had severed completely the neck structures and had cut both main carotid arteries and jugular veins. The depth of the wound was such that it penetrated the spinal column and exposed the underlying spinal cord. Considerable force must have been used to cause these injuries. Death would have been very rapid.

14   In the course of interview after he had been arrested, the offender was clearly very agitated. He sought to explain that he was due to be deported. He was receiving no help as to his immigration status or access to his son. He accepted that he had followed Hassan into the bakery and had confronted the mother, but thereafter claimed that he had been assaulted by members of the public and, fearing for his own safety, picked up the knife which he had found in the shop. He said that he may have cut the mother and the grandmother when lashing out with the knife in order to defend himself, but he could not explain how his son had been killed.

15   The defences raised at trial were accident, self-defence and diminished responsibility based on psychiatric evidence that the offender was suffering from depression. There is no dispute that the offender was suffering from a depressive condition at the time. The evidence before this Court makes it clear that the offender has continued to suffer from depression, that he has made threats to kill himself, that he has attempted to set fire to his cell, and that his actions at times continue to be bizarre.

16   The trial judge, Leveson J., accepted that the offender had been suffering from a mild to moderate depression, even perhaps a moderate depression, at the time of the murder.

17   The Attorney General contends that the crime was aggravated by the following features. First, prior to the offence the offender had armed himself with the knife to which reference has already been made. Secondly, there was a real degree of planning. On the evidence the offender, carrying the knife, had deliberately gone in search of his son. Thirdly, it is contended that the offender intended to kill his son so that no one else could enjoy his company and that the mother would for ever suffer his loss. Fourthly, the victim was extremely young and vulnerable; he was 10 months of age.

18   In his sentencing remarks the judge said that the offender had taken a fearsome knife from the restaurant at which he worked. He added:

> ". . .. I am sure that you deliberately went in search of your son. This is no more than you admitted to the police. On the basis that if you could not see Hassan and were, at any moment, liable to be deported from this country, I am equally sure that you decided that no one should have the pleasure of his company and that you would bring his life to an end. It is no accident that you did not deliberately stab Lorna Martin or her mother. They were left to suffer the loss of Hassan.
>
> I accept that the prospect of your removal from this country and the difficulties which you were having in relation to contact with your son caused you to suffer a mild to moderate depression, even perhaps a moderate depression. This lowers, somewhat your culpability but goes no further."

The judge then referred, as he was required to, to Schs 21 and 22 of the Criminal Justice Act 2003. He added:

> "I must fix the punitive or tariff term which you must serve to meet the requirements of retribution and general deterrence. To that end I have regard to the term which, prior to December 2002, would have been notified by the Secretary of State, and to the guidance set out in a Practice Statement of 31 May 2002."

The judge went on to fix a *starting point* at 15 years. He added:

> "I would not have found any of the aggravating features set out in paragraph 10, although there was a real degree of planning. The only mitigating feature would have been the fact that I accept that you suffer a mental disorder, or suffered a mental disorder, which does not fall within section 2(1) of the Homicide Act 1957."

(That was a reference to the fact that the jury had not regarded this as a case of diminished responsibility.)

> "Bearing in mind all the circumstances, including the difficulties which you will face both in this country and ostracized in your home country, I would have fixed a tariff of 13 years."

He then deducted the appropriate period. He said:

"Going to the law in place before the Act, I am satisfied that a higher starting point than normal would have been appropriate given that the victim is but a baby, and I have come to the conclusion that an identical tariff period would have been appropriate."

The higher tariff point to which the judge referred was the 16 years which was applicable as a starting point under the regime that was in place before the 2003 Act came into force. He added:

". . . .. I have come to the conclusion that an identical tariff period would have been appropriate [under the Practice Direction]. I therefore fix the period at 13 years from which I deduct the period of nine month which effectively represents the period you have spent in custody to date plus the specified part of the sentence for the purposes of section 269(2) of the Act . . .."

Accordingly, the tariff period was 12 years and 3 months. The judge then explained the nature of the offence both to the offender and to the public. The explanation was in accord with the explanation which we gave at the outset of this judgment.

19   From his sentencing remarks it is apparent that the judge considered that there were no statutory aggravating features which applied in this case. In that respect the judge was in error. Schedule 21, which brought in the new regime under the 2003 Act, identified three starting points: an exceptionally high starting point when the appropriate period under the starting point is a whole life order; a period which deals with cases which do not fall within that paragraph but where the offence involves any of the following features: a substantial degree of premeditation or planning, the abduction of the victim, or sexual or sadistic conduct, or the murder of a child involving the abduction of the child, or sexual or sadistic motives, a murder done for the purpose of advancing political, religious or ideological causes, or a murder by an offender previously convicted of murder. In such cases the appropriate starting point is 30 years. Those are particularly serious murders. The Schedule then goes on to identify other cases. In respect of those other cases, if the offender was aged 18 or over when he committed the offence the starting point in determining the minimum term is 15 years.

20   It is agreed by counsel, Mr Horwell on behalf of the Attorney General and Mr Jones QC appearing on behalf of the offender, that this case under Sch.21 justifies a starting point of 15 years. The starting point of 15 years is intended to cover a wide range of offences.

21   The gravity of the offence of murder may vary considerably. On the one hand, there is the sort of murder which justifies a whole life tariff. On the other hand, an offender may be convicted of murder where there may have been no intention to kill, but in defending himself he used excessive force so that he was not entitled to the defence of self-defence. It also covers a loving parent who, because his child has a terminal illness, decides that out of mercy he should unlawfully put the child to death, but who does so only out of mistaken affection for the child and in circumstances where anyone would have the greatest sympathy for them. Although

15 years is a starting point which would apply in such a case, it is clearly a starting point which, in accordance with the approach of both the Home Secretary and of the courts prior to the coming into force of the 2003 Act, would involve a minimum term substantially less than 15 years.

22   The approach with regard to ascertaining the appropriate term was set out in the decision of this Court in *Sullivan* [2004] EWCA Crim 1762; [2005] 1 Cr.App.R.(S.) 67 (p.308).

23   It is important to note that Sch.21 sets out aggravating and mitigating factors. One aggravating factor, which is set out in para.10(a) is a significant degree of planning or premeditation. Mr Horwell accepts that this case would not fall within para.10(a) because there was not a *significant* degree of planning or premeditation, albeit that there was planning and premeditation. Paragraph (b) refers to the fact that the victim was particularly vulnerable because of age or disability. It is clear that the victim in this case was particularly vulnerable because of his age; he was helpless. There are then various provisions which are set out. It is important to note that those aggravating features are not exhaustive. The paragraph commences by making clear that the aggravating factors which are listed are only examples; there may be other aggravating features.

24   The Schedule goes on to identify mitigating features. Subparagraph (c), which is of relevance, provides for an offender who suffers from any mental disorder or mental disability which, although not falling within s.2(1) of the Homicide Act 1957, lowers his degree of culpability.

25   Having regard to those provisions, it is clear that the judge was right to regard as a mitigating factor the depression of the offender; but he was wrong not to have included among the matters he had to consider the aggravating factor, which is identified in para.[10], of vulnerability of the victim to which reference has been made.

26   This case is what has been described as a "transitional case". The offence was committed before the Act came into force. In those circumstances there are provisions contained in Sch.22 which have the consequence of providing a cap on the minimum term which can be imposed by the court. That cap relates to the practice which would be adopted by the Secretary of State prior to the coming into force of the 2003 Act. Regrettably, it is difficult to establish what was the practice of the Secretary of State before the Act came into force. In that regard there have been Practice Directions issued by this court to assist judges generally to comply with that requirement. The matter is dealt with in detail in *Sullivan*; but, taking it shortly, the Practice Directions which are relevant are to be applied as indicating the practice of the Secretary of State. In this case it is agreed that the appropriate Practice Direction is that which was issued by me in 2002. That Practice Direction was based on the advice which the court received from the Sentencing Advisory Panel. Although this is not the case with more serious offences, the approach in this case under that Practice Direction would have been, if anything, more severe than under the 2003 statute. The 2002 Practice Direction sought to divide different categories of murder to a greater extent than those divisions which appear in the 2003 Act. The Practice Direction contains one provision which is particularly relevant to a case of this sort. Paragraph 49.33 refers to a

murder involving a young child and indicates that a term of 20 years and upwards *could* be appropriate. While this paragraph cannot be applied directly to a case which has to be considered under Sch.21 of the 2003 Act it still has to be looked at as providing a general indication of the level of sentence when it suggests a higher sentence since Parliament was not intending in Sch.21 to reduce the length of minimum term applicable.

27   Even offences of murder involving a young child can differ considerably. A young child may be abducted and killed without the murderer having any connection at all with the child. On the other hand, there may be a case such as this where it is reasonably clear that, but for the fact that the offender's relationship with the mother had broken down and he was unable to see the child, it appears unlikely that he would have committed an offence of violence. The offender was unable to deal with the situation in which he found himself, where he was liable to be deported, where in all probability he would never see his child again, and where, for reasons which were no doubt entirely justifiable, the mother felt that it was inappropriate for him to see the child.

28   However, in applying the statutory provisions it is clear that this is a case where the starting point of 15 years would have to be increased to take account of the aggravating features to which we have referred, and then amended in order to take into account the mitigating features. In our view, this was a case where a substantial increase on the period of 15 years was called for. There then had to be the appropriate reduction. It is very difficult to determine the precise position within the bracket to which this court should identify as being the appropriate term for an offence of this nature. It is accepted, as we have already indicated, that this is to be treated as a "normal murder" under the Criminal Justice Act 2003. It does not call for either of the higher periods in the Act.

29   Nonetheless, in our judgment it was a very serious offence, not least because of the effect on the family of the deceased baby, and, in addition, the effect on the members of the public who witnessed the commission of this terrible crime. On the other hand, the court has to bear in mind that the reason the offence was committed was the offender's inability to deal with the situation in which he found himself, other than by resorting to the terrible acts of violence which he committed. It was not a case of diminished responsibility. However, under the provisions of the Act it was nonetheless an offence in respect of which the offender is entitled to a reduction to the appropriate minimum term, having regard to his mental state at the time.

30   The conclusion to which we have come, not without hesitation as to whether an even higher figure would be appropriate, is that the 13 years should be increased to 16 years. From that 16 years there has to be deducted the 9 months. Accordingly the minimum term will be 15 years and 3months. We make no deduction for the fact that the offender is being resentenced because it is made clear by the 2003 Act that there should be no deduction for double jeopardy.

31   Accordingly, the Attorney General's application is allowed. The period of the minimum sentence is increased as we have indicated.

R. v LESLIE JAMES MOULDEN

COURT OF APPEAL (Lord Justice Clarke, Mr Justice Gibbs and Mr Justice Stanley Burnton): October 27, 2004

[2004] EWCA Crim 2715; [2005] 1 Cr.App.R.(S.) 121

(LT) Changes in value; Confiscation orders; Drug trafficking; Procees of crime; Real property

H1 *Confiscation order—proceeds of drug trafficking—property bought with cash derived from drug trafficking—subsequent increase in value of property— whether increased value of property properly treated as a payment or reward in connection with drug trafficking*

H2 **Editor's note:** where a defendant uses money derived from drug trafficking to purchase a property, which subsequently increases in value, the equity in the property at its increased value is a payment or reward received in connection with drug trafficking.

H3 The appellant was convicted of conspiring to supply a Class A controlled drug. It was alleged that he had supplied quantities of ecstasy tablets to another offender who had in turn supplied undercover police officers. Sentenced to 16 years' imprisonment with a confiscation order under the Drug Trafficking Act 1994 in sum of £667,000, with three years imprisonment in default.

H4 **Held:** there were no grounds for giving leave to appeal against the sentence of 16 years' imprisonment. The application for leave to appeal against the confiscation order raised a question of principle. The applicant had acquired a number of properties with cash which the sentencing judge was entitled to find or assume had been derived from drug dealing. In the case of most of the properties, the purchase price had been financed not only from cash derived from drug dealing but from loans made by banks and other financial institutions. The applicant's submission was that the benefit derived from the drug dealing of the applicant was not the property itself but the proportion of the property represented by the deposit which might be assumed to be derived from the proceeds of the drug dealing. It was argued that if £5,000 in cash was applied to a property purchased for £100,000, and a mortgage of £95,000 were taken, and the property doubled in value, the benefit value as at the date of the confiscation order was not £105,000 (the value of the equity in the property) but £5,000 doubled to £10,000. In the Court's judgment that submission was based on a fundamental fallacy, namely that that was what was acquired in the circumstances was an interest of £5,000, rather than the equity in the property subject to the mortgage. In the Court's judgment the Act required the relevant property to be valued as of the date of the confiscation order, subject to any charges, but it was the property which was valued rather than the deposit placed on the property by the defendant. The Court arrived at that conclusion by two possible routes. The first was s.4 of the Act which required the court to assume that any property held by the defendant at any time since his conviction, or transferred to him within the relevant period, was received by him as a payment or reward in connection with drug dealing. The properties concerned had been transferred to the applicant within the relevant period and it followed that the court was required to make the assumption that the properties had been received by him as a payment or reward in connection with drug trafficking and carried on by him. The words "in connection with" were of wide import. They did not necessarily require there to be an immediate and direct connection with drug trafficking. In the Court's judgment, where it was shown that a defendant had acquired property with cash which was itself the proceeds of drug trafficking, s.3(a) required the property to be regarded as a payment or reward in connection with the drug trafficking carried on by the defendant. The assumption was rebuttable if it could be shown to be incorrect or if the court was satisfied that there would be a serious risk of injustice in the defendant's case if the assumption were made. The applicant was unable to establish that the assumption was incorrect. It might have been shown to be incorrect if the property had been purchased by him from monies made quite legitimately, or if the property were a genuine gift or the result of a bequest made by a relative. The Court did not consider that there was a serious risk of injustice if the assumption were to be made. In circumstances where the value of the property in the hands of the defendant exceeded the cash investment he made in it, because the value of the property had risen, there was nothing unjust in the value of the property being taken to be the payment or reward of the defendant made in connection with drug trafficking. It had frequently been said that the legislation was draconian. Its object was to deprive those involved in drug trafficking of the benefit of drug trafficking. Where a deposit had been made of cash monies in order to buy a property, the Court could see nothing unjust and no risk of injustice that if the property which was acquired, which was the equity in the property if there was a mortgage, was taken to be the reward of drug trafficking. In the Court's judgment, it was neither unjust or surprising that where property was bought with a relatively low down payment and a high mortgage and it increased in value, the benefit to the defendant was a sum which might be a multiple of the original deposit. That was because any mortgage remained unchanged by increases in market values, whereas the defendant had acquired the equity in the property, that was to say that he had the property subject only to the mortgage. The same result might be reached by applying the provisions of s.7. If cash which was assumed to be the rewards of drug trafficking was used to purchase a property, then that property represented directly or indirectly the reward. The working of the provisions of the Act were quite clear. The application for leave to appeal against the confiscation order would be refused.

H5   **References:** confiscation order, *Current Sentencing Practice* J 7

H6   *A. Bodnar* for the applicant.

JUDGMENT

1   **Stanley Burnton J.:**   On December 6, 2002 at Newcastle Crown Court, before H.H. Judge Whitburn and a jury, the applicant was convicted by a majority of a single count of conspiracy to supply a class A controlled drug (MDMA) to another in contravention of s.4(1) of the Misuse of Drugs Act 1971. On January 24, 2003 before the same judge he was sentenced to 16 years' imprisonment.

2   On January 30, 2004, before the same judge, a confiscation order was made against him under s.2 of the Drug Trafficking Act 1994 in the sum of £667,000 to be paid within six months, with three years' imprisonment consecutive in default. On February 23 the confiscation order was revised up to the sum of £750,000.

3   He applies for leave to renew his application for leave to appeal against conviction and sentence. He was not represented for that purpose before us. He further seeks leave to appeal against the confiscation order, the Registrar having referred this application to the full court. On that application he was represented by counsel, Mr Bodnar.

4   The brief facts of the case were that in March 2001 the Northumbria Police mounted an undercover operation to target the suppliers of illegal drugs. A shop known as Ace Hardware Store was used as a front. The store was fitted with covert audio and video recording equipment and staffed by undercover police officers who let it be known that they were open to offers to purchase drugs. The police also had access to a flat in nearby Middle Street for some of the transactions.

5   Undercover officers made contact with Edward Wilson from whom they purchased quantities of drugs on various occasions beginning in October 2001. An undercover officer referred to as "Omar" was taken to Wilson's flat by Knowles on October 17, 2001 where he purchased amphetamines and discussed with Wilson the purchase of 5,000 ecstasy tablets. Wilson said he needed to "speak to (his) man".

6   On the following day, two calls were made from a mobile telephone later recovered from Wilson's flat to a mobile telephone subsequently seized by the police from the applicant's home at the time of his arrest.

7   On October 19, Wilson delivered 1,000 ecstasy tablets to an undercover officer called "Sohail". Sohail later contacted Wilson to say he could take another 4,000 tablets. Wilson said he would "ring (his) man and see what he says". Less than 30 minutes later a call was placed from the mobile telephone later found in Wilson's home to the mobile telephone later found at the applicant's home address. Two minutes after that call Wilson called Sohail to confirm the deal. Wilson supplied 5,000 tablets to Sohail later that day. He was driven to the meeting point by Wood.

8   Over the following week there were discussions with Sohail and Wilson as to the supply of a further 5,000 tablets. Wilson supplied these on November 7 at a cost of £6,000.

9   Thereafter undercover officers entered discussions with Wilson for the supply of 15,000 ecstasy tablets. There were a number of telephone calls during this period between the mobile phone later found at Wilson's address and that later

found at the applicant's address. During a discussion with Sohail on December 6, in which Sohail expressed concern as to whether the quantity he wanted was available, Wilson made a call to this applicant's telephone. That telephone call was not in dispute. In the short call he said: "Kid is Edward still there? He is, that's all I wanted to know, I'll be in touch", following which he confirmed that 15,000 tablets would be available for purchase.

10   On December 18, Wilson suggested that the meeting place for the transaction might be at his mate's pub, which was more like a hotel, although in the event this was not the arrangement. That was of some relevance as the applicant owned a pub known as the Ship Inn and it was suggested by the prosecution that that was the venue Wilson was referring to.

11   On December 19 Wilson arrived at the hardware store carrying a large black holdall which contained three heat-sealed packs each containing around 10,000 ecstasy tablets, with a street value of around £100,000. The officers paid £27,000 for the drugs. As he left the store, a call was made from a mobile later found at his home to the mobile later found at the applicant's home. An Audi motorcar seen parked nearby was registered to the applicant. CCTV footage revealed an Audi motorcar leaving the parking area as Wilson walked away.

12   Later the same day Wilson, driven by Wood, met undercover officers and supplied them with amphetamine and ecstasy.

13   Following this applicant's arrest, police found 30 ecstasy tablets bearing the same logo as that on the tablets supplied by Wilson to officers on December 19 in a kitchen drawer at the applicant's home address. A mobile phone was also seized. A large black holdall was found in the cellar at the Ship Inn of which the applicant was the owner.

14   The prosecution case was that the applicant had supplied to Wilson the quantities of ecstasy which Wilson supplied to the undercover officers. The prosecution alleged that he could be directly related to the transactions on October 19 and November 7 by the itemised calls from the mobile telephone found at Wilson's home address to the mobile telephone found at the applicant's home address.

15   It was the Crown's case that the applicant transported Wilson and the drugs to the hardware store in his Audi motorcar on December 19 and that the distinctive markings on the black holdall found in the cellar of the Ship Inn showed it to be identical to that used by Wilson to carry the drugs on that occasion. The Crown relied on evidence from the Dutch manufacturers of the holdall that such holdalls were not actively sold by them in this country.

16   In interview the applicant denied any involvement in a conspiracy to supply class A drugs. He knew Wilson because he drank in his pub. He gave him a lift to the hardware store on December 19 but knew nothing of the drugs. Wilson tended to telephone him when he was drunk to discuss arrangements concerning the pub pool team. The ecstasy tablets found in the kitchen drawer had been handed in at his pub a few days before. He had no knowledge of the holdall found in the cellar at the Ship Inn and it was not his.

17   The defence case was that the applicant was not involved in any conspiracy to supply ecstasy. Wilson had supplied large quantities of cocaine and amphetamine

to the undercover officers. Wood drove Wilson to the meeting point for two such transactions. There was no suggestion that the applicant was the ultimate supplier of these drugs and the defence maintained that if Wilson was being supplied with these drugs by other individuals the jury could not be sure that it was the applicant who had supplied the ecstasy to him. Itemised telephone records showed that Wilson had made telephone calls to Wood and to a man named Lawson during the relevant period, both of whom had convictions for drug matters. It was clear that Wilson was using at least one other mobile telephone at the relevant time for which the itemised calls were not available.

18   The applicant gave evidence and denied any involvement in supplying the ecstasy. His evidence as to the telephone calls was summed up by the judge. His evidence as to the circumstances in which he gave Wilson a lift to the hardware store on December 19 was similarly fairly set out by the judge in the summing-up. His evidence as to the holdall was also summed up. He gave evidence as to the holdall and there was also evidence from Michelle Wilson as to the ecstasy tablets found in the Ship Inn.

19   A man called Edward Leyton also gave evidence. He said that he was a customer at the Ship Inn and knew Wilson. Wilson may have telephoned him at the pub, but he would not have been there during the daytime.

20   The proposed ground of appeal against conviction is that the judge's summing-up was biased against the applicant, in particular that the judge referred to coincidences explained by the applicant in derogatory terms. So far as that is concerned we have carefully considered the summing-up. In our judgment none of the comments made by the judge went beyond those he was entitled to make on the evidence before him. There is no sensible argument that this conviction is unsafe by reason of any derogatory remarks or other prejudice that might arguably be engendered by the terms of the summing-up. It follows that the renewed application for leave to appeal against conviction is refused.

21   So far as sentence is concerned, the applicant had two previous serious convictions for drug offences, albeit they related to class B drugs. The judge said he was quite satisfied that the applicant was the main supplier of ecstasy to Wilson. As the telephone calls demonstrated, he had supplied at least 11,000 other tablets in addition to the 30,000 supplied to Wilson on December 19. Heat sealed packages in which the drugs had been supplied clearly came almost directly from the manufacture into his possession. Given that the judge found, and was entitled to find, that the applicant was a large scale dealer in class A drugs, namely ecstasy, and was close to the source of supply, a substantial sentence of imprisonment was inevitable and indeed that is accepted in the grounds settled by counsel. A sentence of 14 years' imprisonment could not be the subject of any complaint. Here the sentence was one of 16 years' imprisonment. However, that addition was in our judgment well justified by the previous convictions of this applicant. In those circumstances, there is no arguable appeal against the sentence of imprisonment and the application for leave to appeal against that sentence is similarly refused.

22   We turn to the confiscation order. The application for leave to appeal against the confiscation order seeks to raise a question of principle as to the application of

the relevant provisions of the Drug Trafficking Act 1994. The applicant had, on the findings which the judge made and which it is accepted he was entitled to make, acquired a number of properties with cash which the judge was entitled to find, certainly to assume, had been derived from his drug dealing. In the case of all or most of those properties the purchase price had been financed not only from cash derived from the drug dealing, or assumed to be from the drug dealing, but also from loans made by banks and other financial institutions. The submission made on behalf of the applicant in essence is that where that occurs the benefit derived from the drug dealing of the applicant is not the property itself but a proportion of the property represented by the deposit which may be explained or may be assumed to be derived from the proceeds of drug dealing. For example, if £5,000 in cash is supplied to a property purchased for £100,000 and a mortgage of £95,000 is taken and the property doubles in value, the benefit value as at the date of the confiscation order to be taken by the applicant, in his submission, is not £105,000, being the value of the equity in the property, but £5,000 doubled to £10,000.

23   In our judgment that submission is based on a fundamental fallacy, namely that what is acquired in the circumstances to which we have just referred is an interest of £5,000, rather than the equity in the property subject to the mortgage. In our judgment the Act requires that relevant property be valued as at the date of the confiscation order, subject to any charges, but it is the property which is valued rather than the deposit placed on the property by a defendant.

24   We arrive at that result through two possible routes, both of which have exactly the same result. For present purposes we turn first to s.4 of the 1994 Act. Subsection (1) provides:

"For the purpose of this Act—
   (a) any payments or other rewards received by a person at any time (whether before or after the commencement of this Act) in connection with drug trafficking carried on by him or another person are his proceeds of drug trafficking; and
   (b) the value of his proceeds of drug trafficking is the aggregate of the values of the payments or other rewards."

Subsection (2) provides:

"Subject to subsections (4) and (5) below, the Court shall, for the purpose—
   (a) of determining whether the defendant has benefited from drug trafficking, and
   (b) if he has, of assessing the value of his proceeds of drug trafficking, make the required assumptions.
   (3) The required assumptions are—
   (a) that any property appearing to the court—
      (i) to have been held by the defendant at any time since his conviction, or
      (ii) to have been transferred to him at any time since the beginning of the period of six years ending when the proceedings were instituted against him,

was received by him, at the earliest time at which he appears to the court to have held it, as a payment or reward in connection with drug trafficking carried on by him;

(b) that any expenditure of his since the beginning of that period was met out of the payments received by him in connection with drug trafficking carried on by him; and

(c) that, for the purpose of valuing any property received or assumed to have been received by him at any time as such a reward, he received the property free of any other interests in it."

It is undisputed that the various properties which constituted the realisable property of the applicant at the date on the confiscation order were properties which had been transferred to him at a time subsequent to the beginning of the period of six years ending with the proceedings instituted against him referred to in s.4(3)(a)(ii). It follows that the court was required to make the assumption stipulating s.4, namely those properties had been received by him as a payment or reward in connection with drug trafficking carried on by him. The words "in connection with" are of wide input. They do not necessarily require there to be an immediate and direct connection with drug trafficking. In our judgment, where it is shown that a defendant has, with cash which represents the proceeds of drug trafficking, put that money into property, that is acquired property with it, s.3(a) requires the property so acquired be regarded as a payment or reward in connection with the drug trafficking carried out by the defendant.

25   The assumption is a rebuttable assumption. It is rebuttable in the circumstances referred to in s.4(4). That provides:

"The court shall not make any required assumption in relation to any particular property or expenditure if—

(a) that assumption is shown to be incorrect in the defendant's case; or

(b) the court is satisfied that there would be a serious risk of injustice in the defendant's case if the assumption were to be made;

and where, by virtue of this subsection, the court does not make one or more of the required assumptions, it shall state its reasons."

In the present case the applicant was unable to establish that the assumption was incorrect. It might have been shown to be incorrect because a property had been purchased by him from monies made quite legitimately. It might have been shown to have been incorrect if the property were a genuine gift or the result of a request made by relative. He was unable to do anything of that kind. The assumption therefore remained good unless s.4(4)(b) applied. Section 4(4)(b) applies if the court is satisfied that there would be a serious risk of injustice if the assumption were to be made. In circumstances where the value of the property in the hands of the defendant exceeds the cash investment he made in it, because the value of that property has risen, we see nothing unjust or even arguably unjust in the value of the property being taken to be the payment or reward of the defendant made in connection with drug trafficking. It has frequently been said that the legislation is draconian. Its object is to deprive those involved in drug trafficking of the benefit of drug trafficking and in a case such as that which we are considering, where a deposit has been made of cash monies in order to buy a property, we see nothing unjust or arguably unjust and no risk of injustice if the property which is acquired, which we remember is not the deposit but the equity in the property if there is a mortgage, is taken to be the reward of drug trafficking. It is accepted that if the assumptions do apply and the property is assumed and therefore taken to be a payment or reward in connection with drug trafficking, the property is to be valued as at the date of the proceedings resulting in the confiscation order. That is what the judge did. In our judgment it is neither unjust nor surprising that where a property is bought with a relatively low down payment and a high mortgage and it increases in value, the benefit to the defendant is a sum which may be a multiple of the original deposit. That is because, subject to any interest payments, any mortgage remains unchanged by increases in market values, whereas the defendant has acquired the equity in the property, that is to say he has the property subject only to the mortgage. That appears to us to be plain on the wording of s.4 and having regard to the draconian purposes of the Act.

26   A similar result may be reached by applying the provisions of s.7. If cash which is assumed to be the rewards of drug trafficking is used to purchase a property then that property represents directly or indirectly the reward. Section 7(3) provides:

> "Subject to section 8(2) of this Act, if at the material time [the material time relating to confiscation proceedings] the recipient [that is to say the recipient of the properties—in this case the applicant] holds—
> (a) the property which he received (not being cash), or
> (b) property which, in whole or in part, directly or indirectly represents in his hands the property which he received,
> the value referred to in subsection (2)(b) above is the value to him at the material time of the property mentioned in paragraph (a) above or, as the case may be, of the property mentioned in paragraph (b) above so far as it represents the property which he received, but disregarding in either case any charging order."

No question of charging orders arise in the present case. The real properties acquired with cash which were assumed to be, and properly assumed to be, the proceeds of drug trafficking, directly or indirectly represent that cash—that is to say the property which was originally received by the recipient referred to in subs.(3)(b) of s.7 is the cash, and the property applied with it directly or indirectly represents it for the purposes of the Act. If that is so, then the property falls to be valued as at its market value, subject of course to any charging order and it would also be necessary to take into account any outstanding charges or mortgages. That is what the judge did in the case of each relevant property.

27   Our attention has been focused on the Old School Lane project which was the last and most important of the acquisitions made by the applicant. That was a property which was developed. The applicant contributed a relatively small sum, some £40,000 on the judge's findings, to the acquisition of that property. It was acquired and developed by a partnership in which the applicant had a 50

per cent interest. After completion of the development the profit from the partnership was something approaching £1 million and the defendant's 50 per cent of that was some £400,000. The £1 million and the £400,000 were arrived at after deduction of all charges. In our judgment the judge's calculation is precisely that which we would have expected to be made under the provisions of the Act. The fact that the original contribution of the applicant was a relatively small sum and his profit a large sum in no way makes the application of the assumptions in the Act and the requirements of the Act unjust, creates no risk of injustice, nor shows that the assumptions are inaccurate. On the contrary, it is in the public interest that those who traffic in drugs should be deprived of their benefit from drug trafficking viewed in the largest possible way. As we have already observed, this legislation is draconian and intended to be such.

28   It was put to us in favour of Mr Bodnar's submissions that the Crown's interpretation of the Act and that adopted by the judge in this case would lead to bankruptcy of an applicant which is neither a matter stipulated nor intended by the Act. That again is a misapprehension. Whatever may be the calculation of a defendant's benefit from drug trafficking, a confiscation order is limited by the extent of his realisable property and since it is limited to his realisable property, no question arises of a confiscation order being made in a sum which is greater than the value of property available for its satisfaction. Indeed, there are provisions in the Act for reducing the amount of a confiscation order in circumstances where unexpectedly the value of property in practice is not that which a court assumed it to be or found it to be when the confiscation order was made.

29   In our judgment the working of the provisions of the Act are quite clear. The Act has always been applied in the manner we have described and although Mr Bodnar's submissions were worthy of consideration in terms of time, in our judgment they raised no arguable point of appeal. The confiscation order was rightly made and this application is therefore refused.

[Paragraphs [30]–[37] have been omitted.]

R. v ABDIAZIZ WARSAME

COURT OF APPEAL (Lord Justice Rose (Vice President, Court of Appeal Criminal Division), Mr Justice Henriques and Mrs Justice Dobbs): October 28, 2004

[2004] EWCA Crim 2770; [2005] 1 Cr.App.R.(S.) 122

⟨LT⟩ Criminal intent; Minimum term; Murder; Transitional provisions

H1   *Murder—minimum term— Criminal Justice Act 2003 s.269 and Schs 21 and 22*

H2   A minimum term imposed under the Criminal Justice Act 2003, s.269, for murder by stabbing, reduced from 14 years and 4 months to 12 years and 4 months, on the basis that the sentencing judge found that the appellant intended to cause grievous bodily harm but not to kill.

H3 The appellant was convicted of murder. The appellant and the victim were both members of the Somali community and knew each other. The appellant and the victim, together with others, went to a flat to chew khat. The appellant left the flat and returned some time later. He immediately kicked the victim in the chest and produced a large kitchen knife which he used to stab the victim in the back of the right shoulder. The victim managed to escape but was pursued by the appellant who attempted unsuccessfully to stab him again. The appellant discarded the knife in a bin. The victim was taken to hospital where he died the following morning as a result of a single stab wound which had passed through his right lung. The appellant later telephoned the police and said that he had been involved in a fight with the victim. He declined to comment in interview. Sentenced to life imprisonment with a specified period of 14 years and 4 months, derived from a period of 15 years, with the deduction of 8 months spent in custody.

H4 **Held:** the sentencing judge accepted that something must have occurred between the victim and the appellant prior to the murder. The appellant was a man of good character, and violence was out of character. The judge found that there was no intention to kill. The judge rejected the submission that the fact that the appellant's intention was merely to cause grievous bodily harm should be a mitigating feature. The offence was committed in September 2003, and accordingly the transitional provisions set out in the Consolidated Criminal Practice Direction (Amendment No.8) applied. It was submitted for the appellant that, in accordance with the Practice Direction of May 2002, the correct starting point was 12 years and that the offence did not have any of the features required for a higher starting point of 15 to 16 years. The Court agreed with that submission. It was accepted that the sentencer was entitled to regard the fact that the offender had armed himself with a weapon as an aggravating factor but that the judge was wrong not to regard an intention to cause grievous bodily harm rather than to kill as a mitigating factor. It seemed to the Court that the submission was well-founded. If the judge was not sure that there was an intention to kill, it was in accordance with well established authority incumbent on the judge to sentence on the basis more favourable to the defendant. The Court commented that having regard to the appellant's second unsuccessful attempt to stab the victim it might have been possible to conclude that there was an intention to kill, but it was for the judge to determine his view as to the appellant's intention. Bearing in mind that he was not sure one way or the other, the judge misdirected himself as to whether or not mitigation was to be found by reason of intention to cause grievous bodily harm rather than to kill. In those circumstances it was for the Court to assess the aggravating and mitigating factors and the extent to which they should increase or diminish the starting point which should properly been the 12 years. It seemed to the Court that two or three years might properly be regarded as reflecting the aggravation to be found in the pre-arming with a knife, and that one or two years would be regarded as appropriately reflecting the mitigation in relation to the intention to cause grievous bodily harm. When those features were taken into account, the starting point rose from 12 to 13 years. Accordingly the minimum term specified by the judge, having regard to the period served by the defendant on remand, would be reduced to 12 years and 4 months.

H5   **Case cited:** *Sullivan, Gibbs, Elener and Elener* [2005] 1 Cr.App.R.(S.) 67 (p.308)

H6   **References:** murder, *Current Sentencing Practice* B 0–1

H7   **Commentary:** [2005] Crim.L.R. 159.

H8   *P. Rook Q.C.* for the appellant.

JUDGMENT

1   **Rose L.J.:**   On May 14, 2004 at the Central Criminal Court, following a trial before H.H. Judge Gordon, the appellant was convicted of murder and sentenced to life imprisonment, with a specified period of 14 years and 4 months. He appeals against that term by leave of the single judge.

2   The facts can be shortly rehearsed. The appellant and the victim were both members of the Somali community and knew each other. They chewed khat, a habit common among Somali men. They used a flat in Camden Town for that purpose. On September 21, 2003, between about 7.00 and 9.00pm, the appellant went to that flat and chewed khat. The victim arrived at about 9.30 and was there chewing khat with seven other men. The appellant, who had earlier left, returned at about 10.30. Immediately he came into the flat he kicked the victim in the chest and then produced a large kitchen knife which he used to stab the victim in the back of his right shoulder. The victim managed to escape and ran to a taxi company, a few doors away, pursued by the appellant. The appellant tried to stab the victim again, but he was unsuccessful. He ran off. On his way home the appellant discarded the knife in a bin.

3   Passing police officers were flagged down by the victim's associates. Attempts were made to treat him at the scene. He was taken to hospital. He died at 9.00am the following morning as a result of the single stab wound which had passed through his right lung. At about 11.30pm the appellant telephoned the police and said he had been involved in a fight with the victim. He was arrested later, but in interview declined to comment.

4   In passing sentence, the learned judge said that the mandatory sentence was life imprisonment but he was also required to specify a minimum period to be served. The starting point, he said, was 14 years. It was an aggravating factor that the appellant had been home and armed himself with a knife and then gone to attack the victim.

5   By way of mitigation, the judge accepted that something must have occurred between him and the victim prior to the murder to cause the appellant to have strong feelings about it. He was a man of good character, and violence was out of character. The judge said that that reduced but did not eliminate the aggravation of fetching the knife and therefore a period of 1 year should be added to the starting point of 14 years. The minimum period he would serve would therefore be 15 years, less a period of 8 months spent in custody, so the minimum term became 14 years and 4 months.

6   In the course of those sentencing observations, in response to an enquiry by Mr Rook Q.C., then as now appearing for the appellant, the judge reiterated that he did not find that there was an intention to kill. It was submitted to him by Mr Rook that, if the intention was merely to cause grievous bodily harm, this should have been a mitigating feature in relation to sentence. The judge said:

> "No, I indicated to you I think earlier that I was declining to come to a con-
> clusion specifically. There are cases and it seems to me this is what the Act is
> dealing with, it is perfectly clear that there was no intention to kill and where
> that is the position, that clearly ought and always has been reflected in a sen-
> tence. In many murder cases it is not clear one way or the other and it does
> not matter."

7   It is common ground before us that the judge and counsel in the court below did not have the advantage of this Court's decision in *Sullivan and others* [2004] EWCA Crim 1762 [2005] 1 Cr.App.R.(S.) 67 (p.308). The significance of that is this, contrary to the assumption on the basis of which matters proceeded at the Central Criminal Court, the relevant Practice Direction did not indicate that 14 years should be the starting point. That is because of the date on which this offence was committed namely September 2003. In consequence, the tran-sitional provisions set out in Amendment No.8 to the Consolidated Criminal Practice Direction (Mandatory Life Sentences) applied. The correct starting point for the judge, this murder having been committed after May 31, 2002 and before December 18, 2003, was either the normal starting point of 12 years, or the higher starting point of 15 to 16 years.

8   The first submission which Mr Rook makes is that the correct starting point was 12 years. He submits that the offence did not have any of the features requir-ing the higher starting point of 15 to 16 years because of either the exceptionally high culpability of the offender, or the particularly vulnerable position of the vic-tim. Looking at the factors which are exemplified in IV.49.26 of the Practice Direction as giving rise to that higher starting point, we agree with that submis-sion.

9   Mr Rook accepts that the learned judge was entitled to regard as an aggravating factor, justifying an increase from the starting point of 12 years, as identified in VI.49.28C, "arming with a weapon in advance." The judge, as we have said, found that to be an aggravating feature. But, Mr Rook submits that the judge was wrong not to regard as a mitigating factor within IV.49.30A an intention to cause grievous bodily harm rather than to kill. As we have said, the judge declined to come to a conclusion as to the defendant's intention.

10   As it seems to us, Mr Rook's submission on this aspect is well- founded. If the judge was not sure that there was an intention to kill, it was, as it seems to us, in accordance with well- established authority, which it is unnecessary to rehearse, incumbent upon him to sentence on the basis more favourable to the defendant.

11   We comment, in passing, that having regard to the appellant's second unsuc-cessful attempt to stab the victim, it might have been possible to conclude that there was an intention to kill. But it was, in the first place, for the judge to deter-mine his view as to the appellant's intention. Bearing in mind that he was not sure

one way or the other, he, in our judgment, misdirected himself as to whether or not mitigation was to be found by reason of an intention to cause grievous bodily harm rather than to kill.

12   In those circumstances, having regard to the judge's comments in relation to intention, and having regard to our conclusion that he misdirected himself in the light of those comments, it is for this Court to assess, as it seems to us, the aggravating and mitigating factors and the extent to which they should increase or diminish the starting point which, as we have sought to explain, should properly have been 12 rather than 14 as taken by the judge. It seems to us that two or three years might properly be regarded as reflecting the aggravation to be found in the pre-arming with the knife and, it seems to us, one or two years should be regarded as appropriately reflecting the mitigation in relation to the intention to cause grievous bodily harm. When those features are taken into account, the starting point, in our judgment, rises from 12, by reason of aggravation and mitigation, to 13.

13   Accordingly, we quash the term of 15 years specified by the learned judge. We substitute a term of 13 years but, having regard to the 8 months served by the defendant, the term actually to be served would be one of 12 years and 4 months. To that extent this appeal is allowed.

R. v MUNTAZ AHMED, GHULAM QURESHI

COURT OF APPEAL (Lord Justice Latham, Mr Justice Pitchers and Mr Justice Royce): October 28, 2004

[2004] EWCA Crim 2599; [2005] 1 Cr.App.R.(S.) 123

LT Confiscation orders; Discretion; Matrimonial home; Proceeds of crime; Realisable property; Right to respect for home

1   *Confiscation order— Criminal Justice Act 1988 as amended by Proceeds of Crime Act 1995—amount that might be realised—whether judicial discretion to exclude realisable property from calculation*

2   **Editor's note:** in confiscation proceedings under the Criminal Justice Act 1988 as amended by the Proceeds of Crime Act 1995, the sentencing judge has no discretion to disregard realisable property of the defendant, such as the matrimonial home, on the ground that sale of the matrimonial home would expose his wife and children to hardship. Making a confiscation order on the basis that the offender's share in the value of the matrimonial home does not infringe the Convention rights of others entitled to a share in the value of the property.

3   The second appellant pleaded guilty to conspiring to convert cash which he knew or had reasonable grounds to suspect was, or directly or indirectly represented, another person's proceeds from criminal conduct for the purpose of assisting another person to avoid prosecution. The first appellant was convicted

of conspiring to convert cash which he knew or had reasonable grounds to suspect was or, in whole or in part, directly or indirectly represented, another person's proceeds either of drug trafficking or of other criminal conduct, for the purpose of assisting another to avoid prosecution. Confiscation orders were made against both appellants, in the case of the first appellant in the amount of £27,424 and in the case of the second appellant in the amount of £226,152. Each appellant appealed against the confiscation order.

H4   **Held:** in the case of the second appellant, the sentencing judge assessed the appellant's benefit as £12,257,135, and in the case of the first appellant as £1,385,000. The confiscation orders were based on the judge's assessment of the appellants' respective realisable assets. In computing the value of the appellants' realisable assets, the sentencing judge took into account in each case the value of the appellant's half share in his matrimonial home. He accepted evidence that in each case the probability was that the homes would have to be sold to meet the confiscation order. The appellants submitted that the judge had a discretion as to whether or not to include the value of their shares in the matrimonial homes. The sentencing judge accepted the submissions, but concluded that there were no exceptional circumstances which justified his excluding them from the calculation. The appellants argued on appeal that the sentencing judge was correct in concluding that he had a discretion, and that he was wrong in exercising the discretion in the way that he did. The prosecution submitted that the judge had no such discretion and, if he had a discretion, he was entitled to come to the conclusion that he did. There was no doubt that prior to the amendment of the Criminal Justice Act 1988 by the Proceeds of Crime Act 1995, the court had a general discretion in relation to the making of a confiscation order under s.71 of the 1988 Act. If the prosecution applied for a confiscation order, s.71 gave to the court a power to make an order "requiring him to pay such sum as the court thinks fit". Those words clearly gave the court a discretion not only in relation to the amount of the order but also as to whether to make any order at all. The Court had been referred to two cases decided under the original version of the 1988 Act, *Lee* [1996] 1 Cr.App.R.(S.) 135 and *Taigel* [1998] 1 Cr.App.R.(S.) 328. In both cases the sentencing judge had included the value of the appellant's matrimonial home when determining the amount of the confiscation order. In both cases, there was evidence that in order to raise the sum required to be paid by the confiscation order, the matrimonial home of the appellant would have to be sold and, as a result, the family would be rendered homeless. The Court of Appeal held that while there was no justification for a rule precluding a court from taking into account the value of the offender's interest in the matrimonial home, on the facts of those cases, the court in the exercise of its discretion, should not have done so. The Proceeds of Crime Act 1995 made substantial changes to the confiscation provisions of the 1988 Act. Parliament's intention in amending the 1988 Act appeared to be clear. What was a power to make a confiscation order under the original version of the Act was changed to a duty under the amended version the prosecution gave the appropriate notice. Subject to what was said in *Benjafield* [2002] 2 Cr.App.R.(S.) 71 (p.313), the court accordingly had no discretion as to whether to make an

[2005] 1 Cʀ.Aᴘᴘ.R.(S.) 123   705

order. As to the amount of the order, the court was required to make an order calculated in accordance with s.71(6). On its face, this section appeared to preclude
the exercise of any judicial discretion, properly so called. Leaving aside the
assessment of benefit, the assessment of the "amount that might be realised at
the time the order is made" appeared to require the simple application of the provisions of s.74. The Court rejected the submission that the use of the phrase "the
amount appearing to the court" in subs.(6)(b) gave the court a discretion. Both
appellants submitted that the making of a confiscation order was capable of
engaging Art.8 of the European Convention on Human Rights on the ground
that a confiscation order based on inclusion of the offender's share in the matrimonial home which could on the balance of probability be met only if the
matrimonial home was sold would result in interference with the appellant's
Art.8 rights, and the Art.8 rights of innocent members of the family, such as
his wife and children. Accepting that the interference with the offender's rights
could be justified and proportionate under Art.8(2), the appellants submitted that
interference might not be proportionate insofar as it might affect the other members of the family. It was submitted that the phrase "the amount appearing to the
court" should be construed so as to grant the court a discretion so as to ensure
compliance with the Convention. The Court had been referred to *Benjafield*.
The appellants submitted that in the light of that decision the Court should construe the Act so as to ensure that there should be no injustice and that accordingly
s.71(6) should be read so as to import the discretion necessary to achieve this
objective. Since the argument in *Benjafield* was concerned with the possible
impact of Art.6 on the provisions for determining whether the offender had benefited from relevant criminal conduct, the reference in the judgment of Lord
Woolf C.J. in the Court of Appeal, Criminal Division to the discretion given to
the prosecution and to the court seemed to be references to decisions made on
the one hand by the prosecution and on the other by the court under s.71. The present appeals did not concern the question of whether or not there had been any
benefit. The sentencing judge concluded that both appellants had benefited
from criminal activity and that conclusion was not challenged. The Court was
concerned with the next stage of the process, which was the assessment of the
value of all realisable property. It seemed to the Court that that exercise was prescribed by the provisions of the Act. The court was merely concerned with the
arithmetical exercise of computing what was in effect a statutory debt. The process did not involve any assessment of the ways in which the debt might
ultimately be paid. No question therefore arose under Art.8 at this stage in the
process. Different considerations would arise if the debt was not met and the prosecution determined to take enforcement action by obtaining an order for a
receiver. At this stage, the rights of third parties could be taken into account
and resolved. If the court were asked at that stage to make an order for the sale
of the matrimonial homes, Art.8 rights would clearly be engaged and at that
stage the court would have to consider whether or not it would be proportionate
to make an order selling the home in the circumstances of the particular case. That
decision could be made on the facts at the time; the court would undoubtedly
ensure that proper weight was given to the public policy objective behind the

making of confiscation orders, which was to ensure that criminals did not profit from their crimes. The court would have a range of enforcement options available with which to take account of the rights of third parties. For those reasons, the Court considered that the judge's decision was right, albeit that he wrongly concluded that he had a discretion.

H5 **Cases cited:**
Lee [1996] 1Cr.App.R.(S.) 135; *Taigel* [1998] 1 Cr.App.R.(S.) 328; *Benjafield* [2002] 2 Cr.App.R.(S.) 71 (p.313).

H6 **Commentary:** [2005] Crim.L.R. 240

H7 *M. House* for the appellant Muntaz Ahmed.
S. Farrell Q.C. for the appellant Ghulam Qureshi.
M. J. Brompton Q.C. and *J. Weekes* for the Crown.

JUDGMENT

1 **Latham L.J.:** The appellant Qureshi pleaded guilty to two counts of conspiracy to contravene s.93C(2) of the Criminal Justice Act 1988, contrary to s.1(1) of the Criminal Law Act 1977. The particulars were that he, together with others, conspired to convert cash which he knew or had reasonable grounds to suspect was, in whole or in part directly or indirectly or indirectly represented, another persons proceeds from criminal conduct for the purpose of assisting another person to avoid prosecution. The appellant Ahmed was convicted of a conspiracy to contravene s.49(2) of the Drug Trafficking Act 1994 and/or s.93C(2) of the Criminal Justice Act 1988, contrary to s.1(1) of the Criminal Law Act 1977. The particulars were that he together with others conspired to convert cash which he knew or had reasonable grounds to suspect was, or in whole or in part directly represented, another persons proceeds of either drug trafficking or other criminal conduct or both for the purpose of assisting another to avoid prosecution for either a drug trafficking offence or an offence to which Pt VI of the Criminal Justice Act 1988 applied. We have dismissed the appellant Ahmed's appeal against his conviction and allowed in part his appeal against sentence in so far as it related to the sentence of imprisonment which was imposed upon him. On July 8, 2003, the judge made confiscation orders against both appellants. In the case of the appellant Qureshi, he made a confiscation order in the sum of £226,152.90; and in the case of the appellant Ahmed he made a confiscation order in the sum of £27,424.52. In each case he imposed a sentence of imprisonment in default of payment. They both appeal against those orders. At the hearing, we dismissed those appeals and now give our reasons.

2 Each appeal raises a similar question of some practical importance in relation to the application of the confiscation provisions of the Criminal Justice Act 1988, as amended. In the case of the appellant Qureshi, the judge assessed the benefit figure, that is the figure which, in accordance with the Act, was to be taken as the benefit that he had obtained from his criminal activity at £12,257,135.88; and in

the case of the appellant Ahmed he assessed the benefit figure in the sum of £1,385,000. The confiscation orders that he made were based on his assessment of their respective realisable assets. In computing the latter, he took into account the value in each case of the appellant's half share in his matrimonial home. He accepted evidence from the families that in each case the probability was that the homes would have to be sold to meet the confiscation order. The appellants submitted to the judge that he had a discretion as to whether or not to include the value of those shares. The judge accepted those submissions. He nonetheless concluded that there were no exceptional circumstances which justified his excluding them. The appellants submit to us that the judge was correct in concluding that he had a discretion, but that he was wrong in exercising the discretion as he did. The prosecution submit as, as they did to the judge, that he had no such discretion, but that if he had, he was entitled to come to the conclusion that he did.

3   There is no doubt that prior to the amendment of the 1988 Act, the court did have a general discretion in relation to the making of a confiscation order under s.71. If the prosecution applied for a confiscation order, s.71 gave to the court a power to make an order "requiring him to pay such sum as the Court thinks fit". These words clearly gave the court a discretion not merely in relation to the amount of an order but also as to whether to make any order at all. We have been referred to two cases decided by this court under the original provisions of the 1988 Act, *Lee* [1996] 1 Cr.App.R.(S.) 135 and *Taigel* [1998] 1 Cr.App.R.(S.) 328. In both cases the courts were concerned with the same question as that which has been raised before us. In both the judge had included the value of the appellant's interest in the matrimonial home when determining the amount of the confiscation order. In each there was evidence that in order to raise the sum required to be paid by the confiscation order so assessed, the matrimonial home would have to be sold as a result of which the family would be rendered homeless. In both cases, this Court held that while there was no justification for a rule precluding the court from taking into account the value of the offender's interest in the matrimonial home, nonetheless on the facts of those cases, the court, in the exercise of its discretion, should not have done so.

4   The Proceeds of Crime Act 1995, however, made substantial changes to the confiscation provisions of the 1988 Act. Section 71, as amended provided:

> "(1) Where an offender is convicted in any proceedings before the Crown Court or a Magistrates Court, of an offence of a relevant description, it shall be the duty of the court—
> (a) if the prosecutor has given written notice to the court that he considers that it would be appropriate for the court to proceed under this section, or
> (b) if the court considers, even though if it has not been given such notice, that it would be appropriate for it so to proceed,
> to act as follows before sentencing or otherwise dealing with the offender in respect of that offence or any other relevant criminal conduct.

(1A) The court shall first determine whether the offender has benefited from any relevant criminal conduct.

(1B) . . . If the court determines that the offender has benefited from any relevant criminal conduct, it shall then—

    (a) determine in accordance with sub-section (6) below the amount to be recovered in his case by virtue of this section, and

    (b) make an order under this section ordering the offender to pay that amount.

    . . .

(6) . . . .. The sum which an order made by a court under this section requires an offender to pay shall be equal to—

    (a) the benefit in respect of which it is made; or

    (b) the amount appearing to the court to be the amount that might be realised at the time the order is made, whichever is the less.

    . . ."

5   Section 74 of the 1988 Act in its relevant form identifies how the court is to assess "the amount that might be realised". It provides:

"(1) In this Part of this Act, "realisable property" means, subject to sub-section (2) below—

    (a) any property held by a defendant; and

    (b) any property held by a person to whom the defendant had directly or indirectly made a gift caught by this Part of this Act.

    . . . ..

(3) For the purposes of this Part of this Act the amount that might be realised at the time a confiscation order is made is—

    (a) the total of the values at that time of all the realisable property held by the defendant, less

    (b) where there are obligations having priority at that time, the total amounts payable in pursuance of such obligations,

    together with the total of the values at that time of all gifts caught by this Part of this Act.

(4) Subject to the following provisions of this section for the purposes of this Part of this Act the value of property (other than cash) in relation to any person holding the property—

    (a) Where any other person holds an interest in the property, is—

    (i) The market value of the first mentioned person's beneficial interest in the property less

    (ii) The amount required to discharge any encumbrance (other than a charging order) on that interest; and

    (b) And in any other case, is its market value.

    . . .."

6   Parliament's intention in amending the 1988 Act in those terms would appear to be clear. What was a power to make a confiscation order has been changed to a duty where the prosecution gives the appropriate notice. Subject to what was said

in *Benjafield* [2002] 2 Cr.App.R.(S.) 71 (p.313) the court accordingly has no discretion in those circumstances as to whether or not to make an order. As to the amount of the order, the court is required to make an order calculated in accordance with s.71(6). On its face, this also appears to preclude the exercise of any judicial discretion, properly so called. Leaving aside the assessment of benefit, with which we are not concerned in these appeals, the assessment of "the amount that might be realised at the time the order is made" would appear to require a simple application of the provisions of s.74. On behalf of the appellant Ahmed, it was submitted that the court's discretion was retained by the use of the phrase "the amount appearing to the court" in subs.(6)(b). We have little hesitation in rejecting that argument. It seems to us that that phrase is not intended to import any discretion. It merely refers to the evaluation or valuation process which the court has to carry out under s.74.

7   Both appellants submit, however, that the making of a confiscation order is capable of engaging Art.8 of the European Convention on Human Rights. This provides:

"(1) Everyone has the right for respect of his private and family life, his home and his correspondence.

(2) There shall be no interference by a public authority with the exercise of this right except such as is in accordance with the law and is necessary in a democratic society in the interests of National Security, public safety or the economic well being of the country, for the prevention of disorder or crime, for the prosecution of health or morals, or for the protection of the rights and freedoms of others."

8   They submit that where there is evidence, as there was in this case, that a confiscation order based upon the inclusion of the offender's share in the matrimonial home could, on the balance of probabilities, only be met if the matrimonial home was sold, that would result in interference with not just the appellant's Art.8 rights, but the Art.8 rights of innocent members of the family, such as his wife and children. Accepting that the interference with the offender's rights could be justified and proportionate under Art.8(2), they submit that the interference may not be proportionate in so far as it may affect the other members of the family. Accordingly, they submit that the phrase "the amount appearing to the court" should be construed in such a way as to grant to the court a discretion, so as to ensure compliance with the Convention.

9   In support of their submissions, they referred us to *Benjafield* [2002] 2 Cr.App.R.(S.) 71 (p.313). This report deals with two conjoined appeals, by the appellant Benjafield, who was appealing against a confiscation order made pursuant to the Drug Trafficking Act 1994 and the appellant Rezvi, who appealed against a confiscation order made under the provisions with which we are concerned in the 1988 Act as amended. Those appeals raised different issues from the present. Nonetheless, it is submitted, there are statements of principle which support the argument that the court is concerned to ensure that no injustice arises as a result of the making of a confiscation order, and accordingly must retain a discretion in relation to its exercise. The passage to which we have

been referred is contained in para.[15] of the speech of Lord Steyn who was dealing with the argument as to proportionality in the *Rezvi* appeal. He said:

> "It is clear that the 1988 Act was passed in the furtherance of a legitimate
> aim and that the measures are rationally connected with that aim: see *de
> Freitas -v- Permanent Secretary of Ministry of Agriculture, Fisheries,
> Lands and Housing* [1999] 1 AC 69, 80 for the three-stage test. The only
> question is whether the statutory means adopted are wider than is necessary
> to accomplish the objective. Counsel for the appellant submitted that the
> means adopted are disproportionate to the objective in as much as a persuas-
> ive burden is placed on the defendants. The Court of Appeal [2001] 3WLR
> 75, 103 carefully considered this argument and ruled:

'86. The onus which is placed on the defendant is not an evidential one but a
persuasive one, so that the defendant will be required to discharge the burden of proof: see Lord Hope's third category of provisions in *R -v-
Director of Public Prosecutions Ex p Kebilene* [2000] 2 AC 326, 379.
This is therefore a situation where it is necessary to carefully consider
whether the public interest in being able to confiscate the ill-gotten
gains of criminals justifies the interference with the normal presumption
of innocence. While the extent of the interference is substantial, Parliament has clearly made efforts to balance the interest of the defendant
against that of the public in the following respects.

(a) It is only after the necessary convictions that any question of confiscation arises. This is of significance, because the trial which results in
the conviction or convictions will be one where the usual burden and standard of proof rests upon the prosecution. In addition, a defendant who is
convicted of the necessary offence or offences can be taken to be aware
that if he committed the offences of which he has been convicted, he
would not only be liable to imprisonment or another sentence, but he
would also be liable to confiscation proceedings.

(b) The prosecution has the responsibility for initiating the confiscation
proceedings unless the court regards them as inappropriate . . ..

(c) there is also the responsibility placed upon the court not to make a confiscation order when there is a serious risk of injustice. As already
indicated, this will involve the court before it makes a confiscation
order standing back and deciding whether there is a risk of injustice; if
the court decides there is, then the confiscation order will not be made

(d) there is the role of this court on appeal to ensure there is no unfairness.

87. It is very much a matter of personal judgment whether a proper balance
has been struck between the conflicting interests. Into the balance there
must be placed the interests of the defendant as against the interests of the
public, that those who have offended should not profit from their offending
and should not use their criminal conduct to fund further offending. However, in our judgment, if the discretions which are given to the

prosecution, and the court are properly exercised, the solution which Parliament has adopted is a reasonable and proportionate response to a substantial public interest, and therefore justifiable.' (Emphasis supplied.)

For my part I think that this reasoning is correct, notably in explaining the role of the court in standing back and deciding whether there is or might be a risk of serious or real injustice and, if there is, or might be, in emphasising that a confiscation order ought not to be made. The Crown accepted that this is how the court, seized with the question of confiscation, should approach its task. In my view this concession was rightly made."

10   The appellants submit that this makes it clear that the court should construe the Act so as to ensure that there should be no injustice, and that accordingly, this Court should read the words of s.71(6) so as to import the discretion necessary to achieve this objective. But it seems to us that it is important to read the words of Lord Woolf, as approved by Lord Steyn, in their context. The argument in *Rezvi* was concerned with the possible impact of Art.6 on the provisions for determining whether the offender had benefited from the relevant criminal conduct and if he had of assessing the value of that benefit in accordance with s.72AA of the 1988 Act. That section requires the court to make certain assumptions in relation to an offender's property or expenditure unless it is shown to be incorrect in the particular case, or the court is satisfied that there would be a serious risk of injustice if the assumptions were made. The reference to the discretions given to the prosecution and the court in Lord Woolf's judgment seems to us to be clearly references to the decisions made on the one hand by the prosecution under s.71(1)(a), and on the other by the court under s.71(1)(b). Whatever may be the mechanism for the control of the exercise of the prosecution's discretion, that is a discretion capable of review. Further the courts in *Rezvi* considered that where no true benefit could sensibly be said to have been obtained by the offender, it would be inappropriate to make an order. The provisions of s.72AA which entitle the court to decline to make the assumptions where there would be a serious risk of injustice are clearly there for that purpose.

11   But in the present appeals, we are not concerned with the question of whether or not there has been any benefit. The judge concluded that both appellants had benefited from criminal activity and made findings as to the extent of that benefit. There is no appeal against those findings. We are therefore concerned with the next stage of the process, which is the assessment of the value of realisable property. It seems to us that that exercise is prescribed by the provisions of the Act as we have already indicated. The court is merely concerned with the arithmetic exercise of computing what is, in effect, a statutory debt. That process does not involve any assessment, in our judgment, of the way in which that debt may ultimately be paid, any more than the assessment of any other debt. No questions therefore arise under Art.8 at this stage in the process.

12   Different considerations, will, however arise if the debt is not met and the prosecution determine to take enforcement action, for example by obtaining an order for a receiver. As the House of Lords explained in *Norris, Re* [2001] UKHL 34, this is the stage of the procedure in which third party's rights can not only be taken

into account but resolved. If the court is asked at that stage to make an order for the sale of the matrimonial homes, Art.8 rights are clearly engaged. It would be at that stage that the court will have to consider whether or not it would be proportionate to make an order selling the home in the circumstances of the particular case. That is a decision which can only be made on the facts at the time. The court would undoubtedly be concerned to ensure that proper weight is given to the public policy objective behind the making of confiscation orders, which is to ensure that criminals do not profit from their crime. And the court will have a range of enforcements options available with which to take account of the rights of third parties such as other members of the Ahmed family.

13   For these reasons, we consider that the judge's decision was right, albeit that he wrongly concluded that he had a discretion in this case.

R. v JOE BUTLER

COURT OF APPEAL (Lord Justice Rose (Vice President, Court of Appeal Criminal Division), Mr Justice Henriques and Mrs Justice Dobbs): October 28, 2004

[2004] EWCA Crim 2767; [2005] 1 Cr.App.R.(S.) 124

LT Attempts; Grievous bodily harm; Motor vehicles; Resisting arrest; Sentence length

H1   *Attempting to cause grievous bodily harm with intent to resist apprehension— driving car away at speed with police officer on outside—length of sentence*

H2   Ten years' imprisonment upheld for attempting to cause grievous bodily harm with intent to resist apprehension, where the appellant drove his car away at speed on a motorway with a police officer holding on to the outside.

H3   The appellant was convicted of attempting to cause grievous bodily harm, and pleaded guilty to offences of handling stolen goods, making off without payment and doing an act intended to pervert the course of justice. The appellant was driving on a motorway when he was stopped by police due to his excessive speed. A police officer attempted to arrest the appellant for driving while disqualified. The appellant provided a false name. The appellant resisted the officer and punched him twice in the chest. The officer attempted to pull the appellant out of the car. The appellant started the engine and pulled away; the officer had his foot in the driver's foot well and held on to car while it was driven back on to the carriageway. The vehicle gathered speed, reaching about 70 miles per hour, and the appellant veered the vehicle towards the central barrier, shouting threats to the officer. The appellant swerved away from the barrier and braked sharply, causing the officer to release his grip and fall across the motorway. The vehicle then accelerated away. The officer suffered a broken nose and other injuries. Another officer had been dragged for 10 yards before being thrown clear; he sustained bruising to his arm and a cut to his finger. The motor car was found about two hours later. Various items of stolen property were found within the car. Sentenced to 10 years' imprisonment for attempting to cause grievous bodily with intent to resist lawful apprehension and a total of 1 year and 3 months consecutive for the other offences.

H4   **Held:** (considering *Bolster* [1996] 2 Cr.App.R.(S.) 428, *Hall* [1997] 1 Cr.App.R.(S.) 62) the sentencing judge said that the appellant had deliberately used the vehicle as a weapon in circumstances of the utmost danger. The appellant was a very dangerous man who would stop at nothing to achieve its own ends. Having considered the authorities and the facts, the Court had concluded that the sentence of 10 years' imprisonment was fully justified for a clear and deliberate attempt to cause serious injury to a police officer. So far as the other matters concerned, it was rarely appropriate to add comparatively short sentences to lengthy sentence, although there would be occasions when it was appropriate to do so. The other sentences would be ordered to run concurrently to the sentence of 10 years.

H5   **Cases cited:**
Bolster [1996] 2 Cr.App.R.(S.) 428, *Hall* [1997] 1 Cr.App.R.(S.) 62

H6   **References:** causing grievous bodily harm with intent, *Current Sentencing Practice* B 2-2

H7   *G. Fishwick* for the appellant.

JUDGMENT

1   **Henriques J.:**   This appellant appeals with leave of the single judge against a total sentence of 11 years and 3 months' imprisonment, imposed in the Crown Court at Chelmsford by Judge Pearson on September 8, 2003. The appellant had been convicted by a jury of attempting to cause grievous bodily harm with intent to resist or prevent lawful apprehension and was sentenced to 10 years' imprisonment and disqualified from driving for 10 years. For two offences of handling stolen goods, which he had admitted at an earlier hearing, he was sentenced to 9 months' imprisonment in respect of each offence, to run concurrently together but consecutively to the 10-year prison term. For an offence of making off without payment, he was sentenced to a 5-month term of imprisonment to run concurrently and an offence of doing an act intending and intended to pervert the course of justice, namely giving a false name, he was sentenced to 6 months' imprisonment to run consecutively to the earlier sentences, resulting in a total sentence of 11 years and 3 months' imprisonment. In granting leave the single judge indicated that leave to argue totality was the basis of his ground.

2   At about 1.45pm on October 9, 2002 the appellant and his female passenger, Sarah Auld, was stopped by police on the M11 motorway, due to excessive speed. Police Constable Poyser attempted to arrest the appellant for driving while disqualified and he provided a false name. Provision of the false name

was the offence of doing an act to pervert the course of justice. The appellant resisted and punched the officer twice in the chest, before returning to the driver's side of the vehicle. The officer then attempted to pull the appellant out of the car, whilst a fellow officer attempted to remove the ignition key, through the passenger side, to prevent the appellant from driving away. The female passenger, however, leant across and punched Police Constable Poyser in the face several times. An off- duty officer stopped to provide assistance and also tried to pull the appellant out of the vehicle. The appellant then started the engine and pulled away. Police Constable Poyser had his foot on the driver's footwell, and held onto the car whilst it was driven back onto the carriageway. The vehicle gathered speed, possibly up to 70 miles per hour, the appellant veered the vehicle towards the central barrier shouting: "You're going to die you bastard". The appellant then swerved the vehicle away from the barrier and braked sharply, causing Police Constable Poyser to release his grip after approximately half a mile travelling on the car. He tumbled across the motorway. The vehicle then accelerated away.

3   Police Constable Poyser suffered a broken nose, numerous cuts, grazes, bruises and severe body pains. Police Constable Mann had been dragged for 10 yards before he had been thrown clear, and he sustained bruising to his arm and a cut to his finger. The Mercedes Benz motorcar was found approximately two hours later in the car park of a public house in North Weald. Within the vehicle were a briefcase and a printer that had been stolen from a Saab motorcar in West Sussex in October 2002. Those two items were the subject matter of one of two handling stolen goods counts for which nine months' imprisonment was imposed. The other count related to a passport wallet and various cards which had been stolen from a motor vehicle in Bognor Regis in September 2002.

4   In passing sentence the judge indicated that the appellant had been convicted on overwhelming evidence and that the court had a duty to protect police officers from injury. The vehicle was deliberately used as a weapon and that it was difficult to imagine anything more lethal and circumstances of the utmost danger. This was a busy motorway, with traffic moving at speed. Further, the appellant was a disqualified driver carrying stolen property. The judge concluded that there was no mitigation whatsoever and not a word of remorse. He concluded by saying that the appellant was a very dangerous young man, who would stop at nothing to achieve his own ends. The career of a police officer who had served for 24 years had been ended by his conduct. He had regard to totality. Credit was given for the pleas tendered at an earlier stage in relation to the lesser offences.

5   Mr Fishwick, who appears on behalf of the appellant, submits to us that the sentence of 10 years is manifestly excessive. He, in writing, contended that it would be appropriate to have regard to the fact that 10 years was the maximum sentence at the time available for death by dangerous driving. It is also submitted that the principle of totality is offended. We have been referred to two authorities, first, *Bolster* [1996] 2 Cr.App.R.(S.) 428. In that case, nine years' imprisonment for causing grievous bodily harm with intent to prevent apprehension, where the appellant drove his car in such a way as to collide with a police car in the course of a chase, causing grave injury to a police officer, was reduced to seven-and-a-

half years' imprisonment. It should be noted that in that case the appellant pleaded guilty, unlike the present case. Furthermore, the appellant's plea was accepted on the basis that he had not deliberately collided with a police car but had done so recklessly with intent to escape arrest. It was specifically stated in that case that a comparison with the maximum sentence for causing death by dangerous driving was not helpful or appropriate. We have also been referred to the case of *Hall* [1997] 1 Cr.App.R.(S.) 62, in which 12 years' imprisonment was upheld for causing grievous bodily harm with intent, where the driver of a car, taken without authority, drove over a police officer in an attempt to evade arrest. Having considered both those authorities, and having considered the facts of the instant case, we are perfectly satisfied that the sentence of 10 years' imprisonment was fully justified on the facts of this case. This was a very clear and deliberate attempt to cause really serious injury to a police officer. The act of driving up to approximately 70 miles per hour, followed by veering towards the central barriers, shouting at the police officer and then swerving away from the barrier on a busy M11 motorway was very grave conduct indeed. It was no more than good fortune that the police officer's injuries, grave as they were, were not even more serious. This was a deliberate attack upon a police officer. There was no mitigation whatsoever and 10 years could not be described as manifestly excessive.

6   So far as the remaining matters are concerned, while it is clear that the judge did have regard to the principle of totality, it is rarely appropriate to add comparatively short sentences to lengthy sentences, although there will be occasions when it is appropriate to do so. We are minded that the principle of totality can properly be observed by ordering all the sentences in this case to run concurrently. To that extent, this appeal is allowed. The total sentence of 10 years being substituted for 11 years and 3 months.

ATTORNEY GENERAL'S REFERENCE NO.98 OF 2004 (JOEL MEAKIN)

COURT OF APPEAL (Lord Justice Rose (Vice President, Court of Appeal Criminal Division), Mr. Justice Henriques and Mrs.Justice Dobbs): October 28, 2004

[2004] EWCA Crim 2311; [2005] 1 Cr.App.R.(S.) 125

(LT) Actual bodily harm; Detention; Robbery; Undue leniency; Young offender institutions

H1   *Detention in a young offender institution—street robbery by group of youths with gratuitous violence—length of term of detention*

H2   A sentence of 30 months' detention for a street robbery by a group of youths with gratuitous violence increased to four years.

H3   The offender pleaded guilty to one count of robbery and one count of assault occasioning actual bodily harm. The offender was one of a group of youths who approached a man who was standing in a telephone kiosk, having just made a telephone call for a taxi. The man stepped out side the kiosk and the offender and one of his associates attacked the man, punching him to the side of the face and then knocking his spectacles off. The man was knocked to the ground and kicked in his head, shoulder and back. The offender and others searched his pockets and took £64 cash and various other items. The offender and one of the others returned and the offender stamped on the man. The group moved off, but the offender returned and kicked and stamped on the man again. The whole incident was recorded on CCTV. The man went to hospital where it was found that he had deep bruising to the head, back and shoulders. Sentenced to 30 months' detention in a young offender institution for robbery, and 12 months' detention, concurrent, for assault occasioning actual bodily harm. The Attorney General asked the Court to review the sentence on the ground and that it was unduly lenient.

H4   **Held:** (considering *Gordon and Foster* [2001] 1 Cr.App.R.(S.) 58 (p.200), *Attorney General's Reference Nos 4 and 7 of 2002 (Adrian Michael Lobban and Christopher Sawyers)* [2002] 2 Cr.App.R.(S.) 77 (p. 345), *Attorney General's Reference No.23 of 2004 (Fereday)* [2004] EWCA Crim1883) for the Attorney General it was submitted that the robbery was committed by a group of four, it took place at night, shod feet were used as weapons, and gratuitous violence was used. Taking into account the circumstances of the case, the Court would have expected a sentence of at least five years' detention in a young offender institution. It followed that the sentences passed were unduly lenient. Taking account of the element of double jeopardy, the Court would substitute a sentence of four years' detention for the robbery, leaving the sentence for assault undisturbed.

H5 **Cases cited:**
Gordon and Foster [2001] 1 Cr.App.R.(S.) 58 (p.200), *Attorney General's Reference Nos 4 and 7 of 2002 (Adrian Michael Lobban and Christopher Sawyers)* [2002] 2 Cr.App.R.(S.) 77 (p. 345), *Attorney General's Reference No.23 of 2004 (Fereday)* [2004] [2004] EWCA Crim 1883.

H6 **References:** detention in a young offender institution—robbery, *Current Sentencing Practice* E 2–4

H7 *R. Horwell* for the Attorney General.
S. Evans for the offender.

JUDGMENT

1 **The Vice President:** The Attorney-General seeks the leave of the Court, under s.36 of the Criminal Justice Act 1988, to refer sentences said to be unduly lenient. We grant leave. The offender was born in April 1986 and so is 18 years of age. On June 14, 2004 he pleaded guilty to both counts in the indictment; count 1 was robbery and count 2 assault occasioning actual bodily harm. On July 5 he was sentenced by Mr Recorder Carus Q.C., at Manchester Crown Court, to 30 months' detention in a young offender institution on count 1 and 12 months' detention concurrently on count 2. A co-accused, Blanchflower, also charged on count 1, was at that time awaiting trial, but we are told that he has subsequently been convicted.

2 The circumstances of the offence, somewhat unusually, are depicted clearly in CCTV footage which each member of this Court has seen. The offender was in the street at night-time with three others. The victim was alone. He was punched and kicked, not only during the robbery, but also, conspicuously by this offender gratuitously afterwards.

3 The victim was Mr Prince. A little before 2am on February 23, 2004, he was using a public telephone kiosk in Pendleton. He was telephoning for a taxi to take him home. He was told it would be about 15 minutes, so he decided to stay in the kiosk to keep warm. The offender and the three other youths were not far away. As depicted in the video footage, the offender had previously attempted to break into a parked motorcar, but had failed. Thereafter, he and the other three walked towards the kiosk. They saw Mr Prince inside. Mr Prince assumed that they wanted to use the telephone. He stepped outside. Thereupon, the offender and one of the others attacked him, punching him to the side of the face and knocking his spectacles off. He was knocked to the ground and kicked in his head, shoulder and back. At no stage did he offer any resistance. He curled up in a ball in order to protect himself. As he lay on the ground, the offender and others searched his pockets and took £64 in cash, a mobile telephone and a num-

ber of disposable cigarette lighters from him. Thereafter, as we have said, the offender and one of the others returned and the offender stamped on him.

4   The offender and the others walked off. Mr Prince was still lying on the ground and again the offender came back and kicked and stamped on him. Mr Prince said: "Don't you think I've had enough?" That later incident was the subject of count 2, assault occasioning actual bodily harm.

5   Fortunately, not long after this attack, the taxi which Mr Prince had ordered arrived. It took him home. He went to hospital the following morning. He had deep bruising of the head, back and shoulders. Because of what was recorded on the CCTV camera the offender was identified. He was arrested on April 14. In interview he made no comment. He pleaded guilty at the plea and directions hearing on June 14. That was the first occasion when he had the opportunity to do so. Sentence was adjourned to await the outcome of Blanchflower's trial. But, on July 5, that trial was adjourned because he had other matters to face. It was in that context that the learned recorder passed the sentence to which, at the outset, we referred.

6   On May 24, 2001 the offender had been conditionally discharged for 12 months for an offence of having a bladed article in a public place, to which he pleaded guilty. He had been 13 at the time of the offence and 15 at sentence. He had also been cautioned in respect of offences of theft and assault occasioning actual bodily harm when he was 12, and for criminal damage when he was 13. As we have said, he was 18 at the date of sentence. He had been 17 at the time of the offence. The learned recorder, like this Court, had the advantage of seeing the CCTV footage.

7   In passing sentence, the recorder indicated that the plea of guilty would reduce the sentence to be imposed, though he observed that, given the quality of the CCTV evidence, the prospect of a successful contest would have been "virtually zero". The learned recorder also said that, having watched the video, he experienced a sense of revulsion and shock. He indicated that the offender had played the most prominent part in the attack on Mr Prince, who was fortunate not to have sustained serious injuries, despite the offender's best attempts to cause serious injury.

8   On behalf of the Attorney General, Mr Horwell draws attention to what he submits, rightly, are five aggravating features. First, the offence of robbery was committed by a group of four upon a sole individual. Secondly, it took place at night. Thirdly, shod feet were used as weapons. Fourthly, the violence which we have described went beyond that required merely for the purpose of robbery. Fifthly, there was the subsequent further and wholly gratuitous violence used on the victim after the robbery had been committed.

9   Mr Horwell drew attention to the mitigation to be found in the pleas of guilty and the age of the offender. He drew attention to two authorities: *Gordon and Foster* [2001] 1 Cr.App.R.(S.) 58 (p.200), in some respects is similar to the present case, though dissimilar in others. In that case, following a plea of guilty, a sentence of five years was imposed on defendants aged 26 and 28 and that sentence was upheld on appeal to this Court. Mr Horwell also drew attention to *Attorney General's References Nos 4 and 7 of 2002 (Lobban and Ors)*

[2002] 2 Cr.App.R.(S.) 77 (p.345), in particular, para.[5] of the judgment of the Court, where it was accepted that the authorities reveal a sentencing bracket of 18 months to 5 years, subject to the observation that, if offences are committed by an offender who has a number of previous convictions and, if there is a substantial degree of violence, or if there is a particularly large number of offences committed, the 5 year upper limit may not be appropriate. In para.[7] the Court identified as a factor of importance whether a team of offenders was involved.

10   In the present case, as we have said, there were four members of the offender's group, though it is right to point out that one of them took no part in the violence. One of them intervened to reduce the degree of violence and the violence was essentially inflicted by the offender primarily and by one of the other youths secondarily.

11   The submission Mr Horwell makes is that the sentences passed by the learned recorder were unduly lenient and failed to reflect the aggravating features identified and public concern about offences of this kind.

12   On behalf of the offender Mr Evans stresses that the guilty plea on the first occasion is the most powerful aspect of mitigation so far as this offender is concerned. He accepted that the quality of the video made it very difficult to contest the issue of guilt, although he did point out that Blanchflower did contest that issue, albeit he was convicted. Mr Evans conceded that the garment warn by the offender, which bore white stripes, was particularly readily identifiable and he also accepted that the offender's participation in these events was in the forefront of those involved. But, he stresses, the offender was 17 at the time. His only previous involvements with the law, as we have indicated, werewhen he was a good deal younger. As to the offences themselves, Mr Evans stresses that no weapon was used. Bearing in mind the number of those involved and the use which was made of shod feet, that is not, as it seems to us, a particularly powerful point.

13   Mr Evans also drew the Court's attention to *Attorney General's Reference No.23 of 2004 (Fereday)* [2004] EWCA Crim 1883. As was pointed out to Mr Evans in the course of his submissions, individual cases which state no general principle are of limited assistance when approaching sentence, because of the variety of facts which are to be found in the reported cases. Mr Evans' submission, and he said all that could be said on behalf of the offender, is that this was not an unduly lenient sentence and not one with which, in any event, this Court should interfere. That submission we do not accept.

14   Taking into account all the circumstances which we have rehearsed, we would have expected in the court below a sentence of at least five years' detention in a young offender institution for the totality of this criminality. It follows that the sentences passed were unduly lenient. Taking double jeopardy into account, that is the offender is being sentenced a second time, the sentence which we pass is one of fouryears detention in a young offender institution. We pass that sentence in relation to count 1, quashing the sentence of 30 months imposed by the learned recorder and we leave undisturbed the sentence of 12 months concurrent on count 2.

INDEX

[all references are to case number]

Index